Monty Python
SECOND EDITION

Monty Python
A Chronology, 1969–2012

SECOND EDITION

Douglas McCall

McFarland & Company, Inc., Publishers
Jefferson, North Carolina, and London

LIBRARY OF CONGRESS CATALOGUING-IN-PUBLICATION DATA

McCall, Douglas L., 1971–
Monty Python : a chronology, 1969–2012 /
Douglas McCall—2d ed.
p.   cm.
Includes bibliographical references and index.

ISBN 978-0-7864-7811-8
softcover : acid free paper ∞

1. Monty Python (Comedy troupe)—
History—Chronology. I. Title.
PN2599.5.T54M37 2014   791.45'028'0922—dc23   2013036517

BRITISH LIBRARY CATALOGUING DATA ARE AVAILABLE

© 2014 Douglas McCall. All rights reserved

*No part of this book may be reproduced or transmitted in any form
or by any means, electronic or mechanical, including photocopying
or recording, or by any information storage and retrieval system,
without permission in writing from the publisher.*

On the cover: *left to right* Eric Idle, Graham Chapman,
Michael Palin, John Cleese, Terry Jones and Terry Gilliam
in *And Now for Something Completely Different*,
1971 (Columbia Pictures/Photofest)

Manufactured in the United States of America

*McFarland & Company, Inc., Publishers
Box 611, Jefferson, North Carolina 28640
www.mcfarlandpub.com*

To the memory
of Graham Chapman

Table of Contents

Introduction
1

The Chronological Listing
3

Appendix: John Cleese's Business-Training Films for Video Arts, 1972–2012
321

Selected Bibliography
323

Monty Python Sketch and Song Index
325

Eric Idle Solo Sketch and Song Index
334

General Index
337

Introduction

The first edition of *Monty Python: A Chronology*, published in 1991, covered the British comedy troupe's creative output from 1969 — the year *Monty Python's Flying Circus* first appeared on British television — to 1989 — the year of the group's twentieth anniversary and the death of founding member Graham Chapman. At the time it seemed like the end of an era, or at least the end of one brilliantly silly group of British comedians (and one American animator) who somehow made dead parrots, Spam, and even the Spanish Inquisition outrageously funny.

But unlike that famous Norwegian Blue parrot, Python wasn't *quite* dead yet. While it's true that the six-man team responsible for revolutionizing television comedy and creating such classic films as *Monty Python and the Holy Grail* (1975) and *Life of Brian* (1979) may have "ceased to be," the spirit of Python continued on in the solo work of its individual members, none of whom — with the exception of Chapman — have slowed down one bit since that "final" year. Michael Palin turned his one-off 1989 special *Around the World in 80 Days* into a second career as a popular television travel host, taking viewers *Pole to Pole* (1992) and *Full Circle* (1997) and across the *Sahara* (2002) and *Himalaya* (2004). Terry Gilliam expanded his already impressive directorial résumé with films like *The Fisher King* (1991), *12 Monkeys* (1995), and *The Imaginarium of Doctor Parnassus* (2009) while his ambitious — though ultimately unsuccessful — attempt to film *The Man Who Killed Don Quixote* was chronicled in the fascinating documentary *Lost in La Mancha*. Terry Jones, a respected medieval scholar, breathed new life into the history documentary with his television series *Crusades* (1995), *Medieval Lives* (2004), and *Barbarians* (2006) while still continuing to direct and act (*The Wind in the Willows*) and write stories for children (*The Knight and the Squire*). John Cleese, in addition to writing and lecturing (and marrying and divorcing — and marrying again), has appeared — or voiced a character — in more than forty movies since 1990 and found time to host television specials on wine, lemurs, and the human face. And finally, there's Eric Idle who, perhaps more than any other member of the group, has kept the flame of Python alive with his stage tours (*Eric Idle Exploits Monty Python*, *The Greedy Bastard Tour*), a *Brian*-inspired oratorio (*Not the Messiah...He's a Very Naughty Boy*), and the *Holy Grail*–inspired musical *Spamalot*, which premiered on Broadway to great acclaim in 2005.

Even in 2012, which saw the two youngest Pythons (Idle and Palin) enter their 70th years, there were still no signs of slowing. Projects included a one-man stage tour of Australia (Cleese); the play *What About Dick?*, performed for four nights in Los Angeles (Idle); a short opera, *The Owl and the Pussycat*, staged on a London barge (Jones); the filming of *The Zero Theorem* in Romania (Gilliam); and the novel *The Truth* and TV travel series *Brazil* (both Palin). And if all that wasn't enough, the world witnessed a memorable performance (Idle again) of the Python classic "Always Look on the Bright Side of Life" at the closing ceremony of the London Olympic Games.

No, Monty Python's not dead. They're not even "restin'."

This second edition of the chronology aims to celebrate Python's enduring legacy by expanding the original book's twenty-one-year span (1969–1989) by an additional twenty-three years and also providing more detailed information for each entry. This edition also features the addition of two sketch and song indexes— one for Python as a group, the other for Eric Idle on his own.

The information in this book comes from a wide selection of print, television, radio, and internet sources, with special mention going to the works of leading Python chroniclers George Perry (*Life of Python*), Kim "Howard" Johnson (*The First 200 Years of Monty Python*), and Robert Hewison (*Monty Python: The Case Against*), and the publications *The Times (of London)*, *The New York Times*, and *TV Guide*. But perhaps the most valuable information has come from the Pythons themselves, via books and articles, television and radio interviews, etc. The three most important of these sources are *The Pythons: Autobiography by The Pythons* (2003, edited by Bob McCabe) and Michael Palin's two volumes of diaries, *The Python Years* (2006) and *Halfway to Hollywood* (2009), each one an essential reference for any Python addict's library.

Douglas McCall
Fall 2013

THE CHRONOLOGICAL LISTING

1 January 12–February 16, 1969
  The comedy series *The Complete and Utter History of Britain*, written by and starring **Michael Palin** and **Terry Jones**, airs on ITV (produced by London Weekend Television). The six-episode series, which presents historical events and personalities in a modern, television-style manner, is produced by Humphrey Barclay, who had also produced the first series of the children's series *Do Not Adjust Your Set* (co-starring **Palin** and **Jones**) in 1968.

2 January 12–April 6, 1969
  The seventh series of the sketch comedy show *I'm Sorry I'll Read That Again*, co-starring **John Cleese**, airs on BBC Radio 1 & 2. The show, which began as a radio broadcast of the Cambridge Circus revue in 1963, also stars Tim Brooke-Taylor, Graeme Garden, David Hatch, Jo Kendall, and Bill Oddie. **Cleese** has been a regular on the show since 1966 and will continue performing on the program until its final series in 1973. 13 episodes.

3 January 12, 1969
  The Complete and Utter History of Britain (TV episode: ITV/LWT). "From the Dawn of History to the Norman Conquest." This first episode of the series is actually a combination of the first two recorded episodes. The best parts of each episode were edited together to form a single half-hour show. Starring **Michael Palin** and **Terry Jones**, with Colin Gordon (Narrator), Roddy Maude-Roxby (Prof. Weaver), Wallas Eaton, Melinda May, Diana Quick, Ted Carson, Colin Cunningham, John Hughman, and Johnny Vyvyan. Written by **Michael Palin** and **Terry Jones**. Directed by Maurice Murphy.

4 January 19, 1969
  The Complete and Utter History of Britain (TV episode: ITV/LWT). "Richard the Lionheart to Robin the Hood." Second show of the series looks at the 12th century and includes: "Richard I," "Adverts for Water, Food, and Women," "Magna Carta," "Ted Lupini — Royal Court Jester," "Hubert Fitzroy — Food Taster," and "Robin Hood." Starring **Michael Palin** and **Terry Jones**, with Colin Gordon (Narrator), Roddy Maude-Roxby (Prof. Weaver), Wallas Eaton, Diana Quick, Melinda May, Ted Carson, Colin Cunningham, John Hughman, and Johnny Vyvyan. Written by **Michael Palin** and **Terry Jones**. Directed by Maurice Murphy.

5 January 26, 1969
  The Complete and Utter History of Britain (TV episode: ITV/LWT). "Edward the First to Richard the Last." Third show of the series. Starring **Michael Palin** and **Terry Jones**, with Wallas Eaton, Colin Gordon, Roddy Maude-Roxby, Melinda May, and Diana Quick. Written by **Michael Palin** and **Terry Jones**. Directed by Maurice Murphy.

6 February 2, 1969
  The Complete and Utter History of Britain (TV episode: ITV/LWT). "Perkin Warbeck to Bloody Mary." Fourth show of the series. Starring **Michael Palin** and **Terry Jones**, with Wallas Eaton, Colin Gordon, Roddy Maude-Roxby, Melinda May, and Diana Quick. Written by **Michael Palin** and **Terry Jones**. Directed by Maurice Murphy.

7 February 9, 1969
  The Complete and Utter History of Britain (TV episode: ITV/LWT). "The Great and Glorious Age of Elizabeth." Fifth show of the series. Starring **Michael Palin** and **Terry Jones**, with Wallas Eaton, Colin Gordon, Roddy Maude-Roxby, Melinda May, and Diana Quick. Written by **Michael Palin** and **Terry Jones**. Directed by Maurice Murphy.

8 February 12, 1969
Cilla (TV episode: BBC1). Music-variety show hosted by singer Cilla Black. Guest-stars **Graham Chapman**, Tim Brooke-Taylor, and Graeme Garden perform the sketches "Top of the Form" and "Ritual Japanese Wrestling." Black's other guests are Dusty Springfield, Georgie Fame, and Tom Ward. Directed by Vernon Lawrence. Produced by Michael Hurll. Note: **Chapman** and Brooke-Taylor previously co-starred (with **John Cleese**, Marty Feldman, and Aimi MacDonald) in the 1967 series *At Last the 1948 Show*.

9 February 16, 1969
The Complete and Utter History of Britain (TV episode: ITV/LWT). "James the McFirst to Oliver Cromwell." Sixth and last show of the series. Starring **Michael Palin** and **Terry Jones**, with Wallas Eaton, Colin Gordon, Roddy Maude-Roxby, Melinda May, and Diana Quick. Written by **Michael Palin** and **Terry Jones**. Directed by Maurice Murphy.

10 February 19–May 14, 1969
The second series of *Do Not Adjust Your Set* airs on ITV (Thames Television). The children-oriented sketch comedy show stars future Python members **Michael Palin**, **Terry Jones**, **Eric Idle**, and **Terry Gilliam** (animation). Produced by Ian Davidson, the 13-episode series also stars Denise Coffey, David Jason, and The Bonzo Dog Doo-Dah Band (Vivian Stanshall, Neil Innes, et al.). The first series, produced by Humphrey Barclay, aired from Dec. 26, 1967, to Mar. 28, 1968.

11 Spring 1969
Terry Jones marries Alison Telfer in Camberwell, South London. Telfer, a technician in the Botany Department of London University, has since become a successful biochemist specializing in photosynthesis at Imperial College in London. The couple buys a three-story Victorian house in London's Grove Park between Camberwell and Dulwich.

12 March–May 1969
The Magic Christian, a comedy in which **John Cleese** and **Graham Chapman** have small roles (they also contributed to the script), is filmed at Twickenham Studios, England.

13 March 17, 1969
It's Marty Feldman (TV special: BBC2). Special program compiled from episodes of the 1968–69 comedy starring Marty Feldman and featuring material written by **John Cleese**, **Graham Chapman**, **Terry Jones**, and **Michael Palin**. Includes the sketch "A Day in the Life of a Stuntman," written by **Palin** & **Jones**. This show is the BBC entry for the 1969 Golden Rose of Montreux Award. With **Michael Palin**, **Terry Jones**, Tim Brooke-Taylor, John Junkin, Ann Lancaster, and Mary Miller. Written by Marty Feldman and Barry Took, with additional material by **Michael Palin** and **Terry Jones**. Produced by Dennis Main Wilson and Roger Race.

14 April 11–May 30, 1969
The first series of the sitcom/sketch-comedy show *Hark at Barker*, starring Ronnie Barker, airs on ITV (London Weekend Television). **Eric Idle** is one of the writers. Eight episodes.

15 April 17, 1969
Michael Palin begins keeping a diary, a habit he will continue for the next forty-plus years. His diaries will eventually be published in two volumes: *Diaries 1969–1979: The Python Years* (2006) and *Halfway to Hollywood: Diaries 1980–1988* (2009).

16 Early May 1969
A meeting to discuss the start of a new comedy show is held at **John Cleese**'s Basil Street flat in Knightsbridge, London. The meeting is attended by **Cleese**, his writing partner **Graham Chapman**, and *Do Not Adjust Your Set* stars **Michael Palin**, **Terry Jones**, **Eric Idle**, and **Terry Gilliam**. Most of the group had previously worked together on *The Frost Report* (1966–67). **Cleese**, who also appeared with **Chapman** and **Palin** in the 1968 TV special *How to Irritate People*, had previously collaborated with animator **Gilliam** on a photo-shoot for the American humor magazine *Help!* (in 1965).

17 May 23, 1969
Graham Chapman, **John Cleese**, **Terry Gilliam**, **Eric Idle**, **Terry Jones**, **Michael Palin**, directors Ian MacNaughton and John Howard Davies, and Barry Took (writer and comedy advisor to the BBC) gather together in a conference room of BBC Television Centre with Michael Mills, Head of Comedy, to discuss an idea for a new comedy show, which will eventually become *Monty Python's Flying Circus*. During what **Palin** would later call "the world's worst job interview," the future Pythons are unable to answer any of Mills' questions (Will there be music? Will there be guest stars? What's the show called?), but in the end they are given 13 shows.

18 June–September 1969
The Rise and Rise of Michael Rimmer, starring Peter Cook and co-written by Cook, Kevin Billington, **John Cleese** and **Graham Chapman**, is filmed in London. **Cleese** and **Chapman** also have small roles in the film.

19 June 1969
The Best House in London (Feature film: MGM) opens in the U.K. Farce about a government-sponsored brothel in Victorian London. **John Cleese**, in one of his earliest film roles (he had previously appeared in 1968's *Interlude* and *The Bliss of Mrs. Blossom*), plays Jones in a scene with George Sanders. Also starring David Hemmings, Joanna Pettet, Dany Robin, Warren Mitchell, and William Rushton. Written by Denis Norden. Directed by Philip Saville. Produced by Philip Breen and Kurt Unger. Opens in the U.S. on July 30.

20 July 7, 1969
Eric Idle marries Lyn Ashley, an Australian actress, in Kensington, London. She will later appear in episodes of both *Monty Python's Flying Circus* and **Idle**'s *Rutland Weekend Television*.

21 July 8, 1969
First day of filming on *Bunn, Wackett, Buzzard, Stubble, and Boot* (working title for what will become *Monty Python's Flying Circus*). Sketches filmed include "The Wacky Queen" (Oct. 12 episode) and "Bicycle Repair Man" (Oct. 19 episode). The Queen scenes are shot at historic Ham House in London.

22 July 12–October 3, 1969
The first series of the sitcom *Doctor in the House*, based on the novel by Richard Gordon and starring Barry Evans as Dr. Michael Upton, airs on ITV (London Weekend Television). **Graham Chapman** and **John Cleese** write the first episode, while **Chapman** collaborates with Barry Cryer on three later episodes (Aug. 30, Sept. 6 & Oct. 3). **Chapman** and **Cleese** will also write scripts (separately) for the follow-up series, *Doctor at Large*, in 1971.

23 July 12, 1969
Doctor in the House (TV episode: ITV/LWT). "Why Do You Want to Be a Doctor?" After a nerve-wracking interview, Michael Upton is accepted to St. Swithin's, only to have his first day complicated by a dismembered arm. **John Cleese** and **Graham Chapman** wrote this first episode of one of London Weekend Television's most successful comedy series, based on the stories by Richard Gordon. The "Doctor" stories also spawned a series of films (1954–70), the last of which, *Doctor in Trouble*, co-stars **Chapman**. Starring Barry Evans. Directed by David Askey. Produced by Humphrey Barclay.

24 Late July 1969
The BBC informs **Cleese**, **Palin**, **Idle**, et al. that they need to settle on a title for their new comedy series, which has already begun filming. Working titles have so far included: "Owl Stretching Time," "Bunn, Wackett, Buzzard, Stubble and Boot," "A Horse, a Spoon and a Basin," and "The Toad Elevating Moment." The group gathers in **Cleese**'s Basil Street flat (in Knightsbridge) for a brainstorming session. They agree on "Flying Circus" (a title the BBC favors) but still need to decide *whose* "Flying Circus" it will be. They play around with various names, like "Arthur Megapode" and "Gwen Dibley" (a real person's name, which **Palin** had seen in a magazine), until someone (probably **Cleese**) comes up with "Python" as a surname. With the addition of "Monty" (probably from **Idle**), the show's title —*Monty Python's Flying Circus*— is born.

25 August 18, 1969
The *Flying Circus* sketch "Confuse-A-Cat" (Nov. 16 episode) is filmed at Edenfield Gardens, Worcester Park, Surrey.

26 August 30, 1969
The recordings for the first series of *Monty Python's Flying Circus* begin at BBC Television Centre in London. The first episode recorded is "Sex & Violence," which includes the sketches "Flying Sheep" and "A Man with Three Buttocks." It is the second show aired (on Oct. 12).

27 August 30, 1969
Doctor in the House (TV episode: ITV/LWT). "The War of the Mascots." A rival medical school steals St. Swithins' mascot. Eighth show of the first series. Starring Barry Evans. Written by **Graham Chapman** and Barry Cryer. Directed by Maurice Murphy.

28 September 6, 1969
Doctor in the House (TV episode: ITV/LWT). "Getting the Bird." Upton is set up on a date with a nurse nicknamed "Rigor Mortis" (Helen Fraser). Ninth show of the first series. Starring Barry Evans. Written by **Graham Chapman** and Barry Cryer. Directed by Maurice Murphy.

29 September 7, 1969
Episode 1 ("Whither Canada") of *Monty Python's Flying Circus* is recorded. It is the second show recorded but the first aired (on Oct. 5).

30 September 14, 1969
Episode 3 ("How to Recognise Different Types of Trees from Quite a Long Way Away") of *Monty Python's Flying Circus* is recorded.

31 September 21, 1969
Episode 4 ("Owl-Stretching Time") of *Monty Python's Flying Circus* is recorded.

32 October 3, 1969
Episode 5 ("Man's Crisis of Identity in the Latter Half of the Twentieth Century") of *Monty Python's Flying Circus* is recorded.

33 October 3, 1969
Doctor in the House (TV episode: ITV/LWT). "Pass or Fail." Panic sets in as exam day approaches. Thirteenth (and last) show of the first series. Starring Barry Evans. Written by **Graham Chapman** and Barry Cryer. Directed by Bill Turner.

34 October 5–26, November 23, 1969–January 11, 1970
The first series of *Monty Python's Flying Circus* is aired on BBC1. This ground-breaking comedy program features a mixture of sketches, filmed sequences, and animation (provided by American member **Terry Gilliam**). Memorable sketches in the first series include "The Pet Shop," "Nudge, Nudge," "Restaurant Sketch," "The Upper-Class Twit of the Year," "Crunchy Frog," and "The Lumberjack Song." Each of this series' 13 episodes begins with the one-word introduction "It's...," uttered by **Michael Palin**'s hermit character, followed by the show's theme music (Sousa's "Liberty Bell" march) accompanying **Gilliam**'s animated title sequence. Directors on the show are John Howard Davies (first four shows only) and Ian MacNaughton. Recorded Aug. 30, 1970–Jan. 4, 1970.
Awards: BAFTA-winner, Special Award and Television Graphics (**Terry Gilliam**).
Reviews: Norman Hare (*Daily Telegraph*, Oct. 6, 1969): "*Monty Python's Flying Circus* came to town last night on BBC 1 television. Most circuses get by without scriptwriters but this one had five, doubling up as clowns performing what they had written under the ringmastership of Ian McNaughton. The comedy was sophisticated and had much of the delightful absurdity which has not been seen on television since the Marty show"; Richard Last (*The Sun*, Oct. 6, 1969): "...it might have been worse. That title, I mean. Anyway, I hope M. Python and associates will prove a winner"; *The Observer* (Oct. 26, 1969): "This new ... show on BBC 1, television comedy that's actually funny, is rapidly becoming cult viewing. It has been described as the first successful attempt at visual Goonery..."; Henry Raynor (*The Times* [London], Nov. 29, 1969): "Many of our activities and convictions need only a slight nudge to the left to become patently lunatic, and *Monty Python* nudges vigorously but unobtrusively."

35 October 5, 1969
Monty Python's Flying Circus (TV episode: BBC1). "Whither Canada?" (Episode 1). The first show of the first series is aired at 10:55 on a Sunday night. Though it is the first show aired, it was actually the second to be recorded (on Sept. 7). In fact, five shows had been recorded (between Aug. 30 and Oct. 3) before the series premiered. Includes: "It's Wolfgang Amadeus Mozart: Famous Deaths," "Italian Lesson," "Whizzo Butter," "It's the Arts: Sir Edward Ross/Arthur 'Two Sheds' Jackson/Picasso-Cycling Race," "Sit Up/Dancing Soldiers/Falling Pig [anim]," and "The Funniest Joke in the World." Conceived, written & performed by **Graham Chapman, John Cleese, Terry Gilliam, Eric Idle, Terry Jones,** and **Michael Palin**. With Carol Cleveland. Animations by **Terry Gilliam**. Film direction by Ian MacNaughton. Produced & directed by John Howard Davies.

36 October 10, 1969
Episode 7 ("You're No Fun Any More") of *Monty Python's Flying Circus* is recorded. It is the sixth show recorded.

37 October 12, 1969
Monty Python's Flying Circus (TV episode: BBC1). "Sex and Violence" (Episode 2). Second show of the first series, but the first recorded (on Aug. 30). Includes: "Flying Sheep," "French Lecture on Sheep-Aircraft," "Pepperpots Discuss French Philosophers," "The Thinker [anim]," "A Man with Three Buttocks," "A Man with Two Noses," "Musical Mice," "Marriage Guidance Counsellor," "The Wacky Queen," "Working-Class Playwright," "Flying Sheep [anim]," "The Wrestling Epilogue (A Question of Belief)," "Cowboy/Grave/Defacement/Baby Carriage/Musical Statue [anim]," and "The World Around Us: The Mouse Problem." Conceived, written & performed by **Graham Chapman, John Cleese, Terry Gilliam, Eric Idle, Terry Jones,** and **Michael Palin**. With Carol Cleveland. Animations by **Terry Gilliam**. Film direction by Ian MacNaughton. Produced & directed by John Howard Davies.

38   October 19, 1969

Monty Python's Flying Circus (TV episode: BBC1). "How to Recognise Different Types of Trees from Quite a Long Way Away" (Episode 3). Third show of the first series (recorded Sept. 14). Includes: "Court Room (Mrs. Fiona Lewis/Witness in Coffin/Cardinal Richelieu/Dim of the Yard)," "The Larch," "Bicycle Repair Man," "Commie-Hater," "Storytime," "Animals and Clergy [anim]," "Donkey Rides," "Restaurant Sketch (Dirty Fork)," "Purchase a Past [anim]," "Seduced Milkmen," "Stolen Newsreader," "Children's Interview," and "Nudge, Nudge." Conceived, written & performed by **Graham Chapman, John Cleese, Terry Gilliam, Eric Idle, Terry Jones,** and **Michael Palin**. With Ian Davidson. Animations by **Terry Gilliam**. Film direction by Ian MacNaughton. Produced & directed by John Howard Davies. Note: The book **Idle** is holding in the "Storytime" sketch is actually Richard Scarry's *What Do People Do All Day?* (1968).

39   October 26, 1969

Monty Python's Flying Circus (TV episode: BBC1). "Owl Stretching Time" (Episode 4). Fourth show of the first series (recorded Sept. 21). Includes: "Live from the Cardiff Rooms, Libya (song: "And Did Those Teeth…")," "Art Gallery," "An Art Critic (Edible Paintings)," "Colonel (It's a Man's Life in the Modern Army)," "Taking Your Clothes Off in Public," "Colonel," "Self-Defense Against Fresh Fruit," "Changing on the Beach (Sedan Chair)," "Rustic Monologue/Colonel," and "Lemming of the BDA." Conceived, written & performed by **Graham Chapman, John Cleese, Terry Gilliam, Eric Idle, Terry Jones,** and **Michael Palin**. With Dick Vosburgh, Carol Cleveland, and Katya Wyeth. Animations by **Terry Gilliam**. Film direction by Ian MacNaughton. Produced & directed by John Howard Davies.

40   October 27, 1969
John Cleese turns 30.

41   November 1969

Cry of the Banshee (Feature film). **Terry Gilliam** designed the animated title sequence for this horror tale starring Vincent Price as a 16th-century English magistrate whose life is imperiled by a vengeful witch. Directed by Gordon Hessler. Released in U.S. July 22, 1970 (American International Pictures).

42   November 5, 1969

Episode 6 ("It's the Arts") of *Monty Python's Flying Circus* is recorded. It is the seventh show recorded.

43   November 16, 1969

Monty Python's Flying Circus (TV episode: BBC1). "Man's Crisis of Identity in the Latter Half of the 20th Century" (Episode 5). Fifth show of the first series (recorded Oct. 3). Includes: "Confuse-A-Cat Ltd.," "The Smuggler," "A Duck, a Cat, and a Lizard (discussion)," "Man in the Street Interviews," "Police Raid," "Newsreader Arrested," "Erotic Film," "Charles Fatless [anim]," "Silly Job Interview," "Careers Advisory Board," and "Burglar/Encyclopedia Salesman." Conceived, written & performed by **Graham Chapman, John Cleese, Terry Gilliam, Eric Idle, Terry Jones,** and **Michael Palin**. With Carol Cleveland. Animations by **Terry Gilliam**. Film direction by John Howard Davies. Produced & directed by Ian MacNaughton.

44   November 23, 1969

Monty Python's Flying Circus (TV episode: BBC1). "It's the Arts" (Episode 6). Sixth show of the first series (recorded Nov. 5). Includes: "Arthur Figgis," "It's the Arts: Johann Gambolputty … of Ulm," "David and the Fig Leaf [anim]," "Non-Illegal Robbery," "Crunchy Frog," "The Dull Life of a City Stockbroker," "Superhero [anim]," "Red Indian in Theatre," "A Scotsman on a Horse," "Vicious Baby Carriage [anim]," and "Twentieth-Century Vole (Irving C. Saltzberg)." Conceived, written & performed by **Graham Chapman, John Cleese, Terry Gilliam, Eric Idle, Terry Jones,** and **Michael Palin**. With Ian Davidson. Animations by **Terry Gilliam**. Produced & directed by Ian MacNaughton.

45   November 25, 1969

Episode 8 ("Full Frontal Nudity") of *Monty Python's Flying Circus* is recorded.

46   November 30, 1969

Episode 10 ("Untitled") of *Monty Python's Flying Circus* is recorded. It is the ninth show recorded.

47   November 30, 1969

Monty Python's Flying Circus (TV episode: BBC1). "You're No Fun Any More" (Episode 7) Seventh show of the first series (recorded Oct. 10). Includes: "Camel Spotting," "You're No Fun Anymore," "The Audit," and "Science Fiction Sketch: Man Turns into Scotsman, Angus Podgorny, Police Station, Blancmanges Playing Tennis." Conceived, written & performed by **Graham Chapman, John Cleese, Terry Gilliam, Eric Idle, Terry Jones,** and **Michael Palin**. With Donna Reading. Animations by **Terry Gilliam**. Produced & directed by Ian MacNaughton.

48 December 7, 1969
Episode 9 ("The Ant, an Introduction") of *Monty Python's Flying Circus* is recorded. It is the tenth show recorded.

49 December 7, 1969
Monty Python's Flying Circus (TV episode: BBC1). "Full Frontal Nudity" (Episode 8). Eighth show of the first series (recorded Nov. 25). Includes: "Leaving the Army/Army Protection Racket/Colonel (Silly)," "Full Frontal Nudity [anim]," "An Art Critic (The Place of the Nude)," "Buying a Bed," "Colonel (Silly)," "Hermits/Colonel (Silly)," "Meat Grinder/Venus Dancing [anim]," "The Pet Shop (Dead Parrot)," "The Flasher," and "Hell's Grannies/Colonel (Silly)." Conceived, written & performed by **Graham Chapman, John Cleese, Terry Gilliam, Eric Idle, Terry Jones,** and **Michael Palin**. With Carol Cleveland, Kathja Wyeth, and Rita Davies. Animations by **Terry Gilliam**. Produced & directed by Ian MacNaughton.

50 December 11, 1969
The Magic Christian (Feature film: Commonwealth United/Grand Films), world premiere in London. Comedy about an eccentric millionaire (Peter Seller) and his adopted son (Ringo Starr) who go about proving that people will do anything for money. **John Cleese** plays Mr. Dougdale, a director in Sotheby's. **Graham Chapman** plays an Oxford stroke. Also starring Richard Attenborough, Lawrence Harvey, Christopher Lee, Spike Milligan, Yul Brynner, Roman Polanski, Raquel Welch, and Wilfrid Hyde-White. Written by Terry Southern, Joseph McGrath and Peter Sellers, with additional material by **John Cleese** and **Graham Chapman**. Directed by Joseph McGrath. Premieres in the U.S. in January 1970.

51 December 14, 1969
Episode 11 ("The Royal Philharmonic Orchestra Goes to the Bathroom") of *Monty Python's Flying Circus* is recorded.

52 December 14, 1969
Monty Python's Flying Circus (TV episode: BBC1). "The Ant, an Introduction" (Episode 9). Ninth show of the first series (recorded Dec. 7). Includes: "Llamas," "A Man with a Tape Recorder Up His Nose," "Kilimanjaro Expedition (Sir George Head)," "A Man with a Tape Recorder Up His Brother's Nose," "Clergyman Selling Encyclopedias [anim]," "Homicidal Barber/The Lumberjack Song," "Gumby Crooner," "The Refreshment Room at Bletchley," "Brian Islam and Brucie [anim]," "Hunting Film," and "The Visitors." Conceived, written & performed by **Graham Chapman, John Cleese, Terry Gilliam, Eric Idle, Terry Jones,** and **Michael Palin**. With Carol Cleveland, Connie Booth, and The Fred Tomlinson Singers. Animations by **Terry Gilliam**. Produced & directed by Ian MacNaughton. Note: Connie Booth, who plays the lumberjack's sweetheart in this episode, is the wife of **John Cleese**. They were married in February 1968.

53 December 21, 1969
Episode 12 ("The Naked Ant") of *Monty Python's Flying Circus* is recorded.

54 December 21, 1969
Monty Python's Flying Circus (TV episode: BBC1). "Untitled" (Episode 10). Tenth show of the first series (recorded Nov. 30). Includes: "Walk-On Part in Sketch," "Bank Robber in Lingerie Shop," "David Unction," "It's a Tree (Arthur Tree)," "Wooden Impressions [anim]," "Vocational Guidance Counsellor," "David Unction," "Ron Obvious (The First Man to Jump the Channel)," "Pet Conversions," "Gorilla Librarian," "Letters to 'Daily Mirror,'" "Strangers in the Night," and "Animals Eating [anim]." Conceived, written & performed by **Graham Chapman, John Cleese, Terry Gilliam, Eric Idle, Terry Jones,** and **Michael Palin**. With Barry Cryer, Carolae Donoghue, and Ian Davidson. Animations by **Terry Gilliam**. Produced & directed by Ian MacNaughton.

55 December 28, 1969
Monty Python's Flying Circus (TV episode: BBC1). "The Royal Philharmonic Orchestra Goes to the Bathroom" (Episode 11). Eleventh show of the first series (recorded Dec. 14). Includes: "The Royal Philharmonic Orchestra Goes to the Bathroom," "Letters," "The World of History (interruptions)," "Hearses Racing," "Agatha Christie Sketch (Inspector Tiger)," "Undertakers," "Jimmy Buzzard Interview," "Undertakers," "Ladies/Open War [anim]," "Interesting People," "Undertakers," "More Jimmy Buzzard," "Gravediggers," "Coffins [anim]," "The World of History: Social Legislation in the 18th Century, The Battle of Trafalgar, The Batley Townswomens' Guild's Re-enactment of The Battle of Pearl Harbor," and "Undertakers." Conceived, written & performed by **Graham Chapman, John Cleese, Terry Gilliam, Eric Idle, Terry Jones,** and **Michael Palin**. With Carol Cleveland, Ian Davidson, and Flanagan. Animations by **Terry Gilliam**. Produced & directed by Ian MacNaughton.

56 1969
Beauty and the Beast (Pantomime) opens at the Watford Palace Theatre. Written by **Michael Palin** and **Terry Jones**, who had previously penned the 1968 pantomime, *Aladdin*, also for the Watford Palace Theatre.

57 January 1970
John Cleese meets with Victor Lownes (head of the *Playboy* Organization in the U.K.) at the Playboy Club in London. Lownes, an American and a fan of *Flying Circus*, suggests the idea of making a film of the show's best bits as a way of introducing Python to America. A deal is made and Lownes agrees to put up £100,000 to finance the film. Filming begins in October 1970 on what will be called *And Now for Something Completely Different*.

58 January 4, 1970
Episode 13 ("Intermission"), the last show of the first series of *Monty Python's Flying Circus*, is recorded.

59 January 4, 1970
Monty Python's Flying Circus (TV episode: BBC1). "The Naked Ant" (Episode 12). Twelfth show of the first series (recorded Dec. 21, 1969). Includes: "A Signalbox Somewhere Near Hove," "Falling from Building," "Falling People/Magician/Opening Titles [anim]," "Spectrum," "Mr. Hilter/The North Minehead Bye-Election," "Police Station (Silly Voices)," "The Upper-Class Twit of the Year," "Smoking a Pipe [anim]," "Ken Shabby," and "How Far Can a Minister Fall? (A Party Political Broadcast by the Wood Party)." Conceived, written & performed by **Graham Chapman**, **John Cleese**, **Terry Gilliam**, **Eric Idle**, **Terry Jones**, and **Michael Palin**. With Connie Booth and Flanagan. Animations by **Terry Gilliam**. Produced & directed by Ian MacNaughton.

60 January 11, 1970
Monty Python's Flying Circus (TV episode: BBC1). "Intermission" (Episode 13). Thirteenth and last show of the first series (recorded Jan. 4). Includes: "Intermission," "Intermission [anim]," "Restaurant (Abuse/Cannibalism)," "Pearls for Swine (adverts): Soho Motors/La Gondola Restaurant," "Albatross," "Come Back to My Place," "Me, Doctor," "Gumbys," "Historical Impersonations," "Wishes (Schoolboys/Businessmen Interview)," "Probe Around (Police Fairy Stories)," "Mr. Attila the Hun," "Letters," "Psychiatrist (Dr. Larch)," and "Operating Theatre (Squatters)." Conceived, written & performed by **Graham Chapman**, **John Cleese**, **Terry Gilliam**, **Eric Idle**, **Terry Jones**, and **Michael Palin**. With Carol Cleveland and David Ballantyne. Animations by **Terry Gilliam**. Produced & directed by Ian MacNaughton.

61 January 12, 1970
Late Night Line Up (TV talk show: BBC2). Hosted by Joan Bakewell, Michael Dean, Tony Bilbow, and Sheridan Morley. Guests: **John Cleese**, **Graham Chapman**, **Terry Gilliam**, **Eric Idle**, and Carol Cleveland. Produced by Mike Fentiman.

62 February 15–May 10, 1970
The eighth series of the sketch-comedy show *I'm Sorry I'll Read That Again*, co-starring **John Cleese**, airs on BBC Radio 2 (13 episodes). The show also stars Tim Brooke-Taylor, Graeme Garden, David Hatch, Jo Kendall, and Bill Oddie.

63 March 30, 1970
Marty Amok (TV special: BBC1). Comedy special starring Marty Feldman, with John Junkin, Robert Dhéry, Tim Brooke-Taylor, Mary Miller, and others. Sketches include "Bookshop," which Feldman originally performed with **John Cleese** on *At Last the 1948 Show* (1967). Written by Marty Feldman, Barry Took, John Mortimer, Brian Cook, **Terry Jones**, and **Michael Palin**. Directed by Roger Race. Produced by Michael Mills.

64 April 30, 1970
An episode from the first series of *Monty Python's Flying Circus* is shown in the non-competitive section of the 1970 Montreux Television Festival. The following year the Pythons will assemble a special edition of the program to compete in the festival.

65 May 2, 1970
The Pythons record their first record album before a small audience at Camden Theatre in Camden Town, London. The record, containing material from the first series of *Monty Python's Flying Circus*, is produced on a small budget by BBC Enterprises.

66 May 11–22, 1970
The Pythons spend two weeks in the town of Torquay, in Devon, England, filming bits for the TV show. During the filming **John Cleese** and **Eric Idle** stay at the Gleneagles Hotel near Torquay, which is run by a man named Donald Sinclair who, as **Cleese** put it years later, "was wonderfully rude." **Cleese** uses this character in a *Doctor at Large* episode he writes in 1971 and again, more famously, in his celebrated sitcom *Fawlty Towers* (1975, 79).

67 May 19–21, 1970
The Pythons film the sketch "Scott of the Antarctic/Sahara" (Episode 23 of *Flying Circus*) at Goodrington Sands in Paignton, Devon. The episode is recorded before a studio audience on July 2 and airs Dec. 1.

68 June 16, 1970
Doctor in Trouble (Feature film: Rank Organisation) opens in the U.K. Comedy about a doctor's misadventures on an ocean liner. **Graham Chapman**, a frequent writer on the "Doctor" TV series (*Doctor in the House*, *Doctor at Large*, etc.), plays Roddy the photographer in this seventh (and last) entry in the "Doctor" film series, which began in 1954. Starring Leslie Phillips, Harry Secombe, Angela Scoular, Irene Handl, Robert Morley, and Simon Dee. Written by Jack Davies. Directed by Ralph Thomas. Produced by Betty Box and Ralph Thomas.

69 June 25, 1970
The recordings for the second series of *Monty Python's Flying Circus* begin. The first show recorded is "Spam" (episode 25), which will air Dec. 15.

70 June 28, 1970
Oh Hampstead (Stage show). The Pythons perform in this benefit show staged at St. Pancras Town Hall, London. Sketches include "Pet Shop" (**John Cleese** and **Michael Palin**) and "Minister Whose Legs Fall Off" (**Graham Chapman** and **Terry Jones**). The show is a fundraiser for Labour MP Ben Whitaker of Hampstead. Directed by John Neville.

71 July 2, 1970
Episodes 23 ("Scott of the Antarctic") and 15 ("The Spanish Inquisition") of *Monty Python's Flying Circus* are recorded.

72 July 4, 1970
The Clever Stupid Game (Radio show: BBC Radio 4). Guest: **John Cleese**.

73 July 9, 1970
Episode 14 ("Face the Press") of *Monty Python's Flying Circus* is recorded.

74 July 16, 1970
Episode 16 ("Déjà Vu") of *Monty Python's Flying Circus* is recorded.

75 July 23, 1970
Episode 24 ("How Not to Be Seen") of *Monty Python's Flying Circus* is recorded.

76 August 1970
The Pythons form their own company, Python Productions Ltd.

77 August 5, 1970
Nationwide (TV show: BBC1). News magazine. Brian Ash talks to **Terry Gilliam** about his animation work on *Flying Circus*. **Gilliam** demonstrates the process by showing how he created "David and the Fig Leaf" (from Episode 6).

78 Fall 1970
Monty Python's Flying Circus (Record: BBC Records REB 73M) is released in the U.K. Python's first record album, consisting of material from the TV show's first series, was recorded in mono before a live audience at Camden Theatre (on May 2). Tracks: "Flying Sheep," "Television Interviews (A Man with Three Buttocks)," "Trade Description Act (Whizzo Chocolates)," "Nudge, Nudge," "The Mouse Problem," "Buying a Bed," "Interesting People," "The Barber (Homicidal Barber/Lumberjack Song)," "An Art Critic (The Place of the Nude)," "Interviews (Sir Edward Ross)," "More Television Interviews (Arthur 'Two Sheds' Jackson)," "Children's Stories (Storytime)," "The Visitors," "The Cinema (Albatross)," "The North Minehead Bye-Election," "Me, Doctor," "Pet Shop," and "Self-Defense." Written & performed by **Graham Chapman**, **John Cleese**, **Terry Gilliam**, **Eric Idle**, **Terry Jones**, and **Michael Palin**, with Carol Cleveland and The Fred Tomlinson Singers. Sleeve design by **Terry Gilliam**. Produced by Ian MacNaughton and BBC Television. Released in the U.S. on Pye Records PYE 12116 (1975). Note: Unhappy with the results of this BBC-produced recording, the group signs with Charisma Records in 1971.

79 Fall 1970
Monty Python's Flying Circus begins airing on the Canadian Broadcasting Corporation (CBC).

80 September 10, 1970
Episodes 18 ("Live from the Grill-O-Mat") and 19 ("It's a Living") of *Monty Python's Flying Circus* are recorded.

81 September 12–December 5, 1970
The third and final series of the sitcom *No, That's Me Over Here* airs on ITV (produced by London Weekend Television). The show, which stars Ronnie Corbett and Rosemary Leach, was created in 1967 by **Graham Chapman**, Barry Cryer & **Eric Idle**. The first two series (in 1967 & 1968) consisted

of six episodes each. The third series, written by Cryer and **Chapman**, consists of 13 episodes.

82 September 15–29, October 20–December 22, 1970

The second series of *Monty Python's Flying Circus* airs on BBC1. It consists of thirteen shows and features many of Python's most memorable sketches, including "The Ministry of Silly Walks," "The Spanish Inquisition," "World Forum," "Bruces," "Spam," "The Piranha Brothers," "The Architect Sketch," and "Undertaker Sketch." The pre-title introductions on this series are made by **John Cleese**'s announcer seated behind a desk ("And now for something completely different"), followed by **Michael Palin**'s hermit ("It's..."). Recorded June 25–Oct. 16, 1970.

Awards: Winner of the Silver Rose (second place) at the 1971 Montreux Television Festival.

Reviews: Stanley Reynolds (*The Times* [London], Sept. 16, 1970, p. 13): "...undoubtedly the funniest British comedy series since the old *Goon Show* ... this is not a cheap show to mount. It would, however, still be an incredible bargain to the BBC at twice the price"; Milton Shulman (*Evening Standard*, Dec. 23, 1970): "A wondrous example of nonsense and anarchic humour ... its success depends upon a blissful disregard of all the rules of TV humour."

83 September 15, 1970

Monty Python's Flying Circus (TV episode: BBC1). "Face the Press" (Episode 14). First show of the second series (recorded July 9). Includes: "Face the Press," "New Cooker Sketch," "Flying European Monarchs/Shaving [anim]," "Prostitute Advert," "The Ministry of Silly Walks," and "Ethel the Frog: The Piranha Brothers." Conceived, written & performed by **Graham Chapman, John Cleese, Terry Gilliam, Eric Idle, Terry Jones,** and **Michael Palin**. With David Ballantyne, John Hughman, and Stanley Mason. Animations by **Terry Gilliam**. Produced & directed by Ian MacNaughton.

84 September 18, 1970

Episode 17 ("The Buzz Aldrin Show") of *Monty Python's Flying Circus* is recorded.

85 September 20, 1970

The Pythons perform in a charity concert (for Medical Aid for Vietnam) at the Questors Theatre in Ealing, London. Other performers include classical guitarist John Williams and the Scottish music duo The Humblebums (Gerry Rafferty and Billy Connolly).

86 September 22, 1970

Monty Python's Flying Circus (TV episode: BBC1). "The Spanish Inquisition" (Episode 15). Second show of the second series (recorded July 2). Includes: "Man-Powered Flight," "The Spanish Inquisition," "Novelty Salesman," "Animated Head [anim]," "Tax on Thingy," "Photos of Uncle Ted/Comfy Chair (Spanish Inquisition)," "I Confess [anim]," "The Semaphore Version of Wuthering Heights/Julius Caesar on an Aldis Lamp," and "Court Room (Charades/Spanish Inquisition)." Conceived, written & performed by **Graham Chapman, John Cleese, Terry Gilliam, Eric Idle, Terry Jones,** and **Michael Palin**. With Carol Cleveland and Marjorie Wilde. Animations by **Terry Gilliam**. Produced & directed by Ian MacNaughton.

87 September 25, 1970

Episode 22 ("How to Recognize Different Parts of the Body") of *Monty Python's Flying Circus* is recorded.

88 September 29, 1970

Monty Python's Flying Circus (TV episode: BBC1). "Déjà Vu" (Episode 16). Third show of the second series (recorded July 16). Includes: "A Bishop Rehearsing," "Flying Lessons," "BALPA Spokesman," "Hijacked Plane (to Luton)," "The Poet McTeagle," "Highland Spokesman," "Growing Hands/Cowboy [anim]," "Psychiatrist Milkman," "Complaints," and "It's the Mind (Déjà Vu)." Conceived, written & performed by **Graham Chapman, John Cleese, Terry Gilliam, Eric Idle, Terry Jones,** and **Michael Palin**. With Carol Cleveland and Jeannette Wild. Animations by **Terry Gilliam**. Produced & directed by Ian MacNaughton.

89 October 2, 1970

Episode 20 ("The Attila the Hun Show") of *Monty Python's Flying Circus* is recorded.

90 October 9, 1970

Episode 21 ("Archaeology Today") of *Monty Python's Flying Circus* is recorded.

91 October 15, 1970

Radio Times (Magazine/U.K.). "The Idea is That Everyone Interferes with Everyone Else's Business," by Anne Chisholm. Behind-the-scenes look at the creation of an episode of *Flying Circus*.

92 October 16, 1970

Episode 26 ("Royal Episode 13"), the last show of the second series of *Monty Python's Flying Circus*, is recorded.

93 October 20, 1970
Monty Python's Flying Circus (TV episode: BBC1). "The Buzz Aldrin Show" (Episode 17). Fourth show of the second series (recorded Sept. 18). Includes: "Metamorphosis [anim]," "Gumbys," "The Architect Sketch," "How to Recognize a Mason," "Anti-Masonic Therapy [anim]," "Gumbys," "Insurance Sketch," "The Bishop," "Living Room on Pavement," "Poets in the Home," "Nude Man," "The Five Frog Curse [anim]/Gumbys," "The Chemist Sketch," "Words Not to Be Used Again," "After-Shave," and "Police Constable Pan-Am." Conceived, written & performed by **Graham Chapman, John Cleese, Terry Gilliam, Eric Idle, Terry Jones,** and **Michael Palin.** With Sandra Richards and Stanley Mason. Animations by **Terry Gilliam.** Produced & directed by Ian MacNaughton.

94 October 22, 1970
The Pythons attend a party at the Playboy Club in London to celebrate the start of production on *And Now for Something Completely Different.*

95 October 26–December 9, 1970
And Now for Something Completely Different, the Pythons' first feature film, is shot over a five-week period in various locations around London on a low budget of £80,000. Most of the interiors are filmed in a former milk depot, A1 Dairy, in Whetstone, North London.

96 October 27, 1970
Monty Python's Flying Circus (TV episode: BBC1). "Live from the Grill-O-Mat" (Episode 18). Fifth show of the second series (recorded Sept. 10). Includes: "Live from the Grill-O-Mat Snack Bar," "Blackmail," "The Royal Society for Putting Things on Top of Other Things," "Escape from Film," "Escape [anim]," "Current Affairs," "Escape continues [anim]," "Accidents Sketch," "Seven Brides for Seven Brothers," "Piggy Bank Hunting [anim]," "The Rude/Polite Butcher," "Ken Clean-Air System (boxer doc)," and "Host on Bus." Conceived, written & performed by **Graham Chapman, John Cleese, Terry Gilliam, Eric Idle, Terry Jones,** and **Michael Palin.** With Carol Cleveland, Ian Davidson, Connie Booth, and Mrs. Idle. Animations by **Terry Gilliam.** Produced & directed by Ian MacNaughton.

97 November 3, 1970
Monty Python's Flying Circus (TV episode: BBC1). "It's a Living" (Episode 19). Sixth show of the second series (recorded Sept. 10). Includes: "It's a Living," "The Time on BBC1," "School Prize-Giving," "Films of L.F. Dibley: If, Rear Window, Finian's Rainbow," "Foreign Secretary," "Book-of-the-Month Club Dung," "Timmy Williams' Coffee Time," "Raymond Luxury-Yacht Interview," "Sexual Athletes [anim]," "Marriage Registry Office," "The Prince and the Black Spot [anim]," and "Election Night Special (Silly and Sensible Parties)." Conceived, written & performed by **Graham Chapman, John Cleese, Terry Gilliam, Eric Idle, Terry Jones,** and **Michael Palin.** With Rita Davies and Ian Davidson. Animations by **Terry Gilliam.** Produced & directed by Ian MacNaughton. Note: In the original version of **Gilliam**'s animation "The Prince and the Black Spot," the Prince dies of cancer. When the show is repeated, BBC censors replace the word "cancer" with "gangrene."

98 November 10, 1970
Monty Python's Flying Circus (TV episode: BBC1). "The Attila the Hun Show" (Episode 20). Seventh show of the second series (recorded Oct. 2). Includes: "The Attila the Hun Show," "Attila the Nun," "Secretary of State Striptease," "Political Groupies," "Ratcatcher/Killer Sheep," "Sheep Bank Robbers" [anim], "The News for Parrots," "Today in Parliament," "The News for Wombats," "Attila the Bun [anim]," "Village Idiots," "Test Match/Epsom Furniture Race," and "Take Your Pick (The Blow on the Head)." Conceived, written & performed by **Graham Chapman, John Cleese, Terry Gilliam, Eric Idle, Terry Jones,** and **Michael Palin.** With Carol Cleveland and Ian Davidson. Animations by **Terry Gilliam.** Produced & directed by Ian MacNaughton.

99 November 12, 1970
The Rise and Rise of Michael Rimmer (Feature film: Warner-Pathé) premieres in the U.K. Satirical comedy about an efficiency expert who, after taking over an advertising agency, soon becomes an MP, a cabinet minister, and eventually Prime Minister. **John Cleese** and **Graham Chapman** co-wrote the script (started in 1966 while they were still working on *The Frost Report*) and also appear in small roles. **Cleese** plays Pumer, a tango-dancing advertising executive; **Chapman** plays Fromage, a client of the agency. Filmed in June–September 1969. Starring Peter Cook, Vanessa Howard, Arthur Lowe, Ronald Fraser, Denholm Elliott, Harold Pinter, Ronnie Corbett, and Valerie Leon. Written by **John Cleese, Graham Chapman,** Peter Cook, and Kevin Billington. Directed by Kevin Billington. Produced by Harry Fine. Executive produced by David Frost.

100 November 12, 1970
The Pythons attend the premiere of *The Rise and Rise of Michael Rimmer* at the Warner Rendezvous cinema in Leicester Square, London.

101 November 14, 1970
John Cleese is elected rector of St. Andrews University in Scotland. He polled 1,072 votes, while the runner-up, broadcaster-journalist Alistair Cooke, polled 656 votes. **Cleese**, who succeeds Lord Learie Constantine, will be installed as rector on Apr. 21, 1971.

102 November 17, 1970
Monty Python's Flying Circus (TV episode: BBC1). "Archaeology Today" (Episode 21). Eighth show of the second series (recorded Oct. 9). Includes: "BBC Previews," "Archaeology [anim]," "Archaeology Today (Flaming Star)," "An Appeal for Sanity (Silly Vicar)," "An Appeal on Behalf of the National Truss (Leapy Lee)," "Registrar of Marriages (Wife Swap)," "Dr. Darling (abandoned sketch)," "Eggs Diamond/Book Ad [anim]," "The Gits," "Mosquito Hunters," "The Judges," "Mrs. Thing and Mrs. Entity," "Beethoven's Mynah Bird," "Colin Mozart (Ratcatcher)," and "Judges Again." Conceived, written & performed by **Graham Chapman, John Cleese, Terry Gilliam, Eric Idle, Terry Jones,** and **Michael Palin**. With Carol Cleveland. Animations by **Terry Gilliam**. Produced & directed by Ian MacNaughton.

103 November 19, 1970
Michael Palin's son, William, is born.

104 November 22, 1970
Terry Gilliam turns 30.

105 November 24, 1970
Monty Python's Flying Circus (TV episode: BBC1). "How to Recognize Different Parts of the Body" (Episode 22). Ninth show of the second series (recorded Sept. 25). Includes: "Bikini-Clad Women & Announcer," "How to Recognize Different Parts of the Body," "Bruces," "Naughty Bits," "Man Who Contradicts People," "Raymond Luxury-Yacht (Plastic Surgery)," "Camp Army Drills," "Dance of the Sugar Plum Fairy/Bus Stop/The Killer Cars [anim]," "The Verrifast Plane Company," "The Batley Townswomen's Guild's Re-enactment of the First Heart Transplant," "Underwater Productions," "Racing Car [anim]," "The Death of Mary Queen of Scots," "Penguin on the TV," "There's Been a Murder," "Sgt. Duckie's Song (song)," and "Bing Tiddle Tiddle Bong (song)." Conceived, written & performed by **Graham Chapman, John Cleese, Terry Gilliam, Eric Idle, Terry Jones,** and **Michael Palin**. With Carol Cleveland, The Fred Tomlinson Singers, Vincent Wong, Roy Gunson, Alexander Curry, Ralph Wood, and John Clement. Animations by **Terry Gilliam**. Produced & directed by Ian MacNaughton.

106 December 1, 1970
Monty Python's Flying Circus (TV episode: BBC1). "Scott of the Antarctic" (Episode 23). Tenth show of the second series (recorded July 2). Includes: "French Subtitled Film (Le Fromage Grand)," "Scott of the Antarctic/Sahara," "Conrad Poohs and His Dancing Teeth [anim]," "Fish License," "Derby Council v. All Blacks," and "Bournemouth Gynaecologists v. Watford Long John Silver Impersonators." Conceived, written & performed by **Graham Chapman, John Cleese, Terry Gilliam, Eric Idle, Terry Jones,** and **Michael Palin**. With Carol Cleveland and Mrs. Idle. Animations by **Terry Gilliam**. Produced & directed by Ian MacNaughton.

107 December 3, 1970
The Listener (Magazine/U.K.). "The Meaning of 'Monty Python,'" by John Carey, p. 791. Article on *Monty Python's Flying Circus*, "at present the funniest comedy programme available." The cover features **Terry Gilliam** art.

108 December 8, 1970
Monty Python's Flying Circus (TV episode: BBC1). "How Not to Be Seen" (Episode 24). Eleventh show of the second series (recorded July 23). Includes: "Conquistador Coffee Campaign," "Repeating Groove," "Ramsay MacDonald Striptease," "Job Hunter," "Chinese Communist Conspiracy/American Defense/Crelm Toothpaste/Shrill Petrol [anim]," "Agatha Christie Sketch (Railway Timetables)," "Neville Shunt," "Theatre Critic (Gavin Millarrrrrrrr)," "Film Director (Teeth)," "City Gents," "Crackport Religions," "How Not to Be Seen," "Crossing the Atlantic on a Tricycle," "Interview in Filing Cabinet," "Yummy, Yummy, Yummy, I've Got Love in My Tummy (pop song performed in packing crates)," and "20-Second Episode Replay." Conceived, written & performed by **Graham Chapman, John Cleese, Terry Gilliam, Eric Idle, Terry Jones,** and **Michael Palin**. With Carol Cleveland. Animations by **Terry Gilliam**. Produced & directed by Ian MacNaughton. Note: A piece of animation featuring Satan and the image of Jesus crucified on a telephone pole

was later cut from the show. The 30-second piece linked "Crackpot Religions" with "How Not to Be Seen."

109   December 14, 1970
The Times (London) (Newspaper/U.K.). "The Rise and Rise of Monty Python," by Stanley Reynolds, p. 6. Article on Python's growing popularity. Includes a piece of **Terry Gilliam**'s art.

110   December 15, 1970
Monty Python's Flying Circus (TV episode: BBC1). "Spam" (Episode 25). Twelfth show of the second series (recorded June 25). Includes: "The Black Eagle," "Hungarian Phrase Book," "Court Room (Phrase Book)," "Protestors/2001 [anim]," "World Forum (Communist Quiz)," "Ypres 1914 (abandoned)," "Art Gallery Strike," "Ypres 1914," "Hospital for Over-Acting," "Gumby Flower-Arranging," and "Spam (song: Spam Song)." Conceived, written & performed by **Graham Chapman**, **John Cleese**, **Terry Gilliam**, **Eric Idle**, **Terry Jones**, and **Michael Palin**. With The Fred Tomlinson Singers. Animations by **Terry Gilliam**. Produced & directed by Ian MacNaughton.

111   December 22, 1970
Monty Python's Flying Circus (TV episode: BBC1). "Royal Episode 13" (Episode 26). Thirteenth and last show of the second series (recorded Oct. 16). Includes: "The Queen Will Be Watching," "Coal Mine (Historical Argument)," "The Toad Elevating Moment: Roundabout Speaker and Ends/Beginnings/Middles of Words," "Crelm Toothpaste [anim]," "Commercials," "Fish Club: How to Feed a Goldfish," "Man Who Collects Bird-Watcher's Eggs," "The Insurance Sketch/Queen Tunes In," "Hospital Run by RSM," "The Exploding Version of 'The Blue Danube,'" "Girls' Boarding School," "Submarine (Pepperpots)," "Lifeboat (Cannibalism)," "Cannibalism [anim]," and "Undertaker Sketch." Conceived, written & performed by **Graham Chapman**, **John Cleese**, **Terry Gilliam**, **Eric Idle**, **Terry Jones**, and **Michael Palin**. With Carol Cleveland and Ian Davidson. Animations by **Terry Gilliam**. Produced & directed by Ian MacNaughton.

112   December 24, 1970
Aladdin (Pantomime) opens at the Citizens' Theatre in Glasgow, Scotland. Christmas pantomime show written by **Michael Palin** and **Terry Jones**, originally staged in 1968 for the Palace Theatre in Watford, England. The show runs until Jan. 23, 1971. **Palin** and **Jones** attend the Jan. 8 performance. Starring Phil McCall, Patti Love, and David Hayman. Directed by Giles Havergal. Note: **Palin** and **Jones** also wrote *Beauty and the Beast* for the Watford Palace Theatre in 1969.

113   January 1971
The Statue (Feature film: Cinerama). Comedy starring David Niven as a language professor who suspects his sculptress wife of infidelity when she makes an 18-foot statue of him — with someone else's private parts. **John Cleese** plays Niven's psychiatrist, Harry. **Graham Chapman** also appears briefly as a news reader. Also starring Virna Lisi, Robert Vaughn, and Ann Bell. Written by Denis Norden, based on a play by Alec Coppel. Directed by Rod Amateau. Produced by Anis Nohra.

114   January 5, 1971
John Gould One-Man Show (Stage show) begins a two-week engagement at the Jeannetta Cochrane Theatre, London. Music-comedy show starring pianist-comedian John Gould with written contributions from **John Cleese**, **Graham Chapman**, **Michael Palin** & **Terry Jones**. Directed by Jonathan Lynn.

115   January 8, 1971
Graham Chapman turns 30.

116   January 31–February 2, 1971
Monty Python give their first live stage performances when they do three midnight shows (Sunday to Tuesday, all sold-out) at the Belgrade Theatre in Coventry, England, as part of the Lanchester Arts Festival. The show is about 90 minutes long and consists of familiar TV sketches, like "Gumby Flower Arranging," "Albatross," and "Pet Shop," each one met with great cheers from the enthusiastic audience of mostly students (many dressed as Gumbys themselves). The group will eventually take the show on the road with a tour of Great Britain and Canada in 1973. Other artists performing at the festival include Andre Previn and Elton John.

117   February 1971
John Cleese's daughter, Cynthia, is born.

118   February 1971
The CBC in Canada drops *Monty Python's Flying Circus* from its schedule, which leads to protest demonstrations by angry fans in Montreal, Toronto, and Winnipeg.

119   February 1971
Ask Aspel (TV show: BBC1). Hosted by Michael

Aspel. The Pythons appear on this program which presents TV clips requested by young viewers. *Flying Circus* is one of the most requested shows. Recorded Feb. 10.

120   February 5, 1971

Six Dates with Barker (TV episode: ITV/LWT). "1971: Come In and Lie Down." While waiting for his first patient, a psychiatrist talks with the gasman (actually the patient) about his problems. **John Cleese** wrote this fifth episode of the six-part comedy series starring Ronnie Barker. For London Weekend Television. Also starring Michael Bates and Linda Beckett. Directed by Maurice Murphy.

121   February 28–September 12, 1971

The sitcom *Doctor at Large*, a sequel to *Doctor in the House* (1969–70) starring Barry Evans, airs on ITV (London Weekend Television). **Graham Chapman** co-writes (with Bernard McKenna) nine episodes, while **John Cleese** writes six. **Cleese** took the writing job after losing quite a bit of money investing in an unsuccessful health club.

122   February 28, 1971

Doctor at Large (TV episode: ITV/LWT). "Now Dr. Upton..." Dr. Upton works in Ear, Nose and Throat. Starring Barry Evans. Written by **Graham Chapman** and Bernard McKenna. Directed by David Askey.

123   March 1971

Monty Python's Flying Circus is chosen as the BBC entry for the Montreux Television Festival in Switzerland. A special edition of the show will be screened on BBC1 on Apr. 16 before competing in May for the festival's top prize, the Golden Rose of Montreux.

124   March 5, 1971

Woman's Hour (Radio show: BBC Radio 4). Guest: **John Cleese**.

125   March 7, 1971

Doctor at Large (TV episode: ITV/LWT). "You've Really Landed Me in It This Time." Upton is left in charge of his friend's practice — and his man-hungry receptionist (Patsy Rowlands). Starring Barry Evans. Written by **Graham Chapman** and Bernard McKenna. Directed by David Askey.

126   March 20, 1971

The Ronnie Barker Yearbook (TV special: BBC1). Sketch-comedy show starring Ronnie Barker, with support from guest-stars Ronnie Corbett, **John Cleese**, Billy Dainty, and Noel Dyson. Followed next week by a special starring Corbett (the other half of the "Two Ronnies"). Written by **Graham Chapman**, **John Cleese**, **Eric Idle**, Ronnie Barker, Barry Cryer, and Dick Vosburgh.

127   March 27, 1971

Ronnie Corbett in Bed (TV special: BBC1). Comedy special starring Ronnie Corbett, with Ronnie Barker, and Howard Keel. Written by **Eric Idle**, Barry Cryer, John Antrobus, David Nobbs, Doug Fisher, Spike Mullins, and Dick Vosburgh. Produced by Terry Hughes.

128   March 29, 1971

John Cleese and **Michael Palin** film "The Fish-Slapping Dance" at Teddington Lock in London. This celebrated, 20-second piece of Python silliness is part of the group's contribution to the May Day special *Euroshow '71*. It will later reappear in Episode 28 (Oct. 26, 1972) of *Flying Circus*.

129   April 10–May 29, 1971

The first series of the sketch-comedy show *The Two Ronnies*, starring Ronnie Barker and Ronnie Corbett, airs on BBC1. **Eric Idle**, **Terry Jones**, and **Michael Palin** contribute material to the series and **John Cleese** appears in two episodes (May 15 & 29) representing the upper-class in the "Class" sketch.

130   April 16, 1971

Montreux Special Programme (TV special: BBC1). This special edition of *Monty Python's Flying Circus*, compiled from various episodes (with newly-recorded links and other material), is the BBC entry for the Golden Rose at the 1971 Montreux Television Festival. The show wins the Silver Rose, an honor that helps to secure a third Python series. Includes: "Scott of the Sahara," "The Time on BBC1," "Face the Press," "The Gas Cooker Sketch," "Nude Woman [anim]," "Conrad Poohs and His Dancing Teeth [anim]," "It's the Arts: Deflating Chair, Semaphore Version of Wuthering Heights, Julius Caesar on an Aldis Lamp, The Exploding Version of 'The Blue Danube,' Deflated Chair," "David and the Fig Leaf [anim]," "Newspaper Shop," "The Ministry of Silly Walks," "Man-Powered Flight," "Metamorphosis [anim]," "Blackmail," "Newsreader Arrested," "Match of the Day (Romantic Movie)," "Batley Townswomen's Guild," and "Ramsay MacDonald Stiptease." Conceived, written & performed by **Graham Chapman**, **John Cleese**, **Terry Gilliam**, **Eric Idle**, **Terry Jones**, and **Michael Palin**. With Carol Cleveland, David Ballantyne, Helena Clayton, Daphne Davey, John

Hughman, and Stanley Mason. Animations by **Terry Gilliam**. Produced & directed by Ian MacNaughton.

131   April 21, 1971

John Cleese is installed as rector of St. Andrews University in Scotland. Conferred upon him is the honorary degree of LL.D. **Cleese** was elected rector on Nov. 14, 1970.

132   April 24, 1971

John Cleese, **Michael Palin**, and **Terry Jones** perform two cabaret shows at Younger Hall, St. Andrews University (in Scotland), where **Cleese** was recently installed as rector. Material includes Python items like "Pet Shop," "World Forum," and "The Lumberjack Song" and also **Palin**'s "I Don't Go Out Much Nowadays" (from the 1965 Oxford Revue at Edinburgh).

133   April 25, 1971

Doctor at Large (TV episode: ITV/LWT). "Lock, Stock & Beryl." Upton, Collier, and Stuart-Clark attempt to return an inebriated nurse (Philippa Markham) to the nurses home. Starring Barry Evans. Written by **Graham Chapman** and Bernard McKenna. Directed by Bill Turner.

134   May 1, 1971

Euroshow '71 (TV special: BBC2) Monty Python appears in this hour-long May Day special showcasing the best of European TV variety. Python's contribution is a six-minute piece describing traditional May Day celebrations in England, including "The Fish-Slapping Dance" (replayed on the Oct. 26, 1972, episode of *Flying Circus*), "The Gavotte of the Long John Silvers," "The Annual Return of the Overdue Library Book," "Nun-Boiling Week," and "The Spring Dance of the Futures Brokers." This rarely-seen Python sequence was shown again (with a re-constituted soundtrack) on Oct. 9, 1999, as part of BBC2's "Python Night." Directed by Hans-Bernhard Theopold.

135   May 6, 1971

Monty Python's Flying Circus, the BBC's entry for the Golden Rose at the 11th Annual Montreux Television Festival in Montreux, Switzerland, wins the Silver Rose (second place). The winner of the Golden Rose is the Austrian show *Lodynski's Flohmarkt Company*.

136   May 8, 1971

The Two Ronnies (TV episode: BBC1). Includes the "Party Sketch (Loo)," written by **Michael Palin** and **Terry Jones**. Fifth episode of the first series. Starring Ronnie Corbett and Ronnie Barker. Written by Gary Chambers, Tony Hare, **Eric Idle**, David McKellar, Spike Mullins, David Nobbs, **Michael Palin** & **Terry Jones**, Peter Vincent, Bill Solly, Dick Vosburgh, and Gerald Wiley [pseud. of Ronnie Barker]. Produced by Terry Hughes.

137   May 9, 1971

Doctor at Large (TV episode: ITV/LWT). "Saturday Matinee." Left in charge of Dr. Whiteland's private practice, Dr. Upton must cope with a Cabinet Minister (Basil Henson) and a hysterical, sexually-aggressive woman (Maureen Lipman). Starring Barry Evans. Written by **John Cleese**. Directed by Alan Wallis.

138   May 15, 1971

The Two Ronnies (TV episode: BBC1). **John Cleese** is the special guest, portraying the upper-class in the "Class" sketch alongside Ronnie Barker (middle-class) and Ronnie Corbett (lower-class). Sixth episode of the first series. Written by Peter Vincent, Gerald Wiley [pseud. of Ronnie Barker], Spike Mullins, and David Nobbs. Produced by Terry Hughes. Note: **Cleese**, Barker, and Corbett first performed the "Class" sketch on *The Frost Report* in 1966.

139   May 22, 1971

Aquarius (TV arts show: ITV/LWT). Hosted by Humphrey Burton. Includes a spoof football report from Wembley featuring **John Cleese** and **Eric Idle**. As host of *On the Ball*, **Idle** introduces an interview with Colin Buzzard (**Cleese**, reprising his dim-witted footballer, Jimmy Buzzard, from the Python series). Also, **Cleese** gives a report from Iceland and (as Jimmy Hill) interviews a cut-out of Sir Alf Ramsey.

140   May 26–November 10, 1971

Jokers Wild (TV game show: ITV/YTV–Yorkshire Television). **John Cleese** appears on episodes of the fifth and sixth series of this 1969–74 panel game in which comedians compete by telling jokes on a randomly selected topic. His fellow panelists include Les Dawson, Ray Cameron, Clement Freud, Ray Martine, Ted Ray, Albie Keen, David Nixon, and Arthur Askey. Hosted by Barry Cryer/Michael Bentine.

141   May 29, 1971

The Two Ronnies (TV episode: BBC1). **John Cleese** returns as the special guest, again taking the role of the upper-class in the "Class" sketch alongside Ronnie Barker (middle-class) and Ronnie Corbett (lower-class). Eighth episode of the first series. Written by **Eric Idle**, Peter Vincent, Gerald Wiley [pseud. of Ronnie Barker], Spike Mullins, David Nobbs, and Dick Vosburgh. Produced by Terry Hughes.

142   May 30, 1971
Doctor at Large (TV episode: ITV/LWT). "No Ill Feeling!" Dr. Upton stays at a hotel where he is driven to distraction by the resident funny man (Roy Kinnear). In this **John Cleese**-scripted episode, Timothy Bateson plays ill-mannered hotelier Mr. Clifford, a Basil Fawlty (*Fawlty Towers*) prototype. Starring Barry Evans. Directed by Alan Wallis.

143   June 1971
The Pythons' second LP, *Another Monty Python Record*, is recorded at Marquee Studios in London.

144   June 1, 1971
Tuesday's Documentary (TV special: BBC1). "That Well-Known Store in Knightsbridge." Documentary on Harrod's department store, narrated by **John Cleese** and featuring Sir John Betjeman, Marjorie Proops, and Graham Turner. Written by Patrick O'Donovan. Produced by Harry Hastings.

145   June 6, 1971
Doctor at Large (TV episode: ITV/LWT). "Let's Start at the Beginning." Upton is mistaken for a patient at a psychiatric clinic. Starring Barry Evans. Written by **Graham Chapman** and Bernard McKenna. Directed by Bill Turner.

146   June 8, 1971
Tuesday's Documentary (TV special: BBC1). "The Great 20th-Century Love Affair (aka The Car Versus the People)." Man's love for his motor car is explored in this hour-long special hosted by Julian Pettifer. Includes sketches from **Michael Palin** and **Terry Jones**. Written & produced by David Gerrard. Directed by Edward Mirzoeff.

147   June 13, 1971
Doctor at Large (TV episode: ITV/LWT). "It's All in the Mind." At a party, Upton meets Audrey Watt (Patricia Routledge), who claims to be a witch with healing powers. Starring Barry Evans. Written by **John Cleese**. Directed by Alan Wallis.

148   June 20, 1971
Doctor at Large (TV episode: ITV/LWT). "Cynthia Darling." An over-bearing mother (Hattie Jacques) insists that Dr. Upton treat her daughter (Moira Foot), who is perfectly healthy. Starring Barry Evans. Written by **John Cleese**. Directed by Bill Turner.

149   July 1971
The Pythons film their first TV show in Germany, at Bavaria Studios in Munich, delivering their lines phonetically in German. The show is brought about by German producer — and Python fan — Alfred Biolek. Filming locations include Nymphenburg Palace (in Munich).

150   July 11, 1971
Doctor at Large (TV episode: ITV/LWT). "Operation Loftus." Prof. Loftus (Ernest Clark) returns to St. Swithins. Starring Barry Evans. Written by **Graham Chapman** and Bernard McKenna. Directed by Alan Wallis.

151   July 17, 1971
Desert Island Discs (Radio show: BBC Radio 4). Roy Plomley's castaway is **John Cleese**, whose choice of records includes "Simon Smith & His Amazing Dancing Bear" (Alan Price) and "Nimrod, from *Enigma Variations*" (Sir Edward Elgar). His luxury item is a life-size model of Margaret Thatcher and a baseball bat; his book *Vincent Price's Cookery Book*.

152   July 18, 1971
Doctor at Large (TV episode: ITV/LWT). "Mother and Father Doing Well." Dr. Huw Evans (Martin Shaw), a former medical student at St. Swithins, returns to the hospital with his pregnant wife (Ursula Barclay). Starring Barry Evans. Written by **John Cleese**. Directed by Bill Turner.

153   July 25, 1971
Doctor at Large (TV episode: ITV/LWT). "A Joke's a Joke." Upton and Collier become anatomy demonstrators. Starring Barry Evans. Written by **Graham Chapman** and Bernard McKenna. Directed by Alan Wallis.

154   August 8, 1971
Doctor at Large (TV episode: ITV/LWT). "It's the Rich Wot Gets the Pleasure." Stuart-Clark is left a small fortune by a rich uncle, and a wild celebration ensues. Starring Barry Evans. Written by **Graham Chapman** and Bernard McKenna. Directed by Alan Wallis.

155   August 15, 1971
Doctor at Large (TV episode: ITV/LWT). "Things That Go Mump in the Night." Upton comes down with mumps and is admitted to Bingham's ward. Starring Barry Evans. Written by **Graham Chap-

man and Bernard McKenna. Directed by Bill Turner.

156 August 22, 1971
Doctor at Large (TV episode: ITV/LWT). "Mr. Moon." A convalescing Dr. Upton stays at a health farm run by the strict disciplinarian Mr. Moon (John Le Mesurier). Starring Barry Evans. Written by **John Cleese**. Directed by Alan Wallis.

157 August 29, 1971
Doctor at Large (TV episode: ITV/LWT). "The Viva." Upton's car breaks down in the country forcing him to take his oral exam over the phone. Starring Barry Evans. Written by **Graham Chapman** and Bernard McKenna. Directed by Alan Wallis.

158 August 30 & September 6, 1971
Sez Les (TV comedy series: ITV/YTV–Yorkshire Television). **John Cleese** appears as a guest performer on these third-series episodes of Les Dawson's sketch-comedy show (1969–76). Dawson-Cleese sketches include "Scotsman & Englishman on a Train" (Aug. 30) and "Walking License" (Sept. 6). Produced & directed by David Mallett.

159 September 10, 1971
A. P. Herbert's Misleading Cases (TV episode: BBC1). "Regina Versus Sagittarius." **John Cleese** guest stars as Mr. Partridge in this episode of the 1967–71 courtroom comedy. Starring Alastair Sim, Roy Dotrice, Thorley Walters, Avice Landone, with Terence Conoley, Gabrielle Drake, June Jago, George Pravda, and Sydney Tafler. Written by Christopher Bond and Michael Gilbert. Produced & directed by John Howard Davies.

160 September 13, 1971
It's a Wacky World (TV special: NBC). **John Cleese** appears on this American comedy-variety special, produced by George Schlatter (*Laugh-In*), featuring performances and filmed segments from around the world. Pilot for a potential series. Also starring Tony Curtis, Jacques Tati, Lulu, Alfonso Arau, and many others.

161 September 28, 1971
And Now for Something Completely Different (Feature film: Columbia Pictures) opens in London. Monty Python's first feature film is an anthology of some of the better sketches from the first two series of *Flying Circus*. Includes: "How Not to Be Seen," "A Man with a Tape Recorder Up His Nose/Brother's Nose," "Hungarian Phrase Book/Court Room," "Growing Hands/Cowboy/Shaving [anim]," "Marriage Guidance Counselor," "Baby Carriage/David and the Fig Leaf [anim]," "Nudge, Nudge," "Self-Defense," "Hell's Grannies/Colonel (Silly)," "Camp Army Drills/Colonel (Silly)," "The Prince and the Black Spot [anim]," "Mountaineering Expedition," "Bikini-Clad Women & Announcer," "Come Back to My Place," "The Flasher," "Chinese Communist Conspiracy/American Defense/Crelm Toothpaste/Shrill Petrol [anim]," "Twentieth-Century Frog [anim]," "Conrad Poohs and His Dancing Teeth [anim]," "Musical Mice," "It's the Arts: Sir Edward Ross," "Seduced Milkmen," "The Funniest Joke in the World," "Bus Stop/The Killer Cars/Venus Dancing [anim]," "The Pet Shop," "The Lumberjack Song," "Restaurant Sketch," "Musical Statue [anim]," "Bank Robber in Lingerie Shop," "Falling from Building," "Metamorphosis [anim]," "Vocational Guidance Counselor," "Blackmail/Colonel," "A Re-enactment of the Battle of Pearl Harbor," "Erotic Film," and "The Upper-Class Twit of the Year." Filmed in October–December 1970. Written by & featuring **Graham Chapman**, **John Cleese**, **Terry Gilliam**, **Eric Idle**, **Terry Jones**, and **Michael Palin**. Animations by **Terry Gilliam**. Directed by Ian MacNaughton. Produced by Patricia Casey. Note: The film's executive producer, Victor Lownes (head of *Playboy* in the U.K.) suggested making the film back in January 1970 as a way of introducing Python to America. Columbia Pictures, however, is reluctant to release the film in the States and shelves it for almost a year. It is finally given a limited release in the U.S. on Aug. 22, 1972.

Reviews: Howard Thompson (*The New York Times*, Aug. 23, 1972, p. C33): "...where's the wit?... One portion about a bird shop is as dead as the parrot in question ... compared to this, *The Beverly Hillbillies* seems downright Shakespearean"; Penelope Gilliatt (*The New Yorker*, Aug. 26, 1972, p. 60): "...a battily funny film ... nothing is sacrosanct, least of all patriotism and any sort of bigotry"; Sally Beauman (*New York*, Aug. 28, 1972, p. 47): "A mad mix of review, whimsy and satire.... Extremely funny and should be seen"; Paul D. Zimmerman (*Newsweek*, Sept. 4, 1972, p. 81): "...*Different* dances gleefully on the grave of upper-crust English institutions and moribund Establishment mores.... It comes at a good time, when the supply of good comedy is so low here that, unfortunately, we must import it"; Stanley Kauffmann (*The New Republic*, Sept. 23, 1972, p. 244): "The best quality in the film is its youthful brashness ... any film by bright people that tries for 100 minutes to make you laugh ought to succeed some of the time, and this does"; Bruce Williamson (*Playboy*, October 1972, p. 28): "Marx Bros. zaniness ... lives up to its title ... comic boners and solid belly laughs."

162 October 1971
Another Monty Python Record (Record: Charisma CAS 1049) is released in the U.K. The Pythons' second album (following 1970's *Monty Python's Flying Circus*) contains material taken mostly from the show's second series and is packaged as a recording of *Beethoven's Symphony No. 2 in D Major* (by The National Philharmonic Orchestra conducted by Dietriech Walther) but with that title crossed out with a crayon and "Another Monty Python Record" scribbled in the top right-hand corner. The record comes with a "Be a Great Actor" kit. Tracks: "Apologies (Pleasures of the Dance)," "The Spanish Inquisition," "Gumby Theatre (The Cherry Orchard)," "Contradiction," "The Architect Sketch," "The Spanish Inquisition Again," "Ethel the Frog: The Piranha Brothers," "The Death of Mary Queen of Scots," "Penguin on the TV," "Comfy Chair/Sound Quiz," "Be a Great Actor," "Theatre Critic (Gavin Millarrrrrrrrr)," "Royal Festival Hall Concert," "Spam (song: Spam Song)," "The Judges," "Stake Your Claim," "Still No Sign of Land (Lifeboat)," "Undertaker Sketch," and "Knees Up, Mother Brown (Spanish Inquisition)." Written & performed by **Graham Chapman**, **John Cleese**, **Terry Gilliam**, **Eric Idle**, **Terry Jones**, and **Michael Palin**, with Carol Cleveland. Produced by **Terry Jones** and **Michael Palin**. Recorded at Marquee Studios, London. Single issued on Charisma CAS 192. The U.S. release (Charisma, distributed by Buddah Records in 1972) also includes "World Forum." Reissued on CD (with four bonus tracks) in 2006.
Review: Michael Wale (*Financial Times*, Oct. 21, 1971, p. 3): "...should become the biggest selling Christmas album for some time."

163 October 1971
Who's There? (Short film). Instructional 16-minute film, produced by the Labour Party and starring the Python team, showing Labour Party workers how to canvass for votes. **John Cleese**, who was asked to do the film by friend Peter Davis, and the rest of the group gave their services for free. The film premieres at the party conference in Brighton. Narrated by Michael Parkinson. Starring **John Cleese, Graham Chapman, Terry Jones, Michael Palin**, and Carol Cleveland. Directed by Mike Wooler.

164 October 1, 1971–January 14, 1972
The Marty Feldman Comedy Machine (TV series: ITV). **Terry Gilliam** provides the opening title sequence and other animations for this comedy-variety show starring Marty Feldman. The series airs in the U.S. Apr. 12–Aug. 23, 1972, on ABC. Directed by John Robins. Produced by Larry Gelbart.

165 November 1971
The Magnificent Seven Deadly Sins (Feature film: Tigon). British comedy comprised of seven different stories, each based on one of the Seven Deadly Sins. **Graham Chapman** co-writes (with Barry Cryer) the "Gluttony" and "Wrath" episodes. Starring Bruce Forsyth, Joan Sims, Roy Hudd, Harry Secombe, Leslie Phillips, Julie Ege, Harry H. Corbett, Spike Milligan, Ian Carmichael, Alfie Bass, Ronald Fraser, Arthur Howard, and Stephen Lewis. Other writers: Bob Larbey, John Esmonde, Dave Freeman, Graham Stark, Marty Feldman, Alan Simpson, Ray Galton, and Spike Milligan. Produced & directed by Graham Stark.

166 November 1, 1971
Monty Python's Big Red Book (Book: Eyre Methuen), edited by **Eric Idle** and designed by Derek Birdsall, is published in the U.K. The Pythons' first book (which, of course, has a blue cover) is a collection of sketches and animation stills, some original, but most of it derived from the TV show. Contents: "Letters of Endorsement from Television Newscasters," "Classified Ads," "Juliette: Ken Shabby and Rosemary," "The End," "Why Accountancy Is Not Boring," "Naughty Pages," "Ads," "Campaign Literature for the Silly Party," "Keyhole for Voyeurs," "Batley Ladies Townswomen's Guild," "E.D. Silly's Page," "Spam Song," "Sports Page: Jimmy Buzzard and Ken Clean-Air System," "Arts Page," "Horace Poem," "The World Encyclopaedia of Carnal Knowledge," "Australian Page," "Children's Page (Storytime)," "Blackmail," "Uncle Sam," "A Song for Europe: 'Bing Tiddle Tiddle Bong,'" "The Importance of Being Earnest—A New Version by Billy Bremner," "Are You Civilized?," "Le Pouff Celebre," "Madame Palm Writes," "Family Tree of Johann Gambolputty...," "The Greatest Upper Class (Twit) Race in the World," "Lumberjack Song," "Do-It-Yourself Story," "Goats' Page," "Hello O.N.s Everywhere," "Whizzo Assortment," "English-Hungarian Phrasebook," "How to Walk Silly," "Johnson's Novelties," "Be a Modern Hermit," "The Poems of Ewen McTeagle," "The Piranha Brothers," "Python Literary Guild," "Letter Retracting the Endorsement of the Book,"

and "Bibliography." Published in the U.S. by Warner Books (1975).

Review: Matthew Coady (*New Statesman*, Dec. 3, 1971, pp. 794–5): "Not all the Python funnies work. Some are frankly tedious.... Even so, the *Big Red Book* embodies the consistently savage view of the universe which characterises the programme at its devastating best."

167   November 1, 1971

The Monty Python Newscaster of the Year Awards (Award ceremony). To celebrate the publication of *Monty Python's Big Red Book*, the Pythons present a mock-award show at the ICA in London. Hosted by Barry Cryer. Awards presented include Best Dressed Radio Newsreader.

168   November 5–December 17, 1971

The first series of the sitcom *Now Look Here...*, starring Ronnie Corbett and Madge Ryan, airs on BBC1. The seven-episode series is written by **Graham Chapman** and Barry Cryer, and produced by Bill Hitchcock. The second series airs in January–March 1973.

169   November 6, 1971

Aquarius (TV arts show: ITV/LWT). Hosted by Humphrey Burton. Includes a report on the *Monty Python Newscaster of the Year Awards*.

170   November 13, 1971

The Sun (Weekend TV Sun) (Newspaper/U.K.). "In the Crazy Court of King Python," by Kenneth Eastaugh. Behind-the-scenes look at a Python script-writing session at **Terry Jones**' house in East London.

171   December 4, 1971

The recordings for the third series of *Monty Python's Flying Circus* begin. The first show recorded is episode 29 ("The Money Programme"), which will air Nov. 2, 1972.

172   December 11, 1971

Episode 30 ("Blood, Devastation, Death, War, and Horror") of *Monty Python's Flying Circus* is recorded.

173   December 18, 1971

Episode 38 ("A Book at Bedtime") of *Monty Python's Flying Circus* is recorded.

174   December 27, 1971

Monty Python (represented by **John Cleese, Michael Palin** & **Terry Jones**) takes part in a "fancy dress" squash match at the Abraxas Squash Club.

175   1971

The Great Birds Eye Peas Relaunch 1971 (Marketing film). The Pythons play various characters — including Gumbys, housewives, Alan Whickers, and The Comparatively Good Fairy (**Idle**) — in this 25-minute short for Birds Eye Frozen Peas. Starring **Graham Chapman, John Cleese, Eric Idle, Terry Jones, Michael Palin**, and Carol Cleveland. Directed by **Terry Jones**.

176   1971

Miracle of Flight (Short film). Five-minute, cut-out animated short from **Terry Gilliam** depicting man's failed attempts at flight. Originally made for TV's *The Marty Feldman Comedy Machine*, the film is later shown theatrically and also featured in some of the Python stage shows. Screened at the 1975 Annecy Film Festival. Voices by **Terry Gilliam** and **Terry Jones**.

177   1971

Graham Chapman becomes guardian to John Tomiczek, a teenage runaway from Liverpool.

178   1971

Eric Idle serves as script editor on early episodes of the BBC sitcom *The Liver Birds*, about two Liverpool girls who share a flat.

179   1971

The Rectorial Address of John Cleese (Book: Epam), written by **John Cleese**, is published. Speech delivered by **Cleese** on Apr. 21, 1971, upon being installed as rector of St. Andrews University in Scotland.

180   January 3, 1972

Monty Python's Fliegender Zirkus (TV special: ARD, in West Germany). The Pythons' first (of two) TV special made especially for German and Austrian television. The show was performed in German, but since none of the group spoke much German, they had to be taught their lines phonetically (their second show for Germany, made in 1972, will be performed in English and dubbed for German audiences). The 45-minutes show was shot entirely on film at Bavarian Film Studios in Munich and on location in Bavaria in July 1971. Includes: "Woman Announcer/Frogmen," "Photograph/Cymbal Smash [anim]," "Live from Athens (Olympic Torch Runner)," "Albrecht Dürer Documentary/Song," "The Merchant of Venice (The Bad Ischl Dairy Herd)," "A Word from a Frenchman," "Doctor Breeding," "Albrecht Dürer doc," "Paintings [anim]," "Theatre Critic," "The

Merchant of Venice (Doctors)," "Flasher Love Story [anim]," "Torch Runner," "Little Red Riding Hood/Heinz the Stuttgart Rapist," "Albrecht Dürer/Torch Runner," "Silly Olympics (Munich 1972)," "Albrecht Dürer Western," "Stake Your Claim," "The Holzfäller Song (Lumberjack Song)/Complaint Letter," "Photographer/Land Eating/Intro [anim]," "Bavarian Restaurant Sketch," "Aristocrat/Sedan Chair," and "Woman Announcer/Frogmen." Conceived, written & performed by **Graham Chapman, John Cleese, Terry Gilliam, Eric Idle, Terry Jones,** and **Michael Palin**. Animations by **Terry Gilliam**. Directed by Ian MacNaughton. Produced by Alfred Biolek. Note: "Flasher Love Story," "Little Red Riding Hood," and "Silly Olympics" will later be shown during the group's stage shows, including their 1980 stint at the Hollywood Bowl (released as a film in 1982).

181 January 7, 1972
Episode 33 ("Salad Days") of *Monty Python's Flying Circus* is recorded.

182 January 14, 1972
Episode 27 ("Whicker's World") of *Monty Python's Flying Circus* is recorded.

183 January 14, 1972
Comedy Playhouse (TV episode: BBC1). "Idle at Work." Ronnie Barker plays George Idle, a man who starts an organization to debunk outspoken individuals, in this first play of the show's twelfth series. Also starring Graham Crowden, Derek Francis, and Mary Merrall. Written by **Graham Chapman** and Bernard McKenna. Directed by Harold Snoad. Produced by James Gilbert.

184 January 21, 1972
Episode 32 ("The War Against Pornography") of *Monty Python's Flying Circus* is recorded.

185 January 28, 1972
Episode 28 ("Mr. and Mrs. Brian Norris' Ford Popular") of *Monty Python's Flying Circus* is recorded.

186 February 1, 1972
Terry Jones turns 30.

187 April 8, 1972
Braden's Week (TV show: BBC1). Hosted by Bernard Braden. Guests include **Graham Chapman**.

188 April 9–October 8, 1972
The first series of the sitcom *Doctor in Charge* airs on ITV (London Weekend Television). **Graham Chapman** and Bernard McKenna write twelve of the series' 27 episodes. The series, a follow-up to *Doctor in the House* (1969–70) and *Doctor at Large* (1971), stars Robin Nedwell (Dr. Duncan Waring), George Layton (Dr. Paul Collier), and Geoffrey Davies (Dr. Dick Stuart-Clark). Produced by Humphrey Barclay.

189 April 9, 1972
Doctor in Charge (TV episode: ITV/LWT). "The Devil You Know." Dr. Waring returns to St. Swithins. First episode of the series. Written by **Graham Chapman** and Bernard McKenna. Directed by Alan Wallis.

190 April 16, 1972
Doctor in Charge (TV episode: ITV/LWT). "The Research Unit." Prof. Loftus commissions a research unit at St. Swithins in the hope that a medical breakthrough will bring him a knighthood. Written by **Graham Chapman** and Bernard McKenna. Directed by Alan Wallis.

191 April 17, 1972
Episode 37 ("Dennis Moore") of *Monty Python's Flying Circus* is recorded.

192 April 23, 1972
Doctor in Charge (TV episode: ITV/LWT). "The Minister's Health." A case of mistaken identity results when a VIP (Very Important Patient), The Minister of Health (Basil Henson), is admitted to St. Swithins. Written by **Graham Chapman** and Bernard McKenna. Directed by Alan Wallis.

193 April 24, 1972
Episode 31 ("The All-England Summarize Proust Competition") of *Monty Python's Flying Circus* is recorded.

194 May 4, 1972
Episode 34 ("The Cycling Tour") of *Monty Python's Flying Circus* is recorded.

195 May 11, 1972
Episode 35 ("The Nude Organist") of *Monty Python's Flying Circus* is recorded.

196 May 18, 1972
Episode 39 ("Grandstand") of *Monty Python's Flying Circus* is recorded.

197 May 25, 1972
The last recording for the third series of *Monty Python's Flying Circus* takes place. It is also **John Cleese**'s last recording for the show (the fourth and final series, in 1974, is made without him). The show, episode 36 ("E. Henry Thripshaw's Disease"), airs Dec. 21.

198 May 28, 1972
The Great Western Express Festival (Stage show). **John Cleese, Terry Jones,** and **Michael Palin** perform sketches at this pop music festival held at Tupholme Hall in Bardney, Lincolnshire, England. They perform before a crowd of more than 35,000 people with the aid of large video screens. Sketches include "Summarize Proust" and "Pet Shop." Other performers at the four-day festival (May 26–29) include The Faces, Joe Cocker, Slade, and The Beach Boys.

199 Summer 1972
Another Monty Python Record is released in the U.S. by Buddah Records.

200 June 1972
Rentadick (Feature film: Rank Films) opens in the U.K. A private-eye spoof, written by **John Cleese** and **Graham Chapman**, about a detective agency hired by a scientist to keep an eye on his beautiful wife and to keep his secret nerve gas formula out of the hands of Japanese spies. The original script, titled *Rentasleuth*, was meant to be directed by Charles Crichton (of *Lavender Hill Mob* fame, and later, *A Fish Called Wanda*), before producer Ned Sherrin acquired the rights to the project and brought in director Jim Clark. Unhappy with the finished version of the film, **Cleese** and **Chapman** had their names removed from the credits. Starring James Booth, Richard Briers, Julie Ege, Donald Sinden, Ronald Fraser, Richard Beckinsale, Spike Milligan, Michael Bentine, and Roy Kinnear. Directed by Jim Clark. Produced by Ned Sherrin and Terry Glinwood.

201 June 11, 1972
Doctor in Charge (TV episode: ITV/LWT). "Mum's the Word." Waring and Bingham apply for a position on the hospital board. Written by **Graham Chapman** and Bernard McKenna. Directed by Alan Wallis.

202 June 18, 1972
Doctor in Charge (TV episode: ITV/LWT). "The Fox." A new matron arrives at the hospital. Written by **Graham Chapman** and Bernard McKenna. Directed by Alan Wallis.

203 June 25, 1972
Doctor in Charge (TV episode: ITV/LWT). "A Night with the Dead." Waring spends a night alone in the mortuary to win a bet. Written by **Graham Chapman** and Bernard McKenna. Directed by Alan Wallis.

204 July 1972
Video Arts, a company that will produce training films for commerce and industry, is founded by **John Cleese**, Antony Jay, Peter Robinson, and Michael Peacock. The aim of the company is to show, through humor, how to improve performance in the workplace. **Cleese**, who will serve as chairman of the company until 1989, will co-write (with Jay) and star in many of the films himself. Other stars appearing in Video Arts films will include Ronnie Corbett, Ronnie Barker, Stephen Fry, Hugh Laurie, Rowan Atkinson, Emma Thompson, Dawn French, Jennifer Saunders, Robert Lindsay, and Ricky Gervais.

205 July 2, 1972
Doctor in Charge (TV episode: ITV/LWT). "This is Your Wife." Bingham (Richard O'Sullivan) and Mary (Helen Fraser) get married in secret on St. Swithin's Day. Written by **Graham Chapman** and Bernard McKenna. Directed by Alan Wallis.

206 July 23, 1972
Doctor in Charge (TV episode: ITV/LWT). "The System." The doctors develop a system to improve efficiency at St. Swithins. Written by **Graham Chapman** and Bernard McKenna. Directed by David Askey.

207 August 6, 1972
Doctor in Charge (TV episode: ITV/LWT). "Amazing Grace." Clumsy medical student Reggie Grace (Tony Robinson) causes problems for Waring and Collier. Written by **Graham Chapman** and Bernard McKenna. Directed by David Askey.

208 August 20, 1972
Doctor in Charge (TV episode: ITV/LWT). "Yellow Fever." A delegation of Chinese communists visits St. Swithins. Written by **Graham Chapman** and Bernard McKenna. Directed by Alan Wallis.

209 August 22, 1972
And Now for Something Completely Different is released in the U.S. almost a year after its British premiere in September 1971. Columbia Pictures, who had shelved the film, finally agreed to give it a limited release at the urging of Buddah Records, the American distributor of the group's album *Another Monty Python Record*. The film, which was originally intended to introduce the Pythons to America, does little business in the States. It won't be until 1974, when the TV show begins airing on PBS stations, that Python finds a U.S. audience.

210 September 1972

Spam Song/The Concert (Record: Charisma CB 192). U.K. single containing tracks off of the album *Another Monty Python Record*: "Spam Song" and "The Concert (aka Royal Festival Hall Concert)."

211 September 1972

Funny Game, Football... (Record: Charisma Perspective CS 4). British comedy LP containing songs and sketches recorded by The Group (**Michael Palin**, **Terry Jones**, Arthur Mullard, Bryan Pringle, Joe Steeples, Bill Tidy, and Michael Wale). Sketches include "The Missionary," "I Remember It Well," and "Floor's the Limit." Written by Steeples, Tidy, and Wale. Music by Neil Innes. Produced by Michael Wale. Single issued on Charisma CB 197.

212 September 10, 1972

Doctor in Charge (TV episode: ITV/LWT). "That's My Uncle!" Prof. Loftus' holiday replacement is Stuart-Clark's easy-going uncle, Jeremy De Quincy (William Franklyn). Written by **Graham Chapman** and Bernard McKenna. Directed by Bill Turner.

213 September 15–October 5, 1972

The Pythons spend three weeks in Munich filming their second television special for Germany. Unlike the first special, this one is performed in English and later dubbed. This will be **John Cleese**'s last time working with Python on television (he recorded his last *Flying Circus* in May).

214 September 23, 1972

The Two Ronnies (TV episode: BBC1). **Michael Palin** and **Terry Jones** contribute a sketch to this episode of the comedy show starring Ronnie Barker and Ronnie Corbett. Second episode of the second series. Produced by Terry Hughes.

215 October 1972

Marketing in Practice, No. 1: Who Sold You This, Then? (Training film: Video Arts). First film from Video Arts, the company co-founded by **John Cleese**, shows how a service engineer (**Cleese**) without proper training can damage a company's relationship with its customers. Produced for £4,000. Remade in 1997. Starring **John Cleese** (as Charlie Jenkins), Jonathan Lynn, Bernard McKenna, and Madge Ryan. Written by Antony Jay and **John Cleese**. Directed by Peter Robinson.

216 October 1, 1972

Doctor in Charge (TV episode: ITV/LWT). "Blackmail." Prof. Loftus' prospects for receiving a knighthood are threatened by an incriminating recording. Written by **Graham Chapman** and Bernard McKenna. Directed by David Boisseau.

217 October 2, 1972

Terry Jones' mother, Dilys Louisa Jones, dies at the age of 59, in Chichester. **Jones** is filming in Germany at the time.

218 October 12 & 13, 1972

The Pythons record their third album, *Monty Python's Previous Record*, at Radio Luxembourg in London.

219 October 19–December 21, 1972, January 4–18, 1973

The third series of *Monty Python's Flying Circus* airs on BBC1. The tension within the group was at its peak with this series, due to **John Cleese**'s increasing boredom with doing Python for television (this would be his last series) and the growing threat of censorship. The series consists of 13 shows and contains such standout sketches as "Argument Clinic," "Dennis Moore," "Cheese Shop," "Dead Bishop on the Landing (Church Police)," "The All-England Summarize Proust Competition," "Travel Agent," "The Fish Slapping Dance," and "Sam Peckinpah's 'Salad Days.'" This series' pre-title introductions begin with organ fanfare by **Terry Jones**' nude organist, followed by **Cleese**'s announcer ("And now...") and **Michael Palin**'s hermit ("It's..."). Recorded Dec. 4, 1971–May 25, 1972.

Awards: BAFTA-winner for Best Light Entertainment Programme for 1972.

Reviews: Barry Norman (*The Times* [London], Oct. 20, 1972): "Monty Python is still the most original and anarchic comedy show to be seen currently on television."

220 October 19, 1972

Monty Python's Flying Circus (TV episode: BBC1). "Whicker's World" (Episode 27). First show of the third series (recorded Jan. 14). Includes: "Njorl's Saga," "Court Room (Multiple Murderer)," "Manhunt [anim]," "Njorl's Saga/North Malden Icelandic Saga Society," "Court Room (Erik Njorl/Police Constable Pan Am)," "Stock Market Report," "Mrs. Premise and Mrs. Conclusion/Mr. and Mrs. Jean-Paul Sartre," and "Whicker Island." Conceived, written & performed by **Graham Chapman**, **John Cleese**, **Terry Gilliam**, **Eric Idle**, **Terry Jones**, and **Michael Palin**. With Mrs. Idle, Connie Booth, Rita Davies, Nigel Jones, and Frank Williams. Animations by **Terry Gilliam**. Produced & directed by Ian MacNaughton.

221   October 26, 1972
Monty Python's Flying Circus (TV episode: BBC1). "Mr. and Mrs. Brian Norris' Ford Popular" (Episode 28). Second show of the third series (recorded Jan. 28). Includes: "Mr. and Mrs. Brian Norris' Ford Popular," "Schoolboys' Life Assurance Company," "How to Do It," "Minister for Overseas Development (Mrs. Niggerbaiter Explodes)," "Vicar/Salesman," "Doctor (Healing with Dynamite)," "Anatomy Chart [anim]," "Farming Club: Life of Tchaikowsky," "Sviatoslav Richter and Rita," "Trim-Jeans Theatre Presents," "Compere Chasing Mouth [anim]," "The Fish-Slapping Dance," "Nazi Fish [anim]," "Women and Children First/The BBC is Short of Money/Puss in Boots/Horse of the Year Show," and "It's" (chat show with guests Lulu and Ringo Starr). Conceived, written & performed by **Graham Chapman**, **John Cleese**, **Terry Gilliam**, **Eric Idle**, **Terry Jones**, and **Michael Palin**. With Julia Breck. Animations by **Terry Gilliam**. Produced & directed by Ian MacNaughton.

222   October 27, 1972
The Pythons and director Ian MacNaughton meet with the BBC's Head of Comedy, Duncan Wood, in his office to discuss their objections to a list of cuts the BBC wants to make to the third series of *Flying Circus*. The proposed cuts include the removal of entire sketches ("Cocktail Bar" and "Wee-Wee Wine Tasting") and the word "masturbating" from the "The All-England Summarize Proust Competition" sketch. **Terry Jones** reportedly argues: "What's wrong with masturbation? I masturbate, you masturbate, we all masturbate!"

223   November 1972
Eric the Half-a-Bee/The Yangtse Song (Record: Charisma CB 200). U.K. single containing songs off of the LP *Monty Python's Previous Record*: "Eric the Half-a-Bee" (sung by **John Cleese**) and "The Yangtse Song."

224   November 2, 1972
Monty Python's Flying Circus (TV episode: BBC1). "The Money Programme" (Episode 29). Third show of the third series (recorded Dec. 4, 1971). Includes: "The Money Programme (song: Money Song)," "Erizabeth L," "Fraud Film Director Squad (Visconti)," "Hands Up [anim]," "Dead Bishop on the Landing (Church Police)," "Bouncing in Jungle [anim]," "Jungle Restaurant," "Ken Russell's 'Gardening Club,'" "The Lost World of Roiurama," "Fraud Film Director Squad (Antonioni)," and "Argument Clinic/Hit on the Head Lessons/Flying Fox of the Yard." Conceived, written & performed by **Graham Chapman**, **John Cleese**, **Terry Gilliam**, **Eric Idle**, **Terry Jones**, and **Michael Palin**. With Rita Davies, Carol Cleveland, and The Fred Tomlinson Singers. Animations by **Terry Gilliam**. Produced & directed by Ian MacNaughton.

225   November 9, 1972
Monty Python's Flying Circus (TV episode: BBC1). "Blood, Devastation, Death, War, and Horror" (Episode 30). Fourth show of the third series (recorded Dec. 11, 1971). Includes: "Blood, Devastation, Death, War, and Horror (Man Who Speaks in Anagrams)," "Anagram Quiz (Beat the Clock)," "Merchant Banker/Pantomime Horses," "Life or Death Struggles," "The House-Hunters [anim]," "Mary Recruitment Office," "Bus Conductor Sketch," "The Man Who Makes People Laugh Uncontrollably," "Army Captain as Clown," "The Bols Story (Gestures to Indicate Pauses)," "Neurotic Announcer," "The News with Richard Baker (Gestures)," and "The Pantomime Horse Is a Secret Agent." Conceived, written & performed by **Graham Chapman**, **John Cleese**, **Terry Gilliam**, **Eric Idle**, **Terry Jones**, and **Michael Palin**. With Carol Cleveland. Animations by **Terry Gilliam**. Produced & directed by Ian MacNaughton.

226   November 16, 1972
Monty Python's Flying Circus (TV episode: BBC1). "The All-England Summarize Proust Competition" (Episode 31). Fifth show of the third series (recorded Apr. 24). Includes: "The All-England Summarize Proust Competition," "Mount Everest (Hairdresser Expedition)," "A Magnificent Festering [anim]," "Fire Brigade/Our Eamonn," "Party Hints by Veronica Smalls," "Communist Revolutions [anim]," "Language Laboratory," "Travel Agent," and "Thrust: Miss Anne Elk." Conceived, written & performed by **Graham Chapman**, **John Cleese**, **Terry Gilliam**, **Eric Idle**, **Terry Jones**, and **Michael Palin**. With Carol Cleveland and The Fred Tomlinson Singers. Animations by **Terry Gilliam**. Produced & directed by Ian MacNaughton. Note: BBC censors removed the words "and masturbating" from the "Summarize Proust" sketch in which **Graham Chapman**'s contestant lists his hobbies ("Golf, strangling animals…").

227   November 18, 1972
Full House (TV special: BBC2). **Eric Idle** performs on this live arts & entertainment program.

228   November 22, 1972
Michael Palin and **Terry Jones** are commissioned

to write a play for a new BBC series called *Black and Blue*. The play they write, *Secrets*, will air Aug. 14, 1973.

229   November 23, 1972
Monty Python's Flying Circus (TV episode: BBC1). "The War Against Pornography" (Episode 32). Sixth show of the third series (recorded Jan. 21). Includes: "The Housewives of Britain (Clean-Up Campaign)," "Gumby Brain Specialist/Surgery," "Speaker [anim]," "Mollusks (Live TV Documentary)," "Baby Suction [anim]," "Today in Parliament (The Minister for Not Listening to People)/Classic Serial/Tuesday Documentary/Children's Story/Party Political Broadcast/Religion Today/Match of the Day (Footballers Kissing)," "Politicians: An Apology," "Expedition to Lake Pahoe," "Royal Navy Advert [anim]," and "Silly Interview (Mr. Badger)." Conceived, written & performed by **Graham Chapman, John Cleese, Terry Gilliam, Eric Idle, Terry Jones,** and **Michael Palin.** With Mrs. Idle. Animations by **Terry Gilliam.** Produced & directed by Ian MacNaughton.

230   November 25, 1972
Full House (TV special: BBC2). **Eric Idle** performs in sketches with Henry Woolf on this live arts & entertainment program. Hosted by Joe Melia. Directed by Vernon Lawrence.

231   November 28, 1972
The Pythons (minus **Terry Gilliam**) participate in a football match as part of the promotion for the Dec. 8 release of *Monty Python's Previous Record*.

232   November 30, 1972
Monty Python's Flying Circus (TV episode: BBC1). "Salad Days" (Episode 33). Seventh show of the third series (recorded Jan. 7). Includes: "Biggles Dictates a Letter," "Flying Sheep/Traffic Accidents [anim]," "Climbing the Uxbridge Road," "Lifeboat," "Old Lady Snoopers," "Lifeboat," "Storage Jars," "TV Is Bad for Your Eyes/The Good Fairy from Program Control [anim]," "The Show So Far," "Cheese Shop," "Philip Jenkinson on Cheese Westerns," "Sam Peckinpah's 'Salad Days,'" "The News with Richard Baker (Storage Jars)," and "Seashore Interlude Film." Conceived, written & performed by **Graham Chapman, John Cleese, Terry Gilliam, Eric Idle, Terry Jones,** and **Michael Palin.** With Nicki Howorth. Animations by **Terry Gilliam.** Produced & directed by Ian MacNaughton.

233   December 1972
Teach Yourself Heath (Record). One-sided 7" flexi-disc with picture sleeve, given away in the December 1972 issue (No. 27) of the British rock magazine *ZigZag*. Using actual bits of Edward Heath's speeches, **Eric Idle** lampoons the Prime Minister's vocal mannerisms. **Michael Palin** introduces the record as No. 14 in the "Home Tutor Language Course" series.

234   December 7, 1972
Monty Python's Flying Circus (TV episode: BBC1). "The Cycling Tour" (Episode 34). Eighth show of the third series (recorded May 4) and the first Python episode to follow a single narrative for the full half-hour. Includes: "Mr. Pither's Bicycle Pump," "Mr. Gulliver/Clodagh Rodgers," "Casualty Department," "Trotsky," "Smolensk YMACA," "Bingo-Crazed Chinese," "Not Secret Police," "Trotsky/Eartha Kitt," "Firing Squad," "Eartha Kitt/Edward Heath," and "Jack in the Box [anim]." Conceived, written & performed by **Graham Chapman, John Cleese, Terry Gilliam, Eric Idle, Terry Jones,** and **Michael Palin.** With Carol Cleveland. Animations by **Terry Gilliam.** Produced & directed by Ian MacNaughton. Note: This episode's theme music is the "Waltz" from Charles Gounod's 1859 opera *Faust*.

235   December 8, 1972
Monty Python's Previous Record (Record: Charisma CAS 1063) is released in the U.K. Python's third album contains both new and familiar material (mostly from the third series of *Flying Circus*). The album design by **Terry Gilliam** features a long arm stretching around the front and back covers, the hand reaching for a multi-breasted butterfly. Tracks: "Embarrassment/A Book at Bedtime," "Dennis Moore," "Money Programme/Money Song," "Dennis Moore Continues," "Australian Table Wines," "Argument Clinic," "How to Do It," "Putting Down Budgies," "Personal Freedom," "Dennis Moore Continues," "Fish License/Eric the Half-a-Bee (song)," "What Do You...? (Radio Quiz Game)," "Travel Agent," "A Massage from the Swedish Prime Minister/Silly Noises (Quiz show)," "Miss Anne Elk," "Yangtse Kiang/We Love the Yangtse (song)," "A Minute Passed," "Eclipse of the Sun/Alistair Cooke Being Attacked by a Duck," "Wonderful World of Sound," "Funerals at Prestatyn," and "A Fairy Tale (Happy Valley) (song: Ya De Bucketty)." Written & performed by **Graham Chapman, John Cleese, Terry Gilliam, Eric Idle, Terry Jones,** and **Michael Palin,** with Carol Cleveland and The Fred Tomlinson Singers. Produced by Andre Jacquemin, **Michael Palin, Terry Jones,** and Alan Bailey. Recorded Oct. 12 & 13 at

Radio Luxembourg, London. Single ("Eric the Half-a-Bee") issued on Charisma CB 200. Released in the U.S. by Buddah Records (1973). Reissued on Virgin CASCD 1063 (1989 CD, U.K.), Virgin VCCD 002 (1994 CD, U.K.), and EMI PYTHCD 2 (2006 CD, with twelve bonus tracks).

236 December 14, 1972
Monty Python's Flying Circus (TV episode: BBC1). "The Nude Organist" (Episode 35). Ninth show of the third series (recorded May 11). Includes: "Bomb on Plane (Mr. Badger)," "Nude Man (Organist)," "Ten Seconds of Sex," "Housing Project Built by Characters from 19th-Century English Literature," "Mystico and Janet (Flats Built by Hypnosis)," "Mortuary Visit," "Animator/Flying Saucers [anim]," "The Olympic Hide-and-Seek Final," "The Cheap-Laughs," "Probe: Bull-Fighting," "Chairman of the British Well-Basically Club," "Pushing Button/Two Growing Trees/Hitler [anim]," "Prices on the Planet Algon," and "Reading the Credits (Mr. Badger)." Conceived, written & performed by **Graham Chapman, John Cleese, Terry Gilliam, Eric Idle, Terry Jones**, and **Michael Palin**. With Carol Cleveland, Marie Anderson, and Mrs. Idle. Animations by **Terry Gilliam**. Produced & directed by Ian MacNaughton.

237 December 17, 1972
The Sunday Times (London) (Newspaper/U.K.). "Atticus: Now for Something Completely Different," by Tom Davies, p. 32. Interview with **Graham Chapman, Terry Gilliam, Terry Jones, Michael Palin**, and (on the phone) **John Cleese**, promoting *Previous Record*. Includes a photo of the group by Stanley Devon.

238 December 18, 1972
Monty Python's Fliegender Zirkus (TV special: ARD, in West Germany). The Pythons' second TV show for German and Austrian television. Unlike the first show, this one was performed in English and later dubbed, much to the team's relief. The 50-minute show was filmed entirely in Germany, with locations including Grünwalder Stadion and the castles of Neueschwanstein and Hohenschwangau. Produced for Bavaria Atelier GmbH. Broadcast in England on Oct. 6, 1973. Includes: "William Tell," "Randy Businessmen," "Sycophancy," "Mouse Preserve (Frank Tutankhamun)," "Mouse Stampede [anim]," "Chicken Mines," "Flea-Buster [anim]," "International Philosophy (Football Match)," "Self-Wrestling," "Ten Seconds of Sex," "International Philosophy Update," "Noisy Traffic [anim]," "Hearing Aid," and "A Fairy Tale (Happy Valley) (song: Ya De Bucketty)." Conceived, written & performed by **Graham Chapman, John Cleese, Terry Gilliam, Eric Idle, Terry Jones**, and **Michael Palin**. With Connie Booth. Animations by **Terry Gilliam**. Directed by Ian MacNaughton. Produced by Thomas Woitkewitsch. Note: "International Philosophy" is later shown during Python stage shows and can be seen in the 1982 film *Monty Python Live at the Hollywood Bowl*.

239 December 21, 1972
Monty Python's Flying Circus (TV episode: BBC1). "E. Henry Thripshaw's Disease" (Episode 36). Tenth show of the third series (recorded May 25). Includes: "Tudor Job Agency," "Pornographic Bookshop," "The Life of Sir Philip Sidney (Elizabethan Pornography Smugglers)," "Gay Boys in Bondage [anim]," "Silly Disturbances (The Rev. Arthur Belling)," "Shooting Gallery [anim]," "The Free Repetition of Doubtful Words," "Is There?... Life After Death?," "Thripshaw's Disease," "Silly Noises," and "Sherry-Drinking Vicar." Conceived, written & performed by **Graham Chapman, John Cleese, Terry Gilliam, Eric Idle, Terry Jones**, and **Michael Palin**. With Carol Cleveland, The Fred Tomlinson Singers, and Rosalind Bailey. Animations by **Terry Gilliam**. Produced & directed by Ian MacNaughton. Notes: This was the last episode recorded for the third series, marking the end of **John Cleese**'s participation with the show. Three sketches are cut from this episode: "Big-Nosed Sculptor," "Cocktail Bar" (performed at Drury Lane in 1974), and "Wee-Wee Wine Tasting."

240 December 25, 1972
Christmas Night with the Stars (TV special: BBC1). The *Two Ronnies* segment of this holiday special includes a sketch written by **Michael Palin** & **Terry Jones**. Starring Ronnie Barker and Ronnie Corbett.

241 1972
John Cleese's father, Reginald, dies at the age of 78. Born Reginald Francis Cheese in 1893, he changed his name to "Cleese" to avoid teasing when he joined the army in 1915.

242 1972
Graham Chapman co-founds the newspaper *Gay News*.

243 1972
It's a 2'6" Above the Ground World (Feature film: British Lion) is released. Comedy about a Roman Catholic couple (Nanette Newman and Hywel Bennett) who decide to go on the pill. **John Cleese**

plays a lecturer on contraceptives. Later re-released as *The Love Ban*. Also starring Milo O'Shea, Angharad Rees, and Nicky Henson. Written by Kevin Laffan, from his play. Directed by Ralph Thomas. Produced by Betty Box and Ralph Thomas.

244 1972
The Great Gas Gala (TV commercials). **Terry Gilliam** animates commercials for the British Gas Board.

245 1972
The Least Bizarre of Monty Python's Comedy Album (Record: Charisma/Buddah CMP-EP). U.S. promo EP containing six tracks off the album *Another Monty Python Record*: "Spam," "Royal Festival Hall Concert," "Stake Your Claim," "World Forum," "Death of Mary Queen of Scots," and "Penguin on the TV." The black-and-white picture sleeve features a cartoon Gumby.

246 1972
Michael Palin and **John Cleese** appear in commercials for Hunky Chunks dog food and Lloyd's Bank.

247 January 1, 1973
Monty Python's Flying Circus wins the Critics' Circle award for Best Comedy Show of the Year.

248 January 3, 1973
The ABC Afterschool Special (TV special: ABC). "William." An introduction to playwright William Shakespeare, with Lynn Redgrave, Sir John Gielgud, Sir Ralph Richardson, Simon Ward, and Paul Jones. Title sequence by **Terry Gilliam**. Taped in London. Directed by Ian MacNaughton.

249 January 4, 1973
Monty Python's Flying Circus (TV episode: BBC1). "Dennis Moore" (Episode 37). Eleventh show of the third series (recorded Apr. 17, 1972). Includes: "Boxing Tonight (Jack Bodell v. Sir Kenneth Clark)," "Dennis Moore (song: Dennis Moore)," "What the Stars Foretell," "Doctor," "Ambulance [anim]," "The Great Debate: TV4 or Not TV4?," "George I, Episode 3/Dennis Moore (Lupins)," "Ideal Loon Exhibition," "Plan 13A [anim]," "Off-License," "Dennis Moore (Stealing from the Poor)," "Prejudice," "Dennis Moore Again," and "Losing Judges." Conceived, written & performed by **Graham Chapman, John Cleese, Terry Gilliam, Eric Idle, Terry Jones,** and **Michael Palin**. With Carol Cleveland and Nosher Powell. Animations by **Terry Gilliam**. Produced & directed by Ian MacNaughton.

250 January 11, 1973
Monty Python's Flying Circus (TV episode: BBC1). "A Book at Bedtime" (Episode 38). Twelfth show of the third series (recorded Dec. 18, 1971). Includes: "A Party Political Broadcast on Behalf of the Conservative and Unionist Party (Choreographed)," "A Book at Bedtime (Redgauntlet)," "McKamikaze Highlanders," "No Time to Lose," "No-Time Tolouse [anim]," "McKamikaze Highlanders," "2001 [anim]," "Frontiers of Medicine: Penguins," "Unexploded Scotsman Disposal Squad," "Spot the Looney," "Rival Documentaries," and "New Comedy Programmes (Dad's Doctor, Dad's Pooves, etc.)." Conceived, written & performed by **Graham Chapman, John Cleese, Terry Gilliam, Eric Idle, Terry Jones,** and **Michael Palin**. Animations by **Terry Gilliam**. Produced & directed by Ian MacNaughton. Note: The opening "Party Political Broadcast" was cut from a repeat broadcast in 1974, possibly out of fear that it could affect voting in that year's General Election.

251 January 18, 1973
Monty Python's Flying Circus (TV episode: BBC1). "Grandstand" (Episode 39). Thirteenth and last show of the third series (recorded May 18, 1972). Includes: "Thames TV Intro," "The British Show Biz Awards," "The Oscar Wilde Sketch," "Powder My Nose/Charwoman [anim]," "David Niven's Fridge," "Pasolini's 'The Third Test Match,'" "New Brain from Curry's," "Blood Donor," "Wife-Swapping," "Credits of the Year," and "The Dirty Vicar Sketch." Conceived, written & performed by **Graham Chapman, John Cleese, Terry Gilliam, Eric Idle, Terry Jones,** and **Michael Palin**. With Carol Cleveland and Caron Gardner. Animations by **Terry Gilliam**. Produced & directed by Ian MacNaughton.

252 January 18, 1973
Comedy Playhouse (TV special: BBC1). "Elementary, My Dear Watson: The Strange Case of the Dead Solicitors." Half-hour. A Sherlock Holmes parody in which the famous detective (**John Cleese**) and Dr. Watson (William Rushton) investigate the deaths of five solicitors. Pilot for a proposed series that never came about. Also starring Bill Maynard, Josephine Tewson, Norman Bird, Chic Murray, Larry Martyn, John Wells, Frank Muir, Dawn Addams, and Alan Coren. Written by N. F. Simpson. Directed by Harold Snoad. Produced by Barry Took. Note: **Cleese** will again play Holmes in 1977's *The Strange Case of the End of Civilisation as We Know It*.

253 January 18, 1973
Real Time (TV talk show: BBC2). Guest **Michael Palin** discusses TV comedy.

254 January 18, 1973
Liesbeth (TV special: KRO). Dutch variety show starring singer-actress Liesbeth List. Includes a film sequence featuring Monty Python performing the sketch "Custard Pie (Japes Lecture)." Directed by Tineke Roeffen.

255 January 24–March 7, 1973
The second series of the sitcom *Now Look Here...*, starring Ronnie Corbett and Rosemary Leach, airs on BBC1. The seven-episode series is written by **Graham Chapman** and Barry Cryer, and produced by Douglas Argent. The first series aired in November–December 1971.

256 January 28, 1973
Up Sunday (TV show: BBC2). **Eric Idle** guest-stars on this satirical late-night comedy-music series. Also with John Wells, Willie Rushton, James Cameron, Judith Greene, and Vivian Stanshall. Directed by Steve Roberts. Produced by Ian Keill.

257 February 8, 1973
Michael Palin, **Terry Jones**, and **Eric Idle** shoot a marketing film for the new Close-Up green toothpaste in the Colindale area of London. In the film, **Palin** plays a tramp transformed into a white-suited Super Salesman. For Elida-Gibbs Limited.

258 February 10, 1973
Full House (TV special: BBC2). **Michael Palin** performs in a sketch with John Bird on this live arts & entertainment program. Hosted by Joe Melia. Directed by Vernon Lawrence.

259 February 28, 1973
The British Screen Awards (Award ceremony). The Society of Film and Television Arts (now known as BAFTA) names *Monty Python's Flying Circus* the Best Light Entertainment Programme for 1972. The award is received by Bill Cotton (the BBC's Head of Light Entertainment). Michael Parkinson and John Mills host the gala event held at the Royal Albert Hall in the presence of Princess Anne.

260 Spring 1973
Eric Idle's son, Carey, is born.

261 March 17, 1973
Full House (TV special: BBC2). **Michael Palin** performs in (and co-writes) a sketch with John Bird on this live arts & entertainment program. Hosted by Joe Melia. Directed by Vernon Lawrence.

262 March 29, 1973
Eric Idle turns 30.

263 April 1, 1973
Weekend World (TV news show: ITV/LWT). **Eric Idle** impersonates host Peter Jay at the start of the program as an April Fool's Day joke.

264 April 1, 1973
Up Sunday (TV show: BBC2). **Eric Idle** appears as a guest on this satirical late-night comedy-music series. Also with John Wells, Willie Rushton, Keith Dewhurst, and Vivian Stanshall. Produced by Ian Keill.

265 April 13, 1973
John Cleese opens the new Students' Union at St. Andrews University in Scotland. Cleese has been rector of the University since April 1971. His term as rector ends this year.

266 April 22, 1973
Up Sunday (TV show: BBC2). Guest-star **Eric Idle** imitates Eamon Andrews in a parody of *This Is Your Life* set at St. Bartholomew's Hospital, London. Also with John Wells, Willie Rushton, Keith Dewhurst, Clive James, Roger Ruskin Spear, and Vivian Stanshall.

267 April 23, 1973
Monty Python's Flying Football Circus v Grimms (Event). The Pythons participate in a charity football match against the pop-rock group Grimms (John Gorman, Andy Roberts, Neil Innes, Roger McGough, et al) at George Payne's Sports Ground in Croydon, South London. Other players include John Peel, Nick Newman, and Keith Moon. The event, presented by *Time Out* magazine, is a benefit for the charity Shelter.

268 April 27–May 24, 1973
Monty Python's First Farewell Tour (Stage show). The Pythons put together a fast-paced stage show that combines live action, film clips and music, and take it on the road for a tour of Britain, performing 30 shows in 13 towns, augmented by Carol Cleveland and musician-composer Neil Innes. The tour takes them to the Gaumont Theatre in Southampton (Apr. 27), The Dome in Brighton (Apr. 28), Capitol Theatre in Cardiff (Apr. 30), New Theatre in Oxford (May 2–3), Hippodrome in Birmingham (May 4–5), Hippodrome in Bristol (May 7–8), Royal Court Theatre in Liverpool (May 10–11), Manchester Opera House (May 12–13), Empire Theatre in Sunderland (May 16), King's Theatre in Edinburgh (May 17–19), King's Theatre in Glasgow

(May 20), Grand Theatre in Leeds (May 22–23), and Royal Theatre in Norwich (May 24). Sketches include "Gumby Flower Arranging," "The Ministry of Silly Walks," "Take Your Pick (The Blow on the Head)," "Nudge, Nudge," "Self-Wrestling," "Llamas," "Mrs. Premise and Mrs. Conclusion," "Ken Shabby," "Pet Shop," "Custard Pie," "Silly Olympics" (film), "Travel Agent," and "Argument Clinic." Written & performed by **Graham Chapman, John Cleese, Terry Gilliam, Eric Idle, Terry Jones**, and **Michael Palin**, with Carol Cleveland and Neil Innes. Organized by concert promoter Tony Smith.

269   May 4–10, 1973

Time Out (Magazine/U.K.). "Monty Python's London Guide." Includes reviews of restaurants and films. Cover art by **Terry Gilliam**.

270   May 5, 1973

Michael Palin turns 30. The occasion is celebrated onstage at the end of the Pythons' performance at the Hippodrome Theatre in Birmingham.

271   May 19–June 2, December 26, 1973

Radio 5 (Radio series: BBC Radio 1). **Eric Idle** writes and stars in this comedy-music series, which consists of four hour-long programs. Sketches include "Missing Persons Bureau" and "A Penny for Your Warts." A second series airs in March–May 1974. Produced by Clive Burrows.

272   May 19–21, 23–27, 1973

The TV play *Secrets*, written by **Michael Palin** and **Terry Jones**, is recorded. It airs Aug. 14 on BBC2.

273   May 23, 1973

Look North (TV news show: BBC Yorkshire). **Graham Chapman, Terry Jones**, and **Michael Palin** are interviewed in Yorkshire during their U.K. tour.

274   May 25, 1973

The second series of *Monty Python's Flying Circus* begins playing on Canadian television (on the CBC).

275   June 4–20, 1973

Monty Python's First Farewell Tour (Stage show) continues in Canada. The Pythons' two-week Canadian tour takes the group from one side of the country to the other, performing at a variety of venues, including the St. Lawrence Centre in Toronto (June 6), Salle Wilfrid-Pelletier/Place des Arts in Montreal (June 7–8), National Arts Centre in Ottawa (June 9), Centennial Concert Hall in Winnipeg (June 13), Jubilee Auditorium in Edmonton, Alberta (June 14), Saskatchewan Centre of the Arts in Regina, Sask. (June 16), and Queen Elizabeth Theatre in Vancouver, B.C. (June 18–20). Written & performed by **Graham Chapman, John Cleese, Terry Gilliam, Eric Idle, Terry Jones**, and **Michael Palin**, with Carol Cleveland and Neil Innes.

276   June 6, 1973

Canada AM (TV show: CTV, in Canada). **Terry Gilliam, Terry Jones**, and **Michael Palin** are guests on this Canadian morning show hosted by Percy Saltzman.

277   June 20, 1973

The Pythons' tour of Canada ends with a final performance at the Queen Elizabeth Theatre in Vancouver, B.C. The group then travels to the U.S. to do some promotion for Buddah Records, the label that released *Another Monty Python Record* in the States in 1972. They spend eight days (June 21–28) in San Francisco and Los Angeles and make appearances (without **John Cleese**) on TV's *Midnight Special* and *Tonight Show*. **Cleese** returns to England on June 22.

278   June 26–27, 1973

The Pythons (without **John Cleese**, but with Neil Innes) record an appearance on NBC's *The Midnight Special* (June 26), a new late-night music program which premiered in February. Their appearance will air Oct. 12. The following day, the group performs on NBC's *The Tonight Show* (airs June 28), guest-hosted by Joey Bishop.

279   June 28, 1973

The Tonight Show Starring Johnny Carson (TV talk show: NBC). Monty Python's first — but not very successful — appearance on U.S. television. The group (minus **John Cleese**) performs "Putting Down Budgies (Pepperpots)" and "News for Parrots." The show was recorded the previous day. Guest-hosted by Joey Bishop. Produced by Fred DeCordova.

280   August 14, 1973

Black and Blue (TV play: BBC2). "Secrets." Television play written by **Michael Palin** and **Terry Jones**, the first presentation of the series *Black and Blue*, concerns a chocolate factory where three men fall into a mixing vat and end up as fillings for chocolates. The play is later adapted for film under the title *Consuming Passions* (1988). Starring Warren Mitchell, Brian Wilde, Hilda Barry, and Gretchen

Franklin. Directed by James Cellan Jones. Produced by Mark Shivas.
Reviews: The Times (London) (Aug. 12, 1973): "... a bitter-sweet, delicious-horrible, very funny story."

281   August 18, 1973
The Times (London) (Newspaper/U.K.). "Oliver Trimble and the Jelly Hound," by Ken Whitmore, with illustration by **Terry Gilliam**, p. 6. First prizewinner in the adult section of *The Times*/Jonathan Cape Children's Story Competition.

282   September 1973
The Monty Python Matching Tie and Handkerchief, the group's fourth album, is recorded at Radio Luxembourg Studios and Maximum Sound Studios, London

283   September 15–December 29, 1973
The second series of the sitcom *Doctor in Charge* airs on ITV. **Graham Chapman** and David Sherlock write two episodes (Sept. 15 & Dec. 8). **Chapman** had co-written (with Bernard McKenna) twelve episodes of the previous series (1972). Produced by Humphrey Barclay.

284   September 15, 1973
Doctor in Charge (TV episode: ITV/LWT). "The Merger." Waring overhears plans for the demolition of St. Swithins. Starring Robin Nedwell. Written by **Graham Chapman** and David Sherlock. Directed by Maurice Murphy.

285   September 27, 1973–January 3, 1974
The third series of the sketch-comedy show *The Two Ronnies*, starring Ronnie Barker and Ronnie Corbett, airs on BBC2. **Graham Chapman**, **John Cleese**, **Terry Jones**, and **Michael Palin** all contribute material to the series.

286   October 1973
Terry Gilliam marries Maggie Weston, makeup artist on the fourth Python series, in Belsize Park, London. Weston's later makeup credits will include both Python and **Gilliam** films.

287   October 6, 1973
Monty Python's Fliegender Zirkus (TV special: BBC2). The Python's second show for German television (performed in English) is shown by the BBC with the subtitle "Schnapps with Everything." Produced by Thomas Woitkewitsch of Bavarian Atelier GmbH Munich for WDR.

288   October 12, 1973
The Midnight Special (TV music show: NBC). The Bee Gees host this edition of the late-night rock music show. With Chuck Berry, Lee Michaels, King Crimson, Apple and Appleberry, Barbara Mason, and comedy from Monty Python. The group (minus **John Cleese**) recorded their sketches ("Gumby Flower Arranging," "Children's Stories," and "Nudge, Nudge") in Los Angeles on June 26 shortly after the end of their Canadian tour.

289   October 14, 1973
Omnibus (TV special: BBC1). "Laughter — Why We Laugh." An investigation into what makes us laugh, written and presented by Barry Took, with **John Cleese**, Les Dawson, and Peter Black joining in the discussion. Produced by Vernon Lawrence.

290   October 21, 1973
Eric Idle, **Terry Jones**, and **Michael Palin** take part in a charity football match in aid of Sunshine Homes for Children.

291   October 25, 1973
The Two Ronnies (TV episode: BBC1). Includes the sketch "Grublian," written by **John Cleese**. Third episode of the third series. Starring Ronnie Corbett and Ronnie Barker. Written by **John Cleese**, Mick Loftus, Spike Mullins, David Nobbs, **Michael Palin** & **Terry Jones**, Peter Vincent, and Gerald Wiley [pseud. of Ronnie Barker]. Produced by Terry Hughes. Note: "Grublian" will later appear on the 1976 album *The Two Ronnies* (BBC Records REB 257).

292   October 28, 1973
Up Sunday (TV show: BBC2). First show of the sketch-comedy's fourth series, from the Traverse Theatre in Edinburgh. **Eric Idle** guest-stars, with John Wells, Willie Rushton, Barry Humphries, Bill Barclay, Clive James, James Cameron, and Madeline Smith.

293   November 1973
The Monty Python Matching Tie and Handkerchief (Record: Charisma CAS 1080) is released in the U.K. Python's fourth comedy album (following 1972's *Previous Record*) contains a mix of new and TV-derived material. The album, described on the label as a "FREE RECORD Given Away with the Monty Python Matching Tie and Handkerchief," is originally released as a three-sided record; that is, one of the sides has two parallel sets of grooves, each containing a different set of tracks. Tracks: "Dead Bishop on the Landing (Church Police)," "Elephantoplasty," "Novel Writing," "Word Association," "Bruces/The Bruces' Philosophers Song," "Adventures of Ralph Melish/Hot Dogs and Knick-

ers," "Cheese Shop," "Wasp Club/Novel Writing/Tiger Club," "A Great Actor," "The Background to History," "First World War Noises in 4," " Boxing Tonight (Jack Bodell vs. Sir Kenneth Clark)," "Minister for Overseas Development," "Oscar Wilde," "Pet Conversions (Taking in the Terrier)," and "Phone-In." Recorded at Radio Luxembourg Studios and Maximum Sound Studios, London. Written & performed by **Graham Chapman**, **John Cleese**, **Terry Gilliam**, **Eric Idle**, **Terry Jones**, and **Michael Palin**, with Carol Cleveland. Music by Neil Innes. Cover design by **Terry Gilliam**. Produced by Andre Jacquemin, Dave Howman, and **Terry Gilliam**. Released in the U.S. on Arista AL 4039 (1975). U.S. single issued on Arista AS 0130. Remastered and reissued in 1997 as part of the "Arista Masters" series. Reissued in 2006 (EMI) with four bonus tracks.

Awards: Grammy-nominated in 1976 for Best Comedy Recording (it loses to Richard Pryor's *Is It Something I Said?*).

Reviews: (*Cue*, Nov. 22, 1975, p. 55): "Both sides of the disc are labeled side two, and one of them has parallel grooves. Depending on where the needle falls, the listener gets either of two programs. Alternatively dry, madcap, outrageous, blase and malignant!"

294   November 1, 1973

The Brand New Monty Python Bok (Book: Eyre Methuen), edited by **Eric Idle**, is published in the U.K. The Pythons' second book (following 1971's *Big Red Book*) is a collection of original comedy material, with only a few television-derived bits. The book's design features a white cover with some realistic inky thumb smears on it and a title beneath the dust jacket that reads: *Tits 'n Bums, A Weekly Look at Church Architecture*. Contents: "Safety Instructions," "The Old Story Teller," "Biggles is Extrememly Silly (1938)," "Biggles and the Naughty Things (1941)," "Notice of the Availability of Film Rights to Page Six," "Llap-Goch, the Secret Welsh Art of Self-Defense," "Edward Woodward's Fish Page," "The Python Book of Etiquette," "Famous First Drafts," "Page 71 Coming Soon/My Garden," "A Puzzle," "The Bigot," "The London Casebook of Detective René Descartes/Wallpapers," "16 Magazine," "Summer Madness," "Masturbation: The Difficult One," "Coming Soon: Page 16," "Python Panel," "The Adventures of Walter the Wallabee," "Mr. April ("I've Got Two Legs")," "Competition Time," "World Record Page," "Invitations," "The Oxfod Simplified Dictionary," "Unfinished Drawing," "Film Review with Philip Jenkinson," "Rat Recipes," "Chez Rat," "Overland to the World," "This Page Is in Colour," "Contents," "African Notebook," "How to…," "15 Pages to Page 71," "Norman Henderson's Diary," "Sex-Craft," "How to Take Your Appendix Out on the Piccadilly Line," "Join the Dots," "Directory," "The British Apathy League," "Let's Talk About Bottoms," "Ads/Hobbies," "Page 71," "Reviews of Page 71," "Alice," "The Hackenthorpe Book of Lies," "Masturbators of History," "Fairy Tale (Happy Valley)," "Ferndean School Report," "The Stratton Indicator," "Play Cheeseshop," "The Official Medallic Commemoration of the History of Mankind," "The Anagrams Gape," "Your Stars," "Hamsters: A Warning," and "Teach Yourself Surgery." Published in the U.S. by Henry Regnery Co. (1976). Published in paperback, as *The Brand New Monty Python Papperbok*, in 1974 (Eyre Methuen).

295   November 4–December 23, 1973

The ninth and final series of the sketch comedy show *I'm Sorry I'll Read That Again*, co-starring **John Cleese**, airs on BBC Radio 2. The show also stars Tim Brooke-Taylor, Graeme Garden, David Hatch, Jo Kendall, and Bill Oddie. 8 episodes.

296   November 4, 1973

Up Sunday (TV show: BBC2). "What Is Life?" **Eric Idle** makes another guest appearance on this late-night comedy program, joining John Fortune and Eleanor Bron with regulars John Wells, William Rushton, Clive James, and James Cameron. Directed by Tom Corcoran. Produced by Ian Keill.

297   November 12, 1973

Late Night Esther (Radio talk show: BBC Radio). Host Esther Rantzen talks to **Michael Palin** about *The Brand New Monty Python Bok*.

298   November 14, 1973

This Country in the Morning (Radio show: CBC Radio, in Canada). **Eric Idle**, **Michael Palin**, and **Terry Jones** speak (on the phone from London) to host Peter Gzowski about today's wedding of Princess Anne to Mark Phillips before an estimated world-wide audience of 500 million. The Pythons claim to have no knowledge of the event. "There's nothing in the papers," **Idle** remarks.

299   November 29, 1973

The Pythons attend a literary lunch to promote *The Brand New Monty Python Bok* at the Norfolk Gardens Hotel in Bradford, Yorkshire, England.

They give readings and afterward sign copies of the book.

300 December 8, 1973
Doctor in Charge (TV episode: ITV/LWT). "Hello Sailor!" Spurned by his girlfriend Annabel (Angharad Rees), Waring decides to join the Navy. Starring Robin Nedwell. Written by **Graham Chapman** and David Sherlock. Directed by Alan Wallis.

301 December 22, 1973
Melody Maker (Newspaper/U.K.). "Monty Python's Flying Circus," by Chris Welch. Interview with the Pythons about their history and current projects, including their new album, *Matching Tie and Handkerchief*.

302 December 24, 1973
The Goodies (TV episode: BBC2). "The Goodies and the Beanstalk." **John Cleese** appears briefly as a genie near the end of this 45-minute Christmas episode of the 1970–80 comedy series starring Tim Brooke-Taylor, Graeme Garden, and Bill Oddie. Written by Garden and Oddie. Produced by Jim Franklin.

303 December 24, 1973
Jokers Wild Christmas Special (TV special: ITV/YTV–Yorkshire Television). **John Cleese** appears as a panelist on this holiday edition of the comedy panel game. The other panelists include Les Dawson, Jack Douglas, Clive Dunn, David Nixon, Alfred Marks, Michael Aspel, and Norman Vaughan. Hosted by Barry Cryer. Produced & directed by David Millard.

304 1973
Marketing in Practice, No. 2: It's All Right, It's Only a Customer (Training film: Video Arts). A look at how customer enquiries can be mishandled by head-office employees. Starring **John Cleese**, Ronnie Barker, and Jonathan Lynn. Written by **John Cleese** and Antony Jay. Directed by Peter Robinson.

305 1973
Marketing in Practice, No. 3: The Competitive Spirit (Training film: Video Arts). A look at the problem of status-seeking, empire-building, and interdepartmental politics in management. Narrated by Keith Barron. Starring **John Cleese**, Peter Bayliss, and Jonathan Lynn. Written by **John Cleese** and Antony Jay. Directed by Peter Robinson.

306 1973
Customer Relations in Practice, No. 1: In Two Minds (Training film: Video Arts). Film for service staff on understanding customers in order to better meet their needs. Narrated by Philip Bond. Starring **John Cleese**, Tim Brooke-Taylor, Connie Booth, Angharad Rees, and June Whitfield. Written by **John Cleese** and Antony Jay. Directed by Peter Robinson.

307 1973
Customer Relations in Practice, No. 2: The Meeting of Minds (Training film: Video Arts). How to remove the barriers that can obstruct communication between seller and customer. Narrated by Philip Bond. Starring **John Cleese**, Tim Brooke-Taylor, Connie Booth, Angharad Rees, and June Whitfield. Written by **John Cleese** and Antony Jay. Directed by Peter Robinson.

308 1973
Customer Relations in Practice, No. 3: Awkward Customers (Training film: Video Arts). The right and wrong ways to deal with three types of awkward customer: angry (Mr. Tiger), talkative (Mrs. Rabbit), and rude (Mr. Warthog). Narrated by Philip Bond. Starring **John Cleese**, Angharad Rees, Gillian Raine, June Whitfield, George A. Cooper, and John Barron. Written by **John Cleese** and Antony Jay. Directed by Peter Robinson.

309 1973
Is This a Record? (Short film: Arthur Guinness Son and Co.). A humorous look at the Guinness Book of Records, presented by Frank Muir with members of Monty Python. Twenty-two-minute British short sponsored by Guinness. Starring Frank Muir, **John Cleese**, **Terry Jones**, **Michael Palin**, Connie Booth, William Rushton, and Liza Goddard. Animation by Bob Godfrey, Bill Sewell, Richard Taylor, and Corona Maher. Written by Barry Took, with additional material by **John Cleese**, **Terry Jones**, **Michael Palin**, and Frank Muir. Music by Stanley Myers. Directed by Digby Turpin. Produced by Peter Fensom.

310 1973
Harmony Hairspray (Marketing film). Biggles (**John Cleese**), of No. 18 RAF Hairspray Squadron, introduces this promotional short for the relaunch of Harmony Hairspray, with **Graham Chapman** (as Ginger), **Michael Palin** (as Algy), and **Eric Idle** (as Peter West, host of *Come Spraying*). Produced for Harmony employees. The team made a similar film in 1971 for Birds Eye Peas.

311 1973
Punch (Magazine/U.K.). "Monty Python's Tour

of Canada," by **Terry Jones** and **Michael Palin**. Humorous diary account of the group's June 1973 tour of Canada. Reprinted in the 1974 collection *Pick of Punch* (Hutchinson & Co.).

312   January 1974
Jimmy Gilbert, Head of Television Comedy at the BBC, offers **John Cleese** a chance to write a sitcom pilot with his wife, Connie Booth. The pilot they write will be based on a rude hotel manager **Cleese** encountered in May 1970 while the Pythons were filming in Devon. The series will be titled *Fawlty Towers*.

313   January 25–August 9, 1974
Sez Les (TV comedy series: ITV/YTV–Yorkshire Television). **John Cleese** appears as a guest performer on the eighth and ninth series of this sketch-comedy show (1969–76) starring Les Dawson. Other regulars include Roy Barraclough and Eli Woods. Produced & directed by David Mallett.

314   February 9, 1974
New Musical Express (Newspaper/U.K.). Monty Python reviews new single releases.

315   February 20–March 27, 1974
Marty Back Together Again (TV series: BBC1). **Graham Chapman** contributes material to this short-lived comedy series starring Marty Feldman. Other writers include Barry Cryer, Tom Lehrer, Ken Hoare, Johnny Speight, and Marty Feldman. Produced by Dennis Main Wilson.

316   February 26–March 23, 1974
Monty Python's First Farewell Tour (Stage show). Monty Python performs at London's Theatre Royal, Drury Lane for what was originally a two-week engagement, but is extended to four weeks due to popular demand. As in their 1973 tour of Britain and Canada, the group performs many Python television classics as well as some pre–Python sketches like "Four Yorkshiremen," and **Graham Chapman**'s "Self-Wrestling." Other sketches include: "The Pet Shop," "Nudge, Nudge," "Llamas," "Travel Agent," "A Fairy Tale," "Election Night Special," "Lumberjack Song," "Secret Service," "Cocktail Bar," "Argument Clinic," "Albatross," "World Forum," and "Gumby Flower Arranging." Written & performed by **Graham Chapman, John Cleese, Terry Gilliam, Eric Idle, Terry Jones,** and **Michael Palin**, with Neil Innes.
Review: B. A. Young (*Financial Times*, Feb. 27, 1974, p. 3): "For aficionados (I am one) the evening is one of almost uninterrupted enjoyment."

317   Spring 1974
Terry Jones' daughter, Sally, is born.

318   Spring 1974
The Department of the Environment for Scotland denies the Pythons permission to use any of the castles they have chosen as filming locations for their next film *Monty Python and the Holy Grail*, calling the film's script "incompatible with the dignity of the fabric of the buildings." Directors **Terry Jones** and **Terry Gilliam** choose instead to shoot at privately-owned Doune Castle (Castle Anthrax, French Castle, and Swamp Castle) and Castle Stalker (Castle Arrrghhh).

319   March 1974
Six episodes of a new comedy series starring **Eric Idle** are commissioned by the BBC. The series, scheduled to start taping in January 1975, will air under the title *Rutland Weekend Television* beginning in May 1975 on BBC2.

320   March 15, 1974
The script for *Monty Python and the Holy Grail* is completed. The last major change to the script is the removal of the "King Brian the Wild" sketch about a mad king who delights in ordering the deaths of close harmony groups.

321   March 18, 1974
William Jordan, the deputy chief veterinary officer of the RSPCA, attends tonight's performance of Monty Python at Drury Lane to see the "Cocktail Bar" sketch in which a barman kills a duck to make a cocktail. Four people complained to the RSPCA thinking it was a real duck.

322   March 30–May 4, 1974
Radio 5 (Radio series: BBC Radio 1). Second series of **Eric Idle**'s comedy-music series, which consists of six hour-long programs. Produced by Clive Burrows.

323   April 1974
A fourth series of *Monty Python's Flying Circus* (without **John Cleese**) is commissioned by the BBC.

324   April 1974
Re-Cycled Vinyl Blues (Record: United Artists UP 35676) is released. Single written and performed by Neil Innes, with **Michael Palin** providing the voice of the shopkeeper in the opening dialogue. Recorded in February 1974.

325   April 8, May 6 & 20, 1974
Jokers Wild (TV game show: ITV/Yorkshire).

John Cleese appears in episodes of the ninth series of the 1969–74 comedy panel game. His fellow panelists include Les Dawson, Lennie Bennett, Mike Goddard, Michael Aspel, and David Nixon. Hosted by Barry Cryer.

326   April 10–May 15, 1974

The sitcom *The Prince of Denmark*, starring Ronnie Corbett, airs on BBC1. The six-episode series is written by **Graham Chapman** and Barry Cryer and produced by Douglas Argent.

327   April 22, 1974

A Place in History (TV special: ITV/Thames). "University of St. Andrews." A look at the history of St. Andrews University in Scotland, hosted by the current rector of the university, **John Cleese**, and the newly-elected rector, Alan Coren. Half-hour special for Thames Television. Produced & directed by Robert Fleming.

328   April 30–May 31, 1974

Monty Python and the Holy Grail, the first Python-produced feature film, is shot in five weeks on a low budget (some of the money being contributed by the rock groups Pink Floyd and Led Zeppelin) on location in Scotland at Doune Castle, Castle Stalker, Killin, Glencoe, Arnhall Castle, Bracklinn Falls, Sherriffmuir, and completed at Twickenham Film Studios, England. Some additional filming takes place in June in Epping Forest outside London ("The Black Knight" scene) and on Hampstead Heath, London (opening shot). The total cost of production is £229,575.

329   April 30, 1974

Filming begins on *Monty Python and the Holy Grail*. The first day of filming ("The Bridge of Death" scene), on a mountain in Glencoe, Scotland, gets off to a rocky start when the camera breaks halfway through the very first shot. Other problems include a visibly shaking **Graham Chapman** (playing King Arthur), who is suffering from the DTs due to alcohol withdrawal, and the refusal of two Pythons (**Chapman** and **John Cleese**) to run across the rope bridge that spans the "Gorge of Eternal Peril."

330   May 2, 1974

The "Castle Arrrghhh" scene from *Holy Grail* is filmed at Castle Stalker in Argyll, Scotland.

331   May 3–6, 1974

The "Rabbit of Caerbannog/Holy Hand Grenade of Antioch" scene from *Holy Grail* is filmed at a cave in Killin, near Loch Tay, in Scotland.

332   May 5, 1974

The Do-It-Yourself Film Animation Show (TV episode: BBC1). "Table-Top and Cut-Outs." Guest **Terry Gilliam** demonstrates the process of cut-out animation in episode three of this Sunday-morning series hosted by Bob Godfrey. Directed by Anna Jackson. Produced by David Hargreaves.

333   May 7, 1974

The "Knights of the Round Table" musical number from *Holy Grail* is filmed in one day at Doune Castle in Scotland.

334   May 8–9, 1974

The "Castle Anthrax" scene (featuring **Michael Palin** as Sir Galahad) from *Holy Grail* is filmed at Doune Castle in Scotland.

335   May 10–11, 1974

The "French Taunter" scene from *Holy Grail* is filmed at Doune Castle. The filming is documented by the BBC program *Film Night* (the show's location report airs Dec. 19 on BBC2).

336   May 13, 1974

The "Bring Out Your Dead" scene from *Holy Grail* is filmed in Scotland.

337   May 16–18 & 23, 1974

The "Swamp Castle" scene (featuring **John Cleese** as Sir Lancelot) from *Holy Grail* is filmed at Doune Castle in Scotland.

338   May 21, 1974

The "Test of a Witch" scene from *Holy Grail* is filmed in Scotland.

339   May 22, 1974

The "Knights Who Say 'Ni'" scene from *Holy Grail* is filmed in Scotland.

340   May 24, 1974

Funny Ha Ha (TV episode: ITV/Thames). "Commander Badman." Upon learning that they are no longer wanted by the police, aging supervillain Commander Badman and his evil cohorts devise an elaborate plan to break the law. **Eric Idle** wrote and narrates this episode of the children's comedy series. Starring Aubrey Woods (title role), David Battley, Henry Woolf, Bridget Armstrong, and Roland MacLeod. Directed by Darrol Blake. Produced by Ruth Boswell. Note: Battley and Woolf will work again with **Idle** as regulars on his 1975 series *Rutland Weekend Television*.

Review: The Sunday Times (London) (May 19, 1974): "**Eric Idle** has written and narrated a ludicrous but frequently sidesplitting yarn."

341 May 25, 1974
The climactic "battle" scene from *Holy Grail* is filmed on a Saturday morning in Sheriffmuir, Scotland. Some 200 students from nearby Stirling University show up to play soldiers in the scene.

342 May 25, 1974
New Musical Express (Newspaper/U.K.). "Hi There, Tiger!," pp. 26–27+. Andrew Tyler interviews the Pythons during the filming of *Holy Grail* in early May. Included with the issue is the flexidisc single *Monty Python's Tiny Black Round Thing*.

343 May 25, 1974
Monty Python's Tiny Black Round Thing (Record: Charisma/NME SO 1259). Flexidisc given away free with the May 25 issue of the British rock magazine *New Musical Express* to promote the Pythons' new LP *Live at Drury Lane*. Contains two tracks from the album—"Election '74" b/w "The Lumberjack Song"—with a new intro by **Michael Palin**.

344 May 28, 1974
The "Three-Headed Knight" scene (featuring **Eric Idle** as Sir Robin) from *Holy Grail* is filmed in the Bluebell Woods outside Doune, Scotland.

345 May 29, 1974
After reading the pilot script for *Fawlty Towers* (written by **John Cleese** and Connie Booth), a BBC script editor sends a memo (dated May 29) to the Head of Comedy and Light Entertainment giving his opinion of the script. The memo reads in part: "I'm afraid I thought this one as dire as its title.... A collection of cliches and stock characters which I can't see being anything but a disaster."

346 May 31, 1974
The "Constitutional Peasants" scene from *Holy Grail* is filmed in the hills overlooking Callander, a small town north of Doune, Scotland. It is the Python team's last day of filming in Scotland.

347 June 1974
Monty Python Live at Drury Lane (Record: Charisma CLASS 4). Recording of some of Python's best bits performed live at The Theatre Royal in Drury Lane, London in March 1974. Tracks: "Introduction," "Llamas," "Gumby Flower Arranging," "**Terry Jones** (Link)," "Secret Service," "Wrestling," "Communist Quiz," "Idiot Song" (Neil Innes), "Albatross/Colonel (Filthy)," "Nudge, Nudge," "Cocktail Bar," "Travel Agent," "Spot the Brain Cell," "Bruces Song," "Argument Clinic/I've Got Two Legs (song)," "Four Yorkshiremen," "Election Special," "Lumberjack Song," "Theme Song (Liberty Bell)," "Parrot Sketch," and "Theme Song (Liberty Bell)." Written & performed by **Graham Chapman**, **John Cleese**, **Terry Gilliam**, **Eric Idle**, **Terry Jones**, and **Michael Palin**, with Neil Innes. Recorded Mar. 23, 1974. Single (*Monty Python's Tiny Black Round Thing*) issued on a flexidisc with the May 25, 1974, issue of *New Musical Express*. Not released in the U.S. until 1994 (Virgin/Caroline). Remastered & reissued in 2006 (EMI).

348 June 6–August 15, 1974
Dean Martin's Comedyworld (TV series: NBC). Summer replacement series featuring performances by new comedy talent from around the world. Several shows include clips from *Monty Python's Flying Circus* (including "A Scotsman on a Horse"). Directed by John Moffitt. Produced by Greg Garrison.

349 June 12, 1974
The "Black Knight" scene from *Holy Grail* is filmed in Epping Forest outside London. For part of the scene **John Cleese**, who plays the increasingly-limbless knight, is doubled by a one-legged man named Richard Burton. It is the last day of a 28-day shoot.

350 August 24, 1974
It's Cliff Richard (TV episode: BBC1). **Michael Palin** and **Terry Jones** contribute material to this music-variety show starring singer Cliff Richard. Produced by Brian Whitehouse.

351 September 1974
Sporting Relations (Book: Eyre Methuen), written by Roger McGough with drawings by **Terry Gilliam**, is published in the U.K. Poetry collection featuring 18 drawings by **Gilliam**. One of **Gilliam**'s few contributions to a book not his own or Python-related. Later editions of the book feature McGough's own artwork. Note: McGough later appears as an interview subject in **Eric Idle**'s 1978 TV film about The Rutles, *All You Need Is Cash*.

352 September 8, 1974
Filming begins on the fourth (and final) *Monty Python* series.

353 October 1974
The Brand New Monty Python Papperbok (Book: Eyre Methuen), edited by **Eric Idle**, is published in the U.K. Paperback reissue of *The Brand New Monty Python Bok* (1973). Almost identical to the original hardcover, except that the quotes from the dust jacket are now on the back cover and the cover

beneath the dust jacket (titled *Tits 'n Bums*) is gone. Published in the U.S. by Warner Books (1976).

354   October 1974

Bert Fegg's Nasty Book for Boys & Girls (Book: Eyre Methuen), written by **Terry Jones** and **Michael Palin**, is published in the U.K. Collection of comic material (much of it originally written for Python) aimed at children and presented by one Dr. Bert Fegg. Includes: "The Wonderful World of Nature," "Across the Andes by Frog," "Soccer My Way by The Supremes," "The Famous Five Go Pillaging," "Exciting War Yarn for Boys: I Was Hitler's Double," "The Modern British Safety Plane," "A Cowboy Story," "Aladdin and His Terrible Problem," and "How to Destroy This Book." Illustrations by Martin Honeysett and others. An expanded American reissue, *Dr. Fegg's Nasty Book of Knowledge*, is published in 1976 (Berkeley Medallion). Revised and reprinted as *Dr. Fegg's Encyclopeadia of All World Knowledge* (1984).

355   October 1974

John Cleese and wife Connie Booth shoot the short film *Romance with a Double Bass* over a ten-day period on location at Wilton House and The Somerley Estate in Wiltshire, England.

356   October 1974

Monty Python's Flying Circus premieres in the U.S. on a Sunday night on KERA (Channel 13), the PBS (Public Broadcasting Service) station in Dallas, Texas. The station's program director, Ron Devillier, had become a strong supporter of the show after requesting tapes from BBC Enterprises and viewing all three series over one weekend. Devillier convinced the station management and other stations in the Eastern Educational Network — including those in New York, Chicago, Pittsburgh, Miami, and Washington, D.C.— to take the show on a trial basis. *Flying Circus* proves to be a ratings success and by the summer of 1975 it is airing on 113 PBS stations. The group's only prior exposure on American television came in their 1973 appearances on *The Midnight Special* and *The Tonight Show* and in clips shown on 1974's summer series *Dean Martin's Comedyworld*.

Reviews: Richard A. Blake (*America*, May 3, 1975, pp. 348–49): "*Flying Circus* threatens to become an authentic hit with American audiences.... It is a voyage into the absurd on a Humean raft. Experience means nothing, since all laws of logical sequence have been suspended"; Cleveland Amory (*TV Guide*, May 17, 1975, P. 32): "...nothing is once over lightly here. Everything is done at least twice — and heavily ... the cast seems to have a longer boring point than we do ... there are funny ideas coming up here.... But don't get your hopes up unless this show gets a new — and tough — writer-editor-critic."

357   October 1, 1974

The Pythons, along with producers and investors, screen a rough cut of *Monty Python and the Holy Grail* at the Hanover Grand Film Theatre in London. The screening is a disaster, due in part to the poor-quality print and the effect of too much noise on the soundtrack.

358   October 12, 1974

The recordings for the fourth series of *Monty Python's Flying Circus* (now titled *Monty Python*) begin. The first show recorded is episode 40 ("The Golden Age of Ballooning").

359   October 19, 1974

Episode 41 ("Michael Ellis") of *Monty Python* is recorded.

360   October 26, 1974

Episode 42 ("Light Entertainment War") of *Monty Python* is recorded.

361   October 26–November 1, 1974

Radio Times (Magazine/U.K.). "Now for Something Entirely Similar," by Russell Miller, p. 6. A look at Monty Python as they begin their fourth series. The issue, which features cover art by **Terry Gilliam**, is held by **Eric Idle** in the upcoming "Mr. Neutron" episode.

362   October 31–December 5, 1974

The fourth and final series of *Monty Python's Flying Circus* airs on BBC2. This series differs from the first three in that: the shows were made without **John Cleese** (though some written material of his was used); it consists of only 6 shows, rather than 13; it airs on BBC2, rather than BBC1; and the words "Flying Circus" have been dropped from the title. Notable sketches from this series include "The Most Awful Family in Britain," "Teddy Salad of the Yukon," "Batsmen of the Kalahari," "Woody and Tinny Words," "Buying an Ant," and "The 'Anything Goes' Courtmartial." Recorded Oct. 12–Nov. 16, 1974.

363   October 31, 1974

Monty Python (TV episode: BBC2). "The Golden Age of Ballooning" (Episode 40). First show of the fourth series (recorded Oct. 12). Includes: "The Golden Age of Ballooning: Montgolfier Brothers,"

"Montgolfier Brothers Wash Each Other [anim]," "TGAOB: The Montgolfier Brothers in Love/Louis XIV," "Decision (discussion)," "TGAOB: The Court of George III/Antoinette/Butler," "Party Political Broadcast on Behalf of the Norwegian Party," "TGAOB: Barry Zeppelin/Ferdinand von Zeppelin/Corpses in Drawing Room," "The Golden Age of Colonic Irrigation [anim]," and "The Mill on the Floss (Ballooning)." Conceived, written & performed by **Graham Chapman**, **Terry Gilliam**, **Eric Idle**, **Terry Jones**, and **Michael Palin**. With Carol Cleveland, Peter Brett, Frank Lester, Bob E. Raymond, and Stenson Falke. Song: "George III" by Neil Innes. Animations by **Terry Gilliam**. Produced & directed by Ian MacNaughton.

364   November 2, 1974

Episode 43 ("Hamlet") of *Monty Python* is recorded.

365   November 7, 1974

Monty Python (TV episode: BBC2). "Michael Ellis" (Episode 41). Second show of the fourth series (recorded Oct. 19). Single-narrative episode which includes material co-written by **John Cleese**, originally intended for *Holy Grail* (the film, in its early stages, included a sequence set in a modern-day department store). Includes: "Department Store," "Michael Ellis/Buying an Ant," "Tiger and Other Pets," "University of the Air: Let's Talk Ant," "The Anatomy of an Ant [anim]," "Victorian Poetry Reading (Ants)," "Toupee Hall," "Complaints," and "End of Show Department." Conceived, written & performed by **Graham Chapman**, **John Cleese** (writer credit only), **Terry Gilliam**, **Eric Idle**, **Terry Jones**, and **Michael Palin**. With Carol Cleveland and John Hughman. Animations by **Terry Gilliam**. Produced & directed by Ian MacNaughton.

366   November 9, 1974

Episode 44 ("Mr. Neutron") of *Monty Python* is recorded.

367   November 10, 1974

The New York Times (Newspaper/U.S.). "*Monty Python's Flying Circus*—A Souffle of Lunacy," by John J. O'Connor, p. B33. Article describing the British comedy series which has just come to the U.S.

368   November 14, 1974

Monty Python (TV episode: BBC2). "Light Entertainment War" (Episode 42). Third show of the fourth series (recorded Oct. 26). Includes: "Up Your Pavement," "RAF Banter," "Trivializing the War," "Courtmartial (Basingstoke/Special Gaiters/Anything Goes In)," "Film Trailer," "The Public Are Idiots," "Programme Planners," "What a Lovely Day [anim]," "Woody and Tinny Words," "Show-Jumping (Musicals)," "Newsflash (Peter Woods)," and "When Does a Dream Begin? (song)." Conceived, written & performed by **Graham Chapman**, **John Cleese** (writer credit only), **Terry Gilliam**, **Eric Idle**, **Terry Jones**, and **Michael Palin**. With Carol Cleveland, Bob E. Raymond, and Marion Mould. Song: "When Does a Dream Begin?" written & sung Neil Innes. Animations by **Terry Gilliam**. Produced & directed by Ian MacNaughton.

369   November 16, 1974

Episode 45 ("Party Political Broadcast"), the last show of the fourth and final series of *Monty Python*, is recorded.

370   November 21, 1974

Monty Python (TV episode: BBC2). "Hamlet" (Episode 43). Fourth show of the fourth series (recorded Nov. 2). Includes: "Bogus Psychiatrists (Hamlet)," "Nationwide: Westminster Bridge/Police Helmets," "Father-in-Law," "Hamlet and Ophelia," "Paratroopers [anim]," "Boxing Match Aftermath (The Killer vs. The Champ)," "Boxing Commentary," "Piston Engine," and "A Room in Polonius's House: Live from Epsom/Jockey Interviews/Queen Victoria Handicap." Conceived, written & performed by **Graham Chapman**, **John Cleese** (writer credit only), **Terry Gilliam**, **Eric Idle**, **Terry Jones**, and **Michael Palin**. With Carol Cleveland, Jimmy Hill, Bob E. Raymond, Connie Booth, and K. Joseph. Animations by **Terry Gilliam**. Produced & directed by Ian MacNaughton.

371   November 26, 1974

Aspel and Company (TV talk show: BBC1). Hosted by Michael Aspel. Guest: **Michael Palin**.

372   November 28, 1974

Monty Python (TV episode: BBC2). "Mr. Neutron" (Episode 44). Fifth show of the fourth series (recorded Nov. 9). This single-narrative episode includes: "Post Box Ceremony," "Mr. Neutron in Suburbia," "F.E.A.R. Headquarters," "Supreme Commander," "Teddy Salad of the Yukon," "Eskimos," "Prime Minister," "Bombings," "Mrs. Scum," and "Conjuring Today." Conceived, written & performed by **Graham Chapman**, **Terry Gilliam**, **Eric Idle**, **Terry Jones**, and **Michael Palin**. With Carol Cleveland, Bob E. Raymond, and Sloopy.

Animations by **Terry Gilliam**. Produced & directed by Ian MacNaughton.

373   December 1974
Films and Filming (Magazine/U.K.). "'He said with incredible arrogance...': Monty Python Challenges Gordon Gow to a Joust Over Art and Life...," by Gordon Gow. Interview with **Graham Chapman, Michael Palin, John Cleese, Terry Gilliam**, and Neil Innes about *Holy Grail*, with photos from the film.

374   December 5, 1974
Monty Python (TV episode: BBC2). "Party Political Broadcast" (Episode 45). Sixth and last show of the fourth series (recorded Nov. 16). Includes: "Most Awful Family in Britain," "Icelandic Honey Week," "Patient Abuse," "Brigadier and Bishop," "Opera Singer [anim]," "An Appeal on Behalf of Extremely Rich People," "The Man Who Finishes Other People's Sentences," "The Walking Tree of Dahomey (David Attenborough)," "The Batsmen of the Kalahari (Cricket Match)," and "Newsreader." Conceived, written & performed by **Graham Chapman, Terry Gilliam, Eric Idle, Terry Jones**, and **Michael Palin**. With Carol Cleveland, Bob E. Raymond, and Peter Brett. Additional material by Douglas Adams and Neil Innes (words & music). Animations by **Terry Gilliam**. Produced & directed by Ian MacNaughton.

375   December 6, 1974
In Vision (TV talk show: BBC2). William Hardcastle talks with Monty Python members **Graham Chapman, Terry Gilliam, Terry Jones**, and **Michael Palin** in this look back over the past five years of *Monty Python's Flying Circus*, with clips from the show. Produced by Peter Foges.

376   December 17, 1974
The Book Programme (TV talk show: BBC2). Book discussion program hosted by Robert Robinson. This episode looks at the marketing of the bestselling novel *Jaws* by Peter Benchley. Guests **Eric Idle** and Monica Dickens discuss their favorite paperbacks of the past year. Directed by Martin L. Bell. Produced by Philip Speight.

377   December 19, 1974
Film Night (TV talk show: BBC2). "And Now for Something Completely Different...." A report on the making of the Pythons' new film *Monty Python and the Holy Grail* on location in Doune, Scotland during the May 1974 filming of the "French Taunter" scene at Doune Castle. Includes on-set interviews with all six Pythons, conducted by Tony Bilbow and Philip Jenkinson. Produced by Margaret Sharp.

378   December 21, 1974
Les Dawson's Christmas Box (TV special: ITV/ YTV–Yorkshire Television). Holiday special starring comedian Les Dawson. **John Cleese**, a frequent guest on Dawson's *Sez Les* series, appears in one sketch as a hotel manager. Written by Barry Cryer and David Nobbs, with additional material by Les Dawson, Alec Gerrard, and **Eric Idle**. Produced & directed by Vernon Lawrence.

379   December 23, 1974
The pilot episode ("A Touch of Class") of *Fawlty Towers*, written by and starring **John Cleese** and Connie Booth, is recorded. The series debuts in September 1975.

380   1974
Customer Relations in Practice, No. 4: More Awkward Customers (Training film: Video Arts). How to deal with three customer types: the knowledgeable (Mrs. Camel), the easily frightened (Mr. Clam), and the double-checker (Mrs. Ferret). Narrated by Philip Bond. Starring **John Cleese**, Patricia Routledge, Bernard Cribbins, Lynn Redgrave, Angharad Rees, Jane Walker, and Helena Clayton. Written by **John Cleese**. Directed by Peter Robinson.

381   1974
Marketing in Practice, No. 4: Prescription for Complaints (Training film: Video Arts). A six-step guide to handling complaining customers. Narrated by Andrew Cruickshank. Starring **John Cleese**, Penelope Keith, Ian Ogilvy, Norman Bird, John Clive, Una Stubbs, and George A. Cooper. Written by Denis Norden. Directed by Peter Robinson.

382   1974
The Show Business: How to Demonstrate a Product (Training film: Video Arts). The right and wrong ways to conduct a sales demonstration. Narrated by George Sewell. Starring **John Cleese**, Fanny Carby, Terrence Hardiman, Bill Maynard, and Una Stubbs. Written by **John Cleese** and Joe Windsor. Directed by Peter Robinson.

383   1974
Man Hunt: The Selection Interview (Training film: Video Arts). A guide for managers on how to improve their interviewing skills. Starring **John Cleese** (as Ethelred the Unready/Ivan the Terrible/William the Silent), Ian Ogilvy, Andrew Sachs,

Norman Bowler, Terence Alexander, and Tony Robinson. Written by **John Cleese** and Antony Jay. Directed by Peter Robinson.

384 1974
Selling in Practice, No. 2: How Not to Exhibit Yourself (Training film: Video Arts). How to sell from an exhibition stand. Starring **John Cleese**, Bernard Cribbins, John Standing, Bill Owen, Desmond Jones, Andrew Sachs, and John Barron. Written by Denis Norden. Directed by Peter Robinson.

385 1974
How to Lie with Statistics, Part 1: The Gee Whiz Graph (Training film: Videological Productions). Animated film narrated by **John Cleese** and featuring Hugh Burnett's "Monk" cartoon character. Based on the 1954 book of the same title by Darrell Huff and Irving Geis. Written by Robert Reid. Animated by Tony Hart. Produced by Antony Jay and Peter Robinson.

386 1974
Romance with a Double Bass (Short film: Cinema International Corp./Anton Films). Based on an 1886 short story by Anton Chekhov, this 41-minute film tells of the romance that ensues when a poor musician and a betrothed princess find themselves stranded in a lake, their clothes stolen. Filmed over ten days in October 1974, this pre–*Fawlty Towers* project starring **John Cleese** and Connie Booth (his wife) also marks **Cleese**'s first collaboration with director Robert Young (*Splitting Heirs*, *Fierce Creatures*). Shown in theaters with the Clint Eastwood film *The Eiger Sanction*. Starring **John Cleese** (as Smychkov) and Connie Booth (as Princess Constanza), with Graham Crowden, Desmond Jones, Freddie Jones, Jonathan Lynn, John Moffatt, and Andrew Sachs. Screenplay adapted from Chekhov by **John Cleese**, Connie Booth, and Robert Young, based on a screenplay by Bill Owen. Directed by Robert Young.

387 1974
Put in a Potterton (Marketing film). **John Cleese** appears in this humorous promotional short for Potterton's "Netaheat" wall-mounted gas boiler. Sponsored by Potter International. Also starring Larry Grayson. Written by Allardyce Hampshire. Directed by William Steward.

388 1974
The Pythons form their own music publishing company, Kay-Gee-Bee Music Ltd.

389 1974
Henry Cleans Up (Training film). A new pub landlord (**Michael Palin**) receives help from a rival publican (**Terry Jones**) on how to clean the pipes that carry beer from the Guinness barrel to the tap. Twelve-minute instructional short sponsored by Guinness. Narrated by Dick Graham. Starring **Michael Palin** (as Henry), **Terry Jones** (as Albert), Carol Cleveland, and Tommy Mann. Written by **Michael Palin** and Peter Fensom. Directed by Digby Turpin. Produced by Peter Fensom.

390 January 13, 1975
Michael Palin's daughter, Rachel, is born.

391 March 1975
Monty Python and the Holy Grail (Trailer). In this "Coming Attraction" trailer for the film, a professional announcer, a bad reader, a Gumby, and a Chinese man audition for the job of trailer narrator. The Chinese man wins and goes on to describe *Holy Grail* as one of "the more run-of-the-mill films like *Herbie Rides Again* and *La Notte*."

392 March 1975
Hello Sailor (Book: Weidenfeld and Nicolson), written by **Eric Idle**, is published in the U.K. **Idle**'s first novel, a satire on sex and politics, includes such characters as the British Prime Minister who is a "bachelor gay"; a dead foreign secretary who functions as efficiently as before with the aid of a taxidermist; Astronaut Sickert who tests a contraceptive in space; a character who seduces the daughters of the entire Cabinet; and much more. Paperback edition published by Futura. Idle's second novel, *The Road to Mars*, is published in 1999.

Review: Jeremy Brooks (*The Sunday Times* [London], Mar. 30, 1975, p. 39): "**Eric Idle** fails by a mile to transfer his anarchic wit from telly screen to printed word.... Funny lines, though by no means in short supply here, are not enough."

393 March 7, 1975
Four of the Pythons—**Graham Chapman**, **Terry Gilliam**, **Terry Jones**, and **Michael Palin**—fly to the U.S. for a two-week publicity tour for *Flying Circus*, visiting PBS stations in New York (WNET), Philadelphia (WHYY), Washington, D.C. (WETA), Los Angeles (KCET), Dallas (KERA), and Chicago (WTTW), giving interviews and helping solicit money from viewers. The Pythons will return to the U.S. next month to promote the release of *Holy Grail*.

394 March 9, 1975
The four visiting Pythons appear on PBS station

WNET (Channel 13) in New York City. They participate in the station's five-hour pledge drive, helping to answer phones and being interviewed by Gene Shalit.

395 March 10, 1975

The Pythons attend a party at Sardi's restaurant in NYC celebrating their signing (on Feb. 20) with Clive Davis' Arista Records, their new American label. Arista's first Python release will be *Matching Tie and Handkerchief* in April.

396 March 14, 1975

Graham Chapman, **Terry Gilliam**, **Terry Jones**, and **Michael Palin** attend the first public showing of *Monty Python and the Holy Grail* at a special midnight showing at the Los Angeles International Film Exposition (Filmex).

397 March 14, 1975

Monty Python and the Holy Grail (Feature film), world premiere in Los Angeles. Monty Python's second feature film (following 1971's TV-derived *And Now for Something Completely Different*) is a collection of medieval sketches loosely tied together by King Arthur's quest for the Holy Grail. Includes: "Moose titles," "The Swallow," "Bring Out Your Dead," "Constitutional Peasants," "The Black Knight," "The Test of a Witch," "The Book of the Film," "Knights of the Round Table (Camelot Song)," "Arthur and God," "The French Taunter," "The Tale of Sir Robin: The Three-Headed Knight (song: Brave Sir Robin)," "The Tale of Sir Galahad: The Castle Anthrax," "Scene 24," "The Knights Who Say 'Ni,'" "The Tale of Sir Lancelot: Swamp Castle," "Roger the Shrubber," "Tim the Enchanter," "The Rabbit of Caerbannog/Holy Hand Grenade of Antioch," "The Cave of Caerbannog," "The Black Beast of Arrrghhh [anim]," "The Bridge of Death," "The Castle Arrrghhh," and "The Final Attack." Written by and featuring **Graham Chapman**, **John Cleese**, **Terry Gilliam**, **Eric Idle**, **Terry Jones**, and **Michael Palin**. With Connie Booth, Carol Cleveland, Neil Innes, Bee Duffell, John Young, Rita Davies, Avril Stewart, and Sally Kinghorn. Animations by **Terry Gilliam**. Songs by Neil Innes. Directed by **Terry Gilliam** and **Terry Jones**. Produced by Mark Forstater and John Goldstone (exec). A Python (Monty) Pictures/Michael White production. Re-released on June 15, 2001.

Awards: Hugo Award nominee for Best Dramatic Presentation.

Reviews: John Coleman (*New Statesman*, Apr. 4, 1975, p. 458): "...the wanton promise of their title is unexpectedly fulfilled.... This *Python* is often hilarious"; Vincent Canby (*The New York Times*, Apr. 28, 1975): "...*Grail* is a marvelously particular kind of lunatic endeavor ... it manages to send up the [King Arthur] legend, courtly love, fidelity, bravery, costume movies, movie violence and ornithology"; Penelope Gilliatt (*The New Yorker*, May 5, 1975, pp. 115–17): "...a cheerfully loused-up reworking of the legend of King Arthur's Grail hunt.... The whole film, which is often recklessly funny and sometimes a matter of comic genius, is a triumph of errancy and muddle"; Paul D. Zimmerman (*Newsweek*, May 19, 1975, pp. 90–91): "...delightful performances by the members of the Python troop, especially **Graham Chapman**'s wonderfully earnest King Arthur ... marvelously zany"; Richard Schickel (*Time*, May 26, 1975, pp. 58): "*Grail* is as funny as a movie can get, but it is also a tough-minded picture — as outraged about the human propensity for violence as it is outrageous in its attack on that propensity"; Hollis Alpert (*Saturday Review*, May 31, 1975, p. 44+): "The Pythons have taken on the entire King Arthur legendry and smashed it into gorgeous bits and skits"; Gene Siskel (*Chicago Tribune*, June 9, 1975, sec. 3, p. 22): "For my money, I wasn't particularly knocked out by *Holy Grail*. For me, it contained about 10 very funny moments and 70 minutes of silence.... I guess I prefer Monty Python in chunks, in its original, television revue format"; P.J. O'Rourke (*Rolling Stone*, June 19, 1975, p. 16): "*Holy Grail* is an enormous relief from every kind of movie and TV humor ... it's a better movie than *Blazing Saddles* or *Young Frankenstein*."

398 March 15, 1975

Graham Chapman, **Terry Gilliam**, **Terry Jones**, and **Michael Palin** (clutching a stuffed armadillo) are interviewed during a live fund-raising event for the PBS station in Dallas, KERA (Channel 13). They are interviewed by the station's program director Ron Devillier, the man responsible for bringing *Monty Python's Flying Circus* to American television for the first time in October 1974.

399 March 29, 1975

The Times (London) (Newspaper/U.K.). "The Complete and Utter **Palin** and **Jones** in a Two Man Python Team," by Sheridan Morley, p. 6. **Michael Palin** and **Terry Jones** talk about Python, *Holy Grail*, and some of their past history. The interview took place in a recording studio above a Chinese take-out restaurant (in Wardour St., London) where the two were working on the *Holy Grail* soundtrack.

400   March 29, 1975
London Bridge (TV show: ITV/LWT). Saturday-morning children's program hosted by Michael Wale. Guests **Michael Palin** and **Terry Jones**, promoting *Holy Grail*, answer questions from children in the audience. Recorded Mar. 26 at London Weekend Studios.

401   March 31, 1975
Newsweek (Magazine/U.S.). "Pythonmania," by Harry F. Waters, pp. 72–73. Article covering Python's background, sketches, and invasion of the U.S.

402   April 1975
The Monty Python Matching Tie and Handkerchief album is released in the U.S. on Arista AL 4039. Single issued on Arista AS 0130.

403   April 3, 1975
Monty Python and the Holy Grail (released by EMI) premieres in London at the Casino Theatre, Old Compton Street. The Pythons attend the screening, then move on to a party at the Marquee Club.

404   April 6, 1975
The second series of *Monty Python's Flying Circus* begins running in the U.S. on more than fifty PBS outlets.

405   April 11, 1975
Open House (Radio show: BBC Radio 2). Pete Murray talks to **John Cleese**.

406   April 18, 1975
Michael Palin is commissioned by the BBC's Head of Comedy, Jimmy Gilbert, to write and star in a comedy pilot which, if successful, will be the first of a series. **Terry Jones** will co-write (and co-star) and Terry Hughes will direct. The show, *Tomkinson's Schooldays*, will air Jan. 7, 1976, and become the first episode of the **Palin-Jones** series *Ripping Yarns*.

407   April 25, 1975
A.M. America (TV news-talk show: ABC). **Graham Chapman**, **Terry Gilliam**, **Eric Idle**, **Terry Jones**, and **Michael Palin** guest co-host this two-hour morning show with host Stephanie Edwards.

408   April 25, 1975
Graham Chapman, **Terry Gilliam**, **Eric Idle**, **Terry Jones**, and **Michael Palin** pose nude (or nearly) for photographer Richard Avedon at his New York studio. The photo is published in the July 1975 issue of *Vogue* and later in *MONTYPYTHONSCRAPBOOK* (1979).

409   April 26, 1975
The New York Times (Newspaper/U.S.). "Monty Python's Flying Circus is Barnstorming Here," by Michael T. Kaufman, p. 29. The Pythons (minus **John Cleese**) talk about their beginnings and influences. The interview was conducted yesterday at the Central Park Zoo.

410   April 27, 1975
Monty Python and the Holy Grail opens in New York. The Pythons attend the premiere at Cinema II on Third Avenue, giving out coconuts to the first 1,000 people who show up. Although the first screening is scheduled for 11 A.M., the cinema has to add a special 9:30 A.M. screening to accommodate the large crowds that are stretching around the block.

411   April 28, 1975
The Pythons attend a party in their honor at Relaxation Plus, a massage parlor located in the Commodore Hotel in New York. Other celebrities there include Andy Warhol, Jeff Beck, and Dick Cavett.

412   May 5, 1975
The Village Voice (Newspaper/U.S.). "I Am Monty Python, King of the Goons," by Richard Goldstein, back & pp. 79–80. Article on the history of Python. The issue also contains an unfavorable review of *Holy Grail* by Andrew Sarris (p. 81–82).

413   May 8, 1975
Rolling Stone (Magazine/U.S.). "Horse Bites Python, Python Bites Back," by Larry Sloman, p. 18+. Article on the Pythons' visit to New York and some of their mishaps: **Terry Gilliam** nearly getting bounced from the Plaza Hotel Bar; **Graham Chapman** getting roughed up at the Le Jardin Discotheque; and **Terry Jones** getting mugged by a horse. Includes a photo of the group answering phones at WNET, the PBS station in New York.

414   May 9, 1975
Arts Forum (Radio talk show: WNYC-FM, New York). Interview with Python members, promoting *Holy Grail*.

415   May 10, 1975
The Washington Post (Newspaper/U.S.). "A Python in the Center Ring," by Tom Zito, p. D1-2. Python article, with a photo of the visiting **Chapman**, **Palin**, **Gilliam**, and **Jones** taken by Ken Fell.

416 May 10–16, 1975
Radio Times (Magazine/U.K.). "The Tiniest Show on TV," by Irma Kurtz. Interview with **Eric Idle** and Neil Innes about their new series *Rutland Weekend Television*. **Idle** also appears on the cover.

417 May 12–June 16, 1975
The first series of **Eric Idle**'s *Rutland Weekend Television* airs on BBC2. The weekly half-hour comedy show features studio interviews, filmed inserts, and musical items by Neil Innes (former member of the Bonzo Dog Doo-Dah Band and frequent Python collaborator). The show is broadcast from the small English county of Rutland which vanished in an organizational shuffle. The first series, produced by Ian Keill, consists of six shows followed by a Christmas special on Dec. 26.
Review: The Sunday Times (London) (May 11, 1975, p. 52): "While [**Idle**] cannot reach the heights of Pythonry on his own (and there's no one else around in remotely the same class), the new ingredient of satirical songs works extremely well."

418 May 12, 1975
Rutland Weekend Television (TV episode: BBC2). "Rutland Weekend Gibberish." First show of the first series. Includes: "Gibberish," "Star of the Sexy Movies" (song), "Hanging," "Trapped Under Clerics," "Saving Fish from Drowning," "Stoop Solo" (song), "The Royal Rutland Fusiliers," "The Major Who Doesn't Understand," and "The Week Ahead on RWT (Churchill Programmes)." Written by **Eric Idle**, and performed by **Eric Idle**, David Battley, Neil Innes, Timothy Carlton, Peter Glidewell, and Henry Woolf. Music & songs by Neil Innes. Directed by Andrew Gosling.

419 May 12, 1975
The New Yorker (Magazine/U.S.). "The Talk of the Town: *Monty Python's Flying Circus*," pp. 35–36. Article describing the individual members of the group and how Python first started catching on in the States.

420 May 19, 1975
Rutland Weekend Television (TV episode: BBC2). "Rutland Weekend Kung-Fu." Second show of the first series. Includes: "Come Dancing," "Say Sorry Again" (song), "Philosophy Corner," "Intelligence Test (Cretin Club)," "Talk About (Great Wit)," "Origami," "Impersonations of Medical Equipment," "Communist Cooking" (song), "Kung Suey," "The Kung and I," "Normal (Arthur Sutcliffe)" (doc), "The Man from the Off-License," "Lie Down and Be Counted" (song), and "Kung Dancing." Written by **Eric Idle**, and performed by **Eric Idle**, David Battley, Gwen Taylor, Neil Innes, and Henry Woolf. Music & songs by Neil Innes. Directed by Andrew Gosling.

421 May 26, 1975
Rutland Weekend Television (TV episode: BBC2). "Rutland Weekend Warning System." Third show of the first series. Includes: "Warning Signs," "Schizophrenia," "The Children of Rock and Roll" (song), "The Homes of the Poets: Mungo Wright (Cramp Bottom)" (doc), "Football" (song), "Comparative Religions/God of the British Army," "Bathtime Theatre: Splash, Kevin Tripp," "Boring" (song), "No Sherry/Buying People," "Television Forecast," and "The Final Word with Tony Bilbow." Written by **Eric Idle**, and performed by **Eric Idle**, Lyn Ashley, David Battley, Neil Innes, Andy Roberts, Wanda Ventham, and Henry Woolf. Music & songs by Neil Innes. Directed by Andrew Gosling.

422 Summer 1975
The Album of the Soundtrack of the Trailer of the Film of Monty Python and the Holy Grail (Record: Charisma CAS 1103) is released in the U.K. Soundtrack album, presented as the "Executive Version," featuring highlights from *Holy Grail* interspersed with original material. Tracks: "Executive Introduction," "The Classic, Silbury Hill," "Premiere of the Film (Live Broadcast from London)," "Rear Stalls," "Bring Out Your Dead," "Constitutional Peasants," "The Test of a Witch," "A Professional Logician," "Knights of the Round Table (Camelot Song)," "Arthur and God," "The Classic, Silbury Hill," "The French Taunter," "Bomb Scare," "Executive Announcements," "The Story of the Film So Far," "Brave Sir Robin (song)," "The Knights Who Say 'Ni,'" "Rear Stalls," "Marilyn Monroe," "Swamp Castle," "Tim the Enchanter," "Drama Critic," "Holy Hand Grenade of Antioch," "Executive Announcement/Sir Kenneth Clark," and "The Castle Arrrghhh." Written & performed by **Graham Chapman, John Cleese, Terry Gilliam, Eric Idle, Terry Jones,** and **Michael Palin**. Recorded and Produced at Sunrise Music and Recording Ltd. by Andre Jacquemin, Dave Howman, **Michael Palin, Terry Jones,** and **Terry Gilliam**. Original film soundtrack recorded by Garth Marshall and mixed by Hugh Strain. Released in the U.S. on Arista AL 4050. Reissued on Charisma CHC 17 (1983). Digitally remastered and reissued in 1997 (with added track: "The Bridge of Death") as part of the "Arista Masters" series. Reissued again in 2006 (EMI) with three bonus tracks.

Reviews: Jon Tiven (*Audio*, December 1975, p. 89): "Python devotees will not be disappointed with this record."

423   June 1975
ABC Television purchases the American broadcast rights for the fourth Python series from Time-Life Films Inc. (the BBC's New York sales agents). The network intends to show the six episodes in two 90-minute installments of its late-night series *Wide World of Entertainment*. The first of the two Python specials airs Oct. 3.

424   June 1975
Film Review (Magazine/U.K.). Includes a review of *Holy Grail* (p. 8) and interview with the group (p. 9).

425   June 2, 1975
Rutland Weekend Television (TV episode: BBC2). "Rutland Weekend Whistle Test." Fourth show of the first series. Includes: "The Old Gay Whistle Test," "Toad the Wet Sprocket," "Mantra Robinson," "Band Wagon" (song), "Dead Singer," "Rutland Weekend Theatre," "Amnesia," "Beauty Queen Farm" (doc), "Yorkshire Showbiz Butchers," "A Penny for Your Warts," "Once We Had a Donkey (Fabulous Bingo Brothers)" (song), and "Protest Song." Written by **Eric Idle** and performed by **Eric Idle**, Bridget Armstrong, David Battley, Bob Harris, Neil Innes, Andy Roberts, and Henry Woolf. Music & songs by Neil Innes. Directed by Andrew Gosling.

426   June 8, 1975
Monty Python and the Holy Grail opens in Chicago at the Carnegie Theatre. **Graham Chapman** and **Terry Jones** attend the premiere, giving out coconuts.

427   June 9, 1975
Rutland Weekend Television (TV episode: BBC2). "Rutland Weekend Rain in Hendon." Fifth show of the first series. Includes: "Solihull Wife-Swapping Club," "Weather Flash (Rain in Hendon)," "TV Jobs for MPs," "Prime Minister," "I'm the Urban Spaceman" (song), "Your Questions Answered," "Weather Flash (Rain in Hendon)," "Holiday 75," "Front Loader" (song), "Rain in Hendon," "Satan in Electrical Shop," and "Rain in Hendon." Written by **Eric Idle** and performed by **Eric Idle**, Lyn Ashley, David Battley, Neil Innes, Philip Jenkinson, Henry Woolf, and Wanda Ventham. Music & songs by Neil Innes. Directed by Andrew Gosling.

428   June 13, 1975
Chicago Tribune (Newspaper/U.S.). "Zeroing in on the Zanies," by Bruce Vilanch, sec. 3, p. 5. **Terry Jones** and **Graham Chapman** are interviewed.

429   June 16, 1975
Rutland Weekend Television (TV episode: BBC2). "Rutland Weekend Budget Cuts." Sixth and last show of the first series. Includes: "Religion Today," "Singing a Song Is Easy" (song), "Incident at Bromsgrove (Carrot)," "Nelson and Hardy," "The Execution of Charles I," "L'Amour Perdu" (song), "Man Alive: Suburban Prisons," "Johnny Cash (Live at Mrs. Fletcher's)" (song), "Religion Today," and "The Song O' the Continuity Announcers" (song). Written by **Eric Idle** and performed by **Eric Idle**, David Battley, Terence Bayler, Neil Innes, and Henry Woolf. Music & songs by Neil Innes. Directed by Andrew Gosling.

430   June 16–July 9, 1975
Michael Palin spends three weeks filming the TV movie *Three Men in a Boat* along the Thames River in London. The film airs Dec. 31 on BBC2.

431   July 1975
Esquire (Magazine/U.S.). "Monty Python's American Diary (notes on our country by an all-wise visitor from utter space)," by **Michael Palin**, pp. 88–89+. **Michael Palin**'s diary account of Python's visit to America in March in which he writes about Fly-Eezi ("the airline that can't afford to crash"), the group's trashing of their New York hotel room, and an American game show called *Gimme the Money You Bastard, or I'll Strangle You*, among other things. Reprinted on the back cover of the group's *Live at City Center* album in 1976.

432   July 1975
Vogue (Magazine/U.S.). "Monty Python Exposed," by Leo Lerman, pp. 82–83. Python article accompanied by a nude photo of the group (with "naughty bits" covered) taken by Richard Avedon (on Apr. 25 in New York). The photo is later reprinted in 1979's *MONTYPYTHONSCRAPBOOK*.

433   July 5, 1975
Graham Chapman and friends (including writer Douglas Adams) perform between acts at a rock festival at Knebworth Park in Hertfordshire, England. Acts appearing include Pink Floyd, The Steve Miller Band, and Captain Beefheart.

434   August 25, 1975
The Summer Show (Radio show: BBC Radio 4). Guest: **John Cleese**.

435 August 29, 1975
The John Cleese Sketchbook (Radio special: BBC Radio 4). New material from **John Cleese** is presented for the first time in this half-hour program. With Bill Maynard. Produced by John Cassels. 25 mins.

436 September 1975
Playboy (Magazine/U.S.). "On the Scene: Monty Python's Flying Circus," pp. 184–85. Article.

437 September 1975
Cineaste (Magazine/U.S.). "The Wondrous Return of the Wacky Monty Python's Flying Circus," by Lenny Rubenstein, pp. 14–18. A drawing of the group (by Bill Plympton) is featured on the cover.

438 September 4–9, 1975
Michael Palin and **Terry Jones** spend four days in New York City (and the weekend of the 6th–7th in West Granby, CT) working on the layout of the new American edition of their 1974 *Bert Fegg* book. The new book, titled *Dr. Fegg's Nasty Book of Knowledge*, is published in 1976.

439 September 19–October 24, 1975
The first series of *Fawlty Towers*, consisting of six episodes, airs on BBC2. This legendary BBC situation comedy—**John Cleese**'s most successful non–Python effort—stars **Cleese** as Basil Fawlty, the hilariously rude owner of a Torquay hotel with the ability to turn the smallest problem into a major catastrophe. The show also features **Cleese**'s wife and writing partner Connie Booth as Polly the maid, Prunella Scales as the always-in-control Sybil Fawlty, and Andrew Sachs as the abused Spanish waiter Manuel. Other regulars are Ballard Berkeley (Major Gowen), Gilly Flower (Miss Tibbs), and Renee Roberts (Miss Gatsby). The character of Basil Fawlty is based on a real-life hotelier **Cleese** encountered in 1970 during his stay at the Gleneagles Hotel near Torquay while filming for Python. The creation of the show sprang from **Cleese**' desire to move away from his Python television work and write something new with Booth. A second series of six shows airs in 1979.
Awards: BAFTA-winner for Best Situation Comedy; BAFTA-nominated for Best Light Entertainment Performance (**Cleese**); Royal Television Society award for Outstanding Creative Achievement; Variety Club Award 1975 to **Cleese** for BBC TV Personality of the Year; Variety Club Award 1976 to Andrew Sachs for Most Promising Artist; Broadcasting Press Guild award for Best Comedy.

440 September 19, 1975
Fawlty Towers (TV episode: BBC2). "A Touch of Class." Basil, eager to attract a higher class of clientele to the hotel, is delighted when a Lord Melbury checks in. Basil fawns over his important guest, never suspecting that Melbury is actually a confidence trickster. First episode of the first series. Recorded Dec. 23, 1974. Starring **John Cleese**, Prunella Scales, Andrew Sachs, Connie Booth, with Michael Gwynn, Robin Ellis, Ballard Berkeley, Martin Wyldeck, David Simeon, Terence Conoley, and Lionel Wheeler. Written by **John Cleese** and Connie Booth. Produced & directed by John Howard Davies.

441 September 26, 1975
Fawlty Towers (TV episode: BBC2). "The Builders." While he and Sybil are away, Basil hires O'Reilly, an amateur builder, to do some construction on the hotel, against strict orders from Sybil. Second episode of the first series. Starring **John Cleese**, Prunella Scales, Andrew Sachs, Connie Booth, with Ballard Berkeley, David Kelly, Gilly Flower, Renee Roberts, James Appleby, George Lee, Michael Cronin, and Michael Halsey. Written by **John Cleese** and Connie Booth. Produced & directed by John Howard Davies.

442 October 1975
The third series of *Monty Python's Flying Circus* begins running on PBS stations in the U.S.

443 October 1975
The TV special *Out of the Trees*, co-written by and starring **Graham Chapman**, is recorded. It will air Jan. 10, 1976, on BBC2.

444 October 3, 1975
Michael Palin records an appearance on the radio game show *Just a Minute* at BBC Studios in London. The two programs recorded will air on BBC Radio 4 on Nov. 18 and Feb. 10, 1976.

445 October 3, 1975
Monty Python's "The Lumberjack Song" is re-recorded for a Christmas single. The recording, by **Michael Palin** and The Fred Tomlinson Mounted Singers, takes place at The Workhouse studio in Old Kent Road, London with former Beatle George Harrison producing (credited on the record as George "Onothimagen" Harrison). The single is released Nov. 14.

446 October 3, 1975
Fawlty Towers (TV episode: BBC2). "The Wedding Party." After Sybil gives a room to an unmar-

ried couple, Basil becomes obsessed with what he sees as immoral behavior among his hotel guests. Third episode of the first series. Starring **John Cleese**, Prunella Scales, Andrew Sachs, Connie Booth, with Ballard Berkeley, Yvonne Gilan, Conrad Phillips, Diana King, Trevor Adams, April Walker, Gilly Flower, Renee Roberts, and Jay Neill. Written by **John Cleese** and Connie Booth. Produced & directed by John Howard Davies.

447   October 3, 1975

Wide World of Entertainment (TV special: ABC). "The Monty Python Show." A compilation of three Python shows: "The Golden Age of Ballooning," "Mr. Neutron," and "Party Political Broadcast." ABC, needing to fill this 90-minute time slot, bought the rights to the fourth Python series — which consists of six half-hour shows — with the intention of airing them in two groups of three. But with commercials, there is only 66 minutes of actual programming left. The Pythons take legal action after viewing a tape of the program on Nov. 25.

448   October 6–November 24, 1975

The eight-part series *The Selling Line* airs on BBC2. The series showcases the business-training films produced by Video Arts and starring **John Cleese**.

449   October 6, 1975

The Selling Line (TV episode: BBC2). "Who Sold You This, Then?" (1972 training film). First episode of the series. Starring **John Cleese**, Bernard McKenna, Jonathan Lynn, and Madge Ryan. Written by **John Cleese** and Antony Jay. Directed by Peter Robinson.

450   October 10, 1975

Fawlty Towers (TV episode: BBC2). "The Hotel Inspectors." Hearing that there are some hotel inspectors in the area, Basil gives royal treatment to two guests (one is an annoying spoon seller) whom he believes to be the inspectors. Fourth episode of the first series. Starring **John Cleese**, Prunella Scales, Andrew Sachs, Connie Booth, with Bernard Cribbins, James Cossins, Ballard Berkeley, Gilly Flower, Renee Roberts, Geoffrey Morris, and Peter Brett. Written by **John Cleese** and Connie Booth. Produced & directed by John Howard Davies.

451   October 13–20, 1975

Tomkinson's Schooldays (currently titled *The Michael Palin Special*), a TV comedy pilot written by and starring **Michael Palin** and **Terry Jones**, is filmed in Dorset and on the Isle of Dogs. Dorset locations include Lulworth Cove and the Milton Abbey School (in Milton Abbas). The show is recorded before a live studio audience on Nov. 1.

452   October 13, 1975

The Selling Line (TV episode: BBC2). "It's Alright, It's Only a Customer" (1973 training film). Second episode of the series. Starring **John Cleese** and Ronnie Barker. Written by **John Cleese** and Antony Jay. Directed by Peter Robinson.

453   October 17, 1975

Fawlty Towers (TV episode: BBC2). "Gourmet Night." Basil's grand plan for a gourmet night at the hotel turns into disaster when the new chef gets drunk and falls in love with Manuel. Fifth episode of the first series. Starring **John Cleese**, Prunella Scales, Andrew Sachs, Connie Booth, with Andre Maranne, Steve Plytas, Allan Cuthbertson, Ann Way, Richard Caldicot, Betty Huntley-Wright, Ballard Berkeley, Gilly Flower, Renee Roberts, Jeffrey Segal, Elizabeth Benson, and Tony Page. Written by **John Cleese** and Connie Booth. Produced & directed by John Howard Davies.

454   October 20, 1975

The Selling Line (TV episode: BBC2). "The Competitive Spirit" (1973 training film). Third episode of the series. Starring **John Cleese** and Peter Bayliss. Written by **John Cleese** and Antony Jay. Directed by Peter Robinson.

455   October 24, 1975

Graham Chapman, **Terry Gilliam**, **Terry Jones**, and **Michael Palin** are interviewed by disc jockey Alan Freeman for his radio show.

456   October 24, 1975

Fawlty Towers (TV episode: BBC2). "The Germans." Sybil's in the hospital leaving Basil to hang a moosehead, organize a fire drill, and play host to a group of German guests. Sixth and last episode of the first series. Starring **John Cleese**, Prunella Scales, Andrew Sachs, Connie Booth, with Ballard Berkeley, Claire Davenport, Gilly Flower, Renee Roberts, Brenda Cowling, Louis Mahoney, John Lawrence, Iris Fry, Willy Bowman, Nick Kane, Lisa Bergmayr, and Dan Gillan. Written by **John Cleese** and Connie Booth. Produced & directed by John Howard Davies.

457   October 27, 1975

The Selling Line (TV episode: BBC2). "In Two Minds" (1973 training film). Fourth episode of the series. Starring **John Cleese** and Tim Brooke-Taylor. Written by **John Cleese** and Antony Jay. Directed by Peter Robinson.

458   November 1, 1975
Tomkinson's Schooldays, starring **Michael Palin** and **Terry Jones**, is recorded. The show will air Jan. 7, 1976, on BBC2.

459   November 3, 1975
The Selling Line (TV episode: BBC2). "Awkward Customers" (1973 training film). Fifth episode of the series. Starring **John Cleese** and Gillian Raine. Written by **John Cleese** and Antony Jay. Directed by Peter Robinson.

460   November 10, 1975
The Selling Line (TV episode: BBC2). "More Awkward Customers" (1974 training film). Sixth episode of the series. Starring **John Cleese**, Patricia Routledge, Bernard Cribbins, and Lynn Redgrave. Written by **John Cleese**. Directed by Peter Robinson.

461   November 14, 1975
The Lumberjack Song (Record: Charisma CB 268). Single featuring the October 1975 re-recording of "The Lumberjack Song" (b/w "Spam Song"), produced by George "Onothimagen" Harrison. Performed by **Michael Palin** and The Fred Tomlinson Mounted Singers. Arranged by Fred Tomlinson. The single fails to chart.

462   November 17, 1975
The Selling Line (TV episode: BBC2). "I'll Think About It" (1973 training film). Seventh episode of the series. Written by Elwyn Jones. Directed by Peter Robinson.

463   November 18, 1975
Just a Minute (Radio game show: BBC Radio 4). **Michael Palin** guest-stars in the first of two episodes (the second airs Feb. 10, 1976) of this quiz program, joining regular panelists Clement Freud, Peter Jones, and Kenneth Williams. Nicholas Parsons hosts. Produced by John Lloyd. Recorded Oct. 3 in London.

464   November 18, 1975
Michael Palin attends a Bruce Springsteen & The E Street Band concert at Hammersmith Odeon in London.

465   November 24, 1975
The Selling Line (TV episode: BBC2). "How Not to Exhibit Yourself" (1974 training film). Eighth episode of the series. Starring **John Cleese** and Bernard Cribbins. Written by Denis Norden. Directed by Peter Robinson.

466   November 25, 1975
The Pythons view a tape of the *Wide World of Entertainment* special (aired Oct. 3 on ABC), which featured edited versions of three Python episodes. They are appalled at the heavy censorship. The 22 minutes of cuts were not made to tighten the shows up or make them funnier, but to remove what the network saw as "offensive" material. The Pythons decide to take ABC to court.

467   December 15, 1975
Monty Python files suit in Federal District Court to prevent ABC-TV from broadcasting the second *Wide World* compilation of edited Python shows on December 26, claiming that ABC has "substantially altered the artistic nature" of their scripts by deleting significant portions and that the remaining excerpts do "not truly represent the entertainment talents" of the group.

468   December 16–19, 1975
Terry Gilliam and **Michael Palin** spend four days in New York City where they are to appear in court for the Python v. ABC case.

469   December 19, 1975
Monty Python v. American Broadcasting Companies, Inc. (Court case). **Michael Palin** and **Terry Gilliam** appear at the United States Courtroom in Foley Square in New York to represent Python in their case against ABC. After viewing ABC's first installment of *Wide World of Entertainment*, the Pythons have filed a million dollar lawsuit for unfair competition against their own unedited shows and copyright infringement, and a permanent injunction against ABC. They also applied to the Federal District Court for a temporary injunction preventing the airing of the December 26th show. The judge is Morris E. Lasker; the Pythons' chief counsel is Robert Osterberg; and ABC's lawyer is Clarence Fried. After a hearing that goes from morning till night, the judge rules that an injunction preventing the broadcast of the second show would cause ABC to suffer an unreasonable financial loss. Lasker does order, however, that the show carry a disclaimer indicating the Python episodes have been edited without the approval of the Pythons. The group appeals and, six months later (on June 30), succeed in keeping their shows from ever being aired by ABC again, and also establish their ownership of the copyright in their scripts.

470 December 21–23, 1975

Graham Chapman emcees for The Who at three Christmas concerts at London's Hammersmith Odeon. **Chapman** is a friend of the band's drummer, Keith Moon. His comedy is not well-received by the impatient Who fans.

471 December 26, 1975

Christmas with Rutland Weekend Television (TV special: BBC2). Special Christmas edition of the **Eric Idle** comedy series. Guest-star George Harrison, eager to perform in a pirate sketch, finally agrees to sing a song—"The Pirate Song." Includes: "Bigamy Sisters, etc.," "Previews," "Testing (Alberto Rewrite Five)" (song), "How to Ski in Your Own Home," "The Christmas Play: Santa Doesn't Live Here Anymore," "I Don't Believe in Santa Anymore" (song), "Christmas Postscript," "Film Night: Scratchy Bit of Film/Sore Throat/Pommy," "Concrete Jungle Boy (from Pommy)" (song), "Film Night: Ann Melbourne," "A Right Royal Rutland Year (Queen of Rutland)," and "George Harrison Sings (The Pirate Song)." Written by **Eric Idle**, and performed by **Eric Idle**, Lyn Ashley, Carinthia West, David Battley, Jeannette Charles, Fatso, Neil Innes, Gwen Taylor, Derek Ware, Henry Woolf, and George Harrison (as Pirate "Bob"). Music by Neil Innes. Directed by Andrew Gosling. Produced by Ian Keill.

472 December 26, 1975

Wide World of Entertainment (TV special: ABC). "The Monty Python Show." This second Python special, which the group tried to prevent ABC from airing, is a compilation of three fourth-season Python episodes: "Light Entertainment War," "Hamlet," and "Michael Ellis." The show is aired with the three-second disclaimer "EDITED FOR TELEVISION BY ABC" shown at the beginning.

473 December 31, 1975

Three Men in a Boat (TV film: BBC2). TV film of Jerome K. Jerome's classic account of three men holidaying on the Thames in the 1890s. The three leads are played by Tim Curry (as Jerome), **Michael Palin** (as Harris), and Stephen Moore (as George). Written by Tom Stoppard. Directed by Stephen Frears. Produced by Rosemary Hill. Note: Stoppard will later co-write **Terry Gilliam**'s *Brazil*.

474 1975–78

John Cleese takes part in group therapy sessions with Dr. Robin Skynner. **Cleese** and Skynner will later collaborate on two psychology self-help books.

475 1975

The Proposal (Training film: Video Arts). How to write a sales proposal. Starring **John Cleese**, George A. Cooper, and Nerys Hughes. Written by Jonathan Lynn and Joe Windsor. Directed by Peter Robinson.

476 1975

Selling on the Telephone: When I'm Calling You (Training film: Video Arts). Five rules for handling incoming calls. Narrated by Andrew Sachs. Starring **John Cleese**, Dilys Watling, Vivienne Martin, Jacqueline Tong, and Norman Bird. Written by Jonathan Lynn and Antony Jay. Directed by Peter Robinson.

477 1975

Selling on the Telephone: Will You Answer True? (Training film: Video Arts). How to handle sales calls. Narrated by Andrew Sachs. Starring **John Cleese**, Norman Bird, Penelope Keith, and April Walker. Written by Jonathan Lynn and Antony Jay. Directed by Peter Robinson.

478 1975

The Single (Record: Arista AS 0130). U.S. single from the *Matching Tie and Handkerchief* album. Includes: "Elephantoplasty," "Minister for Overseas Development," "Pet Conversions," and "Cheese Shop."

479 1975

Eric Idle and wife Lyn Ashley separate. The couple were married in July 1969.

480 January 7, 1976

Tomkinson's Schooldays (TV special: BBC2). Pilot for the *Ripping Yarns* series, **Michael Palin** and **Terry Jones**' first post–Python project. The story is set in 1913 at a public school called Graybridge where new students are forced to fight a grizzly bear and lower classmen are nailed to walls and where a professional school bully is allowed to have unmarried Filipino women in his room. Filmed Oct. 13–20, 1975, mostly in Dorset, and recorded in studio on Nov. 1. Repeated Sept. 20, 1977, at the start of the first series. Starring **Michael Palin** (as Tomkinson/Headmaster/TV Introducer/Mr. Craffitt), with **Terry Jones** (as Mr. Ellis/Bear/Mr. Moodie/Director), Gwen Watford, Ian Ogilvy, John Wentworth, Sarah Grazebrook, Chai Lee, and Terence Denville. Written by **Michael Palin** and **Terry Jones**. Produced & directed by Terry Hughes. Note: This is the only *Yarns* episode in which **Jones** has an acting part. *Review:* Alan Coren (*The Times* [London], Jan. 8, 1976): "**Jones** and **Palin**, who wrote it and performed hilariously in it, with beautifully tuned support from Gwen Watford and Ian Ogilvy, transcended mere parody."

481   January 10, 1976
Out of the Trees (TV special: BBC2). **Graham Chapman** stars in this one-shot comedy half-hour made up of Python-like sketch material. There is some talk of it becoming a series, but the BBC passes on the idea. Sketches include "British Rail," "Genghis Khan," "Fire," and "Peony." Also starring Roger Brierley, Simon Jones, Maria Aitken, Marjie Lawrence, Tim Preece, Mark Wing-Davey, Maggie Henderson, and Jennifer Guy. Written by **Graham Chapman**, Bernard McKenna, and Douglas Adams. Theme music by Neil Innes. Produced by Bernard Thompson.

482   January 11, 1976
Les Rendez-Vous du Dimanche (The Sunday Appointment) (TV talk show: TF1, in France). Hosted by Michel Drucker. Guests: **Eric Idle**, **Terry Gilliam**, **Terry Jones**, Neil Innes, Jean Rochefort, and Mort Shuman. Taped in Paris.

483   January 15, 1976
Michael Palin and **Terry Jones** speak to film students at the National Film School in Beaconsfield, Buckinghamshire, England.

484   January 21, 1976
The Variety Club Awards for 1975 (Award ceremony). **John Cleese** receives (jointly, with Esther Rantzen) the award for BBC TV Personality of the Year at the ceremony held at the Dorchester Hotel, London. Andrew Sachs (Manuel in *Fawlty Towers*) accepts the award on his behalf and shows a clip of **Cleese** in his bathtub. Introduced by Terry Wogan. Airs on BBC1 on Jan. 21.

485   February 5, 1976
The Listener (Magazine/U.K.). "**John Cleese**: A Very Private Joker," by Wilfred De'Ath, p. 141. Interview/article.

486   February 20, 1976
Superspike (Parts 1 & 2) (Record: Bradley's Records BRAD 7606). U.K. single performed by Bill Oddie & The Superspike Squad and featuring **John Cleese** as a manic sports commentator. Released as part of the International Athletes Club's new "Superspike" fund-raising campaign. The record is supported by a film shown at Wembley Pool on Apr. 6. **Cleese** and Oddie gave their services free to the I.A.C. Produced by Bill Oddie and Stephen Shane.

487   February 20, 1976
Tonight (TV talk show: BBC1). Iain Johnstone interviews **John Cleese** about his life and career, from his school days to his most recent television hit *Fawlty Towers*. The half-hour program also includes clips from his TV work and comments from Connie Booth (his wife), David Frost, Antony Jay, Tim Brooke-Taylor, and critic Alan Coren.

488   February 22, 1976
Michael Palin and **Terry Jones** perform in a benefit show at the Old Vic Theatre in London. **Palin**, **Jones**, Ian Davidson, and Willie Rushton perform the "Custard Pie" sketch.

489   Spring 1976
Monty Python's Flying Circus becomes a top-rated TV show in Japan, where it is renamed *The Gay Boys Dragon Show* and followed by a round-table discussion.

490   March 1976
Dr. Fegg's Nasty Book of Knowledge (Book: Berkeley Medallion), written by **Terry Jones** and **Michael Palin**, is published in the U.S. Expanded American reissue of *Bert Fegg's Nasty Book for Boys & Girls* (1974).

491   March 29, 1976
The New Yorker (Magazine/U.S.). "Onward and Upward with the Arts: Naughty Bits," by Hendrik Hertzberg, pp. 69–70+. Detailed account of the Python v. ABC case, with many examples of the kind of cuts that were made on the *Wide World* specials. Reprinted in *The Sunday Times (London)* of June 6, 1976 ("Monty Python's Flying...Lawsuit," pp. 33–34).

492   April 1–3, 1976
A Poke in the Eye (with a Sharp Stick) (Stage show) runs for three nights at Her Majesty's Theatre in London. Benefit show for the human-rights organization Amnesty International bringing together the members of Monty Python (minus **Eric Idle**), Beyond the Fringe (minus Dudley Moore) and The Goodies. Performers at the comedy gala include **John Cleese**, **Graham Chapman**, **Terry Gilliam**, **Terry Jones**, **Michael Palin**, Peter Cook, Alan Bennett, Jonathan Miller, Graeme Garden, Bill Oddie, Tim Brooke-Taylor, Carol Cleveland, Neil Innes, Barry Humphries (as Dame Edna), Jonathan Lynn, Eleanor Bron, John Fortune, and John Bird. Sketches include: "Pet Shop" (**Cleese** & **Palin**), "Court Room" (Pythons, with Cook), "The Last Supper" (**Cleese** & Lynn), "The Japes Lecture" (Py-

thons), "So That's the Way You Like It" (Beyond the Fringe, with **Jones**), and "The Lumberjack Song" (**Palin** & cast). Directed by Jonathan Miller. Produced by Peter Luff and David Simpson. A film of the show, titled *Pleasure at Her Majesty's*, premieres in November and is shown on TV's *Omnibus* on Dec. 29 (BBC1). The show's success leads to further Amnesty benefits, including *The Secret Policeman's Ball* in 1979.

493   April 7, 1976
Terry Gilliam, **Terry Jones**, **Michael Palin**, and Carol Cleveland tape an appearance on *The Mike Douglas Show* at Westinghouse Studios in Philadelphia.

494   April 14–May 2, 1976
Monty Python Live! (Stage show) runs for three weeks at the City Center in New York City. In their first stage show in America, the Pythons perform classic sketches from their TV series as well as college skits like "Custard Pie (Japes Lecture)" and **Graham Chapman**'s "Self-Wrestling," accompanied by film pieces (taken mostly from their German specials made in 1971 and 1972, including "Silly Olympics"). Sketches include: "Gumby Flower Arranging," "Argument Clinic," "Travel Agent," "Nudge, Nudge," "Crunchy Frog," "Llamas," "The Judges," "World Forum," "Albatross," "Pet Shop," "Death of Mary Queen of Scots," "Bruces' Philosophers Song," "Dead Bishop on the Landing (Church Police)," "Four Yorkshiremen," "Blackmail," "The Ministry of Silly Walks," and "Lumberjack Song." Written & performed by **Graham Chapman**, **John Cleese**, **Terry Gilliam**, **Eric Idle**, **Terry Jones**, and **Michael Palin**, with Carol Cleveland and Neil Innes. Filmed sequences directed by Ian MacNaughton. Staged and presented by Monty Python.
Reviews: Clive Barnes (*The New York Times*, Apr. 16, 1976, p. 11): "Pure adulterated madness.... Monty Python truly is the snake in the garden of modern Eden — a child of our time, a reptile of truly significant immediacy ... there is nothing to beat it since Genghis Khan"; Martin Gottfried (*The New York Post*, Apr. 16, 1979, p. 16): "...the maddest and brightest comedy revue to come along since *Beyond the Fringe*"; Iain Johnstone (*The Times* [London], Apr. 23, 1976): "The humour runs from the surreal into the unknown and takes the audience with it every inch of the journey"; T. E. Kalem (*Time*, Apr. 26, 1976, p. 67): "No matter how high the brow or how low, *Monty Python Live!* creases it with jet-propelled mirth"; Julius Novick (*The Village Voice*, Apr. 26, 1976, p. 138): "The offspring of a left-handed marriage between Dada and Charley's Aunt, they do scenarios of liberating anarchy"; Chet Flippo (*Rolling Stone*, June 3, 1976, p. 21): "Many of the revue's funnier moments are familiar from TV ... but work just as well on stage.... Unlike many comedians, their humor can be vulgar without being malicious."

495   April 18, 1976
The New York Times Magazine (Magazine/U.S.). "And Now for Something Completely Different," by Thomas Meehan, pp. 34–36. Article on the history and comedy of Monty Python and their success in America.

496   April 19, 1976
John Cleese is named as BBC Television Personality of the Year by the Television and Radio Industries Club (TRIC).

497   April 20, 1976
The Pythons (**Graham Chapman**, **Terry Gilliam**, **Terry Jones**, **Michael Palin**) and Neil Innes, while visiting the Bronx Zoo in New York, pose for photographs holding a 14-foot Burmese python. **Eric Idle** refuses to participate in the stunt, which is part of a Warner Books promotion.

498   April 20, 1976
Python fan George Harrison makes a guest appearance on stage with Monty Python at the City Center. He joins the Mountie chorus during the "Lumberjack Song" finale.

499   April 21, 1976
Today (TV news-talk show: NBC). Hosted by Barbara Walters and Jim Hartz. Guests: Monty Python, promoting their City Center show, also Mary Carson and Bishop Paul Moore.

500   April 27, 1976
The Mike Douglas Show (TV talk show: Synd.). Hosted by Mike Douglas with Neil Sedaka (guest co-host). Guests: **Terry Gilliam**, **Terry Jones**, **Michael Palin**, and Carol Cleveland, promoting their City Center show, also Gabe Kaplan, David Soul, Ben Vereen, and Margeaux Hemingway. **Jones** sits on David Soul's lap for part of the interview. Taped Apr. 7 in Philadelphia.

501   April 28, 1976
Singer-songwriter Harry Nilsson joins the Mountie chorus during the Pythons' performance of "Lumberjack Song" at City Center, as George Harrison did eight nights earlier. Unlike Harrison, an

apparently inebriated Nilsson makes his presence known by wearing sunglasses, waving, and ultimately falling from the stage into the front row.

502 May 1976
Monty Python Live at City Center (Record: Arista AL 4073) is released in the U.S. Recording of some of the best sketches performed live at the City Center in New York in April. On the back is reprinted "Monty Python's American Diary" by **Michael Palin**, which originally appeared in *Esquire* Magazine (July 1975). Linked by **Michael Palin**. Tracks: "Introduction/The Llama," "Gumby Flower Arranging," "Short Blues" (Neil Innes), "Wrestling," "World Forum," "Albatross/Colonel," "Nudge, Nudge," "Crunchy Frog," "Bruces Song," "Travel Agent," "Camp Judges," "Blackmail," "Protest Song" (Innes), "Pet Shop," "Four Yorkshiremen," "Argument Clinic," "Death of Mary Queen of Scots," "Salvation Fuzz," and "Lumberjack Song." Written & performed by **Graham Chapman, John Cleese, Terry Gilliam, Eric Idle, Terry Jones**, and **Michael Palin**, with Carol Cleveland and Neil Innes. Cover art by **Terry Gilliam**. Produced by Nancy Lewis. Remastered and reissued in 1997 as part of the "Arista Masters" series.

503 May 3, 1976
Sherrye Henry (Radio show: WOR-AM, New York). Guests: **Terry Jones** and **Michael Palin**, promoting the *Live at City Center* LP.

504 May 3, 1976
The Pythons appear at Sam Goody's record store in Rockefeller Center, New York City, promoting their newly-released *Live at City Center* LP.

505 May 9, 1976
King Biscuit Flower Hour (Radio show: WNEW-FM, New York). Dave Herman interviews Monty Python, with excerpts from the *Live at City Center* LP. Presented by DIR Broadcasting Corporation.

506 May 14, 1976
The Royal Television Society Programme Awards (Award ceremony). **John Cleese** is given the award for Outstanding Creative Achievement for *Fawlty Towers* at the annual awards ball held in London.

507 May 18, 1976
The Old Grey Whistle Test (TV music show: BBC2). **Eric Idle**, impersonating host Bob Harris, introduces the program. Daryl Hall & John Oates perform in concert at Television Theatre in London. **Idle** spoofed the program on the June 2, 1975, episode of *Rutland Weekend Television*.

508 May 20, 1976
Their Finest Hours (Stage plays) premieres at the Crucible Theatre in Sheffield, England. Two short plays written by **Michael Palin** and **Terry Jones** specially for the Crucible Theatre. The first, "Underwood's Finest Hour," deals with a doctor who is more interested in listening to cricket than delivering a baby. The second, "Buchanan's Finest Hour," takes place entirely inside a large crate. Future Python-collaborator Charles McKeown (*Life of Brian, Brazil*) appears in both plays. Directed by David Leland. Notes: "Underwood" was originally written in the fall of 1973 for a BBC series (*Group One*) that never made it to air. "Buchanan" is later filmed as *The Box* (1981 short), featuring the voices of **Palin** and **Jones**.

509 June 2, 1976
John Cleese attends the Midsummer Banquet at the Mansion House in London, held in honor of the arts, the sciences, and learning. The event is hosted by the Lord Mayor and Lady Mayoress.

510 June 30, 1976
The U.S. appeal judges in the Monty Python v ABC case rule in the Pythons' favor granting their injunction to stop ABC from airing edited versions of their shows.

511 July 26–late September 1976
Jabberwocky, a medieval comedy directed and co-written by **Terry Gilliam** and starring **Michael Palin**, is filmed at Shepperton Studios and on location in Wales and London. Filming locations include Pembroke Castle and Chepstow Castle, both in Wales. At Shepperton, streets scenes are filmed on the former set of the 1968 film musical *Oliver!*.

512 August 16, 1976
Festival 40 (TV special: BBC2). A repeat of the special 1971 Montreux edition of *Monty Python's Flying Circus*. Also, David Gillard interviews **Graham Chapman**.

513 September 1976
The Rutland Dirty Weekend Book (Book: Eyre Methuen/Two Continents), written and edited by **Eric Idle**, is published. Collection of material based on **Idle**'s BBC comedy series *Rutland Weekend Television*. Includes appearances by Neil Innes and a guest page by **Michael Palin**. Also includes "The Vatican Sex Manual," "The Rutland TV Times," "The Cretin Club," "Who's Who in Rutland," "Rutland Stone," and "The Wonderful World of Sex." The title beneath the dust jacket: *The Wonderful World of Prince Charles*.

514 September 4–October 23, 1976
The fifth series of the sketch-comedy show *The Two Ronnies*, starring Ronnie Barker and Ronnie Corbett, airs on BBC1. **John Cleese**, **Eric Idle**, **Terry Jones**, and **Michael Palin** all contribute material to the series.

515 October 2, 1976
Saturday Night Live (TV comedy show: NBC). Hosted by **Eric Idle**, with musical guest Joe Cocker. **Idle**, hosting for the first of four times (1976–79), appears in a "Killer Bees" sketch, a *Dragnet* send-up, "Drag Racing" (film), "Baby Conversions," and attempts singing "Here Comes the Sun." The show also features the premiere of The Rutles (Idle, Neil Innes, et al.), a Beatles-parody group, singing "I Must Be in Love" in a film clip from a yet-to-be-aired episode of Idle's *Rutland Weekend Television*. Cast: Dan Aykroyd, John Belushi, Chevy Chase, Jane Curtin, Laraine Newman, Gilda Radner, and Garrett Morris. Directed by Dave Wilson. Produced by Lorne Michaels.

516 October 4–14, 26, 1976
"Across the Andes by Frog," a first series episode of the **Michael Palin**–**Terry Jones** comedy *Ripping Yarns*, is filmed at Pinewood Studios and on location in Glencoe, Scotland. It is the second show filmed (following the pilot *Tomkinson's Schooldays*, filmed in October 1975) but the fifth one aired (on Oct. 18, 1977).

517 October 9, 1976
The Two Ronnies (TV episode: BBC1). Includes the sketch "Cricket Commentators," written by **Michael Palin** and **Terry Jones**, and performed by Ronnie Corbett (as John), Ronnie Barker (as Richie), and Moray Watson (as Peter). Sixth episode of the fifth series. Written by Spike Mullins, **Michael Palin** & **Terry Jones**, and Gerald Wiley [pseud. of Ronnie Barker]. Produced by Terry Hughes. Note: "Cricket Commentators" is also included on the 1977 album *The Two Ronnies Vol. 2: "Me and Him"* (BBC Records REB 300).

518 October 15, 25–November 5, 1976
"Murder at Moorstones Manor," a first series episode of *Ripping Yarns*, is filmed in Glencoe, Scotland and at Harefield Grove in Harefield, Middlesex, England. The last of three episodes directed by Terry Hughes (he will work again with **Palin** on the 1982 concert film *Monty Python Live at the Hollywood Bowl*). Jim Franklin will direct the remaining three episodes of the first series.

519 October 19–December 6, 1976
Sez Les (TV comedy series: ITV/LWT). **John Cleese** appears as a guest performer on the 11th series of this sketch-comedy show (1969–76) starring Les Dawson. Other regulars include Roy Barraclough, Julian Orchard, Kathy Staff, and Norman Chappell. Produced & directed by Vernon Lawrence.

520 October 29, 1976
First Impression (Radio show: BBC Radio 4). Guest: **John Cleese**.

521 October 29, 1976
John Cleese appears at a meeting of business executives in London to promote his new Video Arts training film *Meetings, Bloody Meetings*.

522 October 31, 1976
Your Move (TV show: BBC1). Series to help improve adult reading and writing skills. Hosted by Brian Redhead, with **Graham Chapman**, Tim Brooke-Taylor, William Blezard, and Claire Faulconbridge. Narrated by Norman Rossington. Written by Barry Took. Directed by Caroline Pick. Produced by David Hargreaves.

523 November–December 1976
The Pythons begin writing their next movie, which is to be set during the time of Christ. The idea for the film originated from an off-hand remark made by **Eric Idle** at a *Holy Grail* premiere. When asked what the title of the next Python movie would be, he replied: "Jesus Christ — Lust for Glory!" (It is ultimately titled *Monty Python's Life of Brian*).

524 November 1976
Esquire (Magazine/U.S.). "Monty Python's Regards to Broadway — The Wacky Adventures of Seven Men and a Girl on a British Airways Three Week 'Make-U-A-Star' Bargain Holiday," by **Michael Palin**, pp. 80–83. **Palin**'s diary account of Python's visit to America in April to perform at New York's City Center.

525 November 1976
John Cleese passes his driving test.

526 November 1976
Playboy (Magazine/U.S.). "The Vatican Sex Manual," by **Eric Idle**, pp. 134–35. An excerpt from *The Rutland Dirty Weekend Book*.

527 November 1976
Python on Song (Record: Charisma MP 001; CB 268/PY 2). Two-record 45 rpm set containing the

1975 single "Lumberjack Song" (re-recording produced by George "Onothimagen" Harrison), b/w "Spam Song," and "Bruces Song" (from *Drury Lane*, 1974), b/w "Eric the Half-a-Bee" (from *Previous Record*, 1972).

528   November 1976
True Love (Short film). Promotional film for George Harrison's cover of the Cole Porter song (from his album *Thirty Three & ⅓*), directed by Harrison's friend **Eric Idle**. In the film Harrison sings the song while riding in a gondola with his "true love." **Idle** also directed the film of Harrison's "Crackerbox Palace."

529   November 1976
Terry Gilliam's daughter, Amy Rainbow, is born.

530   November 3, 1976
This Song/Learning How to Love You (Record: Dark Horse DRC-8294) is released in the U.S. George Harrison single, off his album *Thirty Three & ⅓*. In "This Song"—Harrison's comment on the "My Sweet Lord"/"He's So Fine" plagiarism lawsuit—**Eric Idle** dubs in two arguing voices saying "Could be 'Sugar Pie Honey Bunch'" and "No, sounds more like 'Rescue Me'!" Released in the U.K. on K 16856.

531   November 12–December 24, 1976
The second and last series of *Rutland Weekend Television*, starring **Eric Idle**, airs on BBC2. The series, produced by Ian Keill, consists of seven shows. One highlight of the series is the introduction of the Beatles-parody group, The Rutles (in show one). The Rutles clip was first shown in the U.S. on *Saturday Night Live* (Oct. 2, 1976).

532   November 12, 1976
Rutland Weekend Television (TV episode: BBC2). "Rutland Weekend Rutles." First show of the second series. Includes: "Announcer Auditions," "Tonight's Drama (Lawyer and Fall-guy)," "Cure for Love" (doc), "I Must Be in Love (The Rutles)" (song), "The Rutles" (aborted doc), "The Entire History of the World: Episode Three, The Creation (Back-Room Boys)," "The Age of Desperation" (song), "Next Week on RWT," "Inflation," "Tobacco," and "That's My Mum." Written by **Eric Idle**. Music by Neil Innes. Performed by **Eric Idle**, Neil Innes, David Battley, Terence Bayler, Gwen Taylor, John Halsey, Bunny May, and Carinthia West. Directed by Andrew Gosling.

533   November 14, 1976
Read All About It (TV show: BBC1). Book program hosted by Melvyn Bragg. Guests Winifred Ewing, Claire Tomalin, and **John Cleese** choose their Paperbacks of the Week.

534   November 19, 1976
Rutland Weekend Television (TV episode: BBC2). "Rutland Weekend Cop Show." Second show of the second series. Includes: "The Razor Blade Four (announcers)," "Quite Interesting People (Sheep Worrier, Madame Butterfly Collector)," "Topless A Go-Go" (song), "Exposé: Car-Swapping," "Godfrey Daniel" (song), "Rutland Five-O," and "Next Week on RWT (Madame Butterfly)." Written by **Eric Idle**. Music by Neil Innes. Performed by **Eric Idle**, Neil Innes, David Battley, Gwen Taylor, Fatso, and Bunny May. Directed by Andrew Gosling.

535   November 20, 1976
Crackerbox Palace (Short film) premieres on *Saturday Night Live* (NBC). **Eric Idle** directed this promotional film for the George Harrison song (off his album *Thirty Three & ⅓*) which was shot entirely on location at Harrison's Friar Park mansion in Henley-on-Thames and stars the former Beatle (as a looney) and also Neil Innes (in drag). The Nov. 20 episode of *SNL* is hosted by Paul Simon and features Harrison as musical guest. **Idle** also directed the film of Harrison's "True Love."

536   November 21, 1976
Film 76 (TV show: BBC1). Includes an on-location report (from August) on the filming of *Jabberwocky* at Shepperton Studios. **Terry Gilliam** and **Michael Palin** are interviewed.

537   November 26, 1976
Rutland Weekend Television (TV episode: BBC2). "Rutland Weekend Sequel." Third show of the second series. Includes: "Lance Corporal (announcer)," "Prisoner Requests Leave," "Saucer of Rancid Milk" (lecture), "Tomorrows Burke (Inside James Burke, Yuri Geller Bending)," "End of Lecture/Caretaker/Documentaries," "I Give Myself to You" (song), "Husband and Wife," "Collier Rides Again," "Crystal Balls" (song), "Restaurant Dress Code," and "Killing People." Written by **Eric Idle**. Music by Neil Innes. Performed by **Eric Idle**, Neil Innes, David Battley, Gwen Taylor, Henry Woolf, Fatso, Carinthia West, and Terence Bayler. Directed by Andrew Gosling.

538   November 27, 1976
Desert Island Discs (Radio show: BBC Radio 4). Roy Plomley's castaway is **Eric Idle**, whose choice

of records includes "Cello Concerto in C Major" (Joseph Haydn), "Marie" (Randy Newman), "Dear One" (George Harrison), and "Nimrod, from *Enigma Variations*" (Sir Edward Elgar). His luxury item is a guitar; his book is a compendium of world philosophy.

539 November 28, 1976
Pleasure at Her Majesty's (Feature film) premieres at the National Film Theatre, London as part of the London Film Festival. Film of the Amnesty International comedy gala *A Poke in the Eye (with a Sharp Stick)* presented in April 1976 at Her Majesty's Theatre, London. The film features highlights from the show plus a look at the behind-the-scenes preparations. Performers include **John Cleese, Graham Chapman, Terry Gilliam, Terry Jones, Michael Palin**, Peter Cook, Alan Bennett, Jonathan Miller, Graeme Garden, Bill Oddie, Tim Brooke-Taylor, Carol Cleveland, Neil Innes, Barry Humphries, Jonathan Lynn, Eleanor Bron, John Fortune, and John Bird. Sketches include: "Pet Shop" (**Cleese & Palin**), "Court Room" (Pythons, with Cook), "The Last Supper" (**Cleese** & Lynn), "The Japes Lecture" (Pythons), "So That's the Way You Like It" (Beyond the Fringe, with **Jones**), and "The Lumberjack Song" (**Palin** & cast). Narrated by Dudley Moore. Produced & directed by Roger Graef. Stage show directed by Jonathan Miller. The film airs in December as an *Omnibus* special on BBC1 and is released theatrically in 1977. The U.S. theatrical version is retitled *Monty Python Meets Beyond the Fringe*.

540 December 1976
Eric Idle spends Christmas in Barbados with Lorne Michaels and Paul Simon.

541 December 3, 1976
Rutland Weekend Television (TV episode: BBC2). "Rutland Weekend Sprimpo." Fourth show of the second series. Includes: "The Ricochet Brothers (announcers)," "Ill Health Food Store," "The Hard to Get" (song), "Sprimpo," "Bad Continuity/Flashbacks," "Classically Bad American Films," "Twenty-Four Hours in Tunbridge Wells" (song), "Exposé: The Massed Flashers of Reigate," and "Tirade Against Critics." Written by **Eric Idle**. Music by Neil Innes. Performed by **Eric Idle**, Neil Innes, David Battley, Gillian Gregory, Samantha Keston, Robin Miller, Gillian Rhind, Gwen Taylor, and Henry Woolf. Directed by Andrew Gosling.

542 December 10, 1976
Rutland Weekend Television (TV episode: BBC2). "Tony Bilbow Theatre." Fifth show of the second series. Includes: "Boring Intro by Tony Bilbow," "The Life and Legend of Michael Hall (starring Tony Bilbow)," "Flag Seller," "Sex Problems," "Special Equipment for Gentlemen," "Non-Voyeur," "The Song O' the Insurance Men" (song), "Accountancy Shanty" (song), "Another Lonely Man (Singing Gynaecologist)" (song), "Travel Agent/Insurance," "Anti-Insurance Film," and "Boring Intro (Take 139)." Written by **Eric Idle**. Music by Neil Innes. Super-starred Tony Bilbow, with **Eric Idle**, Neil Innes, David Battley, Gwen Taylor, Henry Woolf, Fatso, and Carinthia West. Directed by Andrew Gosling.

543 December 17, 1976
Rutland Weekend Television (TV episode: BBC2). "Rutland Weekend Is Innocent." Sixth show of the second series. Includes: "Highwayman/The Lone Accountant," "Eccentric Judge," "Drama on a Saturday Night" (song), "Rutland Safari Park/Safari Car Park" (doc), "Sexist Sketch/Trapped by the Writer," "Wife Swapping Party" (song), and "Nixon is Innocent." Written by **Eric Idle**. Music by Neil Innes. Performed by **Eric Idle**, Neil Innes, David Battley, Gwen Taylor, Henry Woolf, Fatso, Maggie Henderson, and Terence Bayler. Directed by Andrew Gosling.

544 December 24, 1976
Rutland Weekend Television (TV episode: BBC2). "Rutland Weekend Showtime!" Seventh and last show of the second series. Includes: "Censorship," "The Smoke of Autumn Bonfires" (song), "Janitors' Kids" (song), "Soap Opera," "Autocue," "The David Frost Show Again," "The Return of the Pink Panzer," "Joining the AA," "Australian Love Song" (song), "The Slaves of Freedom" (song), "Angel Demonstration" (doc), "William Plastic-Bidet and the Postman," "Sportsbore," and "It's Hard to Make It When You're Straight" (song). Written by **Eric Idle**. Music by Neil Innes. Performed by **Eric Idle**, Neil Innes, David Battley, Gwen Taylor, Terence Bayler, Bunny May, Fatso, and Carinthia West. Directed by Andrew Gosling.

545 December 29, 1976
Omnibus (TV special: BBC1). "Pleasure at Her Majesty's." Film of the April 1976 benefit show for Amnesty International which also captures the rehearsals and backstage moments. The film premiered at the London Film Festival in November. Performers include **John Cleese, Graham Chapman, Terry Gilliam, Terry Jones, Michael Palin,**

Peter Cook, Alan Bennett, and Jonathan Miller. Produced & directed by Roger Graef. Stage show directed by Jonathan Miller.

546 1976
Selling on the Telephone: The Cold Call (Training film: Video Arts). How to make effective sales calls. Narrated by Andrew Sachs. Starring **John Cleese**, Jonathan Lynn, and Linda James. Written by Jonathan Lynn and Antony Jay. Directed by Peter Robinson.

547 1976
Can We Please Have That the Right Way Round?: A Guide to Slide Presentations (Training film: Video Arts). How to use visual aids effectively in a sales presentation. Starring **John Cleese** and James Cossins. Written by Denis Norden. Directed by Peter Robinson.

548 1976
Meetings, Bloody Meetings (Training film: Video Arts). Classic **John Cleese** training film humorously demonstrating how to make meetings shorter and more productive. One of the most widely-used films produced by Video Arts, the company **Cleese** co-founded in 1972. Remade in 1993 and 2012. Starring **John Cleese**, Timothy West, John Grieve, George A. Cooper, Angela Down, Mark Wing-Davey, Keith Buckley, and Ralph Ball. Written by **John Cleese** and Antony Jay. Directed by Peter Robinson.

549 1976
The Fortune Teller (Marketing film: Video Arts). Humorous sales film for Volvo Cars showcasing their new model, the 343. Sponsored by Volvo Concessionaires. Starring **John Cleese**, Jonathan Lynn, Vivienne Martin, and Charlotte Alexandra. Written by Jonathan Lynn. Directed by Peter Robinson.

550 1976
The Rutland Weekend Songbook (Record: BBC Records REB 233) is released in the U.K. Collection of songs and other items from the BBC series *Rutland Weekend Television* starring **Eric Idle** and Neil Innes. Tracks: "L'Amour Perdu," "Gibberish," "Front Loader," "Say Sorry Again," "I Must Be in Love (The Rutles)," "24 Hours in Tunbridge Wells," "The Fabulous Bingo Brothers (Once We Had a Donkey)," "Concrete Jungle Boy," "The Children of Rock and Roll," "Stoop Solo," "The Song O' the Insurance Men," "Closedown (with Nicholas Parsons)," "Testing," "I Give Myself to You," "Communist Cooking," "Johnny Cash," "Protest Song," "Accountancy Shanty," "Football," "Boring," "L'Amour Perdu Cha Cha Cha," "The Hard to Get," and "The Song O' the Continuity Announcers." Written and produced by **Eric Idle** and Neil Innes. Musicians appearing: Roger Rettig, John Halsey, Brian Hodgson, Billy Bremner, Zoot Money, Andy Roberts, Dave Richards, and Roger Swallow. Recorded at The Rutland Weekend Television Centre, Argonaut Studios, and Sunrise Studios, London. Released in the U.S. in November 1976 on ABC/Passport Records PPSD-98018.

551 1976
John Cleese and his wife, Connie Booth, separate (they will divorce in 1978). Despite the split, the two will begin writing the second series of *Fawlty Towers* in 1977.

552 1976
Michael Palin starts a small publishing company in England called Signford Ltd., which specializes in art and poetry books. Signford's first book is *Chris Orr's John Ruskin*, published in June 1976.

553 1976
Terry Jones' son, Bill, is born.

554 1976
A Poke in the Eye (with a Sharp Stick) (Record: Transatlantic TRA 331) is released in the U.K. LP recording of the April 1976 Amnesty show. Tracks include: "A Brief Introduction" (**John Cleese**), "The Last Supper" (**Cleese** & Jonathan Lynn), "Court Room" (Pythons, with Peter Cook, others), "So That's the Way You Like It" (Beyond the Fringe, with **Terry Jones**), and "The Lumberjack Song" (**Michael Palin** & cast). Cover art by **Terry Gilliam**. Produced by Ritchie Gold. Reissued in 1991 (Castle Communications) with previously-unreleased material.

555 1976
The Case of the Sulphuric Acid Plant (Educational film: Video Arts). **John Cleese** lends his voice to the animated narrator ('Holmes') of this 17-minute educational short on the manufacture of sulfuric acid. **Cleese** also appears in live-action scenes as the plant foreman. Drawings & animation by Tony Hart. Written & devised by Robert Reid.

556 1976
The Worst of Monty Python (Record: Buddah Records BDS 5656-2). Two-LP set. Combined U.S. reissue of *Another Monty Python Record* (1971) and *Monty Python's Previous Record* (1972).

557 1976
Eric Idle becomes a vegetarian.

558 1976
How to Win Holes by Influencing People (Educational film). Guide to golfing etiquette. Produced by Trans World International (Mark McCormack). Narrated by Peter Alliss. Starring **John Cleese**, Holly Palance, and Robert Dorning. Written by Dick Hills. Directed by Peter Robinson.

559 January–February 1977
The Strange Case of the End of Civilisation as We Know It, a TV comedy special starring **John Cleese**, is filmed.

560 January 4–February 15, 1977
The Punch Review (TV series: BBC2). Satirical series based on work from the magazine's contributors. Includes material from **Michael Palin** and **Terry Jones**. Starring Robin Bailey and Julian Holloway. Produced by Roger Race.

561 January 30, 1977
Eric Idle meets American model Tania Kosevich, his future wife, at a party at Dan Aykroyd's New York loft following a *Saturday Night Live* broadcast (hosted by Fran Tarkenton). They will marry in 1981.

562 February 20, 1977
Doctor on the Go (TV episode: ITV/LWT). "For Your Own Good..." Gascoigne's wealthy, unpleasant father (Derek Francis) arrives at St. Swithins. Written by **Graham Chapman** and Douglas Adams. Directed by Bryan Izzard. Produced by Humphrey Barclay. Note: Over three years had passed since **Chapman**'s last "Doctor" episode (in December 1973).

563 February 20, 1977
Live from the Mardi Gras, It's Saturday Night on Sunday (TV special: NBC). The Mardi Gras in New Orleans is the setting for this special prime-time edition of the late-night comedy show *Saturday Night Live*. With guests **Eric Idle**, Henry Winkler, Penny Marshall, Cindy Williams, Buck Henry, and Randy Newman. Cast: Dan Aykroyd, John Belushi, Jane Curtin, Garrett Morris, Bill Murray, Laraine Newman, and Gilda Radner. Directed by Dave Wilson. Produced by Lorne Michaels.

564 February 25, 1977
Monty Python and the Holy Grail premieres on American television as The CBS Late Movie. The film was accidentally sold to CBS, who cut out much of the film's bad language and blood. When the Pythons regain the rights to the film, they sell it to PBS, who show it uncut.

565 March 6, 1977
The Sunday Times (London) (Newspaper/U.K.). "Say **Cleese**," by Hunter Davies, pp. 60–71. Profile of **John Cleese**, who is interviewed at his rented Notting Hill home, which he recently moved into (he and his wife, Connie Booth, separated last year). **Cleese**'s mother Muriel, Tim Brooke-Taylor, and Booth are also interviewed. Photographs by David Montgomery. Reprinted in Davies' 1994 collection *Hunting People*.

566 March 27, 1977
The Sunday Times Magazine (London) (Magazine/U.K.). "The Jaws That Bite, the Claws That Catch," by George Perry, pp. 62–64. Interview with **Terry Gilliam** about his new film *Jabberwocky*.

567 March 28, 1977
Jabberwocky (Feature film: Columbia-Warner) premieres in London. **Terry Gilliam**'s first solo directorial effort, vaguely based on Lewis Carroll's poem, concerns a young cooper's apprentice in medieval times who sets off for the city to seek his fortune. There he meets a beautiful princess and becomes squire to a knight chosen to slay a terrifying monster that's been ravaging the countryside. The Jabberwock was designed by Valerie Charlton and Clinton Cavers, based on John Tenniel's 1871 drawing. Starring **Michael Palin** (as Dennis Cooper), Max Wall, Harry H. Corbett, John Le Mesurier, Warren Mitchell, Deborah Fallender, Annette Badland, Bernard Bresslaw, John Bird, Neil Innes, Graham Crowden, Kenneth Colley, Paul Curran, also **Terry Jones** as a poacher (at the beginning of the film) and **Terry Gilliam** in a cameo. Written by Charles Alverson and **Terry Gilliam**. Directed by **Terry Gilliam**. Produced by Sandy Lieberson. Exec produced by John Goldstone.
Reviews: Alan Brien (*The Sunday Times* [London], Apr. 3, 1977, p. 37): "*Jabberwocky* is not such a continuous hoot as *Monty Python and the Holy Grail*.... But it remains an unmistakably individual and eccentric piece of cinema..."; Vincent Canby (*The New York Times*, Apr. 16, 1977, p. 14): "...the most marvelously demented British comedy to come along since *Monty Python and the Holy Grail*.... The movie's gags are nonstop, both verbal and visual.... *Jabberwocky* is very funny, yet it looks like an epic";

Richard Schickel (*Time*, May 9, 1977, p. 89): "**Gilliam** finds it impossible to sustain, let alone develop anything like a consistent comic tone.... It really is marked-down Pythonism..."; Penelope Gilliatt (*The New Yorker*, May 9, 1977, pp. 124–26): "*Jabberwocky* deserves its Lewis Carroll association; he would have rejoiced in its nincompoop wit and the blue-sky reaches of its nonsense. Not often has the rude been so recklessly funny"; Robert Hatch (*The Nation*, May 21, 1977, pp. 633–34): "...I was pleased by the Jabberwock itself.... Unhappily, the star of the film appeared only in the closing sequences."

568   March 28, 1977
The Pythons (minus **John Cleese**) attend the premiere of *Jabberwocky* at the Columbia Cinema in London.

569   March 30, 1977
John Cleese attends the U.K. premiere of *Silver Streak* at the Odeon Theatre, Leicester Square, London. It is the 31st Royal Film Performance, shown in the presence of the Queen Mother. Interviews from the event are shown on ITV (Thames) on Mar. 31.

570   March 31, 1977
Jabberwocky opens in the U.K.

571   March 31, 1977
Tomorrow's World (TV show: BBC1). **Michael Palin** and **Terry Jones** appear in a new comedy segment of the long-running science news series. In their piece, titled "The Broken Bottle," Michael Rodd reports on one glass company's attempts to market their broken bottles as desirable and useful items.

572   April 1, 1977
Nobody's Fools (or Rock with Laughter) (Stage show). **John Cleese**, **Graham Chapman**, **Michael Palin** and **Terry Jones** perform in this comedy-music benefit show staged at the Royal Albert Hall, London. Also appearing are Neil Innes & Fatso, Alan Price, Barbara Dickson, Alberto Y Lost Trios, Paranoias, Grimms, Scaffold, Jasper Carrott, and John Gorman. The show is in aid of the British Institute for the Achievement of Human Potential and Mind (National Association for Mental Health).

573   April 12, 1977
Three Piece Suite (TV play: BBC2). "Every Day in Every Way." **John Cleese** plays a hypochondriacal husband opposite Diana Rigg in the last of three playlets presented in this half-hour program. Last show in a six-episode series starring Rigg in a variety of roles. Starring **John Cleese** (as Kevin) and Diana Rigg. Written by Alan Coren. Produced & directed by Michael Mills.

574   April 15, 1977
Jabberwocky premieres in New York at Cinema One. **Terry Gilliam** and **Michael Palin** attend, giving out potatoes to the first 1,000 moviegoers.

575   April 23, 1977
Michael Palin's father, Edward Moreton Palin, dies at the age of 76.

576   April 23, 1977
Saturday Night Live (TV comedy show: NBC). Hosted by **Eric Idle**, with Neil Innes, Jeannette Charles, and Alan Price. **Idle**, hosting for the second time, helps raise money to "Save Great Britain" in a telethon sketch, with Charles appearing as Queen Elizabeth II. **Idle** also appears in "Irish Interrogation," "The Nixon Interviews" (as David Frost with Dan Aykroyd as President Richard Nixon), "Body Launguage" (film), "The Heavy Wit Championship," "The Battle of Britain," "Plain Talk (Gibberish)," and "Trans Eastern Airlines." Innes (aka Ron Nasty) performs the Rutles song "Cheese and Onions." Cast: Dan Aykroyd, John Belushi, Jane Curtin, Garrett Morris, Bill Murray, Laraine Newman, and Gilda Radner. Directed by Dave Wilson. Produced by Lorne Michaels.

577   April 25–May 11, 1977
"The Testing of Eric Olthwaite," a first series episode of *Ripping Yarns*, is filmed in Beamish and Tow Law in Co. Durham and also North Yorkshire. Locations include the Beamish Industrial Museum and High Force Waterfall (in Teesdale). It is the first episode directed by Jim Franklin (Terry Hughes directed the first three) and will be the second show aired (on Sept. 27, 1977).

578   May 1, 1977
The New York Times (Newspaper/U.S.). "A Python Comes to Grips with Lewis Carroll," by Leticia Kent, p. D15+. **Terry Gilliam** talks about his life and new film *Jabberwocky*; from a recent interview with the director at the Algonquin Hotel in New York.

579   May 8, 1977
An Evening Without Sir Bernard Miles (Stage show), at the Mermaid Theatre in London. This second Amnesty International benefit show, following 1976's *A Poke in the Eye (with a Sharp Stick)*,

stars **John Cleese**, **Terry Jones**, Connie Booth, Julie Covington, Jonathan Miller, Peter Ustinov, Peter Cook, guitarist John Williams, and The Bowles Brothers. Highlights from the show are presented on the TV special *The Mermaid Frolics*, airing Sept. 10. Sketches include: "Bookshop" (**Cleese** & Booth), "Words and Things" (**Cleese** & Miller), and "Forgive Me" (song by **Jones**). Directed by **Terry Jones** and Jonathan Miller. Note: Jones wrote "Forgive Me" in the 1960s for an Oxford revue but had never performed the song himself.

580   May 14, 1977

Eric Idle attends a concert by Dolly Parton at the Bottom Line club in Greenwich Village, New York City, followed by a VIP party at Windows on the World (atop the World Trade Center) in honor of Parton's NYC debut. Other attendees include Mick Jagger, Candice Bergen, John Belushi, Robert Duvall, and Olivia Newton-John.

581   May 16–27, 1977

"Escape from Stalag Luft 112B," a first series episode of *Ripping Yarns*, is filmed at Littleton Down and Tilshead on Salisbury Plain in southern England.

582   Summer 1977

All You Need Is Cash, **Eric Idle**'s Beatle parody featuring the fictional rock group The Rutles, is filmed over five weeks in Liverpool, London, New York, and New Orleans. The idea for the film originated from Neil Innes' song "I Must Be in Love," which was performed as a Beatles parody for **Idle**'s *Rutland Weekend Television* in 1976. A clip of the piece received an enthusiastic audience reaction when shown on *Saturday Night Live* during **Idle**'s hosting stint on Oct. 2, 1976, leading to interest from *SNL* producer Lorne Michaels for a full-length film.

583   June 1977

Eric Idle undergoes an operation to remove his appendix. Ten days later he is rushed back into intensive care at Wellington Hospital (in North London) due to complications.

584   June 8–24, July 4–5, August 8–9, 1977

"The Curse of the Claw," a first series episode of *Ripping Yarns*, is filmed in Rippingale (near Bourne) in Lincolnshire (June 8–22), also at Maidstone and the Medway Estuary (June 23–24), Eastbourne Pier and Ealing Studios (July 4–5), and Chichester (Aug. 8–9).

585   June 18, 1977

A charity football match is played at Wembley Stadium, with Radio One going up against the Showbiz XI. **Graham Chapman**, **Michael Palin**, Alan Price, and Tommy Steele play on the Showbiz team. Players for Radio One include John Peel, Ed Stewart, Kid Jensen, and Paul Burnett. Radio One wins.

586   July 1977

The first series of **John Cleese**'s *Fawlty Towers* begins playing on public television stations in the U.S. The series originally aired in Britain in September–October 1975.

587   July 3, 1977

Terry Gilliam and **Michael Palin** attend a screening of *Jabberwocky* at the 27th Berlin International Film Festival (June 24–July 5) in Berlin, Germany.

588   July 15, 1977

The Pythons gather in a London studio to record a read-through of the draft screenplay for *Life of Brian*. The final screenplay will be completed in January 1978. The recording of the read-through is later included in the 2007 DVD release of the film ("The Immaculate Edition").

589   July 16, 1977

Penrhos Brewery, a micro-brewery co-founded by **Terry Jones**, opens at Penrhos Court, a manor farm in Lyonshall, Herefordshire, England (on the Welsh border). **Jones**' partner in the venture is Penrhos Court's owner, Martin Griffiths. Attendees at the opening include **Jones**, **Michael Palin**, Richard Boston (founder-editor of the magazine *Vole*), and musician Mike Oldfield. The brewery will close in 1983.

590   August 10, 1977

The Muppet Show (TV episode: Synd.). **John Cleese** joins Kermit the Frog and the rest of the Muppets on this second-season episode of their 1976–81 comedy-variety show. In the show, **Cleese** stretches out Gonzo's limbs, plays a pirate who takes over the starship Swinetrek in "Pigs in Space," and refuses to sing "The Impossible Dream." Airs in the U.K. on Oct. 21 (ITV). Muppeteers: Jim Henson, Frank Oz, Jerry Nelson, Richard Hunt, and Dave Goelz. Written by Jerry Juhl, Joseph A. Bailey, Jim Henson, and Don Hinkley. Directed by Philip Casson. Produced by Jim Henson. Note: **Cleese** will later appear in the second Muppet film, *The Great Muppet Caper* (1981).

591 August 28, 1977
Michael Palin films his part in the Rutles mock-documentary *All You Need Is Cash* in Golden Square, Soho, London. In his scene, **Palin** (playing Eric Manchester) talks to a reporter played by George Harrison.

592 September 1977
Monty Python and the Holy Grail (book) (Book: Eyre Methuen), edited by **Terry Jones** and designed by Derek Birdsall, is published in the U.K. Comprehensive book on the making of *Holy Grail*. Includes the first and final drafts of the script, production notes, daily continuity reports, stills and snapshots, animation artwork, correspondence, and a complete statement of the production costs. The first draft of the script includes the sketches "Buying an Ant," "Boxing Match Aftermath," "Bogus Psychiatrists," and "Toupee Hall" — none of which made it to the final draft but would appear in episodes of the fourth Python TV series (in November 1974). The final draft includes the cut sequence "King Brian the Wild."

593 September 1977
Monty Python Meets Beyond the Fringe (Feature film) is released in the U.S. Re-titled American release of the 1976 concert film *Pleasure at Her Majesty's*.

594 September 10, 1977
The Mermaid Frolics (TV special: ITV/LWT). Hour-long special featuring highlights from the one-night-only May 1977 Amnesty International benefit *An Evening Without Sir Bernard Miles*. Starring **John Cleese**, **Terry Jones**, Connie Booth, Jonathan Miller, Peter Cook, Julie Covington, Peter Ustinov, John Williams, The Bowles Brothers, and others.

595 September 14, 1977
Terry Gilliam and **Michael Palin** attend a screening of *Jabberwocky* at the Savoy Cinema in San Sebastian, Spain as part of the 25th annual San Sebastian International Film Festival (Sept. 10–21).

596 September 18, 1977
The Strange Case of the End of Civilisation as We Know It (TV special: ITV/LWT). Comedy starring **John Cleese** and Arthur Lowe as the descendants of Sherlock Holmes and Dr. Watson who match wits against a descendant of the diabolical Prof. Moriarty. Hour-long program for London Weekend Television. Shown in the U.S. (on PBS) in March 1978. Also starring Connie Booth, Ron Moody, Stratford Johns, Joss Ackland, Denholm Elliott, and Holly Palance. Written by **John Cleese**, Jack Hobbs, and Joseph McGrath. Directed by Joseph McGrath. Produced by Humphrey Barclay. Note: **Cleese** had previously played Holmes in the 1973 *Comedy Playhouse* presentation "Elementary, My Dear Watson."

597 September 20–October 25, 1977
The first series of *Ripping Yarns* airs on BBC2. This **Michael Palin–Terry Jones** comedy affectionately parodies the *Boys Own* adventure stories the pair grew up with — tales of British spies, sports heroes, and Indian princes. The first series, consisting of six episodes, includes a war story, a murder mystery, and a horror tale. The theme music is the Fanfare from the *Façade Suite* (1921–22) by Sir William Walton. A second series of three episodes airs in October 1979.
Award: Broadcasting Press Guild Award for Best Comedy Series of 1977.

598 September 20, 1977
Ripping Yarns (TV episode: BBC2). "Tomkinson's Schooldays." The pilot show, which originally aired Jan. 7, 1976, is repeated to begin the first series. Written by and starring **Michael Palin** and **Terry Jones**. Produced & directed by Terry Hughes.

599 September 21, 1977
Terry Jones opens the first Great British Beer Festival (Sept. 21–25) at Alexandra Palace in London by pouring six pints of beer (from his own Penrhos Brewery) over his head.

600 September 27, 1977
Ripping Yarns (TV episode: BBC2). "The Testing of Eric Olthwaite." A spoof of stories about the members of Northern England's mining communities follows the adventures of one Eric Olthwaite, a man so boring that his parents run away from home. Although set in Yorkshire, the show was filmed mostly in Durham (Apr. 25–May 11). Second show of the first series. Starring **Michael Palin** (as Eric/Bank Manager), with Barbara New, John Barrett, Anita Carey, Liz Smith, Reg Lye, Petra Markham, Kenneth Colley, Roger Avon, Clifford Kershaw, Norman Mitchell, Anthony Smee, Marcelle Samett, and Peter Graham. Written by **Michael Palin** and **Terry Jones**. Song: "The Ballad of Eric Olthwaite" by Andre Jacquemin and Dave Howman. Produced & directed by Jim Franklin. Note: Kenneth Colley, who plays the bank robber, will later play Jesus Christ in the opening scene of the Pythons' next film, *Life of Brian* (1979).

601 September 29, 1977
The Strange Case of the End of Civilisation as We Know It (Book: W.H. Allen & Co./Star Books), written by **John Cleese**, Jack Hobbs, and Joseph McGrath, is published in the U.K. The script of the London Weekend Television program starring **John Cleese**, with stills from the production. Published in two editions with two different covers.

602 September 30, 1977
Michael Palin discovers in an old journal the full story of how his great-grandfather Edward Palin met, in 1861, a 19-year-old Irish-born American girl named Brita Gallagher. The story of their meeting (the two would marry in 1867) will become the basis for **Palin**'s 1991 film *American Friends*. **Palin** later searches for Gallagher's Irish roots in a 1994 episode of *Great Railway Journeys*.

603 October 3, 1977
Publishers Weekly (Magazine/U.S.). "New Python (Book) a Treat for Both Film and Design Buffs," by Paul Doebler, p. 78+. Article on the contents and making of the *Monty Python and the Holy Grail (book)*.

604 October 4, 1977
Ripping Yarns (TV episode: BBC2). "Escape from Stalag Luft 112B." The story of P.O.W. Phipps, a stalwart World War I officer whose attempts at escape from a German prison camp include building an airplane out of 1,400 toilet paper rolls. Third show of the first series. Filmed May 16–27 on Salisbury Plain. Starring **Michael Palin** (as Major Errol Phipps/"Chips"), with Roy Kinnear, John Phillips, Timothy Carlton, David Griffin, Julian Hough, David English, Roland MacLeod, Nicholas Day, Hugh Janes, Philip Graham, James Charles, Glen Cunningham, and David Machin. Narrated by Ronald Fletcher. Written by **Michael Palin** and **Terry Jones**. Directed by Jim Franklin.

605 October 11, 1977
Ripping Yarns (TV episode: BBC2). "Murder at Moorstones Manor." A spoof of Agatha Christie murder mysteries which relates the tale of the wealthy Chiddingfold family and their deadly mansion. Fourth show of the first series. Filmed Oct. 15, 25–Nov. 5, 1976, in Glencoe, Scotland and Harefield, England. Starring **Michael Palin** (as Charles/Hugo), with Isabel Dean, Iain Cuthbertson, Frank Middlemass, Harold Innocent, Candace Glendenning, and Anne Zelda. Written by **Michael Palin** and **Terry Jones**. Directed by Terry Hughes.

606 October 18, 1977
Ripping Yarns (TV episode: BBC2). "Across the Andes by Frog." A British explorer, equipped with a legion of frogs, sets out on the first amphibian assault on the Andes. The story was adapted from a piece that first appeared in **Palin** & **Jones**' 1974 book *Bert Fegg's Nasty Book for Boys & Girls*. Fifth show of the first series. Filmed Oct. 4–14 & 26, 1976, at Pinewood Studios and in Glencoe, Scotland. Starring **Michael Palin** (as Capt. Snetterton), with Denholm Elliott, Don Henderson, Eileen Way, Louis Mansi, Charles McKeown, John White, Alan Leith, Kevin Moran, and Brian Nolan. Written by **Michael Palin** and **Terry Jones**. Directed by Terry Hughes.

607 October 25, 1977
Ripping Yarns (TV episode: BBC2). "The Curse of the Claw." A man attempts to return a cursed claw to its rightful owners in this gothic tale of Oriental magic. Sixth and last show of the first series. Filmed June 8–24, July 4–5 & Aug. 8–9, mostly in Rippingale, Lincolnshire. Starring **Michael Palin** (as Sir Kevin Orr/Uncle Jack), with Hilary Mason, Tenniel Evans, Keith Smith, Aubrey Morris, Nigel Rhodes, Judy Loe, Bridget Armstrong, Michael Stainton, Vanessa Furse, and Diana Hutchinson. Written by **Michael Palin** and **Terry Jones**. Directed by Jim Franklin.

608 November 1977
Fawlty Towers (Book: Futura/Contact Publications), written by **John Cleese** and Connie Booth, is published in the U.K. Oversized paperback containing the scripts of three episodes from the show's first series: "The Builders," "The Hotel Inspectors," and "Gourmet Night." Illustrated with many photos.

609 November 1977
John Cleese attends the opening of the Screen on the Hill cinema in Hampstead, London. Other attendees include Peter Cook and Keith Carradine. The event is reported on by BBC2's *Arena* (Nov. 16).

610 November 5, 1977
The Times (London) (Newspaper/U.K.). "Interview: Beastly Basil," by Sheridan Morley, p. 11. Interview with **John Cleese**, who talks about the new *Fawlty Towers* book and the origins of the series.

611 November 13, 1977
Read All About It (TV talk show: BBC1). Book program hosted by Melvyn Bragg. Guest: **John Cleese**, promoting the new *Fawlty Towers* book.

612 November 25, 1977
The Evening Standard (Newspaper/U.K.). "Fawlty Squash with **Cleese**," by Michael Plummer. Article containing a false report about **John Cleese**, who was then practicing for *The Pro-Celebrity Squash Challenge*, causing him to write a series of letters to the paper's editor, Simon Jenkins. Their correspondence is later published in the *MONTY-PYTHONSCRAPBOOK* (1979).

613 December 1977
The Monty Python Instant Record Collection (Record: Charisma CAS 1134) is released in the U.K. Collection of some of Python's greatest hits from their five previous Charisma albums (*Another, Previous, Holy Grail, Drury Lane,* and *Matching Tie*) plus one previously-unreleased recording: "Summarize Proust Competition" (from the 1972 *Previous* sessions). The record cover, designed by **Terry Gilliam**, folds out into a record box. Tracks: "Introductions," "Alistair Cooke," "Nudge, Nudge," "Mrs. Nigger Baiter," "Constitutional Peasants," "Fish License," "Eric the Half-a-Bee," "Australian Table Wines," "Silly Noises," "Novel Writing," "Elephantoplasty," "How to Do It," "Gumby Cherry Orchard," "Oscar Wilde," "Introductions," "Argument Clinic," "French Taunter," "Summarize Proust Competition," "Cheese Emporium," "Funerals at Prestatyn," "Camelot," "Word Association," "Bruces," "Parrot," and "Monty Python Theme." The American version of this album, released in 1982, contains an almost entirely different set of tracks.

614 December 8, 1977–April 1978
The Pro-Celebrity Squash Challenge (Event). **John Cleese** takes part in this pro-celebrity competition being sponsored by Rank Xerox. Other celebrity players include Tommy Steele, Leonard Rossiter, and William Franklyn; the squash pros include Hiddy Jahan, Bruce Browlee, and Mohibullah Khan. The first match is played at Woking Leisure Centre on Dec. 8.

615 December 14, 1977
Pebble Mill at One (TV talk show: BBC1). Hosted by Donny Macleod. Guest: **John Cleese**.

616 December 18, 1977
The Big Match (TV show: ITV). Hosted by Brian Moore, with guest presenters **John Cleese**, Peter Cook, and Elton John. Produced by Bob Gardam for London Weekend Television.

617 December 26, 1977
Graham Chapman stops drinking — cold turkey — on Boxing Day. He spends the next three days in bed experiencing severe withdrawal symptoms. On the third day (Dec. 29), feeling better, he gets up and invites a few friends over. Soon afterward he collapses and is taken to the hospital, where he stays until Jan. 2.

618 1977
How Am I Doing?: The Appraisal Interview (Training film: Video Arts). Management training film on how to prepare and conduct a professional appraisal interview. Starring **John Cleese** (as Ethelred the Unready/Ivan the Terrible/William the Silent), Julian Holloway, and John Wentworth. Written by Jonathan Lynn. Directed by Peter Robinson.

619 1977
The Balance Sheet Barrier (Training film: Video Arts). Film for managers explaining the essentials of business finance. Part of the "Finance for Non-Financial Managers" series. Remade in 1993. Starring **John Cleese** (as Julian Carruthers) and Ronnie Corbett. Written by Antony Jay. Directed by Peter Robinson.

620 1977
The Secretary and Her Boss, Part 1: Try to See It My Way (Training film: Video Arts). First of two films demonstrating the importance of a boss and secretary working as a partnership. Starring **John Cleese**, Adrienne Posta, Rosemary Leach, David Simeon, and April Walker. Animation by Tony Hart. Directed by Peter Robinson.

621 1977
The Secretary and Her Boss, Part 2: We Can Work It Out (Training film: Video Arts). Starring **John Cleese** (as Mr. Becket), Adrienne Posta, Rosemary Leach, Richard Davies, Ralph Ball, and Gary Waldham. Animation by Tony Hart. Directed by Peter Robinson.

622 1977
The Mermaid Frolics (Record: Polydor 2384 101). Highlights from the Amnesty International show *An Evening Without Sir Bernard Miles*, recorded May 8, 1977, at London's Mermaid Theatre, with comedy sketches performed by **John Cleese**, **Terry Jones**, Connie Booth, Peter Cook, Jonathan Miller, and Peter Ustinov, and music selections by Julie Covington, Pete Atkin, John Williams, and The Bowles Brothers Band. Tracks include "Bookshop" (**Cleese** & Booth), "Words...and Things" (**Cleese** & Miller), and "Forgive Me" (song by **Jones**, with Atkin on piano). Produced by Martin Lewis. Mixed & edited at The Manor Studios in July 1977.

623 1977
General Accident (TV commercials). **John Cleese** appears in a series of British ads for the General Accident Insurance Company. In one ad, **Cleese** and another man hit each other when they try to back their cars into the same parking spot. While the other man becomes furious, the insured **Cleese** remains perfectly calm.

624 1977
Jabberwocky (Book: Pan Books), written by Ralph Hoover (pseud. of Paul Spike), is published in the U.K. Paperback novelization of the 1977 **Terry Gilliam** film, adapted from the film script written by **Gilliam** and Charles Alverson.

625 1977
British Is Best (Marketing film: Video Arts). **John Cleese** stars in this humorous sales film on why the British should buy Volvo Cars. Sponsored by Volvo Concessionaires. Written by Jonathan Lynn. Directed by Peter Robinson.

626 1977
Truth and Logic (Marketing film: Video Arts). Humorous sales film for the *TV Times*. Starring **John Cleese**, Connie Booth, Andrew Sachs, George A. Cooper, June Whitfield, and Fulton MacKay. Written by Chris Langham. Directed by Charles Crichton. Produced by Robert Reid.

627 1977
How to Lie with Statistics, Part 2: The Average Chap (Training film: Video Arts). Animated film narrated by **John Cleese**. Based on the 1954 book of the same title by Darrell Huff and Irving Geis. Written by Robert Reid. Animated by Tony Hart. Produced by Peter Robinson.

628 1977
Terry Jones provides financial backing—in partnership with the Dartington Trust—for the publication of the environmental magazine *Vole*, founded and edited by Richard Boston. The magazine publishes until 1980.

629 1977–80
Sony (Radio commercials). **John Cleese** stars in a series of thirty British radio ads for the Sony Corporation. Two of the ads, "Boo-Boo" and "Shiny Objects," win Clio Awards. Written by **Cleese** and Tim Delaney.

630 January 7–21, 1978
The Pythons spend two weeks in Barbados in the West Indies to complete the rewrites on *Life of Brian*. They also do some swimming and water-skiing, and are joined by Mick Jagger, Jerry Hall, Peter Rudge, Keith Moon, Alan Price, Des O'Connor, and **Idle**'s girlfriend, Tania Kosevich.

631 Late January 1978
EMI Films agrees to finance *Life of Brian*.

632 February 1978
The Rutles: All You Need Is Cash (Record: Warner Bros K 56459 [U.K.]; HS 3151 [U.S.]). Soundtrack to **Eric Idle**'s Beatles mockumentary (airing Mar. 22), containing 14 Rutles classics written by Neil Innes and performed by Innes, Ollie Halsall, Rikki Fataar, and John Halsey. Tracks: "Hold My Hand," "Number One," "With a Girl Like You," "I Must Be in Love," "Ouch!," "Living in Hope," "Love Life," "Nevertheless," "Good Times Roll," "Doubleback Alley," "Cheese and Onions," "Another Day," "Piggy in the Middle," and "Let's Be Natural." The full-color, 20-page booklet included with the album highlights the Rutle years with many photos and excerpts from the film. Album/booklet conceived and written by **Eric Idle**. Designed by Basil Pao. Produced by Neil Innes. Recorded at Chappell Studios, London. Reissued on CD in 1990 (Rhino) with six additional songs: "Goose-Step Mama," "Baby Let Me Be," "Blue Suede Schubert," "Between Us," "It's Looking Good," and "Get Up and Go." U.K. singles issued on K 17180 and K 17125 (12-inch EP). U.S. singles issued on WBS 8560 and E 723 (12-inch EP). A second Rutles collection, *The Rutles Archaeology*, is produced in 1996 (without **Idle**'s involvement).

633 February 27, 1978
The Odd Job, a comedy starring, co-written and co-produced by **Graham Chapman**, begins filming. The film is shot on location in London and at Shepperton Studios, Shepperton, Middlesex, England.

634 Late February 1978
EMI pulls its financial backing for *Life of Brian* three days before the film is to start production. The decision comes after the company's chief executive, Lord Bernard Delfont, reads the script and deems it "obscene and sacrilegious." The Pythons are left to find backing elsewhere. But help will soon come in the form of an ex–Beatle.

635 March 22, 1978
All You Need Is Cash (TV film: NBC). **Eric Idle** spoofs Beatlemania with this mock documentary chronicling the history of the fictional rock group

The Rutles (Dirk McQuickly, Ron Nasty, Stig O'Hara, and Barry Wom) from their beginnings at the Rat Keller in Hamburg, to their appearance on *Ed Sullivan*, concert at Che Stadium, films (*A Hard Day's Rut* and *Ouch!*), and finally their breakup and multiple lawsuits. **Idle** plays both Dirk and the film's trench-coated narrator/interviewer Brian Fowl, as well as the smaller role of Stanley J. Krammerhead III, Jr., a pop music historian. The film, which began as a sketch on **Idle**'s *Rutland Weekend Television* in 1976, includes cameos by real-life rock legends and *Saturday Night Live* cast members. Songs: "Goose-Step Mama," "Number One," "Between Us," "With a Girl Like You," "Hold My Hand," "I Must Be in Love," "Living in Hope," "Ouch!," "It's Looking Good," "Another Day," "Good Times Roll," "Love Life," "Nevertheless," "Piggy in the Middle," "Cheese and Onions," "Let's Be Natural," "Get Up and Go," and "Doubleback Alley." Repeated on Dec. 10. Also starring Neil Innes (as Ron), Rikki Fataar (as Stig), John Halsey (as Barry), **Michael Palin** (as Eric Manchester), George Harrison, Mick Jagger, Paul Simon, Bianca Jagger, John Belushi, Dan Aykroyd, Gilda Radner, Bill Murray, Gwen Taylor, Ron Wood, Terence Bayler, Henry Woolf, Jeannette Charles, Roger McGough, and Tania Kosevich (**Idle**'s girlfriend and future wife, in four roles). Conceived & written by **Eric Idle**. Music & lyrics by Neil Innes. Directed by Gary Weis and **Eric Idle**. Produced by Gary Weis and Craig Kellem. Executive produced by Lorne Michaels. A sequel, *The Rutles 2: Can't Buy Me Lunch*, is produced in 2002.

Reviews: Frank Rich (*Time*, Mar. 27, 1978, p. 102): "*All You Need Is Cash*, a frantic spoof of Beatlemania, is 90 minutes long and has about three genuine laughs ... it's just British undergraduate silliness..."; Harry F. Waters (*Newsweek*, Mar. 27, 1978, p. 78): "...a take-off on the Beatle legend that, wondrously enough, is almost as much fun as the original.... As a spoof of Beatlemania, *All You Need Is Cash* will appeal primarily to those who have acquired the taste for a peculiarly British brand of zaniness."

636 March 27, 1978

All You Need Is Cash is shown in Britain on BBC2 (repeated May 27 on BBC1). Besides the U.S. and U.K., the film is sold to Canada, New Zealand, Denmark, Japan, Iceland, The Netherlands, Austria, Sweden, Norway, and Finland.

637 March 30, 1978

The Broadcasting Press Guild Awards (Award ceremony). *Ripping Yarns* wins the award for Best Comedy or Light Entertainment Programme of 1977. **Michael Palin** accepts the award at the ceremony held at International Press Centre, London.

638 April 1978

Eric Idle and producer John Goldstone travel to New York and Los Angeles in search of investors willing to finance the production of *Life of Brian* (EMI pulled out of the deal in February). They meet with musician George Harrison, an avid Python fan and friend of **Idle**'s, at his Hollywood home. The former Beatle agrees to put up $4.5 million, which will require mortgaging his house and London office. Harrison later remarks: "I just wanted to see the film."

639 April 3, 1978

Michael Palin attends an Oscar party at the New York club Studio 54. The party is hosted by Truman Capote and Andy Warhol. Other guests include Salvador Dali, Bianca Jagger, and a 12-year-old Brooke Shields.

640 April 8, 1978

Saturday Night Live (TV comedy show: NBC). Hosted by **Michael Palin**, with musical guest Eugene Record. **Palin** hosts this late-night sketch-comedy series for the first of four times (1978–84). During his opening monologue, **Palin**, playing his manager Sid Biggs, dances to "The White Cliffs of Dover" while putting sea-food salad and two cats down his trousers. He also appears in "IRS Confession" (as a priest), "The Seagull" (as an actor/escape artist), "Nerds Piano Lesson" (as Mr. Brighton), "The Forgotten Memoirs of Sherlock Holmes" (as Holmes), and "Danger Probe" (as an 18th-century fop). Cast: Dan Aykroyd, John Belushi, Jane Curtin, Garrett Morris, Bill Murray, Laraine Newman, and Gilda Radner. Directed by Dave Wilson. Produced by Lorne Michaels.

641 April 21–May 26, 1978

The first series of *Ripping Yarns* is repeated on BBC2.

642 April 26, 1978

Standing Room Only (TV special: Home Box Office). "Double Bananas." **Michael Palin** appears on this special celebrating comedy teams past and present. Hosted by Dan Rowan & Dick Martin. Also with Sid Caesar, Imogene Coca, Senor Wences, and The Ritz Brothers (Harry and Jimmy). Recorded at the Elysee Theater in NYC on Apr. 2.

643 Summer 1978

Terry Jones writes a collection of original fairy

tales for his daughter Sally. The stories are published under the title *Fairy Tales* in October 1981.

644   June 10, 1978

John Cleese plays with the Lord's Taverners (England) in a celebrity cricket match against the Corfu Select XI (Corfu) on the Greek Island of Corfu. The Lord Taverners is a group of actors and professional cricketers who play for children's charities. Other members of the team include William Rushton, Roy Kinnear, and Nicholas Parsons. The match is documented in the short film *Mad Dogs and Cricketers*.

645   June 24, 1978

Snavely (TV special: ABC). Half-hour pilot based on **John Cleese**'s BBC comedy *Fawlty Towers*. Viacom bought the format rights to the BBC show, but after the failure of this pilot, plans for a series are dropped. Starring Harvey Korman (as Henry Snavely) and Betty White.

646   July 1–14, 1978

"Roger of the Raj," an episode from the second series of *Ripping Yarns*, is filmed in High Halden (at Harbourne Hall) and Godington Park in Kent. The episode will air Oct. 24, 1979, on BBC2.

647   August 1978

Ging Gang Goolie/Mister Sheene (Record: EMI 2852). U.K. single from Dirk & Stig (**Eric Idle** and Ricky Fataar) of The Rutles. Songs: "Ging Gang Goolie" (Trad., arr. by **Idle** and Fataar), b/w "Mister Sheene" (**Idle**). Produced by Fataar and **Idle**.

648   September 1978

John Cleese and his wife (and *Fawlty Towers* writing partner), Connie Booth, divorce after ten years of marriage (they wed in 1968).

649   September 7, 1978

Keith Moon, drummer for The Who and good friend of **Graham Chapman**, dies from an overdose of the prescription sedative Heminevrin at the age of 31. He was set to do some acting in *Life of Brian*, which starts filming in only a week.

650   September 16–November 12, 1978

Monty Python's Life of Brian, the group's third feature film, about a man in biblical times who is mistaken for the Messiah, is filmed on location in Tunisia (in Monastir, Sousse, El Hadj, and Matmata). A 41-day shoot. **Terry Jones** directs and **Terry Gilliam** is the production designer.

651   October 1978

The Odd Job (Feature film: Columbia Pictures) is released in the U.K. Black comedy starring **Graham Chapman** as Arthur Harris, a suicidal insurance executive who, unable to take his own life, hires an odd job man (David Jason) to carry out the task. **Chapman**'s first solo film project faced several setbacks before filming started: Cliff Owen, who was originally set to direct, had to be replaced when he broke a thigh; and rock drummer Keith Moon, who was originally going to play the odd job man, was denied the role by director Peter Medak. Also starring Diana Quick, Simon Williams, Edward Hardwicke, Bill Paterson, Michael Elphick, Stewart Harwood, Carolyn Seymour, Joe Melia, and George Innes. Written by Bernard McKenna and **Graham Chapman**, based on a television play by McKenna. Directed by Peter Medak. Produced by Mark Forstater and **Graham Chapman**.

Review: Alan Brien (*The Sunday Times* [London], Oct. 8, 1978): "An attempt at Joe Orton–style black comedy ... it soon falls apart in a welter of mugging close-ups, high-pitched squeals and repetitive slapstick."

652   October 1978

Animations of Mortality (Book: Eyre Methuen), by **Terry Gilliam** with Lucinda Cowell, is published in the U.K. A collection of **Gilliam**'s artwork reproduced in oversized color. Includes a great deal of Python artwork, as well as some of his earlier and later works. Brian the Badger takes the reader through the animation process. Published in the U.S. in 1979 (Routledge).

653   October 1978

The first series of the **Michael Palin–Terry Jones** comedy *Ripping Yarns* begins playing on Public Television stations in the U.S.

654   October 1, 1978

Film 78 (TV show: BBC1). Hosted by Barry Norman. A segment on the film *The Odd Job* includes interviews with star **Graham Chapman**, director Peter Medak, and producer Mark Forstater.

655   October 5, 1978

Comedian Spike Milligan films a cameo appearance in *Life of Brian* in Sousse, Tunisia.

656   October 22, 1978

George Harrison visits the set of *Life of Brian* in Tunisia. Harrison, who is an executive producer on the movie, films a cameo appearance (as Mr. Papadopoulos) in the scene where Brian is received by a roomful of fanatics and incurables.

657 November–December 1978
Post-production on *Life of Brian* is done in London. The last scene shot is a sequence where **Graham Chapman** is inside a spaceship. To film it, **Chapman** flew from L.A. to England where, for tax purposes, he could stay for only twenty-four hours, eight of which he spent in a box being shaken about.

658 November 27, 1978
Start the Week with Richard Baker (Radio talk show: BBC Radio 4). Sandra Harris interviews **Michael Palin**.

659 November 30, 1978
Ripping Yarns (Book: Eyre Methuen), written by **Michael Palin** and **Terry Jones**, is published in the U.K. Collection of the scripts of all six episodes from the first series: "Tomkinson's Schooldays," "The Testing of Eric Olthwaite," "Escape from Stalag Luft 112B," "Murder at Moorstones Manor," "Across the Andes by Frog," and "The Curse of the Claw." Art direction & design by Kate Hepburn. Artwork by Walter Junge. Photographs by Amy Lune and Bertrand Polo. Published in the U.S. by Pantheon (1979).

660 December 9, 1978
Saturday Night Live (TV comedy show: NBC). Hosted by **Eric Idle**, with musical guest Kate Bush. **Idle**, hosting for the third time in three years, appears in the sketches "Madrigal" (singing quartet), "The Woman He Loved" (as Prince Charles), "What Do You?" (game show), "Candy Slice Recording Session," and "Cochise at Oxford." Cast: Dan Aykroyd, John Belushi, Jane Curtin, Garrett Morris, Bill Murray, Laraine Newman, and Gilda Radner. Directed by Dave Wilson. Produced by Lorne Michaels.

661 December 25, 1978
Black Cinderella Two Goes East (Radio special: BBC Radio 2). The cast of radio's *I'm Sorry I'll Read That Again* reunites — joining Peter Cook and others — for this hour-long Christmas pantomime. Starring **John Cleese** (as Fairy Godperson), David Hatch, Jo Kendall, Tim Brooke-Taylor, Graeme Garden, Bill Oddie, Peter Cook, Rob Buckman, Maggie Henderson, Richard Murdoch, and narrated by Richard Baker. Written by Rory McGrath and Clive Anderson. Produced by Douglas Adams and John Lloyd.

662 1978
Decisions, Decisions (Training film: Video Arts). A manager is taught the principles of good decision-making by four of history's great decision-makers: Field Marshal Montgomery, Queen Elizabeth I, Sir Winston Churchill, and Brutus. Starring **John Cleese** (as Alan, also Montgomery/Elizabeth/Brutus/Churchill), Prunella Scales, Nigel Hawthorne, Roger Hume, Conrad Phillips, John Clive, and Blain Fairman. Written by Jonathan Lynn. Directed by Peter Robinson.

663 1978
The Control of Working Capital (Training film: Video Arts). Sequel to *The Balance Sheet Barrier* (1977). Part of the "Finance for Non-Financial Managers" series. Starring **John Cleese** (as Julian Carruthers) and Ronnie Corbett. Written by Antony Jay. Directed by Peter Robinson.

664 1978
I'm Sorry I'll Read That Again (Record: BBC Records REH 342). Compilation of sketches & songs from series 7 and 8 (1969–70) of the BBC radio comedy program starring Tim Brooke-Taylor, **John Cleese**, Graeme Garden, David Hatch, Jo Kendall, and Bill Oddie, with music by The Dave Lee Group. Script by Garden & Oddie. Tracks include: "Home This Afternoon a Go-Go" and "Taming of the Shrew." **Cleese** was a regular on the show from 1966 to 1973.

665 1978
Accurist (TV commercials). **John Cleese** stars in a series of commercials for Accurist watches. In one, he demonstrates the popularity of the watch by grabbing people on the street and forcing them to show the Accurist watch they're wearing, including one woman's "Accur-ankle" watch.

666 1978
Mad Dogs and Cricketers (Short film). Documentary short (33 mins.) about The Lord's Taverners, a group of actors and cricketers who raise money for children's charities. In the film, the Taverners play a cricket match in Corfu on June 10, 1978. Introduced by Eric Morecambe and starring **John Cleese**, William Rushton, John Alderton, and Roy Kinnear. Produced & directed by Nicholas Parsons.

667 January 1, 1979
Grandstand (TV show: BBC1). Guest: **John Cleese**.

668 January 11, 1979
A rough-cut of *Life of Brian* is given a private showing at Audley Square Theatre in London. **John Cleese** and **Michael Palin** are in the audience.

669 January 19, 1979

A screening of *Life of Brian* is held, attended by the Pythons, producer John Goldstone, executive producer George Harrison, and others.

670 January 22, 1979

You and Me (TV show: BBC1). "The Window Cleaner." Schools program for children age 4–5. **Michael Palin** and Fulton Mackay appear in the dramatized story "Mr. Chubb's Glasses." Directed by Eric Mival. Produced by Barbara Parker.

671 January 27, 1979

Saturday Night Live (TV comedy show: NBC). Hosted by **Michael Palin**, with musical guests The Doobie Brothers, also Father Guido Sarducci. **Palin**, hosting for the second time, appears in the sketches "Nerds Piano Lesson" (as Mr. Brighton), "What If Superman Grew Up in Germany?" (as Hitler), "Miles Cowperthwaite, Part One" (as Miles), and "Name the Bats" (as Jerry the host). Cast: Dan Aykroyd, John Belushi, Jane Curtin, Garrett Morris, Bill Murray, Laraine Newman, and Gilda Radner. Directed by Dave Wilson. Produced by Lorne Michaels.

672 February–March 1979

Eric Idle spends five weeks in a suite of the Chateau Marmont in Los Angeles, working day and night to put together the elaborate book of Monty Python's upcoming film, *Life of Brian*.

673 February 17–23, 1979

Radio Times (Magazine/U.K.). Cover story on the return of *Fawlty Towers*.

674 February 17, 1979

Tiswas (TV episode: ITV/ATV). **Michael Palin** and **Terry Jones** guest-star on this popular Saturday-morning children's show. Hosted by Chris Tarrant, Sally James, and John Gorman.

675 February 19–March 26, October 25, 1979

The second and final series of the **John Cleese**–Connie Booth sitcom *Fawlty Towers* airs on BBC2. Like the first series (in 1975), this series consists of six episodes. The recording of the sixth episode is delayed six months due to a strike at the BBC. During the four years between the two series **Cleese** and Booth had gotten a divorce (in 1978) and **Cleese** returned to Python to perform at NYC's City Center (in 1976) and film their next movie, *Life of Brian* (in 1978). Changes to the show include the addition of actor Brian Hall as Terry the cook, and a new director, Bob Spiers.

Awards: BAFTA-winner for Best Situation Comedy and Best Light Entertainment Performance (**Cleese**).

676 February 19, 1979

Fawlty Towers (TV episode: BBC2). "Communication Problems." When Basil secretly bets on the horses and a senile hotel guest loses some money, great complications arise. First show of the second series. Starring **John Cleese**, Prunella Scales, Andrew Sachs, Connie Booth, with Joan Sanderson (as Mrs. Richards), Ballard Berkeley, Brian Hall, Gilly Flower, Renee Roberts, Robert Lankesheer, Johnny Shannon, Bill Bradley, George Lee, and Mervyn Pasco. Written by **John Cleese** and Connie Booth. Directed by Bob Spiers. Produced by Douglas Argent.

677 February 26, 1979

Fawlty Towers (TV episode: BBC2). "The Psychiatrist." Basil becomes nervous when a psychiatrist checks into the hotel and gets caught in compromising situations with an attractive Australian guest. Second show of the second series. Starring **John Cleese**, Prunella Scales, Andrew Sachs, Connie Booth, with Nicky Henson, Basil Henson, Elspet Gray, Ballard Berkeley, Brian Hall, Luan Peters, Aimee Delamain, Gilly Flower, Renee Roberts, and Imogen Bickford-Smith. Written by **John Cleese** and Connie Booth. Directed by Bob Spiers. Produced by Douglas Argent.

678 March 1–10, April 3–6, 10, May 3–4, 1979

"Whinfrey's Last Case," an episode from the second series of *Ripping Yarns*, is filmed in Cornwall and Devon, with an introductory scene filmed at Russell Square in London (Mar. 2). Filming is interrupted in March due to a BBC workers strike, which also delays the recording of the final *Fawlty Towers* episode ("Basil the Rat"). Filming resumes in April in London and at Ealing Studios.

679 March 5, 1979

Fawlty Towers (TV episode: BBC2). "Waldorf Salad." Basil must prepare dinner for a demanding American who checks in after 9 P.M. when the kitchen is closed. Third show of the second series. Starring **John Cleese**, Prunella Scales, Andrew Sachs, Connie Booth, with Bruce Boa, Claire Nielson, Norman Bird, Stella Tanner, Terence Conoley, June Ellis, Brian Hall, Anthony Dawes, Ballard Berkeley, Gilly Flower, Renee Roberts, Beatrice Shaw, and Dorothy Frere. Written by **John Cleese** and Connie Booth. Directed by Bob Spiers. Produced by Douglas Argent.

680 March 12, 1979
Fawlty Towers (TV episode: BBC2). "The Kipper and the Corpse." When a guest dies in his sleep, Basil tries to prepare the room for the next occupant, but moving the body proves more difficult than he thought. Fourth show of the second series. Starring **John Cleese**, Prunella Scales, Andrew Sachs, Connie Booth, with Geoffrey Palmer, Mavis Pugh, Richard Davies, Elizabeth Benson, Ballard Berkeley, Gilly Flower, Renee Roberts, Brian Hall, Derek Royle, Robert McBain, Pamela Buchner, Raymond Mason, Charles McKeown, and Len Marten. Written by **John Cleese** and Connie Booth. Directed by Bob Spiers. Produced by Douglas Argent.

681 March 17–30, 1979
"Golden Gordon," an episode from the second series of *Ripping Yarns*, is filmed in Yorkshire. Locations include Guiseley, Worth Valley Railway, Keighley, Bradley, Kildwick, Bingley, and the Saltaire Football Ground. **John Cleese** films a cameo appearance (as a passerby) on Brontë Street in Keighley on Mar. 28.

682 March 18–April 15, 1979
The five-episode series *Company Account* airs on BBC1. The series features business-training films from Video Arts, some starring the company's co-founder, **John Cleese**. Series producer: Tony Matthews.

683 March 18, 1979
Company Account (TV episode: BBC1). "The Balance Sheet Barrier" (1977 training film). First episode of the series. Starring **John Cleese** and Ronnie Corbett. Written by Antony Jay. Directed by Peter Robinson.

684 March 25, 1979
Company Account (TV episode: BBC1). "The Control of Working Capital" (1978 training film). Second episode of the series. Starring **John Cleese** and Ronnie Corbett. Written by Antony Jay. Directed by Peter Robinson.

685 March 26, 1979
Fawlty Towers (TV episode: BBC2). "The Anniversary." Basil plans an elaborate surprise anniversary party for Sybil, but problems begin when she unexpectedly leaves the hotel. Fifth show of the second series. Taping of this episode was delayed by a week (from Mar. 11 to Mar. 18) due to a BBC strike. Starring **John Cleese**, Prunella Scales, Andrew Sachs, Connie Booth, with Ken Campbell, Una Stubbs, Robert Arnold, Pat Keen, Roger Hume, Denyse Alexander, Christine Shaw, Ballard Berkeley, Gilly Flower, Renee Roberts, and Brian Hall. Written by **John Cleese** and Connie Booth. Directed by Bob Spiers. Produced by Douglas Argent.

686 March 26, 1979
Publishers Weekly (Magazine/U.S.). "PW Interviews: **Michael Palin**," by Sally A. Lodge, pp. 6–7. **Palin** talks about Monty Python and the *Ripping Yarns* book just released in the U.S. The interview took place in January at the Algonquin in New York (**Palin** was in NY to host *Saturday Night Live*).

687 April 22–May 13, 1979
The Office Line, a series of business-training films starring **John Cleese** for Video Arts, airs on BBC1. Four episodes.

688 April 22, 1979
The Office Line (TV episode: BBC1). "The Secretary and Her Boss: Try to See It My Way" (1977 training film). First episode of the series. Starring **John Cleese** and Adrienne Posta. Directed by Peter Robinson.

689 April 27, 1979
The New York Times (Newspaper/U.S.). "This Isle, Scepter'd," by **Michael Palin**, p. A31. **Palin** on the British election.

690 April 29, 1979
The Office Line (TV episode: BBC1). "The Secretary and Her Boss: We Can Work It Out" (1977 training film). Second episode of the series. Starring **John Cleese** and Adrienne Posta. Directed by Peter Robinson.

691 May 1979
The BBC entry for the Golden Rose of Montreux is the *Fawlty Towers* episode "The Kipper and the Corpse."

692 May 6, 1979
The Office Line (TV episode: BBC1). "Selling on the Telephone: When I'm Calling You" (1975 training film). Third episode of the series. Starring Starring **John Cleese** and Dilys Watling. Written by Jonathan Lynn and Antony Jay. Directed by Peter Robinson.

693 May 10, 1979
Michael Palin tapes an interview with actor-comedian Robert Klein for his syndicated radio program *The Robert Klein Hour*, in New York. The other guests on the show are Jerry Garcia and Clive Davis. Note: Klein will later interview **Palin** (along

with the four other surviving Pythons) for the Monty Python reunion at the Aspen Comedy Festival (in 1998).

694   May 11, 1979
Good Morning America (TV news-talk show: ABC). Guests: **Michael Palin**, Howard Jarvis, and Marian Mahoney.

695   May 12, 1979
Saturday Night Live (TV comedy show: NBC). Hosted by **Michael Palin**, with musical guest James Taylor, also Father Guido Sarducci. **Palin**, hosting for the third time, appears in the sketch "Miles Cowperthwaite, Part Two" (as Miles) and plays Margaret Thatcher in a "Weekend Update" interview. Cast: Dan Aykroyd, John Belushi, Jane Curtin, Garrett Morris, Bill Murray, Laraine Newman, and Gilda Radner. Directed by Dave Wilson. Produced by Lorne Michaels.

696   May 13, 1979
The Office Line (TV episode: BBC1). "Selling on the Telephone: Will You Answer True?" (1975 training film). Fourth and last episode of the series. Starring Starring **John Cleese** and Penelope Keith. Written by Jonathan Lynn and Antony Jay. Directed by Peter Robinson.

697   Summer 1979
While visiting George Harrison's Friar Park home, **Terry Gilliam** is shown the former Beatle's collection of *Baron Munchausen* stories written by 18th-century German writer Rudolf Raspe. The stories — and illustrations by Gustave Doré— intrigue **Gilliam**, who will later bring the stories to the big screen with 1989's *The Adventures of Baron Munchausen*.

698   June 2, 1979
A sneak preview of *Monty Python's Life of Brian* is shown in Los Angeles at the Bruin Theater in Westwood. The Pythons attend the preview, which plays to a full house.

699   June 16–22, 1979
Radio Times (Magazine/U.K.). Article by Ernie Eban on Monty Python's 10th anniversary and the BBC documentary *The Pythons*. **Michael Palin**'s hermit character ("It's...") is featured on the cover.

700   June 20, 1979
The Pythons (TV special: BBC1). Documentary film celebrating the tenth anniversary of Monty Python, the "best known British comedy group in the world." Filmed last year in Tunisia on the set of *Life of Brian*, the program features interviews with each Python, who talk about one another and the origins of the group. Includes some vintage Python clips. Produced & narrated by Iain Johnstone.

701   June 21, 1979
Nationwide (TV show: BBC1). News magazine. Guest: **Michael Palin**, promoting *The Secret Policeman's Ball* and *Ripping Yarns*.

702   June 22, 1979
Tonight in Town (TV talk show: BBC1). Host Michael Billington interviews **John Cleese** and **Michael Palin** about the upcoming *Secret Policeman's Ball* gala. They discuss their decision to perform "Cheese Shop" instead of the overly-familiar "Pet Shop" sketch.

703   June 25, 1979
Michael Palin re-shoots part of the "Ex-Leper" sequence from *Life of Brian* at Shepperton Studios in Shepperton, England.

704   June 27–30, 1979
The Secret Policeman's Ball (Stage show), four nights at Her Majesty's Theatre, Haymarket, London. Amnesty International's third comedy gala — following *A Poke in the Eye (with a Sharp Stick)* (April 1976) and *An Evening Without Sir Bernard Miles* (May 1977) — again brings together some of the top names in British comedy with the addition of acoustic music performances by several rock and classical artists. Performers include **John Cleese**, **Terry Jones**, **Michael Palin**, Peter Cook, Rowan Atkinson, Clive James, The Ken Campbell Road Show, Pete Townshend, John Williams, Eleanor Bron, Tom Robinson, Neil Innes, Billy Connolly, and John Fortune. Sketches include "Interesting Facts" (**Cleese** & Cook), "How Do You Do It?" (**Palin** & **Jones**), "The Name's the Game!" (**Cleese** & **Jones**, with Anna Ford, Clive Jenkins & Mike Brearley), "Stake Your Claim" (**Palin** & Atkinson), "Cheese Shop" (**Cleese** & **Palin**, with Chris Beetles & Rob Buckman), "Four Yorkshiremen" (**Cleese**, **Palin**, **Jones** & Atkinson), and "The End of the World" (Cook & cast). The show is filmed for an hour-long special (airing Dec. 22 on ITV) and full-length feature film (premiered in November 1979; released in July 1980). The show is also released on two albums, one featuring only comedy (Island ILPS 9601), the other just music (Island 12WIP 6598). Organized and (slightly) directed by **John Cleese**.

Review: John Barber (*The Times* [London], June 29, 1979, p. 15): "...I could have done with more satire and less dead-pan zaniness.... It is curious to see how much these comics depend on absurdist humour, now quite out of date in the theatre."

705 June 28, 1979
The Listener (Magazine/U.K.). "Monty Python: The Early Years," by Iain Johnstone, p. 873–4. Article on the group's formation and writing process, with comments from the Pythons. Johnstone produced the BBC documentary *The Pythons*, which aired June 20.

706 July 1979
The Ashes Retained (Book: Hodder & Stoughton), written by Mike Brearley and Dudley Doust, is published in the U.K. Book on cricket, with a foreword by **John Cleese**. Brearley, captain of the English cricket team, appeared in a sketch with **Cleese** in June's *Secret Policeman's Ball*.

707 July 3, 1979
Ask Aspel (TV show: BBC1). Host Michael Aspel talks with **Michael Palin** and shows clips from *Tomkinson's Schooldays*. Recorded July 2. Directed by Anne Freer. Produced by Philip Chilvers.

708 July 8, 1979
The Washington Post (Newspaper/U.S.). "Funny 'Fawlties' of British TV," by Bart Mills, sec. L, p. 2. A talk with **John Cleese** in London about *Fawlty Towers*.

709 August 1979
The British Board of Film Censors passes *Monty Python's Life of Brian* without cuts, giving the film an AA certificate, which means it is restricted to those over 14. The Christian pressure group Festival of Light had been lobbying the BBFC to ban the film outright. In the U.S., despite religious protests, Jack Valenti, head of the Motion Picture Association of America, grants the film an "R" rating, allowing those under 17 to see it if accompanied by an adult. Valenti points out that "the function of the rating system is not to place values or take a moral position, but to place the responsibility for guidance on parents."

710 August 17, 1979
Monty Python's Life of Brian (Feature film: Warner Bros.–Orion Pictures), world premiere in New York. Monty Python's most controversial film tells the story of Brian of Nazareth (played by **Graham Chapman**), a contemporary of Christ who is mistaken for the Messiah. While the film is seen by some as a comedic assault on Christ, it is really aimed at his followers. It is an attack, not on faith, but on those who refuse to question faith and allow others to do their thinking for them. Includes: "Three Wise Men," "Brian (song/animated titles)," "Sermon on the Mount (Big Nose)," "Stoning," "The Ex-Leper," "Peoples' Front of Judea (Roman Amphitheatre)," "Romans Go Home," "What Have the Romans Ever Done for Us? (PFJ Meeting)," "The Raid on Pilate's Palace," "Ben, the Old Prisoner," "Pontius Pilate (Thwow Him to the Floor/Biggus Dickus)," "A Passing Spaceship," "Haggling," "Brian, the Prophet," "Brian, the Messiah (The Shoe and the Gourd)," "He's Not the Messiah (He's a Very Naughty Boy)," "Pilate's Passover Addwess/Biggus Dickus," "One Cross Each (Nisus Wettus and Mr. Cheeky)," "The Crucifixion," and "Always Look on the Bright Side of Life (song)." Written by and featuring **Graham Chapman, John Cleese, Terry Gilliam, Eric Idle, Terry Jones**, and **Michael Palin**, with Terence Baylor, Carol Cleveland, Ken Colley, Neil Innes, Charles McKeown, Gwen Taylor, John Young, Sue Jones-Davies, Peter Brett, John Case, Chris Langham, Andrew MacLachlan, Bernard McKenna, and Spike Milligan. Songs: "Brian" (sung by Sonia Jones) and "Always Look on the Bright Side of Life" (sung by **Idle**). Design & animation by **Terry Gilliam**. Directed by **Terry Jones**. Produced by John Goldstone. Executive produced by George Harrison and Denis O'Brien (HandMade Films). Notes: George Harrison, who put up the money to finance the film after EMI backed out, makes a cameo appearance as Mr. Papadopoulos ("the gentleman who's letting us have the Mount on Sunday," says Reg). Six-foot-nine actor John Case, who appears in the film as the haggler's helper, also played Pilate's wife in a scene cut from the film.

Reviews: Vincent Canby (*The New York Times*, Aug. 17, 1979, p. C15): "It is the foulest-spoken biblical epic ever made, as well as the best-humored — a nonstop orgy of assaults, not on anyone's virtue, but on the funnybone"; Veronica Geng (*The New Yorker*, Aug. 27, 1979, p. 74): "It is fun to see the troupe in Biblical costumes. Their stock British policemen, provincials, salesmen, housewives, and politicians transpose nicely to ancient Judeans and Romans..."; J. Hoberman (*The Village Voice*, Aug. 27, 1979, p. 46): "*Brian* should delight Python addicts ... the finale may be the most transcendentally tasteless musical number since Mel Brook's 'Springtime for Hitler'"; David Ansen (*Newsweek*, Sept. 3, 1979, pp. 65–66): "...this British troupe of zanies has made its most sustained movie yet.... Though the pious will blanch, Pythonmaniacs should find this film a treasure-trove of unborn-again humor"; Richard Schickel (*Time*, Sept. 17, 1979, p. 101): "The Pythons' assault on religion is as intense as their attack on romantic chivalry in *Monty Python and the Holy Grail*.... The movie is occasionally undone by the Pythons' resistance to comic coherence..."; Stanley Kauffmann (*The New Republic*, Sept. 22, 1979, p. 40): "I read the script after seeing the film and doubled up all over again.... Even when I wasn't laughing, I was happy, which to me is a sign of really good comedy"; Robert Hatch (*The Nation*, Oct. 6, 1979, p. 314): "...I won't object on religious grounds. But there are still problems of taste, to say nothing of humor"; Patrick Gibbs (*The Times* [London], Nov. 9, 1979, p. 15): "...sophisticated schoolboy sort of humour expected of this team ... it is **Michael Palin** who gets most of the laughs, and most easily, as a Pontius Pilate unable to pronounce his 'Rs'"; John Coleman (*New Statesman*, Nov. 9, 1979, p. 737): "...an incorrigible delight ... this wildest story ever told runs a gamut from fourth-form snook-cocking through inspired, tangential lunacies and fine parodies of the Christ-movie genre right up to high satire"; Gavin Millar (*The Listener*, Nov. 15, 1979): "*Brian* is a brilliant satire, not on the power of religion, but on the frailty of humanity."

711   August 17, 1979
Terry Jones attends the world premiere of *Life of Brian* at Cinema One in New York City, where it will gross $80,529 in its first week.

712   August 26, 1979
Three Jewish organizations — the Rabbinical Alliance of America, the Union of Orthodox Rabbis of the United States and Canada, and the Rabbinical Council of Syrian and Near Eastern Sephardic Communities of America — representing 1,000 rabbis, denounce *Life of Brian* as "blasphemous" and "a crime against religion." Rabbi Abraham B. Hecht, of the Rabbinical Alliance, says that the film "is a vicious attack upon Judaism and the Bible and a cruel mockery of the religious feelings of Christians as well" and that "its continued showing could result in serious violence."

713   August 27, 1979
In response to the recent protests to *Life of Brian*, Warner Bros., the film's co-distributor (with Orion Pictures), issues a statement: "The public has been enthusiastic, having flocked to every theater now playing the picture. It is entertainment and, to many, *Monty Python's Life of Brian* is an enjoyable movie experience. It was never our intention to offend anyone's beliefs, and we certainly regret having done so. The film is a satire, it is a spoof, and it should be viewed in that context."

714   August 28, 1979
The Roman Catholic Archdiocese of New York calls *Life of Brian* "a mockery of Christ's life." Spokesman Eugene V. Clark says, "The picture holds the person of Christ up to comic ridicule and is, for Christians, an act of blasphemy." The Rev. Kenneth Jadoff, a second spokesman for the archdiocese, says, "This is the most blasphemous film I have ever seen and it pretends to be nothing else."

715   Late August 1979
Robert E. A. Lee, head of communications for the Lutheran Council in the USA, comments in his *Cinema Sound* radio review: "If blasphemy is still an operative word in our society, then we must apply it to the outrageous Monty Python film satire *Life of Brian*." He calls the film "crude and rude mockery, colossal bad taste, profane parody ... grossly offensive to those who accept Jesus Christ as Lord and Savior."

716   Fall 1979
Monty Python Examines the Life of Brian (Record: The Warner Bros Music Show WBMS 110). Dave Herman interviews **Graham Chapman**, **Terry Jones**, and **Michael Palin** about *Life of Brian*. Issued as a promotional disc. Produced by Drea Besch.

717   September 10–19, 1979
The Pythons, at the behest of their business manager Denis O'Brien, spend nine days in New York to promote *Life of Brian* and discuss plans for a new movie. They spend the last few days of their visit on Fisher's Island, off Long Island.

718   September 12, 1979
Tomorrow (TV talk show: NBC). Tom Snyder interviews **Graham Chapman**, **Terry Jones**, and **Michael Palin** on this late-night program. They discuss *Life of Brian* and censorship.

719   September 16, 1979
Citizens Against Blasphemy, an interfaith group headed by the Rev. Roger Fulton, holds a large demonstration (with about 250 protesters) against *Life of Brian* outside the Warner Communications building at Rockefeller Center in New York City.

The group charges that the film "debases Christ, Judaism and the Holy Scriptures."

720 September 20, 1979
Life of Brian opens in about 600 U.S. theaters.

721 October 1979
The Dick Cavett Show (TV talk show: PBS). Hour-long interview (shown in two parts) with **John Cleese**, promoting *Life of Brian*. He also talks about working in the Broadway musical *Half-a-Sixpence* (in 1965), the origin of the name Monty Python, offending people, studying law, business-training films, etc.

722 October 1979
Always Look on the Bright Side of Life/Brian (Record: Warner Bros. WBS 49112). U.S. single off of the *Life of Brian* soundtrack. Contains the songs "Always Look on the Bright Side of Life" (sung by **Eric Idle** and chorus) and "Brian" (sung by Sonia Jones). Produced by **Eric Idle** and **Graham Chapman**. Released in the U.K. in November on K 17495.

723 October 8, 1979
Monty Python's Life of Brian (Record: Warner Bros. BSK 3396) is released in the U.S. Original soundtrack recording, with **Eric Idle** helping **Graham Chapman** link the bits together. Tracks: "Introduction (with bagpipes)," "Brian (song)," "Three Wise Men," "Brian (song)," "Sermon on the Mount (Big Nose)," "Stoning," "Ex-Leper," "I'm Not a Roman," "Link," "Peoples' Front of Judea (Roman Amphitheatre)," "Link," "Romans Go Home," "Link," "What Have the Romans Ever Done for Us? (PFJ Meeting)," "Link," "Ben, the Old Prisoner," "Pontius Pilate (Throw Him to the Floor/Biggus Dickus)," "Link," "Prophets," "Haggling," "Link (lobster)," "Brian, the Prophet," "Link," "Holy Man/Brian, the Messiah," "Link," "He's Not the Messiah (He's a Very Naughty Boy)," "Link (lighter)," "Pilate/Biggus Dickus," "One Cross Each (Nisus Wettus and Mr. Cheeky)," "Pilate's Passover Addwess/Biggus Dickus," "Jailer," "Cheeky Is Released," "Mandy to Her Son," "Always Look on the Bright Side of Life," and "Close." Produced by **Eric Idle** and **Graham Chapman**. Engineered, mixed & edited by Andre Jacquemin. Released in the U.K. on Nov. 9 on Warner Bros. K 56751. Singles issued on Warner Bros. WBS 49112 (U.S.), K 17495 (U.K.), and W 7653 (U.K., 1988). Reissued in 2006 (Virgin/EMI) with six bonus tracks.

724 October 10–24, 1979
The second series of the **Michael Palin–Terry Jones** comedy, *Ripping Yarns*, airs on BBC2. Unlike the previous series of six episodes (in 1977), only three episodes were commissioned for the second series owing to financial cutbacks at the BBC. This series also has a new director, Alan J. W. Bell (on two of the episodes).
Award: BAFTA winner for Best Light Entertainment Programme of 1979.

725 October 10, 1979
Ripping Yarns (TV episode: BBC2). "Whinfrey's Last Case." A spy adventure featuring suave Gerald Whinfrey, who is called upon to save Britain from Germany's plot to start World War I a year early, even though it coincides with his fishing holiday in Cornwall. First show of the second series. Filmed Mar. 1–10, Apr. 3–6, 10, and May 3–4 in Cornwall, Devon, and London. Starring **Michael Palin** (as Gerald/TV Introducer), with Maria Aitken, Antony Carrick, Edward Hardwicke, Richard Hurndull, Jack May, Gerald Sim, Ann Way, Michael Sharvell-Martin, Charles McKeown, Anthony Woodruff, Roy Sampson, Phillip Clayton-Gore, Patrick Bailey, and Steve Conway. Written by **Michael Palin** and **Terry Jones**. Directed by Alan J. W. Bell.

726 October 17, 1979
Ripping Yarns (TV episode: BBC2). "Golden Gordon." The story of a loyal football supporter in the 1930s whose team hasn't won a match in six years. Second show of the second series. Filmed Mar. 17–30 in Yorkshire. Starring **Michael Palin** (as Gordon Ottershaw), with Gwen Taylor, Bill Fraser, Teddy Turner, David Leland, John Berlyne, Ken Kitson, Roger Sloman, David Ellison, Colin Bennett, Matthew Scurfield, Charles McKeown, Margot Lawson, Danny O'Dea, Charles Marcelle, Gillian McClements, Peter Graham, members of Salts, Saltaire Football Club, Yorkshire, and **John Cleese** (as Passerby). Written by **Michael Palin** and **Terry Jones**. Directed by Alan J. W. Bell. Note: The team line-up of "Bunn, Wackett, Buzzard, Stubble and Boot" is a reference to the original working title of *Monty Python's Flying Circus*.

727 October 18, 1979
Rolling Stone (Magazine/U.S.). "The Persecution of *Monty Python's Life of Brian*," by Paul Gambaccini, p. 52+. The Pythons talk about *Brian*, the controversy surrounding it, and the history of the group.

728 October 19, 1979
Showings of *Life of Brian* are canceled in Columbia, South Carolina on the same day that the film

opens. Republican senator Strom Thurmond called for the cancellation after his wife received word of the film's content from a local Presbyterian minister.

729 October 20, 1979
Doctor Who (TV episode: BBC1). "City of Death, Part 4." **John Cleese** and Eleanor Bron make cameo appearances as art gallery visitors in this episode of the British sci-fi serial. Starring Tom Baker (as the Doctor), Lalia Ward, Tom Chadbon, Julian Glover, and Catherine Schell. Written by David Agnew. Directed by Michael Hayes.

730 October 20, 1979
Saturday Night Live (TV comedy show: NBC). Hosted by **Eric Idle**, with musical guest Bob Dylan, also Andy Kaufman and Father Guido Sarducci. **Idle**, in his fourth (and last) time hosting, delivers his opening monologue while laying on a stretcher. He also appears in the sketches "Shoe Store" (as salesman), "Prince Charles Tells You How to Pick Up Girls!" (as Prince Charles), "Hardcore II" (as Kevin), and "Heavy Sarcasm" (as Nigel Quist). Cast: Jane Curtin, Garrett Morris, Bill Murray, Laraine Newman, and Gilda Radner. Directed by Dave Wilson. Produced by Lorne Michaels.

731 October 24, 1979
Ripping Yarns (TV episode: BBC2). "Roger of the Raj." Spoof of Rudyard Kipling–type stories tracing the early years of Roger Bartlesham in 20th-century India. Third and last show of the second series. Filmed July 1–14, 1978, in Kent. Starring **Michael Palin** (as Roger), with Richard Vernon, Joan Sanderson, Roger Brierley, John Le Mesurier, Jan Francis, Allan Cuthbertson, David Griffin, Charles McKeown, David Warwick, Michael Stainton, Ken Shorter, Douglas Hinton, and Dorothy Frere. Written by **Michael Palin** and **Terry Jones**. Directed by Jim Franklin.

732 October 25, 1979
Fawlty Towers (TV episode: BBC2). "Basil the Rat." Manuel's pet hamster turns out to be a rat and gets loose in the hotel just before the health inspector arrives. Sixth and last show of the second series. This episode was originally intended to air Apr. 2, but taping of the show was delayed several months due to a strike at the BBC. Starring **John Cleese**, Prunella Scales, Andrew Sachs, Connie Booth, with John Quarmby, Ballard Berkeley, Brian Hall, Gilly Flower, Renee Roberts, David Neville, Sabina Franklyn, James Taylor, Melody Lang, and Stuart Sherwin. Written by **John Cleese** and Connie Booth. Directed by Bob Spiers. Produced by Douglas Argent.

733 October 27, 1979
John Cleese turns 40.

734 October 28, 1979
Sunday Spectacular (TV special: NBC). **Graham Chapman** appears on this variety special, with *Life of Brian* clips. Other performers include Alexander Godunov, Peggy Fleming, Andy Kaufman, and Gallagher. Hosted by Steve Allen and Gary Coleman. Two hours.

735 October 29, 1979
Michael Palin records his appearance on BBC radio's *Desert Island Discs*. The show airs Nov. 17.

736 October 29, 1979
People Weekly (Magazine/U.S.). "Monty Python's **Graham Chapman** Doesn't Walk on Water, and the Devout Call His *Brian* Spoof All Wet," by Sue Reilly, p. 50+. Article on **Chapman** and the *Life of Brian* controversy.

737 October 30, 1979
Not the Nine O'Clock News (TV episode: BBC2). In the program's intro, **John Cleese** appears as Basil Fawlty speaking on the phone at the front desk of Fawlty Towers. He informs the BBC that there isn't going to be a *Fawlty Towers* this week and suggests putting on a "cheap, tatty revue" instead. Starring Rowan Atkinson, Pamela Stephenson, Chris Langham, and Mel Smith. Directed by Bill Wilson. Produced by John Lloyd and Sean Hardie. Note: **Cleese**'s intro was recorded in March to be shown at the start of *NTNON*'s Apr. 2 pilot episode, which was scheduled to air in place of the postponed (until Oct. 25) final episode of *Fawlty Towers*. The pilot, though, never aired owing to political concerns from the BBC.

738 October 30, 1979
Circus (Magazine/U.S.). Includes an interview with the Pythons about *Life of Brian*.

739 November 1979
Monty Python's Life of Brian (Radio commercials). Four radio spots advertising the Nov. 8 release of *Life of Brian* air in the U.K. In one, Muriel Cleese (mother of **John**) reveals that she lives in an old-age home at her son's expense and he won't be able to keep her in the home if the film isn't a success, so she urges everyone to "see the *Life of Brian* now because I'm 102 years old and if I have to leave here it will kill me." The other three spots are presented

by **Eric Idle**'s mother (Norah), **Terry Gilliam**'s mother (Beatrice), and **Michael Palin**'s dentist (Gerry Donovan, appealing to save **Palin**'s teeth). Written by **John Cleese**, **Michael Palin**, and **Terry Gilliam**. Produced by John Goldstone. Agency: Lonsdales, London.
Award: Clio Award winner.

740 November 1979
Away from It All (Short film: Taylor Hyde International/Python Pictures). Spoof travelogue narrated by Nigel Farquhar-Bennett (**John Cleese**), whose bland descriptions of various tourist destinations (Rome, Venice, Ireland, Bulgaria, Austria, New York City, and Acapulco) turn into a rant of frustration and despair. The 13-minute short is shown in U.K. theaters with *Life of Brian*. Written, produced & directed by Clare Taylor and **John Cleese**.

741 November 1979
Playboy (Magazine/U.S.). "The Gospel According to Monty Python," by Reg Potterton, pp. 161+. Interview with all six Pythons about *Life of Brian*. Includes a full-page illustration by Kinuko Y. Craft.

742 November 1, 1979
Gerald Priestland interviews **John Cleese** and **Michael Palin** about *Life of Brian* for the BBC program *Today*.

743 November 2, 1979
Terry Gilliam convinces **Michael Palin** to join him in writing a script for a children's film that **Gilliam** will direct. The project is given the working title "*Time Bandits*." **Gilliam** sets aside work on *Brazil*, the film he had been writing with Charles Alverson.

744 November 2, 1979
Talking Pictures (TV show: BBC2). Gavin Millar interviews **Terry Jones** about *Life of Brian*. **Jones** discusses the difficulties of shooting on location and answers charges that the film is blasphemous.

745 November 5–9, 1979
Hollywood Squares (TV game show: Synd.). **Graham Chapman** makes a week-long guest appearance on this American game show hosted by Peter Marshall. Celebrity guests in the other squares include Valerie Bertinelli, George Gobel, Gordon Jump, Dottie West, and Vincent Price.

746 November 5, 1979
Kaleidoscope (Radio arts show: BBC Radio 4). Guest: **John Cleese**, promoting *Life of Brian*.

747 November 5, 1979
Film 79 (TV show: BBC1). Barry Norman looks at the new film *Life of Brian*.

748 November 8, 1979
Monty Python's Life of Brian opens in the U.K. (released by Cinema International Corporation).

749 November 9, 1979
Friday Night...Saturday Morning (TV talk show: BBC2). Hosted by Tim Rice. **John Cleese** and **Michael Palin** defend their new film *Life of Brian* in a heated discussion with author Malcolm Muggeridge and Dr. Mervyn Stockwood (Bishop of Southwark). Muggeridge calls it "humbug" to suggest that the film "is not a ridiculing of the founder of the Christian religion ... in an extremely cheap and tenth-rate way." **Cleese** argues that the film does not ridicule Christ but rather says "take a critical view ... don't just believe because somebody tells you to ... question it, work it out for yourself." In the end, Stockwood informs the Pythons that they'll get their "thirty pieces of silver." Directed by John Burrowes. Produced by Iain Johnstone and Frances Whitaker. Note: The discussion is parodied on the Nov. 20 episode of *Not the Nine O'Clock News* (BBC2).

750 November 9, 1979
Monty Python's Life of Brian soundtrack album is released in the U.K.

751 November 10, 1979
Melody Maker (Newspaper/U.K.). "Brian Cohen, Superstar (!)," by Michael Watts, pp. 21–24+. Article/interview from the set of *Life of Brian* in Monastir, Tunisia in October 1978. **John Cleese** (in centurion garb) appears on the cover.

752 November 15, 1979
Monty Python's Life of Brian/MONTYPYTHONSCRAPBOOK (Book: Methuen [U.K.]; Fred Jordan Books-Grosset and Dunlap [U.S.]), edited by **Eric Idle**, designed by Basil Pao and Mike Diehl. The first half of this oversized book of the film contains the complete film script, which includes the "Pilate's Wife" and "Otto" scenes cut from the film. *MONTYPYTHONSCRAPBOOK* is made up of photographs, **Terry Gilliam** artwork, diary entries, letters, cartoon strips, and unused material from the first and second drafts of the film. Includes: "About the Book," "How It All Began," "How It Really All Began," "Heron Bay Diaries, by **Terry Jones** and **Michael Palin**," "Monty Python's First Ten Years," "What to Take on Filming," "Brian

Meets the Psychopath," "Python Cinema Quiz," "Dear Lorne," "Python Cinema Quiz," "Brian Feeds the Multitude," "'Forced Sex, I Say!,'" "What to Do If You Win...A Granny!," "Research, Costume & Makeup," "Big Nose," "Sharing a Caravan with John Cleese, by Michael Palin," "The Gilliam Collection of Famous Film Titles," "Creatures," "An Intergalactic Struggle Set in 33 A.D.," "Chap. XXI," "The Healed Loony," "Jerusalem Advocate: Sports," "Otto," "**Cleese** v. The Evening Standard," "Solidarity," "The Pythons," "A Sermon by Brian Cohen," "The Dead Sea Photos: How They Were Discovered," "Solly and Sarah," "Doc **Chapman**'s Medical Page," "Nude Pythons/Monty Python's Flying Circus: An Appreciation by Graham Greene," "The Bruces' Philosophers Song," "A Letter About the Title," "School Chapel," "Martyrdom of St. Brian," "All Things Dull and Ugly," "Monty Python's Life of Brian: Art and Credits," "Cast," "What to Do After the Movie," "A Message to the World," and "How to Increase the Value of Your Book."

753   November 17, 1979
Desert Island Discs (Radio show: BBC Radio 4). Roy Plomley's castaway is **Michael Palin**, whose choice of records includes "Things Ain't What They Used to Be" (Duke Ellington), "Tales of Men's Shirts" (The Goons), "Things We Said Today" (The Beatles), and "Nimrod, from *Enigma Variations*" (Sir Edward Elgar). **Palin**'s luxury item is a feather pillow & bed; his book is *Vanity Fair* by William Makepeace Thackeray. Recorded Oct. 29. Note: The Elgar piece was also chosen by **John Cleese** (1971) and **Eric Idle** (1976).

754   November 22, 1979
The New York Times (Newspaper/U.S.). "Scraps from History's Table," by **Michael Palin**, p. 23. Humorous article presented in the form of excerpts from Puritan Gordon Ottershaw's diary recounting the first Thanksgiving Day.

755   November 28, 1979
The Secret Policeman's Ball (Feature film) premieres at the National Film Theatre, London as part of the London Film Festival. Filmed record of the June 1979 Amnesty International comedy gala at Her Majesty's Theatre in London. Starring **John Cleese**, **Terry Jones**, **Michael Palin**, Peter Cook, Rowan Atkinson, The Ken Campbell Road Show, Pete Townshend, John Williams, Eleanor Bron, and Tom Robinson. Sketches include: "Interesting Facts" (**Cleese** & Cook), "Cheese Shop" (**Cleese** & **Palin**, with Chris Beetles & Rob Buckman), "The Name's the Game!" (**Cleese** & **Jones**, with Anna Ford, Clive Jenkins & Mike Brearley), "Four Yorkshiremen" (**Cleese**, **Palin**, **Jones** & Atkinson), and "The End of the World" (Cook & cast). Directed by Roger Graef. Produced by Graef and Thomas Schwalm. The film airs Dec. 22 on ITV (shortened from 95 mins. to an hour) and receives a general theatrical release in July 1980.

756   November 28, 1979
The Melody Maker Pop Poll Awards (Award ceremony). **Michael Palin** hosts this annual music award ceremony held at London's Waldorf Hotel.

757   December 5, 1979–January 9, 1980
The second series of *Fawlty Towers* is repeated on BBC1.

758   December 9, 1979
The Sunday Times (London) (Newspaper/U.K.). "A Brighter Shade of **Palin**," by Hunter Davies, p. 42. Interview with **Michael Palin**, conducted at his London home on Nov. 28. Part of Davies' "Life's Illusions" series.

759   December 22, 1979
The Secret Policeman's Ball (TV special: ITV). Hour-long concert special filmed in June at Her Majesty's Theatre in London. The comedy gala benefitting Amnesty International stars **John Cleese**, **Terry Jones**, **Michael Palin**, Peter Cook, Rowan Atkinson, and many others. Previously screened as a feature-length film on Nov. 28 at the London Film Festival.

760   December 24, 1979
New York (Magazine/U.S.). "Books: Buried Treasure," by Richard Condon, **Michael Palin**, pp. 66–67. **Palin** reviews the book *The Rhinestone as Big as the Ritz* by Alan Coren.

761   1979
Welcome Customer, Part 1: Have a Nice Stay (Training film: Video Arts). Demonstration of the common mistakes made by hotel/restaurant staff when dealing with customers. Starring **John Cleese**, Dinsdale Landen, and Lindsay Duncan. Written by David Nobbs. Directed by Peter Robinson.

762   1979
Welcome Customer, Part 2: See You Again Soon (Training film: Video Arts). Second film in the two-part series on dealing with customers. Starring **John Cleese**, Dinsdale Landen, and Lindsay Dun-

can. Written by David Nobbs. Directed by Peter Robinson.

763 1979
I'd Like a Word with You: The Discipline Interview (Training film: Video Arts). Management training film on how to conduct a discipline interview. Narrated by Robert Reid. Starring **John Cleese** (as Ethelred the Unready/Ivan the Terrible/William the Silent), Rosemary Leach, Robin Nedwell, Nicky Henson, and Michael Sheard. Written by Jonathan Lynn. Directed by Peter Robinson. Remade (without **Cleese**) in 1996.

764 1979
The Secret Policeman's Ball (Record: Island ILPS 9601) is released in the U.K. Thirteen-track recording of highlights from the June 1979 Amnesty International Comedy Gala starring **John Cleese**, **Terry Jones**, **Michael Palin**, Peter Cook, Billy Connolly, Rowan Atkinson, and others. Tracks include: "Interesting Facts" (**Cleese** & Cook), "How Do You Do It?" (**Palin** & **Jones**), "The Name's the Game!" (**Cleese** & **Jones**), "Stake Your Claim" (**Palin** & Atkinson), "Cheese Shop" (**Cleese** & **Palin**), "Four Yorkshiremen" (**Cleese**, **Palin**, **Jones** & Atkinson), and "The End of the World" (Cook & cast). Produced by Martin Lewis. A second album from the show, featuring only the music, is released on Island 12WIP 6598.

765 1979
Hip Hip Hooray (Marketing film: Video Arts). Comedy sketches linked by the story of a young exec who attempts to climb the marketing ladder at the *TV Times*. Designed to be shown during presentations by *TV Times* executives. Sponsored by Independent Television Productions. Starring **John Cleese**, Andrew Sachs, Bernard Archard, and James Cossins. Written by Chris Langham. Directed by Charles Crichton. Produced by Robert Reid.

766 1979
Everybody's Guide to the Computer, No. 1: What Is a Computer? (Training film: Video Arts). Animated short, featuring Hugh Burnett's "Monk" character, describing the computer and its functions. Narrated by **John Cleese**. Animated by April Johnson. Written & produced by Robert Reid.

767 1979
Fawlty Towers (Record: BBC Records REB 377 [U.K.]; BBC-22377 [U.S.]). The original television soundtrack of the episodes "Communication Problems (aka "Mrs. Richards")" (1979) and "The Hotel Inspectors" (1975). Co-ordinated by John Lloyd, Derek Goom, and William Grierson. Followed by *Fawlty Towers: Second Sitting* (1981).

768 1979
Fawlty Towers Book 2 (Book: Weidenfeld and Nicolson), by **John Cleese** and Connie Booth, is published in the U.K. Contains the scripts of the remaining three shows from the sitcom's first series: "A Touch of Class," "The Wedding Party," and "The Germans."

769 1979
...To Norway—Home of Giants! (TV special: Nrk-Norwegian Broadcasting Co.). **John Cleese** (as Norman Fearless) hosts this irreverent travelogue exploring the country's Viking heritage and the eccentricities of Norwegian life, including the sport of skull-bumping. He also looks at some inedible native delicacies. Filmed in Oslo. Written by Knut Aunbu, Johnny Bergh, Bjørn Sand, and Erik Søby. Directed by Johnny Bergh and Bjørn Sand.
Awards: Special Prize-winner at the Montreux Festival.

770 January 1980
Chaucer's Knight: The Portrait of a Medieval Mercenary (Book: Weidenfeld and Nicolson), written by **Terry Jones**, is published in the U.K. **Jones** brings his love of English poet Geoffrey Chaucer—and of the Middle Ages in general—to this provocative, well-researched book about the knight in Chaucer's *Canterbury Tales*. By studying his subject in historical, rather than literary, terms he has concluded that the knight was not the idealized figure of chivalry as normally depicted, but was instead a bloodthirsty, professional killer. Published in the U.S. by Louisiana State University Press. **Jones** will later revisit Chaucer with his 2003 book *Who Murdered Chaucer?: A Medieval Mystery*.
Reviews: The Economist (Jan. 26, 1980, pp. 103–104): "Leaving Monty Python far behind him, **Terry Jones** shows himself to be an historian of impressive competence.... It is a masterly and exciting book"; J. A. Burrow (*The Times Literary Supplement* [London], Feb. 15, 1980, p. 163): "...lively and readable ... although I believe [**Jones**'] hypothesis to be mistaken, I welcome his thorough and systematic questioning of conventional views."

771 January 15, 1980
Life of Brian is banned in Norway by the country's Film Control Commission, which deems the film to be blasphemous. The ban is later lifted and the film is released on Oct. 31.

772 January 19, 1980
Tiswas (TV episode: ITV/ATV). Saturday-morning children's show hosted by Chris Tarrant, Sally James, and John Gorman. Guests include **Graham Chapman** and **Terry Jones**, and musician Joe Jackson.

773 January 25, 1980
Friday Night...Saturday Morning (TV talk show: BBC2). Hosted by Ned Sherrin. Guests include **Terry Jones**, Marti Webb, Andrew Lloyd Webber, and Peter Nichols. **Jones** talks about his new book *Chaucer's Knight* and participates in a quiz competition.

774 February 9, 1980
Tiswas (TV episode: ITV/ATV). Saturday-morning children's show hosted by Chris Tarrant, Sally James, and John Gorman. Guest: **Terry Jones**.

775 February 24, 1980
Gay Life (TV episode: ITV/LWT). "Gay Parents." Lesbian motherhood and gay adoption are examined in this program. Interviewees include **Graham Chapman**, who talks about being a gay father (to now 23-year-old John Tomiczek). Directed by Nigel Wattis. Produced by Michael Attwell.

776 March 1980
The Merv Griffin Show (TV talk show: Synd.). Guests: **Graham Chapman**, Debby Boone, Donny Most, Barry Van Dyke, and Michael Keaton. **Chapman**, promoting *The Big Show*, also talks about being the on-set physician during filming of *Life of Brian* and his days at medical school.

777 March 4–June 3, 1980
The Big Show (TV variety show: NBC). A weekly variety show on a grand scale featuring comedy, singing, dancing, and skating. The show has a different pair of hosts each week, along with a regular comedy ensemble that includes **Graham Chapman**, Mimi Kennedy, Charlie Hill, Owen Sullivan, Joe Baker, Paul Grimm, and Edie McClurg. Sketches include "Bookshop" (Mar. 18), from 1967's *At Last the 1948 Show*, performed on the show by **Chapman** and Baker. Hosted by Steve Allen & Gary Coleman (Mar. 4), Marie Osmond & Gavin MacLeod (Mar. 11), Dean Martin & Mariette Hartley (Mar. 18), Tony Randall & Herve Villechaize (Mar. 25), Don Rickles & Steve Lawrence (Apr. 8), Victor Borge & Loretta Swit (Apr. 15), Steve Allen & Sarah Purcell (Apr. 22), Barbara Eden & Dennis Weaver (Apr. 29), Gene Kelly & Nancy Walker (May 6), Steve Allen & Shirley Jones (May 13), and Flip Wilson & Sarah Purcell (June 3). 11 episodes. Directed by Walter C. Miller, Steve Binder, and Tony Charmoli. Produced by Nick Vanoff.

778 March 7, 1980
Friday Night...Saturday Morning (TV talk show: BBC2). Hosted by Jane Walmsley. Guests include Zandra Rhodes, Hazel O'Connor, and **Terry Gilliam**, who talks about living in England, Python's success in the U.S., and his next film.

779 March 15, 1980
Saturday Night Live (TV comedy show: NBC). Fifth season show (no host) featuring Paul Simon, James Taylor, David Sanborn, Ralph Nader, **Michael Palin**, and a returning John Belushi. **Palin** appears in the sketch "Talk or Die" as the host of an "action talk show." Cast: Jane Curtin, Garrett Morris, Bill Murray, Laraine Newman, Gilda Radner, Paul Shaffer, and Harry Shearer. Directed by Dave Wilson. Produced by Lorne Michaels.

780 March 20, 1980
The British Academy Awards (Award Ceremony). *Fawlty Towers* wins the BAFTA for Best Situation Comedy and Best Light Entertainment Performance (**John Cleese**). *Ripping Yarns* wins for Best Light Entertainment Programme. The ceremony, hosted by Anna Ford and Edward Fox, is held at Wembley Conference Centre in London. Broadcast on ITV.

781 March 26–29, 1980
The Pythons spend several days in Paris doing promotion.

782 March 30, 1980
Les Rendez-Vous du Dimanche (The Sunday Appointment) (TV talk show: TF1, in France). Hosted by Michel Drucker. Guests: **John Cleese**, **Terry Gilliam**, **Eric Idle**, **Terry Jones**, and **Michael Palin**. Taped in Paris.

783 April 1980
Do They Hurt? (Record: Charisma CAS 1151). **Michael Palin** wrote the humorous liner notes for this album from the jazz fusion band Brand X. The album's title comes from a line spoken by **Palin** in the "Test of a Witch" scene from *Holy Grail*. Released in the U.S. on Passport Records.

784 April 1, 1980
The original *Time Bandits* script, written by **Terry Gilliam** and **Michael Palin**, is completed.

785 May–September 1980
Time Bandits, directed by **Terry Gilliam** from a script by **Gilliam** and **Michael Palin**, is filmed at Lee International Studios and on location in England, Wales, and Morocco. Locations include Ragland Castle (in Monmouthshire, Wales) and Epping Forest (in Essex, England). Shooting is completed just before Monty Python's appearance at the Hollywood Bowl.

786 May 1980
Michael Palin travels 654 miles from Euston, London to Kyle of Lochalsh in Scotland aboard a variety of classic trains. The journey is filmed by the BBC for an episode of *Great Railway Journeys of the World*, which will air Nov. 27.

787 May 26, 1980
The Mike Douglas Show (TV talk show: Synd.). With co-host Larry Wilcox. Guests: **Graham Chapman**, James Coburn, Joan Van Ark, and Bill Anderson.

788 June 9, 1980
Michael Palin and his wife attend a reception at the Royal Geographical Society in London. The event, commemorating the 150th anniversary of the RGS's founding, is also attended by the Queen and Prince Philip. **Palin** will become president of the RGS in 2009.

789 June 18, 1980
A BBC television production of William Shakespeare's *The Taming of the Shrew*, directed by Jonathan Miller and starring **John Cleese** in the role Petruchio, is recorded. **Cleese** spent five weeks rehearsing for the role. The play airs Oct. 23 on BBC2.

790 June 22, 1980
The Observer (Newspaper/U.K.). "The Taming of **John Cleese**," by Tom Davies, p. 40. Interview with **Cleese** on his role as Petruchio in BBC's *Shrew*.

791 June 26, 1980
John Cleese, playing Robin Hood, films his scenes for **Terry Gilliam**'s *Time Bandits* in Epping Forest, Essex, England.

792 June 29, 1980
John Cleese and **Terry Jones** participate in a charity cricket match at Clifton College (**Cleese**'s alma mater) in Bristol, England. **Jones** ends up with his arm in a sling after he dives for a ball and fractures his humerus bone. The event benefits the Bristol Playwrights Company.

793 July 1980
The Secret Policeman's Ball is released in the U.K. The film was first screened in November 1979 at the London Film Festival.

794 July 6, 1980
The Sunday Times (London) (Newspaper/U.K.). "Atticus: How I Stumbled on the Monty Python Crowd at Play...," by Stephen Pile, p. 32. Pile talks to **John Cleese** and **Terry Jones** at a charity cricket match (June 29) and **Michael Palin** in London.

795 July 20, 1980
Michael Palin performs at a benefit concert for Save the Whales at the music club The Venue in Victoria Street, London. His material includes the newly-written comedy monologue "Save the Plankton."

796 July 25, 1980
The Pythons decide to suspend the writing on their next film (which will eventually become *The Meaning of Life*) and agree on a plan to perform at the Hollywood Bowl for four nights in September. They will resume writing on the film in September 1981.

797 August 21, 1980
Michael Palin and **Terry Jones** set off on a publicity tour of Sweden and Denmark to promote the Scandinavian release of *Life of Brian*.

798 August 25, 1980
Life of Brian opens in Sweden and Denmark (the film was banned in Norway on the grounds that it is blasphemous). In Sweden the film is advertised as "So Funny it was Banned in Norway!"

799 September 1980
Monty Python's Contractual Obligation Album (Record: Charisma CAS 1152 [U.K.]; Arista AL 9536 [U.S.]) is released. This 24-cut album contains all-new recordings—more songs (14 in all) than sketches—with most of the material being written expressly for the record (exceptions include the pre–Python sketches "String" and "Bookshop"). The album, which the Pythons owed to their label, Charisma, is their first to crack the Top Twenty Chart. Tracks: "Sit on My Face," "Announcement," "Henry Kissinger," "String," "Never Be Rude to an Arab," "I Like Chinese," "Bishop," "Medical Love Song," "Farewell to John Denver," "Finland," "I'm So Worried," "I Bet You They

Won't Play This Song on the Radio," "Martyrdom of St. Victor," "Here Comes Another One," "Bookshop," "Do Wot John," "Rock Notes," "Muddy Knees," "Crocodile," "Decomposing Composers," "Bells," "Traffic Lights," "All Things Dull and Ugly," and "A Scottish Farewell (Here Comes Another One)." Written & performed by **Graham Chapman**, **John Cleese**, **Terry Gilliam**, **Eric Idle**, **Terry Jones**, and **Michael Palin**, with The Fred Tomlinson Singers. Produced by **Eric Idle**. Recorded at Redwood Recording Studios. U.K. single issued on Charisma CB 374. U.S. singles issued on Arista AS 0578 and Arista SP 101 (promo sampler). Remastered and reissued in 1997 as part of the "Arista Masters" series. Reissued in 2006 with four bonus tracks. Note: The 17-second "Farewell to John Denver" (in which the singer is strangled) is removed from later pressings after Denver takes legal action over the improper use of his song "Annie's Song."

800   September 1980

Britain's Independent Television Companies Association (ITCA) bans television advertising for *Monty Python's Contractual Obligation Album*, calling the album "unacceptable" and "crude in the extreme."

801   September 1980

I Like Chinese/I Bet You They Won't Play This Song on the Radio/Finland (Record: Charisma CB 374). U.K. single containing three songs off of the *Contractual Obligation Album*.

802   September 1980

I Bet You They Won't Play This Song on the Radio (Record: Arista AS 0578). U.S. single containing stereo and mono versions of the **Eric Idle** song from the *Contractual Obligation Album*.

803   September 1980

Flash Harry (Record: Mercury 6302–022) is released in the U.K. This final album from singer-songwriter Harry Nilsson (1941–1994) opens with the song "Harry," written and performed by **Eric Idle** (with Charlie Dore), and closes with Nilsson's cover of **Idle**'s "Always Look on the Bright Side of Life." Never released in the U.S. Produced by Steve Cropper. "Harry" was produced by **Idle**, Trevor Jones (John Du Prez), and Andre Jacquemin.

804   September 14, 1980

Peter Cook & Co. (TV special: ITV/LWT). Hour-long comedy special written by and starring Peter Cook for London Weekend Television, with **John Cleese** and **Terry Jones** among the guest performers. **Cleese** appears in the sketches "Riverside Chat" (as a father having a sex talk with his 42-year-old son) and "Out-Takes of History" (as Neville Chamberlain doing multiple retakes of his "peace in our time" speech). Also starring Rowan Atkinson, Beryl Reid, Robert Longden, and Paula Wilcox. Produced & directed by Paul Smith. Executive producer: Humphrey Barclay.

805   September 26–29, 1980

Monty Python at the Hollywood Bowl (Stage show). Monty Python performs live at the Hollywood Bowl in Los Angeles for four nights before an audience of 8,000 people. As in their earlier stage tours of Britain and Canada (1973) and their City Center shows (1976), their set includes a mix of classic TV sketches, some pre–Python material ("Custard Pie Lecture," "Four Yorkshiremen," and **Graham Chapman**'s "Self-Wrestling"), and film segments from their 1971–72 German specials (including "Silly Olympics" and "Little Red Riding Hood"). The group is doing the show as a way of having a holiday and making some money after three months of writing for their next film. A film of the show is released in June 1982. Other sketches/songs include: "Sit on My Face," "The Last Supper," "Argument Clinic," "Nudge, Nudge," "Crunchy Frog," "The Judges," "World Forum," "Albatross," "Bruces' Philosophers Song," "Travel Agent," "Dead Bishop on the Landing (Church Police)," "The Ministry of Silly Walks," and "Lumberjack Song." Written & performed by **Graham Chapman**, **John Cleese**, **Terry Gilliam**, **Eric Idle**, **Terry Jones**, and **Michael Palin**, with Carol Cleveland and Neil Innes. Filmed sequences directed by Ian MacNaughton. Staged and presented by Monty Python.

806   October 1980

More Ripping Yarns (Book: Eyre Methuen), written by **Michael Palin** and **Terry Jones**, is published in the U.K. Scripts of all three shows from the second series: "Whinfrey's Last Case," "Golden Gordon," and "Roger of the Raj." Art direction & design by Kate Hepburn. Photographs by Bertrand Polo & Amo.

807   October 1980

Terry Gilliam's second daughter, Holly Dubois, is born.

808   October 3, 1980

The Tonight Show Starring Johnny Carson (TV talk show: NBC). Guest-hosted by David Brenner. Guests: **John Cleese** and **Eric Idle**, also Mel Tillis.

809 October 15, 1980
Parkinson (TV talk show: BBC1). Hosted by Michael Parkinson. Guests: **Graham Chapman**, Michael Bentine, Sir Peter Scott, and Alan Price. **Chapman** talks about becoming a doctor, his alcoholism, Keith Moon, etc.

810 October 16, 1980
A Liar's Autobiography Vol. VI (Book: Eyre Methuen), written by **Graham Chapman** (co-authored by David Sherlock, Alex Martin, David Yallop, and Douglas Adams), is published in the U.K. **Chapman**'s comic semi-autobiography is a mostly factual account of his life with, according to **Chapman** (in a 1987 interview), "quite a few extravagant lies and multiple annoying footnotes included to cloud the issue." In the book **Chapman** chronicles his years at Cambridge University, his training to become a doctor, and performing with Python, and writes frankly about his homosexuality and his struggle with alcoholism. **Chapman** has stated that he first began writing the book because he thought he may not live much longer due to his alcohol abuse. Illustrations by Jonathan Hills. Published in the U.S. in March 1981 (Methuen). Paperback edition issued by Magnum Books (1981). Reissued by Mandarin (1991) with an afterword ("A Bit After the End") by **Eric Idle**. Adapted as a 3-D animated feature in 2012, co-produced & co-directed by Bill Jones (son of **Terry**).

811 October 16, 1980
Top of the Pops (TV music show: BBC1). **Michael Palin** makes a guest appearance on the music chart program.

812 October 22, 1980
Parkinson (TV talk show: BBC1). Hosted by Michael Parkinson. Guests: **John Cleese** and Jonathan Miller, promoting tomorrow night's BBC2 presentation of *The Taming of the Shrew*. **Cleese** also talks about Monty Python, **Graham Chapman** announcing he was gay, *Fawlty Towers*, his mother's radio ad for *Life of Brian*, etc.

813 October 23, 1980
BBC Television Shakespeare (TV special: BBC2). "The Taming of the Shrew." Jonathan Miller's production of the classic William Shakespeare comedy about the opportunistic Petruchio who comes to Padua to woo and wed the shrewish Katherina. **John Cleese**, in his first Shakespeare production, performs the role of Petruchio in a less declamatory, swaggering style than is usually performed. Recorded June 18. Also starring Sarah Badel (as Katherina), John Franklyn-Robbins, Susan Penhaligon, Simon Chandler, Anthony Pedley, David Kincaid, and Leslie Sarony. Produced & directed by Jonathan Miller.
Reviews: Michael Ratcliffe (*The Times* [London], Oct. 24, 1980): "...this *Shrew* struck a very nice balance between domesticity, intelligence and tenderness. Much of the credit for this must go to **John Cleese**, a deliberately spectacular piece of casting as Petruchio..."

814 October 31, 1980
Live from Two (TV show: ITV/Granada). Magazine program. **Graham Chapman** is interviewed.

815 November 1980
John Cleese's scene in *The Great Muppet Caper* is filmed in a day-and-a-half. He and Joan Sanderson play an upper-class British couple whose home is used by Miss Piggy to impress Kermit.

816 November 8, 1980
Did You See...? (TV show: BBC2). Ludovic Kennedy hosts this look back at the week in television. Guests include **Graham Chapman**. Directed by Anne Freer. Produced by John Archer.

817 November 13, 1980
Rolling Stone (Magazine/U.S.). "Monty Python's Holiday in the Sun," by Steve Pond, pp. 20–21+. Interview with the Pythons in Los Angeles. The group talks about their appearance at the Hollywood Bowl, their next film, and the *Contractual Obligation Album*. Group photo taken by Bonnie Schiffman.

818 November 17, 1980
Not the Nine O'Clock News (TV episode: BBC2). **John Cleese** guest-stars on this satirical series starring Rowan Atkinson, Pamela Stephenson, Mel Smith, and Griff Rhys Jones. Directed by Bill Wilson. Produced by John Lloyd and Sean Hardie.

819 November 22, 1980
Terry Gilliam turns 40.

820 November 27, 1980
Great Railway Journeys of the World (TV episode: BBC2). "Confessions of a Train Spotter." **Michael Palin** brings his longtime love of trains (he train spotted as a boy at Sheffield Midland Station) to this hour-long travel program, the fourth in a series of seven. Aboard a variety of trains such as the famous "Flying Scotsman" steam locomotive and the "Inter-City 125," **Palin** travels from Euston Station

in London to Kyle of Lochalsh in northwest Scotland on a route that includes visits to the National Railway Museum in York and the grand railway hotels in Edinburgh. **Palin**'s first travel show for the BBC; his second, 1989's *Around the World in 80 Days*, will change the course of his career. **Palin** will make a second *Railway* journey ("Derry to Kerry") in 1994. Written & hosted by **Michael Palin**. Produced by Ken Stephinson. Series produced by Roger Laughton.

821 December 1980–January 1981
Dark Star (Magazine/U.K.). "A Pepperpot Speaks: The **Terry Jones** Interview," by Cliff Ash, pp. 13–20. Interview with **Jones**, conducted at his Camberwell home in September 1980.

822 December 8, 1980
Michael Palin, **Terry Jones**, and **Graham Chapman** hold a book-signing at WH Smith's in Holborn Circus, London to promote their books *More Ripping Yarns* and *A Liar's Autobiography*.

823 December 8, 1980
Eric Idle is in Barbados, holidaying with Paul Simon, when he learns that John Lennon has been shot and killed in New York.

824 1980–81
Eric Idle writes the script for a film version of the Gilbert & Sullivan operetta *The Pirates of Penzance*. The film is not produced, however, after the 1981 Broadway version of the story — starring Linda Ronstadt and Kevin Kline — is brought to the big screen in 1983.

825 1980
When Will They Realise We're Living in the 20th Century? (Training film: Video Arts). Film dramatizing how poor attitudes affect industrial relations. Starring **John Cleese**. Written by Jack Rosenthal. Directed by Peter Robinson.

826 1980
Cost, Profit and Break-Even (Training film: Video Arts). Management training film dealing with business finance. Part of the "Finance for Non-Financial Managers" series. Starring **John Cleese** (as Julian Carruthers) and John Bird. Written by Antony Jay. Directed by Peter Robinson.

827 1980
Depreciation and Inflation (Training film: Video Arts). The basic principles of depreciation are explained. Part of the "Finance for Non-Financial Managers" series. Starring **John Cleese** (as Julian Carruthers) and John Bird. Written by Antony Jay. Directed by Peter Robinson.

828 1980
The Tom Machine (Short film). In a mechanical-driven future society, computer technician Tom begins to question his regimented life. **John Cleese** voices the household computer in this 47-minute sci-fi parable. Starring Donald Sumpter and Pamela Moiseiwitsch. Written & directed by Paul Bamborough.

829 January 8, 1981
Graham Chapman turns 40.

830 January 26, 1981
The Shakespeare Plays (TV special: PBS). "The Taming of the Shrew." The series' third season begins with Jonathan Miller's 1980 BBC production starring **John Cleese** in the lead role of Petruchio. Also starring Sarah Badel and John Franklyn-Robbins. Produced & directed by Jonathan Miller.

831 February 1981
Graham Chapman travels to Australia to promote his book *A Liar's Autobiography*.

832 February 5, 1981
Michael Palin has his portrait painted by English artist John Bratby. The sitting takes place at the artist's home in Hastings, Sussex, England.

833 February 15, 1981
John Cleese marries Barbara Trentham, an American actress/TV producer, in Los Angeles. **Cleese** was previously married to Connie Booth (*Fawlty Towers*) from 1968 to 1978.

834 February 24, 1981
Laverne & Shirley (TV episode: ABC). "I Do, I Do." As a British tax-dodge, two English rock stars seek American citizenship by marrying Laverne and Shirley. Guest-starring **Eric Idle** (as Derek), Peter Noone, and Stephen Bishop. Starring Penny Marshall, Cindy Williams, Michael McKean, and David L. Lander. Song: "Love, Love, Love" by Stephen Bishop (words, music) and **Eric Idle** (words). Written by Lesa Kite and Cindy Begel. Directed by Phil Perez.

835 February 26, 1981
Russell Harty (TV talk show: BBC2). Guests: **Michael Palin**, **Terry Gilliam**, and Aimi MacDonald. **Palin** talks about classic Python sketches ("Dead Parrot" and "Lumberjack Song"), the Pythons' German shows, etc. **Gilliam** talks about the

grotesque characters he played in Python. They also discuss their new film *Time Bandits*.

836 Spring 1981
The Cambridge Review (Magazine/U.K.). "The Myth of Progress," by **Terry Jones**. By comparing medieval times with supposedly more enlightened modern times, **Jones** concludes that the concept of progress is "distinctly chimerical."

837 March–October 1981
Michael Palin writes his next film, *The Missionary*.

838 March 1981
Great Railway Journeys of the World (Book: BBC Publications), written by Michael Frayn, Ludovic Kennedy, Miles Kington, **Michael Palin**, Eric Robson, Brian Thompson, and Michael Wood, is published in the U.K. Companion book to the BBC2 series written by seven writers and broadcasters describing their railway journeys in different parts of the world. Includes the chapter "Confessions of a Train-Spotter" by **Palin**, from his episode (Nov. 27, 1980) of the series. The book, which includes many maps and photos, becomes a best-seller in Britain. Published in the U.S. by E.P. Dutton (September 1982).

839 March 1981
Terry Jones gives a talk on Chaucer's "Knight's Tale" (from *Canterbury Tales*) at the City of Liverpool College of Higher Education.

840 March 5, 1981
Graham Chapman attends a Python screening at Facets Multimedia in Chicago, after which he addresses the audience and answers questions. **Chapman** will go on a tour of U.S. college campuses in October.

841 March 10, 1981
Good Morning America (TV news-talk show: ABC). Guests: **Graham Chapman**, promoting *A Liar's Autobiography*, and Ellen Burstyn.

842 March 15, 1981
The Sunday Times (London) (Newspaper/U.K.). "Monty Python Dons a Mortar Board," by Stephen Pile, p. 32. Article on **Terry Jones**' lecture on Chaucer in Liverpool.

843 March 18, 1981
The Dick Cavett Show (TV talk show: PBS). Interview with **Graham Chapman**, who talks about British and American humor, creating the Python TV series, the working titles for the show ("Owl Stretching Time," etc.), his struggle with alcoholism, etc.

844 March 21, 1981
Tiswas (TV episode: ITV/ATV). Saturday-morning children's show hosted by Chris Tarrant, Sally James, and John Gorman. Guests: **Michael Palin**, Lee Brennan, and Status Quo.

845 March 22, 1981
The New York Times (Newspaper/U.S.). "Marital Tips for Charles," by **Michael Palin**, p. E19. Humorous piece on the upcoming marriage of Prince Charles to Lady Diana Spencer (on July 29).

846 April 15, 1981
Food, Wine and Friends (TV episode: ITV/Thames). Host Robert Carrier is joined by **John Cleese** in this episode demonstrating how to prepare roast beef and select a wine.

847 April 17, 1981
Swap Shop Star Awards (TV special: BBC1). **John Cleese** wins the award for Favourite Man on TV in this award special hosted by Noel Edmonds.

848 May 2, 1981
The Pythons get together for a meeting at The Chewton Glen Hotel in Hampshire during which they agree to sever ties with their manager Denis O'Brien.

849 May 20, 1981
Did You See...? (TV show: BBC2). Host Ludovic Kennedy joins guests **Terry Jones**, Piers Gough, and Jan Murray in reviewing three programs from the past week: *The Kenny Everett Video Cassette*, *The Electric Revolution*, and *Right Royal Company*.

850 May 27, 1981
Paperbacks (TV talk show: BBC1). Literary discussion program hosted by Robert Kee. Guest **Terry Jones** talks about the Buster Keaton biography *Keaton: The Man Who Wouldn't Lie Down* by Tom Dardis. **Jones** will take over as host of the program next week.

851 May 27, 1981
The Merv Griffin Show (TV talk show: Synd.). Guests: **Graham Chapman**, Steve Lawrence, David Brenner, and Jeff Conaway.

852 June 3–July 15, 1981
Terry Jones hosts the new series of the literary discussion program *Paperbacks* on BBC1. The series, previously hosted by Robert Kee, consists of

853 June 3, 1981
Paperbacks (TV talk show: BBC1). Hosted by **Terry Jones**. A discussion about independent publishers, with authors Fidelis Morgan, J. L. Carr, Sally Emerson, and Paul Theroux. **Jones'** "rave of the week" is *Shadow Work* by Ivan Illich. First show of the series. Directed by Nick Brenton.

854 June 10, 1981
Paperbacks (TV talk show: BBC1). Hosted by **Terry Jones**, who undergoes hypnotic regression with the aid of Joe Keeton (*Encounters with the Past*). **Jones** is also joined by author Michael Moorcock (*Great Rock'n' Roll Swindle*). Second show of the series. Directed by Nick Brenton.

855 June 17, 1981
Paperbacks (TV talk show: BBC1). Hosted by **Terry Jones**. The topic is erotica, with authors Angela Carter (*Heroes and Villains*), Jill Tweedie (*In the Name of Love*), Reay Tannahill (*Sex in History*), and Sir Alfred J. Ayer. **Jones** reviews *Falkland Road*, a photograph book about Bombay brothels by Mary Ellen Mark. Third show of the series. Directed by Nick Brenton.

856 June 17, 1981
Live from Two (TV show: ITV/Granada). Magazine program. **Michael Palin** is interviewed by Shelley Rohde.

857 June 22, 1981
Nationwide (TV show: BBC1). News magazine. Frank Bough reports on the new **Terry Gilliam–Michael Palin** film *Time Bandits* and interviews **Palin**.

858 June 24, 1981
Paperbacks (TV talk show: BBC1). Hosted by **Terry Jones**. The themes are the power of multinationals and the threat of nuclear war, with authors Dr. Charles Levinson (*Vodka-Cola*), Prof. Robert Neild (*How to Make Up Your Mind About the Bomb*), and E. P. Thompson. Fourth show of the series. Directed by Nick Brenton.

859 June 26, 1981
The Great Muppet Caper (Feature film: Universal Pictures) opens in the U.S. The Muppets' second film finds them involved in a mysterious London jewel robbery. **John Cleese** and Joan Sanderson play a British couple whose home is "borrowed" by Miss Piggy. Also starring Charles Grodin, Diana Rigg, Robert Morley, Peter Ustinov, and Jack Warden. Directed by Jim Henson. Produced by David Lazer and Frank Oz. Notes: **Cleese** last worked with the Muppets in 1977 when he hosted *The Muppet Show*. Sanderson played Mrs. Richards in the "Communication Problems" episode (1979) of *Fawlty Towers*.

860 July 1981
Time Bandits (Book: Arrow Books), written by Charles Alverson, is published in the U.K. Novelization of the new **Terry Gilliam** film, adapted from the script by **Gilliam** and **Michael Palin**.

861 July 1, 1981
Paperbacks (TV talk show: BBC1). Hosted by **Terry Jones**. A look at children's books, with Rupert Bear artist Alfred Bestall, pop-up book author Jan Pienkowski, and Ben Owen. Fifth show of the series. Directed by Nick Brenton.

862 July 8, 1981
Paperbacks (TV talk show: BBC1). Hosted by **Terry Jones**, who talks to authors Iris Murdoch (*The Sea, The Sea*), Paul Theroux (*Picture Palace*), and Miles Kington (*Let's Parler Franglais!*). Sixth show of the series. Directed by Nick Brenton.

863 July 15, 1981
Time Bandits (Feature film: HandMade Films) opens in London. **Terry Gilliam's** second solo directorial effort (following 1977's *Jabberwocky*) is a comedy-fantasy about an English schoolboy who joins up with a band of thieving dwarves in possession of a stolen map that charts holes in the universe. Their travels through time bring them in contact with such historical/legendary figures as Napoleon (Ian Holm), Robin Hood (**John Cleese**), and Agamemnon (Sean Connery) and climaxes with a lengthy battle between good and evil. The film does only moderate business in Britain, but is a hit in the U.S. (it is released there Nov. 6). Also starring Ralph Richardson, David Warner, Katherine Helmond, Peter Vaughan, Craig Warnock, David Rappaport, Kenny Baker, Jack Purvis, Malcolm Dixon, Mike Edmonds, Tiny Ross, Shelley Duvall and **Michael Palin** (as Vincent). Written by **Michael Palin** and **Terry Gilliam**. Music by George Harrison. Produced & directed by **Terry Gilliam**. Executive produced by George Harrison and Denis O'Brien. A HandMade Films production.
Reviews: Vincent Canby (*The New York Times*, Nov. 6, 1981): "...a cheerfully irreverent lark.... At its best, *Time Bandits* is very, very good. The phys-

ical production is elaborate and lush, and the special effects are marvelously well done"; Richard Corliss (*Time*, Nov. 9, 1981, p. 98): "...the movie undercuts any involvement in the tale by stopping dead for long derisory skits featuring Napoleon, Robin Hood and Agamemnon ... as a traveler on this time flight, the viewer is less welcome than ignored"; David Ansen (*Newsweek*, Nov. 9, 1981, p. 92): "The sheer technical accomplishment — sets, costumes, special effects — is dazzling.... *Bandits* can be very funny in a Pythonesque way ... the sheer bric-a-brac inventiveness of the endeavor is a delight."

864 July 15, 1981
Paperbacks (TV talk show: BBC1). Hosted by **Terry Jones**. Guests: poet Peter Porter (*English Subtitles*), and authors Ronald Blythe (*The View in Winter*) and Quentin Skinner (*Machiavelli*). Also, Robert Kee looks at the works of F. Scott Fitzgerald. Seventh and last show of the series. Directed by Nick Brenton.

865 July 16, 1981
Rush Hour (Radio show: BBC Radio London). Guests include **Michael Palin** and Jackie Collins. Live.

866 July 18, 1981
Clapperboard (TV show: ITV/Granada). Film magazine for young people. Chris Kelly interviews **Terry Gilliam** and **Michael Palin** about *Time Bandits*. Taped June 18.

867 July 25, 1981
Get Set for Summer (TV show: BBC1). Saturday-morning program for young people, hosted by Peter Powell. **Michael Palin** and his sons Thomas (age 12) and William (age 10) appear in a piece on steam trains, at Worth Valley Railway in West Yorkshire.

868 July 31, 1981
Good Morning America (TV news-talk show: ABC). **Graham Chapman** is interviewed from London.

869 August 3–14, 1981
Story Time (Radio series: BBC Radio 4). "First Time Up/The Boob/Biggles Flies North." Adventure stories by Captain W. E. Johns, read by **Michael Palin**. The stories are: "First Time Up" (Aug. 3), "The Boob" (Aug. 4), and "Biggles Flies North," which is presented in eight parts (Aug. 5–14). Adapted by George Hearton and directed by Marilyn Imrie. Recorded July 6–8, 1981, in Edinburgh, Scotland. An abridged version of the recording is released in August 1997 (BBC Radio Collection). The "Biggles" stories were a favorite of **Palin**'s when he was a youth in the 1950s.

870 August 4, 1981
Calendar (TV news show: ITV/YTV–Yorkshire Television). Guest: **Michael Palin**, promoting *Time Bandits*.

871 September 9–12, 1981
The Secret Policeman's Other Ball (Stage show), four nights at the Theatre Royal, Drury Lane, London. The 1981 Amnesty International gala, organized and co-directed by **John Cleese**, follows the successful formula of 1979's *The Secret Policeman's Ball* by bringing together an array of Britain's top comedy and musical talent. Performers include **Cleese**, **Graham Chapman**, Rowan Atkinson, Alan Bennett, Billy Connolly, John Fortune, Alexei Sayle, Pamela Stephenson, John Wells, Sting, Phil Collins, Chris Langham, Victoria Wood, Donovan, Jeff Beck, Eric Clapton, Bob Geldof, Neil Innes, John Bird, Tim Brooke-Taylor, Griff Rhys Jones, and David Rappaport. Sketches include "A Word of Thanks" (**Cleese** & cast), "Beekeeping" (**Cleese** & Atkinson), "Clothes Off" (**Cleese**, Stephenson & **Chapman**), "Top of the Form" (**Cleese**, **Chapman** & others), and "Card Dance" (**Cleese**, **Chapman** & Brooke-Taylor). Directed by Ronald Eyre, assisted by **Cleese**. A film of the show (with a special appearance by **Michael Palin**) is released in theaters in 1982

872 September 28, 1981
The Innes Book of Records (TV episode: BBC2). Neil Innes' music-comedy program returns for a third series (it debuted in 1979) with special guest **Michael Palin**. In one sketch, **Palin** plays a paranoid policeman. Music by Neil Innes. Directed by Andrew Gosling. Produced by Ian Keill.

873 October–December 1981
Graham Chapman tours 23 U.S. (and Canadian) college campuses performing a comedy lecture, which includes stories from his life, clips from *Flying Circus*, and a Q&A. Venues include the Bacchus Theater at the University of Delaware in Newark, DE (Oct. 16), Red River Community College in Winnipeg (Oct. 27), Facets Multimedia in Chicago (Oct), University of California San Diego's Mandeville Center Auditorium (Nov. 5), Tulane University's McAlister Auditorium in New Orleans (Nov. 10), Finney Chapel at Oberlin College in OH (Nov. 14), Gold Coast Room at the

Florida Atlantic University Center (Nov. 20), and Montgomery County Community College in Blue Bell, PA (Dec). The tour is also part promotion for his book *A Liar's Autobiography*.

874   October 1981

Fairy Tales (Book: Pavilion Books/Michael Joseph), written by **Terry Jones** with illustrations by Michael Foreman, is published in the U.K. Jones' first children's book is a collection of 30 original fairy tales that combine fantasy and morality and are particularly suitable for reading aloud. Stories include "The Corn Dolly," "The Wonderful Cake-Horse," "The Fly-By-Night," "The Wooden City," and "The Beast with a Thousand Teeth." **Jones** originally wrote the stories for his daughter Sally in the summer of 1978. Published in the U.S. by Schocken Books (1982). Reprinted by Penguin/Puffin. Read by **Jones** (and others) for the audiobook version recorded in 1982 and released in 2000 (Orion). The stories are later adapted by Neil Innes for the 1988 TV series *East of the Moon*.

Reviews: Brian Alderson (*The Times* [London], Nov. 27, 1981): "...there isn't a single one devoid of dramatic point or lacking a nice turn of phrase, and they make for splendid reading aloud"; Carol Van Strum (*The New York Times Book Review*, Jan. 16, 1983, p. 22): "As a storyteller, Mr. **Jones** is a wizard.... **Jones** and Michael Foreman have conspired to produce a volume of highly original fairy tales that is beautiful to look at and great fun to read aloud."

875   October 1981

The Complete Works of Shakespeare and Monty Python: Volume One—Monty Python (Book: Eyre Methuen) is published in the U.K. Combined reissue of *Big Red Book* (1971) and *Brand New Monty Python Bok* (1973).

876   October 6, 1981

Nationwide (TV show: BBC1). News magazine. Frank Bough and Sue Cook present a report on **Terry Jones** and his new children's book *Fairy Tales*.

877   October 7, 1981

Live from Two (TV show: ITV/Granada). Magazine program hosted by Shelley Rohde. Guests include **Terry Jones**, Alan Bennett, and Ben Elton.

878   October 8, 1981

A Liar's Autobiography, written by **Graham Chapman**, is published in paperback by Magnum Books.

879   October 29–November 21, 1981

Underwood's Finest Hour, **Michael Palin** and **Terry Jones'** 1976 playlet, is revived for a new production at the Lyric Studio, Hammersmith, London. Directed by Alastair Goolden, with the recorded voice of cricket commentator John Arlott.

880   November–December 1981

Film Comment (Magazine/U.S.). "Bandit," by Anne Thompson, pp. 49–54. Interview with **Terry Gilliam** about his life, career, and *Time Bandits*.

881   November 1981

Time Bandits: A Screenplay (Book: Hutchinson [U.K.]; Dolphin Books [U.S.]), written by **Michael Palin** and **Terry Gilliam**, is published. The original, unexpurgated script of the film, with 16 glossy pages of color photos, bad drawings, black-and-white photos, off-camera shots, and a humorous glossary of the script's technical terms. The script includes the "Spider Ladies" scene cut from the film.

882   November 1981

The Dick Cavett Show (TV talk show: PBS). Hour-long interview (shown in two parts) with **Michael Palin**, who talks about Gwen Dibley (the name discarded in favor of Monty Python), his cats-in-trousers bit on *SNL*, performing in a group, English comics in drag, rat-eating, structural engineering, the "Pet Shop" sketch, and *Time Bandits*. Taped Nov. 5 in New York.

883   November 1981

The Secret Policeman's Other Ball (Record: Springtime HAHA 6003) is released in the U.K. LP recording the September 1981 Amnesty show featuring **John Cleese**, **Graham Chapman**, Rowan Atkinson, Alan Bennett, Billy Connolly, John Fortune, Alexei Sayle, and Pamela Stephenson. Tracks include: "A Word of Thanks" (**Cleese** & cast), "Clothes Off" (**Cleese**, Stephenson & **Chapman**), "Beekeeping" (**Cleese** & Atkinson), and "Top of the Form" (**Cleese**, **Chapman** & others). Produced by Martin Lewis. A second LP from the show, featuring only the music, is released on Island/Springtime ILPS 9698 (1982).

884   November 3, 1981

Eric Idle's first stage play, *Pass the Butler*, premieres at the Arts Centre, University of Warwick, Coventry, presented by the Cambridge Theatre Company. The play will then go on tour (venues including the Theatre Royal in Brighton). It will open in London's West End on Jan. 26, 1982 (prevues begin Jan. 20).

885 November 4, 1981
Terry Gilliam and **Michael Palin** attend the Gala U.S. Premiere of *Time Bandits* in New York. Other stars attending include Shelley Duvall and Katherine Helmond.

886 November 5, 1981
Pebble Mill at One (TV talk show: BBC1). Guests: Jenny Agutter and **Eric Idle**, promoting his play *Pass the Butler*.

887 November 5, 1981
Michael Palin tapes an appearance on *The Dick Cavett Show* in New York. The hour-long interview is shown in two parts in November on PBS.

888 November 6, 1981
Friday Night...Saturday Morning (TV talk show: BBC2). Hosted by **Terry Jones**. The first of a new series, with **Jones**' guests including actress Helen Mirren, author Richard Mabey, and Colin MacCabe (Professor of English at Strathclyde University, Glasgow).

889 November 6, 1981
Time Bandits opens in the U.S. (released by Avco Embassy Pictures). The film takes in $6.5 million during its first three days of release.

890 November 11, 1981
Michael Palin performs a one-man show at the Arts Theatre in Belfast, Northern Ireland, as part of the Belfast Festival. **Palin** had been asked to perform by Michael Barnes, director of the festival.

891 November 15, 1981
The Washington Post (Newspaper/U.S.). "**Terry Gilliam**: On the Trail of *Time Bandits*," by Gary Arnold, p. K1+. Interview with **Gilliam** about his new film.

892 November 21, 1981
Terry Jones and illustrator Michael Foreman sign copies of their new book *Fairy Tales* at The Children's Book Centre in Kensington, London.

893 November 25, 1981
Steve Martin's Best Show Ever (TV special: NBC). Hour-long comedy special starring Steve Martin, broadcast live from New York. In a filmed segment (from Rutland Weekend Television) **Eric Idle** plays a scholar speaking from Stonehenge, where he attempts to answer the question: "Did Dinosaurs Build Stonehenge?" (prod, wr & dir by **Idle**). Also starring Dan Aykroyd, John Belushi, Bill Murray, Laraine Newman, Gregory Hines, Lauren Hutton, and Lynn Redgrave. Directed by Dave Wilson. Produced by Lorne Michaels.

894 November 28, 1981
Tiswas (TV episode: ITV/ATV). Saturday-morning children's show hosted by Chris Tarrant, Sally James, and John Gorman. Guests include **Terry Jones**, Cliff Richard, and Bucks Fizz.

895 December 4, 1981
The John Davidson Show (TV talk show: Synd.). Today's theme: "The British are Coming!" Guests include **Graham Chapman**, Stewart Granger, Roger Whittaker, and Jean Marsh.

896 December 11, 1981
The Merv Griffin Show (TV talk show: CBS). Guests include **Graham Chapman**, Eva Gabor, Tom Wolfe, and Madleen Kane. **Chapman** talks about Keith Moon's antics and being a doctor.

897 December 16, 1981
Terry Jones and illustrator Michael Foreman sign copies of *Fairy Tales* at Dillons Bookshop in London.

898 December 21, 1981
People Weekly (Magazine/U.S.). "The Only Yank in Monty Python Stares Down Critics as His *Time Bandits* Steals $24 Million," by Jerene Jones, p. 50+. Article/interview on **Terry Gilliam**'s life and latest film. Photographs — including one of **Gilliam** staring down a Victorian gargoyle — by Terry Smith.

899 1981
You'll Soon Get the Hang of It (Training film: Video Arts). Film on the technique of one-to-one training in business. Starring **John Cleese** and June Whitfield. Written by Antony Jay and **John Cleese**. Directed by Peter Robinson.

900 1981
So You Want to Be a Success at Selling?, Part 1: The Preparation (Training film: Video Arts). An instructional tape (voice of Andrew Sachs) teaches salesman **John Cleese** the importance of preparation in selling. First of four parts. Also starring Nigel Hawthorne, Joan Sanderson, Derek Fowlds, Julian Holloway, Roger Lloyd-Pack, and April Walker. Written by David Nobbs. Directed by Peter Robinson.

901 1981
So You Want to Be a Success at Selling?, Part 2: The Presentation (Training film: Video Arts). Part Two continues the lesson with salesman **John Cleese** again consulting his instructional tape (voice of An-

drew Sachs). Also starring Nigel Hawthorne, Geoffrey Palmer, Joan Sanderson, Derek Fowlds, Julian Holloway, Keith Ladd, and April Walker. Written by David Nobbs. Directed by Peter Robinson.

902 1981
Why Do People Work? (Training film: Video Arts). **John Cleese** explains why people work in this 3-minute short designed to introduce discussions on motivation at work. Directed by Peter Robinson.

903 1981
Hidden Treasure (Educational film: Video Arts). The advantages of factoring to a business. Sponsored by International Factors. Starring **John Cleese**, James Bellini, Zulema Dene, and Julian Holloway. Written by Antony Jay. Directed by Barbara Trentham.

904 1981
Fawlty Towers: Second Sitting (Record: BBC Records REB 405 [U.K.]; BBC-22405 [U.S.]). The original television soundtrack of the episodes "Basil the Rat" (1979) and "The Builders" (1975). Produced by William Grierson. Followed by *Fawlty Towers: At Your Service* (1982).

905 1981
The Box (Short film). Based on the play *Buchanan's Finest Hour*, by **Michael Palin** and **Terry Jones**, staged in Sheffield, England in 1976. Featuring the voices of Richard Vernon, **Terry Jones** (as Harrington), **Michael Palin** (as Frenchman), and Charles McKeown, with Andrew Lodge as Buchanan. Directed by Micky Dolenz. Produced by Michael Hall.

906 1981
Eric Idle marries Tania Kosevich, an American model he met in 1977. The ceremony takes place in Lorne Michaels' New York apartment with guests including Paul Simon, Carrie Fisher, David Bowie, and Mick Jagger. The after-wedding party is held at Simon's apartment.

907 1981
The Secret Policeman's Other Ball (Book: Eyre Methuen) is published in the U.K. A book of scripts and photos from the Amnesty International stage show, with program notes provided by **Michael Palin** and **Terry Jones**. Python-related material includes "Introduction," "Beekeeping," "Top of the Form," and "Clothes Off." Proceeds from the book are donated to Amnesty International.

908 1981
Monty Python: The Case Against (Book: Eyre Methuen [U.K.]; Grove [U.S.]), written by Robert Hewison, is published. An account of the Pythons' various fights against censorship, from their early battles with the BBC on *Flying Circus* to the later ABC court case (in 1975) and *Life of Brian* controversy (in 1979). Includes script excerpts and copies of letters and memos.

909 1981
Braithwaite's Battle with the Banks (Educational film: Video Arts). A young man demonstrates to his reluctant father the benefits of having a bank account in this film for Barclays Bank. Starring **John Cleese**, June Whitfield, and Daniel Abineri. Written by Antony Jay. Directed by Charles Crichton.

910 1981
Postgiro ("Do You Use Giroblauw?") (TV/cinema commercials). In a series of ads for a Dutch bank, **John Cleese** plays a frustrated interviewer accosting people on the streets of Holland asking "Do *you* use Giroblauw?" Written by **Cleese** and Wim Michels. Directed by Robert Young. Agency: Moussault ABH International, Amsterdam.
Award: Clio Award winner.

911 Early 1982
The Monty Python Instant Record Collection (Record: Arista AL 9580) is released in the U.S. American version of a compilation originally released in Britain in 1977. This U.S. edition contains tracks from *Matching Tie, Holy Grail, City Center,* and *Contractual Obligation Album.* Tracks: "The Executive Intro," "Pet Shop," "Nudge, Nudge," "Premiere of the Film (Live Broadcast from London)," "Bring Out Your Dead," "How Do You Tell a Witch," "Camelot," "Argument Clinic," "Crunchy Frog," "The Cheese Shop," "The Phone-In," "Sit on My Face," "Another Executive Announcement," "Bishop on the Landing," "Elephantoplasty," "The Lumberjack Song," "Bookshop," "Blackmail," "Farewell to John Denver," "World Forum," "String," "Wide World of Novel Writing," "Death of Mary Queen of Scots," and "Never Be Rude to an Arab." Project coordinated by Dennis Fine; mastered at Sterling Sound, New York City.

912 January 1982
Starlog (Magazine/U.S.). "Soaring: *Time Bandits* and Scene Stealers," by David Gerrold, No. 54, pp. 52–53+. Interview with **Terry Gilliam**.

913   January 7, 1982
The Christian Science Monitor (Magazine/U.S.). "Laughs and Deep Themes: A Talk with *Time Bandits'* Maker," by David Sterritt. Interview with **Terry Gilliam**.

914   January 10–21, 1982
The Pythons travel to Jamaica to complete the *Meaning of Life* script (originally titled *Monty Python's Fish Film*), staying nearly two weeks. Their main challenge is coming up with a story or theme to tie together all the material they've written so far. Initially, little progress is made and the project comes close to being abandoned until, on the fifth day, they hit upon the idea of the film being the story of someone's life — or *anyone*'s life — which leads to the "Seven Ages of Man" framework.

915   January 26, 1982
Pass the Butler (Stage play) opens at the Globe Theatre in London's West End. **Eric Idle**'s first stage play, a satirical look at British social and political mores, concerns an ailing Minister of Defense whose country home is invaded by relatives and journalists while he lies comatose in a steel coffin on life support. The play, which has a disappointingly short West End run (closing June 7), had its premiere on Nov. 3, 1981, at the University of Warwick, Coventry. Starring William Rushton (as Hugo), John Fortune (as Butler), Madge Ryan, Peter Jones, Annie Lambert, Andrew C. Wadsworth, Terence Bayler, John Saunders, and Beryl Cooke. Written by **Eric Idle**. Directed by Jonathan Lynn.
Reviews: Michael Coveney (*Financial Times*, Jan. 27, 1982, p. 15): "...a cheap reproduction of Joe Orton, combining elements of *Loot* and *What the Butler Saw* in a flagrantly tactless exercise of misguided *hommage*"; *Daily Telegraph*: "An atmosphere of skyborne lunacy ... splendidly nonsensical ... kept its first night audience laughing continuously."

916   January 28, 1982
Michael Palin attends the 40th-anniversary party for radio's *Desert Island Discs* at BBC Broadcasting House. Other attendees include the program's host, Roy Plomley, also Michael Parkinson, Frankie Howerd, Jonathan Miller, and Roald Dahl. **Palin** was a guest on *Discs* in November 1979.

917   February 1982
Pass the Butler (Book: Methuen), written by **Eric Idle**, is published in the U.K. Script of **Idle**'s first stage play.

918   February 1982
Time Bandits (Comic book: Marvel Comics Group). The official comics adaptation of the **Terry Gilliam** film.

919   February 1982
Terry Jones gives a lecture on Chaucer's "Knight's Tale" at Strathclyde University in Glasgow. **Jones** is appearing at the invitation of Strathclyde English Professor Colin MacCabe, who had appeared with **Jones** on the Nov. 6, 1981, edition of TV's *Friday Night...Saturday Morning*.

920   February 1, 1982
Terry Jones turns 40.

921   February 3, 1982
Late Night with David Letterman (TV talk show: NBC). Guests: **Terry Gilliam**, promoting *Time Bandits*, Hank Aaron, and Irving Caesar. It is the third program of Letterman's new *Late Night* series.

922   February 10, 1982
Parkinson (TV talk show: BBC1). Hosted by Michael Parkinson. Guests: Jonathan Miller, **Eric Idle**, and Chris Brasher. **Idle** talks about his new play *Pass the Butler*, also Python's disastrous appearance on the *Tonight Show*, the "Nudge, Nudge" sketch, George Harrison, etc.

923   February 13, 1982
OTT (TV episode: ITV). **Michael Palin** gueststars on this late-night comedy series, appearing in the sketches "Weather Report," "A Party Political Broadcast on Behalf of the Totally Honest Party," "Negotiators on a Train," "The Week's Good Cause," and "Arthur Spendlove's Cookery & Gossip Corner." Seventh show of the series starring Chris Tarrant, John Gorman, Lenny Henry, and Bob Carolgees.

924   February 19, 1982
Friday Night...Saturday Morning (TV talk show: BBC2). Germaine Greer chairs a discussion on sex with guests Mary Whitehouse, Viviane Ventura, David Sullivan, Noel Dilly, and **Graham Chapman**.

925   Spring 1982
Terry Gilliam picks up the script (*Brazil*) he set aside in November 1979 and begins writing again, this time with Tom Stoppard.

926   March–June 1982
The Missionary, written, co-produced by and starring **Michael Palin**, is filmed on a £2 million

budget at Lee International Studios (Shepperton, Eng.) and on location in England, Scotland, and Kenya. Locations include The National Liberal Club (London), Finsbury Circus (London), Longleat House (Wiltshire, Eng.), and Ardverikie House (Scottish Highlands).

927 March 13, 1982
Parkinson (TV talk show: BBC1). Hosted by Michael Parkinson. Guests: Jimmy Savile, **Michael Palin**, Andrew Lloyd Webber, Marti Webb, and Donald Sinden. **Palin** talks about the German Python shows, etc.

928 March 14–April 18, 1982
Whoops Apocalypse (TV mini-series: ITV/LWT). Expensive six-part comedy relating the events that lead to World War III, offering wicked parodies of U.S., Soviet, and British leaders. **John Cleese** co-stars as Lacrobat, a master of disguise. Produced by London Weekend Television. Also starring John Barron, Richard Griffiths, Peter Jones, Bruce Montague, Barry Morse, Geoffrey Palmer, and Ed Bishop. Written by Andrew Marshall and David Renwick. Directed by John Reardon. Produced by Humphrey Barclay.

929 March 18, 1982
The Other Awards (Award ceremony). Spoof award show, held at the Plaza Cinema in Regent Street in London, celebrating the world premiere of the film *The Secret Policeman's Other Ball*. Emcee Peter Cook hands out awards to every performer in the film who showed up at the event, including **John Cleese**, **Graham Chapman**, Billy Connolly, Tim Brooke-Taylor, and Pamela Stephenson. The comedians were denied the use of BAFTA's larger Picadilly theatre. The award show is featured on BBC's *Nationwide* that night, shortly before the BAFTA ceremony is broadcast on ITV.

930 March 18, 1982
Nationwide (TV show: BBC1). News magazine. James Hogg reports on *The Other Awards*, the alternative to the BAFTA's, held today at the Plaza Cinema in London to publicize the release of *The Secret Policeman's Other Ball*. Interviewees include **John Cleese**, **Graham Chapman**, Tim Brooke-Taylor, and Rowan Atkinson.

931 March 18, 1982
The Secret Policeman's Other Ball (Feature film: United International Pictures) opens in the U.K. Film version of the September 1981 Amnesty benefit at the Theatre Royal, Drury Lane. Performers include **John Cleese**, **Graham Chapman**, Rowan Atkinson, Alan Bennett, Billy Connolly, Alexei Sayle, Pamela Stephenson, John Wells, Sting, Phil Collins, Jeff Beck, Eric Clapton, and Tim Brooke-Taylor. Sketches include "A Word of Thanks" (**Cleese** & cast), "Beekeeping" (**Cleese** & Atkinson), "Clothes Off" (**Cleese**, Stephenson & **Chapman**), "Top of the Form" (**Cleese**, **Chapman** & others), "Card Dance" (**Cleese**, **Chapman** & Brooke-Taylor) and a closing credits sequence featuring a special appearance by **Michael Palin** (as a janitor sweeping up after the show). The American version of the film (released May 21) includes highlights from the first *Ball* film (from 1979), which was not released in the U.S. Directed by Julien Temple. Stage show directed by Ronald Eyre, assisted by **John Cleese**. Produced by Martin Lewis and Peter Walker.
Reviews: Alan Brien (*The Sunday Times* [London], Mar. 21, 1982, p. 40): "More genuinely cinematic than its predecessors ... it has about an equal number of hits and misses"; Stephen Schaefer (*Us*, July 20, 1982, pp. 71–72): "This performance film has the amiability and look of a home movie and the ribald richness of a lusty banquet."

932 April 19, 1982
Nationwide (TV show: BBC1). News magazine. Susannah Greenberg reports from Ezra Street in Bethnal Green, London where **Michael Palin**'s *The Missionary* is currently filming. Greenberg interviews **Palin** and his co-star Denholm Elliott. The piece was taped on Apr. 16.

933 May 1982
Privates on Parade, an adaptation of the Peter Nichols play, is filmed at Shepperton Studios in England. **John Cleese** stars as Major Giles Flack. A HandMade Films production.

934 May 1982
Eric Idle directs Robin Williams and Teri Garr in the cable-TV production *The Tale of the Frog Prince*, from his script. The show will air Sept. 11 as the premiere episode of Showtime's *Faerie Tale Theatre*.

935 May 1982
The Secret Policeman's Other Ball (TV commercial). **Graham Chapman** appears in a 25-second commercial for the Amnesty International film. Playing the spokesman for the Oral Majority, he says: "I wish to complain strongly about this disgusting new comedy movie.... This movie must be banned before it turns us all into weirdos." He then

rises from behind his desk to reveal he is wearing a pink tutu, fishnet stockings, and garters. NBC refuses to air the spot, claiming—in a letter to the film's producers (received on May 17)—that the American flag displayed prominently in the ad is "rumpled and appears to be defaced." **Chapman** addresses NBC's concerns in an appearance on the May 22 broadcast of *Saturday Night Live*.

936   May 1982
Twilight Zone (Magazine/U.S.). "**Terry Gilliam**: Finding Comedy on 'the Dark Side of the Coin,'" by James Verniere, pp. 18–23. An interview with **Terry Gilliam** about his life and *Time Bandits*.

937   May 1982
Monty Python: Complete and Utter Theory of the Grotesque (Book: British Film Institute), edited by John O. Thompson, is published in the U.K. Thompson examines the humorous and grotesque art of Monty Python in a historical context. Contains 48 bits and pieces of Python grotesquerie, from "An Astonishingly Dirty Period" to "**Cleese**'s Body: Visual Gestalt Of." Also includes a Pythonography. Published in the U.S. by University of Illinois Press.

938   May 17, 1982
Monty Python Live at the Hollywood Bowl is screened at the Cannes Film Festival.

939   May 21, 1982
The concert film *The Secret Policeman's Other Ball* is released in the U.S. by Miramax Films. Unlike the British version of the film (which opened in March), the U.S. version includes highlights from the first *Ball* film (1979).

940   May 22, 1982
Saturday Night Live (TV comedy show: NBC). **Graham Chapman** appears on the "Newsbreak" segment to discuss the censored *Ball* commercial. After the ad is shown, **Chapman** reads NBC's letter of objection and apologizes for any unintended offense the ad may have caused. Then, re-creating the ad's final shot, he rises to reveal he is wearing fishnet stockings and a star-spangled speedo. **Chapman** also interrupts a sketch as The Colonel. Olivia Newton-John is the host. Directed by Dave Wilson. Produced by Dick Ebersol.

941   June 24, 1982
Graham Chapman and **Terry Gilliam** tape an appearance on *The Uncle Floyd Show* in Newark, NJ.

942   June 24, 1982
Late Night with David Letterman (TV talk show: NBC). Guests: **Graham Chapman** and **Terry Gilliam**, promoting *Hollywood Bowl*, and Ted Nugent.

943   June 25, 1982
Monty Python Live at the Hollywood Bowl (Feature film: Columbia Pictures) opens in the U.S. Concert film of Python's performance at the Hollywood Bowl in September 1980. Originally produced on videotape and then transferred to film. Includes: "Sit on My Face," "Self-Wrestling," "Never Be Rude to an Arab," "The Last Supper," "Silly Olympics" (film), "Bruces' Philosophers Song," "Ministry of Silly Walks," "Camp Judges," "World Forum," "I'm the Urban Spaceman" (Neil Innes), "Crunchy Frog," "Albatross/Colonel," "Nudge, Nudge," "International Philosophy" (film), "Four Yorkshiremen," "Argument Clinic/I've Got Two Legs," "How Sweet to Be an Idiot" (Innes), "Flasher Love Story [anim]" (film), "Travel Agent," "Custard Pie," "Little Red Riding Hood" (film), "Dead Bishop on the Landing (Church Police)," and "The Lumberjack Song." Written & performed by **Graham Chapman**, **John Cleese**, **Terry Gilliam**, **Eric Idle**, **Terry Jones**, and **Michael Palin**, with Carol Cleveland and Neil Innes. Staged & presented by Monty Python. Filmed sequences directed by Ian MacNaughton. Produced & directed by Terry Hughes. A HandMade Films production.

Reviews: Vincent Canby (*The New York Times*, June 25, 1982): "...the familiar material is all the funnier for being well known ... the Python people are great theatrical performers, and their stage work is just as madly effective as their film and television work"; David Ansen (*Newsweek*, July 12, 1982, p. 76): "*Hollywood Bowl* may not reach some of the surreal heights of *Holy Grail* and *Life of Brian*, but it's more consistently uproarious than either of those features"; Stephen Schaefer (*Us*, Aug. 17, 1982, p. 71): "Hysterically amusing, this performance film should have you laughing out loud — if not falling out of your seat.... Python's *Bowl* is an indescribably vicious, minutely nutritious comedic canape"; Michael Sragow (*Rolling Stone*, Sept. 2, 1982, p. 34): "This is yet another fine concert film from the frenetic British farce group — masters of intellectual slapstick, cosmic japes and surreal puns, and inventors of the comedy of anti-manners"; Bruce Williamson (*Playboy*, October 1982, p. 36): "The lads are in fine form ... in some of their classic skits."

944   July 12–September 11, 1982
Monty Python's The Meaning of Life is filmed in

various locations in England and Scotland and at EMI's Elstree Studios (in Borehamwood, England).

945 July 12, 1982
Principal photography on *Monty Python's The Meaning of Life* begins. The filming location is the International University of Europe (formerly the Royal Masonic School), Bushey, Hertfordshire on the outskirts of London. The scene filmed is the rugby match between the boys and masters of St. Anselm's School.

946 July 21–28, 1982
Aquarian (Magazine/U.S.). "**Graham Chapman** and **Terry Gilliam** of Monty Python: What Do the People Want? Who in the Hell are 'The People'?," by Tony Desena. Interview with **Chapman** and **Gilliam**, promoting *Hollywood Bowl*, conducted June 24 at the Parker Meridien Hotel in New York City.

947 Late July 1982
The "Mr. Creosote" scene from *The Meaning of Life* is filmed over four days at Porchester Hall in Queensway, Bayswater, London. The scene features **Terry Jones** as a grossly overweight restaurant patron and **John Cleese** as an obsequious French maître d'. It also features thousands of gallons of vomit (actually a mixture of Russian salad and vegetable soup).

948 August–September 1982
The "Grim Reaper" scene from *The Meaning of Life* is filmed at Elstree Studios and on location on the cold and rainy Malham Moors in Yorkshire (Aug. 16).

949 August 1982
The "Every Sperm Is Sacred" musical sequence from *The Meaning of Life* is filmed at Elstree Studios and on location in Colne, Lancashire.

950 August 2, 1982
People Weekly (Magazine/U.S.). "Bio: Monty Python," by Lewis Grossberger, pp. 46–48+. The Pythons are interviewed at their London office for this six-page Python history, illustrated with many photos. One photo, taken by Nancy Moran, shows the group posing like statues (while wearing bikini bottoms over their pants) in nearby Regent's Park.

951 August 12 & 13, 1982
The "First Zulu War 1879" scene from *The Meaning of Life* is filmed on a mountainside near Strathblane in Scotland. On the first day, the 150 local black students recruited to play the Zulus walk out over objections to their skimpy tribal costumes and have to be bussed back home again. On the second day, the scene is shot at 5:00 P.M. after spending all day browning up and putting wigs on 100 white Glaswegians.

952 August 13, 1982
The Sun (Newspaper/U.K.). "Day the Angry Zulus Blacked **John Cleese**," by Sun reporter. Article on the *Meaning of Life* filming in Scotland. The piece contains a false quote attributed to **Cleese**, causing him to write a series of letters to the paper's editor. Their exchange appears in the 1983 book of the film.

953 August 25, 1982
The "Delivery Room" scene from *The Meaning of Life* is filmed.

954 September–December 1982
Yellowbeard, a star-studded pirate spoof starring **Graham Chapman** (who also co-wrote the script) with **John Cleese** and **Eric Idle** in supporting roles, is filmed in England and Mexico with an $8 million budget. Shooting goes smoothly until the last week of filming, in Mexico, when co-star Marty Feldman suffers a fatal heart attack.

955 September 8, 1982
Michael Palin attends the premiere of the film *Brimstone and Treacle* at The Classic, Haymarket, London.

956 September 11, 1982
The Pythons play fish on the final day of filming on *The Meaning of Life*.

957 September 11, 1982
Faerie Tale Theatre (TV episode: Showtime). "The Tale of the Frog Prince." A very beautiful — and very vain — young princess rejects all of the princes in the land, but is finally charmed by a witty frog who, it turns out, is a bewitched prince himself. **Eric Idle** wrote, directed, and narrates this premiere episode of Shelley Duvall's children's anthology series *Faerie Tale Theatre*. **Idle** will return to the series in 1985 to play the title role in "The Pied Piper of Hamelin." Starring Robin Williams, Teri Garr, Rene Auberjonois, Candy Clark, Roberta Maxwell, Michael Richards, and Donovan Scott. Produced by Jonathan Taplin. Executive produced by Shelley Duvall. Hour.

958 September 18, 1982
The Glasgow Herald (Newspaper/U.K.). "Now for Something Completely Contradictory," by Iain

Wilson, p. 9. Interview with **Graham Chapman**, conducted last month at a hotel in Glasgow (in Scotland), near Strathblane, where the Pythons were filming *The Meaning of Life*.

959   September 23, 1982
Small Harry and the Toothache Pills (Book: Methuen), written by **Michael Palin** with illustrations by Caroline Holden, is published in the U.K. **Palin**'s first book for children, written in 1980. **Palin** will read the story on an October 1984 episode of the TV series *Jackanory*.

960   October 1982
Head for Business (Training film: Video Arts). **John Cleese** plays a skeptical assistant bank manager who tries to discourage his son from setting up his own business. The film, paid for by the Department of Industry to encourage entrepreneurship, is distributed to British schools. Also starring Nicholas Lyndhurst and Terence Alexander. Written by Antony Jay. Directed by Barbara Trentham.

961   Early October 1982
Michael Palin tours U.S. colleges promoting *The Missionary*. The tour includes stops at the University of Maryland (Oct. 4), where he wins a Turtle Award, also Northwestern University near Chicago (Oct. 6), Southern Methodist University in Dallas (Oct. 7), and San Francisco State (Oct. 8).

962   October 8, 1982
Michael Palin gives a radio interview on San Francisco's KQAK ("The Quake").

963   October 24–November 6, 1982
Michael Palin's second U.S. promotional tour for *The Missionary* begins in Seattle and ends in New York. He makes the talk show rounds (*Merv, Letterman*, etc.) and guests on *Saturday Night Live*.

964   October 26, 1982
Michael Palin tapes an appearance on *The Merv Griffin Show* in Los Angeles. The show airs Nov. 17.

965   October 28, 1982
Mike Douglas: People Now (TV talk show: CNN). Guests: **Michael Palin**, promoting *The Missionary*, and Robert Culp.

966   October 30, 1982
Saturday Night Live (TV comedy show: NBC). Hosted by Michael Keaton, with **Michael Palin** and musical guest Joe Jackson. **Palin** appears in the sketches "A Sense of Fear" and "Topol the Idiot." Cast: Robin Duke, Julia Louis-Dreyfus, Mary Gross, Brad Hall, Tim Kazurinsky, Gary Kroeger, Eddie Murphy, and Joe Piscopo. Directed by Dave Wilson. Produced by Dick Ebersol.

967   November 1, 1982
Michael Palin, in Boston promoting *The Missionary*, is interviewed by Michael Blowen of the *Boston Globe*.

968   November 2, 1982
Good Morning America (TV news-talk show: ABC). David Hartman interviews **Michael Palin** (in New York) about *The Missionary*.

969   November 4, 1982
Late Night with David Letterman (TV talk show: NBC). Guest: **Michael Palin**, promoting *The Missionary*.

970   November 5, 1982
The Missionary (Feature film: Columbia Pictures) opens in the U.S. Light comedy about an Edwardian clergyman who, upon returning from Africa, is assigned by the Bishop of London to set up a shelter for fallen women in London's East End. But he must first get the money from the lusty Lady Ames, who is set on changing her stifling upper-class life. **Michael Palin**, in his first solo film project, plays the lead role of the Rev. Charles Fortescue. Also starring Maggie Smith, Trevor Howard, Denholm Elliott, Michael Hordern, Graham Crowden, David Suchet, Phoebe Nicholls, Valerie Whittington, and Neil Innes. Written by **Michael Palin**. Directed by Richard Loncraine. Produced by Neville C. Thompson and **Michael Palin**. Executive produced by George Harrison and Denis O'Brien. A HandMade Films production. Opens in the U.K. on March 3, 1983.
Reviews: Vincent Canby (*The New York Times*, Nov. 5, 1982): "...a charming, buoyant new English comedy.... The film's physical production is amazingly handsome..."; David Denby (*New York*, Nov. 8, 1982, p. 62+): "...a high-style British comedy about virtue and lust ... a calm, steady, beautifully photographed movie, an aesthetically pleasing object that is also very funny..."; David Ansen (*Newsweek*, Nov. 8, 1982, p. 90): "...a comedy as crisp and satisfying as a good English biscuit, **Palin** has finally left his mark.... *The Missionary* is that rare comedy that never strains for a laugh"; David Robinson (*The Times* [London], Mar. 4, 1983, p. 7): "...a superior comedy, as British comedies go, and enormously enjoyable for its performances."

971 November 10, 1982
The Missionary, according to *Variety*, is the second top-grossing film in the U.S. and Canada this week.

972 November 11, 1982
The Boston Globe (Newspaper/U.S.). "**Michael Palin** Takes Comedy Seriously," by Michael Blowen, p. 1 (Arts & Films). Interview with **Palin** (conducted in Boston on Nov. 1) about *The Missionary*.

973 November 14, 1982
Michael Palin attends the Oxford Children's Book Fair at the Randolph Hotel in Oxford, England where he signs copies of his new children's book *Small Harry and the Toothache Pills*.

974 November 17, 1982
The Merv Griffin Show (TV talk show: Synd.). Guests: **Michael Palin**, promoting *The Missionary*, Durk Pearson and Sandy Shaw, Phyllis and David York, and Lee Greenwood. Taped Oct. 26 in Los Angeles.

975 November 26, 1982
Newsnight (TV news show: BBC2). Joan Bakewell presents a report on **Michael Palin**'s new film *The Missionary*. Includes an interview with **Palin**.

976 November 28, 1982
Sunday, Sunday (TV talk show: ITV/LWT). Hosted by Gloria Hunniford. Guests include **Michael Palin**, David Essex, Jill Gascoine, and Derek Nimmo.

977 November 28, 1982
The Missionary is shown at the London Film Festival. **Michael Palin** and **Terry Jones** are among those attending the screening.

978 December 2, 1982
Actor-comedian Marty Feldman dies at age 49 from a heart attack in Mexico City after completing filming on *Yellowbeard*, the pirate comedy co-starring **Graham Chapman**, **John Cleese**, and **Eric Idle**. Feldman (*Young Frankenstein*) had earlier worked with the Pythons on *The Frost Report* (1966–67) and with **Cleese** and **Chapman** on the 1967 sketch comedy series *At Last the 1948 Show*.

979 December 2, 1982
Michael Palin gives a speech at a meeting of the Society of Bookmen at the Savile Club in London.

980 December 3, 1982
Good Morning New York (TV news-talk show: ABC). Guests: **Terry Jones**, promoting *Fairy Tales*, and Jane Alexander.

981 December 3, 1982
Late Night with David Letterman (TV talk show: NBC). Guest: **Terry Jones**, promoting *Fairy Tales*. Jones reads from "The Silly King" and also talks about *The Meaning of Life*, being Welsh, and owning a brewery.

982 December 9, 1982
The Rupert Bear Story—A Tribute to Alfred Bestall (TV special: Channel 4). **Terry Jones** wrote, directed and hosts this affectionate tribute to 89-year-old author-illustrator Alfred Bestall, the man who has drawn the much-loved bear in the woolly sweater and plaid trousers for the *Daily Express* since 1936. **Jones**, a Rupert fan since childhood, recently met Bestall on a July 1981 episode of *Paperbacks*. Interviewees include Paul McCartney, Dr. John Rae, Sir Hugh Casson, George Perry, and Bestall himself at his home in North Wales. **Jones**' children, Sally and Bill, also appear briefly. Produced by Elizabeth Taylor-Mead.

983 December 12, 1982
Sunday, Sunday (TV talk show: ITV). Hosted by Gloria Hunniford and Nigel Rees. Guests: **John Cleese**, Elvis Costello & The Attractions, Suzanne Danielle, and Herbert Lom.

984 December 20, 1982
Film 82 (TV show: BBC1). Iain Johnstone reviews the new Christmas releases. Also, interviews with **John Cleese** and **Michael Palin**, reflecting on the films they've made this year (*The Meaning of Life*, *Yellowbeard*, *Privates on Parade*, and *The Missionary*).

985 1982
Everybody's Guide to the Computer, No. 2: What Is a Word Processor? (Training film: Video Arts). Film explaining the word processor to office workers. **John Cleese** plays the manager of a company that does not have a word processor. Also starring Alison Steadman, Kay Stonham, Carol Hawkins, and narrated by Judi Dench. Written by David Nobbs. Directed by Peter Robinson. Produced by Robert Reid.

986 1982
Everybody's Guide to the Computer, No. 3: What Is a Computer Program? (Training film: Video Arts). **John Cleese** narrates this animated short explaining what a computer program is. Features

Hugh Burnett's "Monk" character. Animated by April Johnson. Written & produced by Robert Reid.

987 1982
Fawlty Towers: At Your Service (Record: BBC Records 449 [U.K.]; BBC-22449 [U.S.]). LP. Original television soundtrack of the episodes "The Kipper and the Corpse" (1979) and "The Germans" (1975). Produced by Andrew Sachs and William Grierson. Followed by *Fawlty Towers: A La Carte* (1983).

988 1982
Callard & Bowser (Radio commercials). **John Cleese** stars in a series of six American radio spots for the British candy Callard & Bowser. Ads include "Get the Name Straight," "Exciting New Flavors," and "Help England Back on Its Feet." Written by **Cleese** and Lynn Stiles. Agency: Lord, Geller, Federico & Einstein, New York.
Award: Clio Award winner.

989 January 10, 1983
Michael Palin sets off on a promotional tour of Australia for *The Missionary*.

990 January 23, 1983
An Evening at Court (Stage show). Benefit show performed at the Theatre Royal, Drury Lane, London. Performers include Peter Cook, **John Cleese**, **Graham Chapman**, Rowan Atkinson, David Frost, Eleanor Bron, Angela Thorne, Barry Took, Tim Brooke-Taylor, Graeme Garden, and Bill Oddie. **Cleese** and Cook perform "Inalienable Rights." The event aids the Adrian Slade Legal Costs Appeal. Directed by Humphrey Barclay.

991 January 25, 1983
Privates on Parade (Feature film: HandMade Films) opens in the U.K. Film of the Royal Shakespeare Company stage hit by Peter Nichols. **John Cleese** plays the pompous Major Giles Flack, who commands a strange song-and-dance platoon in 1948 Malaysia. The platoon consists of a group of campy entertainers led by the aging drag-queen Captain Terry, played by Denis Quilley. Also starring Michael Elphick, Nicola Pagett, Patrick Pearson, and Joe Melia. Written by Peter Nichols. Directed by Michael Blakemore. Produced by Simon Relph. Executive produced by George Harrison and Denis O'Brien. A HandMade Films production. Opens in the U.S. on Apr. 13, 1984. Note: Nigel Hawthorne originated the role of Major Flack in the 1977 stage production.
Review: David Hughes (*The Sunday Times* [London], Jan. 30, 1983, p. 39): "Clipped, highly strung, a tall story on legs, **Cleese** defines nerves, angst, grit, but is always in well-characterised control..."; Vincent Canby (*The New York Times*, Apr. 13, 1984): "The scale of *Privates on Parade* is small, but the effect is large and lethally funny."

992 January 29, 1983
Wogan (TV talk show: BBC1). Hosted by Terry Wogan. Guests: **John Cleese**, promoting *Privates on Parade*, Shirley Conran, Sir Geraint Evans, and Sky.

993 January 31, 1983
John Dunn Show (Radio talk show: BBC Radio 2). Guest: **John Cleese**, promoting *Privates on Parade*.

994 January 31, 1983
Film 83 (TV show: BBC1). Host Barry Norman looks at the latest film releases, including *Privates on Parade* starring **John Cleese**.

995 Late January 1983
Michael Palin and **Terry Gilliam** visit India. Their trip takes them to Delhi, Agra, Jaipur, and Udaipur.

996 Late January 1983
Monty Python's The Meaning of Life has its first American showing at a shopping mall cinema in Yonkers, New York. The two preview screenings were arranged to gauge public reaction to the film. Seventy-five percent of the audience consists of 15 to 18-year-old high school kids. There are 80 walkouts. As a result of the poor screenings, several cuts are made, including the "Adventures of Martin Luther" and "Diana the Waitress" sequences.

997 February 1983
American Express (TV commercials). **John Cleese** begins appearing in ads for American Express, playing a snooty Englishman whose butler qualified for an American Express card while he did not. Directed by Robert Young. Agency: Ogilvy & Mather, New York.

998 February 1983
The Missionary (Book: Methuen), written by **Michael Palin**, is published in the U.K. Screenplay of the 1982 film, with photos by David Farrell.

999 February 1, 1983
Good Morning Britain (TV talk show: ITV/TV-am). Hosted by Robert Kee, Anna Ford, and David Frost. Guest **John Cleese**, in his pajamas, is interviewed by Frost and Ford on the debut of this new

morning program. **Cleese** talks about the "Pet Shop" and "Silly Walks" sketches and *Fawlty Towers*.

1000 February 1, 1983
A Plus (TV talk show: ITV). Mavis Nicholson interviews **John Cleese**.

1001 February 2, 1983
Gloria Hunniford (Radio talk show: BBC Radio 2). Guest: **John Cleese**, promoting *Privates on Parade*.

1002 February 6, 1983
Sunday, Sunday (TV talk show: ITV/LWT). Hosted by Gloria Hunniford and Nigel Rees. Guests: **John Cleese**, Johnny Morris, Spike Milligan, Julie Walters, Noele Gordon, and William Relton.

1003 February 7, 1983
Film 83 (TV show: BBC1). Hosted by Barry Norman. Includes an on-location report from Rye on the making of **Graham Chapman**'s *Yellowbeard*. Reporter Nicholas Shakespeare talks to **Chapman**, Peter Cook, and Michael Hordern.

1004 February 10–March 24, 1983
Amanda's (TV series: ABC). Short-lived American sitcom based on **John Cleese**'s BBC comedy *Fawlty Towers*. Bea Arthur stars. Six episodes.

1005 February 16, 1983
Pebble Mill at One (TV talk show: BBC1). Paul Gambaccini interviews **John Cleese**.

1006 February 16, 1983
Tim Rice (TV talk show: BBC1). The first of a new seven-show series. Guests: **Michael Palin**, Katia & Marielle Labeque, and Bonnie Tyler. **Palin**, promoting *The Missionary*, also talks about the *Life of Brian* controversy and the upcoming film *The Meaning of Life*.

1007 February 20, 1983
Sunday Night (TV talk show: BBC1). Religious program hosted by Eric Robson. Guest: **Michael Palin**, promoting *The Missionary*.

1008 February 23, 1983
Midweek (Radio talk show: BBC Radio 4). Hosted by Henry Kelly. Guests: Brig. George Hardy and **Terry Jones**.

1009 February 24, 1983
Star Sound Extra (Radio show: BBC Radio 2). Guest: **John Cleese**.

1010 February 26, 1983
Good Morning Britain (TV talk show: ITV/TV-am). Hosted by Michael Parkinson and his wife Mary. Guest: **Michael Palin**, promoting *The Missionary*.

1011 February 28, 1983
Film 83 (TV show: BBC1). Hosted by Barry Norman. Guest: **Michael Palin**, promoting *The Missionary*.

1012 Spring 1983
Monty Python's The Meaning of Life (Record: MCA Records MCA-6121 [U.S.]; CBS 70239 [U.K.]). The original film soundtrack, with links by **Michael Palin**. Tracks: "Intro," "Fish Intro," "The Meaning of Life" (song), "Delivery Room," "Link," "Every Sperm Is Sacred" (song), "Protestantism and Sex," "The Adventures of Martin Luther" (intro only), "Sex Lesson," "British Soldiers," "Fish (end of side one)," "**Terry Gilliam** Intro to Side Two," "Accountancy Shanty" (song), "The First Zulu War 1879/Tiger Hunt," "Link," "Dungeon Room (Mr. and Mrs. Hendy)," "Liver Donor," "Galaxy Song" (song), "The Not Noël Coward Song (Penis Song)," "Mr. Creosote," "The Grim Reaper," "Link," "Christmas in Heaven" (song), and "Link (Dedication to Fish)." Produced by Andre Jacquemin and **Michael Palin**. Engineered, mixed, and edited by Andre Jacquemin at Redwood Recording Studios, London. Single issued on CBS Records A/WA 3495. Digitally remastered and reissued in 2006 with 12 bonus tracks.

1013 Spring 1983
Standby...Lights! Camera! Action! (TV episode: Nickelodeon). Hosted by Leonard Nimoy. Includes a look at the making of *The Meaning of Life*.

1014 March 1983
The Face (Magazine/U.K.). **John Cleese** interview and cover photo ("The Private **Cleese**").

1015 March 2, 1983
Breakfast Time (TV news-talk show: BBC1). Guests **Michael Palin** and Maggie Smith talk about their film *The Missionary*, opening tomorrow.

1016 March 2, 1983
Nationwide (TV show: BBC1). News magazine. Susannah Greenberg reports on the making of *The Missionary*.

1017 March 3, 1983
The Missionary opens in the U.K.

1018 March 3, 1983
Strictly Private (TV special: ITV/Thames). Iain Johnstone gives the viewer a behind-the-scenes look at the making of the film *Privates on Parade*. Includes interviews with **John Cleese**, Peter Nichols, Denis Quilley, Michael Blakemore, and others. Directed by Luke Jeans. Produced by Richard Kuttner and Ray Cooper.

1019 March 10, 1983
The Times (London) (Newspaper/U.K.). "And Now for Something Completely Different," by Chris Peachment, p. 9. Interview with **Michael Palin** about his life and new film *The Missionary*.

1020 March 12, 1983
Good Morning Britain (TV talk show: ITV/TV-am). Guest: **Terry Jones**.

1021 March 14, 1983
Late Night with David Letterman (TV talk show: NBC). Guests: Carl Reiner and **John Cleese**, promoting *The Meaning of Life*.

1022 March 15, 1983
Michael Palin meets Princess Margaret after a screening of *The Missionary* at the Classic Haymarket in London.

1023 March 22, 1983
Late Night with David Letterman (TV talk show: NBC). Guests: **Eric Idle**, promoting *The Meaning of Life*, Ray "Boom, Boom" Mancini, and Stanley Anderson.

1024 March 29, 1983
Eric Idle turns 40.

1025 March 30, 1983
Monty Python's The Meaning of Life (Feature film: Universal Pictures) opens in the U.S. Monty Python's final film returns to the sketch format and contains something to offend everyone. It's targets include the medical profession, birth control, sex education, consumerism, greed, religion, American tourists, halibut, and just about everything else. The film is preceded by a 16-minute short feature called *The Crimson Permanent Assurance*, directed by **Terry Gilliam**. The main feature, following an introduction by the Pythons (as fish) and title song, is divided into seven parts: Part 1, The Miracle of Birth: "Delivery Room," "Every Sperm Is Sacred" (song), and "Protestantism and Sex"; Part 2, Growth and Learning: "School Chapel," "Oh Lord Please Don't Burn Us" (song), "Sex Lesson," and "Rugby Match"; Part 3, Fighting Each Other: "British Soldiers," "Marching Up and Down the Square (RSM)," and "The First Zulu War 1879/Tiger Hunt"; The Middle of the Film: "Find the Fish"; Part 4, Middle Age: "Dungeon Room (Mr. and Mrs. Hendy)"; Part 5, Live Organ Transplants: "Liver Donor," "Galaxy Song" (song), and "The Very Big Corporation of America"; Part 6, The Autumn Years: "Penis Song" (song), "Mr. Creosote," and "The Meaning of Life (Gaston the Waiter)"; Part 7, Death: "Arthur Jarrett," "Falling Leaves [anim]," "The Grim Reaper," and "Christmas in Heaven" (song); The End of the Film: "The Meaning of Life." Written by and starring **Graham Chapman**, **John Cleese**, **Terry Gilliam**, **Eric Idle**, **Terry Jones**, and **Michael Palin**, with Carol Cleveland, Simon Jones, Andrew MacLachlan, Mark Holmes, Valerie Whittington, Patricia Quinn, and Judy Loe. Director of animation: **Terry Gilliam**. Choreographed by Arlene Phillips. Directed by **Terry Jones**. Produced by John Goldstone. Released on DVD in 2001 and September 2003 (two-disc special edition).
Awards: Winner of the Special Jury Prize (second highest honor) at the Cannes Film Festival; BAFTA-nominated for Best Original Song ("Every Sperm Is Sacred").
Reviews: Vincent Canby (*The New York Times*, Mar. 31, 1983): "...sometimes hilarious and colossally rude but, as often as it evokes laughs, it overwhelms them by the majesty of its production and special effects"; Richard Schickel (*Time*, Mar. 28, 1983, p. 62): "...most of the film is designed to offend somebody at the very moment it is making someone else fall helplessly about with laughter.... In their assaults on conventional morality, they generate a ferocious and near Swiftian moral gravity of their own ... an exhilarating experience"; Katrine Ames (*Newsweek*, Apr. 4, 1983, p. 74): "...the best movie to date from England's satirical sextet ... their satire has never been more incisive—they've become savagely hilarious observers of the human condition"; David Denby (*New York*, Apr. 4, 1983, pp. 73–74): "...their humor is more fervently violent and obscene than ever.... The sick-up business has been getting out of hand of late, and this (the French restaurant scene) should certainly put a stop to it"; *People Weekly* (Apr. 11, 1983, p. 10+): "There are a few moments when bad taste is raised to high comic art ... viewers of *The Meaning of Life* will be more apt to double over in disgust than in laughter"; Lawrence O'Toole (*Maclean's*, Apr. 11, 1983, p. 69): "...*Life* is satire of Swiftian proportion: scathing, endlessly inventive and as giddy as a room

filled with laughing gas"; Stanley Kauffmann (*The New Republic*, Apr. 18, 1983, pp. 24–25): "*Life* is not their most consistently funny film, but it's the one that is most free in fantasy and most savage.... They are the most dangerous madmen at large, ruthlessly perceptive and torrentially gifted"; Bruce Williamson (*Playboy*, June 1983, p. 27): "...screamingly funny ... there is no company of social satirists to match Monty Python for savagery, effrontery, freewheeling irreverence and throwaway wit"; David Hughes (*The Sunday Times* [London], June 26, 1983, p. 43): "...nothing here is in bad taste. There is simply no taste at all, except in a certain elegance of wit and the timing of the execution."

1026 March 30, 1983
The Crimson Permanent Assurance (Short film: Universal Pictures). The aged employees of the Permanent Assurance Company mutiny against their young, hard-driving corporate managers and set sail in their office building "upon the high seas of international finance." **Terry Gilliam** directed this comedy-adventure short, which was originally intended to be a six-minute sequence in the middle of Monty Python's feature film, *The Meaning of Life*. When the short's length expanded to 16 minutes, it was decided to move the short to the beginning of the film as a supporting featurette. Starring Sydney Arnold, Guy Bertrand, Andrew Bicknell, Ross Davidson, Myrtle Devenish, Tim Douglas, Eric Francis, Matt Frewer, Billy John, Russell Kilmister, Peter Mantle, Len Marten, Peter Merrill, Cameron Miller, Gareth Milne, Larry Noble, Paddy Ryan, Leslie Sarony, John Scott Martin, Eric Stovell, and Wally Thomas, with cameos by **Gilliam** and **Michael Palin** as window washers. Song: "Accountancy Shanty" (w/m: **Eric Idle** and John Du Prez). Produced by John Goldstone.
Awards: BAFTA-nominated for Best Short Film.

1027 April 1983
The Morning Show (TV talk show: WABC-TV, New York). New morning program hosted by Regis Philbin and Cyndy Garvey. Guest: **Michael Palin**, promoting *The Meaning of Life*. Recorded Apr. 1.

1028 April 1, 1983
Late Night with David Letterman (TV talk show: NBC). Guests: **Michael Palin**, promoting *The Meaning of Life*, Nick Lowe, and Teri Garr.

1029 April 6, 1983
Monty Python's The Meaning of Life, according to *Variety*, is the fifth top-grossing film in the U.S. and Canada this week.

1030 April 7, 1983
20/20 (TV show: ABC). News magazine hosted by Hugh Downs. Arts correspondent Tom Hoving reports on the filming last year of *The Meaning of Life*. Includes interviews and a behind-the-scenes look at how the Pythons became fish (on Sept. 11, 1982).

1031 April 9, 1983
Michael Palin appears at a screening of *Time Bandits* at the Screen on the Hill cinema in London.

1032 April 10, 1983
Too Hot to Handle (Stage show), at the Apollo Victoria Theatre, London. **Michael Palin** and **Terry Jones** perform in this music-comedy concert staged to raise funds for the Stop Sizewell B (nuclear power plant) Public Enquiry Fund. Other performers include Neil Innes, Rik Mayall, Pamela Stephenson, Chris Difford, Glen Tilbrook, Hazel O'Connor, Madness, and UB40.

1033 April 11, 1983
The BBC2 Film Competition (TV episode: BBC2). "The Final." Last of a six-part series in which amateur filmmakers from around Britain compete. Jury members are **Terry Gilliam**, Penelope Gilliatt, Michael Winner, and Peter Yates. Hosted by Michael Dean.

1034 April 13, 1983
The Merv Griffin Show (TV talk show: Synd.). Guests: **Graham Chapman**, **Terry Gilliam**, and **Terry Jones**, promoting *The Meaning of Life*, also Genie Francis, Jeff De Hart, Dr. Melvin Silverman, and Gloria Heidi.

1035 April 13, 1983
Late Night with David Letterman (TV talk show: NBC). Guests: **Graham Chapman**, promoting *The Meaning of Life*, and Harry Anderson.

1036 April 25, 1983
John Cleese's complaint against *The Sun*, which falsely attributed an offensive joke to him in August 1982 during the *Meaning of Life* filming, is upheld by the Press Council.

1037 April 25, 1983
Michael Palin is interviewed at his home by Edward Whitley and another young writer for a book about Oxford University and its graduates. Their questioning of the comedian is aggressive and uncomfortable, and after a while **Palin**, losing patience and late for another appointment, abruptly

ends the interview and leaves the house. The book, titled *The Graduates*, is published in May 1986.

1038   May 5, 1983
Michael Palin turns 40.

1039   May 9, 1983
The Pythons (minus **John Cleese**) attend a press conference and gala screening of *The Meaning of Life* at the 36th annual Cannes International Film Festival (May 7–19) in France.

1040   May 12, 1983
Newsnight (TV news show: BBC2). Joan Bakewell presents a report on the reception of *The Meaning of Life* at the Cannes Film Festival. **Terry Jones** is interviewed.

1041   May 15, 1983
The Sunday Times (London) (Newspaper/U.K.). "Video Choice: **Michael Palin** on Great Train Films," by **Michael Palin** (interviewed by Chris Salewicz), p. 24. **Palin** discusses some of the top railway-themed films, including *Brief Encounter* and *Emperor of the North*.

1042   May 19, 1983
At the Cannes Film Festival, *The Meaning of Life*, which was a British competition entry, is awarded the Special Jury Grand Prize, the festival's second highest honor. At the closing-night ceremony, **Terry Jones** thanks the jury members by name and quips, "Your money is behind the wash basin."

1043   May 20, 1983
Pebble Mill at One (TV talk show: BBC1). Guests: Julie Walters and **Michael Palin**. Marjorie Lofthouse talks to **Palin** about his film *The Missionary*.

1044   May 23, 1983
Film 83 (TV show: BBC1). Iain Johnstone presents a location report from the Cannes Film Festival where *The Meaning of Life* is being screened. Includes interviews with **Graham Chapman**, David Bowie, Julie Walters, and others.

1045   May 31, 1983
A Party Election Broadcast: SDP/Liberal Alliance (TV: BBC1/BBC2/ITV/Channel 4). **John Cleese** appears in this broadcast for the Social Democratic Party/Liberal Alliance.

1046   June 1983
Monty Python's The Meaning of Life (Book: Methuen [U.K.]; Grove Press [U.S.]). The complete film script, with many photos and animation stills. Includes the "Adventures of Martin Luther" and "Diana the Waitress" scenes, which were cut from the film; also **John Cleese**'s correspondence with the editor of *The Sun* concerning racially insensitive remarks falsely attributed to him by a reporter during filming in Scotland in August 1982. Designed by James Campus. Stills photography by David Appleby.

1047   June 1983
Monty Python's The Meaning of Life (Radio commercials). Series of U.K. radio ads promoting the June 23 release of the film. In one, **Michael Palin** plays Dino Vercotti; in another, a game show called *Philosopher's Corner* poses the question "What is the Meaning of Life?" (with **Palin**, **Terry Jones**, **John Cleese**, and **Eric Idle**); another ad features **Palin** as a radio announcer who messes up several takes, at first describing the film as an after-shave.
Awards: Radio Award-winner for Best Use of Comedy on a Commercial and Best Entertainment.

1048   June 1983
Galaxy Song/Every Sperm Is Sacred (Record: CBS Records A 3495). U.K single containing the songs "Galaxy Song" and "Every Sperm Is Sacred" from the *Meaning of Life* soundtrack. Also issued as an oversized, fishbowl-shaped picture disc (WA 3495).

1049   June 1983
Group Madness: The Making of Yellowbeard (TV special: Synd./U.S.). Behind-the-scenes look at the making of the pirate comedy *Yellowbeard*. The 45-minute documentary follows the filmmakers to locations in England and Mexico and includes on-set interviews with **Graham Chapman**, **Eric Idle**, **John Cleese**, Marty Feldman, Peter Boyle, Mel Damski, Peter Cook, and Madeline Kahn. Produced & directed by Michael Mileham and Phil Schuman.

1050   June 1983
Footlights!: A Hundred Years of Cambridge Comedy (Book: Methuen), written by Robert Hewison, is published in the U.K. Preface by **Eric Idle**, a former member (1963–65) of Footlights.

1051   June 4, 1983
Footlights! 100 Years of Comedy (TV special: BBC1). Documentary special celebrating the centenary of the Cambridge Footlights revue of which **John Cleese**, **Graham Chapman**, and **Eric Idle** were members in the 1960s. Hosted by Chris Serle and featuring interviews with **Cleese**, David Frost, Peter Cook, Jonathan Miller, Robert Hewison, and others. Produced by Tom Gutteridge.

1052 June 10, 1983
The Times (London) (Newspaper/U.K.). "Python's Meaning of Life Is That Life Makes No Sense," by Michael Watts, p. 12. Interview with **John Cleese**, who talks about *The Meaning of Life*, etc. Includes a large photo of **Cleese** (by John Voos) and a look at how the film came about.

1053 June 13, 1983
Loose Talk (TV talk show: Channel 4). Hosted by Steve Taylor. Guests include **Terry Gilliam**, promoting *The Meaning of Life*, Victor Romero Evans, Steve Machete, and Jools Holland.

1054 June 15, 1983
Calendar (TV news show: ITV/YTV–Yorkshire Television). Guest: **Michael Palin**, promoting *The Missionary*.

1055 June 15, 1983
The News Is the News (TV episode: NBC). First show of a limited-run series — broadcast live from New York — that satirizes the news. Includes an analysis of the British elections by the show's opening-night guest reporter, **Michael Palin**, standing outside No. 10 Downing Street. **Palin**'s piece was taped June 11. Starring Simon Jones, Michael Davis, Charlotte Moore, and Trey Wilson. Produced by Herb Sargent.

1056 June 19, 1983
The Sunday Times (London) (Newspaper/U.K.). "Monty Python: A Hard Act to Follow," by George Perry, pp. 24–27. A look at the Pythons' latest film *The Meaning of Life*, opening in the U.K. this week. Group photo taken by Clive Arrowsmith. Perry's book, *Life of Python*, is being published later this year.

1057 June 20, 1983
Good Morning Britain (TV talk show: ITV/TV-am). Hosted by Anne Diamond and **Terry Jones** (sitting in for Nick Owen).

1058 June 23, 1983
Monty Python's The Meaning of Life opens in the U.K.

1059 June 24, 1983
Yellowbeard (Feature film: Orion Pictures) opens in the U.S. **Graham Chapman** co-wrote this send-up of pirate movies and plays the title role of the foul, incorrigible buccaneer whose quest to reclaim his booty requires breaking out of jail and stowing away on a ship headed for the island where the treasure is buried. Marty Feldman's last film. Also starring **Eric Idle** (as Commander Clement), **John Cleese** (as Blind Pew), Peter Boyle, Cheech and Chong, Peter Cook, Martin Hewitt, Michael Hordern, Madeline Kahn, and James Mason. Written by **Graham Chapman**, Peter Cook, and Bernard McKenna. Directed by Mel Damski. Produced by Carter DeHaven. Released in Britain in September.
Reviews: Lawrence Van Gelder (*The New York Times*, June 24, 1983): "...the frequency of the wit tends to be intermittent and of varying quality and, at its best, to be reminiscent of superior efforts in Python movies"; *People Weekly* (July 11, 1983, p. 10): "They (the cast) all average about a laugh apiece, which, if doesn't make this film a treasure chest of humor, does make it funnier than most film comedies these days"; David Robinson (*The Times* [London], Sept. 16, 1983): "To capture the Monty Python style of comic anarchy requires more than scatology, rude words and funny faces."

1060 July 1983
Prevue (Magazine/U.S.). "Monty Python: Is *Meaning of Life* Their Last Laugh Together?" Python article, with many photos.

1061 July 2, 1983
Desert Island Discs (Radio show: BBC Radio 4). Roy Plomley's castaway is **Terry Jones**, whose choice of records includes "Five Salted Peanuts" (Tony Pastor & His Orchestra), "Serenade No. 10 in B Flat Major" (Mozart), "Penny Lane" (The Beatles), and "Imagine" (John Lennon). His luxury item is a pencil & paper; his book is *The Complete Works of Chaucer*.

1062 July 2, 1983
Michael Palin appears at the Samaritans Gala at the Theatre Royal, Drury Lane, London. Other stars at the event, which is raising money for the counseling service, include Glenda Jackson, Cleo Laine, Susannah York, Julie Covington, and Tim Brooke-Taylor.

1063 July 11, 1983
Ear to the Ground (TV show: Channel 4). Current affairs program for young people, hosted by Julie Hall and David Barrie. Guests include **Michael Palin** and The Lobes.

1064 July 14–August 10, 1983
A Monty Python film festival is held at the Barbican Centre in London. The retrospective includes both Python films and solo projects (including *Time Bandits* and *The Missionary*).

1065 August 1983
The Secret Policeman's Private Parts (Feature film: Miramax Films) is released in the U.S. Compilation of the best bits that didn't make it into the first two *Ball* films as well as material from the 1976 and 1977 Amnesty shows. Starring **John Cleese**, **Michael Palin**, **Graham Chapman**, **Terry Jones**, **Terry Gilliam**, and many others. Directed by Roger Graef and Julien Temple. Created & produced by Martin Lewis. Also released on video.

1066 August 1983
Prevue (Magazine/U.S.). "The Confessions of **Terry Jones**," by Kim "Howard" Johnson, pp. 24–25. **Jones** talks about *The Meaning of Life*.

1067 August 12, 1983
Breakfast Time (TV news-talk show: BBC1). **Michael Palin** talks to Sue Cook about today's headlines and about his *Comic Roots* documentary airing tonight.

1068 August 12, 1983
Comic Roots (TV special: BBC1). "**Michael Palin**." The first in a four-part series of documentaries on the formative years of four British comedians. The half-hour program traces **Michael Palin**'s early life and the roots of his comic talent through personal remembrances, film clips, and interviews with old friends, teachers, and relatives. It looks at his early years in Sheffield, at Brasenose College (Oxford), the Edinburgh Festival, and the influence of the *Goon Show* on his comedy. Starring **Michael Palin**, Mrs. Mary Palin (his mother), Spike Milligan, Robert Hewison, and **Terry Jones**. Written by **Michael Palin**. Produced by Tony Laryea.

1069 September 1983
The Saga of Erik the Viking (Book: Pavilion Books), written by **Terry Jones** with illustrations by Michael Foreman, is published in the U.K. **Jones**' second children's book (following 1981's *Fairy Tales*) concerns a group of Norse sailors on an odyssey to find "the land where the sun goes at night." Each chapter in the book, which **Jones** wrote for his then six-year-old son Bill, tells a new tale of adventure. Published in the U.S. by Schocken Books. *Erik* is also made into a video game (1984) and adapted for the stage by Laurence Sach (1993), and inspires **Jones**' 1989 film, *Erik the Viking*, which tells a different story from the one in the book.
Awards: Winner of the 1984 Children's Book Award (Federation of Children's Book Groups).
Reviews: Carol Van Strum (*The New York Times Book Review*, Oct. 30, 1983, p. 26): "Giants, ogres, graceful mermaids and savage wolves leap from a landscape of mythic grandeur.... As in *Fairy Tales*, their first collaboration, Mr. **Jones** and Mr. Foreman fashion from traditional materials a tale of high deeds and adventure that is startlingly fresh"; Andrew Wawn (*The Times Literary Supplement* [London], Nov. 25, 1983, p. 1310): "The author's engagement with the medieval world and his belief in the therapeutic power of story find renewed expression in this colourful volume"; *The Economist* (Nov. 26, 1983, p. 102): "The best adventure story this year..."

1070 September 10, 1983
Video Video (TV show: Channel 4). A look at recent video releases, hosted by Adam Faith. Guest: **Graham Chapman**.

1071 September 20, 1983
Good Morning Britain (TV talk show: ITV/TV-am). Hosted by Anne Diamond and Nick Owen. Guest: **Terry Jones**.

1072 September 20, 1983
Michael Palin attends an all-star benefit rock concert for The Ronnie Lane Appeal for ARMS (Action for Research into Multiple Sclerosis) at London's Royal Albert Hall.

1073 September 22, 1983
Yellowbeard opens in the U.K.

1074 September 26, 1983
People Weekly (Magazine/U.S.). "Monty Python's **John Cleese** Pursues a Not-So-Silly Walk of Life — Making Business-Training Films," pp. 83–84. Article on **Cleese**'s involvement with Video Arts. Photographs of **Cleese** by Terence Spencer.

1075 September 27, 1983
Loose Talk (TV show: Channel 4). Hosted by Steve Taylor. Guest: **Graham Chapman**.

1076 September 28, 1983
The Times (London) (Newspaper/U.K.). "How a Python Shed His Tortured Skin," by Paul Nathanson, p. 10. Interview with **John Cleese**, who talks about his book *Families*... and his years in psychotherapy.

1077 September 28, 1983
Woman's Hour (Radio show: BBC Radio 4). Guest: **John Cleese**, promoting *Families*....

1078 September 29, 1983
Families and How to Survive Them (Book: Me-

thuen), written by Robin Skynner and **John Cleese**, is published in the U.K. Humorous question-and-answer book by **Cleese** and his former therapist, Dr. Robin Skynner, outlining Skynner's theories and techniques on dealing with problems of marriage, babies, children, and family relationships. Cartoons by Bud Handelsman. Published in the U.S. by Oxford University Press (paperback, 1984). Produced as a radio series in 1990 (BBC Radio 4). **Cleese** and Skynner's follow-up, *Life and How to Survive It*, is published in 1993.

1079   September 29, 1983
Rolling Stone (Magazine/U.S.). "Obit: Luis Buñuel," by **Michael Palin**, p. 108. **Palin** pays tribute to surrealist filmmaker Luis Buñuel, who died July 29th.

1080   October 1983
An Evening with Graham Chapman (Lecture). **Graham Chapman** performs his comedy lecture on a tour of North America. Venues include Dalhousie University in Halifax, Nova Scotia (Oct. 5), Harper College in Palatine, IL (Oct. 14), and University of Akron's Thomas Hall in OH (Oct. 25).

1081   October 4, 1983
A Plus (TV talk show: ITV). Mavis Nicholson interviews **John Cleese** and Robin Skynner about their book *Families and How to Survive Them*.

1082   October 5, 1983
Michael Palin attends the British Film Institute's 50th Anniversary Banquet at the Guildhall in London, where he meets Prince Charles and Orson Welles. At the ceremony Charles presents fellowships to Welles, Michael Powell, and other directors. Highlights are broadcast as *Fifty Years of the BFI* that night on BBC2.

1083   October 13, 1983
Pebble Mill at One (TV talk show: BBC1). Frank Delaney talks to **John Cleese** and Robin Skynner about their book *Families and How to Survive Them*.

1084   October 21, 1983
Pebble Mill at One (TV talk show: BBC1). Paul Coia talks to **Terry Jones** about his new children's book *The Saga of Erik the Viking*.

1085   October 22, 1983
The Saturday Show (TV show: ITV/LWT). Guest: **Terry Jones**, promoting *Erik the Viking*.

1086   November 1983–August 1984
Brazil, **Terry Gilliam**'s nightmare fantasy, is filmed over a nine-month period at Lee International Film Studios in Wembley, England and on location in London and Cumbria, England and Marne-Le-Vallee, France. Locations include Leighton House (London), Mentmore Towers (Mentmore, Buckinghamshire), and Croydon Power Station (South London). Universal Studios and Twentieth Century–Fox are financing the film, which is budgeted at $15 million.

1087   November 1983
Heavy Metal (Magazine/U.S.). "Nahallywood: Graham Chapman Interview," by Ed Naha, pp. 11–12. **Chapman** talks about Python and the problems with *Yellowbeard*.

1088   November 13, 1983
Terry Jones reads from his new book *The Saga of Erik the Viking* in the Children's Bookshop at the Metropolitan Museum of Art in New York City.

1089   November 14, 1983
Live at Five (TV news-talk show: WNBC, New York). Guests: **Terry Jones**, promoting his book *The Saga of Erik the Viking*, and Mariel Hemingway.

1090   November 15, 1983
Terry Jones reads from his book *The Saga of Erik the Viking* at the Cornelia Street Café in Greenwich Village, New York City.

1091   November 16–19, 1983
More Than 35 Minutes with Michael Palin (Stage show). **Michael Palin** performs his one-man show for four nights at the Arts Theatre in Belfast, N. Ireland as part of the Belfast Festival. This is **Palin**'s second time performing at the festival, following his debut there in November 1981.

1092   November 17, 1983
Latenight America (TV talk show: PBS). Hosted by Dennis Wholey. Guest: **Terry Jones**, promoting his book *The Saga of Erik the Viking*.

1093   November 19, 1983
Data Run (TV show: ITV/TV-am). Magazine program for teenagers. Guest: **Terry Jones**.

1094   November 27, 1983
The Washington Post (Newspaper/U.S.). "**Terry Jones** Isn't Grimm," by Michele Slung. Interview.

1095   November 27, 1983
Sunday, Sunday (TV talk show: ITV/LWT). Hosted by Gloria Hunniford and Brian Hayes. Guests include **Terry Jones**, Maureen Lipman, Jean Marsh, and Omar Sharif.

1096 November 28, 1983
Pebble Mill at One (TV talk show: BBC1). Marian Foster talks to **Terry Jones** and Susan Hampshire about current children's books.

1097 December 1983
Life of Python (Book: Pavilion Books), written by George Perry, is published in the U.K. A history of Monty Python, which begins with an examination of British comedy before Python (*The Goon Show, Beyond the Fringe*, etc.), followed by biographies of each individual Python member and then the group as a whole. Illustrated with many rare photos, the book also includes a Pythonography compiled by Lucy Douch. Published in the U.S. in 1984 by Little, Brown and Company. An updated edition of the book is published in 1995 (revised in 2006). Perry is a journalist and friend of the Pythons.

1098 December 3, 1983
All six Pythons attend the wedding of Nancy Lewis, the team's U.S. publicist, to actor Simon Jones (*Hitchhiker's Guide to the Galaxy, The Meaning of Life*) at St. Paul's, Covent Garden, London.

1099 December 14, 1983
Arts Review of the Year (TV special: Channel 4). **John Cleese** participates in this two-hour discussion program celebrating the year in arts. Hosted by Melvyn Bragg and Billy Connolly. Directed by Don Featherstone.

1100 December 24, 1983
Data Run's Christmas Party (TV special: ITV/TV-am). Holiday special with Jeremy Beadle, **Terry Jones**, Tracey Ullman, and Madness.

1101 December 29, 1983
Star Sound Extra (Radio show: BBC Radio 2). Guests include **John Cleese**, Peter Cushing, and Dustin Hoffman.

1102 1983
So You Want to Be a Success at Selling?, Part 3: Difficult Customers (Training film: Video Arts). Sales training film (third in the series) illustrating how to deal with three types of difficult customers: Desperate Ducker, Disorganised Ditherer, and Domineering Dictator. Salesman **John Cleese** again receives the lesson from his instructional tape (voice of Ian Holm). Also starring Alan Bennett, Robin Nedwell, and Diana Quick. Written by David Nobbs. Directed by Charles Crichton.

1103 1983
The Unorganised Manager, Part 1: Damnation (Training film: Video Arts). Overworked manager Richard Lewis (James Bolam) dies and learns lessons in organization from St. Peter (**John Cleese**). First of four films (two in 1983, two in 1985) demonstrating how managers can improve work performance through better organization. Remade in 1996. Written by Jonathan Lynn. Directed by Charles Crichton.

1104 1983
The Unorganised Manager, Part 2: Salvation (Training film: Video Arts). Remade in 1996. Starring **John Cleese** (as St. Peter) and James Bolam. Written by Jonathan Lynn. Directed by Charles Crichton.

1105 1983
Monty Python and the Holy Grail (CED videodisc: RCA VideoDiscs 03040) is released in the U.S. The original British video version of the film, imported by RCA VideoDiscs. Includes the 4-minute "coming attraction" trailer and a bonus 24-second sequence (found during "The Tale of Sir Galahad") never seen before in the U.S. Presented in the widescreen "letterbox" format.

1106 1983
Fawlty Towers: A La Carte (Record: BBC Records 484). LP. Original television soundtrack of the episodes "Waldorf Salad" (1979) and "Gourmet Night" (1975). Produced by Andrew Sachs and William Grierson.

1107 January 1984
Michael Palin begins working on a script for the "First Love" film series for television. The story, which will eventually make it to the screen (in February 1987) as *East of Ipswich*, is based on his first encounter with his wife Helen when they were teenagers on holiday in Southwold, England.

1108 January 7, 1984
Good Morning Britain (TV talk show: ITV/TV-am). Hosted by Michael Parkinson and his wife Mary. Guests: Hayley Mills and **Michael Palin**.

1109 January 15, 1984
The Sunday Times (London) (Newspaper/U.K.). "Fawlty Father," by **John Cleese**, p. 41. **Cleese** writes about his feelings on becoming a father again. His daughter, Camilla, is born on Jan. 24.

1110 January 21, 1984
Saturday Night Live (TV comedy show: NBC). Hosted by **Michael Palin** and Mary Palin, with musical guests The Motels. **Palin**, hosting for the

fourth time, shares the monologue stage with his 80-year-old mother (enjoying her first trip to America), who keeps interrupting to make him fetch her knitting, book, etc. **Palin** appears in the sketches "Mick Pitwhistle Does It All" (as Mick), "Man on Chain" (as salesman), "Would You Believe It?" (as Sally Benjamin), "Save the Plankton," "House of Mutton" (as Mr. Fenner), and "Life on the Mississippi" (as the Captain). Cast: Jim Belushi, Robin Duke, Julia Louis-Dreyfus, Mary Gross, Brad Hall, Tim Kazurinsky, Gary Kroeger, Eddie Murphy, and Joe Piscopo. Directed by Dave Wilson. Produced by Dick Ebersol. Note: Mrs. Palin turned 80 on Jan. 14.

1111 January 24, 1984

John Cleese's second daughter, Camilla Chloe, is born. Her mother is **Cleese**'s second wife, Barbara Trentham. His first daughter, Cynthia, was born in 1971 to his first wife, Connie Booth.

1112 February 6, 1984

People Weekly (Magazine/U.S.). "The Mad, Mad World of Monty Python's **Terry Jones** Is Not for Adults Only," by Andrea Chambers (reported by Jerene Jones), pp. 102–03. Article on **Jones**' writing for children. Includes a photo (by Ian Cook) of **Jones** swinging on a rope next to his daughter Sally and son Bill.

1113 March 18, 1984

Sunday, Sunday (TV talk show: ITV/LWT). Hosted by Gloria Hunniford and Brian Hayes. Guests include **Michael Palin**, Bill Wyman, Su Pollard, and Max Bygraves.

1114 March 25, 1984

The British Academy Awards (Award ceremony). The BAFTA-nominated song "Every Sperm Is Sacred" (from *The Meaning of Life*) loses in the Best Original Song category to "Up Where We Belong" (from *An Officer and a Gentleman*). The ceremony, hosted by Michael Aspel in the presence of Princess Anne, is held at the Grosvenor House Hotel in London. Broadcast live on ITV.

1115 April 1984

Esquire (Magazine/U.S.). "God Save **John Cleese**," by Laurence Shames, pp. 60–62+. Lengthy interview/article. Includes a full-page photo of **Cleese** by Clive Arrowsmith.

1116 April 1984

Fantasy Empire (Magazine/U.S.). "Monty Python—*The Meaning of Life* Interview," by Randy L'Officier, pp. 30–35. Interview with **Graham Chapman**, **Terry Gilliam**, **Eric Idle**, and **Terry Jones**—with a pre-recorded **Michael Palin** on tape—conducted in Los Angeles on Mar. 12, 1983.

1117 April 3, 1984

Late Night with David Letterman (TV talk show: NBC). Guests: **John Cleese**, promoting *Privates on Parade*, and Kathleen Turner.

1118 April 8, 1984

The Money Programme (TV show: BBC2). Mark Rogerson reports on business-training films. Includes an interview with **John Cleese** about his involvement with Video Arts.

1119 April 13, 1984

Privates on Parade, starring **John Cleese**, opens in the U.S.

1120 April 16, 1984

New York (Magazine/U.S.). "Fast Track: **John Cleese**'s Animal House," by Rhoda Koenig, p. 34.

1121 April 30–June 1984

A Private Function, starring **Michael Palin**, is filmed in England on a budget of $1.4 million. Filming takes place in Ilkley and Bradford in West Yorkshire, also Barnoldswick (in Lancashire) and London. **Palin**'s co-stars include Maggie Smith, Denholm Elliott, and a pig named Betty (actually, three different pigs are used).

1122 May 4, 1984

Judi (TV talk show: ITV). Hosted by Judi Spiers. Guests: Antonia Hunt, Leslie Thomas, and **Terry Jones**.

1123 May 15, 1984

Private Lives (TV talk show: BBC2). Maria Aitken hosts this program revealing the private side of famous people. Tonight she talks to **Terry Jones** and Jill Craigie. **Jones** reveals a memorable place (Lambeth Bridge), his favorite place (Wales, where he spent his early childhood), and a T-shirt with special meaning (relating to ABC's censoring of Python shows). Directed by Philip Chilvers. Produced by Frances Whitaker.

1124 May 24, 1984

Everybody Here (TV children's show: Channel 4). **Terry Jones** tells a story about a fish.

1125 May 29, 1984

The Young Ones (TV episode: BBC2). "Nasty." The boys rent a VCR and nasty videos. **Terry Jones** guest-stars as a drunk vicar on this second-season episode of the 1982–84 sitcom starring Adrian Edmondson, Rik Mayall, Nigel Planer, Christopher Ryan, and Alexei Sayle. Written by Ben Elton, Rik Mayall, and Lise Mayer. Produced by Paul Jackson.

1126 July–August 1984
Compaq ("It Simply Works Better") (TV commercials). **John Cleese** stars in a series of four American TV ads for Compaq personal computers. In the ads, which air during the Summer Olympics, **Cleese** plays characters who have made the wrong decision of purchasing PC's from Compaq's competitors. Agency: Ogilvy & Mather, Houston.

1127 Fall 1984
John Cleese is selected by *Advertising Age* as its Star Presenter for 1984. He was chosen from among more than sixty celebrities. Previous winners include John Houseman, Robert Morley, and Bill Cosby.

1128 September–October 1984
The Dress, a short film starring **Michael Palin**, is filmed in London.

1129 September 1984
Michael Palin and **Terry Jones** appear at the Ilkley Literature Festival (Sept. 14–22) in Ilkley, West Yorkshire, England.

1130 September 17, 1984
Fawlty Towers (Vols. 1 & 2) (Videocassettes: BBC Video) is released in the U.K. The **John Cleese** sitcom comes to video in the first two of a four-cassette set. Volume one contains "The Germans," "The Hotel Inspectors," and "A Touch of Class." Volume two contains "The Psychiatrist," "The Builders," and "The Wedding Party." The remaining two volumes will be released in November.

1131 October 1984
The Golden Skits of Wing Commander Muriel Volestrangler FRHS & Bar (Book: Methuen), by Muriel Volestrangler, is published in the U.K. A collection of sketches, ranging from Cambridge to Monty Python, written or co-written by **John Cleese**. Co-writers include **Graham Chapman**, Marty Feldman, Tim Brooke-Taylor, and **Michael Palin**. Contents: "Architects," "Shirt Shop," "Goat," "Sheep," "Top of the Form," "Word Association Football," "Bookshop," "Arthur 'Two Sheds' Jackson," "The Last Supper," "Merchant Banker," "Cricket Commentators," "Fairly Silly Court," "Crunchy Frog," "Regella," "Hearing Aid," "Argument," "The Good Old Days," "Lucky Gypsy," "Mrs. Beulah Premise and Mrs. Wanda Conclusion Visit Mr. and Mrs. J. P. Sartre," "Undertaker," "Railway Carriage," "Cheese Shop," "String," "Chapel," "Ones," "Army Protection Racket," "Slightly Less Silly Than the Other Court," "Courier," "Ethel the Frog," and "Dead Parrot."

1132 October 3, 1984
Where There's Life (TV talk show: ITV/YTV–Yorkshire Television). Medical program hosted by Miriam Stoppard. Guests **John Cleese** and Robin Skynner talk about their book *Families and How to Survive Them*.

1133 October 7, 1984
Rights & Revels: A Benefit for the National Council for Civic Liberties (Stage show). Benefit show at the Aldwych Theatre in London. Performers include **Michael Palin**, **Terry Jones**, John Hurt, Miriam Karlin, Julie Walters, Miriam Margolyes, and Susanna York.

1134 October 15, 1984
Film 84 (TV show: BBC1). Host Barry Norman presents an on-location report from the set of *A Private Function*. Includes interviews with **Michael Palin**, Alan Bennett, Mark Shivas, and Richard Griffiths.

1135 October 17, 1984
Jackanory (TV show: BBC1). "Small Harry and the Toothache Pills." **Michael Palin** reads his 1982 children's story. Directed by Nel Romano. Produced by Angela Beeching.

1136 October 20, 1984
Wogan (TV talk show: BBC1). Hosted by Terry Wogan. Guests: Sophia Loren, **Terry Jones**, Dick Clement and Ian La Frenais, and Bucks Fizz. **Jones** talks about Python, medieval times, realism in films, Real Ale, etc.

1137 October 31, 1984
Breakfast Time (TV news-talk show: BBC1). Frank Bough and Fern Britton interview **Michael Palin** and **Terry Jones** about their new *Dr. Fegg* book. Appearing with a life-size Dr. Fegg dummy, the two also talk about their other recent projects, including **Jones'** book *Chaucer's Knight* and **Palin's** newly-completed film *A Private Function* and a script he's writing for the "First Love" film series.

1138 November 1984
Dr. Fegg's Encyclopeadia of All World Knowledge (Book: Methuen), written by **Terry Jones** and **Michael Palin**, is published in the U.K. Revised reissue of *Dr. Fegg's Nasty Book of Knowledge* (1976), originally put out as *Bert Fegg's Nasty Book for Boys*

& Girls (1974). Published in the U.S. by Peter Bedrick Books (1985).

1139 November 1984
Fantasy Empire (Magazine/U.S.). "**Terry Gilliam**'s *Brazil*," by Bart Mills, pp. 6–7+. "**Terry Jones** of Monty Python Is Turning the World Upside Down," by Neil Gaiman, pp. 23–26+. Two articles on the current projects of **Gilliam** and **Jones**. With a *Meaning of Life* group photo on the front and back cover.

1140 November 5, 1984
BBC Look East (TV news show: BBC East). Guests: **Michael Palin** and **Terry Jones**, promoting *Dr. Fegg*.

1141 November 7, 1984
Calendar (TV news show: ITV/YTV–Yorkshire Television). Guests: **Michael Palin** and **Terry Jones**, promoting *Dr. Fegg*.

1142 November 16, 1984
Opinions (TV show: Channel 4). Late-night program. This week, **Graham Chapman** argues that we should stop worrying about what the neighbors will say. Half-hour. Directed by K. Angus Robertson. Produced by Michael Jones.

1143 November 18, 1984
Good Morning Britain (TV talk show: ITV/TV-am). David Frost interviews **Michael Palin** and **Terry Jones**.

1144 November 18, 1984
Sunday, Sunday (TV talk show: ITV/LWT). Hosted by Gloria Hunniford. Guests include **Michael Palin**, promoting *A Private Function*, Christopher Biggins, Hannah Gordon, and Martin Shaw.

1145 November 21, 1984
A Private Function, starring **Michael Palin**, has a Royal Charity Premiere at the Odeon Haymarket in London in aid of the Save the Children Fund. Princess Anne attends, as does **Palin** and other stars from the film.

1146 November 22, 1984
A Private Function is shown at the National Film Theatre as part of the London Film Festival (Nov. 15–Dec. 2).

1147 November 27, 1984
Late Night with David Letterman (TV talk show: NBC). Guests: **John Cleese**, promoting his book *Families...*, and Eva Gabor.

1148 November 28, 1984
The Courage to Change: Hope and Help for Alcoholics and Their Families (Book: Houghton Mifflin), by Dennis Wholey, is published in the U.S. *New York Times* bestseller in which PBS talk show host Wholey (himself an alcoholic) presents the accounts of 20 well-known personalities — including Pete Townshend, Doc Severinson, and **Graham Chapman**— who relate their battles with alcohol. **Chapman** describes how he came to accept the fact that he was an alcoholic and how he finally quit drinking (in 1977). One major event **Chapman** recalls is the time he experienced the DTs for the first time, which occurred in Scotland on the first day of filming *Holy Grail* (Apr. 30, 1974).

1149 November 30, 1984
A Private Function (Feature film: HandMade Films) opens in the U.K. Comedy set during the food rationing days of post-war England about a meek, small-town foot doctor and his socially ambitious wife who become involved with the black market when they steal an illegal pig. **Michael Palin**, reuniting with his *Missionary* co-star Maggie Smith, plays the chiropodist Gilbert Chilvers. Filmed mainly in Yorkshire and produced by George Harrison's HandMade Films. Also starring Denholm Elliott, Richard Griffiths, Liz Smith, John Normington, and Bill Paterson. Written by Alan Bennett. Directed by Malcolm Mowbray. Produced by Mark Shivas. Executive produced by George Harrison and Denis O'Brien. Released in the U.S. in March 1985.
Awards: BAFTA-winner for Best Actress (Maggie Smith), Best Supporting Actor (Denholm Elliott), and Best Supporting Actress (Liz Smith), nominated for Best Film and Best Original Screenplay; Evening Standard British Film Award for Best Screenplay and Peter Sellers Award for Comedy (**Palin**).
Reviews: David Robinson (*The Times* [London], Nov. 30, 1984, p. 15): "*A Private Function* is, once and for all, a classic of British comedy"; Vincent Canby (*The New York Times*, Mar. 1, 1985): "...a comedy of immense if often scatological charm"; Richard Corliss (*Time*, Mar. 18, 1985, p. 84): "This is an *Animal Farm* that could have used a taste of *Animal Crackers*"; David Ansen (*Newsweek*, Mar. 18, 1985, p. 71): "This droll allegory puts one in the mind of the classic Ealing comedies of the past, without ever quite matching their hilarity"; Scot Haller (*People Weekly*, Apr. 29, 1985, pp. 13–14): "...**Palin** and Smith, who were well matched in *The Missionary*, again work together marvelously."

1150 December 2, 1984
The Dress (Short film) premieres in London. **Michael Palin** takes on a serious role in this short drama about a man who rediscovers his love for his wife when she wears the red dress he bought for his mistress. The 25-minute short is released theatrically in the U.K. on Jan. 25, 1985, accompanying the feature *Beverly Hills Cop*. Also starring Phyllis Logan, Derrick Branche, Dave Hill, Vivienne Ritchie, John Westbrook, Elisabeth Croft, and Rachel Palin (**Palin**'s real-life daughter). Written by Robert Smith. Directed by Eva Sereny. Produced by Clare Downs.
Award: BAFTA-winner for Best Short.

1151 December 2, 1984
Michael Palin attends the premiere of the short film *The Dress*, in which he stars, at the Lumiere Cinema on the last day of the London Film Festival.

1152 December 7, 1984
Dinner at Albert's (Concert). **Graham Chapman** performs at this benefit concert for Ethiopia, held at London's Royal Albert Hall.

1153 December 9, 1984
Stars on Sunday II: The Stage Show (Stage show), at the London Palladium. Charity comedy show organized by Dr. Rob Buckman in aid of the Oncology Club Fund (cancer charity). Starring Buckman, **Michael Palin**, **Terry Jones**, Rik Mayall, Alexei Sayle, Chris Langham, Dawn French, Jennifer Saunders, Mel Smith, Griff Rhys Jones, Neil Innes, Victoria Wood, and others. Airs as a TV special on Dec. 23, 1986, as *Comedians Do It on Stage* (Channel 4).

1154 December 12, 1984
Festival on Film (TV special: BBC2). Christopher Frayling hosts this look back at the 28th London Film Festival with film clips and interviews with filmmakers and critics. **Michael Palin** is among the interviewees.

1155 December 14, 1984
Breakfast Time (TV news-talk show: BBC1). Nick Ross talks to **Terry Jones** about the video game version of his book *The Saga of Erik the Viking*.

1156 1984
Budgeting (Training film: Video Arts). Film presenting the basics of business finance. Part of the "Finance for Non-Financial Managers" series. Starring **John Cleese** (as Julian Carruthers) and John Bird. Written by Graeme Garden. Directed by Peter Robinson.

1157 1984
So You Want to Be a Success at Selling?, Part 4: Closing the Sale (Training film: Video Arts). Salesman **John Cleese** learns valuable lessons from his instructional tape (voice of Andrew Sachs) on how to close the sale. Last of a four-part series. Also starring Andrew Sachs, Richard Davies, Diane Fletcher, Julian Holloway, Colin Jeavons, Andrew MacLachlan, and Don Warrington. Written by David Nobbs. Directed by Peter Robinson.

1158 1984
More Bloody Meetings (Training film: Video Arts). Management-training film on how to prevent time-wasting at meetings. Sequel to *Meetings, Bloody Meetings* (1976). Remade in 1994. Starring **John Cleese**, Diana Quick, Graeme Garden, Rosemary Leach, and Julian Holloway. Written by Antony Jay. Directed by Charles Crichton.

1159 1984
Kronenbourg (Radio commercials). **John Cleese** lends his voice to four American radio spots for Kronenbourg beer in which he lampoons the beer's "better not bitter" slogan. Written by **Cleese**, Jay Taub, and Tod Seisser. Agency: Levine, Huntley, Schmidt & Beaver, New York. **Cleese** does more Kronenbourg commercials in 1985.
Award: Clio Award winner.

1160 1984
Freaky Fables (Book: Methuen), by J.B. Handelsman, is published in the U.K. Collection of columns from *Punch* by writer-cartoonist Handelsman, with a foreword by **John Cleese**. Handelsman illustrated both of **Cleese**'s psychology books, *Families and How to Survive Them* (1983) and *Life and How to Survive It* (1993).

1161 1984
Michael Palin reads the audiobooks *Jack the Giant Killer/ Scrapefoot* (LP 204), *Mowgli's Brothers* (LP 205), and *How Fear Came* (LP 206). The last two are Rudyard Kipling stories.

1162 1984
Terry Jones reads the audiobooks *The Voyages of Sinbad (I to III)* (LP 212), *The Voyages of Sinbad (IV to VI)* (LP 213), and *Aladdin and the Wonderful Lamp* (LP 214).

1163 1984
The Eliza Stories (Book: Pavilion), written by

Barry Pain with an introduction by **Terry Jones**, is published in the U.K. Collection of humorous stories, originally published in 1900–13, about a Victorian suburban couple. Barry Pain (1864–1928) was an English journalist, novelist and short-story writer. Reprinted in 2002 by Prion Books. Published in the U.S. by Beaufort Books.

1164   1984

Terry Gilliam and family move into a 16th-century, three-story house in Highgate Village, North London. The house, also known as the Old Hall, lies above Highgate Cemetery and next door to St. Michaels, Church of England.

1165   1984

The Saga of Erik the Viking (Video game: Mosaic Publishing). Adventure game based on **Terry Jones**' 1983 children's story.

1166   Early 1985

Silverado, a western directed by Lawrence Kasdan in which **John Cleese** plays an English sheriff, is filmed in New Mexico.

1167   January 1985

Terry Gilliam delivers *Brazil* to its U.S. distributor, Universal, 17 minutes too long. The studio demands that he reduce it from its length of 2 hours, 22 minutes to the contracted 2 hours, 5 minutes. They compromise on a 10-minute cut.

1168   January 1, 1985

The Merv Griffin Show (TV talk show: Synd.). Guests: **John Cleese** and Robin Skynner, promoting their book *Families and How to Survive Them*, recently released in the U.S., and Gallagher.

1169   January 2, 1985

The Independent Broadcasting Authority (IBA) bans Channel 4 in Britain from airing *Life of Brian* because it may be offensive to Christians.

1170   January 27, 1985

The Sunday Times (London) (Newspaper/U.K.). "Big Brother and the Python," by George Perry, p. 38. Interview with **Terry Gilliam** about his new film *Brazil*.

1171   February 1985

After a month of re-cutting, **Terry Gilliam** delivers *Brazil* to Universal (the film's U.S. distributor) at 2 hours, 11 minutes. Universal wants to keep cutting.

1172   February 1, 1985

Calendar (TV news show: ITV/YTV–Yorkshire Television). Guests: **Michael Palin** and Alan Bennett, promoting *A Private Function*.

1173   February 1, 1985

Newsnight (TV news show: BBC2). Robin Denselow presents a report on George Harrison's film company, HandMade Films. Includes interviews with Harrison and **Michael Palin**.

1174   February 10, 1985

Royal Gala Concert (Concert). **Graham Chapman** and Spike Milligan are emcees at this gala benefit concert in aid of the National Jazz Centre, held at the London Palladium in the presence of The Princess of Wales. Performers include Alison Moyet, Jools Holland, Will Gaines, and Stan Tracey.

1175   February 19, 1985

Film 85 (TV show: BBC1). Hosted by Barry Norman. Includes an interview with **Terry Gilliam** from the set of his new film *Brazil*.

1176   February 20, 1985

Breakfast Time (TV news-talk show: BBC1). Mike Smith interviews **Terry Gilliam** about his new film *Brazil*.

1177   February 22, 1985

Brazil (Feature film: Twentieth-Century–Fox) opens in the U.K. Comedy-fantasy set in a bleak futuristic society, described by its director and co-writer **Terry Gilliam** as "a post–Orwellian view of a pre–Orwellian world" and "Walter Mitty Meets Franz Kafka." The film tells the story of Sam Lowry (Jonathan Pryce), a day-dreaming clerk for the Ministry of Information Retrieval, who risks his career and personal freedom to save the girl of his dreams from a fateful bureaucratic blunder. **Michael Palin** co-stars as Sam's best friend, Jack Lint, a professional torturer and family man. Also starring Kim Greist, Robert DeNiro, Katherine Helmond, Ian Holm, Peter Vaughan, Bob Hoskins, Ian Richardson, Jim Broadbent, Charles McKeown, Barbara Hicks, Derrick O'Connor, Kathryn Pogson, Bryan Pringle, and Sheila Reid. Written by **Terry Gilliam**, Tom Stoppard, and Charles McKeown. Directed by **Terry Gilliam**. Produced by Arnon Milchan.

Awards: Academy Award-nominated for Best Original Screenplay and Best Art Direction/Set Decoration (Norman Garwood & Maggie Gray); Los Angeles Film Critics Award-winner for Best Picture, Best Director, and Best Screenplay; BAFTA-winner for Best Production Design (Garwood) and Best Special Visual Effects (George Gibbs & Richard Conway); Winner of the Evening Standard British Film Award for Outstanding Technical Achievement (Garwood).

Reviews: Philip Strick (*The Times* [London], Feb. 22, 1985, p. 19): "**Gilliam**'s jokes are black and gory, but his plot is intricately coiled with spectacular adventures and wild fantasies. It's so astonishing to watch..."; Roger Ebert (*Chicago Sun-Times*, Jan. 17, 1986): "The movie is awash in elaborate special effects, sensational sets, apocalyptic scenes of destruction and a general lack of discipline"; David Denby (*New York*, Jan. 27, 1986, pp. 55–56): "The finest things in the movie are just weird comic riffs, and when **Gilliam** turns to plot, he loses his edge.... *Brazil* goes on and on, and after a while, **Gilliam**'s not having anything to say becomes a handicap"; Pauline Kael (*The New Yorker*, Feb. 10, 1986, p. 106+): "What **Gilliam** presents is a vision of the future as the decayed past, and this vision is an organic thing on the screen — which is a considerable accomplishment.... Yet I must admit to a feeling of relief when the film was over.... This image-maker leaves you with nothing but images"; Peter Travers (*People Weekly*, Feb. 17, 1986): "...**Gilliam**'s most daring, demented and demanding film.... **Gilliam** paints his bleak universe with the most astonishing visuals since *Metropolis*.... But the undeniable power of the film is the way its images keep digging into your memory"; Gahan Wilson (*Twilight Zone*, June 1986, pp. 88–90): "*Brazil* is a Monty Python version of *Brave New World* and *1984*, dear readers, and it works; it works terrifyingly well..."; Thomas Doherty (*Cinefantastique*, July 1986, p. 46+): "Visually beautiful and conceptually befuddled.... Next time around **Gilliam** should aim as carefully for the heart as for the eye."

1178 February 22, 1985
Friday People (TV show: BBC1). Includes a report on the premiere of *Brazil* with **Terry Gilliam** and **Michael Palin**.

1179 Late February–early March 1985
Michael Palin visits the U.S. to promote *A Private Function* and the book *Fish Tales*, written by Al Levinson and published by **Palin**'s company, Signford Ltd.

1180 February 1985
Starlog (Magazine/U.S.). "Science Fiction, According to Monty Python, Part One," by Kim "Howard" Johnson, pp. 21–24. Article on sci-fi in the Python shows looks at the sketches "Science Fiction Sketch" and "Bicycle Repair Man," and the episode "Mr. Neutron."

1181 February 27, 1985
Late Night with David Letterman (TV talk show: NBC). Guests: **Michael Palin**, promoting *A Private Function*, and Carol Channing and animal psychic Beatrice Lydecker. **Palin** talks about the film and makes sausages on this special "morning" edition of the program. Directed by Hal Gurnee. Produced by Barry Sand.

1182 March 1985
Michael Palin attends a screening of *A Private Function* at the San Francisco International Film Festival. It is the closing film of the festival.

1183 March 1985
Hot Properties (TV talk show: Lifetime). Hosted by Richard Belzer. Guests: **Michael Palin**, promoting *A Private Function*, and Hector Elizondo. **Palin** talks about the film and takes questions from callers.

1184 March 1985
Live at Five (TV news-talk show: WNBC, New York). Sue Simmons talks to **Michael Palin** about *A Private Function*.

1185 March 1985
Starlog (Magazine/U.S.). "Hello, *Brazil*," by Kim "Howard" Johnson, pp. 54–56. Article on **Terry Gilliam**'s latest film.

1186 March 1, 1985
A Private Function premieres in the U.S. at the Paris Theater in New York.

1187 March 5, 1985
The British Academy Film Awards (Award ceremony). *A Private Function*, starring **Michael Palin**, wins three BAFTA awards: for Best Actress (Maggie Smith), Best Supporting Actor (Denholm Elliott), and Best Supporting Actress (Liz Smith).

1188 March 8, 1985
6 O'Clock Show (TV news magazine: ITV/LWT). **Graham Chapman**, with co-host Andy Price, draws the winner of a free ski trip with the Dangerous Sports Club.

1189 March 14, 1985
A Private Function is the opening film of the Los Angeles International Film Exposition (Filmex).

1190 March 14, 1985
Pebble Mill at One (TV talk show: BBC1). Paul Coia talks to **Terry Gilliam** about *Brazil*.

1191 March 15, 1985
The Tube (TV show: Channel 4). Hosted by Paula Yates and Muriel Gray. Guests include **Terry Gilliam**, promoting *Brazil*, Jools Holland, Glynis Barber, and Tears for Fears.

1192 March 22, 1985
The Merv Griffin Show (TV talk show: Synd.). Guests: **Michael Palin**, promoting *A Private Function*, and Tony Danza.

1193 March 23, 1985
The Brain of Gilliam (Event). **Terry Gilliam** talks about his career and shows clips from his work at the Children's Cinema Club, ICA, London.

1194 March 24, 1985
Did You See...? (TV show: BBC2). Ludovic Kennedy hosts a discussion on the week in television with guests **Michael Palin**, David Lodge, and Dorothy Hobson.

1195 April 1985
Labyrinth, a Jim Henson–directed fantasy for which **Terry Jones** wrote the screenplay, begins filming.

1196 April 1985
Starlog (Magazine/U.S.). "Science Fiction, According to Monty Python, Part Two," by Kim "Howard" Johnson, pp. 43–46. Article on sci-fi in the Python films. Includes the words to "Galaxy Song."

1197 April 1, 1985
Michael Palin attends a screening of *A Private Function* at the Odeon Film Centre in Glasgow, Scotland. **Palin** talks to the audience after the screening and poses for photographers in a pen with two pigs outside the theater.

1198 April 5, 1985
Faerie Tale Theatre (TV episode: Showtime). "The Pied Piper of Hamelin." Cable-TV adaptation of Robert Browning's famous poem stars **Eric Idle** (who replaced original star David Bowie) as both the poet Browning and the medieval piper hired to rid Hamelin of its rats. But when the mayor of Hamelin refuses to pay him his fee, the mystical piper spirits the town's children away as well. **Idle** had written, directed and narrated the first *Faerie Tale Theatre* production, "The Tale of the Frog Prince," in 1982. Also starring Tony Van Bridge, Keram Malicki-Sanchez, Peter Blais, Peter Boretski. Written & directed by Nicholas Meyer. Produced by Bridget Terry and Fredric S. Fuchs. Executive produced by Shelley Duvall. Hour.

1199 April 18, 1985
The Tonight Show Starring Johnny Carson (TV talk show: NBC). Guests: **Michael Palin**, promoting *A Private Function*, and Mariette Hartley.

1200 April 26, 1985
Filming begins on parts three and four of the Video Arts training series *The Unorganised Manager* starring **John Cleese** (as St. Peter) and James Bolam. Parts one and two of the successful series were released in 1983.

1201 May 1985
WXRT-Chicago (TV commercials). The first in a series of six 30-second TV promos starring **Michael Palin** for the radio station WXRT (93 FM) begins airing in Chicago. In one ad **Palin** uses a record and a pizza to demonstrate the difference between WXRT and other rock stations.

1202 May 2, 1985
Are You Taking the Tablets? (TV talk show: Channel 4). "Thou Shall Not Take the Name of the Lord in Vain." Religious discussion program hosted by Phil Martin. Guest **Graham Chapman** discusses blasphemy and bad language. Half-hour.

1203 May 24, 1985
Book Plug (Radio talk show: BBC Radio 4). Sue MacGregor interviews Wing-Commander Muriel Volestrangler (aka **John Cleese**).

1204 June 2–August 1985
Clockwise, a comedy starring **John Cleese**, is filmed over eight weeks in the English towns of Hull, West Bromwich, Birmingham, Stourport, and Shrewsbury. Locations include Hull Paragon railway station and King Edward's School (in Birmingham). The film is budgeted at £4 million.

1205 July 1985
Starlog (Magazine/U.S.). "**John Cleese**: 'Why is *Starlog* Interviewing Me?,'" by Kim "Howard" Johnson, pp. 88–90. **Cleese** talks about his life and current projects.

1206 July 11, 1985
The Listener (Magazine/U.K.). "A Return to Victorian Values?: Fings Ain't What They Used to Be," by **Terry Jones**, p. 11–12+. **Jones** gives his view on Victorian-age values.

1207 July 14, 1985
Options (Radio show: BBC Radio 4). **Terry Jones** hosts the "Victorian Values" segment. Half-hour.

1208 July 17, 1985
The president of Universal Studios, Sid Shein-

berg, informs **Terry Gilliam** that major re-editing of his film *Brazil* will need to be done before the film can be released in the U.S. The alterations Sheinberg has in mind include a more upbeat ending. **Gilliam** rejects the idea. The "Battle of *Brazil*" begins.

1209   July 19, 1985
Silverado (Feature film: Columbia Pictures) opens in the U.S. Sprawling western about four unlikely comrades who band together to fight injustice in the 1800s town of Silverado. **John Cleese** co-stars as Sheriff John Langston. Also starring Kevin Kline, Scott Glenn, Rosanna Arquette, Kevin Costner, Brian Dennehy, Danny Glover, Jeff Goldblum, and Linda Hunt. Written by Lawrence Kasdan and Mark Kasdan. Produced & directed by Lawrence Kasdan.

1210   July 26, 1985
National Lampoon's European Vacation (Feature film: Warner Bros.) opens in the U.S. Clark Griswald and family stumble through Europe in this sequel to the 1983 hit *Vacation*. **Eric Idle** makes a guest appearance as a very polite British cyclist. Starring Chevy Chase, Beverly D'Angelo, Dana Hill, and Jason Lively. Written by John Hughes and Robert Klane. Directed by Amy Heckerling. Produced by Matty Simmons.

1211   August 1985
Cineaste (Magazine/U.S.). "Monty Python Strikes Again: An Interview with **Michael Palin**," by Lenny Rubenstein, pp. 6–9.

1212   August 16–17, 1985
Michael Palin visits Haugesund, Norway where he attends the Norwegian International Film Festival and presents at the festival's first Amanda Awards (for TV & film) ceremony.

1213   September 1985
Terry Gilliam screens his American cut of *Brazil* at the 11th annual American Film Festival in Deauville, France.

1214   September 3, 1985
The Pythons (minus **Idle**) and Carol Cleveland gather together at the BBC in London for a lunch/reception to promote the release of *Monty Python's Flying Circus* on video.

1215   September 13, 1985
Newsnight (TV news show: BBC2). Joan Bakewell reports on re-discovered Ealing Studios director Charles Crichton, currently working with **John Cleese** on Video Arts training films.

1216   October 1985
Nicobobinus (Book: Pavilion Books/Michael Joseph), written by **Terry Jones** with illustrations by Michael Foreman, is published in the U.K. **Jones**' third children's book (and third collaboration with Foreman), following *Fairy Tales* (1981) and *The Saga of Erik the Viking* (1983), is an adventure story concerning a boy named Nicobobinus who sets off with his friend Rosie on a journey to find the Land of the Dragons. Issued in paperback by Puffin Books (1987). Published in the U.S. by Peter Bedrick Books (1986).
Awards: Parents' Choice Silver Seal Award.
Reviews: Heather O'Donoghue (*The Times Literary Supplement* [London], Feb. 14, 1986, p. 174): "The illustrations are good and the narrative is funny, exciting and extraordinarily inventive"; Elizabeth Ward (*Washington Post Book World*): "...a fantasy tale of a high order"; *Parents* (1986): "...a first-rate adventure story — inspired, quirky, and filled with a cast of unforgettable characters"; Beverly Lyon Clark (*The New York Times Book Review*, Aug. 24, 1986, p. 21): "...an irreverent, parodic, often witty romp ... [the story] reads rather like a Monty Python script, minus the onstage gore."

1217   October 1985
Graham Chapman moves from his Highgate, London residence to a house in Maidstone in the county of Kent.

1218   October 2, 1985
Terry Gilliam places a full-page plea in *Daily Variety* to the president of Universal's parent company, MCA: "Dear Sid Sheinberg: When are you going to release my film, *Brazil*?"

1219   October 4, 1985
Did You See...? (TV show: BBC2). Ludovic Kennedy reviews the week in television with **Graham Chapman**, Shirley Cooklin, and Ken Russell. Directed by Philip Chilvers.

1220   October 5, 1985
Saturday Superstore (TV children's show: BBC1). Guests: **Michael Palin**, promoting his new book *Limericks*, Karin Foster, and Midge Ure.

1221   October 10, 1985
Breakfast Time (TV news-talk show: BBC1). Frank Bough and Debbie Greenwood talk to **Michael Palin** about his new book *Limericks*. The

book's illustrator, Tony Ross, also appears and draws while **Palin** reads from the book.

1222   October 10, 1985
Limericks (Book: Hutchinson Publishing), written by **Michael Palin** with illustrations by Tony Ross, is published in the U.K. A collection of original limericks for children. Reprinted by Red Fox in September 1986 and September 1998 (revised edition). Also released as an audiobook (Random House, 1998), read by **Palin**.

1223   October 11, 1985
Pebble Mill at One (TV talk show: BBC1). Bob Langley talks to **Michael Palin** about his new book *Limericks*.

1224   October 11, 1985
Calendar (TV news show: ITV/YTV–Yorkshire Television). Guest: **Michael Palin**, promoting *Limericks*.

1225   October 13, 1985
Sunday, Sunday (TV talk show: ITV/LWT). Hosted by Gloria Hunniford. Guests include **Michael Palin**, Michael Brandon, Cilla Black, Maureen Lipman, and Nigel Havers.

1226   October 18, 1985
Terry Gilliam appears at the Norris Theater at the University of Southern California with the intention of giving a speech to film students and presenting a screening of his American cut (2 hrs, 11 mins) of *Brazil*. Shortly before the event, however, Universal's Sid Sheinberg calls USC to inform them that the screening has not been authorized and that Universal owns the exclusive rights to exhibit and distribute the film in America. Later that night, **Gilliam** successfully screens the film at the California Institute of the Arts.

1227   October 20, 1985
Michael Palin takes part in "Improvisathon," a 12-hour marathon of improvised theater, presented by Actor Aid and performed at the Donmar Warehouse in London. Other performers include Jonathan Pryce, Robbie Coltrane, Hayley Mills, Ian Charleson, and Kenneth Branagh. The event raises funds for famine relief.

1228   October 21, 1985
The CBS Morning News (TV news-talk show: CBS). Maria Shriver talks to guests **Terry Gilliam** and actor Robert DeNiro about their film *Brazil*. When asked about the problem he's having with the studio, **Gilliam** responds that he only has a problem with one man — Sid Sheinberg (head of Universal) — and he holds an 8 × 10 glossy of Sheinberg up to the camera.

1229   October 30, 1985
Animation at Cambridge (TV special: Channel 4). **Terry Jones** presents the first of three selections from next week's Cambridge Animation Festival.

1230   November 11, 1985
Calendar (TV news show: ITV/YTV–Yorkshire Television). Guest: **Terry Jones**.

1231   November 15, 1985
Michael Palin participates in a 24-hour fast as part of Oxfam's second "Hunger for Change" campaign.

1232   November 20–23, 1985
Michael Palin performs his one-man show at the Arts Theatre in Belfast, N. Ireland as part of the Belfast Festival (Nov. 6–23). It is his third time performing at the festival since 1981.

1233   November 22, 1985
Children in Need (TV appeal: BBC1). Sean Rafferty interviews **Michael Palin** — who is in Belfast performing at the Belfast Festival — for this annual fundraising appeal.

1234   December 1985
Terry Jones attends a sex party hosted by Cynthia Payne at her house in Amble-side Avenue, Streatham in southwest London as part of his research for his next film, *Personal Services*.

1235   December 1985
ZigZag (Magazine/U.K.). "Just **Gilliam**," by Tom Vague, pp. 32–34. Interview with **Terry Gilliam** about Python and his latest film *Brazil*.

1236   December 3, 1985
A Party Political Broadcast: Social Democratic Party (TV: BBC1/ITV/BBC2). **John Cleese** appears in this party political broadcast (which he also wrote) on behalf of the Social Democratic Party, explaining the advantages of proportional representation. Although it is only 10 minutes long, **Cleese** spent 14 hours at Shepperton Studios recording it due to camera problems.

1237   December 5, 1985
Breakfast Time (TV news-talk show: BBC1). Frank Bough and Selina Scott talk to **John Cleese** about his SDP broadcast, his training films for Video Arts, *Fawlty Towers*, etc.

1238 December 6, 1985
Spies Like Us (Feature film: Warner Bros) opens in the U.S. Comedy about two bumbling government agents sent as decoys on a counter-espionage mission. **Terry Gilliam** makes a cameo appearance as a German doctor. Starring Chevy Chase, Dan Aykroyd, and Donna Dixon. Directed by John Landis. Produced by Brian Grazer and George Folsey, Jr.

1239 December 9, 1985
Wogan (TV talk show: BBC1). Hosted by Terry Wogan. Guests: **John Cleese**, Michael Quinn, Delia Smith, and Whitney Houston. **Cleese** talks about his role in *Silverado*, the success of *Fawlty Towers*, and his recent SDP broadcast.

1240 December 12, 1985
Breakfast Time (TV news-talk show: BBC1). Mike Smith talks to **Terry Jones** about Monty Python, the *Life of Brian* controversy, and writing books for children. Also, Debbie Greenwood talks to **Jones** and author Don Lusher about Frank Sinatra, who is celebrating his 70th birthday today.

1241 December 14, 1985
The Los Angeles Film Critics vote *Brazil* Best Picture of 1985, along with Best Director (**Terry Gilliam**) and Best Screenplay (**Gilliam**, Tom Stoppard, and Charles McKeown). After this, Universal releases **Gilliam**'s own re-edit of the film for one week in New York and Los Angeles to qualify for Oscar consideration. **Gilliam** travels around the country promoting it.

1242 December 16, 1985
Names and Games (TV game show: BBC2). Four teams of celebrities compete for charity. Participants include **Graham Chapman**, Suzi Quatro, and Toni Arthur. Hosted by Sandra Dickinson and Lennie Bennett.

1243 December 17, 1985
Film 85 (TV show: BBC1). Host Barry Norman reviews *Silverado* starring **John Cleese**. Also, Iain Johnstone interviews **Cleese** about the film.

1244 December 18, 1985
A week-long showing of *Brazil* in New York begins.

1245 December 20, 1985
Pebble Mill at One (TV talk show: BBC1). Bob Langley interviews **Michael Palin** about his book *Limericks*.

1246 December 25, 1985
A week-long showing of *Brazil* in Los Angeles begins.

1247 December 25, 1985
The Mind of David Berglas (TV special: Channel 4). Christmas special hosted by magician David Berglas. His special guests are **Graham Chapman**, Britt Ekland, Freddie Jones, and Stephanie Lawrence. Directed by Royston Mayoh.

1248 1985
The Unorganised Manager, Part 3: Lamentations (Training film: Video Arts). Third entry in a four-part series (parts 1 & 2 were released in 1983) on improving organization in management. Remade in 1997. Starring **John Cleese** (as St. Peter) and James Bolam. Written by Andrew Marshall and David Renwick. Directed by Charles Crichton.

1249 1985
The Unorganised Manager, Part 4: Revelations (Training film: Video Arts). Remade in 1997. Starring **John Cleese** (as St. Peter) and James Bolam. Written by Andrew Marshall and David Renwick. Directed by Charles Crichton.

1250 1985
Return on Investment (Training film: Video Arts). Film for managers on the principle of return investment. Part of the "Finance for Non-Financial Managers" series. Starring **John Cleese** (as Julian Carruthers) and John Bird. Written by Graeme Garden. Directed by Peter Robinson.

1251 1985
What Is Brazil? (TV special). Half-hour documentary on the making of **Terry Gilliam**'s *Brazil*, with behind-the-scenes footage and interviews with **Gilliam**, **Michael Palin**, Jonathan Pryce, Tom Stoppard, Katherine Helmond, Charles McKeown, Kim Greist, and others. Later included on the laserdisc/DVD release of the film. Written by Rob Hedden and Janice Miller. Produced & directed by Rob Hedden.

1252 1985
Graham Chapman begins re-writing — with David Sherlock — the film script for *Ditto*, which he and **John Cleese** wrote 15 years ago for director Carlo Ponti. The film is meant to be **Chapman**'s directorial debut, but the project is never realized.

1253 1985
Terry Jones writes a story outline for *Gremlins 2* (subtitled "The Forgotten Rule"), a proposed sequel to the 1984 horror-comedy directed by Joe Dante.

1254 1985
Graham Chapman joins the Dangerous Sports Club for their winter sports in St. Moritz, Switzerland. **Chapman** participates in one dangerous stunt: riding a 15-foot-long wooden gondola down a ski slope.

1255 January–February 1986
John Cleese goes on a two-week tour of the U.S. appearing before businessmen and personnel trainers to promote his training-film company Video Arts, which is opening an office in Chicago in an effort to expand the company's presence in the States. He hosts screenings of the films in New York, Boston, Chicago, Seattle, Los Angeles, and other cities.

1256 January 1986
Michael Palin is elected chairman of Transport 2000, a pressure group seeking to improve British transport. His work with the group leads to his involvement in the documentaries *Car Sick* (1994) and *The Road to Hell* (2001). **Palin**'s chairmanship ends on Nov. 21, 1987. He then becomes president of the organization in 1988.

1257 January 1986
Starlog (Magazine/U.S.). "Bye, Bye, *Brazil*?," by Kim "Howard" Johnson, pp. 46–47. Article on **Terry Gilliam**'s struggle to get the film released in the U.S.

1258 January 5, 1986
Michael Palin reads from his books, including *Small Harry* and *Limericks*, at the Purcell Room, South Bank, London. Part of the GLC's (Greater London Council) "10 Day Wonder" event (Dec. 27–Jan. 5) for children.

1259 January 12, 1986
The South Bank Show (TV arts show: ITV/LWT). "**John Cleese**." Host Melvyn Bragg offers an intimate portrait of the comic actor. Includes an in-depth interview with **Cleese**, who reflects on his humor and the characters he has portrayed, accompanied by clips from his films and TV series. A London Weekend Television production. Edited & presented by Melvyn Bragg. Produced & directed by David Hinton.

1260 January 20, 1986
What Have They Given Us? (TV commercial: BBC1). **John Cleese** plays a man in a pub grumbling about his TV license fee and asking "What has the BBC ever given us for 58 quid?" The 2½-minute ad, based on the "What Have the Romans Ever Done for Us?" scene in *Life of Brian*, features a large cast of BBC stars (Michael Hordern, David Attenborough, Alan Whicker, Ronnie Corbett & Ronnie Barker, Bob Geldof, etc.) answering **Cleese**'s question. First shown during an episode of *Wogan*. Written by **John Cleese**. Directed by Alan Parker (*Midnight Express*). Agency: Lowe Howard-Spink, London.

1261 January 24, 1986
Did You See...? (TV show: BBC2). Raymond Snoddy reports on the making of **John Cleese**'s *What Have They Given Us?* commercial for the BBC.

1262 January 25, 1986
Saturday Review (TV show: BBC2). Weekly arts magazine hosted by Russell Davies. **Terry Jones**, Diana Holman-Hunt, and Louise Page discuss the film *Dreamchild*.

1263 January 26, 1986
The Evening Standard British Film Awards (Award ceremony). **Michael Palin** receives the Peter Sellers Award for Comedy (for *A Private Function*) at the film award ceremony held at the Savoy Hotel in London. The award is presented by Joanna Lumley. *A Private Function* also wins for Best Screenplay (Alan Bennett and Malcolm Mowbray) and **Terry Gilliam**'s *Brazil* wins for Outstanding Technical Achievement (Norman Garwood). The Special Award goes to George Harrison's HandMade Films (*Life of Brian*, *A Private Function*, etc.). Barry Norman intros and Anna Ford hosts the event, which is broadcast on BBC1.

1264 January 27, 1986
Good Morning Britain (TV talk show: ITV/TV-am). Guest: **Michael Palin**.

1265 January 28, 1986
Late Night with David Letterman (TV talk show: NBC). Guest: **John Cleese**. The show is taped on the same day as the *Challenger* disaster.

1266 February 1986
The World of Interiors (Magazine/U.K.). "Biggles on the Home Front," by **Michael Palin**. **Palin** explores the room (in Park House, Hampton Court) where "Biggles" author Captain W. E. Johns (1893–1968) worked in his later years.

1267 February 1986
ZigZag (Magazine/U.K.). "**Terry Jones**," by Tom Vague, pp. 18–20. Interview with **Jones** about *The Meaning of Life*, writing children's books, Chaucer, etc.

1268 February 9, 1986
Philadelphia Enquirer (Newspaper/U.S.). "A Zany Guy Has a Serious Rave Movie," by Rick Lyman. Interview with **Terry Gilliam** about his fight to release *Brazil*.

1269 February 14, 1986
Brazil opens in the U.S. nationwide (Universal Pictures).

1270 March 1986
Photoplay (Magazine/U.K.). "Fawlty Goods," by N. Norman, pp. 4–6. Interview with **John Cleese**.

1271 March 3, 1986
The Times (London) (Newspaper/U.K.). "Struggling to Escape from a Familiarly Fawlty Image," by Paul Nathanson, p. 8. Interview with **John Cleese** about his new film *Clockwise* and other current projects.

1272 March 10, 1986
The Oregonian (Newspaper/U.S.). "Python on the Loose," by Jeff Kuechle, p. C1+. Interview with **John Cleese** conducted at the Alexis Hotel in Portland when he was in Oregon promoting Video Arts.

1273 March 12, 1986
The 1985 BAFTA Craft Awards (TV special: Channel 4). Highlights from the awards ceremony. Introduced by David Frost. Mark Shivas, Peter Barkworth, and **Terry Jones** discuss the works of the winners.

1274 March 14, 1986
Clockwise (Feature film: Universal Pictures) opens in the U.K. Comedy starring **John Cleese** as Brian Stimpson, an obsessively punctual middle-school headmaster who has been named chairman of the National Headmasters Conference, but whose trip to the conference to make a speech is marked by a series of disasters beginning when he accidentally boards the wrong train. Also starring Penelope Wilton, Sharon Maiden, and Stephen Moore. Written by Michael Frayn. Directed by Christopher Morahan. Produced by Michael Codron. A Thorn EMI Screen Entertainment/Moment Films production. Opens in the U.S. on Oct. 10.
Reviews: David Robinson (*The Times* [London], Mar. 14, 1986, p. 15): "It has a classic comic form, the escalation of misfortunes; but after a cheerful start the misfortunes become too numerous and too painful for laughter"; Clancy Sigal (*The Listener*, Mar. 20, 1986, p. 36): "Even in a not-so-brilliant film, with a surprisingly weak script by Michael Frayn, **John Cleese** is terrifyingly funny..."; Bruce Williamson (*Playboy*, November 1986): "Although stretched pretty far, *Clockwise* is downright hilarious at least half the time, which earns it better than passing grades"; Ira Hellman (*People Weekly*, Nov. 10, 1986, p. 10): "...a delightfully jaunty farce.... With **Cleese** in top form, *Clockwise* is 96 minutes and four seconds of fun."

1275 March 17–21, 1986
Jackanory (TV episodes: BBC1). "Charlie and the Chocolate Factory." **Michael Palin** reads the Roald Dahl story in five parts: 1. "Mr. Wonka's Mystery Workers" (Mar. 17); 2. "The Golden Tickets" (Mar. 18); 3. "Inside the Gates" (Mar. 19); 4. "Goodbye Veruca and Violet" (Mar. 20); and 5. "The Great Glass Lift" (Mar. 21). Recorded Mar. 3. Directed by Marilyn Fox. Produced by Angela Beeching. Note: **Palin** previously read his own story, *Small Harry and the Toothache Pills*, in an October 1984 episode.

1276 March 17, 1986
Wogan (TV talk show: BBC1). Hosted by Terry Wogan. Guests: **Michael Palin**, Sir Geraint Evans, Eugene Lambert, and Bronski Beat. **Palin** talks about Python, *A Private Function*, and the pressure group Transport 2000, of which he is now chairman.

1277 March 17, 1986
People Weekly (Magazine/U.S.). "With an Eye Out for Trouble, **Terry Gilliam** Does Battle Over *Brazil* and Wins an Oscar Nod," by Jeff Yarbrough, pp. 141–43. Article/interview on **Gilliam**'s life and struggle with Universal. Photographs by Terry Smith.

1278 March 18, 1986
Film 86 (TV show: BBC1). Host Barry Norman reviews *Clockwise* starring **John Cleese**.

1279 March 19, 1986
Pebble Mill at One (TV talk show: BBC1). Magnus Magnusson interviews **John Cleese** about his new film *Clockwise*.

1280 March 22, 1986
Aspel & Company (TV talk show: ITV). Hosted by Michael Aspel. Guests: **John Cleese**, Yoko Ono, and Boy George.

1281 March 24, 1986
Wogan (TV talk show: BBC1). Hosted by Terry Wogan. Guests: **Terry Gilliam**, Maria Aitken, and Paul Shane. **Gilliam** talks about *Brazil* being the only British film nominated for this year's Oscars.

1282 March 24, 1986
The 58th Annual Academy Awards (Award ceremony). **Terry Gilliam**'s *Brazil* is up for two Oscars, in the categories Best Original Screenplay (**Gilliam**, Tom Stoppard, and Charles McKeown) and Best Art Direction (Norman Garwood and Maggie Gray), but loses to *Witness* and *Out of Africa*, respectively. Broadcast live on ABC.

1283 March 26, 1986
A Party Political Broadcast: Social Democratic Party (TV: BBC1/ITV/BBC2). **John Cleese** introduces a party political broadcast on behalf of the Social Democratic Party. With Dr. David Owen and the animated character SD Pete.

1284 April 1986
Spin (Magazine/U.S.). "Kicking Ass," by Jack Mathews, pp. 97–98. Article on **Terry Gilliam**'s fight for *Brazil*'s release, with photos of **Gilliam** by Josh Cheuse.

1285 April 1, 1986
Man's Hour (Radio show: BBC Radio 4). **Terry Jones** hosts this April Fool's Day edition of *Woman's Hour*.

1286 April 4, 5 & 6, 1986
Comic Relief (Stage show), at the Shaftesbury Theatre, London. **Graham Chapman**, **Michael Palin**, **Terry Gilliam**, and **Terry Jones** are among the British comedians and musicians who come together on stage to support the work of Save the Children and Oxfam in the Sudan and Ethiopia. Sketches include "Biggles Goes to See Bruce Springsteen" (reading by **Palin**) and "Custard Pie" (**Chapman**, **Palin**, others). Also, Stephen Fry, Bob Geldof, and Midge Ure perform the Python sketch "Merchant Banker" (written by **Chapman** & **John Cleese**). Also starring The Young Ones, Ben Elton, Rowan Atkinson, French and Saunders, Billy Connolly, and Kate Bush. Directed by Rowan Atkinson. Airs as an *Omnibus* special on Apr. 25 (BBC1).

1287 April 7–May 1986
Personal Services, directed by **Terry Jones**, is filmed on location in London and Spain, and at Jacob Street Studios in London.

1288 April 19, 1986
Spike (TV special: Channel 4). Profile of comedian Spike Milligan (*The Goon Show*) with clips of his work. Milligan is interviewed, as are **Michael Palin**, Harry Secombe, Michael Foot, and Denis Norden. Hosted by Shelley Rohde. Directed by Mike Healey. Produced by Trish Kinane.

1289 April 22, 1986
Sound Waves for Greenpeace (Stage show). **Graham Chapman**, **Michael Palin**, and Neil Innes perform at one of a series of charity concerts (Apr. 21–25) at London's Royal Albert Hall. Other performers include Spike Milligan, Mike Oldfield, The Cure, Pamela Stephenson, and Andrew Sachs.

1290 April 23, 1986
Wogan (TV talk show: BBC1). Hosted by Kenneth Williams (sitting in for Terry Wogan). Guests: **Michael Palin**, promoting his book *Limericks*, Barbara Windsor, Steven Hollings, and Stephen Fry.

1291 April 25, 1986
Omnibus (TV special: BBC1). "Comic Relief." Taped record of the Apr. 4–6 benefit show at London's Shaftesbury Theatre, with **Graham Chapman**, **Michael Palin**, **Terry Gilliam**, **Terry Jones**, and many others. Directed by Geoff Posner and Philip Chilvers. Produced by Roger Graef.

1292 May–June 14, 1986
East of Ipswich, a TV film written by **Michael Palin**, is filmed in the seaside town of Southwold, England. The film will air Feb. 1, 1987, on BBC2.

1293 May 1986
Neighborhood Tales (Book: George Braziller), written by Norman Rosten, is published. Includes the chapter "Flash: **Michael Palin** Crosses the Brooklyn Bridge," in which Rosten, the poet laureate of Brooklyn, recounts a day he spent with his friend **Michael Palin**.

1294 May 1986
The Graduates (Book: Hamish Hamilton), edited by Edward Whitley, is published in the U.K. Collection of interviews with Oxford graduates, including Indira Gandhi, Iris Murdoch, Dudley Moore, and **Michael Palin**. The interview with **Palin** was conducted on Apr. 25, 1983.

1295 May 1986
Starlog (Magazine/U.S.). "**Terry Jones**: Creating the Wonders of *Labyrinth*," by Kim "Howard" Johnson, pp. 32–33+. Article on how **Jones** became involved in the Jim Henson film. Includes a photo of **Jones** surrounded by Goblins from the film.

1296 May 25, 1986
Sport Aid (Event). **Graham Chapman** participates in a "dangerous sport" for this Bob Geldof benefit event held in Hyde Park, London. He is put into a climbing harness and popped into the air "130 feet

or so, where I floated around for what seemed like an age," he remembers.

1297   May 30, 1986
The home of Cynthia Payne, the celebrated British madam upon whom **Terry Jones**' *Personal Services* is based, is raided a second time during a sex party on the night **Jones** is shooting the 1978 raid sequence for the film.

1298   Summer 1986
Michael Palin attends the exhibition "Dreams of a Summer Night" (July 10–Oct. 5), featuring work by Scandinavian artists, at the Hayward Gallery in London. It is here that **Palin** is introduced to the work of Danish painter Vilhelm Hammershøi. In 2005 **Palin** will explore the enigmatic painter's life and work in the documentary *Michael Palin and the Mystery of Hammershøi*.

1299   June 1986
Town and Country Planning (Magazine/U.K.). "Public Transport — Indignation, Despair and Hope," by **Michael Palin**, pp. 180–81. Humorous article on public transportation.

1300   June 21, 1986
A View from the Boundary (Radio sports show: BBC Radio 3). Brian Johnston talks to **John Cleese** about his career and interest in cricket (he's a Somerset supporter).

1301   June 27, 1986
Labyrinth (Feature film: TriStar Pictures) opens in the U.S. Fantasy from Muppet creator Jim Henson about a teenage girl whose baby brother is kidnapped by the King of the Goblins (played by David Bowie) and in order to rescue him she must navigate a devilish labyrinth. Also starring Jennifer Connelly and Toby Froud. Written by **Terry Jones** (and Elaine May). Designed by Brian Froud. Directed by Jim Henson. Produced by Eric Rattray. Executive produced by George Lucas.
Reviews: Ralph Novak (*People Weekly*, July 7, 1986, p. 10): "The writer — with uncredited help from Elaine May — is Monty Python alumnus **Terry Jones**, whose affection for the perverse removes any danger that this film will turn treacly"; Iain Johnstone (*The Sunday Times* [London], Dec. 7, 1986, p. 46): "...lacks the edge that might have given it a more classic status, and probably a wider following."

1302   July 31, 1986
Terry Jones speaks about Chaucer's Knight at the Chaucer Festival (July 24–Aug. 3) in Canterbury, England.

1303   August 8, 1986
The Transformers: The Movie (Feature film: De Laurentiis Entertainment) opens in the U.S. Animated feature starring the popular children's toy characters. **Eric Idle** voices Wreck Gar. Other voices by Orson Welles, Robert Stack, Leonard Nimoy, Judd Nelson, and Lionel Stander. Directed by Nelson Shin. Produced by Joe Bacal and Tom Griffin.

1304   September 27, 1986
The Mikado (Light opera) premieres at the London Coliseum. Jonathan Miller staged this innovative production of Gilbert & Sullivan's 1885 operetta for The English National Opera, shifting the operetta's setting from old Japan to a 1920s English seaside resort. **Eric Idle** makes his operatic debut as Ko-Ko, the Lord High Executioner. The production runs until November, then returns for another season in February–April 1987. Airs Dec. 30, 1987, on ITV. Also starring Bonaventura Bottone (as Nanki-Poo), Lesley Garrett (as Yum-Yum), Felicity Palmer (Katisha), Richard Angas (The Mikado), Richard Van Allan (Pooh-Bah), Mark Richardson (Pish-Tush), Jean Rigby (Pitti-Sing), and Susan Bullock (Peep-Bo). Music by Arthur Sullivan. Words by W.S. Gilbert, with "Little List" rewritten by **Eric Idle**. Chorus & orchestra conducted by Peter Robinson. Produced & directed by Jonathan Miller.
Review: Hilary Finch (*The Times* [London], Sept. 29, 1986): "Jonathan Miller's new production of *The Mikado* ... has put the work back where it belongs: on its toes in the brightest footlights of musical theatre."

1305   October 1986
The Mirrorstone (Book: Jonathan Cape), written by **Michael Palin** and illustrated by Alan Lee, is published in the U.K. Children's story about an English schoolboy named Paul who is brought into another world by a wizard named Salaman and forced on a dangerous quest to retrieve the priceless Mirrorstone. The book, which was conceived and designed by Richard Seymour, contains seven holograms.
Reviews: Edward Sorel (*The New York Times Book Review*, Dec. 7, 1986, p. 77): "Mr. **Palin** has done a splendid job.... *The Mirrorstone* is an exciting, handsomely produced book"; Lachlan Mackinnon (*The Times Literary Supplement* [London], Dec. 26,

1986, p. 1458): "...magical fantasy ... gripping and imaginatively expansive. The book is quite good enough not to need its gimmick, seven holograms printed on to the page."

1306 October 1986

The Goblins of Labyrinth (Book: Pavilion [U.K.]; Owl Books [U.S.]), by Brian Froud and **Terry Jones**, is published. The myriad, malevolent Goblins that populate the film *Labyrinth* are brought to life through the imaginative drawings of conceptual designer Brian Froud. **Terry Jones**, co-author of the film's screenplay, provides the witty text for this collector's item. Reissued in April 1996 as *The Goblin Companion*. A deluxe 20th Anniversary Edition is published in 2006. Froud and **Jones** will collaborate again on *Lady Cottington's Pressed Fairy Book* (1994).

1307 October 1986

The Utterly Utterly Merry Comic Relief Christmas Book (Book: Fontana Press), edited by Douglas Adams and Peter Fincham, is published in the U.K. Comedy book for charity. Includes: "Biggles and the Groupies" by **Michael Palin** (with an introduction by George Harrison), "A Christmas Fairly Story" by **Terry Jones** and Douglas Adams, and "The Private Life of Genghis Khan" by Adams (adapted from a sketch by Adams and **Graham Chapman** for the 1976 TV special *Out of the Trees*).

1308 October 1986

Graham Chapman takes his comedy lecture on an 11-day tour of the U.S. and Canada. Venues include the Humanities Theatre at the University of Waterloo in Ontario (Oct. 19) and the Ingman Room at the University of Toledo Student Union in Toledo, OH (Oct. 28).

1309 October 6, 1986

Today (TV news-talk show: NBC). Guests: **John Cleese**, promoting *Clockwise*, Yoko Ono, and Dwight Gooden.

1310 October 7, 1986

Breakfast Time (TV news-talk show: BBC1). Penny Bustin interviews **Eric Idle** about his operatic debut in Jonathan Miller's production of *The Mikado*.

1311 October 7, 1986

The CBS Morning News (TV news-talk show: CBS). Guest: **John Cleese**, promoting *Clockwise*.

1312 October 7, 1986

Late Night with David Letterman (TV talk show: NBC). Guests: **John Cleese**, promoting *Clockwise*, and Dennis Miller.

1313 October 10, 1986

Clockwise, starring **John Cleese**, opens in the U.S (released by Universal Pictures). The film premiered in Britain in March.

1314 October 11 & 12, 1986

The album of Jonathan Miller's *The Mikado*, featuring **Eric Idle** as Ko-Ko, is recorded at Abbey Road EMI Studios, London.

1315 October 20, 1986

Time (Magazine/U.S.). "Monty Python in the Boardroom," by Janice Castro, p. 65. Article on **John Cleese**'s business-training films.

1316 November 1986

Cyril and the Dinner Party (Book: Pavilion), written by **Michael Palin** with illustrations by Caroline Holden, is published in the U.K. Children's book about a three-year-old with the power to turn people into other things. Written in October 1980.

1317 November 1986

Cyril and the House of Commons (Book: Pavilion), written by **Michael Palin** with illustrations by Caroline Holden, is published in the U.K. **Palin**'s second *Cyril* story. Written in the fall of 1985.

1318 November 1986

John Cleese is voted the funniest man in Britain in a poll conducted by BBC Radio One in England. Lenny Henry comes in second, followed by Michael Barrymore, Ben Elton and Rik Mayall.

1319 November 1986

Personal Services, a new film directed by **Terry Jones**, is withdrawn from the London Film Festival on the insistence of the defense lawyers for famed madam Cynthia Payne, who will go on trial again in January. They feel that the film, which is loosely based on Payne's life, could prejudice her case.

1320 November 1, 1986

That's Television Entertainment (TV special: BBC1). The BBC celebrates its 50th anniversary with this three-hour extravaganza featuring clips selected by guest stars **John Cleese**, **Terry Jones**, **Michael Palin**, David Frost, Ringo Starr, Les Dawson, Roger Moore, Cliff Richard, Ernie Wise, and many others. Produced by Colin Strong.

1321 November 6, 1986

Breakfast Time (TV news-talk show: BBC1). Debbie Greenwood interviews **Michael Palin**.

1322 November 19–24, 1986
Michael Palin and **Terry Gilliam** travel to Moscow for British Film Week with their films *Jabberwocky* and *Brazil*. They then go on to Leningrad, staying in the Soviet Union for five days.

1323 November 21, 1986
Boston Phoenix (Newspaper/U.S.). "The Life of Terry," by Owen Gleiberman. Interview with **Terry Gilliam** about *Brazil*.

1324 November 24, 1986
The Anti-Heroin Project: It's a Live-In World (Album: EMI AHP LP 12) is released in the U.K. Two-record various-artist compilation with proceeds going to the Phoenix House Charity. Includes the comedy song "Naughty Atom Bomb," performed by **John Cleese**, Bill Oddie, and Ringo Starr (written by Kenny Craddock & Colin Gibson). Recorded in August 1986.

1325 December 1986
The Illustrated London News (Magazine/U.K.). "Double Trouble," by George Perry, p. 11. Article on **Terry Jones**' latest film projects, *Labyrinth* and *Personal Services*.

1326 December 1986
Gabereau (Radio talk show: CBC Radio, in Canada). Hosted by Vicki Gabereau. Guest **Michael Palin**, promoting his book *The Mirrorstone*, also talks about his interest in history, eating mud in *Holy Grail*, dressing in drag, etc.

1327 December 1, 1986
The Prince and Princess of Wales attend the Royal Charity premiere of *Labyrinth*, written by **Terry Jones**, in England.

1328 December 2, 1986
Labyrinth opens in the U.K. The film premiered in the U.S. on June 27.

1329 December 3, 1986
Paramount Home Video begins releasing *Monty Python's Flying Circus* on video in the U.S. with three 60-minute volumes, each containing two shows linked thematically, not chronologically. Two more tapes, each priced at $24.95, will be released about every three months. The Pythons decided to sign with Paramount after Python representatives met with Timothy Clott, the company's head of home video. Clott, whose carefully packaged and advertised *Star Trek* videos had been very successful, says "They were encouraged, and they were happy with our marketing plans." All 45 episodes of the show will be released on 22 volumes between now and June 1991. The series was released by BBC Video in Britain in 1985.

1330 December 3, 1986
The First Monty Python's Flying Circus Videocassette (Videocassette: Paramount Home Video 12543). Contains: "The Buzz Aldrin Show" (Ep. 17, 1970) and "Face the Press" (Ep. 14, 1970).

1331 December 3, 1986
The Second (in Sequence, Not Quality) Monty Python's Flying Circus Videocassette (Videocassette: Paramount Home Video 12544). Contains: "The Money Programme" (Ep. 29, 1972) and "The Spanish Inquisition" (Ep. 15, 1970).

1332 December 3, 1986
The Third (but Still Drastically Important and Absolutely Necessary to Have) Monty Python's Flying Circus Videocassette (Videocassette: Paramount Home Video 12545). Contains: "The Attila the Hun Show" (Ep. 20, 1970) and "The All-England Summarize Proust Competition" (Ep. 31, 1972).

1333 December 3, 1986
Made in New York (TV talk show: WNYW-TV, New York). Guest: **Michael Palin**, promoting *Ripping Yarns* on video.

1334 December 3, 1986
Nightlife (TV talk show: Synd.). Hosted by David Brenner. Guest: **Michael Palin**, promoting *Ripping Yarns* on video.

1335 December 4, 1986
The Tonight Show Starring Johnny Carson (TV talk show: NBC). Guest-hosted by Jay Leno. Guests: Amy Irving, Eva Marie Saint, and **Michael Palin**, promoting *Ripping Yarns* on video.

1336 December 5, 1986
CBS/Fox Video, in connection with Britain's BBC Video line, releases all 12 episodes of *Fawlty Towers* and all 9 episodes of *Ripping Yarns* on video in the U.S. as part of the BBC's 50th anniversary celebration. Each videotape contains three episodes.

1337 December 5, 1986
The Late Show (TV talk show: Fox). Hosted by Joan Rivers. Guests: Tyne Daly, John Parr, and **Michael Palin**, promoting *Ripping Yarns* on video.

1338 December 6, 1986
Saturday Night Live (TV comedy show: NBC). Hosted by Chevy Chase, Steve Martin, and Martin Short, with **Eric Idle** appearing in one sketch,

"Halsey & Roarke, British Customs," in which he and Dana Carvey play British customs officers. Directed by Paul Miller. Produced by Lorne Michaels. Note: **Idle** hosted *SNL* four times (1976–79).

1339   December 7, 1986
David Frost on Sunday (TV show: ITV/TV-am). David Frost interviews Norman Tebbit and **Terry Jones**.

1340   December 7, 1986
Sunday, Sunday (TV talk show: ITV/LWT). Hosted by Gloria Hunniford. Guests: **John Cleese**, Tony Adams, Leslie Thomas, Roy Hudd, Pamela Stephenson, Melvyn Bragg, and Anthony Hopkins.

1341   December 7, 1986
Censorama: The Official Secrets Ball (Stage show). **Terry Gilliam** is among the stars appearing at this benefit — held at London's Piccadilly Theatre — for the Campaign for Press & Broadcasting Freedom and the Campaign for Freedom of Information.

1342   December 22, 1986
Late Night with David Letterman (TV talk show: NBC). Guests: **Michael Palin** and chef Julia Child. **Palin**, promoting *Ripping Yarns* on video, also talks about his trip to Russia. Recorded Dec. 3 in New York.

1343   December 23, 1986
Comedians Do It on Stage (TV special: Channel 4). Recording of the December 1984 charity concert *Stars on Sunday II: The Stage Show* organized by Dr. Rob Buckman. Starring Buckman, **Michael Palin**, **Terry Jones**, Dawn French, Jennifer Saunders, Griff Rhys Jones, Neil Innes, Chris Langham, Victoria Wood, Mel Smith, and others. The event benefits the Oncology Club Fund. Directed by David MacMahon. Produced by Paul Smith.

1344   1986
Telephone Behaviour: The Power and the Perils (Training film: Video Arts). Staff-training film illustrating the pitfalls of using the telephone. Starring **John Cleese**, Diane Fletcher, Miranda Richardson, Art Malik, and Patsy Rowlands. Written by Peter Spence. Directed by Peter Robinson.

1345   1986
Inside the Labyrinth (TV special). Hour-long documentary on the making of the fantasy film *Labyrinth*. Includes interviews with director Jim Henson, star David Bowie, designer Brian Froud, and writer **Terry Jones**. Airs in the U.K. on Jan. 2, 1987 (BBC1). Later included on the 1999 DVD release of the film. Directed by Des Saunders. Produced by Arthur Solomon and Anthony Goldsmith.

1346   Early 1987
The Pythons form Prominent Features, "an umbrella company for all our individual projects," says **Terry Jones**. The company's first projects include **Terry Gilliam**'s *The Adventures of Baron Munchausen*, **John Cleese**'s *A Fish Called Wanda*, **Terry Jones**' *Erik the Viking*, and **Michael Palin**'s *American Friends*. The company's headquarters is to be built in Camden Town, London. **Eric Idle** serves as chairman.

1347   January 23, 1987
Inner London Crown Court hears testimony at the trial of madam Cynthia Payne that **Terry Jones** had attended two sex parties hosted by Payne at her London home. He was there doing research for his yet-to-be-released film *Personal Services*. The court testimony is reported on the following day in the tabloid *The Sun* with the front-page headline: "TV Python Comic at Sex Orgies."

1348   January 25, 1987
The Evening Standard British Film Awards (Award ceremony). At the annual awards show, held at the Savoy Hotel in London, **John Cleese** receives the Peter Sellers Award for Comedy for his role in *Clockwise*. Unable to appear in person, **Cleese** accepts the award in a humorous video message. Shown on BBC1. Note: **Michael Palin** won the Peter Sellers Award last year for his role in *A Private Function*.

1349   January 28, 1987
Wogan (TV talk show: BBC1). Hosted by Terry Wogan. Guests: Donald Soper, Jeffrey Archer, and **Michael Palin**, promoting *East of Ipswich*.

1350   January 30, 1987
Breakfast Time (TV news-talk show: BBC1). Jeremy Paxman talks to **Michael Palin** about his TV film *East of Ipswich*.

1351   January 31, 1987
The Times (London) (Newspaper/U.K.). "Bright and Beached Memoirs," by Peter Waymark, p. 16. **Michael Palin** talks about the TV film *East of Ipswich*, which he wrote.

1352   February–April 1987
Jonathan Miller's hit production of *The Mikado* for The English National Opera stages thirteen shows for another season at the London Coliseum. The production, starring **Eric Idle** as Ko-Ko, pre-

miered in September 1986. In addition to **Idle**, the cast includes Bonaventura Bottone (Nanki-Poo), Susan Bullock (Yum-Yum), Ann Howard (Katisha), Richard Van Allan (Pooh-Bah), Eric Shilling (Pish-Tush), and Dennis Wicks (The Mikado).

1353 February 1, 1987
Screen Two (TV film: BBC2). "East of Ipswich." Comedy-drama, penned by **Michael Palin**, about a teenage boy's sexual awakening during a family vacation in seaside Norfolk in 1957. The film, based on **Palin**'s own childhood experience, was shot in Southwold in May–June 1986 (it was in Southwold in 1959 that **Palin** first met his future wife, Helen). Starring Edward Rawle-Hicks, John Nettleton, Pat Heywood, Oona Kirsch, Pippa Hinchley, John Wagland, Joan Sanderson, Allan Cuthbertson, and Graham Crowden. Written by **Michael Palin**. Directed by Tristram Powell. Produced by Innes Lloyd.
Awards: BAFTA-nominated for Best Single Drama; 1988 ACE Award winner for Writing for a Movie or Miniseries.
Review: Sally Payne (*The Sunday Times* [London], Feb. 1, 1987, p. 56): "**Michael Palin**'s brilliantly observed script breathes new and exquisitely English life into the vastly over-subscribed field of teenage 'love,' circa 1957."

1354 February 3, 1987
The Variety Club Awards for 1986 (Award ceremony). **John Cleese** receives the Film Actor of the Year award (accepting on film, in his office) at the 35th Annual Show Business Awards presented by the Variety Club of Great Britain and held at London's Hilton Hotel. Hosted by Terry Wogan and Ray Moore. Broadcast on BBC1.

1355 February 16, 1987
Cross Wits (TV game show: ITV). The celebrity guests are **Graham Chapman** and Adrienne Posta. Hosted by Barry Cryer.

1356 February 18, 1987
Woman's Hour (Radio show: BBC Radio 4). Host Sue MacGregor talks to **Terry Gilliam**.

1357 February 20, 1987
Wogan (TV talk show: BBC1). Hosted by Terry Wogan. Guests: **Eric Idle**, talking about *The Mikado*, Jan Leeming, and Boy George.

1358 February 23–27, 1987
The TV drama *Troubles*, starring **Michael Palin** as Major Archer, films for five days before the production is cancelled (on Mar. 3) due to a strike. The film co-stars Rachel Kempson; the director is Charles Sturridge. Filming re-starts in October with Ian Charleson playing Archer.

1359 February 26, 1987
Breakfast Time (TV news-talk show: BBC1). Sally Magnusson talks to **Terry Gilliam** about the formation of the Pythons' new production company, Prominent Features.

1360 March 1987
The Mikado (Record: That's Entertainment TER 1121; CD: CDTER 1121). Studio recording of Jonathan Miller's hit production of the Gilbert & Sullivan operetta starring **Eric Idle**, made less than four weeks after the show's first night. Contains the entire first act, with considerable cuts made in the second act. Issued in the U.S. on MCA Classics MCAD-6215 (1987).

1361 March 1987
Terry Jones' new film, *Personal Services*, is banned in Ireland. **Jones**' two previous films, *Life of Brian* and *The Meaning of Life*, were also banned from Irish cinemas.

1362 March 1987
Video Review (Magazine/U.S.). "**Michael Palin** Spins His Yarn," by Maury Z. Levy, p. 76. Interview with **Michael Palin** about his humor and *Ripping Yarns*.

1363 March 5, 1987
Cheers (TV episode: NBC). "Simon Says." Diane persuades a noted marriage counselor to have a session with her and Sam, and then refuses to accept his prognosis for their impending marriage. **John Cleese** guest-stars as the marriage counselor, Dr. Simon Finch-Royce. Starring Ted Danson, Shelley Long, Kelsey Grammer, and Woody Harrelson. Directed by James Burrows. Produced by David Angell. Airs in the U.K. on June 19 (Channel 4).
Award: Emmy Award for Outstanding Guest Performer in a Comedy Series (**Cleese**).

1364 March 20, 1987
Nightlife (TV talks show: Synd.). Hosted by David Brenner. Guests: **Terry Jones** and Stacey Lattisaw. **Jones**, promoting *Personal Services*, also talks about muggings and ladies' underwear.

1365 March 26–29, 1987
The Secret Policeman's Third Ball (Stage show). British and American musicians and comedians perform for four evenings at the London Palladium in aid of Amnesty International. In one comedy bit, Stephen Fry and Hugh Laurie present **John**

Cleese with the "Silver Dick" life achievement award (named after Dick Emery) for his long service to comedy. Cleese's surprise appearance comes after initially declining to take part in the show due to prior commitments. Other performers include Joan Armatrading, Mark Knopfler, Chet Atkins, Jackson Browne, Kate Bush, Duran Duran, Spitting Image, and Peter Gabriel. Comedy stage direction by Paul Jackson. A film of the show is released theatrically in September.

1366 March 30, 1987
Wogan (TV talk show: BBC1). Hosted by Terry Wogan. Guests: **Terry Jones**, promoting *Personal Services*, Ian Botham, and Malcolm Turnbull.

1367 March 30, 1987
Graham Chapman is a guest VJ on MTV-Music Television.

1368 March 31, 1987
Personal Services, directed by **Terry Jones**, is screened at a Gala Preview in London. Those attending include **Jones, Michael Palin, Terry Gilliam**, and Cynthia Payne, upon whom the film is based.

1369 April–May 1987
Graham Chapman goes on a month-long, 33-date tour of colleges and clubs throughout the U.S. and Canada performing his comedy lecture, in which he shares stories, shows clips, and does some generally silly things (like tossing dead fish into the audience and inviting them to give him "one minute of abuse" before starting). Venues include The Ritz in Manhattan, NY (Apr. 9), The Comedy Corner in West Palm Beach, FL (Apr. 10), Ryerson Theatre in Toronto (Apr. 12), Comedy Factory Outlet in Philadelphia (Apr. 13 & 27), Park West in Chicago (Apr. 18), Syracuse University in NY (Apr. 28), and The Channel in Boston (Apr. 29).

1370 April 1987
Personal Services (Feature film: United International Pictures), opens in the U.K. Provocative comedy-drama — based loosely on the life of celebrated English madam, Cynthia Payne — pokes fun at society's hypocritical attitude toward sex with its story of a working-class-girl-turned-madam who runs a "kinks and costume" brothel. **Terry Jones'** first non–Python directorial effort. Starring Julie Walters, Alec McCowen, Shirley Stelfox, Danny Schiller, and Victoria Hardcastle. Written by David Leland. Directed by **Terry Jones**. Produced by Tim Bevan. Opens in the U.S. on May 15.

Award: BAFTA-nominated for Best Actress (Walters) and Screenplay (Leland).
Reviews: Janet Maslin (*The New York Times*, May 15, 1987): "Mr. **Jones** has a keen eye for the ludicrousness of certain situations, and keeps the film fast and funny when he sticks to specifics"; Mike McGrady (*Newsday*, May 15, 1987, p. 3): "...*Services* is rescued from total triviality by Julie Walters, playing the madam"; Johanna Steinmetz (*Chicago Tribune*, May 29, 1987, p. 8): "Director **Terry Jones** wrings more from this tale than most filmmakers get out of three times as much footage." David Denby (*New York*, June 1, 1987, pp. 95–96): "Some of *Personal Services* is rude, disorderly fun ... it has the gift of temperament and vividness."

1371 April 1987
Terry Jones begins writing columns for the *Young Guardian* (supplement of the British newspaper *The Guardian*). A collection of his columns will be published in the book *Attacks of Opinion* in November 1988.

1372 April 1, 1987
A Party Political Broadcast: Social Democratic Party (TV: BBC1/ITV/BBC2). **John Cleese** presents a party political broadcast on behalf of the Social Democratic Party.

1373 April 3, 1987
Breakfast Time (TV news-talk show: BBC1). Guy Michelmore reports on **Terry Jones'** new film *Personal Services*. Includes interviews with **Jones**, Julie Walters, and Cynthia Payne.

1374 April 3, 1987
Newsnight (TV news show: BBC2). Joan Bakewell reports on **Terry Jones'** new film *Personal Services*. Includes interviews with **Jones**, David Leland, Julie Walters, and Cynthia Payne.

1375 April 3, 1987
The Last Resort with Jonathan Ross (TV talk show: Channel 4). Guests: **Eric Idle**, Lulu, David Cassidy, and Fanny Cradock.

1376 April 5, 1987
Still Crazy Like a Fox (TV film: CBS). This made-for-TV film, an off-shoot of the 1984–86 detective series *Crazy Like a Fox*, finds Harry and Harrison Fox on a working holiday in London, where Harry is framed for the murder of the Duke of Trent. **Graham Chapman** plays Detective Inspector Palmer. Filmed in England. Also starring Jack Warden, John Rubinstein, James Faulkner, and Catherine Oxenberg. Directed by Paul Krasny.

1377 April 6, 1987
Financial Times (Newspaper/U.K.). "Something Completely Different," by Michael Skapinker, p. 16. Interview with **John Cleese** about his work with Video Arts and interest in psychology.

1378 April 10, 1987
The Last Resort with Jonathan Ross (TV talk show: Channel 4). Guests: Dawn French, Dr. Ruth Westheimer, and **Terry Gilliam**, who talks about his next film, *The Adventures of Baron Munchausen*, and his last film, *Brazil*.

1379 April 12, 1987
The Sunday Times (London) (Newspaper/U.K.). "Whipping Up a Poster Storm," by Mark Brennan, p. 51. A talk with **Terry Jones** about censorship, particularly on the trouble he had finding a *Personal Services* poster that the Society of Film Distributors would pass.

1380 April 16, 1987
Nightlife (TV talks show: Synd.). Hosted by David Brenner. Guest: **Graham Chapman**, talking about the Dangerous Sports Club, etc.

1381 April 19, 1987
The 1984 short film *The Dress*, starring **Michael Palin**, airs on Channel 4 in Britain.

1382 May 1, 1987
Personal Services: The Making of a Celebrity (TV special: BBC2). Joan Bakewell interviews former madam Cynthia Payne, upon whom the film *Personal Services* is based. The film's director, **Terry Jones**, is also interviewed.

1383 May 6, 1987
Graham Chapman and **Michael Palin** attend a memorial service for Tony Stratton-Smith, founder of Charisma Records (Monty Python's record label since 1971). The service takes place at St. Martin-in-the-Fields, London.

1384 May 12, 1987
West 57th Street (TV news show: CBS). **John Cleese** is interviewed by Steve Kroft about his life and work with business-training films. Includes a behind-the-scenes look at **Cleese** making a training film. Repeated on Aug. 8. Produced by Dan Chaykin.

1385 May 13, 1987
The Fourth (Eagerly Awaited, Impatiently Anticipated, Ardently Sought After, Raring-to-Go and Real Good) Monty Python's Flying Circus Videocassette (Videocassette: Paramount Home Video 12560). Contains: "How to Recognize Different Parts of the Body" (Ep. 22, 1970) and "Mr. and Mrs. Brian Norris' Ford Popular" (Ep. 28, 1972).

1386 May 13, 1987
Monty Python's Fifth (Symphony) Videocassette (Videocassette: Paramount 12561). Contains: "Spam" (Ep. 25, 1970) and "The War Against Pornography" (Ep. 32, 1972).

1387 May 15, 1987
The film *Personal Services*, directed by **Terry Jones**, opens in the U.S. (Vestron Pictures).

1388 May 29, 1987
Michael Palin's sister, Angela Herbert, takes her own life at the age of 52. She had been suffering from depression for years.

1389 Summer 1987
Graham Chapman films links for his upcoming Cinemax series *The Dangerous Film Club*. In the links **Chapman** plays an assortment of strange characters in a variety of locations, including New York's Central Park.

1390 June 15, 1987
The Grand Knockout Tournament (Event). **John Cleese** and **Michael Palin** participate in this feudal trash-sport competition for charity. The event, organized by Prince Edward, is held at Alton Towers amusement park in Staffordshire. The 48 cavorting celebrities that attended are divided up into four teams led by Princess Anne, The Duke and Duchess of York, and Prince Edward. **Cleese** plays on Prince Edward's yellow team and **Palin** on The Duke of York's green team. Other celebrities taking part include John Travolta, Meat Loaf, Cliff Richard, and Tom Jones. Airs in the U.K. on June 19 (BBC1) and the U.S. on Aug. 12 (USA-Cable).

1391 June 19, 1987
The Grand Knockout Tournament, with **John Cleese** and **Michael Palin**, airs in the U.K. on BBC1.

1392 June 19, 1987
The "Simon Says" episode of *Cheers*, guest-starring **John Cleese**, airs in the U.K. on Channel 4.

1393 July 1987
Graham Chapman performs his comedy lecture in another tour of the U.S. The lecture, which begins with 30 seconds of abuse from the audience, includes stories about Keith Moon and the Dangerous Sports Club, an update on his current projects, and clips from *Flying Circus*. Venues include

the Guthrie Theater in Minneapolis (July 20), University of Washington in Seattle (July 24), Masonic Temple in Portland, OR (July 25), Comedy & Magic Club in Hermosa Beach, CA (July 26–28), Laughs Unlimited in Sacramento, CA (July 30), and City Gardens in Trenton, NJ (July 31).

1394 July 1987
TV Lite (TV talk show: KCRA, Sacramento). Hosted by Jack Gallagher. Guest: **Graham Chapman**, who talks about his involvement with the Dangerous Sports Club.

1395 July 1987
The Battle of Brazil (The Real Story of Terry Gilliam's Victory Over Hollywood to Release His Landmark Film with Annotated Screenplay) (Book: Crown Books), written by Jack Mathews, is published. Well-documented account of the struggle between **Terry Gilliam** and Universal president Sid Sheinberg over the release of *Brazil*. Includes the film's script and a look at its making. Revised edition published in 1998 (Applause Books).

1396 July 1987
Spin (Magazine/U.S.). "Moving Images: It's...," by Glenn Rechler, pp. 71–73. Article on **Graham Chapman**'s life and recent lecture tour of the U.S.

1397 July 6, 1987
Wogan (TV talk show: BBC1). Hosted by Terry Wogan. Guests: Mike Yarwood, **Graham Chapman**, Dr. Clive Graymore and his wife Kay Graymore.

1398 July 13–September 1987
A Fish Called Wanda, a comedy written by and starring **John Cleese** with **Michael Palin** in a supporting role, is filmed (on a budget of $7.3 million from MGM) at Twickenham Studios and on location in London and Oxford. Locations include Hatton Garden, The Inns of Court, London Central Criminal Court, Oxbridge Town Hall, New Concordia Wharf, and a pet cemetery in Surrey.

1399 July 18, 1987
Just for Laughs (Comedy festival). **Graham Chapman** is among the headliners at the fifth annual *Just for Laughs* comedy festival (July 9–19) in Montreal. Chapman performs his comedy lecture, at the conclusion of which he tosses dead fish into the audience.

1400 July 20, 1987
Happy Holidays: The Golden Age of Railway Posters (Book: Pavilion), introduced by **Michael Palin**, is published in the U.K. Collection of posters from the Railway Age.

1401 August–December 1987
The comedy series *The Dangerous Film Club* airs on Cinemax. The show, hosted by **Graham Chapman**, is a monthly collection of unusual film clips, including home movies, animation, and newsreels. The series consists of five episodes.

1402 August 1987
The Dangerous Film Club (TV episode: Cinemax). The first show of the series includes "A Trip Through the Brooks' Home" and "Dog Baseball." Hosted by **Graham Chapman**. Directed by Paul Fuentes. Produced by Mary Frances Shea and Andrea Cvirko.

1403 August 1987
The Secret Policeman's Third Ball (Book: Sidgwick and Jackson), edited by Terence Blacker, is published in the U.K. Book of the March 1987 Amnesty show. Contains the show's script, including **John Cleese**'s bit accepting the "Silver Dick" award.

1404 August 1987
Q (Magazine/U.K.). "Goon Squad," by Andy Gill. Eight-page interview with the Pythons about the group's history and current solo projects.

1405 August 4, 1987
The Tonight Show Starring Johnny Carson (TV talk show: NBC). Guests: **Graham Chapman** and Midori. **Chapman** talks about the Dangerous Sports Club and shows footage of their winter sports event.

1406 August 10, 1987
Michael Palin and **Terry Jones** are among the celebrities giving public readings from the book *Spycatcher*, by Peter Wright, at Conway Hall, Red Lion Square, London. The book has been banned by the British government.

1407 August 12, 1987
The Grand Knockout Tournament, with **John Cleese** and **Michael Palin**, is shown in the U.S. on USA-Cable.

1408 August 18, 1987
John Cleese is among the celebrities attending Madonna's *Who's That Girl* concert at Wembley Stadium in London.

1409 September 1987
The Secret Policeman's Third Ball (Feature film:

Virgin Vision). Film version of the March 1987 Amnesty International benefit concert at the London Palladium. Performers include **John Cleese** (receiving the "Silver Dick" award), Stephen Fry, Hugh Laurie, Kate Bush, Chet Atkins, Mark Knopfler, and Peter Gabriel. Also, Ruby Wax conducts backstage interviews. Directed by Ken O'Neill. Produced by Neville Bolt and Tony Hollingsworth.

1410   September 1987
The Dangerous Film Club (TV episode: Cinemax). The second show includes "Snack of the Dead," "Sweet Sal," and "Hold the Mayo." Hosted by **Graham Chapman**. Directed by Paul Fuentes. Produced by Mary Frances Shea and Andrea Cvirko.

1411   September 1987
When We Were Young: Memories of Childhood (Book: Graham Tarrant/David and Charles) is published in the U.K. A collection of childhood reminiscences of sixty celebrities, including Barbara Cartland, Roald Dahl, Princess Margaret, Twiggy, Barry Took, and **Terry Jones**, whose contribution is one of his first school papers titled "My Family." All profits from the book are paid to the National Society for the Prevention of Cruelty to Children.

1412   September 1987
Rock 'n' Roll (Record: GWR). Album from the British rock band Motörhead, with **Michael Palin** making an uncredited appearance delivering a mock sermon ("Bless thou these people from Motörhead") at the end of side one.

1413   September 7, 1987
The BBC offers **Michael Palin** the opportunity of writing and presenting a documentary series that would have him follow the route Phileas Fogg took in Jules Verne's *Around the World in 80 Days*. If he accepts (and he does), he will be embarking on the journey a little more than a year from now. BBC executives pitch the project to **Palin** by telling him he was the best man for the job. **Palin** later learns that he was offered the job only after Alan Whicker, Clive James, Miles Kington, and Noel Edmonds turned it down.

1414   September 13, 1987
Graham Chapman and **Michael Palin** perform in a benefit show for the AIDS charity Frontliners at the Piccadilly Theatre in London. **Palin** performs "Biggles" and "The Martyrdom of Brian."

1415   September 16, 1987
Monty Python's Flying Circus: Volume Six and Violence (Videocassette: Paramount Home Video 12582). Contains: "Salad Days" (Ep. 33, 1972) and "How Not to Be Seen" (Ep. 24, 1970).

1416   September 16, 1987
Monty Python's Flying Circus: Volume 7 Pipe Dreams (Videocassette: Paramount Home Video 12583). Contains: "Live from the Grill-O-Mat" (Ep. 18, 1970) and "The Nude Organist" (Ep. 35, 1972).

1417   September 18, 1987
The Last Resort with Jonathan Ross (TV talk show: Channel 4). Guests: **Graham Chapman**, John Hurt, Sarah Miles, and Paul Young.

1418   September 20, 1987
The 39th Annual Emmy Awards (Award ceremony). **John Cleese** wins an Emmy Award for Outstanding Guest Performer in a Comedy Series for his performance on *Cheers* (Mar. 5). He is not there to accept the award. Broadcast live on Fox.

1419   September 21, 1987–March 1988
The Adventures of Baron Munchausen, directed by **Terry Gilliam** and co-starring **Eric Idle**, is filmed at Cinecitta Studios in Rome and on location in Almeria and Belchite, Spain, with miniature work done at London's Pinewood Studios. Originally budgeted at $23.5 million, the film will ultimately cost about $48 million. Problems during the troubled production include: the film crew speaking four different languages; African Horse Fever breaking out in Spain, preventing **Gilliam** from bringing four specially-trained horses into the country; David Puttnam (who greenlit the film) being replaced as head of Columbia Pictures; Film Finances Inc. forcing **Gilliam** to make major cuts in the script due to the spiraling budget; and Sean Connery walking off the film because of the cuts made to his Moon King sequence. One bonus for **Gilliam** is meeting with director Federico Fellini and working with Fellini veterans.

1420   October 1987
The Dangerous Film Club (TV episode: Cinemax). The third show includes "Spontaneous Combustion," "Doggie Doo Check," and "Horror Brunch." Hosted by **Graham Chapman**. Directed by Paul Fuentes. Produced by Andrea Cvirko.

1421   October 1, 1987
MTV-Music Television begins playing *Monty Python's Flying Circus*.

1422 October 27–November 1987

Graham Chapman performs his comedy lecture on a six-date tour of the U.S. Includes stops in Boston (Oct. 27) and Iowa City (Nov. 3).

1423 October 27, 1987

Graham Chapman appears as a guest VJ on MTV-Music Television.

1424 October 30, 1987

The Morning Program (TV news-talk show: CBS). Guest **Graham Chapman** talks with Mariette Hartley about Python, the Dangerous Sports Club, and the Comedy Crusade Against Diabetes.

1425 October 30, 1987

Celebrity Hour with Roger Rose (TV show: VH1). Guest: **Graham Chapman**.

1426 October 31, 1987

MTV Halloween Costume Party (TV special: MTV). **Graham Chapman** appears on this MTV special dressed in a mouse costume that has "Splunge?" written across the front.

1427 November 1987

Monty Python: The Final Rip Off (Record: Virgin MPD1; CD: CDMP1). Two-disc collection of Python's best bits, released by Virgin Records, who now own the rights to the group's material on record after purchasing Charisma Records in 1983. The album's design (by George Rowbottom) features a graphic image of spilling guts on the cover and the packaging contains a humorous Python history and many pictures. All of the songs have been remixed and **Michael Palin** provides some new links. Includes: "Introduction," "Constitutional Peasants," "Fish License," "Eric the Half-a-Bee," "Finland," "Travel Agent," "Are You Embarrassed Easily?," "Australian Table Wines," "Argument," "Henry Kissinger," "Parrot (Oh, Not Again)," "Sit on My Face," "Undertaker," "Novel Writing," "String," "Bells," "Traffic Lights," "Cocktail Bar," "Four Yorkshiremen," "Election Special," "Lumberjack Song," "I Like Chinese," "Spanish Inquisition Part 1," "Cheese Shop," "Cherry Orchard," "Architect Sketch," "Spanish Inquisition Part 2," "Spam," "Spanish Inquisition Part 3," "Comfy Chair," "Famous Person Quiz," "You Be the Actor," "Nudge, Nudge," "Cannibalism," "Spanish Inquisition Revisited (Knees Up, Mother Brown)," "I Bet You They Won't Play This Song on the Radio," "Bruces/Bruces' Philosophers Song," "Bookshop," "Do Wot John," "Rock Notes," "I'm So Worried," "Crocodile," "French Taunter," "Marilyn Monroe," "Swamp Castle," "French Taunter Part 2," and "Last Word." Produced by Andre Jacquemin. Remixed at Redwood Studios.

1428 November 1987

The Dangerous Film Club (TV episode: Cinemax). The fourth show includes "Brides," "Croutons and You," and "Is We Is?" Hosted by **Graham Chapman**. Directed by Paul Fuentes. Produced by Andrea Cvirko.

1429 November 1987

John Cleese and his second wife, Barbara Trentham, separate. **Cleese** moves into an apartment five-minutes walking distance from their Holland Park home in London. The couple were married in February 1981.

1430 November 2, 1987

The First Annual Comedy Crusade Against Diabetes (Stage show). Comedy clubs across the U.S. join together to kick off National Diabetes Month with this "comedy crusade." Comedian Tom Parks, who has diabetes, heads the main event at the Warner Theater in Washington, D.C. Other performers include **Graham Chapman**, Kip Addotta, Franklyn Ajaye, and Nora Dunn. Ticket proceeds go to diabetes research.

1431 November 7–23, 1987

Filming on **Terry Gilliam**'s *The Adventures of Baron Munchausen* is halted for two weeks by the film's insurance company in an effort to keep the film from going further over budget. The shooting schedule is reorganized and **Gilliam** is forced to make major cuts in the script.

1432 November 26, 1987

Michael Palin performs his one-man show at the Arts Theatre in Belfast, N. Ireland as part of the 25th Belfast Festival (Nov. 10–28). It is his fourth time performing at the festival since November 1981.

1433 November 27–December 18, 1987

Assert Yourself (TV series: Channel 4). **John Cleese** participates in this four-part documentary series on assertiveness training, based on a book by Anne Dickson. The program, presented by Andrew Sachs (Manuel in *Fawlty Towers*) with Dickson, also features Robin Skynner, **Cleese**'s former therapist and collaborator on the 1983 book *Families and How to Survive Them*. Directed by Julian Aston and Michael Rolfe. Produced by Maureen Harter.

1434 December 1987

The Importance of Mistakes (Lecture). **John Cleese**

lectures on the value of making mistakes (and learning from them) at the Training & Personnel '87 Conference in New York. Recorded and released as a training film by Video Arts.

1435   December 1987
The Dangerous Film Club (TV episode: Cinemax). The fifth and final show includes "The Homecoming Queen's Got a Gun" and "Pervasive Percussion." Hosted by **Graham Chapman**. Directed by Paul Fuentes. Produced by Andrea Cvirko.

1436   December 6, 1987
What on Earth Is Going On? (TV show: Channel 4). Monthly environmental series hosted by Paul Heiney. Includes *The Chairman*, a film illustrating the concerns of the pressure group Transport 2000, written by and starring the group's chairman, **Michael Palin**.

1437   December 11, 1987
Way Off Broadway (TV talk show: Lifetime). Hosted by Joy Behar. Guests: **Graham Chapman**, Steve Earle, and Dennis Wolfberg.

1438   December 12, 1987
The Times (London) (Newspaper/U.K.). "Funny How People Change," by Bryan Appleyard, p. 11. Interview with **John Cleese** conducted at his Holland Park (London) office and at the 15th birthday party of Video Arts at a West End hotel. The party is also attended by Prunella Scales and Stephen Fry.

1439   December 18, 1987
The Last Resort with Jonathan Ross (TV talk show: Channel 4). Guests: **Michael Palin**, Janet Street-Porter, and Midge Ure.

1440   December 20, 1987
Windmill (TV show: BBC2). "Journeys." Chris Serle presents a program on the theme of journeys and interviews his guest, **Michael Palin**, as they travel on the Docklands Light Railway (opened in August). Clips from the BBC archives feature **Palin** in *Flying Circus* ("The Cycling Tour"), *Three Men in a Boat*, *Great Railway Journeys of the World*, etc. Directed by Alison Hagger.

1441   December 29, 1987
A Source of Innocent Merriment (TV special: ITV/Thames). Documentary following the rehearsals for Jonathan Miller's production of *The Mikado* performed by the English National Opera and featuring **Eric Idle** as Ko-Ko. Produced & directed by John Michael Phillips.

1442   December 30, 1987
The Mikado (TV special: ITV/Thames). Jonathan Miller's 1986 production of Gilbert & Sullivan's operetta for The English National Opera is shown on television in Britain. It is the first sponsored program on the ITV network. Starring **Eric Idle** (as Ko-Ko), Lesley Garrett, Bonaventura Bottone, Felicity Palmer, Richard Van Allan, Richard Angas, Mark Richardson, and Ethna Robinson. Produced & directed for television by John Michael Phillips. Airs in the U.S. in October 1988 on *Great Performances* (PBS).

1443   1987
Can You Spare a Moment?: The Counselling Interview (Training film: Video Arts). How to deal with workers who have personal problems. Remade in 2001. Starring **John Cleese**, Prunella Scales, Art Malik, and Joanne Whalley-Kilmer. Written by **John Cleese** and Antony Jay. Directed by Charles Crichton.

1444   1987
The Importance of Mistakes (Training film: Video Arts). Live recording of **John Cleese**'s address at the Training & Personnel '87 Conference in New York (in December 1987). Written by & starring **John Cleese**.

1445   1987
Branchline Railway (Video: BBC Enterprises). Railway enthusiast **Michael Palin** introduces this video presentation of a 1963 BBC documentary written & narrated by Sir John Betjeman; also sequences from two BBC newsreels (1951/1960).

1446   January 1988
Sean Connery drops out of **Terry Gilliam**'s *The Adventures of Baron Munchausen* after major cuts are made to his part as King of the Moon. **Gilliam** was forced to make the cuts in November due to the film's soaring budget. Connery is replaced in the role by Robin Williams.

1447   January 3, 1988
An Audience with Peter Ustinov (TV special: Channel 4/LWT). Actor-raconteur Peter Ustinov entertains with humorous anecdotes and observations in this hour-long special. **John Cleese** is among the celebrities that comprise the audience. Directed by Alasdair MacMillan. Produced by Helen Fraser.

1448   January 24, 1988
The Evening Standard British Film Awards (Award ceremony). **Michael Palin** appears at the ceremony

held at the Savoy Hotel in London. Broadcast on Channel 4.

1449 January 28, 1988
40 Minutes (TV special: BBC2). "Scarfe's Follies." Political cartoonist Gerald Scarfe presents a tour of British follies (including a garden maze and mini-pyramid) built by eccentrics over the centuries. With Jane Asher (Scarfe's wife), Ian McKellen, **Terry Jones**, Bob Geldof, and others. Written & directed by Gerald Scarfe.

1450 February 1988
Business This Morning (TV series: Synd.). **John Cleese** appears regularly in a brief segment on this syndicated business show, which premieres this month. In each segment **Cleese** teaches business skills with his usual brand of humor.

1451 February 4, 1988
Michael Palin attends an Eric Clapton concert at the Royal Albert Hall in London.

1452 February 5, 1988
A Night of Comic Relief (TV special: BBC1). **Michael Palin** participates in this eight-hour, star-studded benefit show to raise money for famine relief in Ethiopia and Sudan. **Palin** plays his manager, Dino Vercotti, who explains to Jonathan Ross why his client is unable to appear on the show. Hosted by Lenny Henry and Griff Rhys Jones.

1453 February 12, 1988
Punch (Magazine/U.K.). "See You in Court," by **Michael Palin**, p. 35. **Palin** on Python's copyright infringement lawsuit against ABC-TV in 1975.

1454 March 7–11, 1988
Jackanory (TV episodes: BBC1). "Nicobobinus." Tony Robinson reads **Terry Jones'** 1985 children's story in five parts. Directed by Richard Kelly. Produced by Angela Beeching.

1455 March 14, 1988
The pilot for a new series called *Jake's Journey* begins shooting in England. The show, inspired by Mark Twain's *A Connecticut Yankee in King Arthur's Court*, is co-written and produced by **Graham Chapman**, who also stars as a curmudgeonly old knight named Sir George. Also starring Chris Young (as Jake) and Peter Cook (as King Arthur). **Chapman** co-wrote the pilot with his partner, David Sherlock. Hal Ashby directs.

1456 March 20, 1988
The British Academy Film Awards (Award ceremony). Monty Python is presented with The Michael Balcon Award for Outstanding British Contribution to Cinema at the BAFTA awards ceremony held at London's Grosvenor's House Hotel. Princess Anne, who is president of the British Academy, presents the award to **Graham Chapman**, **Terry Gilliam**, **Terry Jones**, and **Michael Palin**. Also that evening, **Palin's** film, *East of Ipswich*, loses in the Best Single Drama category. Hosted by Michael Aspel. Broadcast live on ITV.

1457 April 1988
Graham Chapman goes on another month-long tour of colleges and clubs throughout the U.S. performing his comedy lecture. Venues include Mac-Phie Pub, Tufts University in Medford, MA (Apr. 7), Grafton-Stovall Theater at James Madison University in Harrisonburg, VA (Apr. 13), O'Connell Center in Gainesville, FL (Apr. 14), Sayles Hall at Brown University in Providence, RI (Apr. 15), University of Maine at Orono (Apr. 16), Kansas University's Hoch Auditorium in Lawrence, KS (Apr. 18), Student Center Ballroom at Georgia Tech. University in Atlanta (Apr. 25), and Indiana University (Apr. 26).

1458 April 2, 1988
The Film Club (TV show: BBC2). **Michael Palin** introduces two films on the theme of life after death: *Heaven* (1986) and *A Matter of Life and Death* (1946).

1459 April 3, 1988
Terry Gilliam's son, Harry Thunder, is born. **Gilliam** also has two daughters, Amy and Holly.

1460 April 3, 1988
The Birth of "Brazil" (TV special: BBC2). Ian Holm narrates this 15-minute documentary on the making of **Terry Gilliam's** *Brazil*, which airs tomorrow on BBC2. Includes interviews with **Gilliam**, Charles McKeown, and George Perry. Produced by Nick Jones.

1461 April 6, 1988
Consuming Passions (Feature film: Samuel Goldwyn Co./Euston Films Ltd.) opens in New York. British black comedy—based on the 1973 television play *Secrets* by **Michael Palin** and **Terry Jones**—about a trio of Chumley Chocolate maintenance workers who are accidentally dumped into a vat of chocolate and end up in candy bars. Released in the U.K. in October. Starring Vanessa Redgrave, Jonathan Pryce, Tyler Butterworth, Freddie Jones, Sammi Davis, Prunella Scales, and

Thora Hird. Written by Paul D. Zimmerman and Andrew Davies. Directed by Giles Foster.

1462 April 8, 1988
Changing Transport (Lecture). **Michael Palin**, as president of Transport 2000, gives the Macmillan Education Lecture at the Annual Conference of the Geographical Association. In his lecture **Palin** discusses how transport in Britain has changed over the years and the prospects for future changes. The lecture is published in the October 1988 issue of the Association's journal *Geography*.

1463 April 10–May 22, 1988
The children's series *East of the Moon* airs on Channel 4. Each half-hour program contains two adaptations (one live-action, the other animated) of stories penned by **Terry Jones**, from his 1981 collection *Fairy Tales*. Neil Innes (*Rutland Weekend Television*) wrote the scripts and songs and also narrates. The seven-episode series is produced by Joy Whitby.

1464 April 10, 1988
East of the Moon (TV episode: Channel 4). "The Witch and the Rainbow Cat (live-action)/The Sea Tiger (animated)." First show in the series. Based on the children's stories by **Terry Jones**. Starring Neil Innes. Music & script by Neil Innes. Animation by Alison De Vere. Directed by Marc Evans.

1465 April 15, 1988
Michael Palin reads for a part in Frank Oz's new film *King of the Mountain* (later retitled *Dirty Rotten Scoundrels*), co-starring Steve Martin, in New York. The part later goes to Michael Caine.

1466 April 17, 1988
East of the Moon (TV episode: Channel 4). "The Big Noses (live-action)/The Ship of Bones (animated)." Based on the children's stories by **Terry Jones**. Music & script by Neil Innes. Animation by Alison De Vere.

1467 April 20, 1988
Monty Python's Flying Circus: Behind the (Volume) 8 Ball (Videocassette: Paramount Home Video 12600). Contains: "Royal Episode 13" (Ep. 26, 1970) and "E. Henry Thripshaw's Disease" (Ep. 36, 1972).

1468 April 20, 1988
Monty Python's Flying Circus: Silly Party and Other Favors Volume 9 (Videocassette: Paramount Home Video 12601). Contains: "It's a Living" (Ep. 19, 1970) and "Whicker's World" (Ep. 27, 1972).

1469 April 24, 1988
East of the Moon (TV episode: Channel 4). "The Boat That Went Nowhere (live-action)/Why Birds Sing in the Morning (animated)." Based on the children's stories by **Terry Jones**. Music & script by Neil Innes. Animation by Alison De Vere.

1470 May 1, 1988
East of the Moon (TV episode: Channel 4). "The Silly King (live-action)/The Corn Dolly (animated)." Based on the children's stories by **Terry Jones**. Starring **Terry Jones** (as King Herbert), Dafydd Hywel. Music & script by Neil Innes. Animation by Alison De Vere. Directed by Marc Evans.

1471 May 2, 1988
The New Yorker (Magazine/U.S.). "Height's Delight," by Penelope Gilliatt, pp. 41–42+. A lengthy, in-depth profile of **John Cleese**.

1472 May 4, 1988
Midweek (Radio talk show: BBC Radio 4). Hosted by Ronald Eyre. Guest: **Michael Palin**.

1473 May 8, 1988
East of the Moon (TV episode: Channel 4). "Jack One-Step (live-action)/The Wonderful Cake-Horse (animated)." Based on the children's stories by **Terry Jones**. Music & script by Neil Innes. Animation by Alison De Vere. Directed by Marc Evans.

1474 May 11–23, 1988
Michael Palin, **Terry Jones**, **Terry Gilliam**, and **Eric Idle** attend the Cannes Film Festival in France. Jones is able to find financing for his next film *Erik the Viking*; **Palin**, however, is not able to get the money for his film *American Friends*, the shooting of which has been postponed until next spring.

1475 May 15, 1988
East of the Moon (TV episode: Channel 4). "Faraway Castle (live-action)/Three Raindrops (animated)." Based on the children's stories by **Terry Jones**. Starring Hugh Thomas, Iona Banks, Jim Carter, and **Terry Jones** (as Second Elf in the "Quiet Talks" segment). Animation by Alison De Vere. Music, script & direction by Neil Innes.

1476 May 16, 1988
Forbes (Magazine/U.S.). "No More Mistakes and You're Through," pp. 126+. Excerpts from **John Cleese**'s "The Importance of Mistakes" speech made at the Training & Personnel '87 Conference in New York last year.

1477 May 17, 1988
The Second Annual American Comedy Awards (TV special: ABC). **John Cleese** appears briefly at the beginning of this live award show. Executive producer: George Schlatter.

1478 May 22, 1988
John Cleese delivers the keynote address at the American Society of Training and Development convention in Dallas, TX. A few months later a training film based on the speech, *Humour Is Not a Luxury*, is shot for Video Arts.

1479 May 22, 1988
East of the Moon (TV episode: Channel 4). "The Island of Purple Fruits (animated)/The Fly-By-Night (live-action)." Based on the children's stories by **Terry Jones**. Starring Sara Evans and Rowlant Thomas. Music & script by Neil Innes. Animation by Alison De Vere. Directed by Marc Evans.

1480 May 24, 1988
Film 88 Special (TV show: BBC1). Barry Norman reports from the Cannes Film Festival, where he interviews **Michael Palin**, **Terry Jones**, and **Eric Idle**.

1481 Summer 1988
A Fish Called Wanda (Book: Methuen), written by **John Cleese** and Charles Crichton, is published in the U.K. Screenplay of the film, with photos. Published in the U.S. by Applause Theatre & Cinema Books.

1482 June 6, 1988
Film 88 (TV show: BBC1). Barry Norman reports from London's Heathrow Airport on the making of the new comedy *A Fish Called Wanda*. Includes interviews with **John Cleese**, **Michael Palin**, others.

1483 June 11, 1988
Nelson Mandela: 70th Birthday Tribute (Concert), at Wembley Stadium in England. **Graham Chapman** and **Michael Palin** both speak at this music concert paying tribute to the anti-apartheid leader. **Palin** delivers his "Save the Plankton" speech. The 10-hour event is broadcast live on BBC2.

1484 July–September 1988
John Cleese (with daughter Cynthia) and **Michael Palin** tour the U.S. promoting *A Fish Called Wanda*.

1485 July 1988
Graham Chapman, with David Sherlock and other writers, begins writing more episodes of *Jake's Journey* for CBS, who have commissioned more episodes after initially shelving the show.

1486 July 1988
Larry King Live (TV talk show: CNN). Guest: **John Cleese**, promoting *Wanda*.

1487 July 1988
CBS News Nightwatch (TV talk show: CBS). **John Cleese** is interviewed. He talks about *Wanda*, his daughter Cynthia, film-making, acting, management-training films, and comedy.

1488 July 4, 1988
The Food Programme (Radio show: BBC Radio 4). Host Derek Cooper talks to **Terry Jones** on this special edition of the program focusing on whiskey, brandy, and beer.

1489 July 5, 1988
Late Night with David Letterman (TV talk show: NBC). Guests: **John Cleese** and Allan Havey. **Cleese** talks about British holidays, cricket, fish, and *Wanda*.

1490 July 7, 1988
A Fish Called Wanda has a special screening at the Bruno Walter Auditorium, Lincoln Center in New York City. Those attending include **John Cleese**, **Michael Palin**, Jamie Lee Curtis, Liza Minelli, Margot Kidder, Brooke Shields, Melanie Griffith, Rosanna Arquette, and Deborah Harry. All the stars have high praise for the film.

1491 July 7, 1988
The Big Picture (TV news show: MTV). Hosted by Chris Connelly. Guest: **John Cleese**, promoting *Wanda*, also talks about Beyond the Fringe and Python.

1492 July 8, 1988
Showbiz Today (TV news show: CNN). **Michael Palin** is interviewed about *Wanda* by Cheryl Washington, in New York.

1493 July 13, 1988
A Fish Called Wanda has a special benefit screening at the Academy Theatre in Beverly Hills, CA. Those attending include **John Cleese** with daughter Cynthia, **Michael Palin**, Jamie Lee Curtis with mother Janet Leigh, Michael Shamberg, Steve Abbott, Peter Cook, and Dudley Moore. After the screening, the stars attend a reception to raise money for the hearing-impaired.

1494 July 13, 1988
Entertainment Tonight (TV news show: NBC).

John Cleese, promoting *Wanda*, is interviewed at New York's Aquarium in Brooklyn by Ahmad Rashad.

1495 July 15, 1988

A Fish Called Wanda (Feature film: Metro-Goldwyn-Mayer) opens in New York. Black comedy written by **John Cleese**, who also stars as Archibald Leach, a reputable London barrister whose world is turned upside down when he becomes involved with three jewel thieves: Otto West (Kevin Kline), an American, Nietzsche-loving, psychopathic, ex-CIA operative; Wanda Gershowitz (Jamie Lee Curtis), a maneuvering femme fatale with whom Archie falls in love; and Ken Pile (**Michael Palin**), an animal-loving, small-time English hood with a terrible stutter and a pet fish also called Wanda. Also starring Maria Aitken, Tom Georgeson, Patricia Hayes, Geoffrey Palmer, and Cynthia Caylor. Written by **John Cleese**; story by **John Cleese** and Charles Crichton. Directed by Charles Crichton. Produced by Michael Shamberg. Executive produced by Steve Abbott and **John Cleese**. A Michael Shamberg/Prominent Features production. Note: Leach's daughter Portia is played by **Cleese**'s real-life daughter, 17-year-old Cynthia Caylor.

Awards: Academy Award winner for Best Actor (Kline), also nominated for Best Original Screenplay (**Cleese** and Crichton) and Best Director (Crichton); BAFTA winner for Best Actor in a Leading Role (**Cleese**) and Best Actor in a Supporting Role (**Palin**), also nominated for Best Film, Original Screenplay, Lead Actor (Kline), Lead Actress (Curtis), Supporting Actress (Aitken), Editing, and Direction; Golden Globe nominated for Best Motion Picture Comedy and Best Performance by an Actor (**Cleese**) and Actress (Curtis) in a Motion Picture Comedy; Evening Standard British Film Award for Best Film; Variety Club Show Business Award for Film Actor of 1988 (**Cleese**).

Reviews: Richard Schickel (*Time*, July 18, 1988, p. 73): "The movie blithely places live actors in situations usually the exclusive preserve of drawn figures.... *Wanda* defies gravity, in both senses of the word, and redefines a great comic tradition"; David Denby (*New York*, July 18, 1988, p. 44): "*Wanda* is completely uneven — uproarious in a few scenes, crude and inept in others ... a noisily assertive British-American hybrid.... At its core, *Wanda* is a transatlantic romantic comedy and a scruffy contrast in manners"; Peter Travers (*People Weekly*, July 18, 1988, p. 17): "**John Cleese** may be the funniest man on earth.... Putting heart and heat into a film that could have easily slid by on silliness, **Cleese** proves himself a master actor"; Terence Rafferty (*The New Yorker*, July 25, 1988, p. 78): "...**Cleese**, Curtis, and **Palin** are all fun to watch ... and Kevin Kline gives what must be one of the oddest comic performances ever"; David Robinson (*The Times* [London], Oct. 13, 1988, p. 22): "It is fast, and elegant even in its slapstick; and although a little too long, it is streets ahead of most comedies of recent decades"; George Perry (*The Sunday Times* [London], Oct. 16, 1988, p. C9): "Monty Python meets Ealing comedy, and in spite of the age difference they get on splendidly."

1496 July 17, 1988

The New York Times (Newspaper/U.S.). "*Wanda*: From Idea to Reality," by Benedict Nightingale, p. 23+. Article explaining how *A Fish Called Wanda* evolved. Includes "After the Circus," a rundown of what the individual Pythons have been up to.

1497 July 18, 1988

The Tonight Show Starring Johnny Carson (TV talk show: NBC). Guest-hosted by Jay Leno. Guest **John Cleese** talks about *Wanda* and jokingly puts down the other stars of the film.

1498 July 19, 1988

John Cleese, **Michael Palin**, Jamie Lee Curtis, and Kevin Kline, promoting *Wanda*, tape an hour-long appearance on *Phil Donahue*. **Palin** and Kline are in the studio in New York, while **Cleese** and Curtis appear via satellite from Los Angeles. The show airs Aug. 2.

1499 July 19, 1988

Late Night with David Letterman (TV talk show: NBC). Guests: **Michael Palin**, promoting *Wanda*, and Brian Setzer. **Palin** also talks about the vacations of his youth, his family, and Python's first U.S. appearance.

1500 July 20, 1988

John Cleese, **Michael Palin**, producer Michael Shamberg, and Cynthia Caylor (**Cleese**'s daughter) meet the Boston Press at the Omni Parker House Hotel in Boston, MA to talk about their film *A Fish Called Wanda*.

1501 July 21, 1988

CBS strengthens its defense against the writers' strike by announcing four new writer-proof television show commitments — including the half-hour **Graham Chapman** comedy *Jake's Journey* — to fill out its depleted fall prime-time schedule. A CBS release describes the show as a "comedy/

fantasy about an American teenager (Chris Young) in England with his family who discovers a parallel fantasy world and a cranky old knight named Sir George (**Chapman**)."

1502   July 21, 1988
Paul W. Smith and Company (Radio talk show: WMCA-AM, New York). Guest: **Michael Palin**, promoting *Wanda*.

1503   July 21, 1988
John Cleese is a guest DJ, with Elliott Forrest, on WNCN-FM, a classical music radio station in New York.

1504   July 24, 1988
Chicago Tribune (Newspaper/U.S.). "A *Wanda*ful Life," by Iain Blair, sec. 13, p. 8. **John Cleese** talks about his life and *Wanda*.

1505   July 26, 1988
Showbiz Today (TV news show: CNN). **John Cleese** is interviewed by Dennis Michael. He talks about *Wanda* and says there is little chance of another Python film.

1506   July 27, 1988
Crook and Chase (TV talk show: TNN-The Nashville Network). Kip Kerby interviews *Wanda* stars **John Cleese**, **Michael Palin**, and Jamie Lee Curtis together, in New York via satellite.

1507   July 28, 1988
Today (TV news-talk show: NBC). **John Cleese** is interviewed by Jane Pauley in New York. He talks about names, both his and those in *Wanda*.

1508   July 28, 1988
The Boston Globe: Calendar (Newspaper/U.S.). "A Proud Father of *A Fish Called Wanda*," by Betsy Sherman, p. 14. Taken from the July 20 Parker House interview with **John Cleese**, **Michael Palin**, Cynthia Caylor, and Michael Shamberg.

1509   July 29, 1988
A Fish Called Wanda opens in the U.S. nationwide.

1510   July 29, 1988
Good Morning America (TV news-talk show: ABC). **John Cleese** and **Michael Palin** are interviewed by Chantal. They talk about *Wanda*, **Palin**'s writing for children, and their view of Americans.

1511   July 29, 1988
Goldmine (Newspaper/U.S.). "The Rutles: It Was Ten and a Third Years Ago Today," by Jeff Tamarkin, pp. 14–16+. Lengthy article on the fictional story of The Rutles and the real story of **Eric Idle**'s Beatle parody. Includes a Rutles discography.

1512   July 31, 1988
The Washington Post (Newspaper/U.S.). "You're a Loony, **John Cleese**!; The Ex-Python on Wigs, *Wanda* and All Seriously Funny Things." **Cleese** is interviewed by Hal Hinson.

1513   August 1, 1988
The Wall Street Journal (Newspaper/U.S.). "Serious Talk About Humor in the Office," by **John Cleese**, p. 16. Article on the importance of humor in the workplace.

1514   August 2, 1988
Phil Donahue (TV talk show: NBC). Daytime program hosted by Phil Donahue. The cast of *A Fish Called Wanda* are the guests for the full hour. **Michael Palin** and Kevin Kline are in Donahue's New York studio, while **John Cleese** and Jamie Lee Curtis appear live via satellite from Los Angeles. They answer questions from the audience and clips from the film are shown. Taped July 19. Directed by Bryan Russo.

1515   August 3, 1988
Funny People (TV show: NBC). **John Cleese**'s life is profiled via clips and an interview. He then appears on stage with hosts Leeza Gibbons and Rita Rudner. Produced by George Schlatter.

1516   August 6, 1988
Hersey's Hollywood (TV show: WSBK-Boston). **John Cleese** and **Michael Palin**, acting as schoolboys, talk about their film *A Fish Called Wanda*. Hosted by Dana Hersey. Produced & directed by Bob Ecker.

1517   August 8, 1988
Newsweek (Magazine/U.S.). "Help, Help Me, Wanda," by Cathleen McGuigan, pp. 68–69. Article on **John Cleese**'s life, including his involvement with Monty Python, business-training films, and *A Fish Called Wanda*.

1518   August 15, 1988
People Weekly (Magazine/U.S.). "His Life May Be Fawlty, but **John Cleese** is Reeling in Cash and Kudos with *A Fish Called Wanda*," by Michael Alexander, pp. 62–64+. Article on **Cleese**'s personal life, his career, and success with *Wanda*.

1519   August 20, 1988
A Fish Called Wanda has its first British showing when it is screened as part of a Charles Crichton retrospective at the 42nd Edinburgh International

Film Festival (Aug. 14–Sept. 5) in Edinburgh, Scotland. The film opens in the U.K. on Oct. 14.

1520 August 23, 1988
Forth Fiesta (TV show: BBC2). Muriel Gray talks to **John Cleese** and Charles Crichton, star and director of *A Fish Called Wanda*, in a report from the Edinburgh Festival.

1521 Fall 1988
Sight & Sound (Magazine/U.K.). "The Mad Adventures of **Terry Gilliam**," by David Morgan, pp. 238–42. On-set interview with **Gilliam** during the making of *Baron Munchausen* in Rome in December 1987.

1522 September 1988
The Curse of the Vampire's Socks and Other Doggerel (Book: Pavilion Books), written by **Terry Jones** with illustrations by Michael Foreman, is published in the U.K. Illustrated collection of poetry for children, written in doggerel style. Poems (32 in all) include "The Revolt of the Clothes," "Frank Carew MacGraw," and "The Day the Animals Talked." Issued in paperback by Puffin Books (1990). Also released as an audiobook, read by **Jones**, in 2002 (Orion Audio Books).

1523 September 1988
PM Magazine (TV news show: Synd.). **John Cleese** is interviewed.

1524 September 1988
Life (Magazine/U.S.). "Snapshots: This Man is Not Fishing for Compliments," p. 7. Photo of **John Cleese** with a fish hanging out of his mouth (taken by Albert Watson), and a brief article.

1525 September 2, 1988
Crook and Chase (TV talk show: TNN-The Nashville Network). Reporter Jimmy Carter interviews **John Cleese** about *Wanda*.

1526 September 4, 1988
The Sunday Times (London) (Newspaper/U.K.). "The Wonder of Wanda," by Stephen Davis and Alex Sutherland, p. C7. Report on the success of *A Fish Called Wanda* in the U.S.

1527 September 6, 1988
Today (TV news-talk show: NBC). **John Cleese** is interviewed via satellite from Venice, Italy, where he is promoting *Wanda*. David Frost is the interviewer.

1528 September 7–14, 1988
Time Out (Magazine/U.K.). Interview with **John Cleese** by John Morrish, with cover photo ("How I Became a Sex Symbol").

1529 September 10, 1988
The Moving Image (TV special: BBC2). **Terry Gilliam** visits London's South Bank to preview The Museum of the Moving Image (MOMI), opening Sept. 15. Directed by Elizabeth Sussex.

1530 September 12, 1988–Early 1989
Erik the Viking, an adventure-comedy written and directed by **Terry Jones** and featuring **Jones** and **John Cleese**, is filmed at Shepperton Studios, England and on location in Malta (for four weeks).

1531 September 12, 1988
Wogan (TV talk show: BBC1). Hosted by Terry Wogan. Guests: Baroness Jane Ewart-Biggs, Olivia Newton-John, Robert Morley, and **Michael Palin**.

1532 September 23, 1988
George Harrison's HandMade Films (*Life of Brian*, *Time Bandits*, etc.) celebrates its ten-year anniversary with a dinner at the Old House, Shepperton Studios, England. **Michael Palin** is the master of ceremonies. Footage from the dinner is later featured in the documentary *The Movie Life of George*, which airs in January 1989.

1533 September 24, 1988
Aspel & Company (TV talk show: ITV). Hosted by Michael Aspel. Guests: Barry Norman, **Terry Jones**, and Julie Christie. **Jones** talks about the "Silly Olympics," *Erik the Viking*, his father, his wife Alison, and reads a poem ("Frank Carew MacGraw") from his book *The Curse of the Vampire's Socks*.

1534 September 25–December 12, 1988
Michael Palin travels around the world to find out if the route described in Jules Verne's 1873 novel *Around the World in 80 Days* can still be accomplished today. He will document the trip in a book and TV series for the BBC. The seven-part series will air Oct. 11–Nov. 22, 1989, on BBC1.

1535 September 26, 1988
Start the Week (Radio talk show: BBC Radio 4). Hosted by Melvyn Bragg. Guests: Norman Tebbit, Betty Carter, George Melly, and **Terry Jones**, promoting *The Curse of the Vampire's Socks*.

1536 September 27, 1988
Half Hour Comedy Hour (TV episode: MTV-Music Television). **Michael Palin** guest-hosts this show, which features new stand-up comics, and has

some "Undersea Adventures." Produced & directed by Bill Aiken and Eileen Katz.

1537 September 30, 1988
The Last Resort with Jonathan Ross (TV talk show: Channel 4). Guests include **Terry Jones** and Ilona Staller.

1538 October 1988
Traveling Wilburys: Volume One (Record: Wilbury/Warner Bros. 25796). First release from George Harrison's supergroup. The album's liner notes, providing the "history" of the group, are written by Hugh Jampton E. F. Norti-Bitz Reader in Applied Jacket, Faculty of Sleeve Notes, University of Krakatoa (East of Java) (aka **Michael Palin**).

1539 October 1988
John Cleese moves back into his Holland Park home (in London), which he moved out of last year when he and his wife, Barbara, separated. She is moving into a house nearby.

1540 October 1988
John Cleese gives $140,000 to Sussex University, England to finance a three-year study of a psychological phenomenon **Cleese** finds particularly interesting: projection and denial. **Cleese** hopes to write a book on the subject with Robin Skynner.

1541 October 8, 1988
Aspel & Company (TV talk show: ITV). Hosted by Michael Aspel. Guests: **John Cleese**, Norman Tebbit, and Julio Iglesias. **Cleese** talks about *Wanda*, the current state of health of the other Pythons, and his hair transplants.

1542 October 9, 1988
The Media Show (TV talk show: Channel 4). Presented by Muriel Gray. Includes an interview with **Terry Gilliam**, who talks about the use of *Brazil* scenes by British admen.

1543 October 10, 1988
Film 88 (TV show: BBC1). Hosted by Barry Norman. Includes a look at *A Fish Called Wanda* starring **John Cleese** and **Michael Palin**.

1544 October 12, 1988
Breakfast Time (TV news-talk show: BBC1). Gill Hornby interviews **John Cleese** about *Wanda*.

1545 October 14, 1988
A Fish Called Wanda opens in the U.K.

1546 October 16, 1988
The Sunday Times (London) (Newspaper/U.K.).

"Profile: **John Cleese**—Tormented Fawlty Finds an Analyst's Couch in Comedy," p. A15. "The *Wanda*-ful World of J Otto **Cleese**," by Iain Johnstone, p. C9. Article on **Cleese**'s life and comedy, with comments by **Terry Gilliam** and **Graham Chapman**, and a drawing of **Cleese**. The second article is about **Cleese** and *Wanda*, with a photo of **Cleese** and director Charles Crichton. Johnstone also directed the BBC1 profile *John Cleese's First Farewell Performance* airing Oct. 18.

1547 October 18, 1988
John Cleese's First Farewell Performance (TV special: BBC1). An in-depth profile of **John Cleese**, made during the filming of *A Fish Called Wanda*. The behind-the-scenes footage also features **Michael Palin** and other cast members. Later included as a bonus feature on the 2006 DVD release of the film. Directed by Iain Johnstone.

1548 October 23, 1988
Sunday Premiere (TV play: BBC1). "Number 27." **Michael Palin**'s second television play concerns a greedy young property developer whose heart is changed by a gentle 90-year-old lady he had planned to evict. A tragi-comedy about conflicting morals in modern Britain. Adapted for the stage in 1991, by Gillian Plowman, as *Crooked Wood*. Starring Nigel Planer, Joyce Carey, Helena Michell, and Alun Armstrong. Written by **Michael Palin**. Directed by Tristram Powell. Produced by Innes Lloyd. Note: Powell and Lloyd were also the director and producer of **Palin**'s first TV play, *East of Ipswich*, in 1987. Powell will go on to direct **Palin**'s 1991 feature film *American Friends*.

1549 October 28, 1988
Great Performances (TV episode: PBS). "The Mikado." This music, drama and dance showcase series' 16th season opens with The English National Opera's 1986 production of Gilbert & Sullivan's operetta. Starring **Eric Idle** as Ko-Ko, with Lesley Garrett and Bonaventura Bottone. Stage direction by Jonathan Miller. Produced & directed by John Michael Phillips. Series producer: David Horn.

1550 November 1988
Graham Chapman experiences pain in his throat following a dental checkup. An exploratory operation in December reveals a tumor on his tonsils. The beginning of his fight with cancer.

1551 November 1988
Playboy (Magazine/U.S.). "20 Questions: **John Cleese**," by Dick Lochte, pp. 128–30+. **Cleese** is

interviewed in a hotel suite in Southern California. Includes a photo of **Cleese** in a 150-pound suit made of 400 African cichlid fish, taken by Geof Kern.

1552   November 3, 1988
Attacks of Opinion (Book: Penguin), written by **Terry Jones** with illustrations by Gerald Scarfe, is published in the U.K. A collection of 29 editorial columns in which **Jones** gives his opinion on various issues of the day. The pieces were written between Apr. 8, 1987, and May 13, 1988, for the *Young Guardian* "Input" column.

1553   November 6, 1988
Michael Palin attends a cocktail reception at The 1997 club in Hong Kong celebrating the half-way point (actually day 43) in his *Around the World in 80 Days* journey.

1554   November 17, 1988
Rolling Stone (Magazine/U.S.). "**Graham Chapman**'s Journey," by Jim Yoakum, p. 47+. Article on **Chapman** and his TV series *Jake's Journey*.

1555   December 1988
Monty Python's Flying Circus: Blood, Devastation, Death, War, Horror and Other Humorous Events, Volume 10 (Videocassette: Paramount Home Video 12652). Contains: "Déjà Vu" (Ep. 16, 1970) and "Blood, Devastation, Death, War, and Horror" (Ep. 30, 1972).

1556   December 1988
Monty Python's Flying Circus: Dirty Vicars, Poofy Judges, and Oscar Wilde, Too!, Volume 11 (Videocassette: Paramount Home Video 12653). Contains: "Grandstand" (Ep. 39, 1973) and "Archaeology Today" (Ep. 21, 1970).

1557   December 1988
Monty Python's Flying Circus: Kamikaze Highlanders, Volume 12 (Videocassette: Paramount Home Video 12654). Contains: "Dennis Moore" (Ep. 37, 1973) and "A Book at Bedtime" (Ep. 38, 1973).

1558   December 1988
CBS decides not to produce **Graham Chapman**'s fantasy-sitcom *Jake's Journey* fearing the show's British humor wouldn't work with a mainstream American audience.

1559   December 8, 1988
The Adventures of Baron Munchausen (Feature film), world premiere in West Germany. **Terry Gilliam**'s big-budget fantasy about the 18th-century adventurer and teller of tall tales, Baron Karl Friedrich Hieronymus von Munchausen. In the film, the 80-year-old baron (John Neville), accompanied by young Sally Salt (Sarah Polley), rounds up the super-human companions of his youth to save a baroque European city under siege by the Turks. Their adventures include: a trip to the moon in a balloon made of ladies' knickers; a visit with the lusty war god Vulcan (Oliver Reed) in the heated bowels of Mount Etna; an aerial waltz with the love goddess Venus (Uma Thurman) in a waterfall ballroom; being swallowed by a giant sea monster; and an escape from a mechanized three-headed griffin. The film earns a disappointing $1.6 million in Germany, where distribution costs are put at $2.5 million. Also starring **Eric Idle** (as Berthold), Jonathan Pryce, Valentina Cortese, Robin Williams (uncredited), Winston Dennis, Jack Purvis, Charles McKeown, Bill Paterson, Peter Jeffrey, and Sting. Song: "The Torturer's Apprentice" by Michael Kamen and **Eric Idle**. Written by Charles McKeown and **Terry Gilliam**. Directed by **Terry Gilliam**. Produced by Thomas Schuhly. A Prominent Features & Laura-Film production. Opens in the U.S. on Mar. 10 and in Britain on Mar. 17.

Awards: Academy Award–nominated for Art Direction (Dante Ferretti & Francesca Lo Schiavo), Costume Design (Gabriella Pescucci), Visual Effects (Kent Houston & Richard Conway), and Make-Up (Maggie Weston & Fabrizio Sforza); BAFTA-winner for Production Design, Costume Design, and Make-Up, and BAFTA-nominated for Special Effects.

Reviews: Richard Corliss (*Time*, Mar. 13, 1989, p. 82): "Everything about *Munchausen* deserves exclamation points.... A lavish fairy tale for bright children of all ages. Proof that eccentric films can survive in today's off-the-rack Hollywood"; Jack Kroll (*Newsweek*, Mar. 13, 1989, p. 69): "*Munchausen* is flawed but fascinating, a Pythonesque fantasy with awesome special effects.... **Gilliam** is one of those rare directors who can create an entire world"; Scot Haller (*People Weekly*, Mar. 13, 1989, p. 15): "Its intellectual intent and the physical production seem disconnected, leaving a film that bedazzles the eye even as it bedevils the mind"; J. Hoberman (*The Village Voice*, Mar. 14, 1989, p. 57): "Droll and clamorous, **Terry Gilliam**'s latest epic suggests the overamplified confluence of Federico Fellini and Ronald Searle, a gibbering, capering merry-go-round, full of wacky wigs, funny accents, and throwaway grottiness"; Iain Johnstone (*The

Sunday Times [London], Mar. 19, 1989, p. C8): "This is a firework display of a film, constantly exploding with a vaulting visual imagination that few other directors could match — or producers afford to match"; Bruce Williamson (*Playboy*, April 1989, p. 22): "Wondrous is the word for *Munchausen*, a one-of-a-kind movie that slightly jaded children might recommend to incurable innocents of all ages."

1560   December 12, 1988

Michael Palin completes his trip *Around the World in 80 Days* arriving in London on the 79th day of his journey.

1561   December 25, 1988

The New York Times Magazine (Magazine/U.S.). "**Cleese** Up Close," by Bill Bryson, pp. 14–17+. Lengthy interview/profile of **John Cleese**, "the funniest man in Britain." Photographs of **Cleese** by Julio Donoso.

1562   Late December 1988

Graham Chapman undergoes an exploratory operation on his throat which reveals he has cancer of the tonsils.

1563   1988

Managing Problem People: Rulebound Reggie (Training film: Video Arts). **John Cleese** plays the inflexible, by-the-book title character in this first film of a six-part series designed to show managers how to improve the performance of problem people (the other titles are: "Moaning Minnie," "Big Mouth Billy," "Wimpy Wendy," "Silent Sam," and "Lazy Linda"). Also starring Stephen Fry, Geoffrey Palmer, Julian Holloway, and Christopher Asante. Written by Stephen Fry. Directed by Charles Crichton.

1564   1988

Managing Problem People: Moaning Minnie (Training film: Video Arts). A genie comes to the aid of a manager with a problem employee who delivers nothing but excuses. Starring **John Cleese** (as the Genie of the Lamp), Stephen Fry, and Emma Thompson. Written by Stephen Fry. Directed by Charles Crichton.

1565   1988

Managing Problem People: Big Mouth Billy (Training film: Video Arts). A manager is burdened with an employee who always promises but never delivers. Starring **John Cleese**, Stephen Fry, and Rik Mayall. Written by Stephen Fry. Directed by Charles Crichton.

1566   1988

Humour Is Not a Luxury (Training film: Video Arts). Film on the importance of humor in the workplace. Based on **John Cleese**'s May 1988 keynote address at the American Society of Training and Development convention in Dallas, TX. Written by and starring **John Cleese**. Directed by Peter Robinson.

1567   1988

All Change (The Management of Change), Part 1: Change for the Better (Training film: Video Arts). First of a two-part series starring **John Cleese** as H. G. Wells, who uses his time machine to show the bleak future for businesses that refuse to accept change. He then explains the three stages for successful change management. Also starring Simon Cadell, Geoffrey Palmer, and Carol Royle. Written by Graeme Garden. Directed by Robert Knights.

1568   1988

All Change (The Management of Change), Part 2: The Shape of Things to Come (Training film: Video Arts). H. G. Wells (**John Cleese**) shows three managers how to work with staff during a period of change. Also starring Simon Cadell, Geoffrey Palmer, and Carol Royle. Written by Graeme Garden. Directed by Robert Knights.

1569   1988

The Screwtape Letters (Audio book: Audio Literature [U.S.]; HarperCollins Audiobooks [U.K.]). **John Cleese** reads this three-hour, two-cassette version of C. S. Lewis' 1942 novel in which the devil Screwtape instructs his nephew Wormwood in the art of tempting souls. Part of the "Spiritual Classics on Cassette" series.

Awards: Grammy-nominated for Best Spoken Word Album.

1570   1988

The Complete Fawlty Towers (Book: Methuen), written by **John Cleese** and Connie Booth, is published in the U.K. The complete and unexpurgated scripts of all 12 episodes of the celebrated situation comedy. Includes eight pages of black-and-white photos from the show. Published in the U.S. by Pantheon (1989).

1571   1988

Can I Play with Madness (Music video). Video for the Iron Maiden single featuring a guest appearance by **Graham Chapman** as a strict schoolmaster. The song is from the heavy metal group's album *Seventh Son of a Seventh Son*. Included in the 1992 video compilation *Iron Maiden: From There to Eternity.*

1572 January 1989
Vogue (Magazine/U.S.). "Sharp **Cleese**," by Vicki Woods, p. 230+. A talk with **John Cleese** in Holland Park, London where he is photographed by Max Vadukul.

1573 January 1989
Universal Pictures releases their own edited version of **Terry Gilliam**'s nightmare fantasy *Brazil* on American television. The studio's 93-minute recut of **Gilliam**'s 131-minute version shortens the film by 38 minutes and changes the story, giving the film a happy ending.

1574 January 8, 1989
The Movie Life of George (TV special: ITV). Hour-long documentary on the history of George Harrison's production company, HandMade Films, which is celebrating its tenth anniversary this year. Includes footage from the September 1988 celebration dinner at Shepperton Studios, emceed by **Michael Palin**, as well as clips from *Life of Brian* (the film that launched the company), *Time Bandits, The Missionary, Mona Lisa,* and many others. Also includes interviews with Harrison, Denis O'Brien (Harrison's business partner), **Graham Chapman, John Cleese, Terry Gilliam, Eric Idle, Michael Palin,** Bob Hoskins, Michael Caine, and others. Produced & directed by Charles Brand.

1575 January 9, 1989
Today (TV news-talk show: NBC). A look at the making of *Erik the Viking* includes talks with director **Terry Jones** and **John Cleese**, who has a small part in the film.

1576 January 16, 1989
The English Programme (TV special: Channel 4). "Models of Writing: Argument and Persuasion." Writer-presenter **Terry Jones** discusses the columns he wrote for the *Young Guardian* which were collected in the book *Attacks of Opinion.* A Thames Television production. Directed by Adrian Brown and Greg Lanning.

1577 January 25, 1989
John Cleese wins libel damages from *The Daily Mirror* in an out-of-court settlement approved by the High Court. In August 1987, the newspaper quoted an unidentified "friend" as saying that **Cleese** had increasingly come to resemble his *Fawlty Towers* character, Basil Fawlty — a claim that **Cleese**'s lawyer, Roderick Dadak, calls absurd. In the settlement, **Cleese** receives undisclosed "substantial" damages from Robert Maxwell's Mirror Group Newspapers to be donated to a charity of his choice. The newspaper will also pay **Cleese**'s legal costs and publish an apology.

1578 January 28, 1989
The 46th Annual Golden Globe Awards (Award ceremony). **John Cleese** and Jamie Lee Curtis attend the Golden Globe Awards, presented by the Hollywood Foreign Press Association for excellence in motion pictures and television, at the Beverly Hilton Hotel in Los Angeles. Their film *A Fish Called Wanda,* nominated for Best Motion Picture Comedy, loses to *Working Girl;* **Cleese** and Curtis, nominated for Best Performance by an Actor and Actress in a Motion Picture Comedy, lose to Tom Hanks and Melanie Griffith. Broadcast live on TBS.

1579 January 29, 1989
The Evening Standard British Film Awards (Award ceremony). **John Cleese**'s *A Fish Called Wanda* receives the award for Best Film of 1988 at the annual award show held at the Savoy Hotel, London. Also, *Wanda* director Charles Crichton receives the Peter Sellers Award for Comedy. **Michael Palin** attends the ceremony, which is hosted by Michael York. Shown Jan. 30 on ITV.

1580 January 31, 1989
The Directors Guild of America announces this year's five nominees for its film directing award. Charles Crichton (*A Fish Called Wanda*) is one of them. He was nominated once before, in 1952, for *The Lavender Hill Mob.* The ceremony is held on Mar. 11.

1581 February 5, 1989
Link (TV show: ITV). Tim Newark discusses the treatment of handicaps in comedy with **Michael Palin**, who played a stutterer in *A Fish Called Wanda.*

1582 February 7, 1989
The Variety Club Awards for 1988 (Award ceremony). **John Cleese** (in a filmed acceptance) receives the Film Actor of the Year award (for *Wanda*) at the 37th Annual Show Business Awards presented by the Variety Club of Great Britain and held at the Hilton Hotel, London. Hosted by Terry Wogan. **Cleese** accepts the award by replaying his acceptance of the same award two years earlier (for 1986). Broadcast on BBC1.

1583 February 13–25, 1989
The Museum of Broadcasting in Manhattan, New York presents *Twenty Years of Monty Python*, a two-week retrospective of the British comedy group, who are celebrating their 20th anniversary this year. Part of the museum's New York World Television Festival (Jan. 17–Feb. 25).

1584 February 13, 1989
Twenty Years of Monty Python (Seminar). "A Monty Python Seminar." The Museum of Broadcasting's salute to Monty Python begins with a seminar with **Terry Gilliam**, **Eric Idle**, and **Terry Jones**, who screen highlights of their Python and pre–Python shows, and answer questions from the audience. Hosted by Andy Halper (curatorial director) and moderated by Robert M. Batscha (Museum president).

1585 February 13, 1989
Terry Gilliam, **Eric Idle**, and **Terry Jones** attend a party at New York's Hard Rock Cafe, kicking off the Museum of Broadcasting's ten-day salute to Monty Python. Other guests attending include Malcolm Forbes, Uma Thurman, Lauren Hutton, and Penny Marshall.

1586 February 14, 1989
Breakfast Time (TV news-talk show: BBC1). Includes a report on the Pythons' 20th-anniversary celebration at the Museum of Broadcasting in New York.

1587 February 14, 1989
Twenty Years of Monty Python (Screenings) continues. "Pre-Python." A compilation of the group's early work, including **Graham Chapman** with the Cambridge Circus (1964); a **John Cleese** sketch on *The Frost Report* (1966); a complete episode of the sketch-comedy series *At Last the 1948 Show* (1967) with **Cleese** and **Chapman**; and *Do Not Adjust Your Set* (1968) with **Michael Palin**, **Terry Jones**, and **Eric Idle**.

1588 February 14, 1989
The New York Times (Newspaper/U.S.). "Celebrating Two Mad Decades of Pythonmania," by Glenn Collins, p. C1. Article on the Python seminar at the Museum of Broadcasting.

1589 February 15 & 16, 1989
Twenty Years of Monty Python (Screenings) continues. "Python Highlights and Remembrances." A compilation of interviews with the Pythons, with highlights of their work sprinkled throughout. Screened in its entirety is the BBC documentary *The Pythons* from 1979.

1590 February 17 & 24, 1989
Twenty Years of Monty Python (Screenings) continues. "The German Monty Python." The American premiere of the two German-produced Python television specials, both titled *Monty Python's Fliegender Zirkus*. One special was made in English, the other in German.

1591 February 18, 1989
Twenty Years of Monty Python (Screenings) continues. "The Monty Python Marathon — Part One." The Museum of Broadcasting screens episodes 1–22 of *Monty Python's Flying Circus*, following the sequence in which the episodes were originally broadcast in Britain. Episodes 23–45 are screened the following Saturday (Feb. 25).

1592 February 21, 1989
Twenty Years of Monty Python (Screenings) continues. "More Pre-Python." More early work by the Pythons is presented, including film inserts by **Michael Palin** and **Terry Jones** for *Twice a Fortnight* (1967); sketches from the **Palin-Jones** series *The Complete and Utter History of Britain* (1969); another episode of *Do Not Adjust Your Set* (1968); and rare animation work by **Terry Gilliam**.

1593 February 22 & 23, 1989
Twenty Years of Monty Python (Screenings) continues. "Post-Python." A two-hour compilation of post–Python projects, including a complete episode of **Eric Idle**'s *Rutland Weekend Television*; **John Cleese**'s training film *Managing Problem People* (directed by Charles Crichton); the "Roger of the Raj" episode of the **Michael Palin-Terry Jones** series *Ripping Yarns* (1979); and assorted guest appearances on American television.

1594 February 23, 1989
A Fish Called Wanda (Videocassette: CBS/Fox Video). Video release of the 1988 comedy starring **John Cleese** and **Michael Palin**. The film is preceded by a commercial message for Schweppes (featuring **Cleese**). Released in the U.K. in August (MGM-UA).

1595 February 23, 1989
Schweppes (A Very Public Service Message from John Cleese) (Video commercial). **John Cleese** stars in a 96-second spot spoofing subliminal advertising. **Cleese** also co-wrote (with Helayne Spivak) and directed the ad, which precedes *A Fish Called*

Wanda on the videocassette of the film. Agency: Ammirati & Puris, New York.

Award: Winner of the Gold Lion at the Cannes International Advertising Film Festival.

1596   February 25, 1989
Twenty Years of Monty Python (Screenings) concludes. "The Monty Python Marathon — Part Two." The Museum of Broadcasting screens episodes 23–45 of *Monty Python's Flying Circus*.

1597   February 28, 1989
Late Night with David Letterman (TV talk show: NBC). Guests: **Terry Gilliam** and Shelley Long. **Gilliam** talks about his animation, Python, and *Baron Munchausen*.

1598   Spring 1989
Terry Gilliam announces that his next project will be directing a film adaptation of Alan Moore's graphic novel *Watchmen* for producer Joel Silver (*Die Hard*). **Gilliam** says, "There really is a climate now for these comic book properties." The film's original script, penned by Sam Hamm in 1988, is rewritten by **Gilliam** collaborator Charles McKeown, but the project later stalls due to a lack of funding. **Gilliam** ultimately concludes that Moore's story is too big and complex to be produced as a two-and-a-half hour film and leaves the project.

1599   Spring 1989
The Adventures of Baron Munchausen: The Screenplay (Book: Methuen [U.K.]; Applause Theatre Books [U.S.]), written by **Terry Gilliam** and Charles McKeown, is published. Screenplay, with photos. Includes material cut from the film.

1600   Spring 1989
The Adventures of Baron Munchausen (Book: Methuen/Mandarin [U.K.]; Applause Theatre Books [U.S.]), written by **Terry Gilliam** and Charles McKeown, is published. Novelization of the film.

1601   March 1989
The Adventures of Baron Munchausen is the number one film in France, which Columbia Tri-Star Film Distributors credit to the print and broadcast appearances by **Terry Gilliam** and Uma Thurman in Paris. **Gilliam** has also appeared in Belgium to promote the film.

1602   March 1989
American Film (Magazine/U.S.). "Earth to Gilliam," by Jack Mathews, pp. 34–39+. Article on **Terry Gilliam** and *Baron Munchausen*.

1603   March 4, 1989
Hersey's Hollywood (TV show: WSBK-Boston). **Terry Gilliam** is interviewed about *Baron Munchausen*, *Brazil*, and selling a movie idea to a studio. Hosted by Dana Hersey. Produced & directed by Bob Ecker.

1604   March 8, 1989
The Adventures of Baron Munchausen, directed by **Terry Gilliam**, premieres in the U.S. at the 32nd San Francisco International Film Festival.

1605   March 8, 1989
Terry Gilliam promotes *Baron Munchausen* on the TV entertainment programs *Showbiz Today* (CNN) and *Crook and Chase* (TNN).

1606   March 10, 1989
The Adventures of Baron Munchausen opens in the U.S. (released by Columbia Pictures).

1607   March 10, 1989
Good Morning America (TV news-talk show: ABC). **Terry Gilliam** is interviewed about *Baron Munchausen*.

1608   March 10, 1989
Weekend Live (TV news show: ITV/LWT). News/current affairs program. The theme this week is "Traffic." Mike Smith interviews **Michael Palin**, president of Transport 2000.

1609   March 11, 1989
The 41st Annual Directors Guild of America Awards (Award ceremony). *A Fish Called Wanda* stars **John Cleese** and Jamie Lee Curtis, and director Charles Crichton attend the ceremony held at the Beverly Hilton Hotel in Beverly Hills, CA. Crichton, nominated for Outstanding Directorial Achievement in Motion Pictures, loses to Barry Levinson (for *Rainman*).

1610   March 12, 1989
The Sunday Times (London) (Newspaper/U.K.). "Hail Munchausen," by George Perry, pp. 36–40. **Terry Gilliam** is interviewed for this report on his new film, *The Adventures of Baron Munchausen*.

1611   March 12, 1989
Entertainment Tonight (TV show: Synd.). Includes a look at *Baron Munchausen*, with **Terry Gilliam** and **Eric Idle**.

1612   March 12, 1989
The Other Side of Midnight (TV arts show: ITV/Granada). Hosted by Anthony Wilson. Guests in-

clude **Terry Gilliam**, promoting *Baron Munchausen*, and Anthony Burgess.

1613   March 13, 1989
The Times (London) (Newspaper/U.K.). "Money, Magic and Mischief," by Anne Billson, p. 20. Interview with **Terry Gilliam** about *Baron Munchausen*.

1614   March 13, 1989
Start the Week (Radio talk show: BBC Radio 4). Host Melvyn Bragg talks to **Terry Gilliam** about *Baron Munchausen*.

1615   March 13, 1989
Kaleidoscope (Radio talk show: BBC Radio 4). **Terry Gilliam** is interviewed about *Baron Munchausen*.

1616   March 13, 1989
Wogan (TV talk show: BBC1). Hosted by Terry Wogan. Guests: **Terry Gilliam**, promoting *Baron Munchausen*, and Bruce Forsyth & his daughter Julie Grant.

1617   March 13, 1989
Hot Air and Fantasy: The Adventures of Terry Gilliam (TV special: BBC1). Half-hour documentary on the making of *Baron Munchausen*. Includes interviews with **Terry Gilliam**, **Eric Idle**, John Neville, Charles McKeown, Sarah Polley, and others. Narrated by David Castell. Produced by David Castell and Colin Burrows.

1618   March 13, 1989
The New Yorker (Magazine/U.S.). "Python Scholars," pp. 28–29. Article on the marathon showing of *Monty Python's Flying Circus* episodes at the Museum of Broadcasting.

1619   March 14, 1989
John Cleese receives the 12th Annual Jack Benny Award for his comedy career. The award—whose past recipients include George Burns, Johnny Carson, Robin Williams, and Steve Martin—is presented to him by the University of California (UCLA) in Los Angeles. In his acceptance speech **Cleese** thanks everyone from Diana Ross and the Supremes to Wile E. Coyote.

1620   March 14, 1989
Open Air (TV show: BBC1). Eamonn Holmes interviews **Terry Gilliam** about *Baron Munchausen*.

1621   March 14, 1989
Film 89 (TV show: BBC1). Hosted by Barry Norman. Paul Freedman reports on the making of **Terry Gilliam**'s *Baron Munchausen*.

1622   March 16, 1989
01-for London (TV show: ITV/Thames). Magazine program. **Terry Gilliam** is interviewed about *Baron Munchausen*.

1623   March 17, 1989
Breakfast Time (TV news-talk show: BBC1). Gill Hornby interviews **Terry Gilliam** about *Baron Munchausen*.

1624   March 17, 1989
The Adventures of Baron Munchausen opens in the U.K.

1625   March 18, 1989
Going Live! (TV talk show: BBC1). **Eric Idle** is a guest on this Saturday-morning magazine show. Hosted by Phillip Schofield and Sarah Greene.

1626   March 19, 1989
Sunday, Sunday (TV talk show: ITV/LWT). Hosted by Gloria Hunniford. Guests include **Eric Idle**, Twiggy, and Leigh Lawson.

1627   March 19, 1989
The British Academy Film Awards (Award ceremony). **John Cleese** receives the Best Actor award for *A Fish Called Wanda*, which he accepts via satellite from Los Angeles. **Michael Palin** receives, in person, the Best Supporting Actor award. Also, *Wanda* director Charles Crichton receives The Michael Balcon Award for Outstanding British Contribution to Cinema. The ceremony is held at the Grosvenor House Hotel in London. Broadcast live on BBC1.

1628   March 29, 1989
The 61st Annual Academy Awards (Award ceremony). **John Cleese** attends the Academy Award gala at the Shrine Auditorium in Los Angeles where *A Fish Called Wanda* is up for three Oscars. **Cleese** and Charles Crichton lose the Best Original Screenplay award to Ronald Bass and Barry Morrow for *Rainman*, and Crichton loses the Best Director award to Barry Levinson (*Rainman*). But *Wanda* co-star Kevin Kline wins the Best Supporting Actor award, beating out Sir Alec Guinness and Martin Landau, among others. Kline thanks those who worked on *Wanda*, including **Cleese** and **Michael Palin**, and also Phoebe Cates, whom he recently married. The show is produced by Allan Carr and broadcast live on ABC.

1629   April 1989
Starlog (Magazine/U.S.). "**Terry Gilliam**'s Marvelous Travels and Campaigns," by Kim "Howard" Johnson, pp. 37–40+. Article on *Baron Mun-*

chausen, with many pictures. John Neville riding the cannonball is featured on the cover.

1630 April 1989
Spin (Magazine/U.S.). "The Edge: **Gilliam**'s Island," by Graham Fuller, pp. 84–85+. Article on **Terry Gilliam** and *Baron Munchausen*.

1631 April 1989
Premiere (Magazine/U.S.). "Bye, Bye *Brazil*," by Michael Shulan, pp. 98–102. Shulan's account of his visit to the set of **Terry Gilliam**'s *Baron Munchausen*, with many color photos.

1632 April 3, 1989
Us (Magazine/U.S.). "**Idle** Time," by Bridget Byrne, pp. 40–43. Article on **Eric Idle** and his current projects, with many color photos.

1633 April 6, 1989
Showbiz Today (TV news show: CNN). Dennis Michael interviews **Eric Idle** about his current projects.

1634 April 10–June 1989
Nuns on the Run, starring **Eric Idle** and Robbie Coltrane, is filmed in England at Lee Shepperton Studios in Surrey and on location in London and Hertfordshire, for HandMade Films on a budget of $7 million.

1635 April 10–May 1, 1989
Nearly Departed, a short-lived American sitcom starring **Eric Idle**, airs on NBC. **Idle** plays Grant Pritchard, a snobbish professor who, with his wife Claire, is killed in a rockslide and forced to share his home with its new residents, the ill-mannered Dooley family. Only four of the six episodes recorded are aired. Produced by Jack Seifert. Created and executive produced by John Baskin and Roger Shulman.

1636 April 10, 1989
Nearly Departed (TV episode: NBC). "Grant Meets Grandpa." In the series' opener, Grant and Claire are having a hard time adjusting to the afterlife but discover that they can communicate with the Dooleys' grandfather. First of four episodes. Starring **Eric Idle**, Caroline McWilliams, Stuart Pankin, Wendy Schaal, Jay Lambert, Henderson Forsythe, with guest-star Janet Dubois. Executive consultant: **Eric Idle**. Written by John Baskin and Roger Shulman. Directed by John Rich.

1637 April 13–15, 17, 1989
Entertainment Tonight (TV news show: synd.). **Eric Idle**, armed with a video camera, provides a series of reports from the set of *Around the World in 80 Days* during its filming in Macau, Hong Kong, and Thailand.

1638 April 16, 1989
Around the World in 80 Days (TV mini-series: NBC). Part One. A lavish, three-part TV adaptation of Jules Verne's 1873 novel about Phileas Fogg (Pierce Brosnan), a meticulous, enigmatic Englishman who goes on an around-the-world trek after a boastful wager. Accompanied by his resourceful French valet, Passepartout (**Eric Idle**), Fogg travels by hot-air balloon, steamship, train and elephant caravan, rescuing a beautiful Indian princess and being pursued by the relentless Detective Fixx, who is convinced that Fogg robbed the Bank of England to fund his journey. A colorful mini-series featuring cameos by 19 stars. Also starring Julia Nickson, Peter Ustinov, Roddy McDowall, Robert Morley, Lee Remick, and Arielle Dombasle. Directed by Buzz Kulik. Produced by Renee Valente.
Reviews: John Leonard (*New York*, Apr. 17, 1989, p. 75): "…[the film] usually enjoys itself, and so did I…. But what it should have been is a musical"; John Stark (*People Weekly*, Apr. 17, 1989, p. 13): "…this six-hour miniseries seems more like *Around the World in 80 Years* … overall, this *80 Days* presents a rather flat view of the world."

1639 April 16, 1989
Michael Palin attends a gala screening of the 1931 film *City Lights* at the Dominion Theatre in London. The screening, celebrating the 100th birthday of Charlie Chaplin, is also attended by Princess Diana.

1640 April 17, 1989
Nearly Departed (TV episode: NBC). "Adventures in Babysitting." Problems arise when Grandpa asks Grant to babysit Derek. Second of four episodes. Starring **Eric Idle**, Caroline McWilliams, Stuart Pankin, Wendy Schaal, Jay Lambert, Henderson Forsythe, with guest-stars Shonda Whipple, Randy Irwin, and Al Berry. Executive consultant: **Eric Idle**. Written by John Baskin and Roger Shulman. Directed by John Rich.

1641 April 17, 1989
Around the World in 80 Days (TV mini-series: NBC). Part Two. After doing battle with kidnapping bandits in Burma, Fogg and company go on a perilous sea voyage to Japan. Starring Pierce Brosnan, **Eric Idle**, Julia Nickson, and Peter Ustinov. Directed by Buzz Kulik. Produced by Renee Valente.

1642 April 18, 1989
Around the World in 80 Days (TV mini-series: NBC). Conclusion. Crossing the U.S., Fogg and company have close encounters with Jesse James and Indians. Starring Pierce Brosnan, **Eric Idle**, Julie Nickson, and Peter Ustinov. Directed by Buzz Kulick. Produced by Renee Valente.

1643 April 19, 1989
A Royal Gala in Aid of the Prince's Trust (Stage show). The annual benefit concert, featuring a mix of comedy and music, is held at London's Palladium in the presence of The Prince and Princess of Wales. Sean Connery serves as Master of Ceremonies. Performers include **Michael Palin**, Dame Edna (Barry Humphries), French and Saunders, Kiri Te Kanawa, Nigel Havers, Jools Holland, Jerry Hall, Steven Wright, and Rita Rudner. Broadcast in the U.S. (as *The Prince's Trust: A Rock and Royal Gala*) on July 12 (TBS) and in the U.K. on July 30 (ITV).

1644 April 24, 1989
Nearly Departed (TV episode: NBC). "Altared States." Claire discovers that Grant was still married to his first wife on their wedding day. Third of four episodes. Starring **Eric Idle**, Caroline McWilliams, Stuart Pankin, Wendy Schaal, Jay Lambert, Henderson Forsythe, with guest-stars Robert Rockwell, Brian L. Green, and Courtney Gebhart. Executive consultant: **Eric Idle**. Written by Sy Dukane and Denise Moss. Directed by John Rich.

1645 April 24, 1989
People Weekly (Magazine/U.S.). "Puzzling Out His Post-Python Life Leaves **Eric Idle** with Hands Full," by Susan Schindehette and Michael Alexander, p. 59–63. Article/interview on **Idle**'s life and current projects. Photographs by Terry Smith.

1646 May 1989
Cinefantastique (Magazine/U.S.). "*The Adventures of Baron Munchausen*," pp. 24–28+; "*Munchausen*: The Historical Facts," p. 29+; "*Munchausen*: Special Effects," pp. 32–33; "*Munchausen*: The Budget Debacle," p. 37+, by Alan Jones. Four articles covering every aspect of the **Terry Gilliam** film, with many photos throughout.

1647 May 1, 1989
Nearly Departed (TV episode: NBC). "TV or Not TV." When Derek is pushed around by the school bully, Grant and Claire decide to pay a visit to the junior high. Last of four episodes. Starring **Eric Idle**, Caroline McWilliams, Stuart Pankin, Wendy Schaal, Jay Lambert, Henderson Forsythe, with guest-stars Bobby Jacoby and Anita Dangler. Executive consultant: **Eric Idle**. Written by Neil Alan Levy. Directed by John Rich.

1648 May 5, 1989
Clive Anderson Talks Back (TV talk show: Channel 4). Guests: **Michael Palin** and Peter Bateman.

1649 May 25, 1989
The Big Picture (TV show: MTV-Music Television). Includes a behind-the-scenes look at *Nuns on the Run*, starring **Eric Idle**.

1650 June 1, 1989
John Cleese and his girlfriend, Alyce Faye Eichelberger, attend a dinner at 10 Downing Street, London, hosted by Prime Minister Margaret Thatcher and Mr. Denis Thatcher in honor of President (and Mrs.) George Bush.

1651 June 5, 1989
John Cleese attends the annual dinner of the Royal Academy of Arts at Burlington House, Piccadilly, London.

1652 June 14, 1989
Monty Python's Flying Circus: I'm a Lumberjack, Volume 13 (Videocassette: Paramount Home Video 12736). Contains: "The Ant, an Introduction" (Ep. 9, 1969) and "Whither Canada" (Ep. 1, 1969).

1653 June 14, 1989
Monty Python's Flying Circus: Chocolate Frogs, Baffled Cats and Other Tasty Treats, Volume 14 (Videocassette: Paramount Home Video 12737). Contains: "Man's Crisis of Identity in the Latter Half of the Twentieth Century" (Ep. 5, 1969) and "It's the Arts" (Ep. 6, 1969).

1654 June 14, 1989
Monty Python's Flying Circus: Dead Parrots Don't Talk and Other Fowl Plays, Volume 15 (Videocassette: Paramount Home Video 12738). Contains: "Full Frontal Nudity" (Ep. 8, 1969) and "You're No Fun Anymore" (Ep. 7, 1969).

1655 June 14, 1989
Monty Python's Flying Circus: A Man with Three Cheeks or Butt Naught for Me, Volume 16 (Videocassette: Paramount Home Video 12739). Contains: "Sex & Violence" (Ep. 2, 1969) and "The Royal Philharmonic Orchestra Goes to the Bathroom" (Ep. 11, 1969).

1656 June 14, 1989
Monty Python's Flying Circus: The Upper-Class

Twit Competition, Volume 17 (Videocassette: Paramount Home Video 12740). Contains: "Intermission" (Ep. 13, 1970) and "The Naked Ant" (Ep. 12, 1970).

1657   June 18, 1989
The Sunday Times (London) (Newspaper/U.K.). "Who's Reading Whom: **Michael Palin**," p. G2. **Palin** comments on the books he has been reading: Patrick Leigh Fermor's *A Time of Gifts* and John Updike's *Self-Consciousness*.

1658   July 1989
Terry Gilliam receives an honorary doctorate from the Royal College of Art.

1659   July 1989
Starlog (Magazine/U.S.). "Those Notorious Norsemen in Their Luxurious Long Ships," by Kim "Howard" Johnson, pp. 55–59. "Confessions of the World's Greatest Liar," by Lynne Stephens, pp. 73–75+. Articles on **Terry Jones**' *Erik the Viking* and actor John Neville of **Terry Gilliam**'s *Baron Munchausen*, with color photos from each film.

1660   July 12, 1989
The Prince's Trust: A Rock and Royal Gala (TV special: TBS Superstation). U.S. airing of the April 19 Prince's Trust gala hosted by Sean Connery and featuring **Michael Palin**, Jerry Hall, Steven Wright, Kiri Te Kanawa, Rita Rudner, and many others.

1661   July 27, 1989
The Birthday Show: 21 Years of Variety from Thames Television (TV special: ITV). Special celebrating Thames Television's 21st birthday (it debuted in July 1968), with appearances by **John Cleese**, Tommy Cooper, Ken Dodd, Benny Hill, Eric Sykes, and others. Hosted by Edward Woodward. Produced & directed by Philip Jones.

1662   July 30, 1989
A Royal Gala in Aid of the Prince's Trust (TV special: ITV/LWT). The Prince's Trust benefit concert recorded in April at London's Palladium. Hosted by Sean Connery, with **Michael Palin**, Dame Edna (Barry Humphries), Jerry Hall, Nigel Havers, and others. Directed by Alasdair MacMillan. Produced by Trevor Hopkins.

1663   August 1989
Terry Jones' *Erik the Viking*, delayed by post-production, is withdrawn from the 43rd Edinburgh International Film Festival opening Aug. 12.

1664   August 2–9, 1989
Time Out (Magazine/U.K.). Article on Monty Python's 20th anniversary. The cover features a dead parrot hanging upside down from its perch.

1665   August 30–September 2, 1989
The Secret Policeman's Biggest Ball (Stage show). British comedians and musicians perform at London's Cambridge Theatre for Amnesty International for the fourth *Ball* benefit in ten years, putting a greater emphasis on comedy this time around. Starring **John Cleese**, **Michael Palin**, Peter Cook, Dudley Moore, Lenny Henry, Robbie Coltrane, Dawn French, Ben Elton, Mel Smith, Griff Rhys Jones, Stephen Fry, Hugh Laurie, Chris Langham, Eleanor Bron, Willie Rushton, John Williams, Jeff Beck, Nigel Planer, Helen Lederer, Jim Broadbent, Patrick Barlow, Rory Bremner, Adrian Edmondson, Jimmy Mulville, and Spitting Image. The reunited team of Cook and Moore perform their classic sketches "One-Legged Tarzan" and "Frog and Peach." Other sketches include "Pet Shop" (**Cleese** & **Palin**, in a new, abbreviated version of the Python classic), "Argument Clinic" (**Cleese**, **Palin**, French & Langham), "The Last Supper" (**Cleese** & Edmondson), "Biggles Goes to See Bruce Springsteen" (**Palin**, reading), and "Crunchy Frog" (Python sketch performed by Coltrane, Henry & Mulville). Airs as a TV special on Oct. 28 (ITV). Directed by **John Cleese** and Jennifer Saunders.

1666   September 1989
Entertainment Tonight (TV show: Synd.). **Graham Chapman**, in one of his last interviews, speaks optimistically about his battle with cancer and the progress he's made in regaining control of his muscles. **Chapman** is shown undergoing physical therapy at a London hospital.

1667   September 1989
Video Arts, the business-training film company co-founded by **John Cleese** in 1972, is sold for £44 million in a management buyout. The deal, finalized on Dec. 6, makes **Cleese** and each of his four partners—Antony Jay, Peter Robinson, Michael Peacock, and Robert Reid—about £8 million richer. **Cleese**'s original investment was a mere £1,000. He will continue making new films for the company.

1668   September 1989
The Making of the Prefident 1789: The Unauthorized Campaign Biography (Book: Harper & Row), written by Marvin Kitman with a foreword by **John Cleese**, is published in the U.S. Humorous

biography of George Washington. Published in the U.K. by Weidenfeld & Nicolson.

1669 September 1, 1989
Terry Jones' *Erik the Viking* has its world premiere in Stockholm, Sweden at the Svensk Film-Industri Look cinema.

1670 September 3, 1989
The Pythons, including an ailing **Graham Chapman**, reunite to film some new comedy material with Steve Martin for the BBC documentary *Parrot Sketch Not Included: Twenty Years of Monty Python* (airing Nov. 18). One of the scenes they film — a sketch which featured Martin and the group playing schoolchildren — does not appear in the final program. Disappointed by the quality of the sketch, which they did not write, the Pythons decide to cut it. The other scene filmed is a cameo appearance by the group inside a cupboard.

1671 September 10, 1989
Terry Jones attends the London premiere of his film *Erik the Viking* at the Cannon Cinema. Prince Edward also attends.

1672 September 12, 1989
Film 89 (TV show: BBC1). Hosted by Barry Norman. Includes a location report from the set of *Erik the Viking* in Malta, featuring interviews with **Terry Jones**, **John Cleese**, Tim Robbins, and others.

1673 September 15, 1989
The Big Picture (Feature film: Columbia Pictures) opens in the U.S. A romance-fantasy-satire about the life of a film school graduate in Hollywood. **John Cleese** has a cameo role as a bartender. Starring Kevin Bacon, Emily Longstreth, J. T. Walsh, and Jennifer Jason Leigh. Directed by Christopher Guest. Produced by Michael Varhol.

1674 September 17, 1989
The Sunday Telegraph (Newspaper/U.K.). "Twenty Years of Silly Walks," by Sue Summers, pp. 13–16. The six members of Monty Python discuss the history of the group on its 20th anniversary. Includes a group photo taken by Gered Mankowitz.

1675 September 18, 1989
Hysteria 2 (Stage show). Benefit concert marking World AIDS Day. Comedy highlights include **John Cleese**'s introduction for Tina Turner. Proceeds from the concert, held at the Sadler's Wells Theatre in London, go to the Terrence Higgins Trust. Starring Stephen Fry (host), **John Cleese**, Hugh Laurie, Rowan Atkinson, Tina Turner, Lenny Henry, Robbie Coltrane, Jerry Hall, Adrian Edmondson, and Joss Ackland. Directed by Stephen Fry. Airs Dec. 1 on Channel 4.

1676 September 18–20, 1989
The Sun (Newspaper/U.K.). Series of three articles in which **Graham Chapman**, speaking exclusively to *The Sun*, discusses his battle with cancer and other struggles he's faced in his life. In the first article, "I Knew It Was Cancer" (by Mike Housego and Jean Ritchie, p. 17), **Chapman** tells the tabloid how he used his medical training to diagnose his spinal cancer, details his first bout with cancer in late '88–early '89, and denies rumors he has AIDS. In the final article, "I Nearly Died on Three Bottles of Gin a Day," **Chapman** recounts his years as an alcoholic and how he finally quit drinking in December 1977.

1677 September 22, 1989
Erik the Viking (Feature film) premieres in the U.S. at the Cinetex Film Festival in Las Vegas. A Pythonesque fantasy-adventure-comedy written and directed by **Terry Jones**, inspired by his 1983 children's story. Drawing on elements of Norse and Celtic mythology, the story concerns Erik, a Viking who believes there must be more to life than raping and pillaging. To bring an end to the dark and violent Age of Ragnarok, he and his crew must travel to the land of Hy-Brasil and find the Horn Resounding. By blowing the Horn three times, peace, love and the sun will return. Meanwhile, certain businessmen and arms manufacturers, who find Ragnarok to be profitable, set out to stop the expedition. A re-edited version of the film by **Jones'** son Bill, subtitled *The Director's Son's Cut*, is released in 2006. Starring Tim Robbins, Gary Cady, **Terry Jones** (as King Arnulf), Eartha Kitt, Mickey Rooney, **John Cleese** (as Halfdan the Black), Tsutomu Sekine, Antony Sher, John Gordon Sinclair, Imogen Stubbs, Samantha Bond, Freddie Jones, Tim McInnerny, and Charles McKeown. Music by Neil Innes. Written & directed by **Terry Jones**. A John Goldstone/Prominent Features production.
Reviews: David Robinson (*The Times* [London], Sept. 28, 1989, p. 20): "There is a perilous indecision about *Erik the Viking*, which neither takes off into full-blown Monty Python comedy, nor seems confident enough in its epic and mythical ambitions"; Ralph Novak (*People Weekly*, Nov. 20, 1989, p. 27+): "...**Jones** seems to be driving clumsily at a moral.... **Jones** neither makes his point nor gets the laughs this film could easily have earned."

1678 September 22, 1989
Showbiz Today (TV news show: CNN). Lorne Michaels, Chevy Chase, Martin Short, and **Eric Idle** are interviewed by Bill Tush during a rehearsal for the upcoming *Saturday Night Live* anniversary special.

1679 September 23, 1989
Saturday Matters with Sue Lawley (TV talk show: BBC1). Guests: **Terry Jones**, promoting *Erik the Viking*, Neil Sedaka, Enoch Powell, and Jacqueline Bisset.

1680 September 26, 1989
Film 89 (TV show: BBC1). Barry Norman looks at **Terry Jones'** new film *Erik the Viking*, co-starring **John Cleese**.

1681 September 29, 1989
Erik the Viking opens in the U.K.

1682 September 30, 1989
Melody Maker (Newspaper/U.K.). "Monty Python's Flying Circus," by Allan Brown, p. 50. Interview with **Michael Palin** and **Terry Gilliam** on the group's 20th anniversary.

1683 October 1989
Around the World in 80 Days (Book: BBC Books), written by **Michael Palin**, is published in the U.K. **Palin**'s account of his trip around the world following the route taken by Phileas Fogg in Jules Verne's classic story. This companion book to the TV series becomes a No. 1 bestseller.

1684 October 1989
The First 200 Years of Monty Python (Book: Thomas Dunne), written by Kim "Howard" Johnson, is published. A celebration of the group's 20-year career that includes exclusive interviews, detailed guides to the Python shows, films, books, records, and stage shows, many rare photos, and individual profiles of each Python member.

1685 October 1989
The 3rd International Film Festival in Leeds, England presents a special 20th-anniversary tribute to Monty Python.

1686 October 1, 1989
Sunday, Sunday (TV talk show: ITV/LWT). Hosted by Gloria Hunniford. Guests include **Terry Jones**, John Sessions, and Susan Hampshire.

1687 October 3, 1989
Graham Chapman, his condition worsening, is rushed from his home in Hermitage Lane, Maidstone to Maidstone Hospital.

1688 October 4, 1989
Graham Chapman dies at the age of 48 from cancer of the throat and spine at Maidstone Hospital near London, England. By his side were **Michael Palin** and **John Cleese**. **Terry Jones** had also been with him that day. He had undergone two operations after the disease was detected less than a year ago and was thought to be recovering. Only a month earlier he took part in a Python reunion TV special (*Parrot Sketch Not Included*). **Chapman**'s last wish was that those who admired his work contribute money in his name to the cancer research organization of their choice. It is a very sad day in Python history. His death comes on the eve of the group's 20th anniversary. A party that had been planned to celebrate the anniversary was canceled due to **Chapman**'s illness. **Terry Jones** comments "I think it's the worst case of party pooping I've ever come across. But seriously, we will all miss him — we loved him very much."

1689 October 5, 1989
Monty Python's 20th anniversary. It was 20 years ago today that the first episode of *Monty Python's Flying Circus* was aired on the BBC.

1690 October 5, 1989
Monty Python's Flying Circus: Just the Words (Vols 1 & 2) (Book: Methuen) is published in the U.K. Two-volume collection of the scripts of all 45 Python shows (1969–74), published in celebration of the group's 20th anniversary. The U.S. version, titled *The Complete Monty Python's Flying Circus: All the Words*, is published by Pantheon on Nov. 12.

1691 October 6, 1989
The Guardian (Newspaper/U.K.). "The Life of Graham," by **Michael Palin**, p. 39. Palin pays tribute to his friend and fellow Python, **Graham Chapman**.

1692 October 7–13, 1989
Radio Times (Magazine/U.K.). Article on **Michael Palin**'s new BBC series *Around the World in 80 Days*. The cover features **Palin** seated on a globe ("The World at My Feet").

1693 October 8, 1989
The Sunday Times (London) (Newspaper/U.K.). "Missing That Talent to Amuse," by Iain Johnstone, p. C9. Brief tribute to **Graham Chapman**.

1694 October 11–November 22, 1989
The seven-part travel series *Around the World in 80 Days* airs on BBC1. In the series, filmed in September–December 1988, writer-host **Michael**

Palin travels around the world following the 1872 route of Jules Verne's fictional character, Phileas Fogg, in an attempt to prove that the journey can still be accomplished today. **Palin** traveled with only a five-person film crew (his Passepartout) and was not allowed the use of airplanes. The series, produced by Clem Vallance, airs in the U.S. in January 1990 (A&E).

Reviews: Patrick Stoddart (*The Sunday Times* [London], Nov. 26, 1989, p. C20): "My only regret is that this most amiable and amusing of travelling companions made it within the time limit. If he'd failed, **Palin** might have gone around again, and we could all have gone with him."

1695 October 11, 1989

Wogan (TV talk show: BBC1). Hosted by Joanna Lumley (sitting in for Terry Wogan). Guests: **Michael Palin**, promoting *Around the World in 80 Days*, Willy Russell, and Douglas Adams.

1696 October 11, 1989

Around the World in 80 Days (TV episode: BBC1). "The Challenge." **Michael Palin** takes up the BBC's challenge to replicate Phileas Fogg's 1872 journey and sets out from Victoria Station in London on Sept. 25, 1988. Pythons **Terry Gilliam** and **Terry Jones**, acting as referees, see him off. Day 1-6 of his journey includes a ride on the Orient Express and stops in Venice and Athens. First episode in a seven-part series. Written & hosted by **Michael Palin**. Directed by Roger Mills.

1697 October 13, 1989

Family and friends gather at the chapel at Vinters Park Crematorium in Maidstone, Kent for the funeral of **Graham Chapman**. Flowers were sent by The Rolling Stones with "thanks for all the laughs," and there is a large boot-shaped floral arrangement from "the other five Pythons with all our love. P.S. Stop us if we're getting too silly."

1698 October 16, 1989

U.S. News & World Report (Magazine/U.S.). "Now for Something Completely...," by Alvin P. Sanoff, p. 105. Interview with **John Cleese**.

1699 October 18, 1989

Around the World in 80 Days (TV episode: BBC1). "Arabian Frights." Day 7-14 takes **Michael Palin** to Alexandria, Egypt, then on to Cairo and the Pyramids in Giza, followed by a two-day trip across the Red Sea to Jeddah, Saudi Arabia. While in Egypt, **Palin** makes a cameo appearance (as Man in Elevator) in the film *Inar Gahined* (Hellfire). Second episode in a seven-part series. Written & hosted by **Michael Palin**. Produced & directed by Clem Vallance.

1700 October 25, 1989

Around the World in 80 Days (TV episode: BBC1). "Ancient Mariners." Day 14-25 finds **Michael Palin** on a dhow called the *Al Shama*, operated by an 18-man crew, on an eight-day journey across the Arabian Sea from Dubai to Bombay. Twenty years later, **Palin** will return to the region and reunite with the crew of the *Al Shama*. The reunion is filmed for the BBC documentary special *Around the World in 20 Years*, which airs in December 2008. Third episode in a seven-part series. Written & hosted by **Michael Palin**. Produced & directed by Clem Vallance.

1701 October 27, 1989

John Cleese turns 50.

1702 October 27, 1989

Erik the Viking opens in the U.S. (released by Orion Pictures).

1703 October 27, 1989

Showbiz Today (TV news-talk show: CNN). Guest **Terry Jones** talks with Bella Shaw in Hollywood about *Erik the Viking* and pays tribute to **Graham Chapman**.

1704 October 28–November 3, 1989

TV Times (Magazine/U.K.). **John Cleese** interview and cover photo.

1705 October 28, 1989

The Secret Policeman's Biggest Ball (TV special: ITV). Recording of the fourth *Ball* benefit for Amnesty International, held in August–September 1989. Sketches performed include "Pet Shop" (with a new 1989 punchline), "Argument Clinic," and "The Last Supper." Starring **John Cleese**, **Michael Palin**, Peter Cook, Dudley Moore, Lenny Henry, Robbie Coltrane, Dawn French, Ben Elton, and many others. Stage direction by **John Cleese** and Jennifer Saunders. Directed by Mike Holgate. Produced by Judith Holder.

1706 October 28, 1989

Saturday Night at the Movies (TV show: ITV). Cinema magazine program hosted by Tony Slatterey. Includes a report by **Terry Gilliam** from the Bristol Animation Festival.

1707 October 30, 1989

People Weekly (Magazine/U.S.). "Mourning Monty Python Lays to Rest Silly, Brave, Unique **Graham**

Chapman," by Susan Schindehette and Janine Di Giovanni, pp. 52–54. Tribute to **Chapman**.

1708   October 31, 1989
Daytime Live (TV show: BBC1). Magazine program. Judi Spiers interviews **Michael Palin** about his journey in *Around the World in 80 Days*. Live.

1709   November 1989
Prevue (Magazine/U.S.). "**Terry Jones** Whips Up a Wild Hurricane Film Fantasy ... *Erik the Viking*," by Stan Timmons, pp. 28–29+. Interview with **Jones** about his latest film.

1710   November 1, 1989
Around the World in 80 Days (TV episode: BBC1). "A Close Shave." Day 25–38 finds **Michael Palin** in Bombay, then going on to Madras (in southern India). From there, he boards a Yugoslav freighter that takes him across the Bay of Bengal to Singapore. Fourth episode in a seven-part series. Written & hosted by **Michael Palin**. Directed by Roger Mills.

1711   November 2, 1989
This Morning (TV show: ITV). Magazine program hosted by Richard Madeley and Judy Finnigan. Guest: **Michael Palin**, promoting *Around the World in 80 Days*.

1712   November 3, 1989
The Mikado (Light opera) opens at the Wortham Theater Center in Houston, Texas. Jonathan Miller's version of the Gilbert & Sullivan operetta is staged by the Houston Grand Opera and features **Eric Idle** as Ko-Ko, a role he first performed with The English National Opera when Miller's production premiered in September 1986 at the London Coliseum. *The Mikado* is the last of three works presented during the HGO's British Opera Festival. The Duchess of York attends the opening night performance. Nine more performances are given through Nov. 17. Also starring David Eisler, Sheryl Woods, Marvellee Cariaga, Ian Caddy, John Stephens, Will Roy, and Lee Merrill. Conducted by Ward Holmquist.

1713   November 4–December 2, 1989
The Film Club (TV series: BBC2). **Terry Jones** introduces a new season, celebrating the work of writer-director Preston Sturges, beginning with his 1941 film *The Lady Eve*. In the coming weeks, **Jones** introduces the Sturges classics *Sullivan's Travels* (Nov. 11), *The Palm Beach Story* (Nov. 18), *The Miracle of Morgan's Creek* (Nov. 25), and *Hail the Conquering Hero* (Dec. 2).

1714   November 7–15, 1989
The Art of Travel (TV series: BBC2). **Michael Palin** hosts this series of imaginary train journeys based on famous railway posters of the 1920s & '30s, from the collection at the National Railway Museum in York. The series consists of six ten-minute shows: "London Midland and Scottish Railway" (Nov. 7), "Southern Railway" (Nov. 8), "London and North Eastern Railway" (Nov. 9), "Great Western Railway" (Nov. 13), "London Underground" (Nov. 14), and "British Railways" (Nov. 15). Directed by John Metherall and Denise Winterburn. Produced by Trevor Hearing.

1715   November 8, 1989
Around the World in 80 Days (TV episode: BBC1). "Oriental Express." Day 39–46 follows **Michael Palin**'s journey across the South China Sea, from Singapore to Hong Kong. After meeting up with his friend, photographer Basil Pao, in Cheung Chow the two travel on to Guangzhou (in China), then take a train to Shanghai. Fifth episode in a seven-part series. Written & hosted by **Michael Palin**. Produced & directed by Clem Vallance.

1716   November 11, 1989
Calendar (TV news show: ITV/YTV–Yorkshire Television). Guest: **Michael Palin**, promoting *Around the World in 80 Days*.

1717   November 12, 1989
The Complete Monty Python's Flying Circus: All the Words is published in the U.S. by Pantheon Books.

1718   November 15, 1989
Around the World in 80 Days (TV episode: BBC1). "Far East and Farther East." Day 47–58. **Michael Palin** travels from Shanghai to Yokohama (in Japan), then takes the *Shin-Kensan* (Bullet Train) to Tokyo. After spending the night in a capsule hotel, he boards a container ship that takes him across the Pacific Ocean on an 11-day journey to America. Sixth episode in a seven-part series. Written & hosted by **Michael Palin**. With Basil Pao. Directed by Clem Vallance and Roger Mills.

1719   November 18–24, 1989
Radio Times (Magazine/U.K.). "This Is Getting Too Silly!," by Tony Bilbow, pp. 4–5. Python tribute.

1720   November 18, 1989
Parrot Sketch Not Included: Twenty Years of Monty Python (TV special: BBC1). Highlights from the four series of *Monty Python's Flying Circus* are compiled in this celebration of the group's 20th an-

niversary. Hosted by Steve Martin, the 72-minute special concludes with a brief appearance by all six Pythons inside a cupboard. Filmed in September, about a month before **Graham Chapman**'s death. Produced by Charles Brand and Anne James. Premieres in the U.S. on Mar. 17, 1990 (Showtime).

1721   November 22, 1989

Around the World in 80 Days (TV episode: BBC1). "Dateline to Deadline." Day 63–79. **Michael Palin** travels across America, from Los Angeles to New York, stopping in Colorado to ride in a hot-air balloon and dog sled. Finally, he takes a Danish container ship across the Atlantic (an 8-day trip), arriving in London in the seventh hour of the 79th day of his journey (Dec. 12, 1988). Seventh and last episode of the series. Written & hosted by **Michael Palin**. With **Terry Gilliam**. Directed by Roger Mills.

1722   November 23, 1989

Open Air (TV show: BBC1). Eamonn Holmes interviews **Michael Palin** about *Around the World in 80 Days*. **Palin** also answers questions from viewers.

1723   December 1989

Monty Python Sings (Record: Virgin MONT 1; CD: MONTD 1). Compilation of songs from Python TV series, films, and records. Includes one new track, "Oliver Cromwell" (sung by **John Cleese** and **Eric Idle**). Tracks: "Always Look on the Bright Side of Life," "Sit on My Face," "Lumberjack Song," "Penis Song (Not the Noël Coward Song)," "Oliver Cromwell," "Money Song," "Accountancy Shanty," "Finland," "Medical Love Song," "I'm So Worried," "Every Sperm Is Sacred," "Never Be Rude to an Arab," "I Like Chinese," "Eric the Half-a-Bee," "Brian Song," "Bruces' Philosophers Song," "The Meaning of Life," "Knights of the Round Table (Camelot Song)," "All Things Dull and Ugly," "Decomposing Composers," "Henry Kissinger," "I've Got Two Legs," "Christmas in Heaven," "Galaxy Song," and "Spam Song." Produced by Andre Jacquemin and **Eric Idle**.

1724   December 1, 1989

Hysteria 2 (TV special: Channel 4). Two-hour benefit concert marking World AIDS Day. **John Cleese** gives a lengthy comedic intro for Tina Turner. Proceeds from the concert, recorded Sept. 18 at Sadler's Wells in London, go to the Terrence Higgins Trust. Starring Stephen Fry (host), **John Cleese**, Hugh Laurie, Rowan Atkinson, Tina Turner, Lenny Henry, Robbie Coltrane, Jerry Hall, Adrian Edmondson, and Joss Ackland. Stage show directed by Stephen Fry. Directed by David G. Croft. Produced by Trevor Hopkins.

1725   December 2, 1989

Michael Palin joins dozens of authors taking part in a "signathon," benefitting four charities, at Dillons Bookstore in London.

1726   December 3, 1989

A memorial service for **Graham Chapman** is held in the Great Hall at St. Bartholomew's Hospital in London. **John Cleese** delivers a memorable eulogy in which he invokes the "Dead Parrot" sketch, stating that **Chapman** has "ceased to be, bereft of life, he rests in peace" and, in a spirit the late Python would have appreciated, goes on to say "Good riddance to him, the freeloading bastard. I hope he fries." Also attending are **Michael Palin**, **Eric Idle**, **Terry Gilliam**, **Terry Jones**, David Sherlock (**Chapman**'s partner), Jonathan Miller, Alan Bennett, Tim Brooke-Taylor, and others. The Fred Tomlinson Singers sing "Jerusalem" and **Idle** leads the singing of "Always Look on the Bright Side of Life." Filmed portions of the service are included in the 1990 TV special *Life of Python*.

1727   December 7, 1989

Reruns of *Monty Python's Flying Circus* begin airing on BBC2.

1728   December 11, 1989

Live with Regis and Kathie Lee (TV talk show: Synd.). Hosted by Regis Philbin and Kathy Lee Gifford. Guest: **Michael Palin**, promoting *Around the World in 80 Days*.

1729   December 14, 1989

The Tonight Show Starring Johnny Carson (TV talk show: NBC). Guests: **Michael Palin**, Jon Serl, and band Restless Heart. **Palin** talks about *Around the World in 80 Days* and **Graham Chapman**'s memorial service.

1730   December 22, 1989

Walkie Talkie (TV talk show: Channel 4). Host Muriel Gray talks with guest **Eric Idle** as they stroll around Stratford-on-Avon. Directed by Hamish Barbour.

1731   December 25, 1989

I'm Sorry I'll Read That Again (Radio special: BBC Radio 2). Twenty-fifth anniversary special reuniting the original cast of the classic radio comedy program: Tim Brooke-Taylor, **John Cleese**, Graeme Garden, David Hatch, Jo Kendall, and Bill Oddie. Hour.

1732 December 27, 1989
Woman's Hour (Radio show: BBC Radio 4). Monica Dickens, Sarah Greene, Jeremy Hardy, and **Terry Jones** perform in "Shivering Peaks," written by Sue Limb.

1733 1989
This Is Going to Hurt Me More Than It Hurts You: The Bad News Interview (Training film: Video Arts). Management training film on how to give employees bad news. Starring **John Cleese**, Maria Aitken, Prunella Scales, and Richard Wilson. Written by Sean Hardie. Script editor: **John Cleese**. Directed by Charles Crichton.

1734 1989
How to Lose Customers Without Really Trying (Training film: Video Arts). Film demonstrating the right and wrong ways of dealing with customers. Starring **John Cleese**, Dawn French, Jennifer Saunders, Stephen Fry, and Hugh Laurie. Written by Dawn French, Graeme Garden, Antony Jay, Chris Langham, Jim Pullin, and Jennifer Saunders. Directed by Nick Mallett.

1735 1989
Erik the Viking: The Book of the Film of the Book (Book: Methuen Drama), written by **Terry Jones**, is published in the U.K. Screenplay of the film. Published in the U.S. by Applause Theatre Books (1990).

1736 1989–91
Talking Pages (TV commercials). **John Cleese** stars in a series of British TV ads for BT's Talking Pages. The ads show him in a variety of situations, from searching for an antique diamond ring to finding a locksmith for his parents who cannot get into their car.

1737 January 1990
Michael Palin's mother, Mary Rachel Lockhart (Ovey) Palin, dies at the age of 86. Mrs. Palin cohosted *Saturday Night Live* with her son in January 1984, shortly after her 80th birthday. **Palin**'s father, Edward, died in April 1977.

1738 January 1, 1990
The A–Z of TV (TV special: Channel 4). Three-hour history of British television presented in 26 parts by 26 presenters, including **Michael Palin** ("Ally Pally" segment), Michael Hordern, and Beryl Reid. Directed by Philip McDonald. Produced by Linda Zuck.

1739 January 3, 1990
Signals: Anything for a Quiet Life (TV special: Channel 4). **Terry Gilliam** introduces a comedy about office politics performed by the Théâtre de Complicité. Directed by Andy Wilson.

1740 January 4, 1990–November 20, 2000
The TV series *One Foot in the Grave* airs on BBC1. **Eric Idle** wrote and performed the theme song for this British sitcom starring Richard Wilson and Annette Crosbie. **Idle** also appears in the Dec. 30, 1991, episode "The Man in the Long Black Coat."

1741 January 4, 1990
Schweppes (Video commercial). **John Cleese** narrowly avoids various attempts on his life in this James Bond spoof advertising Schweppes soft drinks. Featured on the videocassette release of the Bond film *License to Kill*. **Cleese** previously appeared in a Schweppes ad for the February 1989 video release of *A Fish Called Wanda*.

1742 January 5, 1990
Good Morning America (TV news-talk show: ABC). Joan Lunden talks to **Michael Palin** about *Around the World in 80 Days*.

1743 January 7–February 18, 1990
Michael Palin's seven-part travel series, *Around the World in 80 Days*, airs in the U.S. on cable's Arts & Entertainment Network.

1744 January 7, 1990
A&E Premieres (TV show: A&E). Host Jack Perkins talks to **Michael Palin** following the U.S. TV premiere of the first episode of **Palin**'s travel series *Around the World in 80 Days*.

1745 January 19, 1990
Behind the Headlines (TV talk show: BBC1). Hosted by Kathy Lette. Guests: **Michael Palin**, Julie T. Wallace, Carlo Gebler, and Margaret Greaves. **Palin** talks about *Around the World in 80 Days*.

1746 January 23, 1990
Friends of **Graham Chapman** gather in Los Angeles for a memorial service/cocktail party held at the St. James' Club. Attendees include David Sherlock (**Chapman**'s partner), Harry Nilsson, Timothy Leary, and Martin Lewis. Hosted by the L.A. chapter of the British Academy of Film and Television Arts (BAFTA).

1747 January 27, 1990
Saturday Night Clive (TV talk show: BBC2). Hosted by Clive James. Guests: **Michael Palin** and Vitali Vitaliev.

1748 February 24, 1990
The Times (London) (Newspaper/U.K.). "A Childhood: **Michael Palin**," by Ray Connolly, p. 35. In-depth article on **Palin**'s early years.

1749 March 1990
The Big Picture (TV news-talk show: MTV). **Eric Idle**, promoting *Nuns on the Run*, is interviewed at a bar by host Chris Connelly.

1750 March 13, 1990
The Arsenio Hall Show (TV talk show: Fox). Guests: **Eric Idle**, promoting *Nuns on the Run*, Miss USA, and Don Cornelius. **Idle** also talks about the *Life of Brian* controversy, the Cambridge Footlights revue, the origins and popularity of Monty Python, and The Rutles.

1751 March 16, 1990
Nuns on the Run (Feature film: HandMade Films) opens in the U.S. Comedy starring **Eric Idle** and Robbie Coltrane as two petty crooks, Brian Hope and Charlie McManus, who find themselves hiding out in a convent disguised as nuns. Produced by George Harrison's HandMade Films. Also starring Janet Suzman, Camille Coduri, Doris Hare, Lila Kaye, Robert Patterson, and Robert Morgan. Written & directed by Jonathan Lynn. Produced by Michael White and Simon Bosanquet. Executive produced by George Harrison and Denis O'Brien.
Reviews: Vincent Canby (*The New York Times*, Mar. 16, 1990): "It has something of the cheerful licentiousness of *A Fish Called Wanda* without that film's exhausting intensity"; Iain Johnstone (*The Sunday Times* [London], May 6, 1990): "...not the sort of movie that builds up crescendos of laughter by brilliant layering ... but a film that leaves you with a pleasing grin on your face throughout."

1752 March 16, 1990
Life of Python (TV special: Showtime). The history of Monty Python is detailed in this 20th-anniversary special through clips and interviews with the five surviving Pythons: **John Cleese, Terry Gilliam, Eric Idle, Terry Jones,** and **Michael Palin**. Also includes comments from Carol Cleveland, Barry Took, Steve Martin, Dan Aykroyd, Chevy Chase, and others. Produced & directed by Mark Redhead. *Parrot Sketch Not Included* airs on Showtime the following night. A British version of the special, presented by John Lloyd, airs in the U.K. on Oct. 5 (BBC1) as an *Omnibus* special.

1753 March 17, 1990
The 1989 compilation special *Parrot Sketch Not Included: Twenty Years of Monty Python* airs in the U.S. on Showtime as part of the cable channel's "Monty Python: 20 Odd Years" celebration.

1754 March 18, 1990
Step Up to Wordpower (TV show: BBC1). "Signs, Charts, and Maps." Hosted by Chris Serle. Guests: **Michael Palin** and Sandra Salter. Directed by John Lane. Produced by Elizabeth Cretch.

1755 March 26, 1990
The 62nd Annual Academy Awards (Award ceremony). **Terry Gilliam** and his wife, Maggie Weston, attend the ceremony at the Dorothy Chandler Pavilion in Los Angeles where his film *The Adventures of Baron Munchausen* is up for four Oscars, including one for Weston (and Fabrizio Sforza) for Best Make-Up (loses to *Driving Miss Daisy*). The film is also nominated for Art Direction (loses to *Batman*), Costume Design (loses to *Henry V*), and Visual Effects (loses to *The Abyss*). Broadcast live on ABC.

1756 Late March 1990
Eric Idle slips at home breaking one of his lower vertebrae. The injury prevents him from completing filming on *Too Much Sun* for several weeks. Filming wraps in May.

1757 April 11, 1990
Today (TV news-talk show: NBC). Guests: **Eric Idle** and Robbie Coltrane, promoting *Nuns on the Run*.

1758 April 17, 1990
Fresh Air from WHYY (Radio talk show: NPR). Terry Gross interviews **Michael Palin**.

1759 April 21, 1990
Aspel & Company (TV talk show: ITV/LWT). Hosted by Michael Aspel. Guests: Princess Anne, **Michael Palin**, and Nigel Kennedy.

1760 April 23, 1990
The New Republic (Magazine/U.S.). "It's...: *The Complete Monty Python's Flying Circus: All the Words*, 2 Vols.," by Veronica Geng. The cover of the issue features a painting (by Bryan Leister) depicting the "Nudge, Nudge" sketch. Geng reviewed *Life of Brian* for *The New Yorker* in 1979.

1761 April 29, 1990
Eric Idle's radio play, *Behind the Crease*, is recorded before a live studio audience at BBC Paris Studios in London. It is broadcast July 28, 1990, on BBC Radio 2.

1762 April 30, 1990
Michael Palin attends the launch party for the

book *Elena: A Life in Soho*, by maîtres' d' Elena Salvoni, at the restaurant L'Escargot in Soho, London.

1763   May 1990
John Cleese and his second wife, Barbara Trentham, divorce after nine years of marriage. The couple had been separated since 1987.

1764   May 4, 1990
Nuns on the Run opens in the U.K. (released by Palace Pictures).

1765   May 4, 1990
Viz: The Documentary (TV special: Channel 4). Hour-long documentary on *Viz* comic, with comments from **Michael Palin**, Harry Enfield, others. Directed by Philip Morrow.

1766   May 12, 1990
Aspel & Company (TV talk show: ITV/LWT). Hosted by Michael Aspel. Guests: Princess Stephanie of Monaco, Bob Geldof, and **Eric Idle**.

1767   May 15, 1990
The Importance of Mistakes (Lecture). **John Cleese** gives a talk on the value of making mistakes at the Palmer House in Chicago as part of a reception benefit for the Wisdom Bridge Theatre.

1768   May 17 & 24, 1990
How Far Can You Go? (Radio talk show: BBC Radio 4). **John Cleese** participates in a discussion on art and blasphemy. With Fay Weldon, Martin Scorsese, Mary Whitehouse, Arnold Wesker, and others. Hosted by Barry Norman. Produced by David Coomes. Recorded Apr. 5.

1769   May 29–July 19, 1990
American Friends, a $5 million period drama starring (and co-scripted by) **Michael Palin**, is filmed in Switzerland and England. Locations include New College in Oxford. **Palin** started writing the script in September of 1986, basing the story on events in the journal of his great-grandfather, Edward Palin.

1770   May 31, 1990
The Complete Ripping Yarns (Book: Methuen), written by **Michael Palin** and **Terry Jones**, is published in the U.K. Collection containing the scripts of all nine episodes of the 1975–79 series. The scripts were previously collected in *Ripping Yarns* (1978) and *More Ripping Yarns* (1980).

1771   May 31, 1990
Daytime Green: The Green Life Guide (TV show: ITV/Granada). Environmental program hosted by Dilly Barlow and Alistair MacDonald. **Michael Palin** is interviewed.

1772   Summer 1990
Eric Idle's daughter, Lily, is born. She is his second child, after his son, Carey, who was born in 1973.

1773   June 2, 1990
The 8.15 from Manchester (TV show: BBC1). **Terry Jones** is a guest on this Saturday-morning children's program hosted by Ross King and Charlotte Hindle.

1774   June 6, 1990
Wogan (TV talk show: BBC1). Hosted by Terry Wogan. Guests: **Terry Jones**, Daniel J. Travanti, and Edna O'Brien.

1775   June 9, 1990
A View from the Boundary (Radio sports show: BBC Radio 3). Brian Johnston talks to **Eric Idle** about his career and interest in cricket. From Trent Bridge cricket ground.

1776   July 28, 1990
Behind the Crease (Radio special: BBC Radio 2). Radio musical by **Eric Idle** and John Du Prez. Originally written for the stage (earlier titles were *The Back Page* and *Sticky Wicket*), this satirical musical follows a famous cricketer (Gary Wilmot) and a seedy tabloid journalist (**Idle**) who covers him on a tour of the West Indies. Recorded Apr. 29. Also starring Brian Bowles, Vicky Licorish, Flaminia Cinque, Ann Howard, Julian Littman, Charlie Dore, and Robert Broadbent. Produced by Harry Thompson.

1777   August 13, 1990
Funny That Way (Radio show: BBC Radio 4). Barry Cryer presents a profile of **John Cleese**. Part two in the series. Produced by Tim Sturgeon.

1778   September 16, 1990
John Cleese speaks on constitutional reform at a rally at the Liberal Democrats Party conference in Blackpool, England.

1779   October 1990
John Cleese gives a series of lectures in the U.S. on creativity and business.

1780   October 1990
A Fish Called Wanda is named Best British Video of the Year and Best Comedy at the British Videogram Association Awards.

1781 October 5, 1990
Omnibus (TV special: BBC1). "Life of Python." Documentary chronicling the history of Monty Python through clips and interviews with the five surviving Pythons. The show, originally planned to mark the group's 20th anniversary in 1989, was postponed due to **Graham Chapman**'s death. An American version of the special aired in the U.S. on Mar. 16, 1990 (Showtime). The U.K. version is hosted by John Lloyd and includes interviews with Stephen Fry and Ben Elton. Directed by Mark Redhead and Mark Chapman. Produced by Mark Chapman.

1782 October 10–December 1990
The comedy *Missing Pieces*, starring **Eric Idle** and Robert Wuhl, is filmed in New York City.

1783 October 10, 1990
Too Much Sun (Feature film: CineTel Films) premieres at the Mill Valley Film Festival in Cal. Comedy about a millionaire who dies and leaves his money to his gay son and lesbian daughter, but only if one of them can give him a grandchild. The son and daughter are played by **Eric Idle** (as Sonny) and Andrea Martin (as Bitsy). Filmed in Los Angeles in the spring of 1990. Also starring Howard Duff, Jim Haynie, Robert Downey, Jr., Ralph Macchio, Leo Rossi, and Laura Ernst. Written by Robert Downey, Sr., Laura Ernst, and Al Schwartz. Directed by Robert Downey, Sr. Produced by Lisa M. Hansen. Released nationally in January 1991.

1784 October 20, 1990
The Economist (Magazine/U.K.). "And Now for Something...," p. 86. Article on **John Cleese** and his U.S. lecture series on the importance of creativity in business.

1785 October 20, 1990
Showbiz Today (TV news show: CNN). **Eric Idle** is interviewed.

1786 October 28, 1990
The Sunday Times Review (London) (Newspaper/U.K.). "Casting Around for a New Comic Catch," by George Perry, pp. 22–28. Interview with **John Cleese** about his career post–*Wanda*.

1787 November 1990
John Cleese and **Michael Palin** both give talks at the Save the Young Vic Festival (Oct. 28–Nov. 4), which raises money for the Young Vic Theatre in London.

1788 November 2, 1990
Bullseye! (Feature film: 21st Century Film Corp.) opens in the U.K. Comedy starring Michael Caine and Roger Moore. **John Cleese** makes a brief guest appearance as Man on the Beach in Barbados Who Looks Like John Cleese. Written by Leslie Bricusse, Laurence Marks, and Maurice Gran. Directed by Michael Winner.

1789 November 8, 1990
Grime Goes Green: Your Business and the Environment (Training film: Video Arts) premieres in London. Un-green factory manager James Grime (**John Cleese**) is visited by two environmental advisors whom he believes to be advance men for a royal visit. Prince Charles, who conceived the idea for the film, guest stars. The video is part of a campaign by the organization Business in the Community (of which The Prince is president). Also starring Peter Davison. Written by Peter Spence. Directed by Nick Mallett.

1790 November 22, 1990
Terry Gilliam turns 50.

1791 November 25, 1990
The New York Times (Newspaper/U.S.). "I Just Flew into New York and...," by **Eric Idle**, p. E11. Idle on filming in New York City.

1792 December 2, 1990
Talking Poetry (Radio show: BBC Radio 5). Poetry on the theme of conflict. Guest: **Terry Jones**.

1793 December 6, 1990
Bookshelf (Radio talk show: BBC Radio 4). Host Nigel Forde talks to **John Cleese**.

1794 December 12, 1990–January 16, 1991
Families and How to Survive Them (Radio series: BBC Radio 4). Six-part radio series presented by **John Cleese** and psychiatrist Robin Skynner, based on their 1983 book of the same name. Episodes: "Why Do We Fall in Love?" (Dec. 12); "For Better or Worse — Which Way Will the Marriage Go?" (Dec. 19); "Mothering and Paranoia" (Dec. 26); "The Astonishing Stuffed Rabbit — and Depression" (Jan. 2); "Fathering — and Authority" (Jan. 9); and "Why Good Sex Is Important" (Jan. 16). Produced by Rachel Yorke and Jonathan James-Moore.

1795 December 14, 1990
Wogan (TV talk show: BBC1). Hosted by Terry Wogan. Guests: **John Cleese** and Robin Skynner, Jamie Lee Curtis (via satellite), and Paul McCartney.

1796   December 31, 1990
Tonight with Jonathan Ross (TV talk show: Channel 4). Guests: **Michael Palin** and Lisa Stansfield.

1797   1990
The Helping Hand: Coaching Skills for Managers (Training film: Video Arts). Management-training film on the essentials of employee coaching. Starring **John Cleese**, Robert Lindsay, and Jan Ravens. Written by Chris Langham. Script editor: **John Cleese**. Directed by Nick Mallett.

1798   1990
The Unorganised Salesperson, Part 2: Valuing Yourself (Training film: Video Arts). A salesman learns how, by valuing himself and his time, he can win the respect and trust of customers. Sequel to *Valuing Your Customers* (1990). Narrated by Graeme Garden. Starring **John Cleese** (as John Thompson), Harry Enfield, Miranda Richardson, Burt Caesar, Diane Fletcher, and Bridget Thornborrow. Written by Sean Hardie. Directed by Peter Robinson.

1799   1990
Rail for the Future: A Development Strategy for the Railways (Book: Railway Development Society) is published. Foreword by **Michael Palin**.

1800   1990
Time to Talk (Video). Program on stammering, hosted by **Michael Palin**. Produced & directed by Luke Jeans.

1801   1990
Everything You Wanted to Know About Buying and Selling a Used Car but Were Afraid to Ask (Educational video). **Idle** plays a sleazy car seller in this hour-long video for inexperienced car buyers. Co-starring Dexter Fletcher. Written & directed by Sheldon Greenberg. Produced by Robert Page.

1802   1990
John Cleese appears in a print ad for American Express, dressed as a woman and holding two small dogs ("**John Cleese**. Cardmember since 1971.").

1803   1990
Schweppes ("Straight Schweppes") (TV commercials). **John Cleese** stars in a series of British TV ads for Schweppes Tonic Water to persuade viewers to drink the tonic on its own. The first several ads, which feature only **Cleese**'s voice, deal mainly with figuring out the slogan ("Straight Schweppes has got citric bite") and finalizing **Cleese**'s contract. The main ad — the one **Cleese** has "been waiting to make all my life" — shows him frolicking shirtless on a beach in the Caribbean with bikini-clad girls. Agency: Saatchi & Saatchi, London.

1804   1990
The Line That Refused to Die (Book: Leading Edge Books), written by Stan Abbott and Alan Whitehouse with a foreword by **Michael Palin**, is published in the U.K. Story of the successful campaign to save England's Settle and Carlisle railway line.

1805   January 1, 1991
1001 Nights of TV (TV special: Channel 4). **Michael Palin** hosts this three-hour compilation of TV highlights. Written by Dick Fiddy. Directed by Steve Connelly. Produced by Linda Zuck.

1806   January 7, 1991
First Bite (TV special: BBC2). **Terry Gilliam** presents six animated films, the winning entries of the 1990/91 "First Bite" Student Animation Competition. Directed by Sebastian Scott. Produced by Jenny Barrett.

1807   January 13, 1991
The 12th Annual Ace Awards (Award ceremony). **Michael Palin** and actress Blair Brown present the award for Best Comedy Series to the creators of *It's Garry Shandling's Show* at the ceremony honoring cable excellence. The ceremony, held at the Wiltern Theatre in Los Angeles and hosted by James Woods, is broadcast on eight cable channels.

1808   January 23, 1991
Creativity in Management (Lecture). **John Cleese** gives a speech on the importance of creative thinking in management to an international audience (via satellite) at the Grosvenor House Hotel, London. The speech is recorded and released as a training film by Video Arts.

1809   January 27, 1991
Everyman (TV special: BBC1). "They Shoot Children, Don't They?" Documentary on the plight of street children in Guatemala. Introduced by **Michael Palin**. Directed by Judy Jackson.

1810   February 12, 1991
Michael Palin attends a press conference at Sheraton Park Tower (in Knightsbridge, London) to launch the Association for Research into Stammering in Childhood. The main goal of the association, of which **Palin** is vice-president, is the creation of a speech therapy center for stammering children.

1811 March 1991
Wilbury Twist (Music video). **Eric Idle** appears (with John Candy) in this video for the Traveling Wilburys' "Willbury Twist," from the supergroup's 1990 album *Traveling Wilburys Vol. 3*.

1812 March 9, 1991
The Times (London) (Newspaper/U.K.). "A Python's Travels in the Joke-Free Zone," by Andrew Davidson, p. 16–17. Interview with **Michael Palin**, conducted at his home in Gospel Park, North London. **Palin** talks about his new film *American Friends*.

1813 March 10, 1991
Naked Hollywood (TV episode: BBC2). "Good Cop, Bad Cop." Includes a look at the work of producers Lynda Obst and Debra Hill in bringing *The Fisher King* to the screen. **Terry Gilliam** is interviewed. Shown in the U.S. on A&E. Directed by Alan Lewens. Produced by Nicolas Kent.

1814 March 12, 1991
Film 91 (TV show: BBC1). Hosted by Barry Norman. **Michael Palin** is interviewed during a location report on his new film *American Friends*.

1815 March 14, 1991
The hotel used in exterior shots for **John Cleese**'s sitcom *Fawlty Towers* is gutted by fire. The former Wooburn Grange Country Club in Buckinghamshire, England — which briefly operated as a hotel in the late 1980s — had been empty for the past three years.

1816 March 15, 1991
6 O'Clock Live (TV show: ITV/LWT). Hosted by Frank Bough. Guests: Cilla Black, Tom Jones, and **Michael Palin**.

1817 March 17, 1991
The Sunday Times (London) (Newspaper/U.K.). "A Comedy of Mild Manners," by Iain Johnstone, p. 11. Interview with **Michael Palin** about his new film *American Friends* and his reputation as a nice guy.

1818 March 22, 1991
American Friends (Feature film: Palace Pictures) opens in the U.K. In this period romance, **Michael Palin** plays the Rev. Francis Ashby, a stuffy Oxford University tutor who meets and falls in love with a young Irish-American girl while on holiday in Switzerland. The film is based on actual events in the life of **Palin**'s great-grandfather, Edward Palin (1825–1903), who, in 1861, was a 35-year-old Oxford tutor when he fell in love (and later married) a 19-year-old Irish-American girl named Brita Gallagher. **Palin** discovered the story in his great-grandfather's journal in September 1977. Also starring Trini Alvarado, Connie Booth, Alfred Molina, Simon Jones, Bryan Pringle, and Charles McKeown. Written by **Michael Palin** and Tristram Powell. Directed by Tristram Powell. Produced by Steve Abbott and Patrick Cassavetti. A Prominent Features production. Released in the U.S. in April 1993.
Award: Winner of the 1991 Writers Guild of Great Britain Award for Best Screenplay.
Reviews: Geoff Brown (*The Times* [London], Mar. 21, 1991, p. 23): "...this attractive if languorous romance, inspired by the diaries of **Palin**'s great-grandfather, keeps its jokes swathed in extreme refinement ... the film survives, just about, on good taste and charm."

1819 March 23, 1991
Aspel & Company (TV talk show: ITV/LWT). Hosted by Michael Aspel. Guests: **Michael Palin**, promoting *American Friends*, Maureen Lipman, and Wendy James.

1820 April–August 31, 1991
A Salute to Monty Python, a series of retrospective screenings, runs at the Museum of Television and Radio in New York City.

1821 April 14, 1991
A Present from the Past: The Making of American Friends (TV special: BBC1). Half-hour documentary on the making of **Michael Palin**'s new film *American Friends*. Includes interviews with **Palin**, Connie Booth, Tristram Powell, and Alfred Molina. Produced by Colin Burrows and David Castell.

1822 April 15, 1991
Scene Today (TV show: BBC1). Guests: **Michael Palin**, Deborah Moggach, and Gloria Estefan. **Palin** talks to host Judi Spiers about his new film *American Friends*.

1823 May 1991
Missing Pieces (Feature film: Orion) is shown at the Cannes Film Festival in France. Comedy starring **Eric Idle** (Wendel) and Robert Wuhl (Lou) as a pair of misfits who attempt to solve a riddle that will lead them to Wendel's inheritance while being pursued by various shady characters. Filmed in late 1990, the film is never given a U.S. theatrical release. Also starring Lauren Hutton and Richard Belzer. Written & directed by Leonard Stern.

1824 May–June 1991
Arena (Magazine/U.K.). "**Michael Palin**— Too Good to Be True?," by John Williams, pp. 66–69. **Palin** is interviewed for this British men's magazine.

1825 May & July–December 1991
Michael Palin goes on a 141-day journey from the North Pole to Antarctica, visiting 16 countries along the way. His journey is documented for the BBC travel series *Pole to Pole*, which will air Oct. 21–Dec. 9, 1992, on BBC1.

1826 May 1991
What's So Funny? (Lecture). **Michael Palin** and **Terry Jones** talk about comedy writing at the Hay-on-Wye Festival of Literature (May 24–June 2) in Wales.

1827 June 1991
Monty Python's Flying Circus: Despicable Families, Naughty Complaints, and Killer Fruit, Volume 18 (Videocassette: Paramount Home Video 12765). Contains: "Owl-Stretching Time" (Ep. 4, 1969) and "Party Political Broadcast" (Ep. 45, 1974).

1828 June 1991
Monty Python's Flying Circus: Nudge, Nudge, Wink, Wink, Volume 19 (Videocassette: Paramount Home Video 12766). Contains: "How to Recognise Different Types of Trees..." (Ep. 3, 1969) and "Hamlet" (Ep. 43, 1974).

1829 June 1991
Monty Python's Flying Circus: Pet Ants, Dead Poets & the Mysterious Michael Ellis, Volume 20 (Videocassette: Paramount Home Video 12767). Contains: "Untitled" (Ep. 10, 1969) and "Michael Ellis" (Ep. 41, 1974).

1830 June 1991
Monty Python's Flying Circus: Scott of the Antarctic, Volume 21 (Videocassette: Paramount Home Video 12768). Contains: "Scott of the Antarctic" (Ep. 23, 1970) and "Light Entertainment War" (Ep. 42, 1974).

1831 June 1991
Monty Python's Flying Circus: Mr. Neutron's Balloonish Bicycle Tour, Volume 22 (Videocassette: Paramount Home Video 12770). Contains: "The Cycling Tour" (Ep. 34, 1972), "The Golden Age of Ballooning" (Ep. 40, 1974), and "Mr. Neutron" (Ep. 44, 1974). Last tape in the series.

1832 June 4, 1991
We All Have Tales (TV episode: Showtime). "Jack and the Beanstalk." Re-telling of the old English folktale, narrated by **Michael Palin** to illustrations by Edward Sorel. Adapted by Eric Metaxas. Music by Dave Stewart. Directed by C. W. Rogers. Produced by Ken Hoin.

1833 June 6–July 18, 1991
The seven-part mini-series *G.B.H.* (Great British Holiday) airs on Channel 4. This political satire— about a corrupt Labor leader in a northern town and the mild-mannered schoolmaster who opposes him—was written by Alan Bleasdale and stars Robert Lindsay (as Labor council member Michael Murray) and **Michael Palin** (as schoolmaster Jim Nelson). Also starring Lindsay Duncan, Dearbhla Molloy, Andrew Schofield, Tom Georgeson, Philip Whitchurch, Alan Igbon, David Ross, Jimmy Mulville, Daniel Massey, Anna Friel, and Julie Walters. Produced by David Jones and Alan Bleasdale. Released on DVD in June 2006.
Awards: BAFTA-winner for Best Actor (Lindsay) and Best Original Television Music (Elvis Costello, Richard Harvey), also nominated for Best Drama Serial, Best Actor (**Palin**), Best Actress (Duncan), Makeup (Annie Spears), Film/Video Editor (Anthony Ham, Oral Norrie Ottey), Film/Video Photography (Peter Jessop), and Graphics (Debby Mendoza).

1834 June 6, 1991
G.B.H. (TV episode: Channel 4). "It Couldn't Happen Here." Jim Nelson (**Michael Palin**), a teacher at a school for handicapped children, comes into conflict with new city council leader Michael Murray (Robert Lindsay) when he fails to take part in Murray's city-wide strike. First episode in the seven-part series. Written by Alan Bleasdale. Directed by Robert Young.

1835 June 13, 1991
G.B.H. (TV episode: Channel 4). "Only Here on a Message." Second episode in the seven-part series. Starring Robert Lindsay and **Michael Palin** (as Jim Nelson). Written by Alan Bleasdale. Directed by Robert Young.

1836 June 20, 1991
G.B.H. (TV episode: Channel 4). "Send a Message to Michael." Third episode in the seven-part series. Starring Robert Lindsay and **Michael Palin** (as Jim Nelson). Written by Alan Bleasdale. Directed by Robert Young.

1837 June 27, 1991
G.B.H. (TV episode: Channel 4). "Message Sent."

Fourth episode in the seven-part series. Starring Robert Lindsay and **Michael Palin** (as Jim Nelson). Written by Alan Bleasdale. Directed by Robert Young.

1838   June 28, 1991
Late Night with David Letterman (TV talk show: NBC). Guests: **Michael Palin** and Reggae Sunsplash.

1839   July 4, 1991
G.B.H. (TV episode: Channel 4). "Message Received." Jim Nelson's troubles follow him as he and his family vacation at the Woodlands Holiday Complex. Fifth episode in the seven-part series. Starring Robert Lindsay and **Michael Palin** (as Jim Nelson). Written by Alan Bleasdale. Directed by Robert Young.

1840   July 8, 1991
The Much Loved Friend?: A Portrait of the National Gallery (TV special: BBC2). Documentary on the history and work of the National Gallery in London. With comments from **Terry Gilliam**, Prince Charles, and others. Directed by Nicholas Rossiter.

1841   July 11, 1991
G.B.H. (TV episode: Channel 4). "Message Understood." Sixth episode in the seven-part series. Starring Robert Lindsay and **Michael Palin** (as Jim Nelson). Written by Alan Bleasdale. Directed by Robert Young.

1842   July 14–August 25, 1991
Michael Palin's popular 1989 travel series, *Around the World in 80 Days*, is repeated on BBC1.

1843   July 16, 1991
Without Walls: Film Talk (TV arts show: Channel 4). Guests **Terry Gilliam** and Lynda La Plante discuss the week's new film releases. Directed by Kathy Myers and Hamish Barbour.

1844   July 18, 1991
G.B.H. (TV episode: Channel 4). "Over and Out." Jim Nelson (**Michael Palin**) returns from his holiday to make his final stand against Michael Murray (Robert Lindsay). Seventh and last episode of the series. Written by Alan Bleasdale. Directed by Robert Young.

1845   September–October 1991
Film Comment (Magazine/U.S.). "**Terry Gilliam**'s Guilty Pleasures," by **Terry Gilliam**. Gilliam discusses some of his favorite movies, including *One-Eyed Jacks* and *Pinocchio*.

1846   September 1991
Always Look on the Bright Side of Life (Record: Virgin PYTH1; CD: PYTHD1). U.K. single containing the title song (sung by **Eric Idle**), b/w "I'm So Worried" (sung by **Terry Jones**) and "I Bet You They Won't Play This Song on the Radio" (sung by **Idle**). The CD single includes the additional track "Holzfäller Song" (German version of "The Lumberjack Song"). Produced by Andre Jacquemin.

1847   September 10, 1991
Terry Gilliam's new film *The Fisher King* has its world premiere at the Venice International Film Festival (Sept. 3–14). It is the official U.S. entry to the festival.

1848   September 13, 1991
The Fisher King is shown at the 16th annual Toronto International Film Festival (Sept. 5–14). For his work on the film **Terry Gilliam** receives the People's Choice Award, the festival's highest honor.

1849   September 16, 1991
The Fisher King, directed by **Terry Gilliam**, has its Los Angeles premiere at the Academy of Motion Picture Arts and Sciences in Beverly Hills. **Gilliam** attends, along with the film's stars (including Robin Williams and Jeff Bridges), writer, and producers. The charity screening benefits Comic Relief and The End Hunger Network.

1850   September 20, 1991
The Fisher King (Feature film: TriStar Pictures) opens in the U.S. **Terry Gilliam**'s follow-up to 1989's *The Adventures of Baron Munchausen* is a smaller-scale Hollywood production and the first film he has directed where he did not also contribute to the script. Robin Williams plays a homeless New Yorker, haunted by his wife's violent death, who goes in search of the Holy Grail, which he believes has been hidden in a Park Avenue mansion. Aiding him in his quest is a suicidal former radio DJ (Jeff Bridges) seeking redemption. Also starring Mercedes Ruehl, Amanda Plummer, and Michael Jeter. Written by Richard LaGravenese. Directed by **Terry Gilliam**. Produced by Lynda Obst and Debra Hill.

Awards: Academy Award winner for Best Supporting Actress (Ruehl), also nominated for Best Actor (Williams), Original Score (George Fenton), Set Decoration (Mel Bourne, Cindy Carr), and Screenplay; BAFTA-nominated for Best Supporting Actress (Plummer) and Screenplay; Golden

Globe winner for Best Actor (Williams) and Actress (Ruehl), also nominated for Best Director, Best Picture, and Best Actor (Bridges); Winner of the People's Choice Award (**Gilliam**) at the Toronto International Film Festival.

Reviews: Roger Ebert (*Chicago Sun-Times*, Sept. 20, 1991): "...a disorganized, rambling and eccentric movie that contains some moments of truth, some moments of humor, and many moments of digression"; David Ansen (*Newsweek*, Sept. 23, 1991): "Working within the constraints of a big studio film has brought out **Gilliam**'s best: he's become a true storyteller and a wonderful director of actors"; Ralph Novak (*People*, Sept. 23, 1991): "**Gilliam** may be a yarn-spinner who doesn't know when to stop, but he gives you your money's worth"; George Perry (*The Sunday Times* [London], Nov. 10, 1991): "[**Gilliam**'s] is one of the most fertile and original imaginations at work in mainstream cinema, and his new film thankfully eradicates the unfairly assigned reputation for excessive self-indulgence that plagued him after his last film, *The Adventures of Baron Munchausen*."

1851   October 6, 1991

The South Bank Show (TV arts show: ITV/LWT). "**Terry Gilliam**." The American Python is interviewed at his Highgate, North London home for this hour-long profile. He also makes a family video in his garden and shows off his collection of movie memorabilia. **Michael Palin** is also interviewed. Edited & presented by Melvyn Bragg. Produced & directed by Frances Dickenson. Note: **John Cleese** was the subject of a January 1986 episode of this long-running arts program.

1852   October 11, 1991

Sixthirtysomething (TV show: Channel 4). **Eric Idle** is interviewed on this movie magazine show hosted by Ann Bryson and Maria McErlane.

1853   October 17, 1991

Top of the Pops (TV music show: BBC1). **Eric Idle** performs "Always Look on the Bright Side of Life," now a hit single in the U.K., in this installment of the long-running pop chart show. From BBC's Elstree Studio. Produced & directed by Stanley Appel.

1854   October 18, 1991

Pebble Mill (TV talk show: BBC1). Hosted by Alan Titchmarsh. Guests: **Eric Idle**, Martha Holmes, Mike DeGruy, Robert Powell, Natalia Makarova, and Level 42.

1855   October 29, 1991

Film 91 (TV show: BBC1). Hosted by Barry Norman. Tom Brook presents a report on *The Fisher King* featuring interviews with **Terry Gilliam**, Robin Williams, Jeff Bridges, and Mercedes Ruehl.

1856   November 1991

Losing the Light: Terry Gilliam and the Munchausen Saga (Book: Applause Books), written by Andrew Yule, is published. Behind-the-scenes look at the troubled production of **Gilliam**'s 1989 film *The Adventures of Baron Munchausen*.

1857   November 4, 1991

Third Ear (Radio talk show: BBC Radio 3). Allan Hunter talks to **Terry Gilliam** about filmmaking and his new film *The Fisher King*.

1858   November 8, 1991

The Fisher King, directed by **Terry Gilliam**, opens in the U.K.

1859   November 22, 1991

An American Tail: Fievel Goes West (Feature film: Universal Pictures) opens in the U.S. Animated feature, sequel to the 1986 hit. **John Cleese** voices Cat R. Waul. Voice cast also includes Phillip Glasser, James Stewart, Erica Yohn, Dom DeLuise, and Amy Irving. Written by Flint Dille. Directed by Phil Nibbelink and Simon Wells.

1860   November 25, 1991

The Royal Variety Performance (Stage show). Gala evening at Victoria Palace Theatre in London, hosted by David Frost, with the Queen and the Duke of Edinburgh in attendance. **Eric Idle** interrupts an operatic performance by Ann Howard to sing "Always Look on the Bright Side of Life." Other performers include Diana Ross, Michael Ball, Jackie Mason, and Les Dawson. This 62nd Royal Variety Performance benefits the Entertainment Artists' Benevolent Fund.

1861   November 29, 1991

A Profile of Jonathan Miller (Book: Cambridge University Press), edited by Michael Romain, is published in the U.K. Romain explores the work of theater/opera director Jonathan Miller. Includes conversations with Miller collaborators **John Cleese** (1980's *The Taming of the Shrew*) and **Eric Idle** (1986's *The Mikado*).

1862   November 30, 1991

The Royal Variety Performance (TV special: ITV/LWT). Telecast of the Nov. 25 gala at Victoria Palace Theatre in London. **Eric Idle** performs "Always Look on the Bright Side of Life." Hosted by David Frost. Directed by Alasdair MacMillan.

1863 December 1991
John Cleese attends a Christmas party hosted by *The Sunday Times* at the Victoria and Albert Museum in London.

1864 December 4, 1991
Wogan (TV talk show: BBC1). Hosted by Terry Wogan. Guests: **Terry Jones**, Saskia Wickham, Bobby Davro, and Dannii Minogue.

1865 December 6, 1991
So This Is Progress? (TV special: BBC2). Half-hour documentary examining whether technological advances have really improved man's happiness and quality of life. Written & hosted by **Terry Jones**. Produced by Clare Richards and David Souden.

1866 December 30, 1991
One Foot in the Grave (TV episode: BBC1). "The Man in the Long Black Coat." Victor learns that the horse manure he recently purchased may have been contaminated with radioactivity. **Eric Idle**, who wrote & performed the theme song for the 1990–2000 comedy series, appears in this episode as Mervyn Whale, a health official who inspects Victor's manure. Starring Richard Wilson, Annette Crosbie, and Angus Deayton. Written by David Renwick. Directed by Susan Belbin.

1867 December 31, 1991
Chain Reaction (Radio talk show: BBC Radio 5). Cartoonist Ralph Steadman interviews **John Cleese** on the first program of this host-less series in which one night's guest becomes the next night's interviewer.

1868 1991
Think or Sink (Training film: Video Arts). Film on team decision skills in management. Starring **John Cleese**, Robert Lindsay, Alex Jennings, Michael Percival, and Josette Simon. Written by Antony Jay. Directed by Peter Robinson.

1869 1991
Straight Talking: The Art of Assertiveness (Training film: Video Arts). Film demonstrating the benefits and techniques of assertive behavior in the workplace. Starring **John Cleese**, Peter Capaldi, and Jennifer Saunders. Written by **John Cleese**, Hugh Laurie, and Sean Hardie. Directed by Sean Hardie.

1870 1991
Creativity in Management (Training film: Video Arts). Film on the importance of creative thinking in management. Recording of a speech delivered by **John Cleese** at Grosvenor House Hotel, London on Jan. 23, 1991.

1871 1991
Eric Idle's song "Always Look on the Bright Side of Life" (from 1979's *Life of Brian*) experiences a resurgence in popularity when English football fans begin singing it during games. Reissued on Virgin Records, the song reaches No. 3 on the U.K. charts.

1872 1991
Magnavox ("Magnavox. Smart. Very Smart") (TV commercials). **John Cleese** stars in a series of ads for Magnavox electronics (TV, CD player, camcorder, etc.). Directed by Bryan Loftus.

1873 January 1, 1992
Chain Reaction (Radio talk show: BBC Radio 5). **John Cleese**, who was interviewed on the first program, takes the interviewer chair and chooses as his guest the screenwriter William Goldman.

1874 January 29, 1992
Midweek (Radio talk show: BBC Radio 4). Guests: **Terry Jones**, John Diamond, and Gordon Haycock.

1875 February 1, 1992
Terry Jones turns 50.

1876 Spring 1992
John Cleese and his fiancée, Alyce Faye Eichelberger, host a three-week cruise down the Nile in Egypt. Among the 45 invited friends are **Eric Idle**, Peter Cook, Stephen Fry, and Kevin and Rachel Billington.

1877 March 5, 1992
Michael Palin attends the premiere of the film *Benjamin Huntsman* in Sheffield, England. The film tells the story of Sheffield steel-making pioneer Benjamin Huntsman (1704–1776). Sheffield native **Palin** is an executive producer on the film.

1878 March 29, 1992
The Sunday Times (London) (Newspaper/U.K.). "Yes, Britain Could Get Politics in Proportion," by **John Cleese**, p. 4. **Cleese** explains why he is voting LibDem.

1879 April 7, 1992
Grand Tour (Radio show: BBC Radio 4). "Fez." **Terry Gilliam** visits the city of Fez in Morocco.

1880 May 9, 1992
And God Blew (TV special: BBC2). **Terry Jones** hosts this half-hour special examining the role the

weather has played in protecting Britain from invasion and insurrection. Directed by Alan Ereira.

1881   Summer 1992
Splitting Heirs, a comedy written by and starring **Eric Idle** (and co-starring **John Cleese**), is filmed in the South of France, at Lee International Studios (in Shepperton, Eng.), and at Longleat House (in Wiltshire, Eng.). Longleat was also a filming location for **Michael Palin**'s *The Missionary* in May 1982.

1882   June 6, 1992
Eric Idle attends the wedding ceremony of David Bowie and Iman at St. James Episcopal Church in Florence, Italy. Other guests include Yoko Ono, Bono, and Brian Eno.

1883   July 24, 1992
Mom and Dad Save the World (Feature film: Warner Bros.) opens in the U.S. Comedy about a suburban California couple who are abducted and brought to an alien planet. **Eric Idle** plays King Raff, the deposed ruler of the planet. Also starring Teri Garr, Jeffrey Jones, Jon Lovitz, Kathy Ireland, and Wallace Shawn. Written by Chris Matheson and Ed Solomon. Directed by Greg Beeman. Produced by Michael Phillips.

1884   July 24, 1992
6 O'Clock Live (TV show: ITV/LWT). **Michael Palin**, **Terry Gilliam**, and other celebrities discuss their opposition to the demolition of The Parkway Cinema in Camden. Reported by Jeni Barnett.

1885   July 30, 1992
John Cleese is awarded a £25,000 settlement in his libel suit against the British tabloid *The Sun*. **Cleese** sued over allegations the paper made about his sex drive in two articles published in March. *The Sun* also publishes an apology on July 31. **Cleese** plans to donate the money to the Fulbright Foundation, saying: "All the money is going toward scholarships for British screenwriters to study in the United States for a year, and I'm delighted *The Sun* has been able to help."

1886   August 1992
The Man (Audio book: Random Century Tellastory TS 472). **Michael Palin** voices the title character of Raymond Briggs' latest children's story about a boy's relationship with a six-inch-tall man who arrives in his bedroom one morning naked and hungry. With William Puttock as the boy. Adapted by the author.

1887   September 1992
Esquire (Magazine/U.K.). "**Cleese** Encounter," by Melvyn Bragg, pp. 46–55. **John Cleese** article with cover photo.

1888   October 1992
Pole to Pole (Book: BBC Books), written by **Michael Palin** with photographs by Basil Pao, is published in the U.K. Companion book to the new BBC travel series which follows **Palin**'s journey from the North Pole to the South Pole. Illustrated with photos and maps.
Award: British Book Award for Travel Writer of the Year (**Palin**).

1889   October 1, 1992
Fantastic Stories (Book: Pavilion Books), written by **Terry Jones** with illustrations by Michael Foreman, is published in the U.K. Stories include "The Dragon on the Roof," "The Improving Mirror," "The Cat with Two Tails," and "The Slow Ogre." **Jones**' first collection of children's stories, *Fairy Tales*, was published in 1981. The two books are published together in 1997 (Pavilion) and 2003 (Chrysalis Children's Books).
Review: Susan Hill (*The Sunday Times* [London], Dec. 6, 1992, p. 9): "**Jones** takes traditional elements — talking creatures, minstrels and jesters, ogres and devils and two-tailed cats — and makes them his own in these varied and inventive stories..."

1890   October 3, 1992
Going Live! (TV talk show: BBC1). **Terry Jones**, promoting *Fantastic Stories*, is a guest on this Saturday-morning magazine show for children. Hosted by Phillip Schofield and Sarah Greene.

1891   October 4, 1992
Sunday Brunch (Radio show: BBC Radio 5). Guest: **Terry Jones**, promoting *Fantastic Stories*.

1892   October 6, 1992
Terry Jones promotes his book *Fantastic Stories* on TV's *Good Morning Britain* (ITV), hosted by Mike Morris and Lorraine Kelly, and on radio's *Kaleidoscope* (BBC Radio 4).

1893   October 7, 1992
This Morning (TV show: ITV/Granada). Magazine program hosted by Richard Madeley and Judy Finnigan. Guest: **Terry Jones**, promoting *Fantastic Stories*.

1894   October 12, 1992
The Young Indiana Jones Chronicles (TV episode:

ABC). "Barcelona, May 1917." **Terry Jones** directs this episode of the 1992–93 adventure series and also co-stars as Marcello, one of a trio of spies who join up with Indy (Sean Patrick Flanery) during his spy mission in Barcelona in 1917. Also starring George Hall, Amanda Ooms, Timothy Spall, Kenneth Cranham, Harry Enfield, William Hootkins, and Charles McKeown. Written by Gavin Scott.

1895   October 17–23, 1992
Radio Times (Magazine/U.K.). Article on **Michael Palin**'s new series, *Pole to Pole*. **Palin** is featured on the cover.

1896   October 19, 1992
Start the Week (Radio talk show: BBC Radio 4). Hosted by Melvyn Bragg and Zoe Heller. Guests: **Michael Palin**, promoting *Pole to Pole*, Anthony Burgess, and Harold Prince.

1897   October 21–December 9, 1992
The eight-part travel series *Pole to Pole* airs on BBC1. In this follow-up to his successful 1989 series *Around the World in 80 Days*, **Michael Palin** travels 12,500 miles from the North Pole to the South Pole, following the line of longitude 30-degrees East down through Scandinavia, Russia, the Middle East, Africa, and Antarctica, visiting a total of 16 countries. Filmed in May & July–December 1991. Series producer: Clem Vallance. Airs in the U.S. in January 1993 (A&E).
Awards: BAFTA Crafts-winner for Best Factual Photography; CableAce-winner for Recreation or Leisure Special or Series, also nominated for Documentary Host (**Palin**).
Reviews: Joe Joseph (*The Times* [London], Oct. 22, 1992, p. 39): "**Palin** is the perfect surrogate to do your travelling for you. He seems keen to tackle any challenges, but he never seems to be enjoying himself so much that you feel jealous."

1898   October 21, 1992
Pole to Pole (TV episode: BBC1). "Cold Start." **Michael Palin** begins his journey with a dicey plane landing on a piece of floating ice at the North Pole. From there, he takes a supply ship across the Barents Sea to Norway, where he pans for gold (in Karasjok). In Finland, he visits Santa Claus (Rovaniemi) and enjoys a sauna (Helsinki), then moves on to Tallinn in Estonia. First episode of the eight-part travel series. Written & narrated by **Michael Palin**. Directed by Roger Mills and Clem Vallance.

1899   October 23, 1992
Clive Anderson Talks Back (TV talk show: Channel 4). Guests: **Michael Palin**, promoting *Pole to Pole*, David Mellor, and Kenneth Branagh.

1900   October 28, 1992
Pole to Pole (TV episode: BBC1). "Russian Steps." In Leningrad (shortly before the fall of the Soviet Union), **Michael Palin** is shown around by a Lenin impersonator, witnesses a christening, and attempts to buy vodka. From there he moves on to Novgorod, where he meets a film-maker/vodka-maker. In the Ukraine, he visits a contaminated area near Chernobyl (Narodichi) and enjoys a mud bath (Odessa). Second episode of the eight-part travel series. Written & narrated by **Michael Palin**. Directed by Roger Mills.

1901   November 1992
The Adventures of Baron Munchausen: The Criterion Collection (Laserdisc: Criterion Collection 144/Columbia TriStar). **Terry Gilliam**'s 1989 fantasy is released on a three-disc set. Bonus features include audio commentary by **Gilliam**, deleted scenes, storyboards, production history, and the original theatrical trailer. Distributed by The Voyager Company. **Gilliam**—with co-screenwriter Charles McKeown—will record a new commentary track for the 2008 20th-anniversary DVD release of the film.

1902   November 4, 1992
Pole to Pole (TV episode: BBC1). "Mediterranean Maze." Beginning in Istanbul, where he enjoys a Turkish bath, **Michael Palin** continues southward to the Greek island of Rhodes and the island country of Cyprus, where he visits an RAF base (Akrotiri) and attends a wedding (Polemi). In Egypt, **Palin** takes a cruise down the Nile and visits the Valley of the Kings (near Luxor). Third episode of the eight-part travel series. Written & narrated by **Michael Palin**. Directed by Roger Mills and Clem Vallance.

1903   November 11, 1992
Pole to Pole (TV episode: BBC1). "Shifting Sands." In the Sudan, **Michael Palin** travels south by train from Wadi Halfa, crossing the Nubian Desert, then takes a bus to Khartoum. From there, he travels on a difficult road to the Ethiopian border. Fourth episode of the eight-part travel series. Written & narrated by **Michael Palin**. Directed by Clem Vallance.

1904   November 18, 1992
Pole to Pole (TV episode: BBC1). "Crossing the Line." **Michael Palin**'s journey through Ethiopia

takes him to Gondar, Lake Tana and the capital city of Addis Ababa. From the border town of Moyale, he continues south through Kenya to the village of Lerata (where **Palin** filmed part of *The Missionary* in June 1982) and on to the Equator line. Then, after gearing up in Nairobi, he heads off on safari in Masai Mara National Park. Fifth episode of the eight-part travel series. Written & narrated by **Michael Palin**. Directed by Roger Mills and Clem Vallance.

1905 November 21, 1992
Going Live! (TV talk show: BBC1). **Michael Palin** talks to Sarah Greene about his series *Pole to Pole* on this Saturday-morning magazine show for children. Hosted by Greene and Phillip Schofield.

1906 November 25, 1992
Pole to Pole (TV episode: BBC1). "Plains and Boats and Trains." **Michael Palin** watches animals from a hot-air balloon over Masai Mara in Kenya, then moves south into Tanzania, passing through Serengeti National Park, to the capital of Dodoma. From there he takes a train west to Kigoma, followed by a visit to Ujiji, where Livingstone met Stanley in 1871. He then travels by ferry down Lake Tanganyika to Mpulungu in Zambia. Sixth episode of the eight-part travel series. Written & narrated by **Michael Palin**. Directed by Clem Vallance.

1907 December 1992–1995
Health Education Authority (Anti-Smoking) (TV/radio commercials). **John Cleese** stars in a series of British TV & radio ads urging people to quit smoking as part of a campaign run by the Health Education Authority. Titles include "Withdrawal Symptoms," "Relax," "Juggling," "Morgue," "Smoking Machine," "Ash," "Preach," "Children," "Robot," "Coughing," "Disgusting Habits," "Over," "Tempted," and "Quitline." The ads are given a regional trial before going national in 1994–95. Written by Richard Foster. Directed by Robert Young. Agency: Abbott Mead Vickers BBDO, London.

1908 December 2, 1992
Pole to Pole (TV episode: BBC1). "Evil Shadow." In Zambia, **Michael Palin** consults a witch doctor (in Mpulungu), visits an English-style estate (Shiwa), and goes white-water rafting on the Zambezi River (on the border with Zimbabwe). In South Africa, he visits a gold mine and a Soweto hostel (Johannesburg). He finally makes it to the southern tip of Africa (Cape Town), but the supply ship bound for Antarctica has no available spaces. Seventh episode of the eight-part travel series. Written & narrated by **Michael Palin**. Directed by Roger Mills.

1909 December 4, 1992
Record Breakers (TV show: BBC1). Roy Castle interviews **Michael Palin** about his journey in *Pole to Pole*.

1910 December 7, 1992
Live with Regis and Kathie Lee (TV talk show: Synd.). Hosted by Regis Philbin and Kathie Lee Gifford. Guests include **Michael Palin**, promoting *Pole to Pole*, and Kenny Rogers.

1911 December 8, 1992
Late Night with David Letterman (TV talk show: NBC). Guests: **Michael Palin**, promoting *Pole to Pole*, Rich Hall, and Christy Turlington.

1912 December 9, 1992
Pole to Pole (TV episode: BBC1). "Bitter End." Unable to sail from South Africa, **Michael Palin** is forced to leave the 30-degree meridian and fly to Santiago in Chile, then down to Punta Arenas on the tip of South America. From there, he takes a plane to Antarctica, reaching the South Pole on day 141 of his journey. Eighth and final episode of the travel series. Written & narrated by **Michael Palin**. Directed by Clem Vallance.

1913 December 11, 1992
Prisoners of Conscience (TV episode: BBC2). **John Cleese** presents this profile of Tibetan doctor Dr. Nyarongsha Jampa Ngodrup, who has been imprisoned by the Chinese. Directed by Deborah Wearn. Produced by Rex Bloomstein.

1914 December 14, 1992
Start the Week (Radio talk show: BBC Radio 4). Hosted by Melvyn Bragg. Guests: Heather Couper, **Terry Jones**, Michael Bywater, and W. J. West.

1915 December 20, 1992
Funny Business (TV episode: BBC2). "A Question of Taste." **John Cleese** appears in this mock-documentary. Fifth episode of a six-part series on comedy. Written & directed by Mark Chapman. Produced by Sarah Williams.

1916 December 24, 1992
In the Beginning (TV special: BBC2). Ten-minute animated version of the Creation and the Fall. Voiced by **John Cleese** (as the Serpent), Harry Enfield (Adam), Janet McTeer (Eve), and Michael Hordern (God). Created & written by Bud Han-

delsman. Directed by Steve Billinger. Produced by Peter Armstrong.

1917 December 28, 1992
John Cleese marries his third wife, Alyce Faye Eichelberger, an American-born psychotherapist, in Barbados. **Cleese** had previously been married to Connie Booth [1968–78] and Barbara Trentham [1981–90], both American. **Cleese** and Eichelberger will also divorce (in 2008).

1918 1992
Terry Jones works on bringing *Gargantua*, a musical spectacular he's written based on the 16th-century novels *Gargantua and Pantagruel* by François Rabelais, to the West End stage. The production, which will include "acrobatics, juggling, stilt-walking and giant puppets," is originally set to open in the fall, but due to lack of funds is postponed until the spring. The project is eventually shelved.

1919 1992
Schweppes (TV commercial). **John Cleese** stars in this parody of Calvin Klein's arty, black & white "Obsession" ads. Directed by Paul Weiland. Agency: Saatchi & Saatchi, London.
Award: Winner of the Gold Lion at the 40th Cannes International Advertising Film Festival.

1920 1992
John Cleese starts writing the script for *Fierce Creatures*, his follow-up to *A Fish Called Wanda*, in collaboration with former film critic Iain Johnstone.

1921 January 1993
Monty Python and the Holy Grail: The Criterion Collection (Laserdisc: Criterion Collection 168/Columbia TriStar). Laserdisc release of the 1975 comedy. Bonus features: audio commentary by **Terry Gilliam** and **Terry Jones**, original theatrical trailer, the missing "24 seconds" (from "Castle Anthrax"), photo gallery, and a Japanese-dubbed version of the film. Distributed by The Voyager Company. Re-released (with more bonus features) on DVD in October 2001.

1922 January 1, 1993
First Night on Meridian (TV special: ITV/Meridian). Special hosted by **Michael Palin** on the New Year's Day launching of Meridian TV, ITV's franchise holder in southern England. **Palin**, a co-founder of Meridian, travels across the Meridian region, from Brighton to the Isle of Wight, conducting interviews with the public and previewing upcoming programs (including *A Class Act*, co-starring **Palin** and Tracey Ullman). Later in the year **Palin** returns to the Isle of Wight to film his four-part series *Palin's Column* for Meridian.

1923 January 8, 1993
Terry Wogan's Friday Night (TV talk show: BBC1). Hosted by Terry Wogan. Guests: **Michael Palin**, Arthur Smith, Neil Kinnock, and Sheila Hancock.

1924 January 9, 1993
Tracey Ullman: A Class Act (TV special: ITV/Meridian). Tracey Ullman plays multiple characters in this comedic take on the British class system. **Michael Palin** co-stars in the vignettes "37 Up," about three children whose lives are documented into adulthood, and "Hethers," in which Ullman and **Palin** play parents who sacrifice greatly to send their daughter to a posh girls' school. With Timothy Spall and Susan Wooldridge. Written by Dick Clement, Ian La Frenais, Kim Fuller, Gary Howe, and Richard Preddy. Directed by Les Blair. Produced by Jo Wright. Airs in the U.S. on Nov. 23, 1993 (HBO).

1925 January 10, 1993
Michael Palin's eight-part series, *Pole to Pole*, begins airing in the U.S. on A&E.

1926 January 29, 1993
The Times (London) (Newspaper/U.K.). "The Shrink and the Shrunken," by Valerie Grove, p. 12. Interview with **John Cleese**.

1927 February 1993
The British Book Awards (Award ceremony). **Michael Palin** is named Travel Writer of the Year for his book *Pole to Pole*.

1928 February 1, 1993
The play *The Dresser* is recorded for radio with **Michael Palin** playing the role of Norman. The play airs Mar. 29 on BBC Radio 4.

1929 February 1, 1993
Jackanory (TV show: BBC1). "Fantastic Stories: The Slow Ogre." Read by **Terry Jones**, from his 1992 children's book *Fantastic Stories*. First of three.

1930 February 8, 1993
Start the Week (Radio talk show: BBC Radio 4). Hosted by Melvyn Bragg and Brenda Maddox. Guests: **John Cleese**, Robin Skynner, Fay Weldon, and Shirley Reynolds.

1931 February 8, 1993
Jackanory (TV show: BBC1). "Fantastic Stories:

The Star of the Farmyard." Read by **Terry Jones**, from his 1992 children's book *Fantastic Stories*. Second of three.

1932   February 11, 1993
Life and How to Survive It (Book: Methuen), written by Robin Skynner and **John Cleese**, is published in the U.K. In this follow-up to their bestselling 1983 book *Families and How to Survive Them*, Skynner and **Cleese** extend their study to our behavior in society, as individuals and as groups. Like *Families*, the book is written in dialogue form, with cartoons by Bud Handelsman. Paperback issued in October 1994 (Mandarin). Published in the U.S. in January 1995 (W.W. Norton & Co.).
Review: Polly Toynbee (*The Times* [London], Oct. 1, 1994, p. 15): "This is not the kind of *How To* book that makes you want to hurl it into the fireplace after a few pages, nauseated by a know-it-all superciliousness nor with an overly chummy tone."

1933   February 22, 1993
Film 93 (TV show: BBC1). Hosted by Barry Norman. A location report from the set of *Splitting Heirs* at Longleat House (in Wiltshire, England) includes interviews with stars **Eric Idle** and Catherine Zeta Jones and director Robert Young.

1934   February 24, 1993
John Cleese and Robin Skynner, authors of the new book *Life and How to Survive It*, join moderator Brian Redhead at a forum on relationships outside the family at the Institute of Education in London. The event is sponsored by *The Times* and Dillons bookshops.

1935   March 2, 1993
Michael Palin opens the Michael Palin Centre for Stammering Children in the Finsbury Health Centre in London. The Centre was established by the ARSC (Association for Research into Stammering in Childhood) and the local NHS trust. **Palin**'s involvement with the ARSC (launched in February 1991) came about through his own personal experience with stammering: his father had suffered from a life-long stammer. He also played the stammering character, Ken, in 1988's *A Fish Called Wanda*. The Centre is re-located to Pine Street in September 2011.

1936   March 8, 1993
Jackanory (TV show: BBC1). "Fantastic Stories: The Ship of Fools." Read by **Terry Jones**, from his 1992 children's book *Fantastic Stories*. Last of three.

1937   March 20, 1993
The Bore of the Year Awards (TV special: BBC2). **Michael Palin** receives the Alan Whicker International Award for Travel Bore of the Year on this first televised Private Eye "BOFTY" Awards. **Palin** appears in a film preview of a new travel show, *Curb to Curb with Palin*, in which he attempts to cross a London street. Hosted by Angus Deayton. Directed by Janet Fraser-Crook.

1938   March 28, 1993
Aspel & Company (TV talk show: ITV/LWT). Hosted by Michael Aspel. Guests: **Eric Idle**, promoting *Splitting Heirs*, Jackie Collins, Peter Gabriel, and Gary Webster.

1939   March 29, 1993
Eric Idle turns 50.

1940   March 29, 1993
The Monday Play (Radio play: BBC Radio 4). "The Dresser." Adaptation for radio of Ronald Harwood's 1980 stage play about the devoted assistant of an aging actor touring with a Shakespearean company during World War II. **Michael Palin** plays Norman (the dresser) in his radio drama debut. Freddie Jones plays "Sir," the role he created on stage. Adapted & directed by David Blount. Recorded Feb. 1.

1941   April 1993
Splitting Heirs, starring **Eric Idle** and **John Cleese**, is selected as one of five British entries in competition at the Cannes Film Festival in France.

1942   April 1993
Dick Cavett (TV talk show: CNBC). Guest **Michael Palin**, promoting *American Friends*, also talks about his reputation for being nice, Python's lack of topicality, *Pole to Pole*, and **John Cleese** prank-calling him in a Scandinavian accent.

1943   April 1, 1993
Today (TV news-talk show: NBC). Guest: **Michael Palin**, promoting *American Friends*.

1944   April 1, 1993
Late Night with David Letterman (TV talk show: NBC). Guests: **Michael Palin**, promoting *American Friends*, Calvin Trillin, and Jonathan Solomon.

1945   April 2, 1993
Splitting Heirs (Feature film: Universal Pictures) opens in the U.K. In this comedy, which he also wrote and executive-produced, **Eric Idle** plays Tommy Henry Butterfly Rainbow Peace Patel, a commodities broker raised in a poor Pakistani fam-

ily who discovers that he had been switched with another baby and is really the 15th Duke of Bournemouth. **John Cleese** co-stars as Tommy's attorney, Raoul P. Shadgrind, who suggests murder as the only way for Tommy to obtain his rightful title. **Idle** also wrote and performs the songs "Someone Stole My Baby" and "La Mére" (music by Michael Kamen). Also starring Rick Moranis, Barbara Hershey, Catherine Zeta Jones, and Sadie Frost. Directed by Robert Young. Produced by Simon Bosanquet and Redmond Morris. A Prominent Features production. Opens in the U.S. on Apr. 30.

Reviews: Geoff Brown (*The Times* [London], Apr. 1, 1993): "**Eric Idle** wrote a script that manages perhaps three good jokes in 89 minutes..."; Ralph Novak (*People*, May 24, 1993): "Despite the pleasure and promise of the onscreen reunion of Monty Pythonites **Cleese** and **Idle** ... this labored farce, written by **Idle**, drags painfully."

1946   April 3, 1993
Going Live! (TV talk show: BBC1). **Eric Idle** is a guest on this Saturday-morning magazine show for children. Hosted by Phillip Schofield and Sarah Greene.

1947   April 4, 1993
The Sunday Times (London) (Newspaper/U.K.). "Idle He Isn't," by Iain Johnstone, p. 15 (sect. 9). Interview with **Eric Idle** about his new film *Splitting Heirs*, his friendships with rock stars, etc.

1948   April 7, 1993
The Tonight Show with Jay Leno (TV talk show: NBC). Guests: **Michael Palin**, promoting *American Friends*, Jack Coen, and Wendy Moten. **Palin**, his voice hoarse from laryngitis, talks about *Pole to Pole*, visiting Russia, etc.

1949   April 9, 1993
American Friends, co-written by and starring **Michael Palin**, opens in select U.S. cities (Castle Hill Productions). The film was originally released in the U.K. in March 1991.

1950   April 15, 1993
CBS This Morning (TV news-talk show: CBS). Guest **Michael Palin**, promoting *American Friends*, also talks about making travel documentaries.

1951   April 16, 1993
Late Night with David Letterman (TV talk show: NBC). Guest: **Eric Idle**, promoting *Splitting Heirs*, also talks about "Always Look on the Bright Side of Life" being a No. 1 hit in Britain last year.

1952   April 23, 1993
Robin Williams: Acting Funny (TV special: Channel 4). Profile of actor-comedian Robin Williams, with comments from **Terry Gilliam** (who directed Williams in *Baron Munchausen* and *The Fisher King*), Robert Altman, and others. Produced & directed by Chris Rodley.

1953   April 25, 1993
The Boston Globe (Newspaper/U.S.). "**Eric Idle**'s Karmic Reward," by Matthew Gilbert, p. B31. Interview with **Idle** about his latest film *Splitting Heirs*.

1954   April 26, 1993
Film 93 (TV show: BBC1). Hosted by Barry Norman. **John Cleese**, Alan Parker, Kenneth Branagh, and others comment on the state of the British film industry.

1955   April 26, 1993
Splitting Heirs stars **Eric Idle** and Catherine Zeta Jones appear at New York's Planet Hollywood where, to publicize the film, they donate a baby blanket used in the production to the club's collection of film memorabilia.

1956   Late April 1993
CBS This Morning (TV news-talk show: CBS). Guest **Eric Idle** talks about *Splitting Heirs*, Python, and The Rutles.

1957   April 30, 1993
Splitting Heirs, starring **Eric Idle** and **John Cleese**, opens in the U.S.

1958   May 1993
Eric Idle attends the Cannes Film Festival in France where his film *Splitting Heirs* is the British entry.

1959   May 5, 1993
Michael Palin turns 50.

1960   May 7, 1993
The Tonight Show with Jay Leno (TV talk show: NBC). Guests: **Eric Idle**, promoting *Splitting Heirs*, Paulina Porizkova, and Poison. **Idle** also talks about censorship on the Python TV series, performing in *The Royal Variety Performance* (in November 1991), and tells a story about the Queen and a flatulent horse.

1961   May 26, 1993
Film 93 Special (TV show: BBC1). Barry Norman, reporting from the Cannes Film Festival, interviews **Eric Idle** about his film *Splitting Heirs*.

1962 Late May 1993
Michael Palin and Terry Jones appear at the Hay-on-Wye Festival of Literature (May 28–June 6) in Wales. Palin gives a talk on the South Pole.

1963 May 31–June 7, 1993
Making Hay (TV series: Channel 4). Three-part series in which Terry Jones reports from the Hay-on-Wye Festival of Literature. Produced by Jeremy Bugler.

1964 June 8, 1993
Four-Mations: Aspects of Comedy (TV special: Channel 4). "Bob Godfrey: A Life in Shorts." Profile of animator Bob Godfrey. Interviewees include Terry Gilliam, Michael Bentine, Ann Jolliffe, and Stan Hayward. Directed by Paul Madden. Note: Gilliam appeared with Godfrey on an episode of his *Do-It-Yourself Film Animation Show* in May 1974.

1965 June 11, 1993
Gabereau (Radio talk show: CBC Radio, in Canada). Vicki Gabereau talks to John Cleese about his new book *Life and How to Survive It*.

1966 June 30, 1993
Michael Palin announces the winners of the Carnegie and Kate Greenaway Medals (children's book awards) at a ceremony held at South Bank Centre in London. Presented by the British Library Association.

1967 July 1993
Did I Ever Tell You How Lucky You Are? (Audiobook cassette: Random House). John Cleese narrates Dr. Seuss' 1973 children's story. Cleese's narration was also used to accompany Seuss' drawings on a 1993 video version (Random House Home Video), part of the "Dr. Seuss Video Classics" series. Produced by Sharon Lerner.
Award: Grammy-nominated for Best Spoken Word Album for Children.

1968 July 15, 1993
Under the Sun (TV special: BBC2). "The Cat and the Mouse." John Cleese talks to the Dalai Lama in India about the Chinese occupation of Tibet. Written & produced by John Paul Davidson. Note: Michael Palin meets the Dalai Lama in the second episode (Oct. 10, 2004) of his series *Himalaya*.

1969 July 16, 1993
Eric Idle and his wife attend a "Bastille Day"–themed costume party in London celebrating the 50th birthday (on July 26) of singer Mick Jagger. The party, thrown by Jagger's wife Jerry Hall, is held at Walpole House at St. Mary's University College. Other attendees include Keith Richards, Ron Wood, Bill Wyman, Charlie Watts, and Peter Cook.

1970 August 2, 1993
Financial Times (Newspaper/U.K.). "Acting the Guru," by Lucy Kellaway, p. 9. Interview with John Cleese about his management training videos and what makes a healthy company.

1971 August 27–November 12, 1993
Michael Palin writes four guest columns (published Aug. 27, Sept. 24, Oct. 22 & Nov. 12) for the *Isle of Wight County Press* newspaper in Isle of Wight, off England's southern coast. Palin's experiences during his four weeks on the island are also chronicled in a four-part travelogue, *Palin's Column*, which airs in January 1994 on Meridian TV.

1972 August 30, 1993
Frost in the Air (TV episode: BBC2). "Supertelevisionman." Part two of a three-part biography of Sir David Frost. John Cleese, who worked with Frost on *The Frost Report* (1966–67) is among the interviewees. Produced by John Bush.

1973 October 1993–1995
Cellnet (TV commercials). John Cleese and Ronnie Corbett appear in British ads for Cellnet mobile phones. In one ad Cleese and Corbett (both in drag) queue up for Joanna Lumley look-alike auditions. In another ad ("Operations") they play army surgeons. Agency: Abbott Mead Vickers BBDO, London.

1974 October 1993
Michael Palin reads a poem for BBC2's *Poems on the Box* series.

1975 October 9, 1993
Danny Baker After All (TV talk show: BBC1). Guests include Terry Gilliam, Tony Collins, and Lloyd Grossman.

1976 November 6, 1993
The Times Magazine (London) (Magazine/U.K.). "A Childhood: Terry Gilliam," by Guy Walters, p. 70. Gilliam talks about growing up in Minnesota and (from 1951) California.

1977 December 4, 1993
The 1993 European Film Awards (Felix Awards) (Award Ceremony). Terry Jones is a presenter at the 6th annual awards held at the Babelsberg Studios in Potsdam, Germany. Jones recently became a member of the European Film Academy.

1978 December 14, 1993
Michael Palin opens the newly refurbished London Transport Museum in Covent Garden and delivers a speech ("Time for a Change").

1979 December 16, 1993
Big City (TV show: ITV/Carlton). Hosted by Gordon Kennedy and Carolyn Marshall. **Michael Palin** is interviewed about the reopening of the London Transport Museum.

1980 December 19, 1993
Devout Sceptics (Radio show: BBC Radio 4). Host Bel Mooney talks to **John Cleese** about the nature of belief.

1981 December 27, 1993
The Best of Rutland Weekend Television (TV special: BBC2). Half-hour compilation of clips from **Eric Idle**'s 1975-76 comedy series.

1982 December 27, 1993
Last of the Summer Wine (TV episode: BBC1). "Welcome to Earth." **John Cleese** makes a guest appearance in this fifteenth season episode of the long-running (1973–2010) British sitcom starring Peter Sallis, Bill Owen, and Brian Wilde. Written by Roy Clarke. Produced & directed by Alan J. W. Bell.

1983 1993–2000
What You Really Need to Know About… (Video series: Video Arts). Series of videos providing medical information for patients, conceived by **John Cleese** in collaboration with Toronto-based oncologist Dr. Robert Buckman (former comedy partner of Chris Beetles). The videos are introduced by **Cleese**, written & presented by Buckman, and directed by Graeme Garden. The 45+ titles produced for the "Videos for Patients" series cover high blood pressure (1993), breast cancer (1993), depression (1993), shingles (1993), migraine (1993), chronic bronchitis and emphysema (1993), asthma (1993), Crohn's disease (1993), rheumatoid arthritis (1993), epilepsy (1994), hepatitis (1994), cystic fibrosis (1994), stress (1994), strokes (1996), heart attacks (1996), diabetes (1996), cholesterol (1996), prostate cancer (1996), anxiety, phobias and panic attacks (1996), schizophrenia (1996), bladder problems (2000), Parkinson's disease (2000), etc. The series is produced by Video Arts, the business-training film company **Cleese** co-founded in 1972. The videos also spawned a series of books published in 2000 by Lebhar-Friedman, written by Buckman with introductions by **Cleese**.
Awards: 1993 Evian Health Award for Medical Information; 1994 British Medical Association Silver Award & Bronze Award.

1984 1993
Meetings, Bloody Meetings (Training film: Video Arts). Remake of the classic 1976 film (and remade again in 2012). Starring **John Cleese**, Robert Hardy, Jeremy Child, Alphonsia Emmanuel, Michael Fenton Stevens, Kulvinder Ghir, Julian Holloway, Ian Hogg, Lesley Nightingale, Michael Percival, Don Warrington, and Diana Weston. Written by **John Cleese** and Antony Jay. Directed by Peter Robinson.

1985 1993
The Balance Sheet Barrier (Training film: Video Arts). Remake of the 1977 film. Starring **John Cleese** (as Julian Carruthers) and Dawn French. Written by Antony Jay. Directed by Peter Robinson.

1986 1993
It's Your Choice: Selection Skills for Managers (Training film: Video Arts). How to conduct a successful selection interview. Starring **John Cleese** (as Ivan the Terrible), Hugh Laurie, Dawn French, Simon Shepherd, Philip Franks, and Meera Syal. Written by **John Cleese** and Antony Jay. Directed by Robert Young.

1987 January 5–26, 1994
The four-part TV documentary series *Palin's Column* airs on Meridian TV (ITV south/southeast region). In these four half-hour shows, **Michael Palin** visits the Isle of Wight, off the south coast of England, in search of material for the four guest columns he is to write for the local *Isle of Wight County Press* newspaper. Filmed in the summer & fall of 1993. The series is re-broadcast June 6–27 on Channel 4.

1988 January 5, 1994
Palin's Column (TV episode: ITV/Meridian). "Black and Wight Magic." **Michael Palin** investigates stories of black magic on the Isle of Wight. First episode in the four-part series. Written & hosted by **Michael Palin**. Produced & directed by Roger Mills.

1989 January 6, 1994
The Big Breakfast (TV talk show: Channel 4). Hosted by Gaby Roslin and Paul Ross. Guest: **Michael Palin**.

1990 January 11, 1994
John Cleese receives the 1993 Jack Oakie Award for Comedy in Motion Pictures (2nd annual) from

the Screen Actors Guild Foundation at a charity dinner held at the Regent Beverly Wilshire Hotel in Beverly Hills. **Michael Palin, Eric Idle**, and Jamie Lee Curtis are among the speakers at the event.

1991 January 12, 1994
Palin's Column (TV episode: ITV/Meridian). "A Gap in the Market." **Michael Palin** visits a collector of dinosaur fossils. Second episode in the four-part series. Written & hosted by **Michael Palin**. Produced & directed by Roger Mills.

1992 January 14, 1994
The Unpleasant World of Penn & Teller (TV episode: Channel 4). **John Cleese** participates in a magic trick involving a water tank and a deck of cards on this British show starring American magician-comedians Penn & Teller. Produced by Peter Orton.

1993 January 19, 1994
Palin's Column (TV episode: ITV/Meridian). "Old Haunts." **Michael Palin** visits the Needles Lighthouse off the west coast of the Isle of Wight and the supposedly haunted sites of Golden Hill Fort and Ventnor's Botanic Gardens. Third episode in the four-part series. Written & hosted by **Michael Palin**. Produced & directed by Roger Mills.

1994 January 19, 1994
The Late Show (TV show: BBC2). Music/arts program hosted by Tracey MacLeod. Guest **Terry Jones** talks about books.

1995 January 22, 1994
Eric Idle and his wife attend the *51st Annual Golden Globe Awards* at the Beverly Hilton Hotel in Beverly Hills, CA.

1996 January 24, 1994
Jesting Pilate: The Diary of a Journey (Book: Flamingo Modern Classic), written by Aldous Huxley, is published in the U.K. Reissue of Huxley's 1926 book, with a foreword by **Michael Palin**. One of 26 Huxley books reissued this year to celebrate the centenary of the author's birth.

1997 January 26, 1994
Palin's Column (TV episode: ITV/Meridian). "I Came, I Saw, I Conkered." **Michael Palin** participates in an Isle of Wight conker tournament and visits Parkhust prison. Fourth episode in the four-part series. Written & hosted by **Michael Palin**. Produced & directed by Roger Mills.

1998 February 3, 1994
Great Railway Journeys (TV episode: BBC2). "Derry to Kerry." In his second *Great Railway* journey (following 1980's "Confessions of a Train Spotter"), **Michael Palin** travels from Derry in Northern Ireland to Kerry in the south on a quest to trace the roots of his great-grandmother, Brita Gallagher. Along the way he visits Lord O'Neill (at Shane's Castle), his friend Michael Barnes (in Belfast), The Edge (of U2), and writer Molly Keane (in Co. Waterford). He also enjoys a performance of The All-Priest Show in Dublin, travels on the "Peace Train," and takes a ride on a Harley Davidson. Written & hosted by **Michael Palin**. Produced & directed by Ken Stephinson.

1999 February 22, 1994
Pole to Pole (Lecture). **Michael Palin** speaks at the Royal Geographical Society in London as part of the *Sunday Times*' "Lunchtime Lectures" series.

2000 February 23, 1994
Open Space (TV special: BBC2). "Car Sick." Documentary, hosted by **Michael Palin**, examining the adverse environmental and health effects of increasing car traffic on Britain's roadways. **Palin** is president (since 1988) of the pressure group Transport 2000. Directed by Mike MacCormack. Produced by Gavin Dutton.

2001 February 26, 1994
Live and Kicking (TV show: BBC1). Saturday-morning children's show hosted by Andi Peters, Emma Forbes & John Barrowman. Guests include **Michael Palin**, Shane Richie, and The Proclaimers. **Palin** talks about his *Great Railway Journeys* episode.

2002 February 27, 1994
Sunday Night Clive (TV talk show: BBC1). Hosted by Clive James. Guests: **Michael Palin**, Ruby Wax, and Latoya Jackson. **Palin** talks about playing football at school, dancing lessons, playing conkers, Marlon Brando, and acting with a pig in *A Private Function*.

2003 March 15, 1994
Michael Palin's first stage play, *The Weekend*, premieres at the Yvonne Arnaud Theatre in Guildford, England. The play will run there until Mar. 26, then tour for several more weeks (in Brighton, Wimbledon, Sheffield, and Crawley) before opening in London's West End on May 3.

2004 April 1994
Michael Palin launches an appeal to raise money

for the Whirlow Hall Farm Trust, a children's charity, in his home town of Sheffield, England.

2005   April 9, 1994
Arena (TV arts show: BBC2). "Philip K. Dick: A Day in the Afterlife." Documentary on science-fiction author Philip K. Dick (1928–1982). **Terry Gilliam** is among the interviewees. Directed by Nicola Roberts.

2006   April 17, 1994
An Evening with Michael Palin (Lecture). **Michael Palin** gives a talk at the Cambridge Theatre in London. The event benefits the Michael Palin Centre for Stammering Children.

2007   April 21, 1994
The Frost Programme (TV talk show: ITV). Hosted by David Frost. Guest: **Michael Palin**, promoting his play *The Weekend*.

2008   April 22, 1994
This Morning (TV show: ITV/Granada). Magazine program hosted by Richard Madeley and Judy Finnigan. Guest: **Michael Palin**, promoting *The Weekend*.

2009   April 24, 1994
Michael Palin attends the memorial service for his friend, cartoonist Mel Calman, at the National Museum of Cartoon Art in London. Calman died on Feb. 10 at age 62.

2010   April 24, 1994
The Sunday Times Magazine (London) (Magazine/U.K.). "More Mr. Nice Guy," by Sally Vincent, pp. 56–61. Interview with **Michael Palin** about his family, career, and new play *The Weekend*. Photographs by Tim Richmond.

2011   April 26, 1994
Michael Palin's play *The Weekend* opens in previews at The Strand Theatre in London's West End.

2012   April 26, 1994
The Big Breakfast (TV talk show: Channel 4). Guests: **Michael Palin** and Richard Wilson, author and star of the new play *The Weekend*, are interviewed by puppets Zig and Zag.

2013   April 26, 1994
Kaleidoscope at 21 (Radio show: BBC Radio 4). Guest: **Michael Palin**, promoting *The Weekend*.

2014   May 1994
The first seven episodes of the first season of *Monty Python's Flying Circus* are released on video for the first time in Britain. The entire series will be released throughout the year. Previously, only seasons two and three have been available on video.

2015   May 2, 1994
The Times (London) (Newspaper/U.K.). "A Weekend in the Life of...," by Kate Bassett, p. 29. Interview with **Michael Palin**, conducted at the Waldorf, on the eve of the opening of his new play *The Weekend*.

2016   May 3, 1994
The Independent (Newspaper/U.K.). "Theatre: A Month and a Half in the Country," by **Michael Palin**. Diary account of **Palin**'s experiences during rehearsals and tryouts for his play *The Weekend*.

2017   May 3, 1994
The Weekend (Stage play), written by **Michael Palin**, opens at The Strand Theatre in London's West End. **Palin**'s first full-length stage play, written in 1979, is a comedy-drama about a cantankerous old man and his long-suffering wife whose daughter (and family) comes to visit for the weekend. The cast includes Richard Wilson (of TV's *One Foot in the Grave*) as Stephen Febble and Angela Thorne as his wife, Virginia. The play premiered Mar. 15 at the Yvonne Arnaud Theatre in Guildford. Closes July 9. Directed by Robin Lefevre. Note: **Palin**'s previous plays, *Secrets* (1973, co-written with **Terry Jones**), *East of Ipswich* (1987), and *Number 27* (1988), were all written for television.
Reviews: Benedict Nightingale (*The Times* [London], May 5, 1994, p. 38): "*The Weekend* often looks and sounds like the first stage play it reportedly is. It lacks economy, tension, momentum, control of mood, sureness of tone"; Alastair Macaulay (*Financial Times*, May 5, 1994, p. 23): "Most of **Michael Palin**'s first play, *The Weekend*, feels just like a TV sitcom.... How disappointing to find [**Palin**] writing so conventional a comedy, and so creakily constructed a play."

2018   May 13, 1994
Emergency Appeal for Rwanda (TV appeal: BBC1). **Michael Palin** delivers a 3-minute appeal on behalf of the Disasters Emergency Committee working to aid victims of the war in Rwanda. Written & produced by Jill Dawson.

2019   May 16, 1994
The Weekend (Book: Methuen Drama), written by **Michael Palin**, is published in the U.K. **Palin**'s first stage play, produced at The Strand Theatre in May 1994.

2020 May 25, 1994
The Independent (Newspaper/U.K.). "Dead Parrots and All That," by Michael Leapman. Interview with **Michael Palin** about his attempt at writing a newspaper column for his series *Palin's Column*.

2021 May 29, 1994
The Sunday Times (London) (Newspaper/U.K.). "A Funny Thing, Humour," by Mark Edwards, pp. 14–15. As Monty Python celebrates its 25th anniversary, Edwards takes a closer look at their place in the evolution of comedy.

2022 June 6–27, 1994
Michael Palin's four-part TV documentary series *Palin's Column* airs on Channel 4. The series originally aired on Meridian TV in January.

2023 June 9, 1994
Esio Trot (Audiobook: HarperCollins Audio). Audio version of Roald Dahl's 1990 children's story, read by **Michael Palin**. Released on one 33-minute cassette. Note: **Eric Idle** reads Dahl's *Charlie and the Chocolate Factory* and *Charlie and the Great Glass Elevator* for audiobooks in 2002 and 2004, respectively.

2024 June 12, 1994
Comedy Tonight!: A Tribute to Roy Kinnear (Stage show). **Michael Palin** appears at this comedy event in aid of The Roy Kinnear Trust, at the Olivier Theatre in London. Also starring David Frost, Peter Ustinov, Tim Brooke-Taylor, Peter O'Toole, Millicent Martin, Eddie Izzard, and many others.

2025 June 27, 1994
Eric Idle attends a memorial service for Australian actress Madge Ryan at St. James, Piccadilly, London. Ryan, who died on Jan. 9 at age 75, was the mother of **Idle**'s first wife, Lyn Ashley, and the grandmother of their son, Carey. Lyn and Carey also attend, as does **Idle**'s wife (Tania) and mother (Norah).

2026 August 21, 1994
Poetry Please! (Radio show: BBC Radio 4). Guest **Terry Jones** discusses Chaucer.

2027 September 1994
Monty Python's Complete Waste of Time (CD-ROM: 7th Level). Monty Python's first CD-ROM computer game. Features include a Desktop Pythonizer (for Windows desktop), screensavers, classic sketches & songs from *Flying Circus*, **Terry Gilliam**'s original art, also newly-written material and vocal contributions from the surviving Pythons (except **John Cleese**), and the chance to "Solve the Secret to Intergalactic Success." Produced by Mark Finkel and Valerie Grant. Executive produced by **Terry Gilliam** and Bob Ezrin. Followed in 1996 by *Monty Python & the Quest for the Holy Grail* (also 7th Level).
Award: CODiE Award for Best Strategy Program.

2028 September 1994
The Instant Monty Python CD Collection (CD: Virgin Records CDBOX3). Six-disc set compiling all of the group's recorded output, including some tracks previously unreleased in the U.S.

2029 Early September 1994
John Cleese makes a citizen's arrest near his home in Notting Hill (West London). Wearing a dressing gown and slippers, **Cleese** chases down a 14-year-old boy after the youth snatched a woman's handbag.

2030 Early September 1994
Terry Gilliam, **Eric Idle**, and **Terry Jones** attend a party celebrating Python's 25th anniversary at the British Consul General's home in Los Angeles.

2031 September 8, 1994
The Los Angeles Times (Newspaper/U.S.). "Why Michael Palin's M.I.A. at Python Festival," by **Michael Palin**, p. F4. **Palin** explains in a humorous open letter why he is unable to attend the Python 25th-anniversary festival in Los Angeles.

2032 September 9–13, 1994
Monty Python: Lust for Glory! (Screenings). Five-day film & television festival celebrating the 25th anniversary of Monty Python, held at the Directors Guild Theatre in Los Angeles. The festival, organized by Martin Lewis and co-sponsored by the American Cinematheque and the British Academy of Film and Television Arts, features both group and solo work, including a 12-hour marathon screening of episodes of *Monty Python's Flying Circus*. Also screened is "Life of Graham," a tribute to **Graham Chapman** shown on opening night. Three Pythons—**Terry Gilliam**, **Eric Idle**, and **Terry Jones**—and Python collaborators Neil Innes and Carol Cleveland attend the festival and take part in post-screening discussions.

2033 September 18, 1994
The Radio 2 Arts Programme (Radio show: BBC Radio 2). "The Life of Python." A look back at 25 years of Monty Python, with **Michael Palin**, **Terry Jones**, and Barry Took.

2034 September 21, 1994
John Cleese, Terry Gilliam, Michael Palin, and **Terry Jones** reunite to celebrate the 25th anniversary of Monty Python at an event held at the Museum of the Moving Image in London.

2035 September 21, 1994
The Times (London) (Newspaper/U.K.). "Pythons Still Flying High," by Patrick Stoddart, p. 23. Article on Monty Python's debut 25 years ago.

2036 October 1994
The Ultimate Monty Python Rip Off (CD: Virgin Records CDV 2748). Compilation of previously-released sketches and songs.

2037 October 1994
Python Periphery (Screenings). Month-long showing of lesser-known work by Monty Python, at The National Film Theatre in London, in celebration of the group's 25th anniversary.

2038 October 1, 1994
The Fairly Incomplete & Rather Badly Illustrated Monty Python Song Book (Book: Methuen) is published in the U.K. Compilation of 44 Python songs from their TV series, films and records, including "Lumberjack Song" and "Always Look on the Bright Side of Life." Foreword by "Elvis Presley." Designed by Gary Marsh. Illustrated by **Terry Gilliam**, Gary Marsh, and John Hurst. Music edited by John Du Prez. Published in the U.S. by HarperPerennial (1994). Reissued Oct. 10, 2005 (Methuen).

2039 October 7, 1994
Clive Anderson Talks Back (TV talk show: Channel 4). Guests: Melvyn Bragg, Damon Hill, and **Terry Jones**.

2040 October 9, 1994
The Big Byte (Radio show: BBC Radio 5 Live). **Terry Gilliam** talks about the new interactive CD-ROM *Monty Python's Complete Waste of Time*.

2041 October 9, 1994
Terry Gilliam participates in a live America Online chat to promote *Monty Python's Complete Waste of Time*.

2042 October 10, 1994
Lunchtime Show (Radio show: BBC Radio 1). Emma Freud talks to **Terry Jones**.

2043 October 13, 1994
Lady Cottington's Pressed Fairy Book (Book: Pavilion), written by **Terry Jones** with illustrations by Brian Froud, is published in the U.K. **Jones** and Froud, who had previously collaborated on *The Goblins of Labyrinth* (1986), re-teamed for this volume which claims to be a reproduction of a journal used by Lady Angelica Cottington to capture the psychic images of the fairies that populated her garden. Published in the U.S. by Turner Publishing. A 10th-anniversary edition is published in 2005 with a new introduction and bonus DVD. Followed by a sequel, *Strange Stains and Mysterious Smells: Quentin Cottington's Journal of Faery Research* (1996).
Awards: Hugo Award for Best Original Art Work.

2044 October 18, 1994
Late Night with Conan O'Brien (TV talk show: NBC). Guests: Brian Benben and **Terry Jones**, promoting *Lady Cottington's Pressed Fairy Book*. **Jones** shows a clip of Lady Cottington as a girl and also talks about Python's influence, directing in the nude, and the banning of his films in Ireland.

2045 October 22, 1994
Eric Idle and his wife attend the West Coast premiere of Steve Martin's play *Picasso at the Lapin Agile* at the Westwood Playhouse in Westwood, CA.

2046 October 25, 1994
Omnibus (TV special: BBC1). "Quentin Tarantino: Hollywood's Boy Wonder." Profile of film director Quentin Tarantino (*Pulp Fiction*), with comments from **Terry Gilliam**, Brian De Palma, Harvey Keitel, and others. Directed by David Thompson.

2047 October 25, 1994
It's Alive: The True Story of Frankenstein (TV special: A&E). Documentary on the *Frankenstein* story and its screen adaptations. **John Cleese**, who co-stars in the new film *Mary Shelley's Frankenstein*, is among those interviewed. Hosted by Roger Moore. Narrated by Eli Wallach. Written & directed by Richard Brown.

2048 October 27, 1994
Crusades (Book: BBC Books), written by **Terry Jones** and Alan Ereira, is published in the U.K. History of the Christians' crusade to free the Holy Land from Islam. Companion book to the upcoming BBC documentary series (airing in January 1995 on BBC2). Reprinted by Penguin Books in 1996. Published in the U.S. by Facts on File (1995).

2049 October 29, 1994
Eric Idle attends Cricket Aid, a pro-celebrity

cricket match, at Will Rogers State Park in Pacific Palisades, CA. The event is a benefit for Tuesday's Child and the Sunlight Mission.

2050 Late October 1994
Tom Snyder (TV talk show: CNBC). Guest: **Terry Jones**, promoting *Lady Cottington's Pressed Fairy Book*. **Jones** shows a clip of Lady Cottington (**Jones**) from the 1930s and talks about writing for Python.

2051 November 1994
Calman's Savoy Sketchbook (Book: Aztec Design), drawn by Mel Calman and edited by Claire Calman, is published in the U.K. Limited-edition volume, the last work of *Times* cartoonist Mel Calman, who died in February. Introduction by friend **Michael Palin**.

2052 November 1994
Honey, I Shrunk the Audience (Short film) opens at Epcot Center in Florida. **Eric Idle** stars in this 18-minute, interactive 3-D film shown at Disney theme parks. In the film **Idle** plays Dr. Nigel Channing, head of the Imagination Institute, where Prof. Wayne Szalinski (Rick Moranis) is presented with the Inventor of the Year award for his shrinking ray. Based on the *Honey, I Shrunk the Kids* film series. Written by Bill Prady and Steve Spiegel. Directed by Randal Kleiser. Note: **Idle** also appears in the spin-off short *Journey into Your Imagination* (1999).

2053 November 3, 1994
John Cleese attends the London premiere of *Mary Shelley's Frankenstein*, in which he co-stars, on the opening night of the London Film Festival.

2054 November 4, 1994
Mary Shelley's Frankenstein (Feature film: TriStar Pictures) opens in the U.S. and Britain. Retelling of Mary Shelley's horror classic starring Robert DeNiro as the monster. **John Cleese** plays Professor Waldman, Dr. Frankenstein's mentor. Also starring Kenneth Branagh and Helena Bonham Carter. Written by Steph Lady and Frank Darabont. Directed by Kenneth Branagh. Note: **Cleese**'s Prof. Waldman dies at the hands of Robert DeNiro's character early in the film, making him the second Python (after **Michael Palin** in *Brazil*) to be killed on screen by DeNiro.

2055 November 18, 1994
The Swan Princess (Feature film: New Line Cinema) opens in the U.S. Animated musical fairy tale. **John Cleese** voices Jean-Bob, a French frog. Voice cast also includes Jack Palance, Michelle Nicastro, Liz Callaway, and Steven Wright. Written by Brian Nissen. Directed by Richard Rich.

2056 December 5, 1994
Film 94 (TV show: BBC1). **John Cleese** is interviewed about the film script he is currently writing, which will be his follow-up to 1988's *A Fish Called Wanda*.

2057 December 25, 1994
The Jungle Book (Feature film: Buena Vista Pictures) opens in the U.S. Based on the Rudyard Kipling story. **John Cleese** plays Dr. Julien Plumford. Also starring Jason Scott Lee, Cary Elwes, Lena Headey, and Sam Neill. Written by Stephen Sommers, Ronald Yanover, and Mark D. Geldman. Directed by Stephen Sommers.

2058 December 30, 1994
New York & Company (Radio show: WNYC-AM, New York). Guest: **Terry Jones**, promoting his book *Lady Cottington's Pressed Fairy Book*.

2059 1994
More Bloody Meetings (Training film: Video Arts). Remake of the 1984 film on improving the productivity of meetings. Sequel to 1993's *Meetings, Bloody Meetings*. Starring **John Cleese** (as Tim), Robert Hardy, Julian Holloway, Caroline Quentin, Danny John-Jules, Tessa Peake-Jones, and Karen Tomlin. Written by Antony Jay. Directed by Peter Robinson.

2060 1994
Great Railway Journeys (Book: BBC Books), written by Clive Anderson, Natalia Makarova, Rian Malan, **Michael Palin**, Lisa St. Aubin de Teran, and Mark Tully, is published in the U.K. Companion book to the 1994 BBC TV series. Includes the chapter "From Derry to Kerry," by **Palin**, from his February 1994 episode.

2061 1994
Eric Idle, with his wife Tania and daughter Lily, moves from England to the San Fernando Valley in California.

2062 1994
The Last Machine: Early Cinema and the Birth of the Modern World (Book: British Film Institute/BBC), written by Ian Christie with a foreword by **Terry Gilliam**, is published. Companion book to the 1995 BBC2 series hosted by **Gilliam**.

2063 January 1995
The 1993 book *Life and How to Survive It*, written

by Robin Skynner and **John Cleese**, is published in the U.S. by W.W. Norton & Co.

2064 January 7–February 4, 1995
The Last Machine, a five-part documentary series on early cinema, airs on BBC2. The series is hosted by **Terry Gilliam** and written by film historian Ian Christie, who will later author the 1999 book *Gilliam on Gilliam*. A companion book for the series was published in 1994 with a foreword by **Gilliam**.

2065 January 7, 1995
The Last Machine (TV episode: BBC2). "The Space and Time Machine." A look at the dawn of motion pictures in the 19th century. First episode of a five-part documentary series hosted by **Terry Gilliam**. Written by Ian Christie. Directed by Richard Curson Smith.

2066 January 9, 1995
Comedian Peter Cook dies of a gastrointestinal hemorrhage at the age of 57. Cook, a member of the influential 1960s satirical group Beyond the Fringe and comedy partner of Dudley Moore (*Not Only...but Also*), worked with the Pythons in four Amnesty International benefit shows between 1976 and 1989 and in the films *The Rise and Rise of Michael Rimmer* (1970, with **John Cleese** and **Graham Chapman**) and *Yellowbeard* (1983, with **Chapman**, **Cleese**, and **Eric Idle**). **Cleese** and **Terry Jones** also appeared on Cook's 1980 TV special *Peter Cook & Co.*

2067 January 10–31, 1995
The four-part documentary series *Crusades* airs on BBC2. The series, co-written and hosted by **Terry Jones**, takes an irreverent look at the 200-year religious conflict (begun in 1096). Airs in the U.S. June 5–8, 1995, on The History Channel and A&E. A companion book was published in October 1994 by BBC Books.
Review: Lynne Truss (*The Times* [London], Jan. 11, 1995, p. 47): "**Terry Jones** is an excellent storyteller, and the subject became surprisingly television-friendly in his hands"; David Hiltbrand (*People*, June 5, 1995, p. 16): "Visually thin but often imaginative, this odd, discursive project is as much a satirical essay as it is history."

2068 January 10, 1995
Crusades (TV episode: BBC2). "Pilgrims in Arms." The Turks' conquest of Constantinople and the Byzantine emperor's appeal for help to Pope Urban II. First episode of the four-part documentary series hosted by **Terry Jones**. Written by **Terry Jones** and Alan Ereira. Produced & directed by David Wallace and Alan Ereira.

2069 January 13, 1995
Pebble Mill (TV talk show: BBC1). Hosted by Gloria Hunniford. Guests: **Terry Jones**, promoting *Crusades*, Nigel Le Vaillant, Lionel Bart, and Georgie Fame & The Blue Flames.

2070 January 14, 1995
The Last Machine (TV episode: BBC2). "Real Lives." A look at early news and documentary films. Second episode of a five-part documentary series hosted by **Terry Gilliam**. Written by Ian Christie. Directed by Richard Curson Smith.

2071 January 15, 1995
The Guardian (Newspaper/U.K.). "Beyond the Final Fringe — Now Is the Time to Say Goodbye," by **Michael Palin**, p. 5. Palin pays tribute to the late Peter Cook.

2072 January 17, 1995
Crusades (TV episode: BBC2). "Jerusalem." The sieges at Antioch and the Holy City of Jerusalem. Second episode of the four-part documentary series hosted by **Terry Jones**. Written by **Terry Jones** and Alan Ereira. Produced & directed by David Wallace and Alan Ereira.

2073 January 21, 1995
The Last Machine (TV episode: BBC2). "The Body Electric." A look at the earliest images of women on film. Third episode of a five-part documentary series hosted by **Terry Gilliam**. Written by Ian Christie. Directed by Richard Curson Smith.

2074 January 24, 1995
Crusades (TV episode: BBC2). "Jihad." The Arab response to the Crusades and the rise of Saladin. Third episode of the four-part documentary series hosted by **Terry Jones**. Written by **Terry Jones** and Alan Ereira. Produced & directed by David Wallace and Alan Ereira.

2075 January 28, 1995
The Last Machine (TV episode: BBC2). "Tales from the City." A look at how early films portrayed the modern city. Fourth episode of a five-part documentary series hosted by **Terry Gilliam**. Written by Ian Christie. Directed by Richard Curson Smith.

2076 January 31, 1995
Crusades (TV episode: BBC2). "Destruction." The crusade of Richard the Lionhart. Fourth

episode of the four-part documentary series hosted by **Terry Jones**. Written by **Terry Jones** and Alan Ereira. Produced & directed by David Wallace and Alan Ereira.

2077   February 4, 1995
The Last Machine (TV episode: BBC2). "The Waking Dream." Early examples of fantasy in film. Last episode of a five-part documentary series hosted by **Terry Gilliam**. Written by Ian Christie. Directed by Richard Curson Smith.

2078   February 8–May 6, 1995
Terry Gilliam's new film, *12 Monkeys*, is shot over three months in Philadelphia and Baltimore, followed by six months of editing. Production on the $29 million sci-fi thriller began in November. For this follow-up to 1991's *The Fisher King*, **Gilliam** is again working as a director-for-hire within the Hollywood system, from a script not his own, and with a big-name cast (Bruce Willis, Brad Pitt, Madeleine Stowe). The filming is chronicled by documentarians Keith Fulton and Louis Pepe (the resulting doc, *The Hamster Factor and Other Tales of Twelve Monkeys*, is released in October 1996).

2079   February 27, 1995
John Cleese promotes his book *Life and How to Survive It* on the TV show *Today* (NBC) and radio show *New York & Company* (WNYC-AM, New York).

2080   February 28, 1995
Live with Regis and Kathie Lee (TV talk show: Synd.). Hosted by Regis Philbin and Kathy Lee Gifford. Guest: **John Cleese**, promoting *Life and How to Survive It*.

2081   March 1, 1995
John Cleese talks to Charlie Rose about his book *Life and How to Survive It* before an audience at the 92nd Street Y in New York City.

2082   March 2, 1995
Charlie Rose (TV talk show: PBS). Guests: **John Cleese**, promoting *Life and How to Survive It*, Peter Brook, and Robert Wright.

2083   March 17, 1995
Oliver 2: Let's Twist Again (TV special: BBC1). **Michael Palin** co-stars in this black-and-white Charles Dickens spoof shown in three parts during BBC1's "Night of Comic Relief." Also starring Diana Rigg, Jeremy Irons, Stephen Fry, Oliver Reed, and Ron Moody. Written by Richard Curtis.

2084   March 20, 1995
Eric Idle attends a celebrity screening of the TV special *A Comedy Salute to Andy Kaufman* at the Improv in West Hollywood, CA.

2085   March 24, 1995
The Washington Post (Newspaper/U.S.). "The Real **John Cleese**. No Fooling. He Writes About Life and Love. Funny Thing Is, He's Serious," by Paula Span. Interview with **Cleese** about *Life and How to Survive It*, recently published in the U.S.

2086   April 3, 1995
Hemingway's Chair (Book: Methuen), written by **Michael Palin**, is published in the U.K. **Palin**'s first novel concerns a mild-mannered postmaster's assistant in a small English village who has an obsession with writer Ernest Hemingway. Published in the U.S. by Thomas Dunne Books/St. Martin's Press in May 1998. Also released as an audiobook (Reed Audio), read by **Palin**. Note: **Palin** will further explore the life of Hemingway in his 1999 TV documentary series *Hemingway Adventure*.
Reviews: Francisca Goldsmith (*Library Journal*, April 1998): "...a tale of frustration that is both gentle and snappy, human to the core"; Bruce Weber (*The New York Times*, May 24, 1998): "The book's strengths ... its dry, deftly understated wit; its careful plot and character construction; its hearty, well-formed sentences; its clever, on-the-money dialogue"; Reviewer (*Publishers Weekly*): "...**Palin** brings a light touch to this yarn, treating his characters and their many weaknesses with an affection that will have readers rooting for his unlikely hero."

2087   April 3, 1995
Start the Week (Radio talk show: BBC Radio 4). Hosted by Melvyn Bragg. Guests: **Michael Palin**, Allison Pearson, and Mike Newell.

2088   April 12, 1995
Calendar (TV news show: ITV/YTV–Yorkshire Television). Guest: **Michael Palin**, promoting *Hemingway's Chair*.

2089   April 15–21, 1995
Radio Times (Magazine/U.K.). Andrew Duncan interviews **Michael Palin** (pp. 17–20) in connection with the upcoming mental health program *Don't Fence Me In*. **Palin** discusses his sister Angela's suicide (in 1987) and his thoughts on depression and madness.

2090   April 18, 1995
Don't Fence Me In (Radio special: BBC Radio 4). Documentary on mental illness, hosted by **Michael**

Palin. This *States of Mind* program is part of the BBC's Mental Health Week. Produced by Clare McGinn.

2091 May 1, 1995

John Cleese and **Michael Palin** attend a memorial service for Peter Cook at St. John's Church in Hampstead, North London. Other attendees include Dudley Moore, Spike Milligan, Alan Bennett, Willie Rushton, Hugh Laurie, Mel Smith, Griff Rhys Jones, Dave Allen, Sir David Frost, Barry Humphries, Terry Wogan, and Clive Anderson. Cook died on Jan. 9.

2092 May 12, 1995

Turns of the Century (Radio show: BBC Radio 3). Robert Cushman looks at the life and comedy of **John Cleese**.

2093 May 14, 1995

The Independent (Newspaper/U.K.). "Arts: To Hell with Basil," by Andrew Davidson. Interview with **John Cleese** on the creation and legacy of *Fawlty Towers*.

2094 May 14–July 30, 1995

All twelve episodes of **John Cleese**'s 1975/79 sitcom *Fawlty Towers* are re-broadcast on BBC1 in celebration of the show's 20th anniversary.

2095 May 15, 1995

Filming begins on *Fierce Creatures* (working title: *Death Fish II*), an $18 million comedy co-written by and starring **John Cleese**. The film reunites the cast of *A Fish Called Wanda* (Cleese, **Michael Palin**, Jamie Lee Curtis, and Kevin Kline) for a new story set in a zoo. Filmed at Pinewood Studios in England and on location at the Marwell Zoological Park (in Hampshire, Eng.) and Jersey Zoo (in Jersey, Channel Islands). A 77-day shoot.

2096 May 18, 1995

The Times (London) (Newspaper/U.K.). "A Comedian on the Constitution," by **John Cleese** (interviewed by Lucy Bailey), p. 19. **Cleese** explains how humor can be used to inform people and improve Britain's flawed political system.

2097 May 18, 1995

Late Show with David Letterman (TV talk show: CBS). **John Cleese** appears via videotape on this episode recorded during Letterman's week of shows in London. **Cleese** reads the Top Ten List "Reasons **John Cleese** Could Not Be on Our Program."

2098 May 20–June 4, 1995

The series *Look at the State We're In!* airs on BBC2. The satirical series, co-produced by Video Arts (the company **John Cleese** founded in 1972) and Roger Graef's Sisyphus Productions, consists of six ten-minute films examining the current state of Britain. **Cleese** stars in two episodes. The series, which was filmed in the summer of 1994, is sponsored by Charter 88 (of which **Cleese** is a signatory), a pressure group advocating constitutional change.

2099 May 21, 1995

Look at the State We're In! (TV episode: BBC2). "Secrecy." Harold Kingsby (**John Cleese**) runs into bureaucratic red tape when he attempts to view his own government file. Also starring Dawn French. Written by Chris Langham. Director Robert Knights. Produced by Roger Graef and Margaret Tree.

2100 May 21, 1995

Eric Idle and family attend the world premiere of the film *Casper*, in which he co-stars, at the Cinerama Dome Theater in Universal City, CA.

2101 May 22–June 2, 1995

Book at Bedtime (Radio show: BBC Radio 4). **Michael Palin** reads his new novel *Hemingway's Chair* in ten parts.

2102 May 26, 1995

Casper (Feature film: Universal Pictures) opens in the U.S. Fantasy-comedy about a girl (Christina Ricci) who befriends a ghost named Casper after she and her widowed father move into a haunted mansion. **Eric Idle** plays Paul "Dibbs" Plutzker, the lawyer of the house's villainous owner. Also starring Malachi Pearson (voice of Casper), Bill Pullman, and Cathy Moriarty. Written by Sherri Stoner and Deanna Oliver. Directed by Brad Silberling.

2103 June 4, 1995

Rabbit Ears Radio (Radio show: Public Radio International). "Tom Thumb." **John Cleese** narrates the classic children's story, with original music by Elvis Costello. The half-hour program is introduced by Meg Ryan. Later released as a book, audiobook, and video.

2104 June 4, 1995

Look at the State We're In! (TV episode: BBC2). "The Status Quo." **John Cleese** plays a politician recording a Party Political Broadcast on behalf of the Status Quo. Last of the series. Also starring Hugh Laurie, Chris Langham, and Sara Stockbridge. Written by **John Cleese**. Directed by Hugh Laurie. Produced by Roger Graef and Margaret Tree.

2105 June 5–8, 1995

The four-part documentary series *Crusades*, co-written and hosted **Terry Jones**, airs in the U.S. on The History Channel (and simulcast on its sister station A&E), presented by Roger Mudd.

2106 June 8, 1995

The Tonight Show with Jay Leno (TV talk show: NBC). Guests: **Eric Idle**, promoting *Casper*, Mike Piazza, and the band Brownstone. **Idle** wearing a **Michael Palin** ("Lumberjack Song") T-shirt, recounts an incident with a dog during an earthquake.

2107 June 22, 1995

Eric Idle attends the premiere of the film *Apollo 13* at the Academy of Motion Picture Arts and Sciences in Los Angeles.

2108 July 13, 1995

Michael Palin hosts a screening of *A Fish Called Wanda* on TNT as part of the cable channel's "Our Favorite Movies: Summer Edition" series.

2109 July 26, 1995

Eric Idle attends the charity London premiere of the film *Casper*, in which he co-stars, at the Empire Theatre in Leicester Square.

2110 August 1995

Filming on *Fierce Creatures* is completed. Poor test screenings later in the year will lead to reshoots next summer.

2111 August 7, 1995

Filming begins on *The Wind in the Willows*, a $15 million live-action adaptation of the Kenneth Grahame story, written and directed by **Terry Jones**. **Jones** also stars in the film (as Toad), along with fellow Pythons **Eric Idle**, **John Cleese**, and **Michael Palin**. Filmed at Shepperton Studios (London) and on location in England. Locations include The Bluebell Railway (in Sussex), Burnham Beeches (in Buckinghamshire), and Kentwell Hall (in Long Melford, Suffolk), which doubles as Toad Hall.

2112 August 28, 1995–Summer 1996

Michael Palin circumnavigates the Pacific Rim for his travel series *Full Circle*. His journey begins on Little Diomede Island in the Bering Strait. Only five days earlier he was in a cupboard with **John Cleese** and a tarantula (filming his last scene for *Fierce Creatures* at Pinewood Studios in Buckinghamshire, England).

2113 October 1995

The Quest for King Arthur (Book: De Agostini Editions), written by David Day with a foreword by **Terry Jones**, is published in the U.K. An examination of the Arthurian legend. Published in the U.S. as *The Search for King Arthur* (Facts on File).

2114 November–December 1995

Sainsbury's (TV commercial). **John Cleese** appears in a British ad for Sainsbury supermarket parodying the store's "celebrity recipe" Christmas spots. **Cleese** will later star in Sainsbury's 1998 "Value to Shout About" campaign. Written by David Abbott. Directed by John S. Clarke. Agency: Abbott Mead Vickers BBDO, London.

2115 November 9, 1995

Look Who's Talking with Mariella Frostrup (TV talk show: ITV/Carlton). Guests: **Terry Gilliam**, Patsy Kensit, and Jack Dee.

2116 November 27, 1995

Close Up (TV show: BBC2). **Terry Gilliam** talks about his favorite movie moment, in Fellini's *8½*.

2117 December 11, 1995

A test screening for **John Cleese**'s new film *Fierce Creatures* is held at the Gotham Cinema in Manhattan, NYC. **Cleese**, co-star Kevin Kline, and co-writer Iain Johnstone attend. The ending of the film tests poorly and as a result reshoots are ordered. Those reshoots will have to wait, however, until **Michael Palin** returns from filming his new travel series *Full Circle*. The reshoots take place in September 1996.

2118 December 25, 1995

The Wind in the Willows (TV special: ITV). Feature-length animated adaptation of Kenneth Grahame's children's classic, produced by TVC London (*The Snowman*). **Michael Palin** voices the role of Rat. A sequel, *The Willows in Winter*, airs in 1996. Other voices by Alan Bennett (Mole), Michael Gambon (Badger), Rik Mayall (Toad), and Vanessa Redgrave (Narrator). Written by Ted Walker. Directed by Dave Unwin. Note: **Palin** will play the smaller role of The Sun in **Terry Jones**' live-action feature version of the story, which will be released in October of next year.

2119 December 27, 1995

12 Monkeys (Feature film: Universal Pictures) premieres in the U.S. (opens nationwide on Jan. 5).

Terry Gilliam's second Hollywood-made film (following 1991's *The Fisher King*) is an apocalyptic sci-fi thriller about a man who is sent back in time, from the plague-ravaged world of 2035 to the pre-plague year of 1996, on a mission to discover how the deadly virus spread. Based on the 1962 French short *La Jetée* directed by Chris Marker. Starring Bruce Willis, Madeleine Stowe, Brad Pitt, Frank Gorshin, Christopher Plummer, David Morse, Jon Seda, and Simon Jones. Written by David Peoples and Janet Peoples. Directed by **Terry Gilliam**. Produced by Charles Roven.

Awards: Academy Award nominated for Best Supporting Actor (Pitt) and Best Costume Design (Julie Weiss); Golden Globe winner for Best Supporting Actor (Pitt); Empire Award winner for Best Director (**Gilliam**).

Reviews: Janet Maslin (*The New York Times*, Dec. 27, 1995): "*12 Monkeys* is fierce and disturbing, with a plot that skillfully resists following any familiar course ... directed by Mr. **Gilliam** with great flair for keeping his audience off balance..."; Kenneth Turan (*Los Angeles Times*, Dec. 27, 1995): "*12 Monkeys* is baffling and difficult to decipher at times, but it's never a standard brand ... it shows what happens when an unconventional talent meets straightforward material"; Owen Gleiberman (*Entertainment Weekly*, Jan. 12, 1996): "...**Gilliam**, for the first time since *Brazil* (1985), indulges his crackpot imagination at full throttle."

2120   December 27, 1995
Late Show with David Letterman (TV talk show: CBS). Guests: Mandy Patinkin and **Terry Gilliam**, promoting *12 Monkeys*. **Gilliam** also talks about his horse-riding accident and his studio battles over *Time Bandits* and *Brazil*.

2121   December 28, 1995
Fierce and Gentle Creatures (TV special: Channel 4). Hour-long documentary on animal conservation efforts at Jersey Zoo in the Channel Islands. Hosted by **John Cleese** with help from his *Fierce Creatures* co-stars Jamie Lee Curtis and Kevin Kline. Also with Lee Durrell (widow of the zoo's founder, Gerald Durrell). Directed by Karl Sabbagh and Celia Lowenstein. Produced by Karl Sabbagh.

2122   1995
Discworld (Computer game: Psygnosis). **Eric Idle** voices the wizard Rincewind in this game based on Terry Pratchett's best-selling books. **Idle** will reprise the role for the 1996 sequel *Discworld II: Mortality Bytes!*. Other voices by Jon Pertwee and Tony Robinson. Designed by Teeny Weeny Games.

2123   January 1996
Norwich Union Direct (TV commercial). **John Cleese** appears in the first of a series of British TV ads for the insurance service Norwich Union Direct.

2124   January 1996
Michael Palin's wife, Helen, undergoes brain surgery to remove a benign tumor while **Palin** is in Kuching, Malaysia, filming his travel series *Full Circle*. After the successful operation, **Palin** breaks away from his journey and flies home to be with her.

2125   January 4, 1996
Terry Gilliam participates in a live online chat to promote *12 Monkeys*.

2126   January 4, 1996
Charlie Rose (TV talk show: PBS). Guest: **Terry Gilliam**, promoting *12 Monkeys*.

2127   January 6–21, 1996
Fairy Tales for Adults: A Terry Gilliam Retrospective (Screenings), at the Museum of the Moving Image in New York City. Retrospective of **Terry Gilliam**'s film career and early animation work. **Gilliam** introduces a screening of *12 Monkeys* on opening night, followed by a Q&A. He speaks again the next night (Jan. 7) following a screening of *Brazil*.

2128   January 7, 1996
The 61st New York Film Critics Circle Awards (Award ceremony). **Terry Gilliam** presents Nicolas Cage with the Best Actor award (for *Leaving Las Vegas*) at the ceremony held at the Rainbow Room in Manhattan, New York.

2129   February 1996
Terry Gilliam attends the 46th Berlin International Film Festival (Feb. 15–26) in Berlin, Germany where his film *12 Monkeys* is nominated for the Golden Bear award.

2130   February 2, 1996
Space Ghost Coast to Coast (TV talk show: Cartoon Network). "Explode." Space Ghost (voice of George Lowe) talks to guests **Terry Jones** and Glen Phillips.

2131   February 20, 1996
Michael Palin films a cameo appearance (as a surfer) in the Australian soap opera *Home and Away*. **Palin** is in Sydney filming his travel series *Full Circle*.

2132 February 22–May 6, 1996
Spellbound: Art and Film (Art exhibition). **Terry Gilliam** contributes a work of art to this exhibition celebrating one hundred years of British cinema, at the Hayward Gallery in London. His piece, called "The Road to Monkey Heaven is a: Paved b: Littered c: Barricaded with Good Intentions!," features a wall of filing cabinets obscuring a screen upon which **Gilliam**'s *12 Monkeys* is being projected. Other contributors include directors Ridley Scott and Peter Greenaway.

2133 February 27, 1996
The Rutles: All You Need Is Cash (Videocassette: Rhino Home Video). Video release of **Eric Idle**'s 1978 Beatles parody. Previously released on video by Pacific Arts (in 1983).

2134 March 6, 1996
Ken Hom's Hot Wok (TV cooking show: BBC2). Chef Ken Hom demonstrates wok cooking with **John Cleese** at the Jersey Zoo, where **Cleese** is filming *Fierce Creatures*. Produced & directed by Kate Kinninmont.

2135 March 8, 1996
Terry Gilliam's *12 Monkeys* is the opening film of the 14th annual Brussels International Festival of Fantasy, Thriller and Science Fiction Films (Mar. 8–23) in Brussels, Belgium. **Gilliam** attends the screening and also cuts the ribbon to open the festival.

2136 March 12, 1996
Frasier (TV episode: NBC). "High Crane Drifter." Frasier is driven to the brink by people's rude and inconsiderate behavior. **Eric Idle** voices the role of Chuck, a caller to Frasier's radio show. Starring Kelsey Grammer. Written by Jack Burditt. Directed by Philip Charles MacKenzie.

2137 March 18, 1996
Film 96 (TV show: BBC1). Hosted by Barry Norman. Includes a location report from the set of **John Cleese**'s *Fierce Creatures*.

2138 March 25, 1996
Eric Idle and his wife attend the *Vanity Fair* Oscar Party at Morton's Restaurant in West Hollywood, CA.

2139 April 1996
Sight & Sound (Magazine/U.K.). "Time and the Machine," by Nick James, pp. 14–16. Interview with **Terry Gilliam** about *12 Monkeys*.

2140 April 1, 1996
Michael Palin's 1995 novel, *Hemingway's Chair*, is released in paperback in the U.K. by Mandarin.

2141 April 2, 1996
Good Morning with Anne and Nick (TV talk show: BBC1). Hosted by Anne Diamond and Nick Owen. **Terry Jones** is interviewed about his new book *The Goblin Companion*.

2142 April 5, 1996
The Times (London) (Newspaper/U.K.). "Still in the Python's Embrace," by Valerie Grove, p. 17. Interview with **Michael Palin** at his North London home. **Palin** talks about his novel *Hemingway's Chair*, his wife's brain surgery, traveling, Python, etc.

2143 April 9, 1996
Moving Pictures (TV show: BBC2). Film program hosted by Howard Schuman. **Terry Gilliam** is interviewed about *12 Monkeys*.

2144 April 13, 1996
Saturday Night Special (TV episode: Fox). **Eric Idle** appears as Fox owner Rupert Murdoch in the premiere episode of this six-week sketch-comedy series. Hosted by Roseanne (the show's executive producer), with musical guests Bush and Melissa Etheridge.

2145 April 14, 1996
The Sunday Times Magazine (London) (Magazine/U.K.). "**Gilliam** the Barbarian," by Joan Goodman, pp. 34–38. Interview with **Terry Gilliam** about his career and new film *12 Monkeys*. Photographs by Nigel Parry.

2146 April 15, 1996
The Times (London) (Newspaper/U.K.). "How to Succeed in Monkey Business," by Stephanie Billen, p. 14. Interview with **Terry Gilliam** about his new film *12 Monkeys*.

2147 April 15, 1996
Omnibus (TV special: BBC1). "Spike." Documentary on the life and career of comedian Spike Milligan (*The Goon Show*). Interviewees include Milligan, Harry Secombe, Michael Bentine, **John Cleese**, and many others. Directed by Alan Lewens. Produced by Jo Lustig and Martin Smith.

2148 April 15, 1996
Film 96 (TV show: BBC1). Hosted by Barry Norman. Includes a report on *12 Monkeys* featuring interviews with **Terry Gilliam**, Bruce Willis, and Brad Pitt.

2149 April 18, 1996
The Big Breakfast (TV talk show: Channel 4). Hosted by Mark Little and Gillian Taylforth. Guest: **Terry Gilliam**, promoting *12 Monkeys*.

2150 April 19, 1996
12 Monkeys opens in the U.K.

2151 April 19, 1996
Good Morning with Anne and Nick (TV talk show: BBC1). Hosted by Anne Diamond and Nick Owen. **Terry Gilliam** is interviewed about *12 Monkeys*.

2152 April 25, 1996
The Goblin Companion (Book: Thorsons), by Brian Froud and **Terry Jones**, is published. Abridged reissue of *The Goblins of Labyrinth* (1986). Published in the U.S. by Turner Publishing.

2153 April 28, 1996
Celebrity Choice (Radio show: Classic FM). Hosted by Paul Callan. Guest: **Michael Palin**.

2154 May 7, 1996
Home and Away (TV episode). **Michael Palin** makes a cameo appearance as a surfer in this Australian soap opera. Filmed while **Palin** was in Sydney in February filming his travel series *Full Circle*. Directed by Dave Gould.

2155 May 18, 1996
The Times (London) (Newspaper/U.K.). "Fan Fare from the Little Man," by **Michael Palin**, p. 15. **Palin** pays tribute to his friend, the late cartoonist Mel Calman, upon the release of the new Calman collection *A Little Light Worrying*.

2156 June 1996
A Little Light Worrying: The Best of Mel Calman (Book: Methuen), by Mel Calman, is published in the U.K. A collection of cartoons by the late Mel Calman (1931–1994), edited by his daughter Claire Calman with a preface by his friend **Michael Palin**.

2157 June 6–August 29, 1996
Blazing Dragons (TV series: ITV). First series (13 episodes) of a British animated comedy-adventure for children set in the dragon kingdom of Camelhot. **Terry Jones** co-created the show (with Gavin Scott) and also serves as one of the executive producers. Co-produced by the studios of Nelvana Limited (Canada) and Ellipse Animation (France). A second series of 13 episodes airs Jan. 8–Oct. 2, 1998. A video game based on the series (and featuring the voice of **Jones**) is released in October 1996. Directed by Lawrence Jacobs. Produced by Jocelyn Hamilton.

2158 July 1996
Monty Python & the Quest for the Holy Grail (CD-ROM: 7th Level). The Pythons' 1975 medieval comedy is the basis for this interactive CD-ROM game, the group's second from Texas-based 7th Level following *Monty Python's Complete Waste of Time* (1994). The player, charged with the task of finding the Holy Grail, must navigate through nine of the film's locations (Plague Village, Camelot, Castle Anthrax, etc.) collecting objects, companions, and clues. Includes video and audio clips from the film, new animation and voice-overs (from the surviving Pythons, except **John Cleese**), and arcade/puzzle games like "Burn the Witch," "Drop Dead," "Knights in Kombat," and "Spank the Virgin." Also features an animated version of "King Brian the Wild," a sequence that was cut from the final script and never filmed. Followed in 1997 by *Monty Python's The Meaning of Life*. Produced by Charles Otte. Executive produced by **Eric Idle** and Bob Ezrin.
Reviews: Ty Burr (*Entertainment Weekly*, July 26, 1996, p. 58): "...*Quest* wholly reworks the movie into a multimedia game that pokes brutal, welcome fun at ... multimedia games"; Tim Wapshott (*The Times* [London], Aug. 17, 1996, p. 21): "The game looks and feels exceptionally good. The animations, sound effects and music score all combine to produce well-honed computer entertainment."

2159 July 1996
PythOnline is launched. The website was created by **Eric Idle** and 7th Level, makers of the *Holy Grail* CD-ROM.

2160 July 1996
The Wind in the Willows (Audiobook: Dove Kids Audio). **Terry Jones** reads Kenneth Grahame's 1908 story (unabridged). Released on four cassettes. **Jones** also wrote, directed & starred in the 1996 film adaptation of the story.

2161 July 1996
John Cleese attends a lecture ("The Four Noble Truths") given by the Dalai Lama at the Barbican Hall in London.

2162 September 1996
Reshoots on *Fierce Creatures* take place over three weeks. The reshoots, which include a new opening and a new ending, were ordered following poor test screenings but had to wait until **Michael Palin** returned from filming his travel series *Full Circle*. The reshoots are directed by Fred Schepisi, as the film's

original director, Robert Young, had become unavailable.

2163 September 1996
River of Mirrors: The Fantastic Art of Judson Huss (Book: Morpheus International), by Judson Huss, is published in the U.S. Collection of paintings by fantasy artist Huss. Foreword by **Terry Gilliam**.

2164 September 1, 1996
The Radio 2 Arts Programme (Radio show: BBC Radio 2). "The Once and Future King." **Terry Jones** explores the legend of King Arthur.

2165 September 5, 1996
Eric Idle participates in a live chat in the Oldsmobile Celebrity Circle on America Online.

2166 September 12, 1996
Eric Idle and his wife attend a fund-raising dinner and concert for President Bill Clinton at the Greenacres estate (former home of silent-film star Harold Lloyd) in Beverly Hills, CA. Performers at the gala event include The Eagles, Chicago, The Neville Brothers, and Barbra Streisand, with Tom Hanks serving as emcee. During the concert the Idles are seated directly behind the President and First Lady.

2167 September 23, 1996
The Los Angeles Times (Newspaper/U.S.). "My Dinner with Bill: Hold the Spam," by **Eric Idle**, p. 3. **Idle** on the Clinton fund-raiser he attended on Sept. 12th.

2168 September 25, 1996
John Cleese launches the Liberal Democrats' new poster campaign.

2169 September 26, 1996
Terry Gilliam attends a lavish party in Shepherd's Bush, West London, celebrating the opening of fashion designer Donna Karan's new store in Bond Street, London.

2170 October 1996
The revised, re-edited version of **John Cleese**'s *Fierce Creatures* is test-screened at a cinema near Hicksville on Long Island, NY. The new ending receives a positive response but the new opening tests poorly. After more re-editing of the opening the film receives a much higher rating in subsequent test screenings.

2171 October 1996
The Quite Remarkable Adventures of the Owl and the Pussycat (Book: Dove Kids), written by **Eric Idle** with illustrations by Wesla Weller, is published. Children's book based on the classic 1871 poem "The Owl and the Pussycat" by Edward Lear. **Idle** originally adapted Lear's poem as an animated musical with songs co-written with John Du Prez. When he couldn't get the film made, the story became a book instead. Also released as an audiobook (Dove Audio), read by **Idle** and featuring ten songs, including "Shopping," "Revenge Is Sweet," and "I Like Dinosaurs."
Award: Grammy-nominated for Best Spoken Word Album for Children.

2172 October 1996
Blazing Dragons (Video game: Crystal Dynamics). Adventure game, based on the TV series, in which the player (in the role of a young dragon named Flicker) competes against rival dragons in a grand tournament for the hand in marriage of the lovely Princess Flame. Created by **Terry Jones**, who also voices Sir Loungealot. For Sony PlayStation and Sega Saturn.

2173 October 1, 1996
Film Education (TV show: BBC2). "Wind in the Willows: The Filming of Mr. Toad." A look at **Terry Jones**' big-screen adaptation of *The Wind in the Willows*. Narrated by Sally James.

2174 October 3, 1996
Brazil: The Criterion Collection (Laserdisc: Criterion Collection 196). Five-disc set containing **Terry Gilliam**'s director's cut (142 mins) of his 1985 comedy-fantasy, digitally remastered under **Gilliam**'s supervision, and the studio-edited "Love Conquers All" version (94 mins) created with the intent of making the film more commercial. Special features include audio commentary by **Gilliam**, *What Is Brazil?* (1985 doc), "The Battle of *Brazil*: A Video History" (1996 doc by writer-critic Jack Mathews, based on his book), The Production Notebook (script, designs, costumes, etc.), and the original theatrical trailer. Distributed by The Voyager Company. Re-released on DVD in 1999 and 2006 and on Blu-ray in 2012.

2175 October 9, 1996
Kaleidoscope (Radio show: BBC Radio 4). Includes a report from the set of **Terry Jones**' new film *The Wind in the Willows*.

2176 October 11, 1996
The Late Jonathan Ross (TV talk show: ITV/LWT). Guests: **Terry Gilliam**, Frank Skinner, Tamara Beckwith, and Piers Morgan.

2177 October 11, 1996
Late Night with Conan O'Brien (TV talk show: NBC). Guests: **Eric Idle**, Peter Gallagher, and Los Lobos. **Idle**, promoting *Owl and the Pussycat*, also talks about PythOnline and sings "Shopping," then ends the interview prematurely to catch a plane to London.

2178 October 12, 1996
Live and Kicking (TV show: BBC1). **Terry Jones** and Steve Coogan are interviewed about *The Wind in the Willows* on this Saturday-morning magazine program for children. Hosted by Zoe Ball and Jamie Theakston.

2179 October 14, 1996
The Times (London) (Newspaper/U.K.). "The Wind-Up in the Willows," by Sue Summers, p. 21. Interview with **Terry Jones** about his new film *The Wind in the Willows*.

2180 October 14, 1996
The Pier on Film (TV arts show: ITV/Meridian). **Terry Jones** is interviewed about *The Wind in the Willows*.

2181 October 14, 1996
Something Like Fire: Peter Cook Remembered (Book: Methuen), edited by Lin Cook (Peter's widow), is published in the U.K. Collection of tributes to the late British comic includes contributions from **Eric Idle** ("The Funniest Man in the World"), **John Cleese** ("Peter Amadeus Cook"), and **Michael Palin** ("I Had That Peter Cook in the Back of My Car").

2182 October 14, 1996
Eric Idle, **Terry Jones**, and **Michael Palin** attend a book party for *Something Like Fire: Peter Cook Remembered* at Tramp nightclub in London.

2183 October 16, 1996
This Morning (TV show: ITV/Granada). Magazine program. Guests include **Terry Jones** and **Eric Idle**, promoting *The Wind in the Willows*.

2184 October 17, 1996
The Daily Mirror (Newspaper/U.K.). "Groan with the Wind; **Terry**'s Toad Catches Wife on the Hop," by Brigit Grant, p. 2. Interview with **Terry Jones** about his new film *The Wind in the Willows*.

2185 October 18, 1996
The Wind in the Willows (Feature film: Pathé) opens in the U.K. Live-action adaptation of Kenneth Grahame's 1908 story in which Mr. Toad's mania for motor cars gets him into all sorts of trouble. Written and directed by **Terry Jones**, who also stars (as Toad) alongside fellow Pythons **Eric Idle** (Rat) and, in smaller roles, **John Cleese** (Toad's Lawyer) and **Michael Palin** (The Sun). **Jones** also wrote the lyrics for the songs "Messing About on the River" (music by Tony Hatch) and "Miracle of Friends" (music by Dave Howman & Andre Jacquemin). Filmed at Shepperton Studios (London) and on location in England. **Palin** had previously voiced the role of Rat in an animated TV production in 1995. Also starring Steve Coogan, Antony Sher, Nicol Williamson, Stephen Fry, Bernard Hill, Nigel Planer, Julia Sawalha, and Victoria Wood. Produced by John Goldstone and Jake Eberts. An Allied FilmMakers production. The film's U.S. distributor, Disney, loses the theatrical rights in a settlement to Columbia, who give the film a limited release on Oct. 31, 1997, in New York and Los Angeles. Disney retains the video rights, releasing the film on video as *Mr. Toad's Wild Ride* in December 1998.
Awards: Best of the Fest award-winner at the Chicago International Children's Film Festival (1998); Winner of the WisKid Award for Best Full-Length Feature at the Wisconsin International Children's Film Festival (2000).
Reviews: Lawrence Van Gelder (*The New York Times*, Oct. 31, 1997): "...brimming with verbal and visual wit and imagination.... In this adaptation, an enchanting book has become an enchanting film."

2186 October 18, 1996
Blue Peter (TV children's show: BBC1). Tim Vincent looks at the making of the new film *The Wind in the Willows* and interviews **Terry Jones**, **Eric Idle**, and Steve Coogan.

2187 October 19, 1996
Go Wild in the Country: The Making of Wind in the Willows (TV special: ITV). Behind-the-scenes look at the making of **Terry Jones**' film adaptation of Kenneth Grahame's *The Wind in the Willows*. Half-hour. Later included on the 2003 DVD release of the film.

2188 October 20, 1996
Clive Anderson All Talk (TV talk show: BBC1). Guests: **Eric Idle**, promoting *The Wind in the Willows*, and Frank Skinner.

2189 October 25, 1996
The Guardian (Newspaper/U.K.). "**Terry Jones** on *Groundhog Day*," by **Terry Jones**, p. 27. **Jones** on why he wishes he had made the Harold Ramis comedy.

2190 October 25, 1996
The Hamster Factor and Other Tales of Twelve Monkeys (Feature film) premieres in Philadelphia. Behind-the-scenes look at the making of **Terry Gilliam**'s 1995 film *12 Monkeys*. Produced, written & directed by Keith Fulton and Louis Pepe, who will later chronicle **Gilliam**'s ill-fated attempt to bring *Don Quixote* to the screen in *Lost in La Mancha* (2002). The 88-minute film is included in the 2004 DVD release of the film.

2191 October 25, 1996
Auntie's TV Favourites: BBC Brings You the World (TV special: BBC1). Host Jill Dando presents the nominations for viewers' favorite BBC presenter. **Michael Palin** discusses his upcoming travel series *Full Circle*.

2192 October 31, 1996
Eric Idle's mother, Norah, age 82, falls and suffers a serious injury to her leg while strolling in the garden at **Idle**'s Los Angeles home. She is taken to the hospital where her condition worsens a few days later after she suffers a minor heart attack.

2193 November 1996
Strange Stains and Mysterious Smells: Quentin Cottington's Journal of Faery Research (Book: Simon & Schuster), written by **Terry Jones** with illustrations by Brian Froud, is published. Sequel to **Jones** and Froud's 1994 volume *Lady Cottington's Pressed Fairy Book*. The journal contains the research of one Quentin Cottington (twin brother of Lady Cottington) analyzing the stains and smells left by pressed fairies.

2194 November 1996
Discworld II: Mortality Bytes! (Computer game: Psygnosis). Sequel to 1995's *Discworld* with **Eric Idle** again voicing the role of the wizard Rincewind. Includes the song "That's Death," written & sung by **Idle**. Developed by Perfect Entertainment.

2195 November 1, 1996
The Tonight Show with Jay Leno (TV talk show: NBC). Guests: Jon Lovitz and **Eric Idle**, promoting *Owl and the Pussycat*. **Idle** also talks about his mother's recent fall, attending a Clinton fundraiser (in September), and sings "Shopping."

2196 November 3, 1996
Auntie's All-Time Greats (TV special: BBC1). Special celebrating the 60th birthday of BBC television, hosted by Michael Parkinson. **Michael Palin** presents the viewers' award for Sitcom Performer to David Jason. **John Cleese** is among the celebrities sending birthday messages.

2197 November 7, 1996
Eric Idle performs songs and signs books at the Storyopolis in Los Angeles in support of his new children's book, *The Quite Remarkable Adventures of the Owl and the Pussycat*. He is accompanied by guitarists John Du Prez and Danny Ferrington.

2198 November 14, 1996
The Terry Gilliam Guardian Interview (Event). **Terry Gilliam** talks to critic Jonathan Romney at the National Film Theatre in London as part of the 40th London Film Festival (Nov. 7–24).

2199 November 17, 1996
Eric Idle and family attend the "Children at Play" fair, a benefit for battered women and children, at Will Rogers State Park in Los Angeles.

2200 November 19, 1996
Eric Idle's mother, Norah Barron (Sanderson) Idle, dies at his Los Angeles home at the age of 82. **Idle**'s father, Ernest, died in December 1945 — when **Idle** was 2½ — in a traffic accident on his way home on Christmas leave from the RAF.

2201 December 3, 1996
Lumberjacks OK! (TV episode: Channel 4). "The Single Bucking Competition." While filming his *Full Circle* travel series, **Michael Palin** stopped in Squamish, B.C. where the annual loggers sports competition is held. **Palin** participates as a celebrity judge in the single bucking competition. Episode three of a six-part series. Hosted by David Jensen and George Spanswick. Produced & directed by Des Bradley.

2202 December 9, 1996
Late Show with David Letterman (TV talk show: CBS). Guest: **John Cleese**, promoting *Fierce Creatures*, also talks about having his hearing tested.

2203 December 15, 1996
Equinox (TV episode: Channel 4). "Dr. Satan's Robot." Documentary on new advances in science and the ethical issues they raise. Interviewees include **Terry Gilliam**.

2204 December 26, 1996
The Willows in Winter (TV special: ITV). Feature-length animated adaptation of William Horwood's 1993 sequel to Kenneth Grahame's children's classic, *The Wind in the Willows* (an animated version of the original story was produced by the same team in 1995). **Michael Palin** reprises

the role of Rat. A TVC London production. Other voices by Alan Bennett (Mole), Michael Gambon (Badger), Rik Mayall (Toad), and Vanessa Redgrave (Narrator). Written by Ted Walker. Directed by Dave Unwin.

2205 1996
The Unorganised Manager, Part 1: Damnation (Training film: Video Arts). Remake of the 1983 film. Starring **John Cleese** (St. Peter), Nigel Lindsay, and Beatie Edney. Written by Jonathan Lynn. Directed by Robert Knights.

2206 1996
The Unorganised Manager, Part 2: Salvation (Training film: Video Arts). Remake of the 1983 film. Followed by Part 3 (*Divine Intervention*) in 1997. Starring **John Cleese** (St. Peter), Nigel Lindsay, and Beatie Edney. Written by Jonathan Lynn. Directed by Robert Knights.

2207 1996
That's Death (CD single: Psygnosis). Single release of the song "That's Death," written & sung by **Eric Idle**, from the computer game *Discworld II: Mortality Bytes!*, in which **Idle** voices the role of Rincewind. Arranged & produced by Tom Scott.

2208 1996
John Cleese declines the title of Commander of the Order of the British Empire (CBE). **Michael Palin** will be made a CBE on New Year's Eve 1999.

2209 1996
The Wind in the Willows: The Complete Illustrated Screenplay (Book: Mandarin/Methuen), written by **Terry Jones**, is published. Screenplay of the 1996 film, based on the story by Kenneth Grahame. Photographs by Keith Hamshere.

2210 January 1997
Today (TV news-talk show: NBC). Matt Lauer interviews **John Cleese** about *Fierce Creatures*.

2211 January 1, 1997
Ronnie Barker: A Life in Comedy (TV special: BBC1). Tribute to the popular British comedian Ronnie Barker (*The Two Ronnies*), now retired. Interviewees include **Michael Palin**, Ronnie Corbett, David Frost, and David Jason.

2212 January 5, 1997
Desert Island Discs (Radio show: BBC Radio 4). Sue Lawley's castaway is **John Cleese**, whose choice of records includes "Rhapsody in Blue" (George Gershwin), "The Meaning of Life" (**Eric Idle**), "Cavatina" (John Williams), and "Easter Hymn, from *Cavalleria Rusticana*" (Pietro Mascagni). His luxury item is **Michael Palin** (stuffed). **Cleese** had previously appeared on the show in July 1971.

2213 January 9, 1997
Late Night with Conan O'Brien (TV talk show: NBC). Guest: **John Cleese**, promoting *Fierce Creatures*, explains why he tries to eat only unintelligent animals.

2214 January 11, 1997
Saturday Night Live (TV comedy show: NBC). Hosted by Kevin Spacey, with musical guest Beck and special guests **John Cleese** (in his *SNL* debut) and **Michael Palin**. In the opening, **Cleese** and **Palin** explain the new TV ratings system. **Palin** also appears in a "Medical Marijuana" sketch (with Spacey and Beck), and later he and **Cleese** perform the "Pet Shop" sketch (ending with "Do you want to come back to my place?"). Cast: Jim Breuer, Will Ferrell, Anna Gasteyer, Darrell Hammond, Chris Kattan, Tracy Morgan, and Molly Shannon. Directed by Beth McCarthy. Produced by Steve Higgins.

2215 January 12, 1997
The Sunday Times (London) (Newspaper/U.K.). "Animal Crackers," by Georgina Howell, pp. 26–33. In-depth interview with **John Cleese** about his life, career, and new film *Fierce Creatures*. Also offering their insights on the man are **Michael Palin** and **Cleese**'s wife, Alyce Faye.

2216 January 13, 1997
Live with Regis and Kathie Lee (TV talk show: Synd.). Hosted by Regis Philbin and Kathy Lee Gifford. Guest: **John Cleese**, promoting *Fierce Creatures*, also talks about his wife and the psychology book she's writing.

2217 January 15, 1997
Des O'Connor Tonight (TV talk show: ITV/Carlton). Guests: **John Cleese**, promoting *Fierce Creatures*, Cliff Richard, and Donna Lewis. **Cleese** also talks about studying law, the hotel owner who inspired *Fawlty Towers*, etc. During the interview he is briefly joined by a lemur. **Cleese** finishes by performing "The Courier Sketch," the first sketch he ever did on TV.

2218 January 15, 1997
The Late, Late Show with Tom Snyder (TV talk show: CBS). Guest: **John Cleese**, promoting *Fierce Creatures*. He also talks about the Royal family, the Dalai Lama, psychotherapy, **Graham Chapman**'s memorial service, surprising **Michael Palin** in his hotel room, etc. and takes questions from callers.

2219 January 16, 1997

John Cleese and his wife attend the world premiere of *Fierce Creatures* at Universal City's Cineplex Odeon Cinemas in Los Angeles. Proceeds from the premiere will benefit the Wildlife Preservation Trust Int. and Greater Los Angeles Zoo Assn.

2220 January 21, 1997

The Daily Show (TV talk show: Comedy Central). Hosted by Craig Kilborn. Guest: **John Cleese**, promoting *Fierce Creatures*. He also talks about the American accent and answers "5 Questions." In response to the question "Why does British food suck?" **Cleese** responds "We had an empire to run."

2221 January 24, 1997

Fierce Creatures (Film: Universal Pictures) opens in the U.S. Comedy reuniting the four leads from *A Fish Called Wanda* tells the story of London zookeepers forced to deal with the changes that come when their failing zoo is bought by a giant conglomerate. Co-star, co-writer & co-producer **John Cleese** based the story on an idea **Michael Palin** and **Terry Jones** developed back in 1968. Starring **John Cleese** (as Rollo Lee) and **Michael Palin** (as Adrian "Bugsy" Malone), with Jamie Lee Curtis, Kevin Kline, Ronnie Corbett, Carey Lowell, Robert Lindsay, Derek Griffiths, and Cynthia Cleese (**John**'s daughter). Written by **John Cleese** and Iain Johnstone. Directed by Robert Young and Fred Schepisi (reshoots). Produced by Michael Shamberg and **John Cleese**. Note: Young had previously directed **Cleese** in *Romance with a Double Bass* (1974) and *Splitting Heirs* (1993) and also in commercials.

Reviews: Desson Howe (*The Washington Post*, Jan. 24, 1997): "[*Creatures*] spends most of its time honoring a banal, farcical storyline. And it often lapses into sophomorically sexual antics which don't always work"; Owen Gleiberman (*Entertainment Weekly*, Jan. 24, 1997): "...*Fierce Creatures* is mostly a mess: toothless when it should be nasty, not so much madcap as merely frantic"; Geoff Brown (*The Times* [London], Feb. 13, 1997, p. 41): "*Fierce Creatures* relies mostly on **Cleese**'s squawks and bluster, on dropped pants and raised eyebrows, plus broad satire on marketing strategies, sponsorship deals and other signs of the times."

2222 January 24, 1997

TFI Friday (TV talk show: Channel 4). Hosted by Chris Evans. Guests: **John Cleese**, promoting *Fierce Creatures*, Gabrielle, Candyskins, and Audioweb. **Cleese** plays "How Far Will John Go?" in order to show a clip from the film.

2223 January 25, 1997

Live and Kicking (TV show: BBC1). **John Cleese** is a guest on this Saturday-morning magazine program for children hosted by Zoe Ball and Jamie Theakston. Answering questions from viewers and audience members, **Cleese** talks about working with animals in *Fierce Creatures*, the living conditions in zoos, and the dullness of movie-making.

2224 January 25, 1997

The National Lottery Live (TV show: BBC1). **John Cleese**, promoting *Fierce Creatures*, talks to host Dale Winton and assists in drawing the winning lottery numbers. Directed by Duncan Cooper. Produced by Peter Estall.

2225 January 28, 1997

Fierce Creatures has its London premiere at the Empire Cinema in Leicester Square. **John Cleese** and **Michael Palin** both attend the gala charity event, the proceeds from which will aid London Zoo, the Marwell Preservation Trust, and Jersey Wildlife Preservation Trust. Other attendees include Sir David Frost and Michael Winner. The film opens in the U.K. on Feb. 14.

2226 January 29, 1997

How Do They Do That? (TV show: BBC1). Includes a behind-the-scenes look at *Fierce Creatures*.

2227 January 30, 1997

Charlie Rose (TV talk show: PBS). Guest: **John Cleese**, promoting *Fierce Creatures*, also talks about comedy writing, focus groups, and experience vs. talent.

2228 January 30, 1997

The Frank Skinner Show (TV talk show: BBC1). Guests: **Michael Palin**, promoting *Fierce Creatures*, Paul Sayce, Isobel Varley, and Kate Wilton. **Palin** also talks about a possible Python reunion, the German Python shows, his travel series, Elvis Presley, and sings "The Lumberjack Song" in German.

2229 January 31, 1997

The Guardian (Newspaper/U.K.). "The Full Monty." Comedian Eddie Izzard interviews **John Cleese**.

2230 February 1997

Empire (Magazine/U.K.). **John Cleese** interview and cover photo ("Hollywood and How to Survive It").

2231 February 9, 1997
The 11th Annual American Comedy Awards (Award ceremony). **Eric Idle** presents the award for Funniest Male in a TV Series to John Lithgow (*3rd Rock from the Sun*). The ceremony, held at the Shrine Auditorium in Los Angeles, is telecast Feb. 17 on ABC.

2232 February 11, 1997
Good Stuff (TV arts show: ITV/Carlton). Hosted by Davina McCall and Rowland Rivron. Guests: Cliff Richard, **Michael Palin**, promoting *Fierce Creatures*, and Paco Pena.

2233 February 14, 1997
Fierce Creatures opens in the U.K.

2234 February 21, 1997
TFI Friday (TV talk show: Channel 4). Hosted by Chris Evans. Guests include **Michael Palin** and John Lenahan.

2235 February 27, 1997
A Party Political Broadcast: Liberal Democrat Party (TV: BBC1/BBC2/ITV) Five-minute party political broadcast presented by **John Cleese** on behalf of the Liberal Democrats.

2236 February 28, 1997
City councilors in Swansea, England, vote to lift a 17-year ban on local showings of Monty Python's controversial comedy *Life of Brian*. The film was refused a license by the city council in 1980.

2237 Spring 1997
The Inferno of Dante (Audiobook: Audio Literature). **John Cleese** reads Robert Pinsky's translation (1995) of the 14th-century epic poem by Dante Alighieri. A three-hour recording released on two cassettes.

2238 March 1997
Arista re-masters and re-releases (in the U.S.) the Python albums *Matching Tie and Handkerchief* (1973), *Holy Grail* (1975), *Live at City Center* (1976), and *Contractual Obligation Album* (1980) on CD as part of their "Arista Masters" series.

2239 March 5, 1997
The 2nd Annual Empire Awards (Award ceremony). The Pythons are honored at this award show hosted by *Empire* magazine and held at the Park Lane Hotel in London. First, **Terry Gilliam** receives the Best Director award for *12 Monkeys*. Later, Elton John presents Monty Python with The Empire Inspirational Award. Accepting in person are **Gilliam**, **Terry Jones**, and **Michael Palin**, with **John Cleese** and **Eric Idle** appearing via satellite from Los Angeles.

2240 March 25, 1997
John Cleese becomes a grandfather for the first time when his daughter Cynthia gives birth to a son, Evan Daniel. The father is screenwriter Ed Solomon (*Men in Black*).

2241 March 26, 1997
Terry Gilliam attends the London premiere of Baz Luhrmann's new film version of *Romeo and Juliet* at the Curzon Cinema in Mayfair.

2242 April 1997
Michael Palin launches an appeal to raise money for the Children's Hospital in his home town of Sheffield, England. The launch takes place at Whirlow Hall Farm.

2243 April 16, 1997
John Cleese lends his support to the campaign of Liberal Democrat Paddy Ashdown by joining him at Church House in Westminster for a live "phone link" with members of the electorate. He asks one caller, a Mr. Brin Dimmot, "Is your name an anagram?"

2244 April 16, 1997
Heroes of Comedy (TV episode: Channel 4). "Les Dawson." British comedian Les Dawson (1931–1993) is profiled. Includes interviews with **John Cleese**, Dave Allen, Barry Cryer, and others. Directed by Tom Atkinson. Produced by John Fisher.

2245 April 22, 1997
John Cleese visits Skansen Zoo in Stockholm, Sweden, where he is promoting *Fierce Creatures*.

2246 April 24, 1997
Sen kväll med Luuk (TV talk show: TV4, in Sweden). Late-night talk show hosted by Kristian Luuk. Guest: **John Cleese**, promoting *Fierce Creatures*.

2247 April 25, 1997
Lo + plus (TV talk show: Canal Plus, in Spain). Guest: **John Cleese**, promoting *Fierce Creatures*.

2248 April 29, 1997
The British Academy Film Awards (Award ceremony). **Michael Palin** presents the BAFTA for Best Comedy Series to *Only Fools and Horses*, at the Royal Albert Hall in London.

2249 May 1997
The five surviving Pythons meet in London to discuss the possibility of making another movie together. Although the meeting — organized by **Eric**

Idle— is an enjoyable reunion, nothing is decided concerning future group projects.

2250 May 7, 1997
Heroes of Comedy (TV episode: Channel 4). "The Goons." The influential British comedy group (Spike Milligan, Peter Sellers, Harry Secombe & Michael Bentine) are profiled. Interviewees include **John Cleese**, **Michael Palin**, Eric Sykes, Eddie Izzard, and others. Produced by John Fisher.

2251 May 10, 1997
Pirates (Short film) premieres at Sea World of Ohio. 3-D comedy adventure written by and co-starring **Eric Idle** (who plays first mate, Pierre). The expensive 17-minute film, aka *Pirates 4D*, premieres at Sea World's new 4-D Theater. Also starring Leslie Nielsen (as Capt. Lucky) and Adam Wylie. Directed by Keith Melton.

2252 May 12, 1997
Ruby (TV talk show: BBC2). Host Ruby Wax discusses European comedy with **Terry Jones**, Eddie Izzard, Raoul Heertje, Babben Larsson, and Leo Bassi.

2253 May 22, 1997
John Cleese (and his wife) and **Michael Palin** attend the annual dinner of the Royal Academy of Arts at Burlington House, Piccadilly, London.

2254 May 30, 1997
Richard and Judy Exclusive (TV talk show: ITV/Granada). Hosted by Richard Madeley and Judy Finnigan. Guests: **Michael Palin**, Rory Bremner, Miriam Margolyes, and Robbie Coltrane.

2255 June 1997
The five surviving Pythons reunite for a meeting at the Cliveden Hotel in Berkshire, England to discuss plans for a project together, possibly a stage show.

2256 June 7, 1997
The Times Magazine (London) (Magazine/U.K.). "**Michael Palin**: Sheffield," by Sue Fox, p. 66. **Palin** reminisces about his home town.

2257 June 10, 1997
John Cleese and his wife attend a lecture by Dr. Robert Buckman at the Royal Society of Medicine in London. **Cleese** and Buckman are collaborators on the "Videos for Patients" series *What You Really Need to Know About...*

2258 June 15, 1997
The Sunday Times Magazine (London) (Magazine/U.K.). "Relative Values," by Sue Fox, pp. 9–12. Interviews with **Michael Palin** and his son, Tom, a music producer and writer. Photograph of father and son by Tim O'Sullivan.

2259 June 22, 1997
Parkinson's Sunday Supplement (Radio show: BBC Radio 2). Hosted by Michael Parkinson. Guest: **Michael Palin**, promoting *Full Circle*.

2260 July 9, 1997
Eric Idle attends the world premiere of *George of the Jungle*, featuring the voice of **John Cleese**, at the San Diego Wild Animal Park.

2261 July 16, 1997
George of the Jungle (Feature film: Buena Vista Pictures) opens in the U.S. Comedy based on the 1960s TV cartoon and starring Brendan Fraser in the title role. **John Cleese** voices Ape, George's animatronic ape pal. **Cleese** reprises the role in the direct-to-video sequel *George of the Jungle 2* (2003). Also starring Leslie Mann and Thomas Haden Church. Written by Dana Olsen and Audrey Wells. Directed by Sam Weisman.

2262 July 23, 1997
Talking Tate (TV episode: BBC2). "**Michael Palin**: Totes Meer." Series of 90-second programs in which art enthusiasts discuss their favorite paintings at the Tate Gallery in London. In this episode **Michael Palin** discusses Paul Nash's "Totes Meer" (1940–41).

2263 August 1997
The Pythons announce that they are planning a reunion, although the date and format are uncertain.

2264 August 1997
Full Circle (Book: BBC Books), written by **Michael Palin** with photographs by Basil Pao, is published in the U.K. **Palin**'s journey around the Pacific Rim is chronicled in this companion book to the BBC TV series.

2265 August 1997
J. R. R. Tolkien: Sir Gawain and the Green Knight (Audiobook: HarperCollins). **Terry Jones** reads J. R. R. Tolkien's translation of the 14th-century poem "Sir Gawain and the Green Knight." On two cassettes. Reissued (with "Pearl" and "Sir Orfeo") in 2006.

2266 August 1997
J. R. R. Tolkien: Pearl and Sir Orfeo (Audiobook: HarperCollins). **Terry Jones** reads J. R. R. Tolkien's

translations of the 14th-century poems "Pearl" and "Sir Orfeo." On two cassettes. Reissued (with "Sir Gawain") in 2006.

2267 August 3–October 1997
The big-screen adaptation of Hunter S. Thompson's *Fear and Loathing in Las Vegas*, directed by **Terry Gilliam**, is filmed over two months (on a budget of $18.5 million), mainly in Las Vegas. Locations include the Stardust Hotel & Casino. **Gilliam** was brought in after the original director and screenwriter, Alex Cox, dropped out of the project in April over artistic differences with producers.

2268 August 10, 1997
The Bookworm (TV show: BBC1). Literary magazine program hosted by Griff Rhys Jones. **Michael Palin** discusses his favorite children's book.

2269 August 24, 1997
The Nation's Favourite Children's Book (TV show: BBC1). "**Michael Palin**: Tales of Arabian Nights." Palin discusses his favorite children's book, *Tales from the Arabian Nights*.

2270 August 30, 1997
The Times: The Directory (London) (Newspaper/U.K.). "Been There, Done That, Got It on Film," by Jason Cowley, p. 9. Interview with **Michael Palin** about his travel programs, including the new *Full Circle*.

2271 August 30, 1997
Loose Ends (Radio show: BBC Radio 4). Host Ned Sherrin talks to **Michael Palin** about his new book & series *Full Circle*.

2272 August 31–November 9, 1997
The ten-part travel series *Full Circle with Michael Palin* airs on BBC1 (except for the first episode, which airs on BBC2). In the series, which was filmed over ten months (a 245-day shoot), **Michael Palin** circumnavigates the Pacific Rim — beginning and ending on Little Diomede Island in the Bering Strait — visiting 18 countries along the way. Palin's third travel series, following *Around the World in 80 Days* (1989) and *Pole to Pole* (1992). The series airs in the U.S. Sept. 15–November 1997 on PBS. Series producer: Clem Vallance.
Awards: Television and Radio Industries Club (TRIC) awards for BBC Programme of the Year and BBC Personality of the Year (**Palin**); National Television Award for Most Popular Documentary.
Review: Matthew Bond (*The Times* [London], Sept. 1, 1997, p. 55): "...a real treat, a skillful blend of the spontaneous and what the suspicious among us might believe was the artfully contrived."

2273 August 31, 1997
The Independent (Newspaper/U.K.). "Python with No Venom; Profile; **Michael Palin**." Hester Lacey interviews **Palin** about the success of his travel series (his latest is *Full Circle*), also Python, politics, his father, etc.

2274 August 31, 1997
The Sunday Times (London) (Newspaper/U.K.). "Profile: In Search of the Python's Tale," by Jonathan Margolis, pp. 8–9. Article on **Michael Palin** by writer Margolis, whose unauthorized biography of **Palin** will be published in November.

2275 August 31, 1997
Full Circle with Michael Palin (TV episode: BBC2). "Alaska and Russia." In this first episode of his ten-part travel series, **Michael Palin** sets off on his journey (in August 1995) from the island of Little Diomede in the Bering Strait. His first stops include Kodiak Island and a former Soviet gulag camp. He also learns a Russian folk song and performs it with the Russian Pacific Fleet Choir. Written & narrated by **Michael Palin**. Produced & directed by Roger Mills.

2276 September 1997
Dad's Army: A Celebration (Book: Virgin Books), written by Richard Webber with a foreword by **Michael Palin**, is published in the U.K. Thirtieth-anniversary tribute to the classic BBC sitcom *Dad's Army* (1968–77).

2277 September 2, 1997
The Jack Docherty Show (TV talk show: Channel 5). Guests: **Michael Palin**, promoting *Full Circle*, Edwyn Collins, and Amanda Donohoe.

2278 September 3, 1997
This Morning (TV show: ITV/Granada). Magazine program hosted by Richard Madeley and Judy Finnigan. Guest: **Michael Palin**, promoting *Full Circle*.

2279 September 7, 1997
The People (Newspaper/U.K.). "'She Thought We All Wore Suits of Armour in London!' I'll Never Forget...My First Penfriend," by **Michael Palin** (told to John Earls). The story of how **Palin** began a correspondence with a 14-year-old Japanese girl named Mayumi in 1975 and how she became his Tokyo guide during his *Full Circle* journey (in the second episode, airing Sept. 14).

2280 September 10, 1997
The Daily Show (TV talk show: Comedy Central). Hosted by Craig Kilborn. Guest: **Michael Palin**, promoting *Full Circle*. He also answers "5 Questions."

2281 September 11, 1997
Charlie Rose (TV talk show: PBS). Guest **Michael Palin** talks about *Full Circle*, Python, and **John Cleese**.

2282 September 11, 1997
Late Night with Conan O'Brien (TV talk show: NBC). Guests: **Michael Palin**, promoting *Full Circle*, and Cyndi Lauper.

2283 September 14, 1997
This Week's Good Cause (Radio appeal: BBC Radio 4). **Michael Palin** appeals on behalf of the World University Service.

2284 September 14, 1997
Full Circle with Michael Palin (TV episode: BBC1). "Japan and Korea." **Michael Palin** visits Sado Island, home of the famous Kodo Drummers, and Tokyo, where he meets for the first time his Japanese pen pal, Mayumi Nobetsu. After Japan he visits Seoul and the North Korean border. Second episode in the ten-part travel series. Written & narrated by **Michael Palin**. Produced & directed by Clem Vallance.

2285 September 15, 1997
Full Circle begins airing in the U.S. on PBS.

2286 September 16, 1997
Actor Brian Hall, who played Terry the cook in the second series (1979) of *Fawlty Towers*, dies of cancer at the age of 59.

2287 September 18, 1997
Michael Palin talks about his journey around the Pacific Rim in *Full Circle* at a forum at Westminster Hall in London. The event is sponsored by *The Times* and Dillons bookshops.

2288 September 21, 1997
Full Circle with Michael Palin (TV episode: BBC1). "China." In China, **Michael Palin** climbs Taishan Mountain, ballroom-dances on the streets of Shanghai, and travels on a steamer down the Yangtse River. Third episode in the ten-part travel series. Written & narrated by **Michael Palin**. Produced & directed by Clem Vallance.

2289 September 21, 1997
Omnibus (TV special: BBC1). "The Film of Reeves & Mortimer." Documentary profiling the British comedy team of Vic Reeves and Bob Mortimer. **Terry Jones** is among the interviewees. Narrated by Sting. Directed by Kevin Hewitt. Produced by Paul Morley.

2290 September 28, 1997
Full Circle with Michael Palin (TV episode: BBC1). "Vietnam and the Philippines." In Vietnam, **Michael Palin** visits the Forbidden Purple City (in Hue) and the Marble Mountains (south of Da Nang). In the Philippines, he visits the cloud-covered Rice Terraces of Banaue, assists a surgeon performing "psychic surgery," and judges a beauty contest. Fourth episode in the ten-part travel series. Written & narrated by **Michael Palin**. Produced & directed by Roger Mills.

2291 September 29, 1997
The Traveller's Handbook (Book: Wexas), edited by Miranda Haines, is published in the U.K. Seventh edition of the travel guide, with a foreword by **Michael Palin**.

2292 October 1997
Michael Palin speaks at the Cheltenham Festival of Literature (Oct. 10–19) in Cheltenham, England.

2293 October 1997
John Cleese is among 18 celebrities appearing in British cinema ads nominating their favorite teachers. The ads are part of a campaign for good teachers launched by The Teacher Training Agency. Other celebs participating include Prime Minister Tony Blair, Joanna Lumley, and Stephen Hawking.

2294 October 1, 1997
The Knight and the Squire (Book: Pavilion), written by **Terry Jones** with illustrations by Michael Foreman, is published in the U.K. Children's story set in 14th-century England about a young boy named Tom who runs away in search of adventure. Paperback edition published by Puffin (1999). Followed by *The Lady and the Squire* (2000).

2295 October 2, 1997
An Alan Smithee Film: Burn Hollywood Burn (Feature film) premieres at the Mill Valley Film Festival in Cal. **Eric Idle** plays film director Alan Smithee (a famous screen pseudonym) in this satire of Hollywood movie-making. Also starring Ryan O'Neal, Sylvester Stallone, and Whoopi Goldberg. Written by Joe Eszterhas. Directed by Alan Smithee (pseudonym for Arthur Hiller, who removed his name

from the credits). The film opens in selected U.S. theaters on Feb. 27, 1998 (Buena Vista Pictures).
Awards: Razzie Award for Worst Film of 1998 (and four other Razzies).

2296   October 2, 1997
Clive Anderson All Talk (TV talk show: BBC1). Guests: **Michael Palin** and Gary Barlow. **Palin** talks about *Full Circle* and the possibility of a Python reunion.

2297   October 4, 1997
Wannabe (TV show: ITV/LWT). **Terry Jones** is a guest on this career advice program.

2298   October 5, 1997
Full Circle with Michael Palin (TV episode: BBC1). "Borneo and Java." In the Borneo jungle **Michael Palin** visits the communal longhouse of the Iban tribe. His stay on the island of Java includes a visit to a tea plantation and the Buddhist temple of Borobudur, and a climb up Mount Bromo (an active volcano). Fifth episode in the ten-part travel series. Written & narrated by **Michael Palin**. Directed by Clem Vallance.

2299   October 10, 1997
Blue Peter (TV children's show: BBC1). Stuart Miles talks to **Michael Palin** about his series *Full Circle*. **Palin** also assists Katy Hill in building a model Jeepney.

2300   October 12, 1997
Full Circle with Michael Palin (TV episode: BBC1). "Australia and New Zealand." In Australia **Michael Palin** visits a crocodile farm (in Katherine), participates in a camel muster (King's Creek), and films a cameo role in the soap *Home and Away* (Sydney). In New Zealand he flies over the Tasman glacier, goes jet-boating (Queenstown), and joins Selwyn College's freshman run (Dunedin). Sixth episode in the ten-part travel series. Written & narrated by **Michael Palin**. Produced & directed by Roger Mills.

2301   October 19, 1997
Full Circle with Michael Palin (TV episode: BBC1). "Chile and Bolivia." From his landing on Cape Horn (southernmost point of the Americas), **Michael Palin** heads north to Chiloe, Santiago (capital of Chile), the Juan Fernandez Islands, the Chuquicamata copper mine, and then crosses the Andes by train (which derails) to La Paz in Bolivia. Seventh episode in the ten-part travel series. Written & narrated by **Michael Palin**. Produced & directed by Roger Mills.

2302   October 21, 1997
The Jack Docherty Show (TV talk show: Channel 5). Guests include **Terry Jones** and Nick Hancock.

2303   October 24, 1997
Good Morning America (TV news-talk show: ABC). Guest **Michael Palin**, promoting *Full Circle*, is interviewed by Lisa McRee and participates in a cooking segment with Graham Kerr.

2304   October 26, 1997
Full Circle with Michael Palin (TV episode: BBC1). "Bolivia and Peru." **Michael Palin** observes reed boat makers on the Bolivian shores of Lake Titicaca. After crossing into Peru he travels north by train to Cuzco (capital of the Inca Empire) and Machu Picchu (lost city of the Incas), then takes a boat up the Urubamba River. Eighth episode in the ten-part travel series. Written & narrated by **Michael Palin**. Produced & directed by Clem Vallance.

2305   October 28, 1997
The Late, Late Show with Tom Snyder (TV talk show: CBS). Guests: **Michael Palin** and Art Garfunkel. **Palin**, promoting *Full Circle*, discusses preparations for the journey, strange foods & drinks, psychic surgery, etc. He also takes questions from callers.

2306   October 31, 1997
Terry Jones' *The Wind in the Willows*, originally released in Britain in October 1996, is given a limited U.S. theatrical release (Columbia) in New York City and Los Angeles. Columbia Pictures won U.S. distribution rights to the film in a lawsuit settlement with Disney (although Disney retained the video rights). The film is released on video (as *Mr. Toad's Wild Ride*) by Disney in December 1998.

2307   November 1997
Graham Crackers: Fuzzy Memories, Silly Bits and Outright Lies (Book: Career Press), edited by Jim Yoakum, is published. Collection of comedy and autobiographical material written (or co-written) by the late **Graham Chapman**, compiled by **Chapman**'s friend, Jim Yoakum. Includes a foreword by **John Cleese**, a backward by **Eric Idle**, and a sideways by **Terry Jones**.

2308   November 2, 1997
Full Circle with Michael Palin (TV episode: BBC1). "Peru and Colombia." From the village of Sepahua **Michael Palin** takes a plane to Iquitos (capital of the Peruvian jungle), then a riverboat down the Amazon. In Colombia **Palin** is given a

tour of the violent streets of Bogota and visits the Cosquez emerald mine. Ninth episode in the ten-part travel series. Written & narrated by **Michael Palin**. Produced & directed by Clem Vallance.

2309   November 2, 1997
The Sunday Times (London) (Newspaper/U.K.). "Books: On Top of the World," by Iain Johnstone, pp. 1–2 (sect. 8). Johnstone reviews Jonathan Margolis' unauthorized biography of **Michael Palin** and remembers working with **Palin** on *Fierce Creatures* (which Johnstone co-wrote with **John Cleese**).

2310   November 5, 1997
Ex-S (TV episode: BBC1 Scotland). "Palin on Redpath." **Michael Palin**'s quest to find out more about his favorite artist, Scottish painter Anne Redpath (1895–1965), takes him to Edinburgh, London, and the South of France. Airs nationally Dec. 15 on BBC2. Written by **Michael Palin**. Directed by Eleanor Yule. Produced by Richard Downes.

2311   November 6, 1997
Lateline (TV show: ABC, in Australia). "Travellers' Tales." Reporter Jonathan Holmes talks to two famous travelers—**Michael Palin** and Redmond O'Hanlon—in this Australian program hosted by Jennifer Byrne. Directed by Janet Collins. Produced by Brett Evans and Janet Carr.

2312   November 9, 1997
Full Circle with Michael Palin (TV episode: BBC1). "Mexico, Western USA, Canada and Alaska." **Michael Palin** observes the Mexican–U.S. border from both sides of the fence, visits Alcatraz prison and the Castro District in San Francisco, and participates in the logging games in Squamish, B.C. **Palin** closes the circle on the 245th day of his journey on a Coast Guard ship just off the coast of Diomede. Tenth episode in the ten-part travel series. Written & narrated by **Michael Palin**. Produced & directed by Roger Mills.

2313   November 18, 1997
Politically Incorrect with Bill Maher (TV discussion show: ABC). Panelists: **Terry Jones** (promoting *Starship Titanic*), Laura Ingraham, Alicia Witt, and Jason Alexander. Topics include the jury system, dyslexia, and the use of "F" for Fail in grading.

2314   November 20, 1997
Late Night with Conan O'Brien (TV talk show: NBC). Guest: **Terry Jones**, promoting *Starship Titanic*. He also talks about voicing the parrot in the *Starship* computer game.

2315   November 30, 1997
Calendar (TV news show: ITV/YTV–Yorkshire Television). **Michael Palin** talks about his efforts to help raise money for the Sheffield Children's Hospital.

2316   November 1997
Douglas Adams's Starship Titanic (Book: Harmony Books), written by **Terry Jones**, is published. Comic sci-fi adventure novel, based on the computer game conceived by Douglas Adams, about three Earthlings trapped aboard a luxurious alien spacecraft. **Jones** also provides the voice of the parrot in the game version. The audio version, read by **Jones**, is released by Simon & Schuster Audio. The computer game will be released next spring.

2317   December 1997
Monty Python's The Meaning of Life (CD-ROM: Panasonic Interactive Media). Monty Python's third CD-ROM, a two-CD comedy-strategy adventure game advertised as "The First Game Devised Exclusively for the Betterment of Humanity," is based on their 1983 film and contains new material from all of the surviving Pythons with **Terry Gilliam** supervising. The game is divided into three acts which the player must navigate in order to discover the meaning of life. Games include "You Don't Know John" (quiz) and "Live Organ Transplants." Developed by 7th Level, makers of the first two Python CD-ROMs, *Monty Python's Complete Waste of Time* (1994) and *Monty Python & the Quest for the Holy Grail* (1996). Produced by David Feldstein. Executive produced by **Terry Gilliam** and Bob Ezrin.

2318   December 1, 1997
Masters of Fantasy (TV episode: Sci-Fi Channel). "Douglas Adams." Half-hour profile of author Douglas Adams (*Hitchhiker's Guide to the Galaxy*, *Starship Titanic*). Interviewees include **Terry Jones** and Joseph Stefano.

2319   December 7, 1997
Point of View (Radio show: WNUA-FM 95.5, Chicago). Charlie Meyerson interviews **Terry Jones** and Douglas Adams, who discuss their book & CD-ROM game *Starship Titanic* and agree that Chaucer was funnier than Shakespeare.

2320   December 17, 1997
Monty Python's Life of Brian: The Criterion Collection (Laserdisc: Criterion Collection 353). Laserdisc release of the 1979 biblical comedy with special features including two commentary tracks—one by **Terry Gilliam**, **Eric Idle**, and **Terry Jones**, one by

John Cleese and **Michael Palin**—the original theatrical trailer, five rare deleted scenes—"Shepherds" (shepherds discussing their love of sheep), "Pilate's Wife," "Otto" (suicide squad leader), "The Sign That Is the Sign," and "Souvenir Salesman"—with commentary, four British radio ads, and the 1979 documentary *The Pythons*. Released on DVD in November 1999.

2321 1997

The Unorganised Manager, Part 3: Divine Intervention (Training film: Video Arts). Manager Richard Lewis returns to heaven for a performance appraisal from St. Peter. Remake. Starring **John Cleese** (as St. Peter), Nigel Lindsay, Beatie Edney, and Ann Bryson. Written by Tony Grounds. Directed by Simon Langton.

2322 1997

Who Sold You This Then? (Training film: Video Arts). **John Cleese** narrates this remake of Video Arts' first business-training film, in which **Cleese** starred in 1972. Starring Hugh Laurie, Hugh Bonneville, Tim McInnerny, Patsy Byrne, and Alphonsia Emmanuel. Written & directed by Sean Hardie.

2323 1997

Telephone Behaviour: The Rules of Effective Communication (Training film: Video Arts). How to improve bad telephone technique. Remake of the 1986 film. Starring **John Cleese**, Rebecca Front, Hugh Bonneville, Lolita Chakrabarti, and Chris Langham. Written by Chris Langham. Directed by Robert Knights.

2324 1997

The Directors: The Films of Terry Gilliam (Documentary). Hour-long doc, part of a series of filmmaker profiles sponsored by the American Film Institute, featuring an interview with **Terry Gilliam**, interspersed with clips from his films and comments from Shelley Duvall, Brad Pitt, Amanda Plummer, David Warner, Madeleine Stowe, and Mercedes Ruehl. Produced, written & directed by Robert J. Emery. Released on video in 2000. Later included in the 2004 special edition DVD release of **Gilliam**'s *Time Bandits*.

2325 1997

Reflections on Success (Book: Lennard), written by Martyn Lewis, is published. **Michael Palin** is one of 67 celebrities interviewed by BBC newsman Lewis on the subject of success.

2326 1997

Graham Chapman: A Six Pack of Lies (CD: Verbatim/Magnum Music CDVB 001). Recording of one of **Graham Chapman**'s comedy lectures made during his U.S. tour in the spring of 1988. Recorded live on Apr. 25, 1988, at Georgia Tech University in Atlanta.

2327 1997

47 Years in Tibet (Documentary). **John Cleese** narrates this short documentary on China's occupation of Tibet. Produced & directed by Camilo Gallardo.

2328 January 16, 1998

Parkinson (TV talk show: BBC1). Hosted by Michael Parkinson. Guests: **Michael Palin**, Stephen Tomkinson, and Elton John. **Palin** talks about The Goons, Python humor, his Yorkshire roots, and losing his temper.

2329 January 19, 1998

Heroes of Comedy (TV episode: Channel 4). "Peter Cook." A profile of comedy great Peter Cook with contributions from **Michael Palin**, **John Cleese**, **Eric Idle**, Lin Cook (his widow), Jonathan Miller, Stephen Fry, Eleanor Bron, and others. Written & Produced by John Fisher. Directed by Tom Atkinson.

2330 February 4–June 4, 1998

Devious Devices (Exhibition). Exhibition of automata at the Croydon Clocktower (in Croydon, South London) featuring 18 pieces (by 18 artists) based on objects chosen by **Terry Gilliam** to symbolize the 20th century. The exhibition will go on tour to Wolverhampton, Manchester, Birmingham, and other towns.

2331 February 7, 1998

An Awfully Big Adventure (TV episode: BBC2). "Kenneth Grahame." Profile of Kenneth Grahame, author of the 1908 classic *The Wind in the Willows*. Includes interviews with **Terry Jones**, Alan Bennett, Griff Rhys Jones, Diana Quick, and others. Second of six documentaries on children's literature. Produced & directed by Sarah Aspinall. Note: **Jones** directed a film version of *Wind in the Willows*, released in 1996.

2332 February 21, 1998

Pinky and the Brain (TV episode: WB). "The Family That Poits Together, Narfs Together." **Eric Idle** voices Pinky's Mom & Dad in this episode of the 1995–98 animated series. Directed by Russell Calabrese.

2333 February 22, 1998

The 12th Annual American Comedy Awards (Award

ceremony). **John Cleese** presents Frank Oz with the Creative Achievement Award and also narrates a six-minute video package covering Oz's TV and film career. Executive producer: George Schlatter. Airs Mar. 17 on Fox.

2334   February 23, 1998

Eric Idle and his wife attend the premiere of *An Alan Smithee Film: Burn Hollywood Burn*, in which he stars, at Mann Village Theatre in Westwood, CA.

2335   Spring 1998

Michael Palin films scenes for the Tom Hanks–Meg Ryan romantic comedy *You've Got Mail* in New York City. **Palin** plays a writer friend of Ryan's character. Director Nora Ephron is later forced to cut certain scenes to shorten the film's length, relegating **Palin**'s entire performance to the cutting-room floor. The film (minus **Palin**) premieres in December.

2336   March 4, 1998

Time Bandits: The Criterion Collection (Laserdisc: Criterion Collection 354). Laserdisc release of **Terry Gilliam**'s 1981 fantasy-comedy. Special features: audio commentaries (recorded separately) by **Gilliam**, **Michael Palin**, **John Cleese**, David Warner, and Craig Warnock and a *Time Bandits* Scrapbook. Released on DVD in March 1999 (Criterion No. 37). A two-disc "Special Edition" DVD (Anchor Bay) is released in January 2004.

2337   March 5, 1998

John Cleese appears at a screening of the *Fawlty Towers* episodes "The Psychiatrist" and "The Kipper and the Corpse" at the Directors Guild of America Theatre Complex as part of the Museum of Television & Radio's 15th Annual William S. Paley Television Festival. **Cleese** talks about the episodes and the creation of the series with moderator (and Museum director) Steven A. Bell and takes questions from the audience.

2338   March 5, 1998

Politically Incorrect with Bill Maher (TV talk show: ABC). Panelists: **Eric Idle**, Dennis Miller, Ariana Huffington, and Jeff Greenfield. Taped at the Wheeler Opera House in Aspen, Colorado. **Terry Jones** appeared in a November 1997 episode.

2339   March 6, 1998

Dennis Miller Live (TV talk show: HBO). "Greed." Guest **John Cleese** talks about tycoons, greed in America vs. England, Python fans, etc. Taped at the Wheeler Opera House in Aspen, Colorado.

2340   March 7, 1998

U.S. Comedy Arts Festival Tribute to Monty Python (Event). The five surviving members of Monty Python—**John Cleese**, **Terry Gilliam**, **Eric Idle**, **Terry Jones**, and **Michael Palin**—and the late **Graham Chapman** (in an urn) reunite on stage at the Wheeler Opera House in Aspen, Colorado as part of the annual U.S. Comedy Arts Festival (Mar. 4–8). Host Robert Klein asks them about the origins of the group's name, censorship on the TV series, Python writing sessions, sketches ("Pet Shop"), the films, stage shows, etc. The biggest laugh of the night comes when **Gilliam** "accidentally" knocks over **Chapman**'s urn, spilling his ashes all over the stage. During the show the Python team is presented the Star Award by the American Film Institute and for the finale **Idle** leads the audience in singing "Always Look on the Bright Side of Life." The interview airs as a one-hour special on Mar. 21 on HBO. After the event there is talk among the Pythons about the possibility of doing a stage show to celebrate the group's upcoming 30th anniversary, but after several months of planning **Michael Palin** backs out. There is also talk of making another movie, possibly a follow-up to *Holy Grail* that would have the knights taking part in the Crusades. But this too fails to materialize.

2341   March 9, 1998

The Pythons take legal action against Paragon Entertainment Corporation, a Toronto-based company that owns the distribution rights for *Life of Brian* and other films previously owned by HandMade Films. The group claims that Paragon allowed cuts to be made to *Brian* without their permission, violated their right to oversee sales and editing, and licensed the film at a rate below the film's worth. The Pythons are also suing Britain's Channel 4 for broadcasting the film under their licensing deal with Paragon after the company's right to distribute the film had been terminated. Paragon bought HandMade Films (founded in 1978 by George Harrison) in 1994.

2342   March 9, 1998

The Times (London) (Newspaper/U.K.). "Python Comeback Rises from the Ashes," by Giles Whittell, p. 3. Article on the Pythons' reunion in Aspen and the possibility of a 30th-anniversary stage tour in 1999.

2343   March 10, 1998

The Television and Radio Industries Club Awards

(Award ceremony). **Michael Palin** receives two awards — for BBC Programme of the Year (*Full Circle*) and BBC Personality of the Year — from the Television and Radio Industries Club (TRIC) in a ceremony held at the Grosvenor House Hotel in London. The second award is presented to **Palin** by Baroness Margaret Thatcher.

2344 March 12, 1998
Michael Palin takes the witness stand in the High Court in London to speak on behalf of the other Pythons in the Python (Monty) Pictures v. Paragon Entertainment Corp. case.

2345 March 21, 1998
U.S. Comedy Arts Festival Tribute to Monty Python (TV special: HBO). Hour-long special from the Mar. 7 event in which host Robert Klein interviews the five surviving Python members on stage at the U.S. Comedy Arts Festival in Aspen, CO. Written by Peter Crabbe. Directed by Paul Miller.

2346 March 23, 1998
Eric Idle attends the *Vanity Fair* Oscar Party at Morton's Restaurant in West Hollywood, CA.

2347 March 23, 1998
U.S. News & World Report (Magazine/U.S.). "Off to the Flying Circus: Comedy's New Stars Silly-Walk in the Footsteps of Monty Python," by Anna Mulrine, p. 64. Article about Python's influence on younger comedians and TV writers.

2348 March 25, 1998
Travel Addiction: Is There a Cure? (Lecture). **Michael Palin** speaks at a Library Evening at the Travellers Club in London.

2349 Late March 1998
WTTW Channel 11 (TV promos). **John Cleese** stars in a series of humorous spots for the PBS station in Chicago promoting an upcoming *Monty Python's Flying Circus* marathon. WTTW was the second PBS station to pick up the show (after Dallas' KERA) in October 1974.

2350 April 1998
John Cleese spends three weeks in Madagascar, off the coast of Africa, for an upcoming documentary on lemurs.

2351 April 1998
Terry Jones films his cameo role (as God) in Albert Dupontel's French comedy *Le Créateur* in Paris. The film is released in June 1999.

2352 April 2, 1998
Starship Titanic (CD-ROM: Simon & Schuster Interactive) is released. Computer game created by best-selling author Douglas Adams (*Hitchhiker's Guide to the Galaxy*), the first project produced by The Digital Village, the company Adams founded in 1996 with Richard Creasey and Robbie Stamp. The sci-fi adventure includes the voices of **Terry Jones** (Parrot) and **John Cleese** (Bomb). **Jones** also wrote the novelization, *Douglas Adams's Starship Titanic*, which was published in the fall of 1997.

2353 April 10, 1998
Coast to Coast (TV episode: BBC2). "A Beast, a Present and a One-Legged Man." Host Janet Street-Porter meets **Terry Jones** in Wales during her coast to coast walk across Britain. Sixth episode of a seven-part documentary series. Directed by John Bush.

2354 April 18–19, 1998
Britain's Paramount Comedy Channel presents a "Monty Python Weekend," two nights of all-Python programming.

2355 April 18, 1998
Spike Milligan: A Loose Cannon (TV special: BBC2). Career retrospective of British comedy great Spike Milligan. Part of BBC2's "Spike Night," celebrating the comedian's 80th birthday. Narrated by Haydn Gwynne. Interviewees include **John Cleese**, **Michael Palin**, **Terry Jones**, Harry Secombe, Billy Connolly, and others. Produced & directed by Dagmar Charlton.

2356 April 19, 1998
David Mellor (Radio show: Classic FM). Guest: **Michael Palin**.

2357 April 26, 1998
The Independent (Newspaper/U.K.). "How We Met: Douglas Adams and **Terry Jones**," by Maggie O'farrell. Interview with the *Starship Titanic* collaborators.

2358 April 28, 1998
3rd Rock from the Sun (TV episode: NBC). "Just Your Average Dick." A new professor arrives at Pendelton State University. **John Cleese** guest-stars in this third-season episode, making the first of his four appearances as Dr. Liam Neesam. Starring John Lithgow, Kristen Johnston, French Stewart, Joseph Gordon-Levitt, and Jane Curtin. Written by Michael Glouberman and Andrew Orenstein. Directed by Terry Hughes.

2359 April 29, 1998
3rd Rock from the Sun (TV episode: NBC). "Dick and the Other Guy." **John Cleese**'s second appear-

ance as Dr. Liam Neesam. **Cleese** will reprise the role for two 2001 episodes (May 8 & 15). Starring John Lithgow, Kristen Johnston, French Stewart, Joseph Gordon-Levitt, and Jane Curtin. Written by Bonnie Turner and Terry Turner. Directed by Terry Hughes.
Awards: Emmy-nominated for Outstanding Guest Actor in a Comedy Series (**Cleese**).

2360   May 1998
The Writers Guild of America rules that screenwriter credit for *Fear and Loathing in Las Vegas* will be given to **Terry Gilliam**, Tony Grisoni, Alex Cox, and Tod Davies. **Gilliam** had objected to an earlier ruling by the WGA giving sole screenwriter credit to Cox (the film's original director) and Davies, even though the screenplay had been rewritten by **Gilliam** and Grisoni. As a result of that ruling **Gilliam** resigned from the Guild.

2361   May 1998
Fear and Loathing in Las Vegas: NOT the Screenplay (Book: Applause Books), written by **Terry Gilliam** and Tony Grisoni, is published. Screenplay of the 1998 **Terry Gilliam** film adapted from the novel by Hunter S. Thompson, illustrated with **Gilliam**'s storyboards. The subtitle pokes fun at The Writers Guild of America's initial decision to credit the film's screenplay solely to Alex Cox and Tod Davies, whose earlier adaptation (to be directed by Cox) had been completely rewritten by **Gilliam** and Grisoni.

2362   May 1998
Michael Palin's 1995 novel *Hemingway's Chair* is published in the U.S. by Thomas Dunne Books.

2363   May 1998
American Cinematographer (Magazine/U.S.). "Unholy Grail," by Stephen Pizzello, pp. 42–47. Interview with **Terry Gilliam** on his career and new film *Fear and Loathing in Las Vegas*. The issue also includes an article ("Gonzo Filmmaking," pp. 30–34+) on the film's cinematographer, Nicola Pecorini.

2364   May 1998
Monty Python Encyclopedia (Book: Batsford), written by Robert Ross, is published in the U.K. Guide to the Python team's work in television, film, books, etc.

2365   May 3, 1998
The New York Times (Newspaper/U.S.). "On Filming a Gonzo Vision: A Gonzo Dialogue." Artist Ralph Steadman talks with his friend **Terry Gilliam** about *Fear and Loathing*. The conversation took place Apr. 5 at Steadman's home in England.

2366   May 3, 1998
Terry Gilliam attends the Los Angeles Comic Book and Science Fiction Convention at the Shrine Auditorium Expo Center. **Gilliam** screens the trailer of his new film *Fear and Loathing in Las Vegas* and answers questions from the audience.

2367   May 11, 1998
Charlie Rose (TV talk show: PBS). Guests: **Terry Gilliam** and Johnny Depp, who discuss their new film *Fear and Loathing in Las Vegas*.

2368   May 15, 1998
Terry Gilliam's new film, *Fear and Loathing in Las Vegas*, premieres at the 51st Cannes Film Festival (May 13–24) in France. **Gilliam** also takes part in a press conference with star Johnny Depp.

2369   May 15, 1998
Quest for Camelot (Feature film: Warner Bros.) opens in the U.S. Animated musical-adventure based on the Arthurian legend. **Eric Idle** voices Devon, one-half of a two-headed dragon (the other half is voiced by Don Rickles). **Idle** and Rickles sing "If I Didn't Have You," written by Carole Bayer Sager and David Foster. Other voices by Pierce Brosnan, Gabriel Byrne, Cary Elwes, Gary Oldman, Jane Seymour, and Sir John Gielgud. Written by Kirk DeMicco, William Schifrin, Jacqueline Feather, and David Seidler. Directed by Frederik Du Chau.

2370   May 18, 1998
Kiss Me Kate (TV episode: BBC1). "Calendar." **John Cleese** appears briefly as himself in this first-series episode of the 1998–2000 British sitcom starring Caroline Quentin, Chris Langham, and Amanda Holden. Written by Chris Langham and John Morton. Directed by John Stroud. Produced by Nick Symons.

2371   May 19, 1998
Terry Gilliam attends the New York premiere of his film *Fear and Loathing in Las Vegas*.

2372   May 20, 1998
Terry Gilliam signs copies of *Fear and Loathing in Las Vegas: NOT the Screenplay* at the Barnes & Noble in Lincoln Center, New York City. After the signing **Gilliam** burns his Writers Guild of America card in protest over the WGA's initial decision to deny him (and co-author Tony Grisoni) screenplay credit.

2373 May 21, 1998
The Pythons win back the distribution rights to their 1979 film *Life of Brian* in a High Court judgment against Canadian distributor Paragon Entertainment Corp. Python sued Paragon for not putting restrictions in their licensing agreements that would prevent broadcasters from cutting or editing the film. Justice Donald Rattee rules that Paragon's licensing deals with a Russian broadcaster (in 1994) and Britain's Channel 4 (in 1995) were invalid and that Channel 4 had paid an "unreasonably low price" (just $100,000) for the film. He also rules that Channel 4, for broadcasting the film under their licensing deal with Paragon, had infringed Python's copyright.

2374 May 21, 1998
Lifeline (TV appeal: BBC1). "Sudan Appeal." **Michael Palin** presents a 4-minute appeal on behalf of those suffering in Sudan on account of civil war and drought. Produced by Jill Dawson.

2375 May 21, 1998
The Best of Southwold (Book: The History Press/Sutton Publishing), edited by John Miller with a foreword by **Michael Palin**, is published in the U.K. Book celebrating the seaside town of Southwold in Suffolk, England. **Palin**'s family used to holiday in Southwold in the 1950s. And it was there that he met his future wife, Helen Gibbins, in 1959 (they married in 1966).

2376 May 22, 1998
Fear and Loathing in Las Vegas (Feature film: Universal Pictures) opens in the U.S. Big-screen adaptation of Hunter S. Thompson's classic 1971 novel about a drug-addled journalist and his Samoan lawyer who have a series of psychedelic adventures while on assignment in Las Vegas. Many attempts to film the novel have been made over the past two decades, with several high-profile directors (Oliver Stone, Alex Cox, et al.) attached, before **Terry Gilliam** came on board. The director had shown interest in the project in the early '90s but was unavailable at the time. Starring Johnny Depp, Benicio Del Toro, Tobey Maguire, Ellen Barkin, Gary Busey, and Christina Ricci. Written by **Terry Gilliam**, Tony Grisoni, Tod Davies, and Alex Cox. Directed by **Terry Gilliam**. Produced by Laila Nabulsi, Patrick Cassavetti, and Stephen Nemeth.
Reviews: Stephen Holden (*The New York Times*, May 22, 1998): "...the closest sensory approximation of an acid trip ever achieved by a mainstream movie and the latest example of Mr. **Gilliam**'s visual bravura"; Geoff Brown (*The Times* [London], Nov. 12, 1998, p. 39): "...the cardinal sin of **Terry Gilliam**'s film is to visually magnify Thompson's excesses without giving the audience any pause for thought, any guide through the jungle or reason for persevering"; Tom Shone (*The Sunday Times* [London], Nov. 15, 1998): "Compared with his baroque spirals of invention for the Pythons, or indeed for his previous films, such as *Time Bandits* and *Brazil,* **Gilliam**'s imaginings here cannot help but look a little ingrown and self-circling."

2377 May 24, 1998
Rolf's Amazing World of Animals (TV episode: BBC1). In this first episode of a six-part wildlife series, host Rolf Harris joins animal lover **John Cleese** at Marwell Zoo in Hampshire, England (where *Fierce Creatures* was partly filmed in 1995). Directed by Bill Morton. Produced by Dale Templar.

2378 May 25, 1998
The New Yorker (Magazine/U.S.). "Profiles: War Games," by Giles Smith. Interview with **Terry Gilliam** conducted at the Four Seasons Hotel in Beverly Hills.

2379 May 26, 1998
Today (TV news-talk show: NBC). Guest: **Michael Palin**, promoting his book *Hemingway's Chair*.

2380 May 26, 1998
Michael Palin takes part in an online chat on Yahoo! Chat, promoting *Hemingway's Chair*.

2381 May 29, 1998
The Late, Late Show with Tom Snyder (TV talk show: CBS). Guest: **Michael Palin**, promoting *Hemingway's Chair*, also talks about being presented the TRIC Award by Margaret Thatcher (in March), the Python reunion in Aspen, losing his voice while performing with Python on stage in NY, etc.

2382 June 1998
Sight & Sound (Magazine/U.K.). "Chemical Warfare," by Bob McCabe, pp. 6–8. Interview with **Terry Gilliam** about *Fear and Loathing*.

2383 June 24, 1998
Funny Women (TV episode: BBC2). "Prunella Scales." Profile of the *Fawlty Towers* star. Interviewees include her *Fawlty* co-stars **John Cleese** and Andrew Sachs. Produced by Louis Heaton.

2384 June 26–September 24, 1998
The Complete and Utter History of Monty Python's Flying Circus (Screenings) is presented by the Museum of Television and Radio in New York and Los Angeles. The screenings are divided into 15 programs, each consisting of *Flying Circus* episodes with pre- and post–Python clips.

2385 June 28, 1998
Fantasy World Cup (TV talk show: ITV/LWT). Hosted by Frank Skinner and David Baddiel. Guests: **Michael Palin** and Caroline Aherne.

2386 July 1998
John Cleese is made an A.D. White Professor-at-Large at Cornell University in Ithaca, NY. The honorary post is named after the university's first president, Andrew Dickson White. **Cleese** will give a lecture about once a year over the course of his six-year term, which is later extended to 2006.

2387 July 6, 1998
Fortune (Magazine/U.S.). "Test: Can You Laugh at His Advice?," by Anne Fisher, pp. 203–04. Interview with **John Cleese** on how laughter and creativity are important in business.

2388 July 20, 1998
Terry Jones conducts a "coroner's inquest" for the International Chaucer Congress at the Sorbonne in Paris in an attempt to determine who murdered 14th-century English poet Geoffrey Chaucer (*The Canterbury Tales*). This event leads to further research and eventually a book, *Who Murdered Chaucer?: A Medieval Mystery*, published in 2003.

2389 July 31, 1998
Twiggy's People (TV talk show: ITV/Granada). Model-actress Twiggy talks to her guest **Eric Idle** about his career, rumors of a Python reunion, the group's beginnings, etc. He also sings a few songs and introduces his daughter Lily and dog Bagel (the Beagle). Fourth show of an eight-episode series.

2390 August 23, 1998
Born to Be Wild: Operation Lemur with John Cleese (TV special: BBC1). Documentary on the endangered primate, the lemur, and the efforts to save them from extinction. Host **John Cleese** travels to the rainforests of Madagascar to view the progress of five lemurs, born in captivity in America, who had been released into the wild five months earlier (in November 1997). The project was partly funded with proceeds from the 1997 London premiere of *Fierce Creatures*. **Cleese** also visits the Jersey Zoo in the Channel Islands. Directed by Justine Kershaw. Produced by Sarah Williams. Premieres in the U.S. as *In the Wild: Lemurs with John Cleese* on Oct. 10, 1999, on PBS.
Awards: BAFTA-nominated for Best Photography (Factual) and Originality.

2391 August 25–26, 1998
Terry Gilliam attends the 52nd Edinburgh International Film Festival (Aug. 16–30) in Scotland where he introduces the U.K. premiere of his film *Fear and Loathing in Las Vegas* (Aug. 25). He also participates in an onstage Q&A with critic Mark Kermode (Aug. 26).

2392 August 25, 1998
Edinburgh Nights (TV episode: BBC2). Coverage of events at the Edinburgh Festival in Scotland. Host Mark Lamarr interviews **Terry Gilliam** about his film *Fear and Loathing in Las Vegas*, which has its U.K. premiere at the festival tonight. Episode four of an eight-part series.

2393 August 31, 1998–March 1999
Hercules (TV series: ABC/synd.). **Eric Idle** voices the role of Parenthesis, a guidance counselor at the Prometheus Academy attended by the young Hercules (voiced by Tate Donovan), in episodes of this Disney animated series based on the 1997 feature film.

2394 Fall 1998
Sainsbury's ("Value to Shout About") (TV commercials). **John Cleese** appears in the first of a series of British TV ads for Sainsbury's supermarket. The ads, in which **Cleese** shouts about the store's low prices, are voted the most irritating of the year in a poll and the campaign is subsequently dropped. **Cleese** previously appeared in a Sainsbury Christmas ad (in 1995). Agency: Abbott Mead Vickers BBDO, London.

2395 September 1998
Terry Gilliam attends the 46th San Sebastian International Film Festival (Sept. 17–26), in San Sebastian, Spain, where he is honored with a film retrospective.

2396 September 3, 1998
A Party Political Broadcast: Liberal Democrat Party (TV: BBC1/BBC2/ITV/Channel 4). **John Cleese** makes the case for proportional representation in a new version of a political ad he made in 1985 (for the Social Democratic Party).

2397 September 10, 1998
The Daily Show (TV talk show: Comedy Central). Hosted by Craig Kilborn. Guest **Terry Jones** talks about *Ancient Inventions* and answers "5 Questions."

2398 September 13, 1998
The three-part documentary series *Ancient Inventions* airs on the Discovery Channel. Co-written & hosted by **Terry Jones**, the hour-long series looks at inventions of the ancient world. Produced by David Souden and Amanda Wilkie.

2399 September 13, 1998
Ancient Inventions (TV episode: Discovery Channel). "City Life." A revealing look at one of man's oldest and greatest inventions—the city. Host **Terry Jones** explores the ancient origins of skyscrapers, fire engines, aqueducts, concrete, taxi meters, street lights, etc. Part one of three. Written by Phil Grabsky, **Terry Jones**, and David Souden. Directed by Phil Grabsky.

2400 September 13, 1998
Ancient Inventions (TV episode: Discovery Channel). "Sex and Love." The origins of kissing, cosmetics, brothels, contraception, etc. are explored. Part two of three. Hosted by **Terry Jones**. Written by **Terry Jones**, Daniel Percival, and David Souden. Directed by Daniel Percival.

2401 September 13, 1998
Ancient Inventions (TV episode: Discovery Channel). "War and Conflict." The surprising sophistication of early weaponry (the bow-and-arrow, tank, flame-thrower, etc.) is examined. Part three of three. Hosted by **Terry Jones**. Written by **Terry Jones**, Daniel Percival, and David Souden. Directed by Daniel Percival.

2402 September 23, 1998
The First Take (TV special: BBC Choice). **Terry Jones** hosts this program celebrating BBC TV firsts. Includes an interview with Wendy Richard. Also with Prof. Robert Winston and Gillian Wearing. **Jones** introduces the first episode of *Monty Python's Flying Circus*. Directed by Elaine Shepherd. Produced by Alex Sumner.

2403 October 14, 1998
Terry Gilliam attends the official launch of DVD Video in the U.K.

2404 October 14, 1998
Terry Gilliam attends a dinner at the Dorchester Hotel in London marking the centenary of Duckworth publishers. Other guests include Dame Iris Murdoch, Twiggy, Malcolm McLaren, and Anthony Andrews.

2405 October 16 & 17, 1998
Terry Jones hosts screenings of his film *The Wind in the Willows* at the Pipers Alley Theater in Chicago as part of the 15th Annual Chicago International Children's Film Festival. He also presents a workshop on the making of the film and takes part in a Q&A session. The film wins the Best of the Fest award.

2406 October 16, 1998
Rudolph the Red-Nosed Reindeer: The Movie (Feature film: Legacy Releasing Corp.) opens in the U.S. Animated tale based on the Robert May story and Johnny Marks song. **Eric Idle** voices Slyly the Fox and sings "It Could Always Be Worse." Other voices by John Goodman, Bob Newhart, Debbie Reynolds, and Richard Simmons. Written by Michael Aschner. Directed by William R. Kowalchuk, Jr.

2407 October 27, 1998
The National Television Awards (Award ceremony). **Michael Palin** attends the 4th annual award ceremony at London's Royal Albert Hall where his TV travel series *Full Circle* wins the award for Most Popular Documentary.

2408 October 30, 1998
TFI Friday (TV talk show: Channel 4). Hosted by Chris Evans. Guest: **Terry Gilliam**, promoting *Fear and Loathing*.

2409 November 1998
The 1998 Sheffield Children's Book Awards (Award ceremony). **Michael Palin** hosts this award show—in which local schoolchildren vote for their favorite children's books—in his home town of Sheffield, England. Author J. K. Rowling accepts the top prize for *Harry Potter and the Philosopher's Stone*.

2410 November 1998
The two Python German shows, *Monty Python's Fliegender Zirkus*, are released on video (VHS) by Guerilla Films.

2411 November 3, 1998
Kiss Kiss Bang Bang (TV show: Channel 4). Film program hosted by Charlie Higson. Guest: **Terry Gilliam**, promoting *Fear and Loathing*.

2412 November 5, 1998
Terry Gilliam participates in an onstage conver-

sation about his career with film critic Stuart Klawans at the Walker Art Center auditorium in Minneapolis (**Gilliam**'s birthplace). It is the final event of a retrospective called *And Now for Something Completely Different: The Films of Terry Gilliam* (Oct. 14–Nov. 5).

2413 November 7, 1998
Recess (TV episode: ABC). "The Girl Was Trouble." **Eric Idle** voices Galileo (a personal computer) in this second-season episode of the Disney animated children's series (1997–2001). **Idle** reprises the role in a November 1999 episode.

2414 November 8, 1998
Big Screen (TV show: ITV/LWT). Anna Richardson interviews **Terry Gilliam** about *Fear and Loathing*.

2415 November 9, 1998
Terry Gilliam and family attend a screening of *Fear and Loathing in Las Vegas* at the Odeon in London.

2416 November 13, 1998
Fear and Loathing in Las Vegas, directed by **Terry Gilliam**, opens in the U.K.

2417 November 14, 1998
The Angry Beavers (TV episode: Nickelodeon). "Open Wide for Zombies/Dumbwaiters." **Eric Idle** voices Spanque in this second-season episode of the animated children's series. Created by Mitch Schauer.

2418 November 18, 1998
John Cleese joins biologist Richard Dawkins for an onstage conversation at the Herbst Theater in San Francisco.

2419 November 28, 1998
Live from the Lighthouse (TV special: Channel 4). Three-hour music-comedy fundraiser marking World AIDS Day. Participants include Stephen Fry (host), **Michael Palin**, Hugh Laurie, Boy George, Graham Norton, and Steve Coogan. Directed by Geoff Posner.

2420 December 8, 1998
Mr. Toad's Wild Ride (Videocassette: Walt Disney). **Terry Jones**' film adaptation of Kenneth Grahame's children's classic — starring **Jones** and **Eric Idle** with **John Cleese** and **Michael Palin** — is released on VHS in the U.S. Released on DVD in March 2004. The film premiered in Britain in 1996 under its original title, *The Wind in the Willows*.

2421 December 22, 1998
The Secret of NIMH II: Timmy to the Rescue (Feature film: MGM) is released on video in the U.S. Direct-to-video sequel to the 1982 Don Bluth animated film. **Eric Idle** voices Timmy's evil older brother, Martin. Other voices by Ralph Macchio, William H. Macy, Dom DeLuise, and Harvey Korman. Written by Sam Graham and Chris Hubbell. Directed by Dick Sebast.

2422 December 30, 1998
What's Eating Johnny Depp? (TV special: Channel 4). Profile of actor Johnny Depp, currently starring in **Terry Gilliam**'s *Fear and Loathing in Las Vegas*. Interviewees include Depp, **Gilliam**, and John Waters. Produced & directed by Adrian Sibley.

2423 1998
Lexus ("The Road Is Calling") (TV commercial). American ad in which the Lexus ES 300 takes on the rain-drenched road to Canterbury in England. **John Cleese** voices the road. Other ads in the series feature different roads voiced by Jeremy Irons (Autobahn), Joe Pesci (Brooklyn Bridge), and others. Written by Rob Schwartz. Directed by David Wagreich. Agency: Team One Advertising, El Segundo, CA.

2424 1998
Michael Palin receives the Ness Award from the Royal Geographical Society in London for his efforts in popularizing geography. **Palin** will become president of the Society in 2009.

2425 1998
Diana: A Dedication in Seven Ages: An Anthology of Poetry with Music (Audiobook: Naxos AudioBooks). Collection of 150 poems read by **John Cleese**, Michael Caine, Dame Judi Dench, Sir Ian McKellen, and many others. **Cleese** reads Edward Lear's "The Owl and the Pussycat," John Whitworth's "Boring," and Robert Frost's "The Road Not Taken." The recording benefits the Princess of Wales Memorial Fund. Two-CD or cassette set. Produced by Sean Murphy. Recorded at Abbey Road Studios in London. Reissued in 2000.

2426 January 22–24, 1999
An Evening with Terry Jones (Event). **Terry Jones** appears at a screening of *Holy Grail* at AMC Glen Lakes Theater in Dallas, TX (Jan. 22) as part of the 29th annual USA Film Festival. Following the screening he takes part in an audience Q&A. Over the weekend (Jan. 23–24) a tribute to **Jones** is pre-

sented at the 15th annual KidFilm Festival with screenings of his films *Erik the Viking* and *The Wind in the Willows* (KidFilm is sponsored by the USA Film Festival). He also gives a reading and signs books.

2427   February 1999
Monty Python is celebrated at the Leicester Comedy Festival (Feb. 12–21) in Leicester, England. The event features new film interviews with **Michael Palin** and **Terry Jones** and a tribute to **Graham Chapman** (who was born in Leicester).

2428   February 1, 1999
John Cleese lectures about decision-making and creativity in business for the keynote address at the Training '99 conference at the Arie Crown Theater in Chicago. The lecture is based on the book *Hare Brain, Tortoise Mind* by Guy Claxton. Recorded and released as a training film (*The Hidden Mind*) by Video Arts.

2429   February 4–6, 1999
John Cleese lectures at Cornell University in Ithaca, NY. It is his first official visit since becoming Cornell's A.D. White Professor-at-Large in 1998. **Cleese** hosts a screening of *Parrot Sketch Not Included: Twenty Years of Monty Python* in Willard Straight Hall (Feb. 5), screens and lectures on *A Fish Called Wanda* in Bailey Hall (Feb. 6), gives a lecture titled "Hare Brain, Tortoise Mind," and conducts a master class on acting.

2430   February 7, 1999
The New York Times (Newspaper/U.S.). "Talking Management With: **John Cleese**," by Adam Bryant. Interview with **Cleese** about what he's learned making business-training films.

2431   February 12, 1999
The Monty Python Reunion Special (TV special: Paramount Comedy Channel). Taping of the Pythons' reunion in Aspen, CO, in March 1998 airs in Britain.

2432   February 25, 1999
Eric Idle and his wife attend the opening of Tennessee Williams' play *Not About Nightingales* at the Circle in the Square, New York City.

2433   March 1999
Gilliam on Gilliam (Book: Faber & Faber), edited by Ian Christie, is published. **Terry Gilliam** reflects on his life and career. Compiled from interviews conducted in 1996 and 1998.

2434   March 12, 1999
Comic Relief: Red Nose Day 1999 — The Record Breaker (TV special: BBC1). **John Cleese** appears on this six-hour fund-raising event for Comic Relief.

2435   March 14, 1999
The Observer (Newspaper/U.K.). "Do Not Adjust Your Set." William Leith interviews **Terry Gilliam** on a train bound for Manchester, England, where **Gilliam** is to give a talk and sign copies of the book *Gilliam on Gilliam*.

2436   March 15–April 28, 1999
Payne (TV series: CBS). This short-lived sitcom — an American version of *Fawlty Towers* — stars John Larroquette as Royal Payne, the Basil Fawlty-like owner of a California inn. Only eight episodes air. Also starring JoBeth Williams, Julie Benz, and Rick Batalla. Note: *Fawlty Towers* was previously adapted for U.S. television as *Snavely* (1978 pilot starring Harvey Korman) and *Amanda's* (1983 series starring Bea Arthur).

2437   March 23, 1999
The Directors (Radio show: BBC Radio 2). Film critic Mark Kermode interviews **Terry Gilliam**.

2438   March 23, 1999
A Fish Called Wanda (DVD: MGM). Single-disc DVD release of **John Cleese**'s 1988 comedy. Re-released in a two-disc "Collector's Edition" in November 2006.

2439   March 24, 31 & April 9, 1999
Omnibus (TV series: BBC1). "Laughter in the House: The Story of British Sitcom." Three-part documentary series examining the history of the British sitcom. Episodes: "The Early Days," "The Sensational Seventies," and "Modern Times." Interviewees include **John Cleese**. Narrated by Julie Walters. Produced by Paul Tilzey.

2440   March 31, 1999
Penn & Teller's Sin City Spectacular (TV episode: FX Channel). **Eric Idle** appears in this episode of the 1998–99 comedy-variety series hosted by magicians Penn & Teller. **Idle** sings "Always Look on the Bright Side of Life" while being suspended over a vat of boiling oil. Taped in January at the MGM Grand Adventures Magic Screen Theatre in Las Vegas.

2441   April 1, 1999
Training (Magazine/U.S.). "**John Cleese** on Cre-

ativity," by Jack Gordon. Interview with **Cleese** conducted in his hotel following his Feb. 1 speech at Training '99 in Chicago.

2442 April 2, 1999

The Out-of-Towners (Feature film: Paramount Pictures) opens in the U.S. Comedy starring Steve Martin and Goldie Hawn as a Midwestern couple who face a series of misfortunes on a trip to New York City. **John Cleese** plays hotel manager Mr. Mersault. Remake of a 1970 film starring Jack Lemmon and Sandy Dennis. Also starring Mark McKinney, Oliver Hudson, and Valerie Perri. Written by Marc Lawrence, based on Neil Simon's original script. Directed by Sam Weisman. Note: **Cleese** had previously worked with Weisman on 1997's *George of the Jungle*.

2443 April 11, 1999

The 51st British Academy Film Awards (Award ceremony). **Michael Palin** presents the BAFTA for Best Original Screenplay to Andrew Niccol (*The Truman Show*) at the annual awards ceremony held at the Business Design Centre in Islington, London.

2444 April 24–25, 1999

Michael Palin appears at the 4th annual Los Angeles Times Festival of Books (Apr. 24–25) on the UCLA campus.

2445 April 26, 1999

Hare Brain, Tortoise Mind (Lecture). **John Cleese** gives a talk on creativity and decision-making on the first day of the Solutions '99 conference, hosted by Hyperion Solutions, in Orlando, FL. The lecture is based on the Guy Claxton book of the same title.

2446 May 1999

Monty Python: How Big Is My IMAX Film? (Short film). Humorous short in which **John Cleese** explains the large-screen IMAX format. The short was created by **Terry Jones** for the opening of the British Film Institute London IMAX Cinema. Written & directed by **Terry Jones**. Produced by John Goldstone.

2447 May 1, 1999–October 7, 2000

Mickey MouseWorks (TV series: ABC). **John Cleese** narrates four cartoons for this Disney animated series: "Around the World in 80 Days" (June 5), "Mickey's Mechanical House" (Sept. 11), "Midsummer Night's Dream" (Sept. 25), and "The Nutcracker" (Oct. 23). Also, **Eric Idle** voices the role of Pluto Angel in two episodes (May 29, 1999, & Jan. 22, 2000). Segments were later repeated on the *House of Mouse* series.

2448 May 14, 1999

Parting Shots (Feature film: United International Pictures) opens in the U.K. British comedy about a man who, upon learning that he has only weeks to live, decides to kill those who wronged him. **John Cleese** plays Maurice Walpole. Filmed in the fall of 1997. Also starring Chris Rea, Felicity Kendal, Bob Hoskins, Diana Rigg, Ben Kingsley, Joanna Lumley, and Oliver Reed. Written by Michael Winner and Nick Mead. Produced & directed by Michael Winner. A Scimitar Films production. Note: **Cleese**, a good friend of Winner's, also appeared briefly in the director's 1990 film *Bullseye!*.

2449 May 14, 1999

Eric Idle takes part in a staged reading of the first draft of *Seussical* in New York City. **Idle**, who co-conceived the show with Lynn Ahrens and Stephen Flaherty, reads the part of the Cat in the Hat.

2450 June 1999

Vanity Fair (Magazine/U.S.). "The Dead Parrot Society," by David Morgan. The five surviving Pythons look back on thirty years of silliness. Highlights from Morgan's new book *Monty Python Speaks!*.

2451 June 1, 1999

Monty Python Speaks! (Book: Spike), by David Morgan, is published in the U.S. Oral history of the group told through interviews with the Pythons themselves, conducted by Morgan in the summer and fall of 1998. Published in the U.K. in October (Fourth Estate).

2452 June 6, 1999

Radio 4 Appeal (Radio appeal: BBC Radio 4). **Michael Palin** appeals on behalf of the Federation of Prisoners' Families Support Groups.

2453 June 8, 1999

Terry Gilliam takes part in a lecture/conversation with journalist Bob McCabe at the Guggenheim Museum in New York City. **Gilliam** is in New York promoting the book *Dark Knights & Holy Fools*, written by McCabe.

2454 June 16, 1999

Le Créateur (English: *The Creator*) (Feature film) is released in France. **Terry Jones** makes a cameo appearance (as God, in a dream sequence) in this

French comedy written and directed by Albert Dupontel, who also stars. **Jones** later appears (with **Terry Gilliam**) in Dupontel's *Enfermés dehors* (2006).

2455 June 19, 1999
John Cleese attends the wedding of Prince Edward to Sophie Rhys-Jones in St. George's Chapel at Windsor Castle in Berkshire, England.

2456 June 30, 1999
South Park: Bigger, Longer & Uncut (Feature film: Paramount Pictures) opens in the U.S. Big-screen version of the popular animated TV series. **Eric Idle** voices Dr. Vosknocker. Also voiced by Trey Parker, Matt Stone, Mary Kay Bergman, and Isaac Hayes. Written by Trey Parker, Matt Stone, and Pam Brady. Directed by Trey Parker.

2457 July 9, 1999
Eric Idle Sings Monty Python Songs (Stage show). **Eric Idle** performs a free concert in the Harold M. Williams Auditorium at the J. Paul Getty Center in Los Angeles, backed by a ten-member band led by conductor-arranger John Du Prez. In addition to Python classics such as "Galaxy Song" and "Always Look on the Bright Side of Life," Idle also performs the original "The Getty Song." The one-night show is recorded for a CD, *Eric Idle Sings Monty Python: Live in Concert* (released in April 2000) and later expanded into a multi-city tour in April–June 2000 called *Eric Idle Exploits Monty Python*.

2458 July 11, 1999
The Mail on Sunday (Newspaper/U.K.). "I've Read My Way Around the World." **Michael Palin** writes about some of the books that have inspired his love of travel.

2459 July 16, 1999
Two Ronnies Night (TV special: BBC1). Second hour of BBC1's two-hour tribute to comedians Ronnie Barker and Ronnie Corbett. Hosted by Barry Cryer, with contributions from **John Cleese**, **Michael Palin**, David Frost, Bob Monkhouse, Terry Wogan, Ben Elton, and others.

2460 July 18, 1999
The Heaven and Earth Show (TV show: BBC1). Psychotherapist Alyce Faye Cleese (wife of John) discusses mothers, with comments from **Michael Palin** and Michael Winner.

2461 July 24, 1999
Michael Palin attends the 18th annual "Papa" Hemingway Look-Alike Contest at Sleepy Joe's Bar in Key West, FL, as part of the celebrations for the 100th birthday (on July 21) of author Ernest Hemingway. **Palin** is filming the event for his documentary series *Hemingway Adventure* (third episode, airing Oct. 31).

2462 July 26, 1999
A Night at the Net (Event). **Eric Idle** performs (with Clint Black) at the annual charity tennis match at UCLA Tennis Center. Players in the pro-celebrity doubles match are Andre Agassi, Pete Sampras, Robin Williams, and Billy Crystal. The event raises money for the charity MusiCares.

2463 August 1999
John Cleese speaks in a video message from the Santa Barbara Zoo on behalf of the World Parrot Trust launching a campaign to save 90 species of parrot in danger of extinction.

2464 August 27, 1999
Dudley Do-Right (Feature film: Universal Pictures) opens in the U.S. Comedy starring Brendan Fraser as a bumbling Canadian Mountie. Based on the popular 1960s TV cartoon. **Eric Idle** plays prospector Kim J. Darling. Also starring Sarah Jessica Parker and Alfred Molina. Written & directed by Hugh Wilson.

2465 August 28, 1999
Eric Idle attends the Men of Lonach Highland Gathering and Games at Strathdon in Aberdeenshire, Scotland. Other kilt-wearing celebrities attending the annual event include Billy Connolly (who lives at nearby Candacraig House), Robin Williams, Dame Judi Dench, and Steve Martin.

2466 September 1999
John Cleese, **Michael Palin**, **Terry Jones**, **Eric Idle**, **Terry Gilliam** film new sketches for a special "Python Night" to air on BBC2 in October in celebration of the group's 30th anniversary.

2467 September 1999
The Road to Mars: A Post Modem Novel (Book: Pantheon Books [U.S.]; Boxtree [U.K.]), written by **Eric Idle**, is published. **Idle**'s second novel (following 1975's *Hello Sailor*), a "comic science-fiction thriller," takes place in the 22nd century and follows the adventures of an interplanetary comedy duo and their robot companion. Based on a film script **Idle** wrote in 1983 with Robin Williams and David Bowie as possible stars. Unable to sell the idea to Hollywood, **Idle** later reworked the story

as a musical (titled *Outta Space*), but that too never sold.

2468   September 2, 1999
Clive Anderson All Talk (TV talk show: BBC1). Guests: Adam Sandler and **Eric Idle**. Idle talks about Python's continuing popularity, his new novel *The Road to Mars*, and sings his new song "The Getty Song," from his recent performance at the Getty Museum.

2469   September 6, 1999
The Big Breakfast (TV talk show: Channel 4). Guest: **Terry Gilliam**.

2470   September 10, 1999
BBC Breakfast News (TV news show: BBC1). Includes a report from Madeleine Holt on **Eric Idle** and the 30th anniversary of Monty Python.

2471   September 13, 1999
Ruby (TV talk show: BBC2). Host Ruby Wax and guests Eddie Izzard and **Terry Gilliam**, seated around a dinner table, discuss various topics.

2472   September 14, 1999
Long Live the Dead Parrot (Radio special: BBC Radio 4). Thirtieth-anniversary special looking back on Monty Python's beginnings and impact on British comedy. Hosted by Carol Cleveland, with insights from **John Cleese**, **Terry Jones**, **Michael Palin**, Harry Secombe, Barry Took, Neil Innes, Stephen Fry, Hazel Pethig, Douglas Adams, and others.

2473   September 14, 1999
Eric Idle attends the *BAFTA/Los Angeles Britannia Awards* at the Beverly Hilton Hotel in Beverly Hills, CA.

2474   September 14, 1999
Film director Charles Crichton dies at his home in London at the age of 89. Crichton, best known for his Ealing Studio comedies of the 1940s & 50s (*The Lavender Hill Mob*, *The Titfield Thunderbolt*), directed and co-wrote **John Cleese**'s 1988 hit comedy *A Fish Called Wanda*, which earned him two Oscar nominations and two BAFTA noms. He also directed **Cleese** in over a dozen Video Arts training films in the 1970s & 80s.

2475   September 15, 1999
The Martin Short Show (TV talk show: Synd.). Guests: **Eric Idle**, Jamie Lee Curtis, and Chad Lowe.

2476   September 20, 1999–December 26, 2000
The fourth season of *Suddenly Susan* airs on NBC in the U.S. In this final season of the 1996–2000 sitcom starring Brooke Shields, **Eric Idle** joins the cast as Ian Maxtone-Graham, the new publisher of *The Gate* (the magazine for which Shields' character works). **Idle** replaces her former boss played by Judd Nelson. 22 episodes.

2477   September 22, 1999
Monty Python's Life of Brian comes in at No. 28 on a list of the top 100 British films of all time, as chosen by more than 400 filmmakers in a survey conducted by the British Film Institute. Also making the list are **John Cleese**'s *A Fish Called Wanda* (No. 39) and **Terry Gilliam**'s *Brazil* (No. 54).

2478   September 22, 1999
Eric Idle participates in an onstage conversation with actress Carrie Fisher at the Writers Guild Theater in Beverly Hills, CA. The event is hosted by Writers Bloc.

2479   September 26, 1999
Eric Idle performs and reads from his new novel, *The Road to Mars*, at the 21st "New York is Book Country" fair in Manhattan.

2480   September 27, 1999
Omnibus (TV special: BBC1). "Steve Martin: Seriously Funny." Profile of actor-comedian Steve Martin. Interviewees include **John Cleese**, **Eric Idle**, Michael Caine, Billy Connolly, and Ron Howard. Produced & directed by Adrian Sibley.

2481   September 28, 1999
Clint Black's cover of **Eric Idle**'s "Galaxy Song" (from *The Meaning of Life*) is released on his album *D'lectrified* (RCA). **Idle** joined Black in writing — and singing — a new intro to the song. It is Black's version of "Galaxy Song" that is played to wake astronauts on the space shuttle *Endeavour* and the International Space Station on May 28, 2011.

2482   September 29, 1999
Late Night with Conan O'Brien (TV talk show: NBC). Guests: **Eric Idle**, Isabella Rossellini, and Tom Shillue.

2483   October 1999
Micronpc.com ("Labyrinth") (TV commercial). **Terry Gilliam**-directed TV ad for the American company Micron Electronics, newly rebranded as Micronpc.com. In the ad, a CEO working at his office late at night makes his way through a laby-

rinth of possessed computers in search of someone to fix his malfunctioning PC. Filmed in London. Written by Mike Gallagher. Produced by Tommy Turtle. Agency: Goldberg Moser O'Neill, San Francisco.

2484   October 1999
Journey into Your Imagination (Short film) opens. Short film accompanying the ride at Disney's Epcot Center. **Eric Idle** hosts, reprising his role as Dr. Nigel Channing from the 1994 film *Honey, I Shrunk the Audience*. In 2002 a new version of the film, *Journey into Imagination with Figment*, debuts.

2485   October 1, 1999
The Times (London) (Newspaper/U.K.). "Farewell to the Admirable Charlie," by **Michael Palin**, p. 48. **Palin** pays tribute to director Charles Crichton (*A Fish Called Wanda*), who died Sept. 14.

2486   October 2, 1999
The Daily Mirror (Newspaper/U.K.). "Bullfights, Elephant Stalking, Car Crashes...I've Had a Busy Day." Sue Blackhall interviews **Michael Palin** about his new series *Hemingway Adventure*.

2487   October 3, 1999
The Heaven and Earth Show (TV show: BBC1). Esther McVey interviews **John Cleese** on the topic of blasphemy.

2488   October 3, 1999
The Sunday Times Magazine (London) (Magazine/U.K.). "A Life in the Day of...," by **Eric Idle** (interviewed by Caroline Scott), p. 78. **Idle** describes an average day at his home in Los Angeles. Photograph of **Idle** by Fergus Greer.

2489   October 5, 1999
Something Completely Different (Radio special: BBC Radio 2). Thirtieth-anniversary documentary on Monty Python narrated by Griff Rhys Jones, with comments from **John Cleese, Terry Jones, Michael Palin, Terry Gilliam**, and others.

2490   October 6, 1999
Fresh Air from WHYY (Radio talk show: NPR). Terry Gross interviews **Eric Idle**, who talks about his new book *Road to Mars* and his father's death at the end of World War II. He also sings "Always Look on the Bright Side of Life," "All Things Dull and Ugly," and "Galaxy Song."

2491   October 7, 1999
Clive Anderson All Talk (TV talk show: BBC1). Guests: **Michael Palin**, promoting *Hemingway Adventure*, and Martin Kemp.

2492   October 7, 1999
Four of the five surviving Pythons—**John Cleese, Terry Gilliam, Terry Jones**, and **Michael Palin**—attend a 20th-anniversay charity screening of *Life of Brian* at the Empire Cinema in Leicester Square, London. The event, which benefits Macmillan Cancer Relief, was organized by the Paramount Comedy Channel and is hosted by Jonathan Ross.

2493   October 8, 1999
30 Years of Python (TV special: Paramount Comedy Channel). Half-hour special. Includes footage cut from 1979's *Life of Brian*: "Shepherds," "Otto," and "Pilate's Wife." The scenes were also included in the 1997 laserdisc release of the film on Criterion. The special is followed by a screening of *Holy Grail*. Narrated by Jonathan Ross. Directed by Chris Loizou.

2494   October 9, 1999
The Independent (Newspaper/U.K.). "Staying In: Travelling Circus." James Rampton interviews **Michael Palin** about his career and new series *Hemingway Adventure*.

2495   October 9, 1999
"Python Night," a four-hour block of all–Python programming celebrating the 30th anniversary of the first broadcast of *Monty Python's Flying Circus*, airs on BBC2. The group (minus **Eric Idle**) and Carol Cleveland perform in new comedy sketches shown throughout the night: "Arthur Ewing/Announcer," "BBC Dumbing Down/Gumbys/Out-Focus-Group/anim/Pepperpots," "*Mastermind* Parody/Talking Apes," "This Is BBC1," "Ken Shabby and Announcer," and "Police Press Conference." **Eric Idle**'s only contribution is a piece (taped in Los Angeles) examining "Who Was Monty Python?" The featured programs are *It's: The Monty Python Story* (doc hosted by Eddie Izzard), *Pythonland* (doc hosted by **Michael Palin**), a screening of *Life of Brian*, "Lost Python" (six-minute short film the Pythons created for the 1971 May Day special *Euroshow '71*), a *South Park* tribute to Monty Python, *From Spam to Sperm: Monty Python's Greatest Hits* (doc hosted by Meat Loaf), and The Peter Sissons Interview (a live, heavily-promoted interview with all five surviving Pythons, which lasts all of 20 seconds). The three documentaries air together in the U.S. as *Life of Python* on A&E in April 2000.

2496 October 9, 1999
It's: The Monty Python Story (TV special: BBC2). Documentary, hosted by comedian Eddie Izzard, telling the group's story through interviews, clips, and a Python family tree created by Pete Frame. Interviewees include **John Cleese**, **Terry Gilliam**, **Terry Jones**, and **Michael Palin**, also Sir David Frost, Ronnie Corbett, Carol Cleveland, Kevin Kline, Trey Parker, and Matt Stone. Produced & directed by Elaine Shepherd.

2497 October 9, 1999
Pythonland (TV special: BBC2). Travel mockumentary in which **Michael Palin** revisits various *Flying Circus* filming locations around London, including the sites for "Seduced Milkmen," "New Cooker Sketch" and "Silly Walks" (Thorpebank Rd, Shepherds Bush), "Climbing the Uxbridge Road" (South Ealing Rd), "Hell's Grannies" (Acton High St), "Bicycle Repair Man" (Acton), "The Fish-Slapping Dance" (Teddington Lock), and the very first "It's" Man intro (Poole Harbour, Dorset). Produced & directed by Ralph Lee.

2498 October 9, 1999
From Spam to Sperm: Monty Python's Greatest Hits (TV special: BBC2). Documentary focusing on the music of Monty Python. Featured songs are "Spam Song," "Lumberjack Song," "Always Look on the Bright Side of Life," and "Every Sperm Is Sacred." Also, **Eric Idle** sings "Galaxy Song." Hosted by Meat Loaf, with comments from the Pythons, also Carol Cleveland, Steve Martin, and others. Produced & directed by Selina Mehta.

2499 October 11, 1999
Michael Palin's Hemingway Adventure (Book: Weidenfeld & Nicolson), written by **Michael Palin** and designed by Basil Pao, is published in the U.K. Companion book to the TV series, assembled from notes and diaries **Palin** kept before, during and after filming, along with plenty of photos. Paperback edition published by Orion (2000). Published in the U.S. by Thomas Dunne Books (St. Martin's Press) in 2000.

2500 October 13, 1999
Michael Palin gives a talk on Ernest Hemingway at the Town Hall in Cheltenham, England, as part of the 50th Cheltenham Festival of Literature (Oct. 8–24).

2501 October 17–November 7, 1999
The four-part documentary series *Michael Palin's Hemingway Adventure* airs on BBC1. In this series, writer-host **Michael Palin** follows in the footsteps of legendary author Ernest Hemingway (1899–1961), a journey that takes him to Chicago, Italy, Spain, Paris, Cuba, Africa, Key West, etc. The project sprung from **Palin**'s love of reading Hemingway as a youth, a love that was reignited while doing research for his 1995 novel *Hemingway's Chair*. The series, produced by Martha Wailes, airs in the U.S. in May 2000 (PBS).
Reviews: Mark Lawson (*The Guardian*, Oct. 10, 1999): "...the itinerary seems to be dictated mainly by the pictures least likely to make the viewer switch off.... There is no sense of the presenter being on a quest"; Paul Hoggart (*The Times* [London], Oct. 18, 1999, p. 47): "...'**Michael Palin** Visits Some Places Mentioned In Hemingway and Pootles Around a Bit' would have been a more honest title"; Mike Davies (*The Birmingham Post*, Oct. 18, 1999): "Hemingway once called Orson Welles an effeminate theatrical and took a chair to him. One suspects **Palin** would have warranted an entire dining table."

2502 October 17, 1999
The Sunday Times (London) (Newspaper/U.K.). "A Funny Fellow in Deadly Ernest," p. 17. Profile of **Michael Palin**.

2503 October 17, 1999
Michael Palin's Hemingway Adventure (TV episode: BBC1). **Michael Palin** travels to Spain, where he observes the annual Running of the Bulls (Pamplona) and attends a bullfight (Valencia). In Kenya, Africa he meets some of the local wildlife and visits the Masai tribe. First episode of the four-part documentary series. Written & narrated by **Michael Palin**. Directed by David F. Turnbull.

2504 October 19, 1999
Donny & Marie (TV talk show: Synd.). Hosted by Donny Osmond and Marie Osmond. Guest: **Eric Idle**.

2505 October 24, 1999
Michael Palin's Hemingway Adventure (TV episode: BBC1). **Michael Palin** visits Oak Park, IL (Hemingway's birthplace), learns how to fire a gun at a shooting range (Chicago), then moves on to north Michigan, where the Hemingways spent their summers. Next, **Palin** investigates the writer's war and post-war experiences, visiting Milan and Paris. Second episode in the four-part documentary series. Written & narrated by **Michael Palin**. Directed by David F. Turnbull.

2506 October 25, 1999
Michael Palin talks about *Hemingway Adventure* at Waterstone's bookstore (High Street) in Birmingham, England, as part of the Birmingham Book Festival (Oct. 15–25).

2507 October 27, 1999
John Cleese turns 60.

2508 October 29, 1999
This Morning (TV show: ITV/Granada). Magazine program hosted by Ruth Langsford and John Leslie. Guest: **Terry Jones**.

2509 October 31, 1999
Michael Palin's Hemingway Adventure (TV episode: BBC1). **Michael Palin** attends a Hemingway look-alike contest in Key West, FL, celebrating the author's 100th birthday (July 21, 1999). He then visits Uganda, where Hemingway survived two successive plane crashes in 1954. In Italy **Palin** dons a Gumby costume for the annual carnival in Venice and joins a duck hunt (in Cáorle). Third episode in the four-part documentary series. Written & narrated by **Michael Palin**. Directed by David F. Turnbull.

2510 November 1999
John Cleese appears in promotional spots for TBS Superstation's "15 Days of 007" James Bond movie festival (beginning Nov. 27). **Cleese** plays R in the new Bond movie *The World Is Not Enough*, premiering this month.

2511 November 1, 1999
Hollywood Greats (TV episode: BBC1). "Cary Grant." Profile of Hollywood leading man Cary Grant. Interviewees include **John Cleese** (who borrowed Grant's real name, Archie Leach, for his character in *A Fish Called Wanda*), Roger Moore, and others. Narrated by Ian McShane. Produced by Richard Downes.

2512 November 4, 1999
A Pocketful of Python: Picked by Terry Jones (Book: Methuen) is published in the U.K. Collection of Python sketches & songs selected by **Terry Jones**, with a preface by **Terry Gilliam**. Includes "Lumberjack Song," "Spam," and "Every Sperm Is Sacred." First book in the series.

2513 November 4, 1999
A Pocketful of Python: Picked by John Cleese (Book: Methuen) is published in the U.K. Collection of Python sketches & songs selected by **John Cleese**, with a preface by **Michael Palin**. Includes "Eric the Half-A-Bee," "The Last Supper," and "Merchant Banker." Second book in the series.

2514 November 5, 1999
The Routes of English (Radio episode: BBC Radio 4). "Evolving English: From the Tabard Inn to Canterbury." **Terry Jones** joins in a discussion on Middle English (as used in Chaucer's *Canterbury Tales*) with Dr. Kathryn Lowe, Dr. Ruth Evans, and Martin Starkie. Episode four in the first series of a program exploring the history of the English language. Hosted by Melvyn Bragg. Produced by Simon Elmes and Tony Phillips.

2515 November 7, 1999
Michael Palin's Hemingway Adventure (TV episode: BBC1). **Michael Palin** travels to Havana, Cuba, where he visits Hemingway's house, takes part in a fishing tournament, and attempts to get an interview with Fidel Castro. Next, he heads back to America, where he visits a dude ranch and a taxidermist (Montana) and, finally, Hemingway's grave (Ketchum, Idaho). Fourth and final episode in the documentary series. Written & narrated by **Michael Palin**. Directed by David F. Turnbull.

2516 November 8, 1999
The World Is Not Enough (Feature film: MGM) premieres in the U.S. James Bond adventure—19th in the series—starring Pierce Brosnan as Bond. **John Cleese** plays R, assistant to Desmond Llewelyn's gadget expert, Q. **Cleese** will take over the role of Q for 2002's *Die Another Day*, replacing Llewelyn, who died in a car accident a month after *World*'s release. The film opens nationwide Nov. 18. Also starring Sophie Marceau, Denise Richards, Robert Carlyle, and Judi Dench. Written by Neal Purvis, Robert Wade, and Bruce Feirstein. Directed by Michael Apted.

2517 November 8, 1999
John Cleese and his wife attend the premiere of *The World Is Not Enough*, in which he plays R, at the Mann Village Theater in Los Angeles.

2518 November 13, 1999
Recess (TV episode: ABC). "That Stinking Feeling." **Eric Idle** voices Galileo (a personal computer) in this third-season episode of the Disney animated children's series (1997–2001). **Idle** first voiced the role in a November 1998 episode.

2519 November 14, 1999
The Sunday Times (London) (Newspaper/U.K.). "Millennium Masterworks: *The Canterbury Tales*,"

by **Terry Jones**, p. 22. **Jones** praises Chaucer's masterwork.

2520   November 15, 1999
Maclean's (Magazine/Can.). "Life After Monty Python: **Eric Idle** Is as Amusing as Ever," p. 120. Interview.

2521   November 15, 1999
Mornings with Margaret Throsby (Radio talk show: ABC Classic FM, in Australia). Margaret Throsby talks to **Michael Palin** about *Hemingway Adventure*.

2522   November 16, 1999
Monty Python's Life of Brian: The Criterion Collection (DVD: Criterion Collection 61). Twentieth-anniversary DVD release containing the same special features from Criterion's 1997 laserdisc release: two commentary tracks by the Pythons, original theatrical trailer, five deleted scenes, four British radio ads, and the 1979 documentary *The Pythons*. The film is re-released on DVD in 2007 in a two-disc "Immaculate Edition."

2523   November 20, 1999
MADtv (TV variety show: Fox). **John Cleese** appears on this late-night comedy show.

2524   November 21, 1999
Open Book (Radio show: BBC Radio 4). A look at children's literature for Christmas, with guests **Terry Jones**, Philip Pullman, and Caroline Horn.

2525   November 22, 1999
Eric Idle reads from his new novel *The Road to Mars* at Chicago Shakespeare Theatre, Navy Pier, Chicago.

2526   November 24, 1999
Michael Palin gives a talk (with slides) on Ernest Hemingway at London's Institute of Education.

2527   November 24, 1999
Terry Gilliam gives a master class and takes part in an interview (with Michael Orpen) in Belfast, N. Ireland. The event is organized by the Northern Ireland Film Commission.

2528   November 29, 1999
People (Magazine/U.S.). "Too **Cleese** for Comfort," by Peter Ames Carlin, pp. 141–46. Article/interview on **John Cleese**'s life and current projects.

2529   December 1999
Michael Palin attends the 2nd annual "Made in Sheffield" dinner in his home town of Sheffield, England.

2530   December 1999
Biography Magazine (Magazine/U.S.). "Stranded on a Desert Island: **Eric Idle**," by David Goldman, p. 38. **Idle** tells Goldman what he would want with him if stranded on a desert island.

2531   December 1999
Eric Idle and Kevin Nealon join musician Clint Black on stage at Caesars Palace in Las Vegas. Wearing black Stetsons, they sing **Idle**'s "Galaxy Song," with Nealon on banjo. Nealon also played banjo on Black's recording of the song on his album *D'lectrified*.

2532   December 12, 1999
Rock 'n' Roll in the Making (TV special: BBC1). Half-hour documentary on the recording of the charity single "It's Only Rock 'n' Roll" by an all-star lineup that includes **Eric Idle**. Hosted by Kathy Burke.

2533   December 13, 1999
It's Only Rock 'n' Roll (Single: Universal ROCK 2). This cover of the Rolling Stones classic, a charity recording in aid of Children's Promise, features an all-star lineup that includes Mick Jagger, Keith Richards, Robin Williams, The Spice Girls, Natalie Imbruglia, James Brown, B.B. King, The Corrs, Annie Lennox, Lionel Ritchie, Iggy Pop, and **Eric Idle**.

2534   December 21, 1999
Hot Pursuits (TV show: BBC Knowledge). "Unusual." **Terry Jones** appears on this careers program hosted by Gill Mills. Produced & directed by Bob Franklin.

2535   December 25, 1999
Aladdin (Radio play: BBC Radio 4). Pantomime adaptation of the classic tale, starring **Terry Jones**, Clive Anderson, Penelope Keith, Robbie Coltrane, Jennifer Ehle, Jeremy Hardy, and others. Written by Stewart Permutt, John Langdon, and Bruce Hyman. Produced & directed by Bruce Hyman.

2536   December 31, 1999–January 1, 2000
2000 Today (TV special: BBC1). Twenty-eight–hour live broadcast from BBC Television Centre covering Millennium Eve celebrations around the world, with **Michael Palin** among the famous names participating (others include Michael Parkinson, David Attenborough, and Cliff Richard).

Throughout the broadcast **Palin** reviews events and provides links and updates.

2537 December 31, 1999
In the Millennium Honors List, **Michael Palin** is awarded the title of Commander of the Order of the British Empire (CBE) for his services to television.

2538 1999
The Hidden Mind (Training film: Video Arts). **John Cleese**'s lecture on creative thinking in business, recorded live Feb. 1, 1999, at the Training '99 conference in Chicago. **Cleese** based his lecture on the book *Hare Brain, Tortoise Mind* by Guy Claxton. Written by and starring **John Cleese**.

2539 1999
A blue plaque dedicated to **Graham Chapman** is unveiled at King Edward VII School in Melton Mowbray, Leicestershire, England. **Chapman** attended the school from 1953 to 1959.

2540 1999
Dark Knights & Holy Fools: The Art and Films of Terry Gilliam (Book: Orion) is published. Book by journalist Bob McCabe, with a foreword by **Terry Gilliam**, covering **Gilliam**'s life and career, including his work as animator for *Monty Python's Flying Circus* and as the director of *Jabberwocky*, *Time Bandits*, *Brazil*, etc. Includes loads of **Gilliam** artwork, scripts, rare photographs, and interviews with **Gilliam**, **John Cleese**, **Terry Jones**, **Michael Palin**, Tom Stoppard, Robin Williams, and others.

2541 1999
OJRIL: The Completely Incomplete Graham Chapman (Book: Batsford [U.K.], Brassey's [U.S.]), written by **Graham Chapman** and edited by Jim Yoakum, is published. Compilation of **Chapman**'s previously unpublished scripts, including a TV special for Ringo Starr (co-written by Douglas Adams) and the pilot script for his unaired series *Jake's Journey*. Foreword by **Eric Idle**. Note: OJRIL is an acronym for "Old Jokes and Ridiculously Irrelevant Links."

2542 1999
Monty Python's Holy Grail Ale, named after the Pythons' 1975 film, is introduced to commemorate the group's 30th anniversary. The label claims that the ale, brewed by the Black Sheep Brewery of North Yorkshire, was "tempered over burning witches."

2543 Early January 2000
Eric Idle visits his friend George Harrison at his Friar Park home (in Henley-on-Thames, England) where Harrison is recuperating from an attack at his home by a knife-wielding intruder (on Dec. 30).

2544 January 3, 2000
Backstage from the Millennium (TV special: BBC Choice). Behind-the-scenes look at the BBC's Millennium Eve broadcast. With Michael Parkinson, Peter Sissons, **Michael Palin**, and others. Hosted by Jon Monie.

2545 January 21, 2000
Trigger Happy TV (TV show: Channel 4). **Terry Gilliam** appears on this comedy series starring Dom Joly. Second of six programs.

2546 January 22, 2000
The Times (London) (Newspaper/U.K.). "Have I Got News for You," by Michael Cable, p. 4. Article on **Michael Palin**'s life in Gospel Oak, the North London neighborhood he's lived in for over 30 years, and his relationship with the local newsagent, Mash Patel.

2547 January 28, 2000
Isn't She Great (Feature film: Universal Pictures) opens in the U.S. Biopic of author Jacqueline Susann (*Valley of the Dolls*) starring Bette Midler in the title role. **John Cleese** plays Susann's publisher, Henry Marcus. Filmed in Montreal in the summer of 1998. Also starring Nathan Lane, Stockard Channing, and David Hyde Pierce. Written by Paul Rudnick. Directed by Andrew Bergman.

2548 February 1, 2000
Trevor McDonald Meets... (TV talk show: ITV2). **Michael Palin** is interviewed.

2549 February 5, 2000
Boy in Darkness (TV special: BBC Choice). **Terry Jones** narrates this half-hour fantasy/drama adapted from a short story by Mervyn Peake. Starring Jack Ryder (as Titus Groan). Directed by Nick Copus.

2550 February 12, 2000
AFI Star Award Tribute to Robin Williams (Stage event). **Eric Idle** hosts this tribute to comedian Robin Williams at the Red Brick Arts and Recreation Center in Aspen, CO. Williams is being honored with the American Film Institute's Star Award at the U.S. Comedy Arts Festival (Feb. 9–13). Monty Python received AFI's Star Award at the festival in March 1998. Note: **Idle** worked with Williams on 1982's *Faerie Tale Theatre* ("Tale of the

Frog Prince") and 1988's *The Adventures of Baron Munchausen*.

2551 March 17, 2000
Late Night with Conan O'Brien (TV talk show: NBC). Guests: Jon Stewart, **Eric Idle**, and Fran Lebowitz. **Idle**, promoting his upcoming album and tour, also talks about St. Patrick's Day and sings "The Bruces' Philosophers Song."

2552 March 22, 2000
The Daily Show with Jon Stewart (TV talk show: Comedy Central). Guest: **Eric Idle**, promoting his upcoming North American tour. **Idle** also sings "Always Look on the Bright Side of Life."

2553 March 26, 2000
John Cleese and his wife attend the *Vanity Fair* Oscar Party at Morton's Restaurant in West Hollywood, CA.

2554 April 7, 2000
Dennis Miller Live (TV talk show: HBO). "The Penis." Guest **Eric Idle** discusses this week's topic and sings, appropriately, the "Penis Song."

2555 April 8, 2000
Michael Palin gives a talk on Ernest Hemingway at the Oxford University Union as part of the Oxford Literary Festival (Apr. 7–9).

2556 April 9, 2000
Life of Python (TV special: A&E). Two-hour compilation of documentaries from 1999 airing in the U.S. on the A&E Network as a "Biography Special" guest-hosted by **Eric Idle**. The documentaries — *It's: The Monty Python Story* (hosted by Eddie Izzard), *From Spam to Sperm: Monty Python's Greatest Hits* (hosted by Meat Loaf), and *Pythonland* (hosted by **Michael Palin**) — originally aired on BBC2 in Britain in October 1999.

2557 April 14, 2000
Astérix & Obélix Take on Caesar (Feature film) is released in the U.K. English-dubbed version of the 1999 French film *Astérix & Obélix Contre César* starring Gerard Depardieu and Christian Clavier in the title roles. **Terry Jones** wrote the English adaptation and also voices Depardieu's role (Obélix). The film is a live-action version of the cartoons created by René Goscinny and Albert Uderzo. Written & directed by Claude Zidi.

2558 April 18, 2000
Eric Idle Sings Monty Python: Live in Concert (CD: Restless Records 73730) is released. The 22-track album was recorded live at the J. Getty Center in Los Angeles in July 1999. In addition to the Python tracks, the album also includes several **Idle** originals and one song from The Rutles. Tracks: "Spam Song," "The Meaning of Life," "Money Song," "Every Sperm Is Sacred," "Accountancy Shanty," "The Meaning of Life Poem," "I Like Chinese," "The Bruces' Philosophers Song," "Men, Men, Men," "Shopping," "Sit on My Face," "Penis Song," "All Things Dull and Ugly," "Eric the Half-a-Bee," "One Foot in the Grave," "I Must Be in Love," "Rock Notes," "Galaxy Song," "Medical Love Song," "Always Look on the Bright Side of Life," "Lumberjack Song (encore)," and "Liberty Bell." Produced by John Du Prez.

2559 April 18, 2000
Terry Jones attends the opening night of the play *Snogging Ken*, a political satire, at the Almeida Theatre in London.

2560 April 20, 2000
TV Guide Online (Website). **Eric Idle** promotes *Eric Idle Sings Monty Python*.

2561 April 22, 2000
Top Ten (TV episode: Channel 4). "Comedy Records." Paul Whitehouse hosts this look at comedy records of the past. **Terry Jones** and **Eric Idle** are interviewed. Directed by Ken McGill.

2562 April 25, 2000
The Unknown Peter Sellers (TV special: American Movie Classics). Hour-long documentary on the life and career of comic star Peter Sellers (1925–1980). Includes interviews with **Michael Palin**, Spike Milligan, Richard Lester, Shirley MacLaine, David Frost, and others. Written & directed by David Leaf and John Scheinfeld.

2563 April 25, 2000
Donny & Marie (TV talk show: Synd.). Hosted by Donny Osmond & Marie Osmond. Guests: **Eric Idle**, Margaret Colin, and Nancy O'Dell.

2564 April 26, 2000
Late Night with Conan O'Brien (TV talk show: NBC). Guest: **Michael Palin**, promoting *Hemingway Adventure* on PBS, talks about the running of the bulls, eating bull's testicles, Cuba, etc.

2565 April 28, 2000
Gladiators: The Brutal Truth (TV special: The Learning Channel). Hour-long documentary, hosted by **Terry Jones,** exploring the history of those trained killers of the Roman Empire who fought and died to entertain the public and to serve

as symbols of Rome's superiority. With insights from Prof. Keith Hopkins, Dr. Shelby Brown, and Dr. Andrew Wallace-Hadrill. Airs in Britain on Aug. 28 as part of BBC2's "Romans' Day." Produced & directed by Alan Ereira.

2566   April 28, 2000
Canned Ham (TV episode: Comedy Central). Eric Idle talks about his career and gives a preview of his upcoming stage tour. With John Du Prez, Peter Crabbe, and Mark Ryan. Written & directed by Natalie Barandes and Andrew Scheer.

2567   April 29–June 29, 2000
Eric Idle Exploits Monty Python: A Rather Stupid Evening of Skits and Songs (Stage show). Eric Idle takes his stage show to over 20 cities in the U.S. and Canada. The show, which evolved from his one-night performance at the Getty Museum in Los Angeles in July 1999, features Python material ("Nudge, Nudge," "The Meaning of Life," "Always Look on the Bright Side of Life," etc.) performed by Idle, accompanied by performers Peter Crabbe, Samantha Harris, and Mark Ryan, and "the Rutland Symphony Orchestra" led by Idle's longtime musical collaborator John Du Prez. Idle's tour takes him to the Orpheum Theatre in Phoenix, AZ (Apr. 29), University of Arizona's Centennial Hall in Tuscon, AZ (Apr. 30), San Diego State University Open Air Theatre (May 2), Sun Theatre in Anaheim, CA (May 3), Universal Amphitheater in Universal City, CA (May 5), Abravanel Hall in Salt Lake City, UT (May 7), Schnitzer Theatre in Portland, OR (May 9), Orpheum Theatre in Vancouver, B.C. (May 12–13), Paramount Theater in Seattle, WA (May 15–16), Warfield Theater in San Francisco, CA (May 18–20), Community Center Theater in Sacramento, CA (May 23), Paramount Theatre in Denver, CO (June 1–2), Fox Theater in Detroit, MI (June 4), Chicago Theatre in Chicago, IL (June 6), Riverside Theatre in Milwaukee, WI (June 7), Orpheum Theater in Minneapolis, MN (June 9), Madison Civic Center in Madison, WI (June 10), Tower Theater in Upper Darby, PA (June 13), Warner Theater in Washington, D.C. (June 14–15), Ohio Theater in Columbus, OH (June 17), Palace Theatre in Cleveland, OH (June 18), Hummingbird Centre in Toronto (June 20–21), New Jersey Performing Arts Center in Newark, NJ (June 25), Carnegie Hall in New York City (June 27–28), and Wang Center in Boston, MA (June 29). Idle will tour again in October–December 2003 with his *Greedy Bastard Tour* of North America.

2568   April 29, 2000
Michael Palin talks about *Hemingway Adventure* at the 5th annual Los Angeles Times Festival of Books (Apr. 29–30) on the UCLA campus.

2569   May 2000
Playboy (Magazine/U.S.). "20 Questions: Michael Palin," by Warren Kalbacker, pp. 126–27+. Palin answers questions concerning the current state of Britain, the comedy of Monty Python, English sex scandals, and Ernest Hemingway.

2570   May 2000
Vanity Fair (Magazine/U.S.). Eric Idle answers the magazine's "Proust Questionnaire."

2571   May 2000
Sight & Sound (Magazine/U.K.). "Preston Sturges Changed My Life," p. 20. Film directors Baz Luhrmann, Peter Farrelly, Clare Kilner, and Terry Jones write about the career of 1940s writer-director Preston Sturges and the impact his films made on them.

2572   May 3 & 10, 2000
The 1999 TV travel series *Michael Palin's Hemingway Adventure* airs in the U.S. on PBS.

2573   May 5, 2000
Quantum Project (Short film) premieres on the internet. Stephen Dorff stars as a physicist exploring the quantum universe in this 32-minute film combining live-action and computer animation. Produced exclusively for distribution on the internet. John Cleese plays Dorff's father, Alexander Pentcho. Also starring Fay Masterson. Written by David Cohen. Directed by Eugenio Zanetti.

2574   May 9, 2000
The View (TV talk show: ABC). Guests: John Cleese and Richard Lewis.

2575   May 11, 2000
Michael Palin attends a reception for the opening of the new Tate Modern art gallery in London.

2576   June 1, 2000
Donny & Marie (TV talk show: Synd.). Hosted by Donny Osmond & Marie Osmond. Guests: John Cleese and Kenny Loggins.

2577   June 6, 2000
Eric Idle takes his show *Eric Idle Exploits Monty Python* to the Chicago Theatre in Chicago, Ill. on the last night of the Chicago Comedy Festival (June 1–6).

2578 June 14, 2000
Morning Edition (Radio show: NPR). Host Bob Edwards interviews **Eric Idle** about his U.S. tour.

2579 June 18, 2000
That's Esther (TV show: ITV/Meridian). Hosted by Esther Rantzen. In this special edition devoted to stammering, Rantzen meets **Michael Palin**, who shows her around the Michael Palin Centre for Stammering Children and talks about his father's stammer.

2580 June 19, 2000
John Cleese and his wife attend the biennial Royal Academy of Arts Mayflower dinner in London.

2581 June 26, 2000
Late Show with David Letterman (TV talk show: CBS). Guests: Tom Brokaw and **Eric Idle**, promoting *Eric Idle Exploits Monty Python*. **Idle** also talks about avoiding the news, having dinner with Prince Charles, etc.

2582 June 27–28, 2000
Eric Idle brings his stage show *Eric Idle Exploits Monty Python* to Carnegie Hall in NYC for two nights as his North American tour draws near to its close. **Terry Jones** attends the performance and also appears on stage for "The Lumberjack Song." Singer Art Garfunkel also makes a surprise appearance, joining **Idle** on "Always Look on the Bright Side of Life" (Garfunkel performed the song on the soundtrack of the 1997 film *As Good as It Gets*).

2583 June 28, 2000
Omnibus (TV special: BBC1). "Wallace and Gromit Go Chicken." Documentary on the making of Aardman Productions' new film *Chicken Run*. Interviewees include Nick Park, **Terry Gilliam**, Ray Harryhausen, and Mel Gibson. Directed by Steven Cole.

2584 July 6, 2000
Michael Palin receives the honorary degree Doctorate of Literature from Queen's University in Belfast, N. Ireland. The degree, presented during the university's graduation ceremonies, is awarded to **Palin** for his services to film, television, and literature.

2585 July 9, 2000
The Facts of Life (TV special: Channel 4). Documentary on sex education in Britain. Includes interviews with **Michael Palin**, Junior Simpson, and John Mortimer. Produced & directed by Jenny De Yong.

2586 August 2000
Michael Palin and **Terry Jones** travel to Scotland to revisit the filming locations (Doune Castle, Loch Tay, Glen Coe, and Castle Stalker) for *Holy Grail*. The resulting documentary, *The Quest for the Holy Grail Locations*, is released on the film's two-disc special edition DVD in October 2001.

2587 August 2000
Erik the Viking (DVD: Arrow Films) is released in the U.K. The British version of **Terry Jones'** 1989 comedy. Re-released on DVD in October 2006 as a two-disc set containing both this version and a new "Director's Son's Cut" edited by **Jones'** son, Bill.

2588 August 2000
Fairy Tales (Audiobook: Orion Audio Books). **Terry Jones** reads stories from his 1981 children's book. Also read by Joan Greenwood, Michael Hordern, Bob Hoskins, Helen Mirren, and Tim Rice. Recorded in 1982.

2589 August 15, 2000
What a Performance! (TV episode: ITV). "Madcap." Hosted by Bob Monkhouse. Program on comedy, with appearances by **Terry Jones**, Spike Milligan, Tim Brooke-Taylor, others. Directed by Charles Boyd.

2590 August 20, 2000
The Sunday Times (London) (Newspaper/U.K.). "History as I Invented It," by **Terry Jones**, p. 4. In this article on the Roman gladiator, **Jones** reflects on how history has often proven to be more surreal than Monty Python.

2591 August 26, 2000
Eric Idle attends the annual Men of Lonach Highland Gathering and Games in Aberdeenshire, Scotland, along with Billy Connolly (host), Robin Williams, Dame Judi Dench, and Steve Martin.

2592 September 2000
Fawlty Towers is voted the greatest British television program of all time in a poll (of TV writers, producers, and critics) conducted by the British Film Institute. *Monty Python's Flying Circus* comes in at No. 5 in the top 100 poll.

2593 September 16, 2000
Night of 1,000 Shows (TV special: BBC1). Michael Parkinson hosts this clip-filled special celebrating the 40th anniversary of BBC Television Centre, with recollections from stars **John Cleese** (about *Fawlty Towers*), Terry Wogan, Bruce Forsyth, Brian

Blessed, Gary Lineker, and Sir David Attenborough. Produced by Kate Phillips.

2594 September 22, 2000
O Happy Day! (Play), written by **Graham Chapman** and Barry Cryer, premieres at Dad's Garage Theatre in Atlanta, GA. This previously-unproduced play, written in the mid-1970s, was discovered several years ago by Jim Yoakum, the Atlanta-based director of the **Graham Chapman** Archives. **John Cleese** and **Michael Palin** serve as consultants on the production, which runs until Nov. 19. Directed by Sean Daniels. Dad's Garage will later adapt a collection of "lost" **Chapman** sketches and perform them under the title *Out of the Trees* (2003).

2595 September 24, 2000
John Cleese's friend and former therapist, Robin Skynner, dies at the age of 78. **Cleese** and Skynner, who first met in 1975, collaborated on two books: *Families and How to Survive Them* (1983) and *Life and How to Survive It* (1993).

2596 September 28, 2000
A launch party is held in London for **Terry Jones**' new film production company, Messiah Pictures. The company, which **Jones** formed in partnership with Julian Doyle, will develop and produce smaller-budgeted feature films.

2597 Late September 2000
After a decade in development, **Terry Gilliam**'s *The Man Who Killed Don Quixote* begins filming in Las Bardenas Reales, north of Madrid, Spain. The film — scripted by **Gilliam** and Tony Grisoni, based on the 1605 story *Don Quixote* by Miguel de Cervantes — is being financed by European investors and stars Johnny Depp (*Fear and Loathing in Las Vegas*) and French actor Jean Rochefort (as Quixote). Filming on the $32 million production, which was set to take place over 17 weeks, is halted after only six days on account of flash floods that wash away the set (on day two) and the worsening condition of 70-year-old Rochefort, who is suffering from a prostate infection. On the fifth day, Rochefort is flown back to Paris for medical attention. When it becomes clear that he will not be able to return, the film is abandoned. The collapse of the production is chronicled in the documentary film *Lost in La Mancha*, which premieres in February 2002.

2598 October 2000
The Lady and the Squire (Book: Pavilion), written by **Terry Jones** with illustrations by Michael Foreman, is published in the U.K. Sequel to *The Knight and the Squire* (1997) continues the medieval adventures of young Tom, now a squire in France. Shortlisted for the Whitbread Children's Book of the Year Award 2001. Paperback edition published by Puffin books (2002).

2599 October–November 2000
Terry Jones talks about — and reads from — his new children's book, *The Lady and the Squire*, at the Newcastle Arts Centre in Newcastle upon Tyne, Eng. (Oct. 14), Waterstone's bookshop in Bath, Eng. (Oct. 18), Orange Tree Theatre in London (Nov. 5), and other venues.

2600 October 2000
Terry Gilliam receives the Time Machine Award at the 33rd Sitges International Film Festival (Oct. 5–14) in Catalonia, Spain. The award honors work in the fantasy genre.

2601 October 5, 2000
John Cleese's mother, Muriel Evelyn (Cross) Cleese, dies on her 101st birthday, in Somerset, England. **Cleese**'s father, Reginald, died in 1972.

2602 October 5, 2000
A Pocketful of Python: Picked by Terry Gilliam (Book: Methuen) is published in the U.K. Collection of Python sketches & songs selected by **Terry Gilliam**, with a preface by **Eric Idle**. Includes "The Meaning of Life (song)." Third book in the series.

2603 October 5, 2000
A Pocketful of Python: Picked by Michael Palin (Book: Methuen) is published in the U.K. Collection of Python sketches & songs selected by **Michael Palin**, with a preface by **John Cleese**. Includes "Cheese Shop" and "The Knights Who Say 'Ni.'" Fourth book in the series.

2604 October 6, 2000
Calendar News (TV news show: ITV/YTV–Yorkshire Television). **Michael Palin** is interviewed.

2605 October 8, 2000
The Sunday Times (London) (Newspaper/U.K.). "Why I Love the Local Colour," by **Michael Palin**, p. 3. Article on the Scottish Colourists.

2606 October 8, 2000
Michael Palin on...The Colourists (TV special: BBC2). Documentary special, hosted by **Michael Palin**, exploring the lives and work of four Scottish painters — John Duncan Fergusson, George Leslie Hunter, Samuel John Peploe, and Francis Camp-

bell Boileau Cadell — known as "The Colourists." **Palin** visits 10 Downing Street, Paris, Edinburgh, the Isle of Iona (off the Scottish coast), Glasgow, and the French Riviera. Produced & directed by Eleanor Yule. Note: **Palin** and Yule previously collaborated on the TV doc *Palin on Redpath* (1997).

2607   October 13–14, 2000
John Cleese visits Cornell University in Ithaca, NY for a second time since being named an A.D. White Professor-at-Large in 1998. During his visit, **Cleese** presents a screening and lecture on *Life of Brian* in Bailey Hall (Oct. 13) and gives a lecture on writing with novelist-screenwriter William Goldman in Rockefeller Hall (Oct. 14).

2608   October 13, 2000
Terry Jones introduces a screening of *Holy Grail* and talks about his career at the Tyneside Cinema in Newcastle upon Tyne, England as part of the Newcastle Film Festival.

2609   October 15, 2000
The Mail on Sunday (Newspaper/U.K.). "East Fife Four, Forfar Five... (or Why a List of Place Names Used to Bring the Nation to a Standstill)," by **Michael Palin**, p. 61. **Palin** recalls his family's ritual of listening to the Saturday football results.

2610   October 25, 2000
Terry Jones gives a talk on the death of Chaucer at the Museum of London.

2611   November 4–December 3, 2000
Watching (TV series: BBC2). Tom Sutcliffe hosts this six-part documentary series on filmmaking. Interviewees include **Terry Gilliam**, John Carpenter, Peter Bogdanovich, Sydney Pollack, Atom Egoyan, and Richard Schickel. Episodes: "Beginnings" (Nov. 4), "Big" (Nov. 11), "Screens" (Nov. 18), "Punch" (Nov. 25), "Unseen" (Dec. 2), and "Freeze" (Dec. 3).

2612   November 12, 2000
An Evening with Michael Palin (Lecture). **Michael Palin** speaks at the Duke of York's Theatre in London in aid of Action for Prisoners' Families.

2613   November 17, 2000
The Scotsman (Newspaper/U.K.). "Master of Middle-Age Mischief," by Aidan Smith. Interview with **Terry Jones**, conducted at his Camberwell, London home.

2614   November 17, 2000
The Beatles Revolution (TV special: ABC). Two-hour documentary on the Fab Four. **Eric Idle** is among the celebrities interviewed. Directed by Rudy Bednar.

2615   November 20, 2000
I Don't Believe It! The "One Foot in the Grave" Story (TV special: BBC1). Documentary looking back on the ten-year run of the popular British sitcom *One Foot in the Grave*. **Eric Idle**, composer and singer of the show's title song, appears. Directed by Gerard Barry.

2616   November 21–22, 2000
Terry Gilliam contributes original artwork to the annual "Secret" postcard exhibition at the Royal College of Art in London. Proceeds from sales of the postcards (contributed by both celebrities and unknown artists) go to the RCA's Fine Art Student Award Fund.

2617   November 22, 2000
Terry Gilliam turns 60. A few days later, he celebrates his birthday with a party at the Cucina restaurant in Hampstead, London, attended by fellow Pythons **Michael Palin** and **Terry Jones**.

2618   November 22, 2000
Michael Palin attends the first gala charity evening for the Peter Cook Foundation in London. Other attendees include Andrew Lloyd Webber, Helen Mirren, Sir David Frost, Bill Wyman, and Ron Wood.

2619   November 22, 2000
102 Dalmatians (Feature film: Buena Vista Pictures) opens in the U.S. Sequel to the 1996 live-action remake of the 1961 Disney animated classic *101 Dalmatians*. **Eric Idle** voices Waddlesworth, a macaw who thinks he's a dog. Starring Glenn Close, Gerard Depardieu, and Ioan Gruffudd. Written by Kristen Buckley, Brian Regan, Bob Tzudiker, and Noni White. Directed by Kevin Lima.

2620   November 29, 2000
Buzz Lightyear of Star Command (TV episode: UPN). "War and Peace and War." **Eric Idle** voices Guzelian in this episode of the animated sci-fi series. Patrick Warburton voices Buzz. Directed by Victor Cook.

2621   November 30, 2000
Seussical opens on Broadway. The musical, by lyricist Lynn Ahrens and composer Stephen Flaherty, is based on the works of children's author Dr. Seuss. Ahrens and Flaherty conceived the work in collaboration with **Eric Idle** in 1998. **Idle** also performed the role of the Cat in the Hat in a staged reading of the show in May 1999.

2622 December 2–23, 2000
The Medieval Ball (Radio series: BBC Radio 4). **Terry Jones** examines medieval thinkers' understanding of the world in this four-part series. Episodes: "A World View" (Dec. 2), "What Have the Romans Ever Done for Us?" (Dec. 9), "The View from the East" (Dec. 16), and "Towards the Age of Discovery" (Dec. 23). Produced by Mark Rickards.

2623 December 2, 2000
A Candlelight Christmas (Concert). **John Cleese** gives a reading of "Twas the Night Before Christmas" at the First Presbyterian Church in Santa Barbara, CA.

2624 December 10, 2000
The Mail on Sunday (Newspaper/U.K.). "A Monty Python and His Holy Trail," by **Terry Jones**, p. 89. Jones writes about his trip (with illustrator Michael Foreman) through France to trace the route of Edward III's 1359–60 campaign.

2625 December 14, 2000
The Magic Pudding (Feature film: 20th Century-Fox Australia) opens in Australia. Animated film, based on the Australian children's classic by Norman Lindsay, starring **John Cleese** as the voice of Albert, the Magic Pudding. Voice cast also includes Sam Neill, Hugo Weaving, and Geoffrey Rush. Written by Harry Cripps, Greg Haddrick, and Simon Hopkinson. Directed by Karl Zwicky.

2626 December 19, 2000
Best of British (TV episode: BBC1). "Ronnie Corbett." Tribute to the comedian, with guests Ronnie Barker, Sir David Frost, **Michael Palin**, and others. Produced & directed by Jo Shinner.

2627 December 28, 2000
Heroes of Comedy (TV episode: Channel 4). "Ronnie Barker." Comedian Ronnie Barker (*The Two Ronnies*) is profiled. Interviewees include **Michael Palin**, Ronnie Corbett, and David Jason. Written & produced by John Fisher. Directed by Tom Atkinson.

2628 December 30, 2000
The Guardian (Newspaper/U.K.). "The Borders of History," by **Michael Palin**. Palin writes about his visits to Poland and Italy for his Radio 4 program on the Iron Curtain, beginning this morning.

2629 December 30, 2000 & January 6, 2001
Excess Baggage (Radio special: BBC Radio 4). "**Michael Palin**'s Iron Curtain." Two-part program in which **Palin** travels to Trieste (in Italy) and Szczecin (in Poland), the two cities immortalized in Winston Churchill's "Iron Curtain" speech of March 1946.

2630 2000
Performance Matters: The Importance of Praise (Training film: Video Arts). Film on the importance of praise as a management tool. Introduced & narrated by **John Cleese**. Starring Andy Taylor and Mina Anwar. Written by Antony Jay. Directed by Sean Hardie.

2631 2000
Performance Matters: The Need for Constructive Criticism (Training film: Video Arts). Film for managers on how to improve employee performance by giving constructive criticism. Introduced & narrated by **John Cleese**. Starring Andy Taylor and Mina Anwar. Written by Antony Jay. Directed by Sean Hardie.

2632 2000
Studies in the Age of Chaucer, Volume 22 (Book: New Chaucer Society, Ohio State University), edited by Larry Scanlon, is published in the U.S. Includes "The Monk's Tale," by **Terry Jones**, pp. 387–97.

2633 2000
Brightness (Short film). Two small-time crooks get a second chance from a mysterious man named Mr. Bix (**Eric Idle**) in this 25-minute short. Also starring Chad Lindberg, Gregory Fawcett, and Fay Masterson. Written by Todd Messegee. Directed by Andrew Tsao.

2634 January 7, 2001
Heroes for the Planet—A Tribute to National Geographic (TV special: National Geographic Channel & CNBC). **John Cleese** appears on this hour-long live broadcast from the Warner Theatre in Washington, D.C. Hosted by Pierce Brosnan.

2635 February 2001–February 2002
Michael Palin's next travel series, *Sahara*, is filmed over four months, taking him across the vast Sahara Desert in Northern Africa. The series will air Oct. 13–Nov. 3, 2002, on BBC1.

2636 February 2, 2001
Blue Peter (TV children's show: BBC1). In this medieval-themed episode **Terry Jones** assists Matt Baker in preparing for a joust.

2637 February 7, 2001
Jeopardy! (TV game show: Synd.). **Eric Idle** competes in this celebrity edition against Dana Delany and Wayne Brady. **Idle** wins the game, earning $15,000 for his charity, Friends of the Los Angeles Free Clinic. Taped at the Las Vegas Hilton. Hosted by Alex Trebek.

2638 March 2001
John Cleese films his scenes as Nearly Headless Nick in *Harry Potter and the Sorcerer's Stone*. The film is released in November.

2639 March 2001
John Cleese is reported to be in negotiations to star in a new American sitcom titled *H.M.O.*, for ABC Television. In the show, which is set at a dysfunctional hospital, **Cleese** would play administrator Dr. Larry King. The pilot is scripted by Peter Tolan.

2640 March 1, 2001
The Human Face (Book: BBC Books), written by Brian Bates with **John Cleese**, is published in the U.K. Companion book to the TV documentary series hosted by **Cleese**, illustrated with many photographs. Published in the U.S. in July (Dorling Kindersley).

2641 March 7–25, 2001
The four-part documentary series *The Human Face* airs on BBC1. The series, hosted with humor by **John Cleese**, explores how facial characteristics and expressions effect our perceptions of personality, beauty, and fame. The series, which costars Elizabeth Hurley (in three episodes) and **Michael Palin** (one episode), airs in the U.S. on Aug. 26 & 27 (The Learning Channel).
Awards: Emmy-nominated for Outstanding Non-Fiction (Informational) Special.

2642 March 7, 2001
The Human Face (TV episode: BBC1). "Face to Face." "Professor" **John Cleese** and his assistant Janet (Elizabeth Hurley) explore how people make and read facial expressions in this first episode of the four-part documentary series. With comments from David Attenborough, Prof. Paul Ekman, and others. Written & hosted by **John Cleese**. Produced & directed by James Erskine.

2643 March 9, 2001
Morning Becomes Eclectic (Radio talk show: KCRW, Santa Monica). Host Nic Harcourt talks to **Eric Idle** about the creation of The Rutles and the DGA screening of *All You Need Is Cash* tonight.

2644 March 9, 2001
Eric Idle introduces a screening of the Rutles film, *All You Need Is Cash* (1978), at the Directors Guild of America Theatre in Los Angeles as part of the Museum of Television & Radio's 18th Annual William S. Paley Television Festival (Feb. 28–Mar. 13). After the screening, **Idle** takes part in a panel discussion (moderated by Museum curator Ron Simon) with his Rutle collaborators Neil Innes, Ricky Fataar, and director Gary Weis.

2645 March 10, 2001
Parkinson (TV talk show: BBC1). Hosted by Michael Parkinson. Tonight's only guest, **John Cleese**, talks about the origins of *Fawlty Towers*, the *Life of Brian* controversy, the sketches "Ministry of Silly Walks" and "Pet Shop," and fame.

2646 March 11, 2001
The Sunday Times Magazine (London) (Magazine/U.K.). "Relative Values: Terry and Bill Jones," pp. 7–9. Caroline Scott interviews **Terry Jones** and his son, film editor Bill Jones (age 24). Photographs of father and son by Zed Nelson. **Michael Palin** and his son, Tom, were also interviewed for "Relative Values" (June 15, 1997).

2647 March 13, 2001
The Rutles: All You Need Is Cash (DVD: Rhino Home Video). **Eric Idle**'s 1978 TV mockumentary is released on DVD with a remastered soundtrack and special features, including an introduction and audio commentary by **Idle**, **Idle**'s memoirs, deleted scenes, and photo gallery.

2648 March 14, 2001
The Human Face (TV episode: BBC1). "Here's Looking at You!" A look at the role the face plays in shaping our identity. Hosted by **John Cleese**, with comments from David Attenborough, caricaturist Tim Watts, and others. Second episode of the four-part documentary series.

2649 March 16, 2001
Comic Relief: Big Red Nose Night (TV special: BBC1). **John Cleese** appeals for donations during this eight-hour TV event in aid of Comic Relief.

2650 March 21, 2001
The Human Face (TV episode: BBC1). "Beauty." An attempt to answer the question "What is beauty?" Hosted by a miniaturized **John Cleese** standing on the face of Elizabeth Hurley. Prunella Scales also co-stars. Interviewees include Candice Bergen, Pierce Brosnan, Dr. Stephen R. Marquardt,

and Prof. Paul Ekman. Third episode of the four-part documentary series.

2651 March 25, 2001
The Human Face (TV episode: BBC1). "Fame." An examination of famous faces. Hosted by **John Cleese**, and guest-starring Elizabeth Hurley and **Michael Palin**, who plays a man applying to become an icon and a lowly peasant who wants his face on a coin. With comments from William Goldman, David Attenborough, Pierce Brosnan, and casting director Mali Finn. Fourth episode of the four-part documentary series. Produced & directed by David Stewart.

2652 March 25, 2001
John Cleese and **Eric Idle** (and their wives) attend the *Vanity Fair* Oscar Party at Morton's Restaurant in West Hollywood, CA.

2653 April 3, 2001
GMTV (TV show: ITV/Carlton). Morning magazine program. Guests: **John Cleese**, Eddie Izzard, and Faith Hill.

2654 April 6, 2001
Eric Idle attends the opening of the exhibition "The Private Collection of Steve Martin" at the Bellagio Gallery of Fine Art in Las Vegas. Other attendees include Martin Short and Martin Mull.

2655 April 13, 2001
An Evening with John Cleese (Event). **John Cleese** hosts a screening of *The Meaning of Life* at Campbell Hall at the University of California Santa Barbara. The event benefits The Arts Fund and UCSB Department of Film Studies.

2656 April 14, 2001
The Archive Hour (Radio show: BBC Radio 4). "Children's Hour." **Terry Jones** hosts this look at 70-plus years of children's radio programs in the English-speaking world. Hour.

2657 April 16, 2001
John Cleese, Benjamin Bottoms, and Margaret Kemp give readings at the Lobero Theatre in Santa Barbara, CA. The readings are part of the "Fine Actors Performing Great Writers" series presented by Speaking of Stories. **Cleese** reads "Sanatorium" by W. Somerset Maugham.

2658 April 19, 2001
Eric Idle attends the opening night of Mel Brooks' Broadway musical *The Producers* at the St. James Theatre in New York City. It was **Idle** who first pitched the idea of a *Producers* musical to Brooks back in the late 1980s, but at the time the director wanted to concentrate on making movies and passed on the project.

2659 April 22–23, 2001
John Cleese speaks at Cornell University in Ithaca, NY. It is his third visit to the university since being named a professor-at-large in 1998. During his visit, **Cleese** delivers a Sunday sermon titled "My First Sermon" at Sage Chapel (Apr. 22), gives a lecture with wildlife preservationist Simon Hicks at the James Law Auditorium (Apr. 22), holds a press conference with local media (Apr. 23), lectures at the McCarthy Reading Room (Libe Café) in Olin Library (Apr. 23), and joins Prof. Stephen Ceci for a talk on "The Human Face" (Apr. 23).

2660 April 24 & May 22, 2001
The Criterion Collection releases on DVD three classic comedies by French filmmaker Jacques Tati — *M. Hulot's Holiday* (1953), *Mon Oncle* (1958), and *Playtime* (1967) — each with a video introduction by Tati fan **Terry Jones**.

2661 April 27, 2001
Terry Gilliam's Desert Island Flicks (Event). **Terry Gilliam** talks about his favorite animated films with writer-critic Mark Kermode as part of the Animated Encounters festival (Apr. 26–29) at the Watershed Media Centre in Bristol, England.

2662 May 2001
Terry Gilliam serves on the jury at the 54th Cannes Film Festival (May 9–20) in France. His fellow jury members include Liv Ullmann, Edward Yang, Charlotte Gainsbourg, and Julia Ormond. **Gilliam** also attends the Amfar AIDS charity dinner at Le Moulin de Mougins (May 17).

2663 May 2001
Speaking Images: Essays in Honor of V. A. Kolve (Book: Pegasus Press), edited by Robert F. Yeager and Charlotte C. Morse, is published. Collection of 26 medieval and Renaissance-themed essays, including "The Image of Chaucer's Knight," by **Terry Jones**, pp. 205–36. The book is presented to retiring professor V. A. Kolve at a banquet in his honor at the University of California, Los Angeles.

2664 May 8, 2001
3rd Rock from the Sun (TV episode: NBC). "Mary Loves Scoochie: Part 1." Dick (John Lithgow) attempts to learn the identity of a mystery man who has been sending love letters to Mary (Jane Curtin). First of two parts. **John Cleese** reprises the role of

Dr. Liam Neesam, whom he first played in two 1998 episodes (Apr. 28 & 29). Also starring Kristen Johnston and French Stewart. Written by Aron Abrams, Gregory Thompson, and Dave Boerger. Directed by Terry Hughes.

2665 May 11, 2001
Author Douglas Adams dies of a heart attack at the age of 49 in Montecito, CA. Adams, best known for his 1978 radio play *The Hitchhiker's Guide to the Galaxy* (later a book & TV series), made several contributions to the fourth series of *Monty Python* in 1974, appearing briefly in sketches and co-writing one sketch ("Patient Abuse") with **Graham Chapman** for the very last show to be broadcast (on Dec. 5). He also collaborated with **Chapman** on the TV special *Out of the Trees* (1976) and the "For Your Own Good..." episode (1977) of *Doctor on the Go*. In 1997 **Terry Jones** wrote the novelization of Adams' computer game *Starship Titanic*. **Jones** later writes two introductions for the U.S. paperback edition (2003) of Adams' posthumous collection *The Salmon of Doubt* (2002).

2666 May 15, 2001
3rd Rock from the Sun (TV episode: NBC). "Mary Loves Scoochie: Part 2." Dick (John Lithgow) learns that Dr. Liam Neesam (**John Cleese**) is only using Mary (Jane Curtin) to further his plot to turn the Earth into a theme park called "Planet Monkey World." Second of two parts. Also starring Kristen Johnston, French Stewart, and Joseph Gordon-Levitt. Written by Will Forte. Directed by Terry Hughes.

2667 May 16–June 23, 2001
Scorched, a comedy co-starring **John Cleese**, is filmed in California.

2668 May 30, 2001
Terry Gilliam attends the annual dinner of the Royal Academy of Art in London.

2669 May 30, 2001
Welcome to South Park (Event). **Eric Idle** hosts this Academy of Television Arts & Sciences event celebrating the hit animated show, *South Park*, held at the Leonard H. Goldenson Theatre in North Hollywood, CA. **Idle** talks to the show's creators, Matt Stone and Trey Parker.

2670 June 3, 2001
An Afternoon with John Cleese (Event). **John Cleese** participates in an onstage discussion with Dr. Stephen Erickson at UC Davis in California as part of the university's Distinguished Speakers Series.

2671 June 13, 2001
The Guardian (Newspaper/U.K.). "'Our Roads? Don't Make Me Laugh,'" by Ros Coward. Interview with **Michael Palin** about his travels and the state of British transport.

2672 June 15, 2001
Monty Python and the Holy Grail (1975) is re-released in selected U.S. theaters. The digitally remastered film will be released on DVD in October. **John Cleese** and **Eric Idle** introduce the film's premiere screening at the Nuart Theater in Los Angeles.

2673 June 15, 2001
The Late Late Show with Craig Kilborn (TV talk show: CBS). Guests: **John Cleese**, promoting the re-release of *Holy Grail*, Jordana Brewster, and Travis.

2674 June 20, 2001
Counterblast (TV special: BBC2). "The Road to Hell." Documentary, hosted by **Michael Palin**, examining the ill effects of road travel on the environment. **Palin**, president of the pressure group Transport 2000, previously visited this subject in the 1994 doc *Car Sick*. Produced & directed by Mike MacCormack.

2675 June 24, 2001
The Sunday Times (London) (Newspaper/U.K.). "Basil Fawlty's Basement," by Cheryl Markosky, pp. 1+ (sect. 12). **John Cleese** is interviewed about his Holland Park, London home. **Cleese** has recently put the Victorian townhouse on the market, priced at £5 million. He purchased the house in 1977.

2676 June 27, 2001
Terry Gilliam receives the second annual Vision Award from the Filmmakers' Alliance at the Director's Guild of America's main theatre in Los Angeles. Presenting the award is **Gilliam**'s *Fisher King* star Mercedes Ruehl.

2677 June 28, 2001
Film 2001 with Jonathan Ross (TV show: BBC1). **Terry Gilliam**, Nick Park, and Jeffrey Katzenberg talk about the future of animation.

2678 June 29, 2001
Monty Python is inducted into the Hollywood Bowl Hall of Fame at the 2nd annual Hall of Fame gala held at the famous Los Angeles venue. **Eric**

Idle accepts the award (from friend Robin Williams) on behalf of the group and sings "The Lumberjack Song," accompanied by the Hollywood Bowl Orchestra (John Mauceri conducting). The other four inductees are Marilyn Horne, Bonnie Raitt, John Raitt, and Stevie Wonder. Python played the Bowl for four nights in September 1980; the film of the performance, *Monty Python Live at the Hollywood Bowl*, was released in 1982. **Idle** will return to the Hollywood Bowl stage in June 2002 to induct the late George Harrison into the Bowl Hall of Fame and again in August 2008 to perform his Python-inspired oratorio *Not the Messiah (He's a Very Naughty Boy)*.

2679   July 2001

John Cleese attends the taping of the pilot episode of *Zum letzten Kliff* (To the Last Cliff), a German version of *Fawlty Towers*, in Cologne, Germany. **Cleese** is serving as a consultant on the show which stars Jochen Busse and Claudia Rieschel as Viktor and Helga Stein, owners of a hotel on the island of Sylt in the North Sea. The pilot is a remake of the first *Fawlty* episode, "A Touch of Class." Produced for Germany's RTL network.

2680   July 3, 2001

On the Ropes (Radio talk show: BBC Radio 4). John Humphrys interviews **Terry Gilliam** about his career and the collapse of his *Don Quixote* film project.

2681   July 6, 2001

The Treatment (Radio talk show: KCRW, Santa Monica). Host/film critic Elvis Mitchell, at the Museum of Television & Radio in New York, interviews **Terry Gilliam** (in Los Angeles).

2682   July 24–August 14, 2001

Best Sellers: The Life and Times of Peter Sellers (Radio series: BBC Radio 4). Four-part documentary on comedian Peter Sellers (*The Goon Show*, *Dr. Strangelove*), hosted by Phill Jupitus. Interviewees include Harry Secombe, Michael Bentine, Shirley MacLaine, Alexander Walker, and **Michael Palin**.

2683   August 2001

Mind the Gap (Book: HarperCollins), photographed & written by Simon James with a foreword by **Michael Palin**, is published. Photographic collection on the London Underground.

2684   August 4, 2001

Omnibus (TV special: BBC2). "Douglas Adams: The Man Who Blew Up the World (aka Life, the Universe and Douglas Adams)." Documentary on the life and work of writer Douglas Adams (*Hitchhiker's Guide to the Galaxy*), who died on May 11. Includes interviews with **Terry Jones**, Stephen Fry, Clive Anderson, Griff Rhys Jones, and others. Presented by Kirsty Wark. Produced & directed by John Bush.

2685   August 10, 2001

Help! I'm a Fish (Feature film) is released in the U.K. English-dubbed version of a 2000 Danish-animated musical adventure about three children who are turned into fish when they drink a potion created by mad Professor MacKrill (voice of **Terry Jones**). **Jones** sings "Fishtastic." Also featuring the voice of Alan Rickman. Written by Stefan Fjeldmark, Karsten Kulerich, and John Stefan Olsen. Directed by Stefan Fjeldmark and Michael Hegner.

2686   August 17, 2001

Rat Race (Feature film: Paramount Pictures) opens in the U.S. Comedy about a Nevada-to-New Mexico race to claim a $2 million prize. **John Cleese** plays casino owner Donald P. Sinclair, who sets up the race. Also starring Breckin Meyer, Amy Smart, Whoopi Goldberg, Rowan Atkinson, Cuba Gooding, Jr., Seth Green, and Jon Lovitz. Written by Andy Breckman. Directed by Jerry Zucker.

2687   August 21, 2001

Today (Radio show: BBC Radio 4). Guest: **John Cleese**, who denies reports that he has left Britain for good.

2688   August 25, 2001

Eric Idle attends the annual Men of Lonach Highland Gathering and Games in Aberdeenshire, Scotland, along with Billy Connolly, Robin Williams, Ewan McGregor, Steve Buscemi, and Aidan Quinn.

2689   August 26 & 27, 2001

John Cleese's four-part documentary series *The Human Face* airs in the U.S. on The Learning Channel. The series first aired in Britain in March on BBC1.

2690   August 26, 2001

The Mail on Sunday (Newspaper/U.K.). "Please Bury Me in Somerset." Caroline Graham interviews **John Cleese** about why he loves California but is still proud to be British.

2691   August 27, 2001

The 100 Greatest Kids TV Shows (TV special:

Channel 4). Countdown of the top 100 children's programs, hosted by Jamie Theakston. **Terry Jones** is among those interviewed.

2692 September 2001
Cineaste (Magazine/U.S.). "Monty Python: Lust for Glory," by David Sterritt and Lucille Rhodes, pp. 18–23. A look at the film and TV work of Monty Python and their influence on comedy.

2693 September 11, 2001
Michael Palin is in Agadez, a remote town in Niger, filming his travel series *Sahara* when he learns of the terrorist attacks on New York City and Washington, D.C.

2694 September 21, 2001
Stammering: A Practical Guide for Teachers and Other Professionals (Book: David Fulton Publishers), written by Lena Rustin, Frances Cook, Willie Botterill, Cherry Hughes, and Elaine Kelman, is published in the U.K. Foreword by **Michael Palin**. Rustin, Cook, Botterill, and Kelman are all speech therapists at the Michael Palin Centre for Stammering Children (founded in 1993).

2695 October 8, 2001
Fawlty Towers (DVD: BBC Video) is released in the U.K. Two-disc set containing all twelve episodes of **John Cleese**'s classic sitcom. Includes interviews with **Cleese** (Basil), Prunella Scales (Sybil), and Andrew Sachs (Manuel), also audio commentaries from the show's director and producer, outtakes, etc.

2696 October 13, 2001
The Big Schmooze (TV show: The Comedy Channel, in Australia). Guest: **Terry Jones**.

2697 October 23, 2001
Monty Python and the Holy Grail: Special Edition (DVD: Columbia TriStar). Two-disc special edition containing the 1975 film presented in high definition wide-screen and 5.1 Dolby Digital sound and including the missing "24 seconds" (during the "Castle Anthrax" scene). To confuse viewers, the film is preceded by the first two minutes of the 1961 film *Dentist on the Job*. The added features include: audio commentaries by **Terry Gilliam** and **Terry Jones** (first track; from the 1993 Criterion Collection laserdisc release) and **John Cleese**, **Eric Idle**, and **Michael Palin** (second track); On-screen screenplay; Singalong; *The Quest for the Holy Grail Locations* (**Palin** & **Jones** revisit the filming locations); "Ministry of Foods: Coconut Information Division" (demonstration by **Michael Palin**); BBC *Film Night* (1974 location report; originally aired Dec. 19, 1974); and the original U.K. trailer (Chinese narrator). Released in the U.K. on Mar. 4, 2002. Followed by a three-disc Extraordinarily Deluxe Edition (in 2006) and a Blu-ray release (in 2012).

2698 October 23, 2001
The Quest for the Holy Grail Locations (Documentary). **Michael Palin** and **Terry Jones** returned to Scotland in August 2000 in search of the filming locations for *Holy Grail*, made 26 years earlier. Locations include Doune Castle ("The Swallow," "Knights of the Round Table," "The French Taunter," "Castle Anthrax," and "Swamp Castle") and Loch Tay ("Rabbit of Caerbannog"). With comments from Julian Doyle (production manager on *Grail*) and Hamish MacInnes (leader of Glencoe Mountain Rescue Team). Released as a special feature on the two-disc special edition DVD of the film.

2699 October 23, 2001
Jabberwocky (DVD: Columbia TriStar) is released in the U.S. **Terry Gilliam**'s 1977 medieval comedy starring **Michael Palin** (with **Terry Jones** in a small role) is presented on DVD with the special features: audio commentary by **Gilliam** and **Palin**, Sketch-to-Screen Comparisons, and theatrical trailer. Released in the U.K. on Feb. 17, 2003.

2700 October 30, 2001
Michael Palin and his wife attend the opening of the Centenary Development extension at the Tate Britain art gallery in London.

2701 November 1, 2001
Victoria Wood's Sketch Show Story (TV special: BBC1). Second of two programs celebrating the sketch show. Hosted by Victoria Wood, with **John Cleese**, Stephen Fry, Hugh Laurie, and others. Produced by Danny Dignan.

2702 November 4, 2001
Harry Potter and the Sorcerer's Stone (Feature film: Warner Bros.) premieres in the U.K. Fantasy story, first in the series based on the best-selling books by J. K. Rowling. **John Cleese** plays Nearly Headless Nick. **Cleese** reprises the role in *Harry Potter and the Chamber of Secrets* (2002). Also starring Daniel Radcliffe, Emma Watson, Rupert Grint, Richard Harris, Robbie Coltrane, Maggie Smith, and John Hurt. Directed by Chris Columbus.

2703 November 4, 2001
The Teaching Awards 2001 (TV special: BBC1).

Award show honoring Britain's best teachers, from the Theatre Royal, Drury Lane, London. Hosted by Carol Smillie, with **John Cleese**, Michael Parkinson, Jonathan Ross, Bryan Ferry, and others. Directed by Steve Smith. Produced by Kaye Godleman.

2704 November 14, 2001
John Cleese and his wife attend the Los Angeles premiere of *Harry Potter and the Sorcerer's Stone*, in which he plays Nearly Headless Nick.

2705 November 24, 2001
MADtv (TV variety show: Fox). **John Cleese** guest-stars on this late-night comedy series.

2706 November 29, 2001
Former Beatle George Harrison dies of cancer at the age of 58. A longtime friend of the Pythons, Harrison provided the financial backing for the group's 1979 film *Life of Brian* after the original backers pulled out. His company, HandMade Films, went on to produce a number of Python solo projects, including *Time Bandits* (1981), *The Missionary* (1982), and *A Private Function* (1984).

2707 November 30, 2001
Newsnight (TV news show: BBC2). Robin Denselow presents a tribute to the late George Harrison. Includes interviews with Paul McCartney, Tony Blair, Tony Gilmour, and **Michael Palin**.

2708 November 30, 2001
Voices for Peace (Book: Scribner), edited by Anna Kiernan, is published in the U.K. Collection of essays reflecting on the tragedy of 9/11 and the military response it provoked. Includes **Terry Jones'** "The Grammar of the War on Terrorism," later reprinted in **Jones'** own 2005 collection *Terry Jones's War on the War on Terror*.

2709 December 1, 2001
The 2001 European Film Awards (Award ceremony). Monty Python is honored with a Lifetime Achievement Award at the 14th annual awards held at the Tempodrom in Berlin, Germany. **Terry Gilliam** and **Terry Jones** are there to accept the award on behalf of the group. Host Mel Smith, disappointed that only two Pythons showed up, attempts to take the award back.

2710 December 1, 2001
'I Love Monty Python,' an evening of all–Python programming, airs on BBC2. The evening begins with repeats of two 1999 documentaries, *It's: The Monty Python Story* and *Pythonland*, followed by two films, *Holy Grail* and **Terry Gilliam**'s *Brazil*.

2711 December 2, 2001
The Independent (Newspaper/U.K.). "George Harrison – 'No CD can bring back his kindness, his generosity or his warmth,'" by **Michael Palin**, p. 21. **Palin** remembers his friend, the late George Harrison.

2712 December 2, 2001
The Observer (Newspaper/U.K.). "George Harrison 1943–2001: George Harrison and Film," by **Michael Palin**, p. 5. **Palin** recalls how Harrison saved *Life of Brian* by putting up the money to make it and founding HandMade Films.

2713 December 6, 2001
Comedy Lab (TV episode: Channel 4). "Knife & Wife." Half-hour animated comedy with **Terry Jones** as the voice of Knife, an angry chicken. Produced by the Welsh animation studio Siriol. Other voices by Jessica Stevenson, Paul Putner, Kevin Eldon, and Brian Murphy. Written by Paul Rose. Directed by Les Orton.

2714 2001
Can You Spare a Moment? (Training film: Video Arts). Remake of the 1987 management-training film on how to deal with workers who have personal problems. Starring **John Cleese** (host), Ricky Gervais, Angus Barnett, Lorraine Brunning, Jaye Griffiths, and Naomie Harris. Written by Antony Jay and **John Cleese**. Directed by Sean Hardie.

2715 2001
Chatter of Choughs (Book: Signal Books), edited by Lucy Newlyn, is published in the U.K. Collection of poems and essays celebrating the Cornish chough (a black crowlike bird) and its association with the college of St. Edmund Hall, Oxford University. **Terry Jones**, an alumnus of the college, contributes the poem "The Unsteady Chough," which will later be made into an animated short (in 2004). **Jones** will contribute another poem ("Untitled") to the second edition of the book (2005).

2716 2001–2008
Titleist (TV commercials). **John Cleese** plays Scottish golf course architect Ian MacCallister in a series of humorous spots for Titleist's NXT golf balls. Titles include: "Press Conference" (2001), "Civil Disobedience" (2001), "Elevator" (2002), "Presentation" (2002), "Dentist" (2003), "Replacement" (2004), "NXT-ivore" (2004), "Painting" (2005), "Statue" (2005), "Intervention" (2006), and "Uncle Sam" (2008). Also starring David Joy

(as Tom Morris) and Robert Trent Jones, Jr. Written by Craig Johnson. Directed by David Kellogg. Agency: Arnold Worldwide, Boston.

2717 January 2002
Terry Jones undergoes an operation to resurface his hip.

2718 January 20, 2002
Hidden History of Egypt (TV special: Discovery Channel). Host **Terry Jones** looks at the daily lives of ordinary citizens in Ancient Egypt. First of three "Hidden History" documentaries. Written by Phil Grabsky, Alan Ereira, and **Terry Jones**. Produced & directed by Phil Grabsky. Airs in the U.K. on Feb. 1, 2003, as *Terry Jones's Hidden Histories: Egypt* (BBC2).

2719 January 20, 2002
Hidden History of the Roman Empire (TV special: Discovery Channel). Host **Terry Jones** examines how the average Roman citizen lived. Second of three "Hidden History" documentaries. Written by Phil Grabsky and **Terry Jones**. Produced & directed by Phil Grabsky. Airs in the U.K. on Feb. 8, 2003, as *Terry Jones's Hidden Histories: Rome* (BBC2). The third doc in the series, *Hidden History of Sex and Love*, airs in the U.K. on Feb. 14, 2003 (Discovery Channel).

2720 January 22, 2002
Terry Jones attends *The 2001 Whitbread Book Awards* ceremony at The Brewery in London. Jones' *The Lady and the Squire* is one of four books nominated for Children's Book of the Year (Philip Pullman wins for his book *The Amber Spyglass*).

2721 January 31, 2002
This Is Your Life (TV talk show: BBC1). "Bill Oddie." Hosted by Michael Aspel. **Michael Palin** and **Eric Idle** appear on this special celebrating the life of comedian Bill Oddie (one-third of The Goodies). They both appear on film, with **Idle** speaking from Pembroke College, Cambridge, where he and Oddie first met as students. Directed by John Gorman and Steve Docherty. Produced by Sue Green.

2722 February 2002
Taking the Wheel (Short film), world premiere at the Berlin International Film Festival. Dark comedy starring **John Cleese** as a man determined to keep his 90-year-old mother off the road. The 10-minute short also stars Patience Cleveland and David Brainard. Written & directed by David Ackerman.

2723 February 2002
Clive James: Talking in the Library (Web show). Australian writer-broadcaster Clive James interviews **Terry Gilliam** for series three of his web program.

2724 February 2002
Michael Palin unveils his new series, *Sahara*, at the annual BBC Showcase television trade show (Feb. 24–27), held at the Brighton Conference Centre in Brighton, England.

2725 February 1, 2002
Terry Jones turns 60.

2726 February 3, 2002
Terry Gilliam and his wife attend the 29th annual *Evening Standard British Film Awards* ceremony at the Savoy Hotel in London.

2727 February 5, 2002
Terry Gilliam and his wife attend the 6th annual *Empire Awards* ceremony at the Dorchester Hotel in London.

2728 February 11, 2002
Lost in La Mancha (Feature film), world premiere in Berlin. Documentary chronicling **Terry Gilliam**'s failed attempt to bring Cervantes' 1605 novel *Don Quixote* to the screen. Filmmakers Louis Pepe and Keith Fulton were allowed to follow **Gilliam** throughout the ill-fated production of *The Man Who Killed Don Quixote* in Spain in 2000. Narrated by Jeff Bridges. Produced by Lucy Darwin. A Quixote Films and Low Key Pictures production. Opens in Britain on Aug. 2 and in New York City and Los Angeles on Jan. 31, 2003.
Awards: Winner of the Peter Sellers Award for Comedy at the Evening Standard British Film Awards.

2729 February 11, 2002
Terry Gilliam attends the world premiere of *Lost in La Mancha* at the 52nd Berlin International Film Festival (Feb. 6–17) in Berlin, Germany.

2730 February 23 & March 2, 2002
George Harrison: The Inner Light (Radio special: BBC Radio 2). Two-part tribute to the late George Harrison. Includes interviews with **Michael Palin**, Ravi Shankar, Jeff Lynne, and many others. Hosted by Bob Harris.

2731 February 28, 2002
The Guardian (Newspaper/U.K.). "Simply Spike," by **Michael Palin**, p. 4. Tribute to the late Spike

Milligan, whose work on radio's *Goon Show* was a major comedic influence on the Pythons.

2732 March 2002
Terry Jones gives a talk on Chaucer's death in Bath, England as part of the Bath Literature Festival (Mar. 2–10).

2733 March 2, 2002
Heroes of Comedy (TV episode: Channel 4). "Spike Milligan." Comedian Spike Milligan (*The Goon Show*) is profiled, with comments from **John Cleese** and **Michael Palin**, who reflect on the influence Milligan and The Goons had on the humor of Monty Python. Directed by Tom Atkinson.

2734 March 3, 2002
The Sunday Telegraph (Newspaper/U.K.). "Spike Changed Britain More Than the Angry Young Men," by **John Cleese**, p. 25. **Cleese** pays tribute to the late Spike Milligan.

2735 March 3, 2002
The Sunday Times (London) (Newspaper/U.K.). "**Cleese** and Izzard on the True King of Comedy," by Stuart Wavell, p. 8 (sect. 5). **John Cleese** and Eddie Izzard pay tribute to their mutual comedy influence, Spike Milligan. "Glorious Delusion of the Golden Age," by Stuart Wavell, p. 9 (sect. 5). **Terry Jones** gives his thoughts on the Renaissance, the subject of his upcoming Radio 4 series, *The Anti-Renaissance Show*.

2736 March 9–23, 2002
The Anti-Renaissance Show (Radio series: BBC Radio 4). **Terry Jones** hosts this series of three half-hour programs challenging the modern view of the Renaissance as a more culturally-advanced period than the Middle Ages. Episodes: "What Did Renaissance Man Ever Do for Us?" (Mar. 9), "Medieval 'Savagery' and Renaissance 'Enlightenment'" (Mar. 16), and "The 19th Century View" (Mar. 23).

2737 March 9, 2002
The Times Magazine (London) (Magazine/U.K.). "Cold Call: **Michael Palin**," p. 8. Alan Jackson interviews **Palin**.

2738 March 24, 2002
John Cleese and his wife attend the *Vanity Fair* Oscar Party at Morton's Restaurant in West Hollywood, CA.

2739 March 24, 2002
The New York Times (Newspaper/U.S.). "The Importance of Being Silly," by Terrence Rafferty, p. A27. Interview with **John Cleese** about his career and the upcoming BBC America tribute *John Cleese Forever*.

2740 March 25, 2002
Good Day Live (TV talk show: Synd.). Guest: **John Cleese**.

2741 March 26, 2002
The Late Late Show with Craig Kilborn (TV talk show: CBS). Guest: **John Cleese**, promoting *Wednesday 9:30*, talks about trying to sell his house, things he dislikes about America, and answers "5 Questions."

2742 March 27–April 3, May 29–June 12, 2002
Wednesday 9:30 (8:30 Central) (TV series: ABC). Short-lived American sitcom co-starring **John Cleese**. The show, created by Peter Tolan (*The Larry Sanders Show*), is set at a television network called IBS. **Cleese** plays Red Lansing, an Australian media mogul who owns the network. Also starring Ivan Sergei, Ed Begley, Jr., Melinda McGraw, James McCauley, and Sherri Shepherd. ABC cancels the show after only two episodes air due to low ratings. Retitled *My Adventures in Television* when the show was relaunched in May. Five episodes air.
Reviews: Terry Kelleher (*People Weekly*, Mar. 25, 2002): "...plays like a laundered *Larry Sanders* with a loud laugh track.... **John Cleese** is a disappointment.... His performance, like his Australian accent, seems half-hearted."

2743 March 29, 2002
John Cleese Forever, a retrospective devoted to **John Cleese**, airs on BBC America. The retrospective includes episodes of *Flying Circus*, *Fawlty Towers*, and the film *Time Bandits*.

2744 March 31, 2002
English writer-comedian Barry Took dies at the age of 73. It was Took who, as comedy advisor for the BBC, facilitated the meeting between the BBC and a group of young British comedians in May 1969 that would lead to the creation of *Monty Python's Flying Circus*.

2745 April–June 2002
Nike ("The Secret Tournament") (TV commercial). **Terry Gilliam** directed this TV ad (and its sequel, "The Rematch") for Nike as part of the company's 2002 World Cup campaign. The ads, filmed in London and Rome in December 2001 and January 2002, take place inside a cargo ship where 24 of the world's greatest football players (in eight teams of three) compete in a secret tournament. Featured

footballers include Eric Cantona, Thierry Henry, Freddie Ljungberg, and Rio Ferdinand. Music: Elvis Presley's "A Little Less Conversation." Written by Tim Wolfe. Agency: Wieden & Kennedy, Amsterdam.

2746 April 11, 2002
The Evening Standard (London) (Newspaper/ U.K.). "So, Has **John Cleese** Lost His Funny Bone?," by Pete Clark, p. 32 (sect. A). Harsh critique of **Cleese** claiming the comedian has stopped being funny since moving to California. **Cleese** sues the paper for libel and in February 2003 wins a £13,500 award.

2747 April 21, 2002
Michael Palin attends the gala re-opening of the newly-refurbished Phoenix Cinema in East Finchley, London.

2748 April 28, 2002
Lifeline (TV appeal: BBC1). "FARM-Africa." **Michael Palin** appears on this monthly charity program appealing on behalf of the FARM-Africa organization (aiding African farmers), of which he is a patron.

2749 May 5, 2002
The Sunday Times (London) (Newspaper/U.K.). "My Hols," by **Michael Palin** (talking to Vanya Kewley), p. 18 (sect. 5). **Palin** describes some of his favorite travel experiences, including visits to the Grand Canyon (with **Terry Jones** in 1972), Southwold, Venice, New York, and the west of Scotland.

2750 May 12–14, 2002
Dinotopia (TV mini-series: ABC). Six-hour TV series set on a mythical island where humans and dinosaurs co-exist. Based on the books by James Gurney, the series combines live-action with computer-generated images. **Terry Jones** voices Messenger Bird. Shown in three parts. Starring Tyron Leitso, Wentworth Miller, Stuart Wilson, Katie Carr, Alice Krige, and David Thewlis. Written by Simon Moore. Directed by Marco Brambilla.

2751 May 17, 2002
Scorched (Feature film) premieres at the Cannes Film Festival in France. Comedy about three bank employees separately plotting to rob the bank on the same night. **John Cleese** plays millionaire Charles Merchant. Released in the U.S. in July 2003, the film is quickly pulled from theaters due to its poor box office performance. Also starring Alicia Silverstone, Rachael Leigh Cook, Woody Harrelson, Paulo Costanzo, and Joseph Leonard. Written by Joe Wein. Directed by Gavin Grazer. Opens in the U.K. on Dec. 9, 2005.

2752 May 18, 2002
Michael Palin opens the Electric Picture Palace, a new, 1912-style cinema in the seaside town of Southwold, England. Southwold had been the site of **Palin**'s summer holidays as a youth and inspired his 1987 TV film *East of Ipswich*.

2753 May 19, 2002
The 2nd Annual World Stunt Awards (Award ceremony). **John Cleese** is a presenter at the ceremony held at Barker Hangar in Santa Monica, CA. Airs May 31 on ABC.

2754 May 22, 2002
Terry Gilliam meets the Queen at a Golden Jubilee celebration of the arts hosted by Her Royal Highness at the Royal Academy of Arts, Piccadilly, London. Other guests include Sir Richard Attenborough, Dame Shirley Bassey, Kate Bush, Joanna Lumley, Jane Asher, Barry Humphries, and Penelope Keith.

2755 May 26, 2002
Banzai! (TV show: Channel 4). **Terry Gilliam** is interviewed by Lady One Question on this comedy-betting show.

2756 June 2, 2002
John Cleese attends the opening of a new three-acre lemur habitat (the Lipman Family Lemur Forest) at the San Francisco Zoo. **Cleese**, a lemur advocate, hosted the 1998 documentary *Born to Be Wild: Operation Lemur with John Cleese*.

2757 June 6, 2002
The Scotsman (Newspaper/U.K.). "**Gilliam**'s Curse," by Stephen Applebaum. Article on **Terry Gilliam**'s ill-fated *Don Quixote* production.

2758 June 10, 2002
John Cleese receives the 2002 Sir Peter Ustinov/ Comedy Network Award at the 23rd annual Banff Television Festival (June 9–14) in Banff, Canada. Appearing on stage with interviewer Ralph Benmergui, **Cleese** discusses his career in comedy.

2759 June 20–26, 2002
John Cleese is a guest-speaker on the Queen Elizabeth 2 ocean liner for its six-night British Comedy-themed transatlantic crossing from New York to Southampton, England.

2760 June 20, 2002
Readers and Writers Roadshow (TV show: BBC4).

Kate Mosse hosts a discussion with authors **Terry Jones** and Terry Pratchett at Hove Town Hall.

2761   June 24, 2002
Maclean's (Magazine/Can.). "Raging with Laughter," by Brian Bergman, p. 54. Interview with **John Cleese** conducted the day after his Banff appearance.

2762   June 28, 2002
Eric Idle posthumously inducts his friend George Harrison into the Hollywood Bowl Hall of Fame at the 3rd annual Hall of Fame gala at the Hollywood Bowl in Los Angeles. **Idle** represented Monty Python when the group was inducted last year (June 29, 2001).

2763   June 28, 2002
John Cleese and his wife, Alyce Faye, unveil two English Heritage Blue Plaques at the Freud Museum in Hampstead, London in honor of Sigmund Freud and his daughter Anna, both pioneers in the field of psychoanalysis. The museum was formerly Freud's London residence.

2764   June 28, 2002
John Cleese and his wife attend the annual James Bond Golf Classic and Gala Dinner at Stoke Park Golf Club in England. The charity event is hosted by the Ian Fleming Foundation. **Cleese** plays Q in the upcoming Bond film *Die Another Day*.

2765   July 3, 2002
John Cleese and **Terry Jones** attend a memorial service for the late writer-comedian Barry Took at St. John's Wood Church in London. Took died on Mar. 31.

2766   July 16, 2002
Michael Palin speaks at the Buxton Festival (July 9–21) in Buxton, Derbyshire, England.

2767   July 20, 2002
Lost in La Mancha, the film documenting **Terry Gilliam**'s attempt to bring *Don Quixote* to the screen, premieres in the U.K. in Cambridge, England as part of the 22nd Cambridge Film Festival (July 11–21). The film had its world premiere in Berlin on Feb. 11.

2768   July 25, 2002
Terry Gilliam and **Michael Palin** attend the London premiere of *Lost in La Mancha* at the Screen on the Green in Islington.

2769   July 30, 2002
Front Row (Radio arts show: BBC Radio 4). Hosted by Mark Lawson. Features a report on the new documentary *Lost in La Mancha*.

2770   August 2, 2002
Lost in La Mancha opens in the U.K.

2771   August 2, 2002
Newsnight (TV news show: BBC2). Includes a report on the documentary *Lost in La Mancha*.

2772   August 16, 2002
The Adventures of Pluto Nash (Feature film: Warner Bros.) opens in the U.S. Sci-fi comedy starring Eddie Murphy in the title role. **John Cleese** plays James, a computerized chauffeur. Also starring Randy Quaid, Rosario Dawson, Jay Mohr, and Pam Grier. Written by Neil Cuthbert. Directed by Ron Underwood.

2773   August 20, 2002
Legends (TV episode: ITV1/Carlton). "Peter Cook." Half-hour profile of the late comedian, with contributions from **Michael Palin**, Ian Hislop, John Bird, and others. Produced & directed by Huda Abuzeid.

2774   August 24, 2002
Eric Idle attends the annual Men of Lonach Gathering and Games in Strathdon, Aberdeenshire, Scotland, along with Billy Connolly, Pamela Stephenson, and Aidan Quinn.

2775   August 28, 2002
Train enthusiast **Michael Palin** unveils the new Virgin Super Voyager high-speed train (number 221130), named in his honor, at Sheffield Train Station in Sheffield, England. He also rides the train to Leeds on its maiden run. A report on the event is shown that night on TV's *Calendar News* (ITV Yorkshire).

2776   August 30, 2002
The documentary *Lost in La Mancha* (featuring **Terry Gilliam**) has its North American premiere at the 29th annual Telluride Film Festival (Aug. 30–Sept. 2) in Telluride, CO. **Gilliam** attends the festival and participates in a conversation with author Salman Rushdie at Telluride Courthouse (Sept. 2). A video recording of their talk is included in the June 2003 DVD release of the film.

2777   August 31, 2002
Financial Times (Newspaper/U.K.). "Lunch with the FT: A Tall Order," by Andrew Davidson, p. III. **John Cleese** is interviewed at a production office in Port Royal, London where he talks about his interest in business and involvement with Video

Arts, which is celebrating its 30th anniversary this year.

2778 September 14–December 2002
Michael Palin tours the U.K. promoting his book & TV series *Sahara*, signing books and giving lectures and readings.

2779 September 14, 2002
The 2002 Primetime Creative Arts Emmy Awards (Award ceremony). **John Cleese** is a presenter at the ceremony held at the Shrine Auditorium in Los Angeles. Broadcast Sept. 21 on E! Entertainment.

2780 September 15, 2002
Michael Palin and **Terry Jones** perform at a charity evening at the Guildhall in London paying tribute to the late Spike Milligan (*The Goon Show*). The event, a fundraiser for The Lord Mayor's Appeal, is broadcast as *Spike Milligan: I Told You I Was Ill...A Live Tribute* on Oct. 5 (BBC2).

2781 September 17, 2002
The Independent (Newspaper/U.K.). "Media: Screen Villains?; What Image of Britain Does Our Television Present Abroad?," by **Michael Palin**.

2782 September 23, 2002
Good Beer Guide 2003 (Book: CAMRA Books), edited by Roger Protz, is published in the U.K. Thirtieth edition of the guide. Includes an article by **Terry Jones**.

2783 September 25, 2002
Michael Palin's new website, *Palin's Travels*, is launched on the 14th anniversary of his departure from Victoria Station for his journey *Around the World in 80 Days*.

2784 September 26, 2002
Sahara (Book: Weidenfeld & Nicolson), written by **Michael Palin** with photographs by Basil Pao, is published in the U.K. Illustrated account of **Palin**'s journey across the vast African desert. This companion book to the 2002 BBC TV series becomes a No. 1 bestseller in Britain. Paperback edition published by Phoenix (2003). Published in the U.S. by Thomas Dunne Books (St. Martin's Press) in April 2003.
Award: British Book Award–winner for Illustrated Book of the Year.

2785 September 26, 2002
Inside Sahara (Book: Weidenfeld & Nicolson), by Basil Pao (photographs) with an introduction by **Michael Palin**, is published in the U.K. Photography book accompanying the **Michael Palin** TV series & book *Sahara*.

2786 September 28, 2002
Parkinson (TV talk show: BBC1). Hosted by Michael Parkinson. Guests: **Michael Palin**, Ricky Gervais, Kate Adie, and Norah Jones. **Palin** talks about *Sahara*, George Harrison, and stammering.

2787 September 29, 2002
Peter Cook: A Post-Humourous Tribute (Stage show), at The Prince of Wales Theatre in London. **Michael Palin** and **Terry Jones** perform at this comedy benefit honoring the late Peter Cook (who died in 1995). Sketches include "How Do You Do It?" (**Palin** & **Jones**). The event raises funds for the Peter Cook Foundation, a charity for mentally-handicapped children. Hosted by Sir David Frost and also starring Rik Mayall, Adrian Edmondson, Griff Rhys Jones, David Baddiel, Jonathan Ross, Harry Enfield, Angus Deayton, Neil Innes, Greg Proops, and Jimmy Carr. Directed by **Terry Jones**. The show is filmed, airing Dec. 28 on BBC2.

2788 September 30, 2002
Michael Palin gives a talk on his new book and series *Sahara* at the Royal Geographical Society in London.

2789 October 2, 2002
Midweek (Radio talk show: BBC Radio 4). Hosted by Libby Purves. Guests: **Michael Palin**, David Bellamy, and Steve Cohen.

2790 October 4, 2002
The Scream Team (TV film: Disney Channel). In this Halloween-themed family comedy, **Eric Idle** plays Coffin Ed, one a trio of bumbling ghosts who try to help two children find their grandfather's lost soul. Filmed in Ontario, Canada. Also starring Tommy Davidson, Kathy Najimy, Mark Rendall, and Kat Dennings. Written by Daniel Berendsen. Directed by Stuart Gillard.

2791 October 5, 2002
Spike Milligan: I Told You I Was Ill...A Live Tribute (TV special: BBC2). Tribute to the late comedian Spike Milligan (who died in February at age 83), recorded live at a charity event on Sept. 15 at London's Guildhall. **Michael Palin** and **Terry Jones** perform some of Milligan's famous *Goon Show* characters and material from his *Q* series. Other performers include John Sergeant (host), Paul Merton, Eddie Izzard, Harry Enfield, Kathy Burke, Dame Cleo Laine, and Eric Sykes. Directed by Dominic Brigstocke. Produced by Cerrie Frost.

2792 October 6, 2002
The New York Times Book Review (Newspaper/U.S.). "Clouseau, Quilty and Sir Jervis Fruit: Peter Sellers managed to invest his most outlandish characters with a measure of dignity," by **Michael Palin**, p. 9. Palin reviews the book *Mr. Strangelove: A Biography of Peter Sellers* by Ed Sikov.

2793 October 8–29, 2002
The Beatles: Across the Universe (Radio special: BBC Radio 2). Four-part retrospective narrated by Robert Lindsay. **Michael Palin** is among those interviewed.

2794 October 8, 2002
Michael Palin signs copies of his new book *Sahara* (tie-in with the TV series) at Hatchards bookshop in London.

2795 October 11, 2002
Michael Palin talks about *Sahara* at the 53rd Cheltenham Festival of Literature (Oct. 11–20) in Cheltenham, England. Followed by a book signing.

2796 October 12, 2002
The Mirror (Newspaper/U.K.). "Follow That Camel," by Tony Purnell. **Michael Palin** describes some highlights from his *Sahara* adventure.

2797 October 13–November 3, 2002
The four-part travel series *Sahara with Michael Palin* airs on BBC1. In the series, filmed over four months between February 2001 and February 2002, **Michael Palin** explores the vast Sahara Desert in northern and western Africa, traveling through the countries of Morocco, Algeria, Mauritania, Senegal, Mali, Niger, Libya, and Tunisia. Shown in the U.S. in April 2003 (Bravo). Series producer: Roger Mills.
Award: BAFTA-winner for Best Photography (Factual) (Nigel Meakin), also nominated for Best Sound (Factual) (John Pritchard & George Foulgham); 2003 TRIC (Television and Radio Industries Club) Award winner for Best Documentary Programme of the Year.
Review: Paul Hoggart (*The Times* [London], Oct. 14, 2002, p. 19): "[Palin's] commentaries are usually relaxed, wry, observant, kindly and informative.... But by now it is beginning to feel as if he is going through the motions, thinking of exotic journeys just to get out of the house for a while"; Claire Stoker (*Liverpool Echo*, Oct. 14, 2002): "The Sahara is not a typical tourist destination, but **Palin**'s ever warm and witty commentary makes it sound a fascinating place."

2798 October 13, 2002
The Sunday Times (London) (Newspaper/U.K.). "Welcome Aboard," by **Michael Palin**, pp. 1–2 (sect. 4). Palin writes of his life-long romance with trains and recalls some particularly memorable railway journeys.

2799 October 13, 2002
Sahara with Michael Palin (TV episode: BBC1). "A Line in the Sand." Starting off in Gibraltar, **Palin** moves on to Tangier (in northern Morocco), then visits the medieval city of Fez and the Berber village of Aremd. After a stop at the Smara Refugee Camp (near Tindouf, Algeria), he travels on to Tfariti (in Western Sahara) and Zouerat (in Mauritania), where he boards the Iron Ore Express. In Atâr, he observes the Paris-Dakar Rally. First episode in a four-part series. Written & narrated by **Michael Palin**. Directed by Roger Mills.

2800 October 14, 2002
Eric Idle attends the premiere of the film *Frida* at the Leo S. Bing Theater in Los Angeles.

2801 October 20, 2002
Sahara with Michael Palin (TV episode: BBC1). "Destination Timbuktu." **Palin** crosses the Senegal River into Senegal, where he visits the town of St-Louis, the island of Goree, and the capital city of Dakar. From there, it's a 43-hour train journey to Bamako, the capital of Mali, followed by visits to the Dogon village of Tirelli and the ancient town of Djenné. He then takes a cargo boat up the Niger River heading for Timbuktu. Second episode in a four-part series. Written & narrated by **Michael Palin**. Directed by John Paul Davidson.

2802 October 23, 2002
The South Bank Tapes (Radio episode: BBC Radio 4). "Early Days of Hollywood." **Terry Jones** hosts this look back at Hollywood's early days. Third episode in a five-part series (Oct. 21–25) celebrating the 50th anniversary of the National Film Theatre.

2803 October 24, 2002
The Times (London) (Newspaper/U.K.). "**John Cleese** Gets Serious — So Don't Mention the Parrot," by Peter Brown, p. 2. Interview with **Cleese** about creativity in business.

2804 October 27, 2002
Sahara with Michael Palin (TV episode: BBC1). "Absolute Desert." **Palin** visits the legendary city of Timbuktu (in Mali), then travels with the nomadic Wodaabe people to Ingal (in Niger), where

he observes the festival of the nomads, Cure Salée. He then joins a Touareg camel train on a five-day trek across the Ténéré Desert. Third episode in a four-part series. Written & narrated by **Michael Palin**. Directed by John Paul Davidson.

2805   October 30, 2002
Michael Palin and **Terry Gilliam** attend the 5th annual *British Independent Film Awards* held at The Pacha Club, Victoria, London. Their late friend George Harrison, founder of HandMade Films (*Life of Brian*, *Time Bandits*), receives a posthumous Lifetime Achievement Award.

2806   October 31, 2002
Open House with Gloria Hunniford (TV show: Five). Guests: **Michael Palin**, promoting *Sahara*, and Lulu.

2807   October 31, 2002
Michael Palin gives an illustrated talk on his new book & TV series *Sahara* at a "Meet the Author" forum at Congress Centre in London. The event is sponsored by *The Times* and Foyles bookshops.

2808   November 2002
Charlie and the Chocolate Factory (Audiobook: Harper Children's Audio). Audio version of Roald Dahl's classic children's story, read by **Eric Idle**. Reissued in 2005 as a tie-in with Tim Burton's film version. **Idle** will later read Dahl's *Charlie and the Great Glass Elevator* for a 2004 audiobook. Note: **Michael Palin** also read the story on TV's *Jackanory* in March 1986.
Awards: Grammy-nominated for Best Spoken Word Album for Children.
Reviews: Rochelle O'Gorman (*Hartford Courant*, Nov. 24, 2002): "Pairing **Eric Idle** with this material was brilliant, as he is an energetic and imaginative narrator; the result is pure magic"; *Publishers Weekly* (Dec. 9, 2002, p. 23): "In a sublime bit of casting, comedic actor **Idle** delivers an inspired rendition of Dahl's classic novel."

2809   November 3, 2002
Sahara with Michael Palin (TV episode: BBC1). "Dire Straits." **Palin** crosses from Niger into Algeria, and from there to Libya, where he attends a last reunion of the Desert Rats of World War II (in Tobruk) and visits the ancient Roman city of Leptis Magna. In Tunisia, he re-visits the locations where *Life of Brian* was filmed in 1978 (El Haddej, Monastir & Sousse). Next, he visits Algiers (in Algeria), the Spanish city of Ceuta, and ends his journey where it began: in Gibraltar. Fourth and final episode of the series. Written & narrated by **Michael Palin**. Directed by John Paul Davidson.

2810   November 3, 2002
Harry Potter and the Chamber of Secrets (Feature film: Warner Bros.) premieres in the U.K. (opens wide Nov. 15 in Britain and the U.S.). Film fantasy, second in the series based on the books by J. K. Rowling. **John Cleese** plays Nearly Headless Nick, a role he first played in *Harry Potter and the Sorcerer's Stone* (2001). Also starring Daniel Radcliffe, Emma Watson, Rupert Grint, Richard Harris, Robbie Coltrane, and Kenneth Branagh. Directed by Chris Columbus.

2811   November 3, 2002
Eric Idle attends the London premiere of *Harry Potter and the Chamber of Secrets* at the Odeon, Leicester Square.

2812   November 8, 2002
The Late Late Show with Craig Kilborn (TV talk show: CBS). Guest: **John Cleese**, promoting *Chamber of Secrets* and *Die Another Day*, talks about being tall, the name Cleese (changed from Cheese by his father), his brief appearances in the Harry Potter films, and his total inability to sing. He also answers "5 Questions."

2813   November 10, 2002
A Centenary Concert for the Mountain Gorillas (Concert). **Michael Palin** performs ("Save the Plankton") at this concert to raise money for the Dian Fossey Gorilla Fund, at the Royal Opera House, Covent Garden, London. Other performers include Bryan Adams, Brian May, Joe Strummer, Jeremy Irons, Sinead Cusack, Terence Stamp, and Alan Bates.

2814   November 12, 2002
The Grierson Documentary Awards 2002 (Award ceremony). **Michael Palin** hosts this award ceremony honoring British documentary filmmakers. The ceremony, held at BAFTA in London, is being televised for the first time (Nov. 13 on BBC4). Directed by Amanda Crayden. Produced by Mark Bell.

2815   November 14, 2002
A Pocketful of Python: Picked by Eric Idle (Book: Methuen) is published in the U.K. Collection of Python sketches & songs selected by **Eric Idle**, with a preface by **Terry Jones**. Includes "The Bruces' Philosophers Song." Fifth book in the series.

2816   November 15–23, 2002
Tilting at Windmills: The Fantastical Worlds of

Terry Gilliam (Screenings). Retrospective of **Terry Gilliam**'s film career presented over two weekends at the Los Angeles County Museum of Art. The retrospective also includes *A Conversation with Terry Gilliam* (Nov. 16) in which the director is interviewed by film critic Elvis Mitchell. The interview airs (in edited form) on IFC's *Independent Focus* in February 2003 and is included (unedited) in the June 2003 DVD release of *Lost in La Mancha*.

2817 November 15, 2002
Richard & Judy (TV talk show: Channel 4). Hosted by Richard Madeley and Judy Finnigan. Guests: **John Cleese** and Sir David Attenborough.

2818 November 17, 2002
E! True Hollywood Story (TV episode: E! Entertainment). "The Bond Girls." Documentary on the "girls" of the James Bond film series. *Die Another Day* co-star **John Cleese** is among the interviewees.

2819 November 18, 2002
Die Another Day (Feature film: MGM) premieres in London (opens in Britain Nov. 20 and in the U.S. Nov. 22). Twentieth film in the James Bond series, starring Pierce Brosnan as Bond (his fourth time in the role). **John Cleese** plays gadget expert, Q, replacing Desmond Llewelyn in the role (Llewelyn died in December 1999). **Cleese** had previously played Q's assistant, R, in 1999's *The World Is Not Enough*. Also starring Halle Berry, Rosamund Pike, Toby Stephens, and Judi Dench. Written by Neal Purvis and Robert Wade. Directed by Lee Tamahori.

2820 November 18, 2002
John Cleese and his wife attend the premiere of *Die Another Day* at London's Royal Albert Hall, held in the presence of the Queen and Prince Phillip. The gala charity event is the Royal Film Performance of 2002.

2821 November 19, 2002
Last Call with Carson Daly (TV talk show: NBC). Guests: **John Cleese** and Good Charlotte.

2822 November 20, 2002
Die Another Day, co-starring **John Cleese**, opens in the U.K.

2823 November 20, 2002
The Human Face of Business (Seminar). The speakers at this business seminar, held at Cass Business School in London, are **John Cleese** (who gives a talk on creativity), Prof. Brian Bates, and Dr. Ken Robinson. Hosted by the London Business Forum.

2824 November 20, 2002
Life on Air (TV special: BBC4). **Michael Palin** hosts this hour-long documentary celebrating the 50-year television career of naturalist Sir David Attenborough. **Palin** narrates and interviews Attenborough at his home. Produced by Brian Leith. Repeats Dec. 5 on BBC1. Note: Attenborough was Director of Programmes at the BBC when *Monty Python's Flying Circus* was commissioned in 1969.

2825 November 22, 2002
Die Another Day, co-starring **John Cleese**, opens in the U.S.

2826 November 29, 2002
Concert for George (Concert). An all-star tribute concert for the late George Harrison held at London's Royal Albert Hall on the one-year anniversary of his death. The event raises money for Harrison's charity, The Material World Charitable Foundation. Participants include fellow Beatles Paul McCartney and Ringo Starr, also Dhani Harrison (George's son), Eric Clapton, Ravi Shankar, Tom Petty, Jeff Lynne, Billy Preston, and four Pythons — **Michael Palin**, **Terry Jones**, **Eric Idle**, and **Terry Gilliam** — who perform "Sit on My Face" (with Neil Innes) and "The Lumberjack Song" (with Tom Hanks as a Mountie). The film of the event premieres in theaters in October 2003 and on TV in March 2004 (PBS).

2827 November 29, 2002
Later with Jools Holland (TV show: BBC2). **Michael Palin** is a guest on this live music program. He talks about his book *Sahara* and friend George Harrison.

2828 December 5, 2002
Forever Ealing (TV special: Turner Classic Movies). Documentary chronicling 100 years of England's Ealing Studios. Interviewees include **Terry Gilliam**, Martin Scorsese, and Richard Attenborough. Airs in Britain on Dec. 30 (Channel 4). Directed by Andrew Snell.

2829 December 5, 2002
Eric Idle and his wife attend the 10th annual "Divine Design" benefit show at Barker Hangar in Santa Monica, CA.

2830 December 10, 2002
TV director Ian MacNaughton dies at the age of 76 in Munich, Germany. The Scottish-born MacNaughton, who started out as an actor (his film credits include *X the Unknown*), directed almost all of Monty Python's TV output between 1969 and

1974, including 41 episodes of *Flying Circus* (the first four were directed by John Howard Davies) and their two German specials in 1971 and 72. He also directed their first feature film, *And Now for Something Completely Different* (1971).

2831 December 14, 2002
The British Comedy Awards (Award ceremony). **Michael Palin** receives the Lifetime Achievement Award (presented by Eric Sykes) at the ceremony held at the Southbank in London. Hosted by Jonathan Ross. Broadcast live on ITV.

2832 December 18, 2002
The funeral of Python director Ian MacNaughton (who died Dec. 10) is held in Glasgow. **Michael Palin** is among the attendees.

2833 December 24, 2002
V Graham Norton (TV talk show: Channel 4). Guests: **Michael Palin** and Roy Wood's Army.

2834 December 25, 2002
Pinocchio (Feature film: Miramax Films) is released in the U.S. The English-dubbed version of the Italian film starring Roberto Benigni in the title role. Benigni also directed and co-wrote the film, which is based on the classic story by Carlo Collodi. The English version features the voices of **John Cleese** (as The Cricket) and **Eric Idle** (as Medoro), also Breckin Meyer, James Belushi, Glenn Close, Topher Grace, Eddie Griffin, Cheech Marin, and David Suchet.

2835 December 27, 2002
The Guardian (Newspaper/U.K.). "Obituary: Ian MacNaughton: Television Director Who Got Monty Python's Circus Flying," by **Terry Jones**, p. 19. **Jones** remembers Python's TV director, Ian MacNaughton, who died Dec. 10.

2836 December 27, 2002
Billy Connolly: A BAFTA Tribute (TV special: BBC1). Tribute to Scottish comedian Billy Connolly. Hosted by Michael Parkinson. Stars celebrating his career include **Eric Idle**, **Michael Palin**, Dame Judi Dench, Robin Williams, Pamela Stephenson, Eddie Izzard, Bob Geldof, and others. Recorded earlier this month. Directed by John L. Spencer.

2837 December 28, 2002
James Bond: A BAFTA Tribute (TV special: BBC1). Tribute to Ian Fleming's superspy, hosted by Michael Parkinson with appearances by four screen Bonds—Roger Moore, Pierce Brosnan, Timothy Dalton, and George Lazenby—and many Bond co-stars, including **John Cleese** (Q in *Die Another Day*), Halle Berry, Christopher Lee, and Ursula Andress. Directed by Stuart McDonald. Produced by Arabella McGuigan.

2838 December 28, 2002
Peter Cook: At a Slight Angle to the Universe (TV special: BBC2). Documentary on the life of comedy great Peter Cook (1937–1995). Includes interviews with **John Cleese**, **Eric Idle**, Jonathan Miller, John Fortune, and others. Followed on BBC2 by *Peter Cook: A Post-Humourous Tribute*. Produced by Lucy Kenwright.

2839 December 28, 2002
Peter Cook: A Post-Humourous Tribute (TV special: BBC2). Recording of the Sept. 29 charity event at The Prince of Wales Theatre in London. Hosted by Sir David Frost and starring **Michael Palin**, **Terry Jones**, Rik Mayall, Adrian Edmondson, Griff Rhys Jones, David Baddiel, Jonathan Ross, Harry Enfield, Angus Deayton, Neil Innes, Greg Proops, and Jimmy Carr. Sketches include "How Do You Do It?" (**Palin & Jones**). Stage show directed by **Terry Jones**. Directed by John L. Spencer. Produced by Sam Donnelly.

2840 2002
Going to a Meeting, Part 1: Messing Up a Meeting (Training film: Video Arts). First of two films on improving meetings. Starring **John Cleese** (host), Lolita Chakrabarti, Felicity Montagu, Andy Taylor, Chris Pavlo, and Ellen Thomas. Written by Antony Jay. Directed by Phil Bowker.

2841 2002
Going to a Meeting, Part 2: Meeting Menaces (Training film: Video Arts). How to deal with five types of meeting menaces: the waffler, the turf warrior, the assassin, the dominator, and the interrupter. Starring **John Cleese** (host), Lolita Chakrabarti, Ralph Ineson, Toby Jones, Dan Mersh, Felicity Montagu, Chris Pavlo, Andy Taylor, and Ellen Thomas. Written by Antony Jay. Directed by Phil Bowker.

2842 2002
A Time to Live (Book: Genesis Publications) is published. Limited-edition, large-format book commemorating the end of the Millennium. Introduction by **Michael Palin**.

2843 January 11, 2003
Heroes and Villains (Radio episode: BBC Radio

4). "Alexander the Great and Attila the Hun." **Terry Jones** re-appraises the reputations of Alexander the Great (as a hero) and Attila the Hun (as a villain). First of a three-part series (Bonnie Greer and Matthew Parris host the next two episodes). Half-hour.

2844 January 18, 2003
Comedians' Comedians (Radio show: BBC Radio 2). "Monty Python." Host Angus Deayton asks comedians Eddie Izzard, Mark Steel, and others about their favorite Python moments.

2845 January 23, 2003
John Cleese gives evidence (via video link from Los Angeles) in the High Court in London in his libel case against the *Evening Standard* newspaper, claiming that the paper's April 2002 article ("So, Has **John Cleese** Lost His Funny Bone?") was "offensive and damaging."

2846 January 30, 2003
Fresh Air from WHYY (Radio talk show: NPR). **Terry Gilliam** is interviewed about the documentary *Lost in La Mancha*.

2847 January 31, 2003
Lost in La Mancha opens in New York and Los Angeles.

2848 Late January–February 2003
Michael Palin visits Australia and New Zealand for a *Sahara* promotional tour.

2849 February 2003
Fear and Loathing in Las Vegas (DVD: Criterion Collection). DVD release of **Terry Gilliam**'s 1998 film. Special features include audio commentaries by Johnny Depp, Benicio Del Toro, and Laila Nabulsi (track 1), **Gilliam** (track 2), and Hunter S. Thompson (track 3). Also deleted scenes and *Hunter Goes to Hollywood* (doc).

2850 February 1, 8 & 14, 2003
The **Terry Jones** documentaries *Hidden History of Egypt* and *Hidden History of the Roman Empire*, which first aired in the U.S. in January 2002 on the Discovery Channel, are shown in the U.K. on BBC2 (Feb. 1 & 8) under the series title *Terry Jones's Hidden Histories*. The third documentary in the series, *Hidden History of Sex and Love*, which did not air in the U.S., is shown in Britain on Valentine's Day (Feb. 14) on the Discovery Channel.

2851 February 2, 2003
Carnival of the Animals (Concert). The 1886 work by Camille Saint-Saëns is performed by **John Cleese** and the West Coast Symphony (Christopher Story VI conducting) at the Lobero Theatre in Santa Barbara, CA. **Cleese** reads the text written by Ogden Nash in 1949.

2852 February 2, 2003
The Evening Standard British Film Awards (Award ceremony). **Terry Gilliam** presents director Stephen Frears with the Best Film Award (for *Dirty Pretty Things*) at the 30th annual awards ceremony, held at the Savoy Hotel in London. Also that night, the **Gilliam**-Quixote documentary *Lost in La Mancha* wins the Peter Sellers Award for Comedy.

2853 February 6, 2003
John Cleese is awarded £13,500 in a libel suit against *The Evening Standard*. The British newspaper, in an April 2002 article ("So, Has **John Cleese** Lost His Funny Bone?"), stated that **Cleese** had stopped being funny since moving to the U.S. **Cleese** told the High Court in London on Jan. 23 that he found the article "offensive and damaging."

2854 February 7, 2003
The Fat (TV sports-talk show: ABC, in Australia). Hosted by Tony Squires. Guests: **Michael Palin**, promoting *Sahara*, Jon Lord, and Kirk Pengilly.

2855 February 8, 2003
The Times: Play (London) (Newspaper/U.K.). "Surreal Deal," by **Terry Gilliam** (interviewed by Dominic Wells), p. 3. **Gilliam** discusses some of his current favorite films, books, etc.

2856 February 11, 2003
An Evening with John Cleese (Seminar). **John Cleese** participates in a seminar on his career at The Museum of Television & Radio in Los Angeles during which he discusses comedy, his work with Python, and takes questions from the audience. Hosted by Museum director Barbara Dixon and moderated by actor Alan Alda.

2857 February 11, 2003
Independent Focus (TV talk show: IFC-Independent Film Channel). Film critic Elvis Mitchell interviews **Terry Gilliam** in November 2002 as part of the Los Angeles County Museum of Art's *Tilting at Windmills* retrospective. Half-hour. Later included (unedited) as a bonus feature in the June 2003 DVD release of *Lost in La Mancha*.

2858 February 14, 2003
Hidden History of Sex and Love (TV special: Discovery Channel/U.K.). **Terry Jones** hosts this documentary looking at sex and love throughout his-

tory and how social and religious attitudes on the subject have changed over time. **Jones** visits locations in Egypt, Italy, Greece, France, and England. Last of three "Hidden History" documentaries produced in 2002. Unlike the first two docs (on Egypt and Roman Empire), which debuted in America in January 2002, "Sex and Love" has not been aired in the U.S. Written by Alan Ereira, Phil Grabsky, and **Terry Jones**. Directed by Alan Ereira and Phil Grabsky. Released on DVD as *The Surprising History of Sex and Love* as part of "The Terry Jones Collection" (2009).

2859   February 24, 2003
The British Book Awards (Award ceremony). **Michael Palin** wins the award (or "Nibbie") for Illustrated Book of the Year for *Sahara*. **Palin** attends the ceremony held at the Grosvenor House Hotel in London.

2860   February 26, 2003
Bitter Jester (Feature film) is released. Documentary about the life and struggles of a New York comic, starring Maija DiGiorgio, Kenny Simmons, Jody Del Giorno, and Heather McConnell. Includes interviews with **Terry Jones**, Joy Behar, George Carlin, Chevy Chase, Richard Belzer, and many others. Written by Maija DiGiorgio and David Burton Levin. Directed by Maija DiGiorgio.

2861   February 28, 2003
Real Time with Bill Maher (TV talk show: HBO). Musical guest **Eric Idle** sings the Rutland Isles' "National Anthem," from his new CD, *The Rutland Isles*.

2862   March 2003
Terry Gilliam's next film, *The Brothers Grimm*—his first since *Fear and Loathing in Las Vegas* in 1998—is greenlit by Bob Weinstein's Dimension Films (a division of Miramax). The company is financing the film in partnership with MGM. Filming begins in June.

2863   March 1, 2003
The USCAF Awards Gala and Comedy Film Honors (Award ceremony). **Eric Idle** presents the Best Theatre Award to Canadian comedienne Sandra Shamas at the gala held in the St. Regis Aspen Ballroom in Aspen, CO. The ceremony takes place on the closing night of the U.S. Comedy Arts Festival.

2864   March 3, 2003
The Daily Show with Jon Stewart (TV talk show: Comedy Central). Guest: **Eric Idle**, promoting his new CD, *The Rutland Isles*. **Idle** also talks about Prime Minister Tony Blair, the George Harrison tribute concert last November, and **Graham Chapman**'s ashes.

2865   March 4, 2003
The Rutland Isles (Album: iMusic/BMG). Mock-travel documentary with music in which host Nigel Spasm (**Eric Idle**) visits the weird and remote Rutland Isles. **Idle** originally conceived of this project as a potential TV series back in the early 1980s, and later tried turning it into a feature film but could not find a studio willing to commit to the project. Tracks: "Intro," "Rock Stars," "Penis Fish," "Rutland Triangle," "National Anthem," "Whoops Look Out Behind You," "Mugger's Day," "Pre-Chewed Food," "Contraception," "Killing for God," "Analogy," "Flipper Minnelli," "Gay Animal Song," "West Pole," "Camouflage Regiment," "General Gucci," "Hey Rita," "Paranoid Jails," "Vacation in Rutland," "Quiz Show (Look Out Behind You)," "Goodbye from Paranoia," "Intermission," "Intro Part II," "Over-Friendly Isles," "Fishing for Compliments," "Muff Diving," "Civil War," "Banana Song," "The Randi," "Homo Semi-Erectus," "Surfing Apes," and "Randi Statistics." Written & directed by **Eric Idle**. Music & lyrics by **Eric Idle** and John Du Prez. Produced by **Eric Idle** and John Du Prez.

2866   March 11, 2003
The Television and Radio Industries Club Awards (Award ceremony). **Michael Palin** receives the award for Best Documentary Programme of the Year (*Sahara*) from the Television and Radio Industries Club (TRIC) in a ceremony held at the Grosvenor House Hotel in London.

2867   March 12, 2003
The Late Late Show with Craig Kilborn (TV talk show: CBS). Guest: **Eric Idle**.

2868   March 13, 2003
This Week (TV news-talk show: BBC1). Hosted by Andrew Neil. Guest **Terry Jones** talks about President Bush's pre-emptive war strategy with Iraq.

2869   March 14, 2003
Comic Relief: Red Nose Night (TV special: BBC1). **John Cleese** appears in this seven-hour TV event in aid of Comic Relief.

2870   March 15, 2003
MADtv (TV variety show: Fox). **Eric Idle** plays

a gay animal trainer in a "Tonight Show" sketch and sings the "Gay Animal Song" (from *The Rutland Isles*).

2871 March 20, 2003
The Wayne Brady Show (TV talk show: Synd.). Guests: **Eric Idle**, Anna Nicole Smith, Poppy Montgomery, Wolfgang Puck, and Bob Wieland.

2872 March 25, 2003
Rove Live (TV talk show: Ten, in Australia). Hosted by comedian Rove McManus. Guest: **John Cleese**.

2873 March 28, 2003
The Caroline Rhea Show (TV talk show: Synd.). Guests: **Eric Idle**, Mariska Hargitay, and Jourdan Urbach.

2874 March 29, 2003
Eric Idle turns 60.

2875 March 30, 2003
The Simpsons (TV episode: Fox). "'Scuse Me While I Miss the Sky." Filmmaker Declan Desmond (voiced by **Eric Idle**) shoots a documentary about Springfield Elementary. **Idle** will reprise the role in the episodes "Fat Man and Little Boy" (2004), "Springfield Up" (2007), and "The Spy Who Learned Me" (2012). Other voices by Dan Castellaneta, Julie Kavner, Nancy Cartwright, Yeardley Smith, Hank Azaria, and Harry Shearer. Written by Dan Greaney and Allen Glazier. Directed by Steven Dean Moore.

2876 March 30, 2003
Michael Palin attends the Broadway opening of *The Play What I Wrote*, directed by Kenneth Branagh, at the Lyceum Theatre in New York City. He also attends the opening-night party afterward at the Blue Fin restaurant in Times Square.

2877 April 2003
Michael Palin's book *Sahara* is published in the U.S. by Thomas Dunne Books (St. Martin's Press).

2878 April 2003
Out (Magazine/U.S.). "Voices: **Eric Idle**," by Michael Musto, p. 65. Interview with **Eric Idle** about *The Rutland Isles*.

2879 April 2003
Spin (Magazine/U.S.). "American **Idle**," by David Peisner. Interview with **Eric Idle**.

2880 April 2003
The Great Outdoors (TV show: Channel 7, in Australia). **John Cleese** guest-stars.

2881 April 1, 2003
W. C. Fields: A Comedian for Politically Incorrect Times (Lecture). **John Cleese** gives an April Fool's Day lecture on the life and career of W. C. Fields in Statler Hall at Cornell University in Ithaca, NY. Also taking part in the lecture is author James Curtis (*W. C. Fields: A Biography*). This is **Cleese**'s fourth lecture at Cornell since being named an A.D. White Professor-at-Large in 1998.

2882 April 1, 2003
The Leonard Lopate Show (Radio talk show: WNYC-FM, New York). Guest **Michael Palin** talks about the filming of *Sahara*.

2883 April 2, 2003
Late Night with Conan O'Brien (TV talk show: NBC). Guest **Michael Palin**, promoting *Sahara* on Bravo, talks about the strange things he's eaten during his journeys.

2884 April 5, 2003
Terry Jones speaks at the 54th Cheltenham Festival of Literature (Apr. 4–6) in Cheltenham, England.

2885 April 5, 2003
The Big Read (TV special: BBC2). Launch program for the BBC's "Big Read" campaign searching for Britain's best-loved book. Those nominating their favorites include **Michael Palin**, Helen Fielding, Sophie Dahl, and Terry Pratchett. Narrated by Joanna Lumley.

2886 April 6, 2003
The four-part 2002 travel series *Sahara with Michael Palin* begins airing in the U.S. on Bravo as *Michael Palin's Travels: Sahara*.

2887 April 10, 2003
Michael Palin talks about the journey he documented in his book *Sahara* at the "Book Soup" event at the Beverly Hills Library in Beverly Hills, CA.

2888 April 14, 2003
Eric Idle attends the premiere of the film *A Mighty Wind* at the Directors Guild in Los Angeles.

2889 April 16, 2003
Michael Palin and the Ladies Who Loved Matisse (TV special: BBC1). Documentary, hosted by **Michael Palin**, telling the story of Etta and Claribel Cone, two wealthy sisters from Baltimore who amassed over a 30-year period one the finest collections of early 20th-century French art. **Palin** vis-

2890 May 2003
Alan Moore: Portrait of an Extraordinary Gentleman (Book: Abiogenesis Press), introduced by **Terry Gilliam**, is published in the U.K. Collection of tributes to comics writer Alan Moore in celebration of his 50th birthday. **Gilliam** was once attached to direct a film adaptation of Moore's *Watchmen*.

2891 May 2003
Time and the Soul (Book: Berrett-Koehler Publishers), written by Jacob Needleman with a foreword by **John Cleese**, is published. Time-management book penned by San Francisco philosophy professor Needleman.

2892 May 2, 2003
Michael Palin launches a new website for the Tate Britain art gallery in London. The website will allow people to view exhibitions from home.

2893 May 5, 2003
Michael Palin turns 60.

2894 May 11, 2003
The BAFTA Craft Awards 2002 (Award ceremony). **Michael Palin** presents at the award ceremony held at the Dorchester Hotel in London. Palin's series *Sahara* wins in the category of Photography Factual (Nigel Meakin). Hosted by Alistair McGowan.

2895 May 12, 2003–April 7, 2004
Michael Palin's new travel series *Himalaya* is filmed over six months. The journey covers 3,000 miles of Himalaya and takes him across Pakistan, India, Nepal, China, and Bangladesh. The six-part series will air in October–November 2004 on BBC1.

2896 May 18, 2003
BBC London News (TV news show: BBC1). Guest: **Michael Palin**.

2897 May 27, 2003
Tubular Bells 2003 (CD: Warner Bros) is released in the U.K. **John Cleese** voices the Master of Ceremonies ("Finale" track) on Mike Oldfield's 30th-anniversary remake of his 1973 album. Vivian Stanshall voiced the MC on the original recording. Released in the U.S. on Rhino Records (Aug. 5).

2898 June 10, 2003
Eric Idle and family attend the premiere of *Hollywood Homicide*, in which he co-stars, at the Mann Village Theater in Westwood, CA.

2899 June 13, 2003
Hollywood Homicide (Feature film: Columbia Pictures) opens in the U.S. Action-comedy starring Harrison Ford and Josh Hartnett as two moonlighting LAPD detectives. **Eric Idle** plays an arrested celebrity. Also starring Lena Olin, Bruce Greenwood, and Isaiah Washington. Written by Robert Souza and Ron Shelton. Directed by Ron Shelton.

2900 June 24, 2003
Lost in La Mancha (DVD: New Video Group) is released. Two-DVD set of Louis Pepe and Keith Fulton's 2002 documentary about **Terry Gilliam**'s ill-fated production of *The Man Who Killed Don Quixote*. Special features include: exclusive interviews with **Gilliam**, et al.; *IFC Focus: Terry Gilliam* (unedited version of a November 2002 interview conducted by Elvis Mitchell); *Salman Rushdie and Terry Gilliam* (conversation from the 2002 Telluride Film Festival); deleted scenes; and theatrical trailer.

2901 June 27, 2003
Charlie's Angels: Full Throttle (Feature film: Columbia Pictures) opens in the U.S. Sequel to *Charlie's Angels* (2000), the big-screen version of the popular TV series, with Drew Barrymore, Lucy Liu, and Cameron Diaz returning in the title roles. **John Cleese** plays Mr. Munday. Also starring Bernie Mac, Crispin Glover, and Demi Moore. Written by John August, Cormac Wibberley, and Marianne Wibberley. Directed by McG.

2902 June 30, 2003
Filming begins on *The Brothers Grimm*, directed by **Terry Gilliam**, in Prague, Czech Republic. The film is budgeted at $75 million (**Gilliam**'s largest film budget to date) and scheduled to shoot over 17 weeks. The production (even before filming begins) is plagued by clashes between **Gilliam** and studio heads Bob and Harvey Weinstein (Dimension Films), clashes over the Weinsteins' refusal to allow **Gilliam** to add a prosthetic bump to star Matt Damon's nose; the Weinsteins' opposition to **Gilliam**'s casting of Samantha Morton in the role of Angelika (the part goes instead to Lena Headey); the firing of **Gilliam**'s director of photography, Nicola Pecorini, six weeks into shooting, and so on.

2903 July 2, 2003
Shrek & Fiona's Honeymoon Storybook (CD-ROM:

DreamWorks). Read-along story based on Universal Studios' theme park attraction *Shrek 4-D*. Narrated by **John Cleese**, who will voice King Harold in 2004's film sequel, *Shrek 2*. A limited-edition CD given away in theaters.

2904   July 7, 2003
Storyville (TV special: BBC4). "Lost in La Mancha." Louis Pepe and Keith Fulton's 2002 documentary chronicling **Terry Gilliam**'s failed attempt to bring *Don Quixote* to the screen.

2905   July 31, 2003
The Way We Travelled (TV episode: BBC2). **Michael Palin** is featured on this last episode of a three-part documentary series about travel on TV over the past 30 years. Narrated by Nick Hancock. Directed by Steve Webb.

2906   August 16, 2003
The Rutles 2: Can't Buy Me Lunch (Film: NBC) premieres at the Don't Knock the Rock film festival in Los Angeles. Hour-long sequel to the 1978 TV film *All You Need Is Cash* finds documentarian Melvin Hall (**Eric Idle**) interviewing various artists on the legacy of The Rutles. Interviewees include David Bowie, Billy Connolly, Steve Martin, Carrie Fisher, Tom Hanks, Conan O'Brien, Jewel, Mike Nichols, Garry Shandling, Salman Rushdie, James Taylor, and Clint Black. Includes footage and outtakes from the original film. Also starring Robin Williams, Jimmy Fallon, Kevin Nealon, Jim Piddock, Catherine O'Hara, and Lily Idle. Produced, written & directed by **Eric Idle**. Music by Neil Innes. Executive produced by Lorne Michaels. Produced in 2002. Released on DVD in March 2005.

2907   August 16, 2003
Eric Idle introduces the world premiere screening of *The Rutles 2: Can't Buy Me Lunch* at the ArcLight Cinema in Los Angeles as part of the Don't Knock the Rock film festival (Aug. 15–17). **Idle** also takes part in a Q&A following the screening.

2908   September 2003
Empire (Magazine/U.K.). "The Pythons: Hall of Fame — Kings of Comedy." Interview with the surviving Pythons, who are inducted into the magazine's Hall of Fame for their contribution to cinema.

2909   September 2, 2003
Monty Python's The Meaning of Life (DVD: Universal Studios) is released in the U.S. Two-disc "Special Edition" marking the 20th anniversary of the 1983 film. Bonus features include an introduction by **Eric Idle**, audio commentary by **Terry Jones** and **Terry Gilliam**, *The Meaning of Making The Meaning of Life* (doc), "Education Tips No. 41: Choosing a Really Expensive School" (six-minute sketch performed by **John Cleese**, **Michael Palin** & **Terry Jones**), *Un Film de John Cleese* (a new **Cleese**-centric promotional trailer for the film created by **Cleese**), "Remastering a Masterpiece" (comic look at how the film was restored, with **Palin**, **Jones**, **Gilliam**, and James C. Katz), *Song and Dance* (doc), "Songs Unsung" (**Eric Idle** sings "Every Sperm Is Sacred" and "Christmas in Heaven" and **Terry Jones** sings "It's the Meaning of Life"), "Virtual Reunion," "What Fish Think," "Soundtrack for the Lonely," promotional spots (trailer, U.K. radio ads, etc.), and deleted scenes (including "The Adventures of Martin Luther" and "Diana the Waitress"). The film was previously released on DVD as a single disc in 2001. Produced by John Goldstone. Released in the U.K. on May 17, 2004.

2910   September 2, 2003
The Meaning of Making The Meaning of Life (Documentary). Forty-nine-minute doc on the making of the film, with comments from all five surviving Pythons. Released as a bonus feature on the two-DVD "Special Edition" of the film.

2911   September 2, 2003
Song and Dance (Documentary). Eleven-minute doc on the making of the musical numbers "Every Sperm Is Sacred" and "Christmas in Heaven" from *The Meaning of Life*, with recollections from director **Terry Jones**, choreographer Arlene Phillips, and actress Jane Leeves (a dancer in "Christmas"). Released as a bonus feature on the two-DVD "Special Edition" of the film.

2912   September 12, 2003
The Business of Commercials (Seminar). **John Cleese** moderates a seminar presented by BAFTA/LA at the Los Angeles Film School.

2913   September 14, 2003
The Sunday Times Magazine (London) (Magazine/U.K.). "Oh What a Circus," by Tony Barrell, pp. 36–41. Python article with many rare photos taken from their new book *The Pythons: Autobiography by The Pythons*.

2914   September 21, 2003
With Friends Like These (TV special: BBC2). "Don't Mention the War." Host Michael Cockerell examines Britain's relationship with Germany in

this second episode of a three-part documentary series. Includes an interview with **John Cleese**, who discusses the "Germans" episode of *Fawlty Towers*.

2915 September 22, 2003
The Pythons: Autobiography by The Pythons (Book: Orion), edited by Bob McCabe, is published in the U.K. Large-sized, lavishly-illustrated chronicle of the group's history, told by the Pythons themselves. The surviving Pythons — and **Graham Chapman**, through previously-published material and contributions from family members and his partner, David Sherlock — offer their recollections of events, with excerpts from the diaries of **Michael Palin** (and **Terry Jones**) sprinkled throughout. Includes photographs (many from the Pythons' private collections) and **Gilliam** artwork. Journalist/film critic Bob McCabe had previously written *Dark Knights & Holy Fools: The Art and Films of Terry Gilliam* (1999). Published in the U.S. by Thomas Dunne Books (St. Martin's Press) on Oct. 7.
Reviews: Barry X. Miller (*Library Journal*, Dec. 15, 2003, p. 120): "...this glorious offering is the bible, the last word, and, yes — the full Monty. One of this season's best offerings; a pox on every library that doesn't acquire it!"; Tom Huntington (*British Heritage*, May 2004, pp. 59–60): "This is a great big book, perhaps as big as the one about how to put your budgie down."

2916 September 24, 2003
Eric Idle attends the premiere of the documentary film *Concert for George* at Warner Bros. Studios in Burbank, CA. Other attendees include Paul McCartney, Ringo Starr, Olivia Harrison and son Dhani, and Yoko Ono. The doc is a filmed record of the November 2002 tribute concert for the late George Harrison.

2917 Late September 2003
Good Morning Canada (TV show: CTV, in Canada). Guest: **Eric Idle**, promoting *The Greedy Bastard Tour*.

2918 October 2003
Football Days (Book: Mitchell Beazley) is published in the U.K. Collection of classic football photographs by Peter Robinson, with text by Will Hoon and foreword by **Michael Palin**.

2919 October 2–December 19, 2003
The Greedy Bastard Tour (Stage show). **Eric Idle** takes his musical revue to 49 cities in the U.S. and Canada. Like in his previous tour (*Eric Idle Exploits Monty Python*) in April–June 2000, **Idle** performs many familiar Python songs and sketches ("The Bruces' Philosophers Song," "Galaxy Song," "Always Look on the Bright Side of Life," etc.), as well as newer solo material ("Fuck Christmas," "Killing for God," etc.), some of it from his recently-released CD *The Rutland Isles*. Accompanying him is his longtime musical collaborator John Du Prez (musical director), also actor/singer Peter Crabbe and actress/singer Jennifer Julian (both veterans of *Idle*'s 2000 tour). Venues: Paramount Theatre in Rutland, VT (Oct. 2), Empire Theatre in Belleville, Ont. (Oct. 5), Centre In the Square in Kitchener, Ont. (Oct. 7), Massey Hall in Toronto (Oct. 8–9), Lac Leamy Casino in Gatineau, Que. (Oct. 11), Centennial Hall in London, Ont. (Oct. 12), St. Denis Theatre in Montreal (Oct. 13), Flynn Center in Burlington, VT (Oct. 16), Bardavon Opera House in Poughkeepsie, NY (Oct. 17), Shubert Theatre in New Haven, CT (Oct. 18), Orpheum Theatre in Boston, MA (Oct. 19), Calvin Theatre in Northampton, MA (Oct. 21), Hart Theatre in Albany, NY (Oct. 22), Count Basie Theatre in Red Bank, NJ (Oct. 23), Williamsport Community Arts Center in Williamsport, PA (Oct. 24), State Theatre in New Brunswick, NJ (Oct. 25), 9:30 Club in Washington, D.C. (Oct. 27), Town Hall Theatre in NYC (Oct. 29–30), Keswick Theatre in Glenside, PA (Oct. 31), Norva Theatre in Norfolk, VA (Nov. 2), Shriver Hall in Baltimore, MD (Nov. 4), Carpenter Center for the Performing Arts in Richmond, VA (Nov. 5), Touhill Performing Arts Center in St. Louis, MO (Nov. 7), University at Buffalo Center for the Arts in Buffalo, NY (Nov. 9), Michigan Theater in Ann Arbor, MI (Nov. 10), Byham Theatre in Pittsburgh, PA (Nov. 11), Southern Theatre in Columbus, OH (Nov. 12), Kalamazoo State Theatre in Kalamazoo, MI (Nov. 14), Adler Theater in Davenport, IA (Nov. 16), Barrymore Theater in Madison, WI (Nov. 18), Pantages Theater in Minneapolis, MN (Nov. 19), Vic Theatre in Chicago (Nov. 21–22), Francis Winspear Centre for Music in Edmonton, Alberta (Nov. 28), Jubilee Auditorium in Calgary, Alberta (Nov. 29), Orpheum Theatre in Vancouver, B.C. (Dec. 1–2), Moore Theatre in Seattle, WA (Dec. 4), Hult Center for the Performing Arts in Eugene, OR (Dec. 5), Egyptian Theatre in Boise, ID (Dec. 6), Met Theatre in Spokane, WA (Dec. 7), Aladdin Theater in Portland, OR (Dec. 8), Fillmore in San Francisco, CA (Dec. 10–11), Flint Center in San Jose, CA (Dec. 12), House of Blues in Las Vegas (Dec. 14), Performing Arts Center in San Luis Obispo, CA

(Dec. 16), Marquee Theatre in Tempe, AZ (Dec. 18), and Henry Fonda Theater in Los Angeles (Dec. 19). **Idle**'s online diary of the tour is later published as a book, *The Greedy Bastard Diary: A Comic Tour of America* (2005).

2920   October 3, 2003
Concert for George (Feature film: ArenaPlex LLC) premieres in the U.S. Documentary film of the November 2002 charity concert at London's Royal Albert Hall paying tribute to the late George Harrison, with appearances by **Michael Palin**, **Terry Jones**, **Eric Idle**, and **Terry Gilliam**. Directed by David Leland.

2921   October 8, 2003
Terry Jones attends the London premiere of the George Harrison tribute documentary *Concert for George* at the Odeon Cinema, Leicester Square, London. Other attendees include Paul McCartney, Ringo Starr, Olivia Harrison and son Dhani, Bill Wyman, and Eric Clapton.

2922   October 13, 2003
Terry Jones attends a party celebrating journalist-broadcaster Joan Bakewell's 70th birthday and the launch of her autobiography, at the Royal College of Physicians in London.

2923   October 19, 2003
Michael Palin witnesses the abduction of a British Gurkha officer by Maoist rebels in the village of Lekhani in Western Nepal. **Palin** is in Nepal filming his new travel series *Himalaya* and at the time was filming a Gurkha recruitment drive in the village. The officer, Lt-Col. Adrian Griffith, is freed unharmed 36 hours later.

2924   October 20, 2003
Who Murdered Chaucer?: A Medieval Mystery (Lecture). **Terry Jones** discusses his investigation into the death of English poet Geoffrey Chaucer at the British Library in London.

2925   October 21, 2003
George of the Jungle 2 (Feature film: Walt Disney) is released. Direct-to-video sequel to 1997's *George of the Jungle*. **John Cleese** voices Ape, reprising his role from the original film. Also starring Christopher Showerman, Julie Benz, Angus T. Jones, and Thomas Haden Church. Written by Jordan Moffet. Directed by David Grossman.

2926   October 22, 2003
BBC Breakfast (TV news show: BBC1). Guest: **Terry Jones**, promoting his new book *Who Murdered Chaucer?*

2927   October 23, 2003
Who Murdered Chaucer?: A Medieval Mystery (Book: Methuen), written by **Terry Jones** with Robert Yeager, Terry Dolan, Alan Fletcher, and Juliette Dor, is published in the U.K. In this historical whodunnit (or "wasitdunnatall"), **Jones** investigates the mystery surrounding the death of the celebrated English poet Geoffrey Chaucer over 600 years ago, shortly after the deposition (in 1399) of Richard II. The project began in July 1998 when **Jones** led a "coroner's inquest" into Chaucer's death at the Sorbonne in Paris. **Jones**' previous book on Chaucer was 1980's *Chaucer's Knight: The Portrait of a Medieval Mercenary*. Published in the U.S. by Thomas Dunne Books (2004).
Reviews: Jonathan Bate (*The Sunday Telegraph*, Nov. 9, 2003): "More of a contextual study than a biography, it contains a great deal of valuable material and intriguing speculation"; Jonathan Myerson (*The Guardian*, Nov. 14, 2003): "...flamboyantly argued, beautifully balanced..."; Alexander Rose (*The Times Literary Supplement* [London], Jan. 16, 2004, p. 24): "Light-hearted, intelligent, panoramic and defiantly unbeholden to conventional interpretations..."; William Grimes (*The New York Times*, Jan. 19, 2005): "...[a] hefty, beautifully illustrated volume ... it sifts through the doctrinal disputes and political rivalries of the time with great zest and close attention to the source material."

2928   October 24, 2003
Who Murdered Chaucer? (Lecture). **Terry Jones** discusses the mysterious death of English poet Geoffrey Chaucer, the subject of his new book, at the Library Theatre in Birmingham, England, as part of the Birmingham Book Festival (Oct. 9–24).

2929   October 29–30, 2003
Eric Idle brings his *Greedy Bastard Tour* to Broadway, playing two nights at the Town Hall Theatre in NYC.

2930   November 2003
James Bond 007: Everything or Nothing (Video game: Electronic Arts). James Bond adventure game. **John Cleese** voices Q, reprising his role from *Die Another Day* (2002). Other voices by Pierce Brosnan, Judi Dench, and Willem Defoe.

2931   November 1, 2003
Parkinson (TV talk show: BBC1). Hosted by Michael Parkinson. Guests: Emma Thompson, **Michael Palin**, Rod Stewart, and Luciano Pavarotti.

2932 November 6, 2003
Will & Grace (NBC). "Heart Like a Wheelchair." Karen (Megan Mullally) tracks husband-stealing Lorraine Finster to a hotel but finds Lorraine's father instead. **John Cleese** plays Lyle Finster in this sixth-season episode of the 1998–2006 sitcom. It is the first of his four appearances in the role (2003–04), which include two two-part episodes in 2004. Also starring Eric McCormack, Debra Messing, and Sean Hayes. Written by Tracy Poust and Jon Kinnally. Directed by James Burrows.
Awards: Emmy-nominated for Outstanding Guest Actor in a Comedy Series (**John Cleese**).

2933 November 13, 2003
From Hollywood to Borehamwood (TV episode: ITV1). "Romance." Episode of the six-part documentary series (Nov. 6–Dec. 18) looking at films made in English studios. Interviewees include **Michael Palin**. Narrated by Nigel Havers. Produced & directed by Caius Julyan.

2934 November 17, 2003
The Boy Who Would Be King (TV special: BBC1). Documentary chronicling—through dramatizations and interviews with historians—the eventful early years of Charles II (1630–1685). **Michael Palin** visits Moseley Hall where, in September 1651, his ancestor helped hide the fugitive future King from Cromwell's soldiers. Produced & directed by Nick Rossiter.

2935 November 19, 2003
Richard & Judy (TV talk show: Channel 4). Hosted by Richard Madeley and Judy Finnigan. Guest: **Terry Jones**.

2936 November 22, 2003
Brits Go to Hollywood (TV episode: Channel 4). "Sean Connery." Profile of the Scottish actor. Last in a four-part series. Interviewees include **Terry Gilliam** (who directed Connery in *Time Bandits*), Diane Cilento, and Harrison Ford. Directed by Christopher Bruce.

2937 November 23, 2003
Terry Jones unveils a blue plaque to Geoffrey Chaucer in front of Copyprints Ltd. in Talbot Yard, Borough High Street, London. The building stands on the site of The Tabard Inn, from where the pilgrims set off in 1386 in Chaucer's *Canterbury Tales*.

2938 November 27, 2003
The Talk Show (TV talk show: BBC4). Hosted by Jonathan Freedland. Guests: Dame Pauline Neville-Jones and **Terry Jones**, promoting his new book *Who Murdered Chaucer?*

2939 November 27, 2003
From Hollywood to Borehamwood (TV episode: ITV1). "Comedy." Third episode of the six-part documentary series (Nov. 6–Dec. 18) looking at films made in English studios. **Terry Jones** and **Terry Gilliam** are among the interviewees. Narrated by Nigel Havers. Produced & directed by Caius Julyan.

2940 November 29, 2003
A recovered episode of the **John Cleese-Graham Chapman**-Tim Brooke Taylor-Marty Feldman sketch-comedy series *At Last the 1948 Show* (1967–68) is screened—with a new introduction by **Cleese**—at the National Film Theatre in London. The screening is part of the 10th anniversary of the BFI's "Missing Believed Wiped" initiative. This "lost" episode, which was re-assembled from various sources, is later aired on BBC4 on Dec. 29 following a *Time Shift* documentary on the subject.

2941 December 2003
The Pythons: Autobiography by The Pythons: The Interviews That Made the Book (Audiobook: Orion). Two-and-a-half hours of interviews and sketches on a two–CD set. The interviews with the surviving Pythons were conducted by Bob McCabe and transcribed for his book *The Pythons: Autobiography by The Pythons* (published in September). Narrated by McCabe with "interjections from **Michael Palin** and **Terry Gilliam**."

2942 December 20, 2003
Christmas Vacation 2: Cousin Eddie's Island Adventure (TV film: NBC). Sequel to 1989's *National Lampoon's Christmas Vacation* starring Randy Quaid as Cousin Eddie. **Eric Idle** reprises his cameo role from 1985's *European Vacation* as an abused Englishman. Also starring Miriam Flynn, Fred Willard, Dana Barron, and Edward Asner. Written by Matty Simmons. Directed by Nick Marck.

2943 December 29, 2003
The Times (London) (Newspaper/U.K.). "Sailing Under the Pole and into History," by **Michael Palin**, p. 6. **Palin** writes about his favorite item in the Royal Geographical Society's Polar Archive: a recording of the USS *Nautilus*' 1958 voyage beneath the North Pole. The piece is written to bring attention to the RGS's "Unlocking the Archive" campaign, supported by *The Times*' Christmas Charity Appeal.

2944   December 29, 2003
Time Shift (TV episode: BBC4). "Missing Believed Wiped." Documentary on the efforts of the BFI's National Film & Television Archive to recover lost British TV programs of the 1960s & '70s that had been wiped from the tapes after broadcast. **Terry Jones**, visiting the archive on Nov. 28, comments on recovered footage from his and **Michael Palin**'s 1969 series *The Complete and Utter History of Britain*, while **John Cleese** comments on the recovery of an episode of his and **Graham Chapman**'s 1967 series *At Last the 1948 Show* (an airing of that episode, with an intro by **Cleese**, follows the documentary). Narrated by Veronika Hyks. Produced & directed by Jo Haywood.

2945   2003
Restoring Balance: Removing the Black Rat from Anacapa Island (Documentary). **John Cleese** narrates this half-hour doc on the efforts to protect the seabirds and other species of Anacapa Island (off the coast of southern California) by removing the island's major predator, the black rat. Written, produced & directed by Kevin White.

2946   2003
John Cleese and writer Kirk DeMicco (*Quest for Camelot*) collaborate on a screen adaptation of Roald Dahl's 1980 children's book *The Twits*, to be produced by Vanguard Animation for Walt Disney Pictures. The project remains in development. Note: **Cleese** will later voice a role in Vanguard's 2005 animated feature *Valiant*.

2947   2003
Terry Jones writes the script for a film adaptation of Roald Dahl's *The BFG (Big Friendly Giant)*.

2948   January 3–24, 2004
The Emmy-nominated, eight-part documentary series *Terry Jones' Medieval Lives* airs on The History Channel (U.S.). Writer and host **Terry Jones** presents an irreverent, myth-debunking look at various archetypes of the medieval world (knight, monk, king, damsel, philosopher, minstrel, outlaw, and peasant). Filmed in Britain, Italy, and France. Airs in the U.K. on Feb. 9–Mar. 29 (BBC2). Series producer: Paul Bradshaw.
Reviews: Josh Wolk (*Entertainment Weekly*, Jan. 9, 2004, p. 76): "With his exuberant delivery and game role-playing (occasionally tossing on a suit of armor), **Jones** is the history teacher you wish you had"; Joe Joseph (*The Times* [London], Feb. 10, 2004, p. 22): "**Jones** makes an engaging companion through this rewardingly informative but reassuringly undemanding history lesson."

2949   January 3, 2004
Terry Jones' Medieval Lives (TV episode: The History Channel). "The Knight." **Terry Jones** debunks the myth of the noble knight in shining armor. First episode in the eight-part documentary series. Airs in the U.K. on Mar. 8 (BBC2). Written & hosted by **Terry Jones**. Directed by Paul Bradshaw.

2950   January 3, 2004
Terry Jones' Medieval Lives (TV episode: The History Channel). "The Monk." **Terry Jones** reveals how the medieval monk's ideal of simplicity, solitude and prayer was corrupted by money and power. Second episode in the eight-part documentary series. Airs in the U.K. on Feb. 16 (BBC2). Written & hosted by **Terry Jones**. Produced & directed by Paul Bradshaw.

2951   January 10, 2004
Terry Jones' Medieval Lives (TV episode: The History Channel). "The King." **Terry Jones** examines the reigns of the English kings Richard I, II and III. Third episode in the eight-part documentary series. Airs in the U.K. on Mar. 29 (BBC2). Written & hosted by **Terry Jones**. Produced & directed by Nigel Miller.

2952   January 10, 2004
Terry Jones' Medieval Lives (TV episode: The History Channel). "The Damsel." **Terry Jones** investigates the myth of the passive "damsel in distress." Fourth episode in the eight-part documentary series. Airs in the U.K. on Feb. 23 (BBC2). Written & hosted by **Terry Jones**. Produced & directed by Nigel Miller.

2953   January 15, 2004
Will & Grace (TV episode: NBC). "The Accidental Tsuris." **John Cleese** returns as Lyle Finster (who first appeared in the Nov. 6, 2003, episode "Heart Like a Wheelchair"). Starring Eric McCormack, Debra Messing, Sean Hayes, Megan Mullally, Geena Davis, and Minnie Driver. Written by Jeff Greenstein. Directed by James Burrows.

2954   January 17, 2004
Terry Jones' Medieval Lives (TV episode: The History Channel). "The Philosopher." **Terry Jones** looks at the discoveries made by medieval scientists, or philosophers as they were then called. Fifth episode in the eight-part documentary series. Airs in the U.K. on Mar. 15 (BBC2). Written & hosted

by **Terry Jones**. Produced & directed by Nigel Miller.

2955 January 17, 2004
Terry Jones' Medieval Lives (TV episode: The History Channel). "The Minstrel." **Terry Jones** shows how being a medieval minstrel could be a dangerous job. His investigation includes a look at the fate of court poet Geoffrey Chaucer, whose mysterious disappearance in 1400 was the subject of **Jones**' 2003 book *Who Murdered Chaucer?* Sixth episode in the eight-part documentary series. Airs in the U.K. on Mar. 1 (BBC2). Written & hosted by **Terry Jones**. Directed by Lucy Cooke.

2956 January 24, 2004
Terry Jones' Medieval Lives (TV episode: The History Channel). "The Outlaw." **Terry Jones** reveals the truth behind the medieval outlaw of legend. Seventh episode in the eight-part documentary series. Airs in the U.K. on Mar. 22 (BBC2). Written & hosted by **Terry Jones**. Directed by Nigel Miller.

2957 January 24, 2004
Terry Jones' Medieval Lives (TV episode: The History Channel). "The Peasant." An examination of the medieval peasant reveals that he may not have been as simple, sickly, and subservient as commonly believed. Last episode in the eight-part documentary series. Airs in the U.K. on Feb. 9 (BBC2). Written & hosted by **Terry Jones**. Produced & directed by Lucy Cooke.
Awards: Emmy-nominated for Outstanding Writing for Nonfiction Programming.

2958 January 24, 2004
Britain's Best Sitcom (TV episode: BBC2). "Fawlty Towers." Host Jack Dee celebrates the classic British sitcom, with comments from **John Cleese**, Prunella Scales, Andrew Sachs, **Terry Jones**, Carol Cleveland, Eddie Izzard, and others. Each episode of the series presents arguments explaining why the featured sitcom should be voted Britain's best. Produced & directed by Matt O'Casey.

2959 January 25, 2004
Eric Idle attends the *61st Golden Globe Awards* and the *In Style* Golden Globe Party afterward at the Beverly Hilton Hotel in Beverly Hills, CA.

2960 January 27, 2004
Time Bandits: Special Edition (DVD: Anchor Bay) is released in the U.S. Two-disc special edition of **Terry Gilliam**'s 1981 fantasy-comedy featuring a new high-definition transfer and bonus material, including an interview with **Gilliam** and co-writer **Michael Palin** (27 mins.), *The Directors: The Films of Terry Gilliam* (AFI program, 60 mins.), theatrical trailers, and a fold-out map of the universe. Previously released by Criterion on laserdisc (1998) and DVD (1999) with audio commentaries by **Gilliam**, **Palin**, **John Cleese**, and others.

2961 January 29, 2004
The Daily Post (Liverpool) (Newspaper/U.K.). "The Journey Back in Time That Led Python Star Home." Graham Keal interviews **Terry Jones** about *Medieval Lives*, his Welsh roots, Python, etc.

2962 January 31, 2004
John Cleese presents director Peter Jackson with the Modern Master Award at the Arlington Theater in Santa Barbara, CA, as part of the 19th Annual Santa Barbara International Film Festival.

2963 February 2004
History Today (Magazine/U.K.). "History with the Boring Bits Put Back," by **Terry Jones**, p. 62. **Jones** explains how the boring bits of Chaucer reignited his interest in history.

2964 February 5, 2004
Terry Jones' Medieval Lives (Book: BBC Books), written by **Terry Jones** and Alan Ereira, is published in the U.K. **Jones** debunks the myths surrounding various medieval archetypes (knight, damsel, minstrel, etc.) in this companion book to the TV series. A No. 1 bestseller in Britain.

2965 February 5, 2004
Today with Des and Mel (TV talk show: ITV). Hosted by Des O'Connor and Melanie Sykes. Guests include **Terry Jones**, promoting *Medieval Lives*, and Dennis Taylor.

2966 February 7, 2004
Ronnie Barker: A BAFTA Tribute (TV special: BBC1). Gala tribute to comedian Ronnie Barker (*The Two Ronnies*) in celebration of his receiving BAFTA's Lifetime Achievement Award. Hosted by Ronnie Corbett, with contributions by **John Cleese**, **Michael Palin**, David Jason, Eric Sykes, Patricia Routledge, and others. Directed by John L. Spencer. Produced by Sam Donnelly.

2967 February 8, 2004
The Observer (Newspaper/U.K.). "The Middle Ages of Reason," by **Terry Jones**, p. 29. **Jones** explains why he made *Medieval Lives* and disputes our common notions of the "ignorant" Middle Ages and the "enlightened" Renaissance.

2968 February 9–March 29, 2004
The eight-part series *Terry Jones' Medieval Lives* airs in the U.K. on BBC2. The series first aired in the U.S. in January on The History Channel.

2969 February 9, 2004
BBC Breakfast (TV news show: BBC1). Guest: **Terry Jones**, promoting *Medieval Lives*.

2970 February 9, 2004
The Terry and Gaby Show (TV talk show: Five). Hosted by Terry Wogan and Gaby Roslin. Guest: **Terry Jones**, promoting *Medieval Lives*.

2971 February 10–13, 2004
John Cleese's Life and Times (Events). **John Cleese** participates in onstage interviews (with film clips) at three California venues: The Rafael Film Center in San Rafael (Feb. 10), The Herbst Theater in San Francisco (Feb. 11), and Spangenberg Theater in Palo Alto (Feb. 13). Michael Krasny is the interviewer for the first two dates, David Kipen for the third. The benefit events will raise funds for the Esalen Institute.

2972 February 12, 2004
The Evening News (Edinburgh) (Newspaper/U.K.). "'History is funny ... that's why I'm so serious about it,'" by Miranda Fettes, p. 26. Interview with **Terry Jones** about his interest in the Middle Ages.

2973 February 18, 2004
The Late Late Show with Craig Kilborn (TV talk show: CBS). Guests: **John Cleese** and Portia de Rossi.

2974 February 18, 2004
Terry Jones reads from his book *Medieval Lives* at the Wycombe Swan Theatre in High Wycombe, England.

2975 February 21, 2004
The Birmingham Post (Newspaper/U.K.). "Comic Trying to Rewrite History," by Simon Evans. Interview with **Terry Jones** about his new book and series *Medieval Lives* and his fascination with the Middle Ages.

2976 February 22, 2004
Special guests **Michael Palin** and Sir David Attenborough are interviewed by Michael Aspel at the Brighton Centre in Brighton, England for the launch of BBC Showcase, a four-day television trade fair.

2977 February 26, 2004
Will & Grace (TV episode: NBC). "Flip-Flop: Part 1." Karen (Megan Mullally) and Lyle Finster (guest-star **John Cleese**) get back together. But things become complicated when Lyle's daughter, Lorraine (Minnie Driver), moves in. Also starring Eric McCormack, Debra Messing, Sean Hayes, and Shelley Morrison. Written by Adam Barr. Directed by James Burrows.

2978 February 29, 2004
Eric Idle and his wife attend the *Vanity Fair* Oscar Party at Morton's Restaurant in West Hollywood, CA.

2979 March 2004
Vanity Fair (Magazine/U.S.). "The Hollywood Portfolio: The League of Extraordinarily Silly Gentlemen," pp. 382–83. Two-page photo spread of the Monty Python team in coffins, taken by Art Streiber. The Pythons were photographed for the "reunion" in separate locations (in December 2003) and then spliced together.

2980 March 3, 2004
Great Performances (TV special: PBS). "Concert for George." Film of the tribute concert to the late George Harrison, held in November 2002 for charity at London's Royal Albert Hall. Includes appearances by **Michael Palin**, **Terry Jones**, **Eric Idle**, and **Terry Gilliam**. The film premiered in October 2003. Airs in Britain on Apr. 2 on BBC1. Directed by David Leland.

2981 March 4, 2004
Will & Grace (TV episode: NBC). "Flip-Flop: Part 2." Lyle Finster (guest-star **John Cleese**) proposes to Karen (Megan Mullally). Also starring Eric McCormack, Debra Messing, Sean Hayes, Shelley Morrison, and Minnie Driver. Written by Alex Herschlag. Directed by James Burrows.

2982 March 6, 2004
The Times (London) (Newspaper/U.K.). "A Python's Tale," by Ed Potton, p. 12. **Michael Palin** interview.

2983 March 17, 2004
X-Play (TV show: TechTV). Video game review program. Guests: Ben Affleck and **John Cleese**.

2984 Late March 2004
Who Murdered Chaucer? (Lecture). **Terry Jones** gives a talk on the mysterious death of English poet Geoffrey Chaucer at The Royal Oak pub in Tabard Street, London, marking the opening of the pub's new Chaucer Room. The lecture is based on his 2003 book of the same name.

2985 April 4, 2004
Lifeline (TV appeal: BBC1). "Motivation." **Michael Palin** presents a 10-minute appeal on behalf of The Motivation Charitable Trust. **Palin** previously appeared on *Lifeline* in 1998 (Sudan Appeal) and 2002 (FARM-Africa). Directed by Jill Dawson.

2986 April 9, 2004
Ella Enchanted (Feature film: Miramax Films) opens in the U.S. Re-imagining of the Cinderella story. Narrated by **Eric Idle**. Starring Anne Hathaway, Hugh Dancy, Cary Elwes, and Joanna Lumley. Written by Laurie Craig, Karen McCullah Lutz, Kirsten Smith, Jennifer Heath, and Michele J. Wolff. Directed by Tommy O'Haver.

2987 April 17, 2004
Eric Idle attends the wedding of author Salman Rushdie and model-actress Padma Lakshmi in New York City.

2988 April 25, 2004
The Los Angeles Times (Newspaper/U.S.). "Recalling the View, Such as It Was," by **Eric Idle**, p. E12. **Idle** recalls the filming of *Life of Brian* and reveals what it's like to be crucified.

2989 April 29, 2004
Will & Grace (TV episode: NBC). "I Do, Oh, No, You Di-in't: Part 1 & 2." Karen and Lyle fly to Las Vegas to elope. **John Cleese**'s final appearance as Lyle Finster, who debuted in a November 2003 episode ("Heart Like a Wheelchair"). Starring Eric McCormack, Debra Messing, Megan Mullally, Sean Hayes, Tim Curry, and Jennifer Lopez. Written by Jeff Greenstein and Jhoni Marchinko (pt 1) and Kari Lizer and Sonja Warfield (pt 2). Directed by James Burrows.

2990 April 30, 2004
Life of Brian is re-released (by Rainbow Films) in New York and Los Angeles to commemorate its 25th anniversary (and also to capitalize on the success of Mel Gibson's *The Passion of the Christ*, released in February).

2991 May & June 2004
Michael Palin and **Terry Jones** record commentaries for the DVD release (Oct. 11) of their 1975–79 series *Ripping Yarns*.

2992 May 5, 2004
The Late Late Show with Craig Kilborn (TV talk show: CBS). Guests: **Eric Idle** and Lauren Holly.

2993 May 8, 2004
John Cleese attends the premiere of *Shrek 2*, in which **Cleese** voices the King, at the Mann Village Theater in Los Angeles.

2994 May 15, 2004
The Times (London) (Newspaper/U.K.). "Every Laugh Is Sacred," by **Terry Jones** (talking to Ed Potton), p. 7. **Jones** talks about the making of *Meaning of Life*, which will be released on DVD in Britain on May 17.

2995 May 16, 2004
VH1 Goes Inside (TV special: VH1). "Shrek." A look at the making of the new *Shrek* film. **John Cleese** is among the interviewees.

2996 May 17, 2004
Monty Python's The Meaning of Life is released on DVD in the U.K.

2997 May 19, 2004
Shrek 2 (Feature film: DreamWorks) opens in the U.S. Animated feature, sequel to the 2001 hit. **John Cleese** voices King Harold, a role he later reprises in *Shrek the Third* (2007). Voice cast also includes Mike Myers, Eddie Murphy, Cameron Diaz, Julie Andrews, and Antonio Banderas. Directed by Andrew Adamson, Kelly Asbury, and Conrad Vernon.

2998 May 30, 2004
Who Murdered Chaucer? (Lecture). **Terry Jones** gives a talk on the mysterious death of poet Geoffrey Chaucer at the Hay-on-Wye literary festival (May 28–June 6) in Wales. The lecture is based on his 2003 book of the same name.

2999 June 16, 2004
Around the World in 80 Days (Feature film: Buena Vista Pictures) opens in the U.S. Steve Coogan plays Phileas Fogg in this big-screen version of the Jules Verne novel. **John Cleese** plays Grizzled Sergeant. Also starring Jackie Chan. Written by David Titcher, David Benullo, and David Andrew Goldstein. Directed by Frank Coraci.

3000 June 21, 2004
Comedy Connections (TV episode: BBC1). "The Goodies." Documentary tracing the origins of the comedy series starring Tim Brooke-Taylor, Bill Oddie, and Graeme Garden. Interviewees include **John Cleese**, who got his start in comedy with the future Goodies in the Cambridge Footlights revue. Narrated by Julia Sawalha. Directed by Angus McIntyre. Produced by Toby Stevens.

3001 June 28, 2004
John Cleese and his wife attend the U.K. premiere of *Shrek 2*, in which Cleese voices the King, at The Empire, Leicester Square, London.

3002 July 2004
Charlie and the Great Glass Elevator (Audiobook: Harper Children's Audio). Audio version of Roald Dahl's children's story, read by Eric Idle. Idle was Grammy-nominated for his reading of Dahl's *Charlie and the Chocolate Factory* in 2002.

3003 July 3, 2004
Wetten, dass..? (Wanna Bet That...?) (TV show: ZDF, in Germany). Hosted by Thomas Gottschalk. Guest: John Cleese. Taped at the Waldbuehne Theater in Berlin.

3004 July 6, 2004
Eric Idle and Kevin Nealon join musician Clint Black on stage at the Civic Arts Plaza in Thousand Oaks, CA, to perform "Galaxy Song" and "The Getty Song," both penned by Idle. Black recorded a cover of "Galaxy Song" in 1999.

3005 July 8–10, 2004
John Cleese and his wife attend the 39th Karlovy Vary International Film Festival (July 2–10) in The Czech Republic where *Shrek 2* is being premiered.

3006 July 23, 2004
John Cleese attends the opening ceremony for the re-constructed Old Bridge in Mostar, Bosnia-Herzegovina. Prince Charles is also among the attendees. The 16th-century bridge was destroyed Nov. 9, 1993, during the Bosnian War. Michael Palin will visit the Old Bridge in 2006 for his travel series *New Europe*.

3007 July 25, 2004
The Independent on Sunday (Newspaper/U.K.). "And Now for Something Completely Different," by Terry Jones. Jones explains his love for Iceland — and sheds.

3008 August 2004
Time Troopers (DVD Game: b EQUAL). Two-disc history trivia game hosted by John Cleese (as Special Agent Wormold). Presented by The History Channel. Directed by Dick Cooper.

3009 August 1, 2004
An Audience with John Cleese (Event). John Cleese participates in an onstage conversation with journalist Robert Hall at the Jersey Opera House on the Isle of Jersey. The event benefits the Durrell Wildlife Conservation Trust.

3010 August 7 & 8, 2004
Terry Jones lectures at English Heritage's Festival of History at Stoneleigh Park in Warwickshire, England.

3011 August 19, 2004
The Birmingham Post (Newspaper/U.K.). "Climb Every Mountain." Emma Pomfret interviews Michael Palin about his *Himalaya* journey.

3012 August 24, 2004
A Valid Path (CD: Artemis). Album from English musician Alan Parsons, with guest spoken vocal by John Cleese on the final track, "Chomolungma." Produced by Alan Parsons.

3013 August 26, 2004
The Late Late Show with Craig Kilborn (TV talk show: CBS). On Craig Kilborn's second to last show, John Cleese is the guest (and Kilborn's last interview). Cleese talks about the animals on his ranch, television executives, and his new website TheJohnCleese.Com (coming in October).

3014 August 31, 2004
Himalaya (Audiobook: RNIB), written & read by Michael Palin, is published. An RNIB (Royal National Institute of Blind People) Talking Book. Special audio version of the companion book (released next month) to the upcoming BBC TV series.

3015 Fall 2004
Terry Jones and his wife, Alison Telfer, separate after 35 years of marriage. Jones' new girlfriend is 21-year-old Oxford University student Anna Söderström, whom he met at a book-signing.

3016 September–October 2004
Terry Jones films in Morocco and other locations for the documentary *The Story of 1*, which will air in September 2005 on BBC1.

3017 September 2004
Terry Jones gives a talk on *Medieval Lives* at Queens' College, Cambridge as part of the second Cambridge History Festival (Sept. 2–5).

3018 September 8, 2004
Eric Idle attends the American opening in Las Vegas of *We Will Rock You*, a British musical built around the music of the rock group Queen. The show is performed at the Paris Las Vegas hotel-casino. Idle attends in a wheelchair, having recently undergone knee surgery.

3019 September 9, 2004
Terry Gilliam Interviews (Book: University Press

of Mississippi), edited by David Sterritt and Lucille Rhodes, is published in the U.S. Collection of interviews with **Terry Gilliam**, previously published in *Film Comment* (1981), *The Christian Science Monitor* (1982), etc.

3020 September 12, 2004
The 2004 Primetime Creative Arts Emmy Awards (Award ceremony). **John Cleese** is a presenter at the ceremony held at the Shrine Auditorium in Los Angeles. Broadcast Sept. 18 on E! Entertainment.

3021 September 20, 2004
Michael Palin attends the U.K. premiere of the film *Wimbledon* in Leicester Square, London, then moves on to the after-party at the Dorchester Hotel.

3022 September 25, 2004
Parkinson (TV talk show: ITV1). Hosted by Michael Parkinson. Guests: **Michael Palin**, promoting *Himalaya* and the DVD release of *Ripping Yarns*, also Julie Andrews, Ant & Dec, Tom Jones, and Jools Holland.

3023 September 26, 2004
The Sunday Times (London) (Newspaper/U.K.). "What's He Up to Now?," by **Michael Palin**, p. 1–2 (sect. 4). **Palin** on his latest travel journey *Himalaya*.

3024 September 27–November 2004
Tideland, directed by **Terry Gilliam**, is filmed on a small budget in the Qu'Appelle Valley and Regina in Saskatchewan, Canada. The film premieres in Toronto in September 2005.

3025 September 27, 2004
Himalaya (Book: Weidenfeld & Nicolson), written by **Michael Palin** with photographs by Basil Pao, is published in the U.K. **Palin** gives his account of his journey across Pakistan, India, Nepal, and other countries of the Himalayas in this companion book to his 2004 BBC travel series. The No. 1 bestseller in Britain for 2004. The audiobook version, read by **Palin**, is released on a six-CD set by BBC Audio. Published in the U.S. on June 17, 2005 (Thomas Dunne Books).
Award: The British Book Award for TV & Film Book of the Year.

3026 September 27, 2004
Inside Himalaya (Book: Weidenfeld & Nicolson), photographed by Basil Pao with foreword by **Michael Palin**, is published. Collection by photographer Pao who accompanied **Palin** on his journey for the BBC TV series and book.

3027 September 28, 2004
Richard & Judy (TV talk show: Channel 4). Hosted by Richard Madeley and Judy Finnigan. Guest: **Michael Palin**, promoting *Himalaya*.

3028 September 29, 2004
BBC Breakfast (TV news show: BBC1). Hosted by Dermot Murnaghan and Natasha Kaplinsky. Guest: **Michael Palin**, promoting *Himalaya*.

3029 September 30, 2004
Michael Palin gives an illustrated talk on his new book & BBC series *Himalaya* at a "Writers & Readers" forum at the Institute of Education in London. Followed by a book-signing. The event is sponsored by *The Times* and Foyles bookshops.

3030 October 2004
Michael Palin signs copies of his book *Himalaya* at bookstores around the U.K., including WH Smith in London (Oct. 6), Waterstone's in London (Oct. 7), Hatchards in London (Oct. 12), Waterstone's at Lancaster University, Eng. (Oct. 13), Ottakar's in Aberdeen, Scot. (Oct. 18), Waterstone's in Edinburgh, Scot. (Oct. 19), Waterstone's in Cardiff, Wales (Oct. 25), and Borders in Oxford, Eng. (Oct. 27).

3031 October 2004
John Cleese launches his own website, TheJohnCleese.Com

3032 October 2004
When We Were Young: A Compendium of Childhood (Book: Bloomsbury Publishing), compiled & illustrated by John Burningham, is published in the U.K. Collection of childhood memories by various writers, with all proceeds going to UNICEF. **Michael Palin** contributes a piece on his family's seaside summer holidays.

3033 October 1, 2004
The Independent (Newspaper/U.K.). "**Michael Palin**: Mountains of the Mind," by Sue Gaisford. Interview with **Michael Palin** about his latest travel series *Himalaya*.

3034 October 1, 2004
Medieval Views of the Cosmos (Book: The Bodleian Library, Oxford), written by Evelyn Edson and Emilie Savage-Smith, is published in the U.K. Foreword by **Terry Jones**.

3035 October 2, 2004
The Times (London) (Newspaper/U.K.). "Climb Every Mountain," by **Michael Palin** (interviewed

by James Jackson), p. 23. **Palin** recalls his journey for the new series *Himalaya*.

3036 October 2, 2004
Excess Baggage (Radio show: BBC Radio 4). Sandi Toksvig talks to **Michael Palin** about his new travel series *Himalaya*.

3037 October 3–November 7, 2004
The six-part travel series *Himalaya with Michael Palin*, airs on BBC1. On this journey (his sixth, following 2002's *Sahara*) **Michael Palin** travels the 1,800-mile length of the mountain range, visiting the countries of Pakistan, India, Nepal, China, and Bangladesh. The series was filmed over six months from May 2003 to April 2004. The book of the series is published in September 2004. Airs in the U.S. on June 20–July 24, 2005, on the Travel Channel.
Awards: BAFTA-nominated for Best Factual Series or Strand, Best Original Television Music, Best Photography (Factual), and Best Sound (Factual); Television and Radio Industries Club (TRIC) award-winner for TV Music and Arts Programme.
Reviews: Paul Hoggart (*The Times* [London], Oct. 4, 2004): "...it promises to be a captivating series, both for the stunning landscape photography and the exotic cultural phenomena."

3038 October 3, 2004
The Sunday Times Magazine (London) (Magazine/U.K.). "A Life in the Day: **Michael Palin**," by **Michael Palin** (interviewed by Danny Scott), p. 78. **Palin** describes his daily routine (when at home), which includes a 50-minute run and a visit to the local art gallery. Photo of **Palin** by Kalpesh Lathigra.

3039 October 3, 2004
Himalaya with Michael Palin (TV episode: BBC1). "North by Northwest." The journey begins at the Khyber Pass on the Pakistan-Afghanistan border. In Pakistan, **Palin** visits a gun seller (Darra) and a dentist (Peshawar), attends a bull race (Taxila), gives an English lesson to the children of the Kalash Valley, and enjoys a polo match on The Shandur Pass. First episode of the six-part travel series. Written & narrated by **Michael Palin**. Produced & directed by Roger Mills.

3040 October 6, 2004
London Tonight (TV news show: ITV1/LNN-Carlton). News magazine hosted by Alastair Stewart. **Michael Palin** talks about *Ripping Yarns* (on DVD) and his new series *Himalaya*.

3041 October 7, 2004
Michael Palin and **Terry Jones** attend the screening of two restored episodes of *Ripping Yarns* at the National Film Theatre in London. The event is a promotion for the launch of the complete series on DVD. Following the screening, **Palin** and **Jones** take part in an onstage interview (with Arthur Smith) and Q&A.

3042 October 9, 2004–October 9, 2005
Super Robot Monkey Team Hyperforce Go! (TV episodes: ABC Family). **Eric Idle** voices Scrapperton in three episodes of the anime series (2004–06): "Magnetic Menace" (Oct. 9, 2004), "Ape New World" (Dec. 4, 2004), and "The Skeleton King Threat" (Oct. 9, 2005).

3043 October 9, 2004
Jonathan Ross (Radio talk show: BBC Radio 2). Guest: **Michael Palin**, promoting *Himalaya*.

3044 October 9, 2004
Terry Jones hosts a screening of his 1996 film *The Wind in the Willows* at the 12th Raindance Film Festival (Oct. 1–10) in London. The screening is followed by a Q&A session.

3045 October 10, 2004
Himalaya with Michael Palin (TV episode: BBC1). "A Passage to India." Before crossing into India, **Palin** attends a flag-lowering ceremony on the Pakistan side of the border. In India, he visits the Golden Temple in the Sikh town of Amritsar, rides the Himalayan Queen railroad, appears on the stage of the Gaiety Theatre in Shimla, and meets with the Dalai Lama in Dharamsala. Second episode of the six-part travel series. Written & narrated by **Michael Palin**. Produced & directed by Roger Mills.

3046 October 11, 2004
The Telegraph Travel Awards (Award ceremony). **Michael Palin** receives the special Global Traveller award at the ceremony held at the Waldorf Hilton in London.

3047 October 11, 2004
The Complete Ripping Yarns (DVD: Network) is released in the U.K. Two-disc set of the complete nine-episode series *Ripping Yarns* (1976–79) starring **Michael Palin** and written by **Palin** and **Terry Jones**. The episodes have been digitally restored. Extras include audio commentaries by **Palin** and **Jones**, a deleted scene from "Murder at Moorstones Manor," also *Comic Roots* (1983 **Palin** doc), *Secrets* (1973 TV play written by **Palin** and **Jones**), and a

commemorative booklet. Released in the U.S. in August 2005 (Acorn Media). Re-released in March 2012 (Network).

3048 October 12, 2004
The Nutcracker and the Mouseking (Feature film: Anchor Bay) is released on video in the U.S. English version of a German animated adaptation (*Nussknacker und Mausekönig*) of the E.T.A. Hoffmann story. **Eric Idle** voices the role of Drosselmeier. Other voices by Leslie Nielsen, Robert Hays, and Fred Willard. Written by Andy Hurst and Ross Helford. Directed by Michael Johnson and Tatiana Ilyina.

3049 October 13, 2004
Who Murdered Chaucer? (Lecture). **Terry Jones** discusses his investigation into the death of 14th-century poet Geoffrey Chaucer at the Victoria and Albert Museum in London. The lecture is based on his 2003 book of the same title.

3050 October 13, 2004
Michael Palin opens the new exhibition "Chris Orr's John Ruskin, and Other Stories" at the Ruskin Library at Lancaster University in Lancaster, England. Earlier **Palin** signed copies of his book *Himalaya* at the Waterstone's bookstore on campus.

3051 October 15, 2004
Who Murdered Chaucer? (Lecture). **Terry Jones** lectures on the death of poet Geoffrey Chaucer at the 55th Cheltenham Literature Festival (Oct. 8–17) in Cheltenham, England.

3052 October 16, 2004
Michael Palin talks about his new book & TV series, *Himalaya*, as part of the "Distant Climes" series at the 55th Cheltenham Festival of Literature (Oct. 8–17) in Cheltenham, England.

3053 October 17, 2004
John Cleese's Wine for the Confused (TV special: The Food Network). Hour-long documentary that guides the inexperienced viewer through the process of wine making and wine selection. Hosted by wine-lover **John Cleese**, who tours several California wineries. Filmed partly at **Cleese**'s ranch in Santa Barbara where a wine-tasting party is held, attended by actor Brendan Fraser, Alyce Faye (**Cleese**'s wife), and others. Written by **John Cleese** and David Kennard. Produced & directed by David Kennard.

3054 October 17, 2004
Himalaya with Michael Palin (TV episode: BBC1).

"Annapurna to Everest." In Nepal, **Palin** has a close encounter with Maoist rebels (in Lekhani), then treks into the mountains to Annapurna Base Camp. In Kathmandu (Nepal's capital), he receives a blessing from the King of Nepal. Then, on his way up to Everest Base Camp, **Palin** visits the highest monastery in the world (in Rongbuk). Third episode of the six-part travel series. Written & narrated by **Michael Palin**. Produced & directed by John Paul Davidson.

3055 October 18, 2004
Eric Idle attends the New York premiere of the film *Alfie* at the Ziegfeld Theatre.

3056 October 22, 2004
What Is Religion?: Musings on the Life of Brian (Lecture). **John Cleese** speaks in Barton Hall at Cornell University, Ithaca, NY. **Cleese** was named A.D. White Professor-at-Large at Cornell in 1998.

3057 October 24, 2004
Himalaya with Michael Palin (TV episode: BBC1). "The Roof of the World." **Palin** crosses the Tibetan Plateau, stopping to visit the country's second largest monastery (in Shigatse) and the Potala Palace and Sera monastery (in Lhasa, the capital), then takes a dip in a hot springs swimming pool (Yangbajing), attempts to milk a dri (a female yak) in Qinghai Province, and attends a horse fair (Yushu). Fourth episode of the six-part travel series. Written & narrated by **Michael Palin**. Produced & directed by John Paul Davidson.

3058 October 29–November 19, 2004
Peter Cook in His Own Words (Radio special: BBC Radio 4). **Michael Palin** hosts this tribute to the late Peter Cook, using the comedian's own writings, interviews, and performances to tell his life story. The four-part program covers the years 1959–65 (Oct. 29), 1966–73 (Nov. 5), 1974–82 (Nov. 12), and 1983–94 (Nov. 19). Released on BBC Audiobooks in October 2005.

3059 October 30, 2004
The 2nd Irish Film and Television Awards (Award ceremony). **John Cleese** presents Pierce Brosnan with the award for Outstanding Irish Contribution to Cinema. The ceremony, hosted by James Nesbitt, is held at The Burlington Hotel in Dublin. Broadcast Nov. 1 on RTE One (Ireland). Directed by John Comiskey.

3060 October 30, 2004
Superman: True Brit (Comic book: DC Comics Elseworlds), written by **John Cleese** and Kim

"Howard" Johnson/illustrated by John Byrne and Mark Farmer, is published in the U.S. Re-imagining of the Superman story in which the Man of Steel grows up, not in Kansas, but in **Cleese**'s home town of Weston-Super-Mare in England. Published in the U.K. by Titan Books.

3061   October 31, 2004
Himalaya with Michael Palin (TV episode: BBC1). "Leaping Tigers, Naked Nagas." In China's Yunnan Province, **Palin** visits with Mosuo singing star Namu (at Lugu Lake), meets famed conductor Xuan Ke (in the city of Lijiang), and visits the Yunnan capital of Kunming. He then travels to the tribal area called Nagaland (in India). In Assam (in India), he visits Tipong Coal Mine, rides an elephant, and stays at a monastery on Majuli Island. Fifth episode of the six-part travel series. Written & narrated by **Michael Palin**. Produced & directed by John Paul Davidson.

3062   November 2004
Michael Palin tours New Zealand and Australia promoting *Himalaya*.

3063   November 2004
Geographical (Magazine/U.K.). "In Conversation: **Michael Palin**." Jessi Tucker interviews **Palin** about his new series *Himalaya*.

3064   November 4, 2004
Poets for Peace (Event). **Terry Jones** gives a reading at this benefit event for the children of Iraq, held at Conway Hall in London. Introduced by Jonathan Pryce. Also with Brian Patten, Adrian Mitchell, Peter Porter, and Jean Binta Breeze.

3065   November 7, 2004
Himalaya with Michael Palin (TV episode: BBC1). "Bhutan to the Bay of Bengal." In the Kingdom of Bhutan, **Palin** attends the Tsechu festival (in Paro), visits a snooker bar (Thimphu), and travels to the Popshika Valley to see the endangered black-neck cranes. In Bangladesh, he visits the ship-breaking yards of Chittagong and meets singer Mahjabeen ("Moni") Khan on a boat ride from Dhaka to Mongla. The journey ends in the Bay of Bengal. Sixth episode of the six-part travel series. Written & narrated by **Michael Palin**. Produced & directed by John Paul Davidson and Roger Mills.

3066   November 16, 2004
Michael Palin gives talks on *Himalaya* in Sydney, Australia, first at the Shangri-La Hotel, then at the Mosman Art Gallery.

3067   November 16, 2004
Rove Live (TV talk show: Ten, in Australia). Hosted by comedian Rove McManus. Guest: **Michael Palin**, promoting *Himalaya*.

3068   November 23, 2004
Good Morning Australia (TV talk show: Ten, in Australia). Hosted by Bert Newton. Guest: **Michael Palin**, promoting *Himalaya*.

3069   November 26, 2004
Michael Palin gives a talk on *Himalaya* at the Lecture Theatre at the University of Queensland in Australia. Followed by a book-signing.

3070   November 27 & 28, 2004
The Ultimate Film (TV special: Channel 4). **John Cleese** hosts this two-part countdown program revealing the 100 most successful movies ever shown in Britain, based on audience figures from the British Film Institute. Narrated by Fay Ripley.

3071   December 3, 2004
The Late Late Show (TV talk show: RTE One, in Ireland). Hosted by Pat Kenny. Guests include **Michael Palin**, promoting *Himalaya*, and Nigella Lawson.

3072   December 4, 2004
Terry Jones introduces two "lost" episodes of his and **Michael Palin**'s 1969 sketch comedy series *The Complete and Utter History of Britain* at the National Film Theatre in London. The episodes, which were recovered through the British Film Institute's "Missing Believed Wiped" initiative, were the first two recorded for the series. The best parts of each show were edited together to form the first broadcast episode (Jan. 12, 1969), meaning that about half of the material from these two episodes has never been seen by the public.

3073   December 6, 2004
Michael Palin gives a talk on his new book and TV series *Himalaya* at the Royal Geographical Society in London.

3074   December 9, 2004
Who Murdered Chaucer?, written by **Terry Jones** et al., is published in the U.S. by Thomas Dunne Books.

3075   December 9, 2004
Arena (TV arts show: BBC4). "Remember the Secret Policeman's Ball?" Documentary celebrating the 25th anniversary of the Amnesty International benefit concert. Includes highlights from the show and recollections from participants **John Cleese**,

Michael Palin, Terry Jones, Terry Gilliam, Rowan Atkinson, Sting, Stephen Fry, Bob Geldof, and others. Narrated by Dawn French. Directed by Margy Kinmonth. Produced by Roger Graef. The special premieres theatrically in June 2009 as part of "The Secret Policeman's Film Festival" in Los Angeles and New York and is also included that year in the three–DVD set *The Secret Policeman's Balls* (Shout! Factory).

3076   December 12, 2004
The Simpsons (TV episode: Fox). "Fat Man and Little Boy." Homer builds a nuclear reactor in this 16th-season episode. **Eric Idle** voices Declan Desmond, host of a TV nature doc Homer watches. **Idle** first voiced the role in the March 2003 episode "'Scuse Me While I Miss the Sky." Other voices by Dan Castellaneta, Julie Kavner, Nancy Cartwright, Yeardley Smith, Hank Azaria, and Harry Shearer. Written by Joel H. Cohen. Directed by Mike B. Anderson.

3077   December 15, 2004
Terry Jones gives a lecture (with slides) on medieval life in Britain at the National Museum and Gallery in Cardiff, Wales. Part of The Annual Christmas Celebrity Lecture series.

3078   December 18, 2004
Let's Hear It for the King of Judea (Radio special: BBC Radio 4). **Terry Jones** re-examines the reign of King Herod in this half-hour program. Produced by Mark Rickards.

3079   December 20, 2004
The New Yorker (Magazine/U.S.). "Sixteen Tons of Fun," by Dave Eggers, pp. 166–174. Interview with **Eric Idle** on the eve of *Spamalot*'s world premiere in Chicago.

3080   December 21, 2004
Eric Idle's new musical *Spamalot*, based on *Monty Python and the Holy Grail*, has its world premiere at the Shubert Theatre in Chicago. **Idle** attends the performance. The show runs there until Jan. 16, 2005, then moves to Broadway in March 2005 (previews begin in February).

3081   December 31, 2004
Tarrant's 2004 (Radio special: BBC Radio 2). Host Chris Tarrant looks back over the past year with guests **Michael Palin**, Katie Melua, Tom Jones, and others.

3082   2004
The Unsteady Chough (Short film). Animated short (part live-action) about an undergraduate's encounter with a drunken bird on his first day at Oxford University. Written by **Terry Jones**, based on his 2001 poem. **Jones** also narrates and voices Father, Barman, Professor, and Priest. Shown May 20, 2006, on BBC4. Produced & directed by Sam Leifer and Jonathan Van Tulleken. Suetonius Productions.

3083   2004
Eric Idle is fined $5,000 by the FCC (Federal Communications Commission) for saying "fuck" on a national American radio broadcast. In response **Idle** composes the ditty "FCC Song (Fuck You Very Much)," which features 14 instances of the offending word. The song is made available for download from the Python website.

3084   January 2005
The Aristocrats (Feature film: THINKFilm) premieres at the Sundance Film Festival. Documentary examining the many versions of the world's dirtiest joke, "The Aristocrats." Comedians appearing include George Carlin, Lewis Black, Kevin Pollack, Bob Saget, and **Eric Idle**. Written by Penn Jillette. Directed by Paul Provenza.

3085   January 2005
Terry Jones's War on the War on Terror (Book: Nation Books), written by **Terry Jones**, is published in the U.S. Collection of 33 columns written by **Jones** between 2001 and 2004 for the British newspapers *The Guardian*, *The Observer*, and *The Independent* criticizing President Bush's "war on terrorism." One of the articles, "The Grammar of the War on Terror," originally appeared in the 2001 collection *Voices for Peace* (Scribner). Illustrations by Steve Bell.

3086   January 1, 2005
The Comedians' Comedian (TV special: Channel 4). Three-hour special counting down the top 50 comedians as selected by their fellow comedians. Among those selected are: **Michael Palin** (No. 30), **Eric Idle** (No. 21), and **John Cleese** (No. 2). Peter Cook is voted No. 1. Hosted by Jimmy Carr.

3087   January 11, 2005
Michael Palin talks about *Himalaya* at The Oldie Literary Lunch at Simpson's-in-the-Strand, London.

3088   January 13, 2005
Michael Palin appears at the Tate Britain art gallery in London to launch "Explore Tate Britain," an interactive, online map of the gallery.

3089 January 18, 2005
The Independent (Newspaper/U.K.). "**Terry Gilliam**: This Python Bites," by Sholto Byrnes. Interview with **Gilliam** at his Soho office.

3090 January 24, 2005
John Cleese speaks at the opening session of IBM's Lotusphere 2005 conference (Jan. 24–26) in Florida.

3091 January 25–February 19, 2005
Monty Python's Flying Circus...at Last, in French (Stage show), at Riverside Studios in London. French stage production featuring Python classics like "Argument Clinic" and "The Lumberjack Song" all performed in French (with English subtitles) by a five-member cast (including one woman). The show, which producer Rémy Renoux first staged in Paris in June–September 2002, was a surprise success at the Edinburgh Festival in August 2003. It is the first and only authorized stage version of Monty Python's television work. Directed by Thomas Le Douarec.

3092 January 28, 2005
Today with Des and Mel (TV talk show: ITV1/Granada). Hosted by Des O'Connor and Melanie Sykes. Guests include **Michael Palin** and **Terry Gilliam**.

3093 January 31, 2005
John Cleese presents his long-time friend, naturalist Sir David Attenborough, with the first Attenborough Nature Filmmaker Award at an event at the Santa Barbara Museum of Natural History (in Santa Barbara, CA) as part of the 20th Santa Barbara International Film Festival (Jan. 28–Feb. 6). The event also includes a screening of the documentary *The Reel Ocean: Tribute to Sir David Attenborough*.

3094 February 2, 2005
Dave Barry's Complete Guide to Guys (Feature film: Labrador Pictures) premieres at the Santa Barbara International Film Festival. Comedy starring columnist Dave Barry, adapted from his book. **John Cleese** plays various roles. Filmed in the fall of 2004. Written & directed by Jeff Arch.

3095 February 2, 2005
John Cleese attends the world premiere of *Dave Barry's Complete Guide to Guys*, in which he co-stars, at the Arlington Theater in Santa Barbara, CA, as part of the Santa Barbara International Film Festival. He also takes part in a Q&A session following the screening.

3096 February 14, 2005
Previews begin at the Shubert Theatre in New York City for the **Eric Idle**–John Du Prez musical *Spamalot*, which opens on Broadway March 17. The previews follow successful tryouts in Chicago in December 2004–January 2005.

3097 February 15, 2005
The Greedy Bastard Diary: A Comic Tour of America (Book: HarperCollins [U.S.]; Weidenfeld & Nicolson [U.K.]), written by **Eric Idle**, is published. **Idle** combines autobiographical material with diary accounts chronicling his 49-city *Greedy Bastard Tour* of North America in October–December 2003. His diary entries were originally posted daily on the internet during the tour.
Reviews: *Publishers Weekly* (Feb. 7, 2005, p. 55): "...writing with wit and honesty.... **Idle** offers a Pythonesque pastiche of goofy observations as he analyzes audiences, dissects his nightly performances and recalls showbiz friendships."

3098 February 15, 2005
The Daily Show with Jon Stewart (TV talk show: Comedy Central). Guest: **Eric Idle**, promoting *Spamalot* on Broadway and his new book *The Greedy Bastard Diary*.

3099 February 19, 2005
Terry Jones reads fairy tales at the Mitchell Library in Glasgow, Scotland, as part of the Aye Write! book festival.

3100 February 21, 2005
Comedy Connections (TV episode: BBC1). "Monty Python's Flying Circus." Documentary on the ground-breaking comedy series covering the Pythons' writing process, **John Cleese**'s departure, battles with the BBC, and the group's various pre- and post–Python projects. **John Cleese**, **Eric Idle**, **Terry Gilliam**, **Michael Palin**, and Carol Cleveland are interviewed. Narrated by Doon Mackichan. Directed by Angus McIntyre. Note: *Ripping Yarns* is the subject of an August 2008 episode.

3101 February 23, 2005
Michael Palin attends the annual Orion Authors' Party at the Tate Britain art gallery in London.

3102 February 25, 2005
NewsNight with Aaron Brown (TV news show: CNN). **Eric Idle** is interviewed.

3103 February 27, 2005
Eric Idle and his wife attend the *Vanity Fair* Oscar Party at Morton's Restaurant in Beverly Hills, CA.

3104 February 28, 2005
Newsweek (Magazine/U.S.). "Spamish Inquisition." Devin Gordon interviews two of the creators of the new Broadway musical *Spamalot*, writer **Eric Idle** and director Mike Nichols.

3105 March 2005
The Rutles 2: Can't Buy Me Lunch (DVD: Warner). **Eric Idle**'s 2002 sequel to his 1978 Beatle parody *All You Need Is Cash*. Hour.

3106 March 2, 2005
Michael Palin is a guest speaker at the Tsunami Appeal Dinner hosted by the magazine *Condé Nast Traveller* and held at The Ballroom of the Four Seasons Hotel, London. Proceeds go to victims of the Asian earthquake and tsunami.

3107 March 4, 2005
John Cleese emcees a live auction at the 6th annual Mission Creek Gala held at the Santa Barbara Museum of Natural History in Santa Barbara, CA.

3108 March 7, 2005
John Cleese's Comedy Heroes (TV special: Five). **John Cleese** talks about some of his favorite comedy stars, including Laurel & Hardy, Alastair Sim, Tony Hancock, Peter Cook, W.C. Fields, Spike Milligan, and Bill Hicks. Includes interviews with **Michael Palin**, Steve Martin, Rik Mayall, and others. Written & presented by **John Cleese**. Directed by J. Dickel.

3109 March 8–22, 2005
Kington's Anatomy of Comedy (Radio series: BBC Radio 4). Three-part series hosted by humorist Miles Kington. Interviewees include **Terry Jones**, Mark Lamarr, and David Quantick.

3110 March 9, 2005
Live with Regis and Kelly (TV talk show: Synd.). Hosted by Regis Philbin and Kelly Ripa. Guests include **Eric Idle**, promoting *Spamalot*.

3111 March 9, 2005
The Tony Danza Show (TV talk show: Synd.). Guests: **Eric Idle**, Phil Keoghan, and George Lopez. **Idle** talks about *Spamalot* and sings "Always Look on the Bright Side of Life."

3112 March 11, 2005
An Evening with Michael Palin (Event). **Michael Palin** talks to moderator Harry Shearer at the Directors Guild of America in Los Angeles as part of the Museum of Television & Radio's 22nd Annual William S. Paley Television Festival (Mar. 2–16).

3113 March 17, 2005
Spamalot (Stage musical) opens on Broadway at New York City's Shubert Theatre. This musical-comedy, "lovingly ripped off" from 1975's *Monty Python and the Holy Grail*, was conceived and written by **Eric Idle** and composer John Du Prez and produced with the blessings of the four other surviving Pythons. The show's score includes "Knights of the Round Table" and "Brave Sir Robin" (both from the original film), "Always Look on the Bright Side of Life" (from *Life of Brian*) and 15 original songs: "Fisch Schlapping Song," "King Arthur's Song," "He Is Not Dead Yet," "Come with Me," "The Song That Goes Like This," "All for One," "Find Your Grail," "Run Away," "You Won't Succeed on Broadway," "The Diva's Lament," "Where Are You?," "Here Are You," "His Name Is Lancelot," "I'm All Alone," and "The Holy Grail." The show is a smash hit, running almost four years (until Jan. 11, 2009). Directed by Mike Nichols (*The Graduate*). Original Broadway cast includes Tim Curry (King Arthur), David Hyde Pierce (Sir Robin, others), Hank Azaria (Sir Lancelot, Knight of "Ni," others), Sara Ramirez (Lady of the Lake), Michael McGrath (Mayor, Patsy, Guard), Christopher Sieber (Sir Galahad, Black Knight, others), with **John Cleese** as the voice of God.

Awards: Winner of the 2005 Tony Award for Best Musical, Best Featured Actress in a Musical (Ramirez), and Best Direction of a Musical (Nichols). Also Tony-nominated for Book (**Idle**), Original Score (**Idle** and Du Prez), Actor in a Musical (Azaria, Curry), Featured Actor in a Musical (McGrath, Sieber), Choreography (Casey Nicholaw), Orchestrations (Larry Hochman), Scenic Design of a Musical (Tim Hatley), Costume Design of a Musical (Hatley), and Lighting Design of a Musical (Hugh Vanstone). Winner of the 2005 Drama Desk Award for Outstanding New Musical, Outstanding Lyrics (**Idle**), and Outstanding Costume Design (Hatley).

Reviews: David Rooney (*Variety*, Mar. 17, 2005): "...the irreverent Arthurian romp's brash, lunatic spirit is impossible to ignore and almost as hard to resist"; Ben Brantley (*The New York Times*, Mar. 18, 2005): "...resplendently silly ... the show is amusing, agreeable, forgettable..."; John Lahr (*The New Yorker*, Mar. 28, 2005): "*Spamalot*'s freewheeling, nonlinear style and wacky non sequiturs are exhilarating because they keep viewers on their toes."

3114 March 17, 2005
John Cleese, Terry Gilliam, Eric Idle, Terry

Jones, and **Michael Palin** attend the Broadway premiere of **Idle**'s *Spamalot* at the Shubert Theatre in New York City. The five Pythons and director Mike Nichols join the cast on stage during the curtain call to sing "Always Look on the Bright Side of Life." Other celebrities attending the premiere include Steve Martin, Candice Bergen, Whoopi Goldberg, Carly Simon, Lauren Hutton, and Ellen Barkin.

3115   March 18–29, 2005
Who Murdered Chaucer?: A Medieval Mystery (Lecture). **Terry Jones**, following his appearance at the *Spamalot* Broadway premiere, takes his lecture (with slideshow) on the death of Geoffrey Chaucer to universities and other venues across the U.S. as part of a promotional tour for the American release of his 2003 book of the same title. Venues include: Lecture Hall South at Pace University, NYC (Mar. 18), Calhoun College at Yale University (Mar. 22), Hamilton College House at the University of Pennsylvania (Mar. 23), Commons Auditorium at the University of West Florida (Mar. 24), and Book Revue in Huntington, Long Island (Mar. 29). He also signs books at Barnes & Noble in New York City (Mar. 28).

3116   March 18, 2005
Today (TV news-talk show: NBC). Guests: **Eric Idle** and the cast of *Spamalot*.

3117   March 18, 2005
Eric Idle signs copies of his book *The Greedy Bastard Diary* at Virgin Megastore in New York City.

3118   March 21–April 8, 2005
Michael Palin films a documentary special exploring the life of Danish painter Vilhelm Hammershøi called *Michael Palin and the Mystery of Hammershøi*. The special, which is filmed over 17 days in London, Amsterdam, and Copenhagen, airs July 14 on BBC1.

3119   March 22, 2005
Good Morning Monterey Bay (Radio talk show: KSCO-AM, Santa Cruz). Guest: **Terry Jones**.

3120   March 23, 2005
The Treatment (Radio talk show: KCRW, Santa Monica). Host/film critic Elvis Mitchell talks to **Eric Idle** about his new book *The Greedy Bastard Diary*, also Python's influence, *Spamalot*, English humor, etc.

3121   March 24, 2005
Eric Idle appears at Dutton's Books in Brentwood, CA, signing copies of his new book *The Greedy Bastard Diary*.

3122   March 25, 2005
Entertainment Weekly (Magazine/U.S.). "The Full Monty," by Chris Nashawaty, pp. 40–47. Interview with all five surviving Pythons on the history of the group. Includes EW's picks of the top 20 Python sketches and a piece ("*Spamalot*'s Opening Knights") on **Eric Idle**'s new Broadway musical.

3123   March 25, 2005
Valiant (Feature film: Entertainment Film Distributors) opens in the U.K. Computer-animated comedy-adventure about a pigeon who joins the London war effort in 1944. **John Cleese** voices Mercury. Voice cast also includes Ewan McGregor, Ricky Gervais, Tim Curry, and Hugh Laurie. Written by Jordan Katz, George Webster, and George Melrod. Directed by Gary Chapman. A Vanguard Animation/Odyssey Entertainment production. Opens in the U.S. on Aug. 19.

3124   March 29, 2005
The Leonard Lopate Show (Radio talk show: WNYC-FM, New York). Guest **Terry Jones** talks about his book *Terry Jones's War on the War on Terror*.

3125   April 2005
Men's Health (Magazine/U.S.). "The Sex God at 62," by **Eric Idle**, p. 84. **Idle**, who turned 62 on March 29, shares his views on aging.

3126   April 1–June 12, 2005
The IN-Complete History of Monty Python (Screenings) is presented by the Museum of Television & Radio in New York City and Los Angeles. The series of screenings consists of five programs: "Sex and Violence" (Apr. 1–14), "Full Frontal Nudity" (Apr. 15–28), "Spam" (Apr. 29–May 12), "Royal Episode Thirteen" (May 13–26), and "Idle Pleasures" (May 27–June 9).

3127   April 3, 2005
The 50 Greatest Comedy Sketches (TV special: Channel 4). Countdown of the best TV comedy sketches as voted on by viewers, with Python making the list five times: "Homicidal Barber/Lumberjack Song" (No. 49), "Nudge, Nudge" (No. 31), "The Ministry of Silly Walks" (No. 15), "The Spanish Inquisition" (No. 12), and "The Pet Shop" (No. 2). Narrated by Tom Baker, with comments from **John Cleese**, **Terry Gilliam**, **Michael Palin**, and others.

3128 April 4, 2005
Risk to Innovate (Lecture). **John Cleese** delivers the keynote address at the Gartner Outsourcing Summit (Apr. 4–6) held at the Westin Century Plaza Hotel in Los Angeles. In his lecture **Cleese** talks about the importance of taking risks and making mistakes.

3129 April 4, 2005
Creativity and the Creative Process (Lecture). **John Cleese** speaks on creativity in an onstage Q&A with screenwriter Ed Solomon at UCLA's James Bridges Theater in Los Angeles. Solomon is **Cleese**'s son-in-law (he married Cynthia Cleese in 1995).

3130 April 11, 2005
The Ellen DeGeneres Show (TV talk show: Synd.). Guests: **Eric Idle**, Brittany Murphy, and Ringside.

3131 April 12, 2005
The Late Late Show with Craig Ferguson (TV talk show: CBS). Guests include **Eric Idle**, promoting *The Greedy Bastard Diary*, and Olympic wrestler Rulon Gardner. **Idle** talks about *Spamalot* star Sara Ramirez, the *Greedy Bastard* tour, and living in the U.S. He also brings cans of Spam (*Spamalot* Collector's Edition by Hormel) for the audience.

3132 April 17, 2005
The British Academy Television Awards (Award ceremony). **Michael Palin** receives a BAFTA Special Award for Outstanding Contribution to Television. Graham Norton hosts the ceremony from the Theatre Royal, Drury Lane, London. Broadcast live on BBC1. **Palin** also attends the after-party at Grosvenor House Hotel.

3133 April 18, 2005
Tavis Smiley (TV talk show: PBS). Guest **Eric Idle** talks about Python, *Spamalot*, his book *The Greedy Bastard Diary*, and the DVD release of *The Rutles 2: Can't Buy Me Lunch*.

3134 April 18, 2005
Sullivan's Travels (DVD: Universal Pictures) is released in the U.K. Preston Sturges' classic 1941 comedy, with audio commentary track by Sturges fan **Terry Jones**. Also sold as part of the seven-disc set *Written and Directed by Preston Sturges*.

3135 April 20, 2005
The British Book Awards (Award ceremony). **Michael Palin** wins the award (or "Nibbie") for TV & Film Book of the Year for *Himalaya*. **Palin**, who attends the ceremony at the Grosvenor House Hotel in London, was also up for the WH Smith Book of the Year prize, which went to Dan Brown's *The Da Vinci Code*. Broadcast Apr. 22 on Channel 4.

3136 April 20, 2005
Terry Jones attends the London premiere of *The Hitchhiker's Guide to the Galaxy*, the film version of Douglas Adams' sci-fi comedy.

3137 April 24, 2005
Eric Idle appears at the 10th annual Los Angeles Times Festival of Books on the UCLA campus where he discusses his new book *The Greedy Bastard Diary*.

3138 April 25, 2005
Animation Nation (TV episode: BBC4). "Something to Say." Part two of a three-part documentary series on the history of British animation. **Terry Gilliam** discusses his work on *Flying Circus*. Also with Bob Godfrey, Gerald Scarfe, and others.

3139 April 26, 2005
Monty Python's Graham Chapman: Looks Like a Brown Trouser Job (DVD: Rykodisc). Recording of **Graham Chapman**'s comedy lecture from his 1988 college tour of the U.S., videotaped under his supervision. Extras include outtakes, interviews, a "Chapmanography," and the Iron Maiden music video for "Can I Play with Madness?" (featuring **Chapman**) from 1988.

3140 April 27, 2005
60 Minutes (TV news show: CBS). In the segment, "A Good Time for Silly," Charlie Rose reports on the Broadway success of *Spamalot*, interviewing **Eric Idle**, Mike Nichols, Tim Curry, David Hyde Pierce, Hank Azaria, and Sara Ramirez. Produced by Elliot Kirschner.

3141 April 27, 2005
Jimmy Kimmel Live! (TV talk show: ABC). Guests: **Eric Idle**, Kevin Nealon, John McEuen, and New Order.

3142 April 30, 2005
The Times (London) (Newspaper/U.K.). "I Could No More Stop Travelling Than I Could Stop Drawing Breath," by **Michael Palin**, p. 2. **Palin** dispels the rumors that he is giving up his TV traveling career.

3143 May 2005
Michael Palin attends the opening of The Watermill, a bookshop-gallery-coffee shop in Aberfeldy, Scotland.

3144 May 3, 2005

Spamalot (CD: Decca Broadway B0004265-02). Original cast recording of **Eric Idle** & John Du Prez's hit Broadway musical. Songs: "Finland/Fisch Schlapping Song," "Come with Me," "The Song That Goes Like This," "All for One," "Knights of the Round Table," "Find Your Grail," "Run Away," "Always Look on the Bright Side of Life," "Brave Sir Robin," "You Won't Succeed on Broadway," "The Diva's Lament (What Happened to My Part?)," "Where Are You?," "His Name Is Lancelot," and "I'm All Alone." Produced by John Du Prez and **Eric Idle**. Recorded Feb. 7 at Right Track Studios in New York City.

Awards: Grammy-winner for Best Musical Show Album (Du Prez and **Idle**).

3145 May 5, 2005

Monty Python's Flying Circus is inducted in the Rose d'Or Hall of Fame at the 45th Rose d'Or (Golden Rose) International Television Festival (May 3–8). **Terry Jones** attends the Hall of Fame ceremony in Lucerne, Switzerland. The show previously won the Silver Rose (1971) and the group itself received the Honorary Rose d'Or at the 1995 festival.

3146 May 10, 2005

Eric Idle's *Spamalot* receives 14 Tony Award nominations, more than any other Broadway show this season. The awards are given out on June 5 in New York City.

3147 May 13, 2005

The 71st Annual Drama League Awards (Award ceremony). **Eric Idle** presents *Spamalot* director Mike Nichols with the Julia Hansen Award for Excellence in Directing. The gala luncheon, hosted by Cherry Jones, is held at the Marriott Marquis Hotel in New York City.

3148 May 15, 2005

For the Roundhouse (Event). **Michael Palin** introduces writer-comedian Alan Bennett (*A Private Function*), who reads from his works and answers questions from the audience. The event, held at the Prince of Wales Theatre, is a fundraiser aiding the renovation of the Roundhouse, a landmark venue in North London.

3149 May 20–21, 2005

John Cleese is a special guest at the "Cooking for Solutions 2005" event sponsored by the Monterey Bay Aquarium. As part of the event **Cleese** presents (with John Ash) a "Wine and **Cleese**" tour of Monterey Bay farms and wineries (May 21).

3150 Summer 2005

The Pythons film new comedy material for a six-episode series titled *Monty Python's Personal Best* in which each member presents their favorite sketches from *Monty Python's Flying Circus*. Filming locations include the Hollywood Bowl in Los Angeles and Teddington Lock in London (where "The Fish-Slapping Dance" was filmed in 1971). The **Eric Idle** and **Michael Palin** episodes will be released on DVD in Aug. The entire series will air on PBS (and released on DVD) in February 2006.

3151 June 5, 2005

The 59th Annual Tony Awards (Award ceremony). **Eric Idle** (and wife) attends the ceremony at Radio City Music Hall in New York City where his musical *Spamalot* is nominated for 14 Tonys. The show wins in three categories: Best Featured Actress in a Musical (Sara Ramirez), Best Direction of a Musical (Mike Nichols), and Best Musical. Also, the *Spamalot* cast performs "Find Your Grail." Broadcast live on CBS.

3152 June 7, 2005

Late Night with Conan O'Brien (TV talk show: NBC). Guests: **Michael Palin**, promoting *Himalaya*, Cedric the Entertainer, and Better Than Ezra. **Palin** talks about his Himalayan Sherpa guide, also eating yak and meeting the Dalai Lama.

3153 June 9–15, 2005

John Cleese and his wife, Alyce Faye, are guest-speakers on the Queen Mary 2 during the ocean liner's transatlantic voyage from New York to Southampton, England.

3154 June 12, 2005

The Sunday Times (London) (Newspaper/U.K.). "On the Whole I Prefer to Drive Spam," by Mark Anstead, p. 3 (sect. 9). Interview with **Terry Jones** about what he drives (a Subaru Legacy) and his first car (a Morris Minor).

3155 June 17, 2005

Himalaya, the book of the series by **Michael Palin**, is published in the U.S. by Thomas Dunne Books.

3156 June 20, 2005

Michael Palin's 2004 travel series, *Himalaya*, begins airing in the U.S. on the Travel Channel.

3157 June 24, 2005

Friday Night with Jonathan Ross (TV talk show: BBC1). Guests: **Michael Palin**, Jennifer Connelly, Nigel Harman, and Moby.

3158 June 25, 2005
Michael Palin talks about his travels at the 2nd annual Borders Book Festival (June 23–26) in Melrose, Scotland.

3159 June 30, 2005
Michael Palin gives a talk at the Museum of Photography, Film and Television in Bradford, Yorkshire, England.

3160 July 1, 2005
Outside Magazine (Magazine/U.S.). "He's Not Dead Yet," by David Rakoff. Interview with **Michael Palin** about his new series *Himalaya*.

3161 July 10, 2005
Terry Gilliam attends the 3rd Annual Ischia Global Film & Music Fest (July 10–15) on the Isle of Ischia, Gulf of Naples, Italy.

3162 July 12, 2005
Unfaithfully Yours (DVD: Criterion). DVD release of the 1948 Preston Sturges comedy starring Rex Harrison with bonus features that include a new 14-minute introduction by Sturges fan **Terry Jones**.

3163 July 14, 2005
Michael Palin and the Mystery of Hammershøi (TV special: BBC1). Hour-long documentary special, hosted by **Michael Palin**, exploring the life and work of Danish painter Vilhelm Hammershøi (1864–1916). **Palin**'s quest to learn more about the enigmatic artist takes him to London, Holland, and Copenhagen. Directed by Eleanor Yule. Produced by Mhairi McNeill.
Awards: BAFTA-nominated for Best Photography Factual (Neville Kidd).

3164 July 19, 2005
Michael Palin's *Himalaya* series is released on DVD by BBC Video.

3165 July 26, 2005
Episodes of the pre–Python TV series *At Last the 1948 Show* (with **John Cleese** and **Graham Chapman**) and *Do Not Adjust Your Set* (with **Eric Idle**, **Terry Jones** and **Michael Palin**) are released on DVD for the first time, in the U.S. (Tango Entertainment) and U.K. (Boulevard Entertainment). Extras include an interview with **Jones**.

3166 July 30, 2005
The Archive Hour (Radio show: BBC Radio 4). Tribute to veteran broadcaster Alan Whicker, with contributions from **Michael Palin**, Michael Parkinson, Jan Morris, Antony Jay, and Michael Grade.

3167 August 2005
Calcium Made Interesting: Sketches, Letters, Essays & Gondolas (Book: Sidgwick & Jackson), written by **Graham Chapman** and edited by Jim Yoakum, is published in the U.K. Collection of previously-unpublished material written or co-written by **Graham Chapman**, compiled by Yoakum, curator of **Chapman**'s archives. Items include sketches, essays, teleplays, letters, and transcripts of **Chapman**'s comedy lectures. Yoakum previously edited 1997's *Graham Crackers* and 1999's *Ojril: The Completely Incomplete Graham Chapman*. Published in paperback by Pan Books (2006).

3168 August 2005
John Cleese undergoes surgery to remove a portion of his colon due to diverticulitis (a digestive ailment). **Cleese** announces that he plans to auction off the removed part, with proceeds to be divided between himself and the surgeon.

3169 August 8, 2005
Terry Gilliam attends the Los Angeles premiere of his film *The Brothers Grimm* at the DGA Theatre.

3170 August 9, 2005
The Piano Tuner of Earthquakes (Feature film) premieres at the Locarno Film Festival in Switzerland. **Terry Gilliam** executive produced this dark fantasy, the second live-action feature from the Quay Brothers (twins Stephen and Timothy), best known for their animated shorts.

3171 August 10, 2005
Terry Gilliam participates in a Q&A with film critic Joel Siegel at the Learning Annex in New York City following a preview screening of his film *The Brothers Grimm*.

3172 August 11, 2005
Here's Your Obituary (TV episode: ITV1 Wales). "**Terry Jones**." **Jones** is interviewed by Hywel Williams, with contributions from **Michael Palin**, John Goldstone, Robert Hewison, Alan Ereira, and Richard Rampton. Produced & directed by Ian Michael Jones.

3173 August 12, 2005
Terry Gilliam attends the 58th Locarno International Film Festival (Aug. 3–13) in Locarno, Switzerland, where he is awarded the Leopard of Honor for his work in film.

3174 August 13, 2005
The Times (London) (Newspaper/U.K.). "Here Be

Wonders," by **Michael Palin**, pp. 12–13 (Books). **Palin** pays tribute to the explorers who inspired him. Extracted from **Palin**'s introduction to *The Explorer's Eye*, out Aug. 25.

3175 August 14, 2005
The Sunday Times: Culture (London) (Newspaper/U.K.). "This is Not a Dead Python," by Jasper Gerard, p. 5 (sect. 5). Interview with **Terry Jones**.

3176 August 21, 2005
The Sunday Times (London) (Newspaper/U.K.). "Crikey! What's That **Terry Gilliam** Gone and Done to The Brothers Grimm, asks Neil Norman," pp. 4–5 (Culture). Interview with **Terry Gilliam** about his new film *The Brothers Grimm*.

3177 August 25, 2005
The Explorer's Eye: First-Hand Accounts of Adventure & Exploration (Book: Weidenfeld & Nicolson), edited by Fergus Fleming and Annabel Merullo, is published in the U.K. Introduction by **Michael Palin**. Published in the U.S. by The Overlook Press (October 2005).

3178 August 26, 2005
The Brothers Grimm (Feature film: Miramax/Dimension Films) opens in the U.S. Comedy-fantasy from **Terry Gilliam** starring Matt Damon and Heath Ledger as Wilhelm and Jacob Grimm, two traveling con-artists in 19th-century Germany who earn their living by ridding villages of evil spirits produced by their own fakery. Their fortunes change, however, when they encounter real supernatural forces in a haunted wood. Filmed in 2003. **Gilliam**'s struggles on *Grimm*—in particular, his differences with Dimension Films head Bob Weinstein—are chronicled in the book *Dreams and Nightmares*, published in November 2005. A delay in the film's release gave **Gilliam** time off to film his next project, *Tideland*. Also starring Monica Bellucci, Jonathan Pryce, Lena Headey, and Peter Stormare. Written by Ehren Kruger. Directed by **Terry Gilliam**. Produced by Charles Roven and Daniel Bobker.
Reviews: Roger Ebert (*Chicago Sun-Times*, Aug. 26, 2005): "...*Grimm* is a work of limitless invention, but it is invention without pattern ... the movie, for all of its fantastic striving, stays on the screen and fails to engage our imagination"; James Christopher (*The Times* [London], Nov. 1, 2005): "*The Brothers Grimm* splutters more than it sparkles, the stars shift uneasily in their boots and you need an ice pick and a Sherpa to negotiate the baffling plot"; Peter Bradshaw (*The Guardian*, Nov. 3, 2005): "...frantic and bombastic, like a multicoloured fairground ride that offers everything but enjoyment."

3179 August 26, 2005
Entertainment Weekly (Magazine/U.S.). "Grimm Tidings." Gillian Flynn interviews **Terry Gilliam** about his latest film *The Brothers Grimm*.

3180 August 27, 2005
Eric Idle attends the annual Lonach Gathering and Games in Strathdon, Aberdeenshire, Scotland, along with Billy Connolly, Eddie Izzard, Brian Cox, Steve Buscemi, and Anna Friel.

3181 August 30, 2005
Monty Python's Flying Circus: Eric Idle's Personal Best (DVD: A&E Home Video). Compilation of Python sketches selected and presented by **Eric Idle** from the Hollywood Bowl. Playing his rain-coated interviewer character, **Idle** talks to his mother (**Idle**), his gynecologist (voice of **Idle**), and Nazi fugitive Otto Rumsfeld (**Idle**). Sketches selected are: "The Holzfäller Song (Lumberjack Song)" (bit), "Sit on My Face," "The Refreshment Room at Bletchley," "The Poet McTeagle" (bit), "World Forum," "Children's Interview," "Nudge, Nudge," "Silly Olympics," "International Philosophy," "Blood, Devastation, Death, War, and Horror (Anagrams)," "Mount Everest (Hairdresser Expedition)," "Travel Agent," "Never Be Rude to an Arab," "Face the Press," "Hermits," "Storytime," "How to Do It," "Camp Army Drills," "Bruces," "Jockey Interviews/Queen Victoria Handicap," "The Money Programme," "Sviatoslav Richter and Rita," "The Judges," "Climbing the Uxbridge Road," "Whicker Island," and "The Lumberjack Song." Written by **Eric Idle**. The show will air on PBS in February 2006 as part of the series *Monty Python's Personal Best*.

3182 August 30, 2005
Monty Python's Flying Circus: Michael Palin's Personal Best (DVD: A&E Home Video). Compilation of Python sketches selected and presented by **Michael Palin** from Teddington Lock in London (where "The Fish-Slapping Dance" was filmed in March 1971). **Palin**'s selections are: "French Lecture on Sheep-Aircraft," "Hungarian Phrase Book," "A Duck, a Cat, and a Lizard (discussion)," "Come Back to My Place," "It's the Arts: Johann Gambolputty ... of Ulm," "David and the Fig Leaf [anim]," "The Chemist Sketch," "Words Not to Be Used Again," "Wishes (Schoolboys/Businessmen Interview)," "Ethel the Frog: The Piranha Brothers,"

"Hearses Racing," "Sexual Athletes [anim]," "Blackmail," "Psychiatrist [anim]," "The Semaphore Version of Wuthering Heights/Julius Caesar on an Aldis Lamp," "A Man with a Tape Recorder Up His Nose," "Leaving the Army," "A Man with a Tape Recorder Up His Brother's Nose," "The Architect Sketch," "A Scotsman on a Horse," "Mosquito Hunters," "Conrad Poohs and His Dancing Teeth," "Wife-Swapping," "Post Box Ceremony (Mr. Neutron)," "Cheese Shop," and "The Fish-Slapping Dance." Written by **Michael Palin**. The show will air on PBS in March 2006 as part of the series *Monty Python's Personal Best*.

3183 September–November 2005
Orange "Gold Spot" (Cinema commercial). **John Cleese** pitches his idea for a war movie to the Orange Film Funding Board. Orange "Gold Spots," shown in U.K. theatres before the feature, are designed to encourage cinema-goers to turn off their mobile phones. Written by Yan Elliott. Directed by Bryan Buckley. Agency: Mother, London.

3184 September 2005
Terry Gilliam attends the 62nd Venice International Film Festival (Aug. 31–Sept. 10) in Venice, Italy where his film *The Brothers Grimm* is being screened (Sept. 4).

3185 September 2005
Intel Centrino ("Entertainment in Your Lap") (TV commercial). **John Cleese** sits on a commuter's lap drinking tea in this TV ad for Intel Centrino mobile technology for laptops. Other celebrity lap-sitters featured in the ad campaign include Tony Hawk, Seal, and Lucy Liu. Agency: McCann-Erickson, New York.

3186 September 9, 2005
Tideland (Feature film), world premiere in Toronto. **Terry Gilliam**'s follow-up to *The Brothers Grimm* (which was released in August after a long delay) is a dark fantasy about a lonely young girl who, neglected by her drug-addicted father, escapes into her imagination. The film, described by **Gilliam** as "a cross between *Alice in Wonderland* and *Psycho*," is met with a mixed critical reaction and spends the next year unable to find a distributor. Starring Jodelle Ferland, Jeff Bridges, Janet McTeer, Brendan Fletcher, and Jennifer Tilly. Written by **Terry Gilliam** and Tony Grisoni, adapted from a story by Mitch Cullin. Directed by **Terry Gilliam**. Produced by Gabriella Martinelli and Jeremy Thomas. Opens in Britain in August 2006, then in selected U.S. theaters in October 2006. Released on DVD on Feb. 27, 2007.
Reviews: J. Hoberman (*The Village Voice*, Sept. 13, 2005): "...almost unwatchable, not altogether unadmirable, and certainly unreleasable..."; Wendy Ide (*The Times* [London], Aug. 10, 2006): "...**Gilliam** is always a fascinating director, and his latest work is among his boldest. Just don't expect an easy ride"; A. O. Scott (*The New York Times*, Oct. 13, 2006): "After a while I started to envy him [Jeff Bridges' character], since duty required me to stay alive and awake for two hours during which misery masqueraded as whimsy and vice versa."

3187 September 9, 2005
Terry Gilliam attends the world premiere of *Tideland* at the Elgin Theatre in Toronto, Canada, as part of the 30th annual Toronto International Film Festival (Sept. 8–17).

3188 September 12, 2005
Michael Palin launches the new Belsize Walk in the London borough of Camden. The walk links Primrose Hill with Parliament Hill.

3189 September 17–19, 2005
Terry Gilliam attends the 11th Lund International Fantastic Film Festival (Sept. 16–25) in Lund, Sweden where he receives the Finn the Giant Award for lifetime achievement and takes part in a Q&A following a screening (on the 18th) of *The Brothers Grimm*.

3190 September 18, 2005
John Cleese is given a silver star on the new Avenue of the Stars, Britain's version of the Hollywood Walk of Fame, located in London. **Cleese** and fellow honoree Ricky Gervais appear together on video (from California) for the opening ceremony in Covent Garden, which airs on ITV.

3191 September 18, 2005
The South Bank Show (TV special: ITV/LWT). "Eric Sykes." Host Melvyn Bragg interviews comedian Eric Sykes about his career. Also appearing are **Michael Palin**, Ken Dodd, Peter Hall, Denis Norden, and others. Produced & directed by Aurora Gunn.

3192 September 19, 2005
Mark Lawson Talks to... (TV talk show: BBC4). "**Michael Palin**." Mark Lawson interviews **Palin** on a wide range of topics (his father, stammering, niceness, religion, Shrewsbury School, Python, etc.) in this hour-long program. Produced & directed by Andrew Thomas. Part of BBC4's "**Palin**

Night," the program is followed by episodes of *Ripping Yarns*, *Himalaya*, etc.

3193 September 20, 2005

What Did ITV Do for Me? (TV special: ITV). Two-hour documentary special celebrating the 50th anniversary of the ITV television channel. Includes appearances by Roger Moore, David Jason, **Michael Palin**, Bruce Forsyth, Chris Tarrant, and others. Narrated by Samantha Bond. Directed by John Kaye Cooper.

3194 September 20, 2005

Terry Gilliam's *Tideland* has its European premiere at the 53rd annual San Sebastian International Film Festival (Sept. 15–24) in Spain, attended by **Gilliam**. Despite a mixed audience reaction (there are many walkouts), the film is awarded the FIPRESCI prize.

3195 September 23, 2005

The "10¾ Anniversary Edition" of *Lady Cottington's Pressed Fairy Book* (1994), by **Terry Jones** and illustrator Brian Froud, is published in the U.K. by Pavilion Books (London). The book includes a new introduction by **Jones** and Froud and a bonus DVD which features a never-before-seen interview with Lady Angelica Cottington (**Jones**). Published in the U.S. in October by Harry N. Abrams Inc. (New York).

3196 September 25, 2005

Michael Palin gives a talk on his life and travels at the Lyceum Theatre in his home tome of Sheffield, England.

3197 September 27 2005

The Complete Monty Python's Flying Circus 16-Ton Megaset (DVD: A&E Home Video). Reissue of the 14-disc set, originally released in 2000, with two bonus discs titled *Monty Python Live!*, containing *Monty Python Live at the Hollywood Bowl* (1982 film), *Live at Aspen* (1998 HBO special), *Parrot Sketch Not Included: Twenty Years of Monty Python* (1989 doc), and *Monty Python's Fliegender Zirkus* (first German special).

3198 September 28, 2005

The Paul O'Grady Show (TV talk show: ITV/Granada). Guests: Jerry Hall, Kelvin Fletcher, and **Terry Jones**. **Jones**, promoting his new BBC doc *The Story of 1*, also talks about writing children's stories, Rupert Bear, and Python.

3199 September 28, 2005

The Story of 1 (TV special: BBC1). Documentary revealing the story behind the world's simplest number. Hosted by **Terry Jones**, who visits Rome, Egypt, Sumeria, Greece, India, and Bletchley. With contributions from mathematician Marcus du Sautoy. Written by Alan Ereira, Nick Murphy and Jasper James. Produced & directed by Nick Murphy. Airs in the U.S. in March 2007 on PBS.

3200 October 2005

The Life of Graham: The Authorised Biography of Graham Chapman (Book: Orion), written by Bob McCabe, is published in the U.K. Biography of the late **Graham Chapman**, written with the full co-operation of **Chapman**'s partner, David Sherlock, and the Pythons. McCabe previously penned the **Terry Gilliam** bio *Dark Knights & Holy Fools* (1999) and edited *The Pythons: Autobiography by The Pythons* (2003).

3201 October 2, 2005

The Sunday Telegraph (Newspaper/U.K.). "Python with the Last Laugh," by Catherine Shoard. Interview with **Eric Idle** on the success of *Spamalot*.

3202 October 9, 2005

The 50 Greatest Documentaries (TV special: Channel 4). Countdown of the top 50 television documentaries — as voted on by a panel of documentary filmmakers — with **Michael Palin**'s *Around the World in 80 Days* coming in at No. 27. Interviewees include **Palin**, David Attenborough, Morgan Spurlock, and Michael Apted. Narrated by Zoë Wanamaker.

3203 October 15, 2005

The Times (London) (Newspaper/U.K.). "A Chinese Epic: If It's Monday It Must Be Inner Mongolia," by **Michael Palin** with photographs by Basil Pao, pp. 4–8 (Travel). **Palin**'s account — exclusive to *The Times* — of his visit to China with his friend, photographer Basil Pao. **Palin** describes their stay in the cities of Hailar and Manzhouli in Inner Mongolia.

3204 October 19, 2005

Eric Idle and his daughter Lily attend a gala screening of George Harrison's *The Concert for Bangladesh* at Warner Bros. Studios in Burbank, CA, celebrating the release of the film on DVD.

3205 October 23, 2005

The 8th Annual Mark Twain Prize (Award ceremony). **Eric Idle** appears at the ceremony, held at Washington, D.C.'s Kennedy Center, honoring recipient Steve Martin. The ceremony is broadcast Nov. 9 on PBS.

3206 October 27, 2005
The Frank Skinner Show (TV talk show: ITV1). Guests: **Terry Gilliam**, promoting *The Brothers Grimm*, George Galloway, and Zoe Ball.

3207 October 31, 2005
Simon Mayo (Radio talk show: BBC Radio 5 Live). Guest: **Terry Gilliam**, promoting *The Brothers Grimm*.

3208 October 31, 2005
Film 2005 with Jonathan Ross (TV talk show: BBC1). Guest: **Terry Gilliam**, promoting *The Brothers Grimm*.

3209 October 31, 2005
The Brothers Grimm, directed by **Terry Gilliam**, premieres in London at the Odeon West End, Leicester Square as part of The Times BFI 49th London Film Festival (Oct. 19–Nov. 3). The Sky Movies gala screening is attended by **Gilliam**, **Michael Palin**, **Terry Jones**, Jonathan Pryce, and others.

3210 October 31, 2005
John Cleese holds a press conference at the Hilton Hotel in Auckland, New Zealand, to promote the upcoming NZ tour of his one-man stage show.

3211 November 2005
The Power of the Sun (Documentary). University of California documentary on solar energy, presented by Nobel Laureates Alan Heeger and Walter Kohn. Hosted & narrated by **John Cleese**. Written by John Perlin and David Kennard.

3212 November 1, 2005
The Times Screen Talk (Event). **Terry Gilliam** talks to Andrew Collins about his career and latest film, *The Brothers Grimm*, at the National Film Theatre as part of the London Film Festival.

3213 November 2, 2005
BBC Breakfast (TV news show: BBC1). Hosted by Bill Turnbull and Sian Williams. Guest: **Terry Gilliam**, promoting *The Brothers Grimm*.

3214 November 3, 2005
Terry Gilliam attends the 19th Leeds International Film Festival in Leeds, England where his new film, *The Brothers Grimm*, is being screened.

3215 November 3, 2005
Terry Jones and **Michael Palin** attend a launch party for cartoonist Gerald Scarfe's new book *Drawing Blood: Forty-Five Years of Scarfe Uncensored* at the Fine Art Society in London.

3216 November 4, 2005
The Brothers Grimm, directed by **Terry Gilliam**, opens in the U.K.

3217 November 6, 2005
Forty Years Without a Proper Job (Lecture). **Michael Palin** gives a talk at London's Prince of Wales Theatre in aid of the Peter Cook Foundation, a charity for mentally-ill children. The talk includes a reading of his comedy piece "Biggles Goes to See Bruce Springsteen." Followed by a Q&A session.

3218 November 7–December 9, 2005
John Cleese — His Life, Times and Current Medical Problems (Stage show). **John Cleese** tours New Zealand with his one-man stage show. The show, directed by Bille Brown, also features appearances by **Cleese**'s 22-year-old daughter/co-writer, Camilla, and actor Jay Bunyan. **Cleese** performs 22 shows in eight cities: Civic Theatre in Invercargill (Nov. 7), Isaac Theatre Royal in Christchurch (Nov. 10–14), Regent Theatre in Dunedin (Nov. 18–19), Opera House in Wellington (Nov. 21–24), Regent on Broadway in Palmerston North (Nov. 26), Municipal Theatre in Napier (Nov. 28–30), Town Hall in Auckland (Dec. 3–7), and TSB Theatre Showplace in New Plymouth (Dec. 9). **Cleese** then takes the tour to California (January–March 2006).

3219 November 7, 2005
Dreams and Nightmares: Terry Gilliam, The Brothers Grimm & Other Cautionary Tales of Hollywood (Book: HarperCollins), written by Bob McCabe, is published. Chronicle of the troubled pre-production and filming of **Terry Gilliam**'s 2005 film *The Brothers Grimm*, told through McCabe's on-set diary accounts and interviews with **Gilliam** and others.

3220 November 10, 2005
Michael Palin speaks at the Environmentally Friendly Vehicles Conference held at the National Motorcycle Museum in Birmingham, England. Organized by the Department for Transport.

3221 November 14, 2005
John Peel's Record Box (TV special: Channel 4). Documentary revealing the favorite records of the late English DJ John Peel (1939–2004), which he kept in a special box. **Michael Palin**, Peel's schoolmate at Shrewsbury School, is among the interviewees. Narrated by Nemone. Directed by Elaine Shepherd.

3222 November 17, 2005
The TV comedy special *Earth to America!*, fea-

turing a performance by **Eric Idle**, is taped at The Colosseum at Caesars Palace in Las Vegas for airing Nov. 20 on TBS.

3223 November 20, 2005
Earth to America! (TV special: TBS). Two-hour comedy special celebrating our planet and raising awareness of global warming. **Eric Idle**, Tom Hanks, and Steve Martin appear together onstage as The Too-Warm Trio, performing Martin's bluegrass number "Tin Roof" and **Idle**'s "Galaxy Song." Taped Nov. 17 at The Colosseum at Caesars Palace in Las Vegas.

3224 November 27, 2005
An Evening with Michael Palin (Lecture). **Michael Palin** gives a talk on his *Himalaya* adventure at the Palace Theatre in London, in aid of the Medical Foundation for the Care of Victims of Torture.

3225 December 8, 2005
The Grammy nominations are announced by the Recording Academy and the *Spamalot* cast recording is among the five nominees for Best Musical Show Album.

3226 December 20, 2005
The Brothers Grimm (DVD: Dimension Home Video). **Terry Gilliam**'s 2005 fantasy-adventure. Special features include audio commentary by **Gilliam**, the making-of featurette *Bringing the Fairy Tale to Life*, and deleted scenes (with optional commentary by **Gilliam**).

3227 2005
John Cleese co-writes — with Kirk DeMicco (*Quest for Camelot*) — the screenplay for *Crood Awakening*, an animated comedy set during the Stone Age. The film is intended to be a co-production between DreamWorks and Britain's Aardman Animation studio. When the two studios end their partnership in 2007, DreamWorks gives the film to writer-director Chris Sanders, who re-writes the script with DeMicco. The film is ultimately released as *The Croods* in March 2013 with **Cleese** receiving a story credit. Note: **Cleese** and DeMicco previously collaborated (in 2003) on a screen adaptation of Roald Dahl's *The Twits*.

3228 2005
Researchers at the University of Zurich in Switzerland name a newly-discovered (in 1990) species of woolly lemur — avahi cleesei — after **John Cleese** in honor of his efforts in bringing attention to the plight of the endangered primate (**Cleese** hosted the 1998 documentary *Born to Be Wild: Operation Lemur with John Cleese*).

3229 2005
Shrek: Totally Tangled Tales (DVD game: b EQUAL/DreamWorks). Interactive family trivia game based on the *Shrek* films. **John Cleese**, reprising his role as King Harold, hosts.

3230 January 1, 2006
The Sunday Times (London) (Newspaper/U.K.). "The World Tells Us to Take the Train," by **Michael Palin**, p. 2 (sect. 4). Extracted from **Palin**'s speech at the Environmentally Friendly Vehicles Conference in November 2005.

3231 January 1, 2006
The 50 Greatest Comedy Films (TV special: Channel 4). Countdown of the 50 greatest film comedies, as voted on by viewers. Making the top ten are *Life of Brian* (at No. 1) and *Holy Grail* (No. 6). Also on the list: *A Fish Called Wanda* (No. 23). Hosted by Stephen Fry, with comments from **Michael Palin**, **Terry Gilliam**, others.

3232 January 7, 2006
An Intimate Evening with John Cleese (Event). **John Cleese** appears at the ANZ Conservation Theatre at the Taronga Zoo in Sydney, Australia. The event raises money for the Taronga Foundation which helps endangered wildlife.

3233 January 27–March 25, 2006
Seven Ways to Skin an Ocelot (Stage show). **John Cleese** tours California (and Arizona) with his one-man stage show. **Cleese** launched the tour, formerly titled *John Cleese—His Life, Times and Current Medical Problems*, in New Zealand in November–December 2005. The show is co-written by his daughter Camilla and directed by Bill Brown. Venues: University of California Santa Barbara's Campbell Hall (Jan. 27–30), Humboldt State University's Van Duzer Theatre in Arcata (Feb. 2), California State University Chico's Laxson Auditorium (Feb. 4), UC Berkeley's Zellerbach Hall in Berkeley (Feb. 8 & 9), Sunset Center in Carmel (Feb. 11), CA Polytechnic State University's Cohan Center in San Luis Obispo (Feb. 12), Pepperdine University's Smothers Theatre in Malibu (Feb. 14), Mandeville Auditorium, UCSD in La Jolla (Mar. 7), Scottsdale Center's Piper Theater in Scottsdale, AZ (Mar. 10 & 11), UCLA's Royce Hall in Los Angeles (Mar. 18), and CA State Long Beach's Carpenter Center in Long Beach (Mar. 24 & 25).

3234 February 4, 2006
Who Is Harry Nilsson (and Why Is Everybody Talkin' About Him?) (Feature film) premieres at the Santa Barbara International Film Festival. Documentary on the life and career of singer-songwriter Harry Nilsson (1941–1994). Includes interviews with **Terry Gilliam**, **Eric Idle** (who also sings "Harry"), Randy Newman, Ringo Starr, Robin Williams, Micky Dolenz, and many others. Written & directed by John Scheinfeld (*The Unknown Peter Sellers*). Opens in New York City on Sept. 10, 2010 (released by Lorber Films). Note: Nilsson, a drinking companion of **Graham Chapman**'s in the 1970s, recorded **Idle**'s "Always Look on the Bright Side of Life" for his 1980 album *Flash Harry*.

3235 February 7, 2006
Medieval Misconceptions (Lecture). **Terry Jones** gives a talk at the Museum of London as part of the "Medieval London" gallery (which opened Nov. 25, 2005). In his lecture, **Jones** makes the case that medieval society was more sophisticated and technologically advanced than previously believed.

3236 February 7, 2006
Man About Town (Feature film: Media 8 Ent.) premieres at the Santa Barbara International Film Festival. Comedy-drama starring Ben Affleck as a successful Hollywood agent reassessing the priorities in his life. **John Cleese** plays Dr. Primkin, the teacher of Affleck's journal-writing class. Also starring Rebecca Romijn, Bai Ling, and Mike Binder. Written & directed by Mike Binder.

3237 February 7, 2006
John Cleese and his wife attend the Santa Barbara International Film Festival.

3238 February 21, 2006
Eric Idle appears at a press event outside the Palace Theatre in London launching the first day of ticket sales for *Spamalot*, which is coming to the Palace Theatre in October.

3239 February 22–March 8, 2006
The six-part series *Monty Python's Personal Best* airs on PBS. Five of these hour-long episodes feature one of the Pythons presenting a compilation of their best moments from Python on TV and film. The sixth, featuring the best of the late **Graham Chapman**, was compiled by the surviving Pythons. The series, produced by John Goldstone, was filmed in the Summer of 2005 in Hollywood (**Idle**), London (**Palin**), Santa Barbara (**Cleese**), and other locations. Four of the shows (**Chapman**, **Cleese**, **Gilliam**, **Jones**) are released on DVD (A&E Home Video) on Feb. 28. The **Palin** and **Idle** shows were released on DVD in August 2005.

3240 February 22, 2006
Monty Python's Personal Best (TV episode: PBS). "**Eric Idle**'s Personal Best." Originally released on DVD in August 2005.

3241 February 22, 2006
Monty Python's Personal Best (TV episode: PBS). "**Graham Chapman**'s Personal Best." Collection of some of **Chapman**'s best sketches, with reminiscences from the surviving Pythons. Sketches selected are: "Colonel (Silly)," "Raymond Luxury-Yacht (Plastic Surgery)," "Agatha Christie Sketch (Inspector Tiger)," "It's the Arts: Sir Edward Ross," "One-Man Wrestling," "Thrust: Miss Anne Elk," "The Fish-Slapping Dance," "The Oscar Wilde Sketch," "Vocational Guidance Counselor," "Mollusks (Live Documentary)," "Ken Shabby," "The Ministry of Silly Walks," "Albatross," "The Pantomime Horse Is a Secret Agent," "The Pet Shop (Dead Parrot)," "Penguin on the TV," "Twentieth-Century Vole (Irving C. Saltzberg)," "Mrs. Premise and Mrs. Conclusion," "Spam," and "Argument Clinic."

3242 February 26, 2006
The Sunday Times: Culture (London) (Newspaper/U.K.). "He Likes to Ham a Lot," by Bryan Appleyard, pp. 6–7. Cover story on **Eric Idle** and *Spamalot*.

3243 March 1, 2006
Monty Python's Personal Best (TV episode: PBS). "**Terry Gilliam**'s Personal Best." **Gilliam**, speaking from his dark basement prison, introduces this compilation of his Python animation. Includes: "Opening titles (3rd series)," "Conrad Poohs and His Dancing Teeth," "The Killer Cars," "Ambulance," "Compere Chasing Mouth/The Fish-Slapping Dance (live-action)/Nazi Fish," "Royal Navy Advert," "Crelm Toothpaste," "Charles Fatless," "Purchase a Past," "Sexual Athletes," "The Prince and the Black Spot," "Powder My Nose/Charwoman," "Baby Carriage/Musical Statue," "What a Lovely Day," "Eggs Diamond," "Hands Up," "Shaving," "Full Frontal Nudity," "Metamorphosis," "No-Time Tolouse," "TV is Bad for Your Eyes/The Good Fairy from Program Control," "The House-Hunters," "Gay Boys in Bondage," and "2001." Written by **Terry Gilliam**. Released on DVD with a 13-minute featurette in which **Gilliam** discusses how he created his cut-out animations.

3244 March 1, 2006

Monty Python's Personal Best (TV episode: PBS). "**John Cleese**'s Personal Best." Dayna Devon interviews a crotchety, 96-year-old **Cleese** at his Santa Barbara ranch. **Cleese**'s selections are: "A Fairy Tale (Happy Valley)," "The Epilogue," "Gumby Brain Surgery," "Self Defense Against Fresh Fruit," "The Exploding Version of 'The Blue Danube,'" "Life or Death Struggles," "Rival Documentaries," "Confuse-A-Cat," "Cheese Shop" (bit), "Raymond Luxury-Yacht Interview," "It's the Arts: Picasso-Cycling Race," "Flying Lessons," "Baby Suction [anim]," "It's Wolfgang Amadeus Mozart: Famous Deaths," "The Batley Townswomens' Guild's Re-enactment of the Battle of Pearl Harbor," "The Fish-Slapping Dance," and "The Upper-Class Twit of the Year." Written by **John Cleese**. Directed by Harry Garvin.

3245 March 2, 2006

Diabolo (Stage show), world premiere at the Noga Hall of the Gesher Theatre in Tel Aviv-Jaffa, Israel. **Terry Gilliam** co-directs this production starring his friend, the celebrated Russian clown Slava Polunin (*Snow Show*). The show runs until March 14. A documentary on the making of the production, titled *Diabolo's Workshop*, is produced in 2009.

3246 March 3, 2006

Michael Palin attends a memorial service for comedian Ronnie Barker (*The Two Ronnies*) at Westminster Abbey in London. Barker died Oct. 3, 2005, at age 76. Other attendees include Ronnie Corbett, Richard Briers, Stephen Fry, David Jason, Donald Sinden, and Terry Wogan.

3247 March 7, 2006

The National Tour of **Eric Idle**'s Broadway musical *Spamalot* begins at The Colonial Theatre in Boston, MA. The tour closes Oct. 18, 2009, in Costa Mesa, CA, after 1,435 performances. The show made its Broadway debut on Mar. 17, 2005.

3248 March 8, 2006

Monty Python's Personal Best (TV episode: PBS). "**Terry Jones**' Personal Best." Hosted by **Jones** who, in his introduction, reveals that it was he who created Monty Python and that the others actually played only minor roles (**Terry Gilliam** was used primarily as a cupboard). **Jones**' selections are: "The Funniest Joke in the World," "Ratcatcher (Killer Sheep)," "The News for Parrots," "Working-Class Playwright," "Housing Project Built by Characters from 19th-Century English Literature," "Mystico and Janet," "Bicycle Repair Man," "The Olympic Hide-and-Seek Final," "Minister for Overseas Development," "The Bishop," "Living Room on Pavement," "Poets in the Home," "The Fish-Slapping Dance," "Clodagh Rodgers (The Cycling Tour)," "The Spanish Inquisition (Comfy Chair)," "Homicidal Barber/The Lumberjack Song," "Up Your Pavement," "RAF Banter," "Trivializing the War," and "Courtmartial (Basingstoke/Special Gaiters/Anything Goes In)." Written by **Terry Jones**.

3249 March 8, 2006

Monty Python's Personal Best (TV episode: PBS). "**Michael Palin**'s Personal Best." Originally released on DVD in August 2005.

3250 March 10, 2006

Michael Palin opens the Davies Alpine House, a new glasshouse at Kew Botanic Gardens in London. The building was designed by architect Wilkinson Eyre.

3251 March 17, 2006

Michael Palin's first grandson, Archie, is born.

3252 March 20, 2006

What I Heard About Iraq (Event). **Terry Jones** participates in a worldwide public reading of Eliot Weinberger's essay at the London Review Bookshop in London.

3253 March 22, 2006

Commemorating *Spamalot*'s first-year anniversary on Broadway, 1,789 fans gather in New York's Shubert Alley to set the Guinness World Record for "World's Largest Coconut Orchestra." Banging two coconut halves together (as the knights in *Spamalot* do to simulate the sound of galloping horses), the fans — led by the *Spamalot* cast — perform the song "Always Look on the Bright Side of Life."

3254 March 25, 2006

Artists and Legends Gala 2006 (Event). **Eric Idle** hosts a charity gala in the Annenberg Theater at the Palm Springs Art Museum in Palm Springs, CA.

3255 March 26, 2006

An Evening with Michael Palin (Lecture). **Michael Palin** gives a talk on his Himalayan journey at the Duke of York's Theatre in London in aid of the Michael Palin Centre for Stammering Children.

3256 April 5, 2006

Enfermés dehors (English: *Locked Out*) (Feature film: UGC Distribution) opens in France. **Terry Jones** and **Terry Gilliam** make cameo appearances in this French comedy starring Albert Dupontel. Written & directed by Albert Dupontel.

3257 April 12, 2006
How Well Do We Know Ourselves? (Lecture). **John Cleese**, A.D. White Professor-at-Large, joins psychology professor David Dunning for a lecture at the Carl Becker House at Cornell University, Ithaca, NY.

3258 April 14, 2006
The Wild (Feature film: Walt Disney Pictures) is released in the U.S. Animated film featuring the song "Really Nice Day," written, produced & performed by **Eric Idle** and John Du Prez. The soundtrack is released on Walt Disney Records.

3259 April 15, 2006
Peter and the Wolf (Concert). **John Cleese** narrates a production of the Sergey Prokofiev work, performed with the Cornell Chamber Orchestra, at the State Theatre in Ithaca, NY. This is **Cleese**'s last public performance as an A.D. White Professor-at-Large at Cornell University, a post he has held since 1998.

3260 April 21, 2006
Eric Idle and composer John Du Prez sign copies of the *Spamalot* CD and **Idle**'s book *The Greedy Bastard Diary* at Borders Book Store on State Street in Chicago.

3261 April 22, 2006
Loose Ends (Radio show: BBC Radio 4). Guest: **Michael Palin**, promoting the Radio 4 adaptation of Gogol's *Dead Souls*.

3262 April 23 & 30, 2006
Classic Serial (Radio drama: BBC Radio 4). "Dead Souls." Two-part adaptation of Nikolai Gogol's satirical 1842 novel, starring **Michael Palin** (as Narrator) and Mark Heap (as Chichikov). Adapted by Dan Rebellato. Produced by Polly Thomas.

3263 April 27, 2006
Terry Jones signs copies of his new book *Terry Jones' Barbarians* at Pace University in New York City.

3264 April 29, 2006
Terry Jones gives a talk on *Barbarians* at the UCLA Hammer Museum in Los Angeles.

3265 May 2006
John Cleese is made Provost's Visiting Professor at Cornell University in Ithaca, NY. The three-year post follows **Cleese**'s previous post at the university, A.D. White Professor-at-Large, which he held from 1998 to 2006.

3266 May 2006
The Idler (Magazine/U.K.). "In Conversation with **Michael Palin**," by Tom Hodgkinson. **Palin** is interviewed at his London office (near Covent Garden).

3267 May 2006
Don't Mention the World Cup (Single), recorded by The First Eleven with **John Cleese**, is released. The World Cup-themed song, written by Dean Whitbread and Ashley Slater, is an appeal for goodwill between English and German football fans. The title was inspired by the line "Don't mention the war" from the "Germans" episode (1975) of *Fawlty Towers*.

3268 May 3, 2006
Terry Jones gives a talk on *Barbarians* in Giffels Auditorium at the University of Arkansas.

3269 May 4, 2006
Terry Gilliam attends the opening of his art installation "Past People of Potsdamer Platz" at the Potsdamer Platz in Berlin, Germany. The installation, which **Gilliam** created in collaboration with several other artists, consists of four headless figures. When a visitor looks into the neck of one of the figures, a photographic image of their face is merged with a face from the past and projected onto the SPOTS light and media facade nearby. The work will be on view until June 8.

3270 May 7, 2006
The Sunday Times (London) (Newspaper/U.K.). "Decline and Fall of the Roman Myth," by **Terry Jones**, p. 2 (sect. 4). **Jones** debunks Roman propaganda that has branded all non–Romans of the ancient world as savage "barbarians."

3271 May 14, 2006
The Sunday Telegraph (Newspaper/U.K.). "What Did the Barbarians Ever Do for Us?" **Terry Jones** (interviewed by Catherine Shoard) talks about some of his favorite Barbarians, also Rupert the Bear and his love of beer.

3272 May 16, 2006–May 4, 2007
Michael Palin's new travel series, *New Europe*, is filmed over a period of five-and-a-half months in 20 countries, including Croatia, Hungary, The Ukraine, and The Czech Republic.

3273 May 18, 2006
Terry Jones' Barbarians (Book: BBC Books), writ-

ten by **Terry Jones** and Alan Ereira, is published. Jones and Ereira present a revealing history of those ancient peoples whom the Romans had written off as uncivilized and barbaric. The authors assert that the Celts, Goths, Persians, and Vandals were more culturally and technologically advanced than Roman propaganda would have us believe. Companion book to the BBC2 TV series. With 24 pages of photos and maps.
Reviews: Publishers Weekly (June 19, 2006): "...readers will go along for a most enjoyable ride and appreciate [**Jones**'] fascinating tale of the barbarians' lost world."

3274 May 19, 2006
The Independent (Newspaper/U.K.). "**Terry Jones**: Blood and Circuses," by Boyd Tonkin. Interview with **Terry Jones** about his upcoming book and TV series *Barbarians*.

3275 May 22, 2006
Start the Week (Radio talk show: BBC Radio 4). Hosted by Andrew Marr. Guests: **Terry Jones**, promoting *Barbarians*, Val Gilbert, Joan Cheever, and Anthony Beevor.

3276 May 24, 2006
Simon Mayo (Radio talk show: BBC Radio 5 Live). Guest: **Terry Jones**, promoting *Barbarians*.

3277 May 24, 2006
The New Paul O'Grady Show (TV talk show: Channel 4). Guests: **Terry Jones**, promoting *Barbarians*, and Laurie Brett.

3278 May 24, 2006
The Brunels' Tunnel (Book: Thomas Telford Ltd), written by Andrew Mathewson, et al., edited by Eric Kentley with a foreword by **Michael Palin**, is published. Story of the 1825–43 construction of the Thames Tunnel undertaken by engineer Marc Brunel and his son, Isambard.

3279 May 25, 2006
Silent Clowns (TV episode: BBC4). "Buster Keaton." British comic Paul Merton profiles silent screen comedian Buster Keaton, with Keaton fan **Terry Jones** commenting on the classic films *Seven Chances* (1925) and *Sherlock Jr.* (1924). First episode in a four-part series. Directed by Tom Cholmondeley.

3280 May 26–June 16, 2006
The four-part documentary series *Terry Jones' Barbarians* airs on BBC2. The series, written & presented by **Terry Jones** and produced by Alan Ereira, takes a fresh look at the Celts, the Goths, the Vandals, and other ancient tribes whom the Romans dismissed as uncivilized and savage. Filming locations include France, Ireland, Romania, and Iran. The companion book, co-authored by Ereira, is published by BBC Books.

3281 May 26, 2006
Terry Jones' Barbarians (TV episode: BBC2). "The Primitive Celts." **Terry Jones** discovers that the "primitive" Celts were more advanced than the Romans in many ways, including road-building, gold-mining, and in their treatment of women. **Jones** visits France, Ireland, and Wales. First episode in the four-part series written & hosted by **Terry Jones**. Produced & directed by Robert Coldstream.

3282 May 26, 2006
The Wright Stuff (TV show: Five). Discussion program hosted by Matthew Wright. **Terry Jones** is a guest panelist.

3283 May 27, 2006
Terry Jones gives a talk on *Barbarians* (his new book and TV series) at the Hay-on-Wye book festival in Wales. **Jones** also screens the "Director's Son's Cut" of his film *Erik the Viking*.

3284 May 28, 2006
Wogan Now and Then (TV talk show: U.K.TV). Hosted by Terry Wogan. Guest: **Terry Jones**, promoting *Barbarians*.

3285 May 30, 2006
John Cleese gives a lecture on creativity at the Oslo Spektrum in Oslo, Norway.

3286 June 2, 2006
Terry Jones' Barbarians (TV episode: BBC2). "The Savage Goths." In this episode, focusing on the "savage" Barbarians of the North, **Terry Jones** looks at the "Romanization" of Germanic hero Hermann (or Arminius, to the Romans), which backfired and led to the slaughter of three Roman legions in the Teutoburg Forest in A.D. 9; the sophistication of Dacian culture and its destruction by the Romans in A.D. 106; and the so-called "Sack of Rome" in A.D. 410 by Alaric, leader of the Goths. **Jones** visits Germany and Romania. Second episode in the four-part series written & hosted by **Terry Jones**. Produced & directed by Robert Coldstream.

3287 June 5, 2006
Terry Jones signs copies of his book *Barbarians* at Waterstone's book shop in Bath, England.

3288 June 6, 2006
Terry Jones gives a talk on *Barbarians* at the Assembly House in Norwich, England.

3289 June 9, 2006
Terry Jones' Barbarians (TV episode: BBC2). "The Brainy Barbarians." **Terry Jones** looks at the enlightened societies of the Persians and the Greeks, whose scientific progress was halted by Roman expansion. This episode examines Archimedes' ingenious inventions used in the defense of the Greek city of Syracuse; Roman general Crassus' ill-fated campaign against the Parthians in 53 B.C.; the military might of the Sassanid Persian Empire; and the discovery of the Antikythera Mechanism, a sophisticated astronomical calculator invented by the Greeks. **Jones** visits Syracuse (in Sicily), Iran, London, and Rhodes. Third episode in the four-part series written & hosted by **Terry Jones**. Produced & directed by David McNab.

3290 June 10, 2006
Eric Idle presents The Del Close Award to comedian Harry Shearer at the 4th Annual Los Angeles Improv Comedy Festival (June 5–10).

3291 June 12, 2006
G.B.H. (DVD: Channel 4). Four-disc set of the 1991 TV series written by Alan Bleasdale and starring Robert Lindsay and **Michael Palin**. Includes audio commentary by Lindsay, **Palin**, and editor Peter Ansorge.

3292 June 15, 2006
Silent Clowns (TV episode: BBC4). "Harold Lloyd." Profile of silent screen comedian Harold Lloyd, presented by Paul Merton, with comments from **Terry Jones**, who had previously appeared in the Buster Keaton episode. Last episode in a four-part series. Produced & directed by Kate Broome.

3293 June 16, 2006
Terry Jones' Barbarians (TV episode: BBC2). "The End of the World." **Terry Jones** looks at the lives of two barbarian leaders — Attila the Hun ("The Scourge of God") and Geiseric, leader of the Vandals — and the roles they played in the destruction of the Roman empire. He also examines the role the Roman Catholic Church played in re-writing history. **Jones** visits Rome, Hungary, and Carthage. Last episode in the four-part series written & hosted by **Terry Jones**. Produced & directed by David Wilson.

3294 June 17, 2006
The Saturday Play (Radio play: BBC Radio 4). "Quartermaine's Terms." **Michael Palin** plays St. John Quartermaine in Simon Gray's 1981 play following the lives and relationships of seven teachers at a Cambridge language school in the 1960s. **Palin**'s first major acting role since 1997's *Fierce Creatures*. Also starring Francesca Faridany, James Fleet, Clive Francis, Andrew Lincoln, David Yelland, and Harriet Walter. Directed by Maria Aitken.

3295 June 21, 2006
L'entente cordiale (Feature film: Warner Bros.) opens in France. French comedy about a former diplomat (Christian Clavier) and his interpreter (Daniel Auteuil) on a secret mission to London. The cast also includes **John Cleese** (as Lord Conrad) and Jennifer Saunders. Written by Fabien Suarez. Directed by Vincent De Brus.

3296 June 27, 2006
The Art of Football (TV special: Sky One). Host **John Cleese**, with comic Tom Konkle, presents the A to Z's of football. Includes interviews with David Stewart, Dennis Hopper, Henry Kissinger, Pelé, Mia Hamm, and Thierry Henry. Shown in the U.S. as *The Art of Soccer*. Written by Chris Langham and Hermann Vaske. Produced & directed by Hermann Vaske. Executive-produced by Bernard Brochand, **John Cleese**, and Nizan Guanaes.

3297 June 30, 2006
Eric Idle and family attend the gala premiere of Cirque du Soleil's Beatle-themed show *Love* at The Mirage Hotel & Casino in Las Vegas. Other attendees include Paul McCartney, Ringo Starr, and Yoko Ono.

3298 July 14, 2006
Michael Palin models an outfit at a presentation of the fashion collection "Demonic Angels, Angelic Demons," by Hungarian designer Katti Zoob, in Budapest, Hungary. **Palin** is in Budapest filming his series *New Europe* (the fashion show appears in Episode 4, first airing Oct. 7, 2007).

3299 July 16, 2006
Radio 4 Appeal (Radio appeal: BBC Radio 4). **John Cleese** delivers a 3-minute appeal on behalf of The British Institute for Brain Injured Children (BIBIC).

3300 July 16, 2006
Eric Idle attends the Toronto premiere of *Spamalot* at The Canon Theatre and appears on stage for the curtain call.

3301 July 16, 2006
Terry Gilliam introduces a screening of his film *Tideland* at the Arts Picturehouse in Cambridge, England on the closing night of the 26th Cambridge Film Festival (July 6–16).

3302 July 21 & 22, 2006
John Cleese appears for the first time at the *Just for Laughs* comedy festival [24th annual] in Montreal. For the July 21st event, *In Conversation with John Cleese*, he participates in an onstage conversation with Ian Hanomansing, followed by an audience Q&A, at Theatre Maisonneuve in Place des Arts. The following night he hosts two galas at the Theatre St. Denis in Montreal. Sketches include "**Cleese** Idol," in which **Cleese** judges a series of **John Cleese** impersonators. Highlights from the festival are later broadcast on CBC television.

3303 July 23, 2006
Mark Lawson Talks to... (TV talk show: BBC4). "**Terry Gilliam**." Mark Lawson interviews **Gilliam** about his life and career in this hour-long program. Directed by Phil Cairney. Produced by Lucie Hass.

3304 August 3, 2006
The Times (London) (Newspaper/U.K.). "Still Swimming Against the Tide," by Wendy Ide, pp. 18–19. Interview with **Terry Gilliam** about his provocative new film *Tideland*.

3305 August 4, 2006
The Daily Telegraph (Newspaper/U.K.). "'I like it when people walk out of my films.'" SF Said interviews **Terry Gilliam** about *Tideland*.

3306 August 5, 2006
Terry Jones gives a talk on *Barbarians* at the Cambridge History Festival (Aug. 3–6) in Cambridge, England.

3307 August 5, 2006
Financial Times (Newspaper/U.K.). "Perfect Weekend: **Terry Gilliam**," p. 50. **Gilliam** writes about some of his favorite London haunts, including Tate Britain (art gallery) and The Wolseley (restaurant).

3308 August 5, 2006
Togas on TV: Visions of Rome (TV special: BBC4). Documentary examining portrayals of Ancient Rome on television. **Terry Jones** comments on past TV historians (Mortimer Wheeler, Kenneth Clark) and on his own series *Barbarians*. Narrated by Mariella Frostrup. Produced & directed by Nick Angel.

3309 August 6, 2006
The Sunday Times Magazine (London) (Magazine/U.K.). "Relative Values: **Terry Gilliam** and His Daughter Amy," pp. 7–9. Beverley D'Silva interviews **Gilliam** and his 29-year-old daughter, Amy, who works as his assistant. Photographs by David Poole.

3310 August 9, 2006
Turn Back Time (TV talk show: BBC2). Hosted by Irish comedian Dara O'Briain. O'Briain's first guest on the series' debut is **Terry Jones**, who looks back on his life and career and ponders what he would do differently if he could "turn back time." Directed by Lissa Evans.

3311 August 11, 2006
Simon Mayo (Radio talk show: BBC Radio 5 Live). Guest-host Phil Williams interviews **Terry Gilliam**.

3312 August 11, 2006
Tideland, directed by **Terry Gilliam**, opens in the U.K.

3313 August 11, 2006
HARDtalk Extra (TV talk show: BBC World). Gavin Esler interviews **Terry Gilliam** about Python, filmmaking, offending people, *Tideland*, etc.

3314 August 12 & 13, 2006
Terry Jones lectures on *Barbarians* at English Heritage's Festival of History at Kelmarsh Hall in Northamptonshire, England.

3315 August 14, 2006
Time Bandits: 25th Anniversary Edition (DVD: Anchor Bay) is released in the U.K. Two-disc edition of **Terry Gilliam**'s 1981 fantasy-comedy. Bonus features include: audio commentary by **Gilliam**, **Michael Palin**, **John Cleese**, and others; two joint interviews with **Gilliam** and co-writer **Palin**, one for the TV show *Clapperboard* from July 1981 (17 mins.), the other more recent (27 mins.); also storyboards, production photos, trailer, etc.

3316 August 19, 2006
Talking Movies (TV show: BBC World News). Hosted by Tom Brook. **Terry Gilliam** talks about his film *Tideland*.

3317 September 4, 2006
EMI Records reissues the Monty Python catalog in the U.K. The eight CDs, all newly-remastered at Abbey Road and Redwood Studios in London, each include a selection of bonus tracks.

3318 September 4, 2006
Another Monty Python Record (CD: EMI Records PYTHCD1) is released in the U.K. Remastered reissue of the Pythons' second album (from 1971), with four bonus tracks: "Treadmill Lager" (alternate version of "Bishop" from *Contractual Obligation Album*), "Bishop at Home (Mr. Stoddard)" (cut from *Contractual*), "Court Room Sketch," and "Undertaker (freelance)."

3319 September 4, 2006
Monty Python's Previous Record (CD: EMI Records PYTHCD2) is released in the U.K. Remastered reissue of the Pythons' third album (from 1972), with twelve bonus tracks: "Baxter's," "Meteorology," "Blood, Devastation, Death, War & Horror (Anagrams)," "The Great Debate (TV4 or Not TV4?)," "Mortuary Visit/Mortuary Hour," "Flying Fox of the Yard," "Is There...Life After Death?," "Teach Yourself Heath" (1972), "The Book Ad," "Big Red Bowl," "Pepperpots," and "Pellagra." The last four tracks are radio ads (from 1971) for *Monty Python's Big Red Book*.

3320 September 4, 2006
The Monty Python Matching Tie and Handkerchief (CD: EMI Records PYTHCD3) is released in the U.K. Remastered reissue of the Pythons' fourth album (from 1973), with four bonus tracks: "Psychopath," "Teleprinter Football Results," "Radio Tuning Radio 4/Radio Time," and "Radio Shop." Released in the U.S. on Arista/Legacy.

3321 September 4, 2006
The Album of the Soundtrack of the Trailer of the Film of Monty Python and the Holy Grail (CD: EMI Records PYTHCD4) is released in the U.K. Remastered reissue of the Pythons' sixth album (from 1975), with three bonus tracks: "Arthur's Song," "**Terry Jones** and **Michael Palin** interview" (from the 2001 doc *The Quest for the Holy Grail Locations*), and "Run Away Song." Released in the U.S. on Arista/Legacy.

3322 September 4, 2006
Monty Python Live at Drury Lane (CD: EMI Records PYTHCD5) is released in the U.K. Remastered reissue of the Pythons' fifth album (from 1974), with the bonus track: "U.K. Tour Interview Promo" (16-min. Python interview).

3323 September 4, 2006
Monty Python's Life of Brian (CD: EMI Records PYTHCD6) is released in the U.K. Remastered reissue of the Pythons' 1979 soundtrack album, with six bonus tracks: "Otto Sketch," "Otto Song," "Otto Song" (demo), "Brian Song" (alternate version), "Record Shop," and "Twice as Good." The last two tracks are radio ads (featuring **Eric Idle** and **Graham Chapman**) for the *Life of Brian* album.

3324 September 4, 2006
Monty Python's The Meaning of Life (CD: EMI Records PYTHCD7) is released in the U.K. Remastered reissue of the 1983 film soundtrack. Includes twelve bonus tracks: "The Meaning of Life" (two alternate versions of the song, sung by **Terry Jones**), "Fat Song" (deleted intro to the "Mr. Creosote" sketch), "Christmas in Heaven" (alternate version), and eight U.K. radio ads.

3325 September 4, 2006
Monty Python's Contractual Obligation Album (CD: EMI Records PYTHCD8) is released in the U.K. Remastered reissue of the Pythons' last album for Charisma Records (from 1980), with four bonus tracks: "Promotional Interview (**Graham Chapman** & **Terry Jones**, from September 1980)," "Radio ad," "Medical Love Song" (alternate demo version), and "I'm So Worried" (demo version).

3326 September 6, 2006
The Daily Telegraph (Newspaper/U.K.). "How I Sold Panto to the Yanks," by **Eric Idle**. Idle on how he came to turn *Monty Python and the Holy Grail* into the hit Broadway musical *Spamalot* (premiering in London next month).

3327 September 16, 2006
The Times Magazine (London) (Magazine/U.K.). "Man of Spam," by Alan Franks, pp. 36–39. Interview with **Eric Idle** on the success of *Spamalot*.

3328 October 2006
Terry Jones is told by doctors that he has early-stage bowel cancer. The 64-year-old **Jones** will undergo surgery to remove the growth later in the month. At the time, **Jones** was in the middle of production on an episode of the TV parody series *Kombat Opera Presents* (which airs Mar. 25, 2007).

3329 October 2006
Terry Gilliam is one of the judges for the 7th annual TCM (Turner Classic Movies) Classic Shorts competition, which is held during The Times BFI 50th London Film Festival (Oct. 18–Nov. 2). Other judges on the panel include Pierce Brosnan, Imelda Staunton, and Matthew Modine. The winner is *Silence Is Golden* directed by Chris Shepherd.

3330 October 2, 2006
Front Row (Radio arts show: BBC Radio 4). Guest **Michael Palin** talks about his new book *The Python Years*.

3331 October 2, 2006
Terry Gilliam talks about his film *Tideland* at The Museum of the Moving Image in New York City.

3332 October 3, 2006
Diaries 1969–1979: The Python Years (Book: Weidenfeld & Nicolson), written by **Michael Palin**, is published in the U.K. **Palin**'s diary, which he started writing in April of 1969, chronicles his day-to-day thoughts and activities from the year of Monty Python's formation to the height of their fame with the release of *Life of Brian* ten years later. Published in the U.S. by Thomas Dunne Books (St. Martin's Press) in September 2007. **Palin**'s second volume of diaries, *Halfway to Hollywood: Diaries 1980–1988*, is published in September 2009.
Reviews: David Baddiel (*The Times* [London], Oct. 7, 2006, p. 3): "It has the useful effect of placing *Python*— a show that perhaps could have flourished only in the 1970s — in historical context, but it also makes anyone who has tried to write a diary feel like a slacker"; Pete Clark (*The Evening Standard*, Oct. 9, 2006): "...we are left with the picture of a man of great ambition and tireless energy. He loves food and the countryside, demands a good night's sleep and worries about his teeth"; Peter Keepnews (*The New York Times*, Dec. 2, 2007): "A voice of (relative) sanity in the eye of a comedic storm, **Palin** paints so vivid a picture that the reader becomes a Python by proxy."

3333 October 3, 2006
Monty Python and the Holy Grail: Extraordinarily Deluxe Edition (DVD: Sony Pictures). The Pythons' 1975 film, previously released in a two-disc Special Edition in 2001, is re-released in a three-disc set with new special features, including a CD of *The Album of the Soundtrack of the Trailer of the Film of Monty Python and the Holy Grail*, "The Holy Grail Challenge" (quizzes), and "A Taste of *Spamalot*" (promo for the CD of the Broadway musical). The film will be re-released again, on Blu-ray, in 2012.

3334 October 4, 2006
Terry Gilliam takes to the streets of New York City carrying a sign that reads "Studio-Less Film Maker — Will Direct for Food" to bring attention to the plight of the independent filmmaker and to promote the Oct. 13 NY opening of his film *Tideland*.

3335 October 5, 2006
Terry Gilliam introduces a screening of *Tideland* at the Smithsonian's Hirshhorn Museum of Art in Washington, D.C., and takes part in a Q&A afterward.

3336 October 7, 2006
Terry Gilliam is interviewed by Mark Askwith at the Toronto Public Library. The interview will air on *HypaSpace* (Oct. 10–14) on the Canadian cable channel Space.

3337 October 7, 2006
Terry Gilliam introduces a screening of the director's cut of *Brazil* at Cinematheque Ontario. Followed by an audience Q&A. The first screening in a **Gilliam** retrospective that runs until Oct. 22.

3338 October 7, 2006
A Culture Show Special: Michael Palin (TV special: BBC2). Special edition of the hour-long program devoted exclusively to **Michael Palin** and his new book *Diaries 1969–1979: The Python Years*. **Palin** is interviewed by Madeleine Holt. Also, Mark Kermode and Matthew Sweet comment on **Palin**'s career.

3339 October 8, 2006
Just for Laughs (TV episode: CBC, in Canada). **John Cleese** hosts an evening of stand-up comedy taped at Montreal's *Just for Laughs* comedy festival in July. First episode of the season.
Awards: Gemini Award-nominee for Best Individual Performance in a Comedy Program or Series (**Cleese**).

3340 October 9–13, 2006
Book of the Week (Radio show: BBC Radio 4). **Michael Palin** reads from his new book *Diaries 1969–1979: The Python Years* in five 10-minute episodes: "The Holy Grail" (Oct. 9), "Branching Out" (Oct. 10), "My Father" (Oct. 11), "Saturday Night Live" (Oct. 12), and "The Life of Brian" (Oct. 13).

3341 October 9, 2006
BBC Breakfast (TV news show: BBC1). Hosted by Dermot Murnaghan and Kate Silverton. Guest: **Terry Jones**, promoting *Erik the Viking* on DVD.

3342 October 9, 2006
The Sharon Osbourne Show (TV talk show: ITV1). Guests: **Terry Jones**, promoting *Erik the Viking* on

DVD, Claire King, Darryn Lyons, and Sean Lennon.

3343 October 9, 2006
Erik the Viking: The Director's Son's Cut (DVD: Arrow Films). Two-disc set containing the new "Director's Son's Cut" (75 mins) of **Terry Jones'** 1989 comedy-adventure, edited by Bill Jones (son of **Terry**). Also includes the U.K. theatrical version (released at 89 mins, cut down from the 100-minute U.S. version) and bonus features: audio commentaries by **Jones**, interview with Terry and Bill (7 mins), *The Making of Erik the Viking* (1989 featurette, 30 mins), cast interviews, and photo gallery.

3344 October 9, 2006
Terry Jones gives a talk on *Barbarians* at the Everyman Theatre in Cheltenham, England as part of the 57th Cheltenham Literature Festival (Oct. 6–15).

3345 October 9, 2006
Terry Gilliam talks with film critic Geoff Pevere at a screening of *Tideland* at the Isabel Bader Theatre in Toronto.

3346 October 10–14, 2006
HypaSpace (TV show: Space, in Canada). Entertainment news program. Mark Askwith interviews **Terry Gilliam** about his career and latest film *Tideland*. The interview was conducted Oct. 7 at the Toronto Public Library.

3347 October 12, 2006
Terry Jones signs copies of the new *Erik the Viking* DVD at Virgin Megastore in London.

3348 October 13, 2006
Tideland, directed by **Terry Gilliam**, opens in New York City. The film premiered in Toronto in September 2005.

3349 October 13, 2006
Terry Gilliam introduces a screening of *Tideland* at the 39th Sitges Film Festival (Festival Internacional de Cinema de Catalunya) (Oct. 6–15) in Sitges, Spain.

3350 October 13 & 14, 2006
John Cleese delivers the keynote speech at Australia's National Commercial Radio Conference which is held at the Crystal Palace Conference Centre at Luna Park in Sydney (Oct. 13). He also presents at the 18th annual Australian Commercial Radio Awards held at Luna Park (Oct. 14).

3351 October 15, 2006
The Sunday Times (London) (Newspaper/U.K.). "Chaos Theory," by Helen Davies, pp. 10–11 (sect. 9). **Terry Gilliam** and his wife, Maggie, describe the renovations they've made to a coach house they purchased in 1991. The property, located near their Highgate home (in North London), is now up for sale.

3352 October 15, 2006
The South Bank Show (TV arts show: ITV1). "Monty Python's Spamalot." A behind-the-scenes look at the hit musical *Spamalot* as it makes the move from Broadway to London. Features exclusive footage of the show's London rehearsals, also interviews with the five surviving Pythons: **Eric Idle**, **Michael Palin**, **Terry Jones**, **Terry Gilliam**, and **John Cleese**. Other interviewees include comedian Eddie Izzard, composer John Du Prez, and members of the cast. Broadcast on the eve of the show's West End debut. Edited & hosted by Melvyn Bragg. Produced & directed by Suzannah Wander.

3353 October 16, 2006
The musical *Spamalot*, which premiered on Broadway to critical acclaim in March 2005, opens to the press at the Palace Theatre in London's West End. The London cast includes Tim Curry (King Arthur, reprising his Broadway role), Hannah Waddingham (Lady in the Lake), and Tom Goodman-Hill (Sir Lancelot). The show ends its run at the Palace Theatre on Jan. 3, 2009.

3354 October 17, 2006
Eric Idle, **Terry Gilliam**, **Terry Jones**, and **Michael Palin** attend the gala London opening of *Spamalot* at the Palace Theatre (**John Cleese** is in Australia). Other guests include Jeremy Irons, Eddie Izzard, Brian May, and Neil Innes.

3355 October 21, 2006
Parkinson (TV talk show: ITV1). Hosted by Michael Parkinson. Guests: **Eric Idle**, Joan Bakewell, Lemar, and Ray Winstone. **Idle** talks about *Spamalot* and the late George Harrison.

3356 October 22, 2006
The Independent on Sunday (Newspaper/U.K.). "The Pythons: Spam, Spam, Spam. A Lot," by Neil Norman. Python profile.

3357 October 22, 2006
Greatest Ever Comedy Movies (TV special: Five). Hosted by Giles Coren. Countdown of the 40 funniest movies, including *A Fish Called Wanda* (No.

18) and *Life of Brian* (No. 1). With comments from **John Cleese**, **Terry Jones**, and others.

3358   October 23, 2006
Hands: A Journey Around the World (Book: Thames & Hudson), by Basil Pao (photographs) with a foreword by **Michael Palin**, is published. Collection of photographs focusing on hands, most of which were taken by Pao as he accompanied **Palin** on his travels for the BBC.

3359   October 27, 2006
HARDtalk Extra (TV talk show: BBC). Gavin Esler interviews **Terry Jones** about his early years, Python, directing, the new re-edit of *Erik the Viking*, *Spamalot*, George W. Bush, etc.

3360   October 31, 2006
Time Out London (Magazine/U.K.). "**Michael Palin**: Interview," by John O'Connell. **Palin** talks about his new book *Diaries 1969–1979: The Python Years* in an interview conducted at his Covent Garden office in April (before he left for Eastern Europe).

3361   November 18, 2006
Parkinson (TV talk show: ITV1). Hosted by Michael Parkinson. Guests: **Michael Palin**, Wendy Richard, Patrick Kielty, and Paolo Nutini.

3362   November 21, 2006
A Fish Called Wanda (DVD: MGM). Two-disc collector's edition of **John Cleese**'s 1988 comedy. Bonus features include audio commentary by **Cleese**, *John Cleese's First Farewell Performance* (1988 TV doc), *Something Fishy* (2003 making-of doc), *Farewell Featurette: John Cleese*, the *Wanda* episode of TV's *On Location* (hosted by Robert Powell), and 26 deleted/alternate scenes. Previously released on DVD in March 1999.

3363   November 28 & 30, 2006
Michael Palin talks about his book *Diaries 1969–1979: The Python Years* (and signs copies) in Logan Hall at the Institute of Education in London (Nov. 28) and at Waterstone's, Deansgate in Manchester (Nov. 30).

3364   December 1, 2006
The Interview (Radio talk show: BBC World Service). **Michael Palin** talks to 12-year-old guest-interviewer Max Syed-Tollan about his love of travel.

3365   December 2, 2006
The Times: The Knowledge (London) (Newspaper/U.K.). "Sketchy Ideas," by **Michael Palin** (interviewed by Ed Potton), p. 6. **Palin** gives his thoughts on comedy writing.

3366   December 2, 2006
A screening of **Graham Chapman** and Douglas Adams' rarely-seen 1976 TV pilot *Out of the Trees*, recently restored from an old video tape, is held at the National Film Theatre in London. The screening is part of the British Film Institute's "Missing Believed Wiped" series.

3367   December 9, 2006
Richard & Judy's Christmas Book Special (TV talk show: Channel 4). Hosts Richard Madeley and Judy Finnigan look at holiday book releases. Guest authors include **Michael Palin**, Gordon Ramsay, and Billie Piper.

3368   December 15, 2006
Charlotte's Web (Feature film: Paramount Pictures) opens in the U.S. Film adaptation of E. B. White's classic children's story. **John Cleese** voices Samuel the Sheep. Also starring Dakota Fanning and the voices of Julia Roberts, Dominic Scott Kay, Oprah Winfrey, Robert Redford, Reba McEntire, and Steve Buscemi. Written by Susannah Grant and Karey Kirkpatrick. Directed by Gary Winick.

3369   December 22, 2006
Front Row (Radio arts show: BBC Radio 4). Mark Lawson interviews **Michael Palin**.

3370   December 24, 2006
Radio 4 Appeal (Radio appeal: BBC Radio 4). **Michael Palin** delivers a Christmas appeal on behalf of the charity FARM-Africa, of which he is a patron.

3371   December 31, 2006
The Independent (Newspaper/U.K.). "How We Met: **Terry Jones** & Geoffrey Burgon." **Jones** and his good friend Geoffrey Burgon (composer of the score for *Life of Brian*) recall their first meeting, which occurred nearly 50 years ago when Burgon became friends with **Jones**' older brother Nigel. Burgon dies in 2010 at age 69.

3372   December 31, 2006
Jools's Annual Hootenanny (TV special: BBC2). **Terry Gilliam** is a guest on Jools Holland's 14th annual New Year's Eve Hootenanny.

3373   2006
Terry Gilliam, a long-time resident and citizen of Great Britain, renounces his American citizenship citing tax issues as the primary reason and dis-

gust with the George W. Bush administration as an added motive.

3374 2006
Medieval Mercenaries: The Business of War (Book: Greenhill Books), written by William Urban, is published. Foreword by **Terry Jones**, who had examined the subject in his own 1980 book *Chaucer's Knight: The Portrait of a Medieval Mercenary*.

3375 January 1, 2007
The Secret Life of Brian (TV special: Channel 4). Hour-long documentary on the making of and controversy surrounding the Pythons' 1979 film *Life of Brian*. Includes interviews with **John Cleese**, **Terry Gilliam**, **Terry Jones**, and **Michael Palin**. The doc—the first program in a night devoted to Python—is followed by a screening of *Life of Brian* and another doc, *What the Pythons Did Next*. Narrated by Richard Dillane. Produced & directed by Will Yapp.

3376 January 1, 2007
What the Pythons Did Next (TV special: Channel 4). Documentary following the Pythons' solo careers. Narrated by Miriam Margolyes. Directed by Jon Riley.

3377 January 1, 2007
Philip Pullman and Enid Jones (Radio special: BBC Radio Wales). **Terry Jones** presents an intimate conversation between best-selling author Philip Pullman and his former teacher Enid Jones. Repeated Mar. 29, 2007, on BBC Radio 4.

3378 January 5, 2007
A New Year at Kew (TV show: BBC2). Includes a report on **Michael Palin** opening the Alpine House at Kew Gardens in London (in March 2006). Narrated by Alan Titchmarsh. Produced by Deborah Perkin.

3379 January 18, 2007
Terry Gilliam attends *The Great Britons Awards* at the Guildhall in London.

3380 January 22, 2007
Eric Idle appears at a press event for the Las Vegas debut of *Spamalot* at The Grail Theater at the Wynn Las Vegas. The show begins previews Mar. 8 and opens Mar. 31.

3381 January 27, 2007
The Comedy Map of Britain (TV episode: BBC2). **Michael Palin** and friend Robert Hewison look back on their college days at Oxford when they first began to write and perform their own comedy material. First episode of the TV documentary series visiting locations around Britain that have inspired great moments in past BBC comedy series. Narrated by Alan Whicker.

3382 February 2, 2007
John Cleese and his wife attend the 22nd Annual Santa Barbara International Film Festival.

3383 February 5, 2007
Richard & Judy (TV talk show: Channel 4). Hosted by Richard Madeley and Judy Finnigan. Guest: **Terry Gilliam**.

3384 February 8, 2007
Frost Tonight (TV talk show: ITV). Hosted by David Frost. Guests: **Terry Gilliam**, discussing his film *Tideland*, Zac Goldsmith, and Steven Berkoff.

3385 February 9, 2007
Anna and the Moods (Short film: Monster Distributes) premieres in Iceland. Icelandic computer-animated film featuring the voice of singer-songwriter Björk. Narrated by **Terry Jones**. Directed by Gunnar Karlsson.

3386 February 15, 2007
Michael Palin attends the annual Orion Authors' Party at the Victoria and Albert Museum in London.

3387 February 17, 2007
The Art Directors Guild Awards (Award ceremony). **Terry Gilliam** receives the Outstanding Contribution to Cinematic Imagery Award at the 11th annual award show, held at the Beverly Hilton Hotel in Beverly Hills, CA.

3388 February 18, 2007
The Simpsons (TV episode: Fox). "Springfield Up." Springfield residents become the subjects of a documentary series in this send-up of Michael Apted's *Seven Up* films. **Eric Idle** voices filmmaker Declan Desmond; his third time voicing the role, following episodes in March 2003 and December 2004. Other voices by Dan Castellaneta, Julie Kavner, Nancy Cartwright, Yeardley Smith, Hank Azaria, and Harry Shearer. Written by Matt Warburton. Directed by Chuck Sheetz.

3389 February 18, 2007
The **Eric Idle**–John Du Prez musical *Spamalot* loses in all categories at *The Laurence Olivier Awards*, the 31st annual British theater awards, held in London. *Spamalot* had received seven nominations including Best New Musical, Best Actor (Tim Curry), and Best Actress (Hannah Waddingham).

At the 2005 *Tony Awards* in NYC the musical — which received 14 Tony nominations — won three awards (including Best Musical).

3390 February 19, 2007
Forty Years Without a Proper Job (Lecture). **Michael Palin** gives a talk (hosted by Samuel West) at the Crucible Theatre in his home town of Sheffield, England. All proceeds from the event go to the Sheffield Theatres Capital Redevelopment Campaign. Earlier in the day, **Palin** was named a Sheffield Legend and honored with a plaque on the Walk of Fame in front of Sheffield Town Hall.

3391 February 25, 2007
John Cleese and his wife attend the *Vanity Fair* Oscar Party at Morton's Restaurant in West Hollywood, CA.

3392 February 27, 2007
Tideland (DVD: THINKFilm). **Terry Gilliam**'s 2005 film is released in a two-disc Collector's Edition that includes audio commentary by **Gilliam** and screenwriter Tony Grisoni, deleted scenes, interviews, and the featurettes *Getting Gilliam* and *The Making of Tideland*.

3393 March 8, 2007
Spamalot begins in previews at The Grail Theater at the Wynn Las Vegas.

3394 March 18, 2007
The Los Angeles Times (Newspaper/U.S.). "The Spread of 'Spam,'" by **Eric Idle**, p. F1. Article on bringing *Spamalot* to Las Vegas.

3395 March 25, 2007
Kombat Opera Presents (TV episode: BBC2). "The South Bragg Show." **Terry Jones** co-directed this parody of the British TV arts series *The South Bank Show* (hosted by Melvyn Bragg), presented in the form of a half-hour opera. Before filming started in October 2006, **Jones** was diagnosed with bowel cancer and had to leave the production. Peter Orton took over as director. The show, originally titled "Children of the Stones," is the last program in a five-episode series of operatic parodies. Written by Richard Thomas and Stewart Lee. Composed by Richard Thomas (*Jerry Springer: The Opera*). Starring Kevin Eldon (Melvynn Bragg). Produced by Stephen Abrahams.

3396 March 25, 2007
The Making of Kombat Opera (TV special: BBC Wales). Documentary on the opera-parody series *Kombat Opera Presents*. Includes interviews with **Terry Jones** and other artists involved in the making of the series. **Jones** explains why he had to pull out of the production of his episode ("The South Bragg Show," which airs Mar. 25) due to the discovery of cancer in his colon. **Jones**' interview takes place shortly before he undergoes surgery in October 2006. Produced & directed by Andy Frith.

3397 March 25, 2007
Eric Idle attends Elton John's 60th Birthday Concert at Madison Square Garden in New York City.

3398 March 31, 2007
Eric Idle, **John Cleese**, and **Terry Gilliam** attend the Las Vegas premiere of *Spamalot* at The Grail Theater at the Wynn Las Vegas. The Vegas production (which is 20 minutes shorter than the Broadway version) features John O'Hurley as King Arthur.

3399 April 2, 2007
The Daily Telegraph (Newspaper/U.K.). "Will *Spamalot* Be Harder in Nevada?," by **Eric Idle**. **Idle** on bringing his hit Broadway musical *Spamalot* to Las Vegas.

3400 April 23, 2007
In honor of *Spamalot*, Python fans gather in London's Trafalgar Square to break the Guinness World Record for "World's Largest Coconut Orchestra" by performing "Always Look on the Bright Side of Life" on coconut halves. Leading the performance are **Terry Jones** and **Terry Gilliam** and the London cast of *Spamalot*, with Michael England conducting. At 4,382 they break the record previously set in New York City on Mar. 22, 2006 (with 1,789 fans). The St. George's Day event is followed by a screening of *Holy Grail*.

3401 May 2007
Candis (Magazine/U.K.). "The **Palin** Effect." Article on **Michael Palin**, with cover photo ("Mr. Nice Guy").

3402 May 1, 2007
An Evening with John Cleese (Event). **John Cleese** hosts a screening of *Life of Brian* at Campbell Hall at the University of California Santa Barbara. The event benefits UCSB's Arts & Lectures Film Series.

3403 May 6, 2007
Eric Idle attends the premiere of *Shrek the Third*, in which he voices Merlin, in Los Angeles.

3404 May 9, 2007
HBO First Look (TV episode: HBO). "The Mak-

ing of *Shrek the Third*." **Eric Idle** is among the interviewees.

3405   May 18, 2007
Shrek the Third (Feature film: Paramount) opens in the U.S. Animated feature, third in the series. **John Cleese** voices the King, a role he first voiced in *Shrek 2* (2004). **Eric Idle** voices Merlin. **Cleese** will voice the king again in *Shrek Forever After* (2010). Voice cast also includes Mike Myers, Eddie Murphy, Cameron Diaz, Julie Andrews, and Antonio Banderas. Written by Jeffrey Price, Peter S. Seaman, Chris Miller, and Aron Warner. Directed by Chris Miller and Raman Hui.

3406   May 18, 2007
Canada AM (TV show: CTV, in Canada). Guest: **Eric Idle**.

3407   May 22–June 7, 2007
John Cleese hosts a festival of his films aboard the ship *Silver Shadow* (Silversea Cruises) during its 16-day Atlantic crossing from New York to Southhampton, England.

3408   May 22, 2007
Michael Palin attends a reception celebrating the 80th anniversary of the Royal Television Society. The event, hosted by The Prince of Wales and Duchess of Cornwall, is held at Clarence House in London. Other guests include Sir David Attenborough, Natasha Kaplinsky, and Lord Melvyn Bragg.

3409   May 27, 2007
Toronto Star (Newspaper/Can.). "**Idle** Thoughts," by **Eric Idle**, p. C6. **Idle** on the upcoming world premiere (in Toronto) of his oratorio *Not the Messiah (He's a Very Naughty Boy)*.

3410   June 1–4, 2007
Not the Messiah (He's a Very Naughty Boy) (Oratorio) has its world premiere at Roy Thomson Hall in Toronto, Canada as part of that city's Luminato festival. **Eric Idle** collaborated with composer John Du Prez — with whom **Idle** had previously adapted *Holy Grail* for the hit Broadway musical *Spamalot* (2005) — to create this comic oratorio, a spoof of Handel's 1741 masterwork *Messiah* which, instead of Jesus, tells the story of Brian Cohen from Monty Python's 1979 film *Life of Brian*. Described by **Idle** as "funnier than Handel," this new work — commissioned by the Luminato festival — includes the original songs: "Chaos and Confusion!," "There Shall Be Monsters," "O God You Are So Big," "Mandy's Song," "Woe Woe Woe!" "We Love Sheep," "Spiritual," "Brian's Dream," "What Have the Romans Ever Done for Us?," "The Peoples' Front of Judea," "I Want to Be a Girl," "The Market Square," "You're the One," "Hail to the Shoe," "Amourdeus," "The Chosen One Has Woken," "When They Grow Up," "Take Us Home," "Not the Messiah," "Individuals," "Find Your Dream," "Arrested," "A Fair Day's Work," and "The Final Song," as well as a sing-along version of "Always Look on the Bright Side of Life" (from the 1979 film). Starring **Eric Idle** as soloist and narrator, and soloists Shannon Mercer (soprano), Jean Stilwell (mezzo-soprano), Christopher Sieber (tenor), and Theodore Baerg (baritone), with Peter Oundjian (**Idle**'s cousin) conducting the Toronto Symphony Orchestra and the Mendelssohn Choir. The oratorio receives its U.S. premiere in Katonah, NY (July 1), followed by performances in Australia and New Zealand (December), Houston (July 2008), The Hollywood Bowl in Los Angeles (August 2008), and The Royal Albert Hall in London (October 2009). Note: Sieber played Sir Galahad in the original Broadway production of *Spamalot* in March 2005.

3411   June 6, 2007
Eric Idle attends "Making Magic Happen," the 3rd Annual Los Angeles Gala for the Christopher and Dana Reeve Foundation at the Century Plaza Hotel. **Idle**'s friend, Robin Williams, is honored at the event for his work with the foundation.

3412   June 13, 2007
The Late Late Show with Craig Ferguson (TV talk show: CBS). Guests include **Eric Idle** and S. Epatha Merkerson. **Idle** talks about *Spamalot* in Las Vegas, younger comedians, and his wife's new hybrid car.

3413   June 16, 2007
Tiswas Reunited (TV special: ITV). Reunion special celebrating the popular British Saturday-morning children's show *Tiswas* (1974–82). **Michael Palin** appears, recalling his and **Terry Jones**' guest-appearance on the show in 1979. Hosted by Chris Tarrant and Sally James.

3414   June 25, 2007
Michael Palin opens the John Murray Archive Exhibition at the National Library in Scotland.

3415   June 27, 2007
Michael Palin receives the honorary degree of Doctor of Letters from Edinburgh University in Scotland in honor of his contributions to literature. The ceremony is held at McEwan Hall.

3416 June 28, 2007
The Wall Street Journal (Newspaper/U.S.). "A Python Grip on Handel," by Barrymore Laurence Scherer, p. D7. Interview with **Eric Idle** about the creation of his comic oratorio *Not the Messiah*.

3417 July 1, 2007
The **Eric Idle**–John Du Prez oratorio *Not the Messiah (He's a Very Naughty Boy)* has its U.S. premiere at The Venetian Theater in Katonah, NY, as part of the Caramoor International Music Festival (June 23–Aug. 5). **Idle**, as soloist and narrator, is joined by soloists Shannon Mercer, Jean Stilwell, Chistopher Sieber, and Theodore Baerg, with Peter Oundjian conducting the Orchestra of St. Luke's and the Collegiate Chorale. The work had its world premiere on June 1 in Toronto.

3418 August 2007
Terry Jones films a new documentary series, *Ogilby's Roads*, in Wales. The series, retitled *Terry Jones' Great Map Mystery*, will air in May–June 2008 on BBC2 Wales.

3419 August 25, 2007
British Film Forever (TV special: BBC2). "Magic, Murder and Monsters: The Story of British Horror and Fantasy." Documentary special, the fifth installment of a seven-part series on British cinema. Includes an interview with **Terry Gilliam**, who talks about British fantasy and his own work in that genre (*Brazil*). Narrated by Jessica Stevenson.

3420 September 2007
Michael Palin's book *Diaries 1969–1979: The Python Years* is published in the U.S. by Thomas Dunne (St. Martin's Press).

3421 September 4–10, 2007
John Cleese is a guest-speaker on the Queen Mary 2 ocean liner during its transatlantic crossing from New York to Southampton, England.

3422 September 4, 2007
The Leonard Lopate Show (Radio talk show: WNYC-FM, New York). Guest **Michael Palin** talks about *Diaries*, the creation of Monty Python, the "Pet Shop" sketch, etc.

3423 September 4, 2007
Talk of the Nation (Radio talk show: NPR). **Michael Palin** is interviewed about *Diaries*.

3424 September 4, 2007
Michael Palin gives a reading from his *Diaries* at the Barnes & Noble book store at Lincoln Center in New York City, and also signs copies of the book.

3425 September 5, 2007
Michael Palin, promoting *Diaries*, talks about his life and career with interviewer Lorne Michaels at the 92nd Street Y in New York City. The event is followed by a book signing.

3426 September 6, 2007
Michael Palin signs copies of *Diaries* at the Free Library in Philadelphia.

3427 September 7, 2007
Michael Palin reads from (and signs copies of) *Diaries* at the First Parish Church Meetinghouse in Cambridge, Mass. The event is sponsored by Harvard Book Store. **Palin** later introduces a screening of *And Now for Something Completely Different* at the Brattle Theatre.

3428 September 8, 2007
Michael Palin speaks at the Hudson Union Society's annual fundraising gala held at the Princeton Club in New York City. During his address he reads from *Diaries* and afterward takes part in a Q&A.

3429 September 8, 2007
British Film Forever (TV special: BBC2). "Sauce, Satire and Silliness: The Story of British Comedy." Last in a seven-part series of documentary specials. **Terry Gilliam** is interviewed.

3430 September 13, 2007
New Europe (Book: Weidenfeld & Nicolson), written by **Michael Palin** with photographs by Basil Pao, is published in the U.K. **Palin**'s account of his visits to Croatia, Romania, Hungary, Albania, Poland, and other former Eastern bloc countries. Companion book to the new BBC travel series. Paperback edition published by Phoenix (2008). Also released as an audiobook (BBC Audiobooks), read by **Palin**, on Oct. 8.

3431 September 14, 2007
The Late Late Show with Craig Ferguson (TV talk show: CBS). Guests include **Eric Idle** and Les Stroud.

3432 September 15, 2007
Parkinson (TV talk show: ITV1). Hosted by Michael Parkinson. Guests: **Michael Palin**, promoting *New Europe*, Dame Diana Rigg, Sir David Frost, and Annie Lennox.

3433 September 16–October 28, 2007
The seven-part travel series *Michael Palin's New*

Europe, written & hosted by **Michael Palin**, airs on BBC1. **Palin**'s seventh travel series takes him to 20 countries in Eastern and Central Europe formerly hidden behind the Iron Curtain. Filmed over a period of five-and-a-half months between May 2006 and May 2007. Airs in the U.S. in January–March 2008 on the Travel Channel.

3434 September 16, 2007
Michael Palin's New Europe (TV episode: BBC1). "War and Peace." **Michael Palin**'s journey through the former Yugoslavia begins in the Julian Alps in Slovenia. He then visits the island of Hvar (Croatia), observes a mine-clearing operation in war-scarred Sarajevo (Bosnia-Herzegovina), and visits Belgrade (Serbia) and Dubrovnik (Croatia). In Albania, he witnesses a sheep sacrifice. First episode in the seven-part travel series. Written & narrated by **Michael Palin**. Produced & directed by John Paul Davidson.

3435 September 19, 2007
Michael Palin signs copies of his new book *New Europe* at Hatchards bookshop in Piccadilly, London.

3436 September 21, 2007
This Morning (TV show: ITV). Magazine program hosted by Ruth Langsford and Phillip Schofield. Guest: **Michael Palin**, promoting *New Europe*.

3437 September 22, 2007
Michael Palin promotes *New Europe* on the radio shows *Jonathan Ross* (BBC Radio 2) and *Excess Baggage* with Sandi Toksvig (BBC Radio 4).

3438 September 23, 2007
Michael Palin's New Europe (TV episode: BBC1). "Eastern Delight." In Bulgaria, **Michael Palin** observes the dance of the White Brotherhood (Rila Mountains) and meets gypsy transvestite singer Azis (Sofia). In Turkey, he watches a display of oil wrestling (Edirne), takes a belly-dancing lesson (Istanbul), attends a camel wrestling festival (Selçuk-Ephesus), and visits a fortune-teller (Göreme, Cappadocia). Second episode in the seven-part travel series. Written & narrated by **Michael Palin**. Produced & directed by John Paul Davidson.

3439 September 24, 2007
The One Show (TV talk show: BBC1). Hosted by Adrian Chiles and Christine Bleakley. Chiles interviews **Michael Palin** about his series *New Europe*.

3440 September 26, 2007
Michael Palin discusses his new book & TV series, *New Europe*, at the Institute of Education in London.

3441 September 30, 2007
Michael Palin's New Europe (TV episode: BBC1). "Wild East." After a visit to the breakaway republic of Transdniester, **Michael Palin** moves on to Moldova's capital, Chisinau. In Romania, he visits the "Merry Cemetery" and rides the lumberjacks' train (Maramures), visits Transylvania and Bran Castle (aka "Dracula's Castle"), then tours the Palace of the People and meets tennis star Ilie Nastase (Bucharest). Third episode in the seven-part travel series. Written & narrated by **Michael Palin**. Produced & directed by John Paul Davidson.

3442 September 30, 2007
A Slice of Cleese — John Cleese In Conversation with James Crathorne (Event). **John Cleese** appears onstage in conversation with his longtime friend James Crathorne at the Georgian Theatre Royal in Richmond, North Yorkshire, England. The event raises money for the theater.

3443 October–November 2007
Michael Palin goes on a book-signing tour of the U.K. to promote *New Europe*.

3444 October 4, 2007
Was Richard II a Tyrant? (Lecture). **Terry Jones** gives a talk in Conron Hall at the University of Western Ontario in London, Ont. In the lecture **Jones** questions the accepted image of English king Richard II as being weak and tyrannical. **Jones**' talk, which is the opening address of the 22nd International Conference on Medievalism, is followed by a screening of *Holy Grail*.

3445 October 6, 2007
Michael Palin talks about his new book & TV series, *New Europe*, at Cheltenham Racecourse as part of the 58th Cheltenham Literature Festival (Oct. 5–14).

3446 October 7, 2007
Michael Palin's New Europe (TV episode: BBC1). "Danube to Dnieper." During his stay in Budapest, Hungary, **Michael Palin** visits the House of Terror Museum and participates in a fashion show. In the Ukraine, he returns to Kiev (which he previously visited in 1991 for *Pole to Pole*) where he meets a fellow Yorkshireman who is married to the Ukranian Prime Minister's daughter. Lastly, he visits the Livadia Palace in Yalta. Fourth episode in the

seven-part travel series. Written & narrated by **Michael Palin**. Produced & directed by Roger Mills.

3447   October 8, 2007
Michael Palin discusses his new book & TV series, *New Europe*, at the Royal Geographical Society in London.

3448   October 8, 2007
Translating Richard II (Was Richard II a Tyrant?) (Lecture). **Terry Jones** speaks in McPherson Lab at Ohio State University. The lecture, in which **Jones** questions Richard's image as a tyrannical king, is presented by the university's Center for Medieval and Renaissance Studies.

3449   October 14, 2007
Michael Palin's New Europe (TV episode: BBC1). "Baltic Summer." **Michael Palin** tours the Baltic States, starting in Estonia, where he witnesses firewalking and receives leech therapy (Tallinn). In Latvia, he participates in the pagan festival of Jani, meets a prominent chef, and sees the Ventspils radio telescope (Riga). In Lithuania, he tours the Museum of Genocide Victims (Vilnius). His last stop is the Russian port city of Kaliningrad. Fifth episode in the seven-part travel series. Written & narrated by **Michael Palin**. Produced & directed by Roger Mills.

3450   October 14, 2007
An Audience with John Cleese (Event). **John Cleese** appears onstage in conversation with journalist Robert Hall at the Jersey Opera House on the Isle of Jersey. Proceeds from the event go to the Durrell Wildlife Conservation Trust.

3451   October 16, 2007
Was Richard II a Tyrant? (Lecture). **Terry Jones** gives his Richard II lecture in the Michael Schimmel Center for the Arts at Pace University in New York City.

3452   October 20, 2007
The Culture Show (TV arts show: BBC2). Newly-published author Karl Pilkington (of the Ricky Gervais podcasts) visits the Cheltenham Literature Festival, where he observes a **Michael Palin** booksigning.

3453   October 21, 2007
Michael Palin's New Europe (TV episode: BBC1). "From Pole to Pole." During his journey through Poland, **Michael Palin** meets Lech Walesa (Gdansk), performs with a famous cabaret group (Elblag), learns to drive a steam locomotive (Poznan to Wolsztyn), tours the former concentration camp Auschwitz I (Oúwiĺcim), visits a salt mine (Wieliczka), and attends the wedding of two ski instructors (Bialka Tatrzanska). Sixth episode in the seven-part travel series. Written & narrated by **Michael Palin**. Produced & directed by Roger Mills.

3454   October 28, 2007
Michael Palin's New Europe (TV episode: BBC1). "Journey's End." In Slovakia, **Michael Palin** learns how to make sausages (Tatra Mountains). In the Czech Republic, he attends Turba's mime class (Brno), visits a health clinic with Miss World 2006, Tatana Kucharova (Karlovy Vary), and enjoys a pedalo ride (Prague). In the former East Germany, **Palin** learns about the Berlin Wall from two actors (Berlin). The journey ends on Rugen Island in the Baltic Sea. Seventh episode in the seven-part travel series. Written & narrated by **Michael Palin**. Produced & directed by John Paul Davidson.

3455   November 2007
Kerri-Anne (TV talk show: Nine Network). Australian daytime talk show hosted by Kerri-Anne Kennerley. Guest: **Michael Palin**, promoting *New Europe*. He also sings "The Lumberjack Song" in German.

3456   November 2007
720 Morning (Radio talk show: ABC Perth, in Australia). Hosted by Geoff Hutchison. Guest: **Michael Palin**, promoting *New Europe* and answering questions from callers.

3457   November 1, 2007
Slices of Cleese: An Evening with John Cleese (Event). **John Cleese** speaks at the Santa Barbara Museum of Natural History in Santa Barbara, CA. The event benefits the Osher Lifelong Learning Institute (**Cleese** is a member of the OLLI's Advisory Board).

3458   November 1, 2007
Late Night Live (Radio talk show: ABC Radio National, in Australia). Hosted by Phillip Adams. Guest: **Michael Palin**, promoting *New Europe*, also talks about Ernest Hemingway, the *Life of Brian* controversy, writing, etc.

3459   November 4, 2007
Rove (TV talk show: Ten, in Australia). Hosted by Rove McManus. Guest: **Michael Palin**, promoting *New Europe*. **Palin** also talks about having to buy underwear in Perth (his luggage arrived late) and his youthful crush on actress Kim Novak.

3460 November 5, 2007
Monty Python's Life of Brian: The Immaculate Edition (DVD: Sony Pictures) is released in the U.K. Two-disc special edition of the 1979 film, previously released on DVD in 1999 (Criterion Collection). This edition includes most of the same special features from the earlier release — minus the 1979 doc *The Pythons*— and adds *The Story of Brian* (hour-long doc, a re-edited version of the recent Channel 4 doc *The Secret Life of Brian*) and an audio recording of the July 1977 table reading by the group of the screenplay in progress. Also released on Blu-ray (Dec. 3). Released in the U.S. in January 2008.

3461 November 5, 2007
John Cleese participates in an onstage conversation with Professor Richard Tarnas at the Lobero Theatre, Santa Barbara, CA. The event is part of the Mind and Supermind Lecture Series.

3462 November 6, 2007
More Boys Who Do Comedy (TV talk show: BBC4). Comedienne Dawn French interviews **John Cleese** about his life in comedy in this premiere episode of her 2007 series. Half-hour. Produced & directed by Ben McPherson.

3463 November 7, 2007
Michael Palin talks about *New Europe* at a literary luncheon at Star City casino in Sydney, Australia.

3464 November 8, 2007
Was Richard II a Tyrant? (Lecture). **Terry Jones** reassesses the reign of King Richard II in a talk at Folkestone Academy in Kent, England as part of the Folkestone Literary Festival (Nov. 2–10).

3465 November 10 & 11, 2007
What About Dick? (Play), written by **Eric Idle** with music by John Du Prez, is presented on two nights at the Ricardo Montalban Theater in Los Angeles. This staged radio play is a work-in-progress based on an unproduced screenplay by **Idle** titled *The Remains of the Piano* (a Merchant-Ivory spoof). The two workshop presentations are performed by **Idle**, Eddie Izzard, Tracey Ullman, Billy Connolly, Emily Mortimer, Tim Curry, Jim Piddock, Tony Palermo, and Jane Leeves.

3466 November 10, 2007
Love Letters (Play). **John Cleese** and Carol Burnett — both residents of Montecito, Cal. (in Santa Barbara County) — give a reading of A. J. Gurney's play at the Lobero Theatre, Santa Barbara. A one-night-only performance benefitting Girls Inc.

3467 November 11–14, 2007
Michael Palin tours New Zealand promoting his book *New Europe*. The tour includes stops in Auckland (Nov. 11) and Wellington (Nov. 13).

3468 November 20, 2007
BBC Breakfast (TV news show: BBC1/News Channel). Hosted by Dermot Murnaghan and Kate Silverton. Guest: **Michael Palin**.

3469 November 20, 2007
Spamalot has its first Australian performance as it begins previews at Her Majesty's Theatre in Melbourne. The musical's official gala opening will take place on Dec. 1.

3470 November 26, 2007
Eric Idle appears on the Australian radio shows *Breakfast* (ABC Radio National) and *Mornings with Margaret Throsby* (ABC Classic FM) to promote *Spamalot* and *Not the Messiah*, which are both making their Australian debuts in early December.

3471 November 26, 2007
Eric Idle attends a party in honor of David Beckham and his team, the LA Galaxy, at Cafe Sydney in Sydney, Australia.

3472 November 28, 2007
Late Night Live (Radio talk show: ABC Radio National, in Australia). Hosted by Phillip Adams. Guest: **Eric Idle**, promoting the Australian premieres of *Spamalot* and *Not the Messiah*, also talks about "Galaxy Song," English comedy, the *Life of Brian* controversy, his love of books, etc.

3473 December 2007
Terry Gilliam begins filming in London on his next film, *The Imaginarium of Doctor Parnassus*, a fantasy starring Heath Ledger and Christopher Plummer (in the title role). Shooting continues in London until Jan. 18, then the production will move to Vancouver. Before filming restarts, however, Ledger is found dead in his New York apartment (on Jan. 22).

3474 December 1, 2007
Spamalot premieres in Australia at Her Majesty's Theatre in Melbourne (previews began Nov. 20). **Eric Idle**, with his wife, attends the gala opening and also joins the cast onstage for the final curtain call. The show will play at the theater until April.

3475 December 4, 2007
Erik the Viking: The Director's Son's Cut (DVD:

MGM) is released in the U.S. The "Director's Son's Cut" of **Terry Jones**' 1989 comedy, by editor Bill Jones (son of Terry), which was first released on DVD in Britain in October 2006. Bonus features include audio commentary by **Jones**, *Behind the Director's Son's Cut* (10-min featurette), *The Making of Erik the Viking* (1989 featurette, 30 mins), photo gallery, and theatrical trailer.

3476 December 5, 2007

The **Eric Idle**–John Du Prez oratorio *Not the Messiah (He's a Very Naughty Boy)* makes its Australian debut at the Lyric Theatre, Queensland Performing Arts Centre in Brisbane. **Eric Idle** appears as narrator and soloist. The work, which premiered in June 2007 in Toronto, will also have performances at the Sydney Opera House (Dec. 9 & 12), The Civic Theatre in Auckland, New Zealand (Dec. 15 & 16), and Perth Concert Hall (Dec. 20 & 21).

3477 December 12, 2007

Michael Palin gives a reading at the Parkinson's Disease Society Christmas Carol Concert at Westminster Cathedral in London.

3478 December 13, 2007

Terry Jones attends a press conference in Fnac Chiado in Lisbon, Portugal for the launch of *The Pythons* autobiography. He also talks about writing fairy tales and his opera *Evil Machines*, which is premiering in Lisbon in January.

3479 December 25, 2007

Robbie the Reindeer in Close Encounters of the Herd Kind (TV special: BBC1). Robbie's fiancée, Donner, is kidnapped by aliens. Third in a series of animated specials featuring Robbie the Reindeer, following *Hooves of Fire* (1999) and *Legend of the Lost Tribe* (2002). **Michael Palin** voices the alien Gariiiiiii. Other voices by Ardal O'Hanlon, Jane Horrocks, Keira Knightly, Ozzy Osbourne, Gillian Anderson, Russell Brand, and Graham Norton. Written by Mark Huckerby and Nick Ostler. Produced & directed by Donnie Anderson.

3480 January 2008

John Cleese separates from his third wife, Alyce Faye.

3481 January 12, 2008

Evil Machines (Opera) premieres at the São Luiz Municipal Theatre in Lisbon, Portugal. The opera, written & directed by **Terry Jones** with music by Luis Tinoco, is a musical fantasy in which household appliances do battle with mankind. The libretto, based on an unpublished work by **Jones**, is later revised and published as a book in November 2011. This work marks the second time that Tinoco has set **Jones**' words to music. In 2005 the composer arranged music for several of **Jones**' children's stories to create the short play *Contos Fantásticos*, also staged at the São Luiz Theatre. The production runs until Feb. 3. Note: **Jones** will write and direct another opera, *The Doctor's Tale*, in April 2011.

3482 January 22, 2008

Actor Heath Ledger dies of an accidental prescription drug overdose in New York City at the age of 28. Ledger, who had previously worked with **Terry Gilliam** on 2005's *The Brothers Grimm*, was about halfway through shooting **Gilliam**'s latest film, *The Imaginarium of Doctor Parnassus*, at the time of his death. He had been filming in London just three days earlier (Saturday) and was scheduled to resume filming in Vancouver at the end of the week. **Gilliam** decides to continue filming using three different actors in the role Ledger originated.

3483 January 28, 2008

Michael Palin's 2007 travel series *New Europe* begins airing in the U.S. on the Travel Channel.

3484 January 31, 2008

Hannity & Colmes (TV news-talk show: Fox News Channel). Guest **John Cleese** talks to pollster Frank Luntz.

3485 February 4, 2008

Movies for Grownups (Award ceremony). **John Cleese** and Dana Delany (replacing Jamie Lee Curtis, who had the flu) host AARP Magazine's 7th annual "Movies for Grownups" awards at the Bel-Air Hotel in Los Angeles. The evening includes a tribute to *A Fish Called Wanda* on its 20th anniversary.

3486 February 10, 2008

Eat Something Sexy (Event). **John Cleese** hosts a workshop on aphrodisiacs at the Santa Barbara Museum of Natural History in Santa Barbara, CA.

3487 February 11, 2008

Terry Jones attends a funeral service for his friend, humorist Miles Kington, at Haycombe Cemetery in Bath, England. Kington died of cancer on Jan. 30.

3488 February 19, 2008

Michael Palin attends a lunchtime reception, hosted by The Prince of Wales and Duchess of Cornwall, celebrating the 60-year legacy of The

Royal Film Performance. The reception, held at Clarence House in London, is also attended by Lord Richard Attenborough and Peter O'Toole. **Palin** later attends the Royal Film Premiere of *The Other Boleyn Girl* at the Odeon, Leicester Square, London.

3489 February 22, 2008
New Hero of Comedy (TV episode: Channel 4). "Ricky Gervais." Comedian Ricky Gervais (*The Office*) is profiled, with comments by **Michael Palin**, others.

3490 February 24, 2008
Filming resumes on **Terry Gilliam**'s *The Imaginarium of Doctor Parnassus* in Vancouver, a month later than planned due to the Jan. 22 death of star Heath Ledger. Three different actors — Johnny Depp, Jude Law, and Colin Farrell — will take over Ledger's role.

3491 February 29, 2008
Michael Palin receives a Lifetime Achievement Award at the opening gala of the 14th annual Bradford International Film Festival (Feb. 29–Mar. 15), held at the National Media Museum in Bradford, West Yorkshire, England. The festival also features a retrospective of **Palin**'s film work.

3492 March 7, 2008
Michael Palin and art historian Tim Marlow give a talk on the Camden Town Group at the Tate Britain gallery in London. The Camden Town Group of the 1910s were a gathering of English post-impressionists that included Walter Sickert and Harold Gilman. **Palin**, an admirer of the group, will return to Tate Britain in 2009 for an episode of *Marlow Meets...*

3493 March 15–21, 2008
Rutlemania, a tribute concert featuring the music of **Eric Idle**'s Beatle-parody group The Rutles, plays five dates at the Ricardo Montalban Theatre in Hollywood, CA. The concert, conceived and directed by **Eric Idle** with music & lyrics by Neil Innes, is performed by Beatles tribute band The Fab Four. The concert then plays four dates (Mar. 26–29) at the Blender Theater at Gramercy in New York City.

3494 March 17, 2008
Entertainment Weekly (Magazine: U.S.). "**Eric Idle** on the Rutles Reunion" by Jamie Reno. Interview with **Eric Idle** on the upcoming Rutles reunion in Los Angeles.

3495 March 17, 2008
Eric Idle takes part in a Rutles reunion at Grauman's Egyptian Theatre in Hollywood celebrating the 30th anniversary of the Beatle-parody group's 1978 TV mockumentary *All You Need Is Cash*. The reunion, part of the Mods & Rockers Film Festival, includes a screening of a restored print of the film followed by a Q&A session with the band members: Dirk (**Idle**), Nasty (Neil Innes), Stig (Ricky Fataar), and Barry (John Halsey), moderated by event organizer Martin Lewis. The band later plays four songs at a reception held in the back room of the Pig 'n Whistle restaurant. It is actually their first performance together, as **Idle** didn't play or sing on the group's original recordings (it was the late Ollie Halsall, rather, who performed in the studio as the fourth Rutle).

3496 March 24, 2008
The Frost Report Is Back! (TV special: BBC4). Two-hour reunion special celebrating the satirical BBC sketch series *The Frost Report* (1966–67), which helped launch the careers of **John Cleese**, **Graham Chapman**, **Terry Jones**, **Michael Palin**, **Eric Idle**, Ronnie Barker, Ronnie Corbett, Tim Brooke-Taylor, and others. Hosted by David Frost, the special includes interviews with **Cleese**, **Jones**, **Palin**, Corbett, Brooke-Taylor, others. Produced & directed by Andrew Fettis.

3497 March 31, 2008
Legends (TV episode: BBC4). "Marty Feldman: Six Degrees of Separation." Documentary on the life and career of writer-comedian Marty Feldman (1934–1982). **John Cleese** and **Michael Palin** are interviewed. Narrated by Nigel Planer. Produced & directed by Jeff Simpson.

3498 April 2008
The Adventures of Baron Munchausen: 20th Anniversary Edition (DVD/Blu-ray: Sony Pictures Home Entertainment). Special edition of **Terry Gilliam**'s 1989 film fantasy. Special features include audio commentary by **Gilliam** and co-screenwriter Charles McKeown, deleted scenes, storyboards, and the new three-part documentary *The Madness and Misadventures of Munchausen*.

3499 April 2008
The Madness and Misadventures of Munchausen (Documentary). Three-part doc (73 mins.) on the making of **Terry Gilliam**'s 1989 film *The Adventures of Baron Munchausen*. Features new interviews with **Terry Gilliam**, John Neville, Sarah Polley, **Eric Idle**, Robin Williams, Charles McKeown, and

others. Released as a special feature on the 20th Anniversary Edition DVD release. Produced by Constantine Nasr.

3500 April 1, 2008
Terry Jones appears as host of a fake nature documentary — about a colony of flying penguins — for an April Fool's Day trailer promoting the BBC iPlayer. Directed by Vince Squibb.

3501 April 5, 2008
Terry Jones introduces a screening of Rene Clair's classic 1931 film *Le Million* at The Courtyard in Hereford, England, as part of the 6th annual Borderlines Film Festival (Mar. 28–Apr. 13).

3502 April 13, 2008
Michael Palin presents an appeal (on BBC Radio 4) on behalf of the international development charity Motivation.

3503 April 15, 2008
Filming ends on Terry Gilliam's *The Imaginarium of Doctor Parnassus*. Post-production won't be completed for nearly a year (in March 2009).

3504 April 17, 2008
Michael Palin opens the "Art in the Age of Steam" exhibition (Apr. 18–Aug. 10) at the Walker Art Gallery in Liverpool, England.

3505 April 24, 2008
John Cleese (and daughter Cynthia) and Eric Idle (and wife Tania) attend the 2nd annual BritWeek launch party at the British Consul General's residence in Los Angeles.

3506 April 26, 2008
The Comedy Map of Britain (TV episode: BBC2). "Scotland." Includes a stop at Doune Castle in Scotland, the main filming location for *Holy Grail*. With comments from *Grail*'s production manager, Julian Doyle. Narrated by Alan Whicker.

3507 April 27, 2008
The Andrew Marr Show (TV talk show: BBC1). Guests: David Cameron, David Miliband, and Michael Palin. Palin talks about the High Tide festival, meeting the Dalai Lama, and the *Timewatch* episode on World War I.

3508 May 2008
Michael Palin attends the High Tide film festival (May 2–5) in Halesworth, England, answering questions after a screening of his 1987 TV film *East of Ipswich*.

3509 May 2008
Terry Jones joins his neighbors, including actor Tom Conti, in a protest against a proposed construction highway near his home in the Hamstead Heath area of London.

3510 May 3, 2008
John Cleese and daughter Camilla attend the opening night performance of *Jersey Boys* at The Palazzo in Las Vegas.

3511 May 9, 2008
Was Richard II a Tyrant? (Lecture). Terry Jones questions King Richard II's reputation as a tyrant in a talk at the 43rd International Congress on Medieval Studies at Western Michigan University in Kalamazoo.

3512 May 13–June 3, 2008
The four-part documentary series *Terry Jones' Great Map Mystery* airs on BBC2 Wales. In the series, host Terry Jones travels four routes through his native Wales following John Ogilby's *Britannia* (1675), the world's first road atlas, in an attempt to discover the real purpose of the map.

3513 May 13, 2008
Terry Jones' Great Map Mystery (TV episode: BBC2 Wales). "The Road to Aberystwyth." Host Terry Jones takes the first route in John Ogilby's 1675 map, traveling from Presteigne, on the English border, to Aberystwyth. First episode in the four-part documentary series. Written, directed & produced by Alan Ereira.

3514 May 15, 2008
An Evening with John Cleese (Event). John Cleese hosts a screening of *Holy Grail* at Campbell Hall at the University of California Santa Barbara. The screening benefits UCSB's Arts & Lectures Cinema Series.

3515 May 19, 2008
Who Murdered Chaucer? (Lecture). Terry Jones speaks at the Hudson Union Society's fundraising gala in New York City. Jones' lecture (with slides) is based on his 2003 book of the same title.

3516 May 19, 2008
Michael Palin attends Press Day at the RHS Chelsea Flower Show 2008 (May 20–24). Also attending are Ringo Starr, George Martin, Brian May, and Felicity Kendal. One of the gardens in the show is "From Life to Life, A Garden for George Harrison," designed by Yvonne Innes.

3517 May 20, 2008
Terry Jones' Great Map Mystery (TV episode: BBC2 Wales). "The Road to St. Davids." Host **Terry Jones** travels from Monmouth to St. Davids. Second episode in the four-part documentary series. Written, directed & produced by Alan Ereira.

3518 May 21, 2008
Terry Jones receives the honorary degree of Doctor of Letters from Pace University during the commencement ceremony for undergraduates held at Radio City Music Hall in New York City. In his acceptance speech, **Jones** gives "bad advice" to the undergraduates.

3519 May 26, 2008
Monty Python's Flying Circus begins airing on the cable channel BBC America.

3520 May 27, 2008
Terry Jones' Great Map Mystery (TV episode: BBC2 Wales). "The Road to Holywell." Host **Terry Jones** travels the route connecting the two Catholic shrines of St. Davids and Holywell. Third episode in the four-part documentary series. Written, directed & produced by Alan Ereira.

3521 May 28, 2008
Michael Palin attends the launch of the Oxford Thinking campaign at the British Academy in London. The campaign raises funds for the University of Oxford, of which **Palin** is an alumnus (1962–65). For the campaign **Palin** filmed the short *Oxford Today*.

3522 May 28, 2008
Oxford Today (Short film). **Michael Palin** presents this 24-minute film on the University of Oxford as part of the school's Oxford Thinking fundraising campaign. Directed by Roger Mills.

3523 June 2008
John Cleese, recently separated from his wife, sells his 15-acre ranch in Montecito, CA, for a reported $16.5 million. **Cleese** will put his second home in Montecito — an ocean-front property — up for sale in October (asking price: $10.75 million).

3524 June 2008
Fourteenth Century England: V (Book: The Boydell Press, Woodbridge), edited by Nigel Saul, is published. Collection of essays, including **Terry Jones'** "Was Richard II a Tyrant? Richard's Use of the Books of Rules for Princes."

3525 June 1, 2008
Was Richard II a Tyrant? (Lecture). **Terry Jones** reassesses Richard II's reign in a lecture at Barclays Wealth Pavilion in Hay-on-Wye, Wales as part of the Hay Literary Festival (May 22–June 1).

3526 June 3, 2008
Terry Jones' Great Map Mystery (TV episode: BBC2 Wales). "The Road to Holyhead." Host **Terry Jones** travels the route from Chester, England (near the Welsh border) to the port town of Holyhead in North Wales. Last episode in the four-part documentary series. Written, directed & produced by Alan Ereira.

3527 June 19 & 20, 2008
Michael Palin gives a talk about *New Europe* at the Showroom Cinema Sheffield in his home town of Sheffield, Yorkshire, England (June 19). The following day he gives a speech (and plants a tree) at Sheffield Botanical Gardens to officially re-open the site following a period of restoration.

3528 June 19, 2008
Was Richard II Mad? (Lecture). **Terry Jones** challenges history's portrayal of Richard II as a mad tyrant in the Historical Association/English Association's annual lecture presented (with slides) at the Bishopsgate Institute in London.

3529 June 23, 2008
Richard & Judy (TV talk show: Channel 4). Hosted by Richard Madeley and Judy Finnigan. Guests: **Michael Palin**, Mary Portas, and Todd Wilbur.

3530 June 25, 2008
Terry Jones and **Michael Palin** introduce a screening of "lost" episodes of their 1969 TV comedy series *The Complete and Utter History of Britain* at an event hosted by the British Film Institute and held at the National Film Theatre in London. The episodes, previously thought to have been wiped from the tapes after their original airing, were recovered through the BFI's "Missing Believed Wiped" initiative (begun in 1993). The screening is followed by a Q&A session.

3531 June 26–27, 2008
The Seventh Python (Feature film), world premiere at the Mods & Rockers Film Festival at the Egyptian Theatre in Hollywood. Documentary about songwriter-musician Neil Innes, former member of The Bonzo Dog Band and the Beatles-parody group The Rutles, often referred to as the "Seventh Python" because of his collaborations with the

group (*Flying Circus, Holy Grail*, stage shows, etc.). Also appearing are **John Cleese, Eric Idle, Terry Jones**, and **Michael Palin**. Directed by Burt Kearns. Innes gives a special concert performance on the second night of the premiere.

3532 June 27, 2008
The One Show (TV talk show: BBC1). Hosted by Adrian Chiles and Christine Bleakley. Guest: **Michael Palin**, promoting his book *New Europe*.

3533 June 28, 2008
Financial Times (Newspaper/U.K.). "'I feel less afraid of the world'—Lunch with the FT: **Michael Palin**," p. 3. Rahul Jacob interviews **Palin** at Wiltons restaurant in London.

3534 July 2008
Michael Palin is awarded an Honorary Fellowship from the School of Oriental and African Studies (SOAS) at the University of London. He is presented the award at the school's graduation ceremonies.

3535 July 2008
Terry Gilliam attends the 6th Annual Ischia Global Film & Music Fest (July 13–20) on the Isle of Ischia, Gulf of Naples, Italy where he takes part in a scriptwriting panel.

3536 July 2, 2008
Michael Palin speaks on the subject of geography at Homerton College, Cambridge University as part of The Prince's Teaching Institute (PTI) Summer School (June 30–July 3).

3537 July 4, 2008
Discovering Hammershøi (Lecture). **Michael Palin** discusses his fascination with the Danish painter Vilhelm Hammershøi at the Royal Academy of Art in London. Part of the "Vilhelm Hammershøi: The Poetry of Silence" exhibition (June 28–Sept. 7). **Palin** hosted the 2005 documentary *Michael Palin and the Mystery of Hammershøi*.

3538 July 7, 2008
Palin on Art (DVD: BBC Worldwide) is released in the U.K. Two-disc set containing three of **Michael Palin**'s four documentaries on great painters: *Palin on Redpath* (1997), *Michael Palin on... The Colourists* (2000), and *Michael Palin and the Mystery of Hammershøi* (2005). The fourth doc, not included here, is *Michael Palin and the Ladies Who Loved Matisse* (2003).

3539 July 9, 2008
John Cleese and **Michael Palin** attend Sir David Frost's annual Summer Garden Party at Frost's residence in London. Other guests include Ronnie Corbett and Bill Wyman.

3540 July 14, 2008
Terry Jones gives a public reading from John Gower's *Confessio Amantis* at an event commemorating the 600th anniversary of the English poet's death (in 1408) at Southwark Cathedral in London.

3541 July 16, 2008
Richard & Judy (TV talk show: Channel 4). Hosted by Richard Madeley and Judy Finnigan. Guests: **John Cleese** and Tracey Emin.

3542 July 16, 2008
The Front Row (Radio arts show: KUHF public radio, Houston). Bob Stevenson talks to **Eric Idle** about tomorrow's Houston premiere of *Not the Messiah*. The interview was conducted backstage at Jones Hall following a rehearsal.

3543 July 17 & 18, 2008
The **Eric Idle**–John Du Prez oratorio *Not the Messiah (He's a Very Naughty Boy)* is performed at Jones Hall in Houston, Texas. **Idle** stars as narrator/soloist, joining soloists Shannon Mercer, Jean Stilwell, William Ferguson, and Theodore Baerg (all, except Ferguson, from the work's original June 2007 production in Toronto), with Du Prez conducting the Houston Symphony and Chorus. Note: **Idle** last performed in Houston in November 1989 in the Jonathan Miller/Houston Grand Opera production of *The Mikado*.

3544 July 23–25, 2008
John Cleese in Conversation with Chris Serle (Events). **John Cleese** participates in three evenings of conversations (with TV host Chris Serle) at The Clifton Pavilion Theatre at Bristol Zoo Gardens in Bristol, England. Proceeds from the events go to funding the Bristol Zoo's conservation programs. **Cleese** used to visit the zoo when he was a student at nearby Clifton College.

3545 July 24, 2008
All Things Considered (Radio talk show: NPR). Robert Siegel interviews **Eric Idle** about *Not the Messiah*.

3546 July 24, 2008
The **Eric Idle**–John Du Prez oratorio *Not the Messiah (He's a Very Naughty Boy)* premieres in the Washington, D.C., area at the Wolf Trap National Park for the Performing Arts near Vienna, VA. **Eric**

Idle stars as narrator and soloist, along with four soloists, the National Symphony Orchestra (conducted by Du Prez), chorus, bagpipers, and sheep.

3547 July 25, 2008
Michael Palin unveils a British Airways plane painted with the special Change for Good logo celebrating the 14-year partnership between BA and UNICEF U.K. which has raised £25 million for charity. The unveiling takes place at Heathrow airport in London.

3548 July 28, 2008
The Late Late Show with Craig Ferguson (TV talk show: CBS). Guest: **Eric Idle**, promoting *Not the Messiah* at the Hollywood Bowl.

3549 August 2008
Michael Palin's 2007 series *New Europe* is censured by the BBC Trust, the governing body of the BBC, for "inaccuracy" relating to statements **Palin** made in the show concerning responsibility for the Balkan wars. **Palin** later calls the action "a stupid decision."

3550 August 1 & 2, 2008
Eric Idle presents his oratorio *Not the Messiah (He's a Very Naughty Boy)* in its West Coast premiere at The Hollywood Bowl in Los Angeles. **Idle** performs as narrator and soloist, while the work's co-creator, composer John Du Prez, conducts the Los Angeles Philharmonic. The production also features soloists Shannon Mercer, Jean Stilwell, William Ferguson, and Theodore Baerg, plus The Pacific Chorale (John Alexander, director), The Los Angeles Scots Pipe Band, and a fireworks display. The oratorio, first performed in Toronto in June 2007, will be presented again in October 2009 at London's Royal Albert Hall with four of the five surviving Pythons participating.

3551 August 8, 2008
Comedy Connections (TV episode: BBC1). "Ripping Yarns." **Michael Palin** and **Terry Jones** look back on the making of their 1976–79 comedy series and the early days of their writing partnership. Narrated by Doon Mackichan. Directed by Maria Stewart. Produced by Paul Gallagher. Note: *Monty Python's Flying Circus* was the subject of a February 2005 episode.

3552 August 24, 2008
Eric Idle attends a surprise 50th birthday party for skater Scott Hamilton in Los Angeles.

3553 Fall 2008
Beautiful Britain (Magazine/U.K.). "Travelling Man." Mark Tully interviews **Michael Palin** at the London Transport Museum.

3554 September 2008
Terry Gilliam suffers a cracked vertebra when he is struck by a car outside a restaurant in Soho, London.

3555 September 3, 2008
Loose Women (TV talk show: ITV). Hosted by Jackie Brambles, Coleen Nolan, Carol McGiffin, and Sherrie Hewson. Guests: Jonathan Wilkes and **John Cleese**, who talks about writing a *Fish Called Wanda* musical with his daughter, his three marriages, his friend Michael Winner, growing old, and California.

3556 September 3, 2008
Michael Palin attends the Foyles Summer Party at Foyles bookshop in Charing Cross Road, London.

3557 September 5, 2008
Icons of England (Book: CPRE/Think Books), introduced by Bill Bryson, is published in the U.K. Anthology celebrating rural England. Contributors include **Michael Palin**, who writes in his piece ("Living on the Edge") about the crags of his native Sheffield. The expanded 2010 edition of the book (Black Swan) also includes a piece by **Terry Jones**, who writes about Hampstead Heath ("View Over London"). Proceeds from the book support the CPRE (Campaign to Protect Rural England).

3558 September 13, 2008
Terry Gilliam attends the 7th Milan Film Festival (Sept. 12–21), which is presenting a retrospective of his work.

3559 September 19, 2008
Michael Palin gives a talk at the Kenton Theatre in Henley-on-Thames, England as part of the Henley Literary Festival (Sept. 19–21).

3560 September 19, 2008
Igor (Feature film: MGM) opens in the U.S. Computer-animated feature. **John Cleese** voices Igor's master, Dr. Glickenstein. Other voices by John Cusack, Steve Buscemi, Molly Shannon, Eddie Izzard, Sean Hayes, Jennifer Coolidge, and Christian Slater. Written by Chris McKenna. Directed by Tony Leondis.

3561 September 30, 2008
Michael Palin attends the launch party for Sir Michael Parkinson's new book, *Parky: My Autobi-*

ography, at the Belvedere Restaurant in Holland Park, London.

3562 October 2008
Michael Palin returns to Dubai (United Arab Emirates) and Mumbai (India) twenty years after his last visit to the region, in October 1988, for his TV travel series *Around the World in 80 Days*. **Palin** also travels to Mandvi (in Kutch, India), where he finds the captain and other crew members of the *Al Shama*, the dhow that transported **Palin** across the Arabian Sea twenty years earlier. **Palin**'s account of his trip is included in the book *Around the World in 80 Days: Special 20th Anniversary Edition* (published Nov. 27). It is also filmed for the TV special *Around the World in 20 Years* (airing Dec. 30).

3563 October 4, 2008
The Times (London) (Newspaper/U.K.). "Richard II: Royal Villain or Victim of Spin?," by **Terry Jones**, p. 13. **Jones** explains why he believes that Richard's usurper, Henry IV, rewrote history in order to justify his treacherous grab for power.

3564 October 5, 2008
The South Bank Show (TV arts show: ITV). "The One Ronnie." Documentary on the career of comedian Ronnie Corbett (one half of the "Two Ronnies"), with contributions from **Michael Palin**, **John Cleese**, Sir David Frost, and others. Hosted & edited by Melvyn Bragg. Produced & directed by Jonathan Levi.

3565 October 11 & 12, 2008
Terry Jones appears at the 59th Cheltenham Festival of Literature (Oct. 10–19) in Cheltenham, England. On Oct. 11 he gives a talk on Richard II at the Book It! Tent; the following day he joins Joanna Lumley and Maureen Lipman in remembering the late humorist Miles Kington for *Miles Kington: A Celebration* at the Main Hall.

3566 October 20–24, 2008
Woman's Hour Drama (Radio series: BBC Radio 4). "How Shall I Tell the Dog?" **Michael Palin** plays Miles Kington in this radio adaptation of the late humorist's final book (he died of cancer in January). Told by his doctors that he has only months to live, Kington suggests a series of increasingly absurd ideas for a book to his agent Gill (played by Anna Massey). Five 15-minute episodes. Produced by Clive Brill.

3567 October 21, 2008
Eric Idle attends the Dream Believe Achieve Inspiration Gala, an event benefitting inner-city youth, at the Ahmanson Ballroom in the Skirball Cultural Center in Los Angeles. Performers include Jackson Browne and Smokey Robinson.

3568 October 30–December 4, 2008
Batteries Not Included (TV series: Dave). **John Cleese**, in his first British TV series since 2001's *The Human Face*, travels around the world testing unusual gadgets. This six-episode series, broadcast on the digital-only channel Dave, was inspired by **Cleese**'s role as gadget expert Q in the James Bond film *Die Another Day* (2002). Also featuring Danny Wallace, Dom Joly, Richard Herring, and others.

3569 October 30, 2008
Travel, Comedy and a Little Bit of Fish (Lecture). **Michael Palin** gives a charity performance at the Irwin Mitchell Oval Hall in his home town of Sheffield, relating stories from his days with Python and his travels around the world. The show raises £40,000 for the local charity, Helen's Trust.

3570 October 31, 2008
Countdown with Keith Olbermann (TV news show: MSNBC). Guest **John Cleese** comments on Sen. John McCain's presidential campaign and reads a poem he wrote about commentator Bill O'Reilly.

3571 October 31, 2008
The Daily Telegraph (Newspaper/U.K.). "**Michael Palin**: My Guilt Over My Great-Uncle Who Died in the First World War," by **Michael Palin**. **Palin** describes his experience making the *Timewatch* special about the last day of World War I (airing Nov. 1 on BBC2) and learning more about his great-uncle, Harry Palin, who was killed in action in 1916.

3572 November 2008
The Pythons launch The Monty Python Channel on YouTube. The site will provide high-quality clips from the group's TV and film archive. The creation of the site is an attempt to combat illegal uploading of Python material to YouTube.

3573 November 2008
Monty Python's Tunisian Holiday: My Life with Brian (Book: Thomas Dunne), written by Kim "Howard" Johnson, is published in the U.S. Behind-the-scenes record of the making of *Life of Brian* from Python chronicler Johnson (*The First 200 Years of Monty Python*), who accompanied the group to Tunisia, where the film was shot in 1978, and kept a diary. Forewords by **John Cleese**, **Eric Idle**, **Terry Jones**, and **Michael Palin**.

3574 November 1, 2008
Timewatch (TV episode: BBC2). "The Last Day of World War One." **Michael Palin** hosts this documentary looking at November 11, 1918, the last day of the First World War, and the thousands of soldiers who died in those final hours after the armistice was signed and before the ceasefire went into effect. **Palin** visits the war's battle and burial sites in France and Belgium. Produced & directed by John Hayes Fisher.

3575 November 2, 2008
The Andrew Marr Show (TV talk show: BBC1). Guests: Prime Minister Gordon Brown, Mark Thompson, and **Michael Palin. Palin** talks about revisiting the *80 Days* series, the *Timewatch* episode on World War I, and Campaign for Better Transport.

3576 November 6, 2008
A Masterclass with Michael Palin (Event). **Michael Palin** is interviewed on stage by travel writer Simon Calder at the Pennine Theatre, Hallam University City Campus in Sheffield (**Palin**'s home town), England as part of Sheffield Doc/Fest (Nov. 5–9). The talk is aided by video clips and followed by an audience Q&A.

3577 November 6, 2008
Eric Idle attends a performance of the first foreign-language production of *Spamalot* at the Teatre Victoria in Barcelona, Spain.

3578 November 7, 2008
The Alan Titchmarsh Show (TV talk show: ITV). Daytime talk show. Gloria Hunniford interviews **Michael Palin**.

3579 November 12, 2008
We Are Most Amused (Stage show). **John Cleese** hosts this comedy gala at London's New Wimbledon Theatre celebrating Prince Charles' 60th birthday (on Nov. 14) and raising money for his charity, The Prince's Trust. The Prince is in attendance, along with his wife, The Duchess of Cornwall, and son, Prince Harry. Other performers include **Eric Idle**, Robin Williams, Rowan Atkinson, Joan Rivers, Bill Bailey, and Andrew Sachs. Sachs reprises his Manuel character (from *Fawlty Towers*) for a short skit with **Cleese**. For the finale, **Idle** leads in the singing of "Always Look on the Bright Side of Life." Televised Nov. 15 on ITV1.

3580 November 13, 2008
Around the World in 80 Ways (Lecture). **Michael Palin** gives a talk at Queen Elizabeth Hall in London. The event raises funds for Campaign for Better Transport (formerly called Transport 2000), of which **Palin** is president.

3581 November 13, 2008
Richard & Judy's New Position (TV talk show: Watch). Hosted by Richard Madeley and Judy Finnigan. Guest: **John Cleese**, who talks about his recent hair transplant.

3582 November 15, 2008
The charity gala *We Are Most Amused*, featuring **John Cleese, Eric Idle**, Robin Williams, and others, airs on ITV1.

3583 November 17, 2008
The Rutles: All You Need Is Cash (30th Anniversary Edition) (DVD: Second Sight Films) is released in the U.K. **Eric Idle**'s 1978 mockumentary, previously released on DVD in 2001, is reissued with new extras, including the documentaries *Get Up & Go: The Making of The Rutles* and *Inside Shabby Road: The Music of The Rutles*.

3584 November 17, 2008
Get Up & Go: The Making of The Rutles (Documentary). The story of The Rutles told through clips from **Eric Idle**'s 1978 film *All You Need Is Cash* and interviews with **Michael Palin** (who played Eric Manchester in the film), Neil Innes (Ron Nasty), John Halsey (Barry Wom), Ricky Fataar (Stig O'Hara), and co-director Gary Weis. Included on the 30th-anniversary DVD release of the film. Half-hour.

3585 November 17, 2008
Inside Shabby Road: The Music of The Rutles (Documentary). Singer-songwriter Neil Innes discusses the music of the Pre-Fab Four and his early music career as a member of The Bonzo Dog Band (who appeared in The Beatles' 1967 TV film *Magical Mystery Tour*). Includes interviews with John Halsey, Ricky Fataar, and **Michael Palin**. Included on the 30th-anniversary DVD release of *All You Need Is Cash*. Half-hour.

3586 November 18, 2008
The Complete Monty Python's Flying Circus: Collector's Edition (DVD set: A&E Home Video) is released. Twenty-one-disc DVD set containing all 45 episodes of *Flying Circus* (14 discs) and the extras (7 discs): *Before the Flying Circus: A Black and White Documentary* (new doc), *Monty Python Conquers America* (new doc), *Animated Gilliam* (short), "Politically Incorrect" (deleted 1973 sketch "A Party Political Broadcast on Behalf of the Conservative

and Unionist Party"), *Monty Python Live at the Hollywood Bowl* (1982 film), *Live at Aspen* (1998 HBO special), *Parrot Sketch Not Included: Twenty Years of Monty Python* (1989 doc), *Monty Python's Fliegender Zirkus* (first German special), and the six *Personal Best* specials (2006). All of the material in this set (except for the two new docs) had been previously released by A&E: The 14-disc *Flying Circus* set (in 2000), the 2-disc *Monty Python Live!* set (in 2001), and the 6-disc *Personal Best* set (in 2006).

3587 November 18, 2008
Before the Flying Circus: A Black and White Documentary (Documentary). Hour-long doc looking back at the Pythons' early years in comedy and how they eventually came together. Includes interviews with the Pythons, also Robert Hewison, Humphrey Barclay, Sir David Frost, Ronnie Corbett, and others. Narrated by Robert Bathurst. Produced & directed by Will Yapp. Executive Producer: John Goldstone. Released on the DVD set *The Complete Monty Python's Flying Circus: Collector's Edition*.

3588 November 18, 2008
Monty Python Conquers America (Documentary). Hour-long doc detailing how Python broke through in the U.S., from their first attempts in 1972 with the film *And Now for Something Completely Different* and Buddah Records' release of *Another Python Record* to their successful run on PBS television (starting in 1974) and hit stage shows (in 1976 and 1980). Includes interviews with the Pythons, also Victor Lownes, Nancy Lewis, Carol Cleveland, Carl Reiner, Tony Smith, John Goldstone, Robert Klein, George Schlatter, Hank Azaria, Jimmy Fallon, David Hyde Pierce, and others. Narrated by Tom Streithorst. Produced & directed by Will Yapp. Executive Producer: John Goldstone. Released on the DVD set *The Complete Monty Python's Flying Circus: Collector's Edition*.

3589 November 19, 2008
John Cleese is a keynote speaker at the World Creativity Forum held at the Lotto Arena in Antwerp, Belgium.

3590 November 24, 2008
Eric Idle attends the Friends of the Saban Free Clinic's 32rd Annual Dinner Gala held at The Beverly Hilton hotel in Beverly Hills, CA.

3591 November 27, 2008
Around the World in 80 Days: Special 20th Anniversary Edition (Book: Weidenfeld & Nicolson), written by **Michael Palin**, is published in the U.K. Updated edition of the 1989 book that accompanied **Palin**'s BBC travel series. Includes new photographs and a new chapter chronicling his return to Dubai and Mumbai in search of the crew of the *Al Shama*, the dhow that carried him across the Arabian Sea twenty years ago. A documentary special about his return visit, *Around the World in 20 Years*, airs Dec. 30.

3592 December 2008
PythOnline is re-launched. The website is operated by **Eric Idle** in partnership with New Media Broadcasting Company (based in Glendale, CA). **Idle** launched the first version of the site in July 1996 (with 7th Level).

3593 December 5, 2008
The New York Times (Newspaper online/U.S.). "The Extended Life of Monty Python," by Douglas Quenqua. Article on **Eric Idle**'s efforts to keep the Python legacy alive, which include the new website PythOnline.

3594 December 8, 2008
Frost Over the World (TV talk show: Al Jazeera English). Hosted by David Frost. Guest: **Michael Palin**, promoting the 20th-Anniversary Edition of his book *Around the World in 80 Days*. He also talks about no longer being the most famous Palin with Alaskan governor Sarah Palin now in the headlines.

3595 December 10, 2008
Michael Palin gives a poetry reading at the annual Parkinson's Disease Society Christmas Carol Concert at the Methodist Central Hall, Westminster, London.

3596 December 12, 2008
The Day the Earth Stood Still (Feature film: Twentieth Century–Fox) opens in the U.S. Remake of the 1951 sci-fi classic. **John Cleese** plays Professor Barnhardt. Also starring Keanu Reeves, Jennifer Connelly, Kathy Bates, Kyle Chandler, and Jaden Smith. Written by David Scarpa. Directed by Scott Derrickson.

3597 December 12, 2008
Delgo (Feature film: Freestyle Releasing) opens in the U.S. Computer-animated fantasy-adventure about a youth who tries to bring peace to two warring alien races. **Eric Idle** voices Spig, servant of the villainous Sedessa. The independently-made film started production back in 1998. Also voiced by Freddie Prinze, Jr., Jennifer Love Hewitt, Anne Bancroft, Val Kilmer, and Burt Reynolds. Written by Patrick J. Cowan, Carl Dream, and Jennifer A.

Jones. Directed by Marc F. Adler and Jason Maurer.

3598 December 15, 2008
The One Show (TV talk show: BBC1). Hosted by Adrian Chiles and Christine Bleakley. Guests: **Michael Palin**, promoting the 20th-Anniversary Edition of his book *Around the World in 80 Days*, and Bette Midler (in New York).

3599 December 16, 2008
Michael Palin signs copies of his new book *Around the World in 80 Days: Special 20th Anniversary Edition* at Waterstone's bookshop in London.

3600 December 22, 2008
Time Shift (TV episode: BBC4). "The Comic Songbook." Documentary on the history of Britain's comic songs. Includes interviews with **Michael Palin**, **Terry Jones**, Neil Innes, Bill Oddie, and others. Produced & directed by Georgina Harvey.

3601 December 26, 2008
The Man Who Made Eric and Ernie (TV special: BBC2). Hour-long tribute to BBC TV exec Sir Bill Cotton (1928–2008), who helped launch the careers of Morecambe & Wise and other British comics. Includes appearances by **Michael Palin**, Ronnie Corbett, Bruce Forsyth, Michael Parkinson, and others. Narrated by Frances de la Tour. Produced & directed by Alexandra Briscoe.

3602 December 30, 2008
Around the World in 20 Years (TV special: BBC1). One-hour documentary celebrating the 20th anniversary of **Michael Palin**'s 1988 journey around the world (broadcast in 1989). In the special, **Palin** returns to Dubai and Mumbai in search of the crew of the dhow that carried him across the Arabian Sea twenty years ago. Written & narrated by **Michael Palin**. Produced & directed by Roger Mills.

3603 2008
Kaupthing Bank ("Thinking Beyond") (TV commercials). **John Cleese** stars in a series of Icelandic ads for Kaupthing Bank playing a banking "expert" speaking at a banking conference. Titles include "E-Card Banking," "Loyalty System," and "Service." Written by Jón Gnarr. Directed by Tim Hamilton. Agency: Ennemm, Reykjavik, Iceland.

3604 2008
John Cleese divorces his third wife, Alyce Faye Eichelberger. The couple were married in December 1992 and separated in January 2008. Eichelberger is awarded a $13 million divorce settlement. **Cleese** must also pay her $1 million a year until 2015.

3605 January 2–March 27, 2009
The Legend of Dick and Dom (TV series: CBBC). First series (13 episodes) of the British children's show. **Terry Jones** narrates the series, which stars Richard McCourt and Dominic Wood as two young princes from the kingdom of Fyredor who set out on a quest to find a cure for the plague ravaging their kingdom.

3606 January 7, 2009
Movie Connections (TV episode: BBC1). "Monty Python and the Holy Grail." Documentary on the making of the 1975 comedy classic. Includes interviews with **John Cleese**, **Terry Gilliam**, **Eric Idle**, **Michael Palin**, Neil Innes, Carol Cleveland, and producers Mark Forstater and John Goldstone. Narrated by Ashley Jensen. Directed by Ewan Torrance.

3607 January 11, 2009
The **Eric Idle**–John Du Prez musical *Spamalot* ends its successful Broadway run at the Shubert Theatre after nearly four years and 1,575 performances. The show opened Mar. 17, 2005.

3608 January 21, 2009
Comedy Chief (Event). **Michael Palin** interviews TV comedy producer Humphrey Barclay about becoming the Development Chief of the African village of Kwahu-Tafo in Ghana. The fundraising event (for Friends of Tafo) takes place at the Royal Geographical Society in London. **Palin** worked with Barclay in the late 1960s on the shows *Do Not Adjust Your Set* and *The Complete and Utter History of Britain*.

3609 January 27, 2009
The Secret Policeman's Balls (DVD: Shout! Factory). Three-DVD set containing the Amnesty International films *Pleasure at Her Majesty's* (1976), *The Secret Policeman's Ball* (1979) and its three sequels (1981–89), plus *Remember the Secret Policeman's Ball?* (2004 doc) and various extras.

3610 January 28, 2009
King Guillaume (Feature film) is released in France. French comedy in which **Terry Jones** appears as an Oxford professor. Starring Florence Foresti, Pierre-François Martin-Laval, and Pierre Richard. Written by Jean-Paul Bathany, Perre-François Martin-Laval, and Fred Proust. Directed by Pierre-François Martin-Laval.

3611 February 2009
Brush with Fame (TV episode: Sky Arts 1). "**John Cleese**." Artist/host John Myatt paints two portraits of **Cleese** in the style of Henri Matisse. The sitting takes place in the Queen's House, Greenwich. Produced & directed by Caz Stuart.

3612 February 3, 2009
BBC Breakfast (TV news show: BBC1/News Channel). Hosted by Bill Turnbull and Sian Williams. Lizo Mzimba interviews **Terry Gilliam**.

3613 February 3, 2009
Jimmy Kimmel Live! (TV talk show: ABC). Guest: **John Cleese**, promoting *The Pink Panther 2*.

3614 February 4, 2009
The Bonnie Hunt Show (TV talk show: Synd.). Guest: **John Cleese**, promoting *The Pink Panther 2*. **Cleese** also talks about his mother's sense of humor, his daughters, his three wives, and his experience working with the late Peter Sellers.

3615 February 5, 2009
Simon Mayo (Radio talk show: BBC Radio 5 Live). Host Simon Mayo and Mark Kermode interview **Terry Gilliam**.

3616 February 6, 2009
The Pink Panther 2 (Feature film: Columbia Pictures) opens in the U.S. Comedy starring Steve Martin as Inspector Clouseau (a role originated by Peter Sellers), sequel to the 2006 re-launch of the series. **John Cleese** plays Chief Inspector Charles Dreyfus. Also starring Jean Reno, Emily Mortimer, Jeremy Irons, and Andy Garcia. Written by Scott Neustadter, Michael H. Weber, and Steve Martin. Directed by Harald Zwart.

3617 February 6, 2009
Chelsea Lately (TV talk show: E! Entertainment). Host Chelsea Handler interviews **John Cleese**, who talks about his age, his daughters, writing a *Fish Called Wanda* musical, and *The Pink Panther 2*.

3618 February 6, 2009
Front Row (Radio arts show: BBC Radio 4). Kirsty Lang talks with **Terry Gilliam** about his reputation as a disaster-prone maverick filmmaker.

3619 February 8, 2009
The Orange British Academy Film Awards (Award ceremony). **Terry Gilliam** is awarded BAFTA's highest honor, The Academy Fellowship, for his outstanding contribution to film. Jonathan Pryce (*Brazil*) presents the award to **Gilliam**, while Jeff Bridges (*The Fisher King*), on video, praises the director and introduces a clip package of career highlights. In his acceptance speech, **Gilliam** thanks his family (who are in the audience) and pays tribute to the late Heath Ledger. The ceremony is hosted by Jonathan Ross from London's Royal Opera House. Broadcast on BBC1 and BBC2.

3620 February 9, 2009
This Morning (TV show: ITV). Magazine program hosted by Phillip Schofield and Fern Britton. **Terry Gilliam** is interviewed.

3621 February 9, 2009
An Evening with John Cleese (Event). **John Cleese** hosts a screening of *A Fish Called Wanda* at Campbell Hall at the University of California Santa Barbara. The event benefits UCSB's Arts & Lectures Cinema Series.

3622 February 13 & 15, March 20 & 22, 2009
The Comic Genius: A Multidisciplinary Approach (Seminar). Two-part seminar taught by **John Cleese** and Prof. Richard Tarnas in Namaste Hall at the California Institute of Integral Studies in San Francisco. The seminar explores the role of comedy in cultural life. **Cleese** and Tarnas became friends in 2003 after **Cleese** attended one of the professor's workshops.

3623 February 18, 2009
Michael Palin attends the annual Orion Authors' Party at the Victoria and Albert Museum in London.

3624 February 20, 2009
The Culture Show Uncut (TV arts show: BBC2). Mark Kermode hosts his own Kermode Awards of 2009, honoring **Terry Gilliam** with the Fellowship Award. Kermode also interviews **Gilliam** about his career and influences.

3625 February 22, 2009
John Cleese and his daughter Camilla attend the *Vanity Fair* Oscar Party at the Sunset Tower Hotel in West Hollywood, CA.

3626 March 2009
John Cleese becomes a contributing editor to the British magazine *The Spectator*. In his first article, "The Real Reason I Had to Join *The Spectator*" (Mar. 28), **Cleese** writes about the consistently bad reviews he has received in *The Spectator* over the years.

3627 March 2009
Michael Palin is a special guest at the 13th Sofia International Film Festival (Mar. 5–15) in Sofia,

Bulgaria where he receives the Sofia Prize for his contribution to film and television. The festival also features screenings of his work.

3628 March 3, 2009
Terry Jones participates in a tribute to his friend, the late humorist Miles Kington, at the Bath Literature Festival (Feb. 28–Mar. 8) in Bath, England.

3629 March 13, 2009
Twenty Years on the Road (Lecture). **Michael Palin** talks about his travels for the BBC in a lecture (with slides) at Assembly Hall in New College, University of Edinburgh in Scotland. The lecture is hosted by the University of Edinburgh and the Royal Scottish Geographical Society (RSGS). Before the lecture **Palin** receives the 2008 Livingstone Medal from the RSGS (presented by the Society's president, Lord Lindsay), along with his Honorary Fellowship of the Society (awarded in 1993). The Livingstone Medal honors outstanding public service in the area of geography.

3630 March 24, 2009
Michael Palin opens a new exhibition at The Portal Gallery in New Cavendish Street, London. The art gallery is celebrating its 50th anniversary.

3631 March 25, 2009
The Ingenious Gentleman Don Quixote: Words and Music from the Time of Cervantes (Concert) is performed by the Los Angeles Guitar Quartet and **John Cleese** with the Santa Barbara Symphony at the Lobero Theatre, Santa Barbara, CA. **Cleese** reads adapted portions from Cervantes' novel while the quartet performs.

3632 March 25, 2009
The Wind in the Willows: A Centenary Celebration (Event). **Terry Jones** attends an evening of readings, conversation and music in appreciation for Kenneth Grahame's classic children's story. The event, hosted by writer Libby Purves, takes place at the British Library in London. **Jones** adapted the story as a live-action film in 1996.

3633 March 26, 2009
Was Richard II a Tyrant? (Lecture). **Terry Jones** gives a talk in defense of King Richard II at the Law and Social Sciences Lecture Theatre at The University of Nottingham, England. Part of the university's Distinguished Speaker Series. **Jones** has given this lecture several times before at venues including Pace University (October 2007) and Western Michigan University (May 2008).

3634 March 27, 2009
Terry Jones gives a talk at the 15th annual Bradford International Film Festival (Mar. 13–28), held at the National Media Museum in Bradford, West Yorkshire, England. The festival also screens **Jones'** post–Python directorial efforts, including *Erik the Viking: The Director's Son's Cut*. **Michael Palin** was honored by the festival in 2008 with a Lifetime Achievement Award.

3635 March 28, 2009
Life of Brian is screened for the first time in the Welsh town of Aberystwyth, with **Terry Jones** and **Michael Palin** attending. The film had been banned in the town since its original release in 1979. The charity screening, which takes place at the Aberystwyth Arts Centre, is also attended by the town's mayor, Sue Jones-Davies, who played Judith in the film. The event is filmed for the TV special *Monty Python in Aberystwyth: A Mayor and Two Pythons*, which airs May 12 on BBC1 Wales. Welsh-born **Jones** previously visited Aberystwyth for the first episode of his 2008 series *Terry Jones' Great Map Mystery*.

3636 April 2009
Terry Jones records an audio guide for visitors to Doune Castle in Scotland. The 14th-century castle was used in much of the filming for *Holy Grail* in May 1974. The audio guide was commissioned by the historical preservation agency Historic Scotland, which has been organizing special "Monty Python Day" events at the castle since 2004.

3637 April 2009
Michael Palin is awarded the Order of Magellan by the Circumnavigators Club.

3638 April 3, 2009
The British Book Awards (Award ceremony). **Michael Palin** receives the Outstanding Achievement Award at the ceremony at the Grosvenor House Hotel in London. It is the fourth "Nibbie" **Palin** has won since 1993. Hosted by Richard Madeley and Judy Finnigan.

3639 April 7, 2009
Michael Palin attends the 70th birthday celebration for Sir David Frost at the Lanesborough Hotel in London. Other guests include Billy Connolly, Ronnie Corbett, Andrew Lloyd Webber, Rory Bremner, Tim Rice, Melvyn Bragg, Sir Roger Moore, and Liam Neeson.

3640 April 14, 2009
The late George Harrison (who died in 2001) re-

ceives a star on the Hollywood Walk of Fame in Los Angeles. His friend **Eric Idle** is among the speakers at the ceremony. Other attendees include Paul McCartney, Tom Hanks, and Tom Petty.

3641 April 15, 2009
The Importance of Creativity (Lecture). **John Cleese** gives a talk on creativity in Laurie Auditorium at Trinity University in San Antonio, TX. Followed by an audience Q&A. Part of the university's Distinguished Lecture Series.

3642 April 19–22, 2009
John Cleese visits Cornell University in Ithaca, NY, where he is currently the Provost's Visiting Professor. During his visit, **Cleese** gives a talk on creativity, politics and psychology in Statler Auditorium (Apr. 19) and, following a screening of the *Fawlty Towers* episode "Waldorf Salad," lectures to Hotel Administration students in the Beck Center about his hotel experiences over the years (Apr. 20).

3643 April 23, 2009
Eric Idle and his wife attend the 3rd annual BritWeek launch party at the British Consul General's residence in Hancock Park, Los Angeles.

3644 April 24, 2009
One on One (TV talk show: Al Jazeera). Riz Khan talks to **Terry Gilliam** about Hollywood, critics, Python, *Don Quixote*, etc.

3645 Late April–May 2009
John Cleese and his daughter, Cynthia, are guests on the Queen Mary 2 ocean liner for its New York-to-Southampton (England) crossing.

3646 May 1, 2009
Michael Palin attends the re-opening of the Pitt Rivers Museum in Oxford, England. The museum, of which **Palin** is a patron, had been closed for ten months for re-modeling.

3647 May 4, 2009
Beyond a Joke (TV episode: ITV3). "A Class Apart." **John Cleese** appears in this first episode of the five-part TV documentary series on British sitcoms of the past. Narrated by Dave Lamb. Produced & directed by Vicky Thomas.

3648 May 6, 2009
The cast of *Fawlty Towers*—**John Cleese**, Connie Booth, Prunella Scales and Andrew Sachs—reunite at a press launch for two upcoming *Fawlty* TV specials (airing May 10 & 17). The event takes place at The Naval and Military Club in London.

3649 May 6, 2009
The Paul O'Grady Show (TV talk show: Channel 4). Guests: Channing Tatum and **John Cleese**. **Cleese**, promoting the two upcoming *Fawlty Towers* documentaries, also talks about the films *Life of Brian* and *A Fish Called Wanda*, and speaking German.

3650 May 7, 2009
In Search of John Gower: Glosses, Recensions, Politics (Discussion). **Terry Jones** participates in a panel discussion on English poet John Gower (a contemporary of Geoffrey Chaucer) at the 44th International Congress on Medieval Studies at Western Michigan University in Kalamazoo. **Jones** gave a lecture on Richard II at the university last May.

3651 May 9 & 10, 2009
Comedy Writing with Terry Jones (Seminars). **Terry Jones** participates in two comedy writing seminars (with interviewer Kim "Howard" Johnson) at Chicago's iO Theatre.

3652 May 9, 2009
Terry Jones attends a "Meet the Maker" screening of *Holy Grail* at the Lakeshore Theater in Chicago. **Jones** introduces the film and takes part in a Q&A session afterward.

3653 May 9, 2009
Eric Idle attends the Westfield Hollywood Ashes Cricket Match between Australia and Britain at Woodley Park Cricket Field in Van Nuys, CA.

3654 May 10, 2009
Fawlty Towers: Re-Opened (TV special: G.O.L.D.). British documentary on the celebrated sitcom *Fawlty Towers*, marking the 30th anniversary of the end of the series' run (in 1979), with comments from the show's stars **John Cleese**, Connie Booth, Prunella Scales, Andrew Sachs, and producer John Howard Davies, also **Michael Palin**, **Terry Jones**, and others. A second documentary, *Fawlty Exclusive: Basil's Best Bits*, compiling the series' best moments, airs the following week. Narrated by Stephen Fry. Directed by Lindsay Jex.

3655 May 12, 2009
Monty Python in Aberystwyth: A Mayor and Two Pythons (TV special: BBC1 Wales). Documentary examining how the controversy surrounding *Life of Brian* in 1979 prompted many towns in Britain to ban the film and how one of those towns, Aberystwyth in Wales, finally lifted the ban thirty years later. Includes interviews with **Terry Jones** and **Michael Palin**, who attended a special screen-

ing of the film in Aberystwyth in March of this year, and Sue Jones-Davies, an actress in the film who became the town's mayor in 2008. Narrated by David Tennant. Written & directed by James Strong.

3656   May 17, 2009
Open Book (Radio show: BBC Radio 4). Mariella Frostrup talks to **Michael Palin**, who selects his "Five of the Best" books (they include *Tales from the Arabian Nights* and *Virginia Woolf Diaries*). Recorded May 5 (**Palin**'s birthday).

3657   May 17, 2009
Fawlty Exclusive: Basil's Best Bits (TV special: G.O.L.D.). Second of two British TV documentaries on the classic sitcom *Fawlty Towers* offers highlights from all twelve episodes as **John Cleese** picks his favorite moments. Also with **Michael Palin**, **Terry Jones**, others. Narrated by Stephen Fry.

3658   May 21, 2009
Spiegel Online (Website). **Michael Palin** is interviewed by Martin Wolf.

3659   May 22, 2009
The Imaginarium of Doctor Parnassus (Feature film), world premiere at the Cannes Film Festival in France. **Terry Gilliam**'s eleventh feature film as director — and his first original screenplay since 1989's *The Adventures of Baron Munchausen* — tells the story of the very old Doctor Parnassus (Christopher Plummer) and his traveling theater troupe who offer customers a chance to explore their imaginations by passing through a magic mirror. When actor Heath Ledger, who plays Tony, died halfway through filming (on Jan. 22, 2008), his role was completed with the help of actors Johnny Depp, Colin Farrell, and Jude Law, who each play a different incarnation of the character after he passes through the mirror. Also starring Lily Cole, Verne Troyer, Andrew Garfield, and Tom Waits. Written by **Terry Gilliam** and Charles McKeown. Songs (lyrics by **Gilliam**): "We Love Violence" and "We Are the Children of the World." Directed by **Terry Gilliam**. Produced by **Terry Gilliam**, Amy Gilliam (daughter of **Terry**), Samuel Hadida, and William Vince. Released in the U.S. on Jan. 8, 2010.
Awards: Academy Award-nominated for Art Direction (Caroline Smith, Anastasia Masaro, and David Warren) and Costume Design (Monique Prudhomme); BAFTA-nominated for Production Design (Smith, Masaro, and Warren) and Make-Up & Hair (Sarah Monzani).

Reviews: Lisa Schwarzbaum (*Entertainment Weekly*, May 22, 2009, p. 59): "...as is so often the case since his Monty Python days, **Gilliam** is best at visual games and weakest at storytelling ... individual scenes are dazzling.... But the assembled moments amount to a portfolio of collages..."; Kenneth Turan (*Los Angeles Times*, Dec. 25, 2009): "...as unusual and idiosyncratic as its one-of-a-kind title. You'd expect no less from **Terry Gilliam**.... *Imaginarium* is one of his most original and accessible works."

3660   May 22, 2009
Terry Gilliam attends the premiere showing of *The Imaginarium of Doctor Parnassus* at the Cannes Film Festival in France. **Gilliam** and the cast take questions from the press corps.

3661   May 23–28, 2009
Michael Palin attends the second Palestine Festival of Literature, or "Palfest." Though a seasoned world traveler, it is **Palin**'s first visit to the Palestine region.

3662   May 30, 2009
Terry Jones talks about *Barbarians* at the Listowel Arms Hotel in Ireland as part of the 39th Listowel Writers Week (May 27–31).

3663   Late May–June 2009
Terry Gilliam attends the 3rd annual Ibiza International Film Festival (May 27–June 3), on the Island of Ibiza in Spain, where he is honored with a film retrospective. **Gilliam** is a patron of the festival.

3664   June 2009
Michael Palin participates in Refugee Action's Simple Acts campaign for Refugee Week (June 15–21). **Palin**'s "simple act" is to learn a few words in another language. His teacher is 26-year-old Somali refugee Musa Ibrahim, whom **Palin** will interview in November for his "Michael Meets..." series for the Royal Geographical Society.

3665   June 1, 2009
Michael Palin is elected president of the Royal Geographical Society for a three-year term. **Palin** has been a Fellow of the Society since 1978 and also had the title of Honorary Vice President of the Society.

3666   June 1, 2009
Michael Palin speaks at the Etonnants Voyageurs International Book and Film Festival in St. Malo, France where he is promoting the French edition of his book *Around the World in 80 Days*.

3667 June 3, 2009
John Cleese and his companion, actress Lisa Hogan, attend the Royal Academy of Arts Summer Exhibition Preview Party 2009 at Burlington House in London.

3668 June 5, 2009
John Cleese speaks about creativity at the 14th Yorkshire International Business Convention, first at the Yorkshire Event Centre in Harrogate, then at Burton Agnes Hall at Bridlington Spa.

3669 June 11–19, 2009
The Secret Policeman's Film Festival (Film screenings). Film festival celebrating the 30th anniversary of Amnesty International benefit show & film *The Secret Policeman's Ball* (1979), presented at the American Cinematheque's Egyptian Theatre in Hollywood. *Ball* and other Amnesty shows brought together the best of British comedy (Monty Python, Peter Cook, Billy Connolly, etc.) and British rock (Pete Townsend, Sting, Donovan, etc.). Films shown during the festival also include *Pleasure at Her Majesty's* (1976), *Mermaid Frolics* (1977), *The Secret Policeman's Ball* (1979), *The Secret Policeman's Other Ball* (1982), and *Remember the Secret Policeman's Ball?* (2004 doc). Curated & produced by *Ball* series co-creator Martin Lewis. The festival also plays at The Paley Center for Media in Beverly Hills (June 24–July 19), The Film Society of Lincoln Center in NYC (June 26–July 1), The Paley Center for Media in Manhattan (July 1–31), and later at the AFI Silver Theatre in Silver Spring, MD (Dec. 10–15).

3670 June 13, 2009
Dermot O'Leary (Radio show: BBC Radio 2). Guest **Michael Palin** selects some of his favorite songs, including Bruce Springsteen's "4th of July, Asbury Park (Sandy)."

3671 June 18, 2009
Michael Palin attends and speaks at the sixth annual Borders Book Festival (June 18–21) at Harmony Gardens in Melrose, Scotland and takes part in the fundraising effort for the literacy charity Book Aid International. **Palin** is promoting the upcoming publication (in September) of his second volume of diaries, *Halfway to Hollywood: Diaries 1980–1988*. While at the festival, **Palin** is interviewed by Stuart McFarlane of Radio Borders for Hotdisc TV. He also talks to Alistair Moffat for *The Radio Café* (Radio Scotland), which airs July 14.

3672 June 19, 2009
Eric Idle attends the opening night gala at the Hollywood Bowl in Los Angeles.

3673 June 25, 2009
The Leonard Lopate Show (Radio talk show: WNYC-FM, New York). Producer Martin Lewis and **Terry Jones** (on the phone) are interviewed about *The Secret Policeman's Film Festival*, opening tomorrow in New York.

3674 June 26, 2009
A Night with Michael Palin: 20 Years of Travelling, 40 Years of Jokes (Lecture). **Michael Palin** gives a talk on his travels for the BBC and his years in comedy. The event, which takes place at the O2 Arena in London, benefits the Medical Foundation for the Care of Victims of Torture.

3675 June 28, 2009
Radio 4 Appeal (Radio appeal: BBC Radio 4). **Michael Palin** delivers a 3-minute appeal on behalf of the Michael Palin Centre for Stammering Children.

3676 July 6, 2009
The Late Late Show with Craig Ferguson (TV talk show: CBS). Guest **Eric Idle** talks about *Spamalot* playing in Los Angeles, *Not the Messiah* playing the Royal Albert Hall in October, and sings his original song "Life Will Get You in the End."

3677 July 8, 2009
Spamalot opens in Los Angeles at the Ahmanson Theater. **Eric Idle** attends, joining the cast onstage at the curtain call. He later attends the rooftop after-party at The Standard Hotel. The production, which features John O'Hurley (King Arthur) and Merle Dandridge (Lady of the Lake), runs until Sept. 6.

3678 July 12, 2009
Toronto Star (Newspaper/Can.). "**John Cleese**: A Towering Force of Funny at *Just for Laughs*," by Rob Salem, p. E1. Interview with **Cleese**, who will be appearing in the upcoming *Just for Laughs* comedy festival.

3679 July 18, 2009
The Globe and Mail (Newspaper/Can.). "Loves Vancouver, Hates Accountants," p. R9. Michael Posner interviews **John Cleese**, who is in Toronto to host tonight's *Just for Laughs* Britcom Galas.

3680 July 18, 2009
John Cleese hosts two BritCom Galas as part of the 3rd Toronto *Just for Laughs* comedy festival (July 15–19) at Massey Hall in Toronto, Canada. Performers include Mark Watson, Gina Yashere,

and Jimmy Carr. **Cleese** devotes his opening monologue to his recent costly divorce settlement and later hosts a telethon for himself. He then moves on to Montreal where he is scheduled to host a *Just for Laughs* gala on July 22. **Cleese** last appeared at the festival in July 2006 (in Montreal).

3681 July 23, 2009
Terry Gilliam appears at Comic-Con International at Hall H in San Diego to discuss — and show clips from — his new film *The Imaginarium of Doctor Parnassus*, which premiered at Cannes in May. Verne Troyer, one of the stars of the film, also appears on the panel. At the start the event **Gilliam** is presented with Comic-Con's Inkpot Award for Achievement in Film Arts.

3682 July 26, 2009
John Cleese hosts two galas on the closing night of the *Just for Laughs* comedy festival at the Theatre St. Denis in Montreal, Canada. He was forced to cancel an earlier performance, on July 22, due to a bout of prostatitis (inflammation of the prostate gland), and was replaced at the last minute by comedian Lewis Black. Poking fun at his illness, **Cleese** appears on stage with an IV pole.

3683 August 3, 2009
New Statesman (Magazine/U.K.). "Diary: **John Cleese**'s Balls-Up," by Mark Watson, p. 8. Comedian Mark Watson writes about his experience working with **Cleese** at the *Just for Laughs* festival.

3684 August 6, 2009
Michael Palin's second grandson, Wilbur Spike, is born.

3685 August 10, 2009
The Daily Post (Liverpool) (Newspaper/U.K.). "The Welsh King of Comedy; Top 30 North Walians Part 8," by Martin Williams, p. 22. Profile of North Wales native **Terry Jones**.

3686 August 29, 2009
George Harrison: What Is Life (Radio documentary: BBC Radio 2). **Michael Palin** narrates this tribute to the late George Harrison. Includes comments from Ringo Starr, Ravi Shankar, Olivia Harrison, and many others. Produced by Kevin Howlett.

3687 September 2009
Terry Jones' daughter, Siri, is born. She is **Jones**' third child, following Sally (now 35) and Bill (now 33). The mother is **Jones**' 26-year-old girlfriend, Anna Söderström.

3688 September 2009
An early 70th birthday party for **John Cleese** is held at the Holland Park, London home of his friend, director Michael Winner, who organized the party. Guests include **Michael Palin** and Leslie Caron. **Cleese** turns 70 on Oct. 27.

3689 September 2009
Marlow Meets... (TV talk show: Sky Arts). "**Michael Palin**." **Palin**, at the Tate Britain gallery in London, talks with host/art historian Tim Marlow about artworks that have inspired him. The six paintings discussed include J. M. W. Turner's "The Fighting Temeraire" (1839) and Joseph Wright's "An Iron Forge" (1772).

3690 September 2009
The Restaurant at the End of the Universe (Book: Pan Books), written by Douglas Adams with a new foreword by **Terry Jones**, is published in the U.K. Reissue of the second volume (1980) in Adams' *Hitchhiker's Guide to the Galaxy* series.

3691 September 14–18, 2009
Book of the Week (Radio show: BBC Radio 4). **Michael Palin** reads from his new book *Halfway to Hollywood*. Five 10-minute episodes.

3692 September 14, 2009
Simon Mayo (Radio talk show: BBC Radio 5 Live). Guest: **Michael Palin**, promoting *Halfway to Hollywood*.

3693 September 17, 2009
Halfway to Hollywood: Diaries 1980–1988 (Book: Weidenfeld & Nicolson), written by **Michael Palin**, is published in the U.K. Second volume of **Palin**'s diaries, following *Diaries 1969–1979: The Python Years* (2006), covers his busiest years as a film actor (in *The Missionary*, *A Private Function*, *Brazil*, etc.), ending in September 1988, just before he was to embark on his first major travel journey for the BBC. Published in the U.S. by Thomas Dunne Books in March 2011.

3694 September 17, 2009
Michael Palin launches his new book *Halfway to Hollywood* with a book-signing at Hatchards in Piccadilly, London. He also appears at a book-signing at Foyles in St. Pancras International, London.

3695 September 19, 2009
Loose Ends (Radio talk show: BBC Radio 4). Clive Anderson talks to **Michael Palin** about his book *Halfway to Hollywood*.

3696 September 22, 2009
Monty Python Live! (Book: Hyperion), edited by **Eric Idle** and Steve Kirwan (art editor) with artwork by **Terry Gilliam**, is published in the U.S. Lavishly-illustrated volume devoted to the group's live performances, from their 1971 shows at the Lanchester Arts Festival in Coventry to the Hollywood Bowl in 1980. Includes recollections from the surviving Pythons (and previously-published thoughts from **Graham Chapman**) and collaborators Carol Cleveland and Neil Innes. Also contains the program and the scripts of every sketch performed at the Hollywood Bowl, appended by other sketches the team has performed on stage. Published in the U.K on Oct. 1 by Simon & Schuster.

3697 September 22, 2009
Film 2009 with Jonathan Ross (TV show: BBC1). Guest: **Michael Palin**, promoting his book *Halfway to Hollywood*.

3698 September 22, 2009
The Paul O'Grady Show (TV talk show: Channel 4). Guests: **Michael Palin**, promoting his book *Halfway to Hollywood*, and the boy band JLS. **Palin**, with O'Grady and the other guests, takes part in a team building exercise.

3699 September 23, 2009
The Daily Telegraph (Newspaper/U.K.). "My Life as a Python," by **Eric Idle**, p. 24. **Idle** recalls the Monty Python years ("Laughter is what I remember most," he writes) and promotes the Oct. 23 Royal Albert Hall performance of *Not the Messiah*.

3700 September 23, 2009
Michael Palin: A Life in Pictures (Event). **Michael Palin** is interviewed by film critic Mark Kermode in Ely Cathedral in Cambridgeshire, England for this special BAFTA event, held as part of the 29th Cambridge Film Festival (Sept. 17–27). **Palin**, promoting his book *Halfway to Hollywood: Diaries 1980–1988*, talks about his boyhood love of cinema, his film career, and George Harrison and HandMade Films.

3701 September 23–October 4, 2009
An Evening Without Monty Python (Stage show) is performed at the Ricardo Montalban Theatre in Los Angeles. Stage revue celebrating the 40th anniversary of Monty Python and featuring some of the group's best sketches and songs. Created by **Eric Idle** and directed by **Idle** and BT McNicholl. Starring Jeff B. Davis, Rick Holmes, Jane Leeves (of *Frasier*), Jim Piddock, and Alan Tudyk. The show moves to NYC for five shows on Oct. 6–10.

3702 September 25, 2009
This Morning (TV show: ITV). Magazine program. Hosts Eamonn Holmes and Ruth Langsford interview **Michael Palin**, who talks about his diaries and his late sister, Angela.

3703 September 26, 2009
Michael Palin delivers the opening speech at an event celebrating the 500th anniversary of the founding of Brasenose College Oxford (his alma mater, 1962–65) at the Sheldonian Theatre in Oxford, England.

3704 September 29, 2009
Conversation Pieces: Michael Palin (Event). **Michael Palin** talks about *Halfway to Hollywood* with host Alistair Moffat at Glasgow Royal Concert Hall in Scotland.

3705 October 2009
ABC News Now (TV news show: ABC). **Terry Gilliam** is interviewed by film critic Peter Travers for the "Popcorn with Peter Travers" segment. He talks about Python reuniting, people's fear of offending, and renouncing his American citizenship (in 2006).

3706 October 2009
Geographical (Magazine/U.K.). "President **Palin** Plots His Course," by Olivia Edward. Interview with **Michael Palin**, the new president of the Royal Geographical Society, conducted at the RGS's Kensington headquarters.

3707 October 1, 2009
From Shrewsbury to the World—A Debt to Darwin (Lecture). **Michael Palin** gives a talk on Charles Darwin in Alington Hall at Shrewsbury School (which **Palin** attended as a youth) in Shrewsbury, England. Proceeds from the lecture go to the Field Studies Council Darwin Scholarship.

3708 October 1, 2009
Terry Jones attends the London gala screening of the Ricky Gervais comedy *The Invention of Lying* at BAFTA. **Jones** tells a reporter that his friendship with Gervais began when the *Office* star saved his dog from drowning while the dog was out for a walk on London's Hampstead Heath with **Jones**' personal assistant.

3709 October 2–10, 2009
A Ludicrous Evening with John Cleese...or How to Finance Your Divorce (Stage show). **John Cleese**

debuts his one-man stage show for a seven-show, nine-day engagement in Norway. The show was necessitated by **Cleese**'s recent divorce, which requires him to pay nearly $20 million in alimony. **Cleese** plays the Oslo Concert House in Oslo (Oct. 2), Maihaugen Hall in Lillehammer (Oct. 3), Olav Hall in Trondheim (Oct. 5), Oseberg Cultural Center in Tønsberg (Oct. 6), Grieg Hall in Bergen (Oct. 8), Stavanger Concert House in Stavanger (Oct. 9), and Oslo Concert House (Oct. 10). **Cleese** brings the show to the U.S. on Oct. 30 as *A Final Wave at the World: The Alimony Tour, Part One*.

3710   October 5, 2009

Terry Gilliam: A Life in Pictures (Event). **Terry Gilliam** is interviewed by film critic Mark Kermode for this special event at BAFTA London. **Gilliam** talks about his films including the soon-to-be-released *The Imaginarium of Doctor Parnassus*.

3711   October 5, 2009

Time Bandits (DVD/Blu-ray: Optimum Home Entertainment) is released in the U.K. Remastered version of **Terry Gilliam**'s 1981 fantasy-comedy. Bonus features include an 18-minute interview with **Gilliam**, production & publicity photos, and trailer.

3712   October 6, 2009

Terry Gilliam signs copies of the remastered *Time Bandits* on DVD/Blu-ray at HMV in Oxford Street, London.

3713   October 6, 2009

Terry Gilliam attends a Q&A for his film *The Imaginarium of Doctor Parnassus* at BAFTA London. Also participating are the film's producers, Amy Gilliam (daughter of **Terry**) and Samuel Hadida, and stars Andrew Garfield, Lily Cole, and Verne Troyer.

3714   October 6, 2009

Terry Gilliam attends the Gala London Premiere of *The Imaginarium of Doctor Parnassus* at the Empire, Leicester Square. **Terry Jones** also attends.

3715   October 6, 2009

Michael Palin talks about his book *Halfway to Hollywood* at the Olivier Theatre in London. Followed by a book-signing.

3716   October 6–10, 2009

The stage revue *An Evening Without Monty Python* is performed at the Town Hall in New York City. The show, created and co-directed by **Eric Idle**, previously played in Los Angeles on Sept. 23–Oct. 4.

3717   October 8, 2009

The One Show (TV show: BBC1). Magazine program hosted by Christine Bleakley and Gethin Jones. Guest **Terry Gilliam** talks about *Doctor Parnassus* and Python's 40th anniversary.

3718   October 9, 2009

The Guardian Books Podcast (Podcast). Claire Armitstead interviews **Michael Palin** about his book *Halfway to Hollywood*.

3719   October 10, 2009

The Times (London) (Newspaper/U.K.). "Douglas, the Last of the Pythons," by **Terry Jones**, p. 42. **Jones** looks back on author Douglas Adams' involvement with Python.

3720   October 10, 2009

The Daily Mail (Newspaper/U.K.). "**Michael Palin**: I'm a Closet Bathrobe Thief," by **Michael Palin** (interviewed by Frances Hardy), p. 7.

3721   October 10, 2009

Michael Palin speaks about his film career in the 1980s as chronicled in *Halfway to Hollywood: Diaries 1980–1988* at Cheltenham Racecourse in Cheltenham, England as part of the 60th Cheltenham Literature Festival (Oct. 9–18).

3722   October 11, 2009

The Observer (Newspaper/U.K.). "My Favorite Table," by **Michael Palin**. **Palin** writes about his dining experiences over the years and gives special praise to his regular haunt, Vasco & Piero's Pavilion restaurant in London.

3723   October 12, 2009

New York (Magazine/U.S.). "Monty Python's Ongoing Circus," by Justin Davidson, p. 16. Interview with **Eric Idle** about the stage revue *An Evening Without Monty Python*.

3724   October 13–November 17, 2009

Around the World in 80 Days (TV series: BBC1). Six-part travel series in which six pairs of celebrities set off on a relay race retracing Phileas Fogg's — and **Michael Palin**'s — epic journey. **Palin** appears in the show, offering advice to the travelers. The program raises money for BBC Children in Need. Produced & directed by Rupert Miles.

3725   October 13, 2009

Film 2009 with Jonathan Ross (TV show: BBC1).

A report on *Doctor Parnassus* includes interviews with **Terry Gilliam**, Verne Troyer, Andrew Garfield, and Lily Cole.

3726   October 14, 2009
Countdown with Keith Olbermann (TV news show: MSNBC). Keith Olbermann interviews **John Cleese**, **Terry Gilliam**, and **Terry Jones**, who discuss the upcoming IFC documentary *Monty Python: Almost the Truth—The Lawyer's Cut*.

3727   October 14, 2009
Late Night with Jimmy Fallon (TV talk show: NBC). Guests: **John Cleese, Terry Gilliam, Eric Idle,** and **Terry Jones**, promoting *Monty Python: Almost the Truth—The Lawyer's Cut*. **Cleese** also takes part in the game "Wheel of Carpet Samples" and **Idle** sings "Always Look on the Bright Side of Life."

3728   October 15, 2009
Live with Regis and Kelly (TV talk show: Synd.). Hosted by Regis Philbin and Kelly Ripa. Guests: **John Cleese, Terry Gilliam, Eric Idle, Terry Jones,** and **Michael Palin**, promoting *Monty Python: Almost the Truth—The Lawyer's Cut*.

3729   October 15, 2009
The five surviving Pythons—**John Cleese, Terry Gilliam, Eric Idle, Terry Jones** and **Michael Palin**—reunite at the Ziegfeld Theater in New York City where they attend a screening of the new IFC documentary *Monty Python: Almost the Truth—The Lawyer's Cut* and afterward take part in a Q&A session, during which **Idle** sings "Galaxy Song." The group also receives a Lifetime Achievement Award from the British Academy of Film and Television Arts (BAFTA). The after party is held at the Le Parker Meridien New York Hotel.

3730   October 16, 2009
The Imaginarium of Doctor Parnassus, directed by **Terry Gilliam**, opens in the U.K.

3731   October 18–23, 2009
The six-part documentary series *Monty Python: Almost the Truth—The Lawyer's Cut* airs on the Independent Film Channel (IFC). The series, commemorating Monty Python's 40th anniversary, chronicles the history of the group through new interviews with the surviving Pythons (and **Graham Chapman** in archived interviews) and clips from their TV series and films. Produced & directed by Ben Timlett and Bill Jones (son of **Terry**).
Awards: Emmy-nominated for Outstanding Nonfiction Series and Outstanding Directing for Nonfiction Programming.

3732   October 18, 2009
Monty Python: Almost the Truth—The Lawyer's Cut (IFC). "The Not-So-Interesting Beginnings." The Pythons reflect on their childhoods, early schooling, college years, working on *The Frost Report*, and the formation of Monty Python. Also discussed is the influence of The Goons and Beyond the Fringe. First episode in a six-part documentary series.

3733   October 18, 2009
Terry Gilliam attends a screening of his film *The Imaginarium of Doctor Parnassus* at the 4th Rome International Film Festival (Oct. 15–23) held at the Auditorium Parco della Musica in Rome, Italy.

3734   October 18, 2009
The National Tour of the Broadway musical *Spamalot* ends following a performance at the Orange County Performing Arts Center in Costa Mesa, CA. The tour has played 1,435 performances in 101 cities since its launch in Boston in March 2006.

3735   October 19, 2009
Monty Python: Almost the Truth—The Lawyer's Cut (IFC). "The Much Funnier Second Episode." The Pythons look back at the debut and growing popularity of *Monty Python's Flying Circus*. Other interviewees include Bill Oddie, Barry Cryer, David Aukin, Phill Jupitus, Bruce Dickinson, Sanjeev Bhaskar, Russell Brand, and Steve Coogan. Second episode in the six-part documentary series.

3736   October 20, 2009
Chiambretti Night (TV variety show: Italy 1). Host Piero Chiambretti interviews **Terry Gilliam** on this Italian late-night program. Taped in Milan.

3737   October 20, 2009
Monty Python: Almost the Truth—The Lawyer's Cut (IFC). "And Now, the Sordid Personal Bits." The Pythons discuss censorship at the BBC, becoming celebrities, and **John Cleese**'s departure from the show. Third episode in the six-part documentary series.

3738   October 20, 2009
Fawlty Towers: The Complete Collection Remastered (DVD: BBC Video) is released. The three-disc set, digitally restored from the original masters, includes: new commentaries recorded by **John Cleese** for all twelve episodes; director commentaries by John Howard Davies (series one) and Bob Spiers (series two); interviews (from the May 2009 TV

doc *Fawlty Towers: Re-Opened*) with **Cleese**, Connie Booth, Prunella Scales, Andrew Sachs, et al.; also outtakes and the short documentary *Torquay Tourist Guide*. BBC Video previously released the complete set on DVD in 2001.

3739   October 21, 2009
Monty Python: Almost the Truth—The Lawyer's Cut (TV episode: IFC). "The Ultimate Holy Grail Episode." A look back at the group's first visit to the U.S. and the making of *Holy Grail*. Fourth episode in the six-part documentary series.

3740   October 21, 2009
The Art Instinct (Event). **John Cleese** participates in a conversation with Prof. Denis Dutton at the Santa Barbara Museum of Art in Santa Barbara, CA.

3741   October 21, 2009
Rolling Stone (Magazine/U.S.). "**John Cleese**'s Towering Legacy," by Eric J. Plosky. Interview with **John Cleese** (by phone from L.A.), who is promoting the new DVD release of *Fawlty Towers*.

3742   October 22, 2009
Monty Python: Almost the Truth—The Lawyer's Cut (TV episode: IFC). "Lust for Glory!" The Pythons discuss the making of *Life of Brian* and the controversy that followed its release. Fifth episode in the six-part documentary series.

3743   October 22, 2009
The Culture Show (TV arts show: BBC2). **Michael Palin**, promoting his new book *Halfway to Hollywood: Diaries 1980–1988*, talks to Mark Kermode and Simon Mayo about his post–Python film career. The interview takes place on stage at the National Film Theatre as part of the London Film Festival.

3744   October 23, 2009
Monty Python: Almost the Truth—The Lawyer's Cut (TV episode: IFC). "Finally! The Last Episode Ever!" The Pythons remember playing the Hollywood Bowl, making their last film *The Meaning of Life*, and **Graham Chapman**'s passing. Final episode of the six-part documentary series.

3745   October 23, 2009
Not the Messiah (He's a Very Naughty Boy) (Oratorio) is performed at the Royal Albert Hall in London. Four of the five surviving Pythons (**John Cleese** was unable to attend) come together in celebration of the group's 40th anniversary to participate in this special presentation of the **Eric Idle**-John Du Prez oratorio based on *Life of Brian*. The work premiered in June 2007 in Toronto, followed by performances in Katonah, NY (July 2007), Australia & New Zealand (December 2007), Houston, TX (July 2008), The Wolf Trap near Vienna, VA (July 2008), and The Hollywood Bowl in Los Angeles (August 2008). Starring **Eric Idle** and soloists Shannon Mercer (soprano, as Judith), Rosalind Plowright (mezzo, as Mandy), William Ferguson (tenor, as Brian), Christopher Purves (bass, as Reg & Biggus Dickus), with special performances by **Michael Palin** (as Mrs. Betty Palin, et al.), **Terry Jones**, and **Terry Gilliam**, and guest appearances by Carol Cleveland, Neil Innes, and Sanjeev Bhaskar. Du Prez conducts the BBC Symphony Orchestra & Chorus. Also with the pipers from the Royal Scots Guard. Directed by Aubrey Powell. Broadcast on BBC Radio 3 on Dec. 26. A film of the performance is released in European theaters on Mar. 25, 2010, and on DVD June 8, 2010.

3746   October 26, 2009
Just for Laughs (TV episode: CBC). Highlights from the Montreal comedy festival. Includes performances by **John Cleese**, Danny Bhoy, and Aisha Tyler.

3747   October 27, 2009
John Cleese turns 70.

3748   October 27, 2009
Monty Python: Almost the Truth—The Lawyer's Cut (DVD/Blu-ray: Eagle Rock Entertainment). The six-part IFC documentary is released on 3-disc DVD and 2-disc Blu-ray sets, with bonus material including classic sketches, extended interviews, bits "From the Cutting Room Floor," and a **Terry Gilliam** picture gallery.

3749   October 27, 2009
Monty Python: The Other British Invasion (DVD: A&E). Two-disc DVD set containing the 2008 documentaries *Before the Flying Circus: A Black and White Documentary* and *Monty Python Conquers America*, both previously released in the 2008 DVD set *The Complete Monty Python's Flying Circus: Collector's Edition*.

3750   October 30–December 11, 2009
A Final Wave at the World: The Alimony Tour, Part One (Stage show). **John Cleese** tours the U.S. west coast with his one-man stage show in which he talks about his divorce, early years, and life in comedy, followed by a Q&A session. **Cleese** debuted the show, originally called *A Ludicrous Evening with*

John Cleese...or How to Finance Your Divorce, in Norway in early October. His U.S. tour takes him to the Gallo Center for the Arts in Modesto, CA (Oct. 30), Newmark Theatre in Portland, OR (Nov. 2), Moore Theatre in Seattle, WA (Nov. 3), McDonald Theatre in Eugene, OR (Nov. 4), John Van Duzer Theatre in Arcata, CA (Nov. 6), Mondavi Center for the Performing Arts, UC Davis in Davis, CA (Nov. 7), Fox Theatre in Redwood City, CA (Nov. 8), Laxson Auditorium in Chico, CA (Nov. 10), Lincoln Theater Napa Valley in Yountville, CA (Nov. 11), Sunset Cultural Center in Carmel, CA (Nov. 13), Alex Theatre in Glendale, CA (Nov. 14), Fred Kavli Theatre in Thousand Oaks, CA (Nov. 15), Carpenter Performing Arts Center in Long Beach, CA (Nov. 17), Spreckels Theatre in San Diego, CA (Nov. 18), and Scottsdale Center for the Performing Arts in Scottsdale, AZ (Dec. 10–11, postponed from Nov. 20–21 due to illness).

3751 November 2009
Vanity Fair (Magazine/U.S.). "Circus Maximus," by Christopher Hitchens. An appreciation of Monty Python on their 40th anniversary. Includes a two-page photo of the Pythons "smoking themselves silly" by Tim Walker.

3752 November 2, 2009
Terry **Gilliam** introduces a screening of *The Imaginarium of Doctor Parnassus* at Grauman's Chinese Theatre in Los Angeles as part of AFI Fest 2009. **Gilliam** is also joined onstage by the film's cast.

3753 November 6–7, 2009
Michael Palin signs copies of his book *Halfway to Hollywood: Diaries 1980–1988* at Eason's in Belfast, N. Ireland (Nov. 6) and Dubray Books in Dublin (Nov. 7).

3754 November 6, 2009
The Late Late Show (TV talk show: RTE One, in Ireland). Hosted by Ryan Tubridy. Guest **Michael Palin** talks about the Pythons' recent reunion in NYC, **John Cleese**, his mother's appearance on *Saturday Night Live*, his sister's suicide, stammering, and his two grandsons.

3755 November 11, 2009
BBC Breakfast (TV news show: BBC1/News Channel). Hosted by Bill Turnbull and Sian Williams. Guest **Michael Palin** talks about Armistice Day and his great-uncle Harry Palin who was killed in World War I.

3756 November 11, 2009
Michael Palin attends the "Passing of a Generation" memorial service, honoring those who fought in the First World War, at Westminster Abbey in London. The service is also attended by the Queen and Prime Minister.

3757 November 13, 2009
Eric Idle attends the opening night of the musical *Baby It's You!* at the Pasadena Playhouse in Pasadena, CA.

3758 November 16, 2009
The Graham Norton Show (TV talk show: BBC1). Guests: Rod Stewart, Dawn French, and **Michael Palin**, who talks about his new book *Halfway to Hollywood*, diary writing, and bringing his mother to America in 1984.

3759 November 18, 2009
Michael Meets...Musa Ibrahim (Event). **Michael Palin** interviews Somali refugee Musa Ibrahim in the first installment of the "Michael Meets..." series held at Ondaatjie Theatre of the Royal Geographical Society (of which **Palin** is president) in London. **Palin** befriended Ibrahim during Refugee Week in June.

3760 November 20, 2009
Planet 51 (Feature film: TriStar Pictures) opens in the U.S. Animated sci-fi comedy with **John Cleese** voicing the role of Professor Kipple, a mad alien scientist. Voice cast also includes Jessica Biel, Gary Oldman, Dwayne Johnson, and Justin Long. Written by Joe Stillman. Directed by Jorge Blanco, Javier Abad, and Marcos Martinez.

3761 November 20, 2009
Vanity Fair.com (Website). "Q&A: **John Cleese** Plans on Living Forever (or at Least Long Enough to Pay Off His Alimony)," by Eric Spitznagel. **Cleese** answers questions on life, death, and politics.

3762 November 21, 2009
Saturday Extra (Radio talk show: ABC Radio National, in Australia). **Michael Palin** is interviewed (by phone from London) about his book *Halfway to Hollywood*.

3763 November 21, 2009
The Guardian (Newspaper/U.K.). "**Michael Palin**'s Hand of Friendship Gives Asylum Seekers a Human Face," by Jamie Doward. Article on **Palin**'s friendship with Somali refugee Musa Ibrahim.

3764 November 23, 2009
Around the World in 80 Ways (Lecture). **Michael Palin** gives a talk at Sheffield City Hall in Sheffield, England. The event raises funds for the Whirlow Hall Farm Trust, of which **Palin** is a patron.

3765 November 23, 2009
Eric Idle attends the Saban Free Clinic's 33rd Annual Dinner Gala held at the Beverly Hilton Hotel in Beverly Hills, CA.

3766 November 24, 2009
Terry Jones speaks at a 30th-anniversary screening of *Life of Brian* in Norway (where the film was banned in 1980) as part of the 19th Oslo International Film Festival (Nov. 19–29). **Jones** is also in Norway promoting his book *Barbarians*.

3767 November 26, 2009
The Alan Titchmarsh Show (TV talk show: ITV). Daytime talk show. Guests: **Michael Palin**, Samantha Bond, and Nick Ferrari.

3768 November 27, 2009
Skavlan (TV talk show: NRK1/SVT1). Norwegian/Swedish program hosted by Fredrik Skavlan. Guests: Mats Sundin, Margot Wallstrom, and **Terry Jones**, who talks about his character Mr. Creosote (from *Meaning of Life*), the Roman Empire, the Middle Ages, his Swedish girlfriend, and baby daughter.

3769 December 2009
Five Minutes with: Michael Palin (Web talk show: BBC News). Matthew Stadlen interviews **Michael Palin** for exactly five minutes. **Palin** talks about Python and modern comedy, and guesses that he's been to about 95 countries.

3770 December 1, 2009
He's Not the Messiah, He's a Very Naughty Boy (Radio special: BBC Radio 2). Special celebrating the 30th anniversary of *Life of Brian*. Hosted by Sanjeev Bhaskar, with remembrances from the Pythons, also Carol Cleveland, producer John Goldstone, and others. Produced by Caroline Hughes.

3771 December 8 & 15, 2009
Monty Python's Wonderful World of Sound (Radio special: BBC Radio 2). Two-part special revisiting the comedy albums of Monty Python. Includes interviews with **Eric Idle**, **Terry Gilliam**, **Terry Jones**, **Michael Palin**, Neil Innes, Andre Jacquemin, Alan Bailey, Dave Howman, and John Du Prez. Hosted by Noel Fielding and Julian Barratt of The Mighty Boosh.

3772 December 8, 2009
Terry Gilliam talks about *The Imaginarium of Doctor Parnassus* after a screening of the film at The Museum of the Moving Image in New York City.

3773 December 14, 2009
Coming Home (TV episode: BBC1 Wales). "**Terry Jones**." **Jones** returns to his native Wales to learn more about his Welsh ancestry, with the help of genealogist Michael Churchill-Jones. **Jones** lived in Colwyn Bay until the age of 4 when his family moved to London. **Jones** visits the railway station in Colwyn Bay where he met his father for the first time, and Gloddaeth Hall in Llandudno where his great-grandmother, Louisa Parry, worked as a servant for the wealthy Mostyn family. Produced by Paul Lewis.

3774 December 17, 2009
The Fabulous Picture Show (TV show: Al Jazeera). **Terry Gilliam** talks to Amanda Palmer about his latest film *The Imaginarium of Doctor Parnassus*.

3775 December 17, 2009
The Hour (TV talk show: CBC, in Canada). Hosted by George Stroumboulopoulos. Guest: **Terry Gilliam**, promoting *Doctor Parnassus*.

3776 December 18, 2009
Vanity Fair.com (Website). "**Terry Gilliam**: The *Vanity Fair* Interview," by Julian Sancton. **Gilliam** discusses his troubled film projects, including his latest, *The Imaginarium of Doctor Parnassus*.

3777 December 20, 2009
All Things Considered (Radio talk show: NPR). Guy Raz talks to **Terry Gilliam** about *Doctor Parnassus*.

3778 December 22, 2009
Fresh Air from WHYY (Radio talk show: NPR). David Bianculli talks to **Terry Gilliam** about *Doctor Parnassus*.

3779 December 23, 2009
HARDtalk (TV talk show: BBC News). Stephen Sackur interviews **Michael Palin**.

3780 December 25, 2009
The Imaginarium of Doctor Parnassus, directed by **Terry Gilliam**, opens in the U.S. in limited release. It will open nationwide on Jan. 8.

3781 Late 2009
John Cleese, recently divorced from his third wife (Alyce Faye Eichelberger), begins dating 39-year-old jewelry designer Jennifer Wade. The two will marry in August 2012.

3782 2009
Traveller: Observations from an American in Exile (Book: Burton & Park), written by Michael Katakis with a foreword by **Michael Palin**, is published in the U.S. Katakis, literary rights manager for Ernest Hemingway's family, served as a consultant on **Palin**'s 1999 series *Hemingway Adventure*.

3783 January–February 2010
Mother Jones (Magazine/U.S.). "Three-Reel Circus: Filmmaker **Terry Gilliam**." Michael Mechanic interviews **Gilliam** about *Don Quixote*, money and movie-making, what inspires him, his childhood, giving up his American citizenship, and Heath Ledger.

3784 January–March 2010
Oxford Today (Magazine/U.K.). "A Python's Progress." Greg Neale interviews **Terry Jones** about his days as a student at Oxford.

3785 January 5, 2010
Up Close with Carrie Keagan (TV show: No Good TV). Carrie Keagan interviews **Terry Gilliam**, Lily Cole, and Verne Troyer about *Doctor Parnassus*.

3786 January 8, 2010
The Imaginarium of Doctor Parnassus, directed by **Terry Gilliam**, opens in the U.S. nationwide.

3787 January 14, 2010
Bristol Evening Post (Newspaper/U.K.). "A Life of Laughter," by Natalie Hale, pp. 6–7. **Michael Palin** interview.

3788 January 20, 2010
Eric Idle attends the opening night of *The Pee-Wee Herman Show* at Club Nokia in Los Angeles.

3789 January 21, 2010
Something ALMOST Completely Different (Event). **Michael Palin** gives a talk onstage (with Graeme Garden) for the Sixth Slapstick Gala at Colston Hall in Bristol, England. The event launches Bristol's four-day Slapstick Silent Comedy Festival. **Palin** also receives the Aardman/Slapstick Award for Excellence in Visual Comedy.

3790 January 21, 2010
Inside Joke with Monty Python's Terry Jones (Event). **Terry Jones** participates in an onstage conversation for "Inside Joke," hosted by Carl Arnheiter, at the Castro Theatre in San Francisco. The event, presented by SF Sketchfest, follows a 35th-anniversary screening of *Holy Grail*. Afterward, **Jones** introduces a screening of *Life of Brian*.

3791 January 22, 2010
A History of the World in 100 Objects (Radio show: BBC Radio 4). "Clovis Spear Point." A 13,000-year-old stone spear point found in Arizona is the object discussed. **Michael Palin** comments on man's desire for movement. Hosted by Neil MacGregor.

3792 January 29, 2010
Singer Roy Orbison receives a posthumous star on the Hollywood Walk of Fame in Los Angeles. Attending the ceremony are **Eric Idle**, Jeff Lynne, Dan Aykroyd, David Lynch, and others.

3793 February 8, 2010
Beatles drummer Ringo Starr receives a star on the Hollywood Walk of Fame in Los Angeles. **Eric Idle** attends the ceremony.

3794 February 16, 2010
Terry Gilliam attends the launch of the Play Station videogame *Heavy Rain* in Paris.

3795 February 18, 2010
Michael Meets...Maan Barua (Event). **Michael Palin** interviews Maan Barua at the Royal Geographical Society in London. Barua guided **Palin** down the Brahmaputra River in India for his *Himalaya* series (in 2004). The second of **Palin**'s "Michael Meets..." conversations (he interviewed Musa Ibrahim in November 2009).

3796 February 21, 2010
The Orange British Academy Film Awards (Award ceremony). **Terry Gilliam** presents the award for Outstanding British Contribution to Cinema to camera technician Joe Dunton at this year's BAFTA ceremony, hosted by Jonathan Ross from London's Royal Opera House. Broadcast on BBC1.

3797 February 22, 2010
Michael Palin attends the annual Orion Authors' Party at the Royal Opera House, Covent Garden, London.

3798 February 24, 2010
Around India in 25 Years (Lecture). **Michael Palin** gives a talk at the Nehru Centre in London in which he discusses his first visit to India in 1982 (with **Terry Gilliam**) and answers questions.

3799 March–April 2010
John Cleese films his role in the movie *Spud* in South Africa. The film premieres in November.

3800 March 2, 2010
GMTV (TV news show: ITV1). Guests **Michael Palin** and Ed Balls (Schools Secretary) talk about

the work of the Michael Palin Centre for Stammering Children and a new fundraising campaign to open a second center in the north of England.

3801 March 2, 2010

Michael Palin attends a reception at Clarence House in London, hosted by The Prince of Wales, for supporters of the Michael Palin Centre for Stammering Children on the 17th anniversary of the Centre's opening. **Palin** uses the event as the launch of the ARSC (Association for Research into Stammering in Childhood) Appeal, which is hoping to raise £2 million to set up a new center in West Yorkshire.

3802 March 3–May 5, 2010

The Legend of Dick and Dom (TV series: CBBC). **Terry Jones** narrates the second series (10 episodes) of the British children's show starring Richard McCourt and Dominic Wood. The series premiered in January 2009.

3803 March 4, 2010

Vanity Fair.com (Website). "**Terry Gilliam**: I don't know what the Oscars represent anymore." Julian Sancton gets **Gilliam**'s perspective on the Academy Awards.

3804 March 7, 2010

Eric Idle attends the *Vanity Fair* Oscar Party at the Sunset Tower Hotel in West Hollywood, CA.

3805 March 8, 2010

Outlook (Radio show: BBC World Service). Guests **Michael Palin** and his friend, Somali refugee Musa Ibrahim, talk about the treatment of asylum seekers in Britain.

3806 March 24, 2010

An Evening with Michael Palin (Lecture). **Michael Palin**, as president of the Royal Geographical Society, speaks at the University of Southhampton, England.

3807 Late March 2010

Michael Palin visits the state of Orissa, in eastern India, staying a week.

3808 April 12 & 13, 2010

Terry Jones returns to his home town of Colwyn Bay, Wales where he attends a benefit screening of *Life of Brian* at Theatre Colwyn (Apr. 12) and gives a talk called "Medieval Lives" in Memorial Hall at Rydal Penrhos College (Apr. 13).

3809 April 14, 2010

Medieval Lives (Lecture). **Terry Jones** gives an illustrated talk at The National Library of Wales in Aberystwyth.

3810 April 16, 2010

A tribute to **Terry Jones** is presented at the 5th Funchal International Film Festival (Apr. 10–17) in Funchal, Madiera, Portugal. **Jones** is prevented from attending the festival by an ash cloud from an Icelandic volcano which has grounded flights out of Britain. He will receive his tribute and award in person at next year's festival (in November 2011).

3811 April 16, 2010

Skavlan (TV talk show: NRK1/SVT1). Norwegian/Swedish program hosted by Fredrik Skavlan. Guests: Robyn, Natascha Illum Berg, and **John Cleese**, who talks about his *Alimony Tour*, his new girlfriend, his failed marriages, and the Catholic church.

3812 April 17, 2010

Due to the volcanic ash cloud disrupting air travel in Europe, **John Cleese** is forced to take a taxi from Oslo, Norway to Brussels, Belgium in order to catch a Eurostar train to London. The 930-mile taxi trip costs him £3,000 (or $5,100). **Cleese** was in Oslo to tape his appearance on the talk show *Skavlan*.

3813 April 22, 2010

Michael Palin and his wife attend a dinner party/sleepover hosted by the Queen and the Duke of Edinburgh at Windsor Castle. **Palin** was invited as president of the Royal Geographical Society. The dinner marks the Queen's 84th birthday (Apr. 21).

3814 April 23, 2010

You and Yours (Radio show: BBC Radio 4). Peter White talks to **Michael Palin** about slow travel.

3815 April 26, 2010

The Graham Norton Show (TV talk show: BBC1). Guests: **John Cleese**, Martin Clunes, Lee Mack, and Jane Turner. **Cleese**, appearing in a wheelchair due to a knee injury, talks about his taxi ride from Oslo to Brussels, his *Alimony Tour*, his new girlfriend, eating dog in Hong Kong, and versions of *Fawlty Towers* in different countries.

3816 April 27, 2010

The Imaginarium of Doctor Parnassus (DVD/Blu-ray: Sony Pictures). **Terry Gilliam**'s 2009 fantasy is released on DVD and Blu-ray. Bonus features include an introduction and audio commentary by **Gilliam**, a deleted scene, interviews, trailer, etc.

3817 May 2010
John Cleese undergoes knee replacement surgery. His knee gave out in April during a night out at a restaurant with Michael Palin. Cleese had his hip replaced in 1999.

3818 May 2010
Terry Gilliam confirms that he plans to start shooting his next film, *The Man Who Killed Don Quixote*, in September with Ewan McGregor and Robert Duvall in the lead roles. Shooting is later postponed when the film's funding falls through. Gilliam's last attempt to film *Quixote*, in 2000 (with Johnny Depp and Jean Rochefort as the leads), fell apart after six days filming (as seen in the 2002 documentary *Lost in La Mancha*).

3819 May 2, 2010
Jarvis Cocker's Sunday Service (Radio show: BBC Radio 6 Music). Guest Michael Palin talks about Sheffield, his start in comedy, hosting the 1960s pop show *Now!*, making travel documentaries, Bruce Springsteen, and Ernest Hemingway (he also reads from Hemingway's *A Moveable Feast*).

3820 May 12, 2010
Eric Idle and his wife attend the 2nd Annual Dream Believe Achieve Gala, an event benefitting ICEF Public Schools, at the Skirball Cultural Center in Los Angeles. Performers include Jackson Browne and Crosby, Stills & Nash.

3821 May 15 & 16, 2010
Terry Gilliam, at the 63rd annual Cannes International Film Festival (May 12–23) in France, attends a star-studded *Vanity Fair*/Gucci party honoring director Martin Scorsese at the Hotel du Cap-Eden-Roc (May 15). The next day he attends the launch of Qatar's Doha Film Institute (DFI) at the Majestic Beach.

3822 May 18, 2010
Front Row (Radio arts show: BBC Radio 4). John Wilson interviews Eric Idle about *Spamalot*, *Not the Messiah*, and his start in comedy.

3823 May 21, 2010
Shrek Forever After (Feature film: Paramount Pictures) opens in the U.S. Animated feature, fourth in the series. John Cleese voices King Harold, a role he first voiced in *Shrek 2* (2004). Voice cast also includes Mike Myers, Eddie Murphy, Cameron Diaz, Julie Andrews, and Antonio Banderas. Directed by Mike Mitchell.

3824 May 24, 2010
The Graham Norton Show (TV talk show: BBC1). Guests: Janet Jackson, Tyler Perry, Marcus Brigstocke, and Eric Idle. Idle talks about *Spamalot*, the Pythons' appearance on the *Tonight Show* in the 1970s, and sings "Always Look on the Bright Side of Life." Note: Comedian Brigstocke will be playing King Arthur in the upcoming U.K. tour of *Spamalot*.

3825 May 25, 2010
Eric Idle and Terry Jones host an Emmy-consideration screening of the IFC documentary *Monty Python: Almost the Truth—The Lawyer's Cut* (a 90-minute version) for members of the Television Academy at the Leonard H. Goldenson Theatre in North Hollywood, CA. They also take part in an onstage conversation with the doc's directors, Bill Jones (son of Terry) and Ben Timlett, and moderator Peter Hammond.

3826 May 27–28, 2010
Michael Palin, visiting Hong Kong as president of the Royal Geographical Society, gives a talk ("Himalaya") at Olympic House, Causeway Bay (May 27). The next day he gives a talk ("Travelling on Television") at a lunch at the Foreign Correspondents' Club (FCC) and another talk ("Around the World in 20 Years") at an RGS fundraising dinner held at the Hong Kong Football Club, Causeway Bay.

3827 May 29, 2010
The U.K. tour of *Spamalot* begins at the New Wimbledon Theatre in London. The cast includes Marcus Brigstocke (King Arthur) and Jodie Prenger (Lady of the Lake).

3828 May 31, 2010
Front Row (Radio arts show: BBC Radio 4). Kirsty Lang talks with Terry Gilliam about his determination to film *Don Quixote*, the recurring themes in his films, and his plan to direct the opera *The Damnation of Faust*.

3829 June 2, 2010
Singer-songwriter Randy Newman is given a star on the Hollywood Walk of Fame. Friend Eric Idle is one of the speakers at the ceremony.

3830 June 2, 2010
Eric Idle attends the opening night performance of *South Pacific* at the Ahmanson Theatre in Los Angeles.

3831 June 4, 2010
The Comedy Café (Radio show: BBC Radio Scotland). Janice Forsyth talks to Eric Idle about *Not the Messiah*.

3832 June 7, 2010
Michael Palin hosts the Royal Geographical Society's Medals and Awards Celebration at the RGS headquarters in London.

3833 June 7, 2010
The Late Late Show with Craig Ferguson (TV talk show: CBS). Guests: **Eric Idle** and Terry Crews. **Idle**, promoting the DVD release of *Not the Messiah*, also talks about playing the Hollywood Bowl, *Spamalot*, etc.

3834 June 8, 2010
The Great British Comedy Event (Event). **Michael Palin**, **Terry Jones**, and **Terry Gilliam** attend the event at Old Billingsgate in London where an original working script for *Life of Brian*—signed by four of the Pythons—is auctioned. The event supports the National Film and Television School.

3835 June 8, 2010
Eric Idle's oratorio *Not the Messiah (He's a Very Naughty Boy)*, filmed live at the Royal Albert Hall in October 2009, is released in the U.S. on DVD. Released in the U.K. on June 14.

3836 June 8, 2010
Talk of the Nation (Radio talk show: NPR). Neal Conan interviews **Eric Idle**, who talks about *Not the Messiah* and takes questions from callers.

3837 June 9, 2010
Talk Asia (TV talk show: CNN). Anjali Rao interviews **Michael Palin** (in Hong Kong) about travel, Python, stammering, his father & mother, and how his travels affect his marriage.

3838 June 10, 2010
The 38th AFI Life Achievement Award (Award ceremony). **Eric Idle** performs at the AFI (American Film Institute) ceremony honoring director Mike Nichols, held at Sony Pictures Studios in Culver City, CA. Dressed as an angel (with a wig and giant wings), **Idle** sings "Always Look on the Bright Side of Life" with the audience—including Oprah Winfrey and Jack Nicholson—singing along. Nichols won a Tony Award in 2005 for his direction of **Idle**'s musical *Spamalot*. The show airs June 26 on TV Land.

3839 June 11–14, 2010
The Directorspective: Terry Gilliam (Screenings). **Terry Gilliam**'s film work is honored at the Barbican Centre in London with screenings of *Brazil*, *Baron Munchausen*, *Fear and Loathing*, and *Doctor Parnassus*.

3840 June 12, 2010
Terry Jones appears at the Theatre Royal in Winchester, England, as part of the Winchester Film Festival 2010 (June 5–13). **Jones** takes part in an interview (with Bernard McKenna) and audience Q&A.

3841 June 12, 2010
Michael Palin attends the 6th Biografilm Festival (June 9–14) in Bologna, Italy, where he takes part in a tribute to comic actor Peter Sellers (*The Goon Show*, *The Pink Panther*). Also attending is John Scheinfeld, co-director of the 2000 doc *The Unknown Peter Sellers*, in which **Palin** also appeared.

3842 June 13, 2010
Terry Jones introduces a screening of *Holy Grail* (on its 35th anniversary) at the Arnolfini Cinema in Bristol, England, as part of Bristol Silents' 10th-anniversary celebration. The screening is followed by a discussion and audience Q&A.

3843 June 17, 2010
Michael Palin promotes the Polish edition of his book *Around the World in 80 Days* at Empik Junior Bookstore in Warsaw, Poland.

3844 June 26, 2010
AFI Life Achievement Award: A Tribute to Mike Nichols (TV special: TV Land). An angel-winged **Eric Idle** performs in this tribute ceremony taped June 10. Directed by Louis J. Horvitz.

3845 June 29, 2010
Terry Gilliam attends the opening of the exhibition "Ray Harryhausen—Myths and Legends," showcasing the work of 90-year-old stop-motion animator Ray Harryhausen, at the London Film Museum in South Bank, London.

3846 July 2010
John Cleese films his role in an episode of HBO's *Entourage*, which will air Sept. 12.

3847 July 8, 2010
Marlow Meets... (TV talk show: Sky Arts). "**Terry Jones**." Host/art historian Tim Marlow talks with **Jones** at the National Gallery of Art in London about the influence of art in his life. The six paintings **Jones** chooses to discuss include Pieter Bruegel the Elder's "The Adoration of the Kings" (1564), Pieter de Hooch's "The Courtyard of a House in Delft" (1658), and J. M. W. Turner's "Rain, Steam and Speed" (1844). **Michael Palin** was featured in a 2009 episode.

3848 July 8, 2010
Michael Palin speaks at the West Cork Literary Festival (July 4–10) in Bantry, Cork, Ireland. He is promoting his book *Halfway to Hollywood: Diaries 1980–1988*, released today in paperback (Phoenix).

3849 July 12, 2010
Simon Mayo Drivetime (Radio talk show: BBC Radio 2). Guest: **Michael Palin**.

3850 July 12, 2010
The One Show (TV show: BBC1). Magazine program hosted by Louise Minchin and Matt Baker. Guest **Eric Idle** talks about *Spamalot*.

3851 July 14, 2010
The Daily Post (Liverpool) (Newspaper/U.K.). "**Idle**'s Light Work Reborn for Liverpool Date." Philip Key interviews **Eric Idle** at the Manchester Opera House about the new touring production of *Spamalot*, which is set to open at the Liverpool Empire Theatre in August.

3852 July 15, 2010
The One Show (TV show: BBC1). Magazine program hosted by Louise Minchin and Matt Baker. Guest **Michael Palin** talks about his book *Halfway to Hollywood* and his role in *A Fish Called Wanda*.

3853 July 18, 2010
Terry Gilliam attends the London premiere of the Pixar-animated film *Toy Story 3* at Empire Leicester Square.

3854 August 5, 2010
The Canadian rock group Arcade Fire performs at Madison Square Garden in New York City. **Terry Gilliam** directs the live worldwide webcast of the show for the series *Unstaged*, sponsored by American Express. **Gilliam** also appears in a behind-the-scenes skit before the concert in which the group members are revealed to be machines under the control of **Gilliam** and his assistant Andrew Garfield.

3855 August 8–14, 2010
John Cleese is a guest-speaker on the Queen Mary 2 ocean liner during its transatlantic crossing from New York to Southampton, England. His talk includes an interview, an audience Q&A, and a screening of the *Fawlty Towers* episode "The Psychiatrist."

3856 August 10, 2010
Simply Absurd (Radio special: BBC Radio 4). **Terry Jones** hosts this half-hour special exploring the Theatre of the Absurd and its influence on modern comedy. Produced by Susan Marling.

3857 August 13, 2010
Home Movie Roadshow (TV episode: BBC2). Kirsty Wark interviews **Terry Jones**, who discusses and shows some the home movies he took with his then-new 8mm camera during the early days of Python. Produced by Stephen Taylor Woodrow.

3858 August 21, 2010
The 2010 Primetime Creative Arts Emmy Awards (Award ceremony). **Terry Jones** presents, with son Bill Jones and Ben Timlett, at the award ceremony held at the Nokia Theatre in Los Angeles. The younger Jones and Timlett were nominated for directing and producing the documentary *Monty Python: Almost the Truth*. Broadcast Aug. 27 on E! Entertainment.

3859 August 24, 2010
Terry Gilliam's *Time Bandits* is released on Blu-ray by Image Entertainment. Special features are an interview with **Gilliam** (18 mins.) and theatrical trailer.

3860 September 2010
Phoenix Pictures announces that a comedy titled *Absolutely Anything*, co-written & directed by **Terry Jones** and starring John Oliver (*The Daily Show*), will begin filming in early 2011. Unfortunately, the project, which was also to feature the voices of **John Cleese** and **Michael Palin**, has trouble getting financing and filming is postponed.

3861 September 2010
Terry Gilliam attends the 36th American Film Festival (Sept. 3–12) in Deauville, France. The festival includes a tribute to **Gilliam** and a screening of *Brazil*.

3862 September 12–October 23, 2010
An Evening with John Cleese— Paying My Ex-Wife, Year Two (Stage show). **John Cleese** tours Scandinavia with his one-man stage show, playing 20 dates. In Norway, **Cleese** plays Grieg Hall in Bergen (Sept. 12), Oslo Concert Hall (Sept. 15–18), Stavanger Concert Hall (Sept. 20), Olavshallen in Trondheim (Sept. 22 & 24), and Ibsen House in Skien (Sept. 25). In Denmark, he plays the Concert Hall in Odense (Sept. 28), Music Hall in Aarhus (Sept. 30), Falconer in Copenhagen (Oct. 2), and Aalborg Hallen (Oct. 22). In Sweden, he plays the Gothenburg Concert House (Oct. 8 & 9), Cirkus in Stockholm (Oct. 11, 12 & 17), Jönköping Concert House (Oct. 14), Linköping Concert & Con-

gress (Oct. 15), Uppsala Concert & Congress (Oct. 18), Västeras Concert House (Oct. 20), and Malmö Concert House (Oct. 23).

3863 September 12, 2010
Entourage (TV episode: HBO). "Lose Yourself." **John Cleese** makes a cameo appearance (as himself) in the seventh-season finale of the 2004–11 comedy-drama. Written by Doug Ellin. Directed by David Nutter.

3864 September 13, 2010
In Conversation (TV talk show: Sky Arts 1). "**Terry Gilliam**." Film critic Derek Malcolm talks with **Gilliam** about his career in film in this first episode of a 12-part series.

3865 September 16, 2010
Senkveld (Late Night) with Thomas and Harald (TV talk show: TV2, in Norway). Guest: **John Cleese**, who talks about humor, his expensive divorce from his third wife, and his new (and much younger) girlfriend.

3866 September 23, 2010
The Guardian (Newspaper/U.K.). "Obituary: Geoffrey Burgon," by **Terry Jones**, p. 38. **Jones** pays tribute to his friend, composer Geoffrey Burgon, who died Sept. 21 at age 69. Burgon's works included the film score for *Life of Brian*.

3867 September 28, 2010
Michael Palin opens a free outdoor exhibition called "Britain from the Air" in Bath City Centre, England. The exhibition, which involves a walk-on map of Britain and over a hundred aerial photographs, was co-created by The Royal Geographical Society, of which **Palin** is president. Before the launch of the exhibition, **Palin** gives a talk (titled "Around the World in 20 Years") in Bath Abbey.

3868 September 30, 2010
BBC Breakfast (TV news show: BBC1/News Channel). Hosted by Bill Turnbull and Sian Williams. Guest: **Michael Palin**.

3869 October 2010
AA Home Emergency Response (Faulty Showers) (TV commercial). **John Cleese** stars in this British TV ad — the launch of a new campaign — playing a man whose daughter has the good sense to call AA Home Emergency Service when their shower pipes break. Agency: McCann-Erickson, London.

3870 October 2010
Terry Gilliam attends the 8th Morelia International Film Festival (Oct. 16–24) in Mexico.

During his visit, **Gilliam** receives the Gold Medal Award in Film from the Film Archive of the National University of Mexico and gives a master class at the University of Michoacan's Public Library.

3871 October 2010
Explorers: Great Tales of Adventure and Endurance (Book: Dorling Kindersley), by the Royal Geographical Society, is published in the U.K. Illustrated guide to the world's greatest explorers. Foreword by Sir Ranulph Fiennes. Introduction by **Michael Palin**, president of the RGS.

3872 October 2010
Geographical (Magazine/U.K.). "One Year On," by **Michael Palin**, p. 20. **Palin** reflects on his first year as president of the Royal Geographical Society.

3873 October 9, 2010
Robins (TV talk show: SVT, in Sweden). Hosted by Robin Paulsson. Guest: **John Cleese**, promoting his stage tour of Scandinavia. To help pay his alimony, **Cleese** accepts a check for 34 krona from the Support **Cleese** Foundation. He also talks about his new girlfriend, *Fawlty Towers*, etc.

3874 October 12, 2010
The Scotsman (Newspaper/U.K.). "Monty Python's **Eric Idle** on His New Musical *Spamalot*." Mark Fisher interviews **Idle**, who is in Edinburgh promoting *Spamalot*'s Oct. 18–23 run at the Playhouse Theatre.

3875 October 20, 2010
An Evening with the President (Event). **Michael Palin**, president of the Royal Geographical Society, speaks at Rattray Lecture Theatre, University of Leicester.

3876 October 25, 2010
John Cleese and his partner, Jennifer Wade, attend an exhibition of The **John Cleese** Collection at The Chris Beetles Gallery in London. The collection consists of 80 English paintings, drawings, and cartoons which **Cleese** will be selling through the gallery from Oct. 26 until Nov. 13. His decision to sell his collection is the result of having sold several homes since his divorce and no longer having the space to display the paintings. Also attending the exhibition are **Terry Jones**, Michael Winner, Barry Cryer, and Chris Beetles.

3877 October 26, 2010
Fable III (Video game: Microsoft). Third installment of the action-adventure role-playing game,

with **John Cleese** voicing Jasper the butler. Other voices by Ben Kingsley, Stephen Fry, and Jonathan Ross. Developed by Lionhead Studios.

3878   October 28, 2010
An Evening with Michael Palin (Lecture). **Michael Palin** gives a talk at Whitla Hall, Queen's University Belfast in Northern Ireland. **Palin**'s talk is part of the Belfast Festival at Queen's (Oct. 15–30). **Palin** will also be funding The Michael Barnes Scholarships and Travel Bursaries for the school's drama students. Barnes — a good friend of **Palin**'s and former director of the Belfast Festival — died in May 2008. **Palin**'s association with the festival began in November 1981 when, at the urging of Barnes, he performed in the first of a series of one-man shows. **Palin** would later receive an honorary degree from Queen's (in July 2000).

3879   October 28, 2010
Dan Dare, Pilot of the Future: The Biography (Book: Orion Books), written by Daniel Tatarsky with an introduction by **Terry Jones**, is published in the U.K. Illustrated biography of the British science-fiction hero who first appeared in *Eagle* comics in 1950.

3880   October 31, 2010
The Legend of Hallowdega (Short film) premieres online. A television host investigates claims that the Talladega Superspeedway race track is haunted. Eighteen-minute short presented by AMP Energy Juice. Starring David Arquette, Justin Kirk, Dale Earnhardt, Jr., and Darrell Waltrip. Written by Aaron Bergeron. Directed by **Terry Gilliam**.

3881   November 2, 2010
Orissa: Temples and Tribes (Lecture). **Michael Palin** gives a talk on Orissa (in India), which he visited in March, at The Clothworkers' Hall in London. **Palin** will repeat the lecture on Apr. 11, 2011, at the Royal Geographical Society.

3882   November 8, 2010
Michael Meets...Raja Shehadeh (Event). **Michael Palin** interviews Palestinian author Raja Shehadeh at the Royal Geographical Society in London. It is the third event in **Palin**'s "Michael Meets..." series for the RGS.

3883   November 11, 2010
Walks on the Wild Side (Event). **Michael Palin** is among the speakers at this Transglobe Expedition Trust Event at the Royal Geographical Society in London. **Palin** talks about "Walking with Camels." Hosted by Paul Heiney.

3884   November 13, 2010
Spud (Feature film: Nu Metro Films) premieres in Johannesburg, South Africa (opens wide Dec. 3). Comedy set in South Africa in 1990, based on the book by John Van De Ruit. **John Cleese** plays Mr. "The Guv" Edly. Also starring Troye Sivan in the title role. Written & directed by Donovan Marsh.

3885   November 13, 2010
John Cleese attends the world premiere of *Spud* at Montecasino in Johannesburg, South Africa.

3886   November 14, 2010
The Sunday Times Magazine (Magazine/U.K.). "So Mr. **Cleese**, Let's Talk About Your Mother." In this six-page article **John Cleese** talks about his bitter divorce, his mother, etc. Cover photo shows **Cleese** peeking out from behind a curtain.

3887   November 18, 2010
The One Show (TV show: BBC1). Magazine program hosted by Chris Evans and Alex Jones. Guest: **John Cleese**, who talks about his one-man stage show.

3888   November 21, 2010
The 24 Hour Plays Celebrity Gala (Stage show). Charity gala hosted by **John Cleese** at London's Old Vic Theatre. The show, which benefits the Old Vic Theatre Trust and Old Vic New Voices, presents six short plays written, rehearsed and performed in just 24 hours.

3889   November 22, 2010
Terry Gilliam turns 70.

3890   November 22, 2010
Eric Idle attends the Saban Free Clinic's 34rd Annual Dinner Gala held at the Beverly Hilton Hotel in Beverly Hills, CA.

3891   November 22, 2010
Michael Palin gives a talk at Nightingale House, a care home in Clapham, South London.

3892   November 23, 2010
Michael Palin talks about *Halfway to Hollywood* at The Oldie Literary Lunch at Simpson's-in-the-Strand, London.

3893   December 2010
Michael Palin completes the first draft his new novel.

3894   December 2, 2010
Terry Jones and **Terry Gilliam** appear at Tower Bridge in London to promote the launch next year

of a new Monty Python video game, *The Ministry of Silly Games*, created by the U.K. company Zattikka. The last Python video game, *Monty Python's The Meaning of Life*, came out in 1997.

3895 December 5, 2010
The British Independent Film Awards (Award ceremony). **Terry Gilliam** and Helen McCrory present the award for Best British Independent Film to Tom Hooper (for *The King's Speech*) at the 13th annual BIFA ceremony held at Old Billingsgate Market in London.

3896 December 9, 2010
Michael Palin attends a gala charity screening of *The King's Speech* at the Curzon Mayfair Cinema, London in aid of the Michael Palin Centre for Stammering Children (founded in 1993).

3897 December 10, 2010
Michael Palin gives a reading at the York Minster Carol Concert in York, England.

3898 December 23, 2010
Being Ronnie Corbett (TV special: BBC2). Documentary on the career of comedian Ronnie Corbett (*The Two Ronnies*), who celebrated his 80th birthday earlier this month. Interviewees include **Michael Palin**, Stephen Merchant, Miranda Hart, Matt Lucas, Catherine Tate, and others. Produced by Andy Humphries.

3899 January 2011
Terry Gilliam directs the short film *The Wholly Family* on location in Naples, Italy. The film is funded by the Italian pasta company Garofalo.

3900 January 2011
Frost Over the World (TV talk show: Al Jazeera English). Hosted by David Frost. Guest: **Michael Palin**, who talks about the film *The King's Speech*, stammering, and his next travel series in Brazil.

3901 January 4, 2011
Michael Palin helps launch the Fair Fares Now campaign, which calls for "cheaper, simpler, fairer train fares," at Charing Cross station in London. Fair Fares Now was organized by Campaign for Better Transport (of which **Palin** is president).

3902 January 6, 2011
Lorraine (TV show: ITV). Host Lorraine Kelly talks to **Michael Palin** about the Centre for Stammering Children.

3903 January 9, 2011
Terry Jones attends an awards ceremony celebrating the 13th birthday of Upstairs at the Gatehouse, a theatre in Highgate, London.

3904 January 9, 2011
That Sunday Night Show (TV talk show: ITV1). Hosted by Adrian Chiles. Guests: **Michael Palin**, Shaun Ryder, Al Murray, Pamela Stephenson, and Darren Gough.

3905 January 11, 2011
The Daily Telegraph (Newspaper/U.K.). "*The King's Speech* Is My Family's Story, Too," by **Michael Palin**. **Palin** describes how the film reminded him of his own experience of growing up with a father who stammered.

3906 January 12, 2011
North West Tonight (TV show: BBC1). **John Cleese** is interviewed by Gordon Burns about his upcoming *Alimony Tour* of the U.K.

3907 January 12, 2011
American Masters (TV special: PBS). "Jeff Bridges: The Dude Abides." Ninety-minute film on the life and career of actor Jeff Bridges. **Terry Gilliam**, who directed Bridges in *The Fisher King* (1991) and *Tideland* (2005), is among the interviewees. Written & directed by Gail Levin.

3908 January 13, 2011
Alex Belfield (Radio talk show: BBC Radio Leeds). **Michael Palin** is interviewed.

3909 January 14, 2011
Yorkshire Evening Post (Newspaper/U.K.). "**John Cleese** in Leeds." Rod McPhee interviews **Cleese** at the Grand Theatre in Leeds. **Cleese** talks about his upcoming tour of the U.K.

3910 January 19–March 23, 2011
The Legend of Dick and Dom (TV series: CBBC). **Terry Jones** narrates the third and final series (10 episodes) of the British children's show starring Richard McCourt and Dominic Wood. The series premiered in January 2009.

3911 February 15, 2011
Michael Palin attends the annual Orion Authors' Party at the Royal Opera House, Covent Garden, London.

3912 February 26, 2011
My Life (TV episode: BBC2). "Stammer School." **Michael Palin** appears in this documentary in which six children go through an intensive two-week course of speech therapy at The Michael Palin Center for Stammering Children (opened in Lon-

don in 1993). Narrated by Andy Akinwolere. Directed by Mick Robertson.

3913 February 27, 2011
Eric Idle and his wife attend the *Vanity Fair* Oscar Party at the Sunset Tower Hotel in West Hollywood, CA.

3914 March 2011
Animal Tales (Book: Pavilion Children's Books), written by **Terry Jones** with illustrations by Michael Foreman, is published. Collection of humorous children's stories, including "The Good Doctor" and "The Ambitious Crocodile." The former story, about a dog doctor, was adapted by **Jones** for the short opera *The Doctor's Tale*, which premieres in London on Apr. 8.

3915 March 2011
An Illustrated History of Bristol Zoo Gardens (Book: The Independent Zoo Enthusiasts Society), written by Tim Brown, Alan Ashby & Christoph Schwitzer, is published in the U.K. Foreword by **John Cleese**. Cleese was a frequent visitor to the zoo when he was a pupil at nearby Clifton College.

3916 March 2011
Independently Animated: Bill Plympton (Book: Universe Publishing), written by Bill Plympton and David B. Levy, is published. Biography of animator Bill Plympton. Foreword by **Terry Gilliam**.

3917 March 2011
Adults Learning (Magazine/U.K.). "And Now for Something Completely Different," by Ed Melia, pp. 30–31. Interview with **Terry Jones** about his new Quick Read book *Trouble on the Heath*.

3918 March 3, 2011
Trouble on the Heath (Book: Accent Press), written by **Terry Jones**, is published. Short story about the trouble that arises from a plan to construct a large, unattractive building in a London suburb. Published on World Book Day as part of the "Quick Reads" series devised to improve adult literacy.

3919 March 5, 2011
Western Mail (Cardiff, Wales) (Newspaper/U.K.). "'I'd rather not be remembered for Python.'" Nathan Bevan interviews **Terry Jones**, who talks about his new book *Trouble on the Heath*, Python, and his early years in Colwyn Bay, Wales.

3920 March 8, 2011
Forty Years Without a Proper Job (Lecture). **Michael Palin** gives the opening talk at the 3rd Emirates Airline Festival of Literature (Mar. 8–12) in Dubai.

3921 March 20, 2011
Terry Gilliam attends the 17th annual Bradford International Film Festival (Mar. 16–27) in Bradford, West Yorkshire, England, where he receives a Fellowship Award for his contribution to film and is honored with a retrospective tribute. Previous guests at the festival include **Michael Palin** (in 2008) and **Terry Jones** (in 2009).

3922 March 20, 2011
Calendar (TV news show: ITV/YTV–Yorkshire Television). Guest: **Terry Gilliam**.

3923 March 25, 2011
The Independent (Newspaper/U.K.). "It's...Monty Python's Flying Opera House," by **Terry Jones**, p. 18. **Jones** on collaborating with composer Anne Dudley on the short opera *The Doctor's Tale* (premiering Apr. 8).

3924 April 2011
Vanity Fair (Magazine/U.S.). "A Dogged Diarist's Dos and Don'ts of Diary Writing," by **Michael Palin**, p. 136. A guide to diary-keeping etiquette.

3925 April 3, 2011
An Afternoon with John Cleese (Event). **John Cleese** hosts a screening of *Life of Brian* at Campbell Hall at the University of California Santa Barbara. Part of the UCSB Arts & Lectures' Student Appreciation Free Event Series.

3926 April 8, 2011
The Doctor's Tale (Opera) premieres at The Linbury Studio Theatre in London. **Terry Jones** directed and wrote the libretto for this short opera composed by Anne Dudley (Oscar-winner for *The Full Monty*). The surreal work, about a respected doctor who is forced to give up his practice because he's a dog, is presented on a double-bill with Stewart Copeland's *The Tell-Tale Heart* as part of the Royal Opera House's "OperaShots" series. **Jones** based his libretto on one of the children's stories ("The Good Doctor") in his recently-published book *Animal Tales*. Cast includes Darren Abrahams as the doctor. The show runs until April 16.

3927 April 10, 2011
The Andrew Marr Show (TV talk show: BBC1). Guests include Danny Alexander, Martin McGuinness, Peter Hain, and **Michael Palin**. Martha Kearney talks to **Palin** about his upcoming travel series on Brazil.

3928 April 10, 2011
Desert Island Discs (Radio show: BBC Radio 4). Kirsty Young's castaway is **Terry Gilliam**, whose choice of records includes "Heartbreak Hotel" (Elvis Presley), "When You Wish Upon a Star" (Cliff Edwards), and "Ein Heldenleben—final movement" (Richard Strauss). **Gilliam** also talks about his life, films, and directing the opera *The Damnation of Faust*. His book is a dictionary; his luxury item is a mirror.

3929 April 11, 2011
Orissa: Temples and Tribes (Lecture). **Michael Palin** gives a talk on Orissa (in India) at the Royal Geographical Society in London. Repeat of his Nov. 2, 2010, lecture at The Clothworkers' Hall.

3930 April 12, 2011
MacAulay and Co. (Radio show: BBC Radio Scotland). Host Fred MacAulay talks to **John Cleese**.

3931 April 15, 2011
Paul O'Grady Live (TV talk show: ITV1). Guests: Charlotte Church, Rupert Everett, Amanda Holden, and **John Cleese**.

3932 April 19, 2011
The One Show (TV show: BBC1). Magazine program hosted by Alex Jones and Matt Baker. Guest: **Terry Jones**, promoting *Animal Tales*.

3933 April 20–22, 2011
An Evening with John Cleese (Stage show). **John Cleese** gives three extra performances of his 2010 one-man stage show at the Cirkus in Stockholm, Sweden. **Cleese** previously played the Cirkus in October 2010.

3934 April 25, 2011
Arena (TV arts show: BBC2). "Produced by George Martin." Documentary on the life of Beatles producer Sir George Martin. Includes a talk with **Michael Palin**. Produced & directed by Francis Hanly.

3935 April 25, 2011
Efter Tio (After Ten) (TV talk show: TV4, in Sweden). Hosted by Malou Von Sivers. Guest: **John Cleese**, who talks about his *Alimony Tour*, his divorce, his new girlfriend, his mother, *Fawlty Towers*, and creativity.

3936 April 26, 2011
Eric Idle and his wife attend the 5th annual BritWeek launch party at the British Consul General's residence in Hancock Park, Los Angeles.

3937 April 27, 2011
John Cleese and his partner, Jennifer Wade, attend a private viewing of an exhibition at the Victoria and Albert Museum in London where bronze sculptures of Wade — created by Jonathan Wylder — are unveiled.

3938 April 27, 2011
Inspirations at NLS: Michael Palin (Event). **Michael Palin** is interviewed on stage by author Alistair Moffat at the National Library of Scotland in Edinburgh.

3939 May 2011
Break Free! (Web videos). **John Cleese** wrote and performs in this series of online videos as part of an ad campaign for the GPS company TomTom and their HD Traffic service. The six comedy vignettes involve **Cleese** trying to pass the time while stuck in traffic. Queen's "I Want to Break Free" is the series' theme song.

3940 May 2011
Saga Magazine (Magazine/U.K.). "Fawlty Tours," by William Langley, pp. 40–43. Interview with **John Cleese** about his *Alimony Tour* of Britain, his expensive divorce, etc.

3941 May 3–July 2, 2011
The Alimony Tour (Stage show). **John Cleese** tours Britain with his one-man stage show. **Cleese** plays 37 dates at 12 venues: Corn Exchange in Cambridge (May 3–7), Hippodrome Theatre in Birmingham (May 9–11), Theatre Royal in Nottingham (May 12–15), Salford Lowry in Manchester (May 24–27), Grand Opera House in York (May 28–29), Liverpool Empire Theatre in Liverpool (May 31–June 1), The Grand Theatre & Opera House in Leeds (June 2–4), Theatre Royal in Glasgow (June 6–8), Festival Theatre in Edinburgh (June 9–11), New Theatre in Oxford (June 17–20), Bristol Hippodrome in Bristol (June 21–23), and Theatre Royal in Bath (June 28–July 2). One of **Cleese**'s last dates in Bath will be recorded for a DVD release in the autumn. Bath is also the city where **Cleese** currently calls home (but for only three months of the year due to tax reasons).

3942 May 3, 2011
BBC Breakfast (TV news show: BBC1/News Channel). Hosted by Bill Turnbull and Sian Williams. Guest: **Terry Jones**.

3943 May 6, 2011
The Damnation of Faust (Opera), directed by **Terry Gilliam**, opens at the London Coliseum.

Gilliam makes his opera directorial debut with this English National Opera production of Hector Berlioz's 1846 work. Leading the cast are Peter Hoare (Faust, tenor), Christopher Purves (Mephistopheles, bass), and Christine Rice (Marguerite, soprano). Edward Gardner conducts the ENO Chorus & Orchestra. *Faust* performs at the Coliseum until June 7. Televised Oct. 14 on BBC4.

Award: South Bank Sky Arts Award for best opera.

3944   May 7, 2011
Monty Python's Fliegender Zirkus! (Radio special: BBC Radio 4). Host Henning Wehn looks back at the making of the two special shows Monty Python produced for German television forty years ago. Interviewees include **Terry Jones**, **Michael Palin**, and producers Alfred Biolek and Thomas Woitkewitsch. Produced by Joe Meek and Marvin Close.

3945   May 9, 2011
Newsnight (TV news show: BBC2). Will Gompertz reports on **Terry Gilliam**'s new production of *The Damnation of Faust*, showing rehearsals and interviewing **Gilliam**, conductor Edward Gardner, others.

3946   May 9, 2011
Simply Shakespeare (Event). **Eric Idle** participates in the 21st Annual "Simply Shakespeare" fundraiser put on by the Shakespeare Center of Los Angeles at Royce Hall, UCLA in Westwood, CA. He and other celebrities give a reading from *The Merry Wives of Windsor*.

3947   May 10, 2011
Michael Meets...Mahjabeen Khan (Event). **Michael Palin** interviews musician-journalist Mahjabeen ("Moni") Khan at the Royal Geographical Society in London. It is the fourth event in **Palin**'s "Michael Meets..." series for the RGS. **Palin** first met Khan in Dhaka, Bangladesh, while filming his *Himalaya* series in 2004 (she appears in episode six).

3948   May 11, 2011
An Evening with the President (Event). **Michael Palin**, president of the Royal Geographical Society, speaks at Wallace Lecture Theatre, Cardiff University, Wales.

3949   May 19, 2011
OxTravels: Meetings with Remarkable Travel Writers (Book: Profile Books), introduced by **Michael Palin**, is published in the U.K. Travel anthology in support of Oxfam.

3950   May 20, 2011
The Chris Evans Breakfast Show (Radio show: BBC Radio 2). Guest: **John Cleese**.

3951   May 20, 2011
The Review Show (TV arts show: BBC2). Hosted by Martha Kearney. Guest **Terry Gilliam** talks about directing the opera *The Damnation of Faust*.

3952   May 25, 2011
Knights, Python, Adventures (Event). **Michael Palin** participates in an onstage conversation with John Murray at The National Concert Hall in Dublin, Ireland as part of the 13th annual Dublin Writers Festival (May 23–29).

3953   May 25, 2011
The Wholly Family (Short film) premieres in Rome, Italy. **Terry Gilliam** wrote and directed this 20-minute short about a boy who enters a strange dream world while he and his parents are vacationing in Naples. Filmed over a week in mid–January on location in Naples, the film was sponsored by the Italian pasta company Garofalo. Starring Cristiana Capotondi, Douglas Dean, Nicolas Connolly, Sergio Solli, and Antonino Iuorio. Produced by Gabriele Oricchio and Amy Gilliam.

Award: European Film Award winner for Best Short Film.

3954   May 26, 2011
Michael Palin attends the launch party for the book *OxTravels* (for which he wrote the intro) at Daunt Books in Marylebone, London.

3955   May 27–29, 2011
Terry Gilliam attends Istancool 2011, the Istanbul International Festival of Culture in Istanbul, Turkey, where he participates in an onstage discussion (at the Vakko Fashion Centre) and a Q&A (at the Pera Museum). There are also screenings of some of his films.

3956   May 28, 2011
Eric Idle's "Galaxy Song," performed by Clint Black, is played to wake the crews of the space shuttle *Endeavour* and the International Space Station.

3957   May 29, 2011
Terry Jones attends the Hay Literary Festival (May 26–June 5) in Hay-on-Wye, Wales, where he helps launch a new reader-supported publishing venture called Unbound. The first book from the publisher is **Jones'** *Evil Machines* (out Nov. 4).

3958   June–July 2011
Michael Palin visits the North-East of Brazil for

the first of four film shoots for his new BBC series *Brazil with Michael Palin*.

3959 June 2011
The Monster of Nix (Short film) premieres at the Annecy Animated Film Festival in France. **Terry Gilliam** voices The Ranger in this 30-minute animated fairy tale by Dutch artist/filmmaker Rosto. Tom Waits voices Virgil (the monster).

3960 June 2, 2011
The Book Show (TV episode: Sky Arts 1). Host Mariella Frostrup talks to **Terry Jones** about his book *Animal Tales* and writing for children.

3961 June 6, 2011
Michael Palin hosts the Royal Geographical Society's Medals and Awards Celebration at the Ondaatjie Theatre of the RGS headquarters in London.

3962 June 13, 2011
Michael Palin and **Terry Jones** participate in an onstage conversation with host Mariella Frostrup (followed by an audience Q&A) at Queen Elizabeth Hall in London. The event is part of Ray Davies' Meltdown festival (June 10–19).

3963 June 14, 2011
Daybreak (TV talk show: ITV1). Hosted by Adrian Chiles and Kate Garraway. Guests: **Terry Jones** and Jennifer Ellison.

3964 June 16, 2011
Terry Gilliam attends the opening of the Persol Magnificent Obsessions exhibition at Center 548 in New York City. The exhibition looks at obsessive craftsmanship in filmmaking.

3965 June 26, 2011
The New York Times (Newspaper online/U.S.). "This May Be Something Completely Different," by Michael Cieply. Article on the making of a new 3-D animated film on the life of **Graham Chapman** for which the other Pythons (except **Idle**) are providing voices.

3966 July 2011
Terry Jones attends The First International Comedy Film Festival (July 4–11) in Albufeira, Portugal.

3967 July 2011
Terry Gilliam attends the 9th Annual Ischia Global Film & Music Fest (July 10–17) on the Isle of Ischia, Gulf of Naples, Italy.

3968 July 11, 2011
The Animal Magic Zoo (TV special: BBC1). Host Terry Nutkins looks at the 175-year history of Bristol Zoo in Bristol, England. Interviewees include **John Cleese** and Nick Park. Produced by Helen Shawcross.

3969 July 15, 2011
Winnie the Pooh (Feature film: Walt Disney Studios) opens in the U.S. Animated film based on A. A. Milne's classic children's story. Narrated by **John Cleese**. Voice cast also includes Jim Cummings, Craig Ferguson, and Tom Kenny. Directed by Stephen Anderson and Don Hall.

3970 July 16, 2011
The Danny Baker Show (Radio show: BBC Radio 5 Live). **Terry Jones** is interviewed.

3971 July 21–31, 2011
Terry Gilliam attends the 11th New Horizons Film Festival in Wroclaw, Poland. The fest includes a retrospective of his films (with Q&A) and the premiere of a new book, *Wunderkamera: Terry Gilliam's Cinema*.

3972 July 21, 2011
Terry Jones hosts a memorial concert by the City of London Sinfonia and the Wellensian Consort celebrating the life and music of composer Geoffrey Burgon (*Life of Brian*) at St. John's Smith Square, London. Burgon, who died in September 2010, would have turned 70 this month.

3973 July 25, 2011
Terry Jones: Animal Tales (Event). **Terry Jones**, in conversation with TV host Carol Bundock, talks about his new book *Animal Tales* at the King's Lynn Arts Centre in King's Lynn, Norfolk, England, as part of the 61st King's Lynn Festival (July 17–30).

3974 July 28, 2011
Michael Palin: In Conversation with Michael Brunson (Event). **Michael Palin** talks with journalist Michael Brunson at the Auden Theatre in Holt, Norfolk, England, as part of the Holt Festival (July 24–30). The talk is followed by an audience Q&A.

3975 July 29, 2011
Q (Radio show: CBC Radio, in Canada). Guest-host Stephen Quinn talks to **Terry Jones** about his book *Evil Machines* (due out in the fall) and the Unbound publishing venture.

3976 August 6, 2011
Ronnie Corbett's Comedy Britain (TV special: ITV1). First of a special two-part series in which

80-year-old Ronnie Corbett (*The Two Ronnies*) looks back on his career and the history of British comedy. Corbett speaks to **John Cleese** (in Oxford), Miranda Hart, Stephen Merchant, Matt Lucas, and David Mitchell. Produced & directed by Nic Guttridge. Note: Corbett and **Cleese** are both veterans of TV's *The Frost Report* (1966–67).

3977 August 14, 2011
Terry Gilliam discusses his career with Dan Jolin at *Empire* magazine's Big Screen event (Aug. 12–14) in London.

3978 August 22, 2011
TV producer-director John Howard Davies dies of cancer at age 72. A former screen child actor (*Oliver Twist*), Davies later directed the first four episodes of *Monty Python's Flying Circus* (in 1969) and the first series of *Fawlty Towers* (in 1975).

3979 August 31, 2011
John Cleese speaks at a press conference at the Sydney Opera House in Sydney, Australia about the upcoming *Just for Laughs* comedy festival, which he will be hosting.

3980 September 3, 2011
John Cleese hosts the International Comedy Gala as part of the *Just for Laughs* comedy festival at the Sydney Opera House in Sydney, Australia. It is the festival's first time in Australia (it originated in Montreal). Other performers include Martin Short, Louis C.K., and Russell Howard. **Cleese** had previously hosted *Just for Laughs* galas in Montreal (in 2006 and 2009) and Toronto (2009).

3981 September 6, 2011
Listen to Me: Buddy Holly (CD: Verve Forecast). Compilation of Buddy Holly songs performed by top music artists, including Ringo Starr, Brian Wilson, Jackson Browne, Stevie Nicks, Linda Ronstadt, and Jeff Lynne. **Eric Idle** performs the bonus track, "Raining in My Heart." Executive produced by Peter Asher.

3982 September 10, 2011
QI Genesis (TV special: BBC2). Documentary on the making of the panel game *QI* (Quite Interesting). **Michael Palin** talks to *QI*'s creator, John Lloyd, recalling why he turned down Lloyd's offer to be the show's moderator (Stephen Fry ultimately got the job). Directed by Ian Lorimer. Produced by Arron Ferster and John Lloyd.

3983 September 11, 2011
Michael Palin: The Good, the Bad, and the Ugly (Lecture). **Michael Palin** gives a talk on architecture he's encountered in his travels, at Sheppey Little Theatre in Sheerness, Isle of Sheppey, England, as part of the Promenade Festival (Sept. 9–11).

3984 September 12, 2011
Michael Palin hosts a dinner at the Pollen Street Social restaurant in London in honor of an expedition team setting off to climb Mount Kilimanjaro in aid of the charity FARM-Africa.

3985 September 13, 2011
Terry Gilliam attends the opening night performance of *No Naughty Bits* at the Hampstead Theatre in London. The play, written by Steve Thompson, tells the story of Monty Python's 1975 legal battle with ABC Television for which **Michael Palin** (played by Harry Hadden-Paton) and **Gilliam** (Sam Alexander) flew to New York to represent the group in court. The show runs until Oct. 15.

3986 September 13, 2011
Michael Palin introduces the premiere of the documentary *The Lost World* for Ibex Earth at the Royal Geographical Society (of which **Palin** is president) in London.

3987 September 15, 2011
Photographs & Words (Book: The British Library), by Michael Katakis and Kris Hardin, is published. Foreword by John Falconer and introduction by **Michael Palin**.

3988 September 24, 2011
John Cleese performs at a comedy gala co-starring Norwegian comics Harald Eia, Atle Antonsen, and Bard Tufte Johansen at the Oslo Spektrum Arena in Oslo, Norway, before an audience of nearly 7,000 fans. **Cleese** brought his one-man stage show to Norway in October 2009 and September 2010.

3989 September 25, 2011
Terry Gilliam attends the 17th International Short Film Festival in Drama, Northern Greece where he accepts the special European Film Academy Prize for his short film *The Wholly Family*.

3990 October 2011
Michael Palin visits Minas Gerais and Rio in Brazil to film part of his new BBC series *Brazil with Michael Palin*.

3991 October 2011
Terry Gilliam attends both the BFI London Film

Festival (Oct. 12–27) and the 5th annual Abu Dhabi Film Festival (Oct. 13–22). His Italian-made short, *The Wholly Family*, is screened at both festivals.

3992 October 2011
Fame in the Frame (TV episode: Sky Arts 1). "**Terry Gilliam**." Artist/host John Myatt paints a portrait of **Gilliam** as "The Buddha" (based on Odilon Redon's 1904 work). Myatt also painted **John Cleese** for his earlier series *Brush with Fame* in February 2009.

3993 October 2011
1001 Comics You Must Read Before You Die (Book: Universe Publishing), edited by Paul Gravett with a foreword by **Terry Gilliam**, is published.

3994 October 2, 2011
Terry Gilliam, **Eric Idle**, and **Michael Palin** attend the U.K. premiere of the documentary *George Harrison: Living in the Material World* at the BFI Southbank, London.

3995 October 4, 2011
Eric Idle and his wife attend the U.S. premiere of the documentary *George Harrison: Living in the Material World* at Alice Tully Hall, Lincoln Center as part of the 49th annual New York Film Festival (Sept. 30–Oct. 16).

3996 October 5–6, 2011
George Harrison: Living in the Material World (Feature film: HBO). Two-part documentary on the life and music of the late former Beatle — and friend of the Pythons — George Harrison. **Eric Idle** and **Terry Gilliam** are interviewed. Directed by Martin Scorsese.

3997 October 6, 2011
Medieval Misconceptions (Lecture). **Terry Jones** gives the Annual Lecture at the Geological Society, Burlington House, Piccadilly, London, in support of The Churches Conservation Trust.

3998 October 6, 2011
John Cleese and his girlfriend Jennifer Wade attend the Build Africa fundraising dinner at the Mandarin Oriental Hotel in London.

3999 October 7, 2011
The One Show (TV show: BBC1). Magazine program hosted by Chris Evans and Alex Jones. Guest **Terry Gilliam** talks about his short *The Wholly Family* and his production of the opera *The Damnation of Faust*, which premiered in May and will air Oct. 14 on BBC4.

4000 October 9, 2011
Dr. Robert Buckman dies at the age of 63. The Toronto-based oncologist, formerly half of a comedy team with Chris Beetles (the two can be seen dancing in the "Cheese Shop" sketch in *The Secret Policeman's Ball*), collaborated with **John Cleese** in the 1990s on the Videos for Patients series. Buckman dies on board a plane flying back to Toronto from London where he had been filming another series of health videos (for MyHealthTips.com), this time with **Terry Jones**.

4001 October 10, 2011
Erik the Viking: The Complete Viking (DVD: Arrow Video) is released in the U.K. Special two-disc edition of the 1989 **Terry Jones** film containing both the 2006 "Director's Son's Cut" and British theatrical versions. Bonus features include audio commentaries by **Jones**, the documentaries *The Making of Erik the Viking* (1989), *The Evolution of a Director*, *The Casting of a Comedy Adventure*, *The Special Effects of Erik the Viking*, *Making Movie Magic on Malta*, *Jones and Cleese: A Grand Reunion*, and *Creating the Look*, also interviews, photo gallery, theatrical trailer, and a collector's booklet.

4002 October 12, 2011
The Guardian (Newspaper/U.K.). "Obituary: Robert Buckman," by **Terry Jones**. Obituary for Dr. Robert Buckman, who had been collaborating with **Jones** on a series of short films in the week before his death.

4003 October 14, 2011
The Damnation of Faust (TV special: BBC4). Berlioz's 1846 opera, directed by **Terry Gilliam** for the English National Opera. Starring Peter Hoare and Christopher Purves.

4004 October 14, 2011
The Big Year (Feature film: Twentieth Century–Fox) opens in the U.S. Comedy starring Steve Martin, Jack Black, and Owen Wilson, with **John Cleese** as Historical Montage Narrator. Directed by David Frankel.

4005 October 15, 2011
Terry Jones cuts the ribbon at the re-opening of the Theatr Colwyn in his home town of Colwyn Bay, Wales. The venue, of which **Jones** is a patron, had been closed for renovations. Afterward there is a benefit screening of *Holy Grail*, followed by an interview with **Jones** (conducted by comedian Phill Jupitus) and a Q&A.

4006 October 15–21, 2011
Radio Times (Magazine/U.K.). **Terry Jones** looks back on the *Life of Brian* controversy.

4007 October 16, 2011
Michael Palin presents an appeal (on BBC Radio 4) on behalf of the international development charity Motivation. His last appeal for the charity in 2008 raised £40,000.

4008 October 18, 2011
Holy Flying Circus (TV special: BBC4). Comedic dramatization of events surrounding the release of Monty Python's controversial film *Life of Brian* in 1979. The Pythons are played by Darren Boyd (**John Cleese**), Charles Edwards (**Michael Palin**), Tom Fisher (**Graham Chapman**), Rufus Jones (**Terry Jones**), Steve Punt (**Eric Idle**), and Phil Nichol (**Terry Gilliam**). Also starring Ben Crispin (Jesus), Simon Greenall (Barry Atkins), Paul Chahidi (Harry Balls), and Stephen Fry (God). Written by Tony Roche. Directed by Owen Harris.

4009 October 18, 2011
The Kid's Speech (TV special: BBC1). Documentary following three children as they undergo intensive speech therapy over a two-week period at The Michael Palin Center for Stammering Children (opened in London in 1993). **Michael Palin** is interviewed. Narrated by Daniel Rigby. Produced & directed by David Brindley.

4010 October 21–29, 2011
The Alimony Tour (Stage show). **John Cleese** brings his one-man show to South Africa, playing the Cape Town International Convention Centre (Oct. 21–22) and the Teatro at Montecasino, Johannesburg (Oct. 25–29). While in Johannesburg, **Cleese** records a radio ad for the online store Takealot.

4011 October 22, 2011
Rupert Bear and Me (Radio special: BBC Radio 4). Mark Radcliffe presents a half-hour tribute to the little white bear of children's comics and talks to Rupert fans **Terry Jones**, John Thompson, and Terence Stamp. Produced by Lorna Skingley. Note: **Jones** wrote, directed & hosted the TV special *The Rupert Bear Story—A Tribute to Alfred Bestall* in 1982.

4012 November 3, 2011
An Evening with the President (Event). **Michael Palin**, president of the Royal Geographical Society, speaks at Merewood Country House Hotel in Windermere, England.

4013 November 4, 2011
Evil Machines (Book: Unbound), written by **Terry Jones**, is published. Collection of 13 darkly-comic tales about machines that turn malevolent. The stories, which include "The Truthful Phone" and "The Lift That Took People to Places They Didn't Want to Go," originally appeared as the libretto for a 2008 opera with music by Luis Tinoco. First book from the reader-funded publisher, Unbound, which **Jones** helped launch at the Hay Festival on May 29.

4014 November 4, 2011
BBC Breakfast (TV news show: BBC1/News Channel). Hosted by Charlie Stayt and Susanna Reid. Guest: **Terry Jones**, promoting *Evil Machines*.

4015 November 4, 2011
Terry Jones attends the launch of his book *Evil Machines* at the Adam Street Private Members Club in London.

4016 November 6, 2011
Sunday Night (TV talk show: Channel 7, in Australia). **John Cleese** talks to interviewer Ross Coulthart about his stage show, divorce, and comedy.

4017 November 8, 2011
Beethoven's Christmas Adventure (Feature film: Universal) is released on video. Holiday children's film starring the loveable St. Bernard, Beethoven. Narrated by **John Cleese**. Starring Curtis Armstrong, Munro Chambers, Robert Picardo, Kyle Massey, and the voice of Tom Arnold. Written by Daniel Altiere and Steven Altiere. Directed by John Putch.

4018 November 11, 2011
Arthur Christmas (Feature film: Sony Pictures) is released in the U.K. This 3-D computer-animated holiday film, a collaboration between Aardman Animations and Sony Pictures Animation, tells the story of Santa's bumbling son, Arthur, and his efforts to deliver one overlooked present on Christmas Eve. **Michael Palin** voices Ernie Clicker. Voice cast also includes James McAvoy (as Arthur), Hugh Laurie, Bill Nighy, Jim Broadbent, Imelda Staunton, and Ashley Jensen. Written by Sarah Smith and Peter Baynham. Directed by Sarah Smith. Produced by Steve Pegram. Opens in the U.S. on Nov. 23.

4019 November 12, 2011
Terry Jones attends the 6th Funchal International

Film Festival (Nov. 12–19) in Funchal, Madeira, Portugal, where he is given an award for his contribution to cinema at the opening night gala at the Teatro Municipal Baltazar Dias. Jones was to have received the award at last year's festival (April 2010) but was unable to attend due to the volcanic ash cloud from Iceland that disrupted air travel in Europe.

4020 November 13, 2011
Open Book (Radio talk show: BBC Radio 4). Hosted by Mariella Frostrup with John Mullen. Guest **Terry Jones** discusses the humor in the work of Chaucer.

4021 November 17, 2011
The Guardian Books Podcast (Podcast). **Terry Jones** is interviewed about writing books for children.

4022 November 17, 2011
John Cleese and his partner, Jennifer Wade, switch on the Christmas lights at a ceremony in Bath, Somerset, England, where the couple are currently residing part-time.

4023 November 19, 2011
Terry Gilliam receives the Premio Fellini (Fellini Award) from the Fellini Foundation in Rimini, Italy.

4024 November 21, 2011
John Cleese Live: The Alimony Tour 2011 (DVD: ITV Studios) is released in the U.K. **John Cleese**'s stand-up show, recorded in Bath on the last day of his U.K. tour.

4025 November 21, 2011
John Cleese, promoting the *Alimony Tour* DVD, appears on the radio shows *The Chris Moyles Show* (BBC Radio 1), *Richard Bacon* (BBC Radio 5 Live), *Dominic King* (BBC Radio Kent), and *Judi Spiers Show* (BBC Radio Devon).

4026 November 21, 2011
The One Show (TV show: BBC1). Magazine program hosted by Matt Baker and Alex Jones. Guest: **John Cleese**, promoting the *Alimony Tour* DVD, also talks about his knee replacement, his teaching days, singing on Broadway, etc.

4027 November 21, 2011
The New Yorker (Magazine/U.S.). "Shouts & Murmurs: Who Wrote Shakespeare?" by **Eric Idle**, p. 65. Humorous essay asserting that lack of evidence is no reason for denouncing a theory.

4028 November 21, 2011
Eric Idle and his wife attend the Saban Free Clinic's 35th Annual Dinner Gala held at the Beverly Hilton Hotel in Beverly Hills, CA.

4029 November 22, 2011
John Cleese, promoting the *Alimony Tour* DVD, appears on the radio shows *The Christian O'Connell Breakfast Show* (Absolute Radio), *Steve Wright in the Afternoon* (BBC Radio 2), and *Shaun Keaveny* (BBC Radio 6 Music).

4030 November 23, 2011
Daybreak (TV talk show: ITV1). Hosted by John Stapleton and Christine Bleakley. Guests: **John Cleese**, promoting his *Alimony Tour* DVD, Russell Grant, Jodie Prenger, and Westlife.

4031 November 30, 2011
Terry Gilliam attends the Hidden Gems photography gala auction held at St. Pancras Renaissance Hotel in London. The event raises funds for Variety, the children's charity.

4032 December 1, 2011
BBC Breakfast (TV news show: BBC1/News Channel). Hosted by Bill Turnbull and Sian Williams. Guest **Terry Gilliam** talks about the battle to get *Brazil* released in the U.S.

4033 December 3, 2011
The 2011 European Film Awards (Award ceremony). **Terry Gilliam** attends the ceremony at the Tempodrom in Berlin, Germany, where his short film *The Wholly Family* wins for Best European Short Film.

4034 December 3, 2011
Buddy Holly: Listen to Me—The Ultimate Buddy Party (TV special: PBS). **Eric Idle** contributes a video message to this tribute concert (recorded Sept. 7), which followed the release of the album *Listen to Me: Buddy Holly* (on which **Idle** performs "Raining in My Heart").

4035 December 5, 2011
BBC Breakfast (TV news show: BBC1/News Channel). Hosted by Charlie Stayt and Susanna Reid. Guest **John Cleese** talks about his stage tour and DVD.

4036 December 5, 2011
This Morning (TV news-talk show: ITV1). Hosted by Phillip Schofield and Holly Willoughby. Guest: **John Cleese**, promoting his *Alimony Tour* DVD.

4037 December 5, 2011
Front Row (Radio arts show: BBC Radio 4). Mark Lawson interviews **John Cleese** about his *Alimony Tour* DVD, his expensive divorce, Python writing sessions, *Life of Brian* controversy, etc.

4038 December 6, 2011
Terry Gilliam is honored with the Golden Star Award at the 11th Annual Marrakech International Film Festival (Dec. 2–10) in Marrakech, Morocco.

4039 December 7, 2011
Film 2011 (TV show: BBC1). Hosted by Claudia Winkleman. **Terry Gilliam** discusses the making of his 1985 film *Brazil*.

4040 December 8, 2011
BBC Breakfast (TV news show: BBC1/News Channel). Guests include **Eric Idle**, Matthew Bourne, and Sir Roger Moore.

4041 December 8, 2011
Michael Palin attends a reception hosted by the Queen and the Duke of Edinburgh celebrating "Exploration and Adventure" at Buckingham Palace in London. Other guests include Sir David Attenborough, mountaineer Sir Chris Bonington, and Bear Grylls.

4042 December 9, 2011
Michael Palin gives a reading at the York Minster Christmas Carol Concert in York, England.

4043 December 10, 2011
Telegraph Magazine (Magazine/U.K.). "The World of: **Terry Jones**." Jones (interviewed by Angela Wintle) discusses his routine, childhood, typewriter, love of Rupert Bear, etc.

4044 December 10, 2011
Loose Ends (Radio talk show: BBC Radio 4). Clive Anderson talks to **Eric Idle** about *Spamalot*'s new U.K. tour.

4045 December 15, 2011
Spamalot's new U.K. tour begins with a four-week residency at The Theatre Royal in Brighton. The production features Marcus Brigstocke (King Arthur) and Jodie Prenger (Lady of the Lake). **Eric Idle** also appears (on film) as God.

4046 December 16, 2011
Front Row (Radio arts show: BBC Radio 4). Mark Lawson interviews **Terry Jones** about Python and his new book *Evil Machines*.

4047 December 24, 2011
The Many Faces of Les Dawson (TV special: BBC2). Profile of British comedian Les Dawson (1931–1993). **John Cleese**, who worked with Dawson on his 1970s series *Sez Les*, is among the interviewees. Narrated by Sally Phillips. Produced & directed by Charlie Stuart.

4048 January 2012
Michael Palin visits Amazônia and Brasília in Brazil to film part of his new BBC series *Brazil with Michael Palin*.

4049 January 2012
Meetings, Bloody Meetings (Training film: Video Arts). Second remake of the best-selling 1976 training film (previously remade in 1993). In this version **John Cleese**, who played the manager in the earlier films, takes the role of the Judge. Also starring Will Smith, Howard Charles, Felix Dexter, Matt Green, Rebecca Johnson, and Susie Kane. Written by **John Cleese** and Antony Jay. Directed by Sean Hardie.

4050 January 2012
Terry Jones is reported to be collaborating with composer-lyricist Jim Steinman on a heavy-metal version of the Tchaikovsky ballet *The Nutcracker*.

4051 January 2, 2012
French and Saunders (Radio special: BBC Radio 2). Hosted by Dawn French and Jennifer Saunders. Guests: **Michael Palin** and Tracey Emin.

4052 January 7, 2012
John Howard Davies: A Life in Comedy (TV special: BBC2). Profile of the late John Howard Davies, who directed episodes of *Monty Python's Flying Circus* (in 1969) and *Fawlty Towers* (in 1975). **John Cleese** is among those paying tribute. Hosted by Penelope Keith. Produced & directed by Hannah Robson.

4053 January 14, 2012
Ken Russell: A Bit of a Devil (TV special: BBC2). Documentary about maverick film director Ken Russell (1927–2011). Interviewees include **Terry Gilliam**, Twiggy, Roger Daltrey, and Glenda Jackson. Hosted by Alan Yentob. Directed by Eleanor Horne. Produced by Allan Campbell.

4054 January 16, 2012
MyHealthTips.com (Web videos). Canadian-made series of videos presented by Dr. Rob Buckman and **Terry Jones**. The five videos, which use comedy to get points across, focus on five different health concerns: "Type 2 Diabetes," "Weight Control," "Asthma," "High Blood Pressure," and "Quitting Smoking." Written by **Terry Jones**. Directed by

Bill Jones (son of **Terry**). Note: Buckman died on Oct. 9 while on board a plane flying back to Toronto from London, where he had just spent a week shooting the videos.

4055   January 19, 2012
Here and Now Toronto (Radio talk show: CBC, in Canada). Laura Di Battista talks with guest **Terry Jones** about the health videos he made with the late Dr. Rob Buckman.

4056   January 19, 2012
George Stroumboulopoulos Tonight (TV talk show: CBC, in Canada). Hosted by George Stroumboulopoulos. Guest **Terry Jones**, promoting the *MyHealthTips.com* videos, talks about his bowel cancer scare (in 2006), working in Python, and how the arms industry drives us into war. Note: **Terry Gilliam** appeared on the show in December 2009 when it was called *The Hour*.

4057   January 19, 2012
The Project (TV talk show: Ten, in Australia). **John Cleese**, speaking from Perth, talks about his Australian tour, also *Fawlty Towers*, Python, etc. He will appear again on the program (in the studio) when his tour comes to Melbourne in March.

4058   January 19, 2012
The Film Programme (Radio show: BBC Radio 4). Host Francine Stock talks to **Terry Gilliam** about his short film *The Wholly Family*.

4059   January 19, 2012
Terry Gilliam discusses his work before a group of film students at the Cantieri Culturali alla Zisa in Palermo, Italy. The talk is followed by a screening of the documentary *Lost in La Mancha*. Gilliam's production of the Berlioz opera *The Damnation of Faust* opens in Palermo on Jan. 22.

4060   January 20, 2012
The Morning Show (TV news-talk show: Global TV, in Canada). Hosted by Liza Fromer. Guest: **Terry Jones**, promoting the *MyHealthTips.com* videos.

4061   January 20, 2012
The Circle (TV talk show: Ten, in Australia). Guest-hosted by Indira Naidoo and Michala Banas. Yumi Stynes talks to **John Cleese** about his career and upcoming Australian tour.

4062   January 22–April 16, 2012
An Evening with John Cleese (Stage show). **John Cleese** tours Australia with his one-man show (previously titled *The Alimony Tour*), performing 54 dates. Venues: Regal Theatre in Perth (Jan. 22–25, 27–Feb. 1, 3), Her Majesty's Theatre in Adelaide (Feb. 6–11), QPAC Concert Hall in Brisbane (Feb. 20–27), The Arts Centre in Gold Coast (Feb. 29 & Mar. 1), Civic Theatre in Newcastle (Mar. 5–7), Comedy Theatre in Melbourne (Mar. 12–17), Princess Theatre in Melbourne (Mar. 19–24, 26, 27), State Theatre in Sydney (Mar. 30–Apr. 2, 4), and Canberra Theatre in Canberra (Apr. 12, 14–16).

4063   January 22, 2012
The opera *The Damnation of Faust*, directed by **Terry Gilliam**, opens at the Teatro Massimo in Palermo, Italy. In this new production, which will run until Jan. 29, Faust is played by Gianluca Terranova; the conductor is Roberto Abbado. The original production, with the English National Opera, premiered at the London Coliseum in May 2011. *Faust* will open in Belgium in September.

4064   January 23, 2012
The Guardian hosts an online screening of **Terry Gilliam**'s short film *The Wholly Family*, with Gilliam participating in a live-blogged interview (with Peter Bradshaw) and post-screening Q&A.

4065   January 27, 2012
BBC Breakfast (TV news show: BBC1/News Channel). Hosted by Charlie Stayt and Susanna Reid. Guest **Terry Jones** discusses his next film project, *Absolutely Anything* (set to feature the voices of **John Cleese**, **Terry Gilliam**, and **Michael Palin**) and silent films.

4066   January 28, 2012
He's Not the Messiah He's...Terry Jones! (Event). **Terry Jones** introduces a screening of *Life of Brian* at Colston Hall in Bristol, England as part of the Slapstick Festival (Jan. 26–29). **Jones** also participates in a discussion about the film with Sanjeev Bhaskar.

4067   January 31, 2012
Afternoons with Gillian O'Shaughnessy (Radio news-talk show: 720 ABC Perth, in Australia). Gillian O'Shaughnessy interviews **John Cleese**, who talks about his early years, working with Python, etc. and takes questions from callers.

4068   February 1, 2012
Terry Jones turns 70.

4069   February 1, 2012
Whitney (TV episode: NBC). "Mind Games." **John Cleese** guest-stars as couples therapist Dr.

Grant in this episode of the new sitcom starring comedian Whitney Cummings. Written by Betsy Thomas and Adrian Wenner. Directed by Linda Mendoza.

4070   February 5, 2012
The Cricklewood Greats (TV special: BBC4). Mock-documentary, directed & hosted by Peter Capaldi, exploring the history of London's "legendary" Cricklewood Film Studios. **Terry Gilliam** plays Terry Gilliam, the director of an out-of-control film project that drove the studio into bankruptcy in the 1980s. Written by Peter Capaldi and Tony Roche. Produced by Adam Tandy.

4071   February 7, 2012
Terry Gilliam attends a lunch at the Savoy Hotel in London celebrating actor John Hurt's BAFTA award for Outstanding British Contribution to Cinema.

4072   February 9, 2012
Eric Idle is among a small gathering of friends and family (and a few lucky fans) attending an intimate concert by Paul McCartney, backed by Diana Krall and others, at Capitol Studios in Los Angeles. The show, which features songs off his new album *Kisses on the Bottom*, is streamed live on iTunes. A few hours earlier McCartney's star was unveiled on the Hollywood Walk of Fame.

4073   February 12, 2012
Terry Gilliam attends the BAFTA Awards after-party at the Grosvenor House Hotel in London.

4074   February 22, 2012
Michael Meets...Michael Katakis (Event). **Michael Palin** interviews writer and photographer Michael Katakis at the Royal Geographical Society in London.

4075   February 23, 2012
An Evening with the President (Event). **Michael Palin**, president of the Royal Geographical Society, speaks at The Hostry, Norwich Cathedral in Norwich, England.

4076   February 27, 2012
Michael Palin attends the BBC Worldwide Showcase at the BT Convention Centre in Liverpool. Among the new BBC programs being promoted at the television festival is the four-part travel series *Brazil with Michael Palin*.

4077   February 27, 2012
The Late Late Show with Craig Ferguson (TV talk show: CBS). Guests: **Eric Idle**, promoting his play *What About Dick?* (coming in April), and Sarah Paulson. **Idle** also plays the harmonica, winning the "Golden Mouth Organ."

4078   February 28, 2012
Eric Idle attends the opening night of *Spamalot* at the Pantages Theatre in Los Angeles.

4079   March 2, 2012
The One Show (TV show: BBC1). Magazine program hosted by Chris Evans and Alex Jones. Guests: **Michael Palin** and **Terry Jones**, promoting the *Ripping Yarns* DVD, also Willem Defoe and Gyles Brandreth.

4080   March 3, 2012
Michael Palin and **Terry Jones** participate in a one-legged "Hopathon" for charity at Hampstead Heath Athletics Track in North London. The event is part of a promotion for the DVD re-release of *Ripping Yarns*. A 30-mile hop was featured in the *Yarns* pilot episode *Tomkinson's Schooldays*.

4081   March 4, 2012
The Secret Policeman's Ball 2012 (Stage show). Amnesty International benefit show staged for the first time in America (the first *Ball*, featuring **John Cleese, Terry Jones & Michael Palin**, was staged in London in June 1979), at Radio City Music Hall in NYC. **Eric Idle, Jones & Palin** appear in pre-recorded video messages. Other stars include Jon Stewart, Eddie Izzard, Kristen Wiig, Mumford & Sons, Russell Brand, Reggie Watts, and Coldplay. Streamed live on Epix in the U.S. and shown Mar. 9 in the U.K.

4082   March 5, 2012
The Complete Ripping Yarns (DVD: Network) is re-released in the U.K. The series was previously released on DVD in 2004. **Michael Palin** and **Terry Jones** sign copies of the DVD at HMV Oxford Street, London.

4083   March 6, 2012
Monty Python and the Holy Grail (Blu-ray: Sony Pictures). The 1975 film — previously released on DVD in a two-disc Special Edition (2001) and a three-disc Extraordinarily Deluxe Edition (2006) — debuts on Blu-ray. New features: "The Holy Book of Days Second Screen Experience," "Lost Animations" (introduced by **Terry Gilliam**), and "Outtakes & Extended Scenes" (introduced by **Terry Jones**).

4084   March 6, 2012
Monty Python: The Holy Book of Days (iPad app).

App giving users the chance to follow the day-by-day filming of *Holy Grail* over 28 days in the spring of 1974. The behind-the-scenes materials include the script (with handwritten notes), outtakes, stills, storyboards, songs, sound effects, **Michael Palin**'s diary entries, etc. Designed to sync with the film's Blu-ray release as a "Second Screen" experience. Produced by Melcher Media.

4085 March 9, 2012
The Secret Policeman's Ball 2012, the Mar. 4 Amnesty International show, airs in the U.K. on Channel 4.

4086 March 9, 2012
The Project (TV talk show: Ten, in Australia). Guest **John Cleese**, appearing live in the studio (in Melbourne), talks about his Australian tour, Python, meeting the Queen, etc.

4087 March 11, 2012
Douglas Adams: The Party (Event). **Terry Jones** participates in an onstage conversation (with Clive Anderson) about the late Douglas Adams, author of *The Hitchhiker's Guide to the Galaxy*, at this event commemorating Adams' 60th birthday. The event, which takes place at the Hammersmith Apollo in London, benefits the Save the Rhino charity. Adams died in 2001.

4088 March 12, 2012
Empire (TV episode: BBC1). "Playing the Game." Third episode in a five-part documentary series telling the story of the British Empire. **Michael Palin** joins host Jeremy Paxman in viewing a scene from the "Roger of the Raj" episode of *Ripping Yarns* and comments on the stories that inspired the series. Directed by Robin Dashwood and David Vincent.

4089 March 14, 2012
Adam Hills in Gordon St. Tonight (TV show: ABC1, in Australia). Guests: **John Cleese**, Tom Green, Lachy Hulme, and Julia Morris. Also, **Cleese** recreates the "Fish-Slapping Dance" with a 15-year-old fan.

4090 March 29, 2012
Terry Jones attends the Teenage Cancer Trust concert, featuring Sir Paul McCartney, at London's Royal Albert Hall.

4091 March 31, 2012
Arena (TV arts show: BBC2). "Jonathan Miller." Profile of comedian, doctor, and theatre/opera/TV director Sir Jonathan Miller. Interviewees include Miller, **Eric Idle** (who starred in Miller's 1986 production of *The Mikado*), Penelope Wilton, Oliver Sacks, and Kevin Spacey. Produced & directed by David Thompson.

4092 April 2012
Michael Palin visits São Paulo and The South of Brazil for the last of four film shoots for his new BBC series *Brazil with Michael Palin*.

4093 April 1, 2012
John Cleese takes part in an interview (with Oscar Hillerstrom) and Q&A following a screening of the 2010 film *Spud*, in which he co-stars, at the Cremorne Orpheum in Sydney, Australia. **Cleese** is touring the country with his one-man show *An Evening with John Cleese*.

4094 April 5, 2012
Terry Gilliam introduces a screening of his short film *The Wholly Family* on the opening night of the 30th Brussels International Fantastic Film Festival (BIFFF) (Apr. 5–17) in Brussels, Belgium. He is also made a "Knight of the Order of the Raven" during the festival's opening ceremony.

4095 April 8, 2012
Perspectives (TV arts show: ITV1). "Sergeant on Spike." Journalist-broadcaster John Sergeant explores the life and career of his comedy idol, Spike Milligan. Sergeant talks to **Michael Palin** (about Milligan's TV work), Eddie Izzard, Noel Fielding, director Richard Lester, and others. Produced & directed by Christopher Bruce.

4096 April 26–29, 2012
What About Dick? (Play), written by **Eric Idle**, runs for four nights at the Orpheum Theater in Los Angeles. Comic play (with music), described by **Idle** as "the decline and fall of the British Empire as seen through the eyes of a piano," starring Russell Brand as Dick, a student of philosophy and gynecology at Oxford who lives in the home of his cousins and alcoholic aunt. A workshop version of the play was presented in November 2007 at the Ricardo Montalban Theater in Los Angeles. Also starring **Idle** (as narrator), Billy Connolly, Tim Curry, Eddie Izzard, Jane Leeves, Jim Piddock, Tracey Ullman, and Sophie Winkleman. Features eight new songs (by **Idle** & composer John Du Prez), including "Arsetrology," "Blow Me (a Kiss in the Moonlight)," "He's Different (Not Gay)," "My Piano," and "The Lament of the Lonely Trout." A film of the play will be made available online Nov. 13.

4097 April 27, 2012
John Le Mesurier: It's All Been Rather Lovely (TV special: BBC2). Profile of the late British character actor John Le Mesurier (*Dad's Army*). **Michael Palin**, who worked with Le Mesurier in the late 1970s (*Jabberwocky, Ripping Yarns*), is among the interviewees. Narrated by Julian Rhind-Tutt. Produced & directed by Lucy Kenwright.

4098 May 2012
The Medieval Python: The Purposive and Provocative Work of Terry Jones (Book: Palgrave Macmillan), edited by Robert F. Yeager and Toshiyuki Takamiya, is published. Collection of essays by various contributors paying tribute to **Terry Jones** for his work as a medieval scholar. Includes "**Terry Jones**: The Complete Medievalist," by **Michael Palin**, pp. 55–58.

4099 May 1, 2012
Michael Meets...Dervla Murphy (Event). **Michael Palin** interviews Irish writer and traveler Dervla Murphy in the last installment of his "Michael Meets..." series for the Royal Geographical Society in London.

4100 May 1, 2012
The South Bank Sky Arts Awards (Award ceremony). The English National Opera production of *The Damnation of Faust*, directed by **Terry Gilliam**, is awarded the prize for best opera at the ceremony held at the Dorchester Hotel in London. **Gilliam** and ENO Artistic Director John Berry accept the award. The ceremony, hosted by Melvyn Bragg, airs on Sky Arts 1.

4101 May 3, 2012
Michael Palin, **Terry Jones**, **Terry Gilliam**, and Carol Cleveland appear at the Regent Street Apple Store in London to introduce the *Monty Python's Flying Circus: Python Bytes* app, which includes 22 sketches from the first series (with commentary). Edith Bowman interviews the Pythons for a "Meet the Comedians" panel discussion.

4102 May 6, 2012
The Simpsons (TV episode: Fox). "The Spy Who Learned Me." **Eric Idle** voices the role of Declan Desmond (for the fourth time since 2003), who presents a *Super Size Me*-style documentary on the dangers of eating Krusty Burgers. Other voices by Dan Castellaneta, Julie Kavner, Nancy Cartwright, Yeardley Smith, Hank Azaria, Harry Shearer, and Bryan Cranston. Written by Marc Wilmore. Directed by Bob Anderson.

4103 May 6, 2012
The 2nd Annual KPFK Hero Awards and Tribute (Award ceremony). **Eric Idle** is a presenter at the benefit event, held at Club Nokia in Los Angeles.

4104 May 7, 2012
It's My Story (Radio show: BBC Radio 4). "White Chief Humphrey." **Michael Palin** introduces the story of how TV comedy producer Humphrey Barclay (*Do Not Adjust Your Set*) became the chief of an African village in Ghana.

4105 May 21, 2012
Terry Gilliam attends the Filmmakers Dinner and award ceremony, during the 65th Cannes Film Festival, at the Hotel du Cap-Eden-Roc in Cap d'Antibes, France. The event is hosted by IWC Schaffhausen (Swiss watchmakers). During the dinner **Gilliam** receives the Finch's Quarterly Filmmaker Award.

4106 May 23–26, 2012
An Evening with John Cleese (Stage show). **John Cleese** brings his one-man show to Dubai for four nights at the First Group Theatre at Souk Madinat Jumeirah.

4107 May 28, 2012
Terry Gilliam presents a street exhibition of his short film *The Wholly Family* in Stoleshnikov Lane at the opening of the summer museum season in Moscow, Russia. The exhibition, which consists of a series of stills and sketches from the film, was organized by Holly Gilliam (the director's daughter).

4108 June 1, 2012
What's So Great About...? (Radio episode: BBC Radio 4). Host Lenny Henry asks: "What's so great about Chaucer?" Medievalist **Terry Jones**, scholar Ardis Butterfield, and playwright Mike Poulton present their cases. Produced by Simon Elmes.

4109 June 7, 2012
The One Show (TV show: BBC1). Magazine program hosted by Matt Baker and Alex Jones. Guest: **Eric Idle**, promoting the new West End production of *Spamalot*.

4110 June 23, 2012
The Daily Telegraph Review (Magazine/U.K.). "**Michael Palin**: 'The Dalai Lama and I have a lot in common,'" by Mick Brown. Interview with **Michael Palin** about his new novel *The Truth*, with cover photo of **Palin**.

4111 June 24 & 25, 2012
Terry Gilliam attends the 58th Taormina Film

Festival (June 22–28) in Taormina, Sicily, where he is presented with the Cubovision Award and hosts a master class titled "The Imagination of Dr. Gilliam."

4112 July 2012
DirectTV (Questions) (TV commercial). **John Cleese** plays a wealthy Englishman who, while appearing in a variety of outlandish costumes and situations, questions himself about DirectTV's "Best Offer of the Year." Directed by Tom Kuntz. Agency: Grey, New York.

4113 July 2012
Terry Gilliam attends the 10th Annual Ischia Global Film & Music Fest (July 7–15) on the Isle of Ischia, Gulf of Naples, Italy, where he receives the Keys to the City (July 10), takes part in a master class on acting and a panel on script writing (July 10), and presents the Ischia Legend Award to directors Paolo and Vittorio Taviani (July 11).

4114 July 2012
John Cleese films *Spud 2*, a sequel to the 2010 film, in South Africa.

4115 July 2–13, 2012
Book at Bedtime (Radio show: BBC Radio 4). "The Truth." Alex Jennings reads **Michael Palin**'s new novel in ten parts. Produced by Joanna Green.

4116 July 2, 2012
Simon Mayo Drivetime (Radio talk show: BBC Radio 2). Guest: **Michael Palin**, promoting *The Truth*.

4117 July 3, 2012
Books and Arts Daily (Radio talk show: ABC Radio National, in Australia). Hosted by Michael Cathcart. Guest **Michael Palin** talks about his book *The Truth*.

4118 July 3, 2012
Michael Palin—The Truth (Event). **Michael Palin** talks to author Joseph Connolly about his life, career, and latest novel *The Truth* at The Gallery at Foyles bookshop, Charing Cross Road, London.

4119 July 4, 2012
This Morning (TV news show: ITV1). Hosted by Phillip Schofield and Holly Willoughby. Guest: **Michael Palin**, promoting *The Truth*.

4120 July 5, 2012
The Truth (Book: Weidenfeld & Nicolson), written by **Michael Palin**, is published. **Palin**'s second novel (following 1995's *Hemingway's Chair*) tells the story of a hack writer, Keith Mabbut, who is commissioned to pen the biography of an elusive environmental activist and humanitarian. Mabbut's assignment takes him to North East India where he finds "the truth" about his subject to be just as elusive.
Reviews: DJ Taylor (*The Guardian*, July 14, 2012, p. 14): "...*The Truth* is immensely well-intentioned, resolutely on the side of the angels and overflowing with wry good humour ... nonetheless the reader may well conclude that the material needed a Paul Theroux or a Justin Cartwright to do it justice"; Rachel Redford (*The Observer*, July 15, 2012, p. 38): "**Michael Palin**'s second novel establishes him as an assured storyteller."

4121 July 6, 2012
Michael Palin talks about his new book, *The Truth*, at the 2012 Telegraph Ways with Words Festival at Dartington Hall in Devon, England.

4122 July 6, 2012
Terry Gilliam and his wife attend the world premiere of a newly-restored version of Alfred Hitchcock's 1929 silent thriller *Blackmail* at the British Museum in London (the film's climax is set on the roof of the Museum). Part of the BFI's "The Genius of Hitchcock" retrospective.

4123 July 8, 2012
Open Book (Radio talk show: BBC Radio 4). Mariella Frostrup talks to **Michael Palin** about his new novel *The Truth*.

4124 July 9, 2012
The Book Café (Radio show: BBC Radio Scotland). Claire English talks to **Michael Palin** about his new novel *The Truth*.

4125 July 13, 2012
The Radio 2 Arts Show with Claudia Winkleman (Radio show: BBC Radio 2). Claudia Winkleman talks to **Michael Palin** about his new book *The Truth*.

4126 July 15, 2012
Understanding Stammering or Stuttering: A Guide for Parents, Teachers and Other Professionals (Book: Jessica Kingsley Publishers), written by Elaine Kelman and Alison Whyte with a foreword by **Michael Palin**, is published. Kelman is a speech therapist at the Michael Palin Centre for Stammering Children.

4127 July 16, 2012
The Times (London) (Newspaper/U.K.). "Why

My Lear Opera is Utterly Runcible," by **Terry Jones**. Article on **Jones**' new opera *The Owl and the Pussycat*.

4128   July 19, 2012
The Hitchhiker's Guide to the Galaxy Radio Show...Live! (Stage show). **Terry Jones** guest stars as the Voice of the Book in a stage production of Douglas Adams' radio serial performed at the Hackney Empire Theatre in London. Also starring Simon Jones (from the original radio & TV versions) as Arthur Dent. Adapted & directed by Dirk Maggs. Other guest stars voicing the book during the production's U.K. tour include Andrew Sachs, John Lloyd, Roger McGough, Phill Jupitus, and Neil Gaiman.

4129   July 20, 2012
Front Row (Radio arts show: BBC Radio 4). Kirsty Lang talks to **Terry Jones** and composer Anne Dudley about their new opera *The Owl and the Pussycat*.

4130   July 20, 2012
The Owl and the Pussycat (Opera) premieres on a canal barge at Brentford Lock, London. Short children's opera based on Edward Lear's 1871 poem, with libretto by **Terry Jones** and music by Anne Dudley, presented in a water-bound production as part of the London 2012 Festival (June 21–Sept. 9). The work, which is being performed throughout July on various London canals and waterways, was commissioned jointly by the Mayor of London and the Royal Opera House with the goal of bringing opera to strange places and new audiences. This is **Jones** and Dudley's second collaboration following their 2011 opera *The Doctor's Tale*. Directed by Martin Constantine. Note: **Eric Idle** had earlier adapted the poem for his 1996 children's book *The Quite Remarkable Adventures of the Owl and the Pussycat*.

4131   July 24–September 9, 2012
Eric Idle's *Spamalot* returns to London's West End for a run at the Harold Pinter Theatre. The production stars Marcus Brigstocke (King Arthur) and Bonnie Langford (Lady of the Lake).

4132   July 24, 2012
The Guardian (Newspaper/U.K.). "**Terry Jones**: The Python, the Owl and the Pussycat," by Stuart Jeffries. Interview with **Jones** (conducted at his Highgate, London, home) about writing the libretto for the opera *The Owl and the Pussycat*.

4133   July 29, 2012
The New Review (The Independent) (Magazine/U.K.). "The Dark Knight Rises: Perhaps **Michael Palin** Isn't the Nicest Chap in Britain After All...," by Robert Chalmers. Interview with **Palin** at his North London home. **Palin** also appears on the cover.

4134   August 2, 2012
John Cleese, 72, marries his girlfriend Jennifer Wade, 41, in a private ceremony on the island of Mustique in the Carribean. *Hello!* magazine is given exclusive access to the event and features the newlyweds on the cover of its Aug. 20 issue. Wade is **Cleese**'s fourth wife, following Connie Booth [1968–78], Barbara Trentham [1981–90], and Alyce Faye Eichelberger [1992–2008].

4135   August 12, 2012
Eric Idle performs "Always Look on the Bright Side of Life" during the closing ceremony of the 2012 Olympic Games in London. The elaborate production number features **Idle** singing the classic Python ditty amid a cast of sexy angels, Indian dancers, and roller-blading nuns.

4136   August 13, 2012
Michael Palin talks to literary agent Jenny Brown about his book *The Truth* in an event at the RBS Main Theatre in Edinburgh, Scotland, as part of the Edinburgh International Book Festival (Aug. 10–26).

4137   August 20, 2012
Hello! (Magazine/U.K.). Cover story on **John Cleese**'s marriage to Jennifer Wade on Aug. 2. The magazine was given exclusive access to the event.

4138   September 2012
John Cleese begins writing his autobiography.

4139   September 6, 2012
Michael Palin, **Terry Jones**, Barry Cryer, and Carol Cleveland gather together to unveil a blue plaque outside the Angel Pub in Highgate, North London. The plaque, created by The British Comedy Society, is dedicated to **Graham Chapman** ("A very naughty boy"), who drank at the pub "often and copiously."

4140   September 8, 2012
A Liar's Autobiography—The Untrue Story of Monty Python's Graham Chapman (Feature film: Epix/Brainstorm Media) premieres in Toronto. 3-D animated adaptation of **Graham Chapman**'s semi-fictionalized 1980 memoir. The film, produced

through the combined efforts of 14 animation studios, uses **Chapman**'s actual voice (taken from audio recordings he made for the book) and those of the other Pythons (minus **Idle**). Airs on EPIX and opens in selected U.S. theaters on Nov. 2. Featuring the voices of **Graham Chapman, John Cleese, Terry Gilliam, Terry Jones, Michael Palin**, Carol Cleveland, Cameron Diaz, and Philip Bulcock. Written & directed by Ben Timlett, Bill Jones, and Jeff Simpson. Produced by Ben Timlett and Bill Jones. Note: Timlett and Jones (son of **Terry**) previously produced the 2009 documentary series *Monty Python: Almost the Truth—The Lawyer's Cut*.

4141   September 8, 2012
Terry Jones attends the world premiere of *A Liar's Autobiography—The Untrue Story of Monty Python's Graham Chapman* at the TIFF Bell Lightbox in Toronto, Canada, as part of the 37th annual Toronto International Film Festival (Sept. 6–16).

4142   September 10, 2012
Writing and Travelling (Event). **Michael Palin** joins author Patrick French for a conversation at the London Jewish Cultural Centre, Ivy House as part of the Hampstead and Highgate Literary Festival (Sept. 9–11). **Palin** talks about his new books *The Truth* and *Brazil*.

4143   September 13, 2012
From Brazil to The Truth (Event). **Michael Palin** talks to Rebecca Jones about his new books *The Truth* and *Brazil* at the Burlington Pavilion, Chiswick House, Chiswick (west London) as a pre-festival event of the 4th Chiswick Book Festival (Sept. 14–16). Followed by a book signing.

4144   September 13, 2012
God Loves Caviar (Feature film), world premiere at the Toronto International Film Festival. Greek/Russian film about the 18th-century Greek pirate and merchant Ioannis Varvakis. **John Cleese** plays McCormick, an English colonial officer. Starring Sebastian Koch, Catherine Deneuve, and Juan Diego Botto. Directed by Yannis Smaragdis. Opens in Greece on Oct. 11.

4145   September 14, 2012
Eric Idle attends the launch party for Salman Rushdie's book *Joseph Anton: A Memoir* at The Collection in London. **Idle** was a guest at the April 2004 wedding of Rushdie and Padma Lakshmi.

4146   September 16, 2012
The opera *The Damnation of Faust*, directed by **Terry Gilliam**, opens in Ghent, Belgium. Faust is played by American tenor Michael Spyres; the conductor is Dmitri Jurowski. The production will play in Ghent until Sept. 23, then move on to Antwerp (Oct. 3–14). The original production premiered in London in May 2011.

4147   September 24, 2012
Searching for Truth (Event). **Michael Palin** talks to Emma Freud about his new novel, *The Truth*, at the Kenton Theatre in Henley-on-Thames, England as part of the Henley Literary Festival (Sept. 24–30).

4148   September 25, 2012
Michael Palin attends the launch party for chef Antonio Carluccio's new memoir *A Recipe for Life* at Carluccio's restaurant in Garrick Street, London.

4149   September 26, 2012
The Province (B.C.) (Newspaper/Can.). "**John Cleese**: Why I Love Having Insurance," by **John Cleese**, p. A16. **Cleese** on the virtues of insurance (his father was an insurance salesman). The article is part of an ad campaign for the Pacific Blue Cross insurance company of British Columbia, for which **Cleese** is a spokesman.

4150   September 28, 2012
Michael Palin is interviewed about his career (and new book *The Truth*) by travel writer Barnaby Rogerson before an audience at the Soho Theatre in London as part of the Soho Literary Festival (Sept. 27–30).

4151   October 2012
Discovering King's Cross: A Pop-Up Book (Book: Cicada Books), illustrated by Lucy Dalzell with texts by **Michael Palin** (foreword) and Dan Cruickshank, is published in the U.K. Pop-up book exploring the 160-year history of King's Cross station in London.

4152   October 2, 2012
Terry Jones attends a gala screening of a restored version of the Beatles' 1967 TV film *Magical Mystery Tour* at The BFI Southbank in London. Paul McCartney also attends.

4153   October 3, 2012
Michael Palin attends the launch for *Discovering King's Cross: A Pop-Up Book*, for which he wrote the foreword, in the Parcel Yard Pub at King's Cross station in London.

4154   October 5, 2012
Mr. Blue Sky: The Story of Jeff Lynne & ELO (TV

special: BBC4). One-hour documentary on musician Jeff Lynne, includes interviews with his friends and collaborators **Eric Idle**, Paul McCartney, Ringo Starr, Dhani Harrison, and others. Written & directed by Martyn Atkins.

4155 October 6, 2012
Western Mail (Cardiff, Wales) (Newspaper/U.K.). "'It's like a re-birth of life.' Not Even Bowel Cancer Could Slow Monty Python Star **Terry Jones** Down...," by Emily Lambert. Interview with **Jones**, who talks about still feeling young at age 70.

4156 October 6, 2012
Brazil (Lecture). **Michael Palin** gives an illustrated talk about his new travel series & book at Cheltenham Racecourse in Cheltenham, England as part of the Times Cheltenham Literature Festival (Oct. 5–14).

4157 October 6, 2012
Arena (TV special: BBC2). "Magical Mystery Tour Revisited." Documentary on the making of the Beatles' 1967 TV film *Magical Mystery Tour*. Interviewees include Paul McCartney, Ringo Starr, **Terry Gilliam**, Martin Scorsese, and Neil Innes. Directed by Francis Hanly. Produced by Jonathan Clyde.

4158 October 10, 2012
Michael Palin gives an illustrated talk about *Brazil* at The Forum in Bath, England as part of the 2012 Bath Autumn Book Festival (Oct. 5–16). The talk, hosted by Topping & Company Booksellers, is followed by a book-signing.

4159 October 11, 2012
Brazil (Book: Weidenfeld & Nicolson), written by **Michael Palin**, is published in the U.K. **Palin**'s account of his visit to South America's largest country. Companion book to the upcoming BBC TV series. Photographed & designed by Basil Pao.

4160 October 12, 2012
The Chris Evans Breakfast Show (Radio show: BBC Radio 2). Guest: **Michael Palin**, promoting his new travel series *Brazil*.

4161 October 15, 2012
The New Yorker (Magazine/U.S.). "Shouts & Murmurs: In Me Own Words," by **Eric Idle**, p. 37. An excerpt from "The Rock and Roll Memoirs of Eff (Stiffie) Steffham."

4162 October 16, 2012
A Liar's Autobiography—The Untrue Story of Monty Python's Graham Chapman has its London premiere at the Empire Cinema in Leicester Square as part of the 56th BFI London Film Festival (Oct. 10–21). **Michael Palin** and **Terry Jones** attend the screening. The two Pythons also appear at a press conference with the film's writer-directors Ben Timlett, Bill Jones, and Jeff Simpson.

4163 October 19, 2012
The Guardian (Newspaper/U.K.). "**Michael Palin**'s *Brazil*." Palin describes the Brazil he discovered making his latest travel series.

4164 October 20, 2012
The Times Magazine (London) (Magazine/U.K.). "What I've Learnt." **Michael Palin** interview.

4165 October 22, 2012
Terry Gilliam begins shooting his next film, *The Zero Theorem*, in Bucharest, Romania. The film, which is being made by MediaPro Studios from a script by Pat Rushin, stars Christoph Waltz, Mélanie Thierry, David Thewlis, Lucas Hedges, Tilda Swinton, and Matt Damon (who previously worked with **Gilliam** on *The Brothers Grimm*). **Gilliam**'s last feature-length film was 2009's *The Imaginarium of Doctor Parnassus*.

4166 October 22, 2012
Daybreak (TV talk show: ITV1). Hosted by Aled Jones and Lorraine Kelly. Guest: **Michael Palin**, promoting *Brazil*.

4167 October 23, 2012
The Alan Titchmarsh Show (TV talk show: ITV). Daytime talk show. Guests: **Michael Palin**, promoting *Brazil*, and The Nolans.

4168 October 24–November 14, 2012
The four-part travel series *Brazil with Michael Palin* airs on BBC1. **Palin** travels to the fifth-largest country on Earth for his first travel program since 2007's *New Europe*. John Paul Davidson is series producer.
Reviews: John Crace (*The Guardian*, Oct. 25, 2012, p. 21): "**Palin** is a thoroughly agreeable companion.... But it did feel a bit like Brazil on valium"; Gerard O'Donovan (*The Daily Telegraph*, Oct. 25, 2012, p. 36): "...a hugely enjoyable introduction to a country that looks all too capable of overwhelming the unsuspecting visitor with its unstoppable zest for life.... **Palin** remained, as ever, a calm and exceptionally charming guide."

4169 October 24, 2012
Brazil with Michael Palin (TV episode: BBC1).

"Out of Africa." **Michael Palin**'s Brazilian journey begins in the North-East region of the country where a mix of races (natives, Portuguese explorers, and African slaves) and cultures produced the Brazil we know today. He witnesses the festival of Bumba Meu Boi (in São Luís), then heads down the coast to Recife, joins a gathering of Brazilian cowboys (or vaqueros) (west of Serrita), and visits the city of Salvador, where he learns how to drum at the Olodum school and observes the martial art of capoeira. Part one of a four-part series. Written & narrated by **Michael Palin**. Directed by Francis Hanly.

4170   October 26, 2012
A photograph of **Terry Gilliam**, posing semi-nude with a spider crab, goes on display at the "Fishlove" exhibition in Soho, London. The exhibition, by the photographer Rankin, is part of a campaign to end over-fishing.

4171   October 31, 2012
Brazil with Michael Palin (TV episode: BBC1). "Into Amazonia." **Michael Palin** travels to a remote village in the Amazon rainforest in North-West Brazil where he visits with the indigenous Yanomami tribe. He also watches a rehearsal of the Amazon Philharmonic Orchestra (in Manaus), views the remains of Henry Ford's ill-fated rubber plantation "Fordlândia" (south of Santarém), meets music producer Priscilla (Belem), visits a Wauja village (Upper Xingu), and meets rock star/activist Dinho Ouro Preto in the capital city of Brasília. Part two of a four-part series. Written & narrated by **Michael Palin**. Directed by John Paul Davidson.

4172   October 31, 2012
Close Up (TV show: TV One, in New Zealand). Mark Sainsbury interviews **Michael Palin** about traveling, Python, being called "nice," etc.

4173   October 31, 2012
Spend an Hour with Michael Palin (Event). **Michael Palin** talks to Finlay Macdonald about *Brazil* and *The Truth* at The Spencer on Byron Hotel in Takapuna, Auckland, New Zealand. Followed by a book-signing.

4174   Late October–November 2012
Michael Palin tours New Zealand and Austalia promoting his new book & TV series *Brazil*.

4175   November–December 2012
Michael Palin visits book stores throughout the U.K. and Ireland signing copies of his new book *Brazil*. Stores include Waterstones Bluewater in Kent (Nov. 22), Eason's in Belfast (Nov. 23), Dubray Books in Dublin (Nov. 24), WH Smith in Guildford (Nov. 26), Waterstones in Staines (Nov. 27), WH Smith in Milton Keynes (Nov. 29), Stanfords in Covent Garden, London (Dec. 5), Blackwells in Oxford (Dec. 6), and Selfridges in London (Dec. 7).

4176   November 1, 2012
Brand X (TV talk show: FX). Guest: **Eric Idle**. Host Russell Brand played the title role in the recent production of **Idle**'s play *What About Dick?*

4177   November 1, 2012
Breakfast (TV news-talk show: TV One, in New Zealand). Morning program hosted by Petra Bagust and Rawdon Christie. Guest **Michael Palin** talks about *Brazil*, traveling, Python, the "Cheese Shop" sketch, etc. He also presents the weather.

4178   November 2, 2012
An Evening with Michael Palin (Event). **Michael Palin** talks about his new book and TV series *Brazil* at Christ's College Auditorium in Christchurch, New Zealand as part of The Press Christchurch Writers Festival.

4179   November 3, 2012
The Late Great Eric Sykes (TV special: BBC2). Tribute to British comedian Eric Sykes, who died on July 4th. Interviewees include **Michael Palin**, Eddie Izzard, and Bruce Forsyth. Produced by Alexandra Briscoe.

4180   November 4, 2012
The Telegraph (Newspaper/U.K.). "**Michael Palin**: Our Very Silly Man in Brazil," by Brian Viner. Interview with **Palin** about his new series *Brazil*, conducted at his London home.

4181   November 5, 2012
Newsweek (Magazine/U.S.). "My Favorite Mistake." **Eric Idle** (interviewed by Sujay Kumar) describes his second wedding — a star-studded ceremony held in Lorne Michaels' apartment — in 1981.

4182   November 7, 2012
Brazil with Michael Palin (TV episode: BBC1). "The Road to Rio." On his way to Rio de Janeiro, **Michael Palin** explores the mining region of Minas Gerais, visiting a gold mine, Serra do Cipo National Park, and the Academy of Coffee (in Belo Horizonte). In Rio, **Palin** views up-close the Christ the Redeemer statue on Corcovado Mountain, visits the Fluminense Football Club, meets artist Vik

Muniz, observes the special ops battalion Bope, rides a cable car, and visits a boxing club and a "love hotel." Part three of a four-part series. Written & narrated by **Michael Palin**. Directed by Francis Hanly.

4183 November 9, 2012
Michael Palin participates in an onstage conversation (with Michael Williams) about his comedy and travel career at Melbourne Town Hall in Melbourne, Australia. The event, hosted by The Wheeler Centre, also includes an audience Q&A and book signing.

4184 November 9, 2012
The Hollywood Reporter (Magazine/U.S.). "Monty Python Alum on American Politics," by **Eric Idle**, p. 18. **Idle** gives his thoughts on the recent American election.

4185 November 9, 2012
The Late Late Show with Craig Ferguson (TV talk show: CBS). Guests include **Eric Idle** and Emily VanCamp. **Idle** discusses *What About Dick?* and sings a Scottish song from the play.

4186 November 10, 2012
The Independent (Newspaper/U.K.). "'I'm just curious about the world.'" Ben Ross interviews **Michael Palin** about his travels and new series *Brazil* at **Palin**'s production offices near Covent Garden in London.

4187 November 10, 2012
The Life of Palin: From Monty Python to Brazil (Event). **Michael Palin** talks about his career with his host Jonathan Biggins in the Concert Hall of the Sydney Opera House in Sydney, Australia.

4188 November 11, 2012
Mornings (TV news-talk show: Channel 9, in Australia). Hosted by David Campbell and Sonia Kruger. Guest: **Michael Palin**, promoting *Brazil*, also talks about stammering, meeting Johnny Cash, and Python.

4189 November 11, 2012
Rove LA (TV talk show: Fox8). Los Angeles–based Australian comedy-talk show hosted by Rove McManus. Guests: **Eric Idle**, promoting *What About Dick?*, Kate Walsh, and Maggie Grace.

4190 November 12, 2012
Midday (Radio show: ABC Classic FM, in Australia). Margaret Throsby interviews **Michael Palin** about *Brazil*, the importance of comedy, his mother's appearance on *SNL*, being a grandfather, etc.

4191 November 13, 2012
Eric Idle's comic play *What About Dick?*, recorded in April, is made available for download from the internet.

4192 November 14, 2012
Brazil with Michael Palin (TV episode: BBC1). "The Deep South." **Michael Palin** experiences a mix of European and Asian cultures in his journey to the deep south. In Parati, he meets a royal heir, then visits the Embraer airplane factory (in São José dos Campos). In the city of São Paulo, **Palin** meets TV soap opera star Carolina Ferraz and former president Fernando Henrique Cardoso. He then visits the German-speaking towns of Blumenau and Pomerode. In the wetlands of The Pantanal, he rides with cowboys and fishes for piranha. **Palin** ends his journey at the Iguazu Falls. Last episode of a four-part series. Written & narrated by **Michael Palin**. Directed by John Paul Davidson.

4193 November 14, 2012
Drive with Richard Glover (Radio show: 702 ABC Sydney, in Australia). Richard Glover interviews **Michael Palin**.

4194 November 16, 2012
Real Time with Bill Maher (TV episode: HBO). Host Bill Maher interviews **Eric Idle** for the show's 10th-season finale. **Idle** last appeared on the show in February 2003.

4195 November 18, 2012
Weekend Wogan (Radio talk show: BBC Radio 2). Host Terry Wogan talks to **Michael Palin** about his new TV series *Brazil*.

4196 November 19, 2012
First Tuesday Book Club (TV show: ABC1, in Australia). Host Jennifer Byrne interviews **Michael Palin** in Melbourne's Athenaeum Library.

4197 November 19, 2012
Eric Idle and his wife attend the Saban Free Clinic's Annual Dinner Gala at the Beverly Hilton Hotel in Beverly Hills, CA.

4198 November 20, 2012
Mornings (TV news-talk show: Channel 9, in Australia). **Eric Idle** talks to Suz Messara about his play *What About Dick?* and his performance at the Olympic closing ceremonies.

4199 November 23, 2012
The Graham Norton Show (TV talk show: BBC1).

Guests: Helena Bonham Carter, Michael Bublé, Jack Whitehall, and **Michael Palin**, promoting *Brazil*.

4200 November 26, 2012
The four-part TV series *Brazil with Michael Palin* is released on DVD & Blu-ray in the U.K.

4201 November 28, 2012
Michael Palin gives a talk on *Brazil* at the Apple Store in Covent Garden, London.

4202 November 30–December 4, 2012
Eric Idle, **Terry Jones**, and **Michael Palin** give evidence during a five-day hearing at the Royal Courts of Justice in London of a lawsuit brought against the Pythons by *Holy Grail* producer Mark Forstater. He is suing the group for royalties he claims to be owed from the hit musical *Spamalot*, which is based on the film. The Pythons' counsel, Richard Spearman QC, tells the court (on Dec. 3): "These are not unpleasant shifty people trying to do people out of their just deserts. They reckoned, and they were right, that he had already got a pretty good deal and here he was, coming back for more, which they weren't prepared to give."

4203 November 30, 2012
This Morning (TV show: ITV). Magazine program. Hosts Eamonn Holmes and Ruth Langsford talk to **Eric Idle** about his play *What About Dick?*.

4204 Early December 2012
Filming is completed, in Romania, on **Terry Gilliam**'s *The Zero Theorem*.

4205 December 2, 2012
An Evening with Michael Palin (Lecture). **Michael Palin** gives a talk on *Brazil* and his comedy career at London's Playhouse Theatre. The talk finishes with a surprise guest appearance by **Eric Idle** (with guitar), who leads the audience in a rendition of "Always Look on the Bright Side of Life." Proceeds from the event go to the Michael Palin Centre for Stammering Children.

4206 December 4, 2012
Brazil: The Criterion Collection (Blu-ray: Criterion Collection). Blu-ray release of Criterion's special edition of **Terry Gilliam**'s *Brazil* containing Gilliam's 142-minute director's cut of the film and special features. First released on laserdisc in 1996.

4207 December 9, 2012
The British Independent Film Awards (Award ceremony). **Terry Gilliam** presents the Variety Award to Jude Law at the 15th annual BIFA ceremony held at Old Billingsgate Market in London.

4208 December 11, 2012
Michael Palin and poet Pam Ayres are guest-speakers at the *Daily Mail* Christmas Literary Lunch at the Lancaster London Hotel. Hosted by Gyles Brandreth.

Appendix: John Cleese's Business-Training Films for Video Arts, 1972–2012

All Change (The Management of Change), Part 1: Change for the Better (1988/act/28 mins)
All Change (The Management of Change), Part 2: The Shape of Things to Come (1988/act/25 mins)
The Balance Sheet Barrier (1977/act/30 mins)
The Balance Sheet Barrier (1993/act/remake/30 mins)
Budgeting (1984/act/30 mins)
Can We Please Have That the Right Way Round? A Guide to Slide Presentations (1976/act/22 mins)
Can You Spare a Moment? (2001/host, co-wr/remake/23 mins)
Can You Spare a Moment? The Counselling Interview (1987/act, co-wr/25 mins)
The Control of Working Capital (1978/act/26 mins)
Cost, Profit and Break-Even (1980/act/23 mins)
Creativity in Management (1991/lecture/36 mins)
Customer Relations in Practice, No. 1: In Two Minds (1973/act, co-wr/18 mins)
Customer Relations in Practice, No. 2: The Meeting of Minds (1973/act, co-wr/15 mins)
Customer Relations in Practice, No. 3: Awkward Customers (1973/act, co-wr/24 mins)
Customer Relations in Practice, No. 4: More Awkward Customers (1974/act, wr/31 mins)
Decisions, Decisions (1978/act/28 mins)
Depreciation and Inflation (1980/act/17 mins)
Everybody's Guide to the Computer: What Is a Computer? (1979/narr/18 mins)
Everybody's Guide to the Computer: What Is a Computer Program? (1982/narr/17 mins)
Everybody's Guide to the Computer: What Is a Word Processor? (1982/act/24 mins)
Going to a Meeting, Part 1: Messing Up a Meeting (2002/host/16 mins)
Going to a Meeting, Part 2: Meeting Menaces (2002/host/21 mins)
Grime Goes Green: Your Business and the Environment (1990/act/30 mins)
Head for Business (1982/act)
The Helping Hand: Coaching Skills for Managers (1990/act/37 mins)
The Hidden Mind (1999 lecture/45 mins)
Hidden Treasure (1981/act)
How Am I Doing? The Appraisal Interview (1977/act/26 mins)
How to Lie with Statistics, Part 1: The Gee Whiz Graph (1974, narr)
How to Lie with Statistics, Part 2: The Average Chap (1977, narr)
How to Lose Customers Without Really Trying (1989/act/32 mins)
Humour Is Not a Luxury (1988/act, wr/40 mins)
I'd Like a Word with You: The Discipline Interview (1979/act/27 mins)

The Importance of Mistakes (1987/lecture/33 mins)
It's Your Choice: Selection Skills for Managers (1993/act, co-wr/34 mins)
Man Hunt: The Selection Interview (1974/act, co-wr/31 mins)
Managing Problem People: Big Mouth Billy (1988/act/16 mins)
Managing Problem People: Moaning Minnie (1988/act/15 mins)
Managing Problem People: Rulebound Reggie (1988/act/12 mins)
Marketing in Practice, No. 1: Who Sold You This, Then? (1972/act, co-wr/23 mins)
Marketing in Practice, No. 2: It's All Right, It's Only a Customer (1973/act, co-wr/29 mins)
Marketing in Practice, No. 3: The Competitive Spirit (1973/act, co-wr/29 mins)
Marketing in Practice, No. 4: Prescription for Complaints (1974/act/21 mins)
Meetings, Bloody Meetings (1976/act, co-wr/30 mins)
Meetings, Bloody Meetings (1993/act, co-wr/remake/34 mins)
Meetings, Bloody Meetings (2012/act, co-wr/remake/34 mins)
More Bloody Meetings (1984/act/27 mins)
More Bloody Meetings (1994/act/remake/25 mins)
Performance Matters: The Importance of Praise (2000/narr/18 mins)
Performance Matters: The Need for Constructive Criticism (2000/narr/19 mins)
The Proposal (1975/act/24 mins)
Return on Investment (1985/act/20 mins)
The Secretary and Her Boss, Part 1: Try to See It My Way (1977/act/28 mins)
The Secretary and Her Boss, Part 2: We Can Work It Out (1977/act/28 mins)
Selling in Practice, No. 2: How Not to Exhibit Yourself (1974/act/30 mins)
Selling on the Telephone: The Cold Call (1976/act/24 mins)
Selling on the Telephone: When I'm Calling You (1975/act/16 mins)
Selling on the Telephone: Will You Answer True? (1975/act/16 mins)
The Show Business: How to Demonstrate a Product (1974/act, co-wr/23 mins)
So You Want to Be a Success at Selling?, Part 1: The Preparation (1981/act/26 mins)
So You Want to Be a Success at Selling?, Part 2: The Presentation (1981/act/25 mins)
So You Want to Be a Success at Selling?, Part 3: Difficult Customers (1983/act/25 mins)
So You Want to Be a Success at Selling?, Part 4: Closing the Sale (1984/act/29 mins)
Straight Talking: The Art of Assertiveness (1991/act, co-wr/27 mins)
Telephone Behaviour: The Power and the Perils (1986/act/29 mins)
Telephone Behaviour: The Rules of Effective Communication (1997/act/remake/32 mins)
Think or Sink (1991/act/25 mins)
This Is Going to Hurt Me More Than It Hurts You: The Bad News Interview (1989/act/28 mins)
The Unorganised Manager, Part 1: Damnation (1983/act/24 mins)
The Unorganised Manager, Part 1: Damnation (1996/act/remake/24 mins)
The Unorganised Manager, Part 2: Salvation (1983/act/26 mins)
The Unorganised Manager, Part 2: Salvation (1996/act/remake/27 mins)
The Unorganised Manager, Part 3: Divine Intervention (1997/act/remake/18 mins)
The Unorganised Manager, Part 3: Lamentations (1985/act/20 mins)
The Unorganised Manager, Part 4: Revelations (1985/act/29 mins)
The Unorganised Salesperson, Part 2: Valuing Yourself (1990/act/21 mins)
Welcome Customer, Part 1: Have a Nice Stay (1979/act/25 mins)
Welcome Customer, Part 2: See You Again Soon (1979/act/23 mins)
When Will They Realise We're Living in the 20th Century? (1980/act/24 mins)
Who Sold You This Then? (1997/narr/remake/20 mins)
Why Do People Work? (1981/act/3 mins)
You'll Soon Get the Hang of It (1981/act, co-wr/29 mins)

Selected Bibliography

BBC Motion Gallery. Archive (Website).
BFI Film & TV Database (Website).
Billboard. Various issues.
Chapman, Graham, et al. *The Complete Monty Python's Flying Circus: All the Words, Vols. 1 & 2*. New York: Pantheon, 1989.
_____. *Monty Python and the Holy Grail*. London: Mandarin, 1992.
_____. *Monty Python Live!* New York: Hyperion, 2009.
_____, edited by Bob McCabe. *The Pythons: Autobiography by The Pythons*. London: Orion, 2003.
Cleese, John, et al., interviewed by David Morgan. *Monty Python Speaks!* New York: Spike, 1999.
Hertzberg, Hendrik. *New Yorker*. "Naughty Bits," pp. 69–70+. March 29, 1976.
Hewison, Robert. *Monty Python: The Case Against*. London: Methuen, 1981.
Idle, Eric. *The Greedy Bastard Diary*. New York: HarperCollins, 2005.
ITN Source. Archive (Website).
Johnson, Kim "Howard." *The First 200 Years of Monty Python*. New York: Thomas Dunne, 1989.
The Los Angeles Times. Various issues.
Mathews, Jack. *The Battle of Brazil*. New York: Crown, 1987
McNeil, Alex. *Total Television, 4th Edition*. New York: Penguin Books, 1996.
Monty Python: The Holy Book of Days. (iTunes app). Melcher Media, 2012.
The New York Times. Various issues.
Palin, Michael. *Around the World in 80 Days*. London: BBC Books, 1989.
_____. *Brazil*. London: Weidenfeld & Nicolson, 2012.
_____. *Diaries 1969–1979: The Python Years*. London: Weidenfeld & Nicolson, 2006.
_____. *Full Circle*. London: BBC Books, 1997.
_____. *Halfway to Hollywood: Diaries 1980–1988*. London: Weidenfeld & Nicolson, 2009.
_____. *Himalaya*. London: Weidenfeld & Nicolson, 2004.
_____. *Michael Palin's Hemingway Adventure*. London: Weidenfeld & Nicolson, 1999.
_____. *New Europe*. London: Weidenfeld & Nicolson, 2007.
_____. *Pole to Pole*. London: BBC Books, 1992.
_____. *Sahara*. London: Weidenfeld & Nicolson, 2002.
Palin's Travels (Website), launched in 2002.
Perry, George. *Life of Python*. Boston/Toronto: Little, Brown, 1983.
Pixley, Andrew. *Ripping Yarns* DVD booklet. "'Plucky' Palin Marches On: A Ripping Tale of BBC2 Comedy Adventure." 2004.
Rolling Stone. Various issues.
Ross, Robert. *Monty Python Encyclopedia*. New York: TV Books. 1997.
The (London) *Times*. Various issues.
TV Guide. Various issues.
Variety. Various issues.
Video Arts Training Catalogue, 1989.

Monty Python Sketch and Song Index

References are to entry numbers.

Accidents Sketch 96
Accountancy Shanty [song, w/m: Idle, John du Prez] 1012, 1026, 1723, 2558
The Adventures of Biggles *see* Biggles Dictates a Letter
The Adventures of Martin Luther [cut] 996, 1012, 1046, 2909
Adventures of Ralph Melish 293
After-Shave 93
Agatha Christie Sketch (Inspector Tiger) 55, 3241
Agatha Christie Sketch (Railway Timetables) 108
Albatross 60, 78, 116, 316, 347, 494, 502, 805, 943, 3241
Albrecht Dürer Documentary/Song 180
Algon *see* Prices on the Planet Algon
Alistair Cooke Being Attacked by a Duck 235, 613
The All-England Summarize Proust Competition [wr: Palin & Jones] 198, 219, 222, 226, 613
All Things Dull and Ugly [song, w: Idle; m: Trad.] 752 (lyrics), 799, 1723, 2490, 2558
Always Look on the Bright Side of Life [song, w/m: Idle] 710, 722, 723, 803, 1723, 1726, 1846, 1853, 1860, 1862, 1871, 1951, 2038, 2340, 2440, 2457, 2490, 2498, 2552, 2558, 2567, 2582, 2919, 3111, 3113, 3114, 3144, 3234, 3253, 3400, 3410, 3579, 3727, 3824, 3838, 4135, 4205
Ambulance [anim] 249, 3243
Anagram Quiz (Beat the Clock) 225
Anatomy Chart [anim] 221
The Anatomy of an Ant [anim] 365
Angus Podgorny *see* Science Fiction Sketch
Animals Eating [anim] 54
Animated Head [anim] 86
Animator/Flying Saucers [anim] 236

Anne Elk *see* Thrust: Miss Anne Elk
Ant Communication *see* University of the Air: Let's Talk Ant
Ant Counter *see* Buying an Ant
Ant Poetry *see* Victorian Poetry Reading (Ants)
Anti-Masonic Therapy [anim] 93
The "Anything Goes" Courtmartial *see* Courtmartial
Anything Goes (In) [song] 368
Apologetic Murderer *see* Court Room (Multiple Murderer)
Apologies (Pleasures of the Dance) 162
An Appeal for Sanity (Silly Vicar) 102
An Appeal on Behalf of Extremely Rich People 374
An Appeal on Behalf of the National Truss (Leapy Lee) 102
Archaeology [anim] 102
Archaeology Today (Flaming Star) 102
The Architect Sketch 82, 93, 162, 1131, 1427, 3182
Are You Embarrassed Easily? *see* Embarrassment
Argument *see* Argument Clinic
Argument Clinic 219, 224, 235, 268, 316, 347, 494, 502, 613, 805, 911, 943, 1131, 1427, 1665, 1705, 3091, 3241
Army Captain as Clown 225
Army Protection Racket 49
An Art Critic (Edible Paintings) 39
An Art Critic (The Place of the Nude) 49, 78
Art Gallery 39
Art Gallery Strike 110
Arthur and God 397, 422
Arthur Ewing *see* Musical Mice
Arthur Figgis 44
Arthur Frampton *see* A Man with Three Buttocks
Arthur Jarrett 1025

Arthur Tree *see* It's a Tree (Arthur Tree)
Arthur "Two Sheds" Jackson *see* It's the Arts: Arthur "Two Sheds" Jackson
Attila the Bun [anim] 98
Attila the Hun *see* Mr. Attila the Hun
The Attila the Hun Show 98
Attila the Nun 98
The Audit 47
Australian Table Wines 235, 613, 1427

Baby Carriage [anim] 37, 161, 3243
Baby Suction [anim] 229, 3244
The Background to History 293
BALPA Spokesman 88
Bank Robber in Lingerie Shop 54, 161
Banter *see* RAF Banter
The Barber *see* Homicidal Barber/Lumberjack Song
Barry Zeppelin (The Golden Age of Ballooning) 363
Basingstoke *see* Courtmartial
The Batley Townswomens' Guild's Re-enactment of the Battle of Pearl Harbor 55, 130, 161, 3244
The Batley Townswomen's Guild's Re-enactment of the First Heart Transplant 105
The Batsmen of the Kalahari (Cricket Match) 362, 374
The Battle of Trafalgar 55
Bavarian Restaurant Sketch 180
Baxter's [cut] 3319
The BBC Is Short of Money 221
BBC Previews 102
Be a Great Actor 162, 1427
Beat the Clock *see* Anagram Quiz (Beat the Clock)
Beethoven's Mynah Bird 102
Being Eaten by a Crocodile *see* Crocodile

325

Bells 799, 1427
Ben, the Old Prisoner [wr: Palin & Jones] 710, 723
Bicycle Repair Man [wr: Palin & Jones] 21, 38, 1180, 2497, 3248
Big Nose see Sermon on the Mount (Big Nose)
Big-Nosed Sculptor [cut] 239
Biggles Dictates a Letter 232
Biggus Dickus see Pontius Pilate (Throw Him to the Floor/Biggus Dickus)
Bikini-Clad Women & Announcer 105, 161
Bing Tiddle Tiddle Bong [song, w: Chapman, m: Fred Tomlinson] 105, 166
Bingo-Crazed Chinese (The Cycling Tour) 234
Birth see Delivery Room
Bishop 799, 3318
The Bishop 93
Bishop at Home [cut] 3318
Bishop on the Landing see Dead Bishop on the Landing (Church Police)
A Bishop Rehearsing 88
The Black Beast of Arrrghhh [anim] 397
The Black Eagle 110
The Black Knight [wr: Cleese & Chapman] 328, 349, 397
Blackmail 96, 130, 161, 494, 502, 911, 3182
Blancmanges Playing Tennis see Science Fiction Sketch
Blood Bank see Blood Donor
Blood, Devastation, Death, War, and Horror (Man Who Speaks in Anagrams) 225, 3181, 3319
Blood Donor 251
Bloody Catholics see Protestantism and Sex
The Blow on the Head see Take Your Pick
Boarding House see Mr. Hilter
Bogus Psychiatrists (Hamlet) 370, 592
The Bols Story (Gestures to Indicate Pauses) 225
Bomb on Plane (Mr. Badger) 236
Bomb Scare 422
Bombings (Mr. Neutron) 372
A Book at Bedtime 235
A Book at Bedtime (Redgauntlet) 250
The Book of the Film 397
Book-of-the-Month Club Dung 97
Bookshop [from *At Last the 1948 Show*, 1967] 63, 579, 622, 777, 799, 911, 1131, 1427
Bouncing in Jungle [anim] 224
Bounder of Adventure see Travel Agent
Bournemouth Gynecologists vs. Watford Long John Silver Impersonators 106
Boxer Documentary see Ken Clean-Air System

Boxing Commentary 370
Boxing Match Aftermath (The Killer vs. The Champ) 370, 592
Boxing Tonight (Jack Bodell vs. Sir Kenneth Clark) 249, 293
Brave Sir Robin [song, w: Idle, m: Neil Innes] 397, 422
Brian [song, w: Palin, m: Andre Jacquemin & Dave Howman] 710, 722, 723, 1723, 3323
Brian Islam and Brucie [anim] 52
Brian, the Messiah (The Shoe and the Gourd) 710, 723
Brian, the Prophet 710, 723
The Bridge of Death 329, 397, 422
Brigadier and Bishop 374
Bright Side of Life see Always Look on the Bright Side of Life
Bring Out Your Dead 336, 397, 422, 911
British Consulate see Bingo-Crazed Chinese (The Cycling Tour)
The British Show Biz Awards 251
British Soldiers (Fighting Each Other) 1012, 1025
Bruces [wr: Cleese & Idle] 82, 105, 293, 613, 1427, 3181
The Bruces' Philosophers Song [song, w/m: Idle] 293, 347, 494, 502, 527, 752, 805, 943, 1427, 1723, 2551, 2558, 2815, 2919
Bruces Song see The Bruces' Philosophers Song
Bull-Fighting see Probe: Bull-Fighting
Burglar/Encyclopedia Salesman 43
Burying the Cat see Mrs. Premise and Mrs. Conclusion
Bus Conductor Sketch 225
Bus Stop [anim] 105, 161
Buying a Bed 49, 78
Buying an Ant 362, 365, 592

Camel Spotting 47
Camelot Song see Knights of the Round Table (Camelot Song)
Camp Army Drills 105, 161, 3181
Camp Judges see The Judges
Cannibalism see Lifeboat (Cannibalism)
Cannibalism [anim] 111
Careers Advisory Board 43
The Castle Anthrax see The Tale of Sir Galahad: The Castle Anthrax
The Castle Arrrghhh 330, 397, 422
The Castle of Guy de Loimbard see The French Taunter
Casualty Department (The Cycling Tour) 234
Caterpillar see Metamorphosis
The Cave of Caerbannog 397
Certified Stiff see Funerals at Prestatyn
Chairman of the British Well-Basically Club 236
The Champ see Boxing Match Aftermath

Changing on the Beach see Taking Your Clothes Off in Public
Changing on the Beach (Sedan Chair) 39
Chapel see School Chapel
Charades see Court Room (Charades/Spanish Inquisition)
Charles Fatless [anim] 43, 3243
Chartered Accountant see Vocational Guidance Counsellor
Charwoman [anim] 251, 3243
The Cheap-Laughs 236
Cheese Emporium see Cheese Shop
Cheese Shop [wr: Cleese-Chapman] 219, 232, 293, 478, 613, 702, 704, 755, 764, 911, 1131, 1427, 2603, 3182, 3244, 4000, 4177
The Chemist Sketch 93, 3182
The Cherry Orchard see Gumby Theatre (The Cherry Orchard)
Chicken Mines 238
Children's Interview 38, 3181
Children's Stories see Storytime
Chinese Communist Conspiracy/ American Defense/Crelm Toothpaste/Shrill Petrol [anim] 108, 161
Chippendale Writing Desk see Wooden Impressions [anim]
Choreographer see A Party Political Broadcast on Behalf of the Conservative and Unionist Party (Choreographed)
Christmas in Heaven [song, w: Jones; m: Idle] 1012, 1025, 1723, 2909, 2911, 3324
Church Police see Dead Bishop on the Landing (Church Police)
The Cinema see Albatross
City Gents 108
The Classic, Silbury Hill 422
Clergyman Selling Encyclopedias [anim] 52
Climbing the Uxbridge Road 232, 2497, 3181
Clock Smuggler see The Smuggler
Clodagh Rodgers (The Cycling Tour) 234, 3248
Coal Mine (Historical Argument) 111
Coal Miner Son see Working-Class Playwright
Cocktail Bar 222, 239, 316, 321, 347, 1427
Coconuts see The Swallow
Coffins [anim] 55
Colin "Bomber" Harris see Self-Wrestling
Colin Mozart (Ratcatcher) 102
Colonel (Filthy) 347, 502, 943
Colonel (It's a Man's Life in the Modern Army) 39
Colonel (Silly) 49, 161, 3241
Come Back to My Place 60, 161, 3182
Comfy Chair (Spanish Inquisition) 86, 162, 1427, 3248
Commie-Hater 38
Communist Quiz see World Forum (Communist Quiz)

Communist Revolutions [anim] 226
Compere Chasing Mouth [anim] 221, 3243
Complaints 88
Complaints (Michael Ellis) 365
The Concert *see* Royal Festival Hall Concert
Confuse-A-Cat Ltd [wr: Cleese & Chapman] 25, 43, 3244
Conjuring Today 372
Conquistador Coffee Campaign 108
Conrad Poohs and His Dancing Teeth [anim] 106, 130, 161, 3182, 3243
Constitutional Peasants 346, 397, 422, 613, 1427
Contradiction *see* Man Who Contradicts People
The Court of George III (The Golden Age of Ballooning) 363
Court Room (Charades/Spanish Inquisition) 86
Court Room (Erik Njorl/Police Constable Pan Am) 220
Court Room (Mrs. Fiona Lewis/Witness in Coffin/Cardinal Richelieu/Dim of the Yard) 38
Court Room (Multiple Murderer) 220
Court Room (Phrase Book) 110, 161
Court Room Sketch [cut] 3318
Courtmartial (Basingstoke/Special Gaiters/Anything Goes In) 362, 368, 3248
Crackport Religions 108
Credits of the Year 251
Crelm Toothpaste [anim] 111, 3243
Cricket Match *see* The Batsmen of the Kalahari (Cricket Match)
Crocodile 799, 1427
Crossing the Atlantic on a Tricycle 108
The Crucifixion 710
Crunchy Frog 34, 44, 78, 494, 502, 805, 911, 943, 1131, 1665
Current Affairs 96
Custard Pie (Japes Lecture) [wr: Jones, Palin, and Robert Hewison, from 1963 revue *Loitering with Intent*] 254, 268, 488, 492, 494, 539, 805, 943, 1286
Customs Inspector *see* The Smuggler

Dance of the Sugar Plum Fairy [anim] 105
David and the Fig Leaf [anim] 44, 77, 130, 161, 3182
David Attenborough *see* The Walking Tree of Dahomey (David Attenborough)
David Niven's Fridge 251
David Unction 54
Dead Bishop on the Landing (Church Police) 219, 224, 293, 494, 502, 805, 911, 943
Dead Indian *see* Book-of-the-Month Club Dung
Dead Parrot *see* The Pet Shop (Dead Parrot)

The Death of Mary Queen of Scots 105, 162, 245, 494, 502, 911
Decision (discussion) 363
Decomposing Composers [song, w/m: Palin] 799, 1723
Déjà Vu *see* It's the Mind (Déjà Vu)
Delivery Room [wr: Cleese & Chapman] 953, 1012, 1025
Dennis Moore 219, 235, 249
Dennis Moore [song] 235, 249
Dennis Moore (Stealing from the Poor) 249
Dental Appendages *see* Film Director (Teeth)
Department Store (Michael Ellis) 365
Derby Council vs. All Blacks 106
The Detective Sketch *see* Agatha Christie Sketch
Diana the Waitress [cut] 996, 1046, 2909
Different Endings *see* End of Show Department (Michael Ellis)
Dim of the Yard *see* Court Room
Dinsdale *see* Ethel the Frog: The Piranha Brothers
Dirty Fork *see* Restaurant Sketch (Dirty Fork)
Dirty Hungarian Phrase Book *see* Hungarian Phrase Book
The Dirty Vicar Sketch 251
Disturbing Vicar *see* Silly Disturbances (Rev. Arthur Belling)
Do Wot John [song, w/m: Idle] 799, 1427
Doctor 249
Doctor Breeding 180
Dr. Darling (abandoned sketch) 102
Doctor (Healing with Dynamite) 221
Dr. E. Henry Thripshaw's Disease *see* Thripshaw's Disease
Dr. Larch *see* Psychiatrist (Dr. Larch)
Double-Vision *see* Kilimanjaro Expedition (Sir George Head)
Drama Critic 422
A Duck, a Cat, and a Lizard (Discussion) 43, 3182
The Dull Life of a City Stockbroker [wr: Idle & Chapman] 44
Dung *see* Book-of-the-Month Club Dung
Dungeon Room (Mr. and Mrs. Hendy) 1012, 1025

Eartha Kitt/Edward Heath (The Cycling Tour) 234
Eclipse of the Sun 235
Education Tips No. 41: Choosing a Really Expensive School [wr: Palin & Cleese] 2909
Edward Ross *see* It's the Arts: Sir Edward Ross
Eggs Diamond/Book Ad [anim] 102, 3243
Election Night Special (Silly and Sensible Parties) 97, 316, 343, 347, 1427

Election '74 *see* Election Night Special
Election Special *see* Election Night Special
Elephantoplasty 293, 478, 613, 911
Elizabethan Pornography Smugglers *see* The Life of Sir Philip Sidney
Embarrassment 235, 1427
Embezzled Penny *see* The Audit
Emigration from Surbiton to Hounslow *see* Mr. and Mrs. Brian Norris' Ford Popular
End of Show Department (Michael Ellis) 365
The Epilogue *see* The Wrestling Epilogue
Eric the Half-a-Bee [song, w/m: Idle & Cleese] 223, 235, 527, 613, 1427, 1723, 2513, 2558
Erizabeth L 224
Erotic Film 43, 130, 161
Escape [anim] 96
Escape from Film 96
Escape from Sack *see* Sviatoslav Richter and Rita
Eskimos (Mr. Neutron) 372
Ethel the Frog: The Piranha Brothers 82, 83, 162, 1131, 3182
Everest Climbed by Hairdressers *see* Mount Everest (Hairdresser Expedition)
Every Sperm Is Sacred [song, w: Palin & Jones; m: Andre Jacquemin & Dave Howman] 949, 1012, 1025, 1048, 1114, 1723, 2498, 2512, 2558, 2909, 2911
Ewan McTeagle *see* The Poet McTeagle
Executive Introduction/Announcements 422, 911
Ex-Leper 703, 710, 723
Expedition to Lake Pahoe 229
Exploding Penguin *see* Penguin on the TV
The Exploding Version of "The Blue Danube" 111, 130, 3244

Face the Press 83, 130, 3181
A Fairy Tale (Happy Valley) [wr: Cleese & Connie Booth] 235, 238, 316, 3244
Falling from Building 59, 161
Falling Leaves [anim] 1025
Falling People/Magician/Opening Titles [anim] 59
Famous Deaths *see* It's Wolfgang Amadeus Mozart: Famous Deaths
Famous Person Quiz *see* Sound Quiz
Farewell to John Denver 799, 911
Farming Club: Life of Tchaikovsky 221
Fat Song [song, cut] 3324
Father-in-Law 370
F.E.A.R. Headquarters (Mr. Neutron) 372
Ferdinand von Zeppelin/Corpses in Drawing Room (The Golden Age of Ballooning) 363

Festival Hall *see* Royal Festival Hall Concert
Fighting Each Other *see* British Soldiers (Fighting Each Other)
Film Director (Teeth) 108
Film Trailer 368
Films of L.F. Dibley: If, Rear Window, Finian's Rainbow 97
The Final Attack 397
Find the Fish 1025
Finland [song, w/m: Palin] 799, 801, 1427, 1723, 3144
Fire Brigade/Our Eamonn 226
Firing Squad (The Cycling Tour) 234
The First Heart Transplant *see* The Batley Townswomen's Guild's Re-enactment of the First Heart Transplant
The First Man to Jump the Channel *see* Ron Obvious
First World War Noises in 4 293
The First Zulu War 1879/Tiger Hunt 951, 1012, 1025
Fish Club: How to Feed a Goldfish 111
Fish License 106, 235, 613, 1427
The Fish-Slapping Dance 128, 134, 219, 221, 2497, 3150, 3182, 3241, 3243, 3244, 3248, 4089
The Five Frog Curse [anim] 93
Flaming Star *see* Archaeology Today (Flaming Star)
The Flasher 49, 161
Flasher Love Story [anim] 180, 943
Flea-Buster [anim] 238
Flower Arrangement *see* Gumby Flower-Arranging
Flying European Monarchs/Shaving [anim] 83
Flying Fox of the Yard 224, 3319
Flying Lessons 88, 3244
Flying Sheep 26, 37, 78
Flying Sheep/Traffic Accidents [anim] 232
Foreign Secretary 97
A Foul-Tempered Rabbit *see* The Rabbit of Caerbannog
Four Yorkshiremen [wr: Chapman, Cleese, Marty Feldman & Tim Brooke-Taylor; from *At Last the 1948 Show*, 1967] 316, 347, 494, 502, 704, 755, 764, 805, 943, 1131, 1427
Fraud Film Director Squad (Antonioni) 224
Fraud Film Director Squad (Visconti) 224
The Free Repetition of Doubtful Words 239
French Castle *see* The French Taunter
French Lecture on Sheep-Aircraft 37, 3182
French Subtitled Film (Le Fromage Grand) 106
The French Taunter 335, 377, 397, 422, 613, 1427, 2698
Fresh Fruit *see* Self-Defense (Against Fresh Fruit)

Le Fromage Grand *see* French Subtitled Film (Le Fromage Grand)
Frontiers of Medicine: Penguins 250
Full Frontal Nudity [anim] 49, 3243
Funerals at Prestatyn 235, 613
The Funniest Joke in the World 35, 161, 3248

Galaxy Song [song, w: Idle; m: Idle & John Du Prez] 1012, 1025, 1048, 1196, 1723, 2457, 2481, 2490, 2498, 2531, 2558, 2919, 3004, 3223, 3472, 3729, 3956
Gardening Club *see* Ken Russell's "Gardening Club"
The Gas Cooker Sketch *see* New Cooker Sketch
Gaston the Waiter *see* The Meaning of Life (Gaston the Waiter)
Gavin Millarrrrrrrrr *see* Theatre Critic (Gavin Millarrrrrrrrr)
Gay Boys in Bondage [anim] 239, 3243
Gay Magistrates *see* The Judges
George I, Episode 3/Dennis Moore (Lupins) 249
George III *see* The Court of George III (The Golden Age of Ballooning)
George III [song, w/m: Neil Innes] 363
Gestures to Indicate Pauses *see* The Bols Story (Gestures to Indicate Pauses)
Girls' Boarding School 111
The Gits 102
The Golden Age of Ballooning *see* Montgolfier Brothers; Louis XIV; The Court of George III; Barry Zeppelin; Ferdinand von Zeppelin
The Golden Age of Colonic Irrigation [anim] 363
La Gondola Restaurant *see* Pearls for Swine (adverts)
The Good Fairy from Program Control [anim] 232, 3243
The Good Old Days *see* Four Yorkshiremen
The Gorge of Eternal Peril *see* The Bridge of Death
Gorilla Librarian 54
Gravediggers 55
A Great Actor 293
The Great Debate: TV4 or Not TV4? 249, 3319
The Great Escape *see* Trim-Jeans Theatre Presents
The Grim Reaper 948, 1012, 1025
Growing Hands/Cowboy [anim] 88, 161
Gumby Brain Specialist/Surgery 229, 3244
Gumby Crooner 52
Gumby Flower-Arranging 110, 116, 268, 288, 316, 347, 494, 502
Gumby Theatre (The Cherry Orchard) 162, 613, 1427
Guy de Loimbard's Castle *see* The French Taunter

Haggling 710, 723
Hairdresser Expedition *see* Mount Everest (Hairdresser Expedition)
Hamlet *see* Bogus Psychiatrists (Hamlet)
Hamlet and Ophelia 370
Hands Up [anim] 224, 3243
Happy Valley *see* A Fairy Tale (Happy Valley)
Hearing Aid [from *At Last the 1948 Show*, 1967] 238, 1131
Hearses Racing 55, 3182
Heinz the Stuttgart Rapist 180
Hell's Grannies 49, 161, 2497
Henry Kissinger [song, w/m: Idle] 799, 1427, 1723
Here Comes Another One [song] 799
Hermits 49, 3181
He's Not the Messiah (He's a Very Naughty Boy) 710, 723
Hide-and-Seek *see* The Olympic Hide-and-Seek Final
Highland Spokesman 88
Hijacked Plane (to Luton) 88
Hilter *see* Mr. Hilter
Historical Impersonations 60
History of the Joke *see* Custard Pie (Japes Lecture)
Hit on the Head Lessons 224
The Holy Hand Grenade of Antioch 331, 397, 422
The Holzfäller Song (Lumberjack Song) 180, 1846, 3181
Homicidal Barber/Lumberjack Song 52, 78, 3127, 3248
Horoscopes *see* What the Stars Foretell
Horse of the Year Show 221
Hospital for Over-Acting 110
Hospital Run by RSM 111
Host on Bus 96
Hot Dogs and Knickers 293
The House-Hunters [anim] 225, 3243
The Housewives of Britain (Clean-Up Campaign) 229
Housing Project Built by Characters from 19th-Century English Literature 236, 3248
How Do You Tell a Witch? *see* The Test of a Witch
How Far Can a Minister Fall? (Party Political Broadcast by the Wood Party) 59
How Not to Be Seen [wr: Palin & Jones] 108, 161
How to Do It 221, 235, 613, 3181
How to Feed a Goldfish *see* Fish Club: How to Feed a Goldfish
How to Put Your Budgie Down *see* Mrs. Premise and Mrs. Conclusion
How to Recognize a Mason 93
How to Recognize Different Parts of the Body 105
Hungarian Phrase Book 110, 161, 3182
Hunting Film 52

I Bet You They Won't Play This Song on the Radio [song, w/m: Idle] 799, 801, 802, 1427, 1846
I Confess [anim] 86
I Like Chinese [song, w/m: Idle] 799, 801, 1427, 1723, 2558
I Like Traffic Lights *see* Traffic Lights
Icelandic Honey Week 374
Icelandic Saga *see* Njorl's Saga
Ideal Loon Exhibition 249
The Idiot in Society *see* Village Idiots
I'm a Lumberjack *see* The Lumberjack Song
I'm So Worried [song, w/m: Jones] 799, 1427, 1723, 1846, 3325, 1723
Inspector Baboon *see* Fraud Film Director Squad (Antonioni)
Inspector Fox *see* Flying Fox of the Yard
Inspector Leopard *see* Fraud Film Director Squad (Visconti)
Inspector Tiger *see* Agatha Christie Sketch (Inspector Tiger)
Insurance Sketch 93
The Insurance Sketch/Queen Tunes In 111
Interesting People 55, 78
Intermission 60
Intermission [anim] 60
International Philosophy (Football Match) 238, 943, 3181
Interview in Filing Cabinet 108
Irving C. Saltzberg *see* Twentieth-Century Vole
Is There?...Life After Death? 239, 3319
It All Happened on the 11:20 from Hainault to Redhill... *see* Agatha Christie Sketch (Railway Timetables)
Italian Lesson 35
It's (Chat Show with Lulu and Ringo Starr) 221
It's a Living 97
It's a Man's Life in the Modern Army *see* Colonel (It's a Man's Life in the Modern Army)
It's a Tree (Arthur Tree) 54
It's the Arts: Arthur "Two Sheds" Jackson 35, 78, 1131
It's the Arts: Johann Gambolputty... of Ulm 44, 3182
It's the Arts: Picasso-Cycling Race 35, 3244
It's the Arts: Sir Edward Ross 35, 78, 161, 3241
It's the Mind (Déjà Vu) 88
It's Wolfgang Amadeus Mozart: Famous Deaths 35, 3244
I've Got Two Legs [song, w/m: Gilliam] 347, 943, 1723

Jack in the Box [anim] 234
Japes Lecture *see* Custard Pie (Japes Lecture)
Jewelry Heist *see* Non-Illegal Robbery
Jimmy Buzzard Interview 55

Job Hunter 108
Jockey Interviews 370, 3181
Johann Gambolputty...of Ulm *see* It's the Arts: Johann Gambolputty...of Ulm
The Judges 102, 162, 494, 502, 805, 943, 3181
Julius Caesar on an Aldis Lamp 86, 130, 3182
Jungle Restaurant 224

Kamikaze Scottish Regiment *see* McKamikaze Highlanders
Ken Clean-Air System (boxer documentary) 96
Ken Russell's "Gardening Club" 224
Ken Shabby 59, 268, 3241
Kilimanjaro Expedition (Sir George Head) [wr: Cleese & Idle] 52, 161
The Killer Cars [anim] 105, 161, 3243
Killer Joke *see* The Funniest Joke in the World
Killer Rabbit *see* The Rabbit of Caerbannog
Killer Sheep 98
King Brian the Wild [cut] 320, 592, 2158
Knees Up, Mother Brown (Spanish Inquisition) 162, 1427
Knights of the Round Table (Camelot Song) [w: Chapman & Cleese; m: Neil Innes] 333, 397, 422, 613, 911, 1723
The Knights Who Say "Ni" 339, 397, 422, 2603

Ladies/Open War [anim] 55
Lake Pahoe *see* Expedition to Lake Pahoe
Language Laboratory 226
The Larch 38
The Last Five Miles of the M2 *see* Programme Planners
The Last Supper 492, 539, 554, 805, 943, 1131, 1665, 1705, 2513
Leapy Lee *see* An Appeal on Behalf of the National Truss (Leapy Lee)
Leaving the Army 49, 3182
Lemming of the BDA 39
Let's Talk Ant *see* University of the Air: Let's Talk Ant
Letters to "Daily Mirror" 54
The Liberty Bell [1893 march, m: John Philip Sousa] 34, 347, 2558
The Life of Sir Philip Sidney (Elizabethan Pornography Smugglers) 239
Life of Tchaikovsky *see* Farming Club: Life of Tchaikovsky
Life or Death Struggles 225, 3244
Lifeboat 232
Lifeboat (Cannibalism) 111, 162, 1427
Lion Tamer *see* Vocational Guidance Counsellor
Little Red Riding Hood 180, 805, 943
Live from Epsom 370
Live from the Cardiff Rooms, Libya 39

Live from the Grill-O-Mat Snack Bar 96
Liver Donor 1012, 1025
Living Room on Pavement 93, 3248
The Llama *see* Llamas
Llamas 52, 268, 316, 347, 494, 502
Logician *see* A Professional Logician
Losing Judges 249
Lost Python *see* May Day in England (Lost Python)
The Lost World of Roiurama 224
Louis XIV (The Golden Age of Ballooning) 363
The Lumberjack Song [w/m: Jones & Palin, Fred Tomlinson] 34, 52, 78, 132, 161, 166, 316, 343, 347, 445, 461, 492, 494, 498, 501, 502, 527, 539, 554, 805, 835, 911, 943, 1427, 1723, 1846, 2038, 2106, 2228, 2498, 2512, 2558, 2582, 2678, 2826, 3091, 3127, 3181, 3248, 3455; *see also* The Holzfäller Song (German version)
Lupins *see* George I, Episode 3/Dennis Moore (Lupins)

A Magnificent Festering [anim] 226
Man in the Street Interviews 43
Man-Powered Flight 86, 130
Man Turns into Scotsman *see* Science Fiction Sketch
Man Who Collects Bird-Watcher's Eggs 111
Man Who Contradicts People 105, 162
The Man Who Finishes Other People's Sentences 374
The Man Who Makes People Laugh Uncontrollably 225
The Man Who Says Things in a Roundabout Way *see* The Toad Elevating Moment
Man Who Speaks in Anagrams *see* Blood, Devastation, Death, War, and Horror
A Man with a Tape Recorder Up His Nose/Brother's Nose 52, 161, 3182
A Man with Three Buttocks 26, 37, 78
A Man with Two Noses 37
Management Training Course Interview *see* Silly Job Interview
Manhunt [anim] 220
Marching Up and Down the Square (RSM) 1025
Marilyn Monroe 422, 1427
Marriage Guidance Counselor 37, 161
Marriage Registry Office 97
Martin Luther *see* The Adventures of Martin Luther
Martydom of St. Victor 799
Mary Recruitment Office 225
Masons *see* How to Recognize a Mason
A Massage from the Swedish Prime Minister 235
Match of the Day (Footballers Kissing) 229

May Day in England (Lost Python) 134
McKamikaze Highlanders 250
Me, Doctor 60, 78
The Meaning of Life [song, w: Idle; m: Idle & John du Prez] 1012, 1025, 1723, 2212, 2558, 2567, 2602, 3324
The Meaning of Life (Gaston the Waiter) 1025
Meat Grinder/Venus Dancing [anim] 49
Mechanical Wings *see* Man-Powered Flight
Medical Love Song [w/m: Idle, John Du Prez & Chapman] 799, 1723, 2558, 3325
Merchant Banker [wr: Cleese & Chapman] 225, 1131, 1286
The Merchant of Venice (The Bad Ischl Dairy Herd) 180
Metamorphosis [anim] 93, 130, 161, 3243
Meteorology [cut] 3319
Michael Ellis 365
Michelangelo and the Pope *see* The Last Supper
Microphone Stealing *see* Rival Documentaries
Milkmen *see* Seduced Milkmen
The Mill on the Floss (Ballooning) 363
The Minister for Not Listening to People *see* Today in Parliament
Minister for Overseas Development (Mrs. Niggerbaiter Explodes) 221, 293, 478, 613, 3248
Ministry of Foods: Coconut Information Division 2697
The Ministry of Silly Walks [wr: Palin & Jones] 82, 83, 130, 268, 494, 805, 943, 999, 2497, 2645, 3127, 3241
A Minute Passed 235
Miss Anne Elk *see* Thrust: Miss Anne Elk
Mr. and Mrs. Brian Norris' Ford Popular 221
Mr. and Mrs. Cheap-Laugh *see* The Cheap-Laughs
Mr. and Mrs. Hendy *see* Dungeon Room (Mr. and Mrs. Hendy)
Mr. and Mrs. Jean-Paul Sartre 220
Mr. Attila the Hun 60
Mr. Badger *see* Silly Interview; Bomb on Plane; Reading the Credits
Mr. Creosote [wr: Palin & Jones, Cleese & Chapman] 947, 1012, 1025, 3324
Mr. Gulliver/Clodagh Rodgers (The Cycling Tour) 234
Mr. Hilter 59
Mr. Neutron in Suburbia 372
Mr. Pither's Bicycle Pump (The Cycling Tour) 234
Mr. Smoke-Too-Much *see* Travel Agent
Mollusks (Live TV Documentary) 229, 3241

The Money Programme 224, 235, 3181
Money Song [w/m: John Gould & Idle] 224, 235, 1723, 2558
Montgolfier Brothers (The Golden Age of Ballooning) 363
The Montgolfier Brothers in Love (The Golden Age of Ballooning) 363
Montgolfier Brothers Wash Each Other [anim] 363
Mortuary Visit 236, 3319
Mosquito Hunters 102, 3182
Most Awful Family in Britain 362, 374
Motor Insurance Policy *see* Insurance Sketch
Mount Everest (Hairdresser Expedition) 226, 3181
Mountaineering Expedition *see* Kilimanjaro Expedition (Sir George Head)
Mouse Organ *see* Musical Mice
Mouse Preserve (Frank Tutankhamun) 238
The Mouse Problem *see* The World Around Us: The Mouse Problem
Mouse Stampede [anim] 238
Movie Writers *see* Twentieth-Century Vole (Irving C. Saltzberg)
Mrs. Niggerbaiter Explodes *see* Minister for Overseas Development
Mrs. Premise and Mrs. Conclusion 220, 235, 268, 279, 1131, 3241
Mrs. Scum (Mr. Neutron) 372
Mrs. Thing and Mrs. Entity 102
Mrs. Zambesi *see* New Brain from Curry's
Muddy Knees [song] 799
Multiple Murderer *see* Court Room (Multiple Murderer)
Murder Solved by Train Schedules *see* Agatha Christie Sketch (Railway Timetables)
Musical Mice 37, 161
Musical Statue [anim] 37, 161, 3243
Mystico and Janet (Flats Built by Hypnosis) 236, 3248

Nationwide: Westminster Bridge/Police Helmets 370
Naughty Bits 105
Nazi Fish [anim] 221, 3243
Neurotic Announcer 225
Never Be Rude to an Arab [song, w/m: Jones] 799, 911, 943, 1723, 3181
Neville Shunt 108; *see also* Theatre Critic (Gavin Millarrrrrrrrr)
New Brain from Curry's 251
New Comedy Programmes (Dad's Doctor, Dad's Pooves, etc.) 250
New Cooker Sketch 83, 130, 2497
The News for Parrots 98, 279, 3248
The News for Wombats 98
The News with Richard Baker (Gestures) 225

The News with Richard Baker (Storage Jars) 232
Newsflash (Peter Woods) 368
Newspaper Shop 130
Newsreader 374
Newsreader Arrested 43, 130
Nisus Wettus *see* One Cross Each (Nisus Wettus and Mr. Cheeky)
Njorl's Saga 220
No Time to Lose 250
No-Time Tolouse [anim] 250, 3243
Noisy Traffic [anim] 238
Non-Illegal Robbery 44
North Malden Icelandic Saga Society 220
The North Minehead Bye-Election [wr: Cleese & Palin] 59, 78
The Not Noël Coward Song *see* Penis Song
Not Secret Police (The Cycling Tour) 234
Novel Writing 293, 613, 911, 1427
Novelty Salesman 86
Nude Man 93
Nude Man (Organist) 236
Nudge, Nudge [wr: Idle] 34, 38, 78, 161, 268, 288, 316, 347, 494, 502, 613, 805, 911, 922, 943, 1427, 1760, 2567, 3127, 3181

Off-License 249
Oh, Lord, Please Don't Burn Us [song, w: Cleese & Chapman; m: Idle & John du Prez] 1025
Old Lady Snoopers 232
Oliver Cromwell [song, w: Cleese; m: Frederic Chopin; adpt of Chopin's Polonaise No. 6 in A Flat Major, Op. 53] 1723
The Olympic Hide-and-Seek Final 236, 3248
Olympic Torch Runner 180
One Cross Each (Nisus Wettus and Mr. Cheeky) 710, 723
One-Man Wrestling *see* Self-Wrestling
Open Field Farming Songs *see* The Background to History
Opera Singer [anim] 374
Operating Theatre (Squatters) 60
The Oscar Wilde Sketch 251, 293, 613, 3241
Otto [cut] 752, 2320, 2493, 3323
Otto Song [song] [cut] 3323
Our Eamonn *see* Fire Brigade/Our Eamonn

The Pantomime Horse Is a Secret Agent 225, 3241
Pantomime Horses 225
Paratroopers [anim] 370
Parrot Sketch *see* The Pet Shop (Dead Parrot)
Party Hints by Veronica Smalls 226
Party Political Broadcast by the Wood Party *see* How Far Can a Minister Fall?
A Party Political Broadcast on Behalf

of the Conservative and Unionist Party (Choreographed) 250
Party Political Broadcast on Behalf of the Norwegian Party 363
Pasolini's "The Third Test Match" 251
A Passing Spaceship 710
Patient Abuse 374
Patient Stabbed by Nurse *see* Patient Abuse
Pearls for Swine (adverts) 60
Penguin on the TV 105, 162, 245, 3241
Penguins *see* Frontiers of Medicine: Penguins
Penis Song (The Not Noël Coward Song) [w/m: Idle] 1012, 1025, 1723, 2554, 2558
Peoples' Front of Judea Meeting *see* What Have the Romans Ever Done for Us?
Peoples' Front of Judea (Roman Amphitheatre) 710, 723
Pepperpots Discuss French Philosophers 37
Personal Freedom 235
Pet Conversions (Taking in the Terrier) 54, 293, 478
The Pet Shop (Dead Parrot) [wr: Cleese & Chapman] 34, 49, 70, 78, 116, 132, 161, 198, 268, 316, 347, 492, 494, 502, 539, 613, 702, 835, 882, 911, 999, 1131, 1427, 1665, 1705, 1726, 2214, 2340, 2645, 3127, 3241, 3422
Philip Jenkinson on Cheese Westerns 232
Philosophers Football Match *see* International Philosophy (Football Match)
Phone-In 293, 911
Photographer/Land Eating/Intro [anim] 180
Photos of Uncle Ted/Spanish Inquisition 86
Picasso-Cycling Race *see* It's the Arts: Picasso-Cycling Race
Piggy Bank Hunting [anim] 96
Pilate's Passover Addwess 710, 723
Pilate's Wife [cut] 752, 2320, 2493
The Piranha Brothers *see* Ethel the Frog: The Piranha Brothers
Piston Engine 370
Plague Village *see* Bring Out Your Dead
Plan 13A [anim] 249
Planet Algon *see* Prices on the Planet Algon
Pleasures of the Dance *see* Apologies (Pleasures of the Dance)
The Poet McTeagle 88, 3181
Poetic Solicitor *see* Off-License
Poetry Reading (Ants) *see* Victorian Poetry Reading (Ants)
Poets in the Home 93, 3248
Police Constable Pan-Am 93
Police Fairy Stories *see* Probe Around
Police Helmets *see* Nationwide: Westminster Bridge/Police Helmets

Police Raid 43
Police Station *see* Science Fiction Sketch
Police Station (Silly Voices) 59
Polite Hijacker *see* Hijacked Plane (to Luton)
Political Groupies 98
Political Peasants *see* Constitutional Peasants
Politicians: An Apology 229
Pontius Pilate (Throw Him to the Floor/Biggus Dickus) 710, 723
Poofy Judges *see* The Judges
The Pope and Michelangelo *see* The Last Supper
Pornographic Bookshop 239
Post Box Ceremony (Mr. Neutron) 372, 3182
Powder My Nose [anim] 251, 3243
Prejudice 249
Premiere of the Film (Live Broadcast from London) 422, 911
Prices on the Planet Algon 236
Prime Minister (Mr. Neutron) 372
The Prince and the Black Spot [anim] 97, 161, 3243
The Princess with Wooden Teeth *see* A Fairy Tale (Happy Valley)
Probe Around (Police Fairy Stories) 60
Probe: Bull-Fighting 236
A Professional Logician 422
Programme Planners 368
Prostitute Advert 83
Protection Money *see* Army Protection Racket
Protestantism and Sex 1012, 1025
Protestors/2001 [anim] 110
Psychiatrist (Dr. Larch) 60
Psychiatrist Milkman 88
Psychopath [cut] 3320
The Public Are Idiots 368
Purchase a Past [anim] 38, 3243
Pushing Button/Two Growing Trees/Hitler [anim] 236
Puss in Boots 221
Putting Down Budgies *see* Mrs. Premise and Mrs. Conclusion

Queen Victoria and Gladstone *see* The Wacky Queen
Queen Victoria Handicap 370, 3181
The Queen Will Be Watching 111

The Rabbit of Caerbannog 331, 397
Racing Car [anim] 105
Radio Quiz Game *see* What Do You...? (Radio Quiz Game)
Radio Shop [cut] 3320
RAF Banter 368, 3248
The Raid on Pilate's Palace 710
Railway Timetables *see* Agatha Christie Sketch (Railway Timetables)
Ralph Melish *see* Adventures of Ralph Melish
Ramsay MacDonald Striptease 108, 130
Randy Businessmen 238

Rat *see* Dead Bishop on the Landing (Church Police)
Ratcatcher *see* Colin Mozart (Ratcatcher)
Ratcatcher (Killer Sheep) 98, 3248
Raymond Luxury-Yacht Interview 97, 3244
Raymond Luxury-Yacht (Plastic Surgery) 105, 3241
Reading Hall *see* Victorian Poetry Reading (Ants)
Reading the Credits (Mr. Badger) 236
Rear Stalls 422
Record Shop *see* First World War Noises in 4
Red Indian in Theatre 44
A Re-enactment of The Battle of Pearl Harbor *see* The Batley Townswomens' Guild's Re-enactment of The Battle of Pearl Harbor
The Refreshment Room at Bletchley 52, 3181
Registrar of Marriages (Wife Swap) 102
Repeating Groove 108
Restaurant (Abuse/Cannibalism) 60
Restaurant in Jungle *see* Jungle Restaurant
Restaurant Sketch *see* Bavarian Restaurant Sketch
Restaurant Sketch (Dirty Fork) 34, 38, 161
The Return of the Native *see* Novel Writing
Richard Baker *see* The News with Richard Baker
Rival Documentaries 250, 3244
Rock Notes 799, 1427, 2558
Roger the Shrubber 397
Roman Amphitheatre *see* Peoples' Front of Judea
Romans Go Home [wr: Cleese & Chapman] 710, 723
Romantic Movie *see* Erotic film
Ron Obvious (The First Man to Jump the Channel) 54
A Room in Polonius's House 370
Royal Festival Hall Concert 162, 210, 245
Royal Navy Advert [anim] 229, 3243
The Royal Philharmonic Orchestra Goes to the Bathroom 55
The Royal Society for Putting Things on Top of Other Things 96
RSM *see* Marching Up and Down the Square (RSM)
Rubbish Dump *see* French Subtitled Film (Le Fromage Grand)
The Rude/Polite Butcher 96
Rugby Match 945, 1025
Rustic Monologue 39

Salad Days *see* Sam Peckinpah's "Salad Days"
Salvation Fuzz *see* Dead Bishop on the Landing (Church Police)

Sam Peckinpah's "Salad Days" 219, 232
Sartre *see* Mr. and Mrs. Jean-Paul Sartre
Scene 24 397
School Chapel 1025, 1131
School Prize-Giving 97
Schoolboys' Life Assurance Company 221
Science Fiction Sketch 47, 1180
A Scotsman on a Horse 44, 348, 3182
Scott of the Antarctic/Sahara 67, 106, 130
A Scottish Farewell (Here Comes Another One) 799
Seashore Interlude Film 232
Secret Service [from *At Last the 1948 Show*, 1967] 316, 347
Secret Service Dentists *see* Lemming of the BDA
Secretary of State Striptease 98
Seduced Milkmen 38, 161, 2497
Self-Defense (Against Fresh Fruit) 39, 78, 161, 3244
Self-Wrestling 238, 268, 316, 347, 494, 502, 805, 943, 3241
The Semaphore Version of Wuthering Heights 86, 130, 3182
Semprini *see* Words Not to Be Used Again
Sermon on the Mount (Big Nose) 710, 723
Seven Brides for Seven Brothers 96
Sex Lesson [wr: Cleese & Chapman] 1012, 1025
Sexual Athletes [anim] 97, 3182, 3243
Sgt. Duckie's Song 105
Shaving [anim] 83, 161, 3243
Sheep Bank Robbers [anim] 98
Shepherds [cut] 2320, 2493
Sherry-Drinking Vicar 239
The Shoe and the Gourd *see* Brian, the Messiah (The Shoe and the Gourd)
Shooting Gallery [anim] 239
Show-Jumping (Musicals) 368
The Show So Far 232
The Sign That Is the Sign 2320
A Signalbox Somewhere Near Hove 59
Silly and Sensible Parties *see* Election Night Special
Silly Disturbances (the Rev. Arthur Belling) 239
Silly Interview (Mr. Badger) 229
Silly Job Interview 43
Silly Noises 239
Silly Noises (Quiz Show) 235, 613
Silly Olympics (Munich 1972) 180, 268, 494, 805, 943, 1533, 3181
Silly Vicar *see* An Appeal for Sanity (Silly Vicar)
Silly Voices *see* Police Station (Silly Voices)
Silly Walks *see* The Ministry of Silly Walks
Sir Edward Ross *see* It's the Arts: Sir Edward Ross

Sir Philip Sidney *see* The Life of Sir Philip Sidney (Elizabethan Pornography Smugglers)
Sit on My Face [song, w: Idle; m: Harry Parr Davies; adpt of "Sing As We Go"] 799, 805, 911, 943, 1427, 1723, 2558, 2826, 3181
Sit Up/Dancing Soldiers/Falling Pig [anim] 35
Smoking a Pipe [anim] 59
Smolensk YMACA (The Cycling Tour) 234
The Smuggler 43
Social Legislation in the 18th Century 55
Soho Motors *see* Pearls for Swine (adverts)
Sound Quiz 162, 1427
Souvenir Salesman 2320
Spam 82, 110, 162, 245, 1427, 2512, 3241
Spam Song [w/m: Palin, Jones & Fred Tomlinson] 110, 162, 166 (lyrics), 210, 245, 461, 527, 1723, 2498, 2558
The Spanish Inquisition [wr: Palin & Jones] 82, 86, 162, 1427, 3127; *see also* Comfy Chair; Knees Up, Mother Brown
Speaker [anim] 229
Special Gaiters *see* Courtmartial
Spectrum 59
The Spot *see* The Prince and the Black Spot
Spot the Brain Cell *see* Take Your Pick (The Blow on the Head)
Spot the Looney 250
Squatters *see* Operating Theatre (Squatters)
Stabbed Patient *see* Doctor Whose Patients are Stabbed by His Nurse
Stake Your Claim 162, 180, 245, 704, 764
Still No Sign of Land *see* Lifeboat (Cannibalism)
Stock Market Report 220
Stolen Newsreader 38
Stolen Wallet *see* Come Back to My Place
Stoning [wr: Cleese & Chapman] 710, 723
Storage Jars 232
The Story of EBW 343 *see* Mr. and Mrs. Brian Norris' Ford Popular
The Story of the Film So Far 422
Storytime 38, 78, 288, 3181
Strangers in the Night 54
Strawberry Tart *see* Dead Bishop on the Landing (Church Police)
String [from *The Frost Report*, 1967] 799, 911, 1131, 1427
Submarine (Pepperpots) 111
Summarize Proust Competition *see* The All-England Summarize Proust Competition
Superhero [anim] 44
Supreme Commander (Mr. Neutron) 372
Sviatoslav Richter and Rita 221, 3181

The Swallow 397
Swamp Castle *see* The Tale of Sir Lancelot: Swamp Castle
Sycophancy 238

Take Your Pick (The Blow on the Head) 98, 268, 347
Taking in the Terrier *see* Pet Conversions
Taking Your Clothes Off in Public 39
The Tale of Sir Galahad: The Castle Anthrax 334, 397
The Tale of Sir Lancelot: Swamp Castle 337, 397, 422, 1427, 2698
The Tale of Sir Robin: The Three-Headed Knight 344, 397
Tax on Thingy 86
Tchaikovsky *see* Farming Club: Life of Tchaikovsky
Teach Yourself Heath 233, 3319
Teddy Salad of the Yukon (Mr. Neutron) 362, 372
Teleprinter Football Results [cut] 3320
Ten Seconds of Sex 236, 238
Test Match/Epsom Furniture Race 98
The Test of a Witch 338, 397, 422, 783, 911
Thames TV Intro 251
Theatre Critic (Gavin Millarrrrrrrrr) 108, 162
The Theatre Sketch *see* Red Indian in Theatre
Theory on Brontosauruses *see* Thrust: Miss Anne Elk
There's Been a Murder 105
The Thinker [anim] 37
Thomas Hardy *see* Novel Writing
The Three-Headed Knight *see* The Tale of Sir Robin: The Three-Headed Knight
Three Wise Men 710, 723
Thripshaw's Disease 239
Throw Him to the Floor *see* Pontius Pilate (Throw Him to the Floor/ Biggus Dickus)
Thrust: Miss Anne Elk 226, 235, 3241
Tiger and Other Pets (Michael Ellis) 365
Tiger Club 293
Tiger Hunt *see* The First Zulu War 1879/Tiger Hunt
Tim the Enchanter 397, 422
The Time on BBC1 97, 130
Timmy Williams' Coffee Time 97
Tired Undertakers *see* Undertakers
The Toad Elevating Moment: Roundabout Speaker and Ends/ Beginnings/Middles of Words 111
Tobacconist *see* Hungarian Phrase Book
Today in Parliament 98
Today in Parliament (The Minister for Not Listening to People) 229
Toothy Film Director *see* Film Director (Teeth)

Torpedo Bay *see* Submarine (Pepperpots)
Tory Housewives Clean-Up Campaign *see* The Housewives of Britain (Clean-Up Campaign)
Toupee Hall 365, 592
Trade Description Act *see* Crunchy Frog
Traffic Lights [song] 799, 1427
Travel Agent [wr: Cleese & Chapman, Idle] 219, 226, 235, 268, 316, 347, 494, 502, 805, 943, 1427, 3181
Treadmill Lager *see* Bishop
Trim-Jeans Theatre Presents 221
Trivializing the War 368, 3248
The Trojan Rabbit *see* The French Taunter
Trotsky (The Cycling Tour) 234
Trotsky/Eartha Kitt (The Cycling Tour) 234
Tudor Job Agency 239
Tudor Porn Merchants *see* Pornographic Bookshop
Tunnelling to Java *see* Ron Obvious
TV Is Bad for Your Eyes [anim] 232, 3243
Twentieth-Century Frog [anim] 161
Twentieth-Century Vole (Irving C. Saltzberg) [wr: Cleese & Chapman] 44, 3241
Two Sheds *see* It's the Arts: Arthur "Two Sheds" Jackson
2001 [anim] 250, 3243

Undertaker (freelance) [cut] 3318
Undertaker Sketch [wr: Cleese & Chapman] 82, 111, 162, 1131, 1427
Undertakers 55
Underwater Productions 105
Unexploded Scotsman Disposal Squad 250
University of the Air: Let's Talk Ant 365
University of Woolamaloo *see* Bruces
Up Your Pavement 368, 3248
The Upper-Class Twit of the Year [wr: Cleese & Chapman] 34, 59, 161, 3244
Urine Donor *see* Blood Donor

Venus Dancing [anim] 49, 161
Vera's Lovers *see* Strangers in the Night
The Verrifast Plane Company 105

The Very Big Corporation of America 1025
A Very Naughty Boy *see* He's Not the Messiah (He's a Very Naughty Boy)
Vicar/Salesman 221
Vicious Baby Carriage [anim] 44
Victorian Poetry Reading (Ants) 365
Village Idiots 98
The Visitors 52, 78
Visitors from Coventry *see* Mr. Hilter
Vocational Guidance Counsellor 54, 161, 3241

The Wacky Queen 21, 37
Wainscotting *see* Ratcatcher (Killer Sheep)
Walk-On Part in Sketch 54
The Walking Tree of Dahomey (David Attenborough) 374
War Noises *see* First World War Noises in 4
Wasp Club 293
We Love the Yangtse [song, w/m: Palin & Jones] 223, 235
Wee-Wee Wine Tasting [cut] 222, 239
Westminster Bridge *see* Nationwide: Westminster Bridge/Police Helmets
What a Lovely Day [anim] 368, 3243
What Do You...? (Radio Quiz Game) 235
What Have the Romans Ever Done for Us? (PFJ Meeting) 710, 723, 1260
What the Stars Foretell [wr: Palin & Jones] 249
When Does a Dream Begin? [song, w/m: Neil Innes] 368
Whicker Island 220, 3181
Whicker's World *see* Whicker Island
Whizzo Butter 35
Whizzo Chocolates *see* Crunchy Frog
The Whizzo Quality Assortment *see* Crunchy Frog
Who Cares? *see* Elephantoplasty
Wide World of Novel Writing *see* Novel Writing
Wife Swap *see* Registrar of Marriages (Wife Swap)
Wife-Swapping 251, 3182

William Tell 238
Wise Men at the Manger *see* Three Wise Men
Wishes (Schoolboys/Businessmen Interview) 60, 3182
Witch Burning *see* The Test of a Witch
Women and Children First 221
Wonderful World of Sound 235
Wooden Impressions [anim] 54
Woody and Tinny Words 362, 368
Word Association 293, 613, 1131
A Word from a Frenchman 180
Words Not to Be Used Again 93, 3182
Working-Class Playwright 37, 3248
The World Around Us: The Mouse Problem [wr: Cleese & Chapman] 37, 78
World Forum (Communist Quiz) 82, 110, 132, 162, 245, 316, 347, 494, 502, 805, 911, 943, 3181
The World of History (interruptions) 55
The World of History *see* Social Legislation in the Eighteenth Century; The Battle of Trafalgar; The Batley Townswomen's Guild Re-enactment of The Battle of Pearl Harbor
World War Noises in 4 *see* First World War Noises in 4
The World's Funniest Joke *see* The Funniest Joke in the World
Wrestling *see* Self-Wrestling
The Wrestling Epilogue (A Question of Belief) 37, 3244

Ya De Bucketty [song from "A Fairy Tale," w/m: Jones] 235, 238
Yangtse Kiang 235
The Yangtse Song *see* We Love the Yangtse
You Be the Actor *see* Be a Great Actor
You're No Fun Anymore 47
Ypres 1914 110
Yummy, Yummy, Yummy, I've Got Love in My Tummy [pop song performed in packing crates] 108

Zeppelin *see* Barry Zeppelin; Ferdinand von Zeppelin/Corpses in Drawing Room (The Golden Age of Ballooning)

Eric Idle Solo Sketch and Song Index

References are to entry numbers in this index to Idle's solo works, the chief among them being *Rutland Weekend Television* and *All You Need Is Cash* (both in collaboration with singer-songwriter Neil Innes), and *Spamalot* and *Not the Messiah (He's a Very Naughty Boy)* (both in collaboration with composer John Du Prez).

Accountancy Shanty [song: Idle-Innes] 542, 550
The Age of Desperation [song: Innes] 532
All for One [song: Idle-Du Prez] 3113, 3144
Amnesia 425
L'Amour Perdu [song: Innes] 429, 550
Amourdeus [song: Idle-Du Prez] 3410
Analogy 2865
Angel Demonstration 544
Ann Melbourne *see* Film Night
Announcer Auditions 532
Another Day (The Rutles) [song: Innes] 632, 635
Another Lonely Man (Singing Gynecologist) [song: Innes] 542
Anti-Insurance Film 542
Arrested [song: Idle-Du Prez] 3410
Australian Love Song [song: Idle-Innes] 544
Autocue 544

Baby Let Me Be (The Rutles) [song: Innes] 632
Back-Room Boys *see* The Entire History of the World: Episode Three, The Creation
Bad Continuity 541
Banana Song [song: Idle-Du Prez] 2865
Band Wagon [song: Innes] 425
Bathtime Theatre: Splash, Kevin Tripp 421
Beauty Queen Farm 425
Between Us (The Rutles) [song: Innes] 632, 635
Bingo Brothers *see* Once We Had a Donkey

Blue Suede Schubert (The Rutles) [song: Innes] 632
Boring [song: Innes] 421, 550
Boring Competitions *see* Sportsbore
Boring Intro by Tony Bilbow 542
Brian's Dream [song: Idle-Du Prez] 3410

Camouflage Regiment 2865
Car-Swapping *see* Exposé: Car-Swapping
Carrot *see* Incident at Bromsgrove (Carrot)
Censorship 544
Chaos and Confusion! [song: Idle-Du Prez] 3410
Cheese and Onions (The Rutles) [song: Innes] 576, 632, 635
The Children of Rock and Roll *see* Good Times Roll
The Chosen One Has Woken [song: Idle-Du Prez] 3410
The Christmas Play: Santa Doesn't Live Here Anymore 471
Christmas Postscript 471
Civil War 2865
Classically Bad American Films 541
Collier Rides Again 537
Come Dancing 420
Come with Me [song: Idle-Du Prez] 3113, 3144
Communist Cooking [sketch/song: Idle-Innes] 420, 550
Comparative Religions 421
Concrete Jungle Boy [song: Innes] 471, 550
Contraception 2865
Cramp Bottom *see* The Homes of the Poets: Mungo Wright (Cramp Bottom)
Cretin Club *see* Intelligence Test (Cretin Club)

Crystal Balls [song: Innes] 537
Cure for Love 532

The David Frost Show Again 544
Dead Singer 425
Did Dinosaurs Build Stonehenge? 893
The Diva's Lament (What Happened to My Part?) [song: Idle-Du Prez] 3113, 3144
Doubleback Alley (The Rutles) [song: Innes] 632, 635
Drama on a Saturday Night [song: Innes] 543

Eccentric Judge 543
The Entire History of the World: Episode Three, the Creation 532
The Execution of Charles I 429
Exposé: Car-Swapping 534
Exposé: The Massed Flashers of Reigate 541

Fabulous Bingo Brothers *see* Once We Had a Donkey
A Fair Day's Work [song: Idle-Du Prez] 3410
FCC Song [song: Idle] 3083
Film Night 471
The Final Song [song: Idle-Du Prez] 3410
The Final Word with Tony Bilbow 421
Find Your Dream [song: Idle-Du Prez] 3410
Find Your Grail [song: Idle-Du Prez] 3113, 3144, 3151
Fisch Schlapping Song [song: Idle-Du Prez] 3113, 3144
Fishing for Compliments [song: Idle-Du Prez] 2865
Flag Seller 542

Flashbacks 541
Flipper Minnelli 2865
Football [song: Idle–Innes] 421, 550
Front Loader [song: Innes] 427, 550
Fuck Christmas [song: Idle–Du Prez] 2919
Fuck You Very Much *see* FCC Song

The Gay Animal Song [song: Idle–Du Prez] 2865, 2870
General Gucci [song: Idle–Du Prez] 2865
Get Up and Go (The Rutles) [song: Innes] 632, 635
The Getty Song [song: Idle] 2457, 2468, 3004
Gibberish 418, 550, 576
Ging Gang Goolie [song: trad., arr. by Idle and Rikki Fataar] 647
God of the British Army 421
Godfrey Daniel [song: Innes] 534
Good Times Roll (The Rutles) [song: Innes] 421, 550, 632, 635
Goodbye from Paranoia 2865
Goose-Step Mama (The Rutles) [song: Innes] 632, 635
Great Wit *see* Talk About (Great Wit)

Hail to the Shoe [song: Idle–Du Prez] 3410
Halsey & Roarke, British Customs 1338
Hanging 418
The Hard to Get [song: Innes] 541, 550
Harry [song: Idle] 803, 3234
He Is Not Dead Yet [song: Idle–Du Prez] 3113
Here Are You [song: Idle–Du Prez] 3113
Hey Rita 2865
Highwayman 543
His Name Is Lancelot [song: Idle–Du Prez] 3113, 3144
Hold My Hand (The Rutles) [song: Innes] 632, 635
Holiday 75 427
The Holy Grail [song: Idle–Du Prez] 3113
The Homes of the Poets: Mungo Wright (Cramp Bottom) 421
Homo Semi-Erectus 2865
How to Ski in Your Own Home 471
Husband and Wife 537

I Am Not Dead Yet *see* He Is Not Dead Yet
I Don't Believe in Santa Anymore [song: Innes] 471
I Don't Want to Fall in Love Again *see* Another Lonely Man
I Give Myself to You [song: Innes] 537, 550
I Like Dinosaurs [song: Idle–Du Prez] 2171
I Must Be in Love (The Rutles) [song: Innes] 515, 532, 550, 582, 632, 635, 2558

I Want to Be a Girl [song: Idle–Du Prez] 3410
If I Didn't Have You [song: Carole Bayer Sager-David Foster] 2369
Ill Health Food Store 541
I'm All Alone [song: Idle–Du Prez] 3113, 3144
I'm the Urban Spaceman [song: Innes] 427, 943
Impersonations of Medical Equipment 420
Incident at Bromsgrove (Carrot) 429
Individuals [song: Idle–Du Prez] 3410
Inflation 532
Inside James Burke *see* Tomorrows Burke
Intelligence Test (Cretin Club) 420
Intermission 2865
Isle of Wight *see* The Royal Rutland Fusiliers
It Could Always Be Worse [song: Al Kasha-Michael Lloyd] 2406
It's Hard to Make It When You're Straight [song: Idle–Innes] 544
It's Looking Good (The Rutles) [song: Innes] 632, 635

Janitors' Kids [song: Innes] 544
Johnny Cash (Live at Mrs. Fletcher's) [song: Idle–Innes] 429, 550
Joining the AA 544

Killing for God [song: Idle–Du Prez] 2865, 2919
Killing People 537
King Arthur's Song [song: Idle–Du Prez] 3113
The Kung and I 420
Kung Dancing 420
Kung Suey 420

Lance Corporal (announcer) 537
Let's Be Natural (The Rutles) [song: Innes] 632, 635
Lie Down and Be Counted [song: Innes] 420
The Life and Legend of Michael Hall (starring Tony Bilbow) 542
Life Will Get You in the End [song: Idle] 3676
Living in Hope (The Rutles) [song: Innes] 632, 635
The Lone Accountant 543
Love Life (The Rutles) [song: Innes] 632, 635
Love, Love, Love [song: Idle-Stephen Bishop] 834

Madame Butterfly Collector *see* Quite Interesting People
Madrigal [song: Idle-John Cameron] 660
The Major Who Doesn't Understand 418
Man Alive: Suburban Prisons 429

The Man from the Off-License 420
Mandy's Song [song: Idle–Du Prez] 3410
Mantra Robinson 425
The Market Square [song: Idle–Du Prez] 3410
The Massed Flashers of Reigate *see* Exposé: The Massed Flashers of Reigate
Men, Men, Men [song: Idle–Du Prez] 2558
La Mère [song: Idle–Michael Kamen] 1945
Mister Sheene [song: Idle] 647
Mrs. Fletcher's *see* Johnny Cash (Live at Mrs. Fletcher's)
Muff Diving [song: Idle–Du Prez] 2865
Mugger's Day [song: Idle–Du Prez] 2865
Mungo Wright *see* The Homes of the Poets: Mungo Wright (Cramp Bottom)

National Anthem (Rutland Isles) [song: Idle–Du Prez] 2861, 2865
Nelson and Hardy 429
Nevertheless (The Rutles) [song: Innes] 632, 635
Nixon Is Innocent 543
No Sherry/Buying People 421
Non-Voyeur 542
Normal (Arthur Sutcliffe) 420
Not the Messiah [song: Idle–Du Prez] 3410
Number One (The Rutles) [song: Innes] 632, 635

O God You Are So Big [song: Idle–Du Prez] 3410
The Old Gay Whistle Test 425
Once We Had a Donkey (Fabulous Bingo Brothers) [song: Idle–Innes] 425, 550
One Foot in the Grave [song: Idle] 1740, 2558
Origami 420
Ouch! (The Rutles) [song: Innes] 632, 635
Over-Friendly Isles 2865

Paranoid Jails 2865
Penis Fish 2865
A Penny for Your Warts 271, 425
The Peoples' Front of Judea [song: Idle–Du Prez] 3410
Philosophy Corner 420
Piggy in the Middle (The Rutles) [song: Innes] 632, 635
The Pirate Song [song: Idle-George Harrison] 471
Plain Talk *see* Gibberish
Pommy *see* Concrete Jungle Boy
Pre-Chewed Food [song: Idle–Du Prez] 2865
Prime Minister 427
Prisoner Requests Leave 537
Protest Song [song: Innes] 425, 502, 550

Queen of Rutland *see* A Right Royal Rutland Year
Quite Interesting People 534
Quiz Show (Look Out Behind You) 2865

Rain in Hendon 427
The Randi 2865
Randi Statistics 2865
The Razor Blade Four (announcers) 534
Really Nice Day [song: Idle–Du Prez] 3258
Religion Today 429
Restaurant Dress Code 537
The Return of the Pink Panzer 544
Revenge Is Sweet [song: Idle–Du Prez] 2171
The Ricochet Brothers (announcers) 541
A Right Royal Rutland Year 471
Rock Stars 2865
The Royal Rutland Fusiliers 418
Run Away [song: Idle–Du Prez] 3113, 3144
Rutland Five-O 534
Rutland Safari Park 543
Rutland Triangle 2865
Rutland Weekend Theatre 425
The Rutles (aborted doc) 532

Safari Car Park 543
Santa Doesn't Live Here Anymore *see* The Christmas Play: Santa Doesn't Live Here Anymore
Satan in Electrical Shop 427
Saucer of Rancid Milk 537
Saving Fish from Drowning 418
Say Sorry Again [song: Innes] 420, 550
Schizophrenia 421
Sex Problems 542
Sexist Sketch 543
Sheep Worrier *see* Quite Interesting People
Shopping [song: Idle–Du Prez] 2171, 2177, 2195, 2558
Showbiz Butchers *see* Yorkshire Showbiz Butchers

Singing a Song Is Easy [song: Innes] 429
The Slaves of Freedom [song: Innes] 544
The Smoke of Autumn Bonfires [song: Idle–Innes] 544
Soap Opera 544
Solihull Wife-Swapping Club 427
Someone Stole My Baby [song: Idle] 1945
The Song O' the Continuity Announcers [song: Idle] 429, 550
The Song O' the Insurance Men [song: Idle–Innes] 542, 550
The Song That Goes Like This [song: Idle–Du Prez] 3113, 3144
Special Equipment for Gentlemen 542
Spiritual [song: Idle–Du Prez] 3410
Sportsbore 544
Sprimpo 541
Star of the Sexy Movies [song: Idle–Innes] 418
Stoop Solo [song: Innes] 418, 550
Suburban Prisons *see* Man Alive: Suburban Prisons
Surfing Apes [song: Idle–Du Prez] 2865

Take Us Home [song: Idle–Du Prez] 3410
Talk About (Great Wit) 420
Television Forecast 421
Testing [song: Innes] 471, 550
That's Death [song: Idle] 2194, 2207
That's My Mum 532
There Shall Be Monsters [song: Idle–Du Prez] 3410
Tirade Against Critics 541
Toad the Wet Sprocket 425
Tobacco 532
Tomorrows Burke 537
Tonight's Drama (Lawyer and Fallguy) 532
Topless a Go-Go [song: Innes] 534
The Torturer's Apprentice [song: Idle–Michael Kamen] 1559
Trapped by the Writer 543

Trapped Under Clerics 418
Travel Agent/Insurance 542
TV Jobs for MPs 427
Twenty-Four Hours in Tunbridge Wells [song: Idle–Innes] 541, 550

Urban Spaceman *see* I'm the Urban Spaceman

Vacation in Rutland 2865

Warning Signs 421
We Love Sheep [song: Idle–Du Prez] 3410
Weather Flash (Rain in Hendon) 427
The Week Ahead on RWT (Churchill Programmes) 418
West Pole 2865
What Have the Romans Ever Done for Us? [song: Idle–Du Prez] 3410
When They Grow Up [song: Idle–Du Prez] 3410
Where Are You? [song: Idle–Du Prez] 3113, 3144
Whoops, Look Out Behind You [song: Idle–Du Prez] 2865
Wife-Swapping Club *see* Solihull Wife-Swapping Club
Wife Swapping Party [song: Idle–Innes] 543
William Plastic-Bidet and the Postman 544
With a Girl Like You (The Rutles) [song: Innes] 632, 635
Woe Woe Woe! [song: Idle–Du Prez] 3410
Worrying Sheep *see* Quite Interesting People

Yorkshire Showbiz Butchers 425
You Won't Succeed on Broadway [song: Idle–Du Prez] 3113, 3144
Your Questions Answered 427
You're the One [song: Idle–Du Prez] 3410
Yuri Geller Bending *see* Tomorrows Burke

General Index

References are to entry numbers.

A&E Premieres (TV) 1744
A Plus (TV) 1000, 1081
AA Home Emergency Response (Faulty Showers) (ad) 3869
Aaron, Hank 921
Abad, Javier 3760
Abbado, Roberto 4063
Abbott, David 2114
Abbott, Stan 1804
Abbott, Steve 1493, 1495, 1818
The ABC Afterschool Special (TV): "William" 248
ABC News Now (TV) 3705
Abineri, Daniel 909
Abrahams, Darren 3926
Abrahams, Stephen 3395
Abrams, Aron 2664
Absolutely Anything (film) 3860, 4065
Abuzeid, Huda 2773
The Abyss (film) 1755
The Academy Awards (ceremony) 1282, 1628, 1755, 3803
Accurist (ads) 665
The Ace Awards (ceremony) 1807
Ackerman, David 2722
Ackland, Joss 596, 1675, 1724
Adam Hills in Gordon St. Tonight (TV) 4089
Adams, Bryan 2813
Adams, Douglas 374, 433, 481, 562, 661, 810, 1307, 1695, 2316, 2318, 2319, 2352, 2357, 2472, 2541, 2665, 2684, 3136, 3366, 3690, 3719, 4087, 4128
Adams, Phillip 3458, 3472
Adams, Tony 1340
Adams, Trevor 446
Adamson, Andrew 2997
Addams, Dawn 252
Addotta, Kip 1430
Adie, Kate 2786
Adler, Marc F. 3597
Adults Learning (magazine) 3917
The Adventures of Baron Munchausen (book) 1600
The Adventures of Baron Munchausen (film) 697, 1346, 1378, 1419, 1431, 1446, 1521, 1559, 1597, 1601–07, 1610–17, 1620–24, 1629–31, 1646, 1659, 1755, 1850, 1856, 1952, 2550, 3498, 3499, 3659, 3839
The Adventures of Baron Munchausen: The Criterion Collection (laserdisc) 1901
The Adventures of Baron Munchausen: The Screenplay (book) 1598
The Adventures of Baron Munchausen: 20th Anniversary Edition (DVD/Blu-ray) 3498
The Adventures of Pluto Nash (film) 2772
Advertising Age (magazine) 1127
Affleck, Ben 2983, 3236
AFI Life Achievement Award [38th] (ceremony) 3838
AFI Life Achievement Award: A Tribute to Mike Nichols (TV) 3844
AFI Star Award Tribute to Robin Williams (stage) 2550
An Afternoon with John Cleese (event) 2670, 3925
Afternoons with Gillian O'Shaughnessy (radio) 4067
Agassi, Andre 2462
Agnew, David 729
Agutter, Jenny 886
Aherne, Caroline 2385
Ahrens, Lynn 2449, 2621
Aiken, Bill 1536
Aitken, Maria 481, 725, 1123, 1281, 1495, 1733, 3294
Ajaye, Franklyn 1430
Akinwolere, Andy 3912
Aladdin (panto) 56, 112
Aladdin (radio) 2535
Aladdin and the Wonderful Lamp (audiobook) 1162
Alan Moore: Portrait of an Extraordinary Gentleman (book) 2890
An Alan Smithee Film: Burn Hollywood Burn (film) 2295, 2334
The Alan Titchmarsh Show (TV) 3578, 3767, 4167
Alberto Y Lost Trios 572
The Album of the Soundtrack of the Trailer of the Film of Monty Python and the Holy Grail (record) 399, 422, 613, 2238, 3321
Alda, Alan 2856
Alderson, Brian 874
Alderton, John 666
Alex Belfield (radio) 3908
Alexander, Danny 3927
Alexander, Denyse 685
Alexander, Jane 980
Alexander, Jason 2313
Alexander, John 3550
Alexander, Michael 1518, 1645
Alexander, Sam 3985
Alexander, Terence 383, 960
Alexandra, Charlotte 549
Alfie (film) 3055
Alice in Wonderland (book) 3186
Alighieri, Dante 2237
The Alimony Tour (DVD) see *John Cleese Live: The Alimony Tour 2011*
The Alimony Tour (stage) 3811, 3815, 3906, 3935, 3940, 3941, 4010, 4062
The Alimony Tour [South Africa, 2011] (stage) 4010
The Alimony Tour [U.K., 2011] (stage) 3906, 3940, 3941
The Alimony Tour [U.S.] see *A Final Wave at the World: The Alimony Tour, Part One*
All Change (The Management of Change), Part 1: Change for the Better (film) 1567
All Change (The Management of Change), Part 2: The Shape of Things to Come (film) 1568
All Things Considered (radio) 3545, 3777
All You Need Is Cash (TV) 351, 582, 591, 632, 635, 636, 2133, 2643, 2644, 2647, 2906, 3105, 3495, 3583–85
Allen, Dave 2091, 2244
Allen, Steve 734, 777
Alliss, Peter 558
Alpert, Hollis 397
Altiere, Daniel 4017
Altiere, Steven 4017

Altman, Robert 1952
Alvarado, Trini 1818
Alverson, Charles 567, 624, 743, 860
Always Look on the Bright Side of Life (record/CD) 1846
Always Look on the Bright Side of Life/Brian (record) 722
A.M. America (TV) 407
Amanda's (TV) 1004, 2436
Amateau, Rod 113
The Amber Spyglass (book) 2720
America (magazine) 356
American Cinematographer (magazine) 2363
The American Comedy Awards (ceremony) 1477, 2231, 2333
American Express (ads) 997, 1802
American Film (magazine) 1602
American Friends (film) 602, 1346, 1474, 1548, 1769, 1812, 1814, 1817–19, 1821, 1822, 1942–44, 1948–50
American Masters (TV): "Jeff Bridges: The Dude Abides" 3907
An American Tail: Fievel Goes West (film) 1859
Ames, Katrine 1025
Amory, Cleveland 356
Ancient Inventions (TV) 2397, 2398; "City Life" 2399; "Sex and Love" 2400; "War and Conflict" 2401
And God Blew (TV) 1880
And Now for Something Completely Different (film) 57, 94, 95, 161, 209, 397, 2830, 3427, 3588
And Now for Something Completely Different: The Films of Terry Gilliam (screenings) 2412
Anderson, Bill 787
Anderson, Bob 4102
Anderson, Clive 661, 2060, 2091, 2535, 2684, 3695, 4044, 4087
Anderson, Donnie 3479
Anderson, Gillian 3479
Anderson, Harry 1035
Anderson, Marie 236
Anderson, Mike B. 3076
Anderson, Stanley 1023
Anderson, Stephen 3969
Andress, Ursula 2837
The Andrew Marr Show (TV) 3507, 3575, 3927
Andrews, Anthony 2404
Andrews, Eamon 266
Andrews, Julie [Dame] 2997, 3022, 3405, 3823
Angas, Richard 1304, 1442
Angel, Nick 3308
Angell, David 1363
The Angry Beavers (TV): "Open Wide for Zombies/Dumbwaiters" 2417
Animal Crackers (film) 1149
Animal Farm (book) 1149
The Animal Magic Zoo (TV) 3968
Animal Tales (book) 3914, 3926, 3932, 3960, 3973
Animation at Cambridge (TV) 1229
Animation Nation (TV): "Something to Say" 3138

Animations of Mortality (book) 652
Anna and the Moods (film) 3385
Annecy Film Festival 176
"Annie's Song" (song) 799
Another Monty Python Record (record) 143, 162, 199, 209, 210, 245, 277, 556, 613, 3318, 3588
Ansen, David 710, 863, 943, 970, 1149, 1850
Ansorge, Peter 3291
Anstead, Mark 3154
Ant & Dec 3022
The Anti-Heroin Project: It's a Live-In World (record) 1324
The Anti-Renaissance Show (radio) 2735, 2736
Antonsen, Atle 3988
Antrobus, John 127
Anwar, Mina 2630, 2631
A. P. Herbert's Misleading Cases (TV): "Regina Versus Sagittarius" 159
Appel, Stanley 1853
Apple and Appleberry 288
Applebaum, Stephen 2757
Appleby, James 441
Appleyard, Bryan 1438, 3242
Apted, Michael 2516, 3202, 3388
Aquarian (magazine) 946
Aquarius (TV) 139, 169
Arau, Alfonso 160
Arcade Fire 3854
Arch, Jeff 3094
Archard, Bernard 765
Archer, Jeffrey 1349
Archer, John 816
The Archive Hour (radio) 3166; "Children's Hour" 2656
Are You Taking the Tablets? (TV) 1202
Arena (magazine) 1824
Arena (TV) 609; "Jonathan Miller" 4091; "Magical Mystery Tour Revisited" 4157; "Philip K. Dick: A Day in the Afterlife" 2005; "Produced by George Martin" 3934; "Remember the Secret Policeman's Ball?" 3075, 3609, 3669
Argent, Douglas 255, 326, 676, 677, 679, 680, 685, 732
The Aristocrats (film) 3084
Arlott, John 879
Armatrading, Joan 1365
Armitstead, Claire 3718
Armstrong, Alun 1548
Armstrong, Bridget 340, 425, 607
Armstrong, Curtis 4017
Armstrong, Peter 1916
Arnheiter, Carl 3790
Arnold, Gary 891
Arnold, Robert 685
Arnold, Sydney 1026
Arnold, Tom 4017
Around India in 25 Years (lecture) 3798
Around the World in 20 Years (lecture) 3826, 3867
Around the World in 20 Years (TV) 1700, 3562, 3591, 3602
Around the World in 80 Days (book) 1683, 3591, 3666, 3843

Around the World in 80 Days (cartoon) 2447
Around the World in 80 Days (film) 2999
Around the World in 80 Days [1989] (TV series) 820, 1413, 1534, 1553, 1560, 1683, 1692, 1694–96, 1699, 1700, 1708, 1710, 1711, 1715, 1716, 1718, 1721, 1722, 1728, 1729, 1742–45, 1842, 1897, 2272, 2783, 3202, 3562
Around the World in 80 Days (TV miniseries) 1637, 1638, 1641, 1642
Around the World in 80 Days [2009] (TV series) 3724
Around the World in 80 Days: Special 20th Anniversary Edition (book) 3562, 3591, 3594, 3598, 3599
Around the World in 80 Ways (lecture) 3580, 3764
Arquette, David 3880
Arquette, Rosanna 1209, 1490
Arrowsmith, Clive 1056, 1115
The Arsenio Hall Show (TV) 1750
The Art Directors Guild Awards (ceremony) 3387
The Art Instinct (event) 3740
The Art of Football (TV) 3296
The Art of Soccer see *The Art of Football*
The Art of Travel (TV) 1714
Arthur, Bea 1004, 2436
Arthur, Toni 1242
Arthur Christmas (film) 4018
Artists and Legends Gala 2006 (event) 3254
Arts Forum (radio) 414
Arts Review of the Year (TV) 1099
As Good as It Gets (film) 2582
Asante, Christopher 1563
Asbury, Kelly 2997
Aschner, Michael 2406
Ash, Brian 77
Ash, Cliff 821
Ash, John 3149
Ashby, Alan 3915
Ashby, Hal 1455
Ashdown, Paddy 2243
Asher, Jane 1449, 2754
Asher, Peter 3981
The Ashes Retained (book) 706
Ashley, Lyn 20, 421, 427, 471, 479, 2025
Ask Aspel (TV) 119, 707
Askey, Arthur 140
Askey, David 23, 122, 125, 206, 207
Askwith, Mark 3336, 3346
Asner, Edward 2942
Aspel, Michael 119, 303, 325, 371, 707, 1114, 1280, 1456, 1533, 1541, 1759, 1766, 1819, 1938, 2721, 2976
Aspel and Company (TV) 371, 1280, 1533, 1541, 1759, 1766, 1819, 1938
Aspinall, Sarah 2331
Assert Yourself (TV) 1433
Astérix & Obélix Contre César (film) 2557
Astérix & Obélix Take on Caesar (film) 2557

Aston, Julian 1433
At Last the 1948 Show (TV) 8, 63, 777, 978, 1587, 2940, 2944, 3165
Atkin, Pete 622
Atkins, Chet 1365, 1409
Atkins, Martyn 4154
Atkinson, Rowan 204, 704, 737, 755, 759, 764, 804, 818, 871, 883, 930, 931, 990, 1286, 1675, 1724, 2686, 3075, 3579
Atkinson, Tom 2244, 2329, 2627, 2733
Attacks of Opinion (book) 1371, 1552, 1575
Attenborough, David [Sir] 1260, 2536, 2593, 2642, 2648, 2651, 2817, 2824, 2976, 3093, 3202, 3408, 4041
Attenborough, Richard [Lord] 50, 2754, 2828, 3488
Attwell, Michael 775
Auberjonois, Rene 957
An Audience with John Cleese (event) 3009, 3450
An Audience with Peter Ustinov (TV) 1447
Audio (magazine) 422
Audioweb 2222
August, John 2901
Aukin, David 3735
Aunbu, Knut 769
Auntie's All-Time Greats (TV) 2196
Auntie's TV Favourites: BBC Brings You the World (TV) 2191
Auteuil, Daniel 3295
Avedon, Richard 408, 432
Average Chap see *How to Lie with Statistics, Part 2: The Average Chap*
Avon, Roger 600
Away from It All (film) 740
An Awfully Big Adventure (TV): "Kenneth Grahame" 2331
Awkward Customers see *Customer Relations in Practice, No. 3: Awkward Customers*
Ayer, Alfred J. [Sir] 855
Aykroyd, Dan 515, 561, 563, 576, 635, 640, 660, 671, 695, 893, 1238, 1752, 3792
Ayres, Pam 4208
The A-Z of TV (TV) 1738
Azaria, Hank 2875, 3076, 3113, 3140, 3388, 3588, 4102
Azis 3438

Baby It's You! (musical) 3757
Bacal, Joe 1303
The Back Page see *Behind the Crease*
Backstage from the Millennium (TV) 2544
Bacon, Kevin 1673
Baddiel, David 2385, 2787, 2839, 3332
Badel, Sarah 813, 830
Badland, Annette 567
Baerg, Theodore 3410, 3417, 3543, 3550
The BAFTA Craft Awards [1985] (TV) 1273

The BAFTA Craft Awards 2002 (ceremony) 2894
BAFTA/Los Angeles Britannia Awards (ceremony) 2473
Bagust, Petra 4177
Bailey, Alan 235, 3771
Bailey, Bill 3579
Bailey, Joseph A. 590
Bailey, Lucy 2096
Bailey, Patrick 725
Bailey, Robin 560
Bailey, Rosalind 239
Baker, Joe 777
Baker, Kenny 863
Baker, Matt 2636, 3850, 3852, 3932, 4026, 4109
Baker, Richard 225, 232, 661
Baker, Tom 729, 3127
Bakewell, Joan 61, 975, 1040, 1215, 1374, 1382, 2922, 3355
The Balance Sheet Barrier [1977] (film) 619, 663, 683
The Balance Sheet Barrier [1993] (film) 1985
Balcon, Michael 1627
Ball, Michael 1860
Ball, Ralph 548, 621
Ball, Zoe 2178, 2223, 3206
Ballantyne, David 60, 83, 130
Balls, Ed 3800
Bamborough, Paul 828
Banas, Michala 4061
Bancroft, Anne 3597
Banderas, Antonio 2997, 3405, 3823
Banks, Iona 1475
Banzai! (TV) 2755
Barandes, Natalie 2566
Barbarians (lecture) 3264, 3268, 3288, 3306, 3314, 3344, 3662
Barbarians (TV) see *Terry Jones' Barbarians*
Barber, Glynis 1191
Barber, John 704
Barbour, Hamish 1730, 1843
Barclay, Bill 292
Barclay, Humphrey 1, 10, 23, 188, 283, 562, 596, 804, 928, 990, 3587, 3608, 4104
Barclay, Ursula 152
Barker, Ronnie 14, 120, 126, 127, 129, 136, 138, 141, 183, 204, 214, 240, 285, 291, 304, 452, 514, 517, 1260, 2211, 2459, 2626, 2627, 2966, 3246, 3496
Barkin, Ellen 2376, 3114
Barkworth, Peter 1273
Barlow, Dilly 1771
Barlow, Gary 2296
Barlow, Patrick 1665
Barnes, Clive 494
Barnes, Michael 890, 1998, 3878
Barnett, Angus 2714
Barnett, Jeni 1884
Baron Munchausen (film) see *The Adventures of Baron Munchausen*
Barr, Adam 2977
Barraclough, Roy 313, 519
Barratt, Julian 3771

Barrell, Tony 2913
Barrett, Jenny 1806
Barrett, John 600
Barrie, David 1063
Barron, Dana 2942
Barron, John 308, 384, 928
Barron, Keith 305
Barrowman, John 2001
Barry, Gerard 2615
Barry, Hilda 280
Barrymore, Drew 2901
Barrymore, Michael 1318
Bart, Lionel 2069
Barua, Maan 3795
Baskin, John 1635, 1636, 1640
Bass, Alfie 165
Bass, Ronald 1628
Bassett, Kate 2015
Bassey, Shirley [Dame] 2754
Bassi, Leo 2252
Batalla, Rick 2436
Bate, Jonathan 2927
Bateman, Peter 1648
Bates, Alan 2813
Bates, Brian [Prof.] 2640, 2823
Bates, Kathy 3596
Bates, Michael 120
Bathany, Jean-Paul 3610
Bathurst, Robert 3587
Batman (film) 1755
Batscha, Robert M. 1584
Batteries Not Included (TV) 3568
The Battle of Brazil (book) 1395
Battley, David 340, 418, 420, 421, 425, 427, 429, 471, 532, 534, 537, 541–44
Bayler, Terence 429, 532, 537, 543, 544, 635, 710, 915
Bayliss, Peter 305, 454
Baynham, Peter 4018
BBC Breakfast (TV) 2926, 2969, 3028, 3213, 3341, 3468, 3612, 3755, 3868, 3942, 4014, 4032, 4035, 4040, 4065
BBC Breakfast News (TV) 2470
BBC London News (TV) 2896
BBC Look East (TV) 1140
BBC Symphony Orchestra 3745
BBC Television Shakespeare (TV): "The Taming of the Shrew" 789, 812, 813, 1861; see also *The Shakespeare Plays*
The BBC2 Film Competition (TV) 1033
The Beach Boys 198
Beadle, Jeremy 1100
The Beatles 531, 753, 1061, 2614, 3531, 3585, 4152, 4157
The Beatles: Across the Universe (radio) 2793
The Beatles Revolution (TV) 2614
Beauman, Sally 161
Beautiful Britain (magazine) 3553
Beauty and the Beast (panto) 56, 112
Beck 2214
Beck, Jeff 411, 871, 931, 1665
Beckett, Linda 120
Beckham, David 3471
Beckinsale, Richard 200

Beckwith, Tamara 2176
Bednar, Rudy 2614
The Bee Gees 288
Beeching, Angela 1135, 1275, 1454
"Beekeeping" (sketch) 871, 883, 907, 931
Beeman, Greg 1883
Beethoven's Christmas Adventure (film) 4017
Beetles, Chris 704, 755, 1983, 3876, 4000
Beevor, Anthony 3275
Before the Flying Circus: A Black and White Documentary (documentary) 3586, 3587, 3749
Begel, Cindy 834
Begley, Ed Jr. 2742
Behar, Joy 1437, 2860
Behind the Crease (radio) 1761, 1776
Behind the Headlines (TV) 1745
Being Ronnie Corbett (TV) 3898
Belbin, Susan 1866
Bell, Alan J. W. 724–26, 1982
Bell, Ann 113
Bell, Mark 2814
Bell, Martin L. 376
Bell, Steve 3085
Bell, Steven A. 2337
Bellamy, David 2789
Bellini, James 903
Bellucci, Monica 3178
Belushi, Jim (James) 1110, 2834
Belushi, John 515, 563, 576, 580, 635, 640, 660, 671, 695, 779, 893
Belzer, Richard 1183, 1823, 2860
Benben, Brian 2044
Benchley, Peter 376
Benigni, Roberto 2834
Benjamin Huntsman (film) 1877
Benmergui, Ralph 2758
Bennett, Alan 492, 539, 545, 871, 877, 883, 931, 1102, 1134, 1149, 1172, 1263, 1726, 2091, 2118, 2204, 2331, 3148
Bennett, Colin 726
Bennett, Hywel 243
Bennett, Lennie 325, 1242
Benny, Jack 1619
Benson, Elizabeth 453, 680
Bentine, Michael 140, 200, 809, 1964, 2147, 2250, 2682
Benullo, David 2999
Benz, Julie 2436, 2925
Berendsen, Daniel 2790
Berg, Natascha Illum 3811
Bergen, Candice 580, 2650, 3114
Bergeron, Aaron 3880
Bergh, Johnny 769
Berglas, David 1247
Bergman, Andrew 2547
Bergman, Brian 2761
Bergman, Mary Kay 2456
Bergmayr, Lisa 456
Berkeley, Ballard 439–41, 446, 450, 453, 456, 676, 677, 679, 680, 685, 732
Berkoff, Steven 3384
Berlin International Film Festival 587, 2129, 2722, 2729

Berlioz, Hector 3943
Berlyne, John 726
Berry, Al 1640
Berry, Chuck 288
Berry, Halle 2819, 2837
Berry, John 4100
Bert Fegg's Nasty Book for Boys & Girls (book) 354, 438, 490, 606, 1138
Bertinelli, Valerie 745
Bertrand, Guy 1026
Besch, Drea 716
The Best House in London (film) 19
Best of British (TV): "Ronnie Corbett" 2626
The Best of Rutland Weekend Television (TV) 1981
The Best of Southwold (book) 2375
Best Sellers: The Life and Times of Peter Sellers (radio) 2682
Bestall, Alfred 861, 982
Betjeman, John [Sir] 144, 1445
Better Than Ezra 3152
Bevan, Nathan 3919
Bevan, Tim 1370
Beverly Hills Cop (film) 1150
Beyond a Joke (TV): "A Class Apart" 3647
Beyond the Fringe 492, 539, 554, 1491, 2066, 3732
Beyond the Fringe (stage) 494, 1097
The BFG (Big Friendly Giant) (book) 2947
Bhaskar, Sanjeev 3735, 3745, 3770, 4066
Bhoy, Danny 3746
Bianculli, David 3778
Bickford-Smith, Imogen 677
Bicknell, Andrew 1026
Biel, Jessica 3760
The Big Breakfast (TV) 1989, 2012, 2149, 2469
The Big Byte (radio) 2040
Big City (TV) 1979
The Big Match (TV) 616
Big Mouth Billy see *Managing Problem People: Big Mouth Billy*
The Big Picture (film) 1673
The Big Picture (TV) 1491, 1649, 1749
The Big Read (TV) 2885
The Big Schmooze (TV) 2696
Big Screen (TV) 2414
The Big Show (TV) 776, 777
The Big Year (film) 4004
Biggins, Christopher 1144
Biggins, Jonathan 4187
Biggles see *Story Time*
"Biggles Goes to See Bruce Springsteen" (Palin sketch) 1286, 1665, 3217
Bilbow, Tony 61, 377, 421, 542, 1719
Billen, Stephanie 2146
Billinger, Steve 1916
Billington, Kevin 18, 99, 1876
Billington, Michael 702
Billington, Rachel 1876
Billson, Anne 1613
Billy Connolly: A BAFTA Tribute (TV) 2836

Binder, Mike 3236
Binder, Steve 777
Biography Magazine (magazine) 2530
Biolek, Alfred 149, 180, 3944
Bird, John 258, 261, 492, 539, 567, 826, 827, 871, 1156, 1250, 2773
Bird, Norman 252, 381, 476, 477, 679
Birdsall, Derek 166, 592
The Birmingham Post (newspaper) 2501, 2975, 3011
The Birth of "Brazil" (TV) 1460
The Birthday Show: 21 Years of Variety from Thames Television (TV) 1661
Bishop, Ed 928
Bishop, Joey 278, 279
Bishop, Stephen 834
Bisset, Jacqueline 1679
Bitter Jester (film) 2860
Björk 3385
Black, Cilla 8, 1225, 1816
Black, Clint 2462, 2481, 2531, 2906, 3004, 3956
Black, Jack 4004
Black, Lewis 3084, 3682
Black, Peter 289
Black and Blue (TV) 228: "Secrets" 228, 280
Black Cinderella Two Goes East (radio) 661
Blacker, Terence 1403
Blackhall, Sue 2486
Blackmail (film) 4122
Blair, Iain 1504
Blair, Les 1924
Blair, Tony [Prime Minister] 2293, 2707, 2864
Blais, Peter 1198
Blake, Darrol 340
Blake, Richard A. 356
Blakemore, Michael 991, 1018
Blanco, Jorge 3760
Blazing Dragons (TV) 2157
Blazing Dragons (video game) 2172
Bleakley, Christine 3439, 3532, 3598, 3717, 4030
Bleasdale, Alan 1833–37, 1839, 1841, 1844, 3291
Blessed, Brian 2593
Blezard, William 522
The Bliss of Mrs. Blossom (film) 19
Bloomstein, Rex 1913
Blount, David 1940
Blowen, Michael 967, 972
Blue Peter (TV) 2186, 2299, 2636
Blythe, Ronald 864
Boa, Bruce 679
Bobker, Daniel 3178
Boerger, Dave 2664
Bogdanovich, Peter 2611
Boisseau, David 216
Bolam, James 1103, 1104, 1200, 1248, 1249
Bolt, Neville 1409
Bond, Christopher 159
Bond, Matthew 2272
Bond, Philip 306–08, 380
Bond, Samantha 1677, 3193, 3767

Bonham Carter, Helena 2054, 4199
Bonington, Chris [Sir] 4041
Bonneville, Hugh 2322, 2323
The Bonnie Hunt Show (TV) 3614
Bono 1882
The Bonzo Dog Doo-Dah Band 10, 417, 3531, 3585
Book at Bedtime (radio): "Hemingway's Chair" 2101; "The Truth" 4115
The Book Café (radio) 4124
Book of the Week (radio): "Diaries 1969–1979: The Python Years" 3340; "Halfway to Hollywood: Diaries 1980–1988" 3691
Book Plug (radio) 1203
The Book Programme (TV) 376
The Book Show (TV) 3960
Books and Arts Daily (radio) 4117
Bookshelf (radio) 1793
The Bookworm (TV) 2268
Boone, Debby 776
Booth, Connie 52, 59, 96, 220, 238, 306, 307, 309, 312, 345, 355, 370, 379, 386, 397, 439–41, 446, 450, 453, 456, 487, 551, 565, 579, 594, 596, 608, 622, 626, 648, 675–77, 679, 680, 685, 732, 768, 833, 1111, 1570, 1818, 1821, 1917, 3648, 3654, 3738, 4134
Booth, James 200
The Bore of the Year Awards (TV) 1937
Boretski, Peter 1198
Borge, Victor 777
"Boring" (poem) 2425
Born to Be Wild: Operation Lemur with John Cleese (TV) 2390, 2756, 3228
Bosanquet, Simon 1751, 1945
Boston, Richard 589, 628
The Boston Globe (newspaper) 967, 972, 1953
The Boston Globe: Calendar (newspaper) 1508
Boston Phoenix (newspaper) 1323
Boswell, Ruth 340
Botham, Ian 1366
Botterill, Willie 2694
Botto, Juan Diego 4144
Bottoms, Benjamin 2657
Bottone, Bonaventura 1304, 1352, 1442, 1549
Bough, Frank 857, 876, 1137, 1221, 1237, 1816
Bourne, Matthew 4040
Bourne, Mel 1850
Bowen-Jones, Rosemary 852
Bowie, David 906, 1044, 1198, 1301, 1345, 1882, 2467, 2906
Bowker, Phil 2840, 2841
Bowler, Norman 383
Bowles, Brian 1776
The Bowles Brothers 579, 594, 622
Bowman, Edith 4101
Bowman, Willy 456
Box, Betty 68, 243
The Box (film) 508, 905
Boy George 1280, 1357, 2419
Boy in Darkness (TV) 2549

The Boy Who Would Be King (TV) 2934
Boyd, Charles 2589
Boyd, Darren 4008
Boyle, Peter 1049, 1059
Braden, Bernard 187
Braden's Week (TV) 187
Bradley, Bill 676
Bradley, Des 2201
Bradshaw, Paul 2948–50
Bradshaw, Peter 3178, 4064
Brady, Pam 2456
Brady, Wayne 2637
Bragg, Melvyn 533, 611, 1099, 1259, 1340, 1535, 1614, 1851, 1887, 1896, 1914, 1930, 2039, 2087, 2514, 3191, 3352, 3395, 3408, 3564, 3639, 4100
The Brain of Gilliam (event) 1193
Brainard, David 2722
Braithwaite's Battle with the Banks (film) 909
Brambilla, Marco 2750
Brambles, Jackie 3555
Branagh, Kenneth 1227, 1899, 1954, 2054, 2810, 2876
Branche, Derrick 1150
Branchline Railway (video) 1445
Brand, Charles 1574, 1720
The Brand New Monty Python Bok (book) 294, 297, 299, 353, 875
The Brand New Monty Python Papperbok (book) 294, 353
Brand X 783
Brand X (TV) 4176
Brandon, Michael 1225
Brandreth, Gyles 4079, 4208
Brantley, Ben 3113
Brasher, Chris 922
Bratby, John 832
Brave New World (book) 1177
Brazil (book) 4142, 4143, 4159, 4173–75, 4178
Brazil (film) 473, 508, 743, 925, 1086, 1139, 1167, 1170, 1171, 1175–78, 1185, 1190, 1191, 1208, 1213, 1218, 1226, 1228, 1235, 1241, 1244, 1246, 1251, 1257, 1263, 1268, 1269, 1277, 1281, 1282, 1284, 1322, 1323, 1378, 1395, 1460, 1542, 1573, 1603, 2054, 2119, 2120, 2127, 2376, 2477, 2540, 2710, 3337, 3419, 3619, 3693, 3839, 3861, 4032, 4039, 4206
Brazil (lecture) 4156, 4158
Brazil: The Criterion Collection (laserdisc/Blu-ray) 2174, 4206
Brazil with Michael Palin (DVD/Blu-ray) 4200
Brazil with Michael Palin (TV) 3958, 3990, 4048, 4076, 4092, 4160, 4163, 4166–69, 4171, 4173–75, 4177, 4178, 4180, 4182, 4186, 4188, 4190, 4192, 4195, 4199–4201, 4205
Break Free! (web videos) 3939
Breakfast (radio) 2470
Breakfast (TV) 4177
Breakfast Time (TV) 1015, 1067, 1137, 1155, 1176, 1221, 1237, 1240, 1310, 1321, 1350, 1359, 1373, 1544, 1586, 1623

Brearley, Mike 704, 706, 755
Breck, Julia 221
Breckman, Andy 2686
Breen, Philip 19
Breeze, Jean Binta 3064
Bremner, Billy 166, 550
Bremner, Rory 1665, 2254, 3639
Brennan, Lee 844
Brennan, Mark 1379
Brenner, David 808, 851, 1334, 1364, 1380
Brenton, Nick 853–55, 858, 861, 862, 864
Bresslaw, Bernard 567
Brett, Laurie 3277
Brett, Peter 363, 374, 450, 710
Breuer, Jim 2214
Brewster, Jordana 2673
Bricusse, Leslie 1788
Bridges, Jeff 1849, 1850, 1855, 2728, 3186, 3619, 3907
Brief Encounter (film) 1041
Brien, Alan 567, 651, 931
Brierley, Roger 481, 731
Briers, Richard 200, 3246
Briggs, Raymond 1886
Brightness (film) 2633
Brigstocke, Dominic 2791
Brigstocke, Marcus 3824, 3827, 4045, 4131
Brill, Clive 3566
Brimstone and Treacle (film) 955
Brindley, David 4009
Briscoe, Alexandra 3601, 4179
Bristol Evening Post (newspaper) 3787
Britain's Best Sitcom (TV): "Fawlty Towers" 2958
The British Academy [Film] *Awards* (ceremony) 780, 1114, 1187, 1456, 1627, 2248, 2443, 3619, 3796
The British Academy Television Awards (ceremony) 3132
The British Book Awards (ceremony) 1927, 2859, 3135, 3638
The British Comedy Awards (ceremony) 2831
British Film Forever (TV): "Magic, Murder and Monsters" 3419; "Sauce, Satire and Silliness" 3429
The British Independent Film Awards (ceremony) 2805, 3895, 4207
British Is Best (film) 625
The British Screen Awards (ceremony) 259
Brits Go to Hollywood (TV): "Sean Connery" 2936
Britton, Fern 1137, 3620
Broadbent, Jim 1177, 1665, 4018
Broadbent, Robert 1776
The Broadcasting Press Guild Awards (ceremony) 637
Brochand, Bernard 3296
Brokaw, Tom 2581
Bron, Eleanor 296, 492, 539, 704, 729, 755, 990, 1665, 2329

Bronski Beat 1276
Brook, Peter 2082
Brook, Tom 1855, 3316
Brooke-Taylor, Tim 2, 8, 13, 62, 63, 295, 302, 306, 307, 457, 487, 492, 522, 539, 565, 661, 664, 871, 929–31, 990, 1062, 1131, 1726, 1731, 2024, 2589, 2940, 3000, 3496
Brooks, Jeremy 392
Brooks, Mel 2658
Broome, Kate 3292
Brosnan, Pierce 1638, 1641, 1642, 2369, 2516, 2634, 2650, 2651, 2819, 2837, 2930, 3059, 3329
The Brothers Grimm (DVD) 3226
The Brothers Grimm (film) 2862, 2902, 3169, 3171, 3176, 3178, 3179, 3184, 3186, 3189, 3206–09, 3212–14, 3216, 3219, 3226, 3482, 4165
Browlee, Bruce 614
Brown, Adrian 1576
Brown, Allan 1682
Brown, Bill 3233
Brown, Bille 3218
Brown, Blair 1807
Brown, Dan 3135
Brown, Geoff 1818, 1945, 2221, 2376
Brown, Gordon [Prime Minister] 3575
Brown, James 2533
Brown, Jenny 4136
Brown, Mick 4110
Brown, Peter 2803
Brown, Richard 2047
Brown, Shelby [Dr.] 2565
Brown, Tim 3915
Browne, Jackson 1365, 3567, 3820, 3981
Browning, Robert 1198
Brownstone 2106
Bruce, Christopher 2936, 4095
Bruegel the Elder, Pieter 3847
Brunel, Isambard 3278
Brunel, Marc 3278
The Brunels' Tunnel (book) 3278
Brunning, Lorraine 2714
Brunson, Michael 3974
Brush with Fame (TV): "John Cleese" 3611, 3992
Bryant, Adam 2430
Brynner, Yul 50
Bryson, Ann 1852, 2321
Bryson, Bill 1561, 3557
Bublé, Michael 4199
Buchanan's Finest Hour (play) 508, 905
Buchner, Pamela 680
Buckley, Bryan 3183
Buckley, Keith 548
Buckley, Kristen 2619
Buckman, Robert [Dr.] 661, 704, 755, 1153, 1343, 1983, 2257, 4000, 4002, 4054, 4055
Bucks Fizz 894, 1136
Buddy Holly: Listen to Me—The Ultimate Buddy Party (TV) 4034
Budgeting (film) 1156
Bugler, Jeremy 1963

Bulcock, Philip 4140
Bullock, Susan 1304, 1352
Bullseye! (film) 1788, 2448
Bundock, Carol 3973
Buñuel, Luis 1079
Bunyan, Jay 3218
Burditt, Jack 2136
Burgess, Anthony 1612, 1896
Burgon, Geoffrey 3371, 3866, 3972
Burke, Kathy 2532, 2791
Burnett, Carol 3466
Burnett, Hugh 385, 766, 986
Burnett, Paul 585
Burningham, John 3032
Burns, George 1618
Burns, Gordon 3906
Burr, Ty 2158
Burrow, J. A. 770
Burrowes, John 749
Burrows, Clive 271, 322
Burrows, Colin 1617, 1821
Burrows, James 1363, 2932, 2953, 2977, 2981, 2989
Burstyn, Ellen 841
Burton, Humphrey 139, 169
Buscemi, Steve 2688, 3180, 3368, 3560
Busey, Gary 2376
Bush 2144
Bush, George H. W. [President] 1650
Bush, George W. [President] 2868, 3085, 3359, 3373
Bush, John 1972, 2353, 2684
Bush, Kate 660, 1286, 1365, 1409, 2754
The Business of Commercials (seminar) 2912
Business This Morning (TV) 1450
Busse, Jochen 2679
Bustin, Penny 1310
Butterfield, Ardis 4108
Butterworth, Tyler 1461
Buzz Lightyear of Star Command (TV): "War and Peace and War" 2620
Bygraves, Max 1113
Byrne, Bridget 1632
Byrne, Gabriel 2369
Byrne, Jennifer 2311, 4196
Byrne, John 3060
Byrne, Patsy 2322
Byrnes, Sholto 3089
Bywater, Michael 1914

Cable, Michael 2546
Caddy, Ian 1712
Cadell, Francis Campbell Boileau 2606
Cadell, Simon 1567, 1568
Cady, Gary 1677
Caesar, Burt 1798
Caesar, Irving 921
Caesar, Sid 642
Caine, Michael 1465, 1574, 1788, 2425, 2480
Cairney, Phil 3303
Calabrese, Russell 2332
Calcium Made Interesting: Sketches,

Letters, Essays & Gondolas (book) 3167
Calder, Simon 3576
Caldicot, Richard 453
Calendar (TV) 870, 1054, 1141, 1172, 1224, 1230, 1716, 2088, 2315, 3922
Calendar News (TV) 2604, 2775
Callan, Paul 2153
Callard & Bowser (ads) 288
Callaway, Liz 2055
Calman, Claire 2051, 2156
Calman, Mel 2009, 2051, 2155, 2156
Calman's Savoy Sketchbook (book) 2051
Cambridge Animation Festival 1229
Cambridge Circus 2, 1587
Cambridge Footlights 1051, 1750, 3000
The Cambridge Review (magazine) 836
Cameron, David 3507
Cameron, James 256, 292, 296
Cameron, Ray 140
Campbell, Allan 4053
Campbell, David 4188
Campbell, Ken 685; *see also* The Ken Campbell Road Show
Can I Play with Madness? (music video) 1571, 3139
Can We Please Have That the Right Way Round?: A Guide to Slide Presentations (film) 547
Can You Spare a Moment? [2001] (film) 2714
Can You Spare a Moment?: The Counselling Interview [1987] (film) 1443
Canada AM (TV) 276, 3406
Canby, Vincent 397, 567, 710, 863, 943, 970, 991, 1025, 1149, 1751
Candis (magazine) 3401
A Candlelight Christmas (concert) 2623
Candy, John 1811
Candyskins 2222
Canned Ham (TV) 2566
Cannes Film Festival 938, 1025, 1039, 1040, 1042, 1044, 1474, 1480, 1823, 1941, 1958, 1961, 2368, 2662, 2751, 3659, 3660, 3681, 3821, 4105
The Canterbury Tales (book) 770, 839, 2388, 2514, 2519, 2937
Cantona, Eric 2745
Capaldi, Peter 1869, 4070
Capote, Truman 639
Capotondi, Cristiana 3953
Captain Beefheart 433
Car Sick (TV) see *Open Space*
Carby, Fanny 382
"Card Dance" (sketch) 871, 931
Cardoso, Fernando Henrique 4192
Carey, Anita 600
Carey, John 107
Carey, Joyce 1548
Cariaga, Marvellee 1712
Carlin, George 2860, 3084
Carlin, Peter Ames 2528

Carlton, Timothy 418, 604
Carluccio, Antonio 4148
Carlyle, Robert 2516
Carmichael, Ian 165
Carnival of the Animals (concert) 2851
Carolgees, Bob 923
The Caroline Rhea Show (TV) 2873
Caron, Leslie 3688
Carpenter, John 2611
Carr, Allan 1628
Carr, Cindy 1850
Carr, J. L. 853
Carr, Janet 2311
Carr, Jimmy 2787, 2839, 3086, 3680
Carr, Katie 2750
Carradine, Keith 609
Carrick, Antony 725
Carrier, Robert 846
Carroll, Lewis 567, 578
Carrott, Jasper 572
Carson, Johnny 1619
Carson, Mary 499
Carson, Ted 3, 4
Carter, Angela 855
Carter, Betty 1535
Carter, Jim 1475
Carter, Jimmy 1525
Cartland, Barbara 1411
Cartwright, Justin 4120
Cartwright, Nancy 2875, 3076, 3388, 4102
Carvey, Dana 1338
Case, John 710
The Case of the Sulphuric Acid Plant (film) 555
Casey, Patricia 161
Cash, Johnny 4188
Casper (film) 2100, 2102, 2106, 2109
Cassavetti, Patrick 1818, 2376
Cassels, John 435
Cassidy, David 1375
Casson, Hugh [Sir] 982
Casson, Philip 590
Castell, David 1617, 1821
Castellaneta, Dan 2875, 3076, 3388, 4102
Castle, Roy 1909
Castro, Fidel 2515
Castro, Janice 1315
Cates, Phoebe 1628
Cathcart, Michael 4117
"Cavatina" (song) 2212
Cavers, Clinton 567
Cavett, Dick 411
Caylor, Cynthia *see* Cleese, Cynthia
The CBS Morning News (TV) 1228, 1311
CBS News Nightwatch (TV) 1487
CBS This Morning (TV) 1950, 1956
Ceci, Stephen [Prof.] 2659
Cedric the Entertainer 3152
Celebrity Choice (radio) 2153
Celebrity Hour with Roger Rose (TV) 1425
Cellnet (ads) 1973
"Cello Concerto in C Major" [Haydn] 538

Censorama: The Official Secrets Ball (stage) 1341
A Centenary Concert for the Mountain Gorillas (concert) 2813
Cervantes, Miguel de 2597, 2728, 3631
Chadbon, Tom 729
Chahidi, Paul 4008
Chain Reaction (radio) 1867, 1873
The Chairman (film) 1436
Chakrabarti, Lolita 2323, 2840, 2841
Chalmers, Robert 4133
Chambers, Andrea 1112
Chambers, Gary 136
Chambers, Munro 4017
Chan, Jackie 2999
Chandler, Kyle 3596
Chandler, Simon 813
Change for the Better see All Change (The Management of Change), Part 1: Change for the Better
Changing Transport (lecture) 1462
Channing, Carol 1181
Channing, Stockard 2547
Chantal 1510
Chaplin, Charlie 1639
Chapman, Gary 3123
Chapman, Mark 1781, 1915
Chappell, Norman 519
Charles, Howard 4049
Charles, James 604
Charles, Jeannette 471, 576, 635
Charles II 2934
Charleson, Ian 1227, 1358
Charlie and the Chocolate Factory (audiobook) 2023, 2808, 3002; see also *Jackanory* (TV)
Charlie and the Great Glass Elevator (audiobook) 2023, 2808, 3002
Charlie Rose (TV) 2082, 2126, 2227, 2281, 2367
Charlie's Angels (film) 2901
Charlie's Angels: Full Throttle (film) 2901
Charlotte's Web (film) 3368
Charlton, Dagmar 2355
Charlton, Valerie 567
Charmoli, Tony 777
Chase, Chevy 515, 1210, 1238, 1338, 1678, 1752, 2860
Chatter of Choughs (book) 2715
Chaucer, Geoffrey 770, 839, 842, 919, 1267, 1302, 2026, 2319, 2388, 2514, 2519, 2610, 2663, 2732, 2924, 2927, 2928, 2937, 2955, 2963, 2984, 2998, 3049, 3051, 3115, 3650, 4020, 4108
Chaucer's Knight: The Portrait of a Medieval Mercenary (book) 770, 773, 1137, 2927, 3374
Cheech and Chong 1059
Cheers (TV): "Simon Says" 1363, 1392, 1418
Cheever, Joan 3275
Chekhov, Anton 386
Chelsea Lately (TV) 3617
Cheuse, Josh 1284
Chiambretti, Piero 3736

Chiambretti Night (TV) 3736
Chicago 2166
Chicago Sun-Times (newspaper) 1177, 1850, 3178
Chicago Tribune (newspaper) 397, 428, 1370, 1504
Child, Jeremy 1984
Child, Julia 1342
Children in Need (TV) 1233
Chiles, Adrian 3439, 3532, 3598, 3904, 3963
Chilvers, Philip 707, 1123, 1219, 1291
Chisholm, Anne 91
Cholmondeley, Tom 3279
The Chris Evans Breakfast Show (radio) 3950, 4160
The Chris Moyles Show (radio) 4025
Chris Orr's John Ruskin (book) 552
The Christian O'Connell Breakfast Show (radio) 4029
The Christian Science Monitor (magazine) 913, 3019
Christie, Ian 2062, 2064, 2065, 2070, 2073, 2075, 2077, 2433
Christie, Julie 1533
Christie, Rawdon 4177
Christmas Night with the Stars (TV) 240
Christmas Vacation 2: Cousin Eddie's Island Adventure (TV) 2942
Christmas with Rutland Weekend Television (TV) 471
Christopher, James 3178
Church, Charlotte 3931
Church, Thomas Haden 2261, 2925
Churchill, Winston [Prime Minister] [Sir] 662, 2629
Churchill-Jones, Michael 3773
Cieply, Michael 3965
Cilento, Diane 2936
Cilla (TV) 8
Cineaste (magazine) 437, 1211, 2692
Cinefantastique (magazine) 1177, 1646
Cinema Sound (radio) 715
Cinque, Flaminia 1776
The Circle (TV) 4061
Circus (magazine) 738
City Lights (film) 1639
City of London Sinfonia 3972
C.K., Louis 3980
Clair, Rene 3501
Clapperboard (TV) 866, 3315
Clapton, Eric 871, 931, 1451, 2826, 2921
Clark, Beverly Lyon 1216
Clark, Candy 957
Clark, Dick 777
Clark, Eugene V. 714
Clark, Jim 200
Clark, Kenneth 3308
Clark, Pete 2746, 3332
Clarke, John S. 2114
Clarke, Roy 1982
Classic Serial (radio): "Dead Souls" 3261, 3262
Clavier, Christian 2557, 3295
Claxton, Guy 2428, 2445, 2538
Clayton, Helena 130, 380
Clayton-Gore, Phillip 725

Cleese, Alyce Faye [wife] *see* Eichelberger, Alyce Faye
Cleese, Camilla [daughter] 1109, 1111, 3218, 3233, 3510, 3625
Cleese, Cynthia [daughter] 117, 1111, 1484, 1487, 1493, 1495, 1500, 1508, 2221, 2240, 3129, 3505, 3645
Cleese, Muriel [mother] 565, 739, 2601
Cleese, Reginald [father] 241, 2601
Clement, Dick 1136, 1924
Clement, John 105
Cleveland, Carol 35, 37, 39, 43, 49, 52, 55, 60, 61, 78, 86, 88, 96, 98, 102, 105, 106, 108, 111, 130, 162, 163, 175, 224–26, 234–36, 239, 249, 251, 268, 275, 293, 363, 365, 368, 370, 372, 374, 389, 397, 492–94, 500, 502, 539, 710, 805, 943, 1025, 1214, 1752, 2032, 2472, 2495, 2496, 2498, 2958, 3100, 3588, 3606, 3696, 3745, 3770, 4101, 4139, 4140
Cleveland, Patience 2722
The Clever Stupid Game (radio) 72
Clinton, Bill [President] 2166
Clive, John 381, 662
Clive Anderson All Talk (TV) 2188, 2296, 2468, 2491
Clive Anderson Talks Back (TV) 1648, 1899, 2039
Clive James: Talking in the Library (web) 2723
Clockwise (film) 1204, 1271, 1274, 1278, 1279, 1309, 1311–13, 1348
Close, Glenn 2619, 2834
Close, Marvin 3944
Close Encounters of the Herd Kind see Robbie the Reindeer in Close Encounters of the Herd Kind
Close Up [U.K.] (TV) 2116
Close Up [New Zealand] (TV) 4172
Closing the Sale see So You Want to Be a Success at Selling?, Part 4: Closing the Sale
"Clothes Off" (sketch) 871, 883, 907
Clott, Timothy 1329
Clunes, Martin 3815
Clyde, Jonathan 4157
Coady, Matthew 166
Coast to Coast (TV) 2353
Coburn, James 787
Coca, Imogene 642
Cocker, Joe 198, 515
Cockerell, Michael 2914
Codron, Michael 1274
Coduri, Camille 1751
Coen, Jack 1948
Coffey, Denise 10
Cohen, David 2573
Cohen, Joel H. 3076
Cohen, Steve 2789
Coia, Paul 1084, 1190
The Cold Call see Selling on the Telephone: The Cold Call
Coldplay 4081
Coldstream, Robert 3281, 3286

Cole, Lily 3659, 3713, 3725, 3785
Cole, Steven 2583
Coleman, Gary 734, 777
Coleman, John 397, 710
Colin, Margaret 2563
Colley, Kenneth 567, 600, 710
Collins, Andrew 3212
Collins, Edwyn 2277
Collins, Glenn 1588
Collins, Jackie 865, 1938
Collins, Janet 2311
Collins, Phil 871, 931
Collins, Tony 1975
Collodi, Carlo 2834
Coltrane, Robbie 1227, 1634, 1665, 1675, 1705, 1724, 1751, 1757, 2254, 2535, 2702, 2810
Columbus, Chris 2702, 2810
The Comedians' Comedian (TV) 3086
Comedians' Comedians (radio) 2844
Comedians Do It on Stage (TV) 1153, 1343
The Comedy Café (radio) 3831
Comedy Chief (event) 3608
Comedy Connections (TV): "Monty Python's Flying Circus" 3100; "Ripping Yarns" 3551; "The Goodies" 3000
Comedy Lab (TV): "Knife & Wife" 2713
The Comedy Map of Britain (TV) 3381, 3506
Comedy Playhouse (TV): "Elementary, My Dear Watson" 252, 596; "Idle at Work" 183
A Comedy Salute to Andy Kaufman (TV) 2084
Comedy Tonight!: A Tribute to Roy Kinnear (stage) 2024
Comedy Writing with Terry Jones (seminars) 3651
Comic-Con International 3681
The Comic Genius: A Multidisciplinary Approach (seminar) 3622
Comic Relief (stage) 1286
Comic Relief: Big Red Nose Night (TV) 2649
Comic Relief: Red Nose Day 1999—The Record Breaker (TV) 2434
Comic Relief: Red Nose Night (TV) 2869
Comic Roots (TV): "Michael Palin" 1067, 1068, 3047
Coming Home (TV): "Terry Jones" 3773
Comiskey, John 3059
Commander Badman (TV) *see Funny Ha Ha*
Company Account (TV) 682–84
Compaq ("It Simply Works Better") (ads) 1126
Competitive Spirit see Marketing in Practice, No. 3: The Competitive Spirit
The Complete and Utter History of Britain (TV) 1, 3–7, 9, 1592, 2944, 3072, 3530, 3608
The Complete and Utter History of

Monty Python's Flying Circus (screenings) 2384
The Complete Fawlty Towers (book) 1570
The Complete Monty Python's Flying Circus: All the Words (book) 1690, 1717
The Complete Monty Python's Flying Circus: Collector's Edition (DVD) 3586–88, 3749
The Complete Monty Python's Flying Circus 16-Ton Megaset (DVD) 3197
The Complete Ripping Yarns (book) 1770
The Complete Ripping Yarns (DVD) 2991, 3022, 3040, 3041, 3047, 4079, 4080, 4082
The Complete Works of Chaucer (book) 1061
The Complete Works of Shakespeare and Monty Python: Volume One—Monty Python (book) 875
Conan, Neal 3836
Conaway, Jeff 851
The Concert for Bangladesh (film) 3204
Concert for George (concert) 2826
Concert for George (film) 2916, 2920, 2921, 2980
Condé Nast Traveller (magazine) 3106
Cone, Etta and Claribel 2889
Confessio Amantis (poem) 3540
Connelly, Chris 1491, 1749
Connelly, Jennifer 1301, 3157, 3596
Connelly, Steve 1805
Connery, Sean 863, 1419, 1446, 1643, 1660, 1662, 2936
Connolly, Billy 85, 704, 764, 871, 883, 929, 931, 1099, 1286, 2355, 2465, 2480, 2591, 2688, 2774, 2836, 2906, 3180, 3465, 3639, 3669, 4096
Connolly, Joseph 4118
Connolly, Nicolas 3953
Connolly, Ray 1748
Conoley, Terence 159, 440, 679
Conran, Shirley 992
Constantine, Learie [Lord] 101
Constantine, Martin 4130
Consuming Passions (film) 280, 1461
Conti, Tom 3509
Contos Fantásticos (play) 3481
The Control of Working Capital (film) 663, 684
Conversation Pieces: Michael Palin (event) 3704
Conway, Richard 1177, 1559
Conway, Steve 725
Coogan, Steve 2178, 2185, 2186, 2419, 2999
Cook, Brian 63
Cook, Frances 2694
Cook, Ian 1112
Cook, Lin 2181, 2329
Cook, Peter 18, 99, 492, 539, 545, 554, 579, 594, 609, 616, 622,

661, 704, 755, 759, 764, 804, 929, 990, 1003, 1049, 1051, 1059, 1455, 1493, 1665, 1705, 1876, 1969, 2066, 2071, 2091, 2181, 2329, 2618, 2773, 2787, 2838, 3058, 3086, 3108, 3217, 3669
Cook, Rachael Leigh 2751
Cook, Sue 876, 1067
Cook, Victor 2620
Cooke, Alistair 101
Cooke, Beryl 915
Cooke, Lucy 2955, 2957
Cooklin, Shirley 1219
Coolidge, Jennifer 3560
Coomes, David 1768
Cooper, Derek 1488
Cooper, Dick 3008
Cooper, Duncan 2224
Cooper, George A. 308, 381, 475, 548, 626
Cooper, John Kaye 3193
Cooper, Ray 1018
Cooper, Tommy 1661
Copeland, Stewart 3926
Coppel, Alec 113
Copus, Nick 2549
Coraci, Frank 2999
Corbett, Harry H. 165, 567
Corbett, Ronnie 81, 99, 126, 127, 129, 136, 138, 141, 168, 204, 214, 240, 255, 285, 291, 326, 514, 517, 619, 663, 683, 684, 1260, 1973, 2211, 2221, 2459, 2496, 2626, 2627, 2966, 3246, 3496, 3539, 3564, 3587, 3601, 3639, 3898, 3976
Corcoran, Tom 296
Coren, Alan 252, 327, 480, 487, 573, 760
Coren, Giles 3357
Corliss, Richard 863, 1149, 1559
Cornelius, Don 1750
Cornell Chamber Orchestra 3259
The Corrs 2533
Cortese, Valentina 1559
Cosby, Bill 1127
Cossins, James 450, 547, 765
Cost, Profit and Break-Even (film) 826
Costanzo, Paulo 2751
Costello, Elvis 1833, 2103
Costello, Elvis & The Attractions 983
Costner, Kevin 1209
Cotton, Bill [Sir] 259, 3601
Coulthart, Ross 4016
Countdown with Keith Olbermann (TV) 3570, 3726
Counterblast (TV): "The Road to Hell" 1256, 2674
Couper, Heather 1914
The Courage to Change: Hope and Help for Alcoholics and Their Families (book) 1148
Covington, Julie 579, 594, 622, 1062
Cowan, Patrick J. 3597
Coward, Ros 2671
Cowell, Lucinda 652
Cowley, Jason 2270

Cowling, Brenda 456
Cox, Alex 2267, 2360, 2361, 2376
Cox, Brian 3180
Crabbe, Peter 2345, 2566, 2567, 2919
Crace, John 4168
Crackerbox Palace (film) 528, 535
Craddock, Kenny 1324
Cradock, Fanny 1375
Craft, Kinuko Y. 741
Craig, Laurie 2986
Craigie, Jill 1123
Cranham, Kenneth 1894
Cranston, Bryan 4102
Crathorne, James 3442
Crayden, Amanda 2814
Creasey, Richard 2352
Le Créateur (film) 2351, 2454
Creativity and the Creative Process (lecture) 3129
Creativity in Management (film) 1870
Creativity in Management (lecture) 1808
Cretch, Elizabeth 1754
Crews, Terry 3833
Cribbins, Bernard 380, 384, 450, 460, 465
Crichton, Charles 200, 626, 765, 909, 1102, 1103, 1104, 1158, 1215, 1248, 1249, 1443, 1481, 1495, 1519, 1520, 1546, 1563–65, 1579, 1580, 1593, 1609, 1627, 1628, 1733, 2474, 2485
The Cricklewood Greats (TV) 4070
The Crimson Permanent Assurance (film) 1025, 1026
Cripps, Harry 2625
Crispin, Ben 4008
Croft, David G. 1724
Croft, Elisabeth 1150
Cronin, Michael 441
Crood Awakening (script) 3227
The Croods (film) 3227
Crook and Chase (TV) 1506, 1525, 1605
Crooked Wood (play) 1548
Cropper, Steve 803
Crosbie, Annette 1740, 1866
Crosby, Stills & Nash 3820
Cross Wits (TV) 1355
Crowden, Graham 183, 386, 567, 970, 1353
Cruickshank, Andrew 381
Cruickshank, Dan 4151
Crusades (book) 2048
Crusades (TV) 2067–69, 2072, 2074, 2076, 2105
Cry of the Banshee (film) 41
Cryer, Barry 22, 27, 28, 33, 54, 81, 126, 127, 140, 165, 167, 168, 255, 303, 315, 325, 326, 378, 1355, 1777, 2244, 2459, 2594, 3735, 3876, 4139
Crystal, Billy 2462
Cue (magazine) 293
Cullin, Mitch 3186
Culp, Robert 965
The Culture Show (TV) 3452, 3743

A Culture Show Special: Michael Palin (TV) 3338
The Culture Show Uncut (TV) 3624
Cummings, Jim 3969
Cummings, Whitney 4069
Cunningham, Colin 3, 4
Cunningham, Glen 604
The Cure 1289
Curran, Paul 567
Curry, Alexander 105
Curry, Tim 473, 2989, 3113, 3123, 3140, 3353, 3389, 3465, 4096
The Curse of the Vampire's Socks and Other Doggerel (book) 1522, 1533, 1535
Curtin, Jane 515, 563, 576, 640, 660, 671, 695, 730, 779, 2358, 2359, 2664, 2666
Curtis, James 2881
Curtis, Jamie Lee 1490, 1493, 1495, 1498, 1506, 1514, 1578, 1609, 1795, 1990, 2095, 2121, 2221, 2475, 3485
Curtis, Richard 2083
Curtis, Tony 160
Cusack, John 3560
Cusack, Sinead 2813
Cushing, Peter 1101
Cushman, Robert 2092
Customer Relations in Practice, No. 1: In Two Minds (film) 306, 457
Customer Relations in Practice, No. 2: The Meeting of Minds (film) 307
Customer Relations in Practice, No. 3: Awkward Customers (film) 308, 459
Customer Relations in Practice, No. 4: More Awkward Customers (film) 380, 460
Cuthbert, Neil 2772
Cuthbertson, Allan 453, 731, 1353
Cuthbertson, Iain 605
Cvirko, Andrea 1402, 1410, 1420, 1428, 1435
Cyril and the Dinner Party (book) 1316
Cyril and the House of Commons (book) 1317

Dadak, Roderick 1577
Dad's Army (TV) 2276, 4097
Dad's Army: A Celebration (book) 2276
Dahl, Roald 916, 1275, 1411, 2023, 2808, 2946, 2947, 3002, 3227
Dahl, Sophie 2885
Daily Express (newspaper) 982
The Daily Mail (newspaper) 3720, 4208
The Daily Mirror (newspaper) 1577, 2184, 2486
The Daily Post (Liverpool) (newspaper) 2961, 3685, 3851
The Daily Show (TV) 2220, 2280, 2397
The Daily Show with Jon Stewart (TV) 2552, 2864, 3098, 3860
The Daily Telegraph (newspaper) 34, 915, 3305, 3326, 3399, 3571, 3699, 3905, 4168

The Daily Telegraph Review (magazine) 4110
Daily Variety (magazine) 1218
Dainty, Billy 126
Dalai Lama 1968, 2161, 2218, 3045, 3152, 3507, 4110
Dalí, Salvador 639
Dalton, Timothy 2837
Daltrey, Roger 4053
Daly, Tyne 1337
Dalzell, Lucy 4151
Dame Edna *see* Humphries, Barry
The Damnation of Faust (opera) 3828, 3928, 3943, 3945, 3951, 3999, 4059, 4063, 4100, 4146
The Damnation of Faust (TV) 4003
Damon, Matt 2902, 3178, 4165
Damski, Mel 1049, 1059
Dan Dare, Pilot of the Future: The Biography (book) 3879
Dancy, Hugh 2986
Dando, Jill 2191
Dandridge, Merle 3677
D'Angelo, Beverly 1210
The Dangerous Film Club (TV) 1389, 1401, 1402, 1410, 1420, 1428, 1435
Dangerous Sports Club 1188, 1254, 1380, 1393, 1394, 1405, 1424
Dangler, Anita 1647
Danielle, Suzanne 983
Daniels, Sean 2594
Danny Baker After All (TV) 1975
The Danny Baker Show (radio) 3970
Danson, Ted 1363
Dante, Joe 1253
Danza, Tony 1192
Darabont, Frank 2054
Dardis, Tom 850
Dark Knights & Holy Fools: The Art and Films of Terry Gilliam (book) 2453, 2540, 2915, 3200
Dark Star (magazine) 821
Darwin, Charles 3707
Darwin, Lucy 2728
Dashwood, Robin 4088
Data Run (TV) 1093
Data Run's Christmas Party (TV) 1100
Dave Barry's Complete Guide to Guys (film) 3094, 3095
The Dave Lee Group 664
Davenport, Claire 456
Davey, Daphne 130
David Frost on Sunday (TV) 1339
David Mellor (radio) 2356
Davidson, Andrew 1812, 2093, 2777
Davidson, Ian 10, 38, 44, 54, 55, 96, 97, 98, 111, 488
Davidson, John Paul 1968, 2801, 2804, 2809, 3054, 3057, 3061, 3065, 3434, 3438, 3441, 3454, 4168, 4171, 4192
Davidson, Justin 3723
Davidson, Ross 1026
Davidson, Tommy 2790
Davies, Andrew 1461
Davies, Geoffrey 188
Davies, Helen 3351

Davies, Hunter 565, 758
Davies, Jack 68
Davies, John Howard 17, 34, 35, 37–39, 43, 159, 440, 441, 446, 450, 453, 456, 2830, 3654, 3738, 3978, 4052
Davies, Mike 2501
Davies, Ray 3962
Davies, Richard 621, 680, 1157
Davies, Rita 49, 97, 220, 224, 397
Davies, Russell 1262
Davies, Tod 2360, 2361, 2376
Davies, Tom 237, 790
Davis, Clive 395, 693
Davis, Geena 2953
Davis, Jeff B. 3701
Davis, Michael 1055
Davis, Peter 163
Davis, Sammi 1461
Davis, Stephen 1526
Davison, Peter 1789
Davro, Bobby 1864
Dawes, Anthony 679
Dawkins, Richard 2418
Dawson, Jill 2018, 2374, 2985
Dawson, Les 140, 158, 289, 303, 313, 325, 378, 519, 1320, 1860, 2244, 4047
Dawson, Rosario 2772
Day, David 2113
Day, Nicholas 604
The Day the Earth Stood Still (film) 3596
Daybreak (TV) 3963, 4030, 4166
Daytime Green: The Green Life Guide (TV) 1771
Daytime Live (TV) 1708
Dead Souls (radio) see *Classic Serial*
Dean, Douglas 3953
Dean, Isabel 605
Dean, Michael 61, 1033
Dean Martin's Comedyworld (TV) 348, 356
"Dear One" (song) 538
De'Ath, Wilfred 485
Deayton, Angus 1866, 1937, 2787, 2839, 2844
De Brus, Vincent 3295
Decisions, Decisions (film) 662
DeCordova, Fred 279
Dee, Jack 2115, 2958
Dee, Simon 68
Defoe, Willem 2930, 4079
DeGruy, Mike 1854
De Hart, Jeff 1034
DeHaven, Carter 1059
de Hooch, Pieter 3847
Delamain, Aimee 677
Delaney, Frank 1083
Delaney, Tim 629
Delany, Dana 2637, 3485
de la Tour, Frances 3601
Delfont, Bernard [Lord] 634
Del Giorno, Jody 2860
Delgo (film) 3597
Del Toro, Benicio 2376, 2849
DeLuise, Dom 1859, 2421
DeMicco, Kirk 2369, 2946, 3227
Dench, Judi [Dame] 985, 2425,

2465, 2516, 2591, 2819, 2836, 2930
Dene, Zulema 903
Deneuve, Catherine 4144
DeNiro, Robert 1177, 1228, 2054
Dennehy, Brian 1209
Dennings, Kat 2790
Dennis, Sandy 2442
Dennis, Winston 1559
Dennis Miller Live (TV) 2339, 2554
Denselow, Robin 1173, 2707
Denver, John 799
Denville, Terence 480
De Palma, Brian 2046
Depardieu, Gerard 2557, 2619
Depp, Johnny 2367, 2368, 2376, 2422, 2597, 2849, 3490, 3659, 3818
Depreciation and Inflation (film) 827
Dermot O'Leary (radio) 3670
de Rossi, Portia 2973
Derrickson, Scott 3596
Des O'Connor Tonight (TV) 2217
Desena, Tony 946
Desert Island Discs (radio) 151, 538, 735, 753, 916, 1061, 2212, 3928
Devenish, Myrtle 1026
De Vere, Alison 1464, 1466, 1469, 1470, 1473, 1475, 1479
Devillier, Ron 356, 398
Devious Devices (exhibition) 2330
Devon, Dayna 3244
Devon, Stanley 237
Devout Sceptics (radio) 1980
Dewhurst, Keith 264, 266
Dexter, Felix 4049
De Yong, Jenny 2585
Dhéry, Robert 63
Diabolo (stage) 3245
Diabolo's Workshop (documentary) 3245
Diamond, Anne 1057, 1071, 2141, 2151
Diamond, John 1874
Diana *see* Princess Diana (of Wales)
Diana: A Dedication in Seven Ages: An Anthology of Poetry with Music (audiobook) 2425
Diaries 1969–1979: The Python Years (book) 15, 3330, 3332, 3338, 3340, 3360, 3363, 3420, 3422–28, 3693
Diaz, Cameron 2901, 2997, 3405, 3823, 4140
Di Battista, Laura 4055
Dick, Philip K. 2005
Dick Cavett (TV) 1942
The Dick Cavett Show (TV) 721, 843, 882, 887
Dickel, J. 3108
Dickens, Charles 2083
Dickens, Monica 376, 1732
Dickenson, Frances 1851
Dickinson, Bruce 3735
Dickinson, Sandra 1242
Dickson, Anne 1433
Dickson, Barbara 572
Did I Ever Tell You How Lucky You Are? (audiobook) 1967

Did You See...? (TV) 816, 849, 1194, 1219, 1261
Die Another Day (film) 2516, 2764, 2812, 2818–20, 2822, 2825, 2837, 2930, 3568
Die Hard (film) 1598
Diehl, Mike 752
Difficult Customers see *So You Want to Be a Success at Selling?, Part 3: Difficult Customers*
Difford, Chris 1032
DiGiorgio, Maija 2860
Di Giovanni, Janine 1707
Dignan, Danny 2701
Dillane, Richard 3375
Dille, Flint 1859
Dilly, Noel 924
Dinner at Albert's (concert) 1152
Dinotopia (TV) 2750
The Directors (radio) 2437
The Directors Guild of America Awards [41st Annual] (ceremony) 1609
The Directors: The Films of Terry Gilliam (documentary) 2324, 2960
The Directorspective: Terry Gilliam (screenings) 3839
DirectTV (Questions) (ad) 4112
Dirk & Stig 647
Dirty Pretty Things (film) 2852
Dirty Rotten Scoundrels (film) 1465
Discovering Hammershøi (lecture) 3537
Discovering King's Cross: A Pop-Up Book (book) 4151, 4153
Discworld (computer game) 2122, 2194
Discworld II: Mortality Bytes! (computer game) 2122, 2194, 2207
Dixon, Barbara 2856
Dixon, Donna 1238
Dixon, Malcolm 863
D'lectrified (CD) 2481, 2531
Do Not Adjust Your Set (TV) 1, 10, 16, 1587, 1592, 3165, 3608, 4104
Do They Hurt? (record) 783
Docherty, Steve 2721
Doctor at Large (TV) 22, 66, 68, 121, 122, 125, 133, 137, 142, 145, 147, 148, 150, 152–57, 188
Dr. Fegg's Encyclopeadia of All World Knowledge (book) 354, 1137, 1138, 1140, 1141
Dr. Fegg's Nasty Book of Knowledge (book) 354, 438, 490, 1138
Doctor in Charge (TV) 188–90, 192, 201–03, 205–08, 212, 216, 283, 284, 300
Doctor in the House (TV) 22, 23, 27, 28, 33, 68, 121, 188
Doctor in Trouble (film) 23, 68
Doctor on the Go (TV) 562, 2665
Doctor Who (TV) 729
The Doctor's Tale (opera) 3481, 3914, 3923, 3926, 4130
Dodd, Ken 1661, 3191
Doebler, Paul 603
Doherty, Thomas 1177

The Do-It-Yourself Film Animation Show (TV) 332, 1964
Dolan, Terry 2927
Dolenz, Micky 905, 3234
Dombasle, Arielle 1638
Dominic King (radio) 4025
Don Quixote (book) 2190, 2597, 2728, 2767, 2904, 3631
Don Quixote (film) see *The Man Who Killed Don Quixote*
Donahue, Phil 1514
Donnelly, Sam 2839, 2966
Donny & Marie (TV) 2504, 2563, 2576
Donoghue, Carolae 54
Donohoe, Amanda 2277
Donoso, Julio 1561
Donovan, 871, 3669
Donovan, Gerry 739
Donovan, Tate 2393
Don't Fence Me In (radio) 2089, 2090
Don't Mention the World Cup (single) 3267
The Doobie Brothers 671
Dor, Juliette 2927
Dore, Charlie 803, 1776
Dorff, Stephen 2573
Dorning, Robert 558
Dotrice, Roy 159
Douch, Lucy 1097
Douglas, Jack 303
Douglas, Mike 500
Douglas, Tim 1026
Douglas Adams: The Party (event) 4087
Douglas Adams's Starship Titanic (book) 2313, 2314, 2316, 2319, 2352, 2357, 2665
Doust, Dudley 706
Doward, Jamie 3763
Down, Angela 548
Downes, Richard 2310, 2511
Downey, Robert Jr. 1783
Downey, Robert Sr. 1783
Downs, Clare 1150
Downs, Hugh 1030
Doyle, Julian 2596, 2698, 3506
Dragnet (TV) 515
Drake, Gabrielle 159
The Drama League Awards [71st Annual] (ceremony) 3147
Drawing Blood: Forty-Five Years of Scarfe Uncensored (book) 3215
Dream, Carl 3597
Dreamchild (film) 1262
Dreams and Nightmares: Terry Gilliam, The Brothers Grimm & Other Cautionary Tales of Hollywood (book) 3178, 3219
The Dress (film) 1128, 1150, 1151, 1381
The Dresser (radio) see *The Monday Play*
Drive with Richard Glover (radio) 4198
Driver, Minnie 2953, 2977, 2981
Driving Miss Daisy (film) 1755
Drucker, Michel 482, 782
Dubois, Janet 1636

Du Chau, Frederick 2369
Duchess of Cornwall 3408, 3488, 3579
Duchess of York (Sarah Ferguson) 1390, 1712
Dudley, Anne 3923, 3926, 4129, 4130
Dudley Do-Right (film) 2464
Duff, Howard 1783
Duffell, Bee 397
Dukane, Sy 1644
Duke, Robin 966, 1110
Duke of Edinburgh see Prince Philip
Duke of York see Prince Andrew
Duncan, Andrew 2089
Duncan, Lindsay 761, 762, 1833
Dunn, Clive 303
Dunn, Nora 1430
Dunning, David [Prof.] 3257
Dunton, Joe 3796
Dupontel, Albert 2351, 2454, 3256
Du Prez, John 803, 1026, 1776, 2038, 2171, 2197, 2457, 2558, 2566, 2567, 2865, 2919, 3096, 3113, 3144, 3258, 3260, 3352, 3389, 3409, 3417, 3465, 3476, 3543, 3546, 3550, 3607, 3745, 3771, 4096
Duran Duran 1365
Durrell, Gerald 2121
Durrell, Lee 2121
du Sautoy, Marcus 3199
D'Silva, Beverley 3309
Dutton, Denis [Prof.] 3740
Dutton, Gavin 2000
Duvall, Robert 580, 3818
Duvall, Shelley 863, 885, 957, 1198, 2324
Dylan, Bob 730
Dyson, Noel 126

E! True Hollywood Story (TV): "The Bond Girls" 2818
The Eagles 2166
Ear to the Ground (TV) 1063
Earle, Steve 1437
Earls, John 2279
Earnhardt, Dale Jr. 3880
Earth to America! (TV) 3222, 3223
East of Ipswich (TV) see *Screen Two*
East of the Moon (TV) 874, 1463, 1464, 1466, 1469, 1470, 1473, 1475, 1479
Eastaugh, Kenneth 170
"Easter Hymn, (*Cavalleria Rusticana*)" [Mascagni] 2212
Eastwood, Clint 386
Eat Something Sexy (event) 3486
Eaton, Wallas 3–7, 9
Eban, Ernie 699
Ebersol, Dick 940, 966, 1110
Ebert, Roger 1177, 1850, 3178
Eberts, Jake 2185
Ecker, Bob 1516, 1603
The Economist (magazine) 770, 1069, 1784
Eden, Barbara 777
The Edge 1998

Edinburgh International Film Festival 1519, 1520, 1663, 2391, 2392
Edinburgh Nights (TV) 2392
Edmonds, Mike 863
Edmonds, Noel 847, 1413
Edmondson, Adrian 1125, 1665, 1675, 1724, 2787, 2839
Edney, Beatie 2205, 2206, 2321
Edson, Evelyn 3034
Edward, Olivia 3706
Edwards, Bob 2578
Edwards, Charles 4008
Edwards, Cliff 3928
Edwards, Mark 2021
Edwards, Stephanie 407
Efter Tio (TV) 3935
Ege, Julie 165, 200
Eggers, Dave 3079
Egoyan, Atom 2611
Ehle, Jennifer 2535
Eia, Harald 3988
Eichelberger, Alyce Faye 1650, 1876, 1917, 2215, 2460, 2763, 3053, 3153, 3480, 3604, 3781, 4134
The Eiger Sanction (film) 386
8½ (film) 2116
The 8:15 from Manchester (TV) 1773
"Ein Heldenleben—final movement" [Strauss] 3928
Eisler, David 1712
Ekland, Britt 1247
Ekman, Paul [Prof.] 2642, 2650
Eldon, Kevin 2713, 3395
The Electric Revolution (TV) 849
Elena: A Life in Soho (book) 1762
Elgar, Edward [Sir] 151, 538, 753
The Eliza Stories (book) 1163
Elizondo, Hector 1183
Ella Enchanted (film) 2986
The Ellen DeGeneres Show (TV) 3130
Ellin, Doug 3863
Ellington, Duke 753
Elliott, Denholm 99, 596, 606, 932, 969, 1121, 1149, 1187
Elliott, Yan 3183
Ellis, June 679
Ellis, Robin 440
Ellison, David 726
Ellison, Jennifer 3963
Elmes, Simon 2514, 4108
Elphick, Michael 651, 991
Elton, Ben 877, 1125, 1286, 1318, 1665, 1705, 1781, 2459
Elwes, Cary 2057, 2369, 2986
Emergency Appeal for Rwanda (TV) 2018
Emerson, Sally 853
Emery, Dick 1365
Emery, Robert J. 2324
Emin, Tracey 3541, 4051
Emmanuel, Alphonsia 1984, 2322
The Emmy Awards (ceremony) 1418
Emperor of the North (film) 1041
Empire (magazine) 2230, 2239, 2908, 3977
Empire (TV): "Playing the Game" 4088
The Empire Awards (ceremony) 2239, 2727

Encounters with the Past (book) 854
"The End of the World" (sketch) 704, 755, 764
Enfermés dehors (film) 2454, 3256
Enfield, Harry 1765, 1798, 1894, 1916, 2787, 2791, 2839
England, Michael 3400
English, David 604
English National Opera 1304, 1352, 1441, 1442, 1549, 1712, 3943, 4003, 4063, 4100
The English Programme (TV) 1576
English Subtitles (book) 864
Eno, Brian 1882
L'entente cordiale (film) 3295
Entertainment Tonight (TV) 1494, 1611, 1637, 1666
Entertainment Weekly (magazine) 2119, 2158, 2221, 2948, 3122, 3179, 3494, 3659
Entourage (TV) 3846; "Lose Yourself" 3863
Ephron, Nora 2335
Equinox (TV): "Dr. Satan's Robot" 2203
Ereira, Alan 1880, 2048, 2068, 2072, 2074, 2076, 2565, 2718, 2858, 2964, 3172, 3199, 3273, 3280, 3513, 3517, 3520, 3526
Eric Idle Exploits Monty Python (stage) 2457, 2567, 2577, 2581, 2582, 2919
Eric Idle Sings Monty Python: Live in Concert (CD) 2457, 2558, 2560
Eric Idle Sings Monty Python Songs (stage) 2457
Eric the Half-a-Bee/The Yangtse Song (record) 223
Erickson, Stephen [Dr.] 2670
Erik the Viking (book) see *The Saga of Erik the Viking*
Erik the Viking (DVD) 2587
Erik the Viking (film) 1346, 1474, 1530, 1533, 1575, 1659, 1663, 1669, 1671, 1672, 1677, 1679–81, 1702, 1703, 1709, 2426
Erik the Viking: The Book of the Film of the Book (book) 1735
Erik the Viking: The Complete Viking (DVD) 4001
Erik the Viking: The Director's Son's Cut (film/DVD) 1677, 2587, 3283, 3341–43, 3347, 3359, 3475, 3634
Ernst, Laura 1783
Erskine, James 2642
Esio Trot (audiobook) 2023
Esler, Gavin 3313, 3359
Esmonde, John 165
Esquire (magazine) 431, 502, 524, 1115, 1887
Essex, David 976
Estall, Peter 2224
Estefan, Gloria 1822
Eszterhas, Joe 2295
Etheridge, Melissa 2144
The European Film Awards (ceremony) 1977, 2709, 4033
European Vacation see *National Lampoon's European Vacation*

Euroshow '71 (TV) 128, 134, 2495
Evans, Barry 22, 23, 27, 28, 33, 121, 122, 125, 133, 137, 142, 145, 147, 148, 150, 152–57
Evans, Brett 2311
Evans, Chris 2222, 2234, 2408, 3887, 3999, 4079
Evans, Geraint [Sir] 992, 1276
Evans, Lissa 3310
Evans, Marc 1464, 1470, 1473, 1479
Evans, Ruth [Dr.] 2514
Evans, Sara 1479
Evans, Simon 2975
Evans, Tenniel 607
Evans, Victor Romero 1053
An Evening at Court (stage) 990
The Evening News (Edinburgh) (newspaper) 2972
The Evening Standard (newspaper) 82, 612, 2746, 2845, 2853, 3332
The Evening Standard British Film Awards (ceremony) 1263, 1348, 1448, 1579, 2726, 2852
An Evening with Graham Chapman (lecture) 1080
An Evening with John Cleese (event) 2655, 3402, 3514, 3621
An Evening with John Cleese (seminar) 2865
An Evening with John Cleese [Australia, 2012] (stage) 4062, 4093
An Evening with John Cleese [Dubai, 2012] (stage) 4106
An Evening with John Cleese [Sweden, 2011] (stage) 3933
An Evening with John Cleese—Paying My Ex-Wife, Year Two [Scandinavia, 2010] (stage) 3862
An Evening with Michael Palin (event/lecture) 2006, 2612, 3112, 3224, 3255, 3806, 3878, 4178, 4205
An Evening with Terry Jones (event) 2426
An Evening with the President (event) 3875, 3948, 4012, 4075
An Evening without Monty Python (stage) 3701, 3716, 3723
An Evening without Sir Bernard Miles (stage) 579, 594, 622, 704
Everett, Rupert 3931
Everybody Here (TV) 1124
Everybody's Guide to the Computer, No. 1: What Is a Computer? (film) 766
Everybody's Guide to the Computer, No. 2: What Is a Word Processor? (film) 985
Everybody's Guide to the Computer, No. 3: What Is a Computer Program? (film) 986
Everyman (TV): "They Shoot Children, Don't They?" 1809
Everything You Wanted to Know About Buying and Selling a Used Car But Were Afraid to Ask (video) 1801
Evil Machines (book) 3481, 3957, 3975, 4013–15, 4046

Evil Machines (opera) 3478, 3481
Ewart-Biggs, Jane 1531
Ewing, Winifred 533
Excess Baggage (radio) 3036, 3437; "Michael Palin's Iron Curtin" 2629
Explorers: Great Tales of Adventure and Endurance (book) 3871
Explorer's Eye: First-Hand Accounts of Adventure & Exploration (book) 3174, 3177
Ex-S (TV): "Palin on Redpath" 2310
Eyre, Ronald 871, 931, 1472
Eyre, Wilkinson 3250
Ezrin, Bob 2027, 2158, 2317

Fable III (video game) 3877
The Fabulous Picture Show (TV) 3774
Façade Suite [Walton] 597
The Face (magazine) 1014
The Faces 198
The Facts of Life (TV) 2585
Faerie Tale Theatre (TV): "The Pied Piper of Hamelin" 1198; "The Tale of the Frog Prince" 934, 957, 2550
The Fairly Incomplete & Rather Badly Illustrated Monty Python Song Book (book) 2038
Fairman, Blain 662
Fairy Tales (audiobook) 2588
Fairy Tales (book) 643, 874, 876, 892, 897, 980, 981, 1069, 1216, 1463, 1889
Fairy Tales for Adults: A Terry Gilliam Retrospective (Screenings) 2127
Faith, Adam 1070
Falconer, John 3987
Falke, Stenson 363
Falkland Road (book) 855
Fallender, Deborah 567
Fallon, Jimmy 2906, 3588
Fame, Georgie 8, 2069
Fame in the Frame (TV): "Terry Gilliam" 3992
Families and How to Survive Them (book) 1078, 1081, 1083, 1132, 1160, 1168, 1433, 1932, 2595
Families and How to Survive Them (radio) 1794
Fanning, Dakota 3368
Fantastic Stories (book) 1889–93, 1929, 1931, 1936
Fantasy Empire (magazine) 1116, 1139
Fantasy World Cup (TV) 2385
Faridany, Francesca 3294
Farmer, Mark 3060
Farrell, Colin 3490, 3659
Farrell, David 998
Farrelly, Peter 2571
The Fat (TV) 2854
Fataar, Ricky (or Rikki) 632, 635, 647, 2644, 3495, 3584, 3585
Fatso 471, 534, 537, 542–44, 572
Faulconbridge, Claire 522
Faulkner, James 1376
Faust (opera) 234
Fawcett, Gregory 2633
Fawlty Exclusive: Basil's Best Bits (TV) 3654, 3657

Fawlty Towers (book) 608, 610, 611
Fawlty Towers (DVD) 2695
Fawlty Towers (record) 767
Fawlty Towers (TV) 66, 142, 312, 345, 379, 386, 439, 484, 487, 506, 551, 586, 645, 648, 673, 675, 708, 737, 757, 780, 812, 833, 999, 1004, 1237, 1240, 1433, 1577, 1815, 2093, 2094, 2217, 2286, 2337, 2383, 2436, 2592, 2593, 2645, 2679, 2743, 2958, 3579, 3648, 3649, 3654, 3815, 3873, 3935, 3978, 4052, 4057; "A Touch of Class" (Ep. 1) 379, 440, 768, 1130; "The Builders" (Ep. 2) 441, 608, 904, 1130; "The Wedding Party" (Ep. 3) 446, 768, 1130; "The Hotel Inspectors" (Ep. 4) 450, 608, 767, 1130; "Gourmet Night" (Ep. 5) 453, 608, 1106; "The Germans" (Ep. 6) 456, 768, 987, 1130, 2914, 3267; "Communication Problems" (Ep. 7) 676, 767, 859; "The Psychiatrist" (Ep. 8) 677, 1130, 2337, 3855; "Waldorf Salad" (Ep. 9) 679, 1106, 3642; "The Kipper and the Corpse" (Ep. 10) 680, 691, 987, 2337; "The Anniversary" (Ep. 11) 685; "Basil the Rat" (Ep. 12) 678, 732, 904
Fawlty Towers (videocassettes) 1130, 1336
Fawlty Towers: A La Carte (record) 987, 1106
Fawlty Towers: At Your Service (record) 904, 987
Fawlty Towers Book 2 (book) 768
Fawlty Towers: Re-Opened (TV) 3654, 3738
Fawlty Towers: Second Sitting (record) 767, 904
Fawlty Towers: The Complete Collection Remastered (DVD) 3738, 3741
Fear and Loathing in Las Vegas (book) 2267
Fear and Loathing in Las Vegas (DVD) 2849
Fear and Loathing in Las Vegas (film) 2267, 2360, 2363, 2365–68, 2371, 2376, 2382, 2391, 2392, 2408, 2411, 2414–16, 2422, 2597, 2862, 3839
Fear and Loathing in Las Vegas: NOT the Screenplay (book) 2361, 2372
Feather, Jacqueline 2369
Featherstone, Don 1099
Feirstein, Bruce 2516
Feldman, Marty 8, 13, 63, 164, 165, 315, 954, 978, 1049, 1059, 1131, 2940, 3497
Feldstein, David 2317
Fell, Ken 415
Fellini, Federico 1419, 1559, 2116
Fensom, Peter 309, 389
Fentiman, Mike 61
Fenton, George 1850
Ferdinand, Rio 2745

Ferguson, Craig 3969
Ferguson, William 3543, 3550, 3745
Fergusson, John Duncan 2606
Ferland, Jodelle 3186
Fermor, Patrick Leigh 1657
Ferrari, Nick 3767
Ferraz, Carolina 4192
Ferrell, Will 2214
Ferretti, Dante 1559
Ferrington, Danny 2197
Ferry, Bryan 2703
Ferster, Arron 3982
Festival 40 (TV) 512
Festival on Film (TV) 1154
Fettes, Miranda 2972
Fettis, Andrew 3496
Fiddy, Dick 1805
Fielding, Helen 2885
Fielding, Noel 3771, 4095
Fields, W. C. 2881, 3108
Fiennes, Ranulph [Sir] 3871
Fierce and Gentle Creatures (TV) 2121
Fierce Creatures (film) 386, 1920, 2095, 2110, 2112, 2117, 2121, 2134, 2137, 2162, 2170, 2202, 2210, 2213, 2215–28, 2232, 2233, 2245–47, 2309, 2377, 2390, 3294
The 50 Greatest Comedy Films (TV) 3231
The 50 Greatest Comedy Sketches (TV) 3127
The 50 Greatest Documentaries (TV) 3202
Fifty Years of the BFI (TV) 1082
Film 76 (TV) 536
Film 78 (TV) 654
Film 79 (TV) 747
Film 82 (TV) 984
Film 83 (TV) 994, 1003, 1011, 1044
Film 84 (TV) 1134
Film 85 (TV) 1175, 1243
Film 86 (TV) 1278
Film 88 (TV) 1482, 1543
Film 88 Special (TV) 1480
Film 89 (TV) 1621, 1672, 1680
Film 91 (TV) 1814, 1855
Film 93 (TV) 1933, 1954
Film 93 Special (TV) 1961
Film 94 (TV) 2056
Film 96 (TV) 2137, 2148
Film 2001 with Jonathan Ross (TV) 2677
Film 2005 with Jonathan Ross (TV) 3208
Film 2009 with Jonathan Ross (TV) 3697, 3725
Film 2011 (TV) 4039
The Film Club (TV) 1458, 1713
Film Comment (magazine) 880, 1845, 3019
Film Education (TV) 2173
Film Night (TV) 335, 377, 2697
The Film Programme (radio) 4058
Film Review (magazine) 424
Films and Filming (magazine) 373
A Final Wave at the World: The Alimony Tour, Part One [U.S., 2009] (stage) 3709, 3750

General Index

Financial Times (newspaper) 162, 316, 915, 1377, 1970, 2017, 2777, 3307, 3533
Finch, Hilary 1304
Fincham, Peter 1307
Fine, Dennis 911
Fine, Harry 99
Finkel, Mark 2027
Finn, Mali 2651
Finnigan, Judy 1711, 1893, 2008, 2254, 2278, 2817, 2935, 3027, 3367, 3383, 3529, 3541, 3581, 3638
The First Annual Comedy Crusade Against Diabetes (stage) 1430
First Bite (TV) 1806
The First Eleven 3267
First Impression (radio) 520
First Love (TV) 1107, 1137
First Night on Meridian (TV) 1922
The First Take (TV) 2402
First Tuesday Book Club (TV) 4196
The First 200 Years of Monty Python (book) 1684, 3573
A Fish Called Wanda (book) 1481
A Fish Called Wanda (DVD) 2438, 3362
A Fish Called Wanda (film) 200, 1346, 1398, 1482, 1484, 1486, 1487, 1489–1500, 1502, 1504–10, 1512, 1514, 1516–20, 1525–27, 1541, 1543–47, 1578–82, 1609, 1627, 1628, 1751, 1786, 1920, 1935, 2056, 2095, 2108, 2221, 2429, 2474, 2477, 2485, 2511, 3231, 3357, 3485, 3555, 3617, 3621, 3649, 3852
A Fish Called Wanda (videocassette) 1594, 1595, 1741, 1780
Fish Tales (book) 1179
Fisher, Anne 2387
Fisher, Carrie 906, 2478, 2906
Fisher, Doug 127
Fisher, John 2244, 2250, 2329, 2627
Fisher, John Hayes 3574
Fisher, Mark 3874
Fisher, Tom 4008
The Fisher King (film) 1813, 1847–50, 1855, 1857, 1858, 1952, 2078, 2119, 2676, 3619, 3907
Fitzgerald, F. Scott 864
Five Minutes with: Michael Palin (web) 3769
"Five Salted Peanuts" (song) 1061
Fjeldmark, Stefan 2685
Flaherty, Stephen 2449, 2621
Flanagan 55, 59
Flanery, Sean Patrick 1894
Flash Harry (record) 803, 3234
Fleet, James 3294
Fleming, Fergus 3177
Fleming, Peggy 734
Fleming, Robert 327
Fletcher, Alan 2927
Fletcher, Brendan 3186
Fletcher, Dexter 1801
Fletcher, Diane 1157, 1344, 1798
Fletcher, Kelvin 3198

Fletcher, Ronald 604
Flippo, Chet 494
Flower, Gilly 439, 441, 446, 450, 453, 456, 676, 677, 679, 680, 685, 732
Flynn, Gillian 3179
Flynn, Miriam 2942
Foges, Peter 375
Folsey, George Jr. 1238
The Food Programme (radio) 1488
Food, Wine and Friends (TV) 846
Foot, Michael 1288
Foot, Moira 148
Football Days (book) 2918
Footlights!: A Hundred Years of Cambridge Comedy (book) 1050
Footlights! 100 Years of Comedy (TV) 1051
For the Roundhouse (event) 3148
Forbes (magazine) 1476
Forbes, Emma 2001
Forbes, Malcolm 1585
Ford, Anna 704, 755, 780, 999, 1263
Ford, Harrison 2899, 2936
Forde, Nigel 1793
Foreman, Michael 874, 892, 897, 1069, 1216, 1522, 1889, 2294, 2598, 2624, 3914
Foresti, Florence 3610
Forever Ealing (TV) 2828
"Forgive Me" (Jones song) 579, 622
Forrest, Elliott 1503
Forstater, Mark 397, 651, 654, 3606, 4202
Forsyth, Bruce 165, 1616, 2593, 3193, 3601, 4179
Forsyth, Janice 3831
Forsythe, Henderson 1636, 1640, 1644, 1647
Forte, Will 2666
Forth Fiesta (TV) 1520
Fortune (magazine) 2387
Fortune, John 296, 492, 539, 704, 871, 883, 915, 2838
The Fortune Teller (film) 549
40 Minutes (TV): "Scarfe's Follies" 1449
47 Years in Tibet (documentary) 2327
Forty Years Without a Proper Job (lecture) 3217, 3390, 3920
Foster, David 2369
Foster, Giles 1461
Foster, Karin 1220
Foster, Marian 1096
Foster, Richard 1907
Foulgham, George 2797
Four-Mations: Aspects of Comedy (TV) 1964
Fourteenth Century England: V (book) 3524
"4th of July, Asbury Park (Sandy)" (song) 3670
Fowlds, Derek 900, 901
Fox, Edward 780
Fox, Marilyn 1275
Fox, Sue 2256, 2258
Frame, Pete 2496

Francis, Clive 3294
Francis, Derek 183, 562
Francis, Eric 1026
Francis, Genie 1034
Francis, Jan 731
The Frank Skinner Show (TV) 2228, 3206
Frankel, David 4004
Franklin, Bob 2534
Franklin, Gretchen 280
Franklin, Jim 302, 518, 577, 600, 604, 607, 731
Franklyn, Sabina 732
Franklyn, William 212, 614
Franklyn-Robbins, John 813, 830
Franks, Alan 3327
Franks, Philip 1986
Fraser, Bill 726
Fraser, Brendan 2261, 2464, 3053
Fraser, Helen [actress] 28, 205
Fraser, Helen [producer] 1447
Fraser, Ronald 99, 165, 200
Fraser-Crook, Janet 1937
Frasier (TV) 3701; "High Crane Drifter" 2136
Frayling, Christopher 1154
Frayn, Michael 838, 1274
Freaky Fables (book) 1160
Frears, Stephen 473, 2852
The Fred Tomlinson Singers 52, 78, 105, 110, 224, 226, 235, 239, 445, 461, 799, 1726
Freedland, Jonathan 2938
Freedman, Paul 1621
Freeman, Alan 455
Freeman, Dave 165
Freer, Anne 707, 816
French and Saunders 1286, 1643
French and Saunders (radio) 4051
French, Dawn 204, 1153, 1343, 1378, 1665, 1705, 1734, 1985, 1986, 2099, 3075, 3462, 3758, 4051
French, Patrick 4142
Frere, Dorothy 679, 731
Fresh Air from WHYY (radio) 1758, 2490, 2846, 3778
Freud, Anna 2763
Freud, Clement 140, 463
Freud, Emma 2042, 4147
Freud, Sigmund 2763
Frewer, Matt 1026
Friday Night...Saturday Morning (TV) 749, 773, 778, 888, 919, 924
Friday Night with Jonathan Ross (TV) 3157
Friday People (TV) 1178
Fried, Clarence 469
Friel, Anna 1833, 3180
Frith, Andy 3396
From Brazil to the Truth (event) 4143
From Hollywood to Borehamwood (TV) 2933, 2939
From Shrewsbury to the World—A Debt to Darwin (lecture) 3707
From Spam to Sperm: Monty Python's Greatest Hits (TV) 2495, 2498, 2556

General Index

Fromer, Liza 4060
Front, Rebecca 2323
Front Row (radio) 2769, 3330, 3369, 3618, 3822, 3828, 4037, 4046, 4129
The Front Row (radio) 3542
Frost, Cerrie 2791
Frost, David [Sir] 99, 487, 576, 990, 999, 1051, 1143, 1273, 1320, 1339, 1527, 1860, 1862, 1972, 2007, 2024, 2091, 2211, 2225, 2459, 2496, 2562, 2618, 2626, 2787, 2839, 3384, 3432, 3496, 3539, 3564, 3587, 3594, 3639, 3900
Frost, Robert 2425
Frost, Sadie 1945
Frost in the Air (TV) 1972
Frost Over the World (TV) 3594, 3900
The Frost Programme (TV) 2007
The Frost Report (TV) 16, 99, 138, 978, 1587, 1972, 3496, 3732, 3976
The Frost Report Is Back! (TV) 3496
Frost Tonight (TV) 3384
Frostrup, Mariella 3308, 3656, 3960, 3962, 4020, 4123
Froud, Brian 1301, 1306, 1345, 2043, 2152, 2193, 3195
Froud, Toby 1301
Fry, Iris 456
Fry, Stephen 204, 1286, 1290, 1365, 1409, 1438, 1563–65, 1665, 1675, 1724, 1734, 1781, 1876, 2083, 2185, 2329, 2419, 2472, 2684, 2701, 3075, 3231, 3246, 3654, 3657, 3877, 3982, 4008
Fuchs, Fredric S. 1198
Fuentes, Paul 1402, 1410, 1420, 1428, 1435
Full Circle (book) 2264
Full Circle (lecture) 2287
Full Circle with Michael Palin (TV) 2112, 2117, 2124, 2131, 2154, 2162, 2191, 2201, 2259, 2270–73, 2275, 2277–82, 2284, 2285, 2288, 2290, 2296, 2298–2301, 2303–05, 2308, 2312, 2343, 2407
Full House (TV) 227, 230, 258, 261
The Full Monty (film) 3926
Fuller, Graham 1630
Fuller, Kim 1924
Fulton, Keith 2078, 2190, 2728, 2900, 2904
Funchal International Film Festival 3810, 4019
Funny Business (TV): "A Question of Taste" 1915
Funny Game, Football... (record) 211
Funny Ha Ha (TV): "Commander Badman" 340
Funny People (TV) 515
Funny That Way (radio) 1777
Funny Women (TV): "Prunella Scales" 2383
Furse, Vanessa 607

Gabereau (radio) 1326, 1965
Gabereau, Vicki 1326, 1965
Gabor, Eva 896, 1147

Gabriel, Peter 1365, 1409, 1938
Gabrielle 2222
Gaiman, Neil 1139, 4128
Gaines, Will 1174
Gainsbourg, Charlotte 2662
Gaisford, Sue 3033
Galaxy Song/Every Sperm Is Sacred (record) 1048
Gallagher 734, 1168
Gallagher, Brita [Palin's great-grandmother] 602, 1818, 1998
Gallagher, Jack 1394
Gallagher, Mike 2483
Gallagher, Paul 3551
Gallagher, Peter 2177
Gallardo, Camilo 2327
Galloway, George 3206
Galton, Ray 165
Gambaccini, Paul 727, 1005
Gambon, Michael 2118, 2204
Gandhi, Indira 1294
Garcia, Andy 3616
Garcia, Jerry 693
Gardam, Bob 616
Garden, Graeme 2, 8, 62, 295, 302, 492, 539, 661, 664, 990, 1156, 1158, 1250, 1567, 1568, 1731, 1734, 1798, 1983, 3000, 3789
Gardner, Caron 251
Gardner, Edward 3943, 3945
Gardner, Rulon 3131
Garfield, Andrew 3659, 3713, 3725, 3854
Garfunkel, Art 2305, 2582
Gargantua (stage) 1918
Gargantua and Pantagruel (books) 1918
Garr, Teri 934, 957, 1028, 1883
Garraway, Kate 3963
Garrett, Lesley 1304, 1442, 1549
Garrison, Greg 348
Garvey, Cyndy 1027
Garvin, Harry 3244
Garwood, Norman 1177, 1263, 1282
Gascoine, Jill 976
Gasteyer, Anna 2214
The Gay Boys Dragon Show [Japan] (TV) 489
Gay Life (TV): "Gay Parents" 775
Gay News (newspaper) 242
G.B.H. (DVD) 3291
G.B.H. (TV) 1833–37, 1839, 1841, 1844
Gebhart, Courtney 1644
Gebler, Carlo 1745
Gee Whiz Graph see *How to Lie with Statistics, Part 1: The Gee Whiz Graph*
Geis, Irving 385, 627
Gelbart, Larry 164
Geldman, Mark D. 2057
Geldof, Bob 871, 1260, 1286, 1296, 1449, 1766, 2836, 3075
General Accident (ads) 623
Geng, Veronica 710, 1760
"Genghis Khan" (Chapman sketch) 481, 1307
Geographical (magazine) 3063, 3706, 3872

Geography (magazine) 1462
George Harrison: Living in the Material World (film) 3994–96
George Harrison: The Inner Light (radio) 2730
George Harrison: What Is Life (radio) 3686
George of the Jungle (film) 2260, 2261, 2442, 2925
George of the Jungle 2 (film) 2261, 2925
George Stroumboulopoulos Tonight (TV) 4056
Georgeson, Tom 1495, 1833
Georgie Fame & The Blue Flames 2069
Gerard, Jasper 3175
German shows see *Monty Python's Fliegender Zirkus*
Gerrard, Alec 378
Gerrard, David 146
Gerrold, David 912
Gershwin, George 2212
Gervais, Ricky 204, 2714, 2786, 3123, 3190, 3452, 3489, 3708
Get Set for Summer (TV) 867
Get Up & Go: The Making of The Rutles (documentary) 3583, 3584
Ghir, Kulvinder 1984
Gibbins, Helen see Palin, Helen (Gibbins)
Gibbons, Leeza 1515
Gibbs, George 1177
Gibbs, Patrick 710
Gibson, Colin 1324
Gibson, Mel 2583, 2990
Gielgud, John [Sir] 248, 2369
Gifford, Kathie Lee 1728, 1910, 2080, 2216
Gilan, Yvonne 446
Gilbert, James (or Jimmy) 183, 312, 406
Gilbert, Matthew 1953
Gilbert, Michael 159
Gilbert, Val 3275
Gilbert, W. S. 1304
Gilbert & Sullivan 824, 1304, 1360, 1442, 1549, 1712
Gill, Andy 1404
Gillan, Dan 456
Gillard, David 512
Gillard, Stuart 2790
Gilliam, Amy [daughter] 529, 1459, 3309, 3659, 3713, 3953
Gilliam, Beatrice [mother] 739
Gilliam, Harry [son] 1459
Gilliam, Holly [daughter] 807, 1459, 4107
Gilliam, Maggie [wife] see Weston, Maggie
Gilliam on Gilliam (book) 2064, 2433, 2435
Gilliatt, Penelope 161, 397, 567, 1033, 1471
Gilman, Harold 3492
Gilmour, Tony 2707
Ging Gang Goolie/Mister Sheene (record) 647

Gladiators: The Brutal Truth (TV) 2565
The Glasgow Herald (newspaper) 958
Glasser, Phillip 1859
Glazier, Allen 2875
Gleiberman, Owen 1323, 2119, 2221
Glendenning, Candace 605
Glenn, Scott 1209
Glidewell, Peter 418
Glinwood, Terry 200
The Globe and Mail (newspaper) 3679
Gloria Hunniford (radio) 1001
Glouberman, Michael 2358
Glover, Crispin 2901
Glover, Danny 1209
Glover, Julian 729
Glover, Richard 4193
GMTV (TV) 2653, 3800
Gnarr, Jón 3603
Go Wild in the Country: The Making of Wind in the Willows (TV) 2187
Gobel, George 745
The Goblin Companion (book) 1306, 2141, 2152
The Goblins of Labyrinth (book) 1306, 2043, 2152
God Loves Caviar (film) 4144
Goddard, Liza 309
Goddard, Mike 325
Godfrey, Bob 309, 332, 1964, 3138
Godleman, Kaye 2703
Godunov, Alexander 734
Goelz, Dave 590
Gogol, Nikolai 3261, 3262
Going Live! (TV) 1625, 1890, 1905, 1946
Going to a Meeting, Part 1: Messing Up a Meeting (film) 2840
Going to a Meeting, Part 2: Meeting Menaces (film) 2841
Gold, Ritchie 554
Goldberg, Whoopi 2295, 2686, 3114
Goldblum, Jeff 1209
The Golden Globe Awards (ceremony) 1578, 1995, 2959
The Golden Skits of Wing Commander Muriel Volestrangler FRHS & Bar (book) 1131
Goldman, David 2530
Goldman, William 1873, 2607, 2651
Goldmine (newspaper) 1511
Goldsmith, Anthony 1345
Goldsmith, Francisca 2086
Goldsmith, Zac 3384
Goldstein, David Andrew 2999
Goldstein, Richard 412
Goldstone, John 397, 567, 638, 669, 710, 739, 1025, 1026, 1677, 2185, 2446, 2909, 3172, 3239, 3587
Gompertz, Will 3945
Good Charlotte 2821
Good Day Live (TV) 2740
Good Morning America (TV) 694, 841, 868, 968, 1510, 1607, 1742, 2303

Good Morning Australia (TV) 3068
Good Morning Britain (TV) 999, 1010, 1020, 1057, 1071, 1108, 1143, 1264, 1892
Good Morning Canada (radio) 2917
Good Morning Monterey Bay (radio) 3119
Good Morning New York (TV) 980
Good Morning with Anne And Nick (TV) 2141, 2151
Good Stuff (TV) 2232
Gooden, Dwight 1309
The Goodies 302, 492, 2721, 3000
The Goodies (TV) 3000; "The Goodies and the Beanstalk" 302
Gooding, Cuba Jr. 2686
Goodman, Joan 2145
Goodman, John 2406
Goodman-Hill, Tom 3353
Goolden, Alastair 879
Goom, Derek 767
The Goon Show (radio) 82, 1968, 1097, 1288, 2147, 2682, 2731, 2733, 2780, 2791, 3841
The Goons 753, 2250, 2328, 2733, 3732
Gordon, Colin 3–7, 9
Gordon, Devin 3104
Gordon, Hannah 1144
Gordon, Jack 2441
Gordon, Noele 1002
Gordon, Richard 22, 23
Gordon-Levitt, Joseph 2358, 2359, 2666
Gorman, John 267, 572, 674, 772, 774, 844, 894, 923, 2721
Gorshin, Frank 2119
Goscinny, René 2557
Gosling, Andrew 418, 420, 421, 425, 427, 429, 471, 532, 534, 537, 541–44, 872
Gottfried, Martin 494
Gottschalk, Thomas 3003
Gough, Darren 3904
Gough, Piers 849
Gould, Dave 2154
Gould, John 114
Gounod, Charles 234
Gow, Gordon 373
Gower, John 3540, 3650
Grabsky, Phil 2399, 2718, 2719, 2858
Grace, Maggie 4189
Grace, Topher 2834
Grade, Michael 3166
The Graduates (book) 1037, 1294
Graef, Roger 539, 545, 755, 1065, 1291, 2098, 2099, 2104, 3075
Graham, Caroline 2690
Graham, Dick 389
Graham, Peter 600, 726
Graham, Philip 604
Graham Chapman: A Six Pack of Lies (CD) 2327
Graham Crackers: Fuzzy Memories, Silly Bits and Outright Lies (book) 2307, 3167
The Graham Norton Show (TV) 3758, 3815, 3824, 4199

Graham, Sam 2421
Grahame, Kenneth 2111, 2118, 2160, 2185, 2187, 2204, 2209, 2331, 2420, 3632
Grammer, Kelsey 1363, 2136
Gran, Maurice 1788
The Grand Knockout Tournament (event) 1390
The Grand Knockout Tournament (TV) 1391, 1407
Grand Tour (radio): "Fez" 1879
Grandstand (TV) 667
Granger, Stewart 895
Grant, Brigit 2184
Grant, Cary 2511
Grant, Julie 1616
Grant, Russell 4030
Grant, Susannah 3368
Grant, Valerie 2027
Gravett, Paul 3993
Gray, Elspet 677
Gray, Maggie 1177, 1282
Gray, Muriel 1191, 1520, 1542, 1730
Gray, Simon 3294
Graymore, Clive [Dr.] 1397
Graymore, Kay 1397
Grayson, Larry 387
Grazebrook, Sarah 480
Grazer, Brian 1238
Grazer, Gavin 2751
Greaney, Dan 2875
The Great Birds Eye Peas Relaunch 1971 (film) 175
The Great British Comedy Event (event) 3834
The Great Britons Awards (ceremony) 3379
The Great Gas Gala (ads) 244
Great Map Mystery see *Terry Jones' Great Map Mystery*
The Great Muppet Caper (film) 590, 815, 859
The Great Outdoors (TV) 2880
Great Performances (TV): "Concert for George" 2980; "The Mikado" 1442, 1549
Great Railway Journeys (book) 2060
Great Railway Journeys (TV): "Derry to Kerry" 602, 820, 1998, 2001
Great Railway Journeys of the World (book) 838
Great Railway Journeys of the World (TV): "Confessions of a Train Spotter" 786, 820, 1440, 1998
Great Rock 'n' Roll Swindle (book) 854
The Great Western Express Festival (stage) 198
Greatest Ever Comedy Movies (TV) 3357
Greaves, Margaret 1745
The Greedy Bastard Diary: A Comic Tour of America (book) 2919, 3097, 3098, 3117, 3120, 3121, 3131, 3133, 3137, 3260
The Greedy Bastard Tour (stage) 2567, 2917, 2919, 2929, 3097, 3131
Green, Brian L. 1644

Green, Joanna 4115
Green, Matt 4049
Green, Seth 2686
Green, Sue 2721
Green, Tom 4089
Greenall, Simon 4008
Greenaway, Peter 2132
Greenberg, Sheldon 1801
Greenberg, Susannah 932, 1016
Greene, Judith 256
Greene, Sarah 1625, 1732, 1890, 1905, 1946
Greenfield, Jeff 2338
Greenstein, Jeff 2953, 2989
Greenwood, Bruce 2899
Greenwood, Debbie 1221, 1240, 1321
Greenwood, Joan 2588
Greenwood, Lee 974
Greer, Bonnie 2843
Greer, Fergus 2488
Greer, Germaine 924
Gregory, Gillian 541
Greist, Kim 1177, 1251
Gremlins 2 (film) 1253
Grier, Pam 2772
Grierson, William 767, 904, 987, 1106
The Grierson Documentary Awards 2002 (ceremony) 2814
Grieve, John 548
Griffin, David 604, 731
Griffin, Eddie 2834
Griffin, Tom 1303
Griffith, Lt-Col. Adrian 2923
Griffith, Melanie 1490, 1578
Griffiths, Derek 2221
Griffiths, Jaye 2714
Griffiths, Martin 589
Griffiths, Richard 928, 1134, 1149
Grime Goes Green: Your Business and the Environment (film) 1789
Grimes, William 2927
Grimm, Paul 777
Grimms 267, 572
Grint, Rupert 2702, 2810
Grisoni, Tony 2360, 2361, 2372, 2376, 2597, 3186, 3392
Grodin, Charles 859
Gross, Mary 966, 1110
Gross, Terry 1758, 2490
Grossberger, Lewis 950
Grossman, David 2925
Grossman, Lloyd 1975
Groundhog Day (film) 2189
Grounds, Tony 2321
The Group 211
Group Madness: The Making of Yellowbeard (TV) 1049
Group One (TV) 508
Grove, Valerie 1926, 2142
Gruffudd, Ioan 2619
Grylls, Bear 4041
Guanaes, Nizan 3296
The Guardian (newspaper) 1371, 1691, 2071, 2189, 2229, 2501, 2628, 2671, 2731, 2835, 2927, 3085, 3178, 3763, 3866, 4002, 4064, 4120, 4132, 4163, 4168

The Guardian Books Podcast (podcast) 3718, 4021
Guest, Christopher 1673
Guinness, Alec [Sir] 1628
Gunn, Aurora 3191
Gunson, Roy 105
Gurnee, Hal 1181
Gurney, A. J. 3466
Gurney, James 2750
Gutteridge, Tom 1051
Guttridge, Nic 3976
Guy, Jennifer 481
Gwynn, Michael 440
Gwynne, Haydn 2355
Gzowski, Peter 298

Hadden-Paton, Harry 3985
Haddrick, Greg 2625
Hadida, Samuel 3659, 3713
Hagger, Alison 1440
Hail the Conquering Hero (film) 1713
Hain, Peter 3927
Haines, Miranda 2291
Hale, Natalie 3787
Half-a-Sixpence (stage) 721
Half Hour Comedy Hour (TV) 1536
Halfway to Hollywood: Diaries 1980–1988 (book) 15, 3332, 3671, 3691–95, 3697–98, 3700, 3704, 3715, 3718, 3721, 3743, 3753, 3758, 3762, 3848, 3852, 3892
Hall, Brad 966, 1110
Hall, Brian 675–77, 679, 680, 685, 732, 2286
Hall, Daryl 507
Hall, Don 3969
Hall, George 1894
Hall, Jerry 630, 1643, 1660, 1662, 1675, 1724, 1969, 3198
Hall, Julie 1063
Hall, Michael 905
Hall, Peter 3191
Hall, Rich 1911
Hall, Robert 3009, 3450
Haller, Scot 1149, 1559
Halper, Andy 1584
Halsall, Ollie 632, 3495
Halsey, John 532, 550, 632, 635, 3495, 3584
Halsey, Michael 441
Ham, Anthony 1833
Hamilton, Jocelyn 2157
Hamilton, Scott 3552
Hamilton, Tim 3603
Hamm, Mia 3296
Hammershøi, Vilhelm 1298, 3118, 3163, 3537
Hammond, Darrell 2214
Hammond, Peter 3825
Hampshire, Allardyce 387
Hampshire, Susan 1096, 1686
Hamshere, Keith 2209
The Hamster Factor and Other Tales of Twelve Monkeys (film) 2078, 2190
Hancock, Nick 2302, 2905
Hancock, Sheila 1923
Hancock, Tony 3108

Handelsman, J. B. (Bud) 1078, 1160, 1916, 1932
Handl, Irene 68
Handler, Chelsea 3617
HandMade Films 710, 863, 933, 943, 970, 991, 1149, 1173, 1263, 1532, 1574, 1634, 1751, 2341, 2706, 2712, 2805, 3700
Hands: A Journey Around the World (book) 3358
Hanks, Tom 1578, 2166, 2335, 2826, 2906, 3223, 3640
Hanly, Francis 3934, 4157, 4169, 4182
Hannity & Colmes (TV) 3484
Hanomansing, Ian 3302
Hansen, Lisa M. 1783
Happy Holidays: The Golden Age of Railway Posters (book) 1400
Harcourt, Nic 2643
Hardcastle, Victoria 1370
Hardcastle, William 375
Hardie, Sean 737, 818, 1733, 1798, 1869, 2322, 2630, 2631, 2714, 4049
Hardiman, Terrence 382
Hardin, Kris 3987
HARDtalk (TV) 3779
HARDtalk Extra (TV) 3313, 3359
Hardwicke, Edward 651, 725
Hardy, Frances 3720
Hardy, George [Brig.] 1008
Hardy, Jeremy 1732, 2535
Hardy, Robert 1984, 2059
Hare, Doris 1751
Hare, Norman 34
Hare, Tony 136
Hare Brain, Tortoise Mind (book) 2428, 2538
Hare Brain, Tortoise Mind (lecture) 2429, 2445
Hargreaves, David 332, 522
Hark at Barker (TV) 14
Harman, Nigel 3157
Harmony Hairspray (film) 310
Harrelson, Woody 1363, 2751
Harris, Bob 425, 507, 2730
Harris, Naomie 2714
Harris, Owen 4008
Harris, Richard 2702, 2810
Harris, Rolf 2377
Harris, Samantha 2567
Harris, Sandra 658
Harrison, Dhani 2826, 2916, 2921, 4154
Harrison, George 445, 461, 471, 498, 501, 527, 528, 530, 535, 538, 591, 635, 638, 656, 669, 697, 710, 863, 922, 970, 991, 1149, 1173, 1263, 1307, 1532, 1538, 1574, 1751, 2341, 2543, 2678, 2706, 2707, 2711, 2712, 2730, 2762, 2786, 2805, 2826, 2827, 2864, 2916, 2920, 2921, 2980, 3204, 3355, 3516, 3640, 3686, 3700, 3996
Harrison, Olivia 2916, 2921, 3686
Harrison, Rex 3162

Harry, Deborah 1490
Harry Potter and the Chamber of Secrets (film) 2702, 2810–12
Harry Potter and the Philosopher's Stone (book) 2409
Harry Potter and the Sorcerer's Stone (film) 2638, 2702, 2705, 2810
Harryhausen, Ray 2583, 3845
Hart, Miranda 3898, 3976
Hart, Tony 385, 555, 620, 621, 627
Harter, Maureen 1433
Hartford Courant (newspaper) 2808
Hartley, Mariette 777, 1199, 1424
Hartman, David 968
Hartnett, Josh 2899
Hartz, Jim 499
Harvey, Georgina 3600
Harvey, Lawrence 50
Harvey, Richard 1833
Harwood, Ronald 1940
Harwood, Stewart 651
Hass, Lucie 3303
Hastings, Harry 144
Hatch, David 2, 62, 295, 661, 664, 1731
Hatch, Robert 567, 710
Hatch, Tony 2185
Hathaway, Anne 2986
Hatley, Tim 3113
Have a Nice Stay see *Welcome Customer, Part 1: Have a Nice Stay*
Havergal, Giles 112
Havers, Nigel 1225, 1643, 1662, 2933, 2939
Havey, Allan 1489
Hawk, Tony 3185
Hawking, Stephen 2293
Hawkins, Carol 985
Hawn, Goldie 2442
Hawthorne, Nigel [Sir] 662, 900, 901, 991
Haycock, Gordon 1874
Haydn, Joseph 538
Hayes, Brian 1095, 1113
Hayes, Isaac 2456
Hayes, Michael 729
Hayes, Patricia 1495
Hayes, Sean 2932, 2953, 2977, 2981, 2989, 3560
Hayman, David 112
Haynie, Jim 1783
Hays, Robert 3048
Hayward, Stan 1964
Haywood, Jo 2944
HBO First Look (TV): "The Making of Shrek the Third" 3404
Head for Business (film) 960
Headey, Lena 2057, 2902, 3178
Healey, Mike 1288
Health Education Authority (Anti-Smoking) (ads) 1907
Heap, Mark 3262
Hearing, Trevor 1714
"Heartbreak Hotel" (song) 3928
Hearton, George 869
Heath, Edward [Prime Minister] [Sir] 233
Heath, Jennifer 2986
Heaton, Louis 2383

Heaven (film) 1458
The Heaven and Earth Show (TV) 2460, 2487
Heavy Metal (magazine) 1087
Heavy Rain (videogame) 3794
Hecht, Abraham B. [Rabbi] 712
Heckerling, Amy 1210
Hedden, Rob 1251
Hedges, Lucas 4165
Heeger, Alan 3211
Heertje, Raoul 2252
Hegner, Michael 2685
Heidi, Gloria 1034
Heiney, Paul 1436, 3883
Helford, Ross 3048
Heller, Zoe 1896
Hellman, Ira 1274
Hello Sailor (book) 392, 2467
Hello! (magazine) 4134, 4137
Helmond, Katherine 863, 885, 1177, 1251
Help! (magazine) 16
Help! I'm a Fish (film) 2685
The Helping Hand: Coaching Skills for Managers (film) 1797
Hemingway Adventure see *Michael Palin's Hemingway Adventure*
Hemingway, Ernest 2086, 2461, 2500, 2501, 2505, 2509, 2515, 2526, 2555, 2569, 3458, 3782, 3819
Hemingway, Margeaux 500
Hemingway, Mariel 1089
Hemingway's Chair (book) 2086, 2088, 2101, 2140, 2142, 2362, 2379–81, 2501, 4120
Hemmings, David 19
Henderson, Don 606
Henderson, Maggie 481, 543, 661
Henry, Buck 563
Henry, Lenny 923, 1318, 1452, 1665, 1675, 1705, 1724, 4108
Henry, Thierry 2745, 3296
Henry Cleans Up (film) 389
Henry V (film) 1755
Henson, Basil 137, 192, 677
Henson, Jim 590, 859, 1195, 1295, 1301, 1345
Henson, Nicky 243, 677, 763
Hepburn, Kate 659, 806
Herbie Rides Again (film) 391
Hercules (TV) 2393
Here and Now Toronto (radio) 4055
"Here Comes the Sun" (song) 515
Here's Your Obituary (TV) 3172
Herman, Dave 505, 716
Heroes and Villains (book) 855
Heroes and Villains (radio): "Alexander the Great and Attila the Hun" 2843
Heroes for the Planet—A Tribute to National Geographic (TV) 2634
Heroes of Comedy (TV): "The Goons" 2250; "Les Dawson" 2244; "Peter Cook" 2329; "Ronnie Barker" 2627; "Spike Milligan" 2733
Herring, Richard 3568
Herschlag, Alex 2981

Hersey, Dana 1516, 1603
Hersey's Hollywood (TV) 1516, 1603
Hershey, Barbara 1945
Hertzberg, Hendrik 491
He's Not the Messiah, He's a Very Naughty Boy (radio) 3770
He's Not the Messiah He's...Terry Jones! (event) 4066
"He's So Fine" (song) 530
Hessler, Gordon 41
Hewison, Robert 908, 1050, 1051, 1068, 3172, 3381, 3587
Hewitt, Jennifer Love 3597
Hewitt, Kevin 2289
Hewitt, Martin 1059
Hewson, Sherrie 3555
Heywood, Pat 1353
Hicks, Barbara 1177
Hicks, Bill 3108
Hicks, Simon 2659
Hidden History of Egypt (TV) 2718, 2850
Hidden History of Sex and Love (TV) 2719, 2850, 2858
Hidden History of the Roman Empire (TV) 2719, 2850
The Hidden Mind (film) 2428, 2538
Hidden Treasure (film) 903
Higgins, Steve 2214
Higson, Charlie 2411
Hill, Benny 1661
Hill, Bernard 2185
Hill, Charlie 777
Hill, Damon 2039
Hill, Dana 1210
Hill, Dave 1150
Hill, Debra 1813, 1850
Hill, Faith 2653
Hill, Jimmy 139, 370
Hill, Katy 2299
Hill, Rosemary 473
Hill, Susan 1889
Hiller, Arthur 2295
Hillerstrom, Oscar 4093
Hills, Dick 558
Hills, Jonathan 810
Hiltbrand, David 2067
Himalaya (audiobook) 3014
Himalaya (book) 3025, 3029, 3030, 3050, 3052, 3073, 3135, 3155
Himalaya (DVD) 3164
Himalaya (lecture) 3029, 3052, 3066, 3069, 3073, 3087, 3826; see also *An Evening with Michael Palin*
Himalaya with Michael Palin (TV) 1968, 2895, 2923, 3011, 3022, 3023, 3027–29, 3033, 3035–37, 3039, 3040, 3043, 3045, 3052, 3054, 3057, 3061–63, 3065–69, 3071, 3073, 3087, 3152, 3156, 3160, 3192, 3795, 3947
Hinchley, Pippa 1353
Hindle, Charlotte 1773
Hines, Gregory 893
Hinkley, Don 590
Hinson, Hal 1512
Hinton, David 1259

Hinton, Douglas 731
Hip Hip Hooray (film) 765
Hird, Thora 1461
Hislop, Ian 2773
A History of the World in 100 Objects (radio): "Clovis Spear Point" 3791
History Today (magazine) 2963
Hitchcock, Alfred 4122
Hitchcock, Bill 168
Hitchens, Christopher 3751
The Hitchhiker's Guide to the Galaxy (film) 3136
The Hitchhiker's Guide to the Galaxy (radio/book/TV) 1098, 2318, 2352, 2665, 2684, 3690, 4087
The Hitchhiker's Guide to the Galaxy Radio Show...Live! (stage) 4128
H.M.O. (TV) 2639
Hoare, Ken 315
Hoare, Peter 3943, 4003
Hobbs, Jack 596, 601
Hoberman, J. 710, 1559, 3186
Hobson, Dorothy 1194
Hochman, Larry 3113
Hodgkinson, Tom 3266
Hodgson, Brian 550
Hoffman, Dustin 1101
Hoffmann, E.T.A. 3048
Hogan, Lisa 3667
Hogg, Ian 1984
Hogg, James 930
Hoggart, Paul 2501, 2797, 3037
Hoin, Ken 1832
Holden, Amanda 2370, 3931
Holden, Caroline 959, 1316, 1317
Holden, Stephen 2376
Holder, Judith 1705
Holgate, Mike 1705
Holland, Jools 1053, 1174, 1191, 1643, 3022, 3372
Hollings, Steven 1290
Hollingsworth, Tony 1409
Holloway, Julian 560, 618, 900, 901, 903, 1157, 1158, 1563, 1984, 2059
Holly, Lauren 2992
Hollywood Bowl Hall of Fame 2678, 2762
Hollywood Greats (TV): "Cary Grant" 2511
Hollywood Homicide (film) 2898, 2899
The Hollywood Reporter (magazine) 4184
Hollywood Squares (TV) 745
Holm, Ian 863, 1102, 1177, 1460
Holman-Hunt, Diana 1262
Holmes, Eamonn 1620, 1722, 3702, 4203
Holmes, Jonathan 2311
Holmes, Mark 1025
Holmes, Martha 1854
Holmes, Rick 3701
Holmquist, Ward 1712
Holt, Madeleine 2470, 3338
Holy Flying Circus (TV) 4008
Hom, Ken 2134
Home and Away (TV) 2131, 2154, 2300
Home Movie Roadshow (TV) 3857

Honey, I Shrunk the Audience (film) 2052, 2484
Honeysett, Martin 354
Hoon, Will 3918
Hooper, Tom 3895
Hootkins, William 1894
Hoover, Ralph *see* Spike, Paul
Hooves of Fire (TV) 3479
Hopkins, Anthony 1340
Hopkins, Keith [Prof.] 2565
Hopkins, Trevor 1662, 1724
Hopkinson, Simon 2625
Hopper, Dennis 3296
Hordern Michael [Sir] 970, 1003, 1059, 1260, 1738, 1916, 2588
Horn, Caroline 2524
Horn, David 1549
Hornby, Gill 1544, 1623
Horne, Eleanor 4053
Horne, Marilyn 2678
Horrocks, Jane 3479
Horvitz, Louis J. 3844
Horwood, William 2204
Hoskins, Bob 1177, 1574, 2448, 2588
Hot Air and Fantasy: The Adventures of Terry Gilliam (TV) 1617
Hot Properties (TV) 1183
Hot Pursuits (TV) 2534
Hough, Julian 604
The Hour (TV) 3775, 4056
Housego, Mike 1676
Houseman, John 1127
Houston, Kent 1559
Houston, Whitney 1239
Hoving, Tom 1030
How Am I Doing?: The Appraisal Interview (film) 618
How Do They Do That? (TV) 2226
"How Do You Do It?" (sketch) 704, 764, 2787, 2839
How Far Can You Go? (radio) 1768
How Fear Came (audiobook) 1161
How Not to Exhibit Yourself see Selling in Practice, No. 2: How Not to Exhibit Yourself
"How Sweet to Be an Idiot" (Neil Innes song) 347, 943
How to Irritate People (TV) 16
How to Lie with Statistics, Part 1: The Gee Whiz Graph (film) 385
How to Lie with Statistics, Part 2: The Average Chap (film) 627
How to Lose Customers without Really Trying (film) 1734
How to Make Up Your Mind About the Bomb (book) 858
How to Win Holes by Influencing People (film) 558
How Well Do We Know Ourselves? (lecture) 3257
Howard, Ann 1352, 1776, 1860
Howard, Arthur 165
Howard, Ron 2480
Howard, Russell 3980
Howard, Trevor 970
Howard, Vanessa 99
Howe, Gary 1924
Howell, Georgina 2215

Howerd, Frankie 916
Howlett, Kevin 3686
Howman, Dave 293, 422, 600, 2185, 3771
Howorth, Nicki 232
Hubbell, Chris 2421
Huckerby, Mark 3479
Hudd, Roy 165, 1340
Hudson, Oliver 2442
Huff, Darrell 385, 627
Huffington, Ariana 2338
Hughes, Caroline 3770
Hughes, Cherry 2694
Hughes, David 991, 1025
Hughes, John 1210
Hughes, Nerys 475
Hughes, Terry 127, 136, 138, 141, 214, 291, 406, 480, 517, 518, 577, 598, 605, 606, 943, 2358, 2359, 2664, 2666
Hughman, John 3, 4, 83, 130, 365
Hui, Raman 3405
Hulme, Lachy 4089
The Human Face (book) 2640
The Human Face (TV) 2641, 2642, 2648, 2650, 2651, 2689, 3568
The Human Face of Business (seminar) 2823
The Humblebums 85
Hume, Roger 662, 685
Humour Is Not a Luxury (film) 1478, 1566
Humphries, Andy 3898
Humphries, Barry (aka Dame Edna) 292, 492, 539, 1643, 1662, 2091, 2754
Humphrys, John 2680
Hunky Chunks (ads) 246
Hunniford, Gloria 976, 983, 1002, 1095, 1113, 1144, 1225, 1340, 1626, 1686, 2069, 3578
Hunt, Antonia 1122
Hunt, Linda 1209
Hunt, Richard 590
Hunter, Allan 1857
Hunter, George Leslie 2606
Hunting People (book) 565
Huntington, Tom 2915
Huntley-Wright, Betty 453
Huntsman, Benjamin 1877
Hurley, Elizabeth 2641, 2642, 2650, 2651
Hurll, Michael 8
Hurndull, Richard 725
Hurst, Andy 3048
Hurst, John 2038
Hurt, John 1133, 1417, 2702, 4071
Huss, Judson 2163
Hutchinson, Diana 607
Hutchison, Geoff 3456
Hutton, Lauren 893, 1585, 1823, 3114
Huxley, Aldous 1996
Hyde-White, Wilfrid 50
Hyks, Veronika 2944
Hyman, Bruce 2535
Hysteria 2 (stage) 1675
Hysteria 2 (TV) 1724
Hywel, Dafydd 1470

I Bet You They Won't Play This Song on the Radio (record) 802
I Don't Believe It! The "One Foot in the Grave" Story (TV) 2615
I Like Chinese/I Bet You They Won't Play This Song on the Radio/Finland (record) 801
Ibrahim, Musa 3664, 3759, 3763, 3795, 3805
Icons of England (book) 3557
I'd Like a Word with You: The Discipline Interview (film) 763
Ide, Wendy 3186, 3304
"Idiot Song" *see* "How Sweet to Be an Idiot"
Idle, Carey [son] 260, 1772, 2025
Idle, Ernest [father] 2200
Idle, Lily [daughter] 1772, 2061, 2389, 2906, 3204
Idle, Mrs. [wife] *see* Ashley, Lyn
Idle, Norah [mother] 739, 2025, 2192, 2200
Idle, Tania [2nd wife] *see* Kosevich, Tania
The Idler (magazine) 3266
Igbon, Alan 1833
Iglesias, Julio 1541
Igor (film) 3560
Ilkley Literature Festival 1129
Illich, Ivan 853
An Illustrated History of Bristol Zoo Gardens (book) 3915
The Illustrated London News (magazine) 1325
Ilyina, Tatiana 3048
I'm Sorry I'll Read That Again (radio) 2, 62, 295, 661, 1731
I'm Sorry I'll Read That Again (record) 664
The Imaginarium of Doctor Parnassus (DVD/Blu-ray) 3816
The Imaginarium of Doctor Parnassus (film) 3473, 3482, 3490, 3503, 3659, 3660, 3681, 3710, 3713, 3714, 3717, 3725, 3730, 3733, 3752, 3772, 3774–78, 3780, 3785, 3786, 3839, 4165
"Imagine" (song) 1061
Iman 1882
Imbruglia, Natalie 2533
The Importance of Creativity (lecture) 3641
The Importance of Mistakes (film) 1444
The Importance of Mistakes (lecture) 1434, 1476, 1767
"The Impossible Dream" (song) 590
Imrie, Marilyn 869
In Conversation (TV): "Terry Gilliam" 3864
In Search of John Gower: Glosses, Recensions, Politics (discussion) 3650
In Style (magazine) 2959
In the Beginning (TV) 1916
In the Name of Love (book) 855
In the Wild: Lemurs with John Cleese (TV) *see* *Born to Be Wild: Operation Lemur with John Cleese*

In Two Minds see *Customer Relations in Practice, No. 1: In Two Minds*
In Vision (TV) 375
Inar Gahined (film) 1699
The IN-Complete History of Monty Python (screenings) 3126
The Independent (newspaper) 2016, 2020, 2093, 2273, 2357, 2494, 2711, 2781, 3033, 3085, 3089, 3274, 3371, 3923, 4186
Independent Focus (TV) 2816, 2857
The Independent on Sunday (newspaper) 3007, 3356
Independently Animated: Bill Plympton (book) 3916
Ineson, Ralph 2841
The Inferno of Dante (audiobook) 2237
The Ingenious Gentleman Don Quixote: Words and Music from the Time of Cervantes (concert) 3631
Ingraham, Laura 2313
Innes, George 651
Innes, Neil 10, 211, 267, 268, 275, 278, 293, 316, 324, 347, 363, 368, 373, 374, 397, 416–18, 420, 421, 425, 427, 429, 471, 481, 482, 492, 494, 497, 502, 513, 515, 532, 534, 535, 537, 539, 541–44, 550, 567, 572, 576, 582, 632, 635, 704, 710, 805, 871, 872, 874, 943, 970, 1032, 1153, 1289, 1343, 1463, 1464, 1466, 1469, 1470, 1473, 1475, 1479, 1677, 2032, 2472, 2644, 2787, 2826, 2839, 2906, 3354, 3493, 3495, 3531, 3584, 3585, 3600, 3606, 3696, 3745, 3771, 4157
Innes, Yvonne 3516
The Innes Book of Records (TV) 872
Innocent, Harold 605
Inside Himalaya (book) 3026
Inside Joke with Monty Python's Terry Jones (event) 3790
Inside Sahara (book) 2785
Inside Shabby Road: The Music of The Rutles (documentary) 3583, 3585
Inside the Labyrinth (TV) 1345
Inspirations at NLS: Michael Palin (event) 3938
The Instant Monty Python CD Collection (CD) 2028
Intel Centrino ("Entertainment in Your Lap") (ad) 3185
"Interesting Facts" (sketch) 704, 755, 764
Interlude (film) 19
The Interview (radio) 3364
An Intimate Evening with John Cleese (event) 3232
The Invention of Lying (film) 3708
Ireland, Kathy 1883
The Irish Film and Television Awards [2nd] (ceremony) 3059
Iron Maiden 1571, 3139
Iron Maiden: From There to Eternity (video) 1571
Irons, Jeremy 2083, 2423, 2813, 3354, 3616
Irving, Amy 1335, 1859

Irwin, Randy 1640
Is This a Record? (film) 309
Ischia Global Film & Music Fest 3161, 3535
Isle of Wight County Press (newspaper) 1971, 1987
Isn't She Great (film) 2547
It's a 2'6" Above the Ground World (film) 243
It's a Wacky World (TV) 160
It's Alive: The True Story of Frankenstein (TV) 2047
It's All Right, It's Only a Customer see *Marketing in Practice, No. 2: It's All Right, It's Only a Customer*
It's Cliff Richard (TV) 350
It's Garry Shandling's Show (TV) 1807
It's Marty Feldman (TV) 13
It's My Story (radio): "White Chief Humphrey" 4104
It's Only Rock 'n' Roll (CD) 2532, 2533
It's: The Monty Python Story (TV) 2495, 2496, 2556, 2710
It's Your Choice: Selection Skills for Managers (film) 1986
Iuorio, Antonino 3953
Izzard, Bryan 562
Izzard, Eddie 2024, 2229, 2250, 2252, 2471, 2495, 2496, 2556, 2653, 2735, 2791, 2836, 2844, 2958, 3180, 3352, 3354, 3465, 3560, 4081, 4095, 4096, 4179

Jabberwocky (book) 624
Jabberwocky (DVD) 2699
Jabberwocky (film) 511, 536, 566–68, 570, 574, 578, 587, 595, 863, 1322, 2540, 4097
Jack and the Beanstalk see *We All Have Tales*
The Jack Docherty Show (TV) 2277, 2302
Jack the Giant Killer/Scrapefoot (audiobook) 1161
Jackanory (TV): "Charlie and the Chocolate Factory" 1275, 2808; "Fantastic Stories: The Slow Ogre" 1929; "Fantastic Stories: The Star of the Farmyard" 1931; "Fantastic Stories: The Ship of Fools" 1936; "Nicobobinus" 1454; "Small Harry and the Toothache Pills" 959, 1135, 1275
Jackson, Alan 2737
Jackson, Anna 332
Jackson, Glenda 1062, 4053
Jackson, James 3035
Jackson, Janet 3824
Jackson, Joe 772, 966
Jackson, Judy 1809
Jackson, Latoya 2002
Jackson, Paul 1125, 1365
Jackson, Peter 2962
Jacob, Rahul 3533
Jacobs, Lawrence 2157
Jacoby, Bobby 1647
Jacquemin, Andre 235, 293, 422,

600, 723, 803, 1012, 1427, 1723, 1846, 2185, 3771
Jacques, Hattie 148
Jadoff, Kenneth [Rev.] 714
Jagger, Bianca 635, 639
Jagger, Mick 580, 630, 635, 906, 1969, 2533
Jago, June 159
Jahan, Hiddy 614
Jake's Journey (TV) 1455, 1485, 1501, 1554, 1558, 2541
James, Anne 1720
James, Clive 266, 292, 296, 704, 1413, 1747, 2002, 2723
James, Jasper 3199
James, Linda 546
James, Nick 2139
James, Sally 674, 772, 774, 844, 894, 2173, 3413
James, Wendy 1819
James Bond: A BAFTA Tribute (TV) 2837
James Bond 007: Everything or Nothing (video game) 2930
James-Moore, Jonathan 1794
Janes, Hugh 604
Jarvis, Howard 694
Jarvis Cocker's Sunday Service (radio) 3819
Jason, David 10, 651, 2196, 2211, 2627, 2966, 3193, 3246
Jay, Antony 204, 215, 304–08, 383, 385, 449, 452, 454, 457, 459, 476, 477, 487, 546, 548, 619, 663, 683, 684, 692, 696, 826, 827, 899, 903, 909, 960, 1158, 1443, 1667, 1734, 1868, 1984–86, 2059, 2630, 2631, 2714, 2840, 2841, 3166, 4049
Jeans, Luke 1018, 1800
Jeavons, Colin 1157
Jebb, Julian 852
Jeffrey, Peter 1559
Jeffries, Stuart 4132
Jenkins, Clive 704, 755
Jenkins, Simon 612
Jenkinson, Philip 377, 427
Jennings, Alex 1868, 4115
Jensen, Ashley 3606, 4018
Jensen, David 2201
Jensen, Kid 585
Jeopardy! (TV) 2637
Jerome, Jerome K. 473
Jerry Springer: The Opera (opera) 3395
Jersey Boys (musical) 3510
"Jerusalem" (song) 1726
Jessop, Peter 1833
Jesting Pilate: The Diary of a Journey (book) 1996
La Jetée (film) 2119
Jeter, Michael 1850
Jewel 2906
Jex, Lindsay 3654
Jillette, Penn 3084
Jimmy Kimmel Live! (TV) 3141, 3613
JLS 3698
Johansen, Bard Tufte 3988
John, Billy 1026

John, Elton 116, 616, 2239, 2328, 3397
John Cleese Forever (TV) 2739, 2743
John Cleese — His Life, Times and Current Medical Problems [New Zealand, 2005] (stage) 3218, 3233
John Cleese in Conversation with Chris Serle (events) 3544
John Cleese Live!: The Alimony Tour 2011 (DVD) 4024–26, 4029, 4030, 4035–37
The John Cleese Sketchbook (radio) 435
John Cleese's Comedy Heroes (TV) 3108
John Cleese's First Farewell Performance (TV) 1546, 1547, 3362
John Cleese's Life and Times (events) 2971
John Cleese's Wine for the Confused (TV) 3053
The John Davidson Show (TV) 895
John Dunn Show (radio) 993
John Gould One-Man Show (stage) 114
John Howard Davies: A Life in Comedy (TV) 4052
John Le Mesurier: It's All Been Rather Lovely (TV) 4097
John Peel's Record Box (TV) 3221
John-Jules, Danny 2059
Johns, Stratford 596
Johnson, April 766, 986
Johnson, Craig 2716
Johnson, Dwayne 3760
Johnson, Kim "Howard" 1066, 1180, 1185, 1196, 1205, 1257, 1295, 1629, 1659, 1684, 3060, 3573, 3651
Johnson, Michael 3048
Johnson, Rebecca 4049
Johnston, Brian 1300, 1775
Johnston, Kristen 2358, 2359, 2664, 2666
Johnstone, Iain 487, 494, 700, 705, 749, 984, 1018, 1044, 1243, 1301, 1546, 1547, 1559, 1693, 1751, 1817, 1920, 1947, 2117, 2221, 2309
Jokers Wild (TV) 140, 325
Jokers Wild Christmas Special (TV) 303
Jolin, Dan 3977
Jolliffe, Ann 1964
Joly, Dom 2545, 3568
Jonathan Ross (radio) 3043, 3437
Jones, Alan 1646
Jones, Aled 4166
Jones, Alex 3887, 3932, 3999, 4026, 4079, 4109
Jones, Angus T. 2925
Jones, Bill [son] 553, 810, 982, 1069, 1112, 1677, 2587, 2646, 3343, 3475, 3687, 3731, 3825, 3858, 4054, 4140, 4162
Jones, Catherine Zeta 1933, 1945, 1955
Jones, Cherry 3147
Jones, David 1833
Jones, Desmond 384, 386
Jones, Dilys Louisa [mother] 217

Jones, Enid 3377
Jones, Freddie 386, 1247, 1461, 1677, 1940
Jones, Gethin 3717
Jones, Griff Rhys 818, 871, 1153, 1343, 1452, 1665, 2091, 2268, 2331, 2489, 2684, 2787, 2839
Jones, Ian Michael 3172
Jones, James Cellan 280
Jones, Jeffrey 1883
Jones, Jennifer A. 3597
Jones, Jerene 898, 1112
Jones, Michael 1142
Jones, Nick 1460
Jones, Nigel [brother] 220, 3371
Jones, Norah 2786
Jones, Paul 248
Jones, Peter 463, 915, 928
Jones, Philip 1661
Jones, Rebecca 4143
Jones, Robert Trent Jr. 2716
Jones, Rufus 4008
Jones, Sally [daughter] 317, 643, 874, 982, 1112, 3687
Jones, Shirley 777
Jones, Simon 481, 1025, 1055, 1098, 1818, 2119, 4128
Jones, Siri [daughter] 3687
Jones, Sonia 710, 722
Jones, Toby 2841
Jones, Tom 1390, 1816, 3022, 3081
Jones, Trevor *see* Du Prez, John
Jones-Davies, Sue 710, 3635, 3655
Jools's Annual Hootenanny (TV) 3372
Jordan, William 321
Joseph, Joe 1897, 2948
Joseph, K. 370
Journey Into Your Imagination (film) 2052, 2484
Joy, David 2716
J. R. R. Tolkien: Pearl and Sir Orfeo (audiobook) 2266
J. R. R. Tolkien: Sir Gawain and the Green Knight (audiobook) 2265
Judi (TV) 1122
Judi Spiers Show (radio) 4025
Juhl, Jerry 590
Julian, Jennifer 2919
Julyan, Caius 2933, 2939
Jump, Gordon 745
Junge, Walter 659
The Jungle Book (film) 2057
Junkin, John 13, 63
Jupitus, Phill 2682, 3735, 4005, 4128
Jurowski, Dmitri 4146
Just a Minute (radio) 444, 463
Just for Laughs [Australia] (festival) 3979, 3980
Just for Laughs [Montreal] (festival) 1399, 3302, 3682
Just for Laughs [Toronto] (festival) 3678–80, 3683
Just for Laughs (TV) 3339, 3746

Kael, Pauline 1177
Kahn, Madeline 1049, 1059
Kalbacker, Warren 2569

General Index

Kaleidoscope (radio) 746, 1615, 1892, 2175
Kaleidoscope at 21 (radio) 2013
Kalem, T. E. 494
Kamen, Michael 1559, 1945
Kane, Madleen 896
Kane, Nick 456
Kane, Susie 4049
Kaplan, Gabe 500
Kaplinsky, Natasha 3028, 3408
Karan, Donna 2169
Karlsson, Gunnar 3385
Kasdan, Lawrence 1166, 1209
Kasdan, Mark 1209
Katakis, Michael 3782, 3987, 4074
Kattan, Chris 2214
Katz, Eileen 1536
Katz, James C. 2909
Katz, Jordan 3123
Katzenberg, Jeffrey 2677
Kauffmann, Stanley 161, 710, 1025
Kaufman, Andy 730, 734
Kaufman, Michael T. 409
Kaupthing Bank ("Thinking Beyond") (ads) 3603
Kavner, Julie 2875, 3076, 3388, 4102
Kay, Dominic Scott 3368
Kay-Gee-Bee Music Ltd. 388
Kaye, Lila 1751
Kazurinsky, Tim 966, 1110
Keagan, Carrie 3785
Keal, Graham 2961
Keane, Molly 1998
Kearney, Martha 3927, 3951
Kearns, Burt 3531
Keaton, Buster 850, 3279, 3292
Keaton, Michael 776, 966
Keaton: The Man Who Wouldn't Lie Down (book) 850
Kee, Robert 850, 852, 864, 999
Keen, Albie 140
Keen, Pat 685
Keepnews, Peter 3332
Keeton, Joe 854
Keill, Ian 256, 264, 296, 417, 471, 531, 872
Keitel, Harvey 2046
Keith, Penelope 381, 477, 696, 2535, 2754, 4052
Kellaway, Lucy 1970
Kelleher, Terry 2742
Kellogg, David 2716
Kelly, Chris 866
Kelly, David 441
Kelly, Gene 777
Kelly, Henry 1008
Kelly, Lorraine 1892, 3902, 4166
Kelly, Richard 1454
Kelman, Elaine 2694, 4126
Kemp, Margaret 2657
Kemp, Martin 2491
Kempson, Rachel 1358
The Ken Campbell Road Show 704, 755
Ken Hom's Hot Wok (TV) 2134
Ken Russell: A Bit of a Devil (TV) 4053
Kendal, Felicity 2448, 3516

Kendall, Jo 2, 62, 295, 661, 664, 1731
Kennard, David 3053, 3211
Kennedy, Gordon 1979
Kennedy, Ludovic 816, 838, 849, 1194, 1219
Kennedy, Mimi 777
Kennedy, Nigel 1759
Kennerley, Kerri-Anne 3455
Kenny, Pat 3071
Kenny, Tom 3969
The Kenny Everett Video Cassette (TV) 849
Kensit, Patsy 2115
Kent, Leticia 578
Kent, Nicolas 1813
Kentley, Eric 3278
Kenwright, Lucy 2838, 4097
Keoghan, Phil 3111
Kerby, Kip 1506
Kermode, Mark 2391, 2437, 2661, 3338, 3615, 3624, 3700, 3710, 3743
Kern, Geof 1551
Kerr, Graham 2303
Kerri-Anne (TV) 3455
Kershaw, Clifford 600
Kershaw, Justine 2390
Keston, Samantha 541
Kewley, Vanya 2749
Key, Philip 3851
Khan, Mahjabeen 3065, 3947
Khan, Mohibullah 614
Khan, Riz 3644
Kidd, Neville 3163
Kidder, Margot 1490
The Kid's Speech (TV) 4009
Kielty, Patrick 3361
Kiernan, Anna 2708
Kilborn, Craig 2220, 2280, 2397, 3013
Kilmer, Val 3597
Kilmister, Russell 1026
Kilner, Clare 2571
Kinane, Trish 1288
Kincaid, David 813
King, B. B. 2533
King, Claire 3342
King, Diana 446
King, Ross 1773
King Biscuit Flower Hour (radio) 505
King Crimson 288
King Guillaume (film) 3610
Kinghorn, Sally 397
The King's Speech (film) 3895, 3896, 3900, 3905
Kingsley, Ben 2448, 3877
Kington, Miles 838, 862, 1413, 3109, 3487, 3565, 3566, 3628
Kington's Anatomy of Comedy (radio) 3109
Kinmonth, Margy 3075
Kinnally, Jon 2932
Kinnear, Roy 142, 200, 604, 644, 666, 2024
Kinninmont, Kate 2134
Kinnock, Neil 1923
Kipen, David 2971
Kipling, Rudyard 731, 1161, 2057

Kirk, Justin 3880
Kirkpatrick, Karey 3368
Kirsch, Oona 1353
Kirschner, Elliot 3140
Kirwan, Steve 3696
Kiss Kiss Bang Bang (TV) 2411
Kiss Me Kate (TV): "Calendar" 2370
Kisses on the Bottom (CD) 4072
Kissinger, Henry 3296
Kite, Lesa 834
Kitman, Marvin 1668
Kitson, Ken 726
Kitt, Eartha 1677
Klane, Robert 1210
Klawans, Stuart 2412
Klein, Calvin 1919
Klein, Robert 693, 2340, 2345, 3588
Kleiser, Randal 2052
Kline, Kevin 824, 1209, 1495, 1498, 1514, 1628, 2095, 2117, 2121, 2221, 2496
Knife & Wife see *Comedy Lab*
The Knight and the Squire (book) 2294, 2598
Knightly, Keira 3479
Knights, Robert 1567, 1568, 2099, 2205, 2206, 2323
Knights, Python, Adventures (event) 3952
Knopfler, Mark 1365, 1409
Koch, Sebastian 4144
Koenig, Rhoda 1120
Kohn, Walter 321
Kolve, V. A. 2663
Kombat Opera Presents (TV): "The South Bragg Show" 3328, 3395, 3396
Konkle, Tom 3296
Korman, Harvey 645, 2421, 2436
Kosevich, Tania [wife of Idle] 561, 630, 635, 906, 2025, 2061, 3505
Kowalchuk, William R. Jr. 2406
The KPFK Hero Awards and Tribute [2nd Annual] (ceremony) 4103
Krall, Diana 4072
Krasny, Michael 2971
Krasny, Paul 1376
Krige, Alice 2750
Kroeger, Gary 966, 1110
Kroft, Steve 1384
Kroll, Jack 1559
Kronenbourg (ads) 1159
Kruger, Ehren 3178
Kruger, Sonia 4188
Kucharova, Tatana 3454
Kuechle, Jeff 1272
Kulerich, Karsten 2685
Kulik, Buzz 1638, 1641, 1642
Kumar, Sujay 4181
Kuntz, Tom 4112
Kurtz, Irma 416
Kuttner, Richard 1018

Labèque, Katia & Marielle 1006
Labyrinth (film) 1195, 1295, 1301, 1306, 1325, 1327, 1328, 1345
Lacey, Hester 2273
Ladd, Keith 901

Lady, Steph 2054
The Lady and the Squire (book) 2294, 2598, 2599, 2720
Lady Cottington's Pressed Fairy Book (book) 1306, 2043, 2044, 2050, 2058, 2193, 3195
Lady Diana *see* Princess Diana (of Wales)
The Lady Eve (film) 1713
Laffan, Kevin 243
La Frenais, Ian 1136, 1924
LaGravenese, Richard 1850
Lahr, John 3113
Laine, Cleo [Dame] 1062, 2791
Lakshmi, Padma 2987, 4145
Lamarr, Mark 2392, 3109
Lamb, Dave 3647
Lambert, Annie 915
Lambert, Emily 4155
Lambert, Eugene 1276
Lambert, Jay 1636, 1640, 1644, 1647
Lancaster, Ann 13
Lanchester Arts Festival 116, 3696
Landau, Martin 1628
Landen, Dinsdale 761, 762
Lander, David L. 834
Landis, John 1238
Landone, Avice 159
Lane, John 1754
Lane, Nathan 2547
Lang, Kirsty 3618, 3828, 4129
Lang, Melody 732
Langdon, John 2535
Langford, Bonnie 4131
Langham, Chris 626, 710, 737, 765, 871, 1153, 1343, 1665, 1734, 1797, 2099, 2104, 2323, 2370, 3296
Langley, Bob 1223, 1245
Langley, William 3940
Langsford, Ruth 2508, 3436, 3702, 4203
Langton, Simon 2321
Lankesheer, Robert 676
Lanning, Greg 1576
La Plante, Lynda 1843
Larbey, Bob 165
Larroquette, John 2436
Larry King Live (TV) 1486
The Larry Sanders Show (TV) 2742
Larsson, Babben 2252
Laryea, Tony 1068
Lasker, Morris E. 469
Last, Richard 34
Last Call with Carson Daly (TV) 2821
The Last Day of World War One see *Timewatch*
The Last Machine (TV) 2064, 2065, 2070, 2073, 2075, 2077
The Last Machine: Early Cinema and the Birth of the Modern World (book) 2062
Last of the Summer Wine (TV): "Welcome to Earth" 1982
The Last Resort with Jonathan Ross (TV) 1375, 1378, 1417, 1439, 1537
The Late Jonathan Ross (TV) 2176
The Late Late Show (TV) 3071, 3754
The Late Late Show with Craig Fer-

guson (TV) 3131, 3412, 3431, 3548, 3676, 3833, 4077, 4185
The Late Late Show with Craig Kilborn (TV) 2673, 2741, 2812, 2867, 2973, 2992, 3013
The Late, Late Show with Tom Snyder (TV) 2218, 2305, 2381
Late Night Esther (radio) 297
Late Night Line Up (TV) 61
Late Night Live (radio) 3458, 3472
Late Night with Conan O'Brien (TV) 2044, 2177, 2213, 2282, 2314, 2482, 2551, 2564, 2883, 3152
Late Night with David Letterman (TV) 921, 942, 969, 981, 1021, 1023, 1028, 1035, 1117, 1147, 1181, 1265, 1312, 1342, 1489, 1499, 1597, 1838, 1911, 1944, 1951
Late Night with Jimmy Fallon (TV) 3727
The Late Show [U.S.] (TV) 1337
The Late Show [U.K.] (TV) 1994
Late Show with David Letterman (TV) 2097, 2120, 2202, 2581
Lateline (TV) 2311
Latenight America (TV) 1092
Later with Jools Holland (TV) 2827
Lathigra, Kalpesh 3038
Lattisaw, Stacey 1364
Laugh-In (TV) 160
Laughton, Roger 820
Lauper, Cyndi 2282
Laurel & Hardy 3108
Laurie, Hugh 204, 1365, 1409, 1665, 1675, 1724, 1734, 1869, 1986, 2091, 2104, 2322, 2419, 2701, 3123, 4018
The Lavender Hill Mob (film) 200, 1580, 2474
Laverne & Shirley (TV): "I Do, I Do" 834
Law, Jude 3490, 3659, 4207
Lawley, Sue 2212
Lawrence, John 456
Lawrence, Marc 2442
Lawrence, Marjie 481
Lawrence, Stephanie 1247
Lawrence, Steve 777, 851
Lawrence, Vernon 8, 230, 258, 261, 289, 378, 519
Lawson, Leigh 1626
Lawson, Margot 726
Lawson, Mark 2501, 2769, 3192, 3303, 3369, 4037
Lawson, Nigella 3071
Layton, George 188
Lazenby, George 2837
Lazer, David 859
Leach, Rosemary 81, 255, 620, 621, 763, 1158
Leaf, David 2562
Leapman, Michael 2020
Lear, Edward 2171, 2425, 4130
Leary, Timothy 1746
The Least Bizarre of Monty Python's Comedy Album (record) 245
Lebowitz, Fran 2551
Led Zeppelin 328
Lederer, Helen 1665

Ledger, Heath 3178, 3473, 3482, 3490, 3619, 3659, 3783
Le Douarec, Thomas 3091
Lee, Alan 1305
Lee, Chai 480
Lee, Christopher 50, 2837
Lee, George 441, 676
Lee, Jason Scott 2057
Lee, Ralph 2497
Lee, Robert E. A. 715
Leeming, Jan 1357
Leeves, Jane 2911, 3465, 3701, 4096
Lefevre, Robin 2017
The Legend of Dick and Dom (TV) 3605, 3802, 3910
The Legend of Hallowdega (film) 3880
Legend of the Lost Tribe (TV) 3479
Legends [BBC4, 2008] (TV): "Marty Feldman: Six Degrees of Separation" 3497
Legends [ITV, 2002] (TV): "Peter Cook" 2773
Lehrer, Tom 315
Leifer, Sam 3082
Leigh, Janet 1493
Leigh, Jennifer Jason 1673
Leister, Bryan 1760
Leith, Alan 606
Leith, Brian 2824
Leith, William 2435
Leitso, Tyron 2750
Leland, David 508, 726, 1370, 1374, 2920, 2980
Lemar 3355
Le Mesurier, John 156, 567, 731, 4097
Lemmon, Jack 2442
Lenahan, John 2234
Lennon, John 823, 1061
Lennon, Sean 3342
Lennox, Annie 2533, 3432
Leno, Jay 1335, 1497
Leon, Valerie 99
Leonard, John 1638
Leonard, Joseph 2751
The Leonard Lopate Show (radio) 2882, 3124, 3422, 3673
Leondis, Tony 3560
Lerman, Leo 432
Lerner, Sharon 1967
Les Dawson's Christmas Box (TV) 378
Leslie, John 2508
Lester, Frank 363
Lester, Richard 2562, 4095
Let's Hear It for the King of Judea (radio) 3078
Let's Parler Franglais! (book) 862
Lette, Kathy 1745
Le Vaillant, Nigel 2069
Level 42 1854
Levi, Jonathan 3564
Levin, David Burton 2860
Levin, Gail 3907
Levinson, Al 1179
Levinson, Barry 1609, 1628
Levinson, Charles [Dr.] 858
Levy, David B. 3916

Levy, Maury Z. 1362
Levy, Neil Alan 1647
Lewens, Alan 1813, 2147
Lewis, C. S. 1569
Lewis, Donna 2217
Lewis, Martin 622, 764, 883, 931, 1065, 1746, 2032, 3495, 3669, 3673
Lewis, Martyn 2325
Lewis, Nancy 502, 1098, 3588
Lewis, Paul 3773
Lewis, Richard 2574
Lewis, Stephen 165
Lexus ("The Road Is Calling") (ad) 2423
A Liar's Autobiography—The Untrue Story of Monty Python's Graham Chapman (film) 4140, 4141, 4162
A Liar's Autobiography Vol. VI (book) 810, 822, 831, 841, 873, 878
Library Journal (magazine) 2086, 2915
License to Kill (film) 1741
Licorish, Vicky 1776
Lieberson, Sandy 567
Liesbeth (TV) 254
Life (magazine) 1524
Life and How to Survive It (book) 1078, 1160, 1932, 1934, 1965, 2063, 2079–82, 2085, 2595
Life of Brian see *Monty Python's Life of Brian*
The Life of Graham: The Authorised Biography of Graham Chapman (book) 3200
The Life of Palin: From Monty Python to Brazil (event) 4187
Life of Python (book) 1056, 1097
Life of Python [1990] (TV) 1726, 1752; see also *Omnibus*
Life of Python [2000] (TV) 2495, 2556
Life on Air (TV) 2824
Lifeline (TV): "FARM-Africa" 2748; "Motivation" 2985; "Sudan Appeal" 2374
Lima, Kevin 2619
Limb, Sue 1732
Limericks (book) 1220–24, 1245, 1258, 1290
Lincoln, Andrew 3294
Lindberg, Chad 2633
Lindsay, Lord 3629
Lindsay, Nigel 2205, 2206, 2321
Lindsay, Norman 2625
Lindsay, Robert 204, 1797, 1833–37, 1839, 1841, 1844, 1868, 2221, 2793, 3291
The Line That Refused to Die (book) 1804
Lineker, Gary 2593
Ling, Bai 3236
Link (TV) 1581
Lipman, Maureen 137, 1095, 1225, 1819, 3565
Lisi, Virna 113
List, Liesbeth 254
Listen to Me: Buddy Holly (CD) 3981, 4034

The Listener (magazine) 107, 485, 705, 710, 1206, 1274
Lithgow, John 2231, 2358, 2359, 2664, 2666
Little, Mark 2149
A Little Light Worrying: The Best of Mel Calman (book) 2155, 2156
Littman, Julian 1776
Liu, Lucy 2901, 3185
Live and Kicking (TV) 2001, 2178, 2223
Live at Five (TV) 1089, 1184
Live from the Lighthouse (TV) 2419
Live from the Mardi Gras, It's Saturday Night on Sunday (TV) 563
Live from Two (TV) 814, 856, 877
Live with Regis and Kathie Lee (TV) 1728, 1910, 2080, 2216
Live with Regis and Kelly (TV) 3110, 3728
Lively, Jason 1210
Liver Birds (TV) 178
Liverpool Echo (newspaper) 2797
Lizer, Kari 2989
Ljungberg, Freddie 2745
Llewelyn, Desmond 2516, 2819
Lloyd, Harold 2166, 3292
Lloyd, Innes 1353, 1548
Lloyd, John 463, 661, 737, 767, 818, 1752, 1781, 3982, 4128
Lloyd-Pack, Roger 900
Lloyd Webber, Andrew 773, 927, 2618, 3639
Lo + plus (TV) 2247
Lo Schiavo, Francesca 1559
The Lobes 1063
Los Lobos 2177
Lochte, Dick 1551
Locked Out see *Enfermés dehors*
Lodge, Andrew 905
Lodge, David 1194
Lodge, Sally A. 686
Lodynski's Flohmarkt Company (TV) 135
Loe, Judy 607, 1025
L'Officier, Randy 1116
Lofthouse, Marjorie 1043
Loftus, Bryan 1872
Loftus, Mick 291
Logan, Phyllis 1150
Loggins, Kenny 2576
Loizou, Chris 2493
Lom, Herbert 983
Loncraine, Richard 970
London Bridge (TV) 400
London Film Festival 539, 545, 755, 759, 793, 977, 1146, 1151, 1154, 1319, 2053, 2198, 3209, 3212, 3329, 3743, 3991, 4162
London Tonight (TV) 3040
Long, Justin 3760
Long, Shelley 1363, 1597
Long Live the Dead Parrot (radio) 2472
Longden, Robert 804
Longstreth, Emily 1673
Look at the State We're In! (TV) 2098; "Secrecy" 2099; "The Status Quo" 2104

Look North (TV) 273
Look Who's Talking with Mariella Frostrup (TV) 2115
Loose Ends (radio) 2271, 3261, 3695, 4044
Loose Talk (TV) 1053, 1075
Loose Women (TV) 3555
Loot (play) 915
Lopez, George 3111
Lopez, Jennifer 2989
Lord, Jon 2854
Lord's Taverners 644, 666
Loren, Sophia 1136
Lorraine (TV) 3902
Los Angeles Guitar Quartet 3631
Los Angeles Philharmonic 3550
The Los Angeles Times (newspaper) 2031, 2119, 2167, 2988, 3394, 3659
The Los Angeles Times Festival of Books 2444, 2568, 3137
Los Lobos 2177
Losing the Light: Terry Gilliam and the Munchausen Saga (book) 1856
Lost in La Mancha (DVD) 2776, 2816, 2857, 2900
Lost in La Mancha (film) 2190, 2597, 2728, 2729, 2767–71, 2776, 2816, 2846, 2847, 2852, 2857, 3818, 4059; see also *Storyville*
The Lost World (documentary) 3986
Louis-Dreyfus, Julia 966, 1110
Love (stage) 3297
Love, Patti 112
The Love Ban (film) see *It's a 2'6" Above the Ground World*
Love Letters (play) 3466
Lovitz, Jon 1883, 2195, 2686
Lowe, Arthur 99, 596
Lowe, Chad 2475
Lowe, George 2130
Lowe, Kathryn [Dr.] 2514
Lowe, Nick 1028
Lowell, Carey 2221
Lowenstein, Celia 2121
Lownes, Victor 57, 161, 3588
Lucas, George 1301
Lucas, Matt 3898, 3976
A Ludicrous Evening with John Cleese...or How to Finance Your Divorce [Norway, 2009] (stage) 3709, 3750
Luff, Peter 492
Luhrmann, Baz 2241, 2571
Lulu 160, 221, 1375, 2806
The Lumberjack Song (record) 461
Lumberjacks OK! (TV) 2201
Lumley, Joanna 1263, 1695, 1973, 2293, 2448, 2754, 2885, 2986, 3565
Lunchtime Show (radio) 2042
Lunden, Joan 1742
Lune, Amy 659
Lusher, Don 1240
Lustig, Jo 2147
Lutz, Karen McCullah 2986
Luuk, Kristian 2246
Lydecker, Beatrice 1181
Lye, Reg 600

Lyman, Rick 1268
Lynch, David 3792
Lyndhurst, Nicholas 960
Lynn, Jonathan 114, 215, 304, 305, 386, 449, 475–77, 492, 539, 546, 549, 554, 618, 625, 662, 692, 696, 763, 915, 1103, 1104, 1751, 2205, 2206
Lynne, Jeff 2730, 2826, 3792, 3981, 4154
Lyons, Darryn 3342

M. Hulot's Holiday (film) 2660
Mabey, Richard 888
Mac, Bernie 2901
Macaulay, Alastair 2017
MacAulay, Fred 3930
MacAulay and Co. (radio) 3930
MacCabe, Colin 888, 919
Macchio, Ralph 1783, 2421
MacCormack, Mike 2000, 2674
MacDonald, Aimi 8, 835
MacDonald, Alistair 1771
Macdonald, Finlay 4173
MacGregor, Neil 3791
MacGregor, Sue 1203, 1356
Machete, Steve 1053
Machiavelli (book) 864
Machin, David 604
MacInnes, Hamish 2698
Mack, Lee 3815
MacKay, Fulton 626, 670
MacKenzie, Philip Charles 2136
Mackichan, Doon 3100, 3551
Mackinnon, Lachlan 1305
MacLachlan, Andrew 710, 1025, 1157
MacLaine, Shirley 2562, 2682
Maclean's (magazine) 1025, 2520, 2761
Macleod, Donny 615
MacLeod, Gavin 777
MacLeod, Roland 340
MacLeod, Tracey 1994
MacMahon, David 1343
MacMillan, Alasdair 1447, 1662, 1862
MacNaughton, Ian 17, 34, 35, 37–39, 43, 44, 49, 52, 54, 55, 59, 60, 78, 83, 86, 88, 93, 96–98, 102, 105, 106, 108, 110, 111, 130, 161, 180, 220–22, 224–26, 229, 232, 234, 236, 238, 239, 248–51, 363, 365, 368, 370, 372, 374, 494, 805, 943, 2830, 2832, 2835
Macy, William H. 2421
Mad Dogs and Cricketers (film) 644, 666
Madden, Paul 1964
Maddox, Brenda 1930
Made in New York (TV) 1333
Madeley, Richard 1711, 1893, 2008, 2254, 2278, 2817, 2935, 3027, 3367, 3383, 3529, 3541, 3581, 3638
Madness 1032, 1100
The Madness and Misadventures of Munchausen (documentary) 3498, 3499
Madonna 1408

MADtv (TV) 2523, 2705, 2870
Maggs, Dirk 4128
The Magic Christian (film) 12, 50
The Magic Pudding (film) 2625
Magical Mystery Tour (TV) 3585, 4152, 4157
Magical Mystery Tour Revisited see *Arena*
Magnavox ("Magnavox. Smart. Very Smart") (ads) 1872
The Magnificent Seven Deadly Sins (film) 165
Magnusson, Magnus 1279
Magnusson, Sally 1359
Maguire, Tobey 2376
Maher, Bill 4194
Maher, Corona 309
Mahoney, Louis 456
Mahoney, Marian 694
Maiden, Sharon 1274
The Mail on Sunday (newspaper) 2458, 2609, 2624, 2690
Makarova, Natalia 1854, 2060
Making Hay (TV) 1963
The Making of Erik the Viking (documentary) 3343, 3475, 4001
The Making of Kombat Opera (TV) 3396
The Making of the Prefident 1789: The Unauthorized Campaign Biography (book) 1668
Malan, Rian 2060
Malcolm, Derek 3864
Malicki-Sanchez, Keram 1198
Malik, Art 1344, 1443
Mallett, David 158, 313
Mallett, Nick 1734, 1789, 1797
The Man (audiobook) 1886
Man About Town (film) 3236
Man Hunt: The Selection Interview (film) 383
The Man Who Killed Don Quixote (film) 2597, 2680, 2728, 2757, 2900, 3644, 3783, 3818, 3828
The Man Who Made Eric and Ernie (TV) 3601
Managing Problem People: Big Mouth Billy (film) 1565
Managing Problem People: Moaning Minnie (film) 1564
Managing Problem People: Rulebound Reggie (film) 1563
Mancini, Ray "Boom, Boom" 1023
Mankowitz, Gered 1674
Mann, Leslie 2261
Mann, Tommy 389
Man's Hour (radio) 1285
Mansi, Louis 606
Mantle, Peter 1026
The Many Faces of Les Dawson (TV) 4047
Maranne, Andre 453
Marceau, Sophie 2516
Marcelle, Charles 726
Marchinko, Jhoni 2989
Marck, Nick 2942
Margolis, Jonathan 2274, 2309
Margolyes, Miriam 1133, 2254, 3376

"Marie" (song) 538
Marin, Cheech 2834
Mark, Mary Ellen 855
Mark Lawson Talks to... (TV): "Michael Palin" 3192; "Terry Gilliam" 3303
The Mark Twain Prize [8th Annual] (ceremony) 3205
Marker, Chris 2119
Marketing in Practice, No. 1: Who Sold You This, Then? (film) 215, 449
Marketing in Practice, No. 2: It's All Right, It's Only a Customer (film) 304, 452
Marketing in Practice, No. 3: The Competitive Spirit (film) 305, 454
Marketing in Practice, No. 4: Prescription for Complaints (film) 381
Markham, Petra 600
Markham, Phillipa 133
Markosky, Cheryl 2675
Marks, Alfred 303
Marks, Johnny 2406
Marks, Laurence 1788
Marling, Susan 3856
Marlow, Tim 3492, 3689, 3847
Marlow Meets... (TV): "Michael Palin" 3492, 3689; "Terry Jones" 3847
Marquardt, Stephen R. [Dr.] 2650
Marr, Andrew 3275
Marsh, Donovan 3884
Marsh, Gary 2038
Marsh, Jean 895, 1095
Marshall, Andrew 928, 1248, 1249
Marshall, Carolyn 1979
Marshall, Garth 422
Marshall, Penny 563, 834, 1585
Marshall, Peter 745
Marten, Len 680, 1026
Martin, Alex 810
Martin, Andrea 1783
Martin, Dean 777
Martin, Dick 642
Martin, George [Sir] 3516, 3934
Martin, John Scott 1026
Martin, Millicent 2024
Martin, Phil 1202
Martin, Steve 893, 1338, 1465, 1619, 1670, 1720, 1752, 2045, 2442, 2465, 2480, 2498, 2591, 2654, 2906, 3108, 3114, 3205, 3223, 3616, 4004
Martin, Vivienne 476, 549
The Martin Short Show (TV) 2475
Martine, Ray 140
Martinelli, Gabriella 3186
Martinez, Marcos 3760
Martin-Laval, Pierre-François 3610
Marty Amok (TV) 63
Marty Back Together Again (TV) 315
The Marty Feldman Comedy Machine (TV) 164, 176
Martyn, Larry 252
Mary Shelley's Frankenstein (film) 2047, 2053, 2054
Masaro, Anastasia 3659
Mascagni, Pietro 2212

Maslin, Janet 1370, 2119
Mason, Barbara 288
Mason, Hilary 607
Mason, Jackie 1860
Mason, James 1059
Mason, Raymond 680
Mason, Stanley 83, 93, 130
Massey, Anna 3566
Massey, Daniel 1833
Massey, Kyle 4017
A Masterclass with Michael Palin (event) 3576
Masters of Fantasy (TV): "Douglas Adams" 2318
Masterson, Fay 2573, 2633
Matheson, Chris 1883
Mathews, Jack 1284, 1395, 1602, 2174
Mathewson, Andrew 3278
Matisse, Henri 3611
A Matter of Life and Death (film) 1458
Matthews, Tony 682
Mauceri, John 2678
Maude-Roxby, Roddy 3–7, 9
Maugham, W. Somerset 2657
Maurer, Jason 3597
Maxwell, Robert 1577
Maxwell, Roberta 957
May, Brian 2813, 3354, 3516
May, Bunny 532, 534, 544
May, Elaine 1301
May, Jack 725
May, Melinda 3–7, 9
May, Robert 2406
Mayall, Rik 1032, 1125, 1153, 1318, 1565, 2118, 2204, 2787, 2839, 3108
Mayer, Lise 1125
Maynard, Bill 252, 382, 435
Mayo, Simon 3615, 3743
Mayoh, Royston 1247
McAvoy, James 4018
McBain, Robert 680
McCabe, Bob 2382, 2453, 2540, 2915, 2941, 3200, 3219
McCain, John [Sen.] 3570
McCall, Davina 2232
McCall, Phil 112
McCarthy, Beth 2214
McCartney, Paul [Sir] 982, 1795, 2707, 2826, 2916, 2921, 3297, 3640, 4072, 4090, 4152, 4154, 4157
McCauley, James 2742
McClements, Gillian 726
McClurg, Edie 777
McConnell, Heather 2860
McCormack, Eric 2932, 2953, 2977, 2981, 2989
McCormack, Mark 558
McCourt, Richard 3605, 3802, 3910
McCowen, Alec 1370
McCrory, Helen 3895
McDonald, Philip 1738
McDonald, Stuart 2837
McDowall, Roddy 1638
McEntire, Reba 3368
McErlane, Maria 1852

McEuen, John 3141
McFarlane, Stuart 3671
McG 2901
McGiffin, Carol 3555
McGill, Ken 2561
McGinn, Clare 2090
McGough, Roger 267, 351, 635, 4128
McGowan, Alistair 2894
McGrady, Mike 1370
McGrath, Joseph 50, 596, 601
McGrath, Michael 3113
McGrath, Rory 661
McGraw, Melinda 2742
McGregor, Ewan 2688, 3123, 3818
McGuigan, Arabella 2837
McGuigan, Cathleen 1517
McGuinness, Martin 3927
McInnerny, Tim 1677, 2322
McIntyre, Angus 3000, 3100
McKean, Michael 834
McKellar, David 136
McKellen, Ian [Sir] 1449, 2425
McKenna, Bernard 121, 122, 125, 133, 145, 150, 153–55, 157, 183, 188–90, 192, 201–03, 205–08, 212, 215, 216, 283, 449, 481, 651, 710, 1059, 3840
McKenna, Chris 3560
McKeown, Charles 508, 606, 680, 710, 725, 726, 731, 905, 1177, 1241, 1251, 1282, 1460, 1559, 1598–1600, 1617, 1677, 1818, 1894, 1901, 3498, 3499, 3659
McKinney, Mark 2442
McLaren, Malcolm 2404
McManus, Rove 2872, 3067, 3459, 4189
McNab, David 3289
McNeill, Mhairi 2889, 3163
McNicholl, BT 3701
McPhee, Rod 3909
McPherson, Ben 3462
McRee, Lisa 2303
McShane, Ian 2511
McTeer, Janet 1916, 3186
McVey, Esther 2487
McWilliams, Caroline 1636, 1640, 1644, 1647
Mead, Nick 2448
Meakin, Nigel 2797, 2894
The Meaning of Life see *Monty Python's The Meaning of Life*
The Meaning of Making The Meaning of Life (documentary) 2909, 2910
Meat Loaf 1390, 2495, 2498, 2556
Mechanic, Michael 3783
Medak, Peter 651, 654
The Media Show (TV) 1542
The Medieval Ball (radio) 2622
Medieval Lives (lecture) 3017, 3808, 3809
Medieval Lives (TV & book) see *Terry Jones' Medieval Lives*
Medieval Mercenaries: The Business of War (book) 3374
Medieval Misconceptions (lecture) 3235, 3997
The Medieval Python: The Purposive

and Provocative Work of Terry Jones (book) 4098
Medieval Views of the Cosmos (book) 3034
Meehan, Thomas 495
Meek, Joe 3944
Meeting Menaces see *Going to a Meeting, Part 2: Meeting Menaces*
Meeting of Minds see *Customer Relations in Practice, No. 2: The Meeting of Minds*
Meetings, Bloody Meetings [1976] (film) 521, 548, 1158
Meetings, Bloody Meetings [1993] (film) 1984, 2059
Meetings, Bloody Meetings [2012] (film) 4049
Mehta, Selina 2498
Melia, Ed 3917
Melia, Joe 230, 258, 261, 651, 991
Mellor, David 1899
Melly, George 1535
Melody Maker (newspaper) 301, 751, 1682
The Melody Maker Pop Poll Awards (ceremony) 756
Melrod, George 3123
Melton, Keith 2251
Melua, Katie 3081
Men in Black (film) 2240
Mendoza, Debby 1833
Mendoza, Linda 4069
Men's Health (magazine) 3125
Mercer, Shannon 3410, 3417, 3543, 3550, 3745
Merchant, Stephen 3898, 3976
Merkerson, S. Epatha 3412
The Mermaid Frolics (record) 622
The Mermaid Frolics (TV) 579, 594, 3669
Merrall, Mary 183
Merrill, Lee 1712
Merrill, Peter 1026
The Merry Wives of Windsor (play) 3946
Mersh, Dan 2841
Merton, Paul 2791, 3279, 3292
Merullo, Annabel 3177
The Merv Griffin Show (TV) 776, 851, 896, 964, 974, 1034, 1168, 1192
Messara, Suz 4198
Messegee, Todd 2633
Messiah (oratorio) 3410
Messiah Pictures 2596
Messing, Debra 2932, 2953, 2977, 2981, 2989
Messing Up a Meeting see *Going to a Meeting, Part 1: Messing Up a Meeting*
Metaxas, Eric 1832
Metherall, John 1714
Metropolis (film) 1177
Meyer, Breckin 2686, 2834
Meyer, Nicholas 1198
Meyerson, Charlie 2319
Michael, Dennis 1505, 1633
Michael Meets... (event): "Dervla Murphy" 4099; "Maan Barua"

3795; "Mahjabeen Khan" 3947; "Michael Katakis" 4074; "Musa Ibrahim" 3664, 3759; "Raja Shehadeh" 3882
Michael Palin: A Life in Pictures (event) 3700
Michael Palin and the Ladies Who Loved Matisse (TV) 2889, 3538
Michael Palin and the Mystery of Hammershøi (TV) 1298, 3118, 3163, 3537, 3538
Michael Palin: In Conversation with Michael Brunson (event) 3974
Michael Palin on...The Colourists (TV) 2606, 3538
Michael Palin: The Good, the Bad, and the Ugly (lecture) 3983
Michael Palin's Hemingway Adventure (book) 2499
Michael Palin's Hemingway Adventure (TV) 2461, 2486, 2491, 2494, 2501, 2503, 2505, 2506, 2509, 2515, 2521, 2564, 2568, 2572, 3782
Michael Palin's Iron Curtain see *Excess Baggage*
Michael Palin's New Europe (TV) 3006, 3272, 3298, 3432–34, 3436–41, 3443, 3445–47, 3449, 3453–56, 3458, 3459, 3463, 3483, 3549, 4168
Michaels, Lee 288
Michaels, Lorne 515, 540, 563, 576, 582, 635, 640, 660, 671, 695, 730, 779, 893, 906, 1338, 1678, 2906, 3425, 4181
Michell, Helena 1548
Michelmore, Guy 1373
Michels, Wim 910
Mickey MouseWorks (TV) 2447
Mickey's Mechanical House (cartoon) 2447
Micronpc.com ("Labyrinth") (ad) 2483
Midday (radio) 4190
Middlemass, Frank 605
Midler, Bette 2547, 3598
Midnight Express (film) 1260
The Midnight Special (TV) 277, 278, 288, 356
Midori 1405
Midsummer Night's Dream (cartoon) 2447
Midweek (radio) 1008, 1472, 1874, 2789
The Mighty Boosh 3771
A Mighty Wind (film) 2888
The Mikado (operetta) 1304, 1310, 1352, 1357, 1441, 1712, 1861, 3543, 4091
The Mikado (record) 1314, 1360
The Mikado (TV) 1442; see also *Great Performances*
Mike Douglas: People Now (TV) 965
The Mike Douglas Show (TV) 493, 500, 787
Milchan, Arnon 1177
Mileham, Michael 1049
Miles, Rupert 3724

Miles, Sarah 1417
Miles, Stuart 2299
Miliband, David 3507
Millar, Gavin 710, 744
Millard, David 303
Miller, Barry X. 2915
Miller, Cameron 1026
Miller, Chris 3405
Miller, Dennis 1312, 2338
Miller, Janice 1251
Miller, John 2375
Miller, Jonathan [Sir] [Dr.] 492, 539, 545, 579, 594, 622, 789, 812, 813, 830, 916, 922, 1051, 1304, 1310, 1314, 1352, 1360, 1441, 1442, 1549, 1712, 1726, 1861, 2329, 2838, 3543, 4091
Miller, Mary 13, 63
Miller, Nigel 2951, 2952, 2954, 2956
Miller, Paul 1338, 2345
Miller, Robin 541
Miller, Russell 361
Miller, Walter C. 777
Miller, Wentworth 2750
Milligan, Spike 50, 165, 200, 655, 710, 1002, 1068, 1174, 1288, 1289, 2091, 2147, 2250, 2355, 2562, 2589, 2731, 2733–35, 2780, 2791, 3108, 4095
Le Million (film) 3501
Mills, Bart 708, 1139
Mills, Gill 2534
Mills, Hayley 1108, 1227
Mills, John [Sir] 259
Mills, Michael 17, 63, 573
Mills, Roger 1696, 1710, 1718, 1721, 1898, 1900, 1902, 1904, 1908, 1988, 1991, 1993, 1997, 2275, 2290, 2300, 2301, 2312, 2797, 2799, 3039, 3045, 3065, 3446, 3449, 3453, 3522, 3602
Milne, A. A. 3969
Milne, Gareth 1026
Minchin, Louise 3850, 3852
The Mind of David Berglas (TV) 1247
The Ministry of Silly Games (video-game) 3894
Minnelli, Liza 1490
Minogue, Dannii 1864
Miracle of Flight (film) 176
The Miracle of Morgan's Creek (film) 1713
Mirren, Helen [Dame] 888, 2588, 2618
The Mirror see *The Daily Mirror*
The Mirrorstone (book) 1305, 1326
Mirzoeff, Edward 146
Missing Pieces (film) 1782, 1823
The Missionary (book) 998
The Missionary (film) 837, 926, 932, 961, 963, 965, 967–72, 974, 975, 977, 984, 989, 1006, 1007, 1010, 1011, 1015–17, 1019, 1022, 1043, 1054, 1064, 1149, 1574, 1881, 1904, 2706, 3693
Mr. Blue Sky: The Story of Jeff Lynne & ELO (TV) 4154

Mr. Strangelove: A Biography of Peter Sellers (book) 2792
Mr. Toad's Wild Ride [video release of *The Wind in the Willows*] (film) 2185, 2306, 2420
Mitchell, Adrian 3064
Mitchell, David 3976
Mitchell, Elvis 2681, 2816, 2857, 2900, 3120
Mitchell, Mike 3823
Mitchell, Norman 600
Mitchell, Warren 19, 280, 567
Mival, Eric 670
Moaning Minnie see *Managing Problem People: Moaning Minnie*
Moby 3157
Modine, Matthew 3329
Moffat, Alistair 3671, 3704, 3938
Moffatt, John 386
Moffet, Jordan 2925
Moffitt, John 348
Moggach, Deborah 1822
Mohr, Jay 2772
Moiseiwitsch, Pamela 828
Molina, Alfred 1818, 1821, 2464
Molloy, Dearbhla 1833
Mom and Dave Save the World (film) 1883
Mon Oncle (film) 2660
Mona Lisa (film) 1574
The Monday Play (radio): "The Dresser" 1928, 1940
Money, Zoot 550
The Money Programme (TV) 1118
Monie, Jon 2544
Monkhouse, Bob 2459, 2589
The Monster of Nix (film) 3959
Montagu, Felicity 2840, 2841
Montague, Bruce 928
Montgomery, David 565
Montgomery, Poppy 2871
Montreux Special Programme (TV) 130
Monty Python see *Monty Python's Flying Circus*
Monty Python: Almost the Truth—The Lawyer's Cut (DVD) 3748
Monty Python: Almost the Truth—The Lawyer's Cut (TV) 3726–29, 3731, 3732, 3735, 3737, 3739, 3742, 3744, 3825, 3858, 4140
Monty Python & the Quest for the Holy Grail (CD-ROM) 2027, 2158, 2159, 2317
Monty Python and the Holy Grail (Blu-ray) 4083
Monty Python and the Holy Grail (Film) 318, 320, 328–31, 333–39, 341, 342, 344, 346, 349, 357, 365, 373, 377, 393, 396, 397, 399, 400, 403, 410, 412, 414, 424, 426, 523, 564, 567, 710, 783, 943, 1148, 1326, 2340, 2426, 2493, 2586, 2608, 2672, 2673, 2710, 3080, 3113, 3231, 3326, 3400, 3410, 3444, 3506, 3514, 3531, 3606, 3636, 3652, 3739, 3790, 3842, 4005, 4084, 4202
Monty Python and the Holy Grail (rec-

General Index

ord) see *The Album of the Soundtrack of the Trailer of the Film of Monty Python and the Holy Grail*
Monty Python and the Holy Grail (trailer) 391
Monty Python and the Holy Grail (videodisc) 1105
Monty Python and the Holy Grail (book) (book) 592, 603
Monty Python and the Holy Grail: Extraordinarily Deluxe Edition (DVD) 3333
Monty Python and the Holy Grail: Special Edition (DVD) 2697
Monty Python and the Holy Grail: The Criterion Collection (laserdisc) 1921
Monty Python at the Hollywood Bowl (stage) 805
Monty Python Channel [YouTube] 3572
Monty Python: Complete and Utter Theory of the Grotesque (book) 937
Monty Python Conquers America (documentary) 3586, 3588, 3749
Monty Python Encyclopedia (book) 2364
Monty Python Examines the Life of Brian (record) 716
Monty Python: How Big Is My IMAX Film? (film) 2446
Monty Python in Aberystwyth: A Mayor and Two Pythons (TV) 3635, 3655
The Monty Python Instant Record Collection [U.K.] (record) 613
The Monty Python Instant Record Collection [U.S.] (record) 911
Monty Python Live! (book) 3696
Monty Python Live! [City Center] (stage) 494, 498–501
Monty Python Live at City Center (record) 431, 502–05, 911, 2238
Monty Python Live at Drury Lane (record) 343, 347, 527, 613, 3322
Monty Python Live at the Hollywood Bowl (film) 238, 518, 938, 942, 943, 946, 2678, 3197, 3586
Monty Python: Lust for Glory! (screenings) 3032
The Monty Python Matching Tie and Handkerchief (record/CD) 282, 293, 301, 395, 402, 478, 613, 911, 2238, 3320
Monty Python Meets Beyond the Fringe (film) 539, 593
The Monty Python Newscaster of the Year Awards (ceremony) 167, 169
The Monty Python Reunion Special (TV) 2431
Monty Python Sings (record/CD) 1723
Monty Python Speaks! (book) 2450, 2451
Monty Python: The Case Against (book) 908
Monty Python: The Final Rip Off (record) 1427

Monty Python: The Holy Book of Days (app) 4084
Monty Python: The Other British Invasion (DVD) 3749
Monty Python v. American Broadcasting Companies, Inc. (court case) 469, 491, 510
Monty Python's Big Red Book (book) 166, 167, 294, 875, 3319
Monty Python's Complete Waste of Time (CD-ROM) 2027, 2040, 2041, 2158, 2317
Monty Python's Contractual Obligation Album (record) 799–802, 817, 911, 2238, 3318, 3325
Monty Python's First Farewell Tour [Britain] (stage) 268
Monty Python's First Farewell Tour [Canada] (stage) 275, 277
Monty Python's First Farewell Tour [Drury Lane] (stage) 239, 316, 321
Monty Python's Fliegender Zirkus [German shows] (TV) 180, 238, 287, 1590, 2410, 3197, 3586
Monty Python's Fliegender Zirkus! (radio) 3944
Monty Python's Flying Circus (record) 65, 78, 162
Monty Python's Flying Circus (TV) 17, 20, 21, 24–26, 34, 57, 64, 65, 69, 77, 79, 82, 91, 107, 118, 119, 123, 130, 135, 161, 171, 197, 213, 219, 222, 235, 247, 259, 274, 323, 348, 352, 356, 358, 362, 367, 375, 393, 398, 404, 419, 423, 442, 489, 512, 726, 873, 908, 1214, 1329, 1393, 1421, 1591, 1596, 1618, 1689, 1690, 1720, 1727, 2014, 2027, 2032, 2349, 2384, 2402, 2495, 2497, 2540, 2592, 2743, 2744, 2824, 2830, 3100, 3138, 3145, 3150, 3519, 3531, 3551, 3586, 3735, 3978, 4052; "Whither Canada?" (ep. 1) 29, 35, 1652; "Sex and Violence" (ep. 2) 26, 37, 1655; "How to Recognise Different Types of Trees from Quite a Long Way Away" (ep. 3) 30, 38, 1828; "Owl Stretching Time" (ep. 4) 31, 39, 1827; "Man's Crisis of Identity in the Latter Half of the 20th Century" (ep. 5) 32, 43, 1653; "It's the Arts" (ep. 6) 42, 44, 1653; "You're No Fun Any More" (ep. 7) 36, 47, 1654; "Full Frontal Nudity" (ep. 8) 45, 49, 1654; "The Ant, an Introduction" (ep. 9) 8, 52, 1652; "Untitled" (ep. 10) 46, 54, 1829; "The Royal Philharmonic Orchestra Goes to the Bathroom" (ep. 11) 51, 55, 1655; "The Naked Ant" (ep. 12) 53, 59, 1656; "Intermission" (ep. 13) 58, 60, 1656; "Face the Press" (ep. 14) 73, 83, 1330; "The Spanish Inquisition" (ep. 15) 71, 86, 1331; Déjà Vu" (ep. 16) 74, 88, 1555; "The Buzz Aldrin Show" (ep. 17) 84, 93,

1330; "Live from the Grill-O-Mat" (ep. 18) 80, 96, 1416; "It's a Living" (ep. 19) 80, 97, 1468; "The Attila the Hun Show" (ep. 20) 89, 98, 1332; "Archaeology Today" (ep. 21) 90, 102, 1556; "How to Recognize Different Parts of the Body" (ep. 22) 87, 105, 1385; "Scott of the Antarctic" (ep. 23) 67, 71, 106, 1830; "How Not to Be Seen" (ep. 24) 75, 108, 1415; "Spam" (ep. 25) 69, 110, 1386; "Royal Episode 13" (ep. 26) 92, 111, 1467; "Whicker's World" (ep. 27) 182, 220, 1468; "Mr. and Mrs. Brian Norris' Ford Popular" (ep. 28) 128, 134, 185, 221, 1385; "The Money Programme" (ep. 29) 171, 224, 1331; "Blood, Devastation, Death, War, and Horror" (ep. 30) 172, 225, 1555; "The All-England Summarize Proust Competition" (ep. 31) 193, 226, 1332; "The War Against Pornography" (ep. 32) 184, 229, 1386; "Salad Days" (ep. 33) 181, 232, 1415; "The Cycling Tour" (ep. 34) 194, 234, 1440, 1831; "The Nude Organist" (ep. 35) 195, 236, 1416; "E. Henry Thripshaw's Disease" (ep. 36) 197, 239, 1467; "Dennis Moore" (ep. 37) 191, 249, 1557; "A Book at Bedtime" (ep. 38) 173, 250, 1557; "Grandstand" (ep. 39) 196, 251, 1556; "The Golden Age of Ballooning" (ep. 40) 358, 363, 447, 1831; "Michael Ellis" (ep. 41) 359, 365, 472, 1829; "Light Entertainment War" (ep. 42) 360, 368, 472, 1830; "Hamlet" (ep. 43) 364, 370, 472, 1828; "Mr. Neutron" (ep. 44) 361, 366, 372, 447, 1180, 1831; "Party Political Broadcast" (ep. 45) 369, 374, 447, 1827
Monty Python's Flying Circus (videocassette) 1214, 1329–32, 1385, 1386, 1415, 1416, 1467, 1468, 1555–57, 1652–56, 1827–31, 2014
Monty Python's Flying Circus...At Last, In French (stage) 3091
Monty Python's Flying Circus: Eric Idle's Personal Best (DVD/TV) 3181
Monty Python's Flying Circus: Just the Words (book) 1690
Monty Python's Flying Circus: Michael Palin's Personal Best (DVD/TV) 3182
Monty Python's Flying Circus: Python Bytes (app) 4101
Monty Python's Flying Football Circus v Grimms (event) 267
Monty Python's Graham Chapman: Looks Like a Brown Trouser Job (DVD) 3139
Monty Python's Holy Grail Ale 2542
Monty Python's Life of Brian (book) 752

Monty Python's Life of Brian (film) 508, 523, 588, 600, 631, 634, 638, 649, 650, 655, 656, 657, 668, 669, 672, 675, 698, 700, 703, 709–21, 727, 728, 734, 736, 738–42, 744, 746–49, 751, 771, 776, 797, 798, 908, 943, 1006, 1169, 1240, 1260, 1263, 1361, 1532, 1574, 1750, 1760, 1871, 2236, 2341, 2373, 2477, 2492, 2493, 2495, 2607, 2645, 2706, 2712, 2805, 2809, 2988, 2990, 3113, 3231, 3332, 3357, 3371, 3375, 3402, 3410, 3458, 3472, 3573, 3635, 3649, 3655, 3742, 3745, 3766, 3770, 3790, 3808, 3834, 3866, 3925, 3972, 4006, 4008, 4037, 4066
Monty Python's Life of Brian (radio ads) 739, 812
Monty Python's Life of Brian (record/CD) 722, 723, 750, 3323
Monty Python's Life of Brian: The Criterion Collection (laserdisc/DVD) 2320, 2522
Monty Python's Life of Brian: The Immaculate Edition (DVD) 2522, 3460
Monty Python's Personal Best (TV) 3150, 3239, 3586; "Graham Chapman's Personal Best" 3241; "John Cleese's Personal Best" 3244; "Terry Gilliam's Personal Best" 3243; "Eric Idle's Personal Best" 3181, 3240; "Terry Jones' Personal Best" 3248; "Michael Palin's Personal Best" 3182, 3249
Monty Python's Previous Record (record/CD) 218, 223, 231, 235, 237, 293, 527, 556, 613, 3319
Monty Python's The Meaning of Life (book) 1046
Monty Python's The Meaning of Life (CD-ROM) 2158, 2317, 3894
Monty Python's The Meaning of Life (DVD) 2909, 2996
Monty Python's The Meaning of Life (film) 796, 914, 944, 945, 947–49, 951–53, 956, 958, 981, 984, 996, 1006, 1013, 1021, 1023, 1025–30, 1034–36, 1039, 1040, 1042, 1044, 1052, 1053, 1056, 1058, 1060, 1066, 1098, 1114, 1116, 1139, 1267, 1361, 2481, 2655, 2911, 2994, 3744, 3768
Monty Python's The Meaning of Life (radio ads) 1047
Monty Python's The Meaning of Life (record/CD) 1012, 1048, 3324
Monty Python's Tiny Black Round Thing (record) 342, 343, 347
Monty Python's Tunisian Holiday: My Life with Brian (book) 3573
Monty Python's Wonderful World of Sound (radio) 3771
MONTYPYTHONSCRAPBOOK (book) 752
Monzani, Sarah 3659
Moody, Ron 596, 2083

Moon, Keith 267, 470, 630, 649, 651, 809, 896, 1393
Mooney, Bel 1980
Moorcock, Michael 854
Moore, Alan 1598, 2890
Moore, Brian 616
Moore, Charlotte 1055
Moore, Demi 2901
Moore, Dudley 492, 539, 1294, 1493, 1665, 1705, 2066, 2091
Moore, Paul [Bishop] 499
Moore, Ray 1354
Moore, Roger [Sir] 1320, 1788, 2047, 2511, 2837, 3193, 3639, 4040
Moore, Simon 2750
Moore, Stephen 473, 1274
Moore, Steven Dean 2875
Morahan, Christopher 1274
Moran, Kevin 606
Moran, Nancy 950
Moranis, Rick 1945, 2052
More Awkward Customers see *Customer Relations in Practice, No. 4: More Awkward Customers*
More Bloody Meetings [1984] (film) 1158
More Bloody Meetings [1994] (film) 2059
More Boys Who Do Comedy (TV) 3462
More Ripping Yarns (book) 806, 822, 1770
More Than 35 Minutes with Michael Palin (stage) 1091
Morecambe, Eric 666
Morecambe & Wise 3601
Morgan, David 1521, 2450, 2451
Morgan, Fidelis 853
Morgan, Piers 2176
Morgan, Robert 1751
Morgan, Tracy 2214
Moriarty, Cathy 2102
Morley, Paul 2289
Morley, Robert 68, 859, 1127, 1531, 1638
Morley, Sheridan 61, 399, 610
Morning Becomes Eclectic (radio) 2643
Morning Edition (radio) 2578
The Morning Program (TV) 1424
The Morning Show [Can.] (TV) 4060
The Morning Show [U.S.] (TV) 1027
Mornings (TV) 4188, 4198
Mornings with Margaret Throsby (radio) 2521, 3470
Morris, Aubrey 607
Morris, Garrett 515, 563, 576, 640, 660, 671, 695, 730, 779
Morris, Geoffrey 450
Morris, Jan 3166
Morris, Johnny 1002
Morris, Julia 4089
Morris, Mike 1892
Morris, Redmond 1945
Morrish, John 1528
Morrison, Shelley 2977, 2981
Morrow, Barry 1628

Morrow, Philip 1765
Morse, Barry 928
Morse, Charlotte C. 2663
Morse, David 2119
Mortimer, Bob 2289
Mortimer, Emily 3465, 3616
Mortimer, John 63, 2585
Morton, Bill 2377
Morton, John 2370
Morton, Samantha 2902
Moss, Denise 1644
Mosse, Kate 2760
Most, Donny 776
The Motels 1110
Moten, Wendy 1948
Mother Jones (magazine) 3783
Motörhead 1412
Mould, Marion 368
A Moveable Feast (book) 3819
Movie Connections (TV): "Monty Python and the Holy Grail" 3606
The Movie Life of George (TV) 1532, 1574
Movies for Grownups (ceremony) 3485
The Moving Image (TV) 1529
Moving Pictures (TV) 2143
Mowbray, Malcolm 1149, 1263
Mowgli's Brothers (audiobook) 1161
Moyet, Alison 1174
Mozart, Wolfgang Amadeus 1061
MTV Halloween Costume Party (TV) 1426
The Much Loved Friend?: A Portrait of the National Gallery (TV) 1840
Mudd, Roger 2105
Muggeridge, Malcolm 749
Muir, Frank 252, 309
Mull, Martin 2654
Mullally, Megan 2932, 2953, 2977, 2981, 2989
Mullard, Arthur 211
Mullen, John 4020
Mullins, Spike 127, 136, 138, 141, 291, 517
Mulrine, Anna 2347
Mulville, Jimmy 1665, 1833
Mumford & Sons 4081
Muniz, Vik 4182
The Muppet Show (TV) 590, 859
Murdoch, Iris [Dame] 862, 1294, 2404
Murdoch, Richard 661
Murdoch, Rupert 2144
Murnaghan, Dermot 3028, 3341, 3468
Murphy, Brian 2713
Murphy, Brittany 3130
Murphy, Dervla 4099
Murphy, Eddie 966, 1110, 2772, 2997, 3405, 3823
Murphy, Maurice 3–7, 9, 27, 28, 120, 284
Murphy, Nick 3199
Murphy, Sean 2425
Murray, Al 3904
Murray, Bill 563, 576, 635, 640, 660, 671, 695, 730, 779, 893
Murray, Chic 252

Murray, Jan 849
Murray, John 3952
Murray, Peter 405
Musto, Michael 2878
My Adventures in Television see *Wednesday 9:30 (8:30 Central)*
My Life (TV): "Stammer School" 3912
"My Sweet Lord" (song) 530
Myatt, John 3611, 3992
Myers, Kathy 1843
Myers, Mike 2997, 3405, 3823
Myers, Stanley 309
Myerson, Jonathan 2927
MyHealthTips.com (web videos) 4000, 4054, 4056, 4060
Mzimba, Lizo 3612

Nabulsi, Laila 2376, 2849
Nader, Ralph 779
Naha, Ed 1087
Naidoo, Indira 4061
Najimy, Kathy 2790
Naked Hollywood (TV): "Good Cop, Bad Cop" 1813
Names and Games (TV) 1242
"The Name's the Game" (sketch) 704, 755, 764
Nash, Ogden 2851
Nash, Paul 2262
Nashawaty, Chris 3122
Nasr, Constantine 3499
Nastase, Ilie 3441
Nathanson, Paul 1076, 1271
The Nation (magazine) 567, 710
National Lampoon's Christmas Vacation (film) 2942
National Lampoon's European Vacation (film) 1210, 2942
The National Lottery Live (TV) 2224
National Symphony Orchestra 3546
The National Television Awards (ceremony) 2407
The Nation's Favourite Children's Book (TV) 2269
Nationwide (TV) 77, 701, 857, 876, 929, 930, 932, 1016
"Naughty Atom Bomb" (song) 1324
Neale, Greg 3784
Nealon, Kevin 2531, 2906, 3004, 3141
Nearly Departed (TV) 1635, 1636, 1640, 1644, 1647
Nedwell, Robin 188, 284, 300, 763, 1102
Needleman, Jacob 2891
Neeson, Liam 3639
Neil, Andrew 2868
Neild, Robert [Prof.] 858
Neill, Jay 446
Neill, Sam 2057, 2625
Nelson, Jerry 590
Nelson, Judd 1303, 2476
Nelson, Zed 2646
Nelson Mandela: 70th Birthday Tribute (concert/TV) 1483
Nemeth, Stephen 2376
Nemone 3221

Nesbitt, James 3059
Nettleton, John 1353
Neustadter, Scott 3616
Neville, David 732
Neville, John 70, 1559, 1617, 1629, 1659, 3499
The Neville Brothers 2166
Neville-Jones, Pauline [Dame] 2938
New, Barbara 600
New Europe (book) 3430, 3435, 3440, 3443, 3445, 3447, 3467, 3532
New Europe (lecture) 3440, 3445, 3447, 3463, 3527
New Europe (TV) see *Michael Palin's New Europe*
New Hero of Comedy (TV): "Ricky Gervais" 3489
New Musical Express (newspaper) 314, 342, 343, 347
New Order 3141
The New Paul O'Grady Show (TV) 3277
The New Republic (magazine) 161, 710, 1025, 1760
The New Review (The Independent) (magazine) 4133
New Statesman (magazine) 166, 397, 710, 3683
A New Year at Kew (TV) 3378
New York (magazine) 161, 760, 970, 1025, 1120, 1177, 1370, 1495, 1638, 3723
New York & Company (radio) 2058, 2079
The New York Film Critics Circle Awards [61st] (ceremony) 2128
The New York Post (newspaper) 494
The New York Times (newspaper) 161, 367, 397, 409, 494, 567, 578, 689, 710, 754, 845, 863, 943, 970, 991, 1025, 1059, 1148, 1149, 1370, 1496, 1588, 1751, 1791, 2086, 2119, 2185, 2365, 2376, 2430, 2739, 2927, 3113, 3186, 3332, 3593, 3965
The New York Times Book Review (newspaper) 874, 1069, 1216, 1305, 2792
The New York Times Magazine (magazine) 495, 1561
The New Yorker (magazine) 161, 397, 419, 491, 567, 710, 1177, 1471, 1495, 1618, 1760, 2378, 3079, 3113, 4027, 4161
Newark, Tim 1581
Newell, Mike 2087
Newhart, Bob 2406
Newlyn, Lucy 2715
Newman, Laraine 515, 563, 576, 640, 660, 671, 695, 730, 779, 893
Newman, Nanette 243
Newman, Nick 267
Newman, Randy 538, 563, 3234, 3829
The News Is the News (TV) 1055
Newsday (newspaper) 1370
Newsnight (TV) 975, 1040, 1173, 1215, 1374, 2707, 2771, 3945

NewsNight with Aaron Brown (TV) 3102
Newsweek (magazine) 161, 397, 401, 635, 710, 863, 943, 970, 1025, 1149, 1517, 1559, 1850, 3104, 4181
Newton, Bert 3068
Newton-John, Olivia 580, 940, 1531
Ngodrup, Nyarongsha Jampa [Dr.] 1913
Nibbelink, Phil 1859
Nicastro, Michelle 2055
Niccol, Andrew 2443
Nichol, Phil 4008
Nicholaw, Casey 3113
Nicholls, Phoebe 970
Nichols, Mike 2906, 3104, 3113, 3114, 3140, 3147, 3151, 3838
Nichols, Peter 773, 933, 991, 1018
Nicholson, Jack 3838
Nicholson, Mavis 1000, 1081
Nicks, Stevie 3981
Nickson, Julia 1638, 1641, 1642
Nicobobinus (book) 1216, 1454
Nielsen, Leslie 2251, 3048
Nielson, Claire 679
A Night at the Net (event) 2462
A Night of Comic Relief (TV) 1452, 2083
Night of 1,000 Shows (TV) 2593
A Night with Michael Palin: 20 Years of Travelling, 40 Years of Jokes (lecture) 3674
Nightingale, Benedict 1496, 2017
Nightingale, Lesley 1984
Nightlife (TV) 1334, 1364, 1380
Nighy, Bill 4018
Nike ("The Secret Tournament") (ad) 2745
Nilsson, Harry 501, 803, 1746, 3234
Nimmo, Derek 976
Nimoy, Leonard 1013, 1303
"Nimrod (*Enigma Variations*)" [Elgar] 151, 538, 753
1984 (book) 1177
Nissen, Brian 2055
Niven, David 113
Nixon, David 140, 303, 325
Nixon, Richard [President] 576
No Naughty Bits (play) 3985
No, That's Me Over Here (TV) 81
Nobbs, David 127, 136, 138, 141, 291, 378, 761, 762, 900, 901, 985, 1102, 1157
Nobetsu, Mayumi 2279, 2284
Noble, Larry 1026
Nobody's Fools (or Rock with Laughter) (stage) 572
Nohra, Anis 113
Nolan, Brian 606
Nolan, Coleen 3555
The Nolans 4167
Noone, Peter 834
Norden, Denis 19, 113, 381, 384, 465, 547, 1288, 3191
Norman, Barry 219, 654, 747, 994, 1003, 1011, 1134, 1175, 1243, 1263, 1278, 1480, 1482, 1533, 1543, 1621, 1672, 1680, 1768, 1814, 1855, 1933, 1954, 1961, 2137, 2148

Norman, Neil 3176, 3356
Normington, John 1149
North West Tonight (TV) 3906
Norton, Graham 2419, 3132, 3479
Norwich Union Direct (ad) 2123
Not About Nightingales (play) 2432
Not Only...But Also (TV) 2066
Not the Messiah (He's a Very Naughty Boy) (DVD) 3833, 3835
Not the Messiah (He's a Very Naughty Boy) (oratorio) 2678, 3409, 3410, 3416, 3417, 3470, 3472, 3476, 3542, 3543, 3545, 3546, 3548, 3550, 3676, 3699, 3745, 3822, 3831, 3836
Not the Nine O'Clock News (TV) 737, 749, 818
La Notte (film) 391
Novak, Kim 3459
Novak, Ralph 1301, 1677, 1850, 1945
Novick, Julius 494
Now! (TV) 3819
Now Look Here... (TV) 168, 255
Nugent, Ted 942
Number 27 (TV) see *Sunday Premiere*
Nuns on the Run (film) 1634, 1649, 1749–51, 1757, 1764
Nussknacker und Mausekönig (film) 3048
The Nutcracker (ballet) 4050
The Nutcracker (cartoon) 2447
The Nutcracker and the Mouseking (film) 3048
Nutini, Paolo 3361
Nutkins, Terry 3968
Nutter, David 3863

O Happy Day! (play) 2594
01-for London (TV) 1622
Oates, John 507
O'Briain, Dara 3310
O'Brien, Conan 2906
O'Brien, Denis 710, 717, 848, 863, 970, 991, 1149, 1574, 1751
O'Brien, Edna 1774
The Observer (newspaper) 34, 790, 2435, 2712, 2967, 3085, 3722, 4120
Obst, Lynda 1813, 1850
O'Casey, Matt 2958
O'Connell, John 3360
O'Connor, Derrick 1177
O'Connor, Des 630, 2965, 3092
O'Connor, Hazel 778, 1032
O'Connor, John J. 367
The Odd Job (film) 633, 651, 654
Oddie, Bill 2, 62, 295, 302, 486, 492, 539, 661, 664, 990, 1324, 1731, 2721, 3000, 3600, 3735
O'Dea, Danny 726
O'Dell, Nancy 2563
O'Donoghue, Heather 1216
O'Donovan, Gerard 4168
O'Donovan, Patrick 144
O'farrell, Maggie 2357
The Office Line (TV) 687, 688, 690, 692, 696

An Officer and a Gentleman (film) 1114
Ogilby, John 3512, 3513
Ogilvy, Ian 381, 383, 480
O'Gorman, Rochelle 2808
O'Hanlon, Ardal 3479
O'Hanlon, Redmond 2311
O'Hara, Catherine 2906
O'Haver, Tommy 2986
O'Hurley, John 3398, 3677
Oh Hampstead (stage) 70
OJRIL: The Completely Incomplete Graham Chapman (book) 2541, 3167
Olbermann, Keith 3726
The Old Grey Whistle Test (TV) 507
Oldfield, Mike 589, 1289, 2897
Oldman, Gary 2369, 3760
Olin, Lena 2899
Oliver! (film) 511
Oliver, Deanna 2102
Oliver, John 3860
Oliver Twist (film) 3978
Oliver 2: Let's Twist Again (TV) 2083
Olsen, Dana 2261
Olsen, John Stefan 2685
Olympic Games [2012] 4135
Omnibus (TV): "Comic Relief" 1286, 1291; "Douglas Adams: The Man Who Blew Up the World" 2684; "The Film of Reeves and Mortimer" 2289; "Laughter in the House: The Story of the British Sitcom" 2439; "Laughter — Why We Laugh" 289; "Life of Python" 1752; "Pleasure at Her Majesty's" 492, 539, 545; "Quentin Tarantino: Hollywood's Boy Wonder" 2046; "Spike" 2147; "Steve Martin: Seriously Funny" 2480; "Wallace and Gromit Go Chicken" 2583
On Location (TV) 3362
On the Ropes (radio) 2680
One Foot in the Grave (TV) 1740, 1866, 2017, 2615
The 100 Greatest Kids TV Shows (TV) 2691
101 Dalmatians (film) 2619
102 Dalmatians (film) 2619
One on One (TV) 3644
The One Show (TV) 3439, 3532, 3598, 3717, 3850, 3852, 3887, 3932, 3999, 4026, 4079, 4109
1001 Comics You Must Read Before You Die (book) 3993
1001 Nights of TV (TV) 1805
O'Neal, Ryan 2295
One-Eyed Jacks (film) 1845
O'Neill, Ken 1409
O'Neill, Lord 1998
Ono, Yoko 1280, 1309, 1882, 2916, 3297
Ooms, Amanda 1894
Open Air (TV) 1620, 1722
Open Book (radio) 2524, 3656, 4020, 4123
Open House (radio) 405

Open House with Gloria Hunniford (TV) 2806
Open Space (TV): "Car Sick" 1256, 2000, 2674
Opinions (TV) 1142
Options (radio): "Victorian Values" 1207
The Orange British Academy Film Awards (ceremony) see *The British Academy [Film] Awards*
Orange "Gold Spot" (ad) 3183
Orbison, Roy 3792
Orchard, Julian 519
The Oregonian (newspaper) 1272
O'Reilly, Bill 3570
Orenstein, Andrew 2358
Oricchio, Gabriele 3953
Orissa: Temples and Tribes (lecture) 3881, 3929
Ormond, Julia 2662
O'Rourke, P.J. 397
Orpen, Michael 2527
Orton, Joe 651
Orton, Les 2713
Orton, Peter 1992, 3395
Osbourne, Ozzy 3479
O'Shaughnessy, Gillian 4067
O'Shea, Milo 243
Osmond, Donny 2504, 2563, 2576
Osmond, Marie 777, 2504, 2563, 2576
Osterberg, Robert 469
Ostler, Nick 3479
O'Sullivan, Richard 205
O'Sullivan, Tim 2258
The Other Awards (ceremony) 929, 930
The Other Boleyn Girl (film) 3488
The Other Side of Midnight (TV) 1612
O'Toole, Lawrence 1025
O'Toole, Peter 2024, 3488
OTT (TV) 923
Otte, Charles 2158
Ottey, Oral Norrie 1833
Oundjian, Peter 3410, 3417
Out (magazine) 2878
Out of Africa (film) 1282
Out of the Trees (stage) 2594
Out of the Trees (TV) 443, 481, 1307, 2665, 3366
Outlook (radio) 3805
The Out-of-Towners (film) 2442
Outside Magazine (magazine) 3160
Outta Space see *Road to Mars*
Owen, Ben 861
Owen, Bill 384, 386, 1982
Owen, Cliff 651
Owen, David [Dr.] 1283
Owen, Nick 1057, 1071, 2141, 2151
"The Owl and the Pussycat" (poem) 2171, 2425
The Owl and the Pussycat (opera) 4127, 4129, 4130, 4132
Oxenberg, Catherine 1376
Oxford Today (film) 3521, 3522
Oxford Today (magazine) 3784
OxTravels: Meetings with Remarkable Travel Writers (book) 3949, 3954
Oz, Frank 590, 859, 1465, 2333

Page, Louise 1262
Page, Robert 1801
Page, Tony 453
Pagett, Nicola 991
Pain, Barry 1163
Palance, Holly 558, 596
Palance, Jack 2055
Palermo, Tony 3465
Palin, Archie [grandson] 3251
Palin, Edward [father] 575, 1737
Palin, Edward [great-grandfather] 602, 1769, 1818
Palin, Harry [great-uncle] 3571, 3755
Palin, Helen (Gibbins) [wife] 1107, 1353, 2124, 2375
Palin, Mary [mother] 1068, 1110, 1737
Palin, Rachel [daughter] 390, 1150
Palin, Sarah [Gov.] 3594
Palin, Thomas [son] 867, 2258
Palin, Wilbur [grandson] 3684
Palin, William [son] 103, 867
Palin Herbert, Angela [sister] 1388, 2089, 3702
Palin on Art (DVD) 3538
Palin's Column (TV) 1922, 1971, 1987, 1988, 1991, 1993, 1997, 2020, 2022
Palin's Travels (website) 2783
The Palm Beach Story (film) 1713
Palmer, Amanda 3774
Palmer, Felicity 1304, 1442
Palmer, Geoffrey 680, 901, 928, 1495, 1563, 1567, 1568
Pankin, Stuart 1636, 1640, 1644, 1647
Pao, Basil 632, 752, 1715, 1718, 2264, 2499, 2784, 2785, 3025, 3026, 3203, 3358, 3430, 4159, 1888
Paperbacks (TV) 850, 852–55, 858, 861, 862, 864, 982
Paranoias 572
Parents (magazine) 1216
Park, Nick 2583, 2677, 3968
Parker, Alan 1260, 1954
Parker, Barbara 670
Parker, Sarah Jessica 2464
Parker, Trey 2456, 2496, 2669
Parkinson (TV) 809, 812, 922, 927, 2328, 2645, 2786, 2931, 3022, 3355, 3361, 3432
Parkinson, Mary 1010, 1108
Parkinson, Michael [Sir] 163, 259, 809, 812, 916, 922, 927, 1010, 1108, 2196, 2259, 2328, 2536, 2544, 2593, 2645, 2703, 2786, 2836, 2837, 2931, 3022, 3166, 3355, 3361, 3432, 3561, 3601
Parkinson's Sunday Supplement (radio) 2259
Parks, Tom 1430
Parr, John 1337
Parris, Matthew 2843
Parrot Sketch Not Included: Twenty Years of Monty Python (TV) 1670, 1688, 1720, 1752, 1753, 2429, 3197, 3586

Parry, Louisa [Jones' great-grandmother] 3773
Parry, Nigel 2145
Parsons, Alan 3012
Parsons, Nicholas 463, 644, 666
Parting Shots (film) 2448
Parton, Dolly 580
A Party Election Broadcast: SDP/Liberal Alliance (TV) 1045
A Party Political Broadcast: Liberal Democrat Party (TV) 2235, 2396
A Party Political Broadcast: Social Democratic Party (TV) 1236, 1283, 1372
Pasco, Mervyn 676
Pass the Butler (book) 917
Pass the Butler (play) 884, 886, 915, 922
The Passion of the Christ (film) 2990
Past People of Potsdamer Platz (art) 3269
Pastor, Tony 1061
Patel, Mash 2546
Paterson, Bill 651, 1149, 1559
Patinkin, Mandy 2120
Patten, Brian 3064
Patterson, Robert 1751
Paul O'Grady Live (TV) 3931
The Paul O'Grady Show (TV) 3198, 3649, 3698
Paul W. Smith and Company (radio) 1502
Pauley, Jane 1507
Paulson, Sarah 4077
Paulsson, Robin 3873
Pavarotti, Luciano 2931
Pavlo, Chris 2840, 2841
Paxman, Jeremy 1350, 4088
Payne (TV) 2436
Payne, Cynthia 1234, 1297, 1319, 1347, 1368, 1370, 1373, 1374, 1382
Payne, Sally 1353
Peachment, Chris 1019
Peacock, Michael 204, 1667
Peake, Mervyn 2549
Peake-Jones, Tessa 2059
Pearson, Allison 2087
Pearson, Durk 974
Pearson, Malachi 2102
Pearson, Patrick 991
Pebble Mill (TV) 1854, 2069
Pebble Mill at One (TV) 615, 886, 1005, 1043, 1083, 1084, 1096, 1190, 1223, 1245, 1279
Pecorini, Nicola 2363, 2902
Pedley, Anthony 813
Peel, John 267, 585, 3221
The Pee-Wee Herman Show (stage) 3788
Pegram, Steve 4018
Peisner, David 2879
Pelé 3296
Pena, Paco 2232
Pengilly, Kirk 2854
Penhaligon, Susan 813
Penn & Teller 1992, 2440
Penn & Teller's Sin City Spectacular (TV) 2440
"Penny Lane" (song) 1061

Penrhos Brewery 589, 599
The People (newspaper) 2279
People (Weekly) (magazine) 736, 898, 950, 1025, 1059, 1074, 1112, 1149, 1177, 1274, 1277, 1301, 1495, 1518, 1559, 1638, 1645, 1677, 1707, 1850, 1945, 2067, 2528, 2742
Peoples, David 2119
Peoples, Janet 2119
Pepe, Louis 2078, 2190, 2728, 2900, 2904
Peploe, Samuel John 2606
Percival, Daniel 2400, 2401
Percival, Michael 1868, 1984
Perez, Phil 834
Performance Matters: The Importance of Praise (film) 2630
Performance Matters: The Need for Constructive Criticism (film) 2631
Perkin, Deborah 3378
Perkins, Jack 1744
Perlin, John 3211
Permutt, Stewart 2535
Perri, Valerie 2442
Perry, George 566, 982, 1056, 1097, 1170, 1325, 1460, 1495, 1610, 1786, 1850
Perry, Tyler 3824
Personal Services (film) 1234, 1287, 1297, 1319, 1325, 1347, 1361, 1364, 1366, 1368, 1370, 1373, 1374, 1379, 1382, 1387
Personal Services: The Making of a Celebrity (TV) 1382
Perspectives (TV): "Sergeant on Spike" 4095
Pertwee, Jon 2122
Pesci, Joe 2423
Pescucci, Gabriella 1559
Peter and the Wolf (concert) 3259
Peter Cook: A Post-Humourous Tribute (stage) 2787
Peter Cook: A Post-Humourous Tribute (TV) 2838, 2839
Peter Cook: At a Slight Angle to the Universe (TV) 2838
Peter Cook & Co. (TV) 804, 2066
Peter Cook in His Own Words (radio) 3058
Peters, Andi 2001
Peters, Luan 677
Pethig, Hazel 2472
Pettet, Joanna 19
Pettifer, Julian 146
Petty, Tom 2826, 3640
Pevere, Geoff 3345
Phil Donahue (TV) 1498, 1514
Philadelphia Enquirer (newspaper) 1268
Philbin, Regis 1027, 1728, 1910, 2080, 2216, 3110, 3728
Philip Pullman and Enid Jones (radio) 3377
Phillips, Arlene 1025, 2911
Phillips, Conrad 446, 662
Phillips, Glen 2130
Phillips, John 604
Phillips, John Michael 1441, 1442, 1549

Phillips, Kate 2593
Phillips, Leslie 68, 165
Phillips, Mark 298
Phillips, Michael 1883
Phillips, Sally 4047
Phillips, Tony 2514
Photographs & Words (book) 3987
Photoplay (magazine) 1270
The Piano Tuner of Earthquakes (film) 3170
Piazza, Mike 2106
Picardo, Robert 4017
Picasso at the Lapin Agile (play) 2045
Pick, Caroline 522
Pick of Punch (book) 311
Picture Palace (book) 862
Piddock, Jim 2906, 3465, 3701, 4096
The Pied Piper of Hamelin see *Faerie Tale Theatre*
Pienkowski, Jan 861
The Pier on Film (TV) 2180
Pierce, David Hyde 2547, 3113, 3140, 3588
Pike, Rosamund 2819
Pile, Stephen 794, 842
Pilkington, Karl 3452
Pink Floyd 328, 433
The Pink Panther (film) 3841
The Pink Panther 2 (film) 3613, 3614, 3616, 3617
Pinky and the Brain (TV): "The Family That Poits Together, Narfs Together" 2332
Pinocchio [1940] (film) 1845
Pinocchio [2002] (film) 2834
Pinsky, Robert 2237
Pinter, Harold 99
Piper, Billie 3367
Pirates (film) 2251
The Pirates of Penzance (film) 824
Piscopo, Joe 966, 1110
Pitt, Brad 2078, 2119, 2148, 2324
Pizzello, Stephen 2363
A Place in History (TV): "University of St. Andrews" 327
Planer, Nigel 1125, 1548, 1665, 2185, 3497
Planet 51 (film) 3760
The Play What I Wrote (play) 2876
Playboy (magazine) 57, 161, 436, 526, 741, 943, 1025, 1274, 1551, 1559, 2569
Playtime (film) 2660
Pleasure at Her Majesty's (film) 492, 539, 593, 3609, 3669; see also *Omnibus*
Plomley, Roy 151, 538, 753, 916, 1061
Plosky, Eric J. 3741
Plowright, Rosalind 3745
Plummer, Amanda 1850, 2324
Plummer, Christopher 2119, 3473, 3659
Plummer, Michael 612
Plympton, Bill 437, 3916
Plytas, Steve 453
PM Magazine (TV) 1523

A Pocketful of Python: Picked by Eric Idle (book) 2815
A Pocketful of Python: Picked by John Cleese (book) 2513
A Pocketful of Python: Picked by Michael Palin (book) 2603
A Pocketful of Python: Picked by Terry Gilliam (book) 2602
A Pocketful of Python: Picked by Terry Jones (book) 2512
Poems on the Box (TV) 1974
Poetry Please! (radio) 2026
Poets for Peace (event) 3064
Pogson, Kathryn 1177
Point of View (radio) 2319
Poison 1960
A Poke in the Eye (with a Sharp Stick) (record) 554
A Poke in the Eye (with a Sharp Stick) (stage) 492, 539, 579, 704
Polanski, Roman 50
Pole to Pole (book) 1888, 1927
Pole to Pole (lecture) 1999
Pole to Pole (TV) 1825, 1895–1900, 1902–06, 1908–12, 1925, 1942, 1948, 2272, 3446
Politically Incorrect with Bill Maher (TV) 2313, 2338
Pollack, Kevin 3084
Pollack, Sydney 2611
Pollard, Su 1113
Polley, Sarah 1559, 1617, 3499
Polo, Bertrand 659, 806
Polunin, Slava 3245
Pomfret, Emma 3011
Pond, Steve 817
Ponti, Carlo 1252
Poole, David 3309
Pop, Iggy 2533
Porizkova, Paulina 1960
Portas, Mary 3529
Porter, Cole 528
Porter, Peter 864, 3064
Posner, Geoff 1291, 2419
Posner, Michael 3679
Posta, Adrienne 620, 621, 688, 690, 1355
Postgiro ("Do You Use Giroblauw?") (ads) 910
Potterton, Reg 741
Potton, Ed 2982, 2994, 3365
Poulton, Mike 4108
Poust, Tracy 2932
Powell, Aubrey 3745
Powell, Enoch 1679
Powell, Michael 1082
Powell, Nosher 249
Powell, Peter 867
Powell, Robert 1854, 3362
Powell, Tristram 1353, 1548, 1818, 1821
The Power of the Sun (documentary) 3211
Prady, Bill 2052
Pratchett, Terry 2122, 2760, 2885
Pravda, George 159
Preddy, Richard 1924
Preece, Tim 481
Premiere (magazine) 1631

Prenger, Jodie 3827, 4030, 4045
Prescription for Complaints see *Marketing in Practice, No. 4: Prescription for Complaints*
A Present from the Past: The Making of American Friends (TV) 1821
Presley, Elvis 2228, 2745, 3928
Preston, Billy 2826
Preto, Dinho Ouro 4171
Previn, André 116
Prevue (magazine) 1060, 1066, 1709
Price, Alan 151, 572, 576, 585, 630, 809
Price, Andy 1188
Price, Jeffrey 3405
Price, Vincent 41, 745
Priestland, Gerald 742
The Primetime Creative Arts Emmy Awards (ceremony) 2779, 3020, 3858
Prince, Harold 1896
Prince Andrew (Duke of York) 1390
Prince Charles (of Wales) 660, 730, 845, 1082, 1789, 1840, 2581, 3006, 3408, 3488, 3579, 3801
Prince Edward 1390, 1671, 2455
Prince Harry 3579
Prince of Denmark (TV) 326
Prince Philip (Duke of Edinburgh) 1860, 3813, 4041
The Prince's Trust: A Rock and Royal Gala (TV) 1643, 1660
Princess Anne 259, 298, 1114, 1145, 1390, 1456, 1759
Princess Diana (of Wales) 845, 1174, 1327, 1639, 1643, 2425
Princess Margaret 1022, 1411
Princess Stephanie of Monaco 1766
Pringle, Bryan 211, 1177, 1818
Prinze, Freddie Jr. 3597
Prisoners of Conscience (TV) 1913
Pritchard, John 2797
A Private Function (film) 1121, 1134, 1137, 1144–46, 1149, 1172, 1179, 1181–84, 1186, 1187, 1189, 1192, 1197, 1199, 1263, 1276, 1348, 2002, 2706, 3148, 3693
Private Lives (TV) 1123
Privates on Parade (film) 933, 984, 991–94, 1001, 1018, 1117, 1119
The Pro-Celebrity Squash Challenge (event) 612, 614
The Proclaimers 2001
The Producers (musical) 2658
A Profile of Jonathan Miller (book) 1861
The Project (TV) 4057, 4086
Prokofiev, Sergey 3259
Prominent Features 1346, 1359, 1495, 1559, 1677, 1818, 1945
Proops, Greg 2787, 2839
Proops, Marjorie 144
The Proposal (film) 475
Protz, Roger 2782
Proust, Fred 3610
Provenza, Paul 3084
The Province (B.C.) (newspaper) 4149
Prudhomme, Monique 3659

General Index

Pryce, Jonathan 1177, 1227, 1251, 1461, 1559, 3064, 3178, 3209, 3619
Pryor, Richard 293
Psycho (film) 3186
Publishers Weekly (magazine) 603, 686, 2086, 2808, 3097, 3273
Puck, Wolfgang 2871
Pugh, Mavis 680
Pullin, Jim 1734
Pullman, Bill 2102
Pullman, Philip 2524, 2720, 3377
Pulp Fiction (film) 2046
Punch (magazine) 311, 1160, 1453
The Punch Review (TV) 560
Punt, Steve 4008
Purcell, Sarah 777
Purnell, Tony 2796
Purves, Christopher 3745, 3943, 4003
Purves, Libby 2789, 3632
Purvis, Jack 863, 1559
Purvis, Neal 2516, 2819
Put in a Potterton (film) 387
Putch, John 4017
Putner, Paul 2713
Puttnam, David 1419
Puttock, William 1886
Python Night (TV) 134, 2466, 2495
Python on Song (record) 527
Python Periphery (screenings) 2037
The Python Years see *Diaries 1969–1979: The Python Years*
Pythonland (TV) 2495, 2497, 2556, 2710
PythOnline (website) 2159, 2177, 3592, 3593
The Pythons (TV) 699, 700, 705, 1589, 2320, 2522, 3460
The Pythons: Autobiography by The Pythons (book) 2913, 2915, 3200, 3478
The Pythons: Autobiography by The Pythons: The Interviews That Made the Book (audiobook) 2941

Q (magazine) 1404
Q (radio) 3975
Q (TV) 2791
QI (TV) 3982
QI Genesis (TV) 3982
Quaid, Randy 2772, 2942
Quantick, David 3109
Quantum Project (film) 2573
Quarmby, John 732
Quartermaine's Terms see *Saturday Play*
Quatro, Suzi 1242
Quay, Stephen 3170
Quay, Timothy 3170
Queen 3018, 3939
Queen Elizabeth II 576, 788, 1860, 1960, 2754, 2820, 3756, 3813, 4041, 4086
Queen Mother 569
Quenqua, Douglas 3593
Quentin, Caroline 2059, 2370
Quest for Camelot (film) 2369, 2946, 3227

The Quest for King Arthur (book) 2113
The Quest for the Holy Grail Locations (doc) 2586, 2697, 2698, 3321
Quick, Diana 3–7, 9, 651, 1102, 1158, 2331
Quilley, Denis 991, 1018
Quinn, Aidan 2688, 2774
Quinn, Michael 1239
Quinn, Patricia 1025
Quinn, Stephen 3975
The Quite Remarkable Adventures of the Owl and the Pussycat (book) 2171, 2177, 2195, 2197, 4130

Rabbit Ears Radio (radio): "Tom Thumb" 2103
Rabelais, François 1918
Race, Roger 13, 63, 560
Radcliffe, Daniel 2702, 2810
Radcliffe, Mark 4011
The Radio 2 Arts Programme (radio): "The Life of Python" 2033; "The Once and Future King" 2164
The Radio 2 Arts Show with Claudia Winkleman (radio) 4125
Radio 4 Appeal (radio) 2452, 3299, 3370, 3675
Radio 5 (radio) 271, 322
Radio Times (magazine) 91, 361, 416, 673, 699, 1692, 1719, 1895, 2089
Radner, Gilda 515, 563, 576, 635, 640, 660, 671, 695, 730, 779
Rae, John [Dr.] 982
Rafferty, Gerry 85
Rafferty, Sean 1233
Rafferty, Terence 1495, 2739
Rail for the Future: A Development Strategy for the Railways (book) 1799
Raine, Gillian 308, 459
Rainman (film) 1609, 1628
Raitt, Bonnie 2678
Raitt, John 2678
Rakoff, David 3160
Ramirez, Sara 3113, 3131, 3140, 3151
Ramis, Harold 2189
Rampton, James 2494
Rampton, Richard 3172
Ramsay, Gordon 3367
Ramsey, Alf [Sir] 139
Randall, Tony 777
Rankin 4170
Rantzen, Esther 297, 484, 2579
Rao, Anjali 3837
Rappaport, David 863, 871
Rashad, Ahmad 1494
Rat Race (film) 2686
Ratcliffe, Michael 813
Rattee, Donald [Justice] 2373
Rattray, Eric 1301
Ravens, Jan 1797
Rawle-Hicks, Edward 1353
Ray, Ted 140
Raymond, Bob E. 363, 368, 370, 372, 374
Raynor, Henry 34
Raz, Guy 3777

Rea, Chris 2448
Read All About It (TV) 533, 611
Readers and Writers Roadshow (TV) 2760
Reading, Donna 47
Real Time (TV) 253
Real Time with Bill Maher (TV) 2861, 4194
Reardon, John 928
Rebellato, Dan 3262
Recess (TV): "That Stinking Feeling" 2518; "The Girl Was Trouble" 2413
Rechler, Glenn 1396
A Recipe for Life (book) 4148
Record Breakers (TV) 1909
The Rectorial Address of John Cleese (book) 179
Re-Cycled Vinyl Blues (record) 324
Redford, Rachel 4120
Redford, Robert 3368
Redgrave, Lynn 248, 380, 460, 893
Redgrave, Vanessa 1461, 2118, 2204
Redhead, Brian 522, 1934
Redhead, Mark 1752, 1781
Redon, Odilon 3992
Redpath, Anne 2310
Reed, Oliver 1559, 2083, 2448
Reel Ocean: Tribute to Sir David Attenborough (documentary) 3093
Rees, Angharad 243, 300, 306–08, 380
Rees, Nigel 983, 1002
Reeves, Keanu 3596
Reeves, Vic 2289
Reflections on Success (book) 2325
Regan, Brian 2619
Reggae Sunsplash 1838
Reid, Beryl 804, 1738
Reid, Robert 385, 555, 626, 627, 763, 765, 766, 985, 986, 1667
Reid, Sheila 1177
Reid, Susanna 4014, 4035, 4065
Reilly, Sue 736
Reiner, Carl 1021, 3588
Relph, Simon 991
Relton, William 1002
Remember the Secret Policeman's Ball? see *Arena*
Remick, Lee 1638
Rendall, Mark 2790
Les Rendez-Vous du Dimanche (TV) 482, 782
Reno, Jamie 3494
Reno, Jean 3616
Renoux, Rémy 3091
Rentadick (film) 200
Renwick, David 928, 1248, 1249, 1866
The Restaurant at the End of the Universe (book) 3690
Restless Heart 1729
Restoring Balance: Removing the Black Rat from Anacapa Island (documentary) 2945
Rettig, Roger 550
Return on Investment (film) 1250
The Review Show (TV) 3951
Reynolds, Burt 3597

Reynolds, Debbie 2406
Reynolds, Shirley 1930
Reynolds, Stanley 82, 109
"Rhapsody in Blue" [Gershwin] 2212
Rhind, Gillian 541
Rhind-Tutt, Julian 4097
The Rhinestone as Big as the Ritz (book) 760
Rhodes, Lucille 2692, 3019
Rhodes, Nigel 607
Rhodes, Zandra 778
Rhys Jones, Griff *see* Jones, Griff Rhys
Rhys-Jones, Sophie 2455
Ricci, Christina 2102, 2376
Rice, Christine 3943
Rice, Tim 749, 2588, 3639
Rich, Frank 635
Rich, John 1636, 1640, 1644, 1647
Rich, Richard 2055
Richard & Judy (TV) 2817, 2935, 3027, 3383, 3529, 3541
Richard & Judy's Christmas Book Special (TV) 3367
Richard & Judy's New Position (TV) 3581
Richard and Judy Exclusive (TV) 2254
Richard, Cliff 350, 894, 1320, 1390, 2217, 2232, 2536
Richard, Pierre 3610
Richard, Wendy 2402, 3361
Richard Bacon (radio) 4025
Richard II 2927, 3444, 3448, 3451, 3464, 3511, 3524, 3525, 3528, 3563, 3565, 3633, 3650
Richards, Clare 1865
Richards, Dave 550
Richards, Denise 2516
Richards, Keith 1969, 2533
Richards, Michael 957
Richards, Sandra 93
Richardson, Anna 2414
Richardson, Ian 1177
Richardson, Mark 1304, 1442
Richardson, Miranda 1344, 1798
Richardson, Ralph [Sir] 248, 863
Richie, Shane 2001
Richmond, Tim 2010
Rickards, Mark 2622, 3078
Rickles, Don 777, 2369
Rickman, Alan 2685
Rieschel, Claudia 2679
Rigby, Daniel 4009
Rigby, Jean 1304
Rigg, Diana [Dame] 573, 859, 2083, 2448, 3432
Right Royal Company (TV) 849
Rights & Revels: A Benefit for the National Council for Civic Liberties (stage) 1133
Riley, Jon 3376
Ringside 3130
Ripa, Kelly 3110, 3728
Ripley, Fay 3070
Ripping Yarns (book) 659, 686, 1770
Ripping Yarns (DVD) *see The Complete Ripping Yarns*
Ripping Yarns (TV) 406, 597, 637, 641, 653, 701, 724, 780, 1362, 2991, 3041, 3047, 3100, 3192, 3551, 4097; "Tomkinson's Schooldays" (Ep. 1) 406, 480, 516, 598, 659, 4080; "The Testing of Eric Olthwaite" (Ep. 2) 577, 600, 659; "Escape from Stalag Luft 112B" (Ep. 3) 581, 604, 659; "Murder at Moorstones Manor" (Ep. 4) 518, 605, 659, 3047; "Across the Andes by Frog" (Ep. 5) 516, 606, 659; "The Curse of the Claw" (Ep. 6) 584, 607, 659; "Whinfrey's Last Case" (Ep. 7) 678, 725, 806; "Golden Gordon" (Ep. 8) 681, 726, 806; "Roger of the Raj" (Ep. 9) 646, 731, 806, 1593, 4088
Ripping Yarns (videocassette) 1333–37, 1342
The Rise and Rise of Michael Rimmer (film) 18, 99, 100, 2066
Risk to Innovate (lecture) 3128
Ritchie, Jean 1676
Ritchie, Lionel 2533
Ritchie, Vivienne 1150
The Ritz Brothers 642
River of Mirrors: The Fantastic Art of Judson Huss (book) 2163
Rivers, Joan 1337, 3579
Rivron, Rowland 2232
"The Road Not Taken" (poem) 2425
The Road to Hell see Counterblast
The Road to Mars: A Post Modem Novel (book) 392, 2467, 2468, 2479, 2490, 2525
Robbie the Reindeer in Close Encounters of the Herd Kind (TV) 3479
Robbins, Tim 1672, 1677
The Robert Klein Hour (radio) 693
Roberts, Andy 267, 421, 425, 550
Roberts, Julia 3368
Roberts, Nicola 2005
Roberts, Renee 439, 441, 446, 450, 453, 456, 676, 677, 679, 680, 685, 732
Roberts, Steve 256
Robertson, K. Angus 1142
Robertson, Mick 3912
Robin, Dany 19
Robin Williams: Acting Funny (TV) 1952
Robins (TV) 3873
Robins, John 164
Robinson, David 970, 1059, 1149, 1274, 1495, 1677
Robinson, Ethna 1442
Robinson, Ken [Dr.] 2823
Robinson, Peter [conductor] 1304
Robinson, Peter [photographer] 2918
Robinson, Peter [producer-director] 204, 215, 304–08, 380–85, 449, 452, 454, 457, 459, 460, 462, 465, 475–77, 546–49, 558, 618–21, 625, 627, 662, 663, 683, 684, 688, 690, 692, 696, 761–63, 825–27, 899–902, 985, 1156, 1157, 1250, 1344, 1566, 1667, 1798, 1868, 1984, 1985, 2059
Robinson, Robert 376
Robinson, Smokey 3567
Robinson, Tom 704, 755
Robinson, Tony 207, 383, 1454, 2122
Robson, Eric 838, 1007
Robson, Hannah 4052
Robyn 3811
Roche, Tony 4008, 4070
Rochefort, Jean 482, 2597, 3818
Rock 'n' Roll (record) 1412
Rock 'n' Roll in the Making (TV) 2532
Rockwell, Robert 1644
Rodd, Michael 571
Rodley, Chris 1952
Roeffen, Tineke 254
Rogers, C. W. 1832
Rogers, Kenny 1910
Rogerson, Barnaby 4150
Rogerson, Mark 1118
Rohde, Shelley 856, 877, 1288
Rolfe, Michael 1433
Rolf's Amazing World of Animals (TV) 2377
Rolling Stone (magazine) 397, 413, 494, 727, 817, 943, 1079, 1554, 3741
The Rolling Stones 1697, 2533
Romain, Michael 1861
Romance with a Double Bass (film) 355, 386, 2221
Romano, Nel 1135
Romeo and Juliet (film) 2241
Romijn, Rebecca 3236
Romney, Jonathan 2198
The Ronnie Barker Yearbook (TV) 126
Ronnie Barker: A BAFTA Tribute (TV) 2966
Ronnie Barker: A Life in Comedy (TV) 2211
Ronnie Corbett in Bed (TV) 127
Ronnie Corbett's Comedy Britain (TV) 3976
Ronstadt, Linda 824, 3981
Rooney, David 3113
Rooney, Mickey 1677
Rose, Alexander 2927
Rose, Charlie 2081, 3140
Rose, Paul 2713
Roseanne 2144
Rosenthal, Jack 825
Roslin, Gaby 1989, 2970
Ross, Ben 4186
Ross, David 1833
Ross, Diana 1619, 1860
Ross, Jonathan 1452, 2492, 2493, 2703, 2787, 2831, 2839, 3619, 3796, 3877
Ross, Nick 1155
Ross, Paul 1989
Ross, Robert 2364
Ross, Tiny 863
Ross, Tony 1221, 1222
Rossellini, Isabella 2482
Rossi, Leo 1783

General Index

Rossington, Norman 522
Rossiter, Leonard 614
Rossiter, Nicholas (or Nick) 1840, 2934
Rosto 3959
The Routes of English (radio) 2514
Routledge, Patricia 147, 380, 460, 2966
Rove (TV) 3459
Rove LA (TV) 4189
Rove Live (TV) 2872, 3067
Roven, Charles 2119, 3178
Rowan, Dan 642
Rowlands, Patsy 125, 1344
Rowling, J. K. 2409, 2702, 2810
Roy, Will 1712
Roy Wood's Army 2833
Royal Gala Concert (concert) 1174
A Royal Gala in Aid of the Prince's Trust (stage) 1643
A Royal Gala in Aid of the Prince's Trust (TV) 1662
Royal Shakespeare Company 991
The Royal Television Society Programme Awards (ceremony) 506
The Royal Variety Performance (stage) 1860, 1960
The Royal Variety Performance (TV) 1862
Royle, Carol 1567, 1568
Royle, Derek 680
Rubenstein, Lenny 437, 1211
Rubinstein, John 1376
Ruby (TV) 2252, 2471
Rudge, Peter 630
Rudner, Rita 1515, 1643, 1660
Rudnick, Paul 2547
Rudolph the Red-Nosed Reindeer: The Movie (film) 2406
Ruehl, Mercedes 1850, 1855, 2324, 2676
Rulebound Reggie see *Managing Problem People: Rulebound Reggie*
Rules of Effective Communication see *Telephone Behaviour: The Rules of Effective Communication*
Rupert Bear and Me (radio) 4011
The Rupert Bear Story — A Tribute to Alfred Bestall (TV) 982
Rupert Bear 982, 3198, 4011, 4043
Rush, Geoffrey 2625
Rush Hour (radio) 865
Rushdie, Salman 2776, 2906, 2987, 4145
Rushin, Pat 4165
Rushton, William (or Willie) 19, 252, 256, 264, 266, 292, 296, 309, 488, 644, 666, 915, 1665, 2091
Russell, Ken 1219, 4053
Russell, Willy 1695
Russell Harty (TV) 835
Russo, Bryan 1514
Rustin, Lena 2694
The Rutland Dirty Weekend Book (book) 513, 526
The Rutland Isles (CD) 2861, 2864, 2865, 2870, 2878, 2919
The Rutland Weekend Songbook (record) 550

Rutland Weekend Television (TV) 20, 319, 340, 417, 418, 420, 421, 425, 427, 429, 507, 513, 515, 531, 532, 534, 537, 541–44, 550, 582, 635, 1463, 1593, 1981
Rutlemania (concert) 3493
The Rutles 351, 515, 531, 532, 550, 576, 582, 591, 632, 635, 647, 1511, 1750, 1956, 2558, 2543, 2644, 2906, 3493–95, 3531, 3584
The Rutles 2: Can't Buy Me Lunch (DVD) 3105, 3133
The Rutles 2: Can't Buy Me Lunch (film) 635, 2906, 2907
The Rutles: All You Need Is Cash (DVD) 2647
The Rutles: All You Need Is Cash (record) 632
The Rutles: All You Need Is Cash (videocassette) 2133
The Rutles: All You Need Is Cash (30th Anniversary Edition) (DVD) 3583–85
Ryan, Christopher 1125
Ryan, Madge 168, 215, 449, 915, 2025
Ryan, Mark 2566, 2567
Ryan, Meg 2103, 2335
Ryan, Paddy 1026
Ryder, Jack 2549
Ryder, Shaun 3904

Sabbagh, Karl 2121
Sach, Laurence 1069
Sachs, Andrew 383, 384, 386, 439–41, 446, 450, 453, 456, 476, 477, 484, 546, 626, 676, 677, 679, 680, 685, 732, 765, 900, 901, 987, 1106, 1157, 1289, 1433, 2383, 2695, 2958, 3579, 3648, 3654, 3738, 4128
Sacks, Oliver 4091
Saga Magazine (magazine) 3940
The Saga of Erik the Viking (book) 1069, 1084, 1085, 1088–90, 1092, 1155, 1216, 1677
The Saga of Erik the Viking (videogame) 1155, 1165
Sager, Carole Bayer 2369
Saget, Bob 3084
Sahara (book) 2778, 2784, 2785, 2794, 2827, 2859, 2877
Sahara (lecture) 2788, 2795, 2807, 2887
Sahara with Michael Palin (TV) 2635, 2693, 2724, 2778, 2785, 2786, 2796, 2797, 2799, 2801, 2804, 2806, 2807, 2809, 2848, 2854, 2866, 2882, 2883, 2886, 2894
Said, SF 3305
Sainsbury, Mark 4172
Sainsbury's (ad) 2114
Sainsbury's ("Value to Shout About") (ads) 2114, 2394
Saint, Eva Marie 1335
St. Andrews University 101, 131, 132, 179, 265, 327
St. Aubin de Teran, Lisa 2060

Saint-Saëns, Camille 2851
Salem, Rob 3678
Salewicz, Chris 1041
Sallis, Peter 1982
The Salmon of Doubt (book) 2665
Salter, Sandra 1754
Saltzman, Percy 276
A Salute to Monty Python (screening) 1820
Salvoni, Elena 1762
Samett, Marcelle 600
Sampras, Pete 2462
Sampson, Roy 725
San Francisco International Film Festival 1182, 1604
Sanborn, David 779
Sancton, Julian 3776, 3803
Sand, Barry 1181
Sand, Bjørn 769
Sanders, Chris 3227
Sanders, George 19
Sanderson, Joan 676, 731, 815, 859, 900, 901, 1353
Sandler, Adam 2468
Sanoff, Alvin P. 1698
Santa Barbara Symphony 3631
Sarducci, Father Guido 671, 695, 730
Sargent, Herb 1055
Sarony, Leslie 813, 1026
Sarris, Andrew 412
Saturday Extra (radio) 3762
Saturday Matters with Sue Lawley (TV) 1679
Saturday Night at the Movies (TV) 1706
Saturday Night Clive (TV) 1747
Saturday Night Live (TV) 515, 531, 535, 561, 563, 576, 582, 635, 640, 660, 671, 686, 695, 730, 779, 935, 940, 963, 966, 1110, 1338, 1678, 1737, 2214, 3754
Saturday Night Special (TV) 2144
The Saturday Play (radio): "Quartermaine's Terms" 3294
Saturday Review (magazine) 397
Saturday Review (TV) 1262
The Saturday Show (TV) 1085
Saturday Superstore (TV) 1220
Saul, Nigel 3524
Saunders, Des 1345
Saunders, Jennifer 204, 1153, 1343, 1665, 1705, 1734, 1869, 3295, 4051
Saunders, John 915
Savage-Smith, Emilie 3034
"Save the Plankton" (Palin sketch) 795, 1110, 1483, 2813
Savile, Jimmy 927
Saville, Philip 19
Sawalha, Julia 2185, 3000
Sayce, Paul 2228
Sayle, Alexei 871, 883, 931, 1125, 1153
Scaffold 572
Scales, Prunella 439–41, 446, 450, 453, 456, 662, 676, 677, 679, 680, 685, 732, 1438, 1443, 1461, 1733, 2383, 2650, 2695, 2958, 3648, 3654, 3738

Scanlon, Larry 2632
Scarfe, Gerald 1449, 1552, 3138, 3215
Scarfe's Follies see *40 Minutes*
Scarpa, David 3596
Scarry, Richard 38
Scene Today (TV) 1822
Schaal, Wendy 1636, 1640, 1644, 1647
Schaefer, Stephen 931, 943
Schauer, Mitch 2417
Scheer, Andrew 2566
Scheinfeld, John 2562, 3234, 3841
Schell, Catherine 729
Schepisi, Fred 2162, 2221
Scherer, Barrymore Laurence 3416
Schickel, Richard 397, 567, 710, 1025, 1495, 2611
Schiffman, Bonnie 817
Schifrin, William 2369
Schiller, Danny 1370
Schindehette, Susan 1645, 1707
Schlatter, George 160, 1477, 1515, 2333, 3588
Schofield, Andrew 1833
Schofield, Phillip 1625, 1890, 1905, 1946, 3436, 3620, 4036, 4119
Schuhly, Thomas 1559
Schuman, Howard 2143
Schuman, Phil 1049
Schwalm, Thomas 755
Schwartz, Al 1783
Schwartz, Rob 2423
Schwarzbaum, Lisa 3659
Schweppes (A Very Public Service Message from John Cleese) (ad) 1594, 1595
Schweppes (ads) 1741, 1919
Schweppes ("Straight Schweppes") (ads) 1803
Schwitzer, Christoph 3915
Scorched (film) 2667, 2751
Scorsese, Martin 1768, 2828, 3821, 3996, 4157
The Scotsman (newspaper) 2613, 2757, 3874
Scott, A. O. 3186
Scott, Caroline 2488, 2646
Scott, Danny 3038
Scott, Donovan 957
Scott, Gavin 1894, 2157
Scott, Peter [Sir] 809
Scott, Ridley 2132
Scott, Sebastian 1806
Scott, Selina 1237
Scott, Tom 2207
Scoular, Angela 68
The Scream Team (TV) 2790
Screen Two (TV): "East of Ipswich" 1107, 1292, 1349–51, 1353, 1456, 1548, 2017, 2752, 3508
The Screwtape Letters (audiobook) 1569
Scurfield, Matthew 726
The Sea, The Sea (book) 862
Seal 3185
Seaman, Peter S. 3405
Searching for Truth (event) 4147
Searle, Ronald 1559

Sebast, Dick 2421
Secombe, Harry 68, 165, 1288, 2147, 2250, 2355, 2472, 2682
The Secret Life of Brian (TV) 3375, 3460
The Secret of NIMH II: Timmy to the Rescue (film) 2421
The Secret Policeman's Ball (film) 755, 793, 931, 939, 3609, 3669, 4000
The Secret Policeman's Ball (record) 764
The Secret Policeman's Ball (stage) 492, 701, 702, 704, 706, 871, 4081
The Secret Policeman's Ball (TV) 759
The Secret Policeman's Ball 2012 (stage) 4081, 4085
The Secret Policeman's Balls (DVD) 3075, 3609
The Secret Policeman's Biggest Ball (stage) 1665
The Secret Policeman's Biggest Ball (TV) 1705
The Secret Policeman's Film Festival (screenings) 3075, 3669, 3673
The Secret Policeman's Other Ball (ad) 935, 940
The Secret Policeman's Other Ball (book) 907
The Secret Policeman's Other Ball (film) 929–31, 939, 3669
The Secret Policeman's Other Ball (record) 883
The Secret Policeman's Other Ball (stage) 871
The Secret Policeman's Private Parts (film) 1065
The Secret Policeman's Third Ball (book) 1403
The Secret Policeman's Third Ball (film) 1409
The Secret Policeman's Third Ball (stage) 1365
The Secretary and Her Boss, Part 1: Try to See It My Way (film) 620, 688
The Secretary and Her Boss, Part 2: We Can Work It Out (film) 621, 690
Secrets (TV) see *Black and Blue*
Seda, Jon 2119
Sedaka, Neil 500, 1679
See You Again Soon see *Welcome Customer, Part 2: See You Again Soon*
Segal, Jeffrey 453
Seidler, David 2369
Seifert, Jack 1635
Seisser, Tod 1159
Sekine, Tsutomu 1677
Self-Consciousness (book) 1657
Sellers, Peter 50, 2250, 2562, 2682, 2792, 3614, 3616, 3841
Selling in Practice, No. 2: How Not to Exhibit Yourself (film) 384, 465
The Selling Line (TV) 448, 449, 452, 454, 457, 459, 460, 462, 465
Selling on the Telephone: The Cold Call (film) 546

Selling on the Telephone: When I'm Calling You (film) 476, 692
Selling on the Telephone: Will You Answer True? (film) 477, 696
Sen kväll med Luuk (TV) 2246
Senkveld with Thomas and Harald (TV) 3865
"Serenade No. 10 in B Flat Major" [Mozart] 1061
Sereny, Eva 1150
Sergeant, John 2791, 4095
Sergeant on Spike (TV) see *Perspectives*
Sergei, Ivan 2742
Serl, Jon 1729
Serle, Chris 1051, 1440, 1754, 3544
Sessions, John 1686
Setzer, Brian 1499
Seuss, Dr. 1967, 2621
Seussical (musical) 2449, 2621
Seven Chances (film) 3279
720 Morning (radio) 3456
Seven Ways to Skin an Ocelot [U.S., 2006] (stage) 3233
The Seventh Python (film) 3531
Seventh Son of a Seventh Son (record) 1571
Severinson, Doc 1148
Sewell, Bill 309
Sewell, George 382
Sex in History (book) 855
Seymour, Carolyn 651
Seymour, Jane 2369
Seymour, Richard 1305
Sez Les (TV) 158, 313, 378, 519, 4047
Sforza, Fabrizio 1559, 1755
Shadow Work (book) 853
Shaffer, Paul 779
Shakespeare, Nicholas 1003
Shakespeare, William 248, 789, 813, 2319, 4027
The Shakespeare Plays (TV): "The Taming of the Shrew" 830
Shalit, Gene 394
Shamas, Sandra 2863
Shamberg, Michael 1493, 1495, 1500, 1508, 2221
Shames, Laurence 1115
Shandling, Garry 2906
Shane, Paul 1281
Shane, Stephen 486
Shankar, Ravi 2730, 2826, 3686
Shannon, Johnny 676
Shannon, Molly 2214, 3560
The Shape of Things to Come see *All Change (The Management of Change), Part 2: The Shape of Things to Come*
Sharif, Omar 1095
The Sharon Osbourne Show (TV) 3342
Sharp, Margaret 377
Sharvell-Martin, Michael 725
Shaun Keaveny (radio) 4029
Shaw, Beatrice 679
Shaw, Bella 1703
Shaw, Christine 685
Shaw, Martin 152, 1144

Shaw, Sandy 974
Shawcross, Helen 3968
Shawn, Wallace 1883
Shea, Mary Frances 1402, 1410
Sheard, Michael 763
Shearer, Harry 779, 2875, 3076, 3112, 3290, 3388, 4102
Sheetz, Chuck 3388
The Sheffield Children's Book Awards (ceremony) 2409
Shehadeh, Raja 3882
Sheinberg, Sid 1208, 1218, 1226, 1228, 1395
Shelton, Ron 2899
Shepherd, Chris 3329
Shepherd, Elaine 2402, 2496, 3221
Shepherd, Sherri 2742
Shepherd, Simon 1986
Sher, Antony 1677, 2185
Sherlock, David 283, 284, 300, 810, 1252, 1455, 1485, 1726, 1746, 2915, 3200
Sherlock Jr. (film) 3279
Sherrin, Ned 200, 773, 2271
Sherrye Henry (radio) 503
Sherwin, Stuart 732
Shields, Brooke 639, 1490, 2476
Shilling, Eric 1352
Shillue, Tom 2482
Shin, Nelson 1303
Shinner, Jo 2626
Shivas, Mark 280, 1134, 1149, 1273
Shoard, Catherine 3201, 3271
Shone, Tom 2376
Short, Martin 1338, 1678, 2654, 3980
"Short Blues" (song) 502
Shorter, Ken 731
The Show Business: How to Demonstrate a Product (film) 382
Showbiz Today (TV) 1492, 1505, 1605, 1633, 1678, 1703, 1785
Showerman, Christopher 2925
Shrek & Fiona's Honeymoon Storybook (CD-ROM) 2903
Shrek Forever After (film) 3405, 3823
Shrek the Third (film) 2997, 3403–05
Shrek: Totally Tangled Tales (DVD game) 3229
Shrek 2 (film) 2903, 2993, 2995, 2997, 3001, 3005, 3405, 3823
Shriver, Maria 1228
Shulan, Michael 1631
Shulman, Milton 82
Shulman, Roger 1635, 1636, 1640
Shuman, Mort 482
Sibley, Adrian 2422, 2480
Sickert, Walter 3492
Sieber, Christopher 3113, 3410, 3417
Siegel, Joel 3171
Siegel, Robert 3545
Sigal, Clancy 1274
Sight & Sound (magazine) 1521, 2139, 2382, 2571
Signals: Anything for a Quiet Life (TV) 1739
Signford Ltd. 552, 1179

Sikov, Ed 2792
Silberling, Brad 2102
Silence Is Golden (film) 3329
Silent Clowns (TV): "Buster Keaton" 3279; "Harold Lloyd" 3292
Silver, Joel 1598
Silver Streak (film) 569
Silverado (film) 1166, 1209, 1239, 1243
Silverman, Melvin [Dr.] 1034
Silverstone, Alicia 2751
Silverton, Kate 3341, 3468
Sim, Alastair 159, 3108
Sim, Gerald 725
Simeon, David 440, 620
Simmons, Kenny 2860
Simmons, Matty 1210, 2942
Simmons, Richard 2406
Simmons, Sue 1184
Simon, Carly 3114
Simon, Josette 1868
Simon, Neil 2442
Simon, Paul 535, 540, 635, 779, 823, 906
Simon, Ron 2644
Simon Mayo (radio) 3207, 3276, 3311, 3615, 3692
Simon Mayo Drivetime (radio) 3849, 4116
"Simon Smith & His Amazing Dancing Bear" (song) 151
Simply Absurd (radio) 3856
Simply Shakespeare (event) 3946
Simpson, Alan 165
Simpson, David 492
Simpson, Jeff 3497, 4140, 4162
Simpson, Junior 2585
Simpson, N. F. 252
The Simpsons (TV): "Fat Man and Little Boy" 3076; "Scuse Me While I Miss the Sky" 2875; "Springfield Up" 3388; "The Spy Who Learned Me" 4102
Sims, Joan 165
Sinclair, Donald 66
Sinclair, John Gordon 1677
Sinden, Donald 200, 927, 3246
The Single (record) 478
Siskel, Gene 397
Sissons, Peter 2495, 2544
Sivan, Troye 3884
Six Dates with Barker (TV): "1971: Come In and Lie Down" 120
6 O'Clock Live (TV) 1816, 1884
6 O'Clock Show (TV) 1188
Sixthirtysomething (TV) 1852
60 Minutes (TV) 3140
Skapinker, Michael 1377
Skavlan (TV) 3768, 3811, 3812
Skavlan, Fredrik 3768, 3811
Skingley, Lorna 4011
Skinner, Frank 2176, 2188, 2385
Skinner, Quentin 864
Sky 992
Skynner, Robin [Dr.] 474, 1078, 1081, 1083, 1132, 1168, 1433, 1540, 1794, 1795, 1930, 1932, 1934, 2063, 2595
Slade 198

Slade, Adrian 990
Slater, Ashley 3267
Slater, Christian 3560
Slatterey, Tony 1706
A Slice of Cleese—John Cleese In Conversation with James Crathorne (event) 3442
Slices of Cleese: An Evening with John Cleese (event) 3457
Sloman, Larry 413
Sloman, Roger 726
Sloopy 372
Slung, Michele 1094
Small Harry and the Toothache Pills (book) 959, 973, 1135, 1258, 1275
Smaragdis, Yannis 4144
Smart, Amy 2686
Smee, Anthony 600
Smillie, Carol 2703
Smith, Aidan 2613
Smith, Anna Nicole 2871
Smith, Arthur 1923, 3041
Smith, Caroline 3659
Smith, Delia 1239
Smith, Giles 2378
Smith, Jaden 3596
Smith, Keith 607
Smith, Kirsten 2986
Smith, Liz 600, 1149, 1187
Smith, Madeline 292
Smith, Maggie 970, 1015, 1121, 1149, 1187, 2702
Smith, Martin 2147
Smith, Mel 737, 818, 1153, 1343, 1665, 2091, 2709
Smith, Mike 1176, 1240, 1608
Smith, Paul 804, 1343
Smith, Richard Curson 2065, 2070, 2073, 2075, 2077
Smith, Robert 1150
Smith, Sarah 4018
Smith, Steve 2703
Smith, Terry 898, 1227
Smith, Tony 268, 3588
Smith, Will 4049
Smith, Yeardley 2875, 3076, 3388, 4102
Snavely (TV) 645, 2436
Snell, Andrew 2828
SNL see *Saturday Night Live*
Snoad, Harold 183, 252
Snoddy, Raymond 1261
Snogging Ken (play) 2559
Snow Show (stage) 3245
The Snowman (TV) 2118
Snyder, Tom 718
So This Is Progress? (TV) 1865
So You Want to Be a Success at Selling?, Part 1: The Preparation (film) 900
So You Want to Be a Success at Selling?, Part 2: The Presentation (film) 901
So You Want to Be a Success at Selling?, Part 3: Difficult Customers (film) 1102
So You Want to Be a Success at Selling?, Part 4: Closing the Sale (film) 1157

General Index

Søby, Erik 769
Söderström, Anna 3015, 3687
Solli, Sergio 3953
Solly, Bill 136
Solomon, Arthur 1345
Solomon, Ed 1883, 2240, 3129
Solomon, Evan Daniel [Cleese's grandson] 2240
Solomon, Jonathan 1944
Something ALMOST Completely Different (event) 3789
Something Completely Different (radio) 2489
Something Fishy (documentary) 3362
Something Like Fire: Peter Cook Remembered (book) 2181, 2182
Sommers, Stephen 2057
Song and Dance (documentary) 2909, 2911
Sony (ads) 629
Soper, Donald 1349
Sorel, Edward 1305, 1832
Souden, David 1865, 2398–2401
Soul, David 500
Sound Waves for Greenpeace (stage) 1289
A Source of Innocent Merriment (TV) 1441
The South Bank Show (TV) 3395; "Eric Sykes" 3191; "John Cleese" 1259; "Monty Python's Spamalot" 3352; "The One Ronnie" 3564; "Terry Gilliam" 1851
The South Bank Sky Arts Awards (ceremony) 4100
The South Bank Tapes (radio): "Early Days of Hollywood" 2802
The South Bragg Show see *Kombat Opera Presents*
South Pacific (musical) 3830
South Park (TV) 2495, 2669
South Park: Bigger, Longer & Uncut (film) 2456
Southern, Terry 50
Souza, Robert 2899
Space Ghost Coast to Coast (TV) 2130
Spacey, Kevin 2214, 4091
Spall, Timothy 1894, 1924
Spam Song/The Concert (record) 210
Spamalot (CD) 3144, 3225, 3260, 3333
Spamalot (musical) 3120, 3131, 3133, 3201, 3242, 3359, 3822, 3833, 3850, 4202; [awards] 3146, 3147, 3151, 3389, 3838; [Australia] 3469, 3470, 3472, 3474; [Broadway] 3096, 3098, 3104, 3110, 3111, 3113–16, 3122, 3140, 3253, 3410, 3607; [Edinburgh] 3874; [Las Vegas] 3380, 3393, 3394, 3398, 3399, 3412; [London] 3238, 3326, 3327, 3352–55, 3400, 4109, 4131; [Los Angeles] 3676, 3677, 4078; [premiere] 3079, 3080; [Spain] 3577; [Toronto] 3300; [U.K. tour] 3824, 3827, 3851, 4044, 4045; [U.S. tour] 3247, 3734
Span, Paula 2085

Spanswick, George 2201
Speaking Images: Essays in Honor of V. A. Kolve (book) 2663
Spear, Roger Ruskin 266
Spearman, Richard 4202
Spears, Annie 1833
The Spectator (magazine) 3626
Speight, Johnny 315
Speight, Philip 376
Spellbound: Art and Film (exhibition) 2132
Spence, Peter 1344, 1789
Spencer, John L. 2836, 2839, 2966
Spencer, Lady Diana *see* Princess Diana (of Wales)
Spencer, Terence 1074
Spend an Hour with Michael Palin (event) 4173
The Spice Girls 2533
Spiegel, Steve 2052
Spiegel Online (website) 3658
Spiers, Bob 675–77, 679, 680, 685, 732, 3738
Spiers, Judi 1122, 1708, 1822
Spies Like Us (film) 1238
Spike (TV) 1288
Spike, Paul 624
Spike Milligan: A Loose Cannon (TV) 2355
Spike Milligan: I Told You I Was Ill... A Live Tribute (TV) 2780, 2791
Spin (magazine) 1284, 1396, 1630, 2879
Spitting Image 1365, 1665
Spitznagel, Eric 3761
Spivak, Helayne 1595
Splitting Heirs (film) 386, 1881, 1933, 1938, 1941, 1945, 1947, 1951, 1953, 1955–58, 1960, 1961, 2221
Sporting Relations (book) 351
Sport Aid (event) 1296
Springfield, Dusty 8
Springsteen, Bruce 464, 3670, 3819
Spud (film) 3799, 3884, 3885, 4093
Spud 2 (film) 4114
Spurlock, Morgan 3202
Spycatcher (book) 1406
Spyres, Michael 4146
Squibb, Vince 3500
Squires, Tony 2854
Sragow, Michael 943
Stack, Robert 1303
Stadlen, Matthew 3769
Staff, Kathy 519
Stainton, Michael 607, 731
Staller, Ilona 1537
Stallone, Sylvester 2295
Stammering: A Practical Guide for Teachers and Other Professionals (book) 2694
Stamp, Robbie 2352
Stamp, Terence 2813, 4011
Standby...Lights! Camera! Action! (TV) 1013
Stander, Lionel 1301
Standing, John 384
Standing Room Only (TV): "Double Bananas" 642
Stansfield, Lisa 1796

Stanshall, Vivian 10, 256, 264, 266, 2897
Stapleton, John 4030
Star Sound Extra (radio) 1009, 1101
Stark, Graham 165
Stark, John 1638
Starkie, Martin 2514
Starlog (magazine) 912, 1180, 1185, 1196, 1205, 1257, 1295, 1629, 1659
Starr, Ringo 50, 221, 1320, 1324, 2541, 2826, 2916, 2921, 3234, 3297, 3516, 3686, 3793, 3981, 4154, 4157
Stars on Sunday II: The Stage Show (stage) 1153, 1343
Starship Titanic (book) see *Douglas Adams's Starship Titanic*
Starship Titanic (CD-ROM) 2318, 2319, 2352, 2357, 2665
Start the Week (radio) 1535, 1614, 1896, 1914, 1930, 2087, 3275
Start the Week with Richard Baker (radio) 658
The Statue (film) 113
Status Quo 844
Staunton, Imelda 3329, 4018
Stayt, Charlie 4014, 4035, 4065
Steadman, Alison 985
Steadman, Ralph 1867, 2365
Steel, Mark 2844
Steele, Tommy 585, 614
Steeples, Joe 211
Stefano, Joseph 2318
Steinman, Jim 4050
Steinmetz, Johanna 1370
Stelfox, Shirley 1370
Step Up to Wordpower (TV) 1754
Stephens, John 1712
Stephens, Lynne 1659
Stephens, Toby 2819
Stephenson, Pamela 737, 818, 871, 883, 929, 931, 1032, 1289, 1340, 2774, 2836, 3904
Stephinson, Ken 820, 1998
Stern, Leonard 1823
Sterritt, David 913, 2692, 3019
Steve Martin's Best Show Ever (TV) 893
The Steve Miller Band 433
Steve Wright in the Afternoon (radio) 4029
Stevens, Michael Fenton 1984
Stevens, Toby 3000
Stevenson, Bob 3542
Stevenson, Jessica 2713, 3419
Steward, William 387
Stewart, Alastair 3040
Stewart, Avril 397
Stewart, Dave (or David) 1832, 3296
Stewart, David 2651
Stewart, Ed 585
Stewart, French 2358, 2359, 2664, 2666
Stewart, James 1859
Stewart, Jon 2551, 4081
Stewart, Maria 3551
Stewart, Rod 2931, 3758
Sticky Wicket see *Behind the Crease*

Stiles, Lynn 988
Still Crazy Like a Fox (TV) 1376
Stillman, Joe 3760
Stilwell, Jean 3410, 3417, 3543, 3550
Sting 871, 931, 1559, 2289, 3075, 3669
Stock, Francine 4058
Stockbridge, Sara 2104
Stockwood, Mervyn (Bishop of Southwark) [Dr.] 749
Stoddart, Patrick 1694, 2035
Stoker, Claire 2797
Stone, Matt 2456, 2496, 2669
Stone, Oliver 2376
Stoner, Sherri 2102
Stonham, Kay 985
Stoppard, Miriam 1132
Stoppard, Tom 473, 925, 1177, 1241, 1251, 1282, 2540
Stormare, Peter 3178
The Story of I (TV) 3016, 3198, 3199
Story Time ["Biggles"] (radio) 869
Storyville (TV): "Lost in La Mancha" 2904
Stovell, Eric 1026
Stowe, Madeleine 2078, 2119, 2324
Straight Talking: The Art of Assertiveness (film) 1869
Strain, Hugh 422
The Strange Case of the End of Civilisation as We Know It (book) 601
The Strange Case of the End of Civilisation as We Know It (TV) 252, 559, 596
Strange Stains and Mysterious Smells: Quentin Cottington's Journal of Faery Research (book) 2043, 2193
Stratton-Smith, Tony 1383
Strauss, Richard 3928
Street-Porter, Janet 1439, 2353
Streiber, Art 2979
Streisand, Barbra 2166
Streithorst, Tom 3588
Strick, Philip 1177
Strictly Private (TV) 1018
Strong, Colin 1320
Strong, James 3655
Stroud, John 2370
Stroud, Les 3431
Stroumboulopoulos, George 3775, 4056
Strummer, Joe 2813
Stuart, Caz 3611
Stuart, Charlie 4047
Stubbs, Imogen 1677
Stubbs, Una 381, 382, 685
Studies in the Age of Chaucer, Volume 22 (book) 2632
Sturgeon, Tim 1777
Sturges, Preston 1713, 2571, 3134, 3162
Sturridge, Charles 1358
Stynes, Yumi 4061
Suarez, Fabien 3295
Suchet, David 970, 2834
Suddenly Susan (TV) 2476
Sullivan, Arthur [Sir] 1304
Sullivan, David 924

Sullivan, Owen 777
Sullivan's Travels (DVD) 3134
Sullivan's Travels (film) 1713
Summers, Sue 1674, 2179
Sumner, Alex 2402
Sumpter, Donald 828
The Sun (newspaper) 34, 170, 952, 1036, 1046, 1347, 1676, 1885
Sunday Brunch (radio) 1891
Sunday Night [Aus.] (TV) 4016
Sunday Night [U.K.] (TV) 1007
Sunday Night Clive (TV) 2002
Sunday Premiere (TV): "Number 27" 1548
Sunday Spectacular (TV) 734
Sunday, Sunday (TV) 976, 983, 1002, 1095, 1113, 1144, 1225, 1340, 1626, 1686
The Sunday Telegraph (newspaper) 1674, 2734, 2927, 3201, 3271
The Sunday Times (London) (newspaper) 237, 340, 392, 417, 491, 565, 567, 651, 758, 794, 842, 931, 991, 1025, 1041, 1056, 1109, 1170, 1301, 1353, 1379, 1495, 1526, 1546, 1559, 1610, 1657, 1693, 1694, 1751, 1817, 1850, 1863, 1878, 1889, 1947, 1999, 2021, 2215, 2274, 2309, 2376, 2502, 2519, 2590, 2605, 2675, 2735, 2749, 2798, 3023, 3154, 3175, 3176, 3230, 3242, 3270, 3351
The Sunday Times Magazine (London) (magazine) 566, 2010, 2145, 2258, 2488, 2646, 2913, 3038, 3309, 3886
Sundin, Mats 3768
Super Robot Monkey Team Hyperforce Go! (TV) 3042
Super Size Me (film) 4102
Superman: True Brit (comic book) 3060
Superspike (record) 486
The Superspike Squad 486
Susann, Jacqueline 2547
Sussex, Elizabeth 1529
Sutherland, Alex 1526
Suzman, Janet 1751
Swallow, Roger 550
The Swan Princess (film) 2055
Swap Shop Star Awards (TV) 847
Sweet, Matthew 3338
Swinton, Tilda 4165
Swit, Loretta 777
Syal, Meera 1986
Syed-Tollan, Max 3364
Sykes, Eric 1661, 2250, 2791, 2831, 2966, 3191, 4179
Sykes, Melanie 2965, 3092
Symons, Nick 2370

Tafler, Sydney 159
Takamiya, Toshiyuki 4098
Taking the Wheel (film) 2722
The Tale of the Frog Prince see *Faerie Tale Theatre*
Tales from the Arabian Nights (book) 2269, 3656
Talk Asia (TV) 3837

Talk of the Nation (radio) 3423, 3836
The Talk Show (TV) 2938
Talking Movies (TV) 3316
Talking Pages (ads) 1736
Talking Pictures (TV) 744
Talking Poetry (radio) 1792
Talking Tate (TV) 2262
Tamahori, Lee 2819
Tamarkin, Jeff 1511
The Taming of the Shrew (TV) see *BBC Television Shakespeare*
Tandy, Adam 4070
Tannahill, Reay 855
Tanner, Stella 679
Taormina Film Festival 4111
Taplin, Jonathan 957
Tarantino, Quentin 2046
Tarnas, Richard [Prof.] 3461, 3622
Tarrant, Chris 674, 772, 774, 844, 894, 923, 3081, 3193, 3413
Tarrant's 2004 (radio) 3081
Tatarsky, Daniel 3879
Tate, Catherine 3898
Tati, Jacques 160, 2660
Tatum, Channing 3649
Taub, Jay 1159
Taviani, Paolo 4113
Taviani, Vittorio 4113
Tavis Smiley (TV) 3133
Taylforth, Gillian 2149
Taylor, Andy 2630, 2631, 2840, 2841
Taylor, Clare 740
Taylor, Dennis 2965
Taylor, DJ 4120
Taylor, Gwen 420, 471, 532, 534, 537, 541–44, 635, 710, 726
Taylor, James [actor] 732
Taylor, James [musician] 695, 779, 2906
Taylor, Richard 309
Taylor, Steve 1053, 1075
Taylor-Mead, Elizabeth 982
Te Kanawa, Kiri 1643, 1660
Teach Yourself Heath (record) 233
The Teaching Awards 2001 (TV) 2703
Tears for Fears 1191
Tebbit, Norman 1339, 1535, 1541
The Telegraph see *The Daily Telegraph*
Telegraph Magazine (magazine) 4043
The Telegraph Travel Awards (ceremony) 3046
Telephone Behaviour: The Power and the Perils (film) 1344
Telephone Behaviour: The Rules of Effective Communication [1997] (film) 2323
The Television and Radio Industries Club Awards (ceremony) 2343, 2866
Telfer, Alison 11, 1533, 3015
The Tell-Tale Heart (opera) 3926
Templar, Dale 2377
Temple, Julien 931, 1065
Tennant, David 3655

Tenniel, John 567
Terranova, Gianluca 4063
Terry, Bridget 1198
The Terry and Gaby Show (TV) 2970
Terry Gilliam: A Life in Pictures (event) 3710
The Terry Gilliam Guardian Interview (event) 2198
Terry Gilliam Interviews (book) 3019
Terry Gilliam's Desert Island Flicks (event) 2661
Terry Jones: Animal Tales (event) 3973
Terry Jones' Barbarians (book) 3263, 3273, 3274, 3287, 3766
Terry Jones' Barbarians (TV) 3273–77, 3280, 3281, 3283, 3284, 3286, 3289, 3293, 3308
Terry Jones' Great Map Mystery (TV) 3418, 3512, 3513, 3517, 3520, 3526, 3635
Terry Jones' Medieval Lives (book) 2964, 2974, 2975
Terry Jones' Medieval Lives (TV) 2948, 2961, 2965, 2967–70, 2975; "The Damsel" 2952; "The King" 2951; "The Knight" 2949; "The Minstrel" 2955; "The Monk" 2950; "The Outlaw" 2956; "The Peasant" 2957; "The Philosopher" 2954
Terry Jones's War on the War on Terror (book) 2708, 3085, 3124
Terry Wogan's Friday Night (TV) 1923
Tewson, Josephine 252
TFI Friday (TV) 2222, 2234, 2408
Thackeray, William Makepeace 753
That Sunday Night Show (TV) 3904
Thatcher, Denis 1650
Thatcher, Margaret [Prime Minister] [Baroness] 151, 695, 1650, 2343, 2381
That's Death (CD) 2207
That's Esther (TV) 2579
That's Television Entertainment (TV) 1320
Theakston, Jamie 2178, 2223, 2691
Théâtre de Complicité 1739
Their Finest Hours (plays) 508
TheJohnCleese.Com 3013, 3031
Theopold, Hans-Bernhard 134
Theroux, Paul 853, 862, 4120
Thewlis, David 2750, 4165
Thierry, Mélanie 4165
"Things Ain't What They Used to Be" (song) 753
"Things We Said Today" (song) 753
Think or Sink (film) 1868
Third Ear (radio) 1857
3rd Rock from the Sun (TV) 2231; "Dick and the Other Guy" 2359; "Just Your Average Dick" 2358; "Mary Loves Scoochie: Part 1" 2664; "Mary Loves Scoochie: Part 2" 2666
Thirty Three & 1/3 (record) 528, 530, 535
30 Years of Python (TV) 2493

This Country in the Morning (radio) 298
This Is Going to Hurt Me More Than It Hurts You: The Bad News Interview (film) 1733
This Is Your Life (TV) 266, 2721
This Morning (TV) 1711, 1893, 2008, 2183, 2278, 2508, 3436, 3620, 3702, 4036, 4119, 4203
This Song/Learning How to Love You (record) 530
This Week (TV) 2868
This Week's Good Cause (radio) 2283
Thomas, Andrew 3192
Thomas, Betsy 4069
Thomas, Ellen 2840, 2841
Thomas, Hugh 1475
Thomas, Jeremy 3186
Thomas, Leslie 1122, 1340
Thomas, Polly 3262
Thomas, Ralph 68, 243
Thomas, Richard 3395
Thomas, Rowland 1479
Thomas, Vicky 3647
Thomas, Wally 1026
Thompson, Anne 880
Thompson, Bernard 481
Thompson, Brian 838
Thompson, David 2046, 4091
Thompson, E. P. 858
Thompson, Emma 204, 1564, 2931
Thompson, Gregory 2664
Thompson, Harry 1776
Thompson, Howard 161
Thompson, Hunter S. 2267, 2361, 2376, 2849
Thompson, John 4011
Thompson, John O. 937
Thompson, Mark 3575
Thompson, Neville C. 970
Thompson, Steve 3985
Thornborrow, Bridget 1798
Thorne, Angela 990, 2017
Three Men in a Boat (TV) 430, 473, 1440
Three Piece Suite (TV): "Every Day in Every Way" 573
Throsby, Margaret 2521, 4190
Thurman, Uma 1559, 1585, 1601
Thurmond, Strom [Sen.] 728
Tideland (DVD) 3392
Tideland (film) 3024, 3178, 3186, 3187, 3194, 3301, 3304, 3305, 3312, 3313, 3316, 3331, 3334, 3335, 3345, 3346, 3348, 3349, 3384, 3907
Tidy, Bill 211
Tilbrook, Glen 1032
Tillis, Mel 808
Tilly, Jennifer 3186
Tilting at Windmills: The Fantastical Worlds of Terry Gilliam (event) 2816, 2857
Tilzey, Paul 2439
Tim Rice (TV) 1006
Time (magazine) 397, 494, 567, 635, 710, 863, 1025, 1149, 1315, 1495, 1559
Time and the Soul (book) 2891

Time Bandits (book) 860
Time Bandits (comic book) 918
Time Bandits (DVD/Blu-ray) 3711, 3712, 3859
Time Bandits (film) 743, 784, 785, 791, 835, 857, 863, 866, 870, 880, 882, 885, 889, 891, 898, 912, 913, 921, 936, 1031, 1064, 1532, 1574, 2120, 2336, 2376, 2540, 2706, 2743, 2805, 2936
Time Bandits: A Screenplay (book) 881
Time Bandits: Special Edition (DVD) 2324, 2960
Time Bandits: The Criterion Collection (laserdisc) 2336
Time Bandits: 25th Anniversary Edition (DVD) 3315
A Time of Gifts (book) 1657
Time Out (magazine) 267, 269, 1528, 1664
Time Out London (magazine) 3360
Time Shift (TV): "The Comic Songbook" 3600; "Missing Believed Wiped" 2940, 2944
A Time to Live (book) 2842
Time to Talk (video) 1800
Time Troopers (DVD game) 3008
The Times (London) (newspaper) 34, 82, 109, 219, 280, 281, 399, 480, 494, 610, 704, 710, 813, 874, 970, 1019, 1052, 1059, 1076, 1149, 1177, 1271, 1274, 1304, 1351, 1438, 1495, 1613, 1677, 1748, 1812, 1818, 1897, 1926, 1932, 1934, 1945, 2015, 2017, 2035, 2067, 2096, 2142, 2146, 2155, 2158, 2179, 2221, 2272, 2287, 2342, 2376, 2485, 2501, 2546, 2797, 2803, 2807, 2943, 2948, 2982, 2994, 3029, 3035, 3037, 3142, 3174, 3178, 3186, 3203, 3304, 3332, 3563, 3719, 4127, 4156
The Times Literary Supplement (London) (newspaper) 770, 1069, 1216, 1305, 2927
The Times Magazine (London) (magazine) 1976, 2256, 2737, 3327, 4164
The Times: Play (London) (newspaper) 2855
The Times Screen Talk (event) 3212
The Times: The Directory (London) (newspaper) 2270
The Times: The Knowledge (London) (newspaper) 3365
Timewatch (TV): "The Last Day of World War One" 3507, 3571, 3574, 3575
Timlett, Ben 3731, 3825, 3858, 4140, 4162
Timmons, Stan 1709
Tinoco, Luis 3481, 4013
Tiswas (TV) 674, 772, 774, 844, 894, 3413
Tiswas Reunited (TV) 3413
Titcher, David 2999
Titchmarsh, Alan 1854, 3378
The Titfield Thunderbolt (film) 2474

Titleist (ads) 2716
Tiven, Jon 422
To Norway— Home of Giants! (TV) 769
Today (radio) 2687
Today (TV) 499, 1309, 1507, 1527, 1575, 1757, 1943, 2079, 2210, 2379, 3116
Today with Des and Mel (TV) 2965, 3092
Togas on TV: Visions of Rome (TV) 3308
Toksvig, Sandi 3036, 3437
Tolan, Peter 2639, 2742
Tolkien, J. R. R. 2265, 2266
The Tom Machine (film) 828
Tom Snyder (TV) 2050
Tom Thumb see *Rabbit Ears Radio*
Tomalin, Claire 533
Tomiczek, John 177, 775
Tomkinson, Stephen 2328
Tomkinson's Schooldays (TV) see *Ripping Yarns*
Tomlin, Karen 2059
Tomlinson, Fred 461
Tomorrow (TV) 718
Tomorrow's World (TV) 571
Tong, Jacqueline 476
Tonight (TV) 487
Tonight in Town (TV) 702
The Tonight Show Starring Johnny Carson (TV) 277–79, 356, 808, 922, 1199, 1335, 1405, 1497, 1729, 3824
The Tonight Show with Jay Leno (TV) 1948, 1960, 2106, 2195
Tonight with Jonathan Ross (TV) 1796
Tonkin, Boyd 3274
The Tony Awards [59th Annual] (ceremony) 3151, 3389
The Tony Danza Show (TV) 3111
Too Hot to Handle (stage) 1032
Too Much Sun (film) 1756, 1783
Took, Barry 13, 17, 63, 252, 289, 309, 522, 990, 1411, 1752, 2033, 2472, 2744, 2765
"Top of the Form" (sketch) 8, 871, 883, 907, 931, 1131
Top of the Pops (TV) 811, 1853
Top Ten (TV): "Comedy Records" 2561
Toronto Star (newspaper) 3409, 3678
Toronto International Film Festival 1848, 1850, 3187, 4141, 4144
Toronto Symphony Orchestra 3410
Torrance, Ewan 3606
Town and Country Planning (magazine) 1299
Townshend, Pete 704, 755, 1148
Toy Story 3 (film) 3853
Toynbee, Polly 1932
Tracey, Stan 1174
Tracey Ullman: A Class Act (TV) 1922, 1924
Training (magazine) 2441
The Transformers: The Movie (film) 1303

Translating Richard II see *Was Richard II a Tyrant?*
Transport 2000 1256, 1276, 1436, 1462, 1608, 2000, 2674, 3580
Travanti, Daniel J. 1774
Travel Addiction: Is There a Cure? (lecture) 2348
Travel, Comedy and a Little Bit of Fish (lecture) 3569
The Traveling Wilburys 1811
Traveling Wilburys: Volume One (record) 1538
Traveling Wilburys: Vol. 3 (record) 1811
Traveller: Observations from an American in Exile (book) 3782
The Traveller's Handbook (book) 2291
Travelling on Television (lecture) 3826
Travers, Peter 1177, 1495, 3705
Travis 2673
Travolta, John 1390
The Treatment (radio) 2681, 3120
Trebek, Alex 2637
Tree, Margaret 2099, 2104
Trentham, Barbara 833, 903, 960, 1111, 1429, 1763, 1917, 4134
Trevor McDonald Meets... (TV) 2548
Trigger Happy TV (TV) 2545
Trillin, Calvin 1944
Trouble on the Heath (book) 3917–19
Troubles (TV) 1358
Troyer, Verne 3659, 3681, 3713, 3725, 3785
"True Love" (song) 528, 535
True Love (film) 528, 535
The Truman Show (film) 2443
Truss, Lynne 2067
The Truth (book) 4110, 4115–21, 4123–25, 4136, 4142, 4143, 4147, 4150, 4173
Truth and Logic (film) 626
Try to See It My Way see *The Secretary and Her Boss, Part1: Try to See It My Way*
Tsao, Andrew 2633
The Tube (TV) 1191
Tubridy, Ryan 3754
Tubular Bells 2003 (CD) 2897
Tucker, Jessi 3063
Tudyk, Alan 3701
Tuesday's Documentary (TV): "That Well-Known Store in Knightsbridge" 144; "The Great 20th-Century Love Affair" 146
Tully, Mark 2060, 3553
Turan, Kenneth 2119, 3659
Turlington, Christy 1911
Turn Back Time (TV) 3310
Turnbull, Bill 3213, 3612, 3755, 3868, 3942, 4032
Turnbull, David F. 2503, 2505, 2509, 2515
Turnbull, Malcolm 1366
Turner, Bill 33, 133, 145, 148, 152, 155, 212
Turner, Bonnie 2359
Turner, Graham 144

Turner, J. M. W. 3689, 3847
Turner, Jane 3815
Turner, Kathleen 1117
Turner, Teddy 726
Turner, Terry 2359
Turner, Tina 1675, 1724
Turns of the Century (radio) 2092
Turpin, Digby 309, 389
Turtle, Tommy 2483
TV Guide (magazine) 356
TV Guide Online (website) 2560
TV Lite (TV) 1394
TV Times (magazine) 626, 765, 1704
Twain, Mark 1455
"'Twas the Night Before Christmas" (poem) 2623
Tweedie, Jill 855
12 Monkeys (film) 2078, 2119, 2120, 2125–27, 2129, 2132, 2135, 2139, 2143, 2145, 2146, 2148–51, 2190, 2239
The 24 Hour Plays Celebrity Gala (stage) 3888
20/20 (TV) 1030
Twenty Years of Monty Python (seminar & screenings) 1582, 1583, 1586, 1588–92, 1595
Twenty Years on the Road (lecture) 3629
Twice a Fortnight (TV) 1591
Twiggy 1411, 1625, 2389, 2404, 4053
Twiggy's People (TV) 2389
Twilight Zone (magazine) 936, 1177
The Twits (book) 2946, 3227
The Two Ronnies (TV) 129, 136, 138, 141, 214, 240, 285, 291, 514, 517, 2211, 2627, 2966, 3246, 3898, 3976
Two Ronnies Night (TV) 2459
2000 Today (TV) 2536
Tyler, Aisha 3746
Tyler, Andrew 342
Tyler, Bonnie 1006
Tzudiker, Bob 2619

UB40 1032
Uderzo, Albert 2557
Ullman, Tracey 1100, 1922, 1924, 3465, 4096
Ullmann, Liv 2662
The Ultimate Film (TV) 3070
The Ultimate Monty Python Rip Off (CD) 2036
The Uncle Floyd Show (TV) 941
Under the Sun (TV): "The Cat and the Mouse" 1968
Understanding Stammering or Stuttering (book) 4126
Underwood, Ron 2772
Underwood's Finest Hour (play) 508, 879
Unfaithfully Yours (DVD) .3162
Unger, Kurt 19
U.S. Comedy Arts Festival 2340, 2345, 2550, 2863
U.S. Comedy Arts Festival Tribute to Monty Python (event) 2340

U.S. Comedy Arts Festival Tribute to Monty Python (TV) 2345
The Unknown Peter Sellers (TV) 2562, 3234, 3841
The Unorganised Manager (film series) 1200
The Unorganised Manager, Part 1: Damnation [1983] (film) 1103
The Unorganised Manager, Part 1: Damnation [1996] (film) 2205
The Unorganised Manager, Part 2: Salvation [1983] (film) 1104
The Unorganised Manager, Part 2: Salvation [1996] (film) 2206
The Unorganised Manager, Part 3: Divine Intervention [1997] (film) 2321
The Unorganised Manager, Part 3: Lamentations [1985] (film) 1248
The Unorganised Manager, Part 4: Revelations [1985] (film) 1249
The Unorganised Salesperson, Part 2: Valuing Yourself (film) 1798
The Unpleasant World of Penn & Teller (TV) 1992
Unstaged (web) 3854
"The Unsteady Chough" (poem) 2715
The Unsteady Chough (film) 3082
Unwin, Dave 2118, 2204
Up Close with Carrie Keagan (TV) 3785
Up Sunday (TV) 256, 264, 266, 292, 296
"Up Where We Belong" (song) 1114
Updike, John 1657
Urban, William 3374
Ure, Midge 1220, 1286, 1439
Us (magazine) 1632
U.S. News & World Report (magazine) 1698, 2347
The USCAF Awards Gala and Comedy Film Honors (ceremony) 2863
Ustinov, Peter [Sir] 579, 594, 622, 859, 1447, 1638, 1641, 1642, 2024
The Utterly Utterly Merry Comic Relief Christmas Book (book) 1307

V Graham Norton (TV) 2833
Vadukul, Max 1572
Vague, Tom 1235, 1267
Valente, Renée 1638, 1641, 1642
Valenti, Jack 709
Valiant (film) 2946, 3123
A Valid Path (CD) 3012
Vallance, Clem 1694, 1699, 1700, 1715, 1718, 1897, 1898, 1902–04, 1906, 1912, 2272, 2284, 2288, 2298, 2304, 2308
Valley of the Dolls (book) 2547
Valuing Yourself see *Unorganised Salesperson, Part 2: Valuing Yourself*
Van Allan, Richard 1304, 1352, 1442
Van Ark, Joan 787
Van Bridge, Tony 1198
Van De Ruit, John 3884
Van Dyke, Barry 776
Van Gelder, Lawrence 1059, 2185
Van Strum, Carol 874, 1069

Van Tulleken, Jonathan 3082
VanCamp, Emily 4185
Vanity Fair (book) 753
Vanity Fair (magazine) 2138, 2346, 2450, 2553, 2570, 2652, 2738, 2978, 2979, 3103, 3391, 3625, 3751, 3804, 3821, 3913, 3924
Vanity Fair.com (website) 3761, 3776, 3803
Vanoff, Nick 777
Vanstone, Hugh 3113
Varhol, Michael 1673
Variety (magazine) 971, 1029, 3113
The Variety Club Awards (ceremony) 484, 1354, 1582
Varley, Isobel 2228
Vaske, Hermann 3296
Vaughan, Norman 303
Vaughan, Peter 863, 1177
Vaughn, Robert 113
Ventham, Wanda 421, 427
Ventura, Viviane 924
Vereen, Ben 500
Verne, Jules 1413, 1534, 1638, 1683, 1694, 2999
Vernierre, James 936
Vernon, Conrad 2997
Vernon, Richard 731, 905
VH1 Goes Inside (TV): "Shrek" 2995
Victoria Wood's Sketch Show Story (TV) 2701
Victorian Values see *Options*
Video Review (magazine) 1362
Video Video (TV) 1070
Videos for Patients see *What You Really Need to Know About...*
The View (TV) 2574
A View from the Boundary (radio) 1300, 1775
The View in Winter (book) 864
Vilanch, Bruce 428
The Village Voice (newspaper) 412, 494, 710, 1558, 3186
Villechaize, Herve 777
Vince, William 3659
Vincent, David 4088
Vincent, Peter 136, 138, 141, 291
Vincent, Sally 2010
Vincent, Tim 2186
Viner, Brian 4180
Virginia Woolf Diaries (book) 3656
Vitaliev, Vitali 1747
Viz: The Documentary (TV) 1765
Vodka-Cola (book) 858
Vogue (magazine) 408, 432, 1572
Voices for Peace (book) 2708, 3085
Vole (magazine) 589, 628
Von Sivers, Malou 3935
Voos, John 1052
Vosburgh, Dick 39, 126, 127, 136, 141
The Voyages of Sinbad (I to III) (audiobook) 1162
The Voyages of Sinbad (IV to VI) (audiobook) 1162
Vyvyan, Johnny 3, 4

Waddingham, Hannah 3353, 3389
Wade, Jennifer 3781, 3876, 3937, 3998, 4022, 4134, 4137

Wade, Robert 2516, 2819
Wadsworth, Andrew C. 915
Wagland, John 1353
Wagreich, David 2423
Wailes, Martha 2501
Waits, Tom 3659, 3959
Waldham, Gary 621
Wale, Michael 162, 211, 400
Walesa, Lech 3453
Walker, Alexander 2682
Walker, April 446, 477, 620, 900, 901
Walker, Jane 380
Walker, Nancy 777
Walker, Peter 931
Walker, Ted 2118, 2204
Walker, Tim 3751
Walkie Talkie (TV) 1730
Walks on the Wild Side (event) 3883
Wall, Max 567
The Wall Street Journal (newspaper) 1513, 3416
Wallace, Danny 3568
Wallace, David 2068, 2072, 2074, 2076
Wallace, Julie T. 1745
Wallace-Hadrill, Andrew [Dr.] 2565
Wallach, Eli 2047
Wallis, Alan 137, 142, 147, 150, 153, 154, 156, 157, 189, 190, 192, 201–03, 205, 208, 300
Wallstrom, Margot 3768
Walmsley, Jane 778
Walsh, J. T. 1673
Walsh, Kate 4189
Walter, Harriet 3294
Walters, Barbara 499
Walters, Guy 1976
Walters, Julie 1002, 1043, 1044, 1133, 1370, 1373, 1374, 1833, 2439
Walters, Thorley 159
Walton, William [Sir] 597
Waltrip, Darrell 3880
Waltz, Christoph 4165
Wanamaker, Zoë 3202
Wander, Suzannah 3352
Wannabe (TV) 2297
Wapshott, Tim 2158
Warburton, Matt 3388
Warburton, Patrick 2620
Ward, Elizabeth 1216
Ward, Lalia 729
Ward, Simon 248
Ward, Tom 8
Warden, Jack 859, 1376
Ware, Derek 471
Warfield, Sonja 2989
Warhol, Andy 411, 639
Wark, Kirsty 2684, 3857
Warner, Aron 3405
Warner, David 863, 2324, 2336
Warnock, Craig 863, 2336
Warren, David 3659
Warrington, Don 1157, 1984
Warwick, David 731
Was Richard II a Tyrant? (lecture) 3444, 3448, 3451, 3464, 3511, 3525, 3633

General Index

Was Richard II Mad? (lecture) 3528
Washington, Cheryl 1492
Washington, George [President] 1668
Washington, Isaiah 2899
The Washington Post (newspaper) 415, 708, 891, 1094, 1512, 2085, 2221
Washington Post Book World (newspaper) 1216
Watching (TV) 2611
Watchmen (comic) 1598, 2890
Waters, Harry F. 401, 635
Waters, John 2422
Watford, Gwen 480
Watling, Dilys 476, 692
Watson, Albert 1524
Watson, Emma 2702, 2810
Watson, Mark 3680, 3683
Watson, Moray 517
Wattis, Nigel 775
Watts, Charlie 1969
Watts, Michael 751, 1052
Watts, Reggie 4081
Watts, Tim 2648
Wavell, Stuart 2735
Wawn, Andrew 1069
Wax, Ruby 1409, 2002, 2252, 2471
Way, Ann 453, 725
Way, Eileen 606
Way Off Broadway (TV) 1437
The Way We Travelled (TV) 2905
Waymark, Peter 1351
The Wayne Brady Show (TV) 2871
W. C. Fields: A Biography (book) 2881
W. C. Fields: A Comedian for Politically Incorrect Times (lecture) 2881
We All Have Tales (TV): "Jack and the Beanstalk" 1832
We Are Most Amused (stage) (TV) 3579, 3582
We Can Work It Out see *The Secretary and Her Boss, Part 2: We Can Work It Out*
We Will Rock You (musical) 3018
Wearing, Gillian 2402
Wearn, Deborah 1913
Weaver, Dennis 777
Weaving, Hugo 2625
Webb, Marti 773, 927
Webb, Steve 2905
Webber, Richard 2276
Weber, Bruce 2086
Weber, Michael H. 3616
Webster, Gary 1938
Webster, George 3123
Wednesday 9:30 (8:30 Central) (TV) 2741, 2742
The Weekend (book) 2019
The Weekend (play) 2003, 2007, 2008, 2010–13, 2015–17
Weekend Live (TV) 1608
Weekend Wogan (radio) 4195
Wehn, Henning 3944
Weiland, Paul 1919
Wein, Joe 2751
Weinstein, Bob 2862, 2902, 3178
Weinstein, Harvey 2902

Weis, Gary 635, 2644, 3584
Weisman, Sam 2261, 2442
Weiss, Julie 2119
Welch, Chris 301
Welch, Raquel 50
Welcome Customer, Part 1: Have a Nice Stay (film) 761
Welcome Customer, Part 2: See You Again Soon (film) 762
Welcome to South Park (event) 2669
Weldon, Fay 1768, 1930
Wellensian Consort 3972
Weller, Wesla 2171
Welles, Orson 1082, 1303, 2501
Wells, Audrey 2261
Wells, Dominic 2855
Wells, H. G. 1567, 1568
Wells, John 252, 256, 264, 266, 292, 296, 871, 931
Wells, Simon 1859
Wences, Senor 642
Wenner, Adrian 4069
Wentworth, John 480, 618
Wesker, Arnold 1768
West, Carinthia 471, 532, 537, 542, 544
West, Dottie 745
West, Samuel 3390
West, Timothy 548
West, W. J. 1914
West 57th Street (TV) 1384
Westbrook, John 1150
Western Mail (Cardiff, Wales) (newspaper) 3919, 4155
Westheimer, Ruth [Dr.] 1378
Westlife 4030
Weston, Diana 1984
Weston, Maggie 286, 1558, 1755, 3351
Whalley-Kilmer, Joanne 1443
What a Performance! (TV) 2589
What About Dick? (play) 3465, 4077, 4096, 4176, 4185, 4189, 4191, 4198, 4203
What Did ITV Do for Me? (TV) 3193
What Do People Do All Day? (book) 38
What Have They Given Us? (TV) 1260, 1261
What I Heard About Iraq (event) 3252
What Is a Computer? see *Everybody's Guide to the Computer, No. 1: What Is a Computer?*
What Is a Computer Program? see *Everybody's Guide to the Computer, No. 3: What Is a Computer Program?*
What Is a Word Processor? see *Everybody's Guide to the Computer, No. 2: What Is a Word Processor?*
What Is Brazil? (TV) 1251, 2174
What Is Religion?: Musings on The Life of Brian (lecture) 3056
What on Earth Is Going On? (TV) 1436
What the Butler Saw (play) 915

What the Pythons Did Next (TV) 3375, 3376
What You Really Need to Know About... (videos) 1983, 2257
What's Eating Johnny Depp? (TV) 2422
What's So Funny? (lecture) 1826
What's So Great About...? (radio) 4108
Wheeler, Lionel 440
Wheeler, Mortimer 3308
When I'm Calling You see *Selling on the Telephone: When I'm Calling You*
When We Were Young: A Compendium of Childhood (book) 3032
When We Were Young: Memories of Childhood (book) 1411
When Will They Realise We're Living in the 20th Century? (film) 825
"When You Wish Upon a Star" (song) 3928
Where There's Life (TV) 1132
Whicker, Alan 175, 1260, 1413, 1937, 3166, 3381, 3506
Whipple, Shonda 1640
Whitaker, Ben 70
Whitaker, Frances 749, 1123
Whitbread, Dean 3267
The Whitbread Book Awards (ceremony) 2720
Whitby, Joy 1463
Whitchurch, Philip 1833
White, Andrew Dickson 2386
White, Betty 645
White, E. B. 3368
White, John 606
White, Kevin 2945
White, Michael 397, 1751
White, Noni 2619
White, Peter 3814
Whitehall, Jack 4199
Whitehouse, Alan 1804
Whitehouse, Brian 350
Whitehouse, Mary 924, 1768
Whitehouse, Paul 2561
Whitfield, June 306–08, 626, 899, 909
Whitley, Edward 1037, 1294
Whitmore, Ken 281
Whitney (TV): "Mind Games" 4069
Whittaker, Roger 895
Whittell, Giles 2342
Whittington, Valerie 970, 1025
Whitworth, John 2425
The Who 470, 649
Who Is Harry Nilsson (and Why Is Everybody Talkin' About Him?) (film) 3234
Who Murdered Chaucer?: A Medieval Mystery (book) 770, 2388, 2926, 2927, 2938, 2955, 2984, 2998, 3049, 3074, 3115, 3515
Who Murdered Chaucer?: A Medieval Mystery (lecture) 2924, 2928, 2984, 2998, 3049, 3051, 3115, 3515
Who Sold You This, Then? [1972]

(film) see *Marketing in Practice, No. 1: Who Sold You This, Then?*
Who Sold You This Then? [1997] (film) 2322
Wholey, Dennis 1092, 1148
The Wholly Family (film) 3899, 3953, 3989, 3991, 3999, 4033, 4058, 4064, 4094, 4107
Whoops Apocalypse (TV) 928
Who's That Girl (concert) 1408
Who's There? (film) 163
Why Do People Work? (film) 902
Whyte, Alison 4126
Wibberley, Cormac 2901
Wibberley, Marianne 2901
Wickham, Saskia 1864
Wicks, Dennis 1352
Wide World of Entertainment ["The Monty Python Show"] (TV) 423, 447, 466, 469, 472
Wieland, Bob 2871
Wiig, Kristen 4081
Wilbur, Todd 3529
Wilbury Twist (music video) 1811
Wilcox, Larry 787
Wilcox, Paula 804
The Wild (film) 3258
Wild, Jeannette 88
Wilde, Brian 280, 1982
Wilde, Marjorie 86
Wilkes, Jonathan 3555
Wilkie, Amanda 2398
Will & Grace (TV): "The Accidental Tsuris" 2953; "Flip-Flop: Part 1" 2977; "Flip-Flop: Part 2" 2981; "Heart Like a Wheelchair" 2932; "I Do, Oh, No, You Di-in't: Part 1 & 2" 2989
Will You Answer True? see *Selling on the Telephone: Will You Answer True?*
Willard, Fred 2942, 3048
Williams, Cindy 563, 834
Williams, Frank 220
Williams, Hywel 3172
Williams, JoBeth 2436
Williams, John [guitarist] 85, 579, 594, 622, 704, 755, 1665, 2212
Williams, John [writer] 1824
Williams, Kenneth 463, 1290
Williams, Martin 3685
Williams, Michael 4183
Williams, Phil 3311
Williams, Robin 934, 957, 1446, 1559, 1619, 1849, 1850, 1855, 1952, 2462, 2465, 2467, 2533, 2540, 2550, 2591, 2678, 2688, 2836, 2906, 3234, 3411, 3499, 3579, 3582
Williams, Sarah 1915, 2390
Williams, Sian 3213, 3612, 3755, 3868, 3942, 4032
Williams, Simon 651
Williams, Tennessee 2432
Williamson, Bruce 161, 943, 1025, 1274, 1559
Williamson, Nicol 2185
Willis, Bruce 2078, 2119, 2148
Willoughby, Holly 4036, 4119

The Willows in Winter (TV) 2118, 2204
Wilmore, Marc 4102
Wilmot, Gary 1776
Wilson, Andy 1739
Wilson, Anthony 1612
Wilson, Bill 737, 818
Wilson, Brian 3981
Wilson, Dave 515, 563, 576, 640, 660, 671, 695, 730, 779, 893, 940, 966, 1110
Wilson, David 3293
Wilson, Dennis Main 13, 315
Wilson, Flip 777
Wilson, Gahan 1177
Wilson, Hugh 2464
Wilson, Iain 958
Wilson, John 3822
Wilson, Owen 4004
Wilson, Richard 1733, 1740, 1866, 2012, 2017
Wilson, Stuart 2750
Wilson, Trey 1055
Wilton, Kate 2228
Wilton, Penelope 1274, 4091
Wimbledon (film) 3021
The Wind in the Willows (audiobook) 2160
The Wind in the Willows (book) 2185, 2187, 2204, 2209, 2331, 3632
The Wind in the Willows (film) 2111, 2173, 2175, 2178–80, 2183–88, 2209, 2306, 2331, 2405, 2420, 2426, 3044, 3632; see also *Mr. Toad's Wild Ride* (video)
The Wind in the Willows (TV) 2118
The Wind in the Willows: A Centenary Celebration (event) 3632
The Wind in the Willows: The Complete Illustrated Screenplay (book) 2209
Windmill (TV) 1440
Windsor, Barbara 1290
Windsor, Joe 382, 475
Wine for the Confused see *John Cleese's Wine for the Confused*
Winfrey, Oprah 3368, 3838
Wing-Davey, Mark 481, 548
Winick, Gary 3368
Winkleman, Claudia 4039, 4125
Winkleman, Sophie 4096
Winkler, Henry 563
Winner, Michael 1033, 1788, 2225, 2448, 2460, 3555, 3688, 3876
Winston, Robert [Prof.] 2402
Winstone, Ray 3355
Winterburn, Denise 1714
Wintle, Angela 4043
Winton, Dale 2224
Wise, Ernie 1320
With Friends Like These (TV): "Don't Mention the War" 2914
Without Walls: Film Talk (TV) 1843
Witness (film) 1282
Witt, Alicia 2313
Wogan (TV) 992, 1136, 1239, 1260, 1276, 1281, 1290, 1349, 1357, 1366,

1397, 1531, 1616, 1695, 1774, 1795, 1864
Wogan, Terry 484, 992, 1136, 1239, 1276, 1281, 1290, 1349, 1354, 1357, 1366, 1397, 1531, 1582, 1616, 1695, 1774, 1795, 1864, 1923, 2091, 2459, 2593, 2970, 3246, 3284, 4195
Wogan Now and Then (TV) 3284
Woitkewitsch, Thomas 238, 287, 3944
Wolf, Martin 3658
Wolfberg, Dennis 1437
Wolfe, Tim 2745
Wolfe, Tom 896
Wolff, Michele J. 2986
Wolk, Josh 2948
Woman's Hour (radio) 124, 1077, 1285, 1356, 1732
Woman's Hour Drama (radio): "How Shall I Tell the Dog?" 3566
Wonder, Stevie 2678
Wong, Vincent 105
Wood, Dominic 3605, 3802, 3910
Wood, Duncan 222
Wood, Michael 838
Wood, Ralph 105
Wood, Ron 635, 1969, 2618
Wood, Victoria 871, 1153, 1343, 2185, 2701
Woodrow, Stephen Taylor 3857
Woodruff, Anthony 725
Woods, Aubrey 340
Woods, Eli 313
Woods, James 1807
Woods, Peter 368
Woods, Sheryl 1712
Woods, Vicki 1572
Woodward, Edward 1661
Wooldridge, Susan 1924
Wooler, Mike 163
Woolf, Henry 230, 340, 418, 420, 421, 425, 427, 429, 471, 537, 541–43, 635
Working Girl (film) 1578
The World Is Not Enough (film) 2510, 2516, 2517, 2819
The World of Interiors (magazine) 1266
The World Stunt Awards [2nd Annual] (ceremony) 2753
The Worst of Monty Python (record) 556
Wright, Jo 1924
Wright, Joseph 3689
Wright, Matthew 3282
Wright, Peter 1406
Wright, Robert 2082
Wright, Steven 1643, 1660, 2055
The Wright Stuff (TV) 3282
Writing and Travelling (event) 4142
Written and Directed by Preston Sturges (DVD set) 3134
WTTW Channel 11 (ads) 2349
Wuhl, Robert 1782, 1823
Wunderkamera: Terry Gilliam's Cinema (book) 3971
WXRT-Chicago (ads) 1201
Wyeth, Katya 39, 49

Wyldeck, Martin 440
Wylder, Jonathan 3937
Wylie, Adam 2251
Wyman, Bill 1113, 1969, 2618, 2921, 3539

X-Play (TV) 2983
X the Unknown (film) 2830

Yallop, David 810
Yang, Edward 2662
Yanover, Ronald 2057
Yapp, Will 3375, 3587, 3588
Yarbrough, Jeff 1277
Yarwood, Mike 1397
Yashere, Gina 3680
Yates, Paula 1191
Yates, Peter 1033
Yeager, Robert F. 2663, 2927, 4098
Yelland, David 3294
Yellowbeard (film) 954, 978, 984, 1003, 1049, 1059, 1073, 1087, 2066
Yentob, Alan 4053
Yoakum, Jim 1554, 2307, 2541, 2594, 3167
Yohn, Erica 1859
York, David 974
York, Michael 1579
York, Phyllis 974
York, Susannah 1062
Yorke, Rachel 1794
Yorkshire Evening Post (newspaper) 3909
You and Me (TV) 670
You and Yours (radio) 3814

You'll Soon Get the Hang of It (film) 899
Young, B. A. 316
Young, Chris 1455, 1501
Young, John 397, 710
Young, Kirsty 3928
Young, Paul 1417
Young Frankenstein (film) 397, 978
Young Guardian (newspaper) 1371, 1552, 1576
The Young Indiana Jones Chronicles (TV): "Barcelona, May 1917" 1894
The Young Ones 1286
The Young Ones (TV): "Nasty" 1125
You've Got Mail 2335

Zanetti, Eugenio 2573